FORGOTTEN HEROES
Zulu & Basuto Wars
Including Complete Medal Roll 1877-8-9

Roy Dutton BSc

First published 1st May 2010 in Great Britain by InfoDial Ltd
PO Box 195
Prenton
CH26 9DF

www.infodial.co.uk

Copyright © 2010 by Roy Dutton

Every effort has been made to locate and contact the holders of copyright material reproduced in this book.

All rights reserved. No part of this book may be reproduced or transmitted in any form or by any means, electronic or mechanical, including photocopying, recording, or by any information storage and retrieval system, without the written permission of the Publisher, except where permitted by law.

Acknowledgements
I would like to thank Chris Poole and Justin Young for proof reading the book. Also Jamie Hughes for his continued support and help in my quest to master InDesign publishing software.

Cover painting -
C.E. Fripps dramatic painting of the last stand of the 24th at Isandlwana.
Courtesy of the National Army Museum.

Contents

4	Introduction and Abbreviations
5	General Order
6	Medal Design
8	Clasps to the South Africa Medal
9	Returned and Re-Issued Medals
10	Medals Issued
11	Colonial Troops
13	Colonial Medal Summary
19	Colonial Troops Medal Roll
179	Colonial Army List July-Aug 1881
185	List of Claimants to Zulu War Medals
186	Imperial Force Medal Summary
190	Imperial Troops Medal Roll
373	The Royal Navy Medal Roll
398	War Service Imperial & Colonial Units
401	Galekas Revolt September 1877-June 1878
403	Ist Invasion 11th January 1879
405	Battles of the Zulu War 1879
406	Isandhlwana - 22 January 1879
412	Rorke's Drift 22-23 January 1879
413	Action at Gingihlovo - 2 April 1879
414	Morosi War 25th March to 20th November 1879
416	Basuto War 1880-1881
419	Appendices
456	Bibliography
4568	Index

Introduction

Introduction

I follow in the foot steps of D.R.Forsyth who compiled the first comprehensive medal roll of the South Africa medal (1877-79) which was a limited duplicator produced edition transcribed via a mechanical typewriter first published in 1978.

There are numerous CD which contain photographs of the rolls, which are difficult to read and make no allowances for the 6,089 returned medals. I have searched in the National Archives at Kew for additional information, together with the Natal Press, Cape of Hope Government Gazette and numerous accounts and publications to add additional data on men that were engaged in the campaigns.

The condition of some of the medal rolls leaves a lot to be desired, some are copies of copies and cannot be relied on as being 100% correct. Spellings are incorrect and initials missing. Most of the errors appear to have occurred in the transcription from the original rolls.

I have compared all the available information to arrive at the most accurate list available to date. The Colonial units (Irregular Regiments) changed their names frequently. Some individuals served in more than one unit and to add to the confusion are listed twice, notes have been made to high light the duplication. I have added numerous individuals that do not appear on the medal roll, but were listed in other documents, using the classification of "Not on medal roll" with additional lists added in the Appendixes.

The Royal Navy Rolls also appear to have been re-written, with various notations added "correct spelling of names cannot be relied on" or "cannot be taken as correct"

The issue of the medals was made to three distinct groups:
1. Imperial Regular Forces. In accordance with General Orders No 103 and 134 issued in 1880.
2. Original Forces. Raised by the Colonial Government, most units in existence before 1879.
3. Colonial Levies. Raised by the General Officer Commanding in the field, and disbanded upon the cessation of hostilities, with poor record keeping, even their Pay Lists were badly kept.

The book is divided into two main parts, the Colonial and Imperial troop medal listings. I have also added information on individuals, auction data, personal accounts and extracts from out of print books.

Numerous unpublished photographs have been added together with contemporary newspaper cuttings. With a brief overview of the campaigns and the location of the various units I hope this book will fill a useful gap in our knowledge of the individuals present during this unrelenting and cruel military campaign.

Abbreviations

The original names and initials have been compiled from the rolls, a name in brackets indicates another spelling of the same surname. Of interest to medal collectors I have selected a number of medals sold by dealers and Auction Houses, especially the rarer and noteworthy.

KIA	Killed in Action (In bold text)	
D/S	Died on Service	
D/W	Died of Wounds	
r	Returned to Woolwich Mint	

If only these Medals could talk. What tales of valour, sacrifice and hope they could tell? The history locked in these small pieces of silver is absolutely amazing, which you will soon discover. Rather than just a name on a medal, I have tried to bring the person back to life.

General Order

On the 8 January 1806, the Battle of Blaauwberg, also known as the Battle of Cape Town, was a turning point in the history of South Africa, when the Dutch, under the command of Lt General Jan Willem Janssens, surrendered the colony of the Cape of Good Hope to a British Force under the command of Sir David Baird. From this point onwards the country has been more or less in a state of warfare between neighbouring tribes, making formidable and dangerous enemies. The Empire rewarded its gallant defenders by the issue of medals. The campaigns of 1877-9, although finally successful, were fraught with disaster and serious loss to the British army. It is interesting to record Colonial Forces Order no. 169 (issued at Kingwilliamstown on 14th Sept 1880, to announce the granting of the medal) stated specifically that 'the Medal will be granted to survivors only.' This proved not to be the case as medals were given to the next-of-kin of men killed in action.

In August, 1880, the following General Order was issued:—

The Queen has been graciously pleased to command that, in consideration of the arduous duties performed and the successful conclusion of the operations referred to in the next paragraph, a Medal be granted to Her Majesty's Imperial forces, and to such of Her Majesty's colonial forces, European or native, as were regularly organised and disciplined as combatants, whether raised by the Colonial Government or by the General Officer commanding. 2. The Medal will be granted to the forces employed against—(a) The Galekas, Gaikas, and other Caffre tribes from the 26th September, 1877, to the 28th of June, 1878, inclusive; (b) against Pokwani, from the 21st to the 28th of January, 1878, inclusive; (c) against the Griquas, from the 24th of April to the 13th of November, 1874, inclusive; (d) against the Zulus, from the 11th of January to the 1st of September, 1879, inclusive; (e) against Secocoeni, from the 11th of November to the 2nd of December, 1879, and including the troops that were stationed at Fort Burghers, Fort Albert Edward, Seven Mile Post, Fort Oliphant, Fort Weeber, and in Secocoeni's Valley; (f) against Moirosi's stronghold. 3. Her Majesty has also been pleased to approve of a Clasp being attached to the same Medal, on which will be indicated the year or years in which the recipients of the Medal were engaged in the late wars, thus—For operations against the Galekas, &c., on Clasp 1877-8; for operations against Pokwani and the Griquas, 1878; for operations in the Zulu and Secocoeni campaigns respectively, or both, 1879; for operations as specified in Paragraph 2 in 1877-8-9, 1877-8-9; for operations as specified in Paragraph 2 in 1878-9, 1878-9—the principle being that the year or years of the Clasp cover all the operations in which the recipient may have been engaged in such year or years. 4. Those troops employed in Natal from the 11th of January to the 1st of September, 1879, but who never crossed the border into Zululand, will be granted the Medal without Clasp. 5. The Medal will be that granted by Her Majesty to commemorate the successful termination of previous wars in South Africa; and those officers, non-commissioned officers and men who are already in possession of this Medal will, if they have been engaged in the operations referred to in Paragraph 2, receive the Clasp with the year or years inscribed thereon, in accordance with Paragraph 3.

November, 1881. Extract from General Order:—

The South African War Medals for the undermentioned corps, raised in Natal for service in the Zulu War, are now ready for issue, viz., the Frontier Light Horse, Baker's Horse, Bettington's Horse, and the Natal Native Contingent (1st and 2nd Battalions, officers only). . . . The Medals for the Cape Colonial Forces are in course of preparation, but are not yet ready for issue.

Medal Design

MEDAL DESIGN

The original Army Order, No 103 of August 1880, made no mention of any change in design from the original earlier 1853 model.

Discussions arose between the War Office and the mint, the later wanted a simple modification to the original South African medal of 1853, see drawings opposite. Also the War Office could not decide on the final format due to the complexities of the different tribes and campaigns as witnessed by the three Royal Warrants. Until finally it was decided on the 1st August 1880 one clasp per medal which would indicate the year or years in which the recipients of the medal were engaged.

Those troops employed in Natal from the 11th January to the 1st September, but who never crossed the border into Zululand, will be granted a medal without a clasp. The General Order which followed set in motion the issue of the medal with one clasp, to be awarded to all officers and men of the Regular and Colonial forces.

Period inclusive	Campaigns Against
26th Sept 1877 - 28th June 1878	Galekas, Gaikas and other Kafir Tribes
21st Jan 1878 - 28th Jan 1878	Chief Pokwane
24th Apr 1878 - 13th Nov 1878	Griguas
11th Jan 1879 - 1st Sep 1879	Zulus
11th Nov 1879 - 2nd Dec 1879	Chief Sekukuni, includes troops stationed at Forts Burgers Albert Edward, Oliphants, & Weeber also Seven Mile Post and in Sekukuni's Valley.
25th Mar 1879 - 20th Nov 1879	Chief Moirosi Stronghold

Of the same basic design as the 1834-53 Kaffir Wars medal but instead of the date 1853, it has a shield and four crossed assegai in the rev. exergue. The obverse of the medal shows the head of Queen Victoria and the legend "VICTORIA REGINA" the reverse a crouching lion and the words "SOUTH AFRICA"

The medal is 36mm in diameter with an ornate swivelling suspension, made from silver. Naming normally engraved in upright or sloping serif capitals, with many variations of style. The ribbon, orange with two outer wide blue stripes, and two inner narrow blue stripes.

Participants in the Zulu War received this medal without a bar if they remained on the Natal side of the Tugela, or with the bar '1879' if they actually saw service in Zululand.

Medal Design

2 August, 1880

Sir,

In reply to Col. Deedes's letter of the 29th of July. I am directed by the Master of the Mint to transmit herewith a drawing of the reverse of the South African War Medal, showing the design which he would propose to substitute for the date "1853", and I am to request that you will move the Secretary of State for War to be so good as to cause him to be informed as soon as possible whether Her Majesty is pleased to approve of the change suggested.

I am further to request that the Drawing may be returned to this Department.

I am, Sir,
Your obedient Servant,
C. Fremantle

The Under Secretary for War,
War Office,
SW

Clasps on the South Africa Medal

South Africa Medal 1877-79

Applicants for the South Africa 1877-79 medal who were in possession of a South Africa 1853 medal were supposed to declare the fact, whereupon they should have received an appropriately dated clasp for attachment to the earlier medal. A very small number were issued with both medals despite volunteering that they held the 1853 award (O.M.R.S. Journal, Winter 1981, G.R. Everson),

Clasps to the medal include 1877, 1877-8, 1877-9, 1877-8-9, 1878, 1878-9 and 1879. The medal was issued with a clasp corresponding to the recipients year or years of service.

Medals issued with a 1877 clasp include, 22 men of the Cape Colonial forces, one in the East London Chalumna Volunteer Cavalry, 13 in the Fort White Mounted Volunteers and 8 in the Sidbury Mounted Rangers, 34 Prince Alfred's Guard Rifle Vols, 70 in Bowkers Rovers, 22 Aliwal North Mounted Volunteers, with anot 19 medals going to volunteer units. A grand total of 167 medals were authorised with 3 awards to Imperial troops.

With 11 recipients of the 1877-9 clasp, The list includes the names of eight men of the 2nd Regiment Cape Mounted Yeomanry, who served in 1877 and again in 1879, but not in 1878. They are listed below:

1. C. 1343 **Sergeant E Craft,** Army Service Corps - Commissariat.
2. **Sergeant C. Mc Gonigle,** Border Horse Reissued in 1914 with the clasp 1877-9
3. 141 **Trooper A. Tweedie,** Bowkers Rovers. Returned to Woolwich Mint
4. **Sergeant Thos. Muldoon,** 2nd Cape Mounted Yeomanry. (K.I.A) Returned to Woolwich Mint
5. **Trumpeter Frank Long,** 2nd Cape Mounted Yeomanry
6. **Trooper William Earle,** 2nd Cape Mounted Yeomanry. Returned to Woolwich Mint
7. **Trooper Alfred Maytham,** 2nd Cape Mounted Yeomanry
8. **Trooper Mathew Maytham,** 2nd Cape Mounted Yeomanry
9. **Trooper John Mc Coll,** 2nd Cape Mounted Yeomanry
10. **Trooper Carl Nel,** 2nd Cape Mounted Yeomanry. Returned to Woolwich Mint
11. **Trooper George James Weatherhead,** 2nd Cape Mounted Yeomanry

Medals not claimed were returned to Woolwich in 1911

Papers in the Public Record Office in Kew give the figures for the medals and clasps issued in the period 1/8/1880 to 30/12/1884 with 4198 medals and clasps supplied on the 12/11/1881, including 8 clasps dated 1877-9 (Requisition No 1908)

Two examples are known to exist of medals with two clasps both being genuine. With one awarded to **Assistant Commissary J. L. Dalton** VC of Rorke's Drift fame.

Both the '1877-8' and '1878-9' clasps are considered scarce while the '1877' clasp is very rare and highly collectable. The most common clasp is that of '1879' for the Zulu War.

An unofficial bar 'ULUNDI' exists with the 1879 date being erased and ULUNDI then engraved on medals awarded to members of the 17th Lancers.

Confusion can occur when faced with a medal bearing the bar '1879', for the same bar was given with the medal for the Moirosi's Mountain campaign in Basutoland, and for the Second Sekukuni War in the North-Eastern Transvaal. The only way to establish whether the bar '1879' was indeed for the Zulu War is to check the service details of the recipient and check that the unit concerned was in Zululand. Within the pages of this book are listed the location of most of the regiments during the different campaigns. With apologies for any errors and omissions.

Returned Medals

THE CAPE OF GOOD HOPE Government Gazette.

Published by Authority

FRIDAY, OCTOBER 14th, 1892.

The Cape of Good Hope Government Gazette dated 14th October 1892 contained within details of 4181 unclaimed medals.
Between 1887 and 1930 medals were returned to the mint at Woolwich, with 4609 medals and 4691 clasps returned in 1911. The majority of the returned medals, well over 5,000 being allocated to the Colonials. The difficulty in tracing the individuals, combined with the badly kept records made the task of issuing medals very difficult.. Returned medals were melted down. The Colonial medal rolls have been re-written, and the errors in transcription have been magnified by the number of foreign sounding names, both native and European.

It was possible for some medals to be re-issued at a later date to the sons and daughters of the original recipient. The naming on such medals would be in whatever style was used at the time.

GOVERNMENT NOTICE.—No 966, 1892.
Colonial Secretary's Office, Cape Town,
Cape of Good Hope, 26th September, 1892.

UNCLAIMED WAR MEDALS.—1877, '78 and '79.

A LIST of Persons who have not yet claimed their South African War Medals, granted them for participation in the Wars that took place during the years 1877, 1878 and 1879, is herewith published for general information.

These Medals are in the care of the Colonial Military Secretary, and can be obtained on application at his Office in Grave Street, Cape Town.

HENRY DE SMIDT,
Under Colonial Secretary.

South African War Medals. (Hansard, 14 July 1903) vol 125 c572. Questions in the House
MAJOR SEELY (Isle of Wight) I beg to ask the Secretary of State for War whether, seeing that large numbers of men in the Army or recently discharged have not yet received South African war medals to which they are entitled, he will say whether this delay is caused by undue centralisation at Woolwich; and, if so, whether he will consider the desirability of despatching the medals to officers commanding units, making them responsible for the engraving and distribution of the medals.
THE FINANCIAL SECRETARY TO THE WAR OFFICE (Lord STANLEY,) Lancashire, Westhoughton.
As I have already explained to the House, considerable time is required for checking the rolls which in many cases were not correct. Up to the 30th June, 390,261 medals and 982,070 clasps had been issued. Commanding officers are now responsible for the distribution, but to make them responsible for the engraving would hardly appear expeditious. The greatest possible efforts have been made to expedite production both at the Mint and Woolwich.

Medals Issued

Medals Issued
South Africa Medals and Clasps Struck at the Royal Mint 1880-86:

Clasp	*Medals	*%	**Loose Clasps	#Medals	#Returned
1877	153	0.42	Nil	171	
1877-8	5822	15.89	5	6081	
1877-8-9	3525	9.62	15	3890	
1877-9	8	0.02	Nil	11	
1878	2009	5.48	Nil	2172	
1878-9	1185	3.23	94	1781	
1879	18332	50.03	668	19573	
No Clasp	5610	15.31	-	5335	
TOTALS	**36644**	**99.99**	**782**	**39014**	**6090**

* From orginal research by Major Townsend of South Africa Medals.
**Most loose clasps were issued in respect of late claims by those who had crossed the border into Zululand.
Totals found on medal roll.

Colonial Troops

After Britain granted the Cape Colony representative government in 1853, the colony was encouraged to take some responsibility for its own defence, and in 1855 the Colonial Parliament formed three separate military organisations: the para-military Frontier Armed and Mounted Police (FAMP); the Burgher Force; and the Volunteer Force.

The FAMP was responsible for maintaining law and order in the outlying districts. The Burgher Force was a district-based militia. The Volunteer Force was also district-based, but consisted of a self-financed and privately-formed force. The first Volunteer corps to be founded in the Colony in November 1855 was the Cape Town Rifle Corps.

Between 1877 and 1881 the Cape forces were deployed in six of the nine wars and campaigns that were fought throughout South Africa. Dozens of volunteer units were formed, but most disbanded once hostilities were over. They were commanded by regular officers, retired officers living in South Africa, or men of standing in the communities. The native levies were often used as a skirmishing screen to trigger off any ambush. After a successful operation by the regular troops they were used to purse the fleeing enemy. With very few fire arms, less than 10% were armed, they were expected to run away at the earliest signs of trouble. Misunderstood by their officers who could really speak their language, they were in an untenable position.

During the period 1877-9 the Volunteer Units were involved in the following hostilities:

        The 9th Kaffir War, August, 1877, to August, 1878.
        The Northern Border War, May, 1878, to July, 1879.
        The Bechuanaland Rebellion, 1878.
        The 1st & 2nd Sekukuni Wars, 1878, 1879.
        The Morosi Rebellion, February to November, 1879.

Volunteers banded together under titles which indicated the districts where the forces were originally raised. Some units took the names of their commanders. A common occurrence with the men as their time expired was to swap between units. During the Zulu War volunteer units were called up to garrison in the Transkei and elsewhere.

The limited number of Imperial troops available led to a proliferation of colonial units. The Natal colonists also played their part. Forces called out on full mobilization to meet the threat of Cetewayo's estimated 40,000 warriors included the Natal Mounted Police (a semi-military formation, and the only 'regulars) and all the Natal Volunteer units then in existence. The Frontier Light Horse and units such as Raaff's Transvaal Rangers and the Kaffrarian Rifles came from the other colonies. Special reserve units were established in Pietermaritzburg and Durban for local garrison duty and large numbers of Natal Natives were enlisted.

Units which earned the medal, but not the bar include:

Carbutt's Border Rangers.
Durban Mounted Reserve.
Durban Volunteer Artillery.
Pietermaritzburg Rifles.
Royal Durban Rifles.
Southey's Rangers.

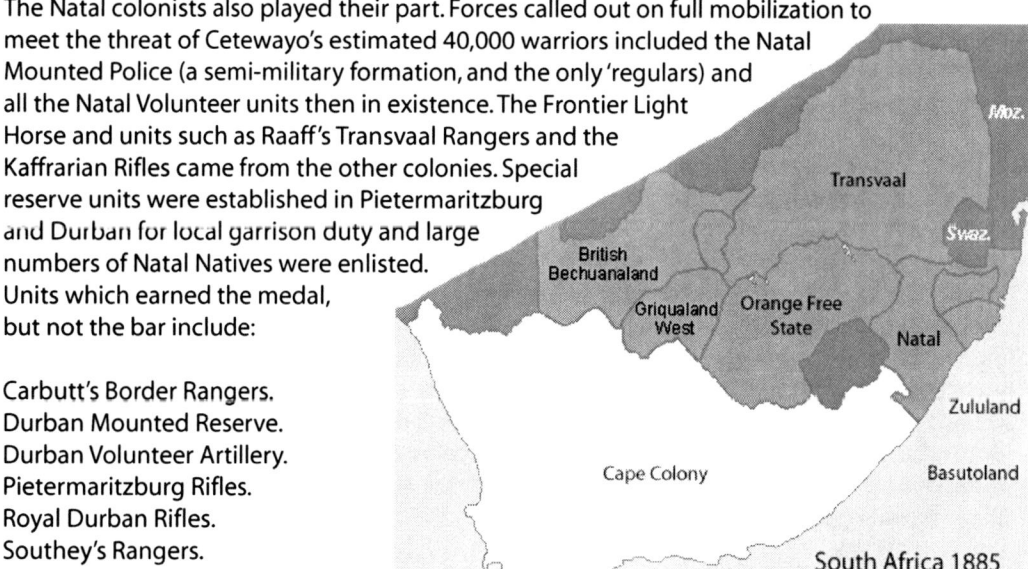

South Africa 1885

Colonial Troops

Colonial Troops
Natal and local units which earned the '1879' bar for the Zulu War.
The Natal government rejected a military force in preference for a system of Volunteer Corps.

Name	Function	Raised	
Alexandra Mounted Rifles.	Natal Volunteers Costal force	Sep	1865
Baker's Horse. (1)	Irregular Cavalry		1878
Bettington's Horse. (2)	Irregular Cavalry	Jan	1879
Border Horse.	Auxiliary Troops	Nov	1878
Buffalo Border Guard.	Natal Volunteers	Oct	1873
Dunn's Scouts. (3)	Foot Scouts	Jan	1879
Durban Mounted Rifles.	Natal Volunteers Costal force		1873
Ferreira's Horse.	Served with Woods Column	Jan	1879
Frontier Light Horse.	Irregular Cavalry		1877
Isipingo Mounted Rifles. (4)	Natal Volunteers Costal force		1878
Kaffrarian Rifles.	With General Wood	Feb	1879
Lonsdale's Horse.	Irregular Cavalry	Feb	1879
Natal Carbineers.	Natal Volunteers		1855
Natal Horse.	Irregular Cavalry		1877
Natal Hussars.	Natal Volunteers Costal force		1865
Natal Light Horse.	Irregular Cavalry	Mar	1879
Natal Mounted Police. (5)	Full time police force not part of the Natal Volunteers	Nov	1878
Natal Native Contingent	Auxiliary Troops (Five Battalions)	Nov	1878
Natal Native Horse. (6)	Joined Woods No 4 Column	Feb	1879
Natal Native Pioneers.	Road repairs, earthworks etc	Nov	1878
Newcastle Mounted Rifles.	Natal Volunteers		1864
Stanger Mounted Rifles.	Natal Volunteers Costal force	Nov	1875
Transvaal Rangers (Raaff's)	Irregular Cavalry	Nov	1878
Uys' Burghers.	Boer Scouts & Cavalry	Jan	1879
Victoria Mounted Rifles.	Natal Volunteers Costal force	Nov	1862
Weenen Yeomanry. (7)	Local Volunteer unit		1873
Woods Irregulars	Auxiliary Troops	Dec	1878

1. Major J.F. Baker, who commanded the unit, raised it three times, (1877-8, 1879, 1880-2).
2. Formed by Captain R. Bettington after the disbanding of the 3rd regiment of NNC after Isandlwana.
3. Dunn's Scouts, were recruited, armed and trained by Dunn, and fought in the Second Invasion of Zululand, also taking part in the battle of Gingindlovu.
4. Sent to the Zululand border in March 1879, together with the Alexandra Mounted Rifles, Durban Mounted Rifles and the Natal Hussars, the Isipingo Mounted Rifles was involved in guard duties. The I.M.R. did not cross the Tugela into Zululand, but half its members volunteered to serve in the composite unit the Natal Volunteer Guides. Captain Stainbank was among those who volunteered and was appointed second in command to Captain Friend Addison in the N.V.G.
5. Placed under military command on the 2nd November 1878, 100 NMP crossed into Zululand.
6. After the defeat at Isandlwana the Natal Native Mounted Contingent was reorganised into the Natal Native Horse.
7. Weenen Yeomanry. B. Units earned the medal, but not the bar.

Colonial Medal Summary

(W/M returned to Woollwich Mint)	Page	W/M	1877	1877-8	1877-9	1877-8-9	1878	1878-9	1879	No Clasp	TOTAL
UNKNOWN UNITS	19			1			1		4		6
ADELAIDE VOLUNTEER CAVALRY	19	42		73		1					74
ALBANY DISTRICT POLICE	19						1				1
ALBANY FINGO LEVY	19	49		53							53
ALBANY MOUNTED POLICE	20						1				1
ALBANY MOUNTED RANGERS	20		3			1					4
ALBANY MOUNTED RIFLES	20			1			1				2
ALBANY MOUNTED VOLUNTEERS	20		3	1							4
ALBANY RANGERS	20	1		48			4		1		53
ALBANY VOLUNTEERS	20						1				1
ALBERT BURGHERS	20	154		264			1				265
ALBERT VOLUNTEERS	22	23	1	41							42
ALBERT DIVISIONAL POLICE	22			1							1
ALEXANDRIA MOUNTED RIFLES	23								29	1	30
ALEXANDRIA MOUNTED RANGERS	23	16		42							42
ALICE LOCAL FINGO LEVY	24						1				1
ALIWAL NORTH BURGHER FORCE	24			2							2
ALIWAL NORTH MOUNTED VOLUNTEERS	24	11	22	1							23
ALIWAL NORTH VOLUNTEERS	24					1					1
AUXILIARY POLICE FORCE	24			1							1
BAKERS HORSE	24	92		1		9	6	2	202		220
BARBERS HORSE	26	61		79			3		1		83
BARKLEY RANGERS	27	38					64				64
BASUTOLAND POLICE	29						1				1
BASUTOLAND CONTINGENT	29								4		4
BEAUFORT RANGERS CAVALRY VOL.	29			60		2					62
BEDFORD BURGHER	30								2		2
BERLIN VOLUNTEER CAVALRY	30			1					1		2
BERLIN VOLUNTEERS (MOUNTED) AND	30										
BERLIN LIGHT INFANTRY	30	44	1	110		11			2		124
BETTINGTONS HORSE	30	53				1		4	107		112
BOLOTWA TEMBUS	31	33		136							136
BOLOTWA VOLUNTEERS	32	5					18				18
BORDER HORSE	32	143			1		1	28	159	58	247
BOWKERS ROVERS	36	101	70	111	1	1	3		1		187
BRABANTS VOLUNTEERS	37	1					1				1
BUCKLEYS NATIVE LEVY	37	46		50							50
BUFFALO BORDER GUARD	38	3							24	1	25
BUFFALO MOUNTED RIFLES	38	1		1							1
BUFFALO VOLUNTEER RIFLES AND LEVY	38	89		198		2	2				202
BURGHER FORCE	40	1					2		6		8
BURGHERSDORP DIVISIONAL POLICE	40					1					1
CAPE FIELD ARTILLERY	40	12		13		39	19	18	3	1	93
CAPE MOUNTED RIFLES AND FRONTIER ARMED AND MOUNTED POLICE	42	191	1	274		173					448

Colonial Medal Summary

(W/M returned to Woollwich Mint)	Page	W/W	1877	1877-8	1877-9	1877-8-9	1878	1878-9	1879	No Clasp	TOTAL
CAPE MOUNTED RIFLEMEN	46	83	1	46		239	4	6	57	2	354
CAPE MOUNTED RIFLEMEN No 6 TROOP	51	16		53		36	1		1		91
CAPE MOUNTED RIFLEMEN No 7 TROOP	51	12		28		64	1				93
CAPE MOUNTED RIFLEMEN No 8 TROOP	52	3		7		11	2	1	1		22
CAPE MOUNTED RIFLEMEN No 9 TROOP	52	29	1	40		69			1		111
CAPE MOUNTED YEOMANRY 1st	53	82				25			282		307
CAPE MOUNTED YEOMANRY 2nd	55	124		1	8	15	1	49	287		361
CAPE MOUNTED YEOMANRY 3rd	59	69		4		48			189	13	254
CAPE NATIVE CONTINGENT	61	1					1				1
CAPE POLICE	61			1							1
CAPE TOWN RIFLES (OR VOLUNTEERS)	61			8		2					10
CARBUTTS BORDER RANGERS	61	12								35	35
CARRINGTONS HORSE	62			4					2		6
CHALUMNA VOLUNTEER CAVALRY	62	6	1	38			6			5	50
CIVIL COMMISSIONER	62			1			1		1		3
CLANWILLIAM VOLUNTEER CORPS	62	31		41			2	1			44
CLARKES POLICE	62							1			1
COLESBERG LIGHT HORSE	62	46		39		4	46	1			90
COLESBERG (PRATTS) VOLUNTEERS	63			1			4				5
COLONIAL CDR'S & LEVY LEADERS	63	9								119	119
COLONIAL CONSTABULARY	64								1		1
CORPS OF GUIDES	65	12					17				17
CRADDOCK BURGHERS	65						3				3
CRADOCK MOUNTED VOLUNTEERS	65	1					2				2
CRADOCK VOLUNTEER RIFLES	65			12		1			2		15
CUYLERVILLE MOUNTED RANGERS	65						1				1
DIAMOND FIELDS HORSE	65	127		156		5	140	7	1		309
DISTRICT NATIVE POLICE	69			8							8
DIVISIONAL POLICE	69	2		2			1				3
DUKE OF EDINBURGH VOL. RIFLES	69	17		60		1	1				62
DURBAN MOUNTED RESERVE	70	5								37	37
DURBAN MOUNTED RIFLES	70									72	72
DURBAN VOLUNTEER ARTILLERY	71									52	52
EAST LONDON BURGHERS	73	10					20				20
EAST LONDON ENGINEERS	73			1			1				2
EAST LONDON VOLUNTEERS	73			1		1					2
ECKERSLEY NATIVES	73								3		3
FERREIRAS HORSE	73	116				2	60	39	100		201
FINGO LEVY	74			4							4
FIRST CITY VOLUNTEER RIFLES	75	30		144							144
FORT BEAUFORT BURGHERS	76	76				1	62		33		96
FORT BEAUFORT HOTTETOT LEVY	76					1					1
FORT BEAUFORT NATIVE POLICE	76						1				1
FORT WHITE MOUNTED VOLUNTEERS	76	28	13	10		2	59				84
FRANKFORT BURGHERS & FINGOE LEVIES	78	28					42				42

Colonial Medal Summary

(W/M returned to Woollwich Mint)	Page	W/M	1877	1877-8	1877-9	1877-8-9	1878	1878-9	1879	No Clasp	TOTAL
FRANKFORT INFANTRY	78								1		1
FRONTIER ARMED AND MOUNTED POLICE	78	30	1	80		74	2		4		161
FRONTIER GUARD	80								1		1
FRONTIER LIGHT HORSE	80	182		29		83	17	7	321	25	482
FRONTIER MOUNTED RIFLEMEN	94	170		261		33	1				295
FROSTS FINGO LEVY	96							1			1
GEORGE MOUNTED VOLUNTEERS	96	17					27				27
GERMAN BURGHER CONTINGENT HORSE and FOOT	96	16		73							73
GERMAN CAPE RIFLES	96						2				2
GERMAN VOLUNTEER RIFLE CORPS and BURGHER CONTINGENT	96	48		79							79
GONOBIE VOLUNTEERS	96		1								1
GRAAFF REINETT VOLUNTEERS	98	12					26				26
GRAHAMSTOWN VOL. HORSE ARTILLERY	98		2	9		5	1	4	7		28
GRAHAMSTOWN VOL. RIFLE CORPS	98	33		104							104
GRIQUALAND WEST CONSTABULARY	99	23					64				64
GRIQUALAND WEST LIGHT INFANTRY	100	85					130				130
GRIQUALAND WEST NATIVE CONTINGENT	101	1					9	1			10
GRIQUALAND WEST VOL. ARTILLERY	101	16					28				28
GRIQUALAND WEST VOL. FIELD FORCE	101			1			2				3
GRIQUATOWN BURGHERS	101						1				1
HARVEYS HORSE	101	1							1		1
HERSCHELS MOUNTED VOLUNTEERS	101	3							59		59
HERSCHELS NATIVE CONTINGENT	101	333							1031		1031
HEYNES FINGO LEVY	108			1							1
HOTTENTOT LEVY No. 1 COY	108	22		104							104
HATTENTOT MILITIA and LEVY	109	6		46		1					47
HUMANSCORP LIGHT HORSE	109			1			1				2
INSIDANJE COLUMN	110			1							1
ISIPINGO MOUNTED RIFLES	110	2							1	39	40
JAMESTOWN MOUNTED VOL. RIFLES	110	21					40	1	1		42
JANSENVILLE YEOMANRY	110	2				1	2	3			6
KAFFRARIAN MOUNTED VOLUNTEERS	110	1	1								1
KAFFRARIAN RANGERS	110	77		122			1	1			124
KAFFRARIAN RIFLES	111	6				2		5	6		13
KAFFRARIAN VOLUNTEERS	111	53	2	132				1			135
KAFFRARIAN VOLUNTEER ARTILLERY	112	3		15							15
KAMAS NATIVE LEVY	112	41		113							113
KAMASTONE FINGO LEVIES	116			1			1				2
KEI ROAD BURGHER FORCE	116	1		1				1			2
KEISKAMA HOEK BURGHER FORCE	116	6		41							41
KEISKAMA HOEK VOL. CORPS INFANTRY	116	4		20							20
KEISKAMA HOEK VOL. MOUNTED CORPS	117	6		57		2	1				60
KIMBERLY HORSE	117	66				2	2	29	81	1	115

Colonial Medal Summary

(W/M returned to Woollwich Mint)	Page	W/M	1877	1877-8	1877-9	1877-8-9	1878	1878-9	1879	No Clasp	TOTAL
KIMBERLY RANGERS	118							1			1
KING WILLIAM'S TOWN VETERAN VOL.	118			29							29
KING WILLIAM'S TOWN VOL. ARTILLERY	118			4			1				5
KOKSTADY VOLUNTEERS	118	1					1				1
KOMGHA FINGO LEVY	118						103				103
LEACHS FINGOES	119	69		94							94
LONSDALES HORSE	119	32				6	1	1	85		93
LONSDALES MOUNTED RIFLES	121	4							10		10
LYDENBURG RIFLES	121	47						4	102		106
MACLEANS FINGO LEVIES	126			1							1
MAFETENG CONTINGENT	126							1			1
MAJOR LARKINS POLICE	126							1			1
MAJOR NESBITTS	126						1				1
MATATIELE FIELD FORCE	126						1				1
MOUNTED EUROPEAN TROOPS	126							1			1
MEDICAL OFFICERS COLONIAL FORCES	126	3		3		2	2	3	5		15
MURRAYS ORANGE ROVERS	126	20		41		1					42
MURRAYSBURG VOL CAVALRY	127	8					34				34
NATAL CARBINEERS	127								75		75
NATAL HORSE	129	9				5		6	20	1	32
NATAL HUSSARS	129								40		40
NATAL LIGHT HORSE	130	33							152	2	154
NATAL MOUNTED INFANTRY	131			1							1
NATAL MOUNTED POLICE & NATIVE POLICE	131	7							166	1	167
NATAL MOUNTED POLICE HEADQUARTERS and RESERVES, includes NATIVE POLICE	133	7								89	89
NATAL NATIVE CONTINGENT	135	16				8	1	11	71	9	100
1st BATTALION	140	1				2			46		48
2nd BATTALION	140							1	75		76
3rd BATTALION	141							2	3		5
4th BATTALION	141					9			25		34
5th BATTALION	141	8				33			17		50
NATAL NATIVE HORSE	142	12							17		17
NATAL NATIVE LEVIES	142								5		5
NATAL NATIVE PIONEERS	142	1						1	11	1	13
NATAL VOLUNTEER FORCE	142								1		1
NATIVE ARTILLERY	142								1		1
NELSONS BURGHERS	142	5		18							18
NESBITTS LIGHT HORSE	142						1				1
NEWCASTLE MOUNTED RIFLES	142	10							37	1	38
NEWCASTLE SCOUTS	143									3	3
NEW ENGLAND CONTINGENT	143			1							1
NORTHERN BORDER HORSE	143	6		10		1		2	2		15
NORTHERN BORDER POLICE FORCE	146	26						56			56
ONE STAR DIAMOND CONTINGENT	146	85					169				169

Colonial Medal Summary

(W/M returned to Woollwich Mint)	Page	W/M	1877	1877-8	1877-9	1877-8-9	1878	1878-9	1879	No Clasp	TOTAL
OUDTSHOORN VOLUNTEERS	147			1			1				2
PANMURE BURGHERS	147			1							1
PEDDIE FINGO LEVY	147	4		8		1	1				10
PEDDIE MOUNTED BURGHER	147	1					2				2
PIETERMARITZBURG RIFLES	147	2								108	108
PONTOON CORPS	148	1							1		1
PORT ELIZABETH MILITIA No. 1 COY	148	28		43							43
PORT ELIZABETH MILITIA No. 2 COY	148	29		53		1	2				56
PORT ELIZABETH MOUNTED RANGERS	149	1		1			2		1		4
PORT ELIZABETH VOLUNTEER HORSE	149	20		56		7					63
PORT ELIZABETH VOLUNTEERS	149					1					1
PRINCE ALFREDS GUARD RIFLE VOL.	149	27	34	85		14		1			134
PRINCE ALFRED'S OWN CAPE VOLUNTEER ARTILLERY	150	6		29			15				44
PULLEINES RANGERS	151	57		43		45	5	1	1	1	96
PULLENS FINGO LEVY	151	45		51							51
QUEENSTOWN BURGHER FORCE	152	115		143							143
QUEENSTOWN DIVISIONAL POLICE	152						1				1
QUEENSTOWN LIGHT HORSE	152						1				1
QUEENSTOWN VOLUNTEER CONTINGENT	153	160	1	328		5	1				335
QUEENSTOWN VOLUNTEER RIFLE CORPS	155	9		30		25			33	1	89
RICHMOND MOUNTED VOLUNTEERS	156	1					3				3
RIVERSDALE MOUNTED BURGHERS	156			2			52				54
ROYAL DURBAN RIFLES	156	8								102	102
RUSTENBURG NATIVE CONTINGENT	157								6		6
SAMSON'S HORSE	157	21		75			1				76
SCHERMBUCKERS HORSE	158	1				1	1	1			3
SHEPSTONES NATIVE HORSE	158	25							89		89
SIDBURY MOUNTED RANGERS	158	12	8	13		1	10				32
SKERSBERG NATIVE CONTINGENT	160							1			1
SHYMANS BURGHERS	160	18					33				33
SIMONSTOWN NATIVE CONTINGENT	160						1				1
SOMERSET EAST BURGHER	160	1							1		1
SOMERSET EAST CONTINGENT	160	51					78				78
SOMERSET EAST VOL. CONTINGENT	160	94		145		1					146
SOUTHEYS RANGERS	161	73		33			2			65	100
STANGER MOUNTED RIFLES	162								54	1	55
STEVENSONS HORSE	162	38		42		28					70
STOCKENSTROOM RANGERS	163	26		27		11			6		44
STOCKENSTROOM RIFLE VOLUNTEERS	163	3				19					19
STOCKENSTROOM VOLUNTEER RIFLES	163	5					2	20	20		42
STREATFIELDS FINGO LEVIES	164			13			1				14
STUTTERHEIM FOOT POLICE	164	27		4			29				33
STUTTERHEIM LIGHT INFANTRY VOL.	164	13		40							40
STUTTERHEIM MOUNTED POLICE	164	16		2			40	5		1	48

Colonial Medal Summary

(W/M returned to Woollwich Mint)	Page	W/M	1877	1877-8	1877-9	1877-8-9	1878	1878-9	1879	No Clasp	TOTAL
SWAMIES KAFFERS	165	7					10				10
SWAZIE CONTINGENT	165	2							7		7
TAMBOOKIELAND DIVISION	165			5							5
TARKASTAD BURGHER CONTINGENT	165	1					1				1
TARKASTAD SOUTH RANGERS	165	7					20				20
TEMBU LEVIES	165			4							4
TRANSKEI FINGOES	165			3		2					5
TRANSKEI (N) FINGO LEVY	165	1		3			1				4
TRANSKEI FINGO MILITIA	165			6							6
TRANSKEI RIFLES	165	87	1	75		34			1	1	112
TRANSPORT SERVICE DEPARTMENT	166								1		1
TRANSVAAL ARTILLERY	166	13					13	4	22		39
TRANSVAAL BORDER HORSE	166								1		1
TRANSVAAL MOUNTED RIFLES	167	73		1			1		158	1	161
TRANSVAAL MOUNTED VOL. FORCES (STAFF)	168			1					12		13
TRANSVAAL RANGERS	168	133					101	20	122		243
TSHUMIE VOLUNTEERS	171	142		153							153
UPINGTONS FOOT	174	19		30							30
UTRECHT BURGHER	174								1		1
UTRECHT NATIVE LEVIES	174								6		6
VAALHOEK MOUNTED VOLUNTEERS	174						1				1
VAN DE VENTERS VOLUNTEER CORPS	174	1							2		2
VICTORIA MOUNTED RIFLES	174								50		50
VICTORIA WEST VOLUNTEERS	177						1				1
VON SUEENBERG RANGERS	177	1		3			4				7
WEENEN YEOMANRY	177	1							19		19
WHITTLESEA MOUNTED RIFLES	177			1							1
WINTERBERG GREYS VOLUNTEERS	177	15					29				29
WODEHOUSE TRUE BLUES	177	55	1	22		6	71	8			108
WOODS IRREGULARS 1st BATTALION	178					1			4		5
WOODS IRREGULARS 2nd BATTALION	178								2		2
ZENIZE MOUNTED CORPS BURGHERS	178								1		1
ZOUTPANSBERG NATIVE CONTINGENT	178								5		5
TOTAL CLASPS AND MEDALS RETURNED TO WOOLWICH/MINT (W/M)		5378	169	5341	10	1243	1821	360	4616	849	14409

Adolf Heinrich Carstensen. SOUTH AFRICA Clasp 1879 / IRON CROSS 2nd CLASS 1870
Sekonde-Lieutenant Carstensen served in the Schleswig-Holsteinisches Feld-Artillerie-Regiment Nr. 9. Commissioned on 21 Sep 1870, he was awarded the EKII for actions during the seige of Metz. He made his way to South Africa and fought in the Zulu War probably Morosi Campaign medal is named to: Lieutenant in the Cape Mounted Yeomanry. In 1880 he joined the Cape Mounted Rifles and fought in the Gun War (MID's and in various books).He left the CMR's after the War in 1881 and died in 1909 in in German S.W Africa . Carstensen kept a keen interest in and contact with Artillery as two documents were found in Pretoria :The first was a letter from Carstensen to General Joubert regarding his trip to the Artillery Camp. The second is a letter from Carstensen to Joubert thanking him for giving his permission for Carstensen to communicate with Krupp. (Information supplied Justin Young)

Adelaide Volunteer Cavalry

UNITS UNKNOWN
CAPTAIN
Campbell   C.C   1878
LIEUTENANT
#Carstensen A   1879
See Cape Mounted Riflemen
Martin   C.J   1879
NO RANK SHOWN
Heathcote J.W   1877-8
Johar   J   1879
TROOPER
Stier   C.M   1879

ADELAIDE VOLUNTEER CAVALRY.
The Commanding Officer was Lt. J. Castleman who was commissioned on 17 September, 1877. The strength in April, 1878, rose to 76, patrols were carried out between Koonap Post and Fort Beaufort The corps was noted in June, 1880, as being in course of disbandment.
CAPTAIN
Holland   F   1877-8
SURGEON
Mathew   T.P.O.   1877-8 r
LIEUTENANT
Castleman J   1877-8
2nd LIEUTENANT
Wood   J   1877-8
SERGEANT
Cross   E   1877-8
Harley   A   1877-8
Mc Master J   1877-8 r
Mills   R   1877-8
Muggleton A.D   1877-8 r
CORPORAL
Mc Master D.H   1877-8
Mathew   A   1877-8 r
Vice   W   1877-8 r
TROOPER
Ainslie   W   1877-8 r
Andrews   W   1877-8 r
Ashton   T   1077-0 r
Beers (Beer) C   1877-8 r
Bishop Snr W   1877-8
Bishop Jnr W   1877-8
Brink   G   1877-8
Brole   C   1877-8
Chipps   T.W   1877-8
Cross   J   1877-8 r
Cross   R   1877-8 r
Dawson   J   1877-8 r
Dawson   W   1877-8 r
De Beer   J.G   1877-8
Delport Snr L   1877-8 r
Delport Jnr L   1877-8 r
Delport   W   1877-8 r

Farr   J.G   1877-8 r
Fell   W   1877-8 r
Fisher   J   1877-8 r
Harcourt   J   1877-8 r
Harley   F   1877-8 r
Hartley   C   1877-8
Hockley   W   1877-8 r
Kemp   R   1877-8 r
Kemp   W   1877-8 r
King   T   1877-8 r
Leppan   E.H   1877-8
Lilford   A   1877-8
Lilford   F   1877-8
Long   J   1877-8
Mathew   C   1877-8-9
Mc Master F.J   1877-8
Mc Master J   1877-8
Mc Master R   1877-8
Meyer   A   1877-8
Niland   J   1877-8 r
Niland   T   1877-8 r
Norton   L   1877-8
O'Brien   J   1877-8
Pedlar   W   1877-8 r
Pehl   G.P   1877-8 r
Potgieter M   1877-8 r
Richards   A   1877-8 r
Robinson   W.S   1877-8
Schutz   W   1877-8
Scott   A   1877-8
Scott   B   1877-8
Smith   W.G   1877-8
Sparks   B.A   1877-8 r
Sparks   K.R   1877-8 r
Sparks   R   1877-8
Stockenstroom Sir
G Henry Bart   1877-8
Van Der Westhuizen C   1877-8
Vice   G   1877-8 r
Vice   J   1877-8 r
Vice   S   1877-8 r
Vice   W   1877-8 r
Viktor   G   1877-8
Webber   W   1877-8 r
Williams   J   1877-8 r
Wynne   M   1877-8 r

ALBANY DISTRICT POLICE
CORPORAL
Arnold   J   1878

ALBANY FINGO LEVY
Loyal Bantu who served under white officers during the Ninth Kaffir War of 1877-78 on the Eastern Cape Frontier.
Corps disbanded 4th July 1878.

COMMANDING OFFICER
Barrett   S   1877-8
LIEUTENANT
Smith   T   1877-8 r
SERGEANT
Logie   J   1877-8 r
Surmon   A.P.   1877-8
CORPORAL
Mncanywa   1877-8 r
Ndzamela   J   1877-8 r
PRIVATE
Andries   J   1877-8 r
Badhlabantu J   1877-8 r
Baliwe   1877-8 r
Barnabas   S   1877-8 r
Bikitsha   J   1877-8 r
Dalani   S   1877-8 r
Dumzela   S   1877-8 r
Feni   N   1877-8 r
Giwa   E   1877-8 r
Giwa   P   1877-8 r
Kandaniso S   1877-8 r
Klabeni   D   1877-8 r
Madnna   1877-8 r
Magonfeni   1877-8 r
Majali   1877-8 r
Makinana   1877-8 r
Manone   T   1877-8 r
Masumpa   T   1877-8 r
Matiwana   1877-8 r
Mbali   1877-8 r
Mbanbo   T   1877-8 r
Mbokela   J   1877-8 r
Meikwane   1877-8 r
Mfanwana   S   1877-8 r
Mgobo   1877-8 r
Mgolombani K   1877-8 r
Mnyawana   N   1877-8 r
Moimbe   S   1877-8 r
Mxrengana   1877-8 r
Ngeantu   1877-8 r
Ngxrobongwana   1877-8 r
Njenjewana D   1877-8
Nikelo   1877 8 r
Nyangaza   1877-8 r
Nzuzu   1877-8 r
Petros   H   1877-8 r
Rolelo   J   1877-8 r
Saul   S   1877-8
Seti   J   1877-8
Sidiwa   1877-8 r
Sika   M   1877-8 r
Simtunzi   J   1877-8 r
Sipika   W   1877-8 r
Yekelo   1877-8 r
Youngman   S   1877-8 r
Zipo   J   1877-8 r
Zulu   D   1877-8 r

Albany Mounted Police

ALBANY MOUNTED POLICE.
STOREKEEPER
Sermon J.J 1878

ALBANY MOUNTED RANGERS.
PRIVATE
Deacon W.R 1877
Thomson J 1877
RANK NOT KNOWN
Kelly J 1877-8-9
Pocock J.T 1877

ALBANY MOUNTED RIFLES.
CAPTAIN
Simkins W.W 1878
Tillard R 1877-8

ALBANY MOUNTED VOLUNTEERS.
SERGEANT
Keen W 1877
TROOPER
Gaw J 1877
Pryce J.J 1877
Tyson A.O 1877-8

ALBANY RANGERS
A body of Salem and Sidbury volunteers. One hundred and twenty mounted Volunteers, were sent off to Stutterheim, under **Captain Gardner** of the Albany Volunteer's. **Captain Gosset** was sent with them as staff-officer, to report and advise. On March 11th 1878 engagement with the enemy, 9 Gaikas killed. Fought in the Gun war (1880), British Bechuanaland 1884.
CAPTAIN
Attwell W.J 1877-8
Gardner J 1877-8
LIEUTENANT
Crouch G.V 1877-8
Hayes F.J 1877-8
2ND LIEUTENANT
Hill G 1877-8
SERGEANT
Berrington J.E 1877-8
Bruce R.M 1877-8
Crosbie R 1877-8
Emslie R 1877-8
Shaw W.A 1877-8
Accidently killed.
CORPORAL
Amm P 1877-8
Emslie G 1877-8

Hancock W 1877-8
Hayton J.E 1877-8
Webber S 1877-8
Wood S 1877-8
BUGLER
Bruce A 1877-8
PRIVATE/TROOPER
Amu E.J 1877-8
Baines S.J 1877-8
Clack T 1877-8
Crosbie W 1877-8
Cross G.W 1877-8
Cyrns H 1877-8
Decroo H.A 1877-8
Emslie C.J 1877-8
Emslie J 1877-8
Emslie S 1877-8
Gardner C 1877-8
Gravett R 1877-8
Gravett W 1877-8
Gunn H 1877-8
Helwig F 1879
Hewson G 1877-8
Hewson J 1877-8
Holliday J 1877-8
Impey D 1877-8
Long C 1877-8
Long E 1877-8
Long J 1877-8
Long W 1877-8
Maree J 1877-8
Maree J.J 1878
Mycock W 1877-8 r
Penny E 1877-8
Penny W 1878
Penny W.G 1878
Powell E.J 1877-8
Richardson W 1877-8
Shaw B.J 1878
Webber W 1877-8
Wilkinson R 1877-8
Willmore H 1877-8
RANK NOT KNOWN
Hayton W 1877-8

ALBANY VOLUNTEERS.
LIEUTENANT
Austin H.A 1878 r

ALBERT BURGHERS.
COMMANDANT
Pelzer T.G.J 1877-8
CAPTAIN
Cloete G.C.J 1877-8 r
Jooste F 1877-8 r

Kruger P 1877-8
Strydom S.J 1877-8
Van Aswegen J 1877-8
Vorster A 1877-8 r
LIEUTENANT
Coetze G.A 1877-8
Coetze H.B 1877-8 r
Greyvensteyn M 1877-8
Kruger J.C 1877-8
KIA 1881
Vorster Jan 1877-8
QUARTERMASTER
Muller M 1877-8 r
SERGEANT
Bothma C.S 1877-8
Brown J.W 1877-8
Grobler P.J 1877-8
Koekemoer A 1877-8 r
Lienbenberg A 1877-8
Mahairy M 1877-8
Olivier C 1877-8
Van Heerden A 1877-8
Vorster Johannes 1877-8
CORPORAL
Albertse J 1877-8
Cloete P.J 1877-8 r
Coetze J.J 1877-8 r
Coetze N 1877-8 r
De Klerk A 1877-8 r
De Klerk A 1877-8
Du Plessis N 1877-8
Greyling B.C.J 1877-8
Hattingh P 1877-8
Havinga A 1877-8
Kruger G.L 1877-8 r
Kruger H.S 1877-8 r
Kruger J 1877-8 r
Smit J 1877-8
Snyman H 1877-8 r
Steyn W 1877-8 r
Van der Walt N 1877-8 r
Van Pletzen A 1877-8
Venter S 1877-8
PRIVATE
Abrahams J 1877-8
Abrahams N 1877-8 r
Albertse B 1877-8
Albertse G.J 1877-8
Aucamp P 1877-8
Benadie G 1877-8 r
Botha Jr J 1877-8
Botha J.D 1877-8 r
Briel H 1877-8 r
Brown S 1877-8 r
Butler W 1877-8 r

Dixons Gazette No47 Autumn 2006 4375 1 clasp, 1877-8. Captain J. Van Aswegen, Albert Burghers. The Albert Burghers was made up of Cape Burghers who volunteered for the Ninth Kaffir War. They also served with the HQ Column in Basutoland in 1880. NEF £650.

Albert Burghers

Albany Mounted Volunteers

Buys	B	1877-8 r
Buys	P	1877-8 r
Buys	S	1877-8 r
Cloete	A	1877-8
Cloete	A.J	1877-8 r
Cloete	P.J	1877-8 r
Coetze	C	1877-8 r
Coetze	Frans	1877-8 r
Coetze	Frans	1877-8
Coetze	G	1877-8 r
Coetze	G	1877-8
Coetze	H	1877-8
Coetze	Jan	1877-8
Coetze	Johannes	1877-8
Coetze	S. P	1877-8 r
Coetze	Jnr P	1877-8 r
Coetzer	B	1877-8 r
Coetzer	D	1877-8 r
Coetzer	J	1877-8 r
Coetzer	W	1877-8
De Beer	Jan	1877-8 r
De Beer	John	1877-8 r
De Beer	Johannes	1877-8 r
De Beer	John	1877-8
De Beer	M	1877-8 r
De Bruin	D.S	1877-8
De Bruin	T	1877-8
De Jager	C	1877-8 r
De Jager	L	1877-8 r
De Klerk	B	1877-8 r
De Klerk	B	1877-8 r
De Klerk	B	1877-8
De Klerk	B	1877-8
De Klerk (Johns/Son)	B	1877-8
De Klerk (W/Son)	B	1877-8
De Klerk	D.W	1877-8
De Klerk	G	1877-8
De Klerk	Jacob	1877-8
De Klerk	Jan	1877-8
De Klerk	J.C	1877-8
De Klerk	W.A	1877-8 r
De Klerk	W.A	1877-8 r
De Kock	H	1877-8 r
Diedericks	F	1877-8 r
Du Plessis	A	1877-8 r
Du Plessis	F	1877-8 r
Du Plessi	S. G	1877-8
Du Plessis	J	1877-8 r
Du Plessis	M	1877-8
Du Plessis	O	1877-8 r
Du Plessis	W	1877-8 r
Duvenhage	J	1877-8 r
Edmonds	W.C.G	1877-8 r
Erlank	A.G	1877-8 r
Erlank	J	1877-8
Fourie	J	1877-8
Fourie	J.L	1877-8
Fourie	L	1877-8 r
Fourie	L	1877-8 r
Gelderblom	B.J	1877-8
Gous	F	1877-8
Gous	W.J	1877-8
Greyvensteyn	B.J	1877-8 r
Greyvensteyn	H	1877-8 r
Greyvensteyn	H	1877-8 r
Greyvensteyn	M	1877-8
Grobler	C	1877-8 r
Grobler	F	1877-8
Grobler	H.M	1877-8
Grobler	N.J	1877-8 r
Haywood	W.J	1877-8
Henning	F	1877-8
Howard	J	1877-8 r
Jansen	S	1877-8 r
Kerkman	J	1877-8
Klaassen	W	1877-8
Kleynhans	H	1877-8 r
Kleynhans	T	1877-8 r
Koekomoer	J	1877-8 r
Kruger	A	1877-8 r
Kruger	A.H	1877-8 r
Kruger	B	1877-8 r
Kruger	C	1877-8 r
Kruger	F	1877-8
Kruger Jnr	F	1877-8 r
Kruger	G	1877-8
Kruger Jnr	G.L	1877-8
Kruger	H	1877-8 r
Kruger Jacob	P	1877-8 r
Kruger	Jacobus	1877-8 r
KrugerJacobus	P	1877-8
Kruger	Johannes	1877-8
Kruger	Johannes	1877-8
Kruger	J.A	1877-8
Kruger	Jonathan	1877-8
Kruger (J/Son)	J.C	1877-8 r
Kruger	P	1877-8 r
Kruger	T	1877-8 r
Labuscagne	A	187-8 r
Labuscagne	J	1877-8 r
Labuscagne	P	1877-8 r
Lambinon	L	1877-8
Lategan	A.W	1877-8 r
Lategan	H	1877-8 r
Lategan	J	1877-8
Lessing	D	1877-8 r
Lessing	J	1877-8
Liebenberg	D	1877-8 r
Liebenberg	F	1877-8 r
Londt	S	1877-8 r
Louw	W	1877-8 r
Louw	W.J	1877-8 r
Marais	B.J	1877-8
Marais	C	1877-8 r
Marais	J.F	1877-8 r

Albert Burghers

Name		Year	Name		Year	Rank/Name		Year
Meyburgh	C	1877-8	Van der Heever	D	1877-8	**QUARTERMASTER**		
Meyburgh	G	1877-8	Van der Heever	D	1877-8	Eaton	F.A	1877-8
Meyburgh	P	1877-8 r	Van der Heever	G.A	1877-8 r	**SERGEANT**		
Nienaber	J	1877-8	Van der Heever	S	1877-8 r	Collary	J	1877-8
Olivier	B	1877-8 r	Van der Linde	J	1877-8 r	Also had Medal for the 1854 War.		
Olivier	C	1877-8	Van der Vyver	S	1877-8 r	Vice	C.J	1877-8 r
Olivier	J	1877-8	Van der Walt	A	1877-8 r	**CORPORAL**		
Olivier	J	1877-8	Van der Walt	B	1877-8	Hartley	F.W	1877-8 r
Oosthuizen	A	1877-8 r	Van der Walt Jnr	J	1877-8	Henker	J.C	1877-8
Pansegrouw	J	1877-8	Van der Walt(M/Son)	N	1877-8 r	Warner	T	1877-8
Pelzer	C	1877-8 r	Van der Walt (S/Son)	N	1877-8 r	**PRIVATE**		
Pelzler	C.J.H	1877-8	Van der Walt	T	1877-8	Adcock	G	1877-8 r
Pelzer	P	1877-8	Van Jaarsveld	J	1877-8 r	Barrable	D	1877-8 r
Peyper	A	1877-8 r	Van Niekerk	C	1877-8 r	Brady	H.J	1877-8
Pienaar	A	1877-8 r	Van Rensburg	J.J	1877-8 r	Brandt	W	1877-8
Pienaar	J	1877-8 r	Van Rooyen	N	1877-8	Bret	C	1877-8 r
Pienaar	J.G	1877-8 r	Van Rooyen	P	1877-8	Brutt	W	1877-8
Pienaar	J.J	1877-8 r	Van Tonder	A	1877-8	Buckley	C	1877-8 r
Potgieter	J	1877-8 r	Van Wyk	A	1877-8	Edmonds	W	1877-8
Pretorius	F	1877-8 r	Van Wyk	B	1877-8 r	Freemantle	J	1877-8
Putter	D	1877-8 r	Van Wyk	Jacob	1877-8 r	Goertz	G	1877-8 r
Putter	J	1877-8 r	Van Wyk	Jacobus	1877-8 r	Graatz	F.L.C	1877-8
Ritchie	J	1877-8 r	Van Wyk	L	1877-8	Haytor	G	1877-8 r
Roelofze	B	1877-8	Van Wyk	L	1877-8 r	Henkes	G	1877-8 r
Roelofze	H	1877-8	Van Wyk	P	1877-8 r	Herman	W	1877-8 r
Roelofze	N	1877-8	Van Wyk	W	1877-8 r	Housley	G	1877-8 r
Roelofze	W	1877-8 r	Van Zyl	G.J	1878	Kannemeyer	H	1877-8 r
Roodt	C	1877-8 r	Venter	A	1877-8	Kay	W	1877-8
Roodt	P	1877-8 r	Venter	B	1877-8 r	Keickhaefir	W	1877-8
Rowch	J	1877-8 r	Venter	C.C.M	1877-8	Knobil	W	1877-8 r
Roux	A	1877-8	Venter	D.E	1877-8	Lendt	A	1877-8 r
Sawer	N	1877-8	Venter	H	1877-8	**Louchlin**	**W**	**1877-8 r**
Sawer	W	1877-8	Venter	Petrus	1877-8 r	KIA Jundwalu		
Schoeman	B.J	1877-8	Venter	Phillipus	1877-8 r	Marron	T	1877-8 r
Schraader	J	1877-8 r	Venter Jnr	P	1877-8	**Moubrey**	**W**	**1877-8 r**
Schraader	W	1877-8 r	Viljoen	H	1877-8	KIA Jundwalu		
Sleebusch	J.L.W	1877-8	Vorster	A	1877-8 r	Murray	C	1877-8 r
Sleebusch	L	1877-8 r	Vorster	B.J	1877-8	Schwaizer	C.A	1877-8
Smit	F	1877-8	Vorster	G	1877-8	Spiller	J	1877-8 r
Smit	F.J	1877-8 r	Vorster	W	1877-8 r	Van Zyl	H	1877-8
Smit	H	1877-8	Zwarts	F	1877-8 r	Van Broombsen	D	1877-8 r
Smit	L	1877-8 r	Zwarts	J	1877-8 r	## Warner	G	1877-8
Smit	J.P	1877-8	Zwarts	J	1877-8 r	Weimer	W	1877-8 r
Stapelberg	F	1877-8 r	Zwarts	P	1877-8 r	**Welsh**	**G**	**1877-8 r**
Steenkamp	H	1877-8 r	Zwarts	W	1877-8 r	KIA Jundwalu		
Steenkamp	P	1877-8 r				West	E	1877-8 r
Steyn	J	1877-8 r	**ALBERT VOLUNTEERS.**			Williams	W	1877-8 r
Swanepoel	J	1877-8 r	CAPTAIN					
Swanepoel	J.J	1877-8	# Brady	H.J	1877-8	**ALBERT DIVISIONAL POLICE.**		
Thomasse	Z	1877-8 r	Also had Medal for the 1854 War.			TROOPER		
Uys	H	1877-8 r	Williams	E	1877	Ford	T.H	1877-8
Van der Berg	T	1877-8 r	LIEUTENANT					
Van der Heever	C	1877-8	Bods	A	1877-8			

Dixons Gazette No36 Winter 2003/4 4018 1 clasp, 1877-8. Captain H.J Brady, Albert Volunteers. Albert Volunteers was raised from Cape Burghers who volunteered for service in the 9th Frontier War. They had thee men killed in the action at Jumdwalu. Fine £550.00

##Dixons Gazette No31 Autumn 2002 3302 1 clasp, 1877-8. Private G. Warner, Albert Volunteers. EF £270.00

Alexandra Mounted Rifles

The Alexandra Mounted Rifles in the 1870s

ALEXANDRA MOUNTED RIFLES.
Founded in 1865. Captain Arbuthnot commanded the unit in Pearson's column.

CAPTAIN
*Arbuthnot W.T   1879
LIEUTENANT
*Cooke   1879
*Kirkman J   No clasp
QUARTERMASTER
*# Kirkman T   1879
SERGEANT MAJOR
*Bru de Wold H.T   1879
*Parkin   Not on medal roll
SERGEANT
*Arbuthnot F.J   1879
*Archibald   Not on medal roll
Fraser   1879
CORPORAL
*Bazley   1879
TRUMPETER
*Arbuthnot St George 1879

TROOPER
*Arbuthnot Mc D   1879
*Arbuthnot N.G   1879
Bazley   G   1879
*Crocker   T   1879
*Crocker   W   1879
Davey   1879
*Fayers   T   1879
*Hawkins   W   1879
*Hawksworth F   1879
*Knox   A   1879
Knox   H   1879
Langton   1879
*Pearce   1879
*Pennington J   1879
*Pigg   C   1879
*Prescott C   1879
*Reynolds C Not on medal roll
*Reynolds S   1879
Ross   1879
*Saunders C Not on medal roll
*Shooter   B.C   1879
*Shooter   W   1879

Sumner   1879
*Thomas S Not on medal roll
* Reported for service in December 1878. Joined the invading British force at the start of the Anglo-Zulu War

ALEXANDRIA MOUNTED RANGERS
CAPTAIN
Drew   A.S   1877-8
LIEUTENANT
Callaghan J.W   1877-8
Dell   B.J   1877-8
SERGEANT
Callaghan W.C   1877-8
Woest   G.H   1877-8 r
CORPORAL
Mackay   W   1877-8
Scheepers F.J   1877-8
TROOPER
Bissinger C.J   1877-8 r
Bissinger J   1877-8 r
Bissinger N.F   1877-8 r
Bruce   W.R   1877-8

City Coins Postal Auction No 58 29th August 2008, Lot No 238. – SAGS no bar Qr. Mr. Thos. Kirkman VF+Hammer price 12,652 Rand. Alexandra Md. Rifles; Union of SA Commemorative Medal 1910 unnamed as issued Kirkman came to Natal from the UK in 1868 and settled on a Government land grant in Alexandra County, where he eventually concentrated on coffee farming. He served in the Volunteer Force for 14 years: this included 8 months active service during the Zulu War. The Hon. Thomas Kirkman was elected to the Legislative Assembly of Natal, representing Alexandra County, when responsible government was granted to the Colony in 1893. He was nominated as one of the 13 Members of the Legislative Council of Natal in 1897 and reappointed in 1907. In this capacity he received the 1910 Union Medal. Sold with copies of medal rolls and biographical data, including a photo of Kirkman.

Alexandra Mounted Rangers

Busschau	W	1877-8 r
Chowles	E	1877-8
Chowles	J.E	1877-8
Deacon	F.C	1877-8
Deacon	W.H	1877-8
Fick	P.H	1877-8
Gibbon	W.H	1877-8

Also medals from two European Wars.

Henderson	M	1877-8 r
Holtzhausen	J.A	1877-8
Holthausen	P.C	1877-8
Holthausen	T.P	1877-8 r
Kock	J.J	1877-8
Krog	C.F	1877-8
Krog	J.C	1877-8
Krog	J.C	1877-8 r
Mackay	J.C	1877-8
Muller	I.J	1877-8 r
Muller	J.H	1877-8 r
Muller	P.C	1877-8 r
Nightingale	J.E	1877-8
Schalkwyk	E	1877-8
Scheepers	C.F	1877-8
Scheepers	C.F.G	1877-8
Scheepers	J.C	1877-8 r
Scheepers	J.C	1877-8 r
Scheepers	J.M	1877-8
Van Niekerk	J.A	1877-8
Van Rooyen	H.O.T	1877-8 r
Van Rooyen	J.C	1877-8
Van Rooyen	J.J	1877-8 r
Woest	P.J	1877-8 r

ALICE LOCAL FINGO LEVY.
CAPTAIN
Nightingale P   1878

ALIWAL NORTH BURGHER FORCE.
QUATERMASTER SERGEANT
Higgins C.A   1877-8
CORPORAL
Philpott K   1877-8

ALIWAL NORTH MOUNTED VOLUNTEERS.
CAPTAIN
Ramsbolton W   1877-8
LIEUTENANT
Parker J.C   1877
See also Captain J.C. Parker 2nd Cape Mtd Yeomanry.
SERGEANT
Stevens C   1877
CORPORAL
Oxford J.S   1877
Phayer E.C   1877
BUGLER
Pocock J   1877 r

See also 2nd Cape Mtd Yeomanry.

TROOPER
Anderson	K	1877 r
Crooks	T.S	1877
Don	H	1877 r
Earle	W	1877 r

See also 2nd Cape Mtd Yeomanry.

Elliott	W	1877 r

See also 2nd Cape Mtd Yeomanry.

Graham	J	1877
Guthrie	A	1877
Matthews	J	1877 r
Mc Coll	J.C	1877

See also 2nd Cape Mtd Yeomanry.

Ritchie	T	1877 r

See also 2nd Cape Mtd Yeomanry.

Sheen	W	1877

See also 2nd Cape Mtd Yeomanry.

Stander	A.C	1877 r
Stockton	W	1877 r
Thomas	J.C	1877
Watts	G	1877 r
Wayland	F	1877
Wright	W.H	1877 r

ALIWAL NORTH VOLUNTEERS.
TROOPER
Ross A   1877-8-9

AUXILIARY POLICE FORCE
RANK NOT KNOWN
Berndt C   1877-8

BAKER'S HORSE.
Those killed in action (KIA) lost their lives at Inhlobane on 28th March 1879.
COMMANDANT
Barker F.J   1877-8-9
CAPTAIN
# Parminter	W.G	1877-8-9
Pickering	W	1877-8-9
Tomasson	W.H	1879
Wilson	W.D	1877-8-9

See also Lt. W.D Wilson below.
LIEUTENANT
Addie	G	1879
Baines	C	1879
Nelson	H	1879
Parkin	W	1877-8-9
Vernon	C	1879 r
Veron	W.H	1879
Wilson	W.D	1878-9

Clasp 1878 & 1879 in error.
REGIMENTAL SERGEANT MAJOR
Miller H   1877-8-9
TROOP SERGEANT MAJOR
Webb T   1879

White D/S	E	1877-8-9

Died in Hospital 25.8.1879
SQUADRON SERGEANT MAJOR
Moore D/S F   1879
Died in hospital July 29th 1879
SERGEANT MAJOR
Close I   1879
White D/S E   1879 r
QUARTERMASTER SERGEANT
Gray G.R   1879
Mc Donald A.M   1879 r
SERGEANT
Butcher	J	1879
Clifford	J	1879 r
Hallack	C	1879
McDonald	J	1879
Pitt	F	1879
Saunders	E	1879 r
Stanford	J	1879
Storey	G	1879
Webb	J	1879 r
Young	G	1879

CORPORAL
Brockett	E	1879
Buckley	W	1877-8-9
Collings	S	1879 r
Freegard	T	1879
Ferguson	C	1879 r
MacBlaine	W	1879
Mitchell	C	1879
Mitten	J	1879
Smith	F	1879

TROOPER
Adams	J	1879
Adams	P	1879 r
Adlam	B	1879
Allport	I	1879 r
Anstey	C	1879 r
Arthur	R	1879
Ashby	G	1879 r

See also Cpl G Ashby Pulleines Rangers.

Barrett	J	1879 r
Baxhforth	W	1879
Becker	J	1879 r
Behrens	A	1879
Behrens	F	1879
Berry	R	1879
Billingham	A	1879 r
Bowles	W	1879
Bracenia	J	1879 r
Bratherson	J	1879 r
Brazil	W	1879
Bunyard	G	1879
Britt	T	1879 r
Bredie	J	1879 r
Burke	J	1879 r
Bushard	R	1877-8

Bakers Horse

 # Major W. G. Parminter Dix Noonan Web Auction Lot 636, 27 Jun 07

A most unusual South Africa 1877-79 campaign service and exploration pair awarded to Major W. G. Parminter, late Baker's Horse: 'A gallant gentleman of the very best English type', he distinguished himself in the actions at Inhlobane Mountain and Ulundi - one witness to his gallant deeds on the former occasion stated that he was worthy of a V.C. - and went on to join Stanley in the Belgian Congo where he lent valuable assistance to the United States Navy Expedition of 1885.

South Africa 1877-79, 1 clasp, 1877-8-9 (Capt. W. G. Parminter, Baker's Horse); Belgium, Congo Free State, Star of Service, 1st type (1889-1910), with Bar (for 3 Years Service), silver, silver-gilt, 30mm. diam., both contained in an old leather, velvet-lined fitted case, the lid with gilt inscription, 'Africa 1877 to 1889', good extremely fine (2) Hammer price £5200

William George Parminter, who was born in Stuttgart, Germany, first witnessed active service as a Captain in the Baker's Horse squadron of the Frontier Light Horse 1877-78, including operations against the BaPedi in the north-eastern Transvaal, but it was in subsequent operations against the Zulus in 1879 that he particularly distinguished himself, not least in the disastrous action at Inhlobane Mountain.

Gallantry at Inhlobane Mountain

A fellow officer, Lieutenant & Adjutant **William H. Tomasson**, the author of With the Irregulars in the Transvaal (London, 1881), later stated that Parminter was the last man to leave the mountain that day and that his deeds were well worthy of a V.C. (see below). In the event, he was not among the five men nominated to receive the Cross, but we may be sure he carried out similarly gallant rescue work. Our casualties amounted to 17 officers and 82 other ranks killed, besides hundreds wounded, most of whom fell in the headlong flight of Buller's force down "The Devil's Pass" - indeed such was the carnage caused by the Zulus' assegais that they renamed Inhlobane the "Stabbing Mountain". Many vivid accounts of the action survive, most of them written by the men of the Frontier Light Horse, including **Captain Cecil D'Arcy** and **Lieutenants Alfred Blane** and **A. Metcalfe-Smith**, but one in particular - that written by **Sergeant George Mossop** - illustrates the desperate nature of the retreat in the "Devil's Pass":

'Some distance ahead I saw a number of horses bunched together, and came to the conclusion that they were abandoned, for I could not see anyone near. Pushing through them to the edge of the Pass and dismounting, I saw one man standing at my side, looking down. I also looked down and my blood turned cold. The Pass was steep and narrow and choked with boulders.

About 20 yards from where we were standing was free from horsemen, or, rather, of men leading their horses, for no one could sit on a horse in such a place. Below that was a complete jam. Zulus, crawling over the rocks on either side, were jabbing at the men and horses. Some of the men were shooting, and some were using clubbed rifles and fighting their way down. Owing to the rocks on either side the Zulus could not charge. The intervening space was almost filled with dead horses and dead men,white and black. No wonder **Colonel Weatherley** had trotted east to look for another opening. It would have been impossible to get down the Pass in time to avoid the great mass of Zulus sweeping round the base of the hill to cut off all retreat. We could see them quite plainly. Many glancing sights had I seen that day of the Zulus with some of our men, who had fallen into their hands - dead or alive. I do not know! It is not good to write about such sights; all I can say is that it was a horror! Perhaps the man at my side has seen that which induced him to act the way he did. I knew him well, but will not mention his name. "Do you think there is any chance of pushing through?" I asked him. I was obliged to shout to make myself heard. The din was terrific. "Not a hope!" he replied, and placing the muzzle of his carbine to his mouth, he pulled the trigger. A lot of brains or other soft stuff splashed over my neck. It was the last straw! I gave one yell, let go the bridle of my pony, and bounded down into the Pass. My feet landed fairly on the smooth rump of a dead horse, slid from under me, and I shot down, coming to rest on my back upon a dead Zulu. On I scrambled, down over dead horses, men and rocks, until I reached the jam of horsemen. Madly, blindly, recklessly, I fought - my only thought to get away from all these horrors.' In such circumstances, therefore, it is all the more remarkable that Parminter should have chosen to stay behind to the very last, and while we have no direct account of his deeds in the engagement at Khambula a day or two later, we do at least have Tomasson's description of him in action at Ulundi on 4 July 1879.

Gallantry at Ulundi

In his history With the Irregulars in the Transvaal, Tomasson states:

'Now **Colonel Buller** comes up, "Send twenty men to ride up close to those fellows, and draw them on, don't let anyone dismount, and mind that dinga to your right." Captain Parminter goes therefore with those twenty men, and we will go with him. On seeing such a small band coming, the Zulus open out, and immediaely set a trap for us. They send a body down the donga Colonel Buller referred to a moment ago. Even playing for such a stake as they were, they cannot help trying for even so small a trick. We ride close up to them and fire at them, more with the idea of enraging them than doing any damage. It succeeds; furious at being bearded by so small a body, they fire at random and advance. Ah! There it is, one fellow, a pigheaded German gets down, in spite of orders, to fire. Terrified at the shouts and rush of the Zulus, the horse plunges and will not let its rider mount; the man himself, nervous enough now, sees the full extent of his danger. Captain Parminter rides to him with another, and helps the man to mount; now they turn, for there's only just time to get away. As they turn to go, the Zulus, some of whom had crept down the donga, redouble their exertions to cut them off, the rest of the men being safe. These last three ride at a furious pace over the ground, knowing that one false step is certain death. The place is pitted with the artificial holes dug and covered by the enemy, and the grass plaited. It seems wonderful, but these were safely crossed without mishap and again they were safe. The rifle shots resound all round the square from the Irregulars as they draw on the enemy. Effectually they have done it now, and turning they ride for the shelter of the square to avoid that storm they have raised. Very pretty the square seemed, lying there so motionless and still in the morning sun. How soon is the change to be made, and the whole face of it flash and grow pale with the volleys of smoke. Already the artillery are at it hard, and the shells scream over our heads as we ride for the square. Squish! Goes a rocket for Ulundi, hit it fairly as I live, and in a second a hut is in a blaze, but is quenched. The shells drop among the advancing enemy, but as they are mostly in skirmishing order the damage done is slight ... '

Bakers Horse

Byrne	M	1879	Hutchings	W	1879 r	Sharman	W	1879
Callaghan	J	1879	Ingram	W	1879	Skelton	J	1879 r
Campbell	John	1879	James	G	1879 r	Small	A	1878
Campbell	**John**	**KIA 1879 r**	Janson	J	1879 r	Smith	C.W	1879 r
Chamberlain	W.H	1879	Jefferson	T	1879	Smith	H	1879
Christianson (Christian) M KIA 1879 r			Johnson	A	1879	Southern	W	1879 r
Clements	G	1879 r	Johnson	E	1879 r	Stahl	W	1879 r
Coetze	W	1879 r	Jones	E	1879	Stanton	T	1879
Cole	G	1879	Jones	H	1879 r	Stevanos	O	1879 r
Coleman	W	1879	Kearn	J	1879 r	Surgina	L	1879 r
Crichten	R	1879	Keen	M	1879	Suter	E	1879
Damarell	H	1879	Kirkman	G	1879 r	Taylor	G	1879
Darlow	R	1879 r	Lawson	J	1879	Taylor	J	1879 r
Darlow	T	1879	Legge	P	1879	Taylor	R	1879 r
Darwin	**J**	**KIA 1879 r**	Lockhead	P	1879	Thompson	A	1879 r
Davis(David) R KIA 1879 r			Lloyd	Robert	1879	Thibault	J	1879
Degret	J	1879	Lloyd	R	1877-8-9	Thorn D/S W.B		1879
See also Frontier L.Hse.			Lumley	J	1879 r	Died April 5th 1879		
De Swart	B	1879 r	Lyllia	R	1879 r	Torbett	J	1879
Didinker	J	1879	Mac Carthy	J	1879	Tuck	J	1879 r
Dillon	C	1879	Macdonald	A	1879	Turner	W	1879
Douglas	W.D	1879	Mac Gilavany	J	1879	Tyler	R	1879
Driscoll	T	1879	Macgregor	M	1879	Tyndale	E	1879 r
Dubois	F	1879 r	**Mackay**	**A**	**1879 r**	Van Niekerk D/W W 1879 r		
Duggan	J	1879 r	KIA with Border Horse.			Wounded 28.3.1879, died 30.3.1879		
Dunbar	**W KIA**	**1879**	Mac Laughlin A		1879	Varley	J	1879
Edwards	H.F	1878	Mac Mamara P		1879	Verity	W	1879 r
118 Elliott	H	1878	Maloney	J	1879	Vivian	J	1879
Ellis	R	1879 r	Miller	W	1879	Wallace	J	1879
Ericson	J	1879 r	Moore	H	1879 r	Wald	L	1879 r
Everleigh	E	1878	Murphy	H	1879 r	**Walters**	**W KIA**	**1879**
98 Fincher	F	1878-9	Musgrove	W	1879	Walther	H	1879
Fitzgibben	W	1879 r	Musthrop	H	1879	**Ward**	**C KIA**	**1879 r**
Forestall	T	1879	Musthrop	H	1879	Wasserfall J		1879
Francis	N	1879 r	Noman	G	1879	Watson	C	1879
Friskin	C	1879	Norden	J	1879	Webster	J	1879 r
Friskin	H	1879	Nitch	L	1879 r	Weir	P	1879
Gemmell	A	1879 r	O' Brien	W	1879	Welsh	A	1879
Giles	G	1879 r	O' Leary	D	1879 r	Welsh	A	1879
Glass	J.W	1879	Oliver	H	1879 r	Wennemark?C.F		1879
Grant	A	1879 r	Olsen	J	1879 r	Westley	A	1879 r
Gray (Ray)	?	1879 r	O' Reilly	A	1879 r	See also Frontier Light Horse.		
Griffiths	R	1879 r	Overend	H	1879	White	J	1879 r
Haigh	G	1879 r	Overton	G	1879 r	White	R	1879 r
Hammond	F	1879	Parkes	T	1879 r	Wilson	F	1879
Hannan	A	1879	Peacock	T	1879	Wilson	J	1879
Hannan	E	1879	Philpott	E	1879	Wroe	J	1879 r
Hart	T	1879 r	Pickham	H	1879 r	RANK NOT KNOWN		
Hart	W	1879	Pilling	E	1879 r	Ashburner F		1878
Hartley	G	1879	Potgieter	S	1879 r	Mc Gilvray J		??
Heddin	L.R	1879	Powers	J	1879			
Henderson	J	1879	Raven	C.R	1879	**BARBERS HORSE.**		
Henderson	W	1879	Robinson	W	1879 r	CAPTAIN		
Hill	C	1879 r	**Rossom (Rossam) G KIA 1879**			Barber	H	1877-8
Hisner	J	1879 r	Salter	H	1879 r	QUARTERMASTER		
Holliday	F	1879	See also Frontier L.H			Dreyer	J	1877-8 r
Holcher	B	1879 r	Savage	R	1879	LIEUTENANT ADJUTANT		
Hudson	J	1879	Schmidt	R	1879 r	Distin	H	1877-8

Barbers Horse

LIEUTENANT
Cowen   C   1877-8
SERGEANT MAJOR
Sanders H.C   1877-8
SERGEANT
Brehen   E.B   1877-8 r
Leisching F   1877-8 r
CORPORAL
Billsow W   1877-8
Distin   A.S   1877-8
Jansen   H   1877-8
Porter   A   1877-8
MEDICAL MAN
Schneider C.A   1877-8 r
PRIVATE
Abbit   T   1877-8 r
Adams   J   1877-8 r
Baker   E.L   1877-8
Barber   H   1878
Blundell A   1877-8 r
Booysen F.J   1877-8 r
Booysen J   1877-8
Clark   W   1877-8 r
Claxton A.B   1877-8 r
Claxton J   1877-8 r
Coleman J   1877-8 r
De Bear H.P   1877-8 r
Du Plessis J   1877-8 r
Distin   W   1877-8
Earl   H   1877-8
Earl   H.P   1878
Enslin   C.T   1877-8
Fischer R   1877-8 r
Fleming C.L   1879?
Garratt T   1877-8 r
Goosen   C   1877-8 r
Havenga J   1877-8
Hoggan   A   1877-8 r
Kok   J.J   1877-8 r
Krog   M   1877-8 r
Kruger   C   1877-8 r
Lake   T   1877-8 r
Le Roux T   1877-8 r
Loggenberg J   1877-8 r
Lynx   7   1877-8 r
Mackintosh D   1877-8
Marsh   T   1877-8 r
Morgan   W   1877-8 r
Muller   J   1877-8 r
Mills   E   1877-8 r
Oosthuizen A   1877-8 r
Oosthuizen W   1877-8 r
Perry   T   1877-8 r
Pieter   ?   1877-8 r
Plessis T   1877-8 r
Porter   J   1877-8 r
Prichard R.A   1877-8 r

Pryra   C   1877-8 r
Rawstorne L   1877-8 r
Renaki   P.D   1877-8 r
Roberts E   1877-8 r
Rubidge C.W   1877-8 r
Saxton   A.B   1877-8 r
Schneider C.A   1877-8 r
See also Medical Man
  C.A. Schneider this Roll
Thackwray C   1877-8 r
Thackwray G   1877-8 r
Theron   P.W   1877-8 r
Van Blerk B   1877-8 r
Van Blerk C   1877-8 r
Van Blerk P   1877-8 r
Van der Merwe D   1877-8 r
Van der Venter J.H 1877-8 r
Van der Venter L 1877-8 r
Van Heerden J   1877-8 r
Venter W   1877-8
Von Bratt C   1877-8 r
Vorster B.J   1877-8
Vorster C   1877-8 r
Vorster D   1877-8 r
Vorster J   1877-8 r
Walters H.C   1877-8
Walters N   1878
Webb   W   1877-8 r
Webster G   1877-8 r
Ysell   G   1877-8 r
Zwaartz J.G   1877-8 r

BARKLEY RANGERS.
COMMANDANT
Ford   J.H   1878 r
CAPTAIN
Bradshaw G.R.K   1878
LIEUTENANT
Patterson   KIA 1878 r
Puddon   J   1878
QUARTERMASTER
Mintern J   1878 r
Sheenan C.G.S   1878 r
SERGEANT MAJOR
Ford   1878 r
Granger R.K   1878
TROOP SERGEANT MAJOR
Kirby   F.E   1878 r
QUARTERMASTER SERGEANT
Clinksenles T.J   1878
COMMISSARIAT SERGEANT
Jefferson T   1878 r
SERGEANT
Blanch   G.R   1878 r
Mintern J   1878 r
Poole   J.G   1878
Rawstorne S   KIA 1878 r

Redding S   1878
Tapscott G.A   1878
Windsor P.F   1878
CORPORAL
Gillings W   1878 r
Glover   J   1878
Mulligan   1878 r
Noble   H.McL   1878
BLACKSMITH
September P   1878 r
BUTCHER
O' Neil   1878 r
DRIVER
Miller   J   1878 r
INTELLIGENCE DEPARTMENT
Bradle   W   1878 r
Chapman E   1878 r
Myer   R   1878
TROOPER
Albrecht   1878
Almendre J   1878 r
Bishop   G.E   1878
Bishop   J   1878
Butler   M   1878 r
Calder   W   1878 r
Campbell C.L.C KIA 1878
Clam   T   1878 r
Coleman H.A   1878
Dawson T   KIA 1878 r
Danduey   1878
Du Toit T.M   1878
Ford   KIA 1878 r
Ford   1878 r
Fowles   W   1878 r
Grobellar N   1878 r
Hockin   1878 r
Lee   1878 r
Leon   T   1878 r
Mc Carthy J   1878
Mc Euckera R   1878
Melville J   1878 r
Miller   L   1878
Miller Jnr W   1878
Nelson   J   1878 r
Percival O   1878
Rawstorne L KIA 1878
Sealey   1878 r
Sinto   W.J   1878
Thompson T   1878 r
Wagner   G   1878 r
Williams A   1878
Williams J   1878 r
Willmore A   1878 r
Woodward   1878 r
Wright   1878 r

Dixons Gazette No39 Autumn 2004 2891 1 clasp, 1877-8. Private W. Venter, Barbers Horse. EF £350.00

Basutoland Contingent

\# Lieutenant-Colonel H.L. Davies, Commandant of the Basuto Contingent
Sale 7012 Lot 118
A Fine South Africa Campaign Group of Four to Lieutenant-Colonel H.L. Davies, Commandant of the Basuto Contingent and Ever Present Throughout Griffith's, Brabant's and Bayly's Command of the Field Force at the Siege and Capture of Morosi's Mountain Stronghold, 1879, Later Commissioner of Cape Police
South Africa 1877-79, one clasp, 1879 (Commdt. H.L. Davies. Basuto. Contingt.), partly officially corrected; Cape of Good Hope General Service 1880-1897, one clasp, Basutoland (Commdt. H.L. Davies. Staff Office), engraved in upright serif capitals; Queen's South Africa 1899-1902, two clasps, Cape Colony, Orange Free State (Lieut:-Col: H.L. Davies. Cape P.D.I.); King's South Africa 1901-02, two clasps (Lt. Col: H.L. Davies. C.P. Dist. I.), last partly officially corrected, good very fine or better, with portrait photograph of recipient (4)
Hammer Price £2300

Lieutenant-Colonel Henry Lee Davies (1851-1912), born King William's Town, South Africa; appointed Assistant Clerk to C. Griffiths (Governor's Agent in Basutoland), 1871; Second Clerk to the Governor's Agent, 1873; Deputy Post Master 1874; First Clerk and Post Master 1876; Resident Magistrate of the Thaba Bosigo District, 1877; he occupied this post as unrest and conflict grew in surrounding districts and territories, in particular with the Gaika and Galeka tribes and then through into Zululand. This unrest manifested itself in Basutoland with the Baphuti tribe. Led by it's tactically astute military commander Morosi, the tribe rose up in defiance of the restrictions being placed upon them by the governing authorities. They were further encouraged by the British disaster at Isandhlwana, persuading the Cape Government to raise a force of two thousand Basuto Levies to quell the rising.

As Magistrate, Davies would have played an organising role in raising the troops and with the rank of Captain he moved (March 1879) with the force to Palmietfontein on the edge of Morosi's territory. The force under the command of Griffiths consisted of Chief Lerothili and Jonathan's men, one hundred Cape Mounted Riflemen, three hundred Cape Mounted Yeomanry, a number of Fingo Levies under Captain McLean and fifty troopers of the Basutoland Mounted Police commanded by Lieutenant Gaffney.

On the 16th March 1879 Griffiths' sent his entire force to move on Morosi's mountain stronghold. The latter had formidable natural defences, combined with loop-holed 'Schantzes' (walls). The Mounted Police and Davies with the Basutoland Contingent acted as scouts, screening the column's advance on the stronghold. Chief Lerothili moved up the north bank of the Orange, skirmishing and capturing cattle along the way, whilst Davies commanded those detached to the right of the column, leading various patrols.

On the 25th of March Griffith's force camped astride the main route up to the mountain. On the 6th of April he was re-enforced with a further troop of the Cape Mounted Rifles, and two seven pounder mountain guns. The assault began at dawn two days later. Despite a sustained period of heavy shelling, the initial full frontal attack on the stronghold was repulsed by heavy rifle fire from within. The defensive strength of the position combined with the attacking force's lack of assault ladders lead to a general retirement at dusk. Griffiths' force had suffered 5 men killed and 17 wounded. Two Cape Mounted Riflemen were awarded the Victoria Cross for there part in the attempted assault.

The besiegers were re-enforced with the arrival **Colonel C.Y. Brabant** and 140 Cape Mounted Yeomanry. Included in the party was a twelve pounder which had been moved into position by 200 burghers. With the arrival of the new mounted troops and the stark failure of the assault, **Griffiths** pursued a different strategy. The crops in the surrounding area were destroyed and the tribe's cattle captured. Davies led many of these raids, 'Started on 22nd for the purpose of recovering certain horses belonging to men of my contingent which had been stolen by the enemy at the Sebapala River. Force: Basutos under Chiefs Bereng and Alexander Letsie, Popoosi Sikuke and Leshuburn, likewise a detachment of the Basuto Police and Volunteers under Chiefs George and Ntsane Moshesh. In all about 750 men. 1st day - reached cave near Sijamolodi's Village, capturing 150 sheep and goats. Camped close to the cave - strongly fortified and apparently well-manned....... The enemy was evidently expecting attack and due to our numbers abandoned the cave during the night, which greatly surprised me when on entering it I found it a large and formidable one. Threw down the fortifications-consisting of "Schansen" built of ironstone boulders....... The left division came on another cave in the river and finding it occupied attacked and got inside...... but as the cave was deep, with many caverns they had to retire with the loss of 1 killed and 1 wounded' (report from Davies to Griffiths headed 'Camp Qoboshianing, 29th April 1879' refers).

On the 15th of May a detachment under **Colonel Brabant** left the Field Force to patrol fifteen miles up the Quthing. Brabant's force consisted of 85 Cape Yeomanry, a seven pounder and 100 Basutos commanded by Davies. Not long into their patrol they found a concentration of enemy forces in a deep gorge running at right angles to the river. Once again the tribesmen had made the most of natural defences - one end of the gorge was too steep to attempt a descent and the other had several cellar like caves, the passages to which were protected by loopholed stone walls. Over the course of three days Brabant's men shelled the position with artillery fire and hurled dynamite in to the entrances of the caves. Davies, due to his knowledge of the local dialect, attempted to induce the natives to surrender by reasoning with them. He eventually succeeded, with both Chief Riza and Letseka's men agreeing terms The Baphuti lost fifteen men killed, eighty-two were made prisoner, ten of this number had been wounded and three hundred women and children accompanied the men. (Davies received a mention in Brabant's report)

Basutoland Police

Continued from previous page.

On the 30th of May. Brabant assumed command of the main field force. He struggled to make an immediate impact however, with Morosi's men undertaking several daring raids outside of their fortified position. A picket of Yeomanry was surprised during the night at the cost 21 killed or wounded. On a similar occasion a C.M.R. patrol was ambushed, with Morosi's men killing one of their number before taking another prisoner. The following morning the prisoner's head was displayed on a pole and his body thrown over the wall.

On the 5th of June another direct assault was attempted, this also ended in failure and ultimately led to the desertion of Chief Lethordi's men from the Basuto Contingent. Davies was made Commandant of the remaining 286 men. With the onset of winter Brabant met Morosi under a flag of truce in September and October, but to no avail. This led to another change of command, with Colonel Bayly of the Cape Mounted Rifles filling the post. The make up of the besieging force also changed with its commander, the Yeomanry, burghers, and many of the levies returned home leaving Bayly, his Regiment and Davies with his force of Basutos.

Bayly conceived a new plan for one final assault on Morosi's stronghold. His troops, complete with 25 scaling ladders were to attack from five different positions. After three days and nights of continuous shelling the assault commenced at midnight on the 19th of November. Fifty of Davies' men were sent in with the 1st and 2nd storming parties. Their role was to carry the scaling ladders. The storming parties were met with a withering fire from inside of the fort, and the assault seemed to be coming to a similar conclusion to its predecessors, with Davies' men capitulating first. The Basutos dropped the ladders they had been entrusted with and ran in the opposite direction. Fortunately the resolve of the Cape Mounted Rifles stayed true, they hoisted the ladders onto their shoulders and pressed home the attack with the point of a bayonet. The rear walls crashed under the weight of the attack and the fort was carried by sunrise. Seventy of Morosi's warriors lay dead, however a great number managed to escape during the melee.

With Morosi's revolt put down, Davies returned to his position as Magistrate. Unrest remained in the territory, however, due to the government's policy to disarm the Basutos. Davies found himself placed in a difficult position, torn between having to carry out his orders and his sympathetic feelings towards the Basuto people, 'I am very heavily handicapped in having now to look out the new order of things:- nor can I fail, under the circumstances of the case, to be partial to the loyals, who have fought side by side with us and risked their lives to save ours. It is therefore in the interests of the Government as well as in my own that I should be removed from Basutoland.' (Letter from recipient to the Acting Governor's Agent, dated 17.11.1881, refers)

Davies' request was granted and he was appointed a Commissioner in the Cape Police, 31.8.1882; Justice of the Peace, 14.10.1882; during the following three years he served as Commissioner of Districts 5, 3 and 6 respectively before moving to District 1 (the Eastern Province) with the re-organisation of the system; with the outbreak of the Boer War the Cape Police were put on a military footing and Davies became Lieutenant-Colonel, seeing active service from November 1899; the 1st Division Cape Police served as part of General Gatacre's 3rd Division, and from June 1901 with Gorringe's Flying Column. Davies retired from the force, 30.6.1904.

BASUTOLAND POLICE.
NO RANK SHOWN
Nesbitt   R.H   1878-9

BASUTOLAND CONTINGENT.
COMMANDANT
Davies   H.L   1879
CAPTAIN
Gafney   W   1879
LIEUTENANT
Gafney   J.H   1879
RANK NOT KNOWN
Surmon   W.N   1879

BEAUFORT RANGERS CAVALRY VOLUNTEERS.
CAPTAIN
Richards   J   1877-8
LIEUTENANT
Pedlar   W.H   1877-8
Solomon   E.P   1877-8
SERGEANT MAJOR
Theron   C   1877-8
SERGEANT
Clayton   T.E   1877-8
Green   A.J   1877-8
CORPORAL
Diesel   C   1877-8

Holliday   J   1877-8
Rochat   E   1877-8
Stokes   G.G   1877-8

TRUMPETER
Holliday   H   1877-8
TROOPER
Ainslie   F   1877-8
Ainslie   J   1877-8
Anderson   H   1877-8
Baker   T   1877-8
Bizuidenhout   G   1877-8
Blakeway   J   1877-8
Booth   M.G   1877-8
Booth   R.G   1877-8
Bulgin   A.J   1877-8
Campbell   G   1877-8
Clarke   W   1877-8
Cochrane   D   1877-8
Cumming   D   1877-8
Dennis   J   1877-8
Diesel   M   1877-8
Dyer   E   1877-8
Dyer   R.H   1877-8
Eade   T.A   1877-8
Elliott   J   1877-8
Farrell   E   1877-8
Gilbert   W   1877-8
Gobey   J   1877-8
Graham   H.W   1877-8
Hacking   W   1877-8
Harley   H   1877-8
Harley   W   1877-8
Harvey   A   1877-8
Holliday   W   1877-8
Keys   H.P   1877-8
King   W.R   1877-8
Lloyd   S.R   1877-8
Mallitt   P.W   1877-8
Mildenhall   E   1877-8
Mildenhall   J   1877-8
Merton   R.A   1877-8
Niland   B   1877-8
Norton   E   1877-8-9
Pedlar   G.H   1877-8
Painter   E.J   1877-8
Painter   W   1877-8
Roberts   S.H   1877-8
Rhodes   C   1877-8
Sampson   D   1877-8-9
Snodgrass   D.W   1877-8
Snodgrass   J   1877-8
Stewart   W   1877-8
Theron   J.J   1877-8
Tidbury   C   1877-8
Vice   E   1877-8
Windell   B   1877-8
Wragg   G   1877-8

Bedford Burghers

BEDFORD BURGHERS.
QUARTERMASTER
Jeffery A 1879
NO RANK SHOWN
Trollip A.J.A 1879

BERLIN VOLUNTEER CAVALRY
PRIVATE
Ahlshager J.C 1877-8 r
TROOPER
Frank W 1879

BERLIN VOLUNTEERS (MOUNTED) & BERLIN LIGHT INFANTRY (ATTACHED).
CAPTAIN COMMANDING
Vincent L.L 1877-8-9
CAPTAIN
Brown J.H 1877-8
Davies D 1877-8
Medal from an earlier Campaign.
LIEUTENANT
Adkins Snr H 1877-8
Brown N.E 1877-8
Coetser S 1877-8
Riggiens J 1877-8 r
Sparks B.J 1877-8
QUARTERMASTER SERGEANT
Carr A 1877-8
ORDERLY ROOM SERGEANT
Hartley H.F 1877-8 r
SERGEANT
Adkins Jnr H 1877-8
Bauer C 1877-8
Erasmus L.K 1877-8
Hartley J.T 1877-8 r
Ninneman W 1877-8
Otto C 1877-8
Van de Merwe P 1877-8
CORPORAL
Ahlshdager 1877-8-9
Blumerick 1877-8
Hartley J.H 1877-8 r
Jones H 1877-8
Nel J 1877-8 r
Schutlz J 1877-8
Sergel W 1877-8
TROOPER
Adkins B 1877-8-9
Adkins W 1877-8
Aydon A 1877-8-9
Bauer R 1877-8 r
Berndt F 1877-8 r
Bindeman 1877-8 r
Botha 1. C 1877-8
Botha 2. C 1877-8

Botha P.E 1877-8
Brack N 1877-8 r
Brown A.A 1877-8
Brown O.R 1877-8
Brown W. 1877 r
Murdered 31/12/77.
Buchner W 1877-8 r
Courtnage J 1877-8 r
Curling J 1877-8 r
Dillen E 1877-8
Engelbrecht 1877-8
Engelbrecht Jnr 1877-8
Engelbrecht C 1877-8
Erasmus D 1877-8
Erasmus P.R 1877-8
Farrel J 1877-8
Farrel C 1877-8
Freitag E 1877-8-9
Geluke F 1877-8
Greyling A 1877-8
Greyling C 1877-8
Greyling J 1877-8
Grobbelaar 1877-8
Hartley A.J 1877-8-9 r
Hartwig H 1877-8
Holl C 1877-8
Holl 1. C.G 1877-8
Holl 2. C.G 1877-8
Holl H 1877-8 r
Holl J 1877-8
Holl J.H 1877-8
Holl L 1877-8
Holl P.G 1877-8
Holl R.F 1877-8
Holzinger 1877-8
Jager C 1877-8 r
Jones ED 1877-8
Keen G 1877-8
Keth W 1877-8
Koch H 1877-8
Koch M 1877-8
Kriedemann C 1877-8
Kriedemann W 1877-8 r
Kursten F 1877-8 r
Lipke A 1877-8
Nel Jan 1877-8 r
Nel Jurie 1877-8 r
Nel P 1877-8 r
Norton T 1877-8 r
Page C.H 1877-8 r
Page C.H 1877-8-9 r
Page O.R 1877-8-9 r
Page R.T 1877-8 r
Page T 1877-8
Page W 1877-8 r

Poole P.G 1877-8
Richter N 1877-8 r
Riggiens G 1877-8 r
Riggiens Jnr J 1877-8 r
Sangerhaus B 1877-8 r
Sangerhaus C 1877-8
Sangerhaus E 1877-8 r
Sansom H 1877-8
Sansom H.F 1877-8
Sansom W 1877-8
Schalkwick P 1877-8
Schultz A 1877-8-9
Schultz F 1877-8 r
Schultz L 1877-8 r
Schwartz H 1877-8 r
Search G 1879 r
Smith J 1877-8
Stevenson J 1877-8-9
Stevenson W 1877-8-9
Stock J 1877-8 r
Strasburg A 1877-8
Strasburg F 1877-8
Tesmer J 1877-8 r
Thies W 1877-8
Van de Merwe Jnr G 1877-8
Van de Merwe Snr G 1877-8
Van de Merwe 1. W 1877-8
Van de Merwe 2. W 1877-8
Van de Merwe W.S 1877-8
Wagener H 1877-8 r
Wagner G 1877-8 r
Walter S 1877-8 r
Warneke F 1877-8
Weyer C 1877-8
Weyer M 1877-8 r
Williams G.H 1879
Winklemen A 1877-8
Winklemen F 1877-8

BETTINGTONS HORSE
CAPTAIN COMMANDING
*Bettington C 1879
LIEUTENANT
*Higginson W 1879
Lambert R.A.A 1879
Long W.B.D 1878-9
SERGEANT MAJOR
Hayes 1879 r
*Mitchell 1879
*Oliver 1879
QUARTERMASTER SERGEANT
*Chilton 1879
*Power 1879

On the 1st of June the Prince Imperial started with Lieutenant Carey of the 98th, and six men of Bettington's Horse, on a reconnoitring expedition, they reached a kraal and unsaddled their horses and rested for an hour. As they were in the act of resaddling, a party of Zulus suddenly sprang out. The Prince Imperial was unable to mount his horse, and was overtaken by the Zulus, and killed.

Bettingtons Horse

SERGEANT
Connor	M	1879
Grey		1879 r
Mac Gilvray		1879 r
Parker		1879
*Smith		1879
*Towel		1879
Zboril	F	1879

CORPORAL
*Elton	F	1879
Fischer	C.V	1879

Duplicate issued 4/5/11.

*Fyfe		1879
Herman		1879 r
*Macwade		1879
*Willis		1879

TRUMPETER
*Hogan	1879
*Mac Evan	1879

TROOPER
Able W	**1878-9**

KIA at Ityotyosi River 1/6/1879

Aiken	1879 r
Anderson	1879 r
*Barbour	1879
Barbourne	1879 r
Bassett	1879 r
Battrass	1879 r
*Blenkinson	1879
Boome	1879
*Bowden	1879
Bowdray	1879 r
Bowman	1879 r
Boyd	1879 r
*Braine	1879
*Broone	1879
Brotherhead	1879 r
Brummer	1879 r
Bunday	1879 r
Charlton	1879 r
Clark	1879 r
Clear	1879 r
Clements	1879
Cochrane	1879 r
Counel	1879 r
*Cuningham	1879

William Cunningham served in the Boer War. Discharged with Ignominy, for drunkenness 7.4.1900 after 168 days service.

*Curtis	1879
Davey	1879 r
*Edwards	1879
*Eyre	1879
Fisher	1879 r
Fitzgibbon	1879 r
Fleming	1879 r
Forbisher	1879 r
*Fraser	1879
Freeth G.W	1877-8-9
Gray G	1878-9
Gregory	1879 r
*Grubb	1879
Gunn	1879 r
Hammond	1879 r
*Hancock	1879
*Herbert	1879
Hardy	1879 r
Harris	1879 r
Herring	1879
Hogan	1879 r
Holman H	1879
Honeychurch	1879 r
Husband	1879 r
Johnson	1879 r
Kilgannon W	1879
*Le Tocq	1879
Lewis	1879 r
Lewis A	1879 r
*Lewis W	1879
*Locke	1879
*Mac Dermot	1879
*Macleod	1879
*Maher	1879
Manuel	1879 r
Mason	1879 r
*Meyer L	1879
*Newman	1879
Morrell	1879 r
Morris	1879 r
Murdock	1879 r
*Pennefather	1879
*Petrie	1879
Reid	1879 r
Rogers G	**1878-9**

KIA at Ityotyosi River 1/6/1879

Rogers	1879 r
Scarmel	1879 r
Schwartz	1879 r
Seacombe	1879
Semple	1879 r
Skinner	1879 r
*Smidt	1879
Smith	1879 r
Sullivan	1879 r
*Taylor	1879
*Titz	1879
*Unger	1879
Wharton	1879 r
Wilcox	1879 r
*Wilkins	1879
*Williams J	1879
*Williams T	1879

NATIVE
Umpatula	1879 r

* From Supplementary Roll

BOLOTWA TEMBUS.
A unit of native troops raised by Robert William Stanford in his capacity as Suprrintendent of Natives at Bolatwa near Queenstown on the Eastern Frontier.

CAPTAIN
Stanfod	R.W	1877-8

LIEUTENANT
Jackson	J.H	1877-8 r
Murphy	J	1877-8
Wakeford	W.E	1877-8

QUARTERMASTER
Dreyer	C	1877-8 r

SERGEANT
Darala	B	1877-8
Darala	J	1877-8
Mati	K	1877-8
Mohweshwl		1877-8
Shadrach		1877-8

CORPORAL
Dalasile		1877-8
Dhlakavoo		1877-8
Dyonta		1877-8 r
Kobocwana		1877-8
Kwahahand		1877-8
Landingive		1877-8
Marill	K	1877-8
Mpiyakl	S	1877-8
Tantsi	J	1877-8
Xwantini		1877-8

TROOPER
Abraham		1877-8
Alfred		1877-8
August		1877-8
Batji		1877-8 r
Bless		1877-8
Boboyi		1877-8
Bokoa (Bokva)		1877-8
Bokwana		1877-8
Boy		1877-8
Cebani		1877-8
Cele	J	1877-8
Celyuve	J	1877-8
Cweza		1877-8
Damana		1877-8
Dike	L	1877-8
Dikl		1877-8
Dupu		1877-8
Dyas		1877-8 r
Elias		1877-8
Foxi		1877-8
Gagayi		1877-8
George		1877-8
Geinomkonto		1877-8
Ggishela		1877-8
Ghert		1877-8
Gosi		1877-8
Hlahll	J	1877-8

Bolotwa Tembus

Jacob		1877-8 r
Jafta		1877-8
Jantyie		1877-8
Jantyie	Y	1877-8 r
January		1877-8
Jardine	K	1977-8 r
Jeremiah		1877-8 r
Joubert	S	1877-8 r
Jubefu	C	1877-8
Kalipa		1877-8
Kase	J	1877-8 r
Kivitshini		1877-8
Klass		1877-8
Kole		1877-8 r
Kolman		1877-8
Kopi		1877-8 r
Kosana	A	1877-8
Kulu	H	1877-8
Lamani		1877-8
Lamani	C	1877-8
Lili		1877-8 r
Lunda	H	1877-8
Lupwana		1877-8 r
Mabeland	N	1877-8
Magiva	S	1877-8 r
Mahasama	S	1877-8
Makina		1877-8
Mapomo		1877-8
Martins		1877-8
Masende		1877-8 r
Mata	J	1877-8 r
Mataba	J	1877-8
Mati		1877-8
Matross	P	1877-8
Matshoba		1877-8
Mayela	K	1877-8
Mbali		1877-8
Mbaza		1877-8
Mdudu		1877-8
Mekula	J	1877-8
Menye	Z	1877-8
Mpetsheni		1877-8
Mpoyi		1877-8
Mquga		1877-8 r
Mququmba	J	1877-8
Nceteto		1877-8
Newton	K	1877-8 r
Nkuku		1877-8
Nobaza	R	1877-8 r
Nontshingo		1877-8
Nqandi	S	1877-8 r
Nyamela	J	1877-8
Nyangive		1877-8
Nyeka		1877-8
Peters	W	1877-8
Piet		1877-8
Piet	G	1877-8
Piet	J	1877-8
Qwelane	K	1877-8

Rabbet		1877-8 r
Sam		1877-8 r
Saul		1877-8
Saul	N	1877-8
Sclingill		1877-8 r
Sepoyo	C	1877-8
Siko		1877-8 r
Sisele		1877-8 r
Soliwe	W	1877-8
Somahono	N	1877-8
Sondhlo	J	1877-8
Stofill		1877-8
Stuurman	H	1877-8
Stuurman		1877-8 r
Sweli		1877-8 r
Tabata	C	1877-8
Tafeni		1877-8
Tambosch		1877-8
Tatand		1877-8
Tivisha	J	1877-8
Tonisi		1877-8
Tuku		1877-8
Tungwana		1877-8 r
Walaza		1877-8
William		1877-8 r
Xamani	S	1877-8 r
Xatyana		1877-8
Zawa		1877-8
Zwartbooy		1877-8
Zwartbooy	F	1877-8 r

BOLOTWA VOLUNTEERS.
CAPTAIN
Wilson J 1878
LIEUTENANT
O'Donnell P 1878
SERGEANT
Kaempfort F 1878
CORPORAL
Howes C 1878
PRIVATE

Carlisle	J	1878
Castens	C	1878
Clayton	G	1878 r
Connock	J	1878
Dick	W	1878
Dreyer	C	1878
Field	W	1878 r
Grunig	W	1878
Hughes	W.J	1878
Kehrt	J	1878
Kupka	W	1878 r
Leonard	H	1878 r
Paepka	A	1878
Prior	E	1878 r

BORDER HORSE.
Those Killed in Action (KIA) lost their lives at Inhlobane. 28/3/1879.
Commanded by Lt Col Weatherley, a Canadian who was farming and gold mining in the Transvaal, and ex-Imperial officer of the 6th Dragoons. The Regiment, 61 strong, lost its commanding officer, and 38 of all ranks killed, and one wounded, at Hlobane. They served under Major Dennison at Kambula and in the Sekukuni campaign. All the Colonial units in Wood's column were commanded by Lt Col Buller.

LIEUTENANT COLONEL COMMANDING
Weatherley F   KIA 1879
COMMANDANT
Dennison C.G   1879
CAPTAIN
Daniell C.W   No clasp r
Dennison H   1879
LIEUTENANT ADJUTANT
Boxwell W   1879
Lys   V.H KIA   1879
LIEUT. PAYMASTER / QUARTERMASTER
Penderel-Longlands H 1878-9
LIEUTENANT
Blyth P.W   No clasp
Davies G.I   1879
Pool (Poole) W   KIA 1879
Rickman W.E   1879
Sanctuary H   1878-9
Weatherly C.P   1879
SUB LIEUTENANT
Parminter H.W   KIA 1879 r
Weatherley R   KIA 1879
REGIMENTAL SERGEANT MAJOR
Brown E.J   KIA 1879 r
Constable R   1879
Law J   1879
Newman H   No clasp r
TROOP SERGEANT MAJOR
Ede A.E   1879
Fisher J.S   KIA 1879 r
Smith F   1879
Taylor H   No clasp r
FARRIER SERGEANT
Francis D   No clasp r
Frieze (Friere) J   KIA 1879 r
Mc Gonigle C   1877-9 r
Re-issued 27/6/1914.
ORDERLY ROOM SERGEANT
Brissenden T.D   KIA 1879 r
PAYMASTER SERGEANT
Edwards S   1879
Johnson A   KIA 1879 r
QUARTERMASTER SERGEANT
Hackett J.M   No clasp

The Laager Method of Defence.

Lord Chelmsford and Staff. Looking at Ulundi

Ernest Grandier - Border Horse

#Among the personal incidents of the Zulu war few are more noteworthy than the escape of **Ernest Grandier.** This man was a trooper in the Irregular Cavalry, who suffered so severely in the surprise at the Zlobane Hill. He was one of the few survivors, and took an exhausted Dutch Boer on his horse. They were, however. presently overtaken by the enemy, who assegaised the Dutchman, and made Grandier their prisoner. He was first taken to the kraal of Umbelini, who resolved to send him as a prize to Cetewayo. His sufferings were intense, as he was lashed to a pole, without cloths, exposed to a burning sun by day and to biting cold by night, he had only mealies to eat, and in the morning his captors beat him with their sticks to restore circulation. After a toilsome journey of seventy miles, Cetewayos' kraal was reached. He was kept for four days more while discussion took place as to the manner of his death. At length the victim was brought into the presence of the King, his councillors, and his people. The latter flocked around him, while the women clapped their hands, jeered him, and spat upon him. Order being restored, Cetewayo, seated on his leopard skin, told him that it had been decided to send him back to Umbelini, who would cut him up bit by bit, until he died, but not before a month elapsed. This decision saved Grandier's life. On the return journey the two Zulus in whose charge he was, allowed him to enter a mealie garden and eat what he could find; his guards meanwhile laying down their arms. Grandier, watching his opportunity, killed one with his own assegai, and carried of the gun of the other, who fled on seeing his late prisoner armed. Grandier hid in a hole, an army of 15,000 Zulus presently passed, but did not perceive him. After he recovered his strength a little he crawled out, and guided by the sun by day and the stars by night, reached Kambuls Camp, fever-stricken and exhausted, after a journey of fifty hours. Grandier, though still under medical treatment when this account was written, bade fair to recover. He is described as a tall, dark, wiry man of twenty-eight, a stone-cutter by trade, and a native of Bordeaux.
Source: The Graphic (London, England), Saturday, July 12, 1879; Issue 502
Grandier captured
Ernest Grandier, a well-made, athletic, and powerful trooper, and **Cramazan Baudoin,** a stout and equally stalwart fellow. Both these men were natives of Bordeaux, and had come out to the colony together about five years before with the intention of trying their fortunes in the wine trade.They had both served their time in the French army, and when the present war commenced could not resist the temptation of seeing service under such a gallant commander as Weatherly, whose knowledge of France and the Continent generally obtained him many excellent French and German recruits. On the day of the Zlobani attack, owing to a thick fog which suddenly came on, ' Colonel "Weatherly's troops missed their road and were unable to effect the junction with Buller ordered by **Colonel Wood.** The Zlobani mountain was successfully carried by Colonel Buller and his horsemen at daylight on the 28th March, and Colonel "Wood, who was with Russell's horsemen a few miles to the west, pushed forward on the same morning with his usual small escort of the 90th mounted men and overtook Weatherly, who had been all night trying to find the path. After the summit of the mountain had been gained, under a heavy fire, during which **Captain Ronald Campbell** and **Mr. Lloyd** were killed...... Weatherly was killed in the endeavour to save his son.... he was overtaken by half-a-dozen savages, and after receiving several severe blows from knobkerries, was seized and pinioned with thongs......

Border Horse

Mc Leed (McLeod) N 1879
KIA at Sekukuni's Town 28/11/1879
Russell F KIA 1879 r
SADDLER SERGEANT
Didcott C.S 1879
  See also Transvaal Rangers
Pretorious W.L 1878-9 r
VETERINARY SERGEANT
Tomlin J No clasp r
SERGEANT
Brown C 1879
Bruce A No clasp r
Colbert J 1879 r
Felt W.H No clasp
Muir J 1879
Murray J 1879
Stewart A KIA 1879 r
Thompson H.T No clasp r
Von Gordon A 1878-9
CORPORAL
Archer J 1879 r
Beard J.B 1879
Blackmore J KIA 1879 r
Coetzee D 1879 r
KIA at Inhlobarie 28/3/1879
Ford B KIA 1879 r
Mayers A.P 1879
Mc Gillivray T No clasp r
Mitchell E.B 1878-9 r
KIA at Sekukuni's Town 28/11/1879
Murton A 1879
Porter H.B KIA 1879 r
Rous A 1879
Shepherd F.R 1879
Thomas K No clasp r
Tillett R 1879
Van Hasselt J.J.C KIA 1879
LANCE CORPORAL
Bernhardt (Burnhard) E KIA 1878-9 r
Green A.L 1878-9 r
GUNNER
Ellwood O 1879 r
Mc Cabe B 1878-9
TRUMPETER
Meredith E.H KIA 1879 r
Reilly (Riley) W KIA 1878-9 r
TROOPER
Adams J No clasp r
Adams W No clasp r
  Deserted.
Andrew W Not on medal Roll
Gazette: Drowned accidentally,
Eerstelling 23/4/1879
Austen J No clasp r
Audibert J No clasp r
Barth L KIA 1879
Bartz (Bart) F.W KIA 1879 r

Bees B 1879
Benson J 1879 r
Bentley J.H No clasp r
  Deserted.
Boggis W No claso r
Bonham H 1879
Boudoin (Bourdoin) C KIA 1879
Bower W No clasp r
Briet J.J.A 1879 r
Brooks P.W KIA 1879 r
Brown J.B No clasp r
Budden T.J 1879 r
Burton J No clasp
Butterworth W.H 1878-9
Cameron J KIA 1879 r
  See also Transvaal Rangers.
Carr H 1879
Carruthers W 1879 r
Cartwright H No clasp
Chandler C 1879
Chasey G 1879
Slightly wounded at Sekukuni's
Town 28/11/1879
Cherry W KIA 1879
  See also Frontier Light Horse.
Clarke W 1879
Collins R 1879 r
Cook W 1879 r
Cornelius A No clasp r
Craney (Crany) B.J KIA 1879 r
Craney P.J No clasp r
Craig J 1879
Craig J.T KIA 1878-9 r
Cumberland B.L 1878-9
  See also Cpl in Ferreiras Horse.
Cunningham J No clasp
Daniells W 1879
Davey (Darcy) J KIA 1879 r
De Beer P.J No clasp r
Devine D 1879 r
Donlin J 1879
Dougherty C 1879
Dowthwaite R 1879
Dwyer J 1879 r
Emmanuel V No clasp r
Evans W KIA 1879 r
Farquharson (Farquarson) KIA 1879 r
Felt R No clasp
Felt W No clasp
Flint A.H 1879
Foster H 1879 r
Fourie J No clasp r
Francis R 1879
Brooks P.W KIA 1879 r
Fraser J.A No clasp r
Freeborn H No clasp
Fry D.J No clasp r
Garrett W No clasp r

Gartrell T.J 1879 r
Germaine A 1879 r
Gibbon J.W No clasp
Gibbs W.H 1879
Gill W 1879 r
Gleeson J 1878-9
Gouws M.J No clasp
Severely W. 25/6/1879 Photo's Kraal
#Grandier (Grandeur) E 1879
Gray J 1879
Green E 1879
Green H.W 1879
Green J 1878-9 r
Hammond A.M 1879 r
Hanneford J 1879
Hartman A KIA 1878-9 r
Hater H 1879 r
Haybittel W 1879
Hettwer T No clasp r
Heugh W 1878-9 r
Hibbert A 1879 r
Hill W 1879 r
Holley E.H 1879 r
Hons J.H 1879 r
Howatson J 1879 r
  See also J.Howardson Transvaal Rangers.
Inglis J No clasp r
Jacobs H 1878? r
Jeffrey F.J KIA 1878-9 r
Jeffries (Jefferys) W KIA 1879 r
Jenkins W 1879 r
Jones Henry 1879 r
Jones H 1879 r
Jones T 1879 r
Kavanagh? 1878-9 r
Kelly J No clasp r
King (2) G KIA 1879 r
King G 1879 r
Kingsley C.G.W 1879 r
Klein P.F 1879
Limkie S 1878-9 r
Lindroth C.P 1879 r
Lotter W 1879 r
Loughran T 1879
Lynch J 1879 r
Lyndon C No clasp r
  Discharged Misbehaviour.
Maloney T 1879 r
  See also T. Mahoney Ferreiras Horse.
Mann (Maun) J.C KIA 1879 r
Martin P KIA 1879
Masters (Mc Master) J.A 1879 r
Dangerously wounded at Sekukuni's
Town 28/11/1879
Maunion B 1879
Mc Naghten T No clasp r
  Discharge Misconduct.
Mc Neil A 1879

Border Horse

Mc Kay	J.A	KIA 1879 r	Sullivan	J	No clasp r	Frank	J	1877
See also A. Mackay Bakers Horse.			Sutherland	J	1878-9 r	Tweedie	A	1877-8
Meilot (Mulot)	F	KIA 1879 r	Swanepoel	A	1878-9	See also Queenstown Vol. Contingent.		
Mellma(Milma)	D	KIA 1879 r	Sweeney	J	1878-9 r	White	G.L	1877-8 r
Michaely	N	No clasp r	Taylor	W	1879 r	**SERGEANT MAJOR**		
Middleton	H	1879 r	Terrin	W	1879 r	Bowker	A	1878
Milton	H.M	No clasp r	Thomas	J	No clasp r	Harty	J	1877 r
Momantz	P	No clasp	**Thompson**		**KIA 1879 r**	James	C	1877-8 r
Morris	J	No clasp r	Thompson	J	1879 r	Vowles	J.B	1877-8-9 r
See also Ferreiras Horse.			Slightly W. 25/6/1879 Photo's Kraal			**QUARTERMASTER SERGEANT**		
Muller	F	1878-9	Thompson	T	No clasp r	Jahre	C	1877-8
Muller	**Jacobus**	**KIA 1879 r**	**Underwood**	**J**	**KIA 1879**	**SERGEANT**		
Muller	**John**	**KIA 1879 r**	Van der Merwe	J.J.J	1879	Barratt	F.A	1877-8
Mullins	M	1878-9 r	Van der Venter	J.L	1879 r	Cumming	H	1877-8 r
Murray	J	1879 r	Van der Venter Snr	W	1879 r	Lang	F	1877-8 r
Newnham	C.D	1879	Van der Venter Jnr	W	1879 r	Whittle	J	1877
See also Frontier Light Horse.			Van der Westhuizen	G	1879	**CORPORAL**		
Newton	H.F	No clasp r	Viljoen	F	1878-9 r	Bosch	P	1877-8 r
Nelan	J	1878-9	Walsh	J	1879	Currie	W	1877-8
O'Reilly	J	1879 r	Watson	A	No clasp r	Ehrke	J	1877
See also Frontier Light Horse.			Watson	R	No clasp r	Farquhar	J	1877 r
Orpen	S	No clasp r	See also Transvaal Artillery.			Harty	J	1877
Parkinson	W	1879	# Weatherley	J	1879	Kelly	T	1877
Peach	G	1879	Weeber	H	No clasp	Kidson		1877-8 r
Pohlson	G	1879	Welsh	W.J	1879	Sell	C	1877-8 r
Powell	T	1879 r	**Westhuisen**	**F.G**	**KIA not on medal roll**	**TROOPER**		
Puddock	G	1879	Wilhelmse	C	No clasp	Adams	J	1877-8 r
Pughe	W.C	1878-9	**Williams**	**?**	**KIA not on medal roll**	Ainslie	F.C	1877 r
Ramsay	R.W	1879 r	Wilson	T	1879 r	Ainslie	J.R	1877
Reid	Alex	1879	Wilson	W	No clasp r	Allan	G	1877-8
Reid (Reed)	**Alfred**	**KIA 1879**	Woolcock	F	1879 r	Auld	W	1877-8
Richards	G	1879	**Wynen (Wynan)**	**S**	**KIA 1879**	Badnitz	A	1877-8 r
Rigg	J.H	1879	**SADDLER**			Barker	G	1877-8 r
Robinson	G	1879	Schmidt	W	1879	Bartle	W	1877-8
Russell	A	No clasp r				Bartram	E	1877-8 r
Deserted.			**BOWKERS ROVERS.**			Bauer	B	1877-8 r
Russell	J	1879 r	**COMMANDANT**			Bauer	D	1877-8
Saunders	J.B	1879 r	Bowker	B.E	1877-8	Bauer	J.W	1877-8 r
Sawyer	L	1879 r	**CAPTAIN**			Bekker	G	1877-8 r
Schenote	G	No clasp r	Douglas	A	1877-8 r	Bekker	N	1877-8 r
Not entitled.			Wainwright	W	1877	Bosch	H	1877-8 r
Schmidt	C	1879 r	**ADJUTANT**			Bosch	J	1877-8 r
Schroeder	H	1878-9 r	Ellis	J.D	1877	Botha	J	1877-8
Schwein	P	1879	**LIEUTENANT & ADJUTANT**			Botha	T.J	1877-8
Sharpe	R.M	1879	Bettington	R.A.A	1877-8	Bowden	W	1877-8 r
Shepherd	**J**	**KIA 1879 r**	Barber	G.H	1877-8 r	Bowker	B	1877-8
Shield	S.B	1879	**QUARTERMASTER**			Bowker	D.C	1877-8
Smith	J	1879 r	Weldon	J	1877	Bowker	G.C	1877-8
Starey	L.B	1879	**LIEUTENANT**			Bowker	J.W	1877-8
Sullivan	F.L	1879	Eade	W	1877-8	Bowker	N	1877-8

Dix Noonan Web Auction Lot 242, 27 Jun 07
South Africa 1877-79, 1 clasp, 1879 (Troopr. J. Weatherley, Border Horse) a few scratches over rank, otherwise nearly extremely fine Hammer price £550. It is interesting to speculate whether the recipient was a relative of his Commanding Officer, Lieutenant-Colonel Frederick Weatherley, and his two sons, both of whom served as officers in the Border Horse. One of them, and the Colonel, fell at Inhlobane Mountain on 28 March 1879, a disastrous encounter that resulted in 17 officers and 82 other ranks being killed, besides many more wounded, most of the fatalities being inflicted on Buller's force during its headlong flight down "The Devil's Pass". Of these fatalities, five were officers and 42 N.C.Os or other ranks from the Border Horse. In fact such was the carnage caused by the Zulus' assegais that they renamed Inhlobane the "Stabbing Mountain".

Bowkers Rovers

Name		Date	Name		Date	Name		Date
Bowker	W.R	1877-8	Kemp	J	1877	Tweedie	A	1877 r
Boyce	L	1877-8 r	Kemp	R	1877	Tweedie	A	1877-9
Breen	W	1877-8 r	Kempsford	?	1877 r	Tois	H.T	1877
Broderick	A	1877-8 r	Kenny	J	1877-8 r	Usher	H	1877 r
Brooks	A	1877 r	Kettles	A	1877-8	Uswell	W	1877-8
Brown	N.E	1877	Klassen	H	1877-8 r	Vanes	T	1877 r
Brown	R	1877	Lang	J	1877 r	Van Rooyen	P	1877-8
Brusson	C	1877-8	Langley	H	1877-8 r	Wainwright	A	1877 r
Buiske	T	1877-8	Landrey	J	1877	Walsh	E	1877-8 r
Burns	W	1877-8 r	Leach	W	1877-8 r	Webster	C	1877-8
Butt	F	1877-8	Lee		1877 r	Welby	R	1877 r
Carrel	J	1877-8 r	Leppan	G	1877-8 r	White		1877
Carney		1877 r	Leyman	O	1877 r	White	A	1877-8 r
Carr	A.W	1877	Leescher	E	1877-8	Whitehead	J	1877-8 r
Clifford	C	1877-8 r	Long	J	1877-8	Wilkins	F	1877-8 r
Coleman	E	1877	Lundell	C	1877 r	Wise	J	1877-8 r
Davis	J	1877 r	Marnietske	W	1877-8 r	Withers	A	1877-8 r
Dell	W	1877 r	Mattig	C	1877-8	Withers	P	1877-8 r
Dicks	B.D	1877-8 r	Mattig	M	1877-8	Wood	M	1877-8 r
Doherty	J	1877-8 r	Maule	W	1877	**RANK NOT KNOWN**		
Donaldson	H	1878	Mc Glashan	P	1877	Wilson	W	1879
Durrant	S.C	1877	Mc Intosh	A	1877 r			
Ebden	A	1877	Mc Min	J	1877-8 r	**BRABANTS VOLUNTEERS.**		
Eade	T.A	1877-8	Mullen	T	1877 r	**TROOPER**		
Ehrke Jnr	C	1877-8	Nelson		1877 r	Pearson	W	1878 r
Ehrke Snr	C	1877-8	Oldham	A.C	1877 r			
Elandveldt	H	1877-8 r	O'Ryan	F	1877-8 r	**BUCKLEYS NATIVE LEVY.**		
Elandveldt	D	1877-8	Page	C	1877 r	**CAPTAIN**		
Faircloth	J	1877-8 r	Page	W	1877 r	Buckley	A	1877-8 r
Ferreira	P	1877-8	Pentland	J	1877 r	**LIEUTENANT**		
Fisher	C	1877-8	Peterson	J	1877-8	Bush	J	1877-8
Fletcher	W	1877-8 r	Preston	R	1877	**PRIVATE**		
Frantz	C	1877-8	Pullen	J	1877 r	Abels	W	1877-8 r
Furnice	T	1877	Pullen	T	1877 r	Antoni		1877-8
Gibson	T	1877-8 r	Reeves		1877 r	Apollus	J	1877-8 r
Gillan		1877	Rennie	C	1877-8 r	Arnns	J	1877-8 r
Goodall	M	1877	Rohrs	W	1878 r	Boy	James	1877-8 r
Graham	J.R	1877	Rooke	G	1877-8	Boy	John	1877-8 r
Graham	R	1877-8 r	Rowley	G	1877-8	Busttella	J	1877-8 r
D/S as a Lt.			Scholt	W	1877-8	Colly	E	1877-8 r
Hall	W.H	1877-8	Schultz	H	1877-8	David	H	1877-8 r
Hanson	W	1877-8 r	Schwartz	A	1877-8	David	W	1877-8 r
Harrower	J	1877 r	Schwartz	H	1877-8	Deidrech	H	1877-8 r
Hey	A	1877	Searle		1877	Dragoons	T	1877-8 r
Hearns	J	1877 r	Sell	C	1877-8 r	Elane	J	1877-8 r
Hearns	T	1877 r	Sell	W	1877-8 r	Exteen	D	1877-8 r
Henry	J	1877-8 r	Smidt	F	1877-8 r	Jacobus	W	1877-8 r
Hillier	A.P	1877-8	Smith	H.T	1877 r	Jansen	D	1877-8 r
Hounslow	T	1877-8 r	Remarks on box "Duplicate K. Wm			Jansen	D.J	1877-8 r
Hughes	T	1877-8	Tn Arty". No trace on that Roll.			Jansen		1877-8
Hughes	W.V	1877 r	Solomon	W.R	1877-8	Jodo	S	1877-8 r
Hunt	T.J	1877-8	Sparks	C	1877-8	Keingo	S	1877-8 r
Hutton	A	1877-8 r	Spires		1877	Kevidore	J	1877-8 r
Hyde	F	1877-8 r	Stander	C	1877-8	Kleinboy	H	1877-8 r
Hyde	T.D	1877-8 r	Stevens	A.B	1877-8	Kock	H	1877-8 r
Jackson	N	1877 r	Stratford	H	1877 r	Leydenberg	A	1877-8 r
Jacoby		1877 r	Trickey	J	1877-8	Mageman	J	1877-8 r
Japp	D	1877-8	Turner	E.S	1877	Martinus	A	1877-8 r
Keightley	J.G.C	1877	Turner	F	1877-8	Martinus	H	1877-8 r

Buckleys Native Levy

Buffalo Border Guard c. 1879.

Martinus	J	1877-8 r
Mickerson	W	1877-8 r
Moffort	C	1877-8 r
Pamar	P	1877-8 r
Petrus		1877-8 r
Plaitjes	J	1877-8 r
Pondula	P	1877-8 r
Rim		1877-8 r
Roberts	W	1877-8 r
Samuel		1877-8 r
Scout	B	1877-8 r
Seaba	C	1877-8 r
Sinxo	J	1877-8 r
Sinxo	John	1877-8 r
Sopoleta		1877-8 r
Swartboy		1877-8
Trumpetter	A	1877-8 r
Wildscruit	J	1877-8 r
Witboy	K	1877-8 r
Wood	B	1877-8 r
Yopo	P	1877-8 r

BUFFALO BORDER GUARD.
Raised on 2 October, 1873 and disbanded in 1880. Its Commanding Officer in Glyn's column was Captain Robson.

LIEUTENANT
*Smith   W.C   1879

QUARTERMASTER
*Mc Phail D   1879
QUARTERMASTER SERGEANT
*Adams   Not on medal roll
SERGEANT MAJOR
*Wilson   1879
SERGEANT
Archer   1879
*Guttridge   1879
*Hepburn   1879
*Money   Not on medal roll
CORPORAL
Pettigrew   ?1879
TROOPER
*Adams Snr   1879
Adams Jnr   1879
*Archer   Not on medal roll
*Coetzee   1879
**De Waal   No clasp
*Dymock (Dimock)   1879
*Eary   **1879 r**
 KIA Isandhlwana .
*Guttridge   1879
 KIA Isandhlwana
Haines   1879
*Lennox   1879
*Marshall   1879
*Pettigrew Not on medal roll
*Posselt   1879

**Robson J   1879
 D/S
**Robson W   1879
*Smith   S   1879
Smith   T   1879 r
*Stretch   1879
*Wehr   **1879 r**
 KIA Isandhlwana.
* Present for duty at Helpmekaar, 16th December 1878,** Troopers to follow. (3) Natal Mercury 21.12.1878

BUFFALO MOUNTED RIFLES.
TROOPER
Zimmer   1877-8 r

BUFFALO VOLUNTEER RIFLES & LEVY.
Note on the re-written Roll:
"Cannot be taken as correct".
COMMANDANT
Von Linsingen   W   1877-8-9
LIEUTENANT
Attwell   G.B   1877-8
Meyer   H.W   1877-8
Selzer   C   1877-8
SUB LIEUTENANT
Weeks   J.C   1877-8 r
QUARTERMASTER
Henderson   T.C   1877-8

BUFFALO BORDER GUARD
The Smiths and their associates were, practically speaking, the Buffalo Border Guard. **Capt. Tom Smith** *commanded;* **Lieut. William Craighead Smith** *was second-in-command;* **Ian Macphail** *was Quartermaster, and* **Gutridge** *and* **Eary** *were troopers. They were a dashing cavalry unit in their black corded breeches and jacket with black velvet facings, with white metal badges and buttons adorned with the fine head of a buffalo. They mustered thirty, which was considerable from such a sparsely populated district.*
As early as Christmas, 1878, they were already in camp at Fort Pine, and in daily contact with the other volunteers, the Newcastle Mounted Rifles, who, along with the Natal Carbineers, were encamped on the heights of Helpmekaar. Smith had solved the water problem at Fort Pine; he had brought out **Robert Marshall** *from "Cleveland," who had dug a well within the fort and had lined it with impeccable brickwork. The Buffalo Border Guard were delighted with their fort. The dry stone walls were twelve feet high and broad in proportion, with double-storied towers at two of the opposite corners. There was:*
"Accomodation for 25 officers and men, stabling for thirty horses, storerooms, offices, and magazines and in fact everything necessary for permanent station or temporary laager.   Extracts from " THE TURBULENT FRONTIER BIGGARSBERG AND BUFFALO AT THE CROSSROADS Mrs Sheila Henderson, M.A.

Buffalo Volunteer Rifles & Levy

COLOUR SERGEANT			Burket	E	1877-8 r	Jorgenson B		1877-8
Ressling	W	1877-8	Butter	J	1877-8 r	Kern	H	1877-8
HOSPITAL SERGEANT			Campbell	C.J	1877-8 r	Kesler	P	1877-8 r
Drummond	D	1877-8	Chapman	J	1877-8	Klose	J	1877-8
QUARTERMASTER SERGEANT			Christinson	Aron	1877-8	Kober	W	1877-8
Chesterton	L.B	1877-8	Christinson	August	1877-8	Krauspe	H	1877-8 r
Crutchley	E.A	1877-8 r	Copeland	W.S	1877-8	Kretzshmar	F	1877-8 r
King	G.A	1877-8	Cowie	J.R	1877-8	Kruger	G	1877-8 r
See also Sgt. G.A king below.			Crosbie	F.W	1877-8	Kruish	F	1877-8
Muller	G	1877-8	Cornhill	W.H	1877-8 r	Kulow	H	1877-8 r
SERGEANT			Daniel	C	1877-8 r	Lambert	W	1877-8 r
Broderick	**M**	**1877-8 r**	Daniel	G	1877-8 r	Lewis Snr	J	1877-8 r
KIA Isandhlwana.			Daniel	N.J	1877-8 r	Lindcostert	A	1877-8
Duritt	F	1877-8	Daniel	S	1877-8 r	Lingsingen	W.L	1877-8
Howard	W.C	1877-8	Daniel	W	1877-8 r	Linz	L	1877-8 r
Keeney	A	1877-8	Death	J	1877-8	Lofs	A	1877-8
King	G.A	1877-8 r	De Klerk	H	1877-8 r	Lucht	R	1877-8 r
See QMS G.A King above.			Eamson	H	1877-8 r	Ludwig	C	1877-8
Lampard	E.J	1877-8	Eckstein	J	1877-8 r	Lundersters	A	1877-8
Lischke	H	1877-8	Ellis	G	1877-8	Maeder	K	1877-8 r
Mackay	J	1877-8	Ellis	W.R	1877-8	Martin	J	1877-8
Rhodin	W	1877-8	Engelbrecht	W	1877-8	Maschke	K	1877-8 r
Schindler	G	1877-8	Feidler	B	1877-8	Mengil	M	1877-8
CORPORAL			Feldmann	J	1877-8 r	Menshausen	J	1877-8 r
Frank	W	1877-8 r	Ferreira	H	1878	Meyr	C	1877-8 r
Hartly	E	1877-8	Fick	E	1877-8 r	Melesch	L	1877-8 r
Langerhausen	H	1877-8 r	Fischer	O	1877-8 r	Muller	M	1877-8
Lunderslist	F	1877-8	Frantzen	S	1877-8 r	Nalder	C	1877-8
Parker	G	1877-8	Fubiger ?	G	1877-8 r	Naushke	H	1877-8
Plotzke	F	1877-8	Gericke	F	1877-8	Nelson	N	1877-8
Plutz	W	1877-8 r	Gibbs	G	1877-8 r	Neumann	E	1877-8
Quirk	J	1877-8	# Gierke	C	1877-8 r	Ohlsen	C	1877-8 r
Sangerhaus	H	1877-8	Goodwin	T.W	1877-8	Osner	F	1877-8
Tillemans	A.J	1877-8	Gratham	J	1877-8 r	Ouvett	C	1877-8
Venn	G	1877-8	Gratz	F	1877-8	Pallcock	J	1877-8 r
LANCE CORPORAL			Gratz	G	1877-8	Panhanrik	W	1877-8 r
Haendike	C	1877-8	Gravett (1)	?	1877-8 r	Parluschke	N	1877-8
BUGLER			Gravett (2)	?	1877-8 r	Peters	H	1877-8 r
George	L.C	1877-8	Grotzahn	W	1877-8 r	Petersen	J	1877-8 r
PRIVATE			Grout	W	1877-8 r	Petersen	O	1877-8 r
Aagesen	F	1877-8 r	Hambley	F	1877-8 r	Petersen	W	1877-8
Aalin	S	1877-8 r	Hambley	R	1877-8	Pettifer	J	1877-8
Albrechtson	A	1877-8	Hannemain	A	1877-8 r	Petzer	H	1877-8 r
Ammann	F	1877-8	Hannuer	T	1877-8 r	Pletschke	E.H	1877-8
Aukiewitz	J	1877-8	Hansen	C	1877-8	Psitzsil	A	1877-8
Back	C	1877-8	Hansen	N	1877-8	Rawlinson	E	1878 r
Baker	O.J	1877-8	Hansen	N	1877-8	Ramsay Snr	D	1877-8
Beaton	C	1877-8 r	Heywood	T.W	1877-8	Ramsay Jnr	D	1877-8
Becker	F.J	1877-8 r	Hildmann	J	1877-8 r	Ramsay	J	1877-8
Berkerling		1877-8	Hoff	A	1877-8	Rensburg	L	1877-8 r
Bratousie	M	1077-0 r	Hoffman	C	1077-0 r	Renshausen	J	1077-0
Brodelet	O.C	1877-8 r	Hopt	W	1877-8 r	Rolandson	R	1877-8 r
Brown	W	1877-8	Holzer	H	1877-8	Roping	R	1877-8
Bruce	C	1877-8	Hulin	A	1877-8 r	Rowers	J	1877-8
Bruce	G.H	1877-8	Jennings	J	1877-8	**Runchuran(Runchwan) C.A 1877-8 r**		
Budge	F	1877-8 r	Jordan	A	1877-8 r	KIA Inhlobane.		

Dix Noonan Web Auction Lot 575, 22 Sep 06
South Africa 1877-79, 1 clasp, 1877-8 (Pte. C. Gierke, Buffalo Md. Vols.) very fine Hammer Price: £270

Buffalo Volunteer Rifles & Levy

Name		Years
Rusch	W	1877-8
Rusel	H	1877-8
Rusendorff	W	1877-8
Rushholtz	H	1877-8
Schmidt	G	1877-8 r
Scholtkapt	H	1877-8 r
Schroder	E	1877-8 r
Schroder	W	1877-8
Schultz	A	1877-8
Schultz	J	1877-8
#Selwitzer (Schwitzer)	J	1877-8
Silvitzer	L	1877-8
Sims	L	1877-8 r
Smith	C	1877-8 r
Smith	H.J	1877-8 r
Snow	G	1877-8
Staffin	W	1877-8 r
Stern	W	1877-8
Stewart	A.E	1877-8
Stickells	W	1877-8 r
Stohr	J	1877-8 r
Suhelschmiedt	J	1877-8
Swain	J	1877-8 r
Tabor	F	1877-8
Taplin	E.G	1877-8
Tapson	J.A	1877-8
Tarluschike?		1877-8 r
Tutton	R.J	1877-8
##Tutton	W.R	1877-8
Van Rhiel	C	1877-8 r
Wahl	C	1877-8
Ward	J	1877-8
Wicks	G	1877-8
Wicks	T	1877-8
Wienand	F	1877-8 r
Williams	C	1877-8 r
Ziehl	T	1877-8

RANK NOT KNOWN

Hanneman	C	1877-8
Holm	A.P	1877-8-9
Pilz	J.A	1877-8

BURGHER FORCE.
Also known as Uys' Burgher Force and Uys' Loyal Burgher Force.

COMMANDANT
Uys Piet
KIA Inhlobane. 28/3/1879.
Rudolph A 1879

CAPTAIN
Rathbone E.F 1879

FIELD CORNET
Rulof T.J 1879 r

TROOPER
Bridenbach Hans not in medal roll wounded at Kambula Hill 10/2/1879
Brown	E	1879
Combrink	G.J	1879
Combrink	**L.S**	**1879**

KIA at Utrecht 26/4/1879
| Gore | J | 1879 |
| Roper | H.B | 1879 |

BURGHERDORP DIVISIONAL POLICE
RANK NOT KNOWN
Holyoak A.F 1877-8-9

CAPE FIELD ARTILLERY.
LIEUTENANT
Cochrane J.P 1877-8-9 r
  See also Cape Mounted Rifles.
Scott VC R.G 1877-8-9
  His VC was for an action at Moirosi' Stronghold 8th April, 1879. In volunteering to throw time fuze shells, wounded in action

SERGEANT MAJOR
Keys R.B 1877-8

FARRIER SERGEANT
Meikeljohn	B	1879 r
Best	J	1877-8-9
Baker	J	1877-8-9
Coxon	H.M	1877-8
Granville	A	1877-8-9 r
White	C.G	1877-8

CORPORAL
| Baker | W | 1877-8 |
| Childe | E | 1877-8-9 |
  See also Cape Mounted Rifles.
Collier	R	1877-8-9
Collingworth	H	1877-8-9
Lodge	F.W	1877-8-9
O'Brien	P	1877-8-9
Pike	W	1877-8-9

GUNNER
Kaeding F 1878

1ST CLASS PRIVATE
Barnett	E.A	1878-9
Brooks	F.A	1878
Brown	H.H	1877-8-9
Butter	A.H	1878-9
Carnegie	G.F	1878-9
Champ	F	1879 r
Cockeran	H.D	1878-9
Collins	H.J	1877-8-9 r
Conway	M	1877-8
Davis	C.E	1877-8-9
Deverell	C.D	1877-8-9
Doland	J	1878 r
Evatt	M.A	1878
Glarbrook	C.E.H	1877-8-9
Graves	W.H	1877-8-9
Handyside	J.R	1878-9
Hare	H.C	1877-8
Harford	A	1877-8-9
Heyman	H.M	1877-8-9
Hobbes	R.D	1877-8-9
Hobson	J	1877-8-9
Jeffery	J	1878-9
Jenkins	D.E	1877-8-9
Kirby	A.C	1877-8
Klockie	W	1877-8-9 r
Koch	C	1878
Liebenn	J	1877-8-9 r
Malcolmson	R.D	1878-9
Mann	H	No clasp?
Mc Munn	E.A	1877-8
Money	G	1877-8-9
Morley	H.W	1877-8-9
Morris	E.W.H	1878-9
Nightingal	G	1877-8-9
Nunns	J.J	1877-8-9
Parke	C	1878-9
Phillips	W.H	1877-8-9
Powell	H	1877-8-9
Robson	J.F	1877-8-9
Schenk	W.M	1878
Smith	H	1878-9
Spencer	J.W	1877-8-9
Staunton	H. de L	1877-8-9
Stewart	R.B	1878-9
Strickland	O	1878
Sutton	R	1878
Taylor	S	1877-8-9
Warren	J	1877-8-9
Whitaker	F.S	1877-8
White	R	1877-8-9
Wood	P	1877-8
Wright	W	1878

2ND CLASS PRIVATE
Briggs	T.P	1878-9
Byrne	W.A	1878-9
Byron	A	1877-8
Davis	G.W	1878

\# Dixons Gazette No13 Spring 1998, 1 clasp, 1877-8. Private J. Schwitzer, Buffalo Volunteer Rifles. 'Selwitzer' on roll which states names are difficult to read. Buffalo Rifle Volunteers the parent corps of the Kaffrarian Rifles raised in East London, Cape in 1876 with a strength of two companies. Disbanded after service in the Kaffir War in September 1880. Wore grey wth black facings. Commanders: Capt. Nettleton and Von Linsingen, Commanding Officer Colonel Brabant. NEF £195.00

\## Dixons Gazette No35 Autumn 2003 4018 1 clasp, 1877-8. Private W.R.Tutton, Buffalo Volunteer Rifles raised in East London, Cape Province in 1876 with a strength of two Companies. Disbanded in 1880 after service in the Frontier Wars. NEF £365.00

The leader of the Boer burghers with no 4 Column, Piet Uys is shown with his four sons, the eldest of whom(right) he died trying to save at Hlobane. Piet Uys had both his brother and his father killed at the battle of Italeni and was keen to avenge their deaths.

FOUR SURVIVORS OF THE BATTLE OF ISANDHLWANA.
DUGALD MacPHAIL, QUARTERMASTER, BUFFALO BORDER GUARD
T.H.CUNNINGHAM, NEWCASTLE MOUNTED RIFLES.
M.McCARTHY, 1st BATTALION, 24th REGIMENT.
Lt COLONEL CLARKE, OBE, NATAL MOUNTED RIFLES.

Cape Field Artillery

Denner	H	1879	309 Cahill	M	1877-8	**PRIVATE**		
Donford	J.S.C	1878-9	479 Cole	A.B	1877-8	190 Adams	A	1877-8 r
Groube	H.F.D	1878-9	317 Dwyer	J.L	1877-8-9	188 Ainsworth	J	1877-8
Hall	S	1878	565 Hilliard	C.H	1877-8-9	192 Allford	W.B	1877-8
Heaphy	H	1877-8-9 r	16 Inman	R	1877-8-9	147 Allwork	R	1877-8
Jacobson	A	1878	182 Jones	W	1877-8-9 r	187 Alveson	C	1877-8 r
Jones	J.O	1878	271 Kendall	J	1877-8-9	143 Andrews	J	1877-8 r
Laslett	R	1878 r	618 Maguire	R	1877-8-9	194 Armil	L.A	1877-8
Mason	H	1877-8	627 Mc Dermot	F	1877-8-9	185 Arnold	D	1877-8 r
Maybury	R	1878-9	589 Mc Gregor	F	1877-8 r	**186 Ashley**	**J**	**1877-8**
Moss	L	1878	Duplicate medal See also Sgt. F			**KIA Moirosi's Stronghold**		
Nunns	E	1878 r	Mc Gregor CMR			189 Austin	E.P	1877-8
Parish	J.V	1878	631 Mc Kenzie	T.L	1877-8-9	372 Bailey	H	1877-8
Parkinson	F	1878	628 Mc Leod	H	1877-8-9	670 Baker	A.J	1877-8 r
Peakman	T.C	1879	626 Meinke	O	1877-8-9	669 Baker	H	1877-8-9 r
Roberts	H	1878	628 Mobbs	J	1877-8-9	671 Banfield	T	1877-8
Rochfort	H	1877-8-9 r	619 Munns	F	1877-8-9	677 Barrett	G	1877-8
Schneider	A	1878-9	630 Murphy	E	1877-8-9 r	680 Bartholomew	E	1877-8
Walker	J	1877-8	629 Myer	H	1877-8-9	664 Beckwith	C	1877-8 r
White	B.L	1877-8-9	240 Ray	R	1877-8-9	663 Behn	W	1877-8 r
			161 Ross	T.G	1877-8	679 Bennett	W.P	1877-8 r
CAPE MOUNTED RIFLES & FRONTIER ARMED AND MOUNTED POLICE.			467 Stewart	S	1877-8 r	655 Berry	J	1877-8 r
			200 Taylor	H.S	1877-8	689 Bescovy	E	1877-8-9
The CMR fought in the Moorosi campaign in 1879, the Basutoland Gun War (1880-1881), the Matabeleland campaign (1893-1894), the Bechuanaland campaign in 1897, and the Second Boer War (1899-1902).			210 Thompson	C	1877-8 r	681 Boucher	H	1877-8
			195 Todd	R	1877-8-9	660 Boucher	R	1877-8-9
			387 Wynne	W	1877-8-9	Wounded at Moirosi's Stronghold		
			CORPORAL			673 Bowman	J	1877-8 r
			193 Albrecht	W	1877-8	678 Boxer	F	1877-8 r
CAPTAIN			659 Bell	J	1877-8-9	683 Boyce	W.S	1877-8 r
Grant	J.M	1877-8-9	668 Brown	G.E.G	1877-8 r	654 Bradshaw	S	1877-8
O'Connor	J.T	1877-8-9	232 Demmer	J	1877-8-9	684 Braine	O	1877-8 r
INSPECTOR			566 Hope	F	1877-8-9	**685 Braine**	**W.H**	**1877-8-9**
Chalmers	E.B	1877-8	194 (191) Jones	A	1877-8-9 r	**KIA Moirosi's Stronghold**		
Surmon	**J**	**1877-8-9**	D/W Moiresi's Stronghold.			**667 Breen KIA**	**J**	**1877-8**
KIA Moirosi's Stronghold			260 Keumm	A	1877-8 r	661 Bremner	A	1877-8
SUB INSPECTOR			18 Lambert	C	1877-8-9	662 Brink	J	1877-8 r
Hamilton	W.E.S	1877-8	**608 Martindale**	**T**	**1877-8-9**	657 Brink	W	1877-8 r
Michell	R	1877-8-9	**KIA Moirosi's Stronghold**			653 Briscoe	R	1877-8 r
LIEUTENANT			616 Manning	T.H	1877-8	505 Brookes	F.A	1877-8 r
Holden	W.S	1877-8	600 Mc Wade	J	1877-8	674 Broome	A	1877-8-9
Maclean	W.A	1877-8-9	40 Schenk	F	1877-8	666 Brown	H	1877-8
Van Ryneveldt	J.H	1877-8-9 r	442 Schnaper ?	R	1877-8	32 Brown VC	P	1877-8-9
Wilde	E.J.J	1877-8-9	371 Scott	H.T	1877-8-9	The VC was for an action at Moirosi's Stronghold, also wounded in action.		
SERGEANT MAJOR			Wounded Moirosi's Stronghold					
686 Burchkard	J	1877-8	440 Steel	J	1877-8 r	658 Browham	J	1877-8 r
318 Darling	A	1877-8	328 Stokes	W	1877-8-9	665 Bunge	F	1877-8 r
276 Kaniesky ?	W	1877-8-9	405 Stoley	H.C	1877-8-9	485 Burgess	G	1877-8
ARMOURER SERGEANT			192 Turner	J.W	1877-8-9	675 Burnside	C.R	1877-8 r
269 Greaves	J	1877-8	194 Turner	W.St J	1877-8-9	676 Burton	C.T	1877-8
468 Smith	W.T	1877-8	155 Taylor	T	1877-8-9	35 Campbell	W.D	1877-8
SERGEANT			198 Terbians	F	1877-8	534 Carton	J	1877-8-9 r
155 Anderson	F	1877-8 r	386 Wentworth	E	1877-8 r	533 Castles	C	1877-8-9
194 Ansell	G	1877-8	294 Wood	P.A.E	1877-8-9	554 Cayton	R	1877-8 r
656 Burgees	H	1877-8	**382 Woodward**	**E**	**1877-8-9**	538 Chamier	H	1877-8-9 r
682 Brooks	A	1877-8	**KIA Moirosi's Stronghold**			539 Chaplin	W	1877-8-9
687 Beeby	J	1877-8-9	**TRUMPETER**			553 Chapman	C.H	1877-8-9
552 Cadle	J	1877-8-9 r	688 Bristner	J	1877-8-9	557 Chauncey	A	1877-8 r
			Medal from earlier war. Clasp Only			542 Cherry	W	1877-8 r

Cape Mounted Rifles & Frontier Armed & Mounted Police

556	Child J	1877-8 r
415	Childe E	1877-8-9 r

See also Col. E. Childe Cape F. Arty.

541	Christman J	1877-8
460	Clarke H	1877-8-9
537	Close H.H	1877-8
544	Clyde J	1877-8
555	Collison D/S J	1877-8 r
549	Compton F	1877-8 r
546	Congdon C	1877-8
532	Coom A	1877-8-9 r

Medal and clasp re-issued 4/7/1930.

535	Coop T.W	1877-8 r
426	Corbett G	1877-8
540	Cousins C	1877-8
550	Coward G	1877-8
536	Cox J	1877-8-9
543	Cox T	1877-8-9
547	Cracknell C	1877-8
545	Crawford H	1877-8

See also Queenstown Vol. Contg.

531	Crosley J	1877-8-9 r
548	Curt H.G	1877-8 r
261	Dalziel R	1877-8-9
311	Davies G.W	1877-8-9 r
241	Davies W.L	1877-8 r
308	Davis A	1877-8
307	Dawson W	1877-8 r
218	Demmer H	1877-8-9 r
316	Demmer J	1877-8-9
310	Derbyshire F	1877-8 r
314	Desfontaine J	1877-8-9 r
359	Devine A	1877-8 r
313	Ditchbourne W	1877-8 r
306	Dixon R	1877-8 r
305	Dobrowsky A	1877-8
315	Domoney H	1877-8-9
303	Dor J	1877-8 r
312	Drayton T	1877-8
301	Dunkin J	1877-8 r
304	Durney H.J	1877-8
302	Dutton H	1877-8
309	Dyer E	1877-8
160	Eastes C	1877-8 r
161	Eastes W	1877-8 r
164	Eaton T	1877-8-9
156	Eiman H	1877-8 r
158	Engelbrecht K	1877-8 r
224	Faircloth J.T	1877-8
236	Falkiner F.R	1877-8-9
235	Farmer C	1877-8-9
229	Ferreira S	1877-8 r
226	Fisher J	1877-8
230	Fowle G.H	1877-8
227	Fowler E	1877-8 r
232	Franks C.R.B	1877-8
225	Franks W	1877-8 r
233	Freeman T.J	1877-8-9
234	Frown R	1877-8-9 r
228	Fuller J	1877-8 r
231	Fyson R	1877-8
261	Garfield J	1877-8
289	**Geise W**	**1877**

KIA Draaibosch 29/12/1877

271	Gherke W.A	1877-8-9
273	Gibson S	1877-8-9
264	Gill H	1877-8
260	Gill T	1877-8-9
270	Gillanm J	1877-8
268	Gimingham? S	1877-8
272	Goddard J	1877-8-9
267	Goldsworthy A	1877-8
266	Gordon F.E	1877-8
262	Gould E	1877-8 r
263	Granthan H	1877-8 r
265	Green W	1877-8 r
553	Halbert T	1877-8
564	Hall S	1877-8
534	Hambley J	1877-8
557	Hamilton C.P	1877-8 r
	Handyside J.R	

Wounded at Moirosi's Stronghold

535	Hannam C	1877-8 r
552	Harris W	1877-8 r
536	Harrison F	1877-8 r
462	Harrison J	1877-8 r
554	Harrison W.H	1877-8 r
532	Harvey W	1877-8 r
539	Haydon W	1877-8 r
550	Hayes R	1877-8 r
233	Hedges W.T	1877-8 r
561	Hedley D	1877-8 r
549	Heine W	1877-8 r
562	Hensworth J.M	1877-8
342	Henderson H	1877-8-9 r
557	Hempel C	1877-8-9
563	Henke P	1877-8 r
555	Hicks W	1877-8
524	Higgins M	1877-8 r
559	Higginson W	1877-8 r
548	Hildebrandt C	1877 r
414	Hilhard C.H	1877-8-9
558	Hillier H.A	1877-8
542	Hingeston C.E	1877-8-9
556	Hodnett T.E	1877-8-9
404	Hobson J	1877-8-9
547	Hoffe P.R	1877-8
541	Hofman G	1877-8-9 r
540	Hopkins C	1877-8-9 r
543	Horne C.W	1877-8-9
407	Horne C.W	1877-8-9
560	How H	1877-8 r
545	Howell A	1877-8 r
546	Hutton S	1877-8 r
131	Jackson J.M	1877-8

CAPE MOUNTED RIFLES.

TO THE EDITOR OF THE DAILY NEWS.

SIR,—I beg to forward you copy of a portion of a letter received from one of the late Cape Mounted Rifles, which might give the information Lord R. Churchill demanded from the Government last night in the House. I am, Sir, yours obediently,

STANLEY LUCAS.

Arts Club, Hanover-square, W.C., Feb. 15.

Jan. 7, 1879.

I daresay that you have read in the papers about the frontier armed and mounted police being changed into the Cape Mounted Rifles, and the extreme dissatisfaction expressed by the men. Instead of being a civil force, we now find we are compelled to serve in a regular cavalry regiment. The authorities argue that they have not changed rules, pay, &c., but without doing that they have changed the whole tone and character of the force, and are in fact making us into soldiers. The Government have broken their contract with us in ever so many respects, but we can obtain no redress, and are told it is no good to fight against Government, as they can do whatever they like, whether just or not. And that they have done. Myself and 19 other men of No. 1 troop refused to serve in the Cape Mounted Rifles, and claimed our discharge, as the frontier armed and mounted police had been abolished. We were made prisoners and subjected to gross ill-treatment, our horses, &c. (our own property), forcibly taken from us, and we made to walk upwards of forty miles towards King William's-town, when, through the kindness of the officer commanding, we were allowed to ride on bullock waggons for the remainder of the journey. After being close prisoners in King William's-town for 14 days we were charged for mutiny and tried by a board of officers (the colonel, adjutant, and captain), and sentenced to six months' hard labour on the breakwater at East London. They would not allow us to try in a civil court whether or not we were bound to serve in the Cape Mounted Rifles, but assumed we were, and sentenced us for mutinying in a force we were never sworn into. We were accordingly sent to the convict station at East London, where men of all crimes and colours are herded together. There were 120 men in the same room with myself. I had a straw bed to sleep on, and was between a Kafir and Hottentot, the one in for killing a man, and the other for cattle stealing. We had to work on the breakwater for 12 hours a day on a pound of brown bread and about half a pound of meat, generally unsuitable for a white man, and a pint of hot water called by courtesy soup. After enduring two months of this modern torture, the Government offered to let us out if we would consent to return to duty, acknowledging ourselves to be Cape Mounted Riflemen. Rather than suffer such fearful misery any longer, we consented, were released, and sent back here again, further off than ever from obtaining redress. There is no doubt we are in the right; even the colonial press says so, but at the same time says the Government cannot afford to disband the forces; and consequently, unless the matter be taken up by the Home Parliament, we shall have to bow to injustice and might.

185	Jacob A	1877-8 r
186	Jennings A.H	1877-8 r
190	Job R	1877-8 r
189	Job W	1877-8 r
183	Johnson B	1877-8-9 r
187	Johnson C	1877-8-9
184	Johnson S.P	1877-8-9
134	Jones J	1877-8-9 r
140	Jones J.O	1877-8-9 r
262	Karg G	1877-8 r
267	Kauntz T.A	1877-8 r
264	Kennedy J	1877-8 r
274	Keumm F	1877-8 r
273	King T	1877-8
268	King W.H	1877-8-9 r
270	Kinsley E.S	1877-8-9
272	Klotke C	1877-8-9
263	Kloke A	1877-8-9 r
240	Kneebone S	1877-8-9 r

Cape Mounted Rifles & Frontier Armed & Mounted Police

265	Knight T.H	1877-8-9	89	Nelson J	1877-8-9	457 Schreiber G	1877-8 r
261	Knorr H	1877-8	84	Nelson W	1877-8-9	444 Schult F	1877-8-9
275	Kreps G	1877-8-9	6	Neville W	1877-8-9 r	448 Schult J	1877-8-9
18	Kunhardt G.A	1877-8-9 r	111	Nicoll H.J.R	1877-8-9	389 Schultz F	1877-8-9
269	Kurtain J	1877-8-9	68	Nightingale G	1877-8-9	339 Scott VC R.G	1877-8-9
266	Kurtain J.W	1877-8	106	Noice G	1877-8-9 r	His VC was for an action at Moirosi's	
229	Lally F	1877-8 r	84	Oakley H.W	1877-8-9	Stronghold.	
233	Langrist W.H	1877-8	85	Ochuyson C	1877-8 r	461 Shaw K	1877-8-9
224	Lawrence W	1877-8-9 r	81	Oliver F.J	1877-8 r	470 Shelton J	1877-8
226	Leary R	1877-8-9 r	83	Osborne R	1877-8	464 Shervington T.R	1877-8
227	Lee C	1877-8	82	Otten C	1877-8	445 Shewan A	1877-8 r
228	Leonard C	1877-8-9 r	271	Paeler? C	1877-8-9	454 Sibley F	1877-8 r
230	Lightfoot F	1877-8 r	269	Paschke (Paskie) J	1877-8-9 r	462 Sloman W.H	1877-8-9 r
225	Lightfoot M	1877-8-9	Mortally Wounded Moirosi's Stronghold.			451 Smith A	1877-8 r
231	Lindam C.O	1877-8	282	Passey C	1877-8 r	**449 Smith KIA C.D.C 1877-8**	
234	Lousada St L	1877-8	276	Patterson J.W	1877-8-9	443 Smith G	1877-8 r
232	Lubba K	1877-8 r	275	Penney F.L	1877-8 r	460 Smith G.A	1877-8 r
223	Luck W	1877-8 r	280	Persch J		463 Smith J	1877-8
235	Lukis W.D	1877-8			1877-8 r	361 Smith R	1877-8 r
166	Luclett R	1877-8 r	270	Perus J.H	1877-8 r	456 Smith T	1877-8
620	Mack A	1877-8-9	**278 Peterson C.W**		**1877-8-9 r**	458 Smythe J.R	1877-8-9
590	Mack D	1877-8-9	**KIA Moirosi's Stronghold**			Wounded at Moirosi's Stronghold	
595	Mack J	1877-8	164	Petry H	1877-8 r	447 Snoer C	1877-8 r
601	Mai G	1877-8	277	Peveritt W.H	1877-8-9 r	448 Snoer P	1877-8 r
597	Malone E	1877-8 r	283	Phillips S	1877-8-9	452 Soarsley W.H	1877-8 r
615	Mansfield W	1877-8	274	Pinckstone A	1877-8 r	450 Stokes J	1877-8 r
596	Marshall H	1877-8 r	273	Pooya C	1877-8 r	459 Sullivan M	1877-8-9
621	Maskell C	1877-8 r	284	Pringle W.W	1877-8-9	455 Suter C	1877-8
591	Master J	1877-8	29	Prior J	1877-8-9	465 Suter C.W	1877-8-9
593	Matheson J	1877-8-9 r	279	Proctor M	1877-8-9 r	471 Sutherland J	1877-8-9
599	Matthews T	1877-8 r	14	Purcell W.H	1877-8-9	365 Swann C	1877-8-9 r
612	Maynier H	1877-8 r	272	Purvis T	1877-8 r	466 Swash T	1877-8-9
603	Mc Dougall S	1877-8	247	Ramsbotton W	1877-8	Mortally Moirosi's Stronghold.	
624	Mc Leod J.E	1877-8-9	239	Rassmussen W	1877-8-9 r	209 Tappenden A	1877-8 r
606	Mc Mullen C	1877-8	252	Rawle F	1877-8 r	196 Tasmer R	1877-8-9
38	Mc Pherson G	1877-8-9	246	Reid B	1877-8	203 Terry A	1877-8
602	Medina C	1877-8 r	236	Revell R	1877-8	202 Thiel C	1877-8
592	Meggersee C	1877-8 r	238	Rich A	1877-8-9	199 Thiel F	1877-8-9
611 Meyerhoffer C.F		**1877-8 r**	242	Richards R	1877-8	193 Thomas F	1877-8-9
KIA near Komgha 30/12/1877			248	Richardson H	1877-8-9 r	205 Thomas R	1877-8 r
598	Middleton J	1877-8	255	Rickette C	1877-8 r	122 Thomas W.E	1877-8
65	Milledge A	1877-8	251	Rigby D/S T.S	1877-8 r	152 Thompson A	1877-8 r
613	Morgan C	1877-8	244	Ristow F	1877-8-9	197 Thompson C	1877-8 r
607	Morkel W	1877-8	192	Roberts H	1877-8 r	208 Thompson J	1877-8
614	Morris E.W.H	1877-8-9 r	254	Robinson H	1877-8-9	206 Thompson W.J	1877-8 r
605	Morris J	1877-8	245	Robinson W	1877-8 r	158 Tremer C.A.C	1877-8 r
622	Morton E	1877-8	243	Roderick W	1877-8	204 Tripp H.S	1877-8
604	Mostert C	1877-8	253	Rogers C.G	1877-8-9	201 Truvin J	1877-8
623	Mostert J	1877-8 r	Wounded at Moirosi's Stronghold			207 Truvin A	1877-8
594	Muller E	1877-8	237	Romain H	1877-8-9	21 Upton C	1877-8
610	Muller W	1877-8 r	195	Ross J.W	1877-8-9 r	544 Van Holst M	1877-8-9
617	Mulvibul J	1877-8-9	Duplicate. See Pts. J.W. Ross CMR			108 Van Neil J	1877-8 r
609	Murphy W	1877-8	250	Rowe H	1877-8-9	109 Van Wyk A	1877-8 r
107	Nantes W.H	1877-8-9 r	249	Russell A.C	1877-8-9	110 Van Wyk W	1877-8 r
110	Neal F	1877-8	235	Russell J	1877-8-9 r	111 Varisfield G	1877-8 r
109	Nebbe B	1877-8 r	21	Ryton A.W	1877-8 r	106 Venn C	1877-8-9
111	Neilson F	1877-8-9 r	441	Sanderson T	1877-8	107 Vermoeter L	1877-8 r
108	Nelson C	1877-8	**453 Schoeppler KIA F 1877-8 r**			395 Wade A	1877-8

Cape Mounted Rifles & Frontier Armed & Mounted Police

Cape Mounted Riflemen		
Colonels	Date	
H.G.Moore, V.C	1878-1879	(1)
Z.S.Bayly, C.M.G	1879-1892	(2)
F.Carrigton, C.M.G.	1880-1884	(3)
E.H Dalgety, C.B	1892-1902	(4)
J.M.Grant	1867-1895	(5)
Majors		
J.C.Waring	1871-1902	(6)
R.F Cantwell	1877-1907	(7)
C.C Bailie	1855-1883	
C.M Sprenger	1868-1900	(8)
Captains		
*H.Carstensen	1880-1905	
C.L.J. Goldsworthy	1876-1	
J.H.Bourne	1870-1886	
M.W.Robertson, C.M.G	1879-1902	
R.B.Stewart	1878-1906	
W.P Straw	1877-1906	
A.Cosgrove	1881-1907	
E.F.Hatton	1871-1899	
H.Sprigg	1882-1894	
*E.A.Taplin	1876-1905	(9)
*J.F.Purcell	1880-1906	
*R.N. Cumming	1880-1913	
J.T. Bowers	1880-1889	
H.T.Fynn	1872-1884	
G.E. Giles	1879-1880	
J.W. Goldsworthy	1877-1882	
J.K. Maclean	1871-1882	
W.McCullum	1877-1884	
H.S. Montague	1876-1883	
C.R. Shervinton	1880-1884	
H.V.Woon	1879-1897	
H.M. Heyman	1877-1889	
R. Watson	1876-1899	
H.W. Goldsworthy	1877-1900	
A.Vizard	1882-1900	
G.D.Ward	1890-1904	
A.S.Boardman	1883-1906	
A.Blaine	1880-1900	
C.D'Arcy, V.C	1880-1881	

*Retired as Major.

Lieutenants			
W. St J.Turner		1877-1881	
C.S.West		1875-1884	
E. Wylde		1871-1879	
F.W.K .Wylde		1859-1879	
L.Winslow		1876-1888	
R.Kennon		1874-1882	
M.E.Knott		1878-1887	
E.Sutherland		1870-1881	
W.Stier		1877-1884	
F.G Shortt		1874-1889	
H.T.Scott		1877-1895	
J.H.van Ryneveld		1870-1880	
N. Neylan		1877-1884	
G.McMullen		1872-1883	
J.C.H.Mahony		1882-1897	
G.Hopkins		1883-1897	
W.C.P.Jones		1880-1897	
R.J.Shaw		1882-1893	
S.R.Style		1880-1896	
C.J Sugden		1882-1896	
T.N.Bailey		1876-1887	
T.C.Birbeck		1868-1881	
J.Best		1874-1880	
W.E. Brownlow		1879-1881	
W.Cruttwell		1876-1884	
R.B. Dent		1877-1884	
D.M. Fraser		1877-1890	
H. Fraser		1890-1897	
G.G.Graves		1880-1884	
H.Heyes		1874-1884	
T.A Clarke		1874-1880	
H.F.B. Taplin		1876-1900	
Paymasters			
W.L.Hutchinson	Major	1859-1894	
J.McCabe	Major	1865-1898	
D.Standin	Captain	1880-1881	
Quartermasters			
J.Leatherland	Major	1856-1896	
W.H.B. Phillips	Major	1876-1908	(10)
W. A. McCarter	Captain	1856-1884	
G.F.Russ	Captain	1875-1898	Died 1898
Medical Officers			
E.B Hartley, V.C	Colonel	1877-1903	(11)
J.F McCrea,	Major	1882-1894	(12)
P.A Green,	Lieut	1881-1884	

(1) Gained V.C 29/12/77 at Draaibosch, Kaffir War 1877-78
(2) Late Norfolk Regt. and O.C. D.E.O.V.R. Cape Town
(3) Formerly South Wales Borderers, commanded left wing, C.M.R, 1880-4. Was severely wounded in the Basuto War, 1881. Served in the Matabele Rebellion, 1893. Commanded the Southern Rhodesian Field Force in the Anglo-Boar War. Later awarded the K.C.B & K.C.M.G.
(4) Late Lieut. Royal Scots Fusiliers 1867-1876
(5) Joined C.M.R 1880. Commissioned 1882, Captain 1898. Major 1900. Brevet Lieut-Colonel, and command of the regiment May 1911.
(6) Severely wounded at Wepener, Anglo-Boer War. April 1900.
(7) Mentioned in dispatches. Anglo-Boer War
(8) Killed at Wepener, April 1900. "nd in command, C.M.R.
(9) Retired as Major. Seriously wounded at Aliwal North.
(10) Had commanded I Squadron C.M.R., took Russ's place in 1898.
(11) Gained V.C Moirosi's Mountain, 5th June 1897.
(12) Before he transferred to the C.M.R, he won the V.C while attached to the 1st Regt. Cape Yeomanry in a battle at Tweefonein,14.01.81
Source Boot & Saddle by P.J.Young. Record of the Cape Mounted Riflemen and Frontier Armed Mounted Police Regiment.

Cape Mounted Rifles & Frontier Armed & Mounted Police

405	Wade A.W.W	1877-8	**CAPTAIN**			Palmer	F.A	1877-8-9
392	Waldron F	1877-8	Grant	J.M	1877-8-9	See also Cpl F.A. Palmer below.		
58	Walker W.B	1877-8 r	Hook	D.B	1877-8-9	Parr	D.B	No clasp
411	Walters C	1877-8 r	Mc Carter	W.A	1877-8-9	Pearce	G	1877-8-9
299	Walton A	1877-8	Shervinton	C.R.St L	1877-8-9	Pitt	J	1878
588	Wardle G	1877-8 r	Waring	J.C	1877-8-9	Richardson J		1877-8-9
381	Wardle J	1877-8-9	**ASSISTANT PAYMASTER**			Ryan	T	1877-8-9
292	Warren J	1877-8 r	Mc Cabe	J	1877-8	Tierney	J.M	1877-8-9
403	Watson A	1877-8 r	**LIEUTENANT**			West	C.R	1877-8-9
391	Watson J	1877-8-9	Birbeck	T.C	1877-8-9	**CORPORAL**		
383	Weir W	1877-8	Cochrane	J.P	1877-8-9	Baker	W	1877-8-9
409	Welch J	1877-8 r	See also Cape Field Artillery.			Childe	E	1877-8-9
404	Wells T	1877-8	Goldworthy	H	1877-8-9	See also Cape Field Artillery.		
384	Wespfahl W	1877-8-9	Kennan	R	1878	Denmer	J	1877-8
393	Whitehead G.S	1877-8-9	Mc Cullum	W	1877-8-9	Hollins	J	1877-8-9 r
401	Whyte H	1877-8	Mc Mullen	G	1877-8-9	Knight	J.H	1877-8-9 r
398	Wild A	1877-8	Montagu	H.S	1877-8-9	# Macpherson G		1877-8-9
385	Wildey G	1877-8-9	Meyland	N	1877-8-9	Matthews	C	1877-8
400	Wilkinson J.R	1877-8	Russ	G.F	1877-8-9	**Murphy**	**E**	**1877-8-9 r**
402	Williams C	1877-8	Sutherland	E	1877-8-9	**KIA Morosi's Stronghold**		
408	Williams H	1877-8	White	G.H	1877-8-9	Palmer	F.A	1877-8-9
407	Williams J	1877-8 r	Williams	G.H	1877-8-9	See also Sgt. F.A. Palmer above.		
396	Williams J	1877-8 r	**SERGEANT MAJOR**			Powell	F	1877-8-9
410	Williams J	1877-8	Burgess	G	1877-8-9	**Sherratt C not on medal roll**		
390	Williams J.L	1877-8-9	Rennick	J	1877-8-9	**KIA at Gwanda Hill 25/9/1877**		
397	**Winkles KIA H**	**1877-8-9 r**	**QUARTERMASTER SERGEANT**			Stokes	W	1877-8-9
353	Woods F.G.M	1877-8-9	Burges	G	1877-8	Taylor	T	1877-8-9
406	Woolward J.D	1877-8	**SERGEANT**			**GUNNER**		
389	Wylie W	1877-8-9	Andrews	J	1877-8-9	Allner	F.O	1877-8
15	Young W	1877-8 r	Berry	N	1877-8-9	Algar	J.E	1877-8-9
16	Young W	1877-8	Cahill	M	1877-8	Butter	A.H	1877-8-9 r
RANK NOT KNOWN			Cazzly	W	1877-8-9	**PRIVATE**		
	Haynes H.W	1877-8-9	Cooley	A.H	1877-8-9	Abbott	C.E	1877-8-9
	Inman P	1877-8-9	**Edwards**	**J**	**1877-8-9**	Adams	W	1877-8-9 r
			KIA Morosi's Stronghold			Allman	A.H	1879
CAPE MOUNTED RIFLEMEN.			Fiveash	J.A	1877-8-9	Anderson	A	1877-8-9
In 1878 it was decided to reorganize the			Graham	H.D	1877-8-9	Andries (Native)		1877-8-9 r
Frontier Armed & Mounted Police as the			Hayes	H	1877-8-9	Anstey	H	1879 r
Cape Mounted Riflemen a decision that			Hilliard	C.H	1877-8-9	Applegren C		1877-8-9
received wide disapproval			Inman	R.P	1877-8-9	Armstrong	A	1877-8-9 r
COMMANDANT			Lock	E	No clasp	Armstrong	H	1879
D'Arcy_ VC C		1877-8-9	Lord	W	1878-9	Atkins	G de V	1877-8-9 r
His VC was for an action at Ulundi.			Mac Gregor	F	1877-8	Avis	A	1877-8-9
Griffith _CMG C.D		1877-8-9	Mc Gregor	T	1877-8-9 r	Ayres	R	1877-8
Clasp only, medal from an earlier			Mc Millan	C.C	1877-8-9	Balach	C	1877-8-9
S.A. War.			Morris	E	1877-8-9	## Balfour E		1877-8-9
SURGEON			Munns	F	1877-8-9	Banks	A	1879
Sharpe LRCS W.A		1877-8	Nelson	R	1877-8-9	Barnett	A.D	1879
						Barnett	S	1879

#Dix Noonan Web Auction Lot 858, 22 Sep 06
Family group: Pair: Sergeant C. G. MacPherson, Natal Police
Queen's South Africa 1899-1902, 2 clasps, Natal, South Africa 1901 (2237 Tpr. C. G. McPherson, Natal Police), unofficial rivets between 1st and 2nd clasps; Natal 1906, 1 clasp, 1906 (2C. Sgt. C. G. MacPherson, Natal Police), note different spelling of name
South Africa 1877-79, 1 clasp, 1877-8-9 (Corpl. G. MacPherson, C.M. Rifles) nearly extremely fine Hammer Price: £490
Footnote: The above, possibly a group to one man?

Dix Noonan Web Auction Lot 400, Lot 571, 7 Dec 05
South Africa 1877-79, 1 clasp, 1877-8-9 (Pte. E. Balfour, C.M. Rifles) very fine Hammer Price: £270

Cape Mounted Riflemen

Barker	C.N	1877-8	Brown	J	1877-8-9	Cullen	E.W	1879 r
Barrett	G	1877-8-9	Bruce	C	1877-8-9	Denmer	H	1879 r
Bayley	A.L	1877-8-9 r	Burr	H	1877-8-9 r	Dent	R.B	1877-8-9
Baylis	E.T	1877-8	Burton	A.L.T	1877-8-9 r	Dick	P	1877-8
Baylıss	E.T	1878	Butt	J	1877-8-9	Dietzsch	P	1877-8
Bell	G	1879	Buttenshaw	F	1877-8-9	Disney	A	1877-8-9 r
Bell	R	1877-8-9	Byrne	W	1879	Doland	J	1877-8
Bennett	B	1877-8-9 r	Byron	A	1877-8	Donough	A	1877-8-9
Benson	J	1877-8-9	Cadle	G	1879	Duplan	J	1877-8-9 r
Bescoby	E	1877-8-9	Cahill	A	1877-8-9	Durant	W	1877-8-9 r
Bickercarten	Adrian	1877-8-9	Cahill	?	1877-8-9	Dwyer	J.C	1877-8-9
Bickercarten	Arnold	1877-8-9	Cheetham	F	1877-8-9	Dyer	E.S	1877-8-9
Biden	A.H	1877-8	Cheetham	F.G	1877-8	Dyson	G	1879
Blabey	G.M	1877-8-9	Clabburn	W	1879 r	Eastwood	J	1877-8-9
Blach	C	1877-8-9 r	Clarke	J	1877-8-9 r	Eastwood	W.F	1877-8-9
Bluhm	F	1877-8-9 r	Clifford	W	1879 r	Edgell	C.H	1879
Bodkin	J	1879	Cloete	H	1877-8-9	Edgeworth	H.E	1877-8-9
Booy (Native)	C.Longa	1877-8-9	Coggin	F.H	1877-8-9	Ellis	J	1877-8-9 r
Bowen	A	1877-8	Cole	F	1877-8-9	England	W.O	1877-8-9
Bowen	Alfred	1877-8	**Cole**	**W (W.F)**	**1877-8-9**	Eyre	A	1877-8-9
Bowen	A.D	1877-8	**KIA Moirosi's Stronghold**			Fatt	F.W	1877-8
Bowler	J	1877-8-9	Collins	A.J	1877-8-9 r	Faulkner	J	1879
Bowler	James	1877-8-9	Corfield	T.W	1877-8-9	Festing	F.W	1877-8-9 r
Brakonji	J	1877-8-9	Wounded at Moirosi's Stronghold.			Finnis	E.J	1877-8-9
Brayshaw	H	1877-8-9	Cornish	W	1879	Fitzpatrick	J	1877-8-9
Brill	F.G	1877-8-9	Corsi	G	1879	Fitzpatrick	P	1877-8
Brown	B	1877-8	Coventry	J	1879	Francis	T.E	1877-8 r
Brown	G.E	1877-8 r	Cruttwell	W	1877-8-9	Frazer	T	1879

CASUALTIES IN THE BASUTOLAND REBELLION (THE GUN WAR) 1880-1881				
Name	Regiment	Rank	Date	Place
Clarke, T. A.	Cape Mounted Riflemen	Lieut.	17/9/1880	Mafeteng
Clover, H. (d)	Cape Mounted Riflemen	Sgt.	17/2/1881	Wepener
Cook, C.	Cape Mounted Riflemen	Pte.	4/10/1880	Mohale's Hoek
Demmer, H. (d)	Cape Mounted Riflemen	Pte.	21/1/1881	Mafeteng
Doland, - (d)	Cape Mounted Riflemen	Pte.	17/3/1881	Mafeteng
Hurst, J.	Cape Mounted Riflemen	Pte.	28/10/1881	Maseru
Kiddy, T. E.	Cape Mounted Riflemen	Pte.	1/12/1880	Mafeteng
Leahy, R. (d)	Cape Mounted Riflemen	Pte.	19/1/1881	Kokstad
Magee, -	Cape Mounted Riflemen	Pte.	17/9/1880	Mafeteng
Morris, E (d)	Cape Mounted Riflemen	Sgt.	4/4/1881	Mafeteng
Murphy, E. P.	Cape Mounted Riflemen	Pte.	13/12/1880	Mafeteng
Rochfort, - (d)	Cape Mounted Riflemen	Pte.	9/3/1881	Mafeteng
Sherratt, -	Cape Mounted Riflemen	Cpl.	31/10/1880	Mafeteng
Trigg, - (d)	Cape Mounted Riflemen	Pte.	8/1/1881	Maseru
White, -	Cape Mounted Riflemen	Pte.	17/9/1880	Mafeteng
CASUALTIES IN THE SIEGE OF MOROSI'S MOUNTAIN IN 1879				
Braine,	Cape Mounted Riflemen	Pte.	8/4/1879	1st Assault
Cole, W. F.	Cape Mounted Riflemen	Sgt.	8/4/1879	1st Assault
Edwards, J.	Cape Mounted Riflemen	Sgt.	8/4/1879	1st Assault
Jones, A.	Cape Mounted Riflemen	Cpl.	5/6/1879	2nd Assault
Martindale, C.	Cape Mounted Riflemen	Cpl.	8/4/1879	1st Assault
Paskie,	Cape Mounted Riflemen	Pte.	8/4/1879	1st Assault
Peterson, R.	Cape Mounted Riflemen	Pte.	6/5/1879	
Schwartz,	Cape Mounted Riflemen		20/11/1879	3rd and Final Assault
Surmon, J.	Cape Mounted Riflemen	Capt	8/4/1879	1st Assault

Extracts from: Military History Journal - Vol 1 No 5, Compiled by Major G. Tyllden ,http://samilitaryhistory.org/vol015gt.html

[by courtesy of Colonel B. C. Judd

F.A.M.P. 1873

Left to right: A trumpeter, Jones, Koch, Sgt.-Major T. Birbeck, Commandant Bowker, Inspector J. M. Grant, Demmer, Luck

CAPE MOUNTED RIFLEMEN (IMPERIAL)
Lieuts. Harvey, Collins, Boyes, Pote, Brabant, and Pasley; Capt. Currie; Majors McConnell and Morant; Vet. Surg. Paton; Lt. Larter; Sgt.-Major McMahon; Riding Master Mories

NCHAYECHIBI WAR (Extracts from Boot & Saddle) by P.J. Young

The Transkei tribal boundaries were constantly disputed, and in 1876 public attention was drawn to Kreli's (chief of the Gcalekas) conquest of the *Tembus. **Governor Barkly** had met Kreli, and a commission had been set up to define the boundaries, but no firm agreement could be reached. The Gcalekas naturally resented the presence of their former servants, the Fingoes, side by side in their own country. They still tried to dominate these people, but the Fingoes would not stand for subjection. Being a kindred race to, the Zulus, they had never been able to submit to it. The conflict between the two tribes was to continue.

At this time **Commandant Bowker** was transferred to the military command in the Transkei, and **Commandant Griffith**, High Commissioner's Agent in Basutoland, was appointed to the command of the F.A.M.P. The force was at that time distributed as follows : No. 1 Troop Queenstown, 2 Kokstad, 3 Komgha, 4 Palmietfontein, 5 King William's Town, 6 Butterworth 7 Peddie, 8 Kenhardt, 9 Ealing Post, 10 Fort Murray. In August 1877 at a beer gatherings a Gcaleka headman had been killed in a fight with the Fingoes, which led to pitched battles with assegais and knobsticks. As the matter was growing worse, a police troop under **Inspector Chalmers** was sent forward on the 26th September from Ibeka towards Idutywa to steady the situation. On the march the police noticed a skirmish between some Fingoes and the Gcalekas near the Gwadana Mountain, and they turned off to aid the Fingoes. During an engagement in which the police gun-carriage broke down, the patrol was obliged to retreat with the loss of one officer — Sub-Inspector Von Hohenau — and six men.

The Gcalekas, encouraged by this success, made an attack on the Ibeka Post, where **Commandant Griffith** had taken up his headquarters. For two days they tried to overcome the garrison, but was unable to get through the defence. Following this attack reinforcements of volunteer units and burgher commandos arrived in the Transkei from the Colony. Consequently, in early October, a general advance on Kreli's kraal took place. During the march the troops went into action at Springs and Gcuwa Valley.

Colonel Griffith, who had been given that rank after the Ibeka affair, detached a force of police and Fingoes to march to the Manubi Forest, and there take up a position to give a column under Griffith time to stem the Gcalekas passing into the Colony. Hardly had the commander, **Inspector Hook**, occupied the position, than the Gcalekas, under Kreli himself, attacked. The fight was difficult and fierce, and a number of the defenders were lost in a few hours. The real heroes of this fight were **Captains William** and **Michael Goss** of the Fingo contingent, who were killed in a gallant attempt to dislodge a party of the enemy who had taken refuge in the Kabakazi Gorge.

Early in December British troops and volunteers were rushed to the frontier. Colonel Griffith was superseded by **Brigadier- General Glynn,** who was placed in command of combined forces under **Sir Arthur Cunnynghame**, K.C.B. Griffith was placed in command of military operations on the Colonial side of the Great Kei River until the arrival of **General Thesiger** (later Lord Chelmsford).

A part of the infantry were trained to mounted work in order to connect them with the cavalry and F.A.M.P. At first there was some friction between the Colonial Ministry and the Governor over the dual control of troops, but later the relative standing of the troops was clearly defined as follows : Imperial troops; Frontier Armed Mounted Police; volunteers and burghers; Native levies. By this order inspectors of the F.A.M.P. were graded as field officers of the local forces, and sub-inspectors as captains of local forces.

Before the year closed Sandile's Gaikas joined forces with the Gcalekas. One notorious act of theirs was the murder of two magistrates, Richard and John Tainton, and Field-Cornet Brown. This was on the 31st December at St. Luke's Mission Station.

Communication between the Kei and Komgha was blocked by the enemy. A notable performance of the F.A.M.P. was the spirited fight against a combined force of the enemy at Draai bosch. In this fight the highest distinction that can be gained on the battle-field — the Victoria Cross — was won by Major Moore of the Connaught Rangers, then attached to the police as second in command. Here is a graphic account of the incident as related by Corporal **John Markham Court** of the F.A.M.P.

"In the Kafir War of 1877-78 **Major Moore** was in command of the troops at Draaibosch. When attacked by the Kafirs, Giese, a member of the F.A.M.P. was in difficulties, his horse having broken away from him. Major Moore, **Sergeant Dan Harber,** and myself went to his assistance, but Giese was assegaied and killed in front of us. Major Moore received an assegai wound through his arm, and he then ordered us to retire. Sergeant Harber carried a man by the name of **Martingale** out of action, his horse having thrown him.

I extracted the assegai from Major Moore and got him to safety, returning with Sergeant Harber to assist others who were in difficulties. Major Moore, Sergeant Harber, and myself were recommended for V.C.s. The decision was Major Moore awarded the V.C. Sergeant Harber and myself promotions". Major Moore enjoyed the distinction of being the first soldier to win the Victoria Cross in South Africa.

Early in January 1878 a fierce attack was made on Forts Warwick and Linsingen. In these actions the loyal Chief Mapassa, with his warriors ,yelling and jumping, came to the aid of the small garrisons, and succeeded in beating off the attackers. Desperately the enemy tried to hang on in the valley, but little by little, inexorable as fate, the troops, with the aid of Native allies, began a creeping movement through the valley, squeezing the enemy out at all points until all their movements were stopped. The valley was cleared of guerrillas .

On 7th February the enemy made a desperate attempt to secure the Quintana Post, but failed. They made another and more serious attempt on the 14th, when their leader, stimulating them to a last effort, led them to within about fifty yards of the trenches around the post. This too, failed, and they retired, leaving many dead behind. In the actual course of the campaign there was some severe fighting at other posts, but the garrisons were not to be moved, and rapidly left the enemy in no doubt of their defeat. The F.A.M.P. distinguished themselves in several of these encounters. Reports of the period testify to this, and also to the substantial assistance rendered by the Pulleine's Rangers, Buffalo Rifles, Carrington's Horse, and various other volunteer units in bringing the campaign to a successful conclusion. Kreli fled into Bomvanaland, and Sandile, the Gaika chief, died of wounds received at the Bawa Forest in a fight with the Fingoes. Among those who received C.M.G. awards for their services in the war were Griffith, Brabant, and Von Linsingen. This was the last of Cape Colony's "Kaffir Wars".

*Nelson Mandela born in 1918 in Umtala in Transkei in South Africa. His father was chief of the Tembus Tribe.

Reference: Boot & Saddle, A narrative record of the Cape Regiment, the British Cape Mounted Riflemen, the Frontier Armed Mounted Police, and the Colonial Cape Mounted Riflemen. P.J.Young.

Cape Mounted Riflemen

Fullerton	A.L	1877-8	Macauley	F.A	1877-8-9	Robinson	H	1877-8
Genth	C	1877-8-9 r	Madden	P	1877-8-9	Robinson	R.H.D	1878
Glynn	J	1879	Maher	W	1879	Rogers	A.D	1877-8-9
Gobey	J	1877-8-9	Marsden	W	1877-8-9	Romain	H	1877-8-9
Gould	K	1879	Mathison	W	1877-8 r	Rosier	J	1878-9
Grarpentein	W	1877-8	Maybury	R	1877-8-9	Ross	J.W	1877-8-9
Greatrex	J.F.R	1879 r	Mc Callum	G	1877-8-9	See also CMP and FAMP		
Green	W	1877-8-9 r	Mc Dermet	F	1877-8-9 r	Ross	W.H	1877-8-9
Green	W	1877-8-9 r	Mc Dougall	S	1877-8	Routh	L	1879 r
Green	W	1877-8-9	Mc Manus	J	1879	Routh	S	1877-8-9 r
Hall	F.J	1877-8-9	McNeil	I	1877-8	Rush	G	1879
Hall	T	1877-8-9 r	Meade	H	1877-8-9	Schenk	W.M	1877-8
Hallifax	G	1877-8-9	Mehew	J	1877-8-9	Schnepel	A	1877-8-9
Hammond	A	1877-8-9	Merrington	H.A	1877-8-9	Schult	G.P.F	1877-8-9 r
Harbor	W.A.H	1877-8-9	See also Duke of Edinburghs Own Rifles.			Schultz	H	1879
Harrington	P.J	1877-8-9 r	Miller	W	1877-8-9 r	September (Native)		1877-8-9 r
Harris	A	1879 r	Misdorp	J	1877-8	Shanahan	W	1877-8-9 r
Hartdegen	L	1879 r	Mons	J	1877-8-9	Sharkey	J.J.L.	1877-8-9
Hatton	E.F	1877-8-9	Morgan	C.W.E	1878-9	Sharp	T	1877-8-9
Hay	C	1877-8-9 r	Morse	T	1879	Shaw	E	1877-8-9
Heaphy	H	1877-8-9 r	Moulden	T	1879	Shaw	J	1879
Henning	C	1877-8-9	Munford	W.H	1879	Shepperson	?	1877-8-9 r
Heskins	J	1877-8-9	Murphy	E	1877-8-9 r	Smallwood	F.H	1879
Heydenrick	C	1877-8-9	Murphy	James	1877-8-9	Smith	E.A	1879
Hill (493)	C.J	1877-8	Murphy	John	1877-8-9	Smith	H	1877-8-9 r
Hobson	G	1877-8-9 r	Murrell	R	1879	Smith	J	1877-8-9
Hocker	C	1879	Nash	F.W	1877-8-9	Smith	W.L	1877-8-9
Hodnett	T.E	1877-8-9	Nebbe	W	1877-8-9 r	Smyth	H.T.C	1879
Hofman	E	1877-8-9	Nelson	W.F	1877-8-9	Spicer	C	1877-8-9
Hoffmann	G.A	1877-8-9	Nesbitt	J	1877-8-9	Stanford	W	1877-8
Hooley	C	1879	Neville	W	1877-8-9	Stanford	W	1877-8
Horne	C.W	1877-8-9	Neville	W	1877-8-9	Stanford	William	1877
Hosmer	E.A.C	1877-8 r	Nightingale	C	1879	Staunton	F	1877-8-9 r
Hudson	A	1877-8-9	Noyes	C	1879	Stone	F	1877-8-9 r
Hughes	H.S	1879	Nunns	E	1877-8-9 r	Storm	F.J	1877-8-9
Jackson	J.M	1877-8	O'Callaghan	J	1879	Strerer	E	1879
Jellicorse	H	1877-8-9	O'Loughlin	J	1879	Strickland	O	1877-8-9 r
Jenner	D	1879	Onken	A	1877-8-9 r	Sullivan	D	1877-8-9 r
Jensen	G	1877-8-9 r	Oxenford	J	1877-8-9	Swift	J	1879
Johnson	H	1877-8-9	Oxley	A	1877-8-9	Swift	J	1879
Johnstone	A	1877-8-9	Owerkirk	W	1877-8	Tanner	H	1877-8-9
Jones	J.D	1879	Palmer	G	1877-8-9	Teadt	J	1877-8-9
Jones	W	1877-8-9 r	Parish	F	1877-8-9	Teeling	T	1877-8-9
Joplin	B.F	1877-8-9	Parish	J.W	1877-8-9 r	Terry	H	1877-8-9
King	T	1877-8-9	Pearce	E	1877-8-9	Thomas	J.V	1877-8-9
Kloks	W	1877-8-9	Pearce	J	1877-8-9	Thompson	A.H	1877-8-9 r
Kirk	T	1877-8 r	Pedgrift	H.A.A	1877-8-9	Thunder	L	1877-8-9 r
Knapp	C	1877-8	Penicud	T	1877-8-9 r	Twiss	C	1877-8
Kock	C	1877-8-9 r	Pratt	J	1877-8-9	Underwood	W	1877-8-9 r
Kunhart	G.O	1877-8-9	Preston	A	1877-8-9 r	Vasey	A.C	1879 r
Lacey	B	1877-8-9	Price	E.W	1877-8-9 r	Vermeiren	C	1877-8-9
Lee	M	1879	Pritchett	G	1877-8-9	Walford	E.A	1877-8-9
Liebenn	J	1877-8-9 r	Purchas	T	1878-9	Walsh	J	1877-8-9
Lindsay	A	1879	Quade	F	1877-8-9	Wardle	James	1877-8
Lischer	E	1877-8	Rich	A	1877-8-9	Wardle	Joseph	1877-8-9
See also 1st Cape Mtd Yeomanry.			Rietveldt	J	1879	Wescomb	W	1877-8-9
Lonsada? (Lonsdalo?) St L 1877-8			Ringsall	J	1877-8-9	Wells	J	1877-8-9 r
Luyt	E.G	1877-8-9 r	Rochfort	H	1877-8-9 r	Wainwright	A.F.H	1877-8-9 r

Cape Mounted Riflemen

Walters	W	1877-8-9 r	Burgenwood	F	1877-8-9	Thompson	M	1877-8 r
White	B	1879	Clarke	J	1877-8 r	Thompson	W	1877-8-9
Whitmore	E.H	1877-8-9	Cockrane	W	1877-8	Toerien	J	1877-8
Whickham	J	1877-8-9	Coombs	H	1877-8	Travis	E	1877-8 r
Wild	H	1877-8	Crutwell	F	1877-8	Underwood	W	1877-8
Williams	J.H	1877-8-9 r	Davies	W	1877-8-9	Upton	H.B	1877-8-9
Williams	J.N	1877-8-9 r	Davis	F	1877-8	Ward	B	1877-8-9
Wilson	M.G.H	1877-8-9	Davis	H	1877-8 r	Ward	F	1877-8-9
Wolhuter	H	1877-8-9 r	De La Harpe	T	1877-8-9	Warrene	R	1877-8
Wood	F.M	1877-8-9	Dogherty	J	1877-8-9	Wells	J	1877-8 r
Wright	A	1879	Domony	J	1877-8	Willard	F	1877-8
Wright	C (H.C)	1878-9	Dougal	O	1877-8-9 r	Williams	C	1877-8
Wright	S.C	1877-8-9 r	Eden	G	1877-8	Worrall	S.J.	1877-8-9
Wright	W.J	1877-8-9 r	Edye	C	1877-8 r	Young	E.A	1877-8
Wright	W.T	1877-8-9	# Evezard	E	1877-8-9			
Wyer	G	1877-8-9	Farrell	E	1878	**CAPE MOUNTED RIFLEMEN No. 7**		
Wynne	G.R	1877-8-9 r	Felton	R	1877-8	**TROOP**		
Yeates	C	1877-8-9	Flynn	W.H	1877-8-9	INSPECTOR		
			Fraser	D McD	1877-8-9	Maclean	J.K	1877-8-9
CAPE MOUNTED RIFLEMEN NO. 6			Fullerton	A	1877-8 r	SUB INSPECTOR		
TROOP			Gaunlett	H	1877-8	Von Hohenan C		**1877-8 r**
CAPTAIN			Goddard	T	1877-8 r	KIA Gwanda		
Blaine	A.E.B	1877-8-9	Graham	G	1877-8	Maclean	A	1877-8-9
LIEUTENANT			Graham	W	1877-8	SERGEANT		
Clarke	T.A	1877-8-9	Greenway	G	1877-8	Buckley	J	1877-8
SERGEANT MAJOR			Harbot	R	1877-8-9	Garstin	F	1877-8-9
Griffen	H	1877-8-9	Head	W.B	1877-8-9	Mc Gregor	J	1877-8-9 r
SERGEANT			Hodnett	T	1877-8-9 r	Nelson	R	1877-8-9
Bell	J	1877-8	Homer	E	1877-8	CORPORAL		
Brady	G.C	1877-8-9	Homer	H	1877-8 r	Ervine	J	1877-8
Freer	A	1877-8-9	Kaufmann	J.B	1877-8	Howell	J	1877-8-9
Keys	R	1877-8	La Chance	C	1877-8 r	Neville	H	1877-8-9
Kockett	F	1877-8	Lambert	E	1877-8 r	Robinson	T	1877-8
Mountain	J	1877-8	Lennon	T	1877-8	PRIVATE		
Phillips	W.H.B	1877-8-9	Lewis	R	1877-8	Adams	W	1877-8
West	E	1877-8-9	Lonergan	E	1877-8	Allen D/S	J	1877-8
CORPORAL			Linnow	A	1877-8	Allison	W	1877-8-9
Bailey	T.N	1879	Lunley D/S	R	1877-8	Auret	J	1877-8-9
Dreyer	W	1877-8	Malley	H	1877-8-9	Baldwin	J	1877-8-9
Matthews	C	1877-8	Maynard	C	1877-8	Bardin	J	1877-8-9
Palmer	A	1877-8-9	Mc Callum	R	1877-8-9	Barr	H	1877-8-9 r
Straw	W.P	1877-8-9	Morris	A	1877-8	Bayley	T	1877-8-9
PRIVATE			Murchison	K	1877-8-9	Bishop	J	1877-8-9
Applin	E	1877 8	Nicolls	L	1877 8	Bragg	T.J	1877 8-9
Bath	W	1877-8-9	Oyns	J	1877-8 r	Brophy	S	1877-8-9
Baum	H	1877-8	Parlaman	W	1877-8-9	Broughton	B	1877-8-9
Beckerson	W	1877-8-9	Robinson	E	1877-8-9	Burrows	W	1877-8
Blatchley	C.A.C	1877-8-9	Shanahan	W	1877-8-9	Carter	P	1877-8-9
Bluhm	F	1877-8	Shepperson		1877-8 r	Caulfield	J	1877-8-9
Booy	G	1877-8	Staunton	F	1877-8	Clarke	H	1877-8
Bull	F	1877-8-9 r	Stepen	A	1877-8	Clarke	J	1877-8-9
Bunn	H.H	1877-8	Swann	C	1877-8-9	Collotte	T	1877-8-9

Dixons Gazette No30 Summer 2002 1454 Private E.H. Evezard, No. 6 Troop Cape Mounted Rifles.
South Africa Medal 1877-1879, 1 clasp, 1877-8-9 (Pte. No. 6 Tp: C.M. Rifles); Cape of Good Hop(• General Service Medal 1880-1897, 2 clasps, Transkei, Basutoland (Pte. C.M. Rif.)(2)
Medals and clasps verified on roll. Edward Haviland Evezard was born in November or December 1855 off the coast of Burma, presumably at sea. He died at East London 3 July 1926. Sold with copy roll pages and death notice which contains his marital status and his eight children's names. Choice EF £575.00

Cape Mounted Riflemen

Cooke	W	1877-8-9	Taylor	H	1877-8-9	Roy	G	1877-8-9
Craigie	A	1877-8-9	Thornton	P	1877-8-9	White	A	1877-8-9
Dalziel	R	1877-8	Trembling	J	1877-8	**CORPORAL**		
Dent	R	1877-8-9	Turner	A	1877-8-9	Bevington	W	1877-8-9
Devine	A	1877-8-9 r	Verity	W	1877-8-9	Goodman	W	1877-8 r
Donaldson T		**1877-8 r**	Waller	E	1877-8	Hawkins	C.B	1877-8-9
KIA Gwanda Hill 25/9/1877			Wardle	J	1877-8-9	Hunt	J	1877-8
Doyle	W	1877-8	Warwick	F.J	1877-8-9	Henderson	B	1877-8-9
Dunn	J	1877-8-9	Watson	J	1877-8-9	Jacob	P.L	1877-8-9
Dyer	M	1877-8 r	Webb	F	1877-8	Kelly	F	1877-8
Dyson	G	1877-8-9	Woods	A	1877-8-9	Knight	F.H	1877-8
Edgell	E	1877-8-9				Mc Arthur	A	1877-8
Elliott	E	1877-8-9	**CAPE MOUNTED RIFLEMEN No. 8**			D/S Ibeka		
Ellis	C	1877-8	**TROOP**			Millwood	R	1877-8 r
Evans C		**1877-8 r**	**LIEUTENANT**			Olver	E	1877-8-9
KIA Gwanda Hill 25/9/1877			Flynn	H	1877-8-9	Petley	A	1877-8-9
Farmer	C	1877-8-9	Sprenger	C.F	1877-8-9	Parkinson	G	1877-8-9
Forst	F.W	1877-8-9	**SERGEANT**			Redmond	P	1877-8-9
Fowler	A	1877-8-9	Court	J.M	1877-8-9	Rowland	G	1877-8 r
Francis	C	1877-8	Kennan	T	1878-9	Rayworth	T	1877-8 r
Garde	H	1877-8	Shortt	F.G	1877-8-9	**Sherratt C**		**1877-8-9**
Garrett	M.W	1877-8-9	**PRIVATE**			KIA Gwanda Hill 25/9/1877		
Gill	S	1877-8-9	Allison	W.H	1877-8-9	Ward	A.F	1877-8-9
Glover	A	1877-8-9	Barnes	E.F.G	1879	**Wesley E**		
Griffin	W	1877-8-9	Bertholomew	W	1877-8-9	KIA Holland's Shop 2/12/1877		
Harrison	J	1877-8	Bortwick	C	1878 r	Wright	W	1877-8-9
Hay	C	1877-8-9	Two medals with clasp 1878 were issued.			**PRIVATE**		
Heydenrich	R	1877-8	Burrows	S	1877-8-9	Anderson	F	1877-8-9
Holmes	A	1877-8-9	Caffyn	R.W	1877-8 r	Arkell	J	1877-8-9
Jacobi	J	1877-8-9	Caldercott	W.T	1878-9 r	Armstrong	F	1877-8-9
Jones	G	1877-8-9	Corbett	G.W	1877-8	Ashworth	W	1877-8-9
Jones	O	1877-8	Hart	F	1877-8-9	Ayre	J	1877-8-9
Keating	R	1877-8-9	Healy	D.G	1877-8	Bartram	J	1877-8-9
Kneebone	S	1877-8-9	Le Sueur	J.S	1877-8	Bennett	W	1877-8
Levis	R	1877-8-9	Luyt	E.G	1877-8	**PRIVATE**		
Mayers	S	1877-8-9	Rawstone	J	1878	Bertholst		1877-8 r
Mayor	J	1877-8-9	Schmidt	F	1877-8-9	Campbell	C.D	1877-8-9
Initially issued with clasp 1877-8. On 2/5/84			Scott	H.T	1877-8-9	Caufield	J	1877-8-9
clasp 1877-8-9 issued as a replacement			Taplin	H.F	1877-8-9	Cole	F	1877-8-9
Mc Aunich W		**1877-8 r**	Terrill	S.J	1877-8	Cooke	C	1877-8-9
KIA Gwanda Hill 25/9/1877						Cooper	E	1877-8 r
Mears	H	1877-8-9	**CAPE MOUNTED RIFLEMEN No. 9**			Corfield	E	1877-8-9
Mulkern	E	1877-8-9 r	**TROOP**			Couper	G	1877-8-9
Murphy	J	1877-8-9	**INSPECTOR**			Crew	C	1877-8-9
Newton	C	1877-8	Bourne	J.H.W	1877-8-9	Curtis	A.P	1877-8
Ockenden	D	1877-8-9	**SUB INSPECTOR**			Davenport	T	1877-8-9
O'Connor	W	1877-8-9	Hatton	E.F	1877-8-9	Deurant	W	1877-8-9 r
O'Reilly	T	1877-8-9	**LIEUTENANT**			Disney	A	1877-8-9
Owens	J	1877-8-9	Goldsworthy	C.L	1879	Dogherty	L	1877-8
Richards	R	1878	**SERGEANT MAJOR**			Driver	W	1877-8-9
Schmidt	F	1877-8	Specht	G	1877-8 r	Ducas	A.W	1877-8
Schnaar	W	1877-8 r	**TROOP SERGEANT MAJOR**			Dyson	G	1877-8-9
Schreiber	C	1877-8-9 r	Schuman	F	1877-8-9	Ellis	F	1877-8 r
Schultz	F	1877-8	**SERGEANT**			Emerson	J	1877-8 r
Short	O	1877-8-9	Higgins	C	1877-8-9	Every	W.A	1877-8-9
Sullivan	D	1877-8 r	Lynn	G	1877-8-9	Fabiernsen	J	1877-8-9
Taplin	E	1877-8-9	Muter	J	1877-8-9	Falkner	W.S	1877-8
Taylor	G	1877-8-9	Palmer	A	1877-8-9	Field	T	1877-8-9 r

Cape Mounted Riflemen

Forbes	E.M.D	1877-8-9
Geyser	H	1877-8-9
Goddard	F	1877-8-9
Green	F	1877-8 r
Hall	T	1877-8 r
Hamilton	E	1877-8
Harrison	T	1877-8
Herman	A	1877-8 r
Heyman	H.M	1877-8-9
Heugh	J	1877-8-9 r
Hobson	G	1877-8-9
Hoffman	E	1877-8 r
Hogen	D	1877-8-9
Holst	H	1877-8 r
Holbeck	R	1877-8-9
Hunter	S	1877-8-9
Jones	M	1877-8-9
Knight	F	1877-8-9
Lambert	H	1877-8 r
Lane	A	1877-8-9
Lukin	L	1877-8-9
Mack	C	1877-8 r
Millbourne	J	1877-8
Milne	G	1877-8-9
Moffatt	H	1877-8
Nicoll	A	1877-8-9
Oakes	G	1877-8-9
Owen	C	1877-8
Paddock	T	1877-8 r
Phelan	J	1877-8-9 r
Price	H	1877-8 r
Probert	R	1877-8-9
Ricard	D	1877-8 r
Rowe	W.L.V	1877-8
Schoenewolf	C	1877-8
Schroeder	H	1877-8-9 r
Sheppard	W	1877-8 r
Stone	T	1877-8 r
Storm	G	1877-8-9
Summerfield	A	1877-8-9
Thomson	L	1877-8-9
Thunder	L	1877-8-9
Trafford	J	1877-8-9
Turner	W	1877-8-9
Walters	W	1877-8
Weatherhead	T	1877-8

Killed KingWilliamsTown.

Westbrook	H	1877-8
Westley	E	1877-8 r
Wesley	**E**	**1877-8 r**

KIA 2/12/1877.

Willcox	J.D	1877-8-9
Wolst	R	1877-8-9 r

1ST CAPE MOUNTED YEOMANRY REGIMENT.
Those Killed in Action (KIA) lost their lives at Moirosi's Stronghold, 29/5/1879.

COLONEL
Brabant CMG	E.Y	1877-8-9

CAPTAIN
Cock	J.W	1877-8-9
Dalgety	E.H	1877-8-9
Dell	S.W	1879
Douglass	A	1879
Duric	W	1879
Nettleton	T.S	1877-8-9
Sprigg	H	1879
Wood	J.G	1879

LIEUTENANT
Brent	T.H	1877-8-9
Gray	J.W	1879 r

Wounded at Quthing 17/5/1879

Ogilvie	H.W	1879
Parker	C.E	1879
Stone	H.M	1879
Smith	H.M	1879

See also Lt. H.M. Smyth Kaffrarian Volunteer Artillery.

2ND LIEUTENANT
Cock	T.T	1879
Purdon	J.T	1877-8-9 r
Van Ryneveldt	W.C	1879

REGIMENTAL SERGEANT MAJOR
Dunn	J.J	1879

SERGEANT MAJOR
Jones	C.R	1879

TROOP SERGEANT MAJOR
Fletcher	A.A	1877-8-9
Hildebrandt	E	1879 r
Marshall	G	1877-8-9
Mc Luckie	J	1879 r
Willmore	W.H	1879 r

ACTING TROOP SERGEANT MAJOR
Berry	J	1879

QUARTERMASTER SERGEANT
Lux	H	1879

1ST CLASS STAFF SERGEANT
Booty	W.F.S	1877-8-9

FARRIER SERGEANT
South KIA	G.H	1877-8-9

SERGEANT
Andendorff	A	1879
Cogan	R	1879
Doyle	W	1879
Gilbert	T	1879
Griffin	J.W	1879 r
Jones	J	1879 r
Krunse	P	1879
Macauley	J	1879
Mc Dougall	A	1879
Petersen KIA	**C**	**1877-8-9**
# Ready	S	1879
Roby	W	1879
Schaunbrauger	A	1879
Vice	E.P	1879 r
Wallis	J	1879

LANCE SERGEANT
Wallis	G.A	1879

CORPORAL
Armstrong	J	1879
Bainbridge	E	1879

Wounded at Morosi's Stronghold
Ballard	W.F	1879
Behrens	J.W	1879 r
Berry	J	1879 r
Blaine	J.R	1879
Currin	R	1879
Dold	W.J	1879
Foxcroft	G	1879 r
Girdlestone	C.H.N	1879
Mack	J	1879

Wounded at Quthing 17/5/1879
Maclean	J.W	1879
Mc Dougall	W	1879 r
Mier	W	1879
Parker	A	1879 r
Ross	C	1879
Skea	H	1879
Wallace	H	1879
Watson KIA	**H.J**	**1879**
Webb	T.K	1879
Warren	G.J	1879

LANCE CORPORAL
Cogan	A	1879
Dell	J.G	1879

TRUMPETER
Boyle	J	1879
Hill	C	1879
Van Wyk	H.J	1879
Young	S	1879

Dixons Gazette No33 Spring 2003 420 1 clasp, 1879. Sergeant S. Ready, 1/Cape Yeomanry. Verified on South Africa War medal roll. 307 medals issued, 282 with 1879 clasp. Cape Yeomanry originally raised as a properly-funded local Militia by the Cape Government in 1878, the Cape Yeomanry was meant to form part of a mobile three for the defence of the eastern frontier of the province. The Government's intention was to raise some 3,000 'gentleman farmers' but never succeeded in recruiting anything like that number. The 1st Cape Yeomanry (approx 300 men) was commanded by Colonel E.Y. Brabant, the 2nd by Lieut Col R.G. Southey (approx 169 men) and the 3rd by Lieut Col T.E. Minto (approx 113 men). The Cape Yeomanry played a leading part in the operations against Moirosi's stronghold in June 1879. All three Regiments were disbanded in 1881. EF £350.00

Cape Mounted Yeomanry

TROOPER								
Adams	R.J	1879	Elliott	J	1879 r	Kennelly	P	1879
Alesbury	J	1879 r	Elton	E	1879	Keogh	S	1879 r
Allwright	T	1877-8-9 r	Evens	A	1879	Kesler	P	1879
Altenkirk	J	1879	Farrell	R.J	1879	Knowles	T	1879
Anke	J	1879 r	Felton	W	1879	## Kock	J.D	1879
Appel Snr	W	1879	Fitzpatrick	G	1879	Krunse	W	1879
Appel Jnr	W	1879	Ford	W.J	1879 r	Kuhn	C	1879
Balmore	S	1877-8-9	Wounded at Morosi's Stronghold			Kuhn	F	1879
Barr	R	1879 r	Foster	J	1879	**Langley KIA**	**G**	**1879**
Belling	C	1879 r	Fo Jnr	W	1879	Laudrey	A.E.P	1879
See also Stuttenhein Foot Police.			Frier	A	1879	Lemyke	J	1879
Belling	J	1879 r	Gardener	T	1879 r	Lennachen	M	1879
See also Stuttenhein Foot Police.			**Glass KIA**	**J.H**	**1879**	Lewis	C	1879
Berg KIA	**H**	**1879 r**	Goby	J	1879 r	**Lewis KIA**	**H**	**1879 r**
Betts	G	1879 r	Goldswain	C	1879	Lewis	O	1879
Bloomer	E	1879	Goldswain	E	1879	Wounded at Morosi's Stronghold		
Bradfield	E.A	1879 r	Grant	J	1879	Lisher	E	1879
Brent	B	1879	**Gravett KIA**	**J.H**	**1879 r**	Deserted. See Cape Mounted Riflemen.		
Brent	C	1879	Gray	W.M	1879 r			
Brent	J	1879 r	Griffiths	C	1879	Luke	E	1879
Brent	W	1879	Haise	T	1879	Lutke	C	1879
Brooks	E	1879	Hambly	F	1877-8-9 r	Lutke	W	1879
Brooks	W.H.L	1879	Hamilton	D	1879	Maclean	A	1879 r
Brotherton	W	1879	Harris	J	1879	**Maclean KIA**	**C**	**1879**
Bruce	C	1879	Harris	T	1879	Macnamee	James	1879
Burger	W	1879 r	Hendricksen	L	1879	Macnamee	Joseph	1879
Campbell	C.J	1877-8-9	Heney	R	1879	Mahoney	J	1879
Carlin	J	1879	Hill	D	1879 r	Mandy	D	1879 r
Carney	A	1879	Hill	J	1879 r	Mandy	S.D	1879 r
Carroll	J	1879	Hodgkinson Jnr	G	1879	Marais	G.H	1877-8-9 r
Carroll	W	1879 r	**# Hoffmeister KIA**	**G**	**1879**	Marais	I	1877-8-9
Causebrock	J	1879	**Medal named Hoffmiestes**			Marillier	H	1879
Clifford	C	1879 r	Hohman	J	1879	Marshall	C.G	1879
Collen	H.W	1879	Holmes	James	1879	Massey	T	1879
Colombel	A	1877-8-9 r	Holmes	John	1879 r	Matthews	A	1879 r
Cooks	J	1879	Howe	Ferdinand	1879	Mc Arthur	J	1879 r
Craig	J	1879	Howe	F	1879	Mc Carty	D	1879
Currin	E.J	1879 r	Howell	G	1879 r	Mc Donald	W	1879
Davies	A	1879	Hulley	T	1877-8-9	Mc Dougall	D	1879
Davies	A.T	1879	Human	J.J	1879	Mc Kay	G	1879
Davies	D.J	1879 r	Hunter	J.W	1879	Mc Namara	A	1879
Davis	T	1879 r	Hurley	J	1879	Mc Quire	E	1879
Day	J	1879	Hurley	P	1879	Moore	W.M	1877-8-9
Deering	C	1879	Hutton	W.H	1879	See also Pulleines Rgs.		
Dent	T	1879	Hyde	F	1879	Moran	E	1879
Dent	W	1879 r	Ingram	N	1879 r	Morris	J	1879
Dixon	W.R	1879	Jacoby	H	1877-8-9	Naudie	J.J	1879
Dobrowsky	F	1879	Jansen	J	1879 r	Nell	L.N	1879
Dunbar	W	1879	Jennings	R	1879 r	Nicholas	B.A	1879 r
Dunn	H	1879	Jennings	S	1879 r	**Nicholas KIA**	**R.P**	**1879**
Eaton	J	1879	Jennings	W	1879 r	Nicholson	A	1877-8-9 r
			Jones	G	1879	Niepert	C	1879

Dixons Gazette No41 Spring 2004
595 1 clasp, 1879. Trooper G. Hoffmeister, 1st Cape Yeomanry. K.I.A. 5.6.1879 Morosis Mountain. See write up for Trooper H.B. Leonard which refers to this action. Choice EF £1600.00

City coins Postal Auction No 58 29th August 2008, Lot No 71 South Africa Medal 1879 (SAGS) bar 1879 Tpr. J.D. Kock 1st Cape Yeory. VF+ 3.500 – 5.000. Hammer Price 4510 Rand

Cape Mounted Yeomanry

Morosi's Mountain from the south

Name	Initial	Year
Norton	J.E	1879 r
Ochlisen	**KIA O**	**1877-8-9 r**
Opitz	T	1879
Orsmond	J.D	1879 r
Orsmond	P	1879
O'Toole	J	1879
Pagel	C	1879
Pearson	T	1879
Petzer	H	1879
Pike	C	1879 r
Pike	C.W	1879
Pike	E	1879
Pike	S	1879
Pocock	W	1879
Powell	S.M	1879
Pratt	W	1879
Purdon	E.A	1879 r
Purdon	T.H	1879
Quate	W.S	1879
Querl	E	1879
Querl	H	1879 r
Quin	J	1879
Rahn	J	1879
Ramer	H	1879
Randall	**KIA W.A**	**1879 r**
Reilly	J	1879 r
Reilly	W	1879 r
Reilly	W.H	1879 r
Rielander	G	1879
Robinson	C	1879
Roebert	C	1879
Rowland	E	1879
Rowly	G	1879
Rusch	W	1879
Wounded at Morosi's Stronghold		
Saymon	J	1877-8-9
Schaefer	F.E	1879
Medal to Lieutenant (Lieut from the 1.12.1878)		
Schaller	F.A	1879 r
Schmidt	J	1879
See also Keiskamahoek Volunteer Force.		
Schnur	W	1879 r
Schroeder	W	1879 r
Shambrock	J	1879
Shamrock	S.J	1879
Shaw	J.W	1879
Shepherd	A	1879 r
Smith	C.R	1879
Smith	S	1879
Spalding	C	1879
Stayl	H	1879
Stone	D.M	1879
Street	I	1879
Strijdoe	J	1879 r
Strutt	R	1879
See Queenstown Volunteer Contingent.		
Stuckman	F	1879
Swailes	T.A	1879
Tarr	D.F	1879 r
Thorsen	**KIA T**	**1879 r**
Toomey	**KIA E**	**1877-8-9 r**
Treasurer	D	1879
Trollip	G	1879 r
Trower	S	1879 r
Tyrell	W	1879
Vandervesthuis	Ch.	1879
Vandervesthuis	Cornelius	1879
Van Rooyen	P.B	1879
Van Wyk	D	1879
Wagner	W	1877-8-9
Warnaki	A	1879
Warren	W.R	1879
Webb	J	1879
Webb	W	1879
Wentworth	W.C	1879
Wesson	**KIA D**	**1879**
Wesson	T	1879
West	T	1879 r
West	W	1879
Whittal	J.F.D	1879 r
Whittall	J.H	1879
Whittall	W.C	1879
Wilford	T	1879
Williams	T	1879 r
Wilmouth	J.P	1879
Wilson	C.F	1879 r
Windsor	C	1879
Wise	T	1879
Wodehouse	W.A	1879
Wollenslager	W	1879
Woolf	G	1879
Wynne	W.J	1879 r

2ND CAPE MOUNTED YEOMANRY REGIMENT.

Those Killed in Action (KIA) lost their lives at Moirosi's Stronghold, 29/5/1879, also *Wounded shown with an asterisk.

COLONEL
| Southey | R.G | 1879 |

COMMANDANT
| Copper | E.R | 1877-8-9 |

SURGEON
| Impey | S.P | 1878-9 |

CAPTAIN
Davis	C	1879
Everitt	H	1879
Fincham	A.W	1879
Fleischer	S	1879

CASUALTIES DURING THE SIEGE OF MOROSI'S MOUNTAIN IN 1879

Name	Regiment	Rank	Date
Muldoon, T.	2nd Cape Mounted Yeomany	Sgt	23/3/1879 During the approach
Robinson, J.	2nd Cape Mounted Yeomany	Sgt	5/6/1879 2nd Assault
Vice, A. J.	2nd Cape Mounted Yeomany	Trooper	5/6/1879 2nd Assault
Wyk, S. van	2nd Cape Mounted Yeomany	Trooper	5/6/1879 2nd Assault

Cape Mounted Yeomanry

#Captain H.Nesbitt   Spink Sale 7012 Lot 140. 19 Apr 2007
South Africa 1877-79, one clasp, 1879 (Capt: H. Nesbitt, Cape Yeory.), extremely fine Hammer Price £1200
Captain Henry Nesbitt (1835-1890), born Cookstown, County Tyrone, Ireland; Henry's father (Alexander Nesbitt) was a Quarter Master serving with the 12th Foot in South Africa in the early 1850's; Alexander was posted on the frontier, with two of his sons living with him (Henry and Charles), the four remaining siblings (Richard, Mary, Elizabeth and Frederick) embarked on H.M.S. Birkenhead with their mother, Anne, at Simon's Bay (24.2.1852), two days before the wreck. Drums of the Birkenhead erroneously gives Mrs. Nesbitt and her two sons, Richard and Henry taking passage on the Birkenhead. Richard Athol Nesbitt (later Colonel and C.B.) was indeed a survivor of the wreck, however as he states in a letter to Mr. J.R. Cocker (the lighthouse-keeper at Danger Point, off which the Birkenhead was lost), 'Captain Nesbitt [Henry], of Barkly West my elder brother. He got his commission in the 12th or Suffolk Regiment, the same regiment as my father. He retired after getting his company in 1865 and started farming near Barkly East..... When the Birkenhead was wrecked he was with my father serving in the Kaffir War of 1852.'

Henry Nesbitt was commissioned Ensign 12th Foot, 1854; Lieutenant 1858 and went to India with the regiment, where he was gazetted Captain; he left the army and went to live in Maclear, South Africa; with the outbreak of the war in South Africa (1877-79), Nesbitt joined the 2nd Cape Mounted Yeomanry as a Captain and after serving during that conflict saw service in 1880-81, 'A great many of our readers will remember that after the treacherous murder of Mr. Hope by Umhlonhlo, the residency of Maclear was invested by the Kaffirs, so that a large number of the inhabitants of the surrounding districts - mostly women and children - (the men had flown to arms to punish the audacious rebels) had fled to the residency for protection and safety, Maclear had become a veritable rat trap to them, they were surrounded by the Kaffirs and were in danger of being either starved to death or because the victims of the rebels. What the latter meant every one of our readers know. It fell to Captain Nesbitt's lot to relieve the beleaguered residents of Maclear, and a relief column was organized under his command - how well he executed his mission, how the starving women, children and officials were relieved by him from a fate which would ultimately been worse than death to the women and certain death to the men, with but the loss of one man on the return march, has become a matter of Colonial history and will be forever remembered by the then residents of Maclear and their descendants.'
(Recipient's Obituary in the Barkly East Reporter, dated 1.2.1890, refers). Henry's nephew, Major R.C. Nesbitt, continued the family's military history by winning the Victoria Cross in 1896, near Salisbury, South Africa.

Name		Years
Hutchons	A	1878-9
Kannemeyer	D.R	1878-9
Kidwell	A.J	1879
See Jamestown Mounted Volunteer Rifles		
# Nesbitt	H	1879
Parker	J.C	1877-8-9
See also Lt. In Aliwal North Mtd. Vols.		
White	H	1879
LIEUTENANT		
Barrable	W	1879
Brady	J	1879
Burnett	G.W	1878-9
Fincham	F.C	1879 r
See Lt F.P. Fincham Jamestown Vol.Rifles		
Gardner	J.G	1879
Kannemeyer	H.M	1878-9
Kemper	C.J	1879
Leach	J.B	1879
Nesbitt	F	1879
White	D	1879
2ND LIEUTENANT		
Austen	W.M	1879
Badger	E	1877-8-9
See also Sgt. E. Badger Wodehouse True Blues.		
Berry	A.W	1879 r
SERGEANT MAJOR		
Cockin R.R		**1879**
KIA at Inhlobane 28/3/1879		
Knight	F	1879
Schweizer	C	1879
Stirton	G	1879
STAFF SERGEANT		
Albrecht	L.W	1877-8-9
FARRIER SERGEANT		
Stuart	R	1879
SERGEANT		
Best	R	1879
See also Col R. Best Wodehouse True Blues.		
Brady	A.R	1879
Caldecott	A.E	1879
Copeland	W.S	1879
De Beer	A	1879
Dixon	W	1879
Foster	W	1879
Freemantle	J	1878-9
Frost	W	1877-8-9
Harding	G	1879 r
Harding	P	1879 r
Jenkinson	E	1878-9
Kidwell	C	1879 r
See Jamestown Mounted Vols.		
Kirkpatrick	W.G	1879
Muldoon	**T**	**1877-9 r**
KIA 23/3/1879		
Pohl	J	1879
Purdon	J.C	1878-9
Quinn	J	1879
Robinson	A	1879
Robinson KIA	**J**	**1879 r**
Robson	T	1879
Scott	J	1879
Thompson	C	1879
Vice	C.J	1878-9
CORPORAL		
Allen	T	1878-9
See also Sgr. T. Allen Wodehouse True Blues.		
Batteson	G.W	1879
Benson	H	1878-9
Connock	R	1877-8-9
Crole	A	1878-9
Cruywagen	C	1879
Ekron	T	1879
Freemantle	H	1879 r
Hattingh	W	1879 r
Henning	G	1878-9
Hooper	R	1877-8
Kelly	T	1879
Lovemore	J	1879 r
O'Brien	G.S	1879
Olivier	P	1879 r
Radford	G	1879
Raeston	L	1879
Ridgway	C	1877-8-9
Ritchie	T	1877-8-9
See also Tpr. T. Ritchie A.N. Mtd. Vols.		
Scaife	J	1879

Cape Mounted Yeomanry

Scanlen	C	1879
Staples	E	1879 r
Symonds	R	1879 r
Trollip	R	1879
Wells	H	1879
Yuill	T	1879 r

TRUMPETER

Andrews	J	1879
Develing	C	1879
James	H	1879 r
Long	F	1877-9
Murfin	W	1879
Passmore	W.H	1879
Pocock	J	1877-8-9 r

See also Aliwal North Mounted Vol.

Prior	W	1879

TROOPER

Adams	L.J	1879
# Anderson	W	1879
Assmuth	C	1879
Austen	H	1879
Barrable	D.S	1878-9
Barrable	W.H	1879
Barry	J.M	1879
Bate	A	1879 r
Bekker	A	1879 r
Bekker	H	1879 r
Bekker	L	1879 r
Bekker	P	1879 r
Bekker	S	1879 r
Bendiman	H	1879
Beukes	G	1879 r
Beukes	J.A	1879
Beukes	S.J	1879
Bishop	E	1879 r
Bleach	G	1879 r
Bolt	L	1879
*Boss	A	1879
Botha	D	1879 r
Botha	F	1879
Botha	H.J	1879
Botha	P	1879
Brady	J	1879
*Broad	J	1879 r
Brown	R	1879 r
Bruns	A	1879
Bruton	A	1879
Bruton	J	1879
Burke	P.J	1879 r
Burnett	G	1879
Clark	G	1879 r
Cloete	A	1879
Cloete	L	1879
Cloete	W	1879
Cockin	F.H	1877-8-9

See also Cpl. F. Cockin Queenstown Vol. Contg.

Coester	B.H	1879
Coetzee	C	1879
*Coetzee	N	1879
Collary	J	1878-9
*Collins	J	1879 r
Cooper	J	1879
De Bruin	D	1879
De Bruin	T	1879
De Clerk	S	1879 r
De Coning	C	1879 r
Deegan	H	1879 r
De la Rosa	F	1879 r
Delport	J.P	1879
De Reuck	P.J	1879 r
De Venter	J	1879
De Wett KIA	**J**	**1879**
Dickson	J	1879 r
Debie	G	1879
Dohse	C	1879
Dugmore	A	1879 r
Durand	J.M	1879 r
Earle	W	1877-9 r

See also Aliwal North Mtd. Vols.

Edwards	W	1879 r
Ekron	M	1878-9
Elliott	W	1877-8-9 r

See also Aliwal North Mtd. Vols.

Ellis	P	1878-9
Eloff	J	1878-9
Erasmus	G.A	1879
Feathers	T	1879
Ferrera	T	1879 r
Fisher	A.J	1879
Flowers	G	1879
Friedrichs	H	1878-9
Frost	A	1878-9
Gav	P	1878-9 r

See Lt. P. Gav Wodehouse True Blues.

Geritzen	W	1879
Gilliard	J	1879
Goddard	W	1878-9
Goosen 1.	C	1879 r
Goosen 2.	C	1879
Goosen	H.W	1879 r
Gould	C	1879
Grant	C	1877-8-9 r
Greyling	H	1879 r
Greyling	J	1879
Greyling	P	1878-9 r
Griffin	H.J	1879 r
Grobelar	J	1879 r
Grobelar	N	1879 r

Grosbendtner	N	1879 r
Gryvenstein	H	1878-9
Haley	J	1878-9
Haley	M.J	1878-9
Haley	W	1878-9 r
Halliday	R	1879
Hamilton	J	1879
*Harding	J.J	1879
Hartslief	J	1879
Haug	C	1878-9
Hersleman	C	1879 r
Heydenreych	W	1879
Heydenreych	W.G	1878-9
Hill	T	1878-9 r
Hollins	J	1879 r
Horn	J.A	1879
Howell	W	1878-9

See Cpl. W. Howell Wodehouse True Blues.

Hulley	R	1878-9
Jakins	S	1878-9
Jenkinson	G	1879
Jenkinson	J	1879 r

See Jamestown Mtd. Volunteer Rifles.

Jenner	O	1879
Johnson	J	1879
Kearney	D.H	1879-9
Kennemeyer	G	1878-9
Kedian	J	1879 r
Kelly	P	1879
Kelly	J	1879
Kelly	W	1879

See also Wodehouse True Blues.

Kemper	C.J	1879
Kemper	J.M	1879
Kemper	W.F	1879
Keys	W.H	1879 r
*Kidwell	T.J	1879 r

See also Tpr. T. Kidwell 2nd Cape Mtd Yeomanry.

Kirton	J	1879 r
Kitter	A	1879
Kleinhans	H	1878-9
Kleinhans	T	1879 r
*Knaust	J	1879
Kotze	J	1879 r
Londt	A	1878-9 r
Lovemore	R	1879 r
Lubbe	A	1879 r
Marshall	T	1879
Maytham	A	1877-9
Maytham	W	1877-9
Mc Cabe	E	1879 r
Mc Coll	J	1877-9

See also Aliwal North Mtd Volunteers.

Dix Noonan Web Auction 25 Jun 08 Lot 75.
South Africa 1877-79, 1 clasp, 1879 (Tpr. W. Anderson, 2nd Cape Yeory.) claw tightened, very fine, hammer price £300

Cape Mounted Yeomanry

Name		Year
Mc Cullum	A	1879
Mc Donald	D.C	1877-8-9
Mc Intyre	E	1878-9
Mc Kenzie	J	1879 r
Medina	C	1877-8-9
Meyburgh	J	1878-9
Meyburgh	P	1879 r
See also Wodehouse True Blues.		
Michaelis	G	1879 r
Miles	A	1879
Mitchley	A.S	1879
Molentzie	W	1879
Montheith	J	1878-9 r
Montjoy	J	1879
Moorcroft	G	1879
Morley	W.W	1879 r
Morrow	J	1879
Mountjoy	G	1879
Murray	R	1879
Nel	C	1877-9 r
Nel	L	1879
Nel	N	1879 r
Nesemann	H	1879
Newson	G	1879 r
Nienaber	B.J	1879
Nienaber	PC	1879
Nienaber	R.J	1879 r
Norman	W	1879 r
Olivier	H	1879 r
Olivier	Piet	1879
Olivier	W.H	1879
Paech	A	1878-9
See also Wodehouse True Blues.		
Peach	P	1878-9
See also Wodehouse True Blues.		
Palmer	B	1879
Palmer	J	1879 r
Palmer	W	1879
Parkes	R	1879 r
Parkin	I	1879
Payne	A	1879 r
Payne	J	1879
Peyper	A	1878-9
Piater	C	1878 r
Pote	F	1879
Potgieter	L.J	1879
Prangley	J	1879 r
Pratt	S	1879
Price	E.E	1879
Prinslow	H	1879
Prinslow	W	1879
Quinn	H	1879
Rheaders	J	1879 r
Ridgway	J	1879
Robinson	T	1879 r
Robinson	T.R	1879 r
Rogers	G	1879 r
Roodt	N	1879 r
Ross	C	1879
Samuels	J	1879
Sawyer	J.C	1879
Schmidt	M	1879
Schroeder	L	1879
Schutte	C	1879 r
Schutte	G	1879 r
Scott	R.A	1879 r
Sheen	W	1877-8-9
Shepperson	F.B	1879
Skea	C	1879
Small	J	1879
Smit	G.C	1879
Smith	G	1879 r
See also Bugler G. Smith Jamestown Mtd. Vol Rifles		
Smithdorp	G	1879
Solomon	J	1879 r
Spiller	R.C	1879
Stelzmer	P	1879 r
Stent	J	1878-9 r
Storey	J	1879
Stretton	G	1879
Stretton	J.K	1879
Stubbs	C	1879
Sutherland	D	1878-9
Sutherland	H.G	1879 r
Swart	C	1879 r
Swart	F	1879
Swart	J	1879 r
Tack	A	1879 r
Tainton	A.P	1878-9
Thompson	J.H	1879
*Thompson	W	1879
Travelyan	E	1879
Tuck	E	1879
Van Aswegen	G	1879
Van Aswegen	P	1879
Van de Merve	J	1879
Van Heerden	H	1879 r
Van Heerden	J.H	1879 r
Van Plaster	A	1879 r
Van Plaster KIA	**R.J**	**1879 r**
Van Staadan	J	1879 r
Van Tonder	F	1879
Van Tonder	J	1879 r
Van Wyk	C	1879 r
Van Wyk	H	1879 r
Van Wyk	P	1879 r
Van Wyk KIA	**S**	**1879 r**
Van Wyk	W.C	1879 r
Van Zyl	H	1878-9 r
Van Zyl	W	1879 r
Venter	A	1879 r
Venter	J	1879 r
Venter	J.J	1879 r
Venter	P.J	1879 r
Verity	R	1879

LIEUT. HERBERT ARTHUR REED, 3RD SOUTH AFRICAN YEOMANRY
Killed in the Attack on Morosi's Mountain, April 8

LIEUTENANT HERBERT ARTHUR REED,

WHO belonged to the Graaff Reinet Troop, 3rd Regiment South African Yeomanry, was the fourth son of Mr. Eardley Reed, of Smethwick, Staffordshire, and was killed on the 8th April, 1879, whilst gallantly leading his troop at the attack on the rebel chief Morosi's Mountain, British Basutoland, South Africa. He had for three years served his Queen and country in the Regular Army, having belonged to the C Battery, A Brigade, R.H.A., in which corps he served in India. After purchasing his discharge he went to reside in South Africa, and during the late Kaffir War against Kreli and Sandili he served with distinction as Lieutenant in a Volunteer Corps raised in the district of Graaff Reinet, while in an engagement two days prior to the attack on Morosi's stronghold, with the enemy under Morosi's son, his troop did good service; Morosi's son being killed by Lieutenant Reed's own hand. In the attack on Morosi's mountain twenty-eight yeomen and police were killed and wounded, and the Colonial forces were compelled to retreat, leaving the mountain in the hands of the rebels.—The photograph from which our portrait is taken is by C. M. Kemp and Co., Graaf Reinet, South Africa.

Name		Year
Vice KIA	**A.J**	**1879 r**
Viljoen	B	1879 r
Viljoen	L	1879 r
Von Broemsen	D	1878-9
Von Metzing	C.W	1879
Vorster	J.P	1879
Vorster	S	1879
Wakeford	O	1879 r
Walker	D	1879 r
Warner	T	1879
Warner	W	1879
Warren KIA	**R**	**1879**
Weatherhead	G.J	1877-9
Webster	E	1879
Webster	H	1879
Webster	W.E	1879
Weimer	S	1879 r
Werdmuller	O	1879
Whitnell	W.H	1879
*Wilson	A	1879 r
Witthuhn	P	1879
Wright	J.C	1878-9
Wyat	J.J	1878-9
Wyat	W	1879

Cape Mounted Yeomanry

3RD CAPE MOUNTED YEOMANRY.
Those Killed in Action (KIA) lost their lives at Moirosi's Stronghold, 29/5/1879.
*Wounded shown with an asterisk.

COLONEL
Minto T.E 1877-8-9

CAPTAIN ADJUTANT
Darwall J.F 1877-8-9 r

CAPTAIN PAYMASTER QUARTERMASTER
Ellis O.H 1877-8-9

CAPTAIN
Bowker J.J.F 1879
Chiappini A.L 1879
Darwall S.F 1877-8-9
Smith R.W 1879 r
Van Niekerk C.J 1877-8-9
Wright W 1879

LIEUTENANT
Bremner C.D 1879
Carstenson A 1879
Ex Pussian Artillery, Iron Cross 2nd Class.
Catton W.T 1879
Heugh P.R 1879
Hudson C.R 1879
Kyd T 1879
Maynier H.F 1877-8-9
Reed KIA H.A 1879
Van Niekerk J.A 1879
Watermeyer F 1879

REGIMENTAL SERGEANT MAJOR
Gill G.E 1879

TROOP SERGEANT MAJOR
Maynier P.G 1877-8-9
Sinclair C.R.B 1879
Zietsman W.L 1877-8-9

STAFF CLERK
Damant W.J 1879

SERGEANT
Anderson R.E 1879
Culley W.H 1879
Flanagan P.J 1879
Gibbon H.J 1879
Meyer P.G 1879
Olivier P.A 1877-8-9
*Parkes W 1879 r
Parkin R.C 1879
Pfingsten E 1879
Slatem W 1879
Smith G 1879
Van Niekerk G.L 1877-8-9
Van Niekerk P.C 1877-8-9
Van Niekerk P.C 1879 r

CORPORAL
Baker G 1877-8-9
Bean L.W 1879
Botha R 1879 r
Cadle C 1877-8-9 r
Carver W.H 1877-8-9
Clarke W 1877-8-9
Damant F.W 1877-8-9
Damant J.S 1879
Ebner H 1877-8
Erasmus P.A 1879
*Essenwien J 1877-8-9
Ferreira D/W P.S 1877-8-9
Ferreira S 1879
Fleischer H.M 1877-8-9 r
Hall T.E 1879 r
Muller A.M 1879 r
Niekerk J.J 1879
Noyce G.T 1879
Rademeyer J 1877-8-9
Rademeyer N.P 1879
Rens P.C 1877-8-9
Roome E 1877-8
Van Coller J.J 1877-8-9 r
Walsh R 1879

CASUALTIES DURING THE SIEGE OF MOROSI'S MOUNTAIN IN 1879

Name	Regiment	Rank	Date
Reed, N.A	3rd Cape Mounted Yeomany	Lieut	8/4/1879 1st Assault
Muldoon, T.	3rd Cape Mounted Yeomany	Sgt.	23/3/1879 During the approach
Ferreira, P.S.	3rd Cape Mounted Yeomany	Corporal/Trooper	29/5/1879 Night Attack
Hannon, W. E.	3rd Cape Mounted Yeomany	Trooper	5/6/1879 2nd Assault
Hastings, A.	3rd Cape Mounted Yeomany	Trooper	29/5/1879 Night Attack Piquet duty
Johnstone, A.	3rd Cape Mounted Yeomany	Trooper	29/5/1879 Night Attack
Johnstone, Thomas	3rd Cape Mounted Yeomany	Trooper	29/5/1879 Night Attack
Kay, W.	3rd Cape Mounted Yeomany	Trooper	29/5/1879 Night Attack
King, W.	3rd Cape Mounted Yeomany	Trooper	No date
Laurens, T. P.	3rd Cape Mounted Yeomany	Trooper	29/5/1879 Night Attack
Leonard, H.	3rd Cape Mounted Yeomany	Trooper	5/6/1879 2nd Assault
Lourens, Cornelius	3rd Cape Mounted Yeomany	Trooper	29/5/1879 Night Attack
Mason, C.	3rd Cape Mounted Yeomany	Trooper	29/5/1879 Night Attack
Meyer, Fred	3rd Cape Mounted Yeomany	Trooper	29/5/1879 Night Attack
Thornton, C	3rd Cape Mounted Yeomany	Trooper	29/5/1879 Night Attack

Cape Mounted Yeomanry

Weeks	W.H	1877-8-9	Cunningham	W	1877-8-9 r	Kritzenger	H	1879 r
BUGLER			Damant	G	1879	Kritzenger	L	1879
Browning	F.W	1877-8-9	De la Harpe	B	1877-8-9	Lane	J	1877-8-9
Heyne	F.A	1879 r	De Villiers	J.G	1879 r	**Laurens**	**C.P KIA**	**1879 r**
Mc Callum	W	1879	Dicks	J	1879	Laurens	P.A	1877-8-9
TROOPER			Du Toit	C.P	1879	Laurens D/W	T.P	1879 r
Ackerman	F	1879	Edmunds	J.W	1879 r	*Leach	J.C	1877-8-9
Adendorp	M.J	1879 r	Evans	G.F	1879 r	# Leonard D/W	H.B	1879
Albertyn	F.J	1879	Ferreira	A.M	1877-8-9	Little	J	1879
Alexander	F.R	1879	Ferreira	A.M	1879 r	Lloyd	G	1879 r
Altenstedt	P	1879	Ferreira	A.M	1879	Lovemore	G	1879
Archer	A	1879	Ferreira	F.G	1879	Macnaby	F	1879
Arendt	O	1879 r	Ferreira	J.M	1879	## Manfield	A.J	1879
Ashley	L.G	1879	Ferreira	T.J	1879	Marley	W.W	1879 r
Aspeling	S.H	1879	Fick	W	1879 r	**Mason**	**C.E KIA**	**No clasp r**
Baker	P.J	1879 r	Fowler	F	1879 r	Mayers	S	1877-8-9 r
Basson	J.S	1877-8-9 r	Gericke	J	1879	Mc Callum	A	1879
*Bean	G.C	1879	Gill	W	1879	Mc Callum	J	1879
Bishop	W	1879	Glover	A	1879 r	Mc Cauley	J	1879
Blunden	T	1879 r	Goss	H	1879 r	Mc Kechnie	W	1879 r
Botha	F	1879	**Hannan**	**W.E KIA**	**1879 r**	Mc Kenzie	A	No clasp r
Botha	J	1879	Harris	J	1879	Mearns	J	1877-8-9
Botha	P.R	1879	**Hasting**	**A.S KIA**	**1879 r**	**Meyer**	**G.F KIA**	**1879**
Brink	J.G	1879	Hawkins	W	1879	*Meyer	P.L	1879
Brown	H.A	1879	Hendricks	M	1877-8-9	Meyer	W.H	1877-8-9
Brown	J	1879	Hendricks	W	1879	Minnie	J.O	1877-8-9
Brown	J	1879	Hosking	R	1879 r	Minnie	M	1879
Brown	J.H	1879	Huggins	R	1879	Minnie	T.C	1879
Browning	A.E.S	1879	Hull	T.E	1879 r	Mirfin	W	1879 r
Butler	C	1879	Hulley	B.S	1879 r	Moolman	P	1879 r
Butler	W.A	1879 r	*Humphreys	A.H	1879	Muller	A.M	1879
Carter	J	1879	Hurley	J	1879	Muller	G	1879
Carton	W	1879	James	G.H	1879	Muller	J	1879
Chaband	L	1879	Jones	D.S	1879 r	Muller	P.J	1879
Clarke	C.E	1879	Jones	T	No clasp	*Munro	J	1877-8-9
Clear	J	1879	Johnson	A	1879 r	Murray	P	1879
*Clear	W	1879	**Johnson**	**A.T KIA**	**1879**	Nicholson	H.M	1879 r
Coetzee	H	1879	Johnson	J	1879	Olivier	C.M	1879
Colling	A	1879	Johnson	J	No clasp	Owen	G	1879
Colling	G	1877-8-9	**Johnson**	**T KIA**	**1877-8-9**	Orsmond	J.W	1879 r
Copeling	R.W	1879	**Kay**	**W KIA**	**1879**	Padoa	J	1877-8 r
Cox	G	1879 r	Kelley	J.F	No clasp	Palmer	J	No clasp r
Cox	J	1879 r	Kemp	P.G	1877-8	Parkin	J	1879

Dixons Gazette No41 Spring 2004
594 1 clasp, 1879, engraved in the correct style, edge bruise at 8 o'clock to reverse. Trooper H.B. Leonard, D/3rd Cape Yeomanry. The Basuto campaign of 1879 against the Baphutis tribe led by the old warrior Chief Moirosi and his son Dodo over their refusal to pay tax led to the tribe retiring to an almost inaccessible mountain near the Orange River. It had three near vertical sides and was strongly fortified by the Baphutis. Moirosi and his people held out for many months during which time several gallant attacks were repulsed. One such attack took place on 5th June 1879 with many casualties. It was in this action that Surgeon Major Hartley won the Victoria Cross for attending to the wounded under fire. Amongst the wounded lay Trooper Hassel B. Leonard of D/3rd Cape Yeomanry with a gunshot wound to his thigh ref W025/3474 and LG 15.8.1879 page 4971. Most other published lists claim his wound as being mortal.
Sold with photocopies of relevant rolls and casualty lists. Medal and clasp verified WO 100/49. VF £1350.00

Spink Sale 7029 Lot 69
The South Africa 1879 Medal to **Trooper A.J. Mansfield**, Cape Yeomanry, Wounded During the Siege of Morosi's Mountain Stronghold South Africa 1877-79, one clasp, 1879 (Tpr. A.J. Mansfield, C/3rd. Cape Yeory.), toned, light scratches to obverse, therefore nearly extremely fine Hammer Price £ 920 . Trooper A.J. Mansfield served in the Graffe Reinet Troop, Cape Mounted Yeomanry during the Zulu War and was wounded by a bullet during the Siege of Morosi"s Mountain stronghold.

Cape Mounted Yeomanry

Pauls	W	1877-8-9
Peacocke	N.F	1879
Perkins	H.M	1879
Pffeuger	A	No clasp
Potgieter	J	1877-8-9
Potgieter	M.E	1879
Potgieteer	P.H	1879
Pringle	J	No clasp r
*Rademeyer	C	1879
Reutenbach	A.J	1879
Rens	A.J	1877-8-9
Restall	H.J	1877-8-9
Roselt	F.J	1879
Royle	C.E	1879
Ruthenberg	W	1879
Ryan	C	1879 r
Saunders	G	1879
Schoenvard	P.J	1879 r
Scott	P.C	No clasp
Siebert	M.W	1877-8-9
Smith	C	1879
Smith	C	1879
*Smith	J.R	1879 r
Smith	S	1879 r
Smith	W	No clasp r
Stanton	W	1879
Stephens	H.G	No clasp r
Stowe	J.C	1879
Tabor	W	1879
Taylor	F	1879
Taylor	G	1879
Terblans	J.W	1879 r
Thornton	**C KIA**	**1879 r**
Towers	J	1879
Van Bloemestein	S	1879
Van Coller	H	1879
*Van Der Hoogen	H	1879
Van der Reit	A	1879 r
Van Der Watt	J.J	1879
Van Der Watt	J.K	1879
Van Der Watt	R	1879
Van Niekerk	A	1877-8-9
Van Niekerk	A.M	1879
Van Niekerk	G	I 1877-8-9
Van Niekerk	J.S	1879 r
Van Niekerk	P.C	1879
Van Niekerk	S	1879 r
Van Niekerk	S.J	1877-8-9
Van Niekerk	T	1877-8-9
Van Onselen	G	1879 r
Van Onselen	G.C	1879
Van Onselen	S	1879
Van Rooyen	J.H	1879 r
Van Rooyen	J.M	1879 r
Vermaak	E	1879 r
Vickers	J.J	No clasp
Waldeck	H.D	1879
Wallace	J	No clasp
Walsh	A.H	1879
Walsh	J	1879
Williams	J.J	1879
Williams	U	1879
Winn	G.D	1879
Wright	E	1879
Zietsman	W.H	1879 r

CAPE NATIVE CONTINGENT.
CORPORAL
Van Blerk	M.J	1878 r

RANK NOT KNOWN
Stubbs	W.R	????
Vercueill	J.M.G	1877-8

CAPE POLICE
CORPORAL
Emanuel	L.K	1877-8

CAPE TOWN RIFLES (OR VOLUNTEERS)
CAPTAIN
De Pass	?	????

SERGEANT
Epps	F	1877-8

PRIVATE
Campling	W.J.B	1877-8
Dever	M	1877-8
Hosman	E.A.C	1877-8-9
Jackson	H	1877-8
Seis	E	1877-8
Vis	T	1877-8

RANK NOT KNOWN
Chavallier	R.E	1877-8
Kelly	J	1878

CARBUTT'S BORDER RANGERS.
Raising was authorised by Govt. Notice No.100 of 15/3/1879 (Natal Govt Gazette of 18/3/1879) for local defence of Klip River County. There was no clasp to these Medals as the Unit did not cross the Border.

CAPTAIN
Carbutt	F.M

LIEUTENANT & ADJUTANT
Rusk	A

MEDICAL OFFICER
Hyde	F

ACTING QUARTERMASTER
Coaker	N

TROOPER
Baillie	A	
Bester	A.J	
Bester	C.J	
Bowes	A	
Brooks	S	
Brown	J	
Brunner	H	
Colling	W	
Cullen	T	r
Dries		
Green	J	r
Griffin	J	
Grubb	J	
Herbert	S	r
King	W	r
Leach	W	r
Lewis	A	
Lloyd	J	
Marshall	W	r
Masters	J	r
Mastert	W	
Mulcahy	M	
Neilson	O	
Russell	C	r
Schwarz	R	r
Score	E.W	r
Shaughnessy	P.O	
Sinclair	T	
Wallace	W	r
Wylde	C	
Yeates	L	r

CARBUTT'S BORDER RANGERS
Discredited by scandals after the Langalibalele affair of 1873, the Natal Frontier Guard faded from military record. However, in 1878, the former Quartermaster, **Thomas Munro Carbutt,** a Yorkshire bachelor in his forties, mustered a group of twenty horsemen and about twenty-two armed natives. **Stephen Pike,** his brother-in-law, was a lieutenant; **Dr. George Clarence Hyde** was M.O., and two of his sons were troopers. Carbutt's Volunteers appear in the records as "Corbet's Scouts", "Corbett's Rangers", and "Carbutt's Mounted Troopers." They established their headquarters in a deserted farmhouse, and keeping up their spirits with a liberal supply of rum, patrolled the Waschbank Valley, the Sundays River drifts, and the approaches to Ladysmith. They were destined to play an invaluable role as guides in the field, where they were the only local unit to serve throughout the War. Five days after the battle of Rorke's Drift, **Thomas Munro** Carbutt and his Rangers rode up to Helpmekaar. Their medical officer **Dr. Hyde,** personally escorted **John Chard** back to Ladysmith and nursed him back to health, in the doctor's Hyde home at "Aller Park". Of the local volunteers, only Carbutt's Rangers

Carringtons Light Horse

CARRINGTONS (LIGHT) HORSE.
SERGEANT
Leslie J   not on medal roll
Slightly wounded at Quintana 7/2/1878
see Frontier Light Horse Trooper J Leslie
TROOPER
Campbell   J   1879
Mulroy   T   not on medal roll
Slightly wounded at Quintana 7/2/1878
see Frontier Light Horse.
PRIVATE
Payne   R   1877-8
RANK NOT KNOWN
Braulo   H   1877-8
Campbell   J   1877-8
Denny   F   1879
Whelan   W.H   1879
Wright   A.P.H.E.S   1877-8

CHALUMNA VOLUNTEER CAVALRY.
Clasp information unreliable.
CAPTAIN
Warren Snr T.H   1877-8
LIEUTENANT
Shone   H   1877-8 r
LIEUTENANT OF LEVIES & TROOPER
Sheard   H.N   1877-8
SERGEANT MAJOR
Rasmussen J   1877-8
SERGEANT
Holl   J.C   KIA 1877-8
CORPORAL
Currin   L   1877-8
Elliott   G   1877-8
Forrester R.W   1877-8
TROOPER
Bentley   M   1877-8
Bowles Snr John   1878
Bowles Jnr John   No clasp
Bowles   J   1878
Bowles   J.H   1877-8
Bowles Snr W   1877-8
Bowles   W.M   1877-8
Bowles   W.T   1877-8
Brooks   A   1877-8
Brooks   C   1877-8
Cooper   T.D   1877-8
   See Cpl. T. Cooper Sansoms Horse.
Currin   A.E   1877-8

Currin   R.W   1877-8
Dredge   S   1877-8
Dredge   S.T   No clasp
Dupree   L   1877-8
Ferguson   H   1878
Forrester J   1878
Gray   J   1877-8
Harty   C   1877-8
Hearns   C   No clasp
Hearns   T   1877-8
Hodgkinson T   1877-8
Holdstock E   1877-8
Holdstock L   1877-8
Holl   C.G   1877-8 r
Holl   J.H   1877-8 r
Holl   J.R.F   1877-8 r
Hurn   R   1877-8
Mountford R   1877-8
Nowel   J.R   1877-8
Rasmussen J.W   No clasp
Sansom   J.E   No clasp r
Sansom   C   KIA 1878 r
Sheard   J   1877-8
Stewart   G.C   1878
Stratford H   1877
Thompson A.D   1877-8
Van der Merwe J.P   1877-8
Venables   J   1877-8
Warren Jnr T.H   1877-8
Wright   A.W   1877-8

CIVIL COMMISSIONER CRADOCK
Ayliff   J   1877-8
Ayliff   J   1879
Two medals to same man ?.
NO DISTRICT SHOWN
Holland   B.H   1878

CLANWILLIAM VOLUNTEER CORPS.
LIEUTENANT
Hayden   T de F.C   1878
CORPORAL
Charles   C   1877-8 r
Fix   J   1877-8
Klaasen   S   1877-8
Straus   A   1877-8
Had the Sir Harry Smith's Medal.
PRIVATE
Adams   W   1877-8 r

Amon   F   1877-8 r
Baatjes   W   1877-8 r
Basson   H   1877-8 r
Basson   J   1877-8 r
Fix   A   1877-8
Fix   S   1877-8
Fransmen   B   1877-8 r
Geering   J   1877-8 r
Goennan   G   1877-8 r
Harvey   W   1878
Jantzes Snr A   1877-8 r
Jantzes   A   1877-8 r
Kamfer   J   1877-8 r
Kalmeyer   T   1877-8 r
Klaasen   S   1877-8 r
Klaasen   W   1877-8 r
Koopman   B   1877-8 r
Kijba   K   1877-8 r
Kajavie   J   1877-8 r
Manel   H   1877-8 r
Manel   J   1877-8 r
Peters   F   1877-8 r
Porter   W   1878-9
Pretorius C   1877-8
Pretorius J   1877-8
Pretorius W   1877-8
Rosant   K   1877-8 r
Scheefers J   1877-8 r
Scheefers J   1877-8
September G   1877-8 r
Strovelot F   1877-8 r
Strovelot W   1877-8
Tampo   H   1877-8 r
Tromp   P   1877-8 r
Tities   G   1877-8 r
Ven der Merwe H   1877-8 r
Williams   B   1877-8 r

CLARKES POLICE
TROOPER
Ohye   W   1878-9

COLESBERG LIGHT HORSE
CAPTAIN
Van Bart   E   1878
LIEUTENANT
Rubidge   R.H   1877-8
Smuts   R   1877-8

Dixons Gazette No34 summer 2003 1617 1 clasp, 1877-8. Trooper T.Hodgkinson, Chalumna Volunteer Cavalry. raised in 1877 with a strenght of only 13, it served with the East London Cavalry in the 9th Frontier War. EF £375.00

Dixons Gazette No13 Spring 1998
76 Trooper A.H. Thompson, Chalumna Volunteer Cavalry and Kingswilliam Town Dist. Mnt Troops.
South Africa Medal 1877-1879, 1 clasp, 1877-8 ((Tpr. Chalumna Vol: Cavy.); Queen's South Africa Medal 1899-1902, no clasp (5 Cpl. K.W.T. D.M.T.)(2)
42 issued. Chalumna Volunteer Cavalry, raised in 1877 and served with a strength of 13 in the Fast London Cavalry in Basutoland on the H.Q. Column. Served with the East London Cavalry in the Ninth Kaffir War. GVF £300.00

Colesberg light Horse

QUARTERMASTER
Murray C 1877-8
SERGEANT MAJOR
Eaton F.A 1877-8
SERGEANT
Hayes D.J 1877-8
Krog M 1877-8
Neser S.A 1877-8 r
Praed J 1877-8
Wallace W 1877-8
CORPORAL
Du Plessis G 1877-8 r
Glass T 1877-8 r
Heath H 1877-8
Owen G 1877-8-9 r
Rait W 1877-8 r
Riordan J de B 1877-8-9
Sauer W 1878 r
Teengs J 1878
White W 1878
Young F 1877-8
PRIVATE
Alexander H 1877-8 r
Arlow J 1878 r
Benade R 1878 r
Bleron J 1878 r
Blignaut Jac 1878 r
Blignaut Jos 1878 r
Bowler C 1877-8
Brandt W 1878
Brookes J 1877-8
Cameron A 1877-8 r
Cheasy E 1878 r
Clark J 1877-8
Coakley J 1878
Conway R 1878 r
Daley C 1877-8
Deane J.A 1877-8
Du Borg C.F 1878
Dutton W 1878
Field W 1878 r
Ford K 1877-8
Francis T 1877-8
Garrot F 1878 r
Gibbon A 1877-8 r
Giraud J 1878 r
Gooding J 1877-8
Harvett J 1878 r
Heppal W 1877-8
Newson E.J 1877-8 r
Hoffmeister W 1877-8 r
Hogan A 1878
Hughes H 1878 r
Jeffery W KIA 1878-9 r
Johns D 1877-8 r
Julien P 1878 r
Kaiser W 1878 r
Kennedy W 1877-8 r

Klaassen J 1878 r
Koen C 1878 r
Koen D 1877-8
Koen J.T 1877-8
Lindstrom F 1878 r
Mac Intyre H 1878 r
Mac Tavish R 1877-8
Martin R 1877-8
Mc Rory W 1878
Melle J 1878 r
Milany M 1878
Miller H 1878 r
Mills E 1878
Muller H 1878 r
Mullins M 1878 r
Nathan H 1878
Poulton F 1878 r
Poulton J 1878 r
Pritchard G 1878 r
Quin T 1878 r
Rawstorne F.A 1878
Risch F 1878 r
Robertson W 1878
Rogers W 1878 r
Sammons F 1877-8-9 r
Samuels W 1877-8
Schammel C 1877-8
Smyth H 1877-8
Towell J 1877-8 r
Uhleman O 1878
Van Blerk J.C 1877-8
Van der Smissen A 1878
Von Kliest W 1877-8-9
Walters C 1878 r

COLESBERG (PRATTS) VOLUNTEERS.
CAPTAIN
Pratt J.C.O. 1878
LIEUTENANT
George C.E 1878
SERGEANT
Murray F.C 1878
NO RANK SHOWN
Du Plissis H.G 1878
Wiilkinson G 1877-8

COLONIAL COMMANDERS &
LEVY LEADERS
All medals appear to have been issued
Without a Clasp.
COLONIAL COMMANDER
MAJ GENERAL
Lloyd ?
  See also Weenen Yeomanry
LIEUTENANT COLONEL
Mitchell (RM) ?
CAPTAIN
Beaumont W.W

Boycott ?
Lucas G.A
Montgomery ?
MISTER
Giles J
Hawkins (RM) A.C
Newcastle R.M
Wheelwright (RM) W.D
MEDICAL OFFICER
Dalzell Dr. ?
STAFF OFFICER
Ashby Mr W.F
see also as Levy Leader
LEVY LEADER
Allison J.S
Ashby W.F
  See as Staff Officer.
Aylward J r
Bailey ?
Barnes E
Bazley E
Bazley W
Beachcroft R
Beachcroft ?
Beahan J
Bennett J
Bennett T.R
Boast E
Brock H
Browne R.O
Buchanan D.F
Clarke ?
Cooke C.B
Crabbe D
Cross J.W
Dawson A.B
De Langa H
De Langa J
Du Bois R
Eastwood J.H
Evatt G.F
Farr R
Ford ?
Frankeish J
Fynn H.F
Gifford W
Gilbert R r
Girvan ? r
Gray W
Gregory ? r
Heathcote H.A r
Hornby C
Household W
Jackson ?
Johnson L
Joyce T
Justice R
Kennedy R

Colonial Commanders & Levy Leaders

A group of Levy Leaders at Umsinga, April 1879.
Top row (left to right): W.C.Warner, H.F.Fynn, Jr.,J.G.Dartnell and N.H. Robinson
Bottom row (left to right): H.E.Kirby, T. Wheeler, J.L. Knight, T.H.Reynolds, R. A Beachcroft and J.Frankish. (Natal Archives Depot)

Kinch	F.K	Pigg	H.G	Umsinga	R.M
King	?	Pigg	W	Van Rooyen Jnr	L.M.J
King	C	Polkinghorne	J.A	Walford	? r
Kirby	H	Potgieter	M.P	Walker	R.W.J
Kirby	H.E	Pretorius Jnr	A	Warner	A.G.B
Knight	J	Pretorius	A		See also Natal Mounted Police.
Knox	F.H	Pretorius	P	Wells	W
Laing	H.J	Randlehoff	W.E	Wheeler	T
Laing	R.H	Rapson	J	Wheeler	T
Lake	G.M	Reynolds	T	Williams	J.E
Leuchars	H.J	Reynolds	T.H	Wood	H
Mare	F	Ritchie	J	Wooley	J.P
Mare	W.W	Ritchie	W	Wooley	R.A
Maree	J	Robindon	N	Wright	T
Martens Jnr	J.T	Robindon	Newman	**CONDUCTOR**	
Masterman	R	Robson	J	Mostert	? X
Maxwell	?	Rock	H	Note: (RM) Resident Magistrate.	
Mearns	R	Searle	?		
Methley	J	Simpson	C.H	**COLONIAL CONSTABULARY.**	
Morrell	?	Smerdon	A	**NO RANK SHOWN**	
Nel	J.S	Smith	W.H	Pattison A	1879
Nosworthy	A.E r	Strydom	G.C		
Ogle	J	Strydom	J.J		
Perry	W.C	Thompson	? r		
Phoenix	J	Threst	T		

Corps of Guides

CORPS OF GUIDES.
CAPTAIN
Opir   J.M   1878
Wittycombo J   1878
LIEUTENANT
Bezuldenhout G   1878 r
Brindenbert W   1878 r
Greathead W.H   1878
Pienaar   A   1878 r
Van Royen   1878 r
SERGEANT
Kotzee   J   1878
TROOPER
Beadle   W   1878 r
Brindenhert W   1878 r
De Boys   W   1878 r
Edwards   S   1878 r
Roux   J   1878
Van Rooyen ?   1878 r
Venter   J   1878 r
Veske   ?   1878 r
CHIEF
Mora   B   1878 r
(In charge of Transport)

NOTE ON ROLL "About 400 Natives but impossible to find their whereabouts."

CRADOCK BURGHERS
LIEUTENANT & ADJUTANT
De Beer   S   1878
NO RANK SHOWN
Hurtir   D   1878
Hurtir   D de W   1878

CRADOCK MOUNTED VOLUNTEERS
QUARTERMASTER
Block   W   1878
PRIVATE
Abbitt   T.A   1878 r

CRADOCK VOLUNTEER RIFLES.
CAPTAIN
Green   F.E   1877-8
SURGEON
Fehrsen   J.McC   1877-8
COLOUR SERGEANT
Palmer   C   1877-8

PRIVATE
Aspinall E   1877-8
Brown   C   1877-8
Cawood   J.E   1877-8
Furvogel A   1877-8
Impey   C   1879
Joslin   T   1877-8
Rochat   E   1877-8
Stevens   A   1877-8
Thackwray C   1879
Thomas   J   1877-8
Webber   S.G.N   1877-8
Woodland L.M   1877-8-9

CUYLERVILLE MOUNTED RANGERS
TROOPER
Hayton   J.A   1878

DIAMOND FIELDS HORSE.
Those Killed in Action (KIA) lost their lives at Gobatse Heights 14/10/1878
LIEUTENANT COLONEL
Warren CMG C   1877-8

Diamond Fields Horse
#Lieut.-General Sir Charles Warren was born at Bangor, North Wales, on 7th February 1840. His early education took place at the Grammar Schools of Bridgnorth and Wem, and at Cheltenham College. He then entered the Royal Military College at Sandhurst, and from that passed through the Royal Military Academy at Woolwich and received a commission as lieutenant in the Royal Engineers on 23rd December 1857. In 1867, Warren went to Palestine with the Palestine Exploration Fund. He conducted the first major excavations of Jerusalem. In 1870, ill-health forced Warren to return to England. He served briefly at the School of Gunnery at Shoeburyness (1871–1873). In 1876, the Colonial Office appointed him special commissioner to survey the boundary between Griqualand West and the Orange Free State. For this work, he was made a Companion of St Michael and St George (CMG) in 1877. In the Transkei War (1877–1878), he commanded the Diamond Fields Horse raised at Kimberley, and was engaged for six months in Kaffraria. He bought his mounts and drilled his men on the way, and infused his own indomitable energy into every member of his command. He took part in numerous engagements, among which may be mentioned the action of Perie Bush in March, when he was badly wounded and the action at Debe Nek on 5th April, where with seventy-five of the Diamond Fields Horse he met 1,200 armed Kafirs of Seyolo's tribe in the open, and gained a complete victory. For this service, he was mentioned in dispatches and promoted to Brevet Lieutenant-Colonel. He was then appointed special commissioner to investigate "native questions" in Bechuanaland and commanded the troops in the rebellion there. In 1879, he became Administrator of Griqualand West. The town Warrenton in the Northern Cape Province of South Africa is named after him. Commended in despatches for ` energy, ability, and resource displayed under most trying circumstances.' He had been promoted to be Major on 10th April 1878, and his services in the campaign were recognised by a brevet-lieutenant-colonelcy, dated 11th November 1878, and the South African medal. In January 1879 Warren succeeded Colonel Lanyon in the civil administration of Griqualand West, and in later life was Commissioner of Police of the Metropolis, the head of the London Metropolitan Police, from 1886 to 1888, during the period of the Jack the Ripper murders. On the outbreak of the Boer War in 1899, he returned to the colours to command the 5th Division of the South African Field Force. From 1908, Warren became involved with Baden-Powell in the creation of the Boy Scout movement. He died of pneumonia, on the 21 January 1927, at his home in Weston-super-Mare, Somerset, and was buried in the churchyard at Westbere, Kent, next to his wife. Extracts from: Sir Charles Warren and Spion Kop, With a Biographical Sketch Smith, Elder and Co., 1902.   http://www.casebook.org/ripper_media/rps.spion.html

Diamond Fields Horse

 # Lieut. Col. David Harris, Kimberley Rifles, Dix Noonan Web Lot 34, 26 Mar 09
Description
Volunteer Officers' Decoration, V.R.I. cypher, reverse inscribed, 'Lieut. Col. David Harris, Kimberley Rifles', hallmarks for Birmingham 1894, lacking brooch bar, good very fine Hammer price £460
Footnote: David Harris was born in the City of London on 12 July 1852 and educated at Coxford's College, City of London. In 1871, at the age of 19, he emigrated to South Africa. Making his way to the 'diamond fields', he invested in a claim in the Dutoitspan Mine, which he worked with moderate success. Meanwhile he learned the business of diamond buying and got employment as a buyer; eventually setting up on his own account. He later acquired new claims and became an associate of Cecil John Rhodes, and in 1897 was made a director of De Beers Consolidated Mines Ltd. He was subsequently Chairman of De Beers, and other mining companies, retiring in 1931
Harris was elected a member for Kimberley in the Cape Legislative Assembly in 1897, and was re-elected in 1904. He retained his seat at the Union in 1910, and retired in 1929 as the longest serving member
Harris was a keen and long serving Volunteer soldier. In 1876 he answered a call for volunteers for the 9th Kaffir War. He became a Sergeant in the Dutoitspan Hussars and went on active service with them. He became Paymaster and Quartermaster in the Diamond Fields Horse in 1877, and Lieutenant in 1878. He served as Adjutant under Sir Charles Warren. He was mentioned in despatches and was awarded the South Africa Medal 1877-79 with a clasp for the Gaika-Gealeka campaign. He subsequently took part in the Griqualand West campaign of 1878. On 13 August 1888, Captain Harris became the Commanding Officer of the Victoria Rifles, until he resigned in October 1890. In December 1890 he became Commanding Officer with the rank of Major, of the Kimberley Rifles. He was promoted to Lieutenant-Colonel in May 1894 and remained C.O. until December 1895.....

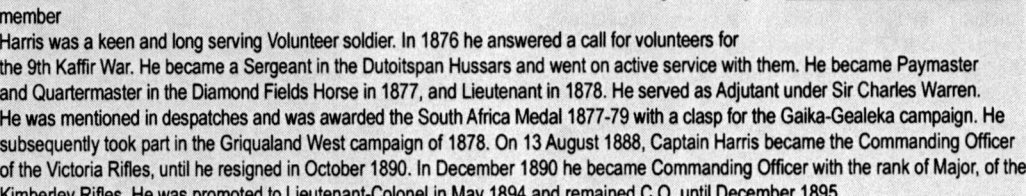

MAJOR		
Rolleston	L.J	1877-8
ADJUTANT		
# Harris	D	1877-8
QUARTERMASTER		
Litkie	E	1878
COMMISSARY GENERAL		
Foggit	M	1878
COMMISSARY		
Graham	W.C	1877-8
CAPTAIN		
Alexander	C	1878
Aston	J	1878 r
Back	G	1877-8
Bellew	W.S	1877-8
Blackbeard	R	1877-8
D'Arcy	R.K.H	1877-8
*Donovan J KIA		1878
Doveton	C.H	1877-8
Doveton	D.E	1878-9
Maxwell	T	1878
Stewart	R	1878
Tyson	T.G	1877-8
LIEUTENANT		
Austin	J.B	1877-8
Bruce	**W** KIA	**1877-8 r**
Dunne	E.E	1878
Humphery	H.J	1878 r
Palliser	KIA	**1877-8 r**
Spencer	H.M	1877-8
***Ward**	**G** KIA	**1877-8 r**
Webb	H.B	1879?
Williams	F	1877-8-9
Wollaston	C.F.B	1878
2ND LIEUTENANT		
Donovan	F	1877-8
Heintz	R.P	1877-8 r
SERGEANT MAJOR		
Green	T	1877-8
Hutchinson	G.W	1877-8
Mc Donald	T	1877-8 r
Norford	R	1877-8
Pole	W	1877-8
Wolff	H.A	1878
TROOP SERGEANT MAJOR		
Master	R.A	1878-9 r
See also Capt. R.A Master Transvaal Rangers.		
FARRIER SERGEANT		
Butler	J	1877-8
QUARTERMASTER SERGEANT		
Brooks	W.E	1878
SERGEANT		
Aburrow	E	1877-8
Adams	F.D	1877-8
Aldum	J	1877-8
Classen	C	1878
Clarkson	A	1877-8
Drysdale	E.R	1878
Easter	F	1877-8
Eggleston	W	1877-8
Haskell	F	1878
Hutton	W.P	1877-8
Levy	J.R	1877-8
Lewis	J.W	1877-8
Ling	B	1878
Masters	A	1878
Mc Donald	A	1877-8 r
Perring	J.R.R	1877-8
Perring	R.C	1877-8
Poole	W.F	1878
Powell	T.H	1877-8
Reilly	J	1877-8
Selby	D	1878
Slade	S	1878
Tinker	J.L	1877-8 r
Turner	A	1877-8
Varrie	J	1877-8
Williams	A	1877-8 r
Winkler	W	1878
Wood	J	1878
CORPORAL		
Adendorff	G	1877-8-9 r
Bayliss	J	1878
Bishop	C.F.G	1878
Bisset	W	1877-8
See also QMS W. Bisset Kimberley Horse		
Black	R	1877-8 r
Clarkson	W	1877-8
Cowell	J.W	1878
Davis	**P** KIA	**1878**
Debbes	E	1878 r
Dunn	W.C	1877-8
Hearle	R.W	1877-8
Hough	W	1878 r
Honeybun	G	1877-8
Jones	W.A	1877-8
Mc Kay	J	1877-8

* **Captain Donovan** and **Lieutenant Ward**, conflicting dates of their demise. There is a vivid description of their ambush in war telegrams, 20-25th March 1878, printed in The Natal Witness, 4 April 1878. Joseph Donovan family was Free State Born, George Walter Ward was an assistant mining surveyor in Kimberley, and a Lieutenant in the Griqualand West Light Infantry.

Capt. Wollaston.   Lieut. Dowing.   Capt. W. Graham.
Major Hamilton-Browne.   Major T. Maxwell.   Capt. Ward.
A GROUP OF OFFICERS OF THE DIAMOND FIELD HORSE.

Diamond Fields Horse

Mc Kay	R.W	KIA 1877-8 r	Brin	T	1877-8 r	Duffy	C	1877-8 r
Mills	J	1877-8 r	Brink	S	1878	Duffy	J	1877-8
Muller	**A**	**KIA 1877-8 r**	Brittain	H	1877-8	Edwards	W	1877-8 r
Payne	**R**	**KIA 1877-8**	Brooker	W	1877-8	Eraser	J	1878
Thornton	**R**	**KIA 1877-8 r**	Brophy	T	1878 r	French	T	1877-8
Vice	E	1877-8 r	Brown	C	1877-8	Garish	E	1878
Vigne	F	1878	Brown	C	1878	Gers	E	1878 r
Wilson	T	1877-8	Brown	J.S	1877-8 r	Gildenhuis	A	1877-8
Wood	A	1878	Bruton	J.S	1877-8 r	Giles	J.G	1878 r
Wriford	G.A.W	1877-8	Burleigh	W.F	1878	Good	G	1878 r
TRUMPETER			Burnett	R.G	1878	Green	E	1877-8 r
Middlecoop	F.J	1878 r	Busby	T	1877-8	Green	H	1878 r
TROOPER			**Campbell**	**E.J**	**KIA 1878**	**Green**	**L**	**KIA 1877-8 r**
Abrahams	J	1878	Carmody	R	1877-8	Green	T.D	1878 r
Action	J	1878 r	Carr	J	1878	**Hailby**	**C**	**KIA 1877-8**
Adler	D	1878	Cawood	H.R	1878	Hailby	W	1877-8
See also Cpl D.J.Adler Transvaal Rangers.			Caynola	C	1878 r	Hammick	Y	1877-8
			Chambers	R	1878 r	Hartzenberg	J.J	1877-8 r
Anderson	J.H	1877-8	Chapman	E.H	1878 r	Hasler	G	1877-8
Anderson	P	1878 r	Chapman	J	1878 r	Hemming	J	1877-8
Anderson	R	1877-8 r	**Chapman**	**W**	**KIA 1878 r**	Henderson	F	1878
Andrias	C	1878 r	Christian	E.J	1877-8 r	Hitge	C.G	1877-8-9
Ansell	C	1878	Clark	P	1878 r	Home	C	1877-8
Armstrong	C.W.P	1878	Clements	A	1877-8	Howse	J	1877-8
Arnold	**A**	**KIA 1877-8 r**	Cloete	G	1878 r	Hulley	D.E	1877-8
Art	T	1877-8	Coakley	T	1878 r	Humphrey	H.J	1878 r
Ashton	J	1878 r	Collins	A	1877-8	Hyman	W.C	1877-8 r
Bacon	H	1877-8 r	Collins	R	1878 r	Jackson	A.W	1878 r
Bamberg not on medal roll Wounded at Debe Nek 30/4/1878			Cook	G	1878 r	Jackson	J.A	1878 r
			Cornish	W	1877-8 r	Jacoby	C.H	1877-8
Banks	E	1878	Cox	W	1878	Jaffray	G	1877-8 r
Barendilla	J.F	1878	Coxen	H	1878 r	Jenkinson	D.H	1877-8
Barrington	**G**	**KIA 1877-8 r**	Coyle	E	1878 r	Jones	C	1877-8 r
Beadle	W	1878 r	See also Transvaal Rangers.			Jones	C	1878
Beard	T	1878 r	Cramer	W	1878 r	Jones	R	1878
Becker	G	1878	Cravat	J	1877-8 r	Johnson	T	1877-8 r
Beddome	R	1878	Cutter	T.G	1877-8	Keeley	J.J	1877-8
Bees		**KIA 1878**	David	C.T	1877-8	Keenan	P	1878 r
Bees	W	1878 r	Deale	H	1877-8	Kerr	W	1877-8 r
Benkes	J	1878 r	Deane	J.A	1877-8	Keys	W.F	1877-8 r
Benville	W	1878 r	D'eath	W	1878	King	F	1878 r
# Blackbeard	C.A	1878	Diaz	H	1878	King	T	1877-8
Bolton	G	1877-8 r	Dillon	D	1878 r	Koch	D	1878
Boly	W	1878	Dispecker	J	1878 r	Kramer	J	1877-8 r
Botha	W	1878 r	Dold	J.H	1877-8 r	Leigh	K	1877-8
Boyce	R	1878 r	Driver	T	1878-9	Litkie	P	1878 r

City Coins Postal Auction No 58 29th August 2008, Lot No 263. SAGS bar: 1878 Tpr. C.A. Blackbeard EF- Hammer price 22,000 Rand Diamond Fds. Hse.; QSA bar: DoK Capt. & Adjt. C.A. Blackbeard Kimberley T.G.; Kimberley Star (complete, mm "a") MiD LG 8 May 1900. Charles Blackbeard was born at Grahamstown in December 1848, the grandson of an 1820 Settler. He came to the Diamond Fields in 1871 and was for years a prominent and successful digger at New Rush (now Kimberley) and Du Toitspan (now Beaconsfield), where he took up residence for more than 30 years. In a cutting from the "Beaconsfield Budget" it is mentioned that "during the so-called Rebellion of 1875 he was one of the volunteers who defended the Gaol at the point of the bayonet against all malcontents; he took part in the suppression of the Griqua Rebellion in 1878 and was present at the fight at Griquatown (Jakkals Vlei)". During the Siege of Kimberley he was Mayor of Beaconsfield as well as Captain and Adjutant of the Beaconsfield Town Guard. He was instrumental in having Kekewich reverse his original decision to abandon Beaconsfield to the Boers if necessary and let the inhabitants retreat to Kimberley. He was mentioned in Col. Kekewich's Despatches (LG 8 May 1900, p. 2919): "Captain C.A. Blackbeard, Beaconsfield Town Guard, has done much good work in connection with the interior economy of the Beaconsfield Town Guard and keeping order in the township of Beaconsfield". Sold with copies of medal rolls and MiD as well as a voluminous copy file of Blackbeard family research.

Diamond Fields Horse

Lockhart	J.A	1878
Lockhart	W.P	1878
Lottering	C	1877-8
Lowrie	J	1877-8
Lucas	W	1877-8 r
Magowan	E	1878
Magowan	E	1878-9
*Mathews	J.W KIA	1878 r
Matthews	F.J	1878 r
Maxwell Jnr	T	1878
Maxwell	W	1877-8
Maynes	J	1878 r
Maynes	J	1878 r
Mc Carthy	C.E	1877-8 r
Mc Cosky	W	1878
Mc Kay	D	1878
Mc Kay	G	1877-8

See also One Star Diamond Contg.

Mc Laghlin	T.P	1877-8 r
Mc Nally	P	1877-8 r
Meyer	J	1877-8
Mills	T	1877-8
Mooney	J	1878
Muller	D	1877-8
Muller	H	1877-8
Murray	J	1877-8 r
Mursner	F	1877-8
Myer	R	1878 r
Myer	R	1878 r
Nicholson	R.G	1877-8

Replacement medal and clasp issued on 28/2/1920.

Nightingale	A	1877-8
Nisbett	G	1878 r
Nisbett	G	1878 r
Onora	G	1877-8 r
Packman	W.K	1878
Paddle	G	1878
Paddock	W	1878
Page	F.W	1878 r
Peacock	A	1877-8 r
Peel	T	1877-8
Perring	C.C	1878
Peters	G	1877 8
Phillips	G	1878 r
Powell	F.J	1878
Quin	P	1877-8
Reilly	F	1878
Reux	D	1877-8 r
Reynolds	W.R	1877-8
Roberts	W.A	1878
Rogers	R.D	1878 r
Rosenthal	L	1878
Saunders	H	1878
Scheepers	F	1878 r
Schoonraad	G	1877-8 r
Shepherd	T	1877-7
Schuler	H	1878 r
Smith	C	1877-8 r
Smith	J.E	1878
Smith	J.P	1877-8
Smith	T	1877-8 r
Smith	T	1878
Snow	T	1877-8
Snyman	M	1877-8
Soar	C.W	1878
Solomon	P	1878
Spencer	F	1878
Spencer	S	1878 r
Springorum	W	1878 r
Stephenson	J	1877-8 r
Stewart	S.J	1877-8
Sullivan	R	1878 r
Summerlee	E	1878
Summers	F	1877-8 r
Thomas	E	1877-8
Thompson	W	1877-8

See also Transvaal Rangers.

Tracey	E	1877-8
Tullis	J	1877-8
Usher	O	1877-8 r
Vecuil	P	1877-8
Waldeck	J	1877-8-9
Walker	J	1877-8 r
Walker	T	1877-8 r
Welby	R	1878
Wepener	F	1878 r
White	E.J	1878 r
White	G.C	1877-8 r
White	H.R	1878 r
White	R.W	1878
White	W	1877-8 r
Williams	**KIA**	**1878 r**
Wilmore	A	1878 r
Wilson	N	1877-8 r
Wright	C.J	1877-8
Young	W.H	1877-8

NO RANK SHOWN

Gorton	C.P	1878-9
Gorton	W.H	1878-9
Hughes	H.S	1878-9
Masters	R.A	????

DISTRICT NATIVE POLICE.
COMMANDER
Blackeway	C.F	1877-8

SUB INSPECTOR
Atmore	T	1877-8
Blakeway	M.J	1877-8
Booth	B	1877-8
Campbell	A.G	1877-8
Chalmers	A	1877-8
Morecroft	W	1877-8

SERGEANT
553 Mc Glashen	W	1877-8

DIVISIONAL POLICE.
SERGEANT
Lotter	W	1877-8 r

CORPORAL
Surmon	E	1877-8 r

PRIVATE
Hansel	F	1878

DUKE OF EDINBURGH VOLUNTEER RIFLES.
(Note on Roll: "No initials given in most cases.")

CAPTAIN
Jones	S.R	1877-8 r

FIELD CAPTAIN
Boyes	J.St G	1878

LIEUTENANT
Furniss	O	1877-8

QUARTERMASTER SERGEANT
Brentnall	E	1877-8

SERGEANT
Flaherty		1877-8 r
Mellon	T	1877-8

CORPORAL
Masters	G	1877-8
Leggett	J	1877-8
Saunder	R	1877-8
Walsh	P	1877-8

BUGLER
Hall	H	1877-8 r

PRIVATE
Adrianse		1877-8
Allen		1877-8
Baker		1877-8 r
Barbier		1877-8
Black		1877-8
Bramwell		1877-8
Brugman		1877-8
Blum		1877-8 r
Carter	G	1877-8
Chambers KIA		**1877-8 r**
Coomer		1877-8
Eager		1877-8
Echardt		1877-8
Edwards		1877-8
Exter		1877-8
Fraser		1877-8 r
Gabriel		1877-8 r
Goslett		1877-8
Gregory		1877-8
Griffin		1877-8 r
Hackett		1877-8
Hayward		1877-8 r
Horsburgh	R	1877-8
Howard		1877-8 r
Jennings		1877-8
King		1877-8
Lambert	W.S	1877-8

Duke of Edinburgh Volunteer Rifles

The Duke of Edinburgh's Own Rifle Volunteer Rifles
About three dozen volunteer units were formed between 1855 and 1861. They included the Cape Rifle Corps (later the Duke of Edinburgh's Own Volunteer Rifles) (1855-); the Port Elizabeth Rifles (later Prince Alfred's Guard) (1856-); the Cape Town Artillery (later Prince Alfred's Own Cape Field Artillery) (1857-); and the Port Elizabeth Volunteer Artillery (1860-1879).
In August, 1877, the corps had a modest strength of 4 officers, 5 sergeants, 4 corporals and 114 privates, who were armed with Sniders of which 50 were Government property and 52 privately owned. The Duke of Edinburgh's Own Rifle Volunteer Rifles was a Volunteer Regiment from Cape Town. They got the "Duke of Edinburgh" title after they supplied a Guard of Honour for him in 1867 and this is when their badge became the Star of the Order of the Thistle surmounted by a royal ducal coronet, and with the regimental title replacing the motto of the Order of the Garter.
In September No. 1 Company had increased to 145 all ranks commanded by Lt. H. Malthouse, rising further in October to 154, of whom 44 were on the frontier. These 44 remained there until January, 1878, reducing to 2 in February. In November, 1877, No. 2 Company was raised with 2 officers and 154 men of whom 44 went to the frontier and the remainder undertook guard duty at Amsterdam Battery. In February there were only 2 on active service. From May, 1878, the returns deal with the whole unit, 28 officers and 557 men, commanded by Col. Z. S. Bayly(6) with Nos. 8 and 9 Companies in course of formation. At the end of the year the Dukes had an authorised establishment of 27 officers and 405 men but an actual strength of 35 and 716. Nos. 1-8 Companies were at Cape Town and No. 9 at Wynberg. Arms were 564 long Sniders and 21 short. The Duke of Edinburgh's Own Rifle Volunteer Rifles was a South African Volunteer Regiment from Cape Town. They got the "Duke of Edinburgh" title after they supplied a Guard of Honour for him in 1867 and this is when their badge became the Star of the Order of the Thistle surmounted by a royal ducal coronet, and with the regimental title replacing the motto of the Order of the Garter.
References: Military History Journal - Vol 1 No 4 Cape Colony Volunteer Units 1877-79 By J. J. Hulme

Name	Years		Name			Name		
Lawrence	1877-8		**SERGEANT MAJOR**			Middelborough	E	
Leslie	1877-8 r		Taylor	W		Pascoe	J	
Luyt	1877-8		**QUARTERMASTER SERGEANT**			Pechey	J M	
Mc Carthy	1877-8		Pinchon	E		Phillips	T	
Mc Dermot	1877-8 r		**SERGEANT**			Sherren	A.G	
Mc Kay	1877-8		Taylor	F.J		Spencer	J.A	
Merrington H.A	1877-8-9		**TROOPER**			Spratt	W	
Middlemost	1877-8		Bassett	A		Whittaker	A	
Miles	1877-8		Boram (Borain)	J				
Newberry	1877-8		Clarence	S		**DURBAN MOUNTED RIFLES.**		
Ormond	1877-8		Crawford	P.O		Raised on 8 November, 1873, The DMR participated in the action at Inyezane, after Isandlwana were sent back to Natal to defend against possible Zulu raids.		
Payne	1877-8 r		Crewe	P.D				
Penfold	1877-8		Culverwell	J				
Pietersen	1877-8		Culverwell	R				
Schroeder	1877-8		Currie	C	r	**CAPTAIN**		
Schultz G	1877-8		Dalgetty	W		Sheptone	W.E	1879
Spolander	1877-8 r		De Rosnay	A	r	**LIEUTENANT**		
Taylor	1877-8		De Rosnnay	O.F	r	Blaine		1879
Thrift	1877-8		De Winter	H	r	Bottomley	J	1879
Turner	1877-8 r		Diamond	F.W	Not on medal Roll	**QUARTERMASTER**		
Van Sittert	1877-8		Doran	R		Adams		1879
Verceuil	1877-8 r		Duberry	H		**SERGEANT MAJOR**		
Wheatley A	1877-8		Elston	C		Shuter		1879
Wilson	1877-8		Elston	F		**QUARTERMASTER SERGEANT**		
			Gibson	A.A		Vause		1879
DURBAN MOUNTED RESERVE.			Green	G.M		Invalided home through illness		
The medals were issued without a clasp.			Green	S.A		**SERGEANT**		
CAPTAIN			Griffiths	C	r	Baker		1879
Escombe H			Groves	E	Not on medal Roll	Evans		1879
LIEUTENANT & QUARTERMASTER			Grix	F	Not on medal Roll	Slatter		1879
Green N			Johnson(Jonsson)	J.G		Voysey	W	1879
LIEUTENANT			Knox	G		**CORPORAL**		
Brunton G			Mann	H	(C.S)	Clarence		1879

From an article in the Natal newspapers dated 28th January 1879, Durban Mounted Reserve at Camp Prospect on patrol and guard duties, they are likely to remain a long time. In addition to the Troopers listed above in the medal roll, the following are mentioned in the article **F Grix, F.W Diamond, E Groves, C.S Mann, and Borain.**

From an article in the Natal newspapers Durban Mounted Reserve. At a shooting contest at Tongaat..**Trooper I .Y Jonsson** 1st; **Trooper Crewe** 2nd; **Staff-clerk Gus Green** 3rd. Heat is extreme, and we are plagued with ticks. Horses are well and the health of the camp is good.

Durban Mounted Rifles

Durban Mounted Rifles

Smith		1879	Fisher		1879	Turner	1879
Watts		1879	Griffith		1879	Tyrell	1879
Wilson		1879	Henwood		1879	Vause	1879
LANCE CORPORAL			Hirron		1879	Voysey	1879
Arnold		1879	Hirst		1879	Wood	1879
Smythe		1879	Hoffman		1879		
TRUMPETER			Kalits		1879	**DURBAN VOLUNTEER ARTILLERY.**	
Lansdell		1879	Kennedy		1879	No clasps were issued to this Unit.	
Palmer		1879	Lapworth		1879	**CAPTAIN**	
TROOPER			Logan	J	1879	Mc Neil	
Acutt		1879	Logan	W.H	1879	**LIEUTENANT**	
Adams		1879	Mann	C.S	1879	Benningfield	
Addison	R.H	1879	Marshall		1879	**QUARTERMASTER**	
Addison	W	1879	Maydon	J.G	1879	Holmes	
Allison		1879	Noble		1879	**SERGEANT MAJOR**	
Beckett		1879	Penfold		1879	Watson	
Behyrens		1879	Povall	H.E	1879	**QUARTERMASTER SERGEANT**	
Bolt		1879	Povall	J.E	1879	Janion	
Invalided home through illness			Proudfoot		1879	**ORDERLY SERGEANT**	
Bransby		1879	Ramsay		1879	Colborne W.W	
Brooke	T	1879	Richardson		1879	**BATTERY SERGEANT**	
Brown		1879	Rippen		1879	Harrison	
Caldwell		1879	Savory		1879	May	
Collins		1879	Smith	C.G	1879	Parfitt	
Invalided home through illness			Invalided home broken leg.			Taylor	
Crompton		1879	Smythe		1879	**BOMBARDIER**	
Cunne		1879	Snell		1879	Bayley	
Currie		1879	Sparks		1879	Upton	
Dacomb	C	1879	Summers		1879	**CORPORAL**	
Died on Service			Thomas		1879	Dove	H
Docomb	L	1879	Tinley		1879	Ingram	J

From an article in the Natal newspapers Durban Volunteer Artillery. The following are the members of this corps who left for the Umgeni encampment on Sunday missing from the above medal roll; Gunner Davis, Zeeman, & Northend.

Durban Mounted Rifles

Capt. W. E. SHEPSTONE
O.C. Durban Mounted Rifles 1876–1881

Durban Mounted Rifles

Formed in 1873, W.E Shepstone was elected first lieutenant, before eventually succeedingas captain in 1876.

On the 2nd January 1879 six members of the DMR, three N.C.O.'s and three troopers had been withdrawn from the Corps to ride dispatches relating to the Zulu reply to Lord Chelmsford's ultimatum; each man travelled a distance of ten to fifteen miles at a gallop.

This important task was given to **Sergeant Evans, Corporals Watts** and **Clarence**, and Troopers **Addison, Kennedy** and **Henwood**.

After crossing the Tugela, while attached to Pearson's Column, their duties included guarding the baggge train, communication between the chain of forts, and guarding the boarder. In July, after only eight months service they were sent back to Durban and released from military duty, some troopers joined the Natal Volunteer Guides

Dissatisfaction over the treatment of war claims. came to a head in February 1880, with most of the members resigning the Corps. The document below was signed by 35 members of the Durban Mounted Rifles, the total muster at the time being 58. Some individuals were absent from the Colony.

On the 28th March 1881, **Captain W.E Shepstone** resigned. **Lieutenant Voysey** acted as Commanding Officer until **Captain Edward F. Tarte** was elected in August 1881.

Referance: The Official Natal Mounted Rifles History, Eric Goetzsche.

Durban Mounted Rifles Resignation. Durban – February, 1880.

W. E. Shepstone, Esq.,
Captain Commanding,
Durban Mounted Rifles.

Sir,

We, the undersigned members of your Corps, have the honour to request that you will accept this our resignation as volunteers in the Durban Mounted Rifles, in support of which we beg to submit the following remarks, and request you will duly bring them to the notice of the Commandant of Volunteers.

1. That during the recent Zulu War the Durban Mounted Rifles, in common with other corps, suffered severe pecuniary loss – a loss in many cases almost irreparable.
2. That after waiting patiently for many months, the members of the Corps are informed through the medium of the Government Gazette of the 17th inst., that a trifling and wholly inadequate recompense is offered them by the Legislative Council.
3. That the undersigned, having been led to expect that some substantial pecuniary compensation would be awarded to them, have continued to remain members of their Corps to the present date.
4. That regarding, as we do, the report of the Select Committee of the Legislative, appointed to consider volunteer's claims, as published in the Gazette of the 17th, as a thorough discouragement to volunteer enterprise, we have no alternative course open to us but to request that His Excellency the Lieutenant-Governor will be pleased to accept our unqualified resignation as members of the volunteer Corps known as Durban Mounted Rifles.
5. We would, *inter alia,* draw your attention to the fact that although Law 17 of 1877 provides that mounted volunteers, when on active service, should only draw pay at the rate of 6/- per diem when rations and forage are found by the Government and foot corps at the rate of 3/- per diem on similar conditions, that the Durban Mounted Reserve and the Royal Durban Rifles drew 12/- and 6/- respectively when rations were provided by the Government. We had deemed the fact above quoted ample precedent for us to base our expectations of extra pay upon. According to Law No. 2 of 1874, we are entitled to fair and reasonable compensation for loss, wear and tear to horses, accoutrement, arms or saddlery: by Law No. 7 of 1878 we are entitled to a payment of £10 for Horse-keep. Under both these headings we have in fact received nothing.
6. We feel bound to observe that had our claims been urged upon the Legislative by resolutions of the Corps or by petition duly setting them forth, the grounds upon which they were based, they would have met with a better reception.

In conclusion, we beg to express our sincere regret at being compelled to take this decided step; but as the inducements held out to volunteers are totally inadequate in every respect – a statement which our recent severe experience fully warrants – we have no alternative but to resign.

Durban Mounted Rifles

Kellar
Vincent C
TRUMPETER
Mahar
Mc Neil
GUNNER
Arbuckle
Blackie
Covan (Cozen)
Crawzen
Davis   Not on medal roll
Dilfhen
Dove S
Elaton (Elston)
Gee J
Gee T
Gooden S
Guillan (Gillan)
Halder
Horne W
Jacques F
Keal J
Kelsall
Leeman
Lewis
Mc Ewan
Middleton
Noble H
Norman
Northend   Not on medal roll
Pitcher
Price
Prince
Robertson
Robinson
Sidderley (Siddeley)
Simmons
Slatter
Squires
Teague
Thompson
Tysack (Tyzack)
Zeeman   Not on medal roll

EAST LONDON BURGHERS
LIEUTENANT
Awdry J.A 1878
SERGEANT
Calder A 1878
Lloyd C 1878
CORPORAL
Sheard W 1878 r
PRIVATE
Baisley W 1878 r
Berry H 1878
Brookhurst H 1878 r
Brookhurst J 1878 r
Charleton H 1878 r

Currin J 1878
   See also Cpl. L. Currin Chalaumann Vol. Cav. Same man.
Finnessey H.J 1878
Gilbert J 1878 r
Hallett F 1878 r
Keene C 1878
Lloyd A 1878
Nelson C 1878
Phillips H 1878 r
Prance F 1878
Preston R 1878 r
Sanderson J.H 1878 r

EAST LONDON ENGINEERS
NO RANK SHOWN
Norton F.J 1877-8
Strathearn G 1878
   See also Frontier Mtd. Rifles Troops Sergeant Major.

EAST LONDON VOLUNTEERS.
TROOPER
Atkin J 1877-8
RANK NOT KNOWN
Frandsen C 1877-8-9

ECKERSLEY NATIVES.
CAPTAIN
Eckersley G 1879
LIEUTENANT
Glinister J.G 1879
Rawlins F.M 1879

FERREIRAS HORSE.
Those Killed in Action (KIA) lost their lives at Sekukuni's Kraal 28/11/1879.
*Wounded shown with an asterisk.
COMMANDANT
Ferreira CMG I.P 1878-9
CAPTAIN
Nourse H 1878-9
15/7/1878 Lieut. Henry Nourse received a buckshot wound to the right thigh
Sampson A.W 1878-9
CAPTAIN AND ADJUTANT
Dow W.K 1878-9
QUARTERMASTER
Gooch A.R 1878
LIEUTENANT QUARTERMASTER
Armstrong T 1878
LIEUTENANT
Mocke C 1878-9
Stewart C.M.D 1878-9
Stockwell W 1878-9
REGIMENTAL SERGEANT MAJOR
Caufield E KIA 1878-9

Wilson R 1878-9 r
KIA at Lebeak's Staadt 14/5/1879
SERGEANT MAJOR
Spring L.F 1878-9 r
TROOP SERGEANT MAJOR
Gorton C.P 1879
*Washborne E.P 1878-9
QUARTERMASTER SERGEANT
*De St Croix A 1879
ORDERLY SERGEANT
Paterson H.McK 1878-9 r
see Transvaal Rangers Lieut.
Potts J.W.W 1878 r
SADDLER SERGEANT
Clarke J 1879 r
SERGEANT
Coston H.J 1879
De Villiers A.J 1879 r
Gibson C.H 1878-9 r
James R.E 1879 r
Taylor W 1878-9 r
Wilson R   Not on medal roll
Slightly W. 14/4/1879 Lebeak's Stadt
CORPORAL
Anderson C 1878
Botts E 1878-9 r
Campbell J 1878 r
Cumberland B.L 1878-9
   See also Pte. Border Horse.
Felix A 1878-9
Gorton W.W 1879 r
Kerswell W 1879
Grant C.P 1879
Potcher C.R 1878 r
Wagener F 1879
Weedon G 1878 r
*Wyndham F 1879
TROOPER
Abrahams W.J 1879
Albinsky A 1879
Arnold J 1879
Badnitz E 1879
Bell C.C 1878 r
Bell J.T.M 1878 r
Berry R 1878-9
*Blackie Henry Not on medal roll
Boje C 1878 r
Bornmann C 1878 r
Boulton J 1879 r
Boyce F.W 1878-9
Brill A.F 1879 r
Brooks C.J 1879 r
Brown G 1879 r
Bruce A.P 1878
Burger W 1878 r
Burns M 1879 r
*Buys P 1879 r
Cameron R 1879 r

Ferreiras Horse

Cayton R	1879 r	
Chippendale H	1879	
Chowles A	**1879 r**	
KIA 26/6/1878		
Crouch H	1878-9 r	
Cubitt J	1878 r	
Cunningham J	1879 r	
Davey R	1878 r	
David E	1878 r	
Davies J	1878 r	
De Beer W	1879	
De Jager L	1879 r	
De Wet A	1878 r	
Doig J.B	1879	
Doyle J	1879	
Du Bois L	1878 r	
Dunsterville F	1879	
Edmunds G.A	1878	
Emerson J	1879 r	
Emery A	1879	
Erasmus L.Z	1879 r	
Erasmus P	1879	
Ford W.H	1878	
Duplicate clasp 1878, issued 23/4/1909. See also Tvl. Rangers.		
Farley N	1879	
Foster J	1879 r	
Foster J.H	1878-9	
Fourie D	1878 r	
Fredericks D	1878 r	
Gorman T	1879 r	
Grant P	1878 r	
Lost on patrol Sekukuni's Kraal 21/11/1879		
Gravett T	1879	
Green C	1879	
Greenell W.C	1878-9	
Greenfield G.W	1878 r	
Grinnell W.E	1879	
Groge T	1879 r	
Gozzer J	1878 r	
Hagan W	1879	
Hall J	1878 r	
Halliday G	1878 r	
Harris S	1878 r	
Helford J	1878 r	
*Hendricksen H	1879	
Henning A	1878-9	
See also Transvaal Rangers.		
Herman G	1878-9	
Hick G	**1878**	
KIA 26/6/1878		
Hinckson H	1879 r	
Hollomby C	1879 r	
Holmes J	1878 r	
Holtzhausen Snr H	1879 r	
Holtzhausen Jnr H	1879 r	
Holtzhausen M	1879 r	
Howard B	1879 r	
Huges H	1878 r	
James A	1879 r	
Johanson P	1878-9	
Jones C.H	1878 r	
Jones H.W	1878-9 r	
Jonke J	1879 r	
Joyce J	1879 r	
Kashagen T	1879 r	
Keely	1879 r	
Kemp R	1879	
Kingswood F	1878	
Konitzky L.B	1877-8-9	
Kreusz A	1879	
Laurence J.S	1878-9 r	
Lazarus G	1878-9 r	
Lea M.B	1879	
Linahan N	1878 r	
*Loescher E	1879 r	
Loescher J.F.E	1878-9	
Maclean A.B	1878-9	
Mahoney T	1878-9	
See also Maloney T. Border Hse. Same man.		
Martin T	1878 r	
Mc Crea F.F	1879 r	
Mc Donald A	1879	
Mc Intyre J	1879 r	
Mc Loughlin J	1879	
Mc Nally B.J	1879	
Meeser F	1878 r	
Morig A	1879 r	
Morris J	1879	
See also Border Horse.		
Neuman O	1879 r	
Nicholson A	1879	
O'Connor J	1877-8-9	
See also Natal Horse.		
Collert J	1879 r	
Oliffe A	1878 r	
O'Rourke T	1878	
Overend H	1878 r	
Packenham C	1879	
Palmer G	1879	
Paul A	1878 r	
Phillips I	1879 r	
Phillipson S	1879 r	
Phillipson T.J	1878 r	
Potcher C.R	1878 r	
Power C	1878 r	
Pretorius C.J	1879	
Quinn T	1879	
Rademeyer J.J	1879	
Rademeyer N	1879	
Rash G	1879 r	
Reiker G	1878-9 r	
Reynolds J	1878	
Robb KIA P	**1878 r**	
Robinson T	1879 r	
Roos H	1879 r	
Roux D.J	1879 r	
Roux M	1879 r	
Russell J.H	1878 r	
Ryan E	1878 r	
Sabotiers J	1878-9 r	
Sansser L	1878 r	
Saunders T	1878-9	
Scheiber C	1879 r	
Schotier N	1878 r	
Scoble F	1879	
Shaw G	1879 r	
Short J.W	1879 r	
Smith J	1879 r	
Stewart W	1879 r	
Summerlee H not on medal roll Severely wounded at Sekukuni's Kraal 28/11/1879.		
Sweetman A	1878-9 r	
Tegetmeyer J	1879	
Thomas G	1879 r	
Towes H.B	1878	
Turner E	1879 r	
Van der Berg J	1878 r	
Van der Berg W	1878 r	
Venn H	1878	
Von Konitzky L.B	1879	
Wagener F	1878-9 r	
Waldek H	1878-9	
Waldek W	1879 r	
Walters C	1879 r	
Warburton J	1878 r	
Warren R	1878 r	
Webber No. 1 H	1879 r	
Webber No. 2 H	1879	
Webster T	1879 r	
Weedon G	1878	
Wemmer S	1879 r	
See also Transvaal Rangers.		
Wentzel J	1879 r	
White T	1879	
Wilkins W	1878 r	
Wille B	1878-9	
Williams J	1879	
Woodgate C.W	1879 r	

FINGO LEVY.
CAPTAIN
Davies A.W.J	1877-8	
Davies D.J	1877-8	
Wienand E.D	1877-8	

RANK NOT SHOWN
O'Connor M	1877-8	

First City Volunteer Rifles

FIRST CITY VOLUNTEER RIFLES.
Including First City Volunteers and First City Mounted Volunteers.
At the end of 1878 the establishment was 3 companies totalling 8 officers and 147 men, In June, 1879, there were 9 officers and 180 men and a band of 18. The information given in July, 1878 (Cape Archives DD 1/7 F-G) states that No. 1 Company was formed on 7th October, 1875, No. 2 on 18th November, 1875, and No. 3 on 15th July, 1876.

CAPTAIN
Greenless	R	1877-8
Nelson	R	1877-8
Sampson	D	1877-8

LIEUTENANT
Clough	T	1877-8
Gilbert	J.G	1877-8
Mc Pherson	J	1877-8
Minto	E	1877-8
#Munday	R	1877-8
Wallace	R	1877-8
Young	G	1877-8

COLOUR SERGEANT
490	Cogan	R.J	1877-8
413	Sampson	W.T	1877-8
563	Wilson	D	1877-8

QUARTERMASTER SERGEANT
245	Guest	H	1877-8
248	Kay	W	1877-8
521	Minto	J	1877-8
	Ray	J	1877-8
223	Reynolds	G	1877-8
415	Sheffield	T	1877-8
564	Wood	S.W	1877-8

CORPORAL
483	Cock	W	1877-8
484	Cookcroft	H	1877-8
486	Copeman	P	1877-8
	Grady	J	1877-8
491	Hardacre	T	1877-8
	Clasp Only		
	Hess	L	1877-8
212	Lloyd	L	1877-8
72	O'Carroll	O	1877-8
408	Sampson	J.C	1877-8
	Saunders	J.W	1877-8
561	Wallace	J	1877-8

PRIVATE/TROOPER
169	Adams	F	1877-8
170	Ainslie	C	1877-8
	Ball	C.R	1877-8
	Ball	S.J	1877-8 r
610	Bartlett	G	1877-8
603	Beadle	C	1877-8
604	Beaust	C	1877-8
605	Berry	W	1877-8
	Bevage	G.T	1877-8
611	Bishop	J	1877-8
612	Blundell	A.S	1877-8
	Bright	W	1877-8
606	Brislin	A	1877-8
	Brooks	L	1877-8 r
607	Brooks	W	1877-8
608	Brookshaw	J	1877-8
	Brookshaw	T	1877-8
	Brookshaw	W	1877-8 r
609	Buckley	J	1877-8 r
	Byrnes	C.R	1877-8
	Byrnes	J.B	1877-8
	Campbell	R	1877-8
480	Capper	T	1877-8
	Cassell	H	1877-8
481	Cherry	T	1877-8
	Cinnamon	J	1877-8
488	Clarke	H	1877-8
491	Copper	H	1877-8
482	Cock	F	1877-8
487	Cox	W	1877-8
269	Demistrataire	P	1877-8 r
	Derracout	W.T	1877-8
270	Dovey	F	1877-8
146	Earle	T	1877-8
	Eaton	A.J	1877-8
	Emms	W	1877-8
209	Fennell	J	1877-8
	Fincham	D	1877-8 r
210	Fletcher	A.R	1877-8
	Fray	C	1877-8
211	Frazer	C	1877-8
242	Galpin	E.E	1877-8
243	Galpin	W.H	1877-8
240	Goldawain	A.H	1877-8
	Grainger	H	1877-8 r
244	Green	W.A	1877-8
	Greenlaws	D	1877-8
488	Hamer	E	1877-8
	Hemming	A.W	1877-8 r
489	Horne	R	1877-8
490	Hurley	J	1877-8
492	Hutchinson	S.G	1877-8
	Hutchinson	T.F	1877-8
165	Jaffray	G	1877-8 r
166	Jansen	J	1877-8
167	Jennings	J	1877-8
	Johnson	J	1877-8 r
	Johnson	R.S	1877-8 r
170	Jordan	J	1877-8 r
249	Keely	M	1877-8
250	Knight	J.W.P	1877-8
211	Lea	A	1877-8
	Lepley	J	1877-8
	Levey	E	1877-8
	Lewis	J	1877-8 r
213	Long	S.W	1877-8
	Lucas	P.J	1877-8
549	Marran	C	1877-8
544	Mc Donald	A	1877-8 r
	Mc Gearry	E	1877-8 r
545	Mc Lean	H	1877-8
550	Mc Leod	A	1877-8
	Milne	J	1877-8 r
	Moore	W	1877-8 r
548	Mullins	W	1877-8
	Murphy	E.J	1877-8
73	Openshaw	D	1877-8
	Painger	H	1877-8 r
259	Parsons	C	1877-8
251	Passmore	F	1877-8
252	Passmore	T	1877-8 r
253	Pearce	W	1877-8
255	Pecock	T	1877-8 r
	Prycel.	J	1877-8
	Quail	J	1877-8 r
222	Redloff	C	1877-8
224	Reynolds	W	1877-8
	Robarts	A.E	1877-8 r
225	Ronald	S	1877-8
	Rowland	J.R	1877-8
	Scott	J	1877-8
414	Sellers	J	1877-8
	Shamuck	C	1877-8
	Shaw	G.C	1877-8
	Smith	W	1877-8 r
416	South	G	1877-8
409	Streak	S	1877-8 r
	Strutt	G.C	1877-8
	Stuart	A	1877-8 r
410	Summers	W	1877-8
411	Surmon	A	1877-8
412	Surmon	E.T	1877-8 r
179	Trotman	W	1877-8
366	Wallor	W	1877 8
	Ward	S.B	1877-8
	Webb	A	1877-8 r
562	Webber	R.J	1877-8
	Wicks	W.S	1877-8
359	Wilkinson	S.J	1877-8 r
	Williams	F.H	1877-8
	Willmore	W	1877-8 r
565	Wynne	W.J	1877-8

#Glendining & Co, Auction 18th March 1981 lot No 45. South Africa 1877-9, One clasp, 1877 (Lieut.R.Mundy, 1st City Vol. Rif.) EF. "The first City Volunteers of Grahamstown", known as the "First City". Mundy was the Adjutant and QM of the First City Volrs, in the 2nd relief contingent in Basuto war of 1881. Died of fever at Mafeking and his name appears on a memorial plaque in Grahamstown Cathedral.

Fort Beaufort Burghers

FORT BEAUFORT BURGHERS.
CAPTAIN
Pope C 1877-8-9
Scott J 1878
  Should have had Clasp only. Also had medal for 1846-7 War as a Cpl. in Royal Engineers.
LIEUTENANT
Ewing W 1878 r
  Also had medal for 1846-7 War. Should have had Clasp only.
SERGEANT MAJOR
Clarke T 1878
Medal for 1846-7 & 1850-53 Wars as Col. Sgt. 60th Foot. Should have Claps only.
SERGEANT
Clarke F 1878
Sampson D 1879
CORPORAL
Garret F 1878
Kidson C 1878 r
Richards A 1879 r
PRIVATE/TROOPER
Anderson M 1878 r
Barker W 1879 r
Botha R 1879 r
Boyce T 1878 r
Bremner J 1878 r
Brodie J 1878 r
Butler J 1878 r
Callaghan W 1878
Cartwright W 1878 r
Curle G 1878
Defrient J.L 1879 r
Defrient P 1879 r
Delport L 1879 r
Delport S 1879 r
Dick W 1878 r
Ellis J 1878 r
Eastment G 1878
Estment W 1878
Flowers F 1879 r
Fraser T 1878 r
Gardiner A 1878 r
Geibeg K 1878 r
Glass E 1878 r

Gilbert R 1878 r
Hanley R 1879 r
Hannah T 1878
Hard R 1878 r
Harvey Snr W 1878 r
Harvey Jnr W 1878 r
Hatton F 1879
Hatting M 1879 r
Hines K 1878 r
Honey J.W 1878 r
Hurley R 1878 r
Jonson C 1878 r
Kelly W 1878 r
Keys W 1878 r
Lambardt A 1878 r
Laurie P 1878 r
Lloyd A.C 1878 r
Lloyd H 1878 r
Lloyd R 1878 r
Lloyd S.R 1878 r
Lloyd W.R 1878 r
Lambard J 1878 r
Lottering L 1879 r
Mathews C 1879 r
Mc Cullum A 1878 r
Meade T 1878 r
Melass G 1878 r
Melass J 1878 r
Meyer M 1879 r
Moss James 1878 r
Moss John 1878 r
Moss W 1878 r
Muller J 1878 r
Mynhart C 1879 r
Mynhart L 1879 r
Nel H 1879
Nel L 1879 r
Norton E 1878 r
Pearce T 1878 r
Pitman F 1878
Qarvel T 1878 r
Rhudens G 1879 r
Roux G 1879 r
Roux J.G 1879 r
Scott G.D 1878
Scott R.H 1878

Scroby W 1879 r
Slater (Sluyter, W) R 1879 r
KIA Moirosi's Stronghold 29/5/1879
Smith J 1878 r
Stuart A 1878 r
Stuart W 1878 r
Styles G.W 1878 r
Sweetman A 1879
Terblanche S 1879 r
Tims C 1878
Vandefyfir J 1879 r
Viljoen H 1879 r
Walker W 1879 r
Ward R.A 1878
Ward T 1878 r
Windell J 1878 r
Wood A 1879 r
Wragg W 1878 r
York H 1879 r

FORT BEAUFORT HOTTENTOT LEVY.
CAPTAIN
Green B 1877-8-9

FORT BEAUFORT NATIVE POLICE.
LIEUTENANT
De Wet C.M 1878

FORT WHITE MOUNTED VOL.
CAPTAIN
Love H.M 1877-8
LIEUTENANT
Murray O.E.E 1877-8-9
  KIA Isandhlwana
Simpson W 1878
SERGEANT MAJOR
Russon G 1878
SERGEANT
Murry J 1877-8-9 r
  KIA Isandhlwana
Whitfield J 1877-8
  See also Kaffrain Rangers.
CORPORAL
Bousfield F.H 1878
Crowe R.J 1877-8

Spink Sale 7012 Lot 138. 19 Apr 2007
South Africa 1877-79, one clasp, 1878 (Capt: J. Scott, Ft. Beaufort Bghs.), nearly extremely fine, scarce Hammer Price £900. Captain James Scott (1821-1890), born Edinburgh, Scotland; enlisted as Private Royal Engineers, 1844; served with the 9th, 10th and 15th Companies during the Second Kaffir War, 1847-48 and the 1850-53 Campaign (entitled to South Africa 1853); Second Corporal 1848; Corporal 1851; discharged 1853 and stayed in South Africa where he married; re-engaged as Captain with the Fort Beaufort Burghers for the 1877-79 conflict, including action against the Gaikas under Macoma in Water Kloof; Officer Commanding 11.12.1877, to their disbandment in May 1879. Approximately 62 '1878' clasps issued to the Fort Beaufort Burghers.
South Africa 1877-79 published roll gives recipient as, 'should have had a clasp only'. Applicants for the South Africa 1877-79 medal who were in possession of a South Africa 1853 medal were supposed to declare the fact, whereupon they should have received an appropriately dated clasp for attachment to the earlier medal. Only 20 men are known to have been in this position. A very small number were issued with both medals despite volunteering that they held the 1853 award (O.M.R.S. Journal, Winter 1981, G.R. Everson), and this appears to be the case with Scott.

Frontier Armed & Mounted Police

Ignatius Philip Ferreira served in the Frontier Armed and Mounted Police under the command of **Sir Walter Currie**, when diamonds were discovered he began a new career as a prospector and staked several claims. He was the founder of Ferreira's Camp, the original site of Johannesburg. In 1876 he was in command of the Middelburg Volunteers during the Pedi Wars against Chief Sekhukhune. During the first occupation of the Transvaal **Colonel Ignatius Ferreira**, CMG, raised three irregular mounted corps at Pretoria The first saw service against Sekukuni in June, 1878. The second, served in Wood's column, and also took part in the capture of Sekukuni's Mountain in 1879. The third corps was known as the Transvaal Horse, and included two 9-pr field guns.

By the middle 1878 there was a large force of Transvaal volunteers under Captain I. P. Ferreira, **Lieutenant P. Raaff,** and **Lieutenant Henry Nourse**.

With the final assault on Sekukuni. taking place on the 27th November, 1879, the Second Sekukuni War was to draw to a close. Colonel Ferreira and his dismounted commando backed by Native contingents, formed the right attack, with the object of taking the kraal. **Major Frederick Carrington** and the rest of the Colonials mounted the left attack, supported by other Native contingents, with the object of clearing the Stad and to prevent reinforcements reaching Sekukuni.

The central position was given to **Lieutenant-Colonel John Murray** and six companies of the 2/21st Regiment (Royal Scots Fusiliers) and the six companies of the 94th Regiment (later designated as the 2nd Battalion, Connaught Rangers), detachments of the 80th Regiment (2nd Battalion, South Staffordshire Regiment), the Royal Engineers, four guns of the Transvaal Artillery and the Rustenburg Contingent. Their mission was to act as a reserve and keep down the fire on the 'Fighting Koppie', which they would eventually storm.

The final action of Ferreira's Horse took place in Leribe, in Northern Basutoland, where it served until disbanded in August, 1881. The Colonel returned to his farming roots and moved to a farm near Louis Trichardt (Makhado). He died in 1921, a relatively poor man.

Referance: family.http://www.zoominfo.com/people/Ferreira_Ignatius_504005777.aspx
The Sekukuni Wars part 11 by H.W. Kinsey http://www.samilitaryhistory.org/vol026nk.html

Lieutenant O'Neill Frontier Armed and Mounted Police.
The Mitchelstown Tragedy Evidence of Capt. Segrave, R.M. Concerns the police firing on an angry protesting mob. Three men were shot by the Irish Constabulary.
Mr O'Neill Segrave giving evidence - I was three years in the Frontier Armed and Mounted Police, and when leaving I was offered a commission if I stopped in the police. I left the police a private. I got a lieutenancy in Basutoland, and there I also got my captaincy. After the war in Basutoland i entered the Cape infantry. After that, as lieutenant, I got instruction direct from the Castle to come here, and I had a letter from Captain Plunkett saying that he had applied for me to go to Mitchelstown as Mr Eaton was engaged on the trial.
Freeman's Journal and Daily Commercial Advertiser (Dublin, Ireland), Saturday, October 8, 1887;

Private Giese, of the Frontier Armed and Mounted Police.
The Gazette of last night states that the Queen has signified her intention to confer the decoration of the Victoria Cross upon **Major (now Brevet Lieutenant-Colonel) Hans Garrett Moore**, of the 88th Regiment, for his gallant conduct in risking his own life in endeavouring to save the life of Private Giese, of the Frontier Armed and Mounted Police on the occasion of the action with the Gaikas, near Komgha, on the 29th of December, 1877.

Charles Duncan Griffith (1830-1906) He succeeded Colonel Bowker as commanding officer of the Frontier Armed and Mounted Police, September 1877. He was congratulated on the apparent defeat of the Galeka by the end of October 1877. With his arrogant attitude and his brusque manner in dealing with subordinates, this combined with excessive caution made him unpopular with his own colonial troops. When he failed to anticipate the return of the Galeka in early December 1877, and inconsequence of the full scale disbanding of colonial volunteers on 19th November 1877. Griffith was sidelined for the remainder of the war.
The Frontier War Journal of Major John Crealock 1878 page 24.

Fort White Mounted Vol.

BUGLER
Kilduff T.J 1878
TROOPER/PRIVATE
Adams T 1877-8 r
Austin A.G 1877
Bain J 1878
Black D 1878 r
Blackbeard F 1877
   See also Sansoms Horse.
Blackbeard W.S 1877
Bolton J.F 1877-8
Bolton T 1877 r
Boulter A 1878
Boys A 1878
Boys F.W 1878
Brown D 1877
Brown J.C 1878
Campbell A 1878 r
Chambers W 1878 r
Cogha ? 1878 r
Cross W 1877
Dieutchman A 1878
Douglass T 1878 r
Elliot W 1878 r
Els J 1878 r
Glover A 1878
Hall W.H 1878 r
Hamilton G 1878 r
Harrison G 1878
Henry ? 1878 r
Hickey C 1877
Hudson J 1878 r
Johnes T.L 1877-8 r
Krangal W 1878
Maclean J 1878
Main J 1878 r
Mc Gilvery J 1877 r
Mc Kay D 1877
Mc Kay H 1878
Mc Namara A 1878
Mc Namara M 1878
Mc Namara J 1878
Mc Tavish C 1878
Mc Tavish D 1878
Mullins J 1878 r
Murray R 1877-8
Nelson A 1878
Nelson F 1878
Nelson J 1878
Pegler C.A 1877
Petzer A 1878 r
Petzer J 1878
Philips J 1878
Pierson J.F 1878 r
Rennie E 1878 r
Rolston S 1878
Russon I 1877-8
Rylfeldt T 1878 r
Sanders J 1878 r
Sansom J 1878 r
Schankucht G 1878
Schultz W 1878
Searle E.W 1878
Smith G 1878 r
Starling H 1878
Tessendorf W 1878
Tranmere S.M 1878 r
Turnbull W 1878
Vickery C 1877 r
Volka E 1878
Volka W 1878
Watchan H 1878
Whitaker ? 1878
Whitaker ? 1878
Whitfield L 1877-8
Whitfield O 1877-8
Wilson J.S 1878
Wingham G.C 1877
Wood C 1878

FRANKFORT BURGHERS AND FINGOE LEVIES.
CAPTAIN
Landrey J.L 1878
See also QMS J.L.Landrey Stutterheim Mounted Police.
LIEUTENANT
Ferreira T 1878 r
Keys H 1878
Keys W.E 1878 r
Turner T.W 1878
QUARTERMASTER
Rahn F 1878
SERGEANT
Klaekers J 1878 r
PRIVATE
Ackerman J.J 1878
Barendt F 1878 r
Burmeister F 1878 r
Burmeister G 1878 r
Boucher F 1878 r
Clive J 1878
Curl J 1878 r
Dettman G 1878 r
Detmann H 1878 r
Emerick H 1878 r
Fleith G 1878 r
Flugh J 1878 r
Gutche H 1878 r
Hill C 1878 r
Keith James 1878 r
Keith Joseph 1878 r
Krause A 1878
Krause F 1878 r
Krienkie F 1878 r
Landrey F.W 1878

Lentz D 1878 r
Moll X 1878 r
Nicholson G 1878
Nicholson J 1878
Pantz H 1878 r
Paskin M 1878
Rasche O 1878 r
Schloedder Martin 1878
Schloedder Matts 1878
Schmidt F 1878 r
Smith S 1878 r
Spain C 1878 r
Sperkie C 1878
Standi W 1878
Swartz W 1878 r

FRANKFORT INFANTRY
RANK NOT KNOWN
Loescher J.F.E 1879

FRONTIER ARMED AND MOUNTED POLICE.
In 1878 it was decided to reorganize the Frontier Armed & Mounted Police as the Cape Mounted Riflemen – a decision that received wide disapproval.
LIEUTENANT COLONEL
Bayly Z.S 1877-8-9
INSPECTOR
Bailie C.C 1877-8-9
Goldsworthy J.W 1877-8-9
INSPECTOR PAYMASTER
Hutchinson W.L 1877-8
INSPECTOR & QUARTERMASTER
Leatherland J 1877-8-9
QUARTERMASTER
Morris W.C 1878 r
SURGEON MAJOR
Hartley VC E.B 1877-8-9
   His VC was for an action at Moirosi's Stronghold. He attended the wounded under fire at the unsuccessful attack at Morosi's Mountain. See also Medical Officers, Colonial Force.
LIEUTENANT
Wylde F.W.K 1877-8
SERGEANT MAJOR
Harber D 1877-8
Lambert H 1877-8-9
SERGEANT
Best J 1877-8-9
#Cantrell (Cantwell) R 1877-8-9
Collins A 1877-8-9
Davie T.B 1877-8
Jerome S 1877-8-9
Lyne W 1877-8-9
Wilson J 1877-8-9

Frontier Armed & Mounted Police

 # Spink Sale 7012 Lot 116. 19 Apr 2007
A South Africa Campaign Group of Four to Lieutenant-Colonel R.F. Cantwell, Cape Mounted Rifles, Late Sergeant Frontier Armed and Mounted Police, A Veteran of the Siege and Capture of Morosi's Mountain Stronghold, 1879, And Later Mentioned in Lord Roberts' Despatches For Wepener, Where He Stoically Commanded the Cape Mounted Rifles Under Appalling Conditions and Heavy Fire
South Africa 1877-79, one clasp, 1877-8-9 (Sergt. R. Cantwell. F.A.M. Police.); Cape of Good Hope General Service 1880-97, one clasp, Basutoland (Regt. Sgt. Maj. R.F. Cantwell.. C.M. Rifn.), engraved in upright serif capitals; Queen's South Africa 1899-1902, four clasps, Cape Colony, Wepener, Transvaal, Wittebergen (Lt: Col: R.F. Cantwell, Cape.M.R.); King's South Africa 1901-02, two clasps (Lieut:-Col: R.F. Cantwell. Cape M.R.), light contacts overall, otherwise good very fine (4)
Hammer Price £3100
Lieutenant-Colonel R.F. Cantwell served in South Africa 1877-79 in the Gaika and the Galeka Campaigns and in the attacks on and subsequent capture of Morosi's mountain stronghold, 16.3.1879-19.11.1879. During the latter siege there were several bloody and unsuccessful assaults on the strongly fortified position, including on the 25th of March, when two Cape Mounted Riflemen won the Victoria Cross. Morosi's stronghold was eventually carried by a night assault on the 19th November, leaving 70 tribesman lying dead. Cantwell saw service with the Cape Mounted Rifles during the Boer War including at Wepener, where his regiment suffered heavy casualties during the defence. Forces at Wepener, under Colonel Dalgety, comprised of: one company of Royal Scots Mounted Infantry; 427 men of the Cape Mounted Rifles; 804 men of the 1st and 2nd Brabant's Horse; 393 men of the Kaffrarian Rifles; 58 men of Driscoll's Scouts; a small number of Royal Engineers and an Artillery Detachment consisting of two 15 pounders, two Naval guns, two 2.5 guns and one Hotchkiss..........
Wepener was relieved on the 24th April, with Cantwell mentioned in Lieutenant-Colonel Dalgety's Report, 29.4.1900, 'Captain Cantwell, after Major Sprenger was killed and Major Waring wounded, on the 9th and 11th respectively commanded in advanced schanzen'. He received a further Mention in Lord Roberts' Despatches, London Gazette 2.4.1901.
Cantwell also proved popular with his men as can be seen from an address given upon his retirement from the post of Adjutant, "It was a painful duty because the occasion of the presenting of the address was his (Captain Cantwell's) retirement from the post of Adjutant, a position which he had held for the last fifteen years, and that in losing him, the N.C.O.'s felt that they were losing a sincere and trusted friend, a friend who was always ready to hear, and when possible, adjust, grievances no matter how trivial. An officer who thoroughly understood his men and took no superficial interest in their welfare; and a man who encouraged by both precept and example all branches of sport and attributes of manliness.' (The Qakamba, relevant pages from issue included in lot refers).
Listed on the published transcription of South Africa 1877-79 roll as 'Cantrell', however correct name of Cantwell is given on the other relevant medal rolls.

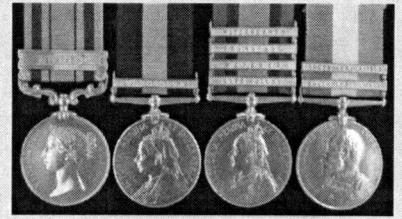

CORPORAL			Cobbett	G	1877-8	Frere	W.K	1877-8 r
Grant	C	1877-8-9	Cole	F	1877-8-9 r	Gardener	J.W	1877-8 r
Harcourt	J	1877-8	Colebrooke	C.F	1877-8-9 r	**Geisse**		**Not on Medal Roll**
Hollins	J	1877-8	Collier	C.O	1877-8	**KIA. Camp Komyha, 29/12/1877**		
Keightly	F	1877-8 r	Collins	H	1877-8-9 r	Givens	G	1879
PRIVATE			Cooke	W.E	1877-8-9	Grasskopf	L	1879
Adkins	G de V	1877-8	Couper	G.J	1877-8-9	Greaves	J	1877-8-9
Alexander	A	1877-8	Cox	E	1877-8-9	Gregg	F	1877-8-9
Allaway	C.E.C.K	1877-8	Crafer	W.C	1877-8 r	Griffen	A.J	1877-8
Allaway	S.A.C.K	1877-8	Dabrowsky	A	1877-8-9	Gurney	A	1877-8
Allen	J	1877-8	Davis	C.E	1877-8 r	Hannan	W.H	1877-8-9
Allwork	W	1877-8-9	Dawson	E	1877-8 r	Hare	H.C	1877-8-9
Armstrong	A	1877-8 r	Dick	D	1877-8	Harrington	F.J	1877-8
Bailey	T	1877-8-9	Dickens	W	1877-8 r	Heaphy	H	1877-8-9
Bartrum	J	1877-8-9	Duplan	S	1877-8 r	Highton	C.E	1877-8 r
Bayley	A.L	1877-8 r	Eaton	R.N	1877-8-9	see Capt E.C.Highton 2/N.N.C		
Beecher	W.A	1877-8	Elton	C.H	1877-8	Hobbes	R	1877-8-9
Brill	F.G	1877-8-9	Emerson	G	1877-8-9	Hobson	A.W	1877-8-9
Bristow	L	1877-8	Evatt	M	1877-8-9	Hobson	G	1877-8-9 r
Brooks	J	1877-8-9	Farrell	E	1877-8-9	Hobson	J	1877-8-9
Brown	H.H	1877-8-9 r	Fenwick	C	1877-8	Hodson	J	1877-8-9 r
Bursey	A	1877-8	Festing	F.W	1877-8	Holden	A.E	1877-8-9
Burton	A.L.T	1877-8 r	Firth	R	1877-8 r	Hull	A.T	1877-8 r
Butler	C.J	1877-8	Fleming	Q	1877-8	Hussey	C.F	1877-8
Calder	A	1877-8 r	Forester	E	1877-8	Jacoby	J	1877-8-9
Chapman	F.T	1877-8-9	Foy	L	1877-8	Jago	T.P	1877-8

Frontier Armed & Mounted Police

Frontier Light Horse

Jeffery J	1877-8-9 r	
Jeremiah J	1877-8	
Jones F.C	1877-8	
Jones J.E	1877-8-9	
Kavanagh W	1877-8	
Keane R	1877-8-9	
Kloke G	1877-8-9	
Knott M.E	1877-8-9	
Kock C	1877-8-9	
Lacey B.M	1877-8-9	
Lambert W	1877-8	
Lankshear H	1877-8	
Liebrus J	1877-8-9	
Macdowall W.D	1877-8-9	
Malconson R de L	1877-8-9	
Marsh C	1877-8-9	
Major H.W	1877-8-9	

Meyhopter J Not on Medal Roll
KIA Camp, Komyha, 31/12/ 1877

Moller C.D	1877-8	
Moyce T.O	1877-8-9	
Neal T	1877-8	
O'Halloran W	1877-8	
Ormerod F	1877-8-9	
Palmer R	1877-8	
Pike J	1877-8-9	
Pitt J	1878	
Preston Alex	1877-8-9	
Preston Augustus	1877-8-9	
Price E.W	1877-8 r	
Reid T	1877-8	
Rinder E.S	1877-8	
Roberts H	1877-8-9	
Robertson M.W	1879	
Robinson C	1877-8	
Sangster A	1877-8-9	
Saunders H	1877-8	
Scheweidsky J	1877-8	
Schneider A	1877-8-9	
Seagrave O.N	1877-8	
Sheffield A	1877-8	
Short H	1879	
Smith H.A	1877-8-9	
Smith R	1877-8-9	
Simpson J.C	1877-8	
Stanford W	1877	
Steward R.B	1877-8-9	
Stier W	1877-8-9	
Swift D	1877-8	
Timpson W	1877-8 r	
Tremeer C	1877-8	
Von Grann C	1877-8	
Wainwright A.F.H	1877-8 r	
Wainwright W	1877-8	
Waters J.W	1877-8	
Watson R	1877-8-9	
Whitham F	1877-8-9	
Willcox J.D	1877-8-9	
Williams E.H.V	1877-8	
Wilmot C	1877-8	
Wills G	1877-8 r	
Wilson A	1877-8-9	
Winslow L	1877-8-9	
Wolhuther H	1877-8	
Wright S.C	1877-8 r	
Wynne G.R	1877-8 r	
Younghusband O	1877-8 r	

RANK NOT KNOWN

Brown G.E	1877-8	
Buckley J	1877-8	
Francis T.E	1877-8	
Fullarton F.L	1877-8	
Mayer J	1877-8-9	

FRONTIER GUARD
CAPTAIN
Barlow Sir Morrison Bt. 1879

FRONTIER LIGHT HORSE
Those Killed in Action (KIA) lost their lives at Inhlobane 28/3/1879.
CAPTAIN
Barton ?   Not on medal roll (Coldstram Guards)
KIA at Inhlobane 28/3/1879

Berry J.H	1877-8-9	
Blaine A	1877-8-9	
Ditrey C	1877-8-9	
Hutton H	1877-8-9	
Jenner H.A	1877-8	

McNagthen not on medal roll
KIA in Perie Bush 8/5/1878

Oldham A.C	1877-8-9	
Whalley W (page 84)	1877-8-9	

LIEUTENANT

Allen H.L	1877-8-9	
Broadbent E.C	1879	
Christian E	1877-8-9	
Everitt C	1877-8-9	
Fenn T.E	1877-8-9	
Hains C	1877-8-9 r	
Hains W	1877-8-9 r	
Hayward G.D	1877-8-9	
Malden H	1877-8-9 r	
Miller T	1879 r	
Paget G	1879	
Pillans E	1877-8	
Pogge L	1877-8-9	
Rutherford J	1879	
#Smith A.M (page82)	1879	
Sparrow R	1879	
Van Cortland A.C	1877-8	

Von Shentercorn   not on medal roll
KIA at Inhlobane 28/3/1879
Williams   not on medal roll
KIA at Inhlobane 28/3/1879

Wright A.P	1877-8	

REGIMENTAL SERGEANT MAJOR

56 Bouffet E	1877-8-9	
5 Winterfelt B	1877-8-9	

TROOP SERGEANT MAJOR

17 Crampton H	1877-8-9	
12 D'Ewes J.A	1877-8-9	

Wounded at Inhlobane 28/3/1879

13 Hendry J	1877-8-9	
6 Hickey C	1877-8-9	
15 Venn C.D	1877-8-9	

On medal roll for Kaffarian Vol. Artillery with 1877-8 clasp.

Frontier Light Horse

Standish William Prendergast Vereker was the third son of the present Viscount Gort, by his marriage with Caroline Harriet, daughter of Viscount Gage. He was born on 23 February 1854, and was educated at Westminster School and Worcester College, Oxford. From 1874-75 he studied at the Royal Agricultural College at Cirencester.

On 22 July 1878, he embarked for South Africa, and a month later arrived at Cape Town. Finding that the war with the Pedi kingdom was still in progress on the Transvaal frontier, he and some friends were determined to join in the action. One of whom was **Metcalfe Smith,** latterly of the Frontier Light Horse whose life was saved by **Major Leet** at Hlobane, an act which earned Leet the Victoria Cross. Vereker enlisted in the Frontier Light Horse on 13 October 1878 under **Colonel Redvers Buller,** participating in the operations against Sekhukhune. He was discharged on 23 December 1878.

On the reorganisation of the army just before the invasion of Zululand. Vereker received a commission in the 3rd, or Lonsdale's Regiment of the Natal Native Contingent, a corps belonging to the Headquarter Column. He subsequently took part in the advance of that force, and was present at the storming of Sihayo's stronghold, in the Batshe Valley.

On the night of 21/22 January 1879, Vereker, **Captain Barry** and No 5 Company of the NNC, of the amaChunu tribe, were positioned on Magaga Knoll to the North of Isandlwana. They were among the first to observe the pockets of Zulus surrounding the camp. Ordered to advance with the Natal Native Horse, the NNC (on foot and armed only with spears) crossed the crest of a hill, only to discover the bulk of the Zulu army in the valley below. The NNH dismounted and fired a volley, before remounting and conducting a fighting retreat back to the camp. Vereker and Barry were helped back to the camp by **Sgt Major Williams** of the NNC, taking turns to ride or hold the stirrups of Williams' horse. Standish Vereker was one of 52 officers out of an estimated 854 Europeans who died at Isandlwana, along with 477 natives – the fate of a further 698 Africans remains unknown. His fate is recorded by **Captain Charles Raw** of the NNC, who was one of the few who survived. "He saw him a few seconds before the retreat," runs the brief record. "I got him a horse, which a native claimed, and which poor Vereker refused to deprive him of; he thus deprived himself of all chance of escape." His sacrifice captured the public imagination.

Four months afterwards Vereker's body was found on the field of battle by Captain Viscount Downe, still unstripped, and was easily identified. According to the account left by journalist **Charles Norris-Newman**, it appears that Vereker perished alongside **Colonel Durnford**, together with most of the Natal Carbineers and Natal Mounted Police. Standish William Prendergast Vereker is commemorated on a memorial tablet in the church at East Cowes, Isle of Wight, and a plaque at the Royal Agricultural College.

The illustration is from "The Boys' Own", published in 1879. An excerpt from "Heroes of modern Africa: True stories of the intrepid bravery and stirring adventures of the pioneers, explorers, and founders of modern Africa" (1911) by **Edward Gilliat**, a former Harrow master. "Two of the young officers who died on that day were known to the writer when they were boys at school. One, the Honourable Captain Vereker, was a Westminster boy, famed at school for leading his comrades to charge the London roughs on the way to Vincent Square. The writer gave him his first lessons in the use of the pistol, little thinking of the dire extremity which should so soon find him, revolver in hand, facing a mob of yelling savages, Vereker, we are told, had just caught a stray horse and was in the act of mounting when a trooper came running up : " Beg pardon, sir, but that is my horse you've got. " Oh ! is it? Here you are, man! jump up quick; I'll manage." So with Irish generosity and pluck the young officer gave up his only chance of safety, and stayed to meet the foe and die.

Information supplied by Peter Weedon.

The medal was sold on eBay in January 2008, it had been in the collection of Don Felipe Hidalgo, a noted Spanish-Filipino collector of antiquities. The medal selling for $4150 US . ebay no 180323946692. The medal had been authenticated

Frontier Light Horse

SOUTH AFRICA Clasp 1879 Lieut. A. M. SMITH, FRONTIER. LIGHT HORSE

A. Metcalfe Smith was a member of the 5th West York Militia before volunteering for service in the Frontier Light Horse, being commissioned into the latter unit as a Lieutenant in December 1878. Present at Inhlobane Mountain In March 1879, he resigned his commission in May of the same year. As stated above, it was the dramatic rescue of Smith by Major Leet of the 13th Light Infantry that resulted in the latter being awarded the V.C. A grateful Smith wrote to The Illustrated London News from Kambula Camp on 31 March 1879, describing the circumstances of his rescue:

'I am most anxious to bring to your notice that, in the retreat from Inhlobane Mountain on 28th inst., Major Leet, of the 13th Light Infantry, who was quite a stranger to me, saved my life, with almost the certainty of losing his own life by doing so. We were going along the top of the mountain, pursued by the Zulus, when **Major Leet** said to **Colonel Buller** that the best way to get the men down was by the right side; and the Colonel said it was, and called out so to the men. However, everyone but Major Leet, myself and one other man, kept on to the front of the mountain; while we began to descend on the right side. Major Leet and the other man were on horseback, but I was on foot, my horse having been shot. When we had got down a little way, a great many Zulus rushed after us, and were catching us up very quickly. The side of the mountain was dreadfully steep and rugged, and there was no pathway at all. They were firing and throwing their assegais at us while they rushed upon us. The third man, whose name is unknown to me, was killed about halfway down. While I was running by myself and trying to catch up, I turned round and shot one with my revolver. I was then quite exhausted and out of breath, and intended to sit down and give up all chance of saving my life, as the Zulus were within a few yards of me; but Major Leet persisted in waiting for me, and called to me to catch hold of the pack-saddle he was riding, which I did. Major Leet then, finding that I could not keep beside the horse, I was so done up and the hill so steep and rugged, insisted, though I told him it was no use, on stopping and dragging me up behind him on the horse, which was also greatly exhausted. By the greatest good luck, he escaped from the bullets and assegais of the Zulus and got near the Colonel's men, coming down the end of the mountain. Had it not been fro Major Leet, nothing could have saved me, and I owe him the deepest gratitude, which I shall feel as long as I live.'

The following announcement of the award of the Victoria Cross to Major William K. Leet, 1st Battalion, 13th Regiment, appeared in The London Gazette of 17 June 1879:

'For his gallant conduct on 28 March 1879, in rescuing from the Zulus, Lieutenant A. M. Smith, of the Frontier Light Horse, during the retreat from Inhlobane. Lieutenant Smith, whilst on foot, his horse having been shot, was closely pursued by the Zulus, and would have been killed, had not Major Leet taken him upon his horse, and rode with him under the fire of the enemy to a place of safety.'

Lt Smith was Mentioned in Dispatches by Buller for his courage during the battle of Hlobane but sent out of camp in disgrace in May 1879 and resigned his Commission From the Times of Natal;

'An unfortunate incident occurred here last night by which a promising young Officer of the Frontier Light Horse by the name of Smith has disgraced himself and thrown unmerited discredit on the fine corps of which he is a part. At 10pm the camp was alarmed by a shot, which caused everyone to stand to their Arms, though the call of 'all right' soon dissipated all fears of Zulu's. ...... Shortly after the same thing was repeated and it turned out that it was the Officer in Question who had drunk himself into a condition of frenzy and defied anyone to approach him. I believe he was only secured without doing damage by the judicious expedient of 'extinguishing' him with his own tent, and he passed the night spread-eagled to the wheels of a wagon. He was a repentant and sorrowful man this morning on finding he was dismissed with disgrace and ordered to be escorted over the Blood River to reflect on the consequences of his want of self control...'

Information suppled by Justin Young

Major William Knox Leet, 1st Battalion 13th (1st Somersetshire) Light Infantry

ON March 28, 1879, the fighting on the Inhlobane Mountain, under Sir Evelyn Wood, was so severe that a retirement was deemed advisable. During the retreat the Zulus continuously harassed our men. The 13th Light Infantry formed part of the small force. Towards evening Lieutenant A. M. Smith, Frontier Light Horse, had his horse shot from under him, and, being closely pursued by the enemy, was on the point of being speared, when Major Leet, galloping to his rescue, took him up behind him, riding with him under rifle-fire and a shower of assagais to a place of safety During the Indian Mutiny General Leet served with marked distinction, both with his battalion under Lord Mark Kerr, and as a Staff Officer to several columns towards the end of the campaign, being twice mentioned in general orders. Served in South Africa, 1878, against Sekukuni, and also in the Expedition to Mandalay, 1886-7, in both latter campaigns being mentioned in despatches. Was in 1887 created a Companion of the Bath, and died on June 29, 1898, aged 65. (Born November 3, 1833.)

Major William Knox Leet

ZULU AGAINST ZULU - CLOSE QUARTERS

"NO SURRENDER" - DEATH OF A ZULU WARRIOR
THE END OF THE ZULU WAR - INCIDENTS AT ULUNDI

Frontier Light Horse

Freeman's Journal and Daily Commercial Advertiser (Dublin, Ireland), Wednesday, October 23, 1878;

HOLDICH—July 30, of typhoid fever, at Komgha, South Africa, Laurence Maydwell Holdich, Troop-Sergeant-Major of the Frontier Light Horse, second son of Charles Walter and Eleanor A. Holdich, of Sleaford, Lincolnshire, aged 33 years.

Light Horse Death Notice Hampshire Telegraph and Sussex Chronicle etc (Portsmouth, England), Saturday, June 15, 1878

MACNAGHTEN—On the 8th ultimo, killed in action, while in command of the Colonial Frontier Light Horse, in the Caffre War, Elliot Macnaghten, late Captain 20th Hussars, and fourth son of the late Francis Macnaghten, Esq., of the Bengal Civil Service.

The Pall Mall Gazette (London, England), Friday, May 9, 1879

PLANTE, Horace P., Light Frontier Horse, in the attack on the Zlobani Mountain, Zululand, aged 38, March 28.

George Hampden Whalley, Captain, Frontier Light Horse. was a British Liberal politician and soldier.
The son of George Hammond Whalley, Member of Parliament for Peterborough, he was born at the family estate of Plas Madoc in 1851. Educated on the training ship Britannia, he afterwards entered the Royal Navy. but following an accident which left him unconscious for 14 days, he was not able to pass his examinations.
Whalley received a lieutenant's commission in the 6th Royal Lancaster Regiment of Militia on 9 March 1871.He resigned his commission on 1 June 1872, and was commissioned a cornet in the Denbighshire Yeomanry on 29 June 1872. Whalley was promoted lieutenant, then captain on 4 December 1878. In 1879, Whalley commanded C Troop of Lonsdale's Horse in the Anglo-Zulu War. A convoy under his command from Fort Tenedos to Fort Chelmsford successfully beat off a Zulu ambush.
Gaika and Gaeleka War 1877-8. Mentioned-in-despatches (LG 26.3.7) for services at Quintana 7.2.78. Wounded in action (severely contused) 8.5.78 whilst assembling the troops for an attack. Mentioned-in-despatches (LG 18.6.7 .
Sekukune operations in the Transvaal 1878. He commanded the Frontier Light Horse at one point. Resigned 10.12.78.
Captain and Adjutant, Baker's Horse 3.2.79. He was ordered to take command of the Pietermaritzburg and Durban Troops of the Frontier Light Horse as one Squadron (NLH). Commandant (Captain) and Commanding Officer, Natal Light Horse 3.5.79. Zulu War 1879. He was mentioned with great praise on 8.7.79 for operations around Fort Evelyn Wood. Mentioned-in-despatches (LG 21.8.79) Captain Whalley, Natal Light Horse, is a brave, straight forward gentleman, whom I have known for the last fifteen months, and who has always done well. . He was described as a regular soldier of fortune
Whalley was elected Liberal MP for Peterborough in 1880, like his father (who had occupied the seat until his death in 1878). He resigned by becoming Steward of the Manor of Northstead in June 1883. He was adjudged bankrupt later that year.In April 1884, Whalley and his wife rented a house in South Kensington. They were evicted in August, after Whalley's draft for the rent had proved uncollectable, but by this time Whalley had broken into a locked room and stolen £200 of the owner's goods and pawned them. He was subsequently convicted of theft at the Old Bailey and sentenced on the 25th October 1884 to nine months hard labor. He arrived in Australia on a ship, the Duke of Buccleuch, in about 1885 or 1886, having changed his surname by deed poll to White. According to shipping records at the State Archives in Brisbane, he arrived with a wife, Eleanor and an infant.
Information supplied Cam Simpson.

Brevet Major (later General Sir) Redvers Henry Buller (1839-1908)
On the 30th January 1878 Buller was sent to South Africa as a special service officer. He succeeded Carrington as commander of Frontier Light Horse in April. He later commanded a detachment of 930 troops, coprising his own Frontier Light Horse, one company of the 24th regiment, Captain Comley's Somerset Volunteer Horse and Allan Maclean's Mfengu. The unit was involved in the last major assault of the Ciskei campaign - the attack in the Pirie bush starting on 8th May, they ran into a rebel stronghold and was forced to fight, suffering 4 killed and 6 wounded in the process. He won the Victoria Cross at Hlobane., In August, 1879 he was repatriated, largely because of his ill-health, his achievements in the Kaffir and Zulu wars were immediately recognised by his appointment as aide-de-camp to Queen Victoria, promotion to full colonel and by being made CMG, A Companion of the Order of St Michael and St George.

Brevet Major (later General Sir) Redvers Henry Buller (1839-1908)

Frontier Light Horse

QUARTERMASTER SERGEANT				Schmidt	H	1877-8	284	Brown	T	1879 r

QUARTERMASTER SERGEANT
  Day   S.F.S   1879
STAFF SERGEANT
  91 Lawson F.C   1877-8-9 r
  9   Macdonald W.H   1877-8-9
FARRIER SERGEANT
      Dyer   H   1879
      See also 16th Lancers.
      Quick   C   1879
      See also 21st Hussars.
SERGEANT
      Ainslie H.J   1878
  85 Blinck   C.F   1879
  229 Clarke   W   1879 r
      Coulson W.F   1879
  304 Ellis   F.M   1879
  26 Gould   J   1877-8-9
      Hayes   D.J   1877-8
  3   Julian   J.T   1877-8-9
  14 Mantle   G   1877-8-9
  189 O'Toole VC E   1877-8-9
      His VC was for an action at Ulundi.
  305 Routh   L.H.T   1879
  250 Tippett (Tibbett) J KIA 1879
CORPORAL
  22 Austee   G.W   1879
  70 Baldy   G   1879
  307 Brussow W   1879
      Wounded in Action Hlobane
  370 Chilman H.R   1879
      Dreyer   C.B   1877-8
  258 Friday   W   1879
  39 Hurrell W   1877-8-9 r
  261 Jones   E   1879
      Kirsten J.M.F   1877-8
  18 Lansdell G   1877-8-9 r
      Leach   F   1877-8
      Mahoney T   1877-8
      Mortimore J.H   1877-8?
      Returned 1887 reissued 21/7/1902.
  142 Muller   H.W   1879
  21 Murray   H   1877-8-9
  124 Ochse   C   1879
  53 Oddy   A   1877-8-9
      Salaman W.H   1879

      Schmidt   H   1877-8
  # 341 Theis   C.A   1879
TROOPER
  172 Acton   V   1879
  59 Allingham W   1879 r
  344 Allinson W   1879 r
  78 Anderson R   1877-8-9
  118 Anderson W   1879 r
  362 Armstrong W   1879
  52 Arthurs   T   1877-8 r
  368 August   G   1879 r
      Axel   L   1877-8
  104 Bailey   W   1879 r
  110 Ban   A   1879 r
  185 Baner   J.H   1879
      Becker   A.R.G   1877-8
  328 Beckham   A   1879
  197 Bedford   W   1879
  207 Behu   H   1879
  303 Bell   J.T.M   1879
  94 Benecky   H.S   1877-8-9
  95 Benecky   J.W   1877-8-9 r
  352 Benson   J   1879
  173 Berry   J   1879
  275 Berry   J   1879
  300 Berry   J   1879
      Berry   J   1878-9
      See also Wodehouse True Blues.
  73 Betlige   J.A.C   1879 r
  280 Blake   G.S   1879
  363 Bold   J   1879
  366 Bold   R   1879
  199 Bostedt   E   1879 r
  47 Boyce   W   1877-8-9
  ## 64 Boyd   W   1877-8-9
  252 Boyes   W   1879
  69 Bran   J   1877-8-9 r
  28 Branagan J   1877-8 r
  287 Briscoe   R   1879
  180 Broadbent E.C   1879
  396 Bronner   C   1879
  253 Broomfield T.O   1879
  54 Brown   G   1877-8-9
  284 Brown   G   1879
  23 Brown DCM R   1877-8-9 r

  284 Brown   T   1879 r
  418 Buckley   F.W   1879 r
  174 Buckley   J   1879 r
  306 Bulmer   F.W   1879
  377 Buonyeat D   1879
  93 Burnett   A   1877-8 r
  55 Burns   M   1877-8-9
  221 Burns   W.J   1879 r
  251 Burton KIA A.J 1879
  361 Byran   W.J   1879
  288 Caffin KIA P.W 1879
  61 Caldicott F   1879 r
  401 Cameron   C   1879 r
  181 Carroll   J   1879
      Carleton C.E   1879 r
  416 Chapman   G   1879
  367 Cherry KIA W 1879 r
  See also Border Horse.
  82 Chilton   G   1879 r
  254 Clarke   F   1879 r
  406 Clarke   J   No clasp
      No medal Deserted.
  27 Clarke   W   1879 r
  310 Clarke   W   1879
  36 Coe   S   1877-8-9
  119 Coleman   J   1879
      See Port Elizabeth Militia No. 1 Coy.
  345 Cook   J   1879
      See Port Elizabeth Militia No. 1 Coy.
  341 Cooper   J   1879
      See also Kaffrarian Rangers.
  386 Corrigan W.H   1879 r
  297 Coutts   J.J   1879
      No medal Deserted.
  255 Coviney   A   1879 r
  333 Crawford H   1879
      Crocker   H   1877-8
  394 Crous   P.A   1879
  49 Cullen   E   1877-8-9
  25 Cullen   T   1877-8-9
  244 Cumming   H   No clasp
      No medal Deserted.
  157 Cunningham W   1879
  347 Currie   C   1879
  257 Daniels   C   1879 r

\# City Coins Postal Auction No 58 29th August 2008, Lot No 393. – bar: 1879 341 Corpl. C.A. Theis Frontr. L. Horse F+
Hammer price 1,925 Rand The medal roll (copy page enclosed) confirms that Theis was only engaged against the Zulus in 1879. Medal poorly removed from obverse brooch mounting and re-suspendered.

\#\# Dix Noonan Web Auction Lot 498, 21 Sep 07
Three: Lance-Corporal W. Boyd, Cookhouse Town Guard, late Frontier Light Horse and Prince Alfred's Volunteer Guard
South Africa 1877-79, 1 clasp, 1877-8-9 (64 Tpr. W. Boyd, Frontr. L. Horse); Cape of Good Hope General Service 1880-97, 2 clasps, Transkei, Basutoland (Pte. W. J. Boyd, P.A.V.G.); Queen's South Africa 1899-1902, no clasp (15 L. Cpl. W. Boyd, Cookhouse T.G.), this last with corrected number, occasional edge bruising, generally very fine or better and rare (3) Hammer price £1100 (Barrett J. Carr Collection)
Footnote; William Boyd was one of 83 men in the Frontier Light Horse to qualify for the "1877-8-9" clasp; one of four in Prince Alfred's Volunteer Guard to qualify for both the "Transkei" and "Basutoland" clasps, and one of around 100 men awarded the Queen's South Africa 1899-1902 for services in the Cookhouse Town Guard.

Frontier Light Horse

The following letters from the pen of **Arthur Dobson** give an insight into the life of an ordinary Trooper in the Frontier Light Horse. Arthur was never to see his homeland again he was killed in action in 1879.

A TASMANIAN IN ZULULAND. (The Sydney Morning Herald Tuesday 7th October 1879)
Believing that many of our readers would be interested in any accounts from the pen of a Tasmanian as to the character of the country of Transvaal for settlement or as to his experiences in campaigning in the South Africa, we applied for, and have had placed at our disposal the following extracts from letters of Mr. Arthur Dobson to members of his family. He left Tasmania in March, 1878,for South Africa, to inspect, report upon, and take up land in Transvaal. On his arrival, the warlike aspect of affairs put an end to any prospect of settling there for some time to come, and in July last he joined the corps of Frontier Light Horse under Colonel (then Major) Buller, now attached to Colonel Evelyn Wood's column.

He saw active service against Secocosni, and subsequently againstthe Zulus. No reasonable doubt can be entertained but that out of the 33 Light Horse who went to the Zoblane Mountain on tho 28th March last, he was one of the 23 who fell victims to the assegais of the Zulus. His experience in pastoral pursuits in Tasmania, and for 13 years in New Zealand, may. perhaps render his observations on the character of the country for settlement of some value.

The Camp, 20 miles from Utrecht,
Wakestrom, November 30,1878

I joined the Frontier Light Horse, in July last,for six months. My time is up on tho 31st January, but I shall never have another opportunity of seeing the country, so I think I shall continue for another six months, Where I have been, and what I have seen, would take a long time to relate. It is astrange country, especially when you get out of civilization, as we were for weeks in Secocosni's country, which is all bush land ; the heat awful, and bad climate, and bad water. The Chief, Seooccceni, has not given in, and his men shot two of our fellows; but we were obliged to retire on account of horse sickness, and no water for the cattle that draw all our provisions and forage. It is a dangerous country to fight in, and it is a wonder that we were not all killed. On my way to the Transvaal I was at Port Elizabeth for two days, and there saw the ostrich feather sale. It was said that £230,000 was realized in the one day's sale. The feathers were all laid out in bunches on long tables, and such a motley crowd of buyers. A proportion of the feather men are well off, but only the old hands, or men who have had large capital to start with. The feathers are nearly as dear here as in England. I went on to Maritzburg. There was nothing to be done, The cost of traveling about to see the country would have been very great, and it would not have been safe to travel in some parts, so I saw Major Buller, and joined the Frontier Light Horse. It's a funny go, isn't it ? However, batter men than myself are in this corps. I will try and give you some insight into the life of a Light Horseman.

You are found with a horse, saddle, and bridle, saddle-bags, spurs, two blankets, a valise, overcoat and cape ; coat and trousers, of chocolate colour, leggings, boots, socks, and shirts a wideawake, with scarlet puggaree, this is our badge, also a Snider rifle, and belt for ammunition, with 30 rounds, water bottle and haversack, and blanked under the saddle. Thus equipped we left Maritaburg in August, the Band of the, 80th Regiment playing us out of town ; we traveled 10 or 17 miles and camped. The horses are turned out till dark; horse guards are on duty to keep them together; they are then fastened by halters to the picket lines. We very seldom have had tents, but sleep with the sky as our roof. We are provided with 1 1/4lbs. of very brown bread, enough coffee, tea and sugar for three portions a day, and 1 lb of meat. We cook for ourselves, and are obliged to buy rations to keep ourselves going. A store wagon follows us, as a rule ; sugar, Is. 6d. per lb. ; tea, 1s. , rice, 2s. small packages of cocoa, 2s. We receive 5s. a day as pay, which enables us to supplement our ration.

The day after we arrived at Burgher's fort, 170 of us were picked out and went on patrol ; we got hold of 147 head of splendid cattle ; we were fired at nearly all night coming home, and a few horses were shot. On the 6th October some 300. of us, including 2 guns of the artillery, and 152 of the 13th Regiment went out, and were fired on, and returned it during most of the day. At dark they attacked our camp, pouring bullets into us, the ring is unpleasant ; we with breechloaders, but principally the soldiers, fired with such rapidity that in 20 minutes all was quiet. This is the second time I have been under heavy fire, hut somehow I have not the least fear, nor do I feel nervous. I was on guard at 2 am next day, when the horses (76) got mixed in the ring, and in trying to separate them I was kicked below the knee, and can only now walk after six days in hospital.

The Frontier Light Horse returned from Secoccgni's frontier on the 22nd October ; after two days' spell, we were ordered back, and on the 27th we attacked Umsosta, a native chief, 60 miles from Lydenberg; we had with us 4 guns of the Artillery, part of the 13th Regiment, and some others. Nine of our men were wounded, and two since dead : the Kaffirs were driven back. We stayed on the field a day, when orders were issued for our return to Lydenburg. Any amount of deserted farms destroyed, and houses burnt. The lemons were ripe in some of the gardens, and very refreshing they were along the line of march. After a few days' halt, we journeyed on, and on the 2nd November we slept at' Comitee River, and got some goods at a store,very dear they were.

On the 4th November we came to Laka Crissio and camped there. This is the only decent sheet of water I have seen up country. It is in the shape of a horse shoe, about 4 miles round. I saw birds and waterfowl of all descriptions on the lake; flamingoes, black geese, etc.-but the water was only two foot deep, and all the wator supply was a little spring; 10 minutes' flow would fill a gallon. Some 20 men were out buck shooting, and they brought five or six into camp. On the day we left Laka Crissie, and three miles on our road we passed two lagoons, the number of birds upon them was wonderful, but I was not near enough to see what they were. This was a gala day for me, as B troop was in front, and I and some six others had some splendid buck shooting, I dropped one ; but I did not think much of the sport after I got two or three. The flesh is first class when properly cooked, and what soup! if you can, get a few vegetables.

On the 7th, we came on to the Vaal River and camped at Robertson's store. Here I first saw an ostrich farm ; some 50- birds enclosed, in a paddock.

Frontier Light Horse

This farm is owned by two brothers, who have had great experience in this country. I was pleased with this place, as some land was being ploughed, and five or six Paddocks were fenced in, and actually a gate into the orchard ; gates are not common in this country, I assure yon, I fenced-in fifty-acre paddocks, out of the question ; no boundary fences ; and, a farm means a kraal made of stones and a bare, house, but on the older farms you see trees. There has been a wonderful drought all over the country this year ; carriage, from Maritzburg to Durban, 50 miles, is 12s, to 16s. per cwt., which used to be 2s. to 3s ; potatoes, 30s. per cwt.

On the 10th still at Robinson's got some milk for 1s, found some mushrooms and had a good meal. Sunday, parade and service. We were complimented by Colonel Rowlands for the week we had done, which was satisfactory. He his Commander-In-Chief at the front. On the 11th, Saddle parade and drill ; lovely day some of the horses got away, and parties, were sent out in search.

12th and 13th. In camp, parties out looking for horses.

15th. Jam and, soap got from Government store; jam, 2s. per pot. 16th. Sugar and white bread; by jove this, was a treat. 17th. Rain this, to me, was a treat. I enjoyed getting wet through served out. 18th November. We left Robertson's and journeyed towards Newcastle,and on 23rd we arrived here, Eland's Neck, and found a camp. A lovely grass country this is, beautiful low hills, also a little bush, very well watered, climate very cold in winter, and for the last few days rain nearly every night. There is a lovely stream within 100 yards of our camp, and some tree ferns,.... Here I gathered some small pieotees, and some leaves of the native vine. The native flowers are voery beautiful, and the grass hills better than I have seen in New Zealand or Tasmania ; the soil in places wherever I have been is wonderful.

I killed a snake when searching for material to make fires with. The Dutch farmers are not well off. They are a lazy set, and think of nothing but money, and live, anyhow. They cut the corn, and then thrash it by driving stook over it, and then toss it in the air on a windy day.

I like some of the country very much, but it is banishment for life. No one. would care about investing much till the war is over ; land will then improve very much in, value at Pretoria. To get goods up the country is something very difficult. The greater part of South Africa is a good

climate; the place reminds me of Tasmania. It will be a wonderful country some day, especially if the Delagoa Bay railway is opened. How long I shall be able to stand this life I don't know. Most of our men are going to leave at the end of two months, when our time is up. I am undecided what I shall do, perhaps stay on with Major Buller. We have certainly very brave officers.

Captain Barton, of the Coldstream Guards, is much liked. Some of our men are educated men, some not so. This sort of life is precarious hard ; sleeping out on wet ground,

etc, Still, if any inducement, I shall fight the Zulu ; that is to say, if I feel well and strong, as at present. The Zulu country is in sight here, and we are on its borders ; how long we stay I know not. I must now close this ; the trumpet sounds, horses in, and stables. It seems so strange to be in this inferior position. I have seen a splendid grass country in its native state, and thousands and thousands of acres of splendid grass land surround's us yes, fifty miles each way. There are a most infernal lot of ants, centipedes, and scorpions in this country. From what I have seen of South Africa, I should say that it will be, in twenty or thirty years, one of the finest countries in the world.

Kaffirs come into camp here with milk and wood! every morning ; every little thing is very expansive. It is a lovely climate in winter, here, and in most of the country I have seen, but too wet in summer. Land can be bought at from 4s, to 10s. acre. The 10s land is worth about £2 and the 4s. about 16s. I find it very difficult writing on the ground, or on my knee in camp.

The Camp, Blood River,
8th January, 1879.

About 10 days ago we, the F. L. Horse, the 13th and 19th Regiments, Artillery and allies met together, about 2,000, under Col. Wood of the 90th Regiment. We are now in Zululand proper, and as we expect every day to be ordered to attack, the border is carefully guarded. All the young men in Natal are volunteers; in fact, are compelled to turn out. Whether I come safe out of the Zulu affair it is difficult to say. If the king does not come to terms, we have 11,000 men against his 40,000, and we expect to give him a licking.

Yesterday I was on patrol with 60 men; we rode 20 miles into the enemy's country. Nearly all the kraals or huts were deserted by the young men ; the women fled up the hills at our approach ; the quantity of cattle and sheep we saw astonished us. We were not molested, as war is not yet actually declared, but when it is there will be hot work for us. I have a very good horse and sundries, but the difficulty is fire, firewood is so scarce-and is a very great drawback. Round about here, the country is composed of hills about half the height of Mount Nelson, with splendid green grass all over them up to the very top, but in places rather rocky.

During our twenty miles ride out, and back by a different route, I only saw one single tree. The grass in South Africa is a lovely green at this time of year, and it will be a lovely country in 50 years' time ; in fact, it is a wonderful place for grass, and far before Australia and New Zealand. Not so hot as Melbourne, on account of the rainy season. It has rained now five days a week from the middle of November ; generally a thunderstorm at night.

We have killed a good many snakes-two in our tent ; as a rule they do not run large, although some kinds are very deadly. There is an absence of birds all about here, and very few wild animals ; the animals are nearly all killed out. Sometimes we see a rare specimen spoken of in books, such as the Kaffir cranes-lovely birds. It is raining very hard, and I am on fatigue duty to-day-which means that I have, with four others, to do the work of the camp. I have a bad cold, and sleeping in damp clothes does not improve it ; especially as we are ordered to sleep with our boots on, in case of an attack- pleasant, is it not? I miss vegetables very much.

We get bread and fresh meat, as a rule ; but, if out for a day, preserved meat and biscuits, also a limited supply of coffee and tea.

Frontier Light Horse

Camp, 12 miles from Blood River,
January 19th, 1879.

Nothing but the Zulu war is talked of, and we are all going into the heart of the country, to advance 10 or 12 miles every fine day. The day before yesterday the Kaffirs were supposed to be 8,000 strong, within 10 miles of the camp. I was on night guard, orders came, every available horseman saddled up at 1 a.m., and we started, taking a piece of bread, some coffee and sugar, and made over the hills, and passed any number of kraals or huts, but all had cleared out, cattle and all. I was one, on the return home, who had to stay with a sick man 10 miles from camp, and just lie down on the wet grass till daylight. Seventy-six miles, with one's rifle and bag on your shoulders and your ammunition round your waist are things to be read of, but actual experience only can prove the hardship. My being so accustomed to the saddle was fortunate, as out of the 200, there were not 10 fresh men. This is what we call " patrol;" we were all very much out up at not having a fight.

Yesterday we shifted camp and came 10 miles towards one of the enemy's kraals. The line of march is a splendid sight, the cavalry (that is our 200), the 90th and its band, the Artillery, the 13th, the Dutch, the Kaffir allies, the ambulances, water carts, etc., extending over 3 miles, mule wagons, goats for milking (officers' property), dogs, etc, in fact, such a host of strange sights that would astonish anyone out of South Africa. Last night some of our Niggers, under two white leaders, opened the ball on our side and had a hand to hand fight, killing seven Zulus ; they assegaied two of our blacks, who are now lying in the hospital in comfortable camp beds. Our doctor wanted them to eat something, but no ; their own Kaffir doctor, a fellow who carries his shop round his neck and waist,; a lot of short pieces of wood and powders, must mix up a drink and give it them on the sly, then they are perfectly satisfied. Some of these Kaffirs are splendid made fellows, and look better in their own dress of a small skin round their waist and one behind than in anything else. A few wear tiger skins, but very few, for wild animals are very scarce all over South Africa. The amount of ants, centipedes, and scorpions up about the wooded country for miles round Burgher's fort was awful ; that is the place for sickness, and our men had such a bad time of it there that one half of them have given notice to leave, as they fancy when this war is over we shall be ordered back there. It is constantly raining here, and thundering. Four nights ago we had a storm ; its equal I have never seen-hailstones bigger than Hobart Town walnuts; the camp washed out. However I have seen something, and when my love of adventure will end I know not. Only give me Tasmania, before all or any of the colonies. The number of black sheep here from England is very great. Modesty is all put aside ; but the Kaffir women are one of the most chaste people as a nation that it is possible to meet. We may fight to-morrow, and all South Africa is awaiting the result of our movements, and thousands and tens of thousands of other Kaffirs are watching the result, as the Zulu King, with his 40,000 men, has never fought against the English.

Camp, 10 miles from Blood River,
January 30th, 1879.

I have led an extraordinary life since I eat my last apple in your garden in March last ; would that we bad a few now. War has been declared against the Zulu king, and the Frontier Light Horse is camped here with Colonel Wood's column. After three fights with the Kaffirs we captured about 4,000 head of cattle and about 2,000 head of sheep and goats during the first few days. On the 10th January we started under Col. Wood, with the 13th and, 19th Regiments, Artillery, and allies, to meet General Lord Chelmsford. We met him about 20 miles from our camp at Blood River, he had 6,000 men ; 4,000 white, the rest black allies. The commanders conversed and he went his way, and we went back. There are three or four columns, and we are about the smallest, only 1,600 soldiers, 200 Light Horse, 40 Dutch, and 600 Native Allies. Gen. Chelmsford's column is about 30 miles from us down the Blood River. Coming home from the meeting we captured 2,300 cattle and 1,400 sheep and goats, and just after the General left us he had a brush with some Kaffirs and killed 30, but the savages shot two of his men.

The Light Horse go out on patrol, and we have had a few engagements, but on the 23rd we left 300 men in camp, and all the rest of us went into the interior some 20 miles. On the 24th we fought and defeated a small force of Kaffirs, about 3,000, having shot 150 of them, when at night a messenger came in with the awful news that the General's camp had been sacked. We have been in great suspense the last few days as every one has friends in the General's camp. The particulars I cannot give you, as there is only one paper in camp, and that is going the rounds of nearly 2,000 men ; but it appears that the General, with a large force under his command, on the 22nd, left the camp, with some 1,000 men in it, and most of the stores and ammunition. When away, the Kaffirs, to the number of 5,000, rushed on the camp in the middle of the day, and then a most fearful hand to hand conflict took place, our friendly natives, volunteers, regulars, and others, all mixed up, and fighting desperately. However, 950 men could do nothing against 10,000. A few escaped to tell the dreadful story. Artillery men killed at their guns, poor little band boys assegaied (an assegaie is a piece of wood about 4 feet long, pointed, with a long iron blade at the end, like butcher's knife, sharpened on both sides). Our poor fellows killed about 4,000, but the scene of the struggle presented a frightful spectacle ; nearly all the white men stripped of every particle of their clothing, and the bodies very much out up; the sick men in the hospital had been stabbed as they lay in bed, and you'll read all this startling news in the papers.

The General returned to the camp when all was over, and the living and the dead slept side by side that night. A most singular affair occurred. The mounted man, whose business it was to carry dispatches, got out of the melee and rode to a small place called **Rorke's Drift,** and was just in time to warn 80 soldiers that the Kaffirs were coming. They immediately set to work and made a small fort of mealy bags (bags full of Indian corn), and these brave fellows kept off 4,000 Kaffirs for eight hours, and shot 1,000 of them, only losing 11 killed and 7 wounded. The niggers then retired. One fortunate circumstance was, that there were a number of casks of rum in the wagons in the General's camp, and the wretches indulged very freely and got drunk, so that only a small number of them went to attack Rorke's Drift. After the news came to us we had a meal, and Colonel Wood said that he felt it his duty to return to our 300 men left in camp. We got within three miles of the camp and went to sleep, and next morning we found them all safe, but we have since learnt that another night away and our camp would have shared the same awful fate as the General.

Frontier Light Horse

Continued from previous page.

We all sleep with clothes on and rifles by our side. It is not pleasant, and the thought of a large army of these black devils coming down upon you at night is, to say the least, annoying ; however, Half of our men, the cavalry, leave in a few days, as our time is up. I said that I would go on a few months longer, and in spite of the danger, I should feel a coward in my heart if I left just now. I may go under; in fact, it is on the cards that if we are attacked one half of us will go, as we are not strong enough. It
is rather hard to be shot, or rather murdered in this infernal country, although the green grass for hundreds of miles round is a lovely sight to any one in my line.

Camp, 16 miles from Blood River,
February 6th, 1879.

"I am at present on a vidette, some three miles way from camp, writing you these few lines. My ??? is on the look out, straining his eyes in the direction of the distant mountains, We got up at 3:30 a.m., and take our meat,and tea and sugar with as, and stay till dark: I can only scribble, as one's knee is not a good place to write upon properly.

Some four days ago our corps went out on patrol, some 15 miles into the interior, and came to Umbelini's kraal, a stronghold. We cantered up the defile, and one by one led our horses down into a large valley surrounded by high rocky hills. We galloped up to the huts and burnt his place, taking 200 head of cattle, and the last part of the way came home in the dark. We did not see any Kaffirs in this valley; a most fortunate thing, for if they had surprised us, few would have come out alive, It is the most dangerous place I have yet been in, and one and all of us dread the thoughts of what might have happened. Reports come in every day, and the latest is that three days ago the Kaffirs made a raid just over the Blood River, and killed men, women, and children belonging to the friendly natives.

If I get through the next four months without being shot or stabbed, I shall leave; there is nothing to be done in my line here, the country is too new. I shall probably try anything I can get, but this life is too trying, the food too much all alike, and lying on the ground for nine months will be enough. I often think how I should feel in a comfortable bed, and a breakfast table, and fresh vegetables. I get on very well with the men and officers, and yesterday I applied to be put in A troop, which was granted ; so I am under Captain Pryor a very nice fellow he is. I lent all the papers you sent me, and got others in return, so I have had a little reading lately. It is getting dark, and our guard is nearly up; the thunder rolls right round us, and it is spitting with rain.

The green hills of Zululand are covered with flowers ; many of them you see in your gardens at home. Here ixias, gladiolus, piccottee, kallow, convolvulus, petunia, are just as common as the wild lilies that used to grow in the fields years ago, when we were children in dear old Tasmania. My happiest days, I fear, have been spent. What memories the 90th band last night brought home to one, as familiar waltzes came into one's ears, whilst cleaning our horses-remembrances only a short 10 months ago.

Our climate here is very similar to Tasmania, and heat about the same-except there is more rain here at this season of the year. Now for the camp. 7tb February.-Just as I arrived in camp last night I had a welcome waiting me in letters, and the Punches and other papers. I thank you immensely. The Punches are now being read by the sick soldiers in the hospital.

Arthur Dobson Frontier Light Horse

Letters from the The Sydney Morning Herald Tuesday 7th October 1879

Lieutenant-Colonel Buller, whose name must be familiar to all who have followed the events of the Zulu war, has with the kindest thoughtfulness written the following letter to one of Mr Dobson's family. Dating from the Flying Column, Zululand, June 15, 1879, he says:

A post has just come in bringing me your letter to your brother Arthur. I did not notice the subscription on the envelope till I had opened it. Having opened it, I glanced at it, and thought you would like to hear the particulars of your poor brother's death. At the end of March the Lieutenant-General Commanding, having to take in a large convoy to relieve the garrison of Ekowe in the South, ordered General Wood to make diversions in the North of the theatre of operations. General Wood accordingly decided to commence a series of offensive movements which culminated on the 28th March in an attack upon Zlobane Mount, a natural fortress of great strength about tewnty miles distant from our then camp.

The mounted men only were employed, and we assaulted the position at early dawn, carrying it brilliantly. Once on the top, we found that, difficult to get up, it was far more difficult to get down, and our descent was moreover rendered al the more difficult by the knowledge that a large zulu army was close at hand, marching to the assistance of those we had attacked. I covered the descent of the mountain with some of my best men, among them your brother. The Zulu closed in on our rear guard, and your brother was among those who fell, and is one of the many friends I lost on that day among those I regret most. He had just seven months with me. I never had occasion to speak anything but commendation to him. Brave, courteous, and obliging, he was a model volunteer, and I deeply sympathise with you in his loss. I am dear sir, yours faithfully, Red. Buller, Lieutenant-Colonel 60th Rifles.

We are also informed that a letter received from Lieutenant and Paymaster Hutton, of the Frontier Light Horse, says that Mr Dobson met his death by a gunshot wound and died instantaneously.

The Hobart Town Mercury of the 30th September 1879.

Frontier Light Horse

109	Darcey	J	1879 r	165	Geeve	C	1879 r	77	Hogan	T	1879 r

109 Darcey J 1879 r
See also D'Arcy Lydenburg Rifles.
291 Davidge R 1879 r
111 Deacon T 1879 r
412 De Gret J 1879
See also Bakers Horse.
96 De Million G 1877-8 r
371 Dennis J.H 1879 r
358 Denton J.F 1879 r
176 De Vere F 1879
Dixon A.C 1877-8-9
228 Dobson A.W KIA 1879
(see letters page 86)
224 Dobson T 1879
19 Dodds W.M 1877-8-9
83 Dodwell G KIA 1879
George T Dodwell died aged 20.
Pall Mall Gazette 26/4/1879
170 Dogherty G No clasp
38 Donovan M No clasp
80 Dowling H 1879 r
103 Dowse D No clasp
102 Dowse F.W 1879
395 Draycott T 1879
256 Drouey M 1879
105 Duffy E 1879
389 Duprez E.P 1879 r
283 Dyer J 1879
220 Earle G 1879 r
282 Eayres J 1879 r
135 Edwards F 1879
198 Elgenn W 1879
315 Elliott E 1879
243 English E 1879 r
4 Errington W 1877-8-9
342 Ewing E.W 1879 r
259 Feather J 1879 r
340 Feenstea A 1879 r
343 Filby M.B 1879 r
20 Fitzgerald J 1877-8-9 r
234 Fitzgerald T.C No clasp r
211 Flower P 1879
204 Flynn P 1879 r
346 Forrest J 1879 r
318 Foster F.J 1879 r
407 France J.E 1879
260 Fraser J 1879
150 Freeman C 1879 r
293 Freeman C 1879 r
Frieslaan A 1877-8-9
178 Frost T 1879
415 Gains J 1878 r
120 Gainsford R 1879
136 Gardiner G 1878?
No medal Deserted.
227 Gebser J KIA 1878-9

165 Geeve C 1879 r
George W 1878
242 Gibson A 1878? r
101 Gibson C 1879 r
313 Gitzman C 1879 r
392 Goodyer D 1879
247 Goodman W KIA 1879 r
Name on casualty roll 247 Gordon
302 Gordon H.P 1879
184 Gordon T 1879
379 Graham J 1879 r
Grant J.W 1877-8-9
163 Green W 1879
164 Green W.A 1879
177 Grills J KIA 1878-9 r
290 Grisseir A.G 1879
193 Grunder A No clasp
217 Grunderson M 1879 r
121 Gunn J 1879 r
122 Gunn P 1879
99 Gunn S 1877-8-9 r
Hahair P 1879
112 Halliday T KIA 1878-9?
134 Hallier G 1879
393 Halvey W.B 1879
Hambly R 1877-8-9
149 Hambly R 1879
402 Hanning C 1879 r
378 Hardie J 1879 r
138 Harding A 1879 r
140 Hardy R 1879 r
417 Harman E 1879 r
298 Harris T.R 1879 r
380 Harvey G 1879 r
Promoted to Native Corps officer
320 Haskins J 1879 r
24 Hassledine J KIA 1878-9?
356 Hay W 1879
408 Haynes E 1879
192 Haynes S.W 1879 r
385 Hebourne H 1879
156 Heck H 1879
200 Helwig H KIA 1878-9? r
301 Hennessey G 1879
Hennan A.I 1877-8-9
Hennan A.J 1878-9
349 Herbert F 1879
381 Herbet H 1879
382 Herne T 1879
84 Hesse L 1879
11 Hewitt C 1877-8-9
332 Higgins E KIA 1879 r
60 Hill H 1877-8-9 r
66 Hitge C.G 1879 r
329 Hoare J 1879
71 Hogan M 1877-8-9 r

77 Hogan T 1879 r
See also Transvaal Mounted Rifles.
7 Holdich L.M 1879 r
33 Holmes A 1877-8-9 r
113 Horn G KIA 1878-9? r
29 Horn W.A 1877-8-9 r
353 Howard B.C 1879
175 Howard J 1879
330 Howett A.C 1879
241 Hughes R.E 1878?
Hulley F.W 1877-8
Hulley J.E 1877-8
166 Humpage E.J 1879
Hunter R 1879 r
123 Huskisson G 1879
30 Ingles J 1877-8 r
323 Irvine D.R 1879
294 Jackson D.K 1879 r
286 Jackson E 1879 r
390 James W 1879 r
81 Jarvis M 1877-8-9 r
98 Jeffers M 1877-89-9
144 Jeskey J 1879
34 Jones H.R 1877-8-9
(Could be alias R. Gardiner)
348 Johnavon W.B 1879 r
387 Johnson H 1879 r
129 Johnson W No clasp
246 Johnson W.H 1879 r
405 Johnston J 1879
205 Jones Peter 1879
215 Jones R.B No clasp
No Medal Deserted.
262 Jostmyer M 1879 r
281 Kaimtze T 1879 r
206 Kearns M 1879
137 Keeley N 1879 r
155 Keeley P 1879 r
398 Keenan E 1879
107 Keblsey A 1879
263 Kennedy R 1879
Keough M 1879 r
87 Kerween J KIA 1878-9?
62 King W 1879 r
148 Kirby H.W 1879
339 Kirchner A 1879
264 Kruger J 1879 r
146 Lambert J No clasp r
231 Lavender J 1879
391 Legg W 1879 r
2 Leslie J 1877-8-9
237 Lethkey J 1879
41 Lewis S 1877-8-9
317 Livingstone W.H KIA 1879 r
223 Lloyd H 1879 r
126 Lloyd J.P 1877-8-9

Records indicate Leslie was wounded in action and was discharged in 1878. Clasp should be 1877-8

Frontier Light Horse

Frontier Light Horse
From the Roll Issued 14.7.81, Frontier Light Horse, List of Officers, Non-Commissioned Officers, and Men entitled to the Medal for military operations in South Africa during 1877-8-9.
*This roll has the following names which are not included in the Medal Roll located at the National Archives.
Captain D'Arcy, C. V.C Date of enrolment 20.12.77 entitlement the 1877-8-9 clasp
341 Corporal C.A Theis Date of enrolment 14.12.78 entitlement the 1879 clasp.
*23 **Trooper Robt. Brown** Date of enrolment 18.12.77 entitlement the 1877-8-9 clasp
*278 **Trooper T Brown** Date of enrolment 9.5.78 date of discharge 15.6.79 entitlement the 1879 clasp
*249 **Trooper C.S Christian** Date of enrolment 14.12.78 date of discharge 4.1.79 Recruit from Baker's Horse, Refused to serve.
*345 **Trooper J Cook** Date of enrolment 13.3.79 entitlement the 1879 clasp.
184 **Trooper J Graham** Date of enrolment 13.3.79 entitlement the 1879 clasp. (See 379 Graham J, different Reg No)
240 **Trooper C.S Shepherd** Date of enrolment 13.10.78 Promoted in other Corps.
152 **Trooper G Stamp** Date of enrolment 25.6.78 date of discharge 7.9.78 Deserter.
132 **Trooper O Stevanus** Date of enrolment 2.7.78 date of discharge 27.8.78, 1879 clasp. Discharged:Maritzburg afterwards N.L.H.
233 **Trooper W.D Vinnicombe** Date of enrolment 27.8.78 date of discharge 12.7.79,Promoted Lieut. N.N.C.
(DCM for Hlobane Mountain)
*222 **Trooper A Von Hagen** Date of enrolment 27.8.78 date of discharge 3.2.79, entitlement the 1879 clasp.
Note when a discharge date is not shown the individual was in the Corps till the end of August 1879.
Frontier Light Horse (1877-9). The regiment was raised within the Cape Colony, for service in the Ninth Cape Frontier War, a mounted unit raised by **Lieutenant Frederick Carrington** of the 2nd/24th Regiment at Kingwilliamstown, Eastern Cape Colony. It is often referred to as the Cape Frontier Light Horse. It was the only cavalry regiment raised by the Imperial Government during the Kaffir Wars.In April 1878 the command passed to Major Redvers Buller, 60th Rifles. At the time a British soldier received one shilling (5p) per day, a trooper in the Frontier Light Horse could expect to receive five shillings (25p) per day with no deductions. In July 1878 the unit of 276 officers and men marched from Kingwilliamstown to Pietermaritzburg and then to Sekhukhuneland for service there. During September and October, 1878 the Regiment saw service against Sekukuni, and in mid-December returned to Natal, to join Wood's No 4 Column. Its strength in the Zulu War was 216.
On the 20th January, Buller took a patrol of Frontier Light Horse and Piet Uys's Boers to try and dislodge the Zulus off a flat topped mountain called Zungwini, this act was to help safeguard his left flank. He was met by an attacking hoard of Zulus who swept down the mountain at speed, and he was nearly surrounded, which forced a hasty retreat. The following day another attempt was made with a much lager force including infantry, this succeeded, forcing the Zulus to abandon their livestock. The success was short lived when a large force of some 4000 plus men were seen drilling on the lower slope of an adjoining mountain. The following day Wood's force marched out of camp and moved swiftly on the Zulu positions, forcing the Zulus to withdraw onto Hlobane Mountain. In the early hours of the morning the column received the news of Isandlwana, and the loss of nearly a full battalion of British troops. Worried by events, Wood searched for a more secure position to form a camp, and on the 31st January moved to Khambula Hill a windswept ridge some fifteen miles from Fort Thinta. From his new base attacks were mounted on the enemy who retaliated by attacking white-owned farms.
On 28 March, 1879, the unit, which acted as a rearguard during the withdrawal from the Hlobane Mountain, lost almost 20% of the 156 of all ranks engaged. The Regiment's Commanding Officer in the column, **Captain Robert Barton** of the Coldstream Guards, was killed at Hlobane, and was succeeded by **Captain Cecil D'Arcy**.
The final battle of the campaign took place on 4 July 1879 and was the last major battle of the Anglo-Zulu War. The military power of the Zulu nation was destroyed the final act being the capture and razing of the capital of Zululand, the royal kraal of Ulundi.Two members of the Frontier Light Horse, **Captain D'Arcy** and **Sergeant Edmund O'Toole** were awarded the Victoria Cross for their acts of valor in endeavoring to save the lives of soldiers during the reconnaissance made before the Battle of Ulundi on 3 July, 1879.

(Various Obituaries from The Times)
Surgeon Paul Bennett Conolly , A.M.S Frontier Light Horse
This young medical officer was born June 28th, 1854.His first experience of war service was in the Russo-Turkish campaign at Bucharest...He was decorated by the King of Romania with the gold cross. He next volunteered for service at the Cape during the Zulu War, and was with Sir E.Woods at the engagements at Zlobani Hill, and the battles of Kambula and Ulundi, as Surgeon to the Frontier Light Horse. He was mentioned in despatches for his gallantry at Zlobani Hill, and at the end of the war received the medal and clasp. Served in the Boer War,and the Egyptian Campaign present at Kassassin and Tel-el-Kebir...Also the Relief Expedition to Gordon... Mr Conolly died, April 8th last, at Shabadood (Handak), on the Nile, of enteric fever.
Hon. Standis ; W.P.Verkker On the 22nd Jan, killed at the battle of Isandula, in Zululand. Lieutenant the Hon. Standis ; W.P.Verkker, Natal Contingent, and previously of the Frontier Light Horse, third son of Viscount Gort, aged 24.
Arthur Gibson, On the 22nd Jan. killed at the battle of Isandula, South Africa, Arthur Gibson, Lieutenant 3rd Natal Native Contingent, and previously of the Frontier Light Horse aged 22, third surviving son of John Gibson, Esq. 11 Westbourne Square,W.
Laurence Maydwell Holdich, July 30th of Typhoid fever, at Komgha, South Africa,Laurence Maydwell Holdich, Troop Sergeant - Major of the Frontier Light Horse, second son of Charles Walter and Eleanor A. Holdich, of Sleaford, Lincolnsire, aged 33 years.
Elliot Macnaghten On the 8th ultimo, killed in action, while in command of the Colonial Frontier Light Horse in the Caffre War, late Captain 20th Hussars, and fourth son of the late Francis Macnaghten, Esq. of the Bengal Civil Service.

Frontier Light Horse

COMMANDANT CECIL D'ARCY, FRONTIER LIGHT HORSE
Recently Awarded the Victoria Cross

COMMANDANT CECIL D'ARCY, V.C.,

Of Frontier Light Horse, is the youngest son of Major D'Arcy, late 18th Royal Irish, and Cape Mounted Rifles, and was born at Wanganni, New Zealand, in 1851. He held an appointment in the Civil Service, which he threw up on the outbreak of the Gaika and Galeka War, when he became a trooper in the Albany Mounted Volunteers. When they were disbanded he was made a Lieutenant in Carrington's, afterwards Buller's, Frontier Light Horse, in which he served all through the wars, taking part in every action in which his regiment was engaged in Zululand, and distinguishing himself by repeated acts of bravery, received the Victoria Cross for giving up his horse to a wounded trooper when hotly pursued by the enemy at Zhlobani Mountain, on the 28th March, while in the Flying Column, under Sir Evelyn Wood, V.C., K.C.B.—Our portrait is from a photograph by Carl Bluhm, King William's Town, Cape Colony.

OFFICERS KILLED IN THE TRANSVAAL.

Colonel Bonar Millett Deane, late of the 19th Foot, and deputy-adjutant and quartermaster-general at the Cape of Good Hope, who is reported as killed in the attack on Lang's Neck Pass, in the Transvaal, was in command of the advance column of Sir George Colley's force, consisting of the 3rd Battalion 60th Rifles and two companies of the 58th Foot, having gone up to Natal on hearing of the outbreak in the Transvaal. Born in 1834, he was gazetted an ensign in the 94th Foot, by purchase, in 1853, but three days afterwards was transferred to the 22nd Foot, then serving in India. He became lieutenant in the 22nd, by purchase, in 1855, and was adjutant to that corps from 1856 till his promotion to the rank of captain, also by purchase, in 1857. The 22nd Regiment returned from India in 1855, and embarked for Malta in 1860. Colonel Deane became major of the 22nd, by purchase, in 1863, but was transferred to the 18th (Royal Irish) in 1864, and to the 19th Foot in 1865. He next served on the Indian staff as assistant quartermaster general at headquarters, Madras, from 1866 to 1871, and received the brevet rank of lieutenant-colonel in 1873. From 1872 till 1875 he was military secretary to Sir Philip Wodehouse, Governor of Bombay, and rejoined his regiment, the 19th Foot, on relinquishing that appointment, as regimental lieutenant-colonel, to which rank he was gazetted in 1875. He continued in command of the 1st Battalion of the 19th at Aldershot and other home stations, until placed on half-pay in 1879, having just before attained the brevet rank of colonel. In the same year he was appointed extra inspector under the Local Government Board in Ireland during the distress of last winter. This post he resigned in order to undertake the duties of deputy-adjutant and quartermaster-general at the Cape of Good Hope in 1880, and he has now fallen in the first action in which he was ever engaged.

Brevet-Major Joseph Ruscombe Poole, also reported as killed, was born in 1843, and educated at the Royal Military Academy. He received his commission in the Royal Artillery in 1861, and was promoted to a captaincy in 1875. He served as brigade-major to Colonel Reilly, R.A., C.B., who commanded the artillery during the Zulu war, and received in July, 1880, a brevet majority. Major Poole was given the charge of King Cetewayo during the period of his captivity, and lived with him at the castle at Cape Town. It is said that Major Poole acquired great influence with Cetewayo, who petitioned when Major Poole was removed from him that he should be permitted to remain.

Lieutenant Edward Inman, 60th Rifles, who is among the killed, was born in 1852. He entered the army as a private soldier in a cavalry regiment, but was discharged as being under age. He again enlisted, and worked his way up to the position of troop sergeant-major. After six years' service in the ranks he received an officer's commission in the 10th Hussars. Having remained in his regiment for some time, he effected an exchange with Lord Alwyne Compton, of the Grenadier Guards. Last year he exchanged again with Lieutenant Archer Crawley, of the 60th Rifles, and it was while serving with his new regiment in the capacity, it is said, of acting adjutant, that he lost his life.

Lieutenant Robert Hamond Elwes was a son of Mr. Robert Elwes, of Congham Hall, King's Lynn, Norfolk. He was born in 1856, was educated at Eton, and entered the 3rd battalion of the Grenadier Guards in 1877. He went out to Natal last year as aide-de-camp to Sir George Pomeroy Colley.

Commandant d'Arcy, who, according to a recent telegram from our Durban correspondent, was shot in one of the patrols from Pretoria, entered the service during the war in the old colony as an officer in Colonel Buller's Frontier Light Horse. He received the command of this corps when the irregular mounted men were formed into a brigade under Colonel Buller in Sir Evelyn Wood's flying column during the Zulu campaign. It will be remembered that it was for saving Captain d'Arcy's life during the retreat from the Hlobane Mountain that Colonel Buller received the Victoria Cross. Captain d'Arcy received that decoration for "his gallant conduct on the 3rd of July, 1879, during the reconnoissance made before Ulundi by the mounted corps in endeavouring to rescue Trooper Raubenheim, of the Frontier Light Horse, who fell from his horse as the troop were retiring. Captain d'Arcy, though the Zulus were close upon them, waited for the man to mount behind him. The horse kicked them both off, and, though much hurt by the fall and quite alone, Captain d'Arcy coolly endeavoured to lift the trooper, who was stunned, on to the horse, and it was only when he found that he had not strength to do so that he mounted and rode off. His escape was miraculous, as the Zulus had actually closed upon him." Colonel Buller, in his despatch after the battle of Ulundi, speaks thus of him:—"Commandant d'Arcy, Frontier Light Horse, reckons neither personal inconvenience nor danger in the execution of any order. He is determined and bold, and has frequently shown great personal gallantry, always showing a fine example to his men." Commandant d'Arcy received the Victoria Cross from the hands of Sir Garnet Wolseley at Pretoria at the time of the Secocoeni war.

Commandant Cecil D'Arcy, VC from The Graphic, Saturday, December 27, 1879; Issue 526.

Officers Killed in the Transvaal from Reynolds's Newspaper, Sunday, February 6, 1881; Issue 1591.

Frontier Light Horse

	Lloyd	G		1879 r
	Lund	A		1877-8
295	**Lyndon (Lynden)**	**C**	**KIA**	**1879 r**
188	Mahon	M		1879
139	Marks	H		1879
265	Martin	C		1879 r
216	Mason	H		1879

See also Natal Light Horse.

	Matthews	H		1877-8
266	**May**	**J**	**KIA**	**1879**
364	Mc Intyre	R		1879 r
202	McKay	L		1879
31	Mc Minn	J		No clasp

No medal Deserted.

312	**Merk**	**C**	**KIA**	**1879 r**
326	Meyer	C		1879 r
309	Meyer	M		1879 r
327	Meyer	T		1879 r
212	Michael	P		1879 r
357	Miller	J.B		1879
351	Mills	J.E		1879
226	Moffit	H		1878?

No medal Deserted.

213	Molineux	G		1878?

No medal Deserted.

218	Moran	P		1879
	Moriarty	J		1877-8 r
419	Mortlock	J		1879
274	Mossop	G		1879
151	Muller	C		1879 r
	Mulroy	T		1877-8
267	Murdoch	W		1879

Returned 1887 but reissued 8/9/1936.

44	Murray Fraser	J		1877-8-9
	Myers	J		1879
268	Mynott	W		1879 r
372	Nelson	H.J		1879
404	Nelson	M		1879
245	Newnhan	C.O.T		1879 r

See also Border Horse.

89	Niestrom	O		1879 r
409	Nightingale	C.A		1879 r
	Ninnemann	A		1877-
183	Nitch	A		1879 r
355	Nixon	C		1879
161	Norton	E.B		1879 r
48	Oalfken	A		1877-8-9
230	O'Connor	J		1879 r
128	Ohlsen	C		1878? r

Deserted.

127	Ohlsen	J		1877 8 9
359	Olivier	R		1879
	O'Neil	J		1878
147	O'Reilly	J		1879 r

See also Border Horse.

365	Paddock	R		1879
383	Paddock	T		1879
74	Parker	F		1877-8 r

130	Patterson	J		No clasp
168	Patterson	W		1879
369	**Patterson**	**G**		**1879**

KIA day before Ulundi.
On Casualty roll 369 Pearce G
KIA near Ulundi 3/7/1879

108	Pearn	W		No clasp
97	Parkins	C		1877-8-9 r
360	Perkins	C.J		1879 r
187	Peterson	F		1879
115	Peterson	T.H (T.N)		1879

Dangerously wounded at Kambula

116	Phillips	G		1879
145	Philpott	H		1879
	Pietersen	F		1878-9
57	**Plante**	**H**	**KIA**	**1878?**
92	Porter	D		1877-8-9
160	Potgister	J		1879 r
354	Potter	J		1879
131	Pound	H		1879 r
296	**Prendergast**	**M**	**KIA**	**1879**
	Pruen	W.B		1879
335	Pugh	W		1879
	Quick	W		1879
235	Raphfeldt	R		1879
269	Randall	J		1879

Wounded at Yungin's Nek 20/1/1879

374	Randall	W		1879
394	Ratwsch	A		1879 r
171	Rennaichs	A		No clasp
10	Richards	H.A		1877-8-9 r
208	Ricks	A		1879
72	Roberts	J		1877-8-9
117	Roberts	T		No clasp
276	Robertson	H		1879 r
320	**Robson**	**D.A**		**No clasp**

KIA Inhlobane.

278	**Rogan**	**W.A**	**KIA**	**1879 r**

Reg. Number on C Roll 248

	Rosher	C.H		1877-8
46	Ross	F		1877-8-9
219	Rosser	A		1879 r
400	Rothwell	J		1879 r
375	**Roubenhamer**	**J.A**		**1879 r**

KIA the day before Ulundi.

16	**Runciman**	**H**	**KIA**	**1879**
100	Rutherford	T		1877-8-9 r
68	Sagaar	T		No clasp
316	Saloman	G		1879
411	Salter	H		1879

See also Bakers Horse.

334	Samson	M		1879 r
63	Saunders	H.W		No clasp
50	Schaper	A		1877-8-9
311	**Schermel**	**A**	**KIA**	**1879 r**
388	Schmidt	G		1879 r
314	Schoff	W		1879 r
154	Searle	T		1879 r

279	Saymour	G	KIA	1879
214	Shearer	L	KIA	1879 r
88	Shemble	A		1877-8-9 r

See also Natal Light Horse.

240	Shepherd	C.S		No clasp
158	Skinner	H		1879
410	Skinner	H.J		1878-9
182	Skinner	J		1879 r
201	Skinner	W		1879
324	Smith	A		1879
141	Smith	C.J		No clasp

No medal Deserted.

289	Smith	H		1879 r

Wounded at Izedingi 11/4/1878

413	Smith	H		1879 r
40	Smith	J		1877-8-9 r
90	Smith	H.F		No clasp

No Medal Deserted.

210	Smith	J.R		1879 r
277	Smith	T		1879 r
285	Snoore	K		1879 r
152	Stamp	G		No clasp

No medal Deserted.

132	Stevanus	O		1879
350	Stevenson	S.W		1879
325	**Stewart**	**A.L**		**1879 r**

KIA Inhlobane. See also
Sgt. A. Stewart Border Horse.

319	Stewart	E		1879 r
	Stewart	W		1879 r
270	Stirling	A		1879 r

Wounded at Isihlingo 5/61879

376	Stoke	R		1879
337	Stone	R		1879 r
37	Stopford	T.A.B		1877-8-9

Wounded in shoulder and jaw fractured, at Kambula

397	Stratton	R		1879 r
125	Sullivan	P		1879
196	Taylor	W		1879 r
133	Temple	J.A		1879 r
410	Thied	J		1879 r
76	Thomas	J		1877-8-9
162	Thoroughgood	C		1879
232	Tinling	J		1879
236	**Tirrill**	**W**	**KIA**	**1879 r**
67	Tolmy	T		1877-8-9
403	Tracy	J		1879 r

Wounded at White Umyolosi 3/7/1879

153	Trusler	H		1879
169	Turner	E		1879 r
143	Turner	F		1879
167	Van der Riet	A.D		1879
336	V Brandis	A		1879 r

See also Lydenburg Rifles.

Frontier Light Horse

# 239 Vereker S KIA 1878	LIEUTENANT			Bloomer	W.E	1877-8-9
See also Lt. The Hon S.W. Vereker	Boys	G	1877-8 r	Blumrick	C	1877-8
Natal Native Contingent. 2nd Btn.	Davis	R.P Beverley	1877-8-9 r	Bodley	C	1877-8
233 Vinnicombe W.D DCM 1879	Keightley	F.W	1877-8 r	Bodley	W	1877-8
See also Natal Native Contingent.	Margary	A.F	1877-8	Bolton	G	1877-8 r
42 Visser J 1877-8-9 r	Welby	R.E	1877-8 r	Boyle	F	1877-8 r
152 Vogel F 1879	Wescomb	W	1877-8-9	Bradshaw	H	1877-8 r
Von Der Decker T 1878-9	Williams	T	1877-8	Brebner	W	1877-8
45 Von Honitzsky L.B 1877-8-9 r	SERGEANT MAJOR			Brittain	H	1877-8 r
79 V Schmidt C 1877-8-9 r	Booty	W.F.S	1877-8-9	Broedelett Jnr	O.C	1877-8 r
338 V Vliet J 1879	TROOP SERGEANT MAJOR			Brown	A	1877-8 r
179 Wagenar C.H 1879	Fordham	F	1877-8 r	**Brown**	**F.L**	**KIA 1877-8 r**
292 Walsh P 1879	Hicken	C.T	1877-8	Bunday	W	1877-8
225 Wanklin W No clasp	**Nagle (Hagle) P KIA 1877-8-9 r**			Burbrow	J.F	1877-8
No Medal Deserted.	Strathearn	G	1877-8	Burke	J.B	1877-8
43 Warne (Lane?) F 1879	See also East London Engineers.			Burke	W.H	1877-8
299 Watts G 1879	Zeitzman	W	1877-8-9	Burt	E	1877-8
271 Webb P 1879 r	QUARTERMASTER SERGEANT			Callaghan	C.J	1877-8 r
272 Webb V 1879	Crutchley	C.E	1877-8 r	Cameron	C	1877-8
322 Weber A 1879	HOSPITAL SERGEANT			Campbell	C.J	1877-8-9
51 Welsh G 1879 r	Roberts	O.E	1877-8 r	Campbell	S.C	1877-8 r
86 Welsh T 1877-8-9 r	SERGEANT			Caughlin	C	1877-8-9
414 Westley A 1879	Daniel Jnr	N.G	1877-8	Cavanagh	A	1877-8
See also Bakers Horse.	Dowling	S.B	1877-8	Chandler	C	1877-8
Whelan W.H 1877-8	Fawcett	W	1877-8-9	Cockles	R	1877-8 r
58 Whitcombe C 1879	Lewis	J	1877-8	Cole	J	1877-8 r
194 White J.W 1877-8	Lobley	C.H	1877-8 r	Collins	S	1877-8 r
209 Whitecross A 1879	Madgwick	A	1877-8	Colombel	A	1877-8-9
273 Williams G KIA 1879	Petrie	A	1877-8-9 r	Cook	J	1877-8
Note on Roll "Captain in W.Y.M."	CORPORAL			Corlees	R.H	1877-8 r
384 Williams J.H 1879 r	Craigie	H.W	1877-8	Cornhill	W	1877-8
65 Wilson D 1879 r	Hayes	R	1877-8 r	Corsterton	C.E	1877-8 r
32 Wilson T No clasp	Head	P	1877-8 r	Cowen	P	1877-8
No Medal Deserted.	**Hunder S.R KIA 1877-8-9 r**			Daly	J	1877-8
373 Woodford G 1879	Lewis	J	1877-8	Daniel	B	1877-8
No Medal Deserted.	Moore	J	1877-8	Daniel	Charles	1877-8 r
186 Woodgate C.W 1879	Nunan	J	1877-8	Daniell	C	1877-8
195 Woolf M No clasp	Peirson	J	1877-8 r	Daniel	J.T	1877-8
RANK NOT KNOWN	Seymour	H	1877-8	Daniel	W.H	1877-8
Boyce W.G 1879	Taplin	E	1877-8 r	De Goede	J	1877-8 r
Harris A.E 1879	Taylor	W	1877-8	Deklerk	B	1877-8 r
Mumford W.H.T 1879	Warden	G	1877-8	Dennis	W	1877-8 r
Pillans C.E 1878	PRIVATE			Denny	E	1877-8
	Allen	J	1877-8	Dickerson	D	1877-8 r
FRONTIER MOUNTED RIFLEMEN.	Duplicate Medal and Clasp			**Doherty J KIA 1877-8-9 r**		
Also known as "Brabant's Horse"	issued 9/9/1917.			Dorehill	V	1877-8
FIELD COMMANDANT	Allen	W	1877-8 r	Draycote	T	1877-8
Brabant E.Y 1877-8-9	Anstiss	W	1877-8 r	Duffy	M	1877-8
MAJOR	Artz	M	1877-8 r	Duprez	J	1877-8 r
Currie C 1877-8 r	Balmour	T	1877-8-9	Duprez	James	1877-8 r
CAPTAIN	Bayham	W	1877-8 r	Duprez	John	1877-8 r
Dalgety E.H 1877-8-9	Berrier	F	1877-8	Duprez	S	1877-8
Macintosh A.F 1877-8 r	Bester	I	1877-8	Ebbe	J	1877-8 r
Sprigg H 1877-8-9	Bester	J.P	1877-8 r	Edwards	W	1877-8 r

The Honourable Standish William Prendergast Vereker was born on 23 February 1854 the third son of Lord Gort. In 1878 he enlisted as a trooper in the Frontier Light Horse for the campaign against the Sekukuni. Commandant Lonsdale offered him a commission in the 2nd Batn NNC for the Zulu Campaign. He died on 22 January 1879 age 24 at Zululand, killed in action. His body was discovered among the heap of men who died with Durnford. See Page 81

Frontier Mounted Riflemen

Egan	A	1877-8 r	Keenan	E	1877-8	Nielson	J	1877-8 r
Eld	P	1877-8 r	Kerr	W	1877-8 r	Nielson	N	1877-8 r
Ellis	W	1877-8	Kesler	P	1877-8-9	Ochllssen	O	1877-8-9
Els	C.A	1877-8 r	Kidean	J	1877-8 r	O'Keiffe	D	1877-8
Els	J.C	1877-8 r	Korumann	B	1877-8 r	Page	P	1877-8 r
Els	N.G	1877-8 r	Krohn	A.F	1877-8	Paulsen	W	1877-8 r
Engelbrecht	A.F	1877-8 r	Lambert	W	1877-8	Pearson	W	1877-8 r
Everitt	A.A	1877-8 r	Lambert	W.C	1877-8 r	Petersen	C.E	1877-8-9
Fergus	D	1877-8	Larsen	A	1877-8 r	Phillips	E.G	1877-8
Fincher	F	1877-8	Lavid	D	1877-8	Pierson	J	1878 r
Fisher	J	1877-8	Lawrence	M	1877-8 r	Pitt	J	1877-8
Freeguard	J	1877-8 r	Lefevre	F	1877-8 r	Pitt	J.R	1877-8 r
Freeman	T	1877-8 r	Leharpe	B	1877-8 r	Pohl	J	1877-8
Freeman	W	1877-8 r	Letocq	N	1877-8 r	Pollock	M.B	1877-8 r
Garde	J.W	1877-8 r	Leonard	E.H	1877-8	Quinton	H	1877-8 r
Garratt	C	1877-8 r	Lewis	?	1877-8 r	Ramsay	D	1877-8
Gibson	E	1877-8 r	Lewis	A	1877-8 r	Ramsay	W	1877-8
Gilbert	T	1877-8	Lind	W	1877-8	Rieter	J	1877-8 r
Gilbert	W	1877-8	Locke	D	1877-8 r	Ring	C	1877-8 r
Gilmour	J	1877-8-9 r	Locke	W	1877-8 r	Roberts	T	1877-8 r
Goldschmidt	J	1877-8 r	Lockier	T	1877-8 r	Robertson G (G.C)		1877-8
Gooch	A	1877-8 r	Louis			Robertson	R.J	1877-8
Graham	J	1877-8	(Known as French Louis)		1877-8 r	Robinson	C	1877-8 r
Grant	A	1877-8 r	Maher	J	1877-8	Rochussen	J.R	1877-8
Green	C	1877-8 r	Main	A	1877-8	Rodgers	H	1877-8
Greyling	C.J	1877-8 r	Marais	C	1877-8	Rushton	D	1877-8 r
Grootjohn	A	1877-8 r	Marais	D.P	1877-8 r	Saymann	J	1877-8-9 r
Hambly	F	1877-8-9	Marais	G	1877-8-9 r	Scammel	C	1877-8-9 r
Hamilton	John	1877-8	Marais	I	1877-8-9 r	Searle	N	1877-8 r
Hamilton	J	1877-8 r	Marais	J	1877-8 r	Sellers	J	1877-8
Hanson	C	1877-8 r	Marcussen	R	1877-8	Seymour	H	1877-8
Harrington	J	1877-8 r	Masters	J.A	1877-8 r	Sheean	M	1877-8 r
Harrington	J.P	1877-8 r	Maxwell	J	1877-8 r	Smith	E	1877-8-9 r
Harrison	J	1877-8 r	Mc Arthur	C	1877-8	Smith	J	1877-8 r
Hearn	T	1877-8 r	Mc Bride	D	1877-8 r	Snyman	D	1877-8
Heathcote	T.M	1877-8 r	Mc Dermott	C	1877-8	Snyman	J	1877-8 r
Heller	A	1877-8 r	Mc Donald	G	1877-8	Soffe	W	1877-8
Henning	J	1877-8 r	Mc Grath	J	1877-8	Medal has 1879 clasp - Lot 85		
Hickman	R	1877-8-9	Mc Gregor	J	1877-8 r	Spinks Auction 5.12.2002		
Hines	J	1877-8	Mc Ilvride	W	1877-8	Spiller	H	1877-8
Hood	D	1877-8	Mc Kenna	W	1877-8 r	Sprenger	C	1877-8 r
Howen	F	1877-8 r	Mc Lachlan	A	1877-8 r	Stalzmann	F	1877-8 r
Hudson	C.D	1877-8 r	Mc Morland	H	1877-8	Starcke	A	1877-8 r
Hullcy	T	1877 8 9	Mc Morland	H.G	1877 8	Starcy	L.B	1877 8
Hunter	W	1877-8	Merk	C	1877-8 r	Steward	D	1877-8 r
Hutton	W	1877-8	Middlebrook	T	1877-8 r	Stokes	C	1877-8 r
Jackson	C	1877-8	Miller	J.A	1877-8 r	Strathearn	G	1878
Jacoby	H	1877-8-9	Mills	G	1877-8 r	See also East London Engineers.		
James	J	1877-8	Mitchell	W	1877-8	Stuart	J	1877-8 r
Jamieson	J	1877-8 r	Moore	H	1877-8 r	**Sturk**	**H**	**KIA 1877-8-9 r**
Jansen	C	1877-8 r	Morgan	T	1877-8	Sullivan	J	1877-8 r
Jarvis	J	1877-8 r	Moyle	H	1877-8 r	Swann	S	1877-8 r
Johansen	P	1877-8 r	Nell	D.B	1877-8	Tamblyn	E	1877-8 r
Johnson	A	1877-8 r	Nell	M.J	1877-8	Thacker	J	1877-8
Jones	H.S	1877-8	Nell	P.J	1877-8	Thomas	C	1877-8 r
Jones	R	1877-8 r	Nelson	J	1877-8 r	Thompson	G	1877-8 r
Jones	W	1877-8 r	Nicholsen	A	1877-8-9	Tolney	B	1877-8 r
Kays	M	1877-8 r	Nieman	P	1877-8 r	Tonzean	B	1877-8 r

Frontier Mounted Riflemen

Toomey	**B**	**KIA**	**1877-8 r**
Tracey	J		1877-8 r
Troye	E.A		1877-8
Tutton	H		1877-8
Valentine	W		1877-8 r
Van Dyk	J		1877-8
Van Rooyen	D.B		1877-8
Van Rooyen	L		1877-8 r
Van Zanteen	T		1877-8
Vietz	J		1877-8
Waddell	J		1877-8 r
Wagner	F		1877-8 r
Wagner	J		1877-8
Wagner	W		1877-8
Walker	F.J.F		1877-8 r
Webstock	B		1877-8
West	A		1877-8
Wieland	W		1877-8 r
Wilkie	A		1877-8 r

See also Kaffrarian Rang.

Williams	J	1877-8
Wilson	J.G	1877-8 r
Zeller	H	1877-8
Zeller	J	1877-8 r

NO RANK SHOWN

Robertson	G.C	1877-8

FROSTS FINGO LEVY
NO RANK SHOWN

White	D	1878-9

GEORGE MOUNTED VOLUNTEERS.
LIEUTENANT

Andrews	J.H	1878
Goldsbury	S	1878

SERGEANT

May	J	1878

PRIVATE

Barker	J	1878 r
Barker	T	1878 r
De Swart	B	1878 r
Ferreira	T.S	1878 r
Green	R	1878
Heine	D	1878
Herman	P	1878 r
Holskampf	C	1878
Jonck	C	1878 r
Marais	G.T	1878 r
Marais	P.W	1878 r
Mc Carthy	C	1878 r
Melville	J.G	1878 r
Meyer	M.D	1878 r
Moore	L	1878
Muller	C	1878 r
Neville	R.F	1878 r
Pedro	J	1878 r
Rensburg	F	1878 r
Russel	W	1878
Style	C	1878 r
Turner	W	1878
Van Schalkwyk	H.S	1878 r
Wass	F	1878

GERMAN BUGHER CONTINGENT.
HORSE.
CAPTAIN

Gerardy	L	1877-8

LIEUTENANT

Kramer	P.C.C	1877-8
Schmidt	A	1877-8

QUARTERMASTER SERGEANT

Rusterberg	T	1877-8

SERGEANT

Brown	J.H	1877-8 r
Scherer	A	1877-8

CORPORAL

Bahlmann	F	1877-8
Lohane	J	1877-8

PRIVATE

Albrecht	F	1877-8
Andrieka	C	1877-8
Andrieka	Z	1877-8
Bartel	A	1877-8
Bartel	J	1877-8
Bartell	N	1877-8
Binie	H	1877-8
Buske	W	1877-8
Busse	W	1877-8
Fick	F	1877-8
Fick	N	1877-8
Fietze	C	1877-8 r
Fietze	L	1877-8
Hempel	F	1877-8
Hofert	F	1877-8 r
Lehmann	Y	1877-8
Luck	A	1877-8
Mauer	A	1877-8
Meinke	C	1877-8
Pantz	H	1877-8
Pentz	C	1877-8 r
Rehfeldt	G	1877-8
Richter	F	1877-8
Schmidt	H	1877-8
Schmidt	L	1877-8 r
Schmidt	R	1877-8 r
Schroder	W	1877-8
Sergel	H	1877-8
Warnicke	H	1877-8
Wegener	J	1877-8
Wiegmann	A	1877-8 r
Zerbe	E	1877-8

GERMAN BURGHER CORPS.
FOOT
LIEUTENANT

Van Riebeck	H	1877-8 r

CORPORAL

Krantz	C	1877-8
Rau	F	1877-8

PRIVATE

Bahlmann	C	1877-8
Bischoff	C	1877-8
Duiterhoft	C	1877-8
Durow	C	1877-8
Hempel	D	1877-8
Hoffart	W	1877-8 r
Homann	F	1877-8
Kock	J	1877-8
Kock	W	1877-8
Korte	G	1877-8
Krause	C.F	1877-8 r
Kretschmer	G	1877-8
Kretschmer	W	1877-8
Kruhse	F	1877-8 r
Leilach	J	1877-8
Luck	H	1877-8
Luck	W	1877-8
Mauer	C	1877-8
Peter	W	1877-8 r
Purchert	F	1877-8 r
Scherer	L	1877-8
Schultz	W	1877-8
Sergel	A	1877-8
Sergel	G	1877-8
Thiele	W	1877-8
Volker	H	1877-8 r
Warnecke	G	1877-8 r
Wietzke	J	1877-8 r
Wittstock	C	1877-8
Wittstock	F	1877-8 r

GERMAN CAPE RIFLES.
NO RANK SHOWN

Neiss	P	1878
Neiss	W	1878

GERMAN VOLUNTEER RIFLE CORPS AND BURGHER CONTINGENT.
CAPTAIN

Fiseher	C	1877-8

LIEUTENANT

Dreyfus	T	1877-8

SERGEANT MAJOR

Rinderle	C	1877-8 r

SERGEANT

Deneke	F	1877-8 r
Lorenz	C	1877-8

CORPORAL

Fischer	H	1877-8
Harmuth	G	1877-8
Keil	F	1877-8
Nleier	W	1877-8 r

BUGLER

Dix	O	1877-8 r

THE PICTORIAL WORLD

AN ILLUSTRATED WEEKLY NEWSPAPER

NEW SERIES—PRICE TWOPENCE.

No. 275. Vol. XI. (No. 49, New Series)　　SATURDAY, JUNE 7th, 1879.　　[Registered at the General Post Office as a Newspaper.]　　TWOPENCE. Per Post, 2½d.

THE ZULU WAR: GRAHAM'S TOWN 1st YEOMANRY LEAVING FOR KING WILLIAM TOWN.
1. A lift on a Material Train.　　2. The Assembly.　　3. On the way to the Border: Horses on the Road.　　4. Captain's Baggage Saddle and Bags.

German Volunteer Rifle Corps

PRIVATE
Andre	C	1877-8
Andreka	J	1877-8 r
Arnhold	A	1877-8 r
Becker	F	1877-8 r
Behrendt	F	1877-8
Bertram	E	1877-8 r
Birkholtz	A	1877-8 r
Birkholtz	F	1877-8 r
Birkholtz	W	1877-8 r
Bode	T	1877-8 r
Boy	A	1877-8 r
Boegenhold	F	1877-8 r
Butt	F	1877-8 r
Braun	C	1877-8 r
Buschmann	A	1877-8 r
Buerger	C	1877-8 r
David	G	1877-8
Dengler	W	1877-8 r
Deutschmann	A	1877-8
Deutschmann	E	1877-8
Dix	R	1877-8
Duerheim	C	1877-8
Franz	C	1877-8 r
Goldschmidt	J	1877-8 r
Grunow	R	1877-8
Hortkopf	H	1877-8 r
Heese	J	1877-8 r
Henning	Jacob	1877-8 r
Henning	Johan	1877-8 r
Hiebert	C	1877-8 r
Igelhoff	F	1877-8
Illenfeld	J	1877-8 r
Jahns	W	1877-8 r
Klee	A	1877-8 r
Keth	J	1877-8
Ketterer	B	1877-8
Kuchardt	W	1877-8
Luck	A	1877-8 r
Ninow	A	1877-8
Ninow	G	1877-8
Nlauer	G	1877-8 r
Nlatz	C	1877-8 r
Nloenning	H	1877-8 r
Nloltenhauer	W	1877-8 r
Pape	A	1877-8
Pape	W	1877-8
Pahl	A	1877-8 r
Peinke	M	1877-8
Peinke	W	1877-8
Pfitzer	C	1877-8 r
Rahn	J	1877-8
Reimers	C	1877-8 r
Roetinger	T	1877-8
Salzmedel	G	1877-8
Schaffner	J	1877-8 r
Schenk	W	1877-8 r
Scherer	T	1877-8 r
Schmidt	H	1877-8 r
Schroeder	F.W	1877-8
Schultz	H	1877-8 r
Schwarts	A	1877-8 r
Sell	J	1877-8 r
Sell	W	1877-8 r
Sergel	A	1877-8 r
Sprenger	A	1877-8
Thiel	W	1877-8 r
Volb	J	1877-8
Warkus	E	1877-8 r
Wolf	R	1877-8

GONOBIE VOLUNTEERS
NO RANK SHOWN
Bennett	G.L	1877

GRAAFF REINET VOLUNTEERS.
LIEUTENANT
Van Coller	J	1878

SERGEANT
De Grandhome	H	1878

PRIVATE
Basson	A	1878
Biroskie	P	1878
Brooks	J	1878 r
Cook	R.T	1878
Coon	T	1878
De Graff	C	1878
Duran	C	1878
Faircloth	J	1878 r
Greef	F	1878 r
Herelinger	W	1878 r
Herelinger Jnr	W	1878 r
Japp	J	1878 r
Kokemoer	J	1878
Liemann	P	1878 r
Libersensie	A	1878 r
Lottering	C	1878 r
Lottering	P	1878
Mc Casker	C	1878
Minnie	J	1878 r
O'Reilly	M	1878
Ryan	W	1878 r
Smith	T	1878
Wagner	A	1878
Wood	M	1878 r

NO RANK SHOWN
Bland	W.C	1877

GRAHAMSTOWN VOLUNTEER HORSE ARTILLERY.

On 22nd January, 1879, Lieutenant Nelson, Sergeant Greenlees, 16 gunners and three drivers left for service in the Northern Border War. In February, 1879, Lieutenant Norton resigned. Strength for that month was three officers and 55 men. Lieutenant Wells resigned in October, 1879. In December, a further officer appears in the returns - Lieutenant Charles Frederick Seigert, commissioned on 29th September, 1879.

CAPTAIN
Nelson	A.E	1879

LIEUTENANT ADJUTANT
Wells	W.H	1877-8

Wells, William Harrison commissioned on 5th December, 1876

SERGEANT MAJOR
Greenless	J.S	1877-8

QUARTERMASTER SERGEANT
Pryce	T.L	1878

SERGEANT
Easton	T.J	1879
Fraser	R.R	1877-8
Fraser	R.R	1877

See also Pte R.R. Fraser below.

CORPORAL
Marden	J	1877-8-9

BOMBARDIER
Hornabrook	G.E	1877-8
Jamieson	J	1879
Smith	S	1877-8-9

GUNNER
Allison	J	1878-9
Anderson	J.L	1877-8
Dezech	A	1879
Emms	W	1879
Erskine	J	1878-9
Hawkins	J	1878-9
Higgins	F	1879
Jamieson	A	1877-8
Mitten	C	1879
Mullholland	D	1877-8-9
Passmore	T	1878-9
Pitt	J	1877-8-9
Scott	F	1877-8-9
Tomlinson	G	1877-8

DRIVER
Hamilton	R	1877-8

PRIVATE
Fraser	R.R	1877

See Sgt. R.R. Fraser above.

TRUMPETER
Gibson	J	1877-8

GRAHAMSTOWN VOLUNTEER RIFLE CORPS.
CAPTAIN
Eddie	C.N de R	1877-8

See also Upingtons Foot.

LIEUTENANT
Eddie	L.A	1877-8

DRUM MAJOR
579 Mc Cabe	J	1877-8

Grahamstown Volunteer Rifle Corps

QUARTERMASTER SERGEANT			507	Helwig H	1877-8 r	**SERGEANT**		
19	Quirk D	1877-8 r	515	Hemming J.W	1877-8 r	Barker	W	1878
BAND SERGEANT			504	Hill W	1877-8	Buckley	R	1878
234	Ryan J	1877-8	516	Hinton W	1877-8	Brooks	R.H	1878
SERGEANT				Hinton W.H	1877-8	Heugh	P	1878
650	Barnett A	1877-8	514	Hunt T	1877-8 r	Igdebski	W.M	1878
	Barnett W	1877-8	508	Hynes P	1877-8 r	Morris	W.C	1878
222	Fielding W	1877-8	175	Janson W	1877-8	Thomson	W	1878
256	Godfrey H	1877-8	176	Jeffries J	1877-8	**ACTING SERGEANT**		
	Mulligan W	1877-8 r		Kating W	1877-8 r	Cook	J	1878 r
	Parsons W	1877-8		Keefe S	1877-8 r	Foster	G	1878 r
20	Quirk J	1877-8	254	Keer R	1877-8	Hill	J	1878
BUGLE CORPORAL			256	Kirk C	1877-8 r	Idensohn	P	1878 r
	Daniells O	1877-8 r	255	Kirwan M	1877-8	Kealey	J	1878
CORPORAL			222	Langley A	1877-8	Martin	G	1878
	Burke T	1877-8		Langley C	1877-8	Osselair	F	1878
527	Cairns J	1877-8		Langley H	1877-8	Polley	A.J	1878
	Hinton W.H	1877-8	221	Limskey M	1877-8	Slade	C	1878 r
	Hunt T	1877-8	584	Maher J	1877-8	**PRIVATE**		
	Jacques W	1877-8	588	Maynes P	1877-8 r	Allard	C	1878
174	Jonson B	1877-8	586	Maynes W	1877-8 r	Antomassive	A	1878
21	Quick D	1877-8		Mc Carthy D	1877-8	Beaufoys	L	1878 r
BUGLER			585	Mc Dermot P	1877-8	Brown	I.C	1878
	Brick W	1877-8	577	Mc Donald F	1877-8	Buckingham	J	1878
	Hill C	1877-8	576	Mc Donald H	1877-8	Clacey	C	1878
PRIVATE			580	Mc Kay E	1877-8	Collin	J	1878
183	Arnold S	1877-8	587	Mc Tavish J	1877-8	Creiney	J	1878
644	Barry M	1877-8		Milligan W	1877-8 r	Delbies	E.E	1878 r
	Barry R	1877-8	581	Mulholland D	1877-8	Earley	E	1878 r
647	Black T	1877-8	582	Mulholland J	1877-8	Flynn	D	1878 r
642	Brick J	1877-8		Mulholland W	1877-8	Frawley	M	1878 r
641	Brick W	1877-8	80	O'Brien W	1877-8	Gallett	G	1878 r
646	Burns C	1877-8		Quinn J	1877-8	Hansen	C	1878 r
643	Burns W	1877-8	18	Quirk M	1877-8	Hibbert	A	1878
649	Burns W.T	1877-8 r	432	Sachel A	1877-8 r	Hodson	R	1878 r
645	Burrows P	1877-8	435	Selby J	1877-8 r	Howe	S	1878
648	Burshske A	1877-8 r	434	Selby J	1877-8 r	# Howe	W	1878
	Carroll J	1877-8	437	Shaw T	1877-8	Johnson	J	1878
525	Casselry J	1877-8 r	433	Smith W.H	1877-8	Jones	G	1878
	Casselry M	1877-8	438	Standermacher B	1877-8	Jones	J	1878 r
529	Cheetham W	1877-8 r		Standermacher G	1877-8 r	Joshua	C	1878 r
528	Cuthbert J	1877-8	436	Sterley W.E	1877-8 r	Larney	B	1878
294	Danniels R	1877-8 r		Townshend J	1877-8	Leo	D	1878
	Danaher J	1877-8		Van Rooyen P	1877-8	Liddiard	T	1878
296	Diggiden J	1877-8	102	Voight F	1877-8 r	Marshall	V.E	1878
295	Diggiden W	1877-8	103	Vonderdacken A	1877-8	Michael	G	1878 r
293	Dunnahar J	1877-8	104	Vonplaster T	1877-8 r	Morris	C	1878 r
223	Fielding J	1877-8	377	Wheelan F	1877-8	Okeden	A.P	1878
257	Gardner G	1877-8 r	378	Wiley W	1877-8 r	Pfeiffer	G	1878
512	Hadley M	1877-8	379	Williams C	1877-8 r	Scard	J	1878
505	Hardie J	1877-8 r	376	Witham G	1877-8 r	Scott	W	1878
506	Harpur W	1877-8 r				Seelig	H	1878 r
510	Hayden P	1877-8	**GRUIQUALAND WEST**			Sharpe	T.H	1878 r
	Healey J	1877-8	**CONSTABULARY.**			Shaw	L	1878 r
	Healey M	1877-8	**INSPECTOR**			Slade	W	1878 r
509	Heck N	1877-8 r		Percy G	1878	Smith	E	1878

Dix Noonan Web Auction Lot 400, 5 Apr 06
South Africa 1877-79, 1 clasp, 1878 (Pte. W. Howe, Griqualand W. Constaby.) about very fine Hammer Price: £290

Griqualand West Constabulary

Sparkling	W	1878 r	Sherwood	T	1878	Gardner	S	1878 r
Walker	H	1878	Wright	G	1878 r	Grace	J	1878 r
Ward	S	1878	CORPORAL			Gray	J	1878 r
Wheelan	E	1878	Adcock	D	1878 r	Hamilton	T	1878 r
Wollfer	G	1878	Bradley	H.H	1878	Harvey	H	1878 r
Wilson	J	1878	Humphries	F.C	1878	Hauser		1878
Wood	J	1878 r	John	H	1878 r	Heineman	H	1878 r
Work	D	1878 r	Kelly	P	1878 r	Hendricks	H.J	1878
Work	J	1878 r	Millar	W	1878 r	Henry	P	1878 r
NO RANK SHOWN			Palvie	S.C	1878	Horne	H	1878
Ellison	T.W	1878	Royer	B	1878 r	Humphries	J.H	1878
			Sims	G	1878	Jeppe	O	1878
GRIQUALAND WEST LIGHT INFANTRY			Suckermeyer		1878 r	Jubber	G.C	1878 r
Note on Roll:- Correct spelling of names on this roll cannot be relied upon.			Webster	A	1878	Koen	J	1878 r
			PRIVATE			Lloyd	F	1878 r
			Adamson	J	1878	Loots	J	1878 r
CAPTAIN			Adier	D	1878 r	**Lubbe**	**G.C**	**KIA 1878 r**
Ling	E	1878	Bacon	H	1878 r	Nittmarney	H	1878 r
Lowe	S.J	1878	Bagley	J.O	1878 r	Marks	T.C	1878 r
Also had Indian Mutiny Medal			Banks	C.W	1878	Mc Gonegal	J	1878
Smart	R	1878	Beukes	J	1878 r	Mc Master		1878
SURGEON			Bezeudenhout	J	1878 r	Mc Master	J	1878 r
Murphy	W	1878	Bezeudenhout	W	1878 r	Muir	J.T	1878 r
SERGEANT MAJOR			Bodley	W	1878	Muller	M	1878 r
Phillips	?	1878 r	**Britz**	**J**	**KIA 1878 r**	Murray	J	1878 r
QUARTERMASTER			Brook	R	1878 r	Norton	J	1878 r
Webster	A	1878	Cairnthers	?	1878 r	O'Brien	?	1878 r
LIEUTENANT			Carey	P	1878 r	Petersen	F	1878
Boag	J.H	1878	Carruthers		1878 r	Pollock		1878
Caseley	J.P	1878	Chapman	J.A	1878 r	Pollock	J.P	1878
Goch	G.H	1878 r	Clarence	W	1878 r	Poulton	H	1878 r
Gordall	J.S	1878 r	Cloete	H.A	1878	Pretorius	A	1878 r
#Parker (Parkin)	H	1878	##Cramp (Camp)	W	1878	Pretorius	M	1878 r
Vickers	G.S	1878	Crube	M.B	1878 r	Pretorius	S	1878 r
SERGEANT MAJOR			Cruse	M.H	1878 r	Prior	C.E	1878
Greenshiel	H.W	1878	Cumbey	G	1878 r	Reilly	J	1878 r
Phillips	?	1878 r	David	P	1878 r	Roets	L	1878 r
QUARTERMASTER SERGEANT			De Lore	C	1878 r	Roets	P	1878 r
Bennett	G.T	1878 r	De Villers	J.A	1878	Routledge	J	1878
Evans	J	1878 r	Doonan	?	1878 r	Roux	D.F	1878 r
SERGEANT			Driver	J	1878 r	Roux	D.S	1878
Bees	J.P	1878	Dunlary	M	1878 r	Roux	J.P.R	1878
Brophy	J.L	1878 r	Du Prez	H	1878 r	Roux	P	1878 r
Colyn		1878	De Prez	J	1878 r	Seitz	H	1878 r
Florence		1878 r	Ede	A	1878	Seitz	H	1878
Mackenzie	J	1878 r	Erasmus	J.H	1878 r	Shannon	T.S	1878
Also had Indian Mutiny Medal			Fisher	A	1878 r	Smit	S	1878 r
Sherwood	H	1878 r	Freeman	J	1878	Smith	W	1878 r

\# Dix Noonan Web Auction Lot 829, 22 Sep 06
Pair: Lieutenant H. Parkin, Griqualand West Light Infantry and Imperial Light Horse
South Africa 1877-79, 1 clasp, 1878 (Lieut., Griqualand West L.I.), claw tightened; Queen's South Africa 1899-1902, 2 clasps, Transvaal, South Africa 1901 (1748 Serjt., Imp. Lt Horse) very fine and better. Hammer Price: £680
H. Parkin (listed as 'Parker' in the published roll) served as Lieutenant in the Griqualand West Light Infantry in the 1878 campaign in South Africa. During the Boer War he served as a Sergeant in the Imperial Light Horse. He died of disease (Pyaemia) at Matjespruit on 22 August 1901 and was interred at Klerksdorp.

\#\# Dixons Gazette No33 Spring 2003 410 1 clasp, 1878. Private W. Camp, Griqualand West Light Infantry. Letters CAM of CAMP officially re-engraved. CRAMP on South Africa War medal roll. 130 '1878' clasp medals issued, 85 returned to Mint. EF £270.00

Griqualand West Light Infantry

Smith	W.A	1878
Somes	H	1878 r
Thwaites	S	1878
Tidmarsh	**T KIA**	**1878**
Tidmarsh Jnr	T	1878
Van der Walt		1878 r
Van Schoorn	F	1878 r
Van Vuren	J	1878 r
Ventura	N	1878 r
Welsh	J	1878 r
Wentzel	J	1878 r
Williams	D	1878 r
Wilson	G	1878 r
Wingrove	J	1878
Wright	**H KIA**	**1878 r**
Zennenberg	J	1878 r

NO RANK SHOWN
Francis	R	1878-9
Paine	P	1878

GRIQUALAND WEST NATIVE CONTINGENT.
CAPTAIN
Bailie	A.C	1878

LIEUTENANT
Humphrey	H.J	1878-9

Medal has 1878 clasp - Lot 88
Spinks Auction 5.12.2002

SERGEANT MAJOR
Inkomoyapi	N	1878

SERGEANT
Abrams	J	1878
Gigmiseni		1878
Gugudela		1878
Manxonyi	M	1878

PRIVATE
John Brown	John	1878
Gabus	Z	1878
Methlo	I	1878 r

GRIQUALAND WEST VOLUNTEER ARTILLERY.
CAPTAIN
Parkin	H	1878

SERGEANT MAJOR
Benson	J	1878 r

QUARTERMASTER SERGEANT
Rogers	J	1878 r

SERGEANT
Brophy	E.K	1878 r
Slatter	W.J	1878

CORPORAL
Chase	G.W	1878
Cusins	T.D	1878
Hartley	J	1878

GUNNER
Andrews	J	1878 r
Carmichael	P	1878 r
Davis	H.D'U	1878 r
Dixon	W.A	1878 r
Fraser	James	1878
Fraser	John	1878
Gibbs	H.R	1878
Harding	G.H	1878
Jacob	L	1878
O'Leary	P	1878 r
Pascall	E.S	1878 r
Runchman	M.S	1878
Sanderson	J	1878
Shaw	R.L	1878 r
Stewart	W	1878 r
Spike	W.H	1878
Sutherland	J	1878
Taylor	J.B	1878 r
Tonkin	A	1878 r
Whelan	W.T	1878 r

DRIVER
Carney	M	1878 r
Ehlert	F	1878 r

RANK NOT KNOWN
Carr	J.A	1878-9

GRIQUALAND WEST VOLUNTEER FIELD FORCE.
BRIGADE MAJOR
Maxwell	T	1878

LIEUTENANT
Thompson	C.W	1877-8
Wright	G.D	1878

GRIQUATOWN BURGHERS.
CAPTAIN
Roper	H.B	1878

PRIVATE
Williams	J	1878

NO RANK SHOWN
Hinton	W.C	1878

HARVEY'S HORSE.
SERGEANT
Walker	R	1879 r

HERSCHELS MOUNTED VOL.
CAPTAIN
Clough	E.J.G	1879

LIEUTENANT
Austen	A.G	1879

SERGEANT
Darnelly (??)	J	1879
Grover (??)	A	1879
Heart	J	1879
Lotreng	A	1879

CORPORAL
Smith	J.C	1879

PRIVATE
Adams	T	1879
Africa	M	1879
Aprial	J	1879
Cock	L	1879 r
Cock	W	1879
Croles	W	1879
Devea	P	1879
Engelbrecht	P	1879
Gallon	T	1879
Godman	J	1879
Godman	L	1879
Godman	L	1879
Heart	J	1879
Jacktymie	C	1879
Jenkinson	C	1879
Jonson	A	1879
Jordan	E	1879
Julie	J	1879 r
Klasea	K	1879
Lotreng	A	1879
Lotreng	A	1879
Lotreng	Jacob	1879
Lotreng	John	1879
Lotreng	P	1879
Macpherson	P	1879
Mentor	A	1879
Mesteros	J	1879 r
November	L	1879
Pennels	J	1879
Pennels	W	1879
Rabie	J	1879
Ruyters	A	1879
Searnit	J	1879
Searnit	P	1879
Seland	B	1879
Seland	G	1879
Sterkes	J	1879
Supke	A	1879
Thomas	J.H	1879
Tron	D	1879
Tron	P	1879
Van der Merwe	J	1879
Vandlenda	H	1879
Vandlende	N	1879
Von Broembsen	**H KIA**	**1879**
Vorie	A	1879
Vorie	A	1879
Vorie	M	1879
Williams	A	1879
Williams	K	1879
Windvogal	J	1879

HERSCHELS NATIVE CONTINGENT.
COMMANDANT
Maclean	A.C	1879

CAPTAIN
Berry	J	1879
Halse	F.W	1879

The Zulu War: On the Road to Ulundi.

Pearson Crossing Tugela

Herschels Native Contingent

Peacock	N	1879 r	Dumela	M	1879	Bongo	M	1879 r
Stevens	H	1879	Dumela	M	1879	Boosuck	N	1879
Tainton	A	1879	Eland	C	1879	Booy	G	1879
LIEUTENANT			Jonas	D	1879	Booy	H	1879
Rieger	F	1879	Khati	G	1879	Booy	J	1879
SERGEANT MAJOR			Leroba	M	1879	Booy	J	1879
Coba	I	1879	Mabasela	J	1879	Booy	L	1879
QUARTERMASTER SERGEANT			Madica	A	1879 r	Booy	N	1879
Mongogo	M	1879	Mangwana	W	1879	Booy	P	1879
Parkies	J	1879	Matewane	M	1879	Booy	V	1879
SERGEANT			Misela	J	1879	Booy	r	1879 r
Bekesane	??	1879	Mkuzangwa	N	1879	Bothloke	B	1879 r
Coba	S	1879	Moelas	J	1879 r	Bovena	O	1879
Dada	Q	1879	Mogina	B	1879 r	Boyabothsea	M	1879
Doba	O	1879	Mogina	M	1879	Boyabothsea	S	1879
Eland	P	1879	Mogina	T	1879	Bukazi	D	1879
Gwanbine	J	1879	Mpekeka	B	1879	Bukula	M	1879 r
Jafta	M	1879 r	Mtrilie	N	1879	Bungwa	B	1879
Jiya	J	1879	Nonben	Z	1879	Bute	N	1879 r
Jolinjana	J	1879 r	Omdidma	G	1879	Buthel	O	1879
Kakudi	M	1879 r	Omgogo	J	1879	Cabie	B	1879
Karasa	M	1879	Pitso	D	1879	Cabie	C	1879
Ketelane	C	1879	Scinelane	M	1879	Catohi	F	1879
Ketelane	W	1879	Thlempe	L	1879	Cekana	M	1879
Magathla	R	1879 r	Tomone	V	1879	Cekiya	Q	1879
Malbone	D	1879 r	Walasa	H	1879 r	Chaba	J	1879 r
Malejane	J	1879	**PRIVATE**			Chabalala	O	1879
May	K	1879	Adonis	J	1879 r	Chebea	I	1879
Mboavo	N	1879	Afrika	M	1879 r	Cheyoti	D	1879 r
Mekomakulu	M	1879	Afrika	S	1879 r	Chicka	S	1879 r
Mkuzangwa	D	1879	Alfan	J	1879	Chie	M	1879 r
Mkuzangwa	T	1879	Andries	M	1879	Chinga	N	1879
Mokwea	M	1879	Antonio	O	1879	Choka	M	1879
Mpangazita	R	1879	Antrisi	M	1879	Choka	N	1879
Nkopane	J	1879	Aprial	N	1879	Choka	O	1879
Nomben	Z	1879	Aprial	O	1879	Chopa	K	1879
Ombobo	W	1879 r	August	B	1879 r	Chutah	F	1879 r
Omdolombo	O	1879	August	K	1879	Chutchwa	H	1879 r
Oathlapo	B	1879	August	O	1879 r	Coba	O	1879 r
Owe	R	1879 r	August	P	1879	Coba	O	1879 r
Pasie	S	1879	Baam	C	1879	Comalo	P	1879
Pitso	J	1879	Baam	H	1879	Comalo	T	1879
Sebenya	S	1879	Baam	O	1879	Dagamjama	O	1879 r
Solocomo	J	1879	Babgigic	T	1879 r	Dakana	M	1879
Sibanya	N	1879	Baguso	S	1879 r	Dakana	M	1879
Thlase	S	1879	Bahulekase	O	1879	Dalie	J	1879 r
Thom	M	1879	Bakenya	W	1879	Daman	M	1879 r
Zelilo	N	1879	Balkie	K	1879 r	Daman	S	1879 r
Zwane	K	1879	Bashols	A	1879 r	Daofa	D	1879
CORPORAL			Bassa	W	1879	Debenonze	M	1879
Afrika	T	1879 r	Basulo	M	1879	Dejantje	G	1879
Aprial	O	1879	Becana	M	1879	Dekane	T	1879 r
Armanese	K	1879 r	Becana	W	1879	Dengilizane	M	1879
Booy	J	1879	Beksane	C	1879	Dewadubena	J	1879
Booy	P	1879	Bintie	M	1879 r	Dhlangayi	N	1879
Branner	J	1879	Boko	O	1879	Dhlangsegandla	M	1879
Cheba	I	1879	Boko	S	1879	Doba	M	1879
Dumela	C	1879	Bongase	P	1879 r	Dobaba	O	1879 r

Herschels Native Contingent

Name		Year	Name		Year	Name		Year
Domane	S	1879	Guso	M	1879 r	Khama	L	1879
Dondolo	N	1879	Gwabine	J	1879	Khumalo	E	1879
Dufa	L	1879 r	Gwabini	G	1879	Kidie	O	1879 r
Dugongo	O	1879 r	Gwabini	N	1879	Kinkie	N	1879
Dukuzana	?	1879	Gwobolanda	D	1879	Klaas	S	1879 r
Duloloman	O	1879 r	Gylane	P	1879	Kobeni	H	1879
Eland	C	1879	Helaway	M	1879 r	Koborhunsana	M	1879
Eland	P	1879	Hlangwa	M	1879	Kokota	J	1879
Fekesolo	M	1879 r	Hobo	B	1879 r	Kolo	S	1879
File	J	1879	Hobo	O	1879	Komtsane	J	1879
Flatela	M	1879	Hokwen	S	1879	Komtsane	P	1879
Flatela	O	1879	Homoye	H	1879	Komyelo	M	1879
Fodoka	O	1879	Ina	P	1879 r	Konong	K	1879
Fokase	M	1879	Inthelela	D	1879 r	Konthlo	M	1879 r
Fufo	M	1879	Jackalas	D	1879	Kontwana	V	1879
Gabasa	G	1879	Jackalase	M	1879 r	Kope	S	1879
Gabasa	G	1879	Jackase	W	1879	Kosa	C	1879
Gabasa	O	1879	Jacob	A	1879 r	Kotwana	G	1879
Gaga	P	1879 r	Jacob	H	1879 r	Kotwana	O	1879
Gagalala	W	1879	Jana	T	1879 r	Kouga	D	1879
Gagana	B	1879	January	S	1879	Kouga	W	1879
Gagane	O	1879 r	Jash	S	1879 r	Kozane	S	1879
Gagane	X	1879 r	Jim John	J	1879 r	Kuche	M	1879 r
Gamana	Z	1879	Jinkie	P	1879	Kukane	S	1879 r
Gane	O	1879 r	Jipajeka	S	1879	Kupo	K	1879 r
Gangane	N	1879	Jiya	C	1879	Lange	B	1879 r
Gangata	K	1879 r	Jobe	C	1879	Langosa	K	1879 r
Ganya	K	1879 r	Jobe	J	1879	Leasia	L	1879 r
Gena	M	1879	Jobe	S	1879	Lebesa	B	1879 r
Getva	R	1879 r	Jodo	M	1879	Lefasa	R	1879 r
Gigimane	A	1879	Jola	O	1879 r	Lefasa	S	1879 r
Gigimane	J	1879	Jonas	M	1879	Legango	N	1879
Gina	L	1879	Jonas	S	1879	Legonja	M	1879 r
Glokelea	P	1879	Jonas	S	1879	Lehoto	P	1879 r
Gobela	S	1879 r	Jonas	T	1879	Leketa	M	1879 r
Gobela	W	1879	Jose	O	1879 r	Lekethla	N	1879
Gobobea	G	1879	Joyane	C	1879	Lekeloa	R	1879 r
Gosi	B	1879	Joyane	M	1879	Lemone	T	1879 r
Gosi	K	1879	Joyane	N	1879	Lepepa	M	1879
Gogela	B	1879	July	M	1879 r	Lepepa	O	1879
Gogela	M	1879	July	S	1879 r	Lepongole	K	1879 r
Gogela	V	1879	July	S	1879 r	Lepotin	L	1879
Golala	B	1879	July	Z	1879	Lepuotane	J	1879
Golala	S	1879	Kabola	M	1879	Leroba	P	1879
Golandan	O	1879	Kakane	G	1879 r	Leseya	L	1879 r
Golongwane	M	1879	Kakane	O	1879 r	Leseya	N	1879 r
Goma	W	1879	Kakudi	J	1879	Leseya	R	1879 r
Gomotsowana	T	1879 r	Kakudi	L	1879 r	Letsego	T	1879
Gonya	R	1879 r	Kakudi	R	1879	Letsika	M	1879
Gotva	H	1879 r	Kane	O	1879	Letuli	N	1879
Goza	M	1879 r	Kanyangwa	N	1879	Letuli	Z	1879
Gubusa	M	1879	Kakyangwa	S	1879	Lewele	M	1879
Gubusa	M	1879	Keba	M	1879 r	Lintsa	M	1879 r
Gubusa	N	1879	Kegane	V	1879	Lithleka	N	1879
Gubusa	M	1879	Kende	N	1879	Lithletha	R	1879
Gubusa	N	1879	Kesa	S	1879	Legogwana	J	1879
Gumate	M	1879	Ketelane	K	1879	Lumate	W	1879
Gumenke	G	1879	Ketelane	N	1879	Lutie	N	1879

Herschels Native Contingent

Name		Year	Name		Year	Name		Year
Lutie	S	1879	Magungala	S	1879	Matafene	P	1879
Mabadene	O	1879	Nagwagwa	P	1879	Matarchi	S	1879
Mabindasa	B	1879 r	Magwara	M	1879	Matetelane	O	1879 r
Mabonsie	B	1879 r	Mahlabani	T	1879	Mathlanga	O	1879 r
Mabozolo	I	1879 r	Mahoye	A	1879 r	Mathlomba	F	1879 r
Macaccumba	G	1879 r	Majolea	E	1879	Mathlwa	O	1879
Macala	F	1879	Majorosa	S	1879 r	Matia	O	1879
Macala	F	1879	Makaliane	H	1879	Matitibala	S	1879
Macala	L	1879	Makana	O	1879	Matobidoba	P	1879 r
Macala	N	1879	Makara	J	1879	Matomba	O	1879 r
Macala	T	1879	Makela	J	1879 r	Matseiso	J	1879 r
Macala	Y	1879	Makelema	M	1879 r	Matula	M	1879
Macala	Z	1879	Makelema	Z	1879 r	Matyesini	B	1879
Macetshana	M	1879	Maketa	M	1879	Matyesini	I	1879
Machiqa	L	1879	Makoelebeta	M	1879	Matyesini	S	1879
Macumba	N	1879 r	Makoke	R	1879 r	Mavongana	B	1879 r
Madhlohlo	M	1879	Makolata	C	1879	Mavondla	X	1879 r
Madiegie	I	1879	Makonsa	J	1879 r	Mawokwene	N	1879
Mafalala	K	1879	Makoru	K	1879	Maxamba	G	1879
Mafalala	W	1879	Makubalo	K	1879	Maybo	S	1879
Mafata	R	1879 r	Malangabe	A	1879	Mazamelela	S	1879
Maga	F	1879 r	Malefane	G	1879	Nazepo	O	1879
Maga	N	1879	Malefane	K	1879	Maziboko	M	1879
Maga	S	1879	Malepea	S	1879 r	Mazikiss	H	1879
Magabalala	G	1879 r	Maloe	N	1879	Maziroa	H	1879
Magabalala	N	1879 r	Maloka	A	1879	Mbaka	G	1879
Magabalala	N	1879 r	Malona	W	1879 r	Mbanga	M	1879 r
Magade	P	1879 r	Maloyl	D	1879	Mbanga	O.K	1879 r
Magadhla	N	1879	Malropea	B	1879 r	Mbati	M	1879
Magadhla	R	1879	Mandinga	M	1879 r	Mbejana	D	1879
Magagla	F	1879	Manga	M	1879	Mbese	B	1879
Magalane	N	1879	Mangana	M	1879 r	Mbilana	M	1879
Magalana	Z	1879	Mangangelele	J	1879 r	Mbo	B	1879
Magantana	B	1879 r	Mangangelele	O	1879 r	Mbomvo	J	1879
Magarie	P	1879 r	Mangena	S	1879 r	Mbombo	N	1879
Magasa	T	1879 r	Mangiekie	F	1879 r	Mbonge	S	1879 r
Magasa	W	1879 r	Mangwana	M	1879	Mdilyana	B	1879
Magathleta	N	1879	Mangwana	W	1879	Mechwana	J	1879 r
Magela	G	1879 r	Mankie	T	1879 r	Mela	M	1879 r
Magelwa	S	1879	Mapetela	O	1879	Melvoswana	K	1879 r
Magipo	T	1879 r	Maposche	F	1879	Menaniso	Z	1879
Magisa	P	1879	Maqmaru	M	1879	Mfanana	N	1879
Magobona	L	1879 r	Maquza	J	1879	Mgala	M	1879
Magobolo	O	1879 r	Maraseni	S	1879	Mgala	V	1879
Magobolo	S	1879 r	Marondla	W	1879 r	Mgamo	M	1879
Madoda	S	1879	Marwapie	G	1879	Mgavu	B	1879
Magodene	L	1879 r	Masai	G	1879	Mgazi	M	1879
Magodene	M	1879 r	Masali	B	1879	Mgebisa	R	1879
Magodene		1879 r	Masboko	M	1879	Mgedlana	K	1879
Magodo	D	1879 r	Masena	L	1879	Mgizi	L	1879
Magogana	O	1879 r	Masesa	G	1879	Mgohlumen	N	1879
Magoloza	Z	1879	Maseso	D	1879	Mgongclea	G	1879
Magomelane	S	1879 r	Mashapa	B	1879	Mgongclea	K	1879
Magone	F	1879 r	Masheyana	F	1879	Mgsiolwa	N	1879
Magongana	J	1879 r	Mashokhoeng	T	1879	Mgwotwa	M	1879
Magotane	F	1879 r	Mashwie	M	1879 r	Mhlahlo	M	1879
Magotane	O	1879 r	Masimans	C	1879	Mhlati	K	1879
Magumba	K	1879 r	Masizane	R	1879	Mhlati	M	1879

Herschels Native Contingent

Name		Year		Name		Year		Name		Year
Mhalati	T	1879		Mosia	L	1879		Ndela	M	1879 r
Mhlengi	T	1879		Mosia	M	1879		Ndela	N	1879
Mhlohlo	P	1879		Mosia	T	1879		Ndhelanga	M	1879
Mhlongetyala	M	1879		Mosinyahi	J	1879		Ndhlangazo	D	1879
Mika	S	1879		Mososa	G	1879		Ndhlangazo	M	1879
Misela	T	1879		Mosotwana	T	1879		Ndleta	M	1879
Mjone	L	1879		Motebkana	S	1879 r		Ndomane	D	1879
Mjulalelwa	G	1879		Moteta	M	1879		Ndowelo	B	1879 r
Mkandwana	T	1879		Mothlabane	N	1879		Ndubane	M	1879
Mkapela	P	1879		Mothlomela	N	1879		Nduku	B	1879
Mkapella	T	1879		Mothlabula	J	1879		Nelea	N	1879 r
Mkombo	J	1879		Motshlwe	R	1879 r		Neyse	K	1879 r
Mkontwana	L	1879		Mowen	L	1879 r		Neyse	W	1879 r
Mkontwana	M	1879		Mpako	L	1879		Ngane	D	1879 r
Mkosi	M	1879		Mpambo	H	1879		Ngazi	F	1879 r
Mkublane	M	1879		Mpambo	N	1879		Ngcepe	S	1879
Mkubukeli	J	1879		Mpete	G	1879		Ngecenge	B	1879 r
Mlambeli	J	1879		Mpepuka	M	1879		Ngesa	N	1879
Mlota	T	1879		Mphakoanyane	B	1879		Ngoko	K	1879
Mnokwa	T	1879 r		Mphakoanyane	K	1879		Ngolo	N	1879
Mobongwena	A	1879		Mphunyetsane	O	1879		Njakela	M	1879 r
Mofagang	M	1879 r		Mphuting	J	1879		Nkane	T	1879 r
Mogena	F	1879 r		Mphuting	J	1879		Nkeso	R	1879 r
Mogiedie	B	1879 r		Mpopo	L	1879 r		Nkopane	J	1879
Mogina	B	1879 r		Mpopoma	M	1879		Nkoyijane	M	1879
Mohanla	L	1879		Mpupuma	M	1879		Nkwali	N	1879
Mohape	L	1879 r		Mpupuma	M	1879		Noa	M	1879
Mohapi	J	1879		Mqaqwa	J	1879		Nobongosa	S	1879
Mohapi	T	1879		Mrayisa	S	1879		Nomadolo	M	1879
Mohier	L	1879		Mrola	B	1879 r		Nomadolo	M	1879
Mohobo	L	1879 r		Mshanga	L	1879		Nomadolo	M	1879
Mokhanya	K	1879		Mshenga	M	1879		Nomban	M	1879
Mokhanya	M	1879		Msobongwana	J	1879		Nomgine	S	1879
Mokhmbane	N	1879		Msutu	M	1879		Nondabula	C	1879
Mokoe	D	1879 r		Mtabane	M	1879		Nongogo	A	1879
Mokotsolane	M	1879		Mtanda	N	1879		Nongola	D	1879
Molal		1879		Mtenjana	K	1879		Nogagane	L	1879
Moleko	F	1879		Mthlamba	O	1879 r		Notanng	R	1879
Moleko	G	1879		Mtrilie	N	1879		Nozoko	G	1879 r
Moletsane	M	1879 r		Mvasani	S	1879		Nqoma	O	1879
Moletsane	N	1879		Mvelase	K	1879		Nqupe	J	1879
Moletwe	A	1879		Mvenyelwa	N	1879		Nquventhe	L	1879
Moletwe	T	1879 r		Mweli	M	1879		Nquventhe	M	1879
Molobali	M	1879		Myamo	N	1879		Ntetya	W	1879 r
Moloye	J	1879 r		Myimbane	S	1879		Nthlemesa	M	1879 r
Monakola	M	1879		Myondeki	W	1879		Ntoyli	L	1879
Monang	G	1879		Mzamo	K	1879		Ntsabana	N	1879 r
Mondi	G	1879		Mzambo	M	1879		Ntuli	L	1879
Mondi	N	1879		Mzambo	N	1879		Ntwana	J	1879
Mondisa	M	1879		Mzebisa	R	1879		Ntwana	K	1879
Mongenia	G	1879		Mzilise	G	1879		Nyangetsimbo	M	1879
Mongia	M	1879 r		Mzungulu	D	1879		Nyelewa	P	1879
Mongwazana	J	1879 r		Nankusane	M	1879		Nyelika	M	1879
Mone	S	1879		Nankusane	S	1879		Nyelike	M	1879
Mongue	T	1879 r		Ndala	B	1879		Nyondhlo	M	1879
Mortengana	M	1879 r		Ndandubani	K	1879		Nyondile	G	1879
Mosea	H	1879		Ndandubani	M	1879		Nyongana	G	1879
Moseso	O	1879 r		Ndandubani	M	1879		Nyongana	M	1879

Herschels Native Contingent

Name	Year	Name	Year	Name	Year
Nyongana V	1879	Omnesia M	1879	Qaba P	1879
Nyongwana M	1879	Omneyla M	1879	Qetoka B	1879
Nyongwana N	1879	Omnokwa G	1879 r	Qetoka M	1879
Nzwa M	1879 r	Omnokwa Q	1879 r	Qiniseli C	1879
Ombagayo H	1879	Omnokwa L	1879 r	Quela J	1879 r
Ombakwa D	1879	Omnokwa S	1879 r	Qunzie A	1879 r
Ombakwa M	1879 r	Omnwana S	1879	Qunzie O	1879 r
Ombana C	1879	Ompiqa O	1879	Rakolazue T	1879
Ombobo W	1879 r	Omsamie A	1879 r	Ramagala N	1879
Ombolwa M	1879	Omsena L	1879	Ramatsapane L	1879 r
Ombonge O	1879	Omsenya K	1879	Ramba P	1879
Ombose M	1879	Omsimbe C	1879 r	Ramoneka M	1879
Ombote V	1879	Omtaki J	1879	Ranaman M	1879 r
Ombotshwa S	1879 r	Omtambo S	1879	Ranchebi M	1879 r
Omchaso D	1879	Omteka A	1879	Rangodo D	1879
Omchaswea O	1879	Omteka K	1879	Rantwena D	1879 r
Omchaswea O	1879	Omteto M	1879 r	Rasanzoatsi M	1879
Omchaswea J	1879	Omtetwa S	1879 r	Rathope P	1879
Omchentha B	1879	Omthlabatsi J	1879 r	Rayisa S	1879
Omcherwea D	1879	Omthlamba M	1879 r	Relane M	1879
Omcombe A	1879	Omthlolo L	1879 r	Rinabane M	1879
Omdabola Z	1879	Omthlovane M	1879	Rogani M	1879
Omdaka M	1879 r	Omtong S	1879	Rogani S	1879
Omdidma G	1879	Omyanise N	1879 r	Rolarola J	1879 r
Omdidma M	1879	Omyolowe O	1879 r	Rorwana M	1879
Omdolombo D	1879	Padenyana S	1879 r	Sabesa O	1879
Omdosea D	1879 r	Pahleni B	1879	Sakamasa M	1879
Omfanekeso J	1879 r	Pakas P	1879 r	Sauga W	1879
Omfatka D	1879	Palashea S	1879 r	Sauli T	1879
Omgabalala D	1879 r	Palweni A	1879 r	Sauli T	1879
Omgabalala W	1879	Parkie A	1879	Schaluza G	1879
Omgabola G	1879 r	Pathlane W	1879	Schlaba P	1879
Omgadana K	1879	Patsibana J	1879	Schosea L	1879 r
Omgena O	1879 r	Patswana R	1879	Sebamba O	1879
Omgesena J	1879 r	Paul S	1879	Sebeso N	1879
Omgesena P	1879 r	Peger U.V	1879	Sebeso N	1879
Omgidiwa A	1879 r	Pekasa L	1879	Sebethla K	1879 r
Omgidma L	1879 r	Penduka P	1879	Seckeka P	1879
Omgidma O	1879 r	Pepea L	1879 r	Secosana D	1879
Omgidma O	1879	Pepea O	1879	Secosana H	1879
Omgogea T	1879 r	Peta H	1879	Sefete D	1879
Omgolea G	1879	Peta M	1879	Segaka N	1879
Omgolea O	1879 r	Pexo D	1879 r	Segebue M	1879
Omgololo O	1879	Phakwe A	1879	Segeni B	1879
Omgoma S	1879 r	Phatlane L	1879	Segobela L	1879 r
Omgothling K	1879	Philips F	1879	Segogililira L	1879 r
Omjeke B	1879 r	Pita R	1879 r	Segubi M	1879
Omjwabi O	1879 r	Pitso A	1879	Sekaja J	1879
Omholeni M	1879	Pofo P	1879	Sekedie V	1879
Omkagala H	1879	Ponapono M	1879 r	Seketie A	1879
Omkela S	1879	Pongwana N	1879 r	Seketie A	1879
Omkontwa S	1879 r	Pongwana O	1879 r	Seketie M	1879 r
Omlindaze J	1879 r	Potongwana N	1879	Seketsie J	1879 r
Omlota L	1879	Puonane A	1879	Sekisane J	1879
Omlota L	1879	Pupama F	1879	Sekisasane G	1879
Omlota S	1879	Pupama M	1879	Sekisasane M	1879
Omnayamene S	1879 r	Putuma M	1879	Sekitea T	1879
Omnela B	1879 r	Puza J	1879	Sekonyana O	1879 r

Herschels Native Contingent

Name		Year	Name		Year	Name		Year
Selecomo	G	1879	Sodoma	A	1879	Tsiane	M	1879
Selecomo	N	1879	Sodoma	S	1879	Tsiane	N	1879
Seleka	M	1879 r	Sogoka	D	1879	Tsiane	S	1879
Selesane	J	1879	Sogogeba	L	1879 r	Tswachi	L	1879
Sello	J	1879	Somatube	G	1879 r	Tswene	M	1879 r
Selona	W	1879 r	Somatube	M	1879 r	Tune	T	1879 r
Selwana	K	1879 r	Somatube	N	1879	Tyali	M	1879
Selwana	K	1879 r	Somfola	K	1879 r	Umvungama	G	1879
Semalane	O	1879	Somo	O	1879	Umvungama	J	1879
Semalane	O	1879	Sondosa	K	1879	Vangana	S	1879 r
Semeso	M	1879	Sondosa	O	1879	Vata	A	1879
Senowana	M	1879	Songeni	M	1879 r	Velokazi	G	1879
Sepamala	S	1879 r	Sontashi	G	1879 r	Veltbeest	L	1879
Sepambo	O	1879	Sqqwasqqwa	Z	1879	Veltbeest	T	1879
Sepaye	O	1879	Steckleye	Z	1879 r	Vondisa	K	1879 r
Sepeka	-	1879 r	Stephanus	R	1879	Vondisa	M	1879 r
Sepeka	A	1879 r	Sufeing	L	1879	Waba	M	1879
Sepeka	O	1879 r	Sufeing	M	1879	Wabendhlane	M	1879
Sepeka	G	1879 r	Swaartbooy	N	1879	Wabosa	H	1879 r
Sepofan	K	1879 r	Swaartbooy	N	1879 r	Wakelema	T	1879 r
Sepola	T	1879 r	Swaartbooy	N	1879 r	Walasa	H	1879 r
September	A	1879 r	Swaartbooy	O	1879 r	Walasa	L	1879 r
September	G	1879	Tabeni	A	1879	Walasa	M	1879 r
September	M	1879	Tabeni	K	1879	Wanga	G	1879 r
September	M	1879	Tabeni	O	1879	Weka	S	1879
Sequash	O	1879	Tala	G	1879 r	Wenglane	M	1879
Sequash	S	1879	Talithla	N	1879	Wenla	N	1879
Sequate	M	1879 r	Talweni	A	1879 r	Wenlane	S	1879
Serwetsa	N	1879 r	Tandalaza	G	1879	Winana	G	1879
Seshea	P	1879	Tepedie	C	1879 r	Wlale	X	1879 r
Seskara	S	1879	Tetea	D	1879	Wnasana	L	1879
Setola	K	1879	Thenanie	N	1879 r	Wnatha	M	1879 r
Setola	S	1879	Thom	N	1879	Wogebelana	G	1879
Setona	P	1879 r	Thlakanyane	S	1879 r	Wongobakase	S	1879
Setona	R	1879 r	Thlapa	B	1879 r	Wwazi	N	1879
Sevoma	M	1879	Thlata	O	1879	Wwazi	S	1879
Sevoma	N	1879	Thlatena	S	1879	Xabaga	J	1879 r
Sevona	N	1879	Thlathene	O	1879 r	Zakana	O	1879
Seyatsha	M	1879	Thlekie	M	1879	Zekandaba	O	1879
Shai	P	1879	Thlempo	K	1879	Zekandaba	O	1879
Shawabetia	O	1879	Thlikakia	S	1879 r	Zekaneze	T	1879 r
Shawpa	S	1879	Thlogana	K	1879	Zelilo	D	1879
Shume	W	1879 r	Thloka	O	1879 r	Zelilo	M	1879
Somane	O	1879 r	Thlokonya	M	1879	Zelilo	O	1879
Sibatu	N	1879	Thlomanglene	B	1879 r	Zelilo	O	1879
Sibidela	W	1879	Thlomanglene	P	1879 r	Zidi	N	1879
Sidyiyo	S	1879 r	Thlooa	P	1879	Zidi	S	1879
Sieng	C	1879	Thlooa	P	1879	Zingwa	O	1879
Sifele	M	1879	Titie	L	1879 r	Ziswana	L	1879
Sigumba	J	1879	Tlabo	B	1879			
Silele	N	1879	Tlasa	K	1879			

HEYNES FINGO LEVY
<u>LIEUTENANT</u>

Hengsberg	J	1877-8

Sinjanye	N	1879	Tobie	S	1879
Skomola	M	1879	Tokela	O	1879 r
Skomola	N	1879	Tsapa	P	1879

HOTTENTOT LEVY. NUMBER 1 COMPANY
<u>CAPTAIN</u>

Soal	T	1879 r	Tsela	N	1879 r
Sobetwa	B	1879	Tsetsalene	S	1879 r
Sobetwa	M	1879	Tsomo	T	1879
Sobosa	O	1879	Tsiane	L	1879

Ernett	W.T.L	1877-8

Hottentot Levy

LIEUTENANT and ADJUTANT
Ernett W.E.C 1877-8
LIEUTENANT
Pearson E 1877-8
SERGEANT MAJOR
Kleynbury K 1877-8
SERGEANT
Camfer P 1877-8
De Boer G 1877-8
Rooy B 1877-8
CORPORAL
Arends J 1877-8
Beukes W 1877-8
Boosman K 1877-8
Dragooner I 1877-8
Forie Snr C 1877-8
Fortuyn Snr J 1877-8
Orange J 1877-8
Pretorius A 1877-8
Vrey P 1877-8
PRIVATE
Appel A 1877-8 r
Appel C 1877-8
Arends A 1877-8 r
Arends F 1877-8
Arends M 1877-8
Baarb D 1877-8
Baarb K 1877-8
Bantum Jnr A 1877-8
Bantum A 1877-8
Bantum P 1877-8
Boosman J 1877-8 r
Booyse S 1877-8
Camfer E 1877-8
Casper M 1877-8 r
Casper W 1877-8
De Boer Jnr G 1877-8
De Boer J 1877-8
De Boer M 1877-8
De Klerk 1877-8
Dragooner J 1877-8
Dragooner P 1877-8
Dragooner S 1877-8
Floris B 1877-8 r
Forie Jnr C 1877-8
Forie D 1877-8 r
Forie J 1877-8
Fortuyn H 1877-8
Fortuyn Jnr J 1877-8
Fortuyn P 1877-8
Geswinb K 1877-8
Glover G 1877-8
Groepe C 1877-8 r
Hendricks J 1877-8
Janmyer A 1877-8
Johannes G 1877-8
Johannes W 1877-8 r
Jonkers A 1877-8 r
Kelvedo J 1877-8
Klaasen D 1877-8
Klaasen S 1877-8
Kleyn D 1877-8
Koopnan J 1877-8
Lyny D 1877-8
Manel K 1877-8
Menljas P 1877-8
Menton D 1877-8 r
Minnie P 1877-8
Mulriel C 1877-8
Pieters A 1877-8
Pikeur B 1877-8 r
Pretorius Snr D 1877-8
Pretorius J.D 1877-8
Pretorius W 1877-8 r
Prins N 1877-8
Prins P 1877-8
Prins R 1877-8
Quly Snr D 1877-8
Quly Jnr D 1877-8
Rensburg H 1877-8
Rory G 1877-8
Rory P 1877-8
Rory R 1877-8
Rooy A 1877-8
Rooy S 1877-8
Ruyters B 1877-8
Schweman W 1877-8
Smit B 1877-8 r
Smit J 1877-8
Smit M 1877-8
Sneyman N 1877-8
Sneyman S 1877-8
Spanger D 1877-8
Spoytor D 1877-8 r
Spoyter Snr K 1877-8
Spoyter Jnr K 1877-8 r
Spoyter P 1877-8
Spoyter S 1877-8
Stoffels K 1877-8 r
Swanepoel A 1877-8 r
Swanepoel C 1877-8
Theunis A 1877-8 r
Van de Venter Snr T 1877-8
Van de Venter Jnr T 1877-8 r
Van Eck S 1877-8
Vrey A 1877-8 r
Wahl A 1877-8 r
Windvogel M 1877-8
Windvogel S 1877 8

HOTTENTOT MILITIA AND LEVY.
CAPTAIN
Boyes C KIA 1877-8
LIEUTENANT
Francke R 1877-8

SERGEANT MAJOR
Argue W 1877-8
Hatha Jnr A 1877-8
Vincent F 1877-8
SERGEANT
Bantum A 1877-8
Branden C 1877-8
Pieters P 1877-8
CORPORAL
Berryman F 1877-8-9
PRIVATE
Ague M KIA 1877-8
Arends I 1877-8
Arends S 1877-8
Bolton H 1877-8
Bolton W 1877-8
Davids A 1877-8
Davids D 1877-8
Davids D 1877-8
Davis S 1877-8 r
De Klerk D/S J 1877-8
Dragooner I 1877-8
Dragooner O 1877-8
Fone C 1877-8 r
Fone I 1877-8
Fritz H 1877-8
Geswinb J 1877-8
Jayers J 1877-8
Jonkers A 1877-8 r
Jonkers P 1877-8
Keyster Snr D 1877-8
Keyster Jnr D 1877-8
Keyster K 1877-8
Keyster P 1877-8
Klaasen A 1877-8 r
Kramer E 1877-8
Loetz P 1877-8
Matioos J 1877-8
Michiel J 1877-8
Peffer F 1877-8
Peffer G 1877-8
Piet A 1877-8
Prins A 1877-8
Willems K 1877-8 r
Windvogel A 1877-8
Windvogel B 1877-8
Windvogel D 1877-8 r
Wiltroy K 1877-8
Zeeland C 1877-8

HUMANSDORP LIGHT HORSE.
SURGEON
Ward W.W 1877-8
TROOPER
Human M.G 1878

Insidanje Column

INSIDANJE COLUMN
COMMANDANT
Fleischer W.M   1877-8

ISIPINGO MOUNTED RIFLES.
The corps stationed at Stanger.
CAPTAIN
Steinbank D
LIEUTENANT
Quested W
QUARTERMASTER
Bower
SERGEANT MAJOR
Murray
QUARTERMASTER SERGEANT
Rockey
SERGEANT
Chapman
CORPORAL
Birkett
Ramsay W.R   1879
A duplicate Medal issued 27/8/1978.
No details as to the clasp awarded.
Served in the New Zealand.
TRUMPETER
Haines
TROOPER
Buxton
Cass   r
Chapman
Clarence   r
Clarkson
Daddy
Fayers Q.R
Fayers W.F
Gilbert
Green
   Accidentally Killed fall from horse..
Hillary
Hogard
Ingle
Kenton
Madore
Mc Donald
Munn
Platt
Prince
Pugh
Robinson
Royston J.B
Skinner
Sinart   Not on medal roll
Smart
Smith T
Smith W
Stainbank
Steel
Stewart

Westley
Westley A.C

JAMESTOWN MOUNTED VOLUNTEER RIFLES.
CAPTAIN
Kindwell A.J   1878-9
   See also 2nd Cape Mounted Yeom.
LIEUTENANT
Fincham F.P   1879
   See also 2nd Cape Mounte Yeom.
Wagenaar J   1878
SERGEANT MAJOR
Schaeffner A   1878
QUARTER MASTER
Gabriel H   1878
SERGEANT
Anderson W.H   1878 r
Ritchie A   1878
Wagenaar A   1878
CORPORAL
De Beer H.G   1878
Wagenaar P   1878 r
TROOPER
Austin H   1878
Austin W   1878
Basson J.H   1878 r
Bekker H   1878 r
Binderman H   1878 r
Botha D.P   1878 r
Botha T.J   1878
De Klerk C   1878 r
Du Preez S   1878
Goosen H   1878 r
Hattingh W   1878 r
Jenkinson G   1878
Jenkinson J   1878
   See also 2nc Cape Mounted Yeom.
Kidwell C   1878
   See also Sgt in Cape Mtd Yeom.
Kidwell T   1878
   See also 2nd Cape Mounted Yeom.
Lang P   1878 r
Lubbe A   1878 r
Lubbe J   1878 r
Olivier P   1878 r
Ralston L   1878
Strydom J   1878
Swart C   1878 r
Usher J   1878 r
Van Hierden Jnr C   1878 r
Van Hierden Snr C   1878 r
Van Vuuren L   1878 r
Walker D   1878 r
Walker J   1878 r
Wagenaar C   1878
Wagenaar J.J   1878 r
Wagenaar N.J   1878

BUGLER
Smith G   1878
   See also Tpr G. Smith 2nd Cape Mounted Yeom.
NO RANK SHOWN
Hagan A.V.M   1877-8-9

JANSEVILLE YEOMANRY.
LIEUTENANT
Payne P.B   1878-9 r
TROOP SERGEANT MAJOR
Luyt F   1878 r
QUARTERMASTER SERGEANT
Kirkman W.N   1878
CORPORAL
Dyason A   1877-8-9
PRIVATE
Loryl F   1878
Payn P.B   1878-9
NO RANK SHOWN
Moran H   1878

KAFFRARIAN MOUNTED VOLUNTEERS.
TRUMPETER
Dix R.A.D   1877 r

KAFFRARIAN RANGERS.
CAPTAIN
Gorman T   1877-8
Murray O   1877-8
LIEUTENANT AND ADJUTANT
Murray J   1877-8
LIEUTENANT
Adams T   1877-8 r
Sheenan J   1877-8
Simpson J.E   1877-8 r
Whitfield J   1877-8
   See also Fort White Mounted Volunteers.
SERGEANT MAJOR
Glover A   1877-8 r
Graddage T   1877-8
Vaines T   1877-8 r
QUARTERMASTER SERGEANT
Ford R   1877-8 r
Peglar C   1877-8 r
SERGEANT
Collins D   1877-8 r
Hearne T   1877-8
Lynch J   1877-8
Sansom I   1877-8
CORPORAL
Coker J   1877-8
Hood R   1877-8
Luyt J   1877-8 r
   See also Sgt J. Luyt Stevensons Horse.
Mc Carthy C   1877-8

Kaffrarian Rangers

Russon	I.C	1877-8	Mc Namara	James	1877-8 r	QUARTERMASTER SERGEANT		
Waggoneer	J	1877-8 r	Mc Namara	James	1877-8 r	Foster	J	1879
TROOPER			Meslim	D	1877-8 r	SERGEANT		
Adams	J	1877-8 r	Morum	W	1877-8 r	Wilson	J.G	1877-8-9 r
Angsorge	G.T	1877-8 r	Mullins	J	1877-8 r	CORPORAL		
Bain	J	1877-8 r	Mullins	P	1877-8	Davies	J	1878-9 r
Beaumont	W	1877-8	Mullins	T	1877-8	PRIVATE		
Berhend	C	1877-8 r	Murray	R	1877-8	Birkoltz	F	1878-9 r
Birkholtz	F	1877-8 r	Nelson	A	1877-8 r	TROOPER		
Birkholtz	W	1877-8 r	O'Driscoll	T	1877-8	Bell	W.W	1879
Campbell	J	1877-8	O'Neal	M	1877-8 r	Buchler	W	1878-9
Chambers	W	1877-8	O'Brien	R	1877-8 r	Enders	G	1878-9
Cheesen	P	1877-8 r	O'Reilly	W	1877-8 r	Gombert	W	1879
Clock	W	1877-8 r	O'Rorke	J	1877-8 r	Johnson	J	1878-9 r
Cockler	C	1877-8 r	Paddock	M	1877-8	Selzwedel	G	1879 r
Collas	C	1877-8 r	Patterbridge	C	1877-8	Wilkie	J.C.O	1879
Colman	W	1877-8 r	Quinn	J	1877-8 r			
Condren	J	1877-8 r	Rennie	E	1877-8 r	**KAFFRARIAN VOLUNTEERS.**		
Connor	J	1877-8 r	Roll	W	1877-8 r	FIELD COMMANDANT		
Cooper	J	1877-8	Rutter	G	1877-8 r	Gray	G	1877-8
See also Frontier Light Horse.			Ryder	F	1877-8	CAPTAIN		
Daniels	S	1877-8	Saunders	G	1877-8 r	Sansom	J	1877-8
See also Sansoms Horse.			Saunders	M	1877-8 r	Sprigg	H	1877-8
Devitt	J.L	1877-8	Saunders	T	1877-8	ACTING SURGEON		
Dilly	J	1877-8	Scott	J	1877-8 r	May	S	1877-8
Driscoll	T.D	1877-8 r	Shafner	C	1877-8 r	LIEUTENANT ADJUTANT		
Duitchman	A	1877-8 r	Simon	L	1877-8 r	Dick	R.J	1877-8
Durraeux	J	1877-8 r	Singleton	J	1877-8	LIEUTENANT		
Elliott	W	1877-8	Smith	C	1877-8 r	Curtes	T	1877-8
Francious	P	1877-8 r	Smith	J	1877-8 r	Manley D/W	J	1877-8 r
Friggens	W.J	1877-8	Smith	W	1877-8 r	Perks	W	1877-8
Gilman	G	1877-8	Stephens	C	1877-8 r	Warren	W.J	1877-8
Glyn	W	1877-8 r	Stevens	O	1877-8 r	Welsh	W.S	1877-8 r
Goddard	F	1877-8 r	Sullivan	T	1877-8 r	SERGEANT		
Goddard	W	1877-8 r	Symons	A	1877-8 r	Cumming	J	1877-8
Goldseller	W	1877-8	Taylor	W	1877-8	Fletcher	A	1877-8 r
Gorman	J.L	1877-8	Thomas	F	1877-8 r	Hall	E.J	1877-8
Hall	H	1877-8 r	Turner	J	1877-8	Keightly	H.T	1877-8
Harrison	G	1877-8 r	Verity	W	1877-8 r	Pascoe	R	1877-8
Hees	J	1877-8	Volker	W	1877-8 r	Reynolds	C.F	1877-8
Hendry	J	1877-8 r	Warren	W	1878-9	Smith	R	1877-8
Herbert	R.S	1878	Wehr	H	1877-8 r	Tweedie	J	1877-8
Higgens	F	1877-8	Whelan	J	1877-8	CORPORAL		
Hurford	W	1877-8 r	White	J	1877 8 r	Forroira	P.J	1877-8
Hutchins	W	1877-8 r	Whitfield	S	1877-8	Rennie	W.C	1877-8
Ingram	T	1877-8 r	Wilkie	A	1877-8 r	Sansom	E.L	1877-8
Jones	W	1877-8 r	See also Frontier Mounted Rifles.			Warren	J	1877-8
Kelly	J	1877-8	Willey	W	1877-8 r	BUGLER		
Kelly	T	1877-8 r	Wilson	J	1877-8 r	Lonsdale	C.B	1877-8
Kerr	A	1877-8	Zentgraf	R	1877-8 r	PRIVATE		
Kerr	J.3	1877-8	NO RANK SHOWN			Beel	A	1877-8
Krabfontein	H	1877-8 r	Driscoll	C.O	1877-8-9	Benning	J	1877-8
Lintekamp	E	1877-8 r				Bennet	M	1877-8
Marryatt	T	1877-8	**KAFFRARIAN RIFLES.(or VANGUARD)**			Blake	W	1877-8 r
Maske	N	1877-8 r	LIEUTENANT			Blakeway	G	1877-8 r
Matthews	H	1877-8 r	Schwarzkoff	A	1877-8-9	**Blakeway**	**W**	**KIA 1877-8 r**
Mc Dermott	H	1877-8 r	FARRIER SERGEANT			Bluhm	H	1877-8
Mc Donald	J	1877-8 r	Richards	F	1879 r	Booth	W	1877-8

Kaffrarian Volunteers

Bourgees	E	1877-8 r
Brown	J.C	1877-8 r
Clack	E	1877-8
Cogho	M	1877-8
Connellan	J	1877-8
Costerlon	C.E	1877-8
Cowie	J.H	1877-8
Cowie	R	1877-8 r
Cumming	W.B	1877-8
Curtes	W	1877-8
Daly	M.H	1877-8
Deary	P	1877
Driver	W.R	1877-8 r
Durheim	A	1877-8
Edwards	G	1877-8 r
Edwards	W.M	1877-8
Fitzgerald	J	1877-8
Fitzgerald	R	1877-8 r
Friegaart	W	1877-8
Gaylard	G	1877-8
Gaylard	P	1877-8 r
Godfrey	W	1877-8 r
Goldsmith	J	1877-8
Green	W	1877-8 r
Hamilton	G.D	1877-8
Handcock	A	1877-8
Harmuth	G	1877-8
Hart	J	1877-8
Harty	John	1877-8 r
Harty	Joshua	1877-8 r
Hayhurst	F.C	1877-8 r
Hayhurst	W	1877-8 r
Heath	T.A	1877 r
Hockey	W	1877-8
Hoole	T	1877-8
Hutchinson	A	1877-8
Hutton	W	1877-8 r
Jacoby	C.H	1877-8
Jacoby	E.L	1877-8
Jordan	T	1877-8
Keightby	S	1877-8
Kettle	J.B	1877-8
Kirk	J	1877-8 r
Kruger	H	1877-8
Lehman	P	1877-8
Lishman	E	1877-8
Lloyd	E	1877-8 r
Lunch	J	1877-8 r
Luyt	J	1877-8 r
Malcomess	C	1877-8
Manley	W	1877-8
Marillier	G	1877-8
Marillier	H	1877-8 r
Marshall	E	1877-8
Marst	A	1877-8 r
Mawais	H	1877-8 r
Mawais	T	1877-8 r
Mc Mabon	W.G	1877-8
Mc Laughlan	H	1877-8 r
Minkley	J	1877-8 r
Nel	D.C	1877-8 r
Nel	J	1877-8
Nelson	A	1877-8
Norten	J	1877-8 r
Owen	H	1877-8
Paddock	I	1877-8 r
Paul	F	1877-8
Preston	M	1877-8 r
Pullen	A	1877-8
Ranger	A	1877-8 r
Ranger	Alex	1877-8
Raubenheimer	C	1877-8
Rawlings	G	1877-8 r
# Reyner	H	1877-8
Robinson	W	1877-8 r
Rossen	A	1877-8 r
Routledge	G	1877-8
Rushmer	J	1877-8
## Sansom	J.E	1877-8
Schermbrucker	E	1877-8
Scully	T	1877-8
Sell	W	1877-8
Sheenan	J	1877-8 r
Sibesy	J	1877-8 r
Smith	A	1877-8 r
Smith	C	1877-8 r
Snyman	G	1877-8 r
Sparks	J.W	1877-8
Spreinger	W	1877-8
Symons	J	1877-8
Thomas	T.B	1877-8
Tilmer	J	1877-8 r
Turner	S	1877-8 r
Voncharrel	R	1877-8
Wainwright	D	1877-8 r
Warren	R	1877-8
Webb	C.E	1877-8
Welbourne	H.W	1877-8
Welch	A	1877-8 r
Welsh	W.S	1878-8
Wellbeloved	W.J.T	1877-8
Yates	J.J	1877-8 r
Zella	?	1877-8 r
Zella	J	1877-8

KAFFRARIAN VOLUNTEER ARTILLERY
LIEUTENANT
Smyth   H.M   1877-8 r
See Lt H.M.Smith 1st Cape Mounted Yeo.
SERGEANT MAJOR
White   W.I   1877-8
SERGEANT
Judd   J.R   1877-8
Tooke   W.H   1877-8
CORPORAL
Bender   W   1877-8
Head   H.F   1877-8
GUNNER
Angrove   H   1877-8
Grandin   P   1877-8
Jarvis   F.J   1877-8
Leask   J   1877-8
Leeshemiunt J   1877-8
Venn   C.D   1877-8 r
see Troop Sgt Maj Frontier Light Horse
Venn   J.L   1877-8
Williams   C   1877-8
Dempster   J   1877-8
NO RANK SHOWN
Bender   B.E   1877-8

KAMAS NATIVE LEVY.
CAPTAIN
Attwell   W.H   1877-8
Fielding   R.M.B   1877-8
   Also served in 1845-53.
LIEUTENANT
Kama   W.S   1877-8
SERGEANT
Bashman   1877-8
Joyi   1877-8
Mbangi   T   1877-8
Minto   1877-8
Tuiteli   D   1877-8
Umsilwaii   G   1877-8
CORPORAL
Joyi   1877-8
Makweio   1877-8 r
Plaate   1877-8
Tyeni   1877-8
PRIVATE
Abram   1877-8
Bam   M   1877-8 r
Barn   J   1877-8 r
Bekime   1877-8
Betso   J   1877-8 r
Bobo   S   1877-8
Boyce   1877-8

\# Dix Noonan Web Auction Lot 400, Lot 109, 7 Dec 05
Description: South Africa 1877-79, 1 clasp, 1877-8 (Pte. H. Reyner, Kaffrarian Vols.) nearly extremely fine Hammer Price: £270

\## Dixons Gazette No34 Summer 2003 4018 1 clasp, 1877-8. Private J.E Sansom, Kaffrarian Volunteers. Raised in Kingwilliamtown in 1870 the unit approx. 170 men served under Captain Lonsdale in the 9th Frontier War. EF £350.00

Martini-Henry Rifle

The Martini-Henry introduced into the army in 1871 was immortalized in the epic film "Zulu" and was a breech loading, single shot lever-actuated rifle It was the first British service rifle that was a true breech-loader using metallic cartridges. There are four classes of the Martini-Henry rifle: Mark I (released in June 1871). There was also an 1877 carbine version with carbine variations (Mark I, Mark II, and Mark III). The Mark IV Martini-Henry rifle ended production in the year 1889, but remained in service throughout the British Empire until the end of the First World War.

But very little has been written about the other important carbine used during the Zulu War the Swinburn Henry. It was manufactured by The Abingdon Works Co. Limited of Birmingham. Operation was similar to the Martini action with a breech lever.

Major Dartnell's report of January 1878, "During the year the change of arms has been completed and the whole of the Volunteer Force is now armed with Swinburn Henry rifles and carbines in place of the Sniders and Enfields."

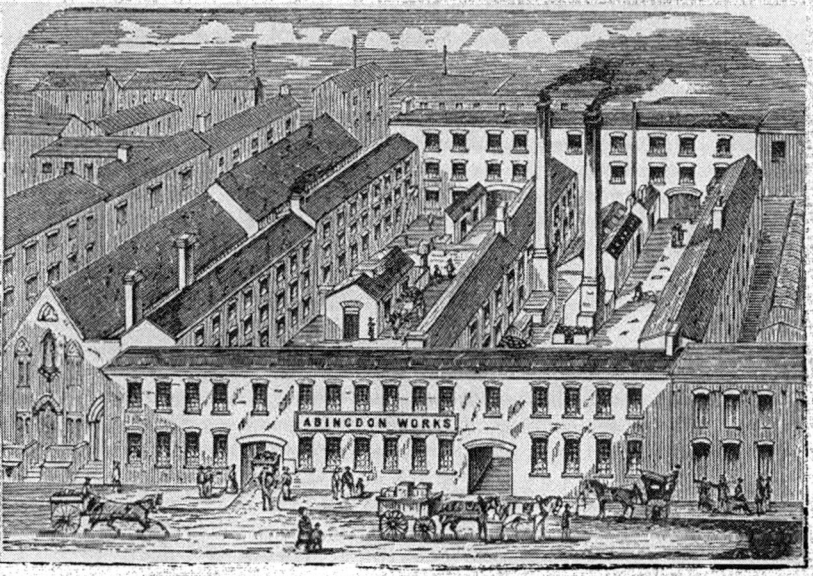

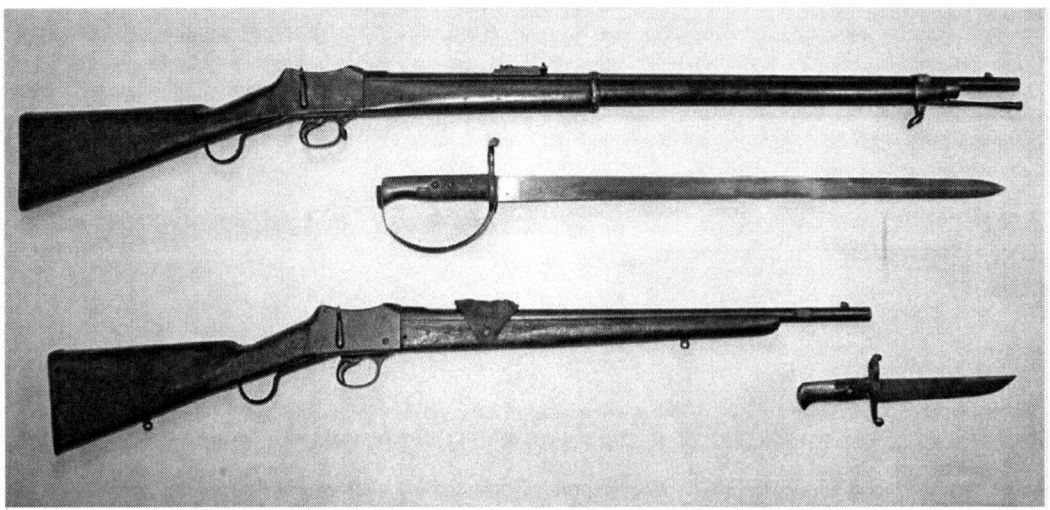

Top Swinburn Henry rifle as supplied to the Natal Volunteer Rifle Regements
Bottom Swinburn Henry carbine the model issued to the Natal Mounted Police.

The Natal Mounted Police were the first unit to be issued with Swinburn Henry carbines, which was of the type that could accept a bayonet. The ordinary carbine being supplied to the Mounted Volunteers.

On the 22nd January the British invaded Zululand in three separate columns. Lord Chelmsford required the services of the Mounted Volunteers, men who knew the country and its people. Their strength was divided between the columns. The centre column under Lord Chelmsford contained men of the Buffalo Border Guard, Natal Carbineers, Newcastle Mounted Rifles, and detachments of the Natal Mounted Police. A British force armed with Martin-Henry rifles and supported by artillery needed only to form up in close order to repel any number of attacking Zulus. That was the prognosis at the time.

These forces were supplemented by the Natal Native Contingent (NNC), composed of poorly equipped local black and white auxiliaries. Chelmsford had split his force, the Zulus had slipped around his flank and fallen on the main camp at Isandlwana. There then followed the attack on the supply depot at **Rorke's Drift.**

The Right Flank column under the command of Colonel Charles Knight Pearson had men from the Alexander, Durban, Isipingo, and Victoria Mounted Rifles, together with troopers from the Natal Hussars. To prevent a possible Zulu invasion into Natal the Isipingo Mounted Rifles were detached to patrol the Tugelea river. On the 22nd January 1879 the Zulu's mounted an ambush near the ford in the Nyezene River. The Natal Mounted Volunteers with the Swinburn Heny's were heavily involved in the action, before advancing to occupy the deserted mission station at Eshowe.

The Left Flank Column under General Evelyn Wood contained 200 Frontier Light Horse raised in King Williams Town, veterans of the 9th Kaffir War, 236 Bakers Horse and 61 men of Frederick Weatherly's Border Horse. Also the Transvaal Rangers formed by Pieter Raaf 138 strong plus a group of 40 Boers led by Piet Uys. All the units were present at the actions of Inholobane mountain and Kambula.

Some of the newly formed mounted units were placed under the command of Major Dartnell. All relied on the Swinburn Henry Rifle.

All rifles, carbines and bayonet purchased had to be inspected by the Ordnance Factory. Returns from the1870's provide some interesting clues as to South African orders and the quantities shipped. All the arms would have an inspection or viewers stamp marked on them, in practice samples were drawn from the consignment, rather than inspecting each individual item.

1875-76 Birmingham...	300 Swinburn Henry rifles viewed
	60 Swinburn Henry carbines viewed
1878-77 Birmingham...	600 Swinburn Henry viewed (rifles or carbines not stated)
1877-78 Birmingham...	1,000 Snider Cavalry carbines viewed
	130 Swinburn Henry carbines with Bowie knives viewed
	500 Swinburn Henry carbines viewed
	100 Swinburn Henry rifles viewed

Acknowledgements:
The Gun Report. The Swinburn Henry by Brian C.Knapp
Engineers and the Zulu War 179 http://www.remuseum.org.uk/campaign/rem_campaign_zuluwar79.htm

Summary of Colonial Forces raised under the authority of this Government during the Zulu War, 1879

Artillery*
Durban Artillery Volunteer   51 men

Infantry Volunteers*
Maritzburn Rifles   105 men
New German Rifles   60 men
Royal Durban Rifles   52 men
* Took no part in the campaign remained in reserve as home defence.
The Ixopo mounted Rifles and 66 troopers of the Natal Mounted Police also stayed in Natal.

Border Defence
Carbutts Border Rangers   36 men   35 Native Scouts
Durban Mounted Reserve   47 men   15 Native Scouts
Newcastle Scouts   -   50 Native Scouts

Mounted Volunteers
On the 23rd November orders were issued to march to the border for active service.
Alexander Mounted Rifles   30 men   proceed to Trigs Post
Buffalo Border Guard   23 men   proceed to Helpmaker
Durban Mounted Rifles   65 men   proceed to Trigs Post
Isipingo Mounted Rifles   36 men
Ixopo Mounted Rifles   29 men
Natal Carbineers   59 men   proceed to Helpmaker
Natal Hussars   59 men   proceed to Trigs Post
Natal Mounted Police   130 men
Newcastle Mounted Rifles   33 men   proceed to Helpmaker
Stranger Mounted Rifles   46 men   proceed to Trigs Post
Victoria Mounted Rifles   47 men
Weenan Yeomanry   19 men

Natal Mounted Police
Quasi military police scattered all over the Colony, drafted into Chelmsfords force.

Border Defence
Carbutts Border Rangers   36 men   35 Native Scouts
Durban Mounted Reserve   47 men   15 Native Scouts
Newcastle Scouts   50 Native Scouts

At Isandlwana the Natal Mounted Police lost 26 troopers, Natal Carbineers 22, Newcastle Mounted Rifles 7, and the Buffalo Border Guard 3.
Trooper Sydney Hunter died at **Rorke's Drift**, while troopers Lugg, Green and Hunter were hospitalized and were all members of the Natal Mounted Police and all in possession of their Swinburns.

Return of Levies called out, or in the Field, or available for the Defence of the Colony

		Name of Col. Commander	Foot	Mntd	Resrv.
District	No1	Major Dartnell	3,507	224	...
District	No2	General Lloyd	35		1,000
District	No3	Major Boycott	129	12	...
District	No4	Mr Hawkins			...
District	No5	Major Giles	.....	...	...
District	No6	Captain Lucas	3,043	10	...
District	No7	Mr Wheelwright	1,492	554	1,500

Acknowledgements:
The Gun Report. The Swinburn Henry by Brian C. Knapp
Engineers and the Zulu War 179 http://www.remuseum.org.uk/campaign/rem_campaign_zuluwar79.htm
Martini-Henry http://en.wikipedia.org/wiki/Martini-Henry

Kamas Native Levy

Name		Year	Name		Year	Name		Year
Charles		1877-8 r	Nokimba		1877-8 r	**SERGEANT**		
Debo	S	1877-8	Ntanta	J	1877-8 r	Hardwich	A	1877-8
Dick		1877-8	Ntanta	S	1877-8	Heinrich	W	1877-8
Durmizwern		1877-8	Ntanta	S	1877-8	**CORPORAL**		
Dyup		1877-8 r	Panti		1877-8 r	Pagel	C	1877-8
Esau		1877-8	Peke		1877-8 r	Schenk	W	1877-8
Fecani		1877-8	Petros		1877-8	**PRIVATE**		
Fityi		1877-8	Pomp		1877-8	Brown	W	1877-8
Fudu	T	1877-8	Quazi		1877-8 r	Bruske	C	1877-8
Galo		1877-8	Rasi		1877-8	Bruske	J	1877-8 r
Ganto		1877-8 r	Schubeyi		1877-8	Buch	A	1877-8
Ggomfa		1877-8 r	Sexwarn		1877-8	Burmeister	F	1877-8 r
Gunta		1877-8	Seya	E	1877-8	Crossman	W	1877-8
Henry		1877-8	Skepe		1877-8 r	Fenner	W	1877-8
Hlobo		1877-8 r	Stephen		1877-8 r	Hamman Snr	W	1877-8
Holoda		1877-8 r	Tabalazo		1877-8 r	Hardwich	H	1877-8
Jack		1877-8 r	Tainto		1877-8	Hoffeld	A	1877-8
Jala		1877-8 r	Tata		1877-8 r	Jacobs	J	1877-8
Jali		1877-8	Tavagi	E	1877-8	Karshagen	F	1877-8
Jantyi		1877-8	Teli	B	1877-8	Keitzman	C	1877-8
Janytyi		1877-8 r	Tempo		1877-8	Kobus	W	1877-8
January		1877-8	Tentile		1877-8	Kuhn	C	1877-8
Jobo		1877-8	Tobi		1877-8	Kumm	W	1877-8
Kolisi		1877-8 r	Tokwe		1877-8	Lange	C	1877-8
Kona		1877-8	Tonke		1877-8	Leverentz	C	1877-8
Leivani		1877-8	Tshali	T	1877-8	Markus	A	1877-8
Libela		1877-8 r	Tshatshube		1877-8	Meyers	A	1877-8
Lolonga		1877-8	Tshayi	J	1877-8	North	W	1877-8
Lufelo		1877-8	Twayi	N	1877-8	Pagel	W	1877-8
Luke		1877-8	Vavani		1877-8 r	Paul	G	1877-8 r
Maclean		1877-8	William		1877-8 r	Ruch	J	1877-8
Mali	C	1877-8	Yape		1877-8 r	Schmidt	A	1877-8
Mangina	T	1877-8 r	Yaya		1877-8 r	Schmidt	J	1877-8
Mangina	F	1877-8 r	Zaye		1877-8	Schroeder	J	1877-8
Maniyo		1877-8 r	Zayo		1877-8	Schwartz Snr	C	1877-8
Manji	S	1877-8				Seibretz Snr	M	1877-8 r
Marnke		1877-8	**KAMASTONE FINGO LEVIES.**			Spitzer	E	1877-8 r
Marona		1877-8 r	**CAPTAIN**			Sternberg	F	1877-8
Matya	J	1877-8	Webster	J.G	1877-8	Sternberg	J	1877-8
Matomela		1877-8	**NO RANK SHOWN**			Sternberg	W	1877-8
Matyeka		1877-8	Anderson	W	1878	Stoltzman	G	1877-8
Mazondo		1877-8 r						
Mfingu		1877-8 r	**KEI ROAD BURGHER FORCE.**			**KEISKAMA HOEK VOLUNTEER CORPS (INFANTRY).**		
Mliko		1877-8 r	**LIEUTENANT**					
Mpalisa		1877-8	Heenon	R.H.H	1877-8	**LIEUTENANT**		
Muleka		1877-8	**PRIVATE**			Kietzmann	C	1877-8
Munije		1877-8	Anderson	J	1878-9 r	**SERGEANT**		
Ncam		1877-8	**NO RANK SHOWN**			Bentz	F	1877-8
Ncanca		1877-8 r	Batras	A	1878-9	**CORPORAL**		
Ndata	J	1877-8	Kincaid	J	?????	Hildebrand	F	1877-8
Ndythyana		1877-8				Ruck	A	1877-8
Ngai		1877-8	**KEISKAMA HOEK BURGHER FORCE.**			**PRIVATE**		
Ngese		1877-8 r	**CAPTAIN**			Beckmann	F	1877-8
Nghubo	J	1877-8 r	Humpel	J.F	1877-8	Bentz	W	1877-8
Ngoutsi		1877-8 r	**LIEUTENANT**			Brown	J	1877-8
Ngxaute		1877-8	Keifer	P	1877-8	Burmeister	A	1877-8
Nizini		1877-8 r	Peter	C	1877-8	Hamann	A	1877-8
Nojoholo		1877-8				Hamann	W	1877-8

Keiskama Hoek Volunteer Corps.

Humpel J	1877-8	
Kable G	1877-8 r	
Krebs H	1877-8	
Myer S	1877-8	
Peinke F	1877-8	
Schenk F	1877-8 r	
Schmidt J	1877-8	
See also 1st Cape Mounted Yeomanry.		
Siebritz M	1877-8 r	
Todd H	1877-8	
Wolf M	1877-8 r	

KEISKAMA HOEK VOLUNTEER MOUNTED CORPS.
CAPTAIN
Nettleton G.A 1877-8
LIEUTENANT
Bodley M 1878 r
Branshaw H 1877-8
Frauenstein G 1877-8
QUARTERMASTER
Lishman J 1877-8
SERGEANT MAJOR
Wambach D 1877-8
SERGEANT
Markus A 1877-8
Schmidt F 1877-8
CORPORAL
Hageman Jnr F 1877-8
Hageman W 1877-8
Hapelt A 1877-8
Kietzmann W 1877-8
Kurtz W 1877-8
TROOPER
Bradshaw J 1877-8
Brown G 1877-8
Brown R 1877-8
Brown W 1877-8
Buchler A 1877-8
Buchler H 1877-8
Buchler H.A 1877-8
Eastes J 1877-8
Ehbert C 1877-8
Ehbert H 1877-8
Frauenstein A 1877-8-9
Hagemann A 1877-8
Hagemann Snr F 1877-8
Hessel H 1877-8
Hessel L KIA 1877-8 r
Hoffeld A 1877-8
Hoffeld P 1877-8
Karshagen C 1877-8 r
Karshagen W 1877-8-9
Kietzmann A 1877-8
Kobus C 1877-8
Kopke F 1877-8
Kreusch C 1877-8 r
Kuhn W 1877-8
Lieverentz C 1877-8

Pagel A 1877-8
Paul C 1877-8
Paul W 1877-8
Peinke A 1877-8
Peter F 1877-8
Peter W 1877-8
Putzser A 1877-8
Putzser W 1877-8
Radloff C 1877-8
Radloff F 1877-8
Radloff G 1877-8 r
Radloff W 1877-8
Schenk F 1877-8
Schmidt A 1877-8
Schmidt G 1877-8
Schroder M.F 1877-8
Schroder W 1877-8
Schwartz C 1877-8
Scott W 1877-8
Sternberg F 1877-8 r
Sternberg W 1877-8
Todd W.J 1877-8

KIMBERLY HORSE.
COMMANDANT
Mac Pherson W.P.G 1878-9
CAPTAIN
Tomes H.B 1878-9
Vyoyen H.S 1879
LIEUTENANT ADJUTANT
Milne J.A 1879
LIEUTENANT QUARTERMASTER
Mc Lean C 1879 r
LIEUTENANT
Hughes H.S 1878-9
Jefferson R 1878-9
Laws H.G.L 1879 r
Thompson W 1879 r
Thompson W 1879 r
  (This medal was unengraved and could be a duplicate).
Tucker W.D 1878-9
REGIMENTAL SERGEANT MAJOR
Fisher H.Mc N 1879
TROOP SERGEANT MAJOR
Driver J 1878-9
Johnston J 1878-9
FARRIER SERGEANT
Mc Leod W 1879
QUARTERMASTER SERGEANT
Bissett W 1877-8-9 r
  See also Cpl W. Bisset Diamond Fields Horse.
SERGEANT
George W 1879 r
Godwin E 1879 r
Hirst E.B No clasp r
  Non Combatant. Butcher
Levi H.M 1879

Joseph H.F 1879 r
Webster T 1879 r
CORPORAL SADDLER
Francis T 1879 r
CORPORAL
Cyrus C.H 1879 r
James W 1879 r
Mc Connichie W 1878-9
Peacock A.P 1878-9 r
Reid J 1878-9
Roberts H 1878-9
TROOPER
Addie D 1878-9 r
Anderson E 1879 r
Andrews G 1879
Andrews J 1878-9 r
Andrews W.S 1879 r
Ashley E.L 1879 r
Bartolomie R 1879 r
Broadlick J 1879 r
Carlson A.J 1879 r
  Reissued 5/4/1929.
Carsten C.B 1878-9
Celler V 1879
Clear D 1879 r
Clist W 1879 r
Cole C 1879
Coleman S.C 1878-9
Connelly P 1879
Cretney J 1878-9 r
Cunningham A 1879 r
Curnow J 1878-9
Davey A 1878-9 r
Davey R 1879 r
De Villiers J.C 1879 r
De Villiers J.D 1879 r
Doonan H 1879 r
Driver T 1878-9
Du Plessis J 1878-9 r
Faillarde E 1879
Fabricius D 1879 r
Farley H 1879 r
Forgie R 1879 r
Fricker R.G 1879
Gabriel A 1879
Genestrille O 1879 r
Gravett T 1878-9 r
Halloway T 1879
Hass C 1879
Haupt E 1878-9 r
Healey J 1879
Heydenrych C.P 1879 r
John H 1878-9
Jones T 1879
Jones W 1879 r
Joseph M 1879 r
Ladyson W.E 1879
Lees J.C 1878
Mc Intyre H 1879 r

Kimberly Horse

Michael	J	1879
Moody	H	1879
Moore	J	1879 r
Mostert	A.B	1879 r
Naylor	J.T	1879 r
Noble	J	1879 r
Obrey	F	1879 r
O'Neill	J	1877-8-9 r
O'Rorke	T	1879 r
Palm	F.W	1879
Patterson	J	1879 r
Patterson	J	1879 r
Peters	L	1879 r
Perry	G	1879
Phillips	T	1879 r
Pickering	T	1879 r
Pooti	T.J	1878
Rule	J	1878-9 r
Scard	J.J	1879
Schultz	C	1878-9 r
Schuman	C	1878-9 r
Smith	H	1879 r
Smith	L	1879 r
Smith	W	1879 r
Snider	J	1879 r
Stewart	J.G	1879
Stewart	S.J	1879 r
Summerlie	H	1879
Symonds	J	1878-9
Timmins	W.H	1878-9
Tucker	S	1879 r
Viljoen	J	1879
Waldek	W.F	1879 r
Walsh	M	1879 r
Webber	H.E	1879 r
Wentzel	J	1878-9 r
Wese	?	1879
White	J	1879
Williams	W	1879
Wilson	L	1879

KIMBERLY RANGERS.
NO RANK SHOWN
Mc Kenzie R.P   1878-9

KING WILLIAM'S TOWN VETERAN VOLUNTEERS.
LIEUTENANT
Wood R   1877-8
  Roll mentions that he had a medal from a previous War.
SERGEANT
Stevenson W   1877-8
CORPORAL
Cresswell G   1877-8
Land J   1877-8
Renney J   1877-8
PRIVATE
Bock P   1877-8

Bradshaw	H	1877-8
Carroll	P.J	1877-8
Cannon	J	1877-8
Clark	E	1877-8
Connolly	R	1877-8
Curling	J.R	1877-8
Dix	O	1877-8
Gilman	G	1877-8
Goodall	W.G	1877-8
Johns	W	1877-8
Kavanagh	W	1877-8
Levey	P	1877-8
Mc Carthy	P	1877-8
Nicholls	T	1877-8

  Role mentions that he had a medal from a previous War.

Radley	R	1877-8
Sherriff	J	1877-8
Tupper	E	1877-8
Vogt	A	1877-8
Walsh	E	1877-8
Walsh	M	1877-8
Watcham	W	1877-8
Webb	C.A	1877-8
Wilmers	H	1877-8

KING WILLIAM'S TOWN VOLUNTEER ARTILLERY
SERGEANT MAJOR
Fuller A.J   1877-8
Morris J.W   1877-8
GUNNER
Honey J.W   1878
Perks T   1877-8
Roach M   1877-8

KOKSTADT VOLUNTEERS.
TROOPER
Grierson H.F   1878 r

KOMGHA FINGO LEVY.
CAPTAIN
Cowie J   1878
LIEUTENANT
Cowie J.H   1878
SERGEANT
Marmanquua   1878
Mqqeuzana V   1878
CORPORAL
Ardonce A   1878
Barlu   1878
Bowler   1878
Boy   1878
Browngee   1878
Dick   1878
Dimmiss   1878
Kungelagissimla   1878
Soldad   1878
Tattani   1878

PRIVATE
Andries		1878
April		1878
Bommala		1878
Carlonie		1878
Chabo		1878
David		1878
Dwango		1878
Farkana		1878
Farlonie		1878
Fourpenny		1878
Furne		1878
Gaduka		1878
George		1878
George	V	1878
Go	J	1878
Guheku (?)		1878
Gwangau		1878
Halfcrown		1878
Jack		1878
Jacob		1878
Jacob		1878
Jacob 2nd		1878
Jacob 3rd		1878
Jacob	F	1878
Jafton		1878
Jim		1878
John		1878
John	M.H	1878
Jonas (1)		1878
Jonas (2)		1878
Jonnie		1878
Jueman		1878
Kambee		1878
Kangayongo		1878
Katuto		1878
Koliotronie		1878
Kondela 1st		1878
Kondela 2nd		1878
Kubars		1878
Kulas		1878
Kuttanie		1878
Lannuane		1878
Lentula		1878
Letta		1878
Maclean		1878
Maclean		1878
Makahusie		1878
Matross		1878
Maqueto		1878
Melusane		1878
Min	J	1878
Moaf		1878
Moaf		1878
Mulgrass		1878
Mungala		1878
Nagola		1878
Nillonie		1878
Nomingane		1878

Komgha Fingo Levy

Patanie	1878	Hlanabi		1877-8 r	Tengu	S	1877-8 r
Pattin	1878	Hlanbula		1877-8 r	Thume	T	1877-8 r
Peater	1878	Ingalwa		1877-8 r	Tinny		1877-8
Peckana	1878	Ingothia		1877-8	Tupie	K	1877-8 r
Pembane	1878	Jack		1877-8 r	Twetoo		1877-8 r
Pimbie	1878	Keker		1877-8	Twetu	B	1877-8 r
Sabata	1878	Kelete		1877-8 r	Umdaga	J	1877-8 r
Sabie	1878	Kidama		1877-8	Umhilini	W	1877-8 r
Sammugisha	1878	Kinkebe		1877-8	Umlandu	A	1877-8 r
Schnpie	1878	Koffee		1877-8 r	Umlandu	J	1877-8 r
Sickle	1878	Kraai	D	1877-8 r	Umquibi		1877-8 r
Skay	1878	Kraai	W	1877-8 r	Umsiklana		1877-8 r
Soktel	1878	Langa	C	1877-8 r	Umzilini	T	1877-8 r
Soldad	1878	Linda		1877-8	Vumazoke		1877-8 r
Stephen	1878	Lopolo	L	1877-8 r	Xeleke	W	1877-8 r
Swartboy	1878	Mabetu	r	1877-8 r	Xobola		1877-8 r
Taka	1878	Machoba		1877-8 r	Xule		1877-8 r
Tamer	1878	Madella	J	1877-8 r	Xumbanie	B	1877-8 r
Togo	1878	Magazole		1877-8 r	Zandenie		1877-8
Tom	1878	Maize	M	1877-8 r			
Tondoni	1878	Malapi	J	1877-8 r	**LONSDALES HORSE.**		
Tubuku	1878	Malowana		1877-8 r	COMMANDANT		
Tunine	1878	Maqazola		1877-8	Lonsdale R.L		
Twonie	1878	Mase		1877-8 r	Note on Role: "Medal already prepared		
Umgatee	1878	Masoka	Jacob	1877-8 r	by WO" See 3rd Battallion N.N.C.		
Van Vellen	1878	Masoka	Jantjie	1877-8	CAPTAIN		
Vetham	1878	Manzana	S	1877-8 r	Burnet	R	1879
Zano	1878	Manzana	J	1877-8 r	Commack	J	1879
Zazela	1878	Matela		1877-8 r	Drury Lowe R.C		1879
Zelliangy	1878	Madella Snr	A	1877-8 r	Gordon	A	1877-8-9
Zondana	1878	Madella Jnr	S	1877-8 r	Hickson	J.C	1879
		Mhlelini	J	1877-8 r	Duplicate medal only returned.		
LEACHS FINGOES.		Mngandi	G	1877-8 r	CAPTAIN ACTING ADJUTANT		
LIEUTENANT		Mnquandie	J	1877-8 r	Reeves	E.H	1879
Barnes W	1877-8	Mokoli		1877-8	LIEUTENANT		
Leach J.B	1877-8	Mona		1877-8	Billinghurst S.F		1879 r
SERGEANT		Mpula	J	1877-8	#Bourchier C.L.J (page 120) 1879		
Barnes W	1877-8 r	Mtanya	U	1877-8 r	Gardner	T.F.K	1879
Shabi S	1877-8	Mtia	G	1877-8 r	Hurt	J	1879
CORPORAL		Mtia	A	1877-8 r	Maunsell	C.S	1879
Hlakusa	1877-8 r	Mtuka		1877-8 r	Myburgh	R.W	1879
Hlati J	1877-8	Mzelini	T	1877-8	Prengerest (Prendergast) A 1879		
Shuba S	1877-8	Mzuzu		1877-8	Robertson D.P		1879
Zufa	1877-8	Panza		1877-8 r	Studd	A.E	1879
PRIVATE		Parass		1877-8	Von Wackerbarth The		
Africa	1877-8 r	Pie	W	1877-8 r	Baron Henry		1879
Baboo	1877-8 r	Platjie		1877-8 r	Webster	A.W	1879 r
Bantisi	1877-8 r	Quinkiwe		1877-8	Werge	W.B	1879
Basuto	1877-8	Quizana		1877-8 r	SERGEANT MAJOR		
Bobeyan	1877-8 r	Scoisana	J	1877-8	Greetham H.T.J		1879
Boopa	1877-8 r	Shume		1877-8 r	# Rampton J		1879
Dabie	1877-8 r	Sibenda	J	1877-8 r	ORDERLY ROOM SERGEANT		
Danibi J	1877-8 r	Silanda	J	1877-8 r	Priestley	S	1879
Daniess	1877-8 r	Silini		1877-8	FARRIER SERGEANT		
Fainaktaba	1877-8 r	Slangani		1877-8	Dood	G	1879 r
Gama J	1877-8 r	Slatama		1877-8	QUARTERMASTER SERGEANT		
					Naylor	T.J	1879

Spink Sale 7012 Lot 1019. 19 Apr 2007
South Africa 1877-79, one clasp, 1879 (Sgt. Maj: J. Rampton, Lonsdales Horse), good very fine Hammer Price £450.

Lonsdales Horse

Lonsdale's Horse SOUTH AFRICA   THE ZULU WAR   THE IRREGULARS.—QUESTION   Hansard HaHC Deb 17 June 1879 vol 247 cc31-2 31

MR. PARNELL asked the Secretary of State for the Colonies, Whether he has received information that, in addition to the Regular Troops and Native Contingent, considerable forces of Irregulars and Volunteers are employed in South Africa, recruited from the floating population of the Colonies and Diamond Fields; whether he has seen the statements in the last Mail News from South Africa that parties of these men, known as "Lonsdale's Horse," have taken to highway robbery in the neighbourhood of Durban; and, whether he is aware that **Sir Arthur Conynghame**, lately commanding in South Africa, has described these Volunteers as enlisting for the purpose of plundering, "fighting, not for Country, but cattle?"

SIB MICHAEL HICKS-BEACH Sir, it is the case that considerable Forces of Irregulars and Volunteers are employed in South Africa, and they have done excellent service. I have not seen the statements in the last Mail News from South Africa quoted by the hon. Member; he has not stated where they are to be found. I have heard nothing at all confirming them; but if any members of "Lonsdale's Horse" had been guilty of highway robbery, which I cannot believe, they could, of course, be made amenable by the civil and military authorities; and I am sure that that efficient and gallant officer, Commandant Lonsdale himself, would be the first to take steps for the purpose. Sir Arthur Cunynghame never, so far as I know, 32 described the Volunteers as enlisting for the purpose of plundering, " fighting, not for country, but cattle." He quotes, in his book, an opinion expressed by a speaker in South Africa to that effect; but he prefaces the quotation by saying that he had always had a high opinion of the Volunteers, and does not altogether agree with it.

MR. PARNELL said, the statement was made by the correspondent of the Eastern Province Herald of Durban, who spoke of the Lonsdale Horse as a desperate set of roughs, who had committed open robbery in public, and defied everybody, including the police. On one night, after having received a month's pay, 20 of them were taken to the station for drunkenness, and three "run in" for theft.

SOUTH AFRICA Clasp 1879 **LIEUT C.L.J BOURCHIER** LONSDALES HORSE   Medal appeared on ebay 19/10/09 Item number: 200392717686

Starting bid: £1,085.00, or buy it now Price: £1,095.00   Lieutenant Bourchier served with Lonsdales Horse from early May 1879.

Lonsdales Horse were formed into four Troops and three of these took part in the second invasion under Maj General Crealock's I Division. After the Battle of Ulundi two troops served with Colonel Clarke's column (C and D Troops) and one troop with Lt Colonel Baker Russell (B Troop). B Troop took part in the capture of the fugitive Zulu King.

I have been unable to establish which Troop Bourchier served with but since A Troop never crossed into Zululand , members to this Troop would not have received the Clasp 1879.   Charles Legendre Johnstone Bourchier. Born August 1851. Queens Cadet. Sub Lieutenant, 35th Regiment 29.12.71.   Sub-Lieutenant, 65th Regiment 26.3.73.   Resigned 2.11.73. Lieutenant, Lonsdales Horse, Zulu War 1879. Captain, Cape Colonial Forces c1880's.   Father; Colonel Legendre Charles Bourchier 98th Regiment – Indian Mutiny veteran.

He was described as being a descendant of William The Conqueror. Nice Irregular Officers medal to confirmed ex imperial Officer

Lonsdales Horse

SERGEANT
Coghill	W.H	1879

Duplicate medal only returned.

Edwards	G.R	1879
Martin	C.A	1879
Rennie	W.A	1879

CORPORAL
Butler	St. J.G	1879
Levins	R	1879 r
Lewis	J	1877-8-9 r
Mayor	J.H	1877-8-9
Wilson	H	1879 r

LANCE CORPORAL
Mc Combie	T.M	1879

TRUMPETER
Ayres	R	1879
Best	J	1879

TROOPER/PRIVATE
Andrews	A	1879
Atkins	J	1879 r
Baldwyn	T	1879
Bates	E.W	1877-8-9
Brodie	A.W	1879
Casper	H.J	1879 r
Chaloner	G	1879
Chapman	H	1879
Christianson	T.H	1879 r
Chubb	W.G	1879
Clarke	J	1879 r
Clinton	I	1879 r
Clayton	J	1879 r
Dixon	J	1879
Draper	F.W	1879 r
Ferguson	J.A	1879 r
Freeman	E	1879 r

Reissued 21/9/1903.

Geingan	M	1879
Griffen	J.J	1879
Hamilton	J	1879 r
Harris	E	1879
Hartley	T	1879
Higgins	C	1879 r
Hollcampf	C.J	1877-8-9
Jenkins	A.P	1879
Kelly	T	1879 r
Kennedy	R.L	1879 r
Kirby	F.V	1879
Lever	J	1879 r
Little	C	1879
Livingston	G	1879
Mc Kenzie	R	1879
Mc Kinnen	H.W	1879
Mc Kinnon	K	1879
Newton	D	1879
Oliver	P	1878-9
Pansey	A	1879
Pickard	H	1879
Pollard	W	1879 r
Pope	F	1879 r
Refenstein	O	1879 r
Rose	W.F	1877-8-9

See also Lonsdale Mounted Rifles.

Rush	T	1879 r
Russel	G	1879
Sadler	T.O	1879
Schenck	A.C	1879
Schmidt	P	1879 r
Sherry	P.T	1879
Shervington	W.M	1879
Teasel	C.A	1879
Tothill	F	1879
Upton	S	1879
Upton	S	1879 r
Walker	R	1879
Warner	J	1879 r
Wilckens	J.H.T	1879 r
Willis	R	1879 r
Yateman	F.W	1879

LONSDALES MOUNTED RIFLES.

CORPORAL
Miller	W.L	1879
Wilson	W	1879 r

TRUMPETER
Smuts	H	1879 r

TROOPER
Davidson	T.L	1879
Dreyer	P	1879 r
Hillier	H	1879 r
Madden	M	1879
Mergenroad	H	1879
Rose	W.F	1879
Stockdale	J	1879

LYDENBURG RIFLES.

COMMANDANT
Owen	L.M	1879

CAPTAIN
# Corrie	E.V	1879
Van de Venter	W	1879 r

LIEUTENANT
Geere	C	1879
Mortimer	B	1879
Wells	F.J	1879

REGIMENTAL SERGEANT MAJOR
Williamson	S	1879 r

TROOP SERGEANT MAJOR
Lewis	M	1879
Nelson	J	1879

SERGEANT MAJOR
Phillips	J.H	1879

QUARTERMASTER SERGEANT
Jackson	S	1879

ARMOURER SERGEANT
Henderson	K	1879

See also Pte Henderson Transvaal Rangers.

QUARTERMASTER
Hepworth	J.C	1879

FARRIER SERGEANT
Hayes	M	1879

See also Cpl Hayes Transvaal Rangers.

ORDERLYROOM SERGEANT
Cossins	G.H	1879

SADDLER SERGEANT
O'Briend	J.M	1879

SERGEANT
Doig	A.E	1879
Lewis	H	1879 r
Thriffs	J	1879

CORPORAL
Brown	P	1879
Brown	W	1879 r
Nelson	J	1879
O'Reilly	J.R	1879 r
Sharrocks	J	1879

As a Trooper with CMR had a Medal from a previous War. The Clasp only may have been issued.

BUGLER
Hopkins	H	1879 r

TROOPER
Addison	H	1879 r
Anderson	J	1879

See also Transvaal Rangers.

Bates	G	1879
Barclay	H	1879
Barker	T.W	1879 r
Blank	C	1879
Bowden	J	1879 r
Brandeo	J	1879 r
Brittain	H	1879
Brooks	W	1879 r
Burton	?	1879 r
Carmesin	H.C	1879

Dix Noonan Web Auction Lot 243, 27 Jun 07
South Africa 1877-79, 1 clasp, 1879 (**Capt. E. V. Corrie,** Lydeng. Rifles), clasp backstrap with brooch fitting, nearly extremely fine. Hammer Price £880 Captain E. V. Corrie, Lydenburg Rifles, clasp confirmed. 106 medals issued to the regiment; 102 with clasp '1879'; 47 returned to Woolwich/Mint. Captain Corrie was the author of the book, The Promised Land, 1884. In it he gives a graphic account of the Second Campaign of the Second Sekukuni War (1879) and of the assault on the Sekukuni's Stad, 28 November 1879, in which the Lydenburg Rifles took part. During the First Boer War, Lydenburg was the scene of a siege, 6 January-30 March 1881; the British Garrison of some 100 men being commanded by **Lieutenant Walter Long**.

Lydenburg Rifles

E. V. Corrie, who was later a member of the Lydenburg Rifles, gives a graphic account in "The Promised Land: Or Nine Years, Gold Mining, Hunting and Volunteering, In the Transvaal (1884) early in the morning of the 28th November 1879 the column under Major Bushman moved into position. His description of the Swazi host leaving Fort Burgers: 'Before we left Fort Burgers, we were joined by a force of nearly 8,000 Swazies, and never can anyone who beheld these natives forget their magnificent appearance. The Swazie is the perfection of a black warrior, and his war-dress even finer than that of the Zulu Kafir, our crowd of 8,000 were magnificently attired in beautifully-dressed leopard skins, and thick head-dresses of black ostrich feathers. When on the march the dusky companies sweep along at a great rate, each warrior on his left arm carries a shield, black, white, or striped, according to his regiment; from his waist hangs a kilt of leopard tails, or twisted strips of fur, and in the right hand is held the short stabbing assegai - a few of the 8,000 had rifles slung across their backs, but in the fighting that ensued most of the Swazies depended on the assegai. The Lydenburg Rifles was the only mounted force with the column, and to us fell the advanced post....The Swazies were led, in addition to their own chiefs, by five white men - **McLeod, Campbell, Walker, Barnett** and another..... On the second day after forming larger, we received orders to hold ourselves in readiness to march four hours before next dawn...The mountain to be climbed was we knew so steep that both hands and feet would have to be used...**Campell** who ran a dead heat with ***George Eckersley** for first up the heights, carried a small Union Jack to plant on the summit in one hand. and a large assrgai in the other. Campbell was brave to recklessness, but what became of him never transpired.... Corrie then mentions other incidents on the march...'At punctually four hours before dawn the whispered order was passed to fall in. The moon was then at the full, and poured a flood of light on the most imposing scene we had ever witnessed. From the host of the Swazies there was hardly a sound as they silently gathered in one dense cloud, from the centre of which started their black column, the Kafirs forming in companies as they marched off over the plain, their bare feet giving back little sound as they trod the ground. 'I cannot describe the wild effect produced by the great host of sable warriors. Their towering head-dresses of black ostrich plumes gave them individually an imposing appearance and fictitious stature, while viewed as a mass, the waving plumes and swinging kilts produced a weird effect of ever-changing and cloud-like mass of shadow. 'Meanwhile the Lydenburg Rifles were falling in, and the shrill neigh of a horse or ringing of a loose stirrup iron as we sprang into our saddles sounded rowdy enough, compared with the silent and ghost-like movements of the natives. As we marched off our horses' feet among the stones made more noise than the thousands of Swazies. The 94th and 80th were about falling-in when we started, and soon we could hear the steady tramp of their advance from the rear...' We presently off-saddled, and having seen the horses knee-haltered and guards posted, I started off with Lieut. Sampson of Fereira's horse, to do a little exploring on our own account... They then went on to discover the cave which was the hiding place of Sicooenie (Sekukuni). Early the following morning, 29th November, 1879, Captain W. G. Lawrell and Captain J. E. Macaulay, together with the four or five other men killed in the previous day's fighting, were buried at the camp with full military honours.

*George Eckersley, born 1851 in Natal, joined Lydenburg Volunteers to fight the Pedi and Sekukuni in 1876. In 1879 raised a Corps of African volunteers for service in the Zulu War as part of Rowland's Column - afterwards became part of the Transvaal Mounted Police.

Killed at the Stad and 'Fighting Koppie' and buried at the camp on the plain:	
Captain W. G. Lawrell	4th Hussars, Wolseley's Staff.
Captain J. E. Macaulay	12th Lancers - in command Transvaal Mounted Rifles.
Cpl P. MacNally	2nd Bn 21st Regiment
Pte H. Donahoe	2nd Bn 21st Regiment
Pte W. Weston	2nd Bn 21st Regiment
Pte Chipps	94th Regiment
Cpl E. Mitchell	Border Horse
Killed on the mountain or at the Stad, but buried at Fort Victoria at the top of the mountain:	
Lt Alister Campbell, R.N.	Swazi Native Contingent
Sgt-Maj. R. Wilson	Ferreira's Horse
Pte Wm. Reston	2nd Bn 21st Regiment
QMS N. McLeod	Border Horse
Tpr Mackay	Border Horse
Tpr P. Matibe	Transvaal Mounted Rifles.

The remains of these 13 men were re-interred at the northern end of the 'Fighting Koppie' by Mr. B. P. Margetson and party of the Northern Transvaal Soldiers' Graves Association on 25th December, 1961. Joseph Lehmann records that three officers were killed and seven wounded; other ranks, seven killed and 43 wounded. Smith records that three officers were killed and five wounded; other ranks, 10 killed and about 30 wounded. In so far as deaths are concerned, the latter figures appear to be correct.

Ref Military History Journal - Vol 2 No 6 THE SEKUKUNI WARS PART II by H.W. Kinsey http://samilitaryhistory.org/vol026nk.html

Lieutenant N.D Black - 1st/1st NNC

Trooper J.A. Blaikie - Natal Carbineers

Captain C.R. Bradstrret - Newcastle Mounted Rifles

Lieutenant - Colonel F.A. Weatherley - Border Horse

Trooper R. Brown - Frontier Light Horse

Captain H.C.D. D'Arcy - Frontier Light Horse

Major J Dartnell - Natal Mounted Police

Captain T.R. Hamilton - Transvaal Rangers

Lieutenant G. Williams - Frontier Light horse

Quartermaster J.R. Mccormack - 1st/3rd NNC

Lieutenant J. Poole - Border Horse

Lieutenant J.L Raines - 2nd/2nd NNC

Lieutenant F.J.D Scott - Natal Carbineers

Lieutenant the Hon. S.W..P. Vereker - 2nd/3rd NNC

Orderly Room Sergeant - F.D Brissenden - Border Horse

Captain J.F. Lonsdale - Ist/3rd NNC

Mr F.O.Brissenden, who was an Orderly Sergeant in Colonel Weatherly's Border Horse, was war correspondent Friend of Free State Gazette, and was also on the staff of Galignam's Messenger. He was but thirty-two years of age when he was killed during the attack on the Zloblane Mountain on March 28.

Captain Thomas Rice Hamilton, a brother of General Hamilton, entered the British Army in 1847, and after serving some time in India, returned to Europe, and volunteered for the Crimea, where he served with local rank as Captain, and as Lieut. Colonel in the turkish Army at Kertch, and was awarded the Turkish medal. In 1855 Captain Hamilton, whilst on leave, was appointed Resident Magistrate at Raglan, New Zealand. He retired from the army in 1867; in January last he settled with his family in South Africa, serving as Assistant Commissary General, first at Pietermaritzburg and afterwards at Pretoria, until appointed Captain in the Transvaal Rangers. He was killed in the disastrous affair upon the Zloblane Mountain, while endeavouring to extricate his troop from the overwhelming mass of Zulu warriors by which it was surrounded.

Captain James Faunce Lonsdale, 1st Battalion, 3rd Regiment Natal Native Contingent, was the eldest son of Mr J.Faunce Lonsdale, Mayor of King William's Town, British Kaffraria. As a member of the Kaffrarian Volunteers, was present at the momoral action of the "Springs" when ninety Kaffrarian Volunteers defeated over 1,500 Galekas, their Fingo allies having failed to come to their support. When war was imminent with the Zulus he accepted a Captaincy under his cousin, Commandant La Trober Lonsdale (late 74th Highlanders). He was in the engagement on the 12th January at Sirayo's Kraal, when the behaviour of the Contigent received the praises of Lord Chelmsford. On the fatal morning at Isandlwhana he was on picquet duty, his company being one of the first to engage the enemy, and fought until their ammunition was expended. Of 120 natives and nine Europeans composing this company, only Lieut. Vanes and three natives escaped.   The Graphic (London, England), Saturday, August 16, 1879; Issue 507

Lydenburg Rifles

Chapman	R	1879	Phew	H	1879 r	Ross	J	1878
Coetzee	?	1879 r	Prex	G	1879	Smith	J.A.J	1877-8
Connor	J	1879 r	Rockbeck	M	1879 r	**CIVILIAN SURGEON**		
Coomis	F	1879	Rodgers	H.W	1879	Ashton	J.E	1879
Cooper	D	1879 r	Rolson		1879	Clapham	J.C.N	1878-9
See also Transvaal Rangers.			Rush	J	1878-9	Wright	H.C	1878-9
Crowley	P	1878-9	Shaw	J.W	1879	**DISPENSER**		
D'Arcy	J	1879	Silow	A.H	1879	Beste	W	1878
See also Frontier Light Horse.			Smith	W	1879			
Darling	W	1879 r	Steel	T.T	1879 r	**MURRAYS ORANGE ROVERS.**		
Davis	W	1879 r	Stein	W.G	1879	**CAPTAIN**		
Day	A	1879 r	Truppel	F	1879 r	#Murray	G	1877-8
De Koza	P	1879 r	Van de Venter	J	1879 r	**LIEUTENANT**		
De Reis	A	1879 r	Von Brandis	A	1879	Combes	L.M	1877-8
Dickens	W	1879 r	See also Frontier Light Horse.			Murray D/S	W	1877-8-9 r
Dorkerill	R.H	1879 r	Walsh	M.L	1879	**QUARTER MASTER SERGEANT**		
Dore	F	1879	Watermeyer	J	1879	Banbridge	?	1877-8
Dos Santos	J	1879 r	Williams	A	1879	**SERGEANT**		
Ehrhard	O	1879 r	Williams	J	1879 r	Charlton	J	1877-8 r
Fagan	J	1879				**CORPORAL**		
Fernandez	J	1879 r	**MACLEANS FINGO LEVIES.**			Glass	T.U	1877-8
Ferreira	L	1879 r	**CORPORAL**			Woest	H.C	1877-8 r
Fluke	G	1879	Moffat	W.A	1877-8	**BUGLER**		
Francis	C	1879				Essex	T	1877-8
Fry	O	1879 r	**MAFETENG CONTINGENT**			**PRIVATE**		
Grace	E	1879	**CAPTAIN**			Ackerman		1877-8
Harris	A.A	1879	Barkly	A.S.C	1879	Bardenhorst		1877-8
Hellier	C	1878-9				Bezuidenhout		1877-8 r
Hendricks	H	1879 r	**MAJOR LARKINS POLICE.**			Bowen		1877-8 r
Hesselbein	N	1879 r	**TROOPER**			Briggs		1877-8 r
Hoey	J	1879 r	Ohye	P.H	1879	Condon	J	1877-8 r
Holmes	P.H	1879				David		1877-8 r
Jackson	C	1879 r	**MAJOR NESBITTS.**			Durant	P.C	1877-8
Joaquin	A	1879 r	**NO RANK SHOWN**			Gentle	J	1877-8 r
Kimlin	J	1879	Wustenhoff	J.H	1878	Glass	E	1877-8
Lamb	?	1879				Gordon		1877-8 r
Lamphere	O.L	1879	**MATATIELE FIELD FORCE**			Green	J	1877-8
Lewis	J.R	1879	**NO RANK SHOWN**			Hanies		1877-8
Lewis	S	1879 r	Liefeldt	S.B	1878	Herman	J	1877-8 r
Loxton	?	1879				Hogan		1877-8 r
Maeder	C	1879 r	**MOUNTED EUROPEAN TROOPS**			Hunt	J	1877-8 r
May	J	1879 r	**NO RANK SHOWN**			Hynes	J	1877-8
Mc Naughton	H	1879	Human	G	1879	Kayton		1877-8 r
Neintjes	B	1879				Leach		1877-8
Miller	J	1879 r	**MEDICAL FORCES COLONIAL FORCES.**			Lewis	C	1877-8 r
Moll	?	1879 r				Mc Can	F	1877-8
Moody	C.S	1879	**SURGEON**			Mc Kenna Jnr	J	1877-8
Wounded at Murengeni Jani Hilr on 9/6/1879 See also Tvl. Rangers.			Chiappini	P.A	1877-8	Odendaal		1877-8
			Clarke	J.H	1879	Pickles		1877-8 r
Nelson	?	1879	Cumming	R.B	1877-8-9	Quirk	T	1877-8
Nicholas	M	1879 r	Daumas	L.C	1879 r	Reeves	W	1877-8 r
Noyes	C	1879	Guild	R.K	1879	Smith	T	1877-8 r
Oats	W	1879	Hall	B.W	1877-8 r	Stewart	D	1877-8 r
Oasthuizen	S	1879 r	Hartley VC E.B 1877-8-9			Stewart	J	1877-8 r
Pauer	M	1878-9 r	VC for an action at Moirosi's Stronghold.			Taylor	G	1877-8
Percival B Not on medal roll			Kennemeyer	D.R	1878-9 r	Thompson		1877-8
Died heart disease 13/6/1879.			Ress	C	1879	Tims	J	1877-8

Glendining's 22nd June 1988, Lot 175, South Africa 1877-79, medal to the officer who raised and commanded Murray's Orange Rovers. 1 clasp, 1877-8-9 (Capt. G. Murray, Murray's Orange Rovers) Capt. G.Murray listed as receiving the 1877-8 clasp, N.EF (£200-£300)

Murraysburg Volunteer Cavalry

Woest JnrF 1877-8
York 1877-8 r

MURRAYSBURG VOLUNTEER CAVALRY.
LIEUTENANT
Joubert J 1878
SERGEANT MAJOR
Van Heerden J.L 1878
SERGEANT
Francis J 1878 r
CORPORAL
Campbell J 1878
Hallier L 1878 r
TRUMPETER
Hogan T 1878
TROOPER
Benadie J 1878
Booysen J 1878 r
Brider D.S 1878
Burger D 1878
Cottman D 1878 r
 Accidentally Killed.
Cruse J.B 1878
Dames H 1878 r
Edwards C 1878 r
Ferguson C 1878
Goutier P 1878
Joubert J 1878
Le Roux M.G 1878
Le Roux J.I 1878
Liebenberg D 1878 r
Van As G 1878
Van Coller J 1878 r
Van de Merwe J 1878
Van der Merwe Iz/Son W 1878
Van der Merwe W's Son 1878
Van der Merwe W.H 1878
Van Heerden D 1878
Van Heerden G 1878
Van Heerden J.L 1878
Van Heerden M.J 1878

MURRAYSBURG VOLUNTEER CAVALRY & SISSISONS HORSE.
CAPTAIN
Lee H 1878
Sissison J 1878
DRIVER
Willemse G 1878
TROOPER
Williams J 1878

NATAL CARBINEERS
Those Killed in Action (KIA) lost their lives at Isandhlwana on 22/1/1879. The Regiment was raised on 15 January, 1855, and gazetted on 13 March of that year. Original troop was recruited

Captain T Shepstone Anglo Boer War Lieutenant. W Royston.

in Pietermaritzburg, troops were soon established in Richmond, Karkloof, Estcourt, Ladysmith, Newcastle, and Dundee. The Carbineers served against Bushmen in the 1850s and I860s, and in 1873 against Langalibalele, incurring casualties. At Isandlwana they lost two officers and nineteen other ranks. Major Dartnell of the Natal Mounted Police commanded the unit in Glyn's column.

CAPTAIN
*Shepstone T 1879
LIEUTENANT
*Royston W 1879
Scott F.J.D KIA 1879
QUARTERMASTER
London W KIA 1879
SERGEANT MAJOR
Methley F 1879
Scott D 1879
QUARTERMASTER SERGEANT
Dullock W (I.C) KIA 1879
SERGEANT
Mac Farlane G.J 1879
*Mc Kenzie ? 1879
Mileman W 1879
*Scott ? Not on medal roll
FARRIER SERGEANT
*Hall ? Not on medal roll
CORPORAL
*Matterson ? Not on medal roll
*Methley ? Not on medal roll
Merryweather ? 1879
*Mileman ? Not on medal roll
Stirton H 1879
*Symons ? Not on medal roll

TRUMPETER
*Scott C 1879
TROOPER
*Badger ? Not on medal roll
*Ball G 1879
*Barker W 1879
*Bissett C 1879
 # *Blaikie J.A KIA 1879
see portrait p122
***Borraine (Bornin) G KIA 1879**
*Brewer H 1879
Brown ? 1879
Burns ? 1879
*Byrne ? Not on medal roll
*Bullock ? Not on medal roll
Christian C.G.S KIA 1879
 See also P.A.G. Rifle Vols.
*Clarence B.C 1879
Collins ? 1879
Comrie P.G 1879
Cook W 1879
*Cowrie ? Not on medal roll
Craik W 1879
Crawford ? 1879
Davis H.W KIA 1879
see page 166
Deane H (J) KIA 1879
Dick ? 1879
Dickinson H KIA 1879
*Edwards W 1879
*Fletcher C 1879
Gibson H 1879
*Granger(Grainger) W1879
*Greene E.M 1879
*Hair A 1879
Haldane(Haldam)) C KIA 1879

Natal Carbineers

1879 Natal Carbineers
Troopers Miller, B.C Clarence, A. Muirhead, W.W.Baker.
Troopers C.Tatham, Corpl H Stirton, Tropper W. Grainger.

Sir E. Wood distributed, before he left Natal, the war medals to the Maritzburg Rifles and the Natal Carabineers, it may be remembered, suffered most severely at the battle of Isandula, where, when the battlefield was afterwards visited by the cavalry brigade under General Marshal, it was found that forty of them had fallen in making a last stand with Colonel Durnford close to where they had all died.
The Belfast News-Letter Saturday 14th 1882, issue 20753.

The Queens Commemoration Diamond Jubilee
The Graphic June 28th 1879
Natal Mounted troops, Natal Carabineers, Umvoti, Natal, and Border Mounted Rifles all Took part in the Colonial Procession.

The Swinburn was purchased in large quantities by Natal, the first ordered in July 1879.They were issued to the Natal Carabineers, Victoria Mounted Rifles, Border Mounted Rifles and similar volunteer units in 1878-9.

On the 22nd Jan. killed at Isandhlwana, in his 20th year. James Adrian Blaikie, Natal Carbineers, eldest son of the late Anthony Adrian Blaikie, and grandson of the late Sir Thomas Blaikie.
The Times, Friday, Mar 07, 1879

Camp, Maritzburg 1887 Natal Carabineers
Tpt-Major A.J.Molyneux, Sergt. Tilney, Sergt. Muir, R-S Major Molyneux, Sergt. Brewer, Sergt Worman,
Sergt Cooke, Sergt Whittaker, Sergt Foxon, Sergt Hair, Sergt Hutton, Sergt Comrie,
Sergt Powell.

Natal Carbineers

*Hawkins V.C (W) KIA 1879
*Hay D/S J 1879
J.B Hay died of Fever 4/5/1879
Hayhow (Haylow) H (C) KIA 1879
Hendenhall W KIA
Not on Medal Roll, On C list
Hilton ? Not on medal roll
Hollington D 1879
Hutton J 1879
***Jackson F KIA 1879**
***Jackson R KIA 1879**
*Keytel ? Not on medal roll
Lavender C 1879
*Little D 1879
Lloyd H 1879
*Lumley W (J) KIA 1879
*McFarlane ? Not on medal roll
Macleroy G.T KIA 1879
Matterson A 1879
Mondenhall W KIA 1879
*Mendenhall on C. list
Miller ? 1879
*Moodie N (M) KIA 1879
Morris ? 1879
*Muirhead A 1879
Pearse A 1879
Pennyfather (Pennefather) H.P 1879
*Rock ? Not on medal roll
*Ross G 1879
***Ross J KIA 1879**
*Shepstone W 1879
*Sibthorne (Sibthorp) W 1879
*Slatter C 1879
*Stirton ? Not on medal roll
***Swift W KIA 1879**
*Symons J 1879
Symonds J.P 1879
***Tarbaton (Tarboton) E KIA 1879**
*Tarbaton (Tarboton) W 1879
Tatham C 1879
Troy ? Not on medal roll
Wales ? 1879
***Whitelaw J (G) KIA 1879**
*Wodehouse (Woodhouse) ? 1879
*List of men at the front, from the Times of Natal, 6th December, 1878.

NATAL HORSE.
Formed from NNC after Isandlwana.
CAPTAIN
De Burgh U.J.R 1879
LIEUTENANT
Purchas F.W 1877-8-9 r
SERGEANT MAJOR
Gray G 1879 r
QUARTERMASTER SERGEANT
Currie W 1879
Fyfe R.B 1879 r
 See also 2nd Natal Native Contg.
Painter J 1879
PAY SERGEANT
Leigh H.B 1879
SERGEANT
Holyoak A 1878-9
##Lane VC T 1879 r
Leeding W 1879
Sheppard F 1879
Sherwood J 1879
CORPORAL
Casselden C 1878-9 r
Evans F 1879
Skea J 1877-8-9
Sweet J 1877-8-9
Tebbs W.A 1877-8-9
TROOPER
Arsorga G.T 1879
Carstens R 1879
Drisley C.R 1879
Frandsen C 1878-9
Green H.J 1879
Could have been issued with the clasp 1877-8-9.
Holm A.P 1878-9
Human G 1879 r
Jebb A.R 1879 r
Johnson P 1879 r
Moore M.T 1879
Moseley N.I 1878-9
O'Connor J 1877-8-9 r
 Also served with F.A.M.P. Two clasps 1877-8 and 1879 could have been issued.
Pietersen (Pte) S 1878-9
Prior J 1879
Ward G No clasp

NATAL HUSSARS.
Original name of the Regiment was the Greytown Mounted Rifles. In 1866 the Natal Hussars was raised by a Major Eastwood. In 1869 the two units amalgamated under the designation of the Natal Hussars. In overall command in Pearson's column was Major Percy Barrow of the 19th Hussars.
CAPTAIN
Norton P 1879
LIEUTENANT
Menne T.C 1879
QUARTERMASTER
Whittaker 1879
QUARTERMASTER SERGEANT
Landsberg 1879
SERGEANT MAJOR
Milner 1879
SERGEANT
Duckham 1879
Preller 1879
CORPORAL
Handley 1879
Player 1879
TRUMPETER
Landsberg 1879
TROOPER
Byloo J 1879
Byloo N 1879
Byrne 1879
Dafel Snr 1879
Dafel Jnr 1879
Dafel J.C 1879
De Waal 1879
Eksteen 1879
Havreman 1879
Harris 1879
Kaufman 1879
Kohler 1879
Markham 1879
Menne 1879
Moore 1879
Newmarch 1879
Niekerk D 1879
Niekerk J.C 1879
Niekerk S 1879

Joseph Lumley initial W on medal roll was born in Yorkshire at Normanby near Scunthorpe on the 8th December 1857 he arrived in South Africa in September 1862. He died on the battlefield of Isandlwana on the 22.01.1879. A small number of the Carbineers had engaged and held the left horn in Durnford's Donga in the middle of the depression in front of Isandlwana Mountain The foot soldiers who were deployed to back them up got caught in hollow ground approaching the Donga where they were overwhelmed and all killed. Durnford and his mounted men had by this time started a retreat up the slope towards the saddle ridge below Isandlwana Mountain. Before they were finally surrounded on the rocky knoll, there they were killed and disembowelled. A monument stands on this spot today. The monument bears the name of J Lumley (Joseph Peter Lumley). David Moon http://www.genealogyworld.net/azwar/

Sergeant T. Lane V.C.
His Victoria Cross was earned on 21/8/1860 at Taku Forts, China while he was serving as Private with 67th Regiment (Hampshire Regiment). This decoration was, however, forfeited by him under Royal Warrant of 7/4/1881. This forfeiture was but one of the total of eight ever recorded. Since 1920 forfeitures were discontinued. His S.A. War Medal with clasp 1879 also appears to have been forfeited.

Natal Hussars

Otto		1879	Barnes	?	1879	Kahns	H.A	1879
Preller	C	1879	Barnes	F	1879		Wounded at Ulundi 4/7/1879
Rabe		1879	Barnes	R.A	1879	Keay	J	1879
Schwegman		1879	Barry	A	1879 r	Kemp	T.E	1879
Taylor		1879	Barry	R.P	1879	Keogh	M	1879
Van de Bosch		1879	Bayley	E	1879		also on roll for Frontier Light Horse
Van Rooyen		1879	Beissner	A	1879	Kuidler	W	1879
Van Zuidam		1879	Brain	W	1879 r	Lavender	H	1879
Vlotman		1879	Brooks	W	1879	Leal	H.H	1879
Wolhuter		1879	Brown	J.S	1879	Marande	F	1879
Younge		1879	Bruce-Ogilvy Hon J		1879	Marriott	F	1879
			Buist	C.M	1879	Jacobson	W.J	1879 r
NATAL LIGHT HORSE.			Carter	J	1879	Mason	H	1879 r
COMMANDANT			Chambers	H	1879	See also Frontier L. Horse.		
Whalley	W.W	1879	Clarke	J	1879 r	Mathieson	J.A	1879
CAPTAIN			Collinge	P.B	1879	Mc Carthy	J	1879 r
Marshall	G	1879	Conway	W	1879	Mc Ewen	E.G	1879
Mc Donald	T	1879	Cozon	E	1879	Mc Ewen	E.J	1879 r
LIEUTENANT			Cradock	C	1879	Mc Laughlin	H	1879 r
Arden	F.H	1879	Cranwell	W.H	1879	Mac Mahon	R.H	1879
colspan=3	Duplicate Medal and Clasp issued 9/7/1910.	Cronin	P	1879	Mesny	P	1879
			Davis D/W	H.E	1879	Mileman	G	1879
Fraser	C.A	1879	Douglas	P	1879 r	Monkman	H	1879
Robertson	W.K	1879	Dupuis	L	1879	Morgan	W	1879 r
Warren	W	1879	Eakins	H.H	1879	Newsome	H	1879
ACTING LIEUTENANT			Egan	D	1879	Nicholson	D	1879 r
Shore	A.D	1879	Emmott	J.H	1879	Nistenmacher	?	No clasp
REGIMENTAL SERGEANT MAJOR			Flynn	P	1879 r	O'Brien	W.J	1879
James	C	1879	Forsyth	D	1879	O'Connor	J.A	1879 r
TROOP SERGEANT MAJOR			Frantz	C	1879 r	O'Connor	P	1879
Burton	G	1879	Full	W	1879	Olmersdahl	F.W	1879
Grant	A.J	1879	Fyfe	D	1879	Parker	J	1879 r
Kerr	W	1879 r	Galloway	F	1879	**Peacock**	**J**	**1879**
FARRIER SERGEANT			colspan=3	Rank corrected on medal to Lieut.	colspan=3	**KIA at Umvolozi River 3/7/1879**
Roberts	W	1879	colspan=3	Lot 96 Spinks Auction 5.12.2002	Payne	G.J.A	1879
QUARTERMASTER SERGEANT			Gandolfe	M	1879	Pescod	?	1879
Lloyd	E.C	1879	Glover	E	1879 r	Pinkerton	J	1879
Stout	A.W	1879	Greenwood	R.B	1879	Richardson	R	1879
SERGEANT			Hallinan	M	1879	Ripley	J	1879
Clabburn	W	1879	Hamilton	A.W	1879 r	Schemble	A	1879 r
Ingle	C	1879	Hanley	J	1879	See also Frontier Light Horse.		
Molyneux	H	1879	Hanrah	R	1879	Scheuble	A	1879
CORPORAL			Harburn	C.R	1879	Seamer	W.F	1879
Farrell	J	1879	Hardon (Duplicate)		1879	Shillson	E	1879
colspan=3	Severely wounded at Ulundi 4/7/1879	Hardon	F.H.H	1879 r	Siems	F.G	1879
Hopton	H.C	1879	Harkson	G.H	1879	Siems	W.G	1879 r
Mc Kinnon	A	1879	Harper	H	1879	Simmons	E	1879 r
colspan=3	Wounded at Isihlingo 5/6/1879	Hassade	H.A	1879	Smith	J.A	1879
North	A	1879	Hayes	J.R	1879	Smith	J.D	1879
Robertson	J	1879	Hodge	W	1879	Smith	J.S	1879
colspan=3	Seamer W.E Not on Medal Roll	Hogan	M	1879 r	Smith	J.V	1879
colspan=3	Wounded at Isihlingo 5/6/1879	Housley	S.S	1879	Sparrow	R.B	1879
Smith	C	1879	Hudson	E.W	1879	Stewart	C	1879
PRIVATE			Jacobson	W.F	1879 r	Swan	R.M	1879
Aboll	S	1879	Jelly	F.S	1879	Tatum	G.L	1879
Addie	G	1879	Josephs	J	1879 r	Terry	J.J	1879
Ambler	P.L	1879	Joughin	C	1879	Thomas	S	1879
Amberley	P.L	1879	Julian	A	1879 r	Toomey	W	1879
Armstrong	H.J	1879	Kahns	A	1879 r	Tuck	E.W	1879

Natal Light Horse

Vine	A.J	1879
Von Kornitski	R.C	1879
Waite	C.A	No clasp
Walker	J	1879 r
Warte	C.A	No clasp
Webb	?	1879
Webber	C	1879
Webster	L	1879
Welsh	T	1879 r
Welyn	F.D	1879
Wilkin	S	1879
Williams	W.C	1879
Wilson	J	1879
Wilson	R	1879 r
Woods	J.G	1879 r
Yendall	J	1879
Young	W.R.C	1879

NATAL MOUNTED INFANTRY.
LIEUTENANT
Lloyd   J   1877-8

NATAL MOUNTED POLICE.
Those Killed in Action KIA lost their lives at Issandhlwana 22/1/79. Formed 1874, in Natal. The Commanding Officer (Major, later Major General Sir John Dartnell), commanded the unit in Glyn's column. In 1894 the title was changed to the Natal Police. The unit sent 80 personnel of all ranks to the Zulu War, of whom 26 were killed at Isandlwana.

COMMANDANT
Dartnell   J.G   1879
   Also had Indian Mutiny Medal.

INSPECTOR
Campbell   F.A   1879
Mansel   G   1879

SUB-INSPECTOR
Phillips   F.L   1879

SERGEANT MAJOR
Stean   W   1879

SERGEANT
Faddy   W.R   1879 r
Hobson   W.H   1879
Maclaren   J.W   1879
Masson   M.A   1879
Mc Queen   D.F   1879
Moor   R   1879

COLOUR SERGEANT
Eaton   R.N   1879
Escaped from Isandhlwana

CORPORAL
Abraham   F.M   No clasp
Campbell   H.F   1879
Capps   H.I   KIA 1879
Carpenter   J   1879
Carter   J   1879
Carter   L   1879
Chaddock D/S   W.S   1879
Died of fever at Helpmakaar
Chappell   S   1879
Clark   H   1879
Clark   J   KIA 1879
Clarke   W   1879
Collier   G   1879
Escaped from Isandhlwana
Cooper   G.J   1879
Corry   ?   1879
Cuming (Cumming) ?   1879
Daniels (Daniels)   S   KIA 1879
Day   E.A   1879 r
De Bathe   T.H   1879
#Doig   D   1879
Dorehill   W.V   1879
Escaped from Isandhlwana
Dorey   C.T   KIA 1879
Eicke   ?   1879
Groschke   A   1879
Hall   M (M.H)   1879
Hamilton   C   1879
Hammond   J.G.C   1879
Jordan   W   1879
Lally   M (H)   KIA 1879
Lyos(Lyons)   E.H   1879
Melville   J.A   1879
Smart   ?   1879

LANCE CORPORAL
Campbell   H.C   KIA 1879 r

TRUMPETER
Angrove   R.S   1879
Haygarth   Jos   1879
Knott   W   1879
Stevens   R.W   1879

TROOPER
Adams   C.F   1879
Allison   M   1879
Babington   G   1879
Bacon   ?   Not on medal roll
Ballech (Balloch)   W   1879
Bampton   ?   Not on medal roll
Banger   G.H   KIA 1879
Bates   F F   1879
Bawtree   W.J.E   1879
Beeby   H   1879

Major Knott. Migrated from Yorkshire to South Africa in 1861, enlisted into the Natal Mounted Police 22nd Oct 1875. Part of the escort of Sir T Shepstone when he annexed the Transvaal in 1877. Also part of the escort in 1880 when Princess Engenie visited the site where her son (Prince Imperial) fell in June 1879. Was RSM in the Natal Carbineers between 1890 and 1894. Major in Royston's Horse during the Zulu uprisings in 1906. It was he who brought the severed head of Chief Bambhata from Mome Gorge to Richmond at the time of the native trials. A Sgt Calverley had removed the head for ease of transport. Information from: Patricia Frykberg Granddaughter of Major William Knott.

Bennett D/S   G   1879
Died of fever at helpmakaar
Berry   H   KIA 1879
Berthold   ?   1879
Billing   ?   1879
Billson   ?   1879
Blakeman   E   KIA 1879
Boik   H   1879
Brown   W.J   1879
Capps J KIA   Not on medal roll
Cooper   B   1879
Davies   C.C   1879
Driemeier (Driemeyer)   W   1879
Murdered at Newcastle
Dryer (Dreyer)   T   1879
Eason   J.A   KIA 1879

A few other survivors of the fight at Isandhlwana also reached **Rorke's Drift**. A Natal Carbineer rode by, leading a spare horse. Without boots, tunic or a gun, he was utterly exhausted, and he took one look at the preparations for another fight and rode on toward Helpmakaar at once. **Troopers Doig and Shannon** of the Natal Mounted Police had also gotten out by Fugitive's Drift, and they rode by to see how their comrades were doing. **Hunter and Green** could not walk, and Lugg could not ride. Too weak to help move the heavy boxes and sacks, **Lugg** was lashing the split stock of his carbine together with an old rein, and he intended to stay and fight. Doig and Shannon also rode on. *The Washing of the Spears by Donld R. Morris. page 397*

NEWCASTLE MOUNTED RIFLES
WHO FELL AT
ISANDHLWANA.

CAPTAIN R. BRADSTREET.

QUARTER MASTER G.E. HITCHCOCK. SERGT A. SWAN.

TROOPERS.
J.W. BARNES. G. GREENBANK. A. MACALISTER.
J. DINKELMAN. A.E. DIXON.

NATAL MOUNTED POLICE.
CORPORAL LALLY. LANCE CORPORAL CAMPBELL.

TROOPERS.
C.H. BANGO. H. BERRY. E. BLAKEMAN. H.S. CAPPS.
J. CLARK. S. DANIEL. C. DOBEY. J. EASON.
W. FLETCHER. H.C. LLOYD. T. MACRAE. C. MEARES.
H. NEIL. A.R. PARSONS. W.T. PEARSE. J.W. PLEYDELL.
A.T. POLLARD. J.W.M. SIDDALL. F. SECRETON. W.E. STINTON.
S. THICKE. C. WHITE. H. WINKLES.

S. HUNTER. RORKE'S DRIFT.

CORPORAL CHADDOCK. HELPMAKAAR.

TROOPERS.
C. BENNETT. W. HAYES. B. INGRAM.
P. NAGLE. H.S. SMITH.

C.J. LOUGHNAN. LADISMITH.

S. GRANT. INTERPRETER N.N.C. ISANDHLWANA.

CONDUCTORS.
L. DuBOIS. D. NOLAN. F.C. DOYLE.
J.P. ARCHBELL. LEROUE.

L.H. BYRNE COMMIS. RORKE'S DRIFT.

C.A. POTTER. N.W.C. HLOBANE.

LLEWELLYN LLOYD. POLITICAL ASSISTANT.

J. FERREIRA. CONDUCTOR KAMBULA.

Deaths Reported in The Times
On the 22nd Jan, killed at the battle of Isandula, in Zululand. Lieutenant the Hon. Standis ; **W.P. Verkker**, Natal Contingent, and previously of the Frontier Light Horse, third son of Viscount Gort, aged 24.
On the 22nd Jan. killed at the battle of Isandula, South Africa, **Arthur Gibson**, Lieutenant 3rd Natal Native Contingent, and previously of the Frontier Light Horse aged 22, third surviving son of John Gibson, Esq. 11 Westbourne Square, W.

Natal Mounted Police

Evans A.J 1879
Fletcher W KIA 1879
Fogg C 1879
Ford J 1879
Fowler A.S 1879
Fuyings(Fugings) ? 1879
Gilmore J 1879
Gleeson D 1879
Green H.C 1879
#Green R 1879
Took part in defence of Rorke's Drift
Haigh L 1879
Hall W 1879
Hall W.G 1879
Hamilton H.R 1879
Harrison G.F 1879
Harrison G 1879
Hayes D/S W (P) 1879
Escaped from Isandhlwana
and died of fever at Helpmakaar.
Hefferman (Hiffernan) N 1879
Heyes H 1879
Hope J.A 1879
Howie G.A 1879
Hughes D/S G 1879
Hughes J 1879
#Hunter S 1879
  KIA Rorkes Drift.
Ingram D/S P.B 1879
Irving F.E 1879
Jones G.W 1879
Kershaw W 1879
Kincade R 1879
Escaped from Isandhlwana
Laughman D/S C.J 1879
Lellyett W 1879
Litton R.T 1879
Lloyd H.C **KIA** 1879
Loftus E 1879
#Lugg E 1879
Took part in defence of Rorke's Drift
Mathiue (Mathie) E.C 1879
Mc Rae T **KIA** 1879 r
Medigan(Madigan) W.E 1879
Meares C.H **KIA** 1879
Molyneux ? 1879
Nagle (Nagles) D/S P 1879
Fever 17/2/1879 Helpmakaar.
Neil H **KIA** 1879 r
Nelson W 1879 r
Nowbold R.W 1879
Newhook H 1879
Owen A 1879
Owens W 1879
Palmer H 1879
Parsons A.B KIA 1879
Patrick ? Not on medal roll
Pearse H.T (John W) KIA 1879
Piers H 1879

Pitt H.J 1879
Pleydell John .W KIA. 1879
Pollard A.F KIA 1879
Read H.T 1879
Reed R 1879
Richardson R 1879
Robinson J.H.T 1879
Robson C 1879
Roffey J.R 1879
Royston C.W 1879
Rummings A 1879
Secretan A.J 1879
Secretan A (F) KIA 1879
#Shannon R.I 1879
Escaped from Isandhlwana
Siddall J.W.M KIA 1879
Singleton C.W 1879
Smith E.G.W 1879 r
Smithe D/S H.W 1879
Suicide 27/2/1879 Helpmakaar.
Smith J.S 1879
Soundy J 1879
Sowerby J.A 1879
Sparks C.M.F 1879
Escaped from Isandhlwana
Steer T.B 1879
Stimpson (Stimson) W.E KIA 1879
Thicke S.C KIA 1879
Turner G.E 1879
Walker J.F 1879
Walker W.B 1879
Wall E 1879
Warner A.G.B 1879
  See also Levy Leader.
Watts ? 1879
White C KIA 1879
White M.H 1879
Winkles (Winkle) H KIA 1879
Wright D 1879

NATIVE POLICE
SERGEANT
Mankawane 1879
CORPORAL
Tintibella 1879
PRIVATE
Boya 1879
Boza 1879
Isufuba 1879
Jantze 1879
Madagan 1879
Magamene 1879
Nyoni 1879
Sobantu 1879
Ujan 1879
Umpini 1879

NATAL MOUNTED POLICE.
Headquarters and Reserves who did not cross the Zulu border. Medal issued without a clasp
SUB INSPECTOR
Jackson S
SERGEANT
Crallan
CORPORAL
Champ r
Jenkins
TRUMPETER
Richardson
TROOPER
Adams J.G
  Accidentally killed.
Bekkeley F
Biggs J.W.F
Blakeman T
Boome H.S r
Bowman J.M r
Bradbury F.G.H
Burgoyne S
Burney A
Camp E
Campbell C.A.M
Charlesworth T
Charlesworth W
Cheesman E
Clarabut H.D
Coates S.W r
Connorton J.G
Cooper G.I
Cunningham A.E
Dalrymple E.C.E
Daw E.M
Dickenson W
Drewcatt W.D
Drury E.T r
Farr R.W
Fry W.W
Gardner W.B
Gill T
Gray J r
Green H
Green H.C
Hamshire E.A
Harris H.D
Harrod P
Haynes A
Hearn H.W
Hearn J.H
Hutton J.M
Libery F
Jenner E.F
Joseph S.H
Langmid H
Lochner F.E
Leslie A.A

Natal Mounted Police

Natal Mounted Police. Henry Lugg

Henry Lugg (generally known as Harry) was born in 1859 at Northlew, Devonshire. Henry aged 19 sailed for Natal on the Roslyn Castle with his future brothers-in-law, Edwin and Fred Camp. To seek their fortune in this new country. With them sailed other young men all intent on adventure and new opportunities. One of whom was W.J.Clarke, later to become Commissioner of the Natal Police. Clarke was present when the body of the Prince Imperial was recovered, Louis Napoleon's death caused an international sensation. The Prince was ritually disemboweled a common Zulu practice to prevent his spirit seeking revenge on his killers in the afterlife. In his diary Clarke records that the body was pickled in salt, and the viscera had been removed and buried in a biscuit tin. He was one of the escort to accompany Princess Eugene to the spot, to recover these remains. The Prince's heart had shriveled to the size of a walnut and was taken back to France for the burial in the Arc de Triomphe, which was French Law that the heart of every Napoleon be disposed of in this manner.

Henry Lugg along with Edwin and Fred Camp decided to seek adventure by joining the Natal Mounted Police in 1878, a body formed by Major John Dartnell in 1874. The force was attached to the Central Column that invaded Zululand via Rorke's Drift. The first engagment of the Mounted Police was the attack on Sihayo's stronghold near Sandlwana, after which Henry was sent with important dispatches a distance of some 113 miles from Helpmekaar to Pietrmaritzburg. He did the trip in less than 11 hours using a total of ten horses in relays. On his return to join his troop, on crossing the Buffalo river his horse fell, crushing his knee against a rock, this is how young Henry found himself in the hospital at Rorke's Drift.

3rd Regt. Natal Native Contingent Colonel Henry Charles Harford.

Colonel Henry Charles Harford C.B. served in the Zulu War of 1879, and was Staff Officer to Commandant Lonsdale of the 3rd Regiment, Natal Native Contingent. He kept a journal in which he recorded his experiences, his eye-witness accounts, writings and sketches have been the subject of two books.. As an experienced Lieutenant Harford participated in a number of important actions during the Zulu War and was at Rorke's Drift where he witnessed and recorded the fortification of the Mission Station prior to the invasion of Zululand. He led the first attack against the local Zulu Chief Sihayo and accompanied Lord Chelmsford on his ill-fated search for the Zulu army which left the main British camp at Isandlwana unprepared for a full Zulu attack the following day. He recorded the chaos and confusion in the hours leading to the Zulu destruction of Chelmsford's main camp. Just days later, he supervised the disbandment of the Natal Native Contingent. After this event Commandant Lonsdale, gave Harford custody of two officer deserters, who had abandoned their men in the action against the Zulus, the whole affair concerning Lieutenants Higginson and Stephenson being highly embarrassing to Harford.

After service in Zululand, Harford remained in the British army and served variously in the UK, Bahamas and India. He retained his interest in collecting rare insect specimens and he meticulously recorded these and sent the best exhibits to the Museum of Natural History in Durban.

He married late in life but tragically lost his new young wife to fever in India. He was left with an infant daughter, Sweetie, and never re-married. Harford died at the age of 86.

He witnessed the aftermath of both the destruction of Isandlwana and the Zulu attack at **Rorke's Drift**.. Following the eventual Zulu defeat on the 4th July 1879 Harford was part of the force that searched for King Cetshwayo and following his capture the King was given into the custody of Harford until his exile to Cape Town. Harford meticulously recorded and sketched his experiences.

References:
The Writings, Photographs & Sketches of Henry Charles Harford CB by Dr David Payne and Emma Payne.
Edited by Dr Adrian Greaves FRGS
Zulu War Journal of Colonel Henry Harford, Pietermaritzburg, 1978,by Daphne Child, (ed.),
http://www.rrw.org.uk/shop/shop.php?action=view&prodid=307

Natal Mounted Police

Liddell	J.T	
Longfield	H	
Macdermott	J	
Macdonald	C.R.G	
Martin	G	
Marsh	E.C	
Marshall	W.P	
Mathie	J.R	
Mattheys	H.F	
Moreland	C.W	
Moscow	F.W.C	
Myers	T.F	
Palmer	R	
Pardy		
Pavy	W.P	
Pearson	W.R	
Peirsin	J	
Penny	W.C	
Pringle	P	
Purcer	E.A	
Richards	G.C	
Russ	A.B	
Secretan	C.C	
Sidney	A.P	
Simons	W	
Steffan	E.C	
Stephens	D.J	
Taylor	W	
Thomson		
Wardrop	H.S	
Watson	J.B	
Widdrington	H.F	
Wignall	T	
Williams	W	
Wingfield	F.W	
Young	A.J	

NATIVE POLICE
PRIVATE
Endengiza   r
Matchlan
Siquesa
Umbedda

NATAL NATIVE CONTINGENT.
Natal Native Contingent formed in 1879. Commanded by European officers and NCOs. After Isandlwana, many of the NCOs transferred to Natal Horse. In some battalions a few men were mounted and were useful as scouts. Corporal Schiess, 3rd Regiment, won the VC at Rorke's Drift.

Officer commanding the unit in Pearson's column was Major Shapland Graves.
CAPTAIN
Cooke	J.W	1879
Davies	R.P.B	1879
De Beer	J.J	1878-9
King	J	1879
Mackintosh	A.J.F	1877-8-9
Margary	A.F	1877-8-9
Muller	C.J	1878-9
# Newman (Neumann)	A.H	1879
(See page 136)		
Penfold	W.C	1879
Pizzeghelli	R	1879
Wunch	R.F	1879

See also Capt. R.F. Wrench 2nd Battn.
LIEUTENANT
Allaway	C.K	1879 r
Barker	C.N	1879
Battye	T	1879 r
Bevis	T	1879
Buchanan	C	1879
Campbell	W.D	1879
Dennis	E.E	1879
Doveton	F.B	1879
Driscoll	C.B	1877-8-9
Eld	P.S.F.E	1877-8-9
Evans	W.G.L	1879
Fairlough	W	1878-9
Halder	A.H	1879
Hicks	W	1879
Innerson	C	1879 r
Maxwell	J	1877-8-9
Morant	H.G	1879
Moreland	E.B	1879
Murphy	G.H	1879
Platterer	G	not in medal roll

KIA at Inyetzane 22/1/1879
#Purvis	T	1879

Severe wound in the arm, Natal Mercury 16.01.1879. (see page 139)
Raines   L   1879
KIA at Inyetzane 22/1/1879
Reynell	H	1879
Shaw	A.P.A	1878-9
Van Palm	H	1879
Vinnicombe	W.D	1878-9

See also Frontier Light Horse Pte. W.D. Vinnicombe.
Walker	F.J	1877-8-9
Whitfield	C	1879 r
Williams	C	1879

Wright	W.J	1879
Wyld	J.H	1879
Wynne	C.F.D	1879
Young	H.C	1879

CHIEF
Jantze		No clasp

SERGEANT MAJOR
Butter	D	1879
Spring	J	1878?

INTREPRETER
Cato	C.A	1879

COLOUR SERGEANT
Fox	T	1879
Wilkins	W	1879

SERGEANT
Baker	T	1879
Bowman	J.N	1879 r
Bulmer	A	1879
Luck	G	1878-9 r
Maidwell	R	1879
Mawbery	G.G	1879
Murphy	F	1879 r
Murphy	F	1879 r
Paton	J	1879
Peters	D	1879
Scharer	H	1879
Swan	C	1879 r
Thornton	F.J	1879
Towle	J.C	1879 r
Unger	**J.W**	**1879 r**

KIA at Inyetzane 22/1/1879
Yeates	L.G	1879

CORPORAL
Balmer	T	1879
Barstow	T	1878-9
Becton	R	1878-9
Besserve	P	1879
Carroll	J.V	1879
Keel	J.C	1879 r
Leichenring	C.W	1879
Mathews	W.B	1878-9
Mc Glew	R	No clasp
Mc Keown	J.F	1879
Mener	E	1879 r
Quinn	E	1879
Reenberg	L.L	1878-9
Robertson	T	1879 r
Schiers	C.F	1877-8-9
Schiess VC	F.C	1879

    His VC was for Rorkes Drift
Thompson	J.H	1879

The Natal Native Contingent was created in 1878 out of the local black population in order to bolster the defences of Natal. In January of 1879 when the British army invaded Zululand black Africans made up more than half of the force, they went on to fight in the battles of Isandlwana, **Rorke's Drift**, and Ulundi. The British invasion force, under the overall command of General Frederick A. Thesiger, soon to be Lord Chelmsford, totalled some 16,800 men, at least 9,000 of whom were Africans. Most NNC troops were drawn from the Basuto and Mponso tribes, which had had long experience of fighting against the Zulus. As many as 1,000, were dissident Zulus warriors whose leaders held a grudge against chief Cetshwayo and were eager to defeat the aggressive Zulu king.

Natal Native Contingent

Spink Sale 7012 Lot 720. 19 Apr 2007.
The Most Interesting South African Pair to Captain A.H. Neumann, South African Light Horse, Late Native Contingent, Famous African Explorer and Big Game Hunter, Author of Elephant Hunting in East Equatorial Africa, and Fondly Known as 'Nyama Yango' by Natives of the East Africa Highlands
South Africa 1877-79, one clasp, 1878 (Capt: A.H. Neumann, Native Contgt.), partially officially corrected; Queen's South Africa 1899-1902, three clasps, Cape Colony, Tugela Heights, Relief of Ladysmith (Lieut: A.H. Neumann, S.A. Lt: Horse.), extremely fine, sold with a copy of the book Hunter Away - the Life and Times of Arthur Henry Neumann 1850-1907 (2)   Hammer price £5,800

Captain Arthur Charles Neumann, born Bedfordshire, 1850; became a coffee planter in Natal aged 18. He later tried cotton, tobacco growing and gold mining in the Transvaal with his brother Charles. Whilst operating a trading post in Swaziland, he became fluent in the local dialects and befriended the King of the Swazis, Ubandeni. He was able to put this friendship to good use with the outbreak of the hostilities with the Zulus, joining one of the Native Contingents as a Captain and an interpreter for Captain Macleod, the then Chief of Swaziland Police. It was feared at the time that the Swazis would join forces with the Zulus against the British, and one day whilst Macleod and Neumann were out riding together near the border they received news from a galloper informing them of the disaster at Isandhlwana. Given the precarious position that they were in with relation to the Swazis they were urged to keep the news from Neumann's friend King Ubandeni. After consultation, however, Macleod considered it a better plan to break the news to the King himself, insisting that a British army would soon come to avenge the defeat. Upon delivering the news to the King, Macleod and Neumann were greeted with complete silence, as the two men would have realised at the time both their lives hung in the balance. Some hours later, native spies confirmed Macleod's report and the King sent for him saying, 'Mafu, you speak the truth and if it takes the whole Zulu army to destroy one English camp, the English will win'. As a result of Macleod's snap decision the Swazis fought with the British against the Zulus and later against the Basutos. In the latter conflict it was the Swazis under Macleod who surrounded Sekukuni and captured him.

Neumann rejoined his brother in a farming venture in 1880 and for the next ten years travelled and hunted along the Limpopo River before being employed by the East African Company to map routes for projected railways. It was whilst in this employment that his camp was attacked in Masai country and he received a spear wound.

For a brief period he was employed as a Magistrate, before going looking for adventure again - this time he travelled North to Mombasa to organise an elephant shooting expedition. In the three years that followed, he spent all his time wandering the unknown interior, amongst the Ndoroba savages by Mount Kenia and the Lorogi Mountains. Here, totally in his element, he learnt the local dialects, traded with the natives and continued to enhance his reputation as a hunter. During this period he mentions shooting a rhino with a horn measuring 40 inches and having killed 11 elephants.
On the 1st of January 1896 his personal servant was carried off before his eyes by a crocodile and shortly afterwards he was himself badly injured by a cow elephant which gored him and knelt on him in the thick bush. He was saved from death only by the springy undergrowth and could not lie in any position except on his back for two months.

He later sold all his his ivory, amongst which were tusks up to nine feet in length. Having made a fortune out of the latter, he then wrote his book Elephant Hunting in East Equatorial Africa and was credited with the discovery of several new animal and insect species. He was revered and loved by the natives of the East African highlands, who knew him as 'Nyama Yango', literally translated as 'My Meat' - the name is said to have been given to him because once he had marked his target, he never missed. J.G. Millais, the famous hunter author, likened Neumann to Selous, Livingstone, Speke, Grant Thomson and Burton, as a man caring little for worldly applause, but bent upon gaining a knowledge of the unknown for benefit of those who came after him. He also stipulates that the achievement of a totally peaceful settlement of the highlands in later years was due entirely to Neumann's way of life and influence on the natives.
In November 1899 Neumann went to South Africa to take part in the Boer War and he assisted Colonel Bethune to raise the South African Light Horse. Here he served as a Lieutenant, alongside one W.L.S. Churchill, taking part in the Relief of Ladysmith and having a very narrow escape at Spion Kop where a bullet passed through his hat and hair.

After the War Neumann returned to Mount Kenia country, but with the advent of the preservation of game, he saw that his days as an elephant hunter were at an end and he returned to England in October 1906. Upon arrival he suffered a severe attack of influenza, from which he never really recovered. Millais records his depression at this stage of his life and on the 29th of May 1907 Neumann used one of his own firearms to take his own life.
In a bizarre twist it was said that upon the day of his death he appeared to his godchild, Noomi Jackson, at her Convent school in Belgium telling her that he was suffering terribly for transgressions whilst on earth and asked her to pray constantly for him. She recorded how he continued to appear to her every day until she left the school and returned to London. The facts of the visitations were put before the Society of Psychical Research and published in their Journal of May 1908.
Published transcription of roll gives recipient's details as 'Captain A.H. Newman Natal Native Contingent', and as being entitled to a '1879' clasp, the medal however appears entirely as issued.

Natal Native Contingent

LIEUT SHARP 1/NATAL NATIVE CONTINGENT
Lieutenant Thomas Sharp Adjutant of 1/NNC previously held the position of Regimental Sergeant Major of 1/1 NNC at the time of the battle of Isandhlwana and accompanied Durnford's Command into Zululand.
General Orders printed in the Natal Witness 29th and 31st May 1879 give the following:
The following Promotions and appointments in the 1st Battalion Natal Native Contingent... Sergeant Major T. Sharp to be Lieutenant 21st May 1879 and Lieutenant T Sharp is appointed Adjutant Vice Wynne retired 21st May 1879
  Sharp left an account of his involvement in the form of a letter written to a relative which was published in the Irish Times 5 May 1879 .
A Survivor of Isandula.
The following letter from Sergeant Major Thomas Sharp, Natal Native ContinTingent, who was present at the battle of Isandula, may interest some of our readers:-

                              Rorke's Drift, Fort Melville,
                              21st March, 1879

I suppose you will be surprised to hear from me after keeping you so long without writing. I have given up baking, and gone to the front, as it is a better paying job, but more dangerous..... I am at present Sergeant-Major of the 1st Battalion of No 3 Column, commanded by Colonel Durnford. We left Petermaritzburg on the 22nd December, and arrived at Kranig Kop, 80 or 90 miles off, two days before New Year's Day. We were stationed there about a month, and then got orders to proceed to **Rorke's Drift**, the crossing place to get into the Zulu country with wagons. We crossed on in January all safe, about 5,000 Europeans and natives. On the 21st General Lord Chelmsford took the main force away, as it was reported the Zulus were some distance off. He proceeded with his force to meet them, but they came round a hill some miles to his right, cut him off from us, and commenced firing on the stores and wagons. Colonel Dunford was in charge of use. We advanced about a mile, threw out skirmishers and commenced banging away; the more we fired and killed the stronger they seemed to appear. At last we had to retire on the Regulars, who were fighting in another direction. Firing continued, for several hours, till at last they came over the hill in front, in rear, and on both sides of us, and we were hemmed in; they were just like a lot of bees. At last we had to give up our position and get ammunition from the wagons, but when we got to the wagons to our great disappointment they were in the hands of the enemy. The six companies of the 24th Regiment stood their ground to the last. ....There were two or three escaped of the six companies; the remainder died like true British soldiers. The loss of the regiment is about 600, including the colonel. I believe the Zulus took the two smallest drummer boys to Cetywayo's Kraal. What he has done with them it is hard to say. I do not suppose the poor little fellows will ever see their comrades any more. In the battalion I am in we lost rather heavily. Out of a thousand there were 6 officers, 14 non-commissioned officers, and 420 natives cut to pieces, including **Colonel Durnford**, who fought with his one arm like a true British officer. The last words he said "Now men this is our last escape: death or glory, God help us." He then gave the word, "Charge" but before he got through a bullet entered his breast, and he was then numbered with the slain. We cut right and left, and managed to clear through. I put spurs to my horse and left the others to follow. The then commandant told me to go and try if I could see anything of the main column. After hunting for miles I returned without finding any sign of it. I only saw about 20,000 more Zulus, which were never brought into action at all. So you see I had a narrow escape. The total loss was about 1,400 to 1,800 on our side, and it is said the enemy lost about 4,000 to 5,000. They captured about 200 wagons and a large quantity of ammunition and rifles, also the General's provisions and a quantity of hard cash that was in the Government wagons. They never saved anything; they burnt all the medicine of the medical staff, set fire to the hospital tents, and killed the sick and wounded that were lying in their beds. They did not leave a single European without cutting him open and letting his entrails out. Some they tied up to trees, took out their eyes, and put empty cartridge cases into the holes. They stripped all the dead of their cloths and wore them themselves. I am thankful to the Almighty I have escaped so far from the wicked brutes. I often think how poor father and mother used to give us 3d or so to put into the plate at--- - Church for the poor heathen in Africa.. Little did I think then that I should be amongst "the poor" so called heathen. It is nothing but the missionaries that make them what they are: once a Kaffir is Christianised he is no use to a white man for labour. He will commence to steal and plunder, and do everything that is bad, whereas a raw Kaffir will do as he is told, or die in the attempt. I have a lot of dealings with the natives lately, and I would sooner have a Kaffir straight from the hut than one who has a knowledge of English. We are at a standstill at present waiting for reinforcements. I expect we shall be hard at it by the time you get this, and I hope we shall take a lot of cattle, as we get a share of the loot. We have captured about 17,000 oxen, sheep and goats. The country is full of them, but there are very few horses, as this country is bad for horses to live in. In the regiment I am the only white non-commissioned officer, and am over about 2,000 natives; the remainder are taken away and made into a mounted troop. I have quite enough to do to keep them in order and see them fed. I get along with them very well. They call me their white chief, and I am getting on with the language very fast. I can talk to them quite easily.

  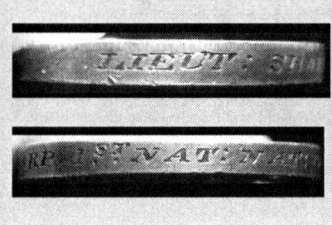 

Information Supplied by Justin Young

Natal Native Contingent

CAPT. J.W.COOKE N.N.C SOUTH AFRICA Clasp 1879
Captain John William Cooke initially served as as a Captain in 2nd Battalion NNC. After the disaster at Isandhlwana many Officers and NCO's were transferred to form the Natal Horse and Captain Cooke was selected to Command No.2 Troop - which was to be known as Cooke's Horse.
COOKE John William. Seaman. Farmer of South Africa. Natal Volunteers. Captain, 2nd Battalion, 2nd Regiment, Natal Native Contingent. Captain and Officer Commanding, No2 Troop (Cooke's Horse), Native Horse 9.3.79. Zulu War 1879 including the actions at Gingindlovu and the relief of Eshowe. Commander of the Turkish Coast Guard service (5 years); operations against slave traders, smuggling and gun running. He received a decoration from the Sultan. Retired 1899. Yacht Master under Sir Rendall Rodd. Died at Cowes 1924 aged 70 years.
Cooke's Horse saw action at Gingindlovu and the relief of Eshowe. It later took part in the second invasion under Maj General Creaclock's I Division before being disbanded after the battle of Ulundi

LIEUT H. HANCOCK N.N.C. SOUTH AFRICA Clasp 1879
The Natal Native Pioneers were formed to assist in engineering tasks, road maintenance etc. Companies of which served with the various invasion columns. Lieutenant Herbert Hancock served in number 3 company Natal Native Pionneers, who were attached to Durnford's No 2 Column.

CAPTAIN E.C.HIGHTON 2/NNC SOUTH AFRICA 1879, CLASP 1879
Edward Claude Goulburn Highton from Oxford was accidentally shot and killed while on parade by one of the Privates 17th Jan 1882 while serving as a Lieutenant in Bakers Horse, he had served with this unit at this Rank since 1881
Copies from SA Archives include; application for SA 1879 medal by his Mother, oddly gives his service with 2 NNC until 1881 when Force disbanded – presumably served with another unit when NNC disbanded in 1879- which?
Information Supplied by Justin Young

A special correspondent of the Daily Telegraph describes the scene at the reception of the body at Pietermaritzburg. he says; Sunday, June 8th will be a day long remembered in the annals of Natal. Since Thursday it has been known that the remains of the Prince Imperial would reach this city yesterday......a company of Major Bengugh's Regiment of Natal Native Contingent, in red jackets and regimental trousers, under the command of Captain Digby Willoughby.
Aberdeen Weekly Journal, Tuesday, July 1, 1879;

Jay May 15th at Fort Pearson, Lower Tugela, South Africa, of dysentery. Lieut. Herbert Valentine Jay, Natal Native Contingent, son of James I Ray of Lewisham, Kent aged 24 years.
Freeman's Journal and Daily Commercial Advertiser (Dublin, Ireland), Wednesday, June 25, 1879;

Native Contingent Looting

Natal Native Contingent

Spink Sale 7012 Lot 1018. 19 Apr 2007
The South Africa 1879 Medal to **Lieutenant T. Purvis,** Natal Native Contingent, Wounded at Sirhayo's Kraal, 12th January, The first officer casualty of the Zululand Campaign, and one of only three military casualties on that day; He was taken with another Casualty, Corporal Scheiss, of V.C. Fame, to the Hospital at Rorke's Drift, discharging himself just before the legendary defence took place.
South Africa 1877-79, one clasp, 1879 (Lieut: T. Purvis Natal Native Contingent.), good very fine Hammer price £3400
Lieutenant Thomas Purvis 1st Battalion 3rd Regiment of Natal Native Contingent, was the first officer and one of only three Military men to be wounded on the first day of the campaign in Zululand, at the capture of Sirhayo's Kraal, 12.1.1879, 'There was a short, sharp melee among the boulders, and then Sirhayo's retainers broke and fled into the depths of the gorge, leaving 20 dead men behind. Two of Mvubi's Zulus had been killed, Lieutenant Purvis had been shot through the arm and **Corporal Mayer** behind the knee, and **Corporal Scheiss** shortly to win a V.C. at Rorke's Drift in the thick of the fight, had been struck by a lunging assegai which ripped his boot open and slashed his calf. They were joined in the ambulance for the trip back to the hospital at Rorke's Drift by two wounded survivors of Sirhayo's party, one with a thigh broken by a rifle bullet.' (The Washing of Spears, refers)
Whilst being nursed at the hospital Purvis also started to suffer from an acute form of dysentery. Luckily for Purvis, however, he left Rorke's Drift with Captain Stevenson's Natal Native Contingent just before the legendary action took place, a statement from **Lieutenant W.R. Higginson** N.N.C. offers further insight, 'We got into Helpmaaker about 7pm. I found that **Captain Stevenson** of the 2nd Battalion 3rd Regiment N.N.C., had brought Lieutenant Purvis up from Rorke's Drift, where he had been wounded in the arm in the cave fighting on Sunday, 12th January; he asked me to help him take Purvis to Ladysmith..... so at 9pm we started for and got to Dundee at 3am, from there we pushed on to Ladysmith and got there on Friday, being obliged to go slowly on account of Purvis. On Saturday morning the General and his staff arrived, and he was kind enough to see me. I told him all that I have stated here. Major Buller then saw Lieutenant Purvis and took a seat for him in the post-cart for Maritzburg.'
At Maritzburg, Purvis had a medical examination (a copy of the proceedings is included with the lot), in which it was concluded that his wound was the equivalent to the loss of a limb and that he would be unlikely to be fit enough for military service again.

#Dix Noonan Web Auction Lot 408, 5 Apr 06
South Africa 1877-79, 1 clasp, 1879 (**Capt. H. Dymes**, 1st Nat. Nat. Contgt.), with ornate silver top bar, claw refixed, slight edge bruising, good very fine Hammer Price: £780
Footnote Ex Don Forsyth Collection; sold with letter from Forsyth concerning the medal, dated 5 December 1988. Also with a note from a later owner speculating that the recipient 'escaped from Isandlwana'. This is not confirmed.
Sold with an old miniature photograph (of the recipient?), in frame, reverse with brooch fitting.

SOUTH AFRICA Clasp 1879 Lieut. BLACK 1st Nat Nat Contnt.
Norman Lister Black born 1857 first Military appointment was as Sub Lieutenant of 33rd Lancashire Rifle Volunteer Corps on 12 May 1875 and by 1876 had been promoted Lieutenant. At some point in 1877 he left for South Africa and obtained a position in the Colonial Engineer's Offices.
7th December 1878 Norman was appointed Lieutenant in Colonel Durnford's 1st Battalion, 1st Regiment NNC, specifically **Captain Nourse's** 'D' Company.
Colonel Durnford, who's brainchild the NNC was, quickly appointed the best recruits to his own Battalion. Many men who had had previous Military Service or Son's of local farmers and gentry who spoke Zulu were what he was after and the Natives themselves were from tribes Durnford personally had worked with before and knew their worth.
On 22nd Jan 1879 Colonel Durnford and his Natal Mounted Contingent of Natives, along with the Rocket Battery under **Major Russell** R.A and two Companies of 1st NNC under **Captain's Stafford** ('E' Company) and Nourse. Joined Pullien's force at Isandhlwana and at once the troops of the Natal Mounted Contingent were sent out to reconnoitre. Durnford took two troops and the Rocket Battery along with him and **Captain Nourse's** Company of NNC as protection for the Battery . Captain Staffords Company had been ordered back along the path they had come to hurry up the baggage.
After going several miles from the camp it was found that the Mounted troops had way out paced the Rocket Battery and NNC and the sound of volley firing could be heard from the direction the other Mounted Troops had gone. Russell had also heard the sound of gun fire and had changed direction he was going towards this sound in the hope of catching the enemy but due to the uneven terrain the Company and Battery became somewhat disorganised. Soon after this a large formation of Zulu's were sighted at very close proximity and the order to prepare for action was given. Apparently only one rocket was fired before the battery was overwhelmed and Russell was killed. Captain Nourse and men from his Company made a stand before either being killed or retreating.
Captain Nourse was picked up by Durnfords Mounted troops on their own retreat on the camp along with a few survivors of his Company. It is not yet known if Lt Black was with him, only the perish at the camp or during the retreat down 'fugitives trail' or if he was killed during the initial stand.
Account of Captain W.H. Stafford, Natal Mercury, 22nd January, 1929:
"After placing **Lieutenant Andrews** in charge of a fresh picket, the rest of the evening was spent over a game of cards. The popular games in those days were "Twenty five" and "all Four". A chap, by name Lieutenant Black, who had not been long out in this Country was the looser [sic] and I remember that officer staking his farm in Zululand against his opponent's prospective piece of ground. I jokingly told him that the only plot of ground he would ever get in Zululand [was] one measuring seven foot by four feet. There is many a true word said in jest and, sad to relate, the poor fellow fell from a Zulu Assegai about thirteen hours later at the Massacre of Isandlwana."
Information Supplied by Justin Young.

Natal Native Contingent

PRIVATE
Barker   N   1879
Mc Keating J   1877-8-9
   See also Cape Town Rifles.
Batras   A   1878-9
Carrol   J.V   1879
Heathcote   H.E.J   1879
Kemp   C   1879 r
Lord   F   1879
Lyon   J.W   1879
Monkman   H   1879
Palmer   R   1879
Pemberton   G   1879 r
NATIVE
Aba   S   No clasp
Buys (2)   No clasp
Litsega (alias Liky)   No clasp
Sambo   No clasp
Tshabala   D   No clasp
Tshabala   S   No clasp
RANK NOT KNOWN
Harber   S.S   1879
Hayes   D.J   1877-8-9
Luyt   J   1879
Vaughan   C.R   1879

NATAL NATIVE CONTINGENT. 1ST BATTALION.
All who were killed in action (KIA) lost their lives at Isandhlwana. 22nd Jan, 1879.
1ST BATTALION COMMANDANT
Montgomery A   1879
Battalion Commander in Durnford's No 2 column. D/S Snakebite
ACTING SURGEON
Bull   F   KIA 1879
Frank William Buee in Casualty roll
QUARTERMASTER
Mc Cormick KIA J 1879
John R McCormack in Casualty roll
INTERPRETER
Grant Mr Samuel KIA 1879
CAPTAIN
Clifton   F.P   1879
Dymes (page 139) H 1879
Krohn   R   KIA 1879
Lonsdale   J.F   KIA 1877-8-9
LIEUTENANT
Avery   S   KIA 1879
##Black (page 139) KIA 1879
Halcraft   F   KIA 1879
Frank Holcraft on Casualty roll
Jamieson   C   KIA 1879
Charles Jameson Casualty roll
Lister   ?   KIA 1879

Mathews   ?   1879
Nurden   ?   1879
Robinson   G.L   1879
CONDUCTOR
Archbell J.P KIA Not on medal roll
Doyle (HW)   KIA 1879
Le Roue (Roux) KIA 1879
PROVOST SERGEANT
Jackson   T   1879
   See also Native Levies.
HOSPITAL SERGEANT
Cane KIA ?   1879
SERGEANT
Atkins   H   KIA 1879
Bryant   G   KIA 1879
Church   H   KIA 1879
Cole   J   KIA 1879
Connock   J   KIA 1879
Donnell   ?   KIA 1879
Golding   W   KIA 1879
Golling   W   KIA 1879
Humphries   W   KIA 1879
Mc Carty   W   KIA 1879
Monkman   H   1879
Patterson   C   KIA 1879
C. Peterson Casualty roll
Russell   W   KIA 1877-8-9
Welsh   J   KIA 1879
CORPORAL
Anderson   W   KIA 1879
Balmore   J   KIA 1879
Davidson   ?   KIA 1879
Duprie   J   KIA 1879
Fyfe   ?   1879
O'Connell   D   KIA 1879
O'Neil (O'Neill) M KIA 1879
Palmer   R   KIA 1879
Pearson   J   KIA 1879
Price   W   KIA 1879
Quinn   J   KIA 1879
Sibley   F   KIA 1879
Willey   W   KIA 1879
COOK
Niel   G   KIA 1879

NATAL NATIVE CONTINGENT. 2ND BATTALION
Those Killed in Action (KIA) lost their lives at Isandhlwana on 22nd January, 1879.
LIEUTENANT COLONEL
Bengough   H.M   1879
Battalion Commander in Durnford's No 2 column. See also 77th Regiment.
SURGEON
Wood   R.E   1879

   See also Army Medical Department
QUARTERMASTER
Chambers   A   KIA 1879
Mc Cracken V   1879
CAPTAIN
Barry   A.T   KIA 1879
Birkett   R.C   1879
Boord   E.H   1879
Dallamore   J.M   1879
Erskine   E   KIA 1879
Galley   J.R   1879
Highton E.C   1879
Murray   O.E KIA 1879
Fort White Mounted Vols
Openshaw   W.T   1879
Spiers   A.T   1879
Willoughby A.H   1879
Wrench   A.F   1879
Wrench   R.F   1879
LIEUTENANT AND ADJUTANT
Greville   B.S   1879
Battye   C.S.A   1879
Bischoff   D.J   1879
Doveton   W.W   1879
Ducat   A   1879
Gibson   A   KIA 1879
Heathcote   G.W   1879
Lukin   H   1879
Slightly wounded at Ulundi 4/7/1879
Moncrieff   L.N   1879
Slightly wounded at Ulundi 4/7/1879
Morphy   J.W.M   1879
Pritchard   R.A KIA 1879
Rivers   H.O KIA 1879
Roberts   G.N   1879
Roberts   J.A   1879
Standish   ?   KIA 1879
Tyrrell   G (O) KIA 1879
Tytler   S.D   1879
Vereker Hon S KIA 1878-9
See also Frontier Light Horse rank Tpr
Wainwright A.T   1879
Wadmore   H.R   1879
Woodfall   C.W   1879
Worsley   A.A   1879
Worsley   D   1879
Young   L.D KIA 1879
SERGEANT MAJOR
Ingram   E   1879
QUARTERMASTER SERGEANT
Farr   A   KIA 1879
Fyffe   A.B   1879
Fyfe   W.W   1879
   See also Natal Force.

Dix Noonan Web Auction Lot 244, 27 Jun 07
South Africa 1877-79, 1 clasp, 1879 (Capt. E. C. Highton, 2nd Bn. Nat: N. Cont.) extremely fine, Hammer Price: £920
Footnote Captain E. Claude Goulburn Highton was accidentally shot and killed in 1882. His name is recorded on a War Memorial at Barford St Michael, Oxfordshire.

Natal Native Contingent

SERGEANT
Allen	J	KIA	1879
Brebner	W	KIA	1879
Broderick	A	KIA	1879
Broderick	M	KIA	1879
Elverson	G	KIA	1879
Hamilton	W	KIA	1879
Kemp	W	KIA	1879
Moore	G	KIA	1879
Mowbray	G	KIA	1879
Murray	W	KIA	1879
Phillips	S	KIA	1879
Schaap	D	KIA	1879

CORPORAL
Allen	W	KIA	1879

See also Sgt. W. Allen 3rd Battalion.

Caufield	J	KIA	1879
Delaharpe	D	KIA	1879
De Villiers	D	KIA	1879
Gier	G		1879
Green	W	KIA	1879
Harrington	T	KIA	1879
Klingstron	C		1879
Laughlin	W	KIA	1879
Pitzer	T	KIA	1879
Schneither	L	KIA	1879
Stapleton	W	KIA	1879
Sturk	H	KIA	1879
Styles	R	KIA	1879
Walker	J	KIA	1879
Welsh	E	KIA	1879
Willis	J	KIA	1879

PRIVATE
Gruppy	W		1879

NATAL NATIVE CONTINGENT. 3RD BATTALION.
COMMANDANT
Lonsdale R de la T		1878-9

CAPTAIN
Cherry	C	1879

Batt. Commander in Durnford's Col. No 2 Column.

LIEUTENANT
Alleway	C.E.C.K	1879

SERGEANT
Allen	W	1879

KIA See also Cpl. W. Allen 2nd Regt.

CORPORAL
Mayor	J.H	1878-9

NATAL NATIVE CONTINGENT. 4TH BATTALLION
CAPTAIN COMMANDING
Barton	W	1879

CAPTAIN
Bartholomew	E	1879
Bartholomew	J.S	1879
Cogan	J	1877-8-9
Costerton	C.E	1877-8-9

Duplicate medal & clap issued 26/10/1908.

De Beer	J	1877-8-9
Garde	H.P	1879
Hill	W	1879
Kettles	R	1877-8-9
Ludwig	H	1879
Mc Taggart	J	1879
Plosh	F	1879
Steiner	F	1879
Thomas	T.B	1879
Wood	E.J.P	1879

LIEUTENANT
Ashington	F	1877-8-9
Carroll	J.W	1879
Du Place	S	1879
Elliott	W	1879
Hiron	L.A	1879
Hungerford	T.H	1879
O'Sullivan	D.J	1879
Jenkins	C	1879
Peverett	J	1877-8-9
Ranger	A.C	1877-8-9
Ranger	A.H	1877-8-9
Russon	G	1879
Starck	A.F	1879
Von Hirschberg Count F		1877-8-9

See also Sgt. Von Herschberg Warehouse Tree Blues.

Wright	W	1879

INTERPRETER
Dick		1879

SERGEANT MAJOR
Larson	A	1879

COOK SERGEANT
Gerard	G	1879

QUATERMASTER SERGEANT
Norgaard	H	1879

NATAL NATIVE CONTINGENT. 5th BATALLION
COMMANDANT
Nettleton	W.J	1877-8-9

See also Port Elizabeth Vol. Horse

CAPTAIN ADJUTANT
Rorke	A.G	1877-8-9
Shervinton	C.R. St. L	1877-8-9
Welsh	A	1877-8-9

CAPTAIN
Bean	W	1877-8-9
Bovey	R	1877-8-9
Burnside	C.R	1877-8-9
Ceck	C	1877-8-9
Cooke	E.W	1877-8-9 r
Crutchley	E.A	1877-8-9
Davis	A.E	1877-8-9
Gough Hon D/S	H.R	1879
Guiney	J	1877-8-9
Hall	W.H	1877-8-9
Hamilton	E.B	1877-8-9
Maclean	R	1877-8-9
Ricketts	A.H	1877-8-9

LIEUTENANT
Armytage	C.A.E	1877-8-9
Baker	J	1879
Birch	E	1879
Blakeney	J	1877-8-9
Bruce	H.M	1879 r
Davis	J.P.	1879-8-9
Doveton	W.W	1877-8-9
Ellis	F.W	1877-8-9
Ferreira	P	1879 r
Ginningham	S	1877-8-9
Gray	W	1879
# Hay	A.B	1877-8-9

City Coins Postal Auction No 58 29th August 2008, Lot No 262. – SAGS bar: 1877-8-9 VF Hammer price 16,610 Rand
Lieut. A.B. Hay 5th Bn. N.N.Infantry; CGHGS 2 bars: Transkei, Basutoland Commry. A.B. Hay; QSA 5 bars: RoL, CC, OFS, Tvl, SA '01 Capt. A.B. Hay C. in C. Bdy. Gd.
On the original SAGS medal roll Hay's service was recorded against the Gaikas, Galekas and other tribes, 1877-8, as well as against the Zulus, 1879. His place of abode was given as Grahamstown. His CGHGS medal is verified on the Forsyth and Owen rolls for service in the Commissariat Department but with rank listed as Deputy Comm. The handwritten Mitchell copy of the Issue Register confirms the rank as Commry. The bars on Angus Hay's QSA are not as issued.
According to the Officers Nominal Roll, he was appointed Captain in Bethune's Mounted Infantry on 19 Oct 1899 and resigned on 5 Jan 1900. The QSA roll for BMI credits him with a bar Natal, and notes that it was issued off the roll of the Commander-in-Chief's Bodyguard. This roll initially credited him with bars for CC, OFS, Tvl and RoL. The CC and RoL were subsequently ruled through and Natal added. A note was added "M + 4 cl. incldg. SA 1901 issued 19.9.06 to P O Box 152, J'burg". The 4 bars would have been OFS, Tvl, Natal, SA '01 but Capt Hay changed them to the 5 bars he preferred to wear (unofficial suspender bar, 2 sets of rivets on carriage).
Sold with copies of SAGS, CGHGS, QSA medal rolls.

Natal Native Contingent

Jay H.W 1879
Jones L.M 1877-8-9
Scrivener C 1879
Shervinton T.R.M 1877-8-9
Spiller H.E 1877-8-9
Stirton J 1877-8-9
Thompson W 1879 r
Welby R.E 1877-8-9
IST CLASS INTERPRETER
Lean F.H 1879
PAYMASTER
Hornabrook G.E 1877-8-9
CLERK AND QUARTERMASTER
Staley W 1879
CLERK
Lamont D 1877-8-9
Milner H 1879
Martin T.D 1879
Mulachy H.W 1879 r
Patterson P.B 1877-8-9
Pigott W.H 1877-8-9
Pohl P
SERGEANT MAJOR
Hanrahan J 1879
QUARTERMASTER SERGEANT
Vanghan C.R 1879
TROOPER
Jeffery J.J 1877-8-9

The following Natal Native Contingent are listed in the Casualty Roll, but not listed in the medal roll, battalion unknown.
LIEUTENANT
Webb H Slightly wounded at Inyetzane 22/1/1879
SERGEANT
Aydenburg O Slightly wounded at Inyetzane 22/1/1879
CORPORAL
Goesh, Carl KIA at Inyetzane 22/1/1879
Meyer J Slightly wounded at Ngudu Mountain 12/1/1879
Miller E KIA at Inyetzane 22/1/1879
Tieper W KIA at Inyetzane 22/1/1879

NATAL NATIVE HORSE.
CAPTAIN
Cochrane W.F.B 1879
See also 32nd Regiment.
Shepstone G.J.P KIA Not on medal roll (See page 421)
LIEUTENANT
Davies H.D 1879
Henderson A.F 1879
See also Shepstones Native Horse
Vance R.W 1879

Wright T 1879
TROOPER
Bags 1879 r
David 1879 r
Itlubi 1879 r
Kambula S 1879 r
Sgt Simron Kambula D.C.M Umfolozi River 3.7.79
Learda 1879 r
TSM Learda D.C.M Kambula 29.3.79
Letser 1879 r
Letser 1879 r
Litseya (Alias Siki) 1879
Sams (Sama) 1979 r
Si 1879 r
Tshabalala D 1879
Tshabalala S 1879
Xaba Solomon 1879 r
Xaba Tomas 1879 r
Zulu John 1879 r

NATAL NATIVE LEVIES.
CAPTAIN
Macrae C 1879
Mc Gregor D 1879
LIEUTENANT
Dacomb H.L 1879
Davey P.F.J 1879
PROVOST SEGEANT
Jackson T 1879
See also 1st NNC.

NATAL NATIVE PIONEERS
Formed in 1879. Overall strength was 273, organized in three companies, one with each of the three invading columns, It was responsible for the repair of roads and tracks, The company in Pearson's column was commanded by Captain Beddoes.
CAPTAIN
Beddoes G.K.E 1879
Nolan W.J 1879
STAFF OFFICER
Allen W 1879
Andrews G.F 1879
Wounded at Ulundi 4/7/1879
Chase F.D 1878-9
Foxon F.E 1879
Grimes G.R 1879
#Hancock H 1879
Hickley H 1879
Wounded at Ulundi 4/7/1879
Peel T.A 1879 r
Southall W 1879
Stevens C.S 1879

CLERK
Michell J.A No clasp

NATAL VOLUNTEER FORCE.
CAPTAIN ADJUTANT
Davey N.E 1879

NATIVE ARTILLERY
RANK NOT KNOWN
Kemp C 1879

NELSONS BURGHERS.
FIELD CORNET
Nelson J.B 1877-8
LIEUTENANT
Adcock W.C 1877-8 r
Owen R 1877-8
BURGHER
Bartness J 1877-8 r
Cory G 1877-8
Hodgkison H 1877-8
Nelson G 1877-8
Nelson J.R 1877-8
Owen R.J 1877-8
Scheepers A 1877-8
Scheepers J.H 1877-8
Scheepers J.J 1877-8
Scheepers S.K. 1877-8
Schaepers T.C 1877-8 r
Wagener W 1877-8 r
Wood J 1877-8 r
Woods W 1877-8

NESBITTS LIGHT HORSE.
MAJOR
Nesbitt R.A 1877-8-9

NEWCASTLE MOUNTED RIFLES
Raised in Northern Natal in 1876, The unit was present at Isandlwana and lost seven men. Major Dartnell of the Natal Mounted Police commanded the unit in Glyn's column. During the course of the war it merged with the Natal Carbineers. Those killed in Action (KIA) lost their lives at Isandlwana 22/1/1879.
CAPTAIN
*Bradstreet Robert KIA 1877
SURGEON
Ward C No clasp
LIEUTENANT
*Dixon (R.F) 1879
*Jones C.J 1879
SERGEANT MAJOR
Napier ? 1879
*Swan ? Not on medal roll

Glendinings Sale 26th March 1998 Lot 114. South Africa 1877-1879, one bar, 1879 (Lieut.H.Hancock. Natal Nat.Contgt.) Extremely fine. Not found on Natal Native Contingent rolls. Estimate £180-220)

Newcastle Mounted Rifles

NEWCASTLE MOUNTED RIFLES
*In 1877, during the British annexation of the Transvaal, Newcastle had been at the hub of affairs. Recognised as a strategically commanding position, the straggling, treeless, dusty and bleak little village had enjoyed the excitement of the troop movements. In July of that year, Lieut. Colonel Amiel arrived with 300 men of the 80th to build a fort and garrison the town. Crowds would turn out to watch the departure of a regiment. A tiny moving caterpillar of red dust and faint brassy music marked their route up past Majuba to Meek's Farm, where the Dutch farmers would crowd in to hear the band play. It was a boom time for innkeepers. Young **Edward Hitchcock**, newly married to Melmoth Osborn's daughter, was expanding his Newcastle Hotel, and winning commendation from the officers and gentlemen of H.M. Forces for his genteel bar and excellent billiard room. As Quartermaster of the newly formed Newcastle Rifles he was kept busy. His C.O. was **Capt. Charles Robert Bradstreet**, the Assistant Magistrate. A gentleman born and bred, Bradstreet had been something of a rolling stone, but had finally joined the Civil Service; being stationed in Newcastle, he had met and married Maud, the daughter of Dr. Scoble of Boscobello. His volunteer company was a bit thin on the ground with a muster of twenty. He had inspanned two of his magisterial staff, **Barnes and McAllister; Swan**, the local wagon-maker, had joined up, as had **John Dinkelman**, the son of the German sawyer at "Beginsel" in Normandien, and young Posselt of the German missionary family who was helping the **Rev. Mr. Prozesky** at "Koenigsberg." **Parsons, Walsh and Boast** were local village troopers.*
Bradstreet had a hectic time. The licentious soldiery were continually giving trouble and there were daily brawls in the canteens. The remount officers came to protest that farmers were fleecing them, demanding £70 to £100 for a horse! Boer farmers rode in to complain about cattle thieving, and native servants came to complain of ill treatment by their masters.
*Bradstreet was profoundly thankful when the Government found a man of the right calibre for the post of Magistrate in this busy garrison town. It was late in 1878 when **William Henry Beaumont** arrived. An Anglo-Indian like Bradstreet, he had a Sandhurst military training and career behind him, but had opted for the Colonial Service at 23. Now 28 and newly married to **Alice Millar**, he was the proud father of a first son. Young, vital, highly intelligent, he galvanised his district for defence. Not only did he shape the Newcastle Mounted Rifles, but he also recruited numbers of loyal natives to the Newcastle Scouts. So ably did he go about his task that, within a very brief time, Beaumont was appointed by Lord Chelmsford as Colonial Commander for District No. 1, which included, not only Newcastle and the Biggarsberg, but also Lady-smith and Klip River, Weenen and Umsinga. His responsibility was heavy.*
Extracts from THE TURBULENT FRONTIER BIGGARSBERG AND BUFFALO AT THE CROSSROADS Mrs Sheila Henderson, M.A.

QUARTERMASTER
*Hitchcook KIA   1879
From Causality Roll George
Earnest Edward Max Hitchcock
QUARTERMASTER SERGEANT
*Parsons   ?   Not on medal roll
SERGEANT
Bierbaum   ?   1879
Swan   A   KIA   1879
*Walsh   ?   1879
TRUMPETER
Horne   ?   1879
CORPORAL
*Bierbaum?   Not on tmedal roll
TROOPER
*Barnes   W.H.J   1879 r
KIA Returned but reissued.
*Bentley   ?   1879 r
Berning   ?   1879 r
*Brown   ?   1879
Burns   ?   1879 r
*Carey   ?   Not on medal roll
Clasen   ?   1879 r
*Cuningham ?   1879
*****Dinkelman   KIA   1879**
Initials from Causality Roll
H.H Dinkelman (Dinkelman)

Dixon   A.E   1879
Dixon   ?   Not on medal roll
Drowned 12/1/1879 rorkes' Drift
Du Barry   ?   1879
Frankeish (Frankish) ? 1879
Gourman   ?   1879 r
Gourzi   ?   1879 r
*Grant   ?   1879
Greenbank KIA   1879 r
Initials from Causality Roll
G.Greenbank
*Grundy   ?   1879
*Hall   ?   1879
*Horn   ?   1879
*Jones   ?   1879
*****Mc Allister KIA   1879**
Causality Roll Alexander McAllister
Mc Intyre   ?   1879
*Moodie   ?   1879
*Napier   ?   Not on medal roll
*Napier   ?   Not on medal roll
Osborn   ?   1879
*Parsons   ?   Not on medal roll
*Parsons   H   Not on medal roll
*Player   ?   1879
*Short   ?   1879
*Simpson   ?   1879
St Clair   ?   1879

*Van Rooyen ?   1879 r
*Present for duty at Helpmakaar,
16th December 1878, (Natal Mercury
21 December.1878)

NEWCASTLE SCOUTS.
The Medals were without a clasp.
HON CAPTAIN
Beaumont (RM) W.W

LIEUTENANT AND ADJUTANT
Austin
LIEUTENANT
Sanlez

NEW ENGLAND CONTINGENT
QUATERMASTER
Bristin   A.C   1877-8

NORTHERN BORDER HORSE
LIEUTENANT COMMANDING
Heineberg J   1877-8
LIEUTENANT
Titman   J.E   1879
CORPORAL
Dall   G.F   1877-8

#Spink Sale 7022 Lot 1362. 19 Jul 2007 The Isandhlwana Casualty Zulu War Medal to Trooper W.H.J. Barnes, Newcastle Mounted Rifles South Africa 1877-79, one clasp, 1879 (Tpr. W.H.J. Barnes. Newcastle M.R.), officially impressed in medium sans-serif capitals, Extremely fine Hammer Price £2400. Trooper W.H.J. Barnes was killed in action at the Battle of Isandhlwana, 22.1.1879. His original medal was returned to Woolwich, and the above medal was applied for and issued c.1920.

NCOs Victoria Mounted Rifles and Stanger Mounted Rifles (KZN Archives, Pietermaritzburg)

Victoria Mounted Rifles

Natal Carbineers - Left to Right Sgt Major D.Scott, Trumpeter C.Scott, and Lt F.J Scott (killed at Isandlwana) family photograph taken prior to departure for the Zulu War.

Natal Carbineers

Durban Mounted Rifles - NCO - Full Dress

Group of officers of the Umzimkulu Mounted Rifles and the Alexandra Mounted Rifles at a combined camp, Marburg Commonage, July 1887.
Front row: Lieut. Fitzjames Arbuthnot (A.M.R.), Capt. H. T. Bru de Wold (U.M.R.), Lieut. H. Lugg (U.M.R.), Lieut. R. Vause (A.M.R.).
Back row: Lieut. F. Rethman (U.M.R.), Lieut. V. W. L. Blake (A.M.R.), Lieut. W. Sangmeister (U.M.R.), Lieut. Barnes (U.M.R.).

1882 Natal Carabineers
Sergt H. Brewer, Corpl. T. Edwards, Trpr C.Tatham, Sergt W. Edwards, Corpl. D McKenzie, Regt. Sergt-Major E.M Greene, Sergt. Geo. Ross, Sergt A. Hair, Sergt H. Stirton, Sergt. W. Barker.

Northern Border Horse

TROOPER								
Betzer	C	1877-8 r	Hanke	P	1878-9 r	**SERGEANT MAJOR**		
Bowhill	T	1877-8	Hoffe	P	1878-9	Clarke	W	1878 r
Chillier	W	1878-9 r	Issacks	J	1878-9 r	**QUARTERMASTER SERGEANT**		
Creed	H.L	1879	Jagers	W	1878-9 r	Bloomfield	W	1878
Dallaine	E	1877-8	Jarson	U	1878-9 r	Tee	W.S	1878
Deals	H	1877-8	Jolliffe	M	1878-9 r	Waterworth	F.E.S	1878
Duffey	G	1877-8 r	Jones	J	1878-9	**SERGEANT**		
Hold	F	1877-8 r	Knight	T	1878-9 r	Armstrong	C	1878
Scobel (Schotel) L		1877-8 r	Links	P	1878-9 r	Ashley	C	1878 r
Listed on roll as "dead". Medal issued to Lieut. L.Schotel, North. Bord.Horse.			Lubbe	K	1878-9	Remarks on roll "Not entitled M/3003"		
			Maher	J	1878-9	##Denys	J.P	1878
Towzaan	B	1877-8	Manning	M	1878-9 r	Dorehill	G	1878
Van Damme A		1877-8	Mc Donald M		1878-9 r	Doyle	G	1878
Williams	J	1878-9 r	Morgenrood F		1878-9 r	Lange	S.E	1878
			Otto	F	1878-9 r	Mc Pherson W.F.G		1878
NORTHERN BORDER POLICE FORCE.			Orian	A	1878-9 r	See also Commandant		
CAPTAIN			Poza	C	1878-9 r	W.P.G Mac Pherson Kimberly Horse		
Blum	A	1878-9	Roberts	J	1878-9	Orpen	C.C.H	1878
# Dyason G.B (W.W) 1878-9			Rossult	J	1878-9	Rube	C	1878 r
KIA at Blamokop 10/4/1879 in Port of Elizabeth Volunteer Horse.			San	J	1878-9	Smith	T	1878 r
			Smit	W	1878-9 r	**CORPORAL**		
FIELD ADJUTANT			Stearens	A	1878-9	Dempster	J	1878
Dorrington N.G		1878-9	Stearens	J	1878-9	Maritz	A.T	1878
Schnackenberg W.C		1878-9	**Tippert**	**J**	**Not in Medal Roll**	Mc Namara	P	1878
SERGEANT			Died of wounds at Rietfontein 6/3/1879			Noir	G	1878
Harper	F	1878-9	Tom		1878-9	Osterloh	P	1878
Grant	D	1878-9	Towzean	B	1878-9	St Ledger F		1878
Gunsy	W	1878-9	Unzomanzie ?		1878-9 r	**TROOPER**		
Newhook E		1878-9	Viljoen	G	1878-9 r	Allkins	S	1878
CORPORAL			Woods	J	1878-9 r	Anderson	A	1878 r
Cilliers	W	1878-9	Zwartbooy G		1878-9 r	Ayers	W.M	1878 r
Mc Evoy	R	1878-9 r	**BUGLER**			Baron	A	1878 r
Schroeder J		1878-9	Chevalier	T	1878-9	Bauman	C	1878 r
Steele	J	1878-9	Wier	W	1878-9 r	Beal	J	1878
Pieto	M	1878-9				Beeby	C	1878
TROOPER			**ONE STAR DIAMOND CONTINGENT.**			Blenkin	T	1878
Adams	Jan	1878-9	Drawn from diamond miners of the Transvaal and Griqualand.			Bowley	W	1878 r
Adams	John	1878-9				Bremner	G	1878 r
Baardt	C	1878-9	**CAPTAIN COMMANDING**			Brittain	J.D	1878 r
Brink	D	1878-9	Ward	W	1878	Brown	J	1878 r
Brins	J	1878-9	**CAPTAIN** Mc Kenna W 1878			Browning		1878 r
Coetzee	D	1878-9 r	**LIEUTENANT**			Burnett	G	1878 r
Eiman	S	1878-9 r	Barratt	S	1878	Carney	?	1878
Farenhinn E		1878-9 r	Benningfield J		1878	Carr	R	1878 r
Firbank	W	1878-9	De Pass	F	1878	Carruthers W.W		1878 r
Francis	L	1878-9	Mc Pherson E.D		1878	Carstens	C	1878 r
Gras	J	1878-9 r	Moses	D.W	1878 r	Carver	T	1878 r
						Chandler	C	1878 r

Spinks 05 Nov 2003 Sale 3016 Lot 538
South Africa 1877-79, no clasp or suspension (Adjt W W Dyason, North: Bord: Police.), contemporarily brooch mounted on obverse, minor edge bruise, otherwise good very fine Hammer Price: £ 850

Dixons Gazette No33 Spring 2003 409 1 clasp, 1878. Lieutenant J.P. Denys, One Star Diamond Contingent.
The medal roll of the One Star Diamond Contingent, a unit drawn from diamond miners of the Transvaal and Griqualand Districts shows Lieut Jacob Peter Denys as one of the six Lieutenants entitled to the South Africa medal 1877-79. There were thirteen officers serving with this unit. The roll also states Denys was engaged against the Pokwane 1878 and the Griquas 1878, his rank at the time the medal was earned was Sgt. A total of 169 medals issued with 1878 clasp, 85 returned. Rank officially corrected on medal from Sgt on roll. Sold with photocopy roll page. NEF £455.00

One Star Diamond Contingent

Chivers	J	1878
Christian	E	1878 r
Cloete	L	1878
Conway		1878 r
Coetzee	J	1878 r
Cooper	E	1878 r
Cousens	F	1878 r
Cox	M.W	1878 r
Cowley	F	1878 r
Davis	G	1878
Deal	A	1878 r
Dodds	D	1878
Donovan	E	1878 r
Du Ploy	P	1878
Du Preez	A	1878 r
Du Preez	J	1878
Edwards	C	1878
Edmunds	W.L	1878
Ellitson	R	1878 r
Enjel		1878 r
Essenwein	F	1878
Ewert	W	1878
Fouchee	J.P	1878
Frames	W.B	1878
Friend		1878
Frost	F	1878 r
Gibbon	A	1878 r
Gifford	P	1878 r
Glass	W	1878
Hartley	C	1878
Hartley	J.W	1878
Harvey	W.F	1878 r
Hawkins	M	1878 r
Hayes	J	1878 r
Healey	M	1878
Heugh	W	1878 r
Hollander	M	1878
Hoskins	P	1878 r
Hughes	J	1878
Jones	J.J	1878
Jubber	E.S	1878 r
Kearne	B.C	1878
Kelly	J	1878 r
Kimble	J	1878
Kleb	J	1878 r
Lake	A.C	1878
Lawson	J	1878 r
Mainzer	M	1878
Makin	L	1878
Marais	B	1878
Marais	P	1878 r
Marshall	J	1878 r
Mathews	G	1878 r
Mc. Conishel	W	1878 r
Mc Farlane	P	1878 r
Mc Mahon	P	1878 r
Mc Kay	G	1878
See D.F. Horse		
Meyers	E	1878-9
Milligan	J	1878
Murray	J.C	1878
Nelson	G	1878
Nicholas	W	1878 r
Nolan	J	1878 r
O'Brien	J	1878
Olliver	W	1878
O'Neil		1878 r
Oppel	H.A	1878
Orpen	C	1878
Osborne	T.G	1878
Parkins	F	1878 r
Pike	J.C	1878
Pohl	H	1878
Pohl	J	1878
Richards	W	1878 r
Richardson	W.S	1878 r
Roach	A.C.F	1878
Rose	N	1878
Rossiter	T	1878 r
Rothwell	G	1878
Rowlands	J	1878 r
Schultz	C.S	1878 r
Shannon	M	1878 r
Shaw	J	1878
Shepherd	P	1878
Simpson	E.C	1878 r
Shears (Snears)	D	1878 r
Soundy	J.E	1878
Soundy	J.W	1878 r
Sparling	W	1878
Steyn	M	1878 r
Stewart	J	1878
Street	F	1878
Stuart	B	1878
Syrus	C.H	1878 r
Roll states "Duplicate Kimberley Horse"		
Thompson	R	1878
Thompson	W	1878 r
Trigs	J	1878
Trutter	L	1878
Tucker	B	1878
Tucker	H.C	1878
Tucker	J.E	1878
Tucker	W.D	1878
Tuder	H	1878 r
Tyrell	S.A	1878 r
Van Blerk	E	1878 r
Van Breda	C	1878 r
Van den Byl	P	1878
Van Hiekerk	C	1878 r
Van Hiekerk	T.R	1878
Viljoen	W	1878 r
Vorster	J	1878
Wallace	J.A	1878
Wienand	F.B.H	1878
Wild	H.W	1878
Whittock	T	1878 r
Williams	A.E	1878 r
Williams	C	1878 r
Wolf	L.J	1878
Wood	H.T	1878
Zigentein	A	1878

OUDTSHOORN VOLUNTEERS.
CAPTAIN
Ferreira   A.H   1878
PRIVATE
Warren   J   1877-8

PANMURE BURGHERS
RANK NOT KNOWN
Norton   J.L   1877-8

PEDDIE FINGO LEVY.
CAPTAIN
Bartholomew I.W.T.A.H 1878
Cogan   J.M   1877-8-9
Lloyd   W   1877-8 r
Maclean   W.A   1877-8 r
Commanding.
Watson   H   1877-8
LIEUTENANT
Crutchfield H   1877-8
Langdon   I   1877-8
Moolwman F   1877-8 r
Nelson   A.V   1877-8
Schultz   F   1877-8 r
RANK NOT KNOWN
Hunt   J.C   1877-8-9

PEDDIE MOUNTED BURGHERS
TROOPER
Elliott   S.M   1878 r
Hasenjaeger F   1878

PIETERMARIZBURG RIFLES
This unit did not cross the Border (Tugela River). Medals were issued without a clasp.
CAPTAIN
Matterson   G.O
LIEUTENANT ADJUTANT
Scoones   T.E
QUARTERMASTER
Halliday   R
Thring   A.L
LIEUTENANT
Horsley   R
QUARTERMASTER SERGEANT
Walker   W.N
SERGEANT
Campbell   P
George   F
Guttridge   J.T
Quirk   A
Wade   F

Pietermarizburg Rifles

CORPORAL
Ballantyne W
Butterfield W.T
Elton P
Gordon V
Mc Kenzie F
Mitchell E.H
Mitchell J.W
Mitchell T

PRIVATE
Armitage G
Baird W.H
Bakewell H
Bakewell J
Ballantyne J
Barry R
Bonham T
Boecock W.H
Burn J.E
Chaplin W.R
Chapman W.F
Cox G.B
Cox P.A.M
Cox S
Crouch C r
Crouch H
Crouch P
Crozen E
Daly W
Drydon H
Edwards T
Farrell W
Ferguson E.H
Ferreira P
Forbes J
Forsyth J
Gass J.C
Geere J.M
Geere M
Gordon G.W
Gordon L.R
Haines W
Hall A
Hamilton D
Harbourn C.R
Harbourn T
Harvey A
Hirst A
Hodson E.G
Holding J.W
Hopkins E
Hutchinson W.H
Ince H
Johnstone A
Judd C
Kinmair R
Kinsman F
Lamb A
Lambert R

Lindsay A
Lindsay D
Lindsay J
Lindsay W
Mc Claren J.M
Mc Crystal H
Mc Mullen G
Mileman A
Munden J.T
Parson H
Patterson D
Patrick G
Payne J.T r
Pewsey F
Quirk P
Radford A
Radford W
Shepherd Jas
Simpson C
Stacey A
Staples W
Stevens F
Stevens T
Stewart A
Stewart P
Terry E
Theobald A
Thring I.L
Tray P
Tucker A.W
Tuffield R
Varty I.B
Varty W
Vincer R
Wallett W.G
Wallet W.H
Walters C.A
Westbrooke W.H
Winter F.S
Winter J.W

PONTON CORPS.
PRIVATE
Finn E   1879 r

PORT ELIZABETH MILITIA. No.1 Co.
CAPTAIN
Dix-Peek G   1877-8
SERGEANT
Blake W.J   1877-8
Crankshaw J.F.W   1877-8 r
CORPORAL
Bailey W   1877-8 r
Hendricks M   1877-8
Milne D   1877-8 r
O'Brien P   1877-8 r
BUGLER
Dix-Peek A   1877-8

PRIVATE
Anderson W   1877-8
Backstrom G.H   1877-8 r
Bates G   1877-8
Bracenga J   1877-8 r
Bradford R   1877-8 r
Bull W   1877-8 r
Coleman J   1877-8 r
See also Frontier L. Horse
Cook J   1877-8 r
See also Frontier L. Horse
Cravett J   1877-8
Discharge for insubordination 1878
Daneif J   1877-8 r
Doig D   1877-8
Gainsford R   1877-8 r
Geary T   1877-8 r
Gunn J   1877-8 r
Henderson J   1877-8 r
Huskisson G   1877-8 r
Johnson E   1877-8 r
Jones J   1877-8 r
Keans J   1877-8 r
Kellsey A   1877-8
Lloyd R   1877-8 r
March H   1877-8 r
Nixon T   1877-8 r
Osche C.H   1877-8 r
Petersen J.H   1877-8 r
Rundle W   1877-8 r
Smith C   1877-8
Stanton T   1877-8
Styles C   1877-8
Swann M   1877-8 r
Tebbs W.A   1877-8 r
Whelan J   1877-8 r
White A.E   1877-8
Woods W   1877-8 r
Wroe J   1877-8 r

PORT ELIZABETH MILITIA. No. 2 Co.
ACTING CAPTAIN
Ronny-Tailyour E.R   1877-8
LIEUTENANT
Cooke E.W   1877-8-9
COLOUR SERGANT
Ashkettle J   1877-8
SERGEANT
Boltenstern A   1877-8
CORPORAL
French T   1877-8 r
Stephens W   1877-8 r
Surr J   1877-8 r
Yates J   1877-8
PRIVATE
Altensted C   1877-8 r
Altensted P   1877-8 r
Barsley T   1877-8 r
Botts E   1877-8

Port Elizabeth Militia No2 Company

Butler	R	1877-8 r		See also 5th Btn. Natal Nat. Contin.			Russell	F.J	1877-8 r
Chowles	A	1877-8 r		LIEUTENANT			Scallan	A	1877-8
Clancy	J	1877-8		Deare	C.R	1877-8	Smith	G	1877-8 r
Coleman	D	1877-8		SERGEANT MAJOR			Snetler	L	1877-8
Compton	F	1877-8 r		Clifton	J.S	1877-8	Stark	A	1877-8
Cooke	F.R	1877-8 r		QUARTERMASTER SERGEANT			Sturk	A	1877-8
Coppard	J	1877-8 r		Hutchinson		E 1877-8	Sutter	J	1877-8 r
Darcy	J	1877-8		SERGEANT			Thomas	W.H	1877-8
Darlow	G	1877-8 r		Crews	W.H	1877-8	Thornton	F.J	1877-8 r
Darlow	T	1877-8 r		Rutherford	J	1877-8-9 r	Tuck	J	1877-8 r
Doble	W	1877-8		CORPORAL			Van Niekerk	J.L	1877-8
Donald	J	1877-8		**Borain**	**H**	**1877-8-9 r**	Van Vunren	L.J	1877-8
Doorley	M	1877-8 r		**KIA Isandhlwana.**			Vermaak	E.S	1877-8
Durville	J	1877-8 r		Ellis	F.W	1877-8-9 r	Vernon	C	1877-8 r
Duthie	J	1877-8		Gibson	O	1877-8 r	Waitt	R	1877-8
Farre	H.C	1877-8		Hill	T	1877-8	Warrington	G	1877-8 r
Friend	E	1877-8 r		Whittuck	J.S	1877-8 r	Whealm	J	1877-8
Gillman	A	1877-8		FARRIER			RANK NOT KNOWN		
Hillery	P	1877-8		Macdonald		J 1877-8	Wilson	W	1878
Hooker	F	1877-8 r		BUGLER					
Howard	J	1877-8		Clayton	J.M	1877-8	**PORT ELIZABETH VOLUNTEERS.**		
Ireland	J	1877-8 r		Murray	T	1877-8	TROOPERS		
Jansen	J	1877-8		PRIVATE			Lee	J	1877-8-9
Johnson	M	1877-8		Baker	D	1877-8	Served in 1879 in F.L. Hse. and		
Kirkman	G	1877-8		Baker	W	1877-8	Pulleins Rangers.		
Lang	S.O	1878-8 r		Ball	J	1877-8 r			
Linicher	M	1878		Bean	F	1877-8	**PRINCE ALFRED GUARD RIFLE VOLUNTEERS.**		
Lloyd	H	1877-8		Banister	J	1877-8 r			
Mathews	J	1877-8 r		Berry	A.H	1877-8	* Wounded in Action at Umzintzani		
Mc Alister	A	1877-8 r		Berry	H	1877-8 r	CAPTAIN		
Mc Alister	T	1877-8 r		See also Prince Alfreds Guard Rifle			Dean	G.R	1877-8-9
Nolan	W	1877-8		Volunteers			LIEUTENANT		
Pound	H	1877-8		Bradley	A	1877-8	O'Flaherty	C.R	1877
Povey	R	1877-8		Brockett	E.J	1877-8-9	SUB-LIEUTENANT		
Shaw	G	1877-8		Butcher	J	1877-8	*Gordon	G	1877-8
Skinner	W	1877-8 r		Colling	G	1877-8 r	SERGEANT MAJOR		
Smith	J	1877-8 r		See also 3rd Cape Mtd. Yeos.			Cameron	W	1877 r
Smith	W	1877-8		Cousins	J.W	1877-8	Had a Medal from a Previous War.		
Thaw	G	1877-8		Cressy	J	1877-8	Wasley	F.C	1877-8
Thompson	F	1877-8 r		Crowder	S	1877-8	COLOUR SERGEANT		
Thorn	W	1877-8		Duffy	C.D	1877-8 r	Palmer	C	1877-8
Wasserfall	J	1877-8 r		Fleischer	A.J	1877-8	SERGEANT		
Wood	A	1877-8 r		Fleischer	H.M	1877-8	Hagon	G. NeD	1877-8
Wright	E	1877-8 r		Frost	J.P	1877-8	Jones	J	1877-8
				Gaskell	T	1877-8-9 r	Leslie	J	1877
PORT ELIZABETH MOUNTED RANGERS / RIFLES.				Goldsmith	G	1877-8-9 r	Mc Kenzie	D.C	1877-8
				Hamilton	J	1877-8	CORPORAL		
TROOPERS				Heath	A	1877-8	Blink	C.F	1877-8
Barendsee	T.H	1878 r		Holland	J	1877-8	Buckland	C.C	1877-8 r
Brown	J.C	1879		Jenkins	C	1877-8	Cannicott	T.R	1877-8
Goodin	W	1878		Lovemore	A	1878-8	Hutchinson	E	1877
Pullin	W.H	1877-8		Lovemore	W	1877-8	Masterton	E	1877
				Marson	A	1877-8	Morgan	J.R	1877-8
PORT ELIZABETH VOLUNTEER HORSE.				Matthews	C.F	1877-8	*Stahlschmidt	H	1877-8
				Matthews	C.F.B	1877-8	Weighton	J	1877-8
CAPTAIN				Matthews	S	1877-8	BUGLER CORPORAL		
Nettleton	W.J	1877-8-9		Matthews	W	1877-8	Gilman	J	1877
Had medal for 1853 War.				Moran	P.P	1877-8	LANCE CORPORAL		
Should have received Clasp only.				Peterson	F	1877-8 r	Holmes	R	1877-8

Prince Alfred Guard Rifle Vols.

BUGLER		
Ferguson A.W	1877-8	
PRIVATE		
Adams A.B	1877-8-9	
Alexander G	1877-8	
Bailey H.C	1877	
Barron H.P	**1877**	
KIA at Umzintzani 2/12/1877		
Baumeister A	1877-8	
Berry H	1877	
See also Port Elizabeth Volunteer Horse.		
Birch E.A	1877-8 r	
Blaine B.W	1877	
Blakeney J	1877-8 r	
Bleakinsop H	1877-8	
Blink W.E	1877-8-9	
Booth R	1877-8 r	
Booth Y.M	1877-8	
Bowhill T	1877-8	
Braidwood A.J	1877-8	
Bremer H.M	1877-8 r	
Brooks E	1877-8	
Brown C.W	1877-8 r	
Brown J	1877-8	
Brown T	1877-8 r	
Burns G.T	1877-8	
Caithness D.S	1877-8	
Caldecott F	1877-8 r	
Calvert L..J	1877-8	
Chase J.E	1877-8-9	
Christian G.C.S	**1877-8-9 r**	
KIA Isandhlwana.22/1/1879		
See also Natal Carbineers.		
Clayton J	1877	
Clifford J.J	1877-8-9	
Crosley H	1877	
Cunningham J	1877-8	
Darcy J.W	1877-8-9 r	
Davie T.W	1877	
Dunn J	1877-8	
Elliott H	1877-8	
Elmer J	1877-8	
Everitt A.P	1877-8	
Faure F.H	1877-8	
Fitzgerald N	1877-8	
Frames W.S	1877-8	
Fraser J	1877-8	
Freeman A	1877	
Froude P.G	1877 r	
Fuller W.H	1877	
Gamble F.F	1877	
Geere C	1877-8	
Glendinning P	1877 r	
Green J	1877-8	
Halladay T.J	**1877-8-9 r**	
KIA Hlobane.		
Hamilton J.C	1877-8	
Hough W.V	1877-8 r	
Hinton F	1877-8	
Holton F.G	1877-8	
Ingram C.H	1877-8	
Jackson C	1877 r	
Jenkins J.R	1877-8	
Jones A.J	1877-8	
Jones A.R.B	1877-8 r	
Johnson H.E	1877	
Johnston T	1877	
Kemp H.C	1877-8	
Kemp J	1878-9	
Lee J	1877-8	
Lewis G	1877 r	
Lloyd E.C	1877-8 r	
*Marshall A	1877-8	
Marshall J	1877-8	
Mc Intosh J	1877	
Mc Kay L.J	1877-8-9	
Mc Lachlan H.F	1877	
Mc Laughlin D	1877-8	
Milne W	1877-8	
Moller E.J	1877-8	
Morgan A	1877	
Morgan C	1877-8-9	
Morgan R.J	1877	
Murray T	1877	
Nash W	1877-8	
Nitsch L.A	1877-8 r	
O'Shaugnessy P.J	1877-8	
*Overweg L	1877-8 r	
Palmer G.E	1877-8	
Parkin F	1877	
Philip H.H	1877-8	
Philpot W	1877-8	
*Pickering E	1877-8	
Pickering W	1877-8-9	
Piercy W.P	1877-8	
*Pillans J.M	1877-8	
Popham H	1877-8 r	
Price T	1877-8 r	
Pridgeon H	1877-8 r	
Purchase F.E	1877-8-9	
Rex G.A	1877-8	
Roberts S	1877	
Sheldrake W	1877-8	
Smith F	1877-8	
Smith G.H	1877-8	
Storey G.R	1877-8-9	
Tailyour E	1877	
Tipper J.C	1877-8	
Tonks S	1877-8	
Tynan J	1877 r	
Valentine A.J	1877	
Von Konitski L.B	1877-8 r	
Wenman W.R.E	1877-8	
Whiley H.C	1877-8	
White R.K	1877-8 r	
Whitehead J.W	1877	
Whitehead R	1877-8	
Wilheim C.L	1877-8 r	
Wolfe A.K	1877-8-9	
Wood J	1877-8	
Wright C.P	1877-8	
RANK NOT KNOWN		
Konitzky L.B	1877-8-9	
PRINCE ALFRED'S OWN CAPE VOLUNTEER ARTILLERY		
LIEUTENANT		
Calf P.J	1877-8	
Stegant P.J	1877-8	
SERGEANT		
Elton C.G	1877-8	
Fell W	1877-8	
Van Breda N	1877-8	
BOMBARDIER		
Rogers C	1877-8	
Silkstone E	1877-8	
Ulrich W	1877-8	
CORPORAL		
Armstrong N	1877-8	
Hinton F	1878 r	
Inglesby W.T	1877-8	
Thompson W	1878 r	
TRUMPETER		
Tennant J.D	1877-8	
GUNNER		
Art W.J	1877-8	
Brittain E	1877-8	
Charters W.G	1877-8	
Campbell J	1878	
Cogill W	1878	
Dix W.A	1878	
Eckard C.S	1877-8	
Flack E.J	1877-8	
Froggart C.H	1877-8 r	
Gibson C	1877-8	
Graham A.B	1878	
Hardy R.J	1877-8 r	
Inglesby T.J.J	1877-8	
Keymed W.E	1877-8	
Lawton J.D	1877-8	
Linderberg J	1878	
Martin C.H	1878	
Murphy E	1877-8	
Payne W.E	1878 r	
Pentz A	1878	
Rennie A.L	1878	
Simpson G.H	1877-8	
Smart J	1878	
Thomas G.F	1877-8	
Thorndike W.J	1877-8	
Timmerman W	1878 r	
Vos P	1878	
Vos R	1878-8	
Whiley R.T	1877-8	
Wolff A.V.H	1878	
Wran-Ruind (?) J	1877-8	

Prince Alfred's Own Cape Vol. Artillerry

PULLEINES RANGERS
CAPTAIN
Barry	D.G	1877-8
Cameron	W.M	1877-8
Mc Taggart	H.E	1877-8

See also Southeys Rangers and Transkei Rifles. Medal from a previous campaign.

LIEUTENANT
Davis	A	1877-8-9 r
Mc Taggart	J	1877-8-9
Paley	W.W	1877-8-9 r
Peck	H.W	1877-8

Two medals were issued to this officer. One was returned.

Ricketts	A.H	1877-8-9 r
Yates	?	1877-8

SERGEANT MAJOR
Stoneham	?	1877-8

COLOUR SERGEANT
Lardner	A	1878

SERGEANT
Aspinall	**J**	**1877-8-9 r**

KIA at Centane 7/2/1878

Jackson	J	1877-8 r
Landsberg	M	1877-8-9
Maidwell	N.J	1877-8-9
Montgomery	P	1878
Morgan	J.A	1877-8 r
Nickelsom	D	1877-8-9 r
Shannon	J.T	1877-8
Thomas	C	1877-8

CORPORAL
Able	J	1877-8 r
Armstrong	W	1877-8
Ashby	G	1877-8-9

See also Tpr G Ashby Bakers Horse.

Brown	W	1877-8 r
Cole	**J**	**1877-8-9 r**

KIA at Centane 7/2/1878

Luck	G	1877-8-9 r
Maitland	R	1877-8 r
Robinson	W	1877-8 r
Russell	W	1877-8-9 r
Seangur	J.W	1877-8 r
Taylor	W	1877-8-9
Turner	W	1877-8-9

Reissued 1908

Whitecross	A	1877-8

PRIVATE
Badrow	T	1877-8 r
Barend	J.F	1877-8
Beaumont	W	1877-8 r
Bennett	**J**	**1877-8-9**

KIA at Centane 7/2/1878

Brazil	T	1877-8 r
Broderock	A	1877-8 r
Brown	J.A	1877-8
Buckley	J	1877-8 r
Burke	W.M	1877-8
Carrahill	J	1877-8
Cross	G	1877-8 r
Carran	W	1877-8-9 r
Dallamau	A.W	1878
Dunstan	J	1877-8-9
Easten	F	1877-8-9 r
Eyre	T.S	1877-8-9
Francis	T	1877-8-9 r
Gorry	J	1877-8-9 r
Harris	A	1877-8-9 r
Hart	W	1877-8-9 r
Hessen	W	1877-8-9
Hinds	H	1877-8-9
Holmes	W	1877-8-9 r
Howard	H	1877-8-9 r
Hyland	B	1877-8-9 r
Ingram	W	1877-8-9 r
Jantje	?	1877-8-9 r
Jordaan	M	1877-8-9 r
Mayers	R	1877-8-9 r
Mc Cartney	J	1877-8-9 r
Mc Kella	A	1877-8-9 r
Mc Nallay	P	1877-8-9 r
Mc Taggart	?	1877-8-9
Melvin	M	1878 r
Moore	W.M	1877-8-9

See also Ist Cape Mounted Yeomanry. It is possible that two clasp viz 1877-8 and 1879 may have been issued.

Morris	J	1877-8-9
O'Gardy	J	1877-8-9
Peters	H.J	1877-8-9
Preslin	W	1877-8-9 r
Saunders	J	1877-8 r
Scott	J	1877-8-9 r
Sheen	J	1877-8-9 r
Sheppard	F	1877-8-9 r
Silver	J	1877-8 r
Skelton	J	1877-8 r
Skinner	H.J	1878-9

See also Frontier Light Horse.

Smith	G	1877-8 r
Sulivan	C	1877-8-9
Sweeney	M	1879 r
Thatan	J	1877-8 r
Thompson	G	1877-8 r
Tucker	W	1877-8
Walsh (1)	J	1877-8 r
Walsh (2)	J	1877-8 r
Watson	R	1877-8
Weir	P.D	1877-8
West	W	No clasp
Whamby	C	1877-8 r
Whandles	G	1877-8 r
Wheeler	W	1877-8 r
Whitcobe	C	1877-8 r
Williams	T	1877-8-9
Wyatt	B	1877-8

RANK NOT KNOWN
Byrne	R.A	1879
Lardner	A	1877-8
Mossely	M.J	1879
Pietersan	S	1877-9-9

PULLENS FINGO LEVY.
CAPTAIN
Pullen	W.O	1877-8 r

SERGEANT
Yowa		1877-8

CORPORAL
John		1877-8

PRIVATE (No rank is shown)
Andries	1877-8 r
Babachie	1877-8 r
Bobejan	1877-8 r
Boniel	1877-8 r
Boya	1877-8 r
Breakfast	1877-8 r
Captain	1877-8 r
Chrisjan	1877-8 r
Cindanie	1877-8 r
Daniel	1877-8 r
Faleine	1877-8
Fuba	1877-8 r
Golosa	1877-8 r
Harsh	1877-8 r
Henry	1877-8
Hermanus	1877-8 r
Issack	1877-8 r
Landana	1877-8 r
Lucas	1877-8
Maguada	1877-8 r
Manners	1877-8
Manzwana	1877-8 r
Palieso	1877-8 r
Pendanie	1877-8 r
Pindie	1877-8 r
Rowan	1877-8
Sasi	1877-8 r
Sahekele	1877-8 r
Sewanga	1877-8 r
Singanie	1877-8 r
Sisi	1877-8 r
Stephanie	1877-8 r
Towbanie	1877-8 r
Thomas	1877-8 r
Tom	1877-8 r
Tois	1877-8 r
Tushu	1877-8 r
Umsaha	1877-8 r
Umtana	1877-8 r
Umtantieso	1877-8 r
Whiteboy	1877-8 r
William (1)	1877-8 r
William (2)	1877-8
Xenga	1877-8 r
Xolo	1877-8 r

Pullens Fingo Levy

Name		Year
Xongp		1877-8
Zashiene		1877-8 r

QUEENSTOWN BURGHER FORCE
COMMANDANT
Bouwer	W.C	1877-8

CAPTAIN
Phillips	E	1877-8 r

SERGEANT
Brown	R	1877-8 r
Herselman	J.C.W	1877-8 r
Smith	C	1877-8 r
Strachan	P	1877-8 r

SERGEANT
Tarr	J	1877-8
Vosleo	G	1877-8 r

CORPORAL
Dell	S	1877-8 r
Herselman	C.L	1877-8 r
Hudson	R	1877-8 r
King	F	1877-8 r
Mundell	P.J	1877-8
Ousthuizen	S	1877-8 r
Pietout	C	1877-8 r
Scott	T	1877-8 r
Smith	W	1877-8 r
Vosloo	G	1877-8
Vosloo	J	1877-8 r

PRIVATE
Armstrong	G	1877-8 r
Bartlett	H	1877-8 r
Bartlett	W	1877-8 r
Betram	J	1877-8 r
Brown	B	1877-8
Brown	B	1877-8 r
Brown	C	1877-8 r
Brown	R	1877-8 r
Coetzee Snr	C	1877-8 r
Coetzee	J	1877-8 r
Coetzee	P	1877-8 r
Cowley	W	1877-8 r
De Bruin	A	1877-8
De Bruin	G	1877-8 r
De Bruin Jnr	G	1877-8 r
De Bruin	P	1877-8 r
De Bruin	P	1877-8 r
De Bruin	W	1877-8 r
De Koning	C	1877-8 r
De Koning	H	1877-8 r
De Koning	P	1877-8
De Lange	M	1877-8 r
Dell	J	1877-8 r
Dell	S	1877-8 r
Dicks	W	1877-8 r
Ferreira	C	1877-8 r
Filmer	B	1877-8 r
Filmer	G	1877-8 r
Filmer	J.G	1877-8 r
Forward	W	1877-8 r
Foxcroft	James	1877-8 r
Foxcroft	Joseph	1877-8 r
Gibbons	W	1877-8 r
Goosen	W	1877-8 r
Gravitt	B	1877-8 r
Gravett	R	1877-8
Hartmann	W	1877-8 r
Henderson	J.R	1877-8 r
Herselman	J	1877-8 r
Hudson Jnr	R	1877-8 r
Jordan	M	1877-8 r
Kerstener	A	1877-8 r
Kilpatrick	C	1877-8 r
Klassen Snr	J	1877-8 r
Klassen Jnr	J	1877-8 r
Laity	R	1877-8 r
Lombard	A	1877-8 r
Lombard	J	1877-8 r
Marx	A	1877-8 r
Marx	G	1877-8 r
Miles	A	1877-8 r
Miles	J	1877-8 r
Miles	Robert	1877-8 r
Miles	Rueben	1877-8 r
Miles	W	1877-8
Muller	A	1877-8 r
Mundell	W	1877-8 r
Oosthuizen	C	1877-8
Oosthuizen Snr.	G	1877-8 r
Oosthuizen Jnr.	G	1877-8 r
Oosthuizen Snr.	J	1877-8
Oosthuizen Jnr.	J	1877-8
Oosthuizen	Jacobus	1877-8
Oosthuizen	Jan H	1877-8 r
Oosthuizen	Jan J	1877-8
Oosthuizen	P	1877-8 r
Opperman	R	1877-8 r
Purdon	David	1877-8
Purdon	D	1877-8 r
Roberts	H	1877-8 r
Selby	W	1877-8
Smiles	J	1877-8 r
Staples	E	1877-8 r
Stubbs	H	1877-8 r
Sutton	J	1877-8
Sutton	R	1877-8
Sutton	W	1877-8
Tarr	H	1877-8
Triegaardt	L	1877-8 r
Trollip	J	1877-8
Trollip	R	1877-8 r
Trollip	William	1877-8 r
Trollip	William	1877-8 r
Van Aardt	F	1877-8 r
Van Gass	F	1877-8
Van Straaten	J	1877-8 r
Van Straaten	W	1877-8 r
Van Vuren	L	1877-8 r
Vogel	G	1877-8 r
Vosloo	Gert	1877-8
Vosloo	Gert	1877-8
Vosloo	Gideon	1877-8
Vosloo	Jacobus	1877-8
Vosloo	Johannes	1877-8 r
Vosloo	M	1877-8 r
Vosloo	W	1877-8 r
Woest	H	1877-8 r
Zeiler	J	1877-8 r

QUEENSTOWN BURGHER FORCE NATIVE LEVY.
QUARTERMASTER
Kerstener	A	1877-8 r

PRIVATE
Aasvogel		1877-8 r
Botha	H	1877-8 r
Botha	J	1877-8 r
Botha	W	1877-8 r
Buwer	J	1877-8 r
Christiaan		1877-8 r
Fletcher	J	1877-8 r
Fletcher	W	1877-8 r
Golding	B	1877-8 r
Jantje		1877-8 r
Johannes		1877-8
Klaas		1877-8
Levysman		1877-8 r
Marcus	P	1877-8 r
Mei		1877-8 r
Morgan	H	1877-8 r
Petrus		1877-8 r
Phillip		1877-8 r
Piet		1877-8 r
Scott	F.J	1877-8 r
Sican		1877-8 r
Soldaat		1877-8 r
Soudekka		1877-8 r
Stefanus		1877-8 r
Stuurman		1877-8 r

QUEENSTOWN DIVISIONAL POLICE
NO RANK SHOW
Mennigko ?	C.F.F	1878

QUEENSTOWN LIGHT HORSE
TROOPER
Webb	C.D	1878

Duplicate medal and clasp issued on 1/7/79

RANK NOT KNOWN
Bell	S.C	????
Melass	A	????
Shepstone	F.W	1877-8

Queenstown Light Horse

FORT PEARSON, LOWER TUGELA, FROM THE WEST.

QUEENSTOWN VOLUNTEER CONTINGENT.

COMMANDER
Frost   J   1877-8

SURGEON
Hull   G.A   1877-8

ACTING COMMANDANT
Harvey   E   1877-8

ADJUTANT
Markel   P.J   1877-8

CAPTAIN
Darmer   F.I   1877-8
Ella   A.N   1877-8
May   G   1877-8
Henman   W.C   1877-8
O'Toole   F.L   1877-8 r

AIDE de CAMP
Frost   A.H   1877-8 r
Tweedie   A   1877-8
See also Bowkers Rovers.

LIEUTENANT
Caffyn   A   1877-8
Erskine   C   1877-8
Hinds   G.H   1877-8
Kelly   T   1877-8
Mc Donald   A.C   1877-8
Ross   C.T   1877-8

Tripp   R.S   1877-8
Webb   A.D   1877-8-9

CONNISSARIAT
Bell   E   1877-8
Brown   J   1877-8 r
Hinds   G.D   1877-8

SERGEANT MAJOR
Stirton   J   1877-8

QUARTERMASTER SERGEANT
Nelson   C.E   1877-8

SERGEANT
Brady   J   1877-8-9 r
Brailsford   E   1877-8
Carney   J   1877-8 r
Fegan   ?   1877-8
Franken   C   1877-8 r
Kidson   F   1877-8
Kilpatrick   J.C   1877-8
Liefeldt   J   1877-8
Mc Tavish   W   1877-8 r
Norval   F   1877-8
Robinson   T   1877-8
Sevier   R.S   1877-8
Strike   J.R   1877-8
Syggs   J   1877-8 r
Symonds   R.H   1877-8
Trollip   J   1877-8 r

CORPORAL
Bestall   C   1877-8
Botha   D   1877-8
Cockin   F   1877-8 r
See also Tpr F. Cockin
2nd Cape Mtd. Yeomanry
Hully   J   1877-8
Kelty   W   1877-8 r
Manawyk   J   1877-8
Martin   J.B   1877-8
Mayberry   W   1877-8
Orwin   ?   1877-8 r
Steadworthy   J   1877-8
Trollip   H   1877-8 r
Wiper   R   1877-8 r

BUGLER
Adams   A   1877-8
Oaten   H   1877-8 r

PRIVATE
Adams   A   1877-8
Alexander   C   1877-8 r
Anderson   T   1877-8 r
Arnott   E   1877-8
Arnott   G   1877-8
August   J   1877-8
Avis   A   1877-8
Bagley   D   1877-8 r

Queenstown Volunteer Contingent

Name		Year	Name		Year	Name		Year
Bagley	T	1877-8 r	Dorsor	C	1877-8 r	Huyer	C	1877-8 r
Bands	S	1877-8	Duffy	C	1877-8 r	Jacobs	J	1877-8
Barnes	R	1877-8 r	Duffy	R	1877-8 r	Jakins	?	1877-8
Barnes	W	1877-8	Dugmore	A	1877-8	James	H	1877-8 r
Beresford	W	1877-8	Du Plessis	?	1877-8 r	Jewell	J	1877-8
Berg	W.F	1877	Duprez	D	1877-8 r	Jewell	W	1877-8
Berry	A	1877-8	Duprez	H	1877-8 r	Johnson	G	1877-8
Bentley	G	1877-8 r	Easton	A	1877-8 r	Johnson	J	1877-8 r
Bentley	W.D	1877-8	Edwards	A	1877-8 r	Joseph	M	1877-8 r
Benville	T	1877-8 r	Ella	P	1877-8	Kemp	G	1877-8 r
Billingham	R	1877-8	Engelbrecht	J	1877-8 r	Kidson	R	1877-8
Blackbeard	J	1877-8 r	Exner	T	1877-8	King	W	1877-8
Blakemore	W	1877-8	Exton	A	1877-8	Kirwin	H.	1877-8 r
Bobana	A	1877-8	Filmer	J.W	1877-8 r	Klempt	F	1877-8
Bold	J	1877-8 r	Flack	J	1877-8 r	Kleinhans	F	1877-8 r
Botha	B	1877-8 r	Floss	W	1877-8 r	Kleinkart	J	1877-8 r
Botha	F	1877-8 r	Fotheringham	W	1877-8	Koekemoer	D	1877-8
Botha	H	1877-8 r	Fox	T	1877-8 r	Koekemoer	F	1877-8
Botha	J	1877-8 r	Foxcroft	J	1877-8 r	Krause	J	1877-8 r
Botha	L	1877-8	Franken	W	1877-8 r	Landt	A	1877-8 r
Botha	R	1877-8	Fuller	C	1877-8 r	Landt	S	1877-8 r
Bradfield	T	1877-8 r	Fuller	D	1877-8 r	Lang	H	1877-8
Bremner	T	1877-8	Fuller	F	1877-8	Lantz	W	1877-8 r
Britzke	T	1877-8	Gallagher	E	1877-8 r	Larter	A.A	1877-8
Bromley	?	1877-8 r	Gaskell	J	1877-8 r	Larter	C.A	1877-8
Broodie	A	1877-8	George	J	1877-8 r	Lee	C.B	1877-8
Bruton	G.E	1877-8 r	Gheel	C	1877-8 r	Le Roux	A	1877-8
Buckley	R	1877-8 r	Glover	W.T	1877-8	Le Roux	L	1877-8
Burke	P	1877-8 r	Gobey	J	1877-8 r	Le Roux	P	1877-8
Burke	T	1877-8 r	Goddard	W	1877-8	Lolo	M	1877-8
Callery	?	1877-8 r	Goosen	H	1877-8	Loser	C	1877-8 r
Cameron	D	1877-8	Grant	C.G	1877-8-9 r	Lovemore	M	1877-8
Cherry	E	1877-8	Greyling	J	1877-8	Maclean	D	1877-8 r
Clothier	W	1877-8 r	Grief	C	1877-8	Manawyk	C	1877-8 r
Cockson	H	1877-8	Grunig	H	1877-8	Manawyk	D	1877-8 r
Cockson	W	1877-8	Gunloch	H	1877-8	Manawyk	T	1877-8
Coleridge	H	1877-8	Hadeke	A	1877-8 r	Marrow	T	1877-8 r
Colombo	B	1877-8 r	Hagan	A	1877-8 r	Matham	M	1877-8
Condon	P	1877-8	Halstead	W	1877-8 r	Maulin	M.J	1877-8
Coombes	F	1877-8	Harris	J	1877-8 r	Maydiam	R	1877-8
Coombes	T	1877-8	Hart	C	1877-8 r	Mc Cabe	J	1877-8 r
Cooper	J	1877-8	Hart	James	1877-8	Mc Donald	D	1877-8
Cornell	G.C	1877-8	Hart	John	1877-8 r	Mc Kenzie	P	1877-8 r
Coutts	C	1877-8	Hart	W	1877-8	Meyer	W	1877-8
Cox	T	1877-8	Hart	W.F	1877-8	Millen	A	1877-8 r
Crawford	H	1877-8 r	Hattangh	H	1877-8	Mills	W	1877-8
See also Cape M.R. and FAMP.			Hendrickes	J	1877-8 r	Mitchley	R	1877-8
Creba	R	1877-8	Henyse	H	1877-8 r	Mitchley	T	1877-8
Cunning	G.M	1877-8 r	Herbst	H	1877- r	Morgan	J.M	1877-8
Cutter	T	1877-8	Hill	J	1877-8 r	Mullajan	A	1877-8 r
Cutter Jnr	T	1877-8	Hillard	J.T	1877-8 r	Mundry	J. r	1877-8 r
Cutter Snr	W	1877-8	Hoffman	D	1877-8 r	Myburg	A	1877-8
Cuyler	J	1877-8 r	Hogen	W	1877-8	Myburg	F	1877-8
De Lange	D	1877-8 r	Holmes	J	1877-8	Myburg	J	1877-8
De Lange	M	1877-8 r	Honor	P	1877-8 r	Myburg	P	1877-8
Dell	A	1877-8 r	Howard	P	1877-8	Myburg	Z	1877-8
Dennis	J	1877-8	Hunt	P	1877-8 r	O'Brien	J	1877-8 r
Desselboom	M	1877-8 r	Hunter	G	1877-8	Oliver	H	1877-8
Dobey	G	1877-8 r	Huyer	A	1877-8 r	Palata	D	1877-8 r

Queenstown Volunteer Contingent

Parsons	A	1877-8	Sweet	J	1877-8 r	LIEUTENANT		
Parsons	T	1877-8	Thomas	?	1877-8	Impey	R.H	1877-8 r
Patmore	G	1877-8	Thompson	L	1877-8 r	Smith	W.T	1879
Payne	T	1877-8 r	Thompson W Rowland		1877-8 r	SERGEANT		
Pedlar	H.C	1877-8 r	Tinman	R	1877-8	Backhouse	P	1877-8
Pedlar	H.W	1877-8	Townsend	J	1877-8	Bell	J.W	1877-8
Piater	A	1877-8 r	Turvey	M	1877-8 r	Bushell	J	1877-8
Pienaar	?	1877-8 r	Tyre	?	1877-8 r	Cronin	C.E	1877-8-9
Platt	W	1877-8 r	Underwood	H	1877-8	Fisher	R.M	1879
Powell	T.M	1877-8 r	Upton	L	1877-8	Newman	A	1877-8
Pringle	J	1877-8	Usher	G	1877-8 r	Palmer	C.T	1877-8-9
Pringle	J.R	1877-8	Van Gaas	H	1877-8	CORPORAL		
Prinsloo	H	1877-8 r	Van Gaas	N	1877-8	Bestall	C.E	1877-8-9
Purvis	T	1877-8	Van Heerden	P	1877-8 r	Mallett	C.N	1879
Quin	F	1877-8 r	Van Hurden	W	1877-8 r	Sole	A.W	1879
Ramsay	W	1877-8-9 r	Van Royen	C	1877-8 r	Wilson	A.D	1879
Rich	R	1877-8 r	Van Staaden	A	1877-8 r	PRIVATE		
Rickliffe	F	1877-8 r	Van Staaden	C	1877-8 r	Anderson	K	1879
Rickliffe	J	1877-8 r	Van Staaden	P.J	1877-8	Arnott	E	1879
Robinson	W	1877-8	Van Wyk	J	1877-8 r	Baker	G	1879
Roderick	F	1877-8	Venter	A	1877-8 r	Bands	J	1879
Rogers	J	1877-8	Venter	J	1877-8 r	Barfield	S.C	1879
Rogers	J.F	1877-8 r	Venter	L	1877-8 r	Barnes	C	1877-8
Ross	A	1877-8	Venter	S	1877-8 r	Bate	A.W	1877-8
Ross	H	1877-8	Wakeford	W	1877-8	Barton	A.S	1877-8
Ross	J.W	1877-8	Wardell	J	1877-8	Beadfield	T	1877-8-9
Rynders	P	1877-8 r	Wasserfal	J	1877-8 r	Bell	W	1877-8
Saunders	W	1877-8 r	Weatherhead	G.J	1877-8 r	Bennett	T.W	1877-8
Sawerthal	N	1877-8 r	Webb	H	1877-8	Bickerton	W.F	1879 r
Schneidel	H	1877-8	Webster	W.G	1877-8 r	# Birdekin	J.E	1879
Schroeder	H	1877-8 r	Wells	H	1877-8	Brown	C.B	1877-8
Schultz	?	1877-8	Whall	G	1877-8	Clift	W.H	1879
Schutte	G	1877-8 r	Wherry	J	1877-8 r	Dale	B	1879
Shaw	W	1877-8 r	Whitehead	V	1877-8 r	Dell	A	1878-8-9
Shepperson	F	1877-8	Whitson	H	1877-8	Denison	?	1877-8
Smith	A	1877	Whitten	F	1877-8	Dugmore	I	1879
Smith	C	1877-8 r	Wiegardt	A	1877-8	Edkins	D.R	1879
Smith	G	1877-8 r	Wiggill	I	1877-8	Edkins	H	1879
Smith	R	1877-8	Williams	J	1877-8 r	Eedes	C	1877-8-9
Snoeke	W	1877-8	Wille	B	1877-8	Eedes	W.H	1877-8
Snyman	W	1877-8	Wilson	A.A	1877-8	Fisher	F	1877-8
Spalding	R	1877-8 r	Wilson	E	1877-8 ?	Fuller	R	1877-8
Spoolander	F	1877-8	Wink	T	1877-8 r	Gilmour	J	1879 r
Steffin	W	1877-8				Goddard	E	1879
Steele	H	1877-8 r	**QUEENSTOWN VOLUNTEER RIFLE**			Green	S	1879
Stone	C	1877-8 r	**CORPS.**			Henderson	G	1877-8
Stone	R	1877-8 r	CAPTAIN			Henry	C.L	1879
Strutt	R	1877-8 r	Davis	C	1877-8	Henry	J.H	1879 r
See also 1st Cape Mounted Yeo.			Dugmore	H.H	1879	Hicks	W	1879
Sutherland	E	1877-8	Jones	F.H	1877-8	Hine	J.B	1879
Sutherland	J.W	1877-8 r	Webb	A.D	1877-8-9	Holgate	C.H	1877-8
Sutton	A	1877-8	SURGEON			Impey	R.H	1877-8-9
Swartz	B	1877-8	Rhind	J	1877-8	Jones	T	1879
Swartz	G	1877-8	See also Tawbookieland Division.			Key	W	1877-8
Swartz	J	1877-8				Klette	J	1877-8-9

Dix Noonan Web Auction Lot 264, 19 Mar 08
South Africa 1877-79, 1 clasp, 1879 (Pte. E. Birdekin, Queenstown Volr. R. Corps) clasp pierced above the number '7', some edge bruising and contact marks, nearly very fine Hammer price £260.   33 '1879' clasps awarded to the Queenstown Volunteer Rifle Corps.

Queenstown Volunteer Rifle Corps

Long	F	1877-8-9
Longden	A.J	1877-8-9
Marshall	T	1877-8 r
Marshall	W	No clasp
Maythan	R	1877-8-9
Midgley	R	1877-8-9
Mushlenback	F.A	1877-8-9
Moore	F.W.G	1877-8-9
Quin	F	1877-8-9
Replacement Issued.		8/5/1922
Rhind	A.L	1877-8
Roberts	H.B	1877-8
Ryan	J	187708
Sawerthal	H	1877-8
Scott	W.B	1877-8
Stone	C	1877-8-9 r
Strike	J.R	1877-8-9
Stirton Jnr	G	1877-8
Taylor	G.J	1877-8
Tiffin	H	1877-8
Trennery	J	1877-8
Trennery	T	1877-8
Townsend	J.W	1877-8
Trollip	G	1877-8-9
Wakeford	O	1877-8
Wakeford	W.J	1877-8-9
Weatherhed	G	1877-8- r
Whitnall	R.W	1879
Wilhelm	G.F	1879
Wilson	J.V	1877-8
Windell	J.C	1879
Wiper	R.A	1877-8-9
Wright	R.M	1879

RICHMOND MOUNTED VOLUNTEERS.
CORPORAL
Hurter	G	1878-

PRIVATE
Atkinson	W.S	1878
Netz	C	1878 r

RIVERSDALE MOUNTED BURGERS.
COMMANDANT
Meurant	L.H	1878

QUARTERMASTER
Newman	C	1878

LIEUTENANT ADJUTANT
Lombaard	W	1878

SERGEANT
La Grange I/Son	M	1878
Lawrence	A	1878
Theunissen	T	1878

CORPORAL
Breslaar	C	1878
Helm	M	1878
La Grange	M	1878
Luyt	D	1878
Theunissen	P	1878

TROOPER
Becker	G	1878
Berg	F	1878
Bredenhaan	G	1878
Bredenhaan	J	1878
Brown	H	1878
Coldrey	F	1878
Cordier	A	1878
Fontaine	E	1878
Golding	G	1878
Hill	J	1878
Keown	J	1878
Kriek	C	1878
Lane	J	1878
Leonard	J	1878
# Lotz	W	1878
Luyt	H	1878
Marais	H	1878
Marcus	H.C	1878-8
Meyer	G	1878
Muller	W	1878
Nothangel	A	1878
Pace	H	1878
Petersen	C	1878
Petersen	G	1878
Purchase	G	1878
Rensburg	A	1878
Rensburg	J	1878
Rice	R	1878
Rothman	L	1878
Saayman D/Son	D	1878
Saayman W/Son	D	1878
Smalberger	H	1878
Smith	W	1878
Tessenaar	H	1878
Van Eeden	G	1878
Van Tonder	P	1878
Van Zyl	P	1878
Vivier	H	1878
Vollenhoven	J	1878
Windt	D	1878
Wolfaardt	G	1877-8
Wolfaart	S	1878

RANK NOT KNOWN
Casseldon	C.S	1878-9

ROYAL DUBRAN RIFLES.
This unit did not cross the Border (Tugela River. The medal had no clasp.

CAPTAIN
Flack	P.S

SURGEON
Schulz	J (M.D)

LIEUTENANT
Nolan	D.J

SERGEANT MAJOR
Goodall	W

QUARTERMASTER SERGEANT
Wheeler	T.D

COLOUR SERGEANT
Archibald	J
King	J.F

ORDERLY SERGEANT
Seymour	V

SERGEANT
Johnson	J.E
Orchard	G
Taylor	A
Tomlinson	A
Rapson	J
Wright	T

CORPORAL
Bates	J
Boast	E
Brewer	H.M
More	F r
Royston	J
Williams	A
Woodroofe	W.S

PIONEER
Elstroom	C
Hodgson	R

BUGLER
Jelly	F
Replacement Issued on 16/6/1917	
Menderson	E
Robinson	T
Williams	T

PRIVATE
Auld	J
Baynes	R
Bird	W
Boast	A
Capel	S
Clark	W
Cullingworth	A.W
Cullis	J
Dalton	T

City Coins Postal Auction No 58 29th August 2008, Lot No 70 South Africa Medal 1879 (SAGS) bar 1878 Tpr. W. Lotz, Riversdale Md. Bgrs. VF+ Hammer price 5500 Rand £366 approx.

From an article in the Natal newspapers dated 27th January 1879, Royal Durban Rifles are now encamped on the flat near the Zingari cricket ground, article includes a list of members at camp, missing from above medal roll.
Corporal J Rapson, Bugler E Manderson, Privates A Johnson, H N Bremer (Corporal H.M Brewer on medal roll) Darcy, W.H Harris, Hanch, Misplon, T Rapson, E Hooker, Gifford, J Smith, R Hutchinson, J Makar, Rose, J L Robertson.

Royal Durban Rifles

D'Arcy	H		Shuter	A		Birkholtz	A	1877-8
Emmett	J r		Slatter	J		Birkholtz	Franz	1877-8
Forrest	A		Smith	H		Birkholz Frederick	1877-8 r
Forrest	J		Smith	A		Birkholtz	W	1877-8
Garner	W		Spring	H		Blackbeard H	1877-8
Gordon	E.C		Stonell	A		Blackbeard F	1877-8 r
Hallowell	T		Taylor	J.P		See also Fort White Mtd. Vol.
Hansch	P r		Taylor	W.T		Blaine	J	1877-8 r
Harris	E r		Tomlinson	W		Brolin	J	1877-8
Harris	W.M		Tyass	W		Brown	T	1877-8
Harvey	J		Watkins	W		Brown	T	1877-8
Heffner	C		Wheeler	J.N		Cavanagh	W	1877-8
Heffner	J r		Wilkinson	L		Coles	J	1877-8 r
Herbert	F		Williams	F		Connoch	J	1877-8
Hewitt	E		Williams	H		Cooper	C	1877-8
Hewitt	T		Willis	C		Cooper	W	1877-8
Horner	J		Wright	J		Daniels	S	1877-8 r
Horner	R					See also Kaffrarian Rangers.
Horner	W		**RUSTENBURG NATIVE CONTINGENT.**		Deklerk	J	1877-8 r
James	E.C		**CAPTAIN**			Devitt	J	1877-8 r
Jefford	E.D		Beeton	W.M		Dick	Q	1877-8
Johnson	G		Wounded at Sekukuni's Kraal 28/11/1879		Edwards	W	1877-8
Johnson	H		Ommanney	E.M		Egelhoff	C	1877-8
Johnson	W.B		**LIEUTENANT & ADJUTANT**		Elliott	D	1877-8 r
Keal	F.G		Dunn	J.F	1879	Fischer	C	1877-8
Leshnick	J		**LIEUTENANT**			Fitzgerald	J	1877-8
Mack	W		Beeton	T.J	1879	Healingfeldt H	1877-8
Maxted			Pistorius	W.E	1879	Hearns	W	1877-8 r
Mc Donald	C r		Powell	D.M.T	1879	Henry	J	1877-8 r
Michel	A					Hess	J	1877-8
Miller	H		**SAMSON HORSE.**			Holdstock	L	1877-8
Misplon	H		**CAPTAIN**			Jacoby	F.W	1877-8
Murphy	W		Mandey	J	1877-8	Kay	E	1877-8
Northern	E		**LIEUTENANT**			Kidson	J	1877-8
Orchard	W		Farquhar	J	1877-8	Kirk	J	1877-8
Pay	W		Harty	J		Kringle	A	1877-8
Payn	A		**SERGEANT**			Kromhout	H	1877-8
Payn	J		Gibson	T	1877-8	Laing	J	1877-8
Pemberton	A		**CORPORAL**			Lehman	S	1877-8
Percival	H		Cooper	T	1877-8 r	Linch	J	1877-8 r
Phillips	W.J		See also Trooper T.D Cooper		Lloyd	H	1877-8 r
Prince	A		Chalunna Volunteer Cavalry.		Logan	T	1877-8 r
Purvis	F.D		Kilfoil	J	1877-8	Macgregor	G	1877-8 r
Raleigh	A		**PRIVATE**			Macmillan	D	1877-8
Rapson	G		Abernethy	H.P	1877-8	Marals	H	1878
Rapson	S		Ashenhurst	J.J	1877-8	Mulligan	L	1877-8
Salmon	G		Batchelor	R	1877-8	Mullins	T	1877-8
Sandall	F r		Beling	W	1877-8	Oostherysen D	1877-8

Dix Noonan Web Auction Lot 398, 5 Apr 06
South Africa 1877-79, 1 clasp, 1877-8 (Pte. **C. Welch**, Sansom's Horse) nearly extremely fine Hammer Price: £420
Footnote Medals named to this unit are very seldom seen, a matter of fact raised by Dr. Frank Mitchell in his article "Sansom's Horse", published in the South African Military History Journal, December 1973. The same source describes a close encounter with the Galekas: On 9 October 1877, a force consisting mainly of Sansom's Horse was encamped at Springs, about six miles on the Transkei side of the Great Kei, south-east of the present Kei Bridge. Early that morning, while most of the men were still asleep, the camp was heavily attacked by a large force of Galekas. Captain Sansom ordered his men to stand fast, and immediately sent a despatch rider for reinforcements. Some of the young recruits were close to panic, but Sansom rallied them - he in fact threatened to shoot the first man to put his foot in a stirrup! - and coolly set about arranging the defence of the camp. The battle continued until after midday, but by the time reinforcements arrived the Galekas had withdrawn, leaving many dead behind. Sansom's Horse had two men wounded.'

Pronger	T	1877-8	Magamuzana		1879 r	Mtimkulu	M	1879
Rolston	G	1877-8	Uanhla		1879 r	Myembi	A	1879
Ryder	F	1877-8	Uasimba		1879 r	Mzondo	P	1879
Saunders	W	1877-8 r	Umgannise		1879 r	Ncobe	M	1879
Schmidt	F	1877-8	Ungolo		1879 r	N'dhleva	T	1879
Shearer	C	1877-8	Uulakusa		1879 r	Ndimande	J	1879
Stevenson	J	1877-8	SERGEANT			Ndimandi	E	1879
Stroudie	C	1877-8	Abraham		1879 r	Ndimandi	M	1879
Symons	A	1877-8	Bob		1879 r	Neinde	D	1879
Symons	S	1877-8	Lutuli		1879 r	Ngomezulu	S	1879
Tarr	M	1877-8 r	Manhla		1879 r	Nkwanantzi	L	1879
Towshend	H	1877-8	Masimba		1879 r	Oumyisa		1879
Vaines	T	1877-8	Mutakusa		1879 r	Saliwa		1879
Vickery	A	1877-8	TROOPER			Sine	J	1879
# Welch	C (page 157) 1877-8		Bantman	A	1879	Tember	S	1879 r
Wellbeloved W		1877-8	Duba	M	1879 r	**Tegingela**	**E KIA**	**1879**
Whittal	J	1877-8	Gale	A	1879	Twala	E	1879
Wright	A	1877-8 r	Gama	J	1879	Unbuyazwe		1879
Young	S	1877-8	Gube	P	1879	Unvele		1879 r
			Gula	J	1879	Vilakazi	L	1879
SCHERMBUCKER HORSE.			Gula	P	1879	Vimbi	J	1879
COMMANDANT			Haba	A	1879	Xaba	A	1879
Schermbucker F		1877-8-9	Habbakuk		1879	Zulu	Jacoh	1879
QUARTERMASTER SERGEANT			Hlati	T	1879	Zulu	John	1879
Foster	J	1877-8	Hlaytwako	M	1879	See also Natal Native Horse.		
CORPORAL			Hlaytwako	S	1879	Zuma	R	1879
Staude	W	1878 r	Incobo	M	1879 r			
			Innyisa		1879 r	**SIDBURY MOUNTED RANGERS.**		
SHEPSTONE NATIVE HORSE			Kambula	M	1879	CAPTAIN		
Reformed as Shepstone's Horse in early			Kambula	S	1879	Gush	J	1877
May 1879, and joined the II Division for the			See also Natal Native Horse.			LIEUTENANT		
second invasion. Also 31 Edendale men			Kaula	L	1879	Howarth	W	1878 r
from Carbutt's Border Rangers transferred			Kingedwana		1879	2nd LIEUTENANT		
in April.1879.All who were killed in action			Knmalo	S	1879	Thomas	W	1878-8 r
(KIA) lost their lives at Ulundi 4/7/1879.			Kontzedwana		1879	SERGEANT MAJOR		
CAPTAIN.			Korda	L	1879	Gush	R	1877 r
Green Thompson J.H		1879	Kulu	J.I	1879	SERGEANT		
LIEUTENANT			Kumalo	H	1879	Thomas	G	1877-8
Fairlie	W.F	1879	Kumalo	L	1879	Wilmot	E.E	1877
Henderson	A.F	1879	Kumalo	P	1879	CORPORAL		
See also Natal Native Horse.			Kumalo Thomas		1879	Short	I	1877
Wyatt	V	1879 r	Kumalo Thimothy		1879	BUGLER		
2nd LIEUTENANT			Kunene	L	1879	Bruce	A.F	1877-8 r
Buys	?	1879	Kunene	M	1879	TROOPER		
NATIVE OFFICER AND CHIEF			Kunene	N	1879	Austin	W.F	1878 r
Myandd		1879	Kunene	U	1879	Cawood	S	1877
Snyanda		1879	Livi	J	1879	Clack	Walter	1877-8
Yamela		1879	Lokotwayo	J	1879	Clack	William	1877-8
NATIVE OFFICER			Lokotwayo	S	1879	Daniell	A	1878 r
Iorroson		1879	**Lopela**	**J KIA**	**1879**	Emsile	J	1878
SERGEANT MAJOR			Mahootsha		1879 r	Emsile	R	1877-8
Jabey M'Lifa		1879	Maliga	S	1879	Gush	G.R	1877-8
INTERPRETER OFFICER			Malinga	M	1879 r	Hannay	J.H	1877-8-9
Jantje		1879 r	Mavinbela	S	1879	Howarth	H.W	1877-8
SERGEANT AND PETTY CHIEF			Mbele	J	1879	Lake	S.M	1877-8
Bangulana		1879	Meimango E		1879	McDermott	J	1877-8 r
Kongane		1879 r	**Mgadi**	**J KIA**	**1879**	Midgeley	P	1877-8
Lacisa		1879	Mini	P	1879	Nosworhty	C	1877 r
Lintuli		1879 r	Mini	S	1879	Nostworthy	H	1877 r

Commandant Schermbrucker

The engraving depicts an incident of the Zulu War, which occurred on Sunday, May 18th. A report having reached the camp that about a hundred Zulus has occupied a kraal on the side of the Pongolo River near Luneberg, where they were said to be harvesting crops, it was decided that **Commandant Schermbrucker** should make a reconnaissance, accompanied by **Captain Moore**, 4th King's Own Regiment, and an orderly, **Trooper L. Laasen** (Schermbrucker's horse). After a while the reconnoitring party found themselves hemmed in by Zulus, who numbers rapidly increased, and who opened fire upon them. Presently the Commandant's horse was shot dead, whereupon he took Laasen's horse, and bade the trooper mount behind him. But the horse refused the double load, and presently it was decided that Laasen should seek safety on foot. The poor fellow, however, never returned to camp. The Zulus were soon after this within 150 yards, and the bullets were flying like hailstones. Moore's horse was shot down. Now came the critical moment shown in our picture. Moore quickly rose, and directed a well-aimed shot at the foremost of his pursuers. It took effect, and the Zulus were momentarily checked. Schermbrucker utilised that moment by urging Moore to mount behind him. They had scarcely adjusted themselves to the double riding when the Zulus renewed their fire. There, was however, an open path before them, the horse proved equal to the occasion, and soon after noon they were safe at Luneberg. In the evening of the same day the Commandant, with an escort, proceeded to search for **Laasen**, but in vain.....The above engravings are from sketches by **Dr, Doyle Glanville**, attached to General Wood's column.
Source: The Graphic (London, England), Saturday, July 12, 1879; Issue 502

BASUTO POLICE

BASUTOLAND is a little territory adjoining the Free State on the north of the Orange River, and at the beginning of last year, previous to the Boer rising, was the scene of a serious rebellion, which, however, was ultimately put down, in a great measure through the energy of Colonel Carrington. The district was proclaimed British territory in 1868, and since that time considerable efforts had been made, and with much success, to civilise the natives, who after a while began to place confidence in the British Government, of which the headquarters were at the magistrate's station, Maseru. This confidence also was increased by the employment of some of the sons of Moshesh, the former chief paramount, and by the formation of a native police force, the members of which, under the command of Colonel Schermbrucker, are shown in our illustration, engraved from a photograph by Mr. F. Armstrong, Bloemfontein, Orange Free State. All went well, the Basutos led a peaceful and industrious life, showing complete loyalty and good faith to the British, until 1878, when the Cape Parliament passed the Native Disarmament Act, to which the Basutos, a warlike race, refused obedience, and, as we have said, broke out into open rebellion under a son of Moshesh, Masupha, and another chief, Lerothodi. Now that peace is once more restored we trust that the "powers that be" in South Africa will refrain from unnecessarily irritating a brave and loyal people who have shown themselves perfectly amenable to judicious government.

Sidbury Mounted Rangers

Rippon	J.C	1878
Rippon	S	1878
Rippon	W.J	1877-8
Short	E	1878 r
Short	W	1878 r
Thomas	J	1877-8
Wedderburn	A	1877
Wilmot	J.C	1878 r
Wilmot	J.E	1877-8

SIMONSTOWN NATIVE CONTINGENT.
RANK NOT KNOWN
de Stadler G.F   1878

SKERSBERG NATIVE CONTINGENT.
LIEUTENANT
Scholefield H   1879

SNYMAN'S BURGHERS
CAPTAIN
Snyman W.D   1878
SERGEANT
Snyman M   1878
FARRIER SERGEANT
Smoeg H   1878 r
CORPORAL
Becker   1878
PRIVATE

Crous	D	1878
Crous	J	1878
Crous	P	1878
De Clerk	H	1878 r
Els	C	1878
Els	F	1878 r
Els	H	1878 r
Els	H	1878 r
Els	J	1878 r
Els	W	1878 r
Engelbrecht	J	1878 r
Hend	N	1878
Keyton	G	1878 r
Koester	A	1878 r
McDaniels Snr	J	1878 r
McDaniels Jnr	J	1878 r
Nel	J	1878
Nel	S	1878 r
Rautenbach	A	1878
Snyman	G	1878 r
Snyman	Jnr G	1878 r
Snyman	Jnr G	1878
Snyman	Snr G	1878 r
Snyman	J	1878
Snyman	Jnr M	1878

See also Transvaal Rangers.
Snyman   M   1878 r
See also Transvaal Rangers.
Snyman   T   1878
Snyman   W   1878
Vilpen   W   1878 r

SOMERSET EAST BURGHERS.
PRIVATE
Byleveld H   1879 r

SOMERSET EAST CONTINGENT.
PRIVATE
Erasmus P   1878
Webster G   1878
DOCTOR
Moolman (MD) H.J   1878 r
QUARTERMASTER
Hannen F.J.H   1878
LIEUTENANT
Else N   1878
Hurter W   1878 r
Jordan G   1878 r
QUATERMASTER SERGEANT
Smith S.C   1878 r
SERGEANT
De Kerk T   1878 r
Van Roeyen W   1878
Webster Jnr J   1878
TROOPER

Bester	T	1878 r
Bolleurs	J	1878 r
Boots	F	1878 r
Bosch	C	1878 r
Bosch	J	1878
Bosch Jnr	M	1878 r
Bosch Snr	M	1878 r
Botha	B	1878
Botha	C	1878 r
Botha	J	1878 r
Botha	P	1878
Botha	P.F	1878
Bouwer	P.F.B	1878 r
Bouwer	W	1878 r
Callaghan	P	1878
Carver	W.H	1878 r
De Lange	C	1878 r
Denny	E	1878 r
De Villiers	A	1878 r
Du Plessis	D	1878 r
Du Randt	A	1878 r
Eales	W	1878 r
Else	J	1878 r
Erasmus	H	1878 r
Erasmus	J	1878
Erasmus	W	1878 r
Fischer	F	1878
Flemner	S	1878 r
Goosen	D	1878 r
Greyling	C	1878
Grobbeelaar	G	1878 r
Grobbeelaar	H	1878 r
Hattingh	H	1878 r
Hayward	A	1878
Jordan	P	1878 r
Jordan	W	1878
Kemp	E	1878
Kemp	P.G	1878 r
Kretzinger	J	1878 r
Kruger	P	1878 r
Landman	J.A	1878
Le Roux	J	1878
Letter	C	1878 r
Marens	P	1878 r
Mare Snr	D	1878 r
Mare	P	1878
Mc Callum	A	1878 r
Mc Kenzie	J	1878 r
Mills	W	1878 r
Moolman	H.J	1878
Muller	A	1878
Nel	A	1878 r
Nel	T	1878 r
Niekerk	A	1878 r
Pedlar	W	1878
Pexter	C	1878 r
Robson	W	1878
Roux	T	1878 r
Ryneveldt	H	1878 r
Smith	D	1878 r
Stroebels	J	1878
Strydom	J	1878 r
Triegardt	L	1878 r
Van Rensburg	A	1878 r
Voslo	F	1878 r
Wade	A	1878 r
Welkens	P	1878 r

SOMERSET EAST VOLUNTEER CONTINGENT.
COMMANDANT
Comley W.C   1878-8
CAPTAIN
Bosch W   1878 r
Leppan T.S   1878 r
Trollip A.T   1877-8 r
ADJUTANT
Nesbitt J.W   1877-8
LIEUTENANT
Bolleurs N   1877-8 r
Comley J.L   1877-8 r
Kyd R   1877-8
Rademeyer H.N   1877-8
Trollip E.W   1877-8 r
SERGEANT
Hayward A   1877-8 r
Hubbard A   1877-8
Jackson J.W   1877-8
Rensburg M   1877-8
CORPORAL
Aggett G   1877-8 r
Arendt O   1877-8
Berry W.J   1877-8-9
Booysen P   1877-8 r

Somerset East Vol. Contingent

Cotton	L.E	1877-8 r	Greyling	J	1877-8 r	Van der Vyver	J	1877-8 r
Eaglestone	W	1877-8 r	Hanley	R	1877-8 r	Van der Vyver	O	1877-8
Hall	G	1877-8	Harvey	G	1877-8	Van der Watt	C	1877-8
Nikoli (Native)	D	1877-8	Hefke (Native)	J	1877-8	Van der Watt	H	1877-8
Nel	P	1877-8	Henning	A	1877-8	Van Duyk	J	1877-8 r
Simon (Native)	M	1877-8 r	Henry	E	1877-8	Van Heerden	I	1877-8
Wilson	G	1877-8	Hollamby	C	1877-8 r	Van Rooyen	G	1877-8 r

TROOPER

			Horne	H	1877-8	Williams (Native)	W	1877-8 r
Allright	R	1877-8	Howard	A	1877-8 r	Wolmerans	I	1877-8 r
Ashman	F	1877-8 r	Huggins	R	1877-8 r	Wragg	G	1877-8 r
Bartman (Native)	F	1877-8 r	Jacobs (Native)	C	1877-8 r	Zwartbooi (Native)	K	1877-8 r
Bartman (Native)	H	1877-8 r	Jaftha (Native)	A	1877-8 r			
Bayn	I	1877-8	Jansen (Native)	H	1877-8 r	**SOUTHEYS RANGERS**		
Bayn	Jacobus	1877-8 r	Jones	J	1877-8	Most medals are without a clasp, see below:		
Bayn	Joseph	1877-8	Kemp	J	1877-8			
Bayn	N	1877-8 r	Laigh	J	1877-8 r	COMMANDANT		
Berry	I	1877-8 r	Leary	D	1877-8	Mc Taggart	H.E	1877-8
Bester	P	1877-8	Liverskine (Native)	C	1877-8 r	See also Pulleins Rangers.		
Bolleurs	J	1877-8 r	Lombard	C	1877-8	LIEUTENANT		
Booysen	D	1877-8 r	Lombard	S	1877-8 r	Cox	F	1877 r
Booysen	H	1877-8 r	Lotter	M	1877-8 r	Crause	P	-
Bosch	Baltazar	1877-8 r	Lottering Snr	B	1877-8 r	Miller	H	-
Bosch	B	1877-8	Lottering	B	1877-8 r	QUARTERMASTER SERGEANT		
Bosch	H	1877-8 r	Magida (Native)	W	1877-8 r	Gower	P	-
Bowden	W	1877-8	Malusie (Native)	P	1877-8 r	SERGEANT		
Bouwer	I	1877-8	Manarie (Native)	O	1877-8 r	Becker	P	- r
Bretten	J	1877-8	Mare	D	1877-8	Grant	D	- r
Bretten	R	1877-8 r	Mazwe (Native)	C	1877-8	Horsberg	R	-
Butler	J	1877-8 r	Mazwe (Native)	J	1877-8 r	Stewart	J	1877-8 r
Butz	A	1877-8 r	Mazwe (Native)	P	1877-8 r	CORPORAL		
Campbell	A	1877-8	Mc Kenzie (Native)	C.J	1877-8 r	Birmingham	G	1878 r
Campbell	J	1877-8 r	Meyer	H	1877-8 r	Mc Evoy	R	1877-8 r
Carver	T	1877-8	Meyer	J	1877-8	Norgenrood	F	-
Coetzee	D	1877-8	Mills	J	1877-8	Newberry	J	1877-8 r
Coetzee	F	1877-8	Moolwan	P	1877-8 r	Schroeder	J	-
Coetzee	H	1877-8	Nel	F	1877-8	Sharply	D	1877-8
Davis	J	1877-8 r	Nel	J	1877-8	Vickers	J	1877-8 r
De Beer	C	1877-8	Nel	W	1877-8 r	PRIVATE		
De Klerk	A	1877- r	Nel	W	1877-8 r	Abramse	C	-
De Klerk	J	1877-8	Petzer	G	1877-8	Amen	S	- r
De Klerk	W	1877-8 r	Plaatjies (Native)	M	1877-8 r	Bannytyne	E	- r
De Villiers	P	1877-8 r	Poke	G	1877-8 r	Barbier	G	- r
De Zeech	A	1877-8 r	Prince (Native)	S	1877-8 r	Bartweck	C	-
Durandt	P	1877-8 r	Prichard	R	1877-8 r	Bartweck	E	-
Eales	C	1877-8	Rademeyr	H	1877-8 r	Booth	J	- r
Erasmus	D	1877-8 r	Ross	W	1877-8 r	Bowden	D	- r
Erasmus	J	1877-8	Ruyter (Native)	S	1877-8 r	Brownlee	A	- r
Erasmus	L	1877-8 r	Ruyter (Native)	W	1877-8 r	Clements	A	- r
Ferreira	I	1877-8 r	Scheepers	F	1877-8 r	Colbert	J	- r
Ferreira	J	1877-8	Scheepers	L	1877-8	Cosgrove	J	- r
Fisher	P	1877-8 r	Schoeman	W	1877-8 r	Dante	J	-
Fortuin (Native)	P	1877-8 r	Smith	P	1877-8 r	Dawson	J	- r
Fourie	H	1877-8 r	Stander (Native)	S	1877-8 r	Dreyer	C	-
Frans	S.H	1877-8	Strijdon	D	1877-8 r	Fairbank	W	- r
Freith	G	1877-8 r	Strijdon	J	1877-8 r	Fitzsimmons	J	- r
Geyer	C	1877-8	Taylor	J	1877-8	Francis	J	-
Greef	C	1877-8 r	Triegardt (Native)	C	1877-8 r	Francis	L	-
Greef	W	1877-8 r	Van der Berg	J	1877-8 r	Geyer	R	- r
Greenlees	W	1877-8	Van der Berg	P	1877-8 r	Gibbons	J	- r

Southeys Rangers

Gobert	J	-	r	Villette	C	1877-8 r	*Fayle	Not on medal roll
Hayden	C	1877-8		Ward	J	1877-8	Freeman	1879
Hitchcock	G	-		Wells	E	-	*Gielink A.B	1879
Hodgson	F	-		White	A	1877-8 r	*Gielink C	No clasp
Howard	J	1877-8 r		Wilson	H	- r	*Gielink G (J.W)	1879
Hueswill	G	-		Wilson	J	- r	*Gielink Johan	Not on medal roll
Hughes	G	-	r	Woods	J	- r	Glenn	1879
Jacobson	E	-	r	Worthington	R	- r	*Green	1879
Joliff	W	1877-8 r		**RANK NOT KNOWN**			*Hoogvorst A	1879
Jones	W	1877-8 r		Nelson	J	1878	*Hoogvorst J (C)	1879
Kingsford	F	-	r				Hoogvorst P	1879
Laeson	H	-	r	**STANGER MOUNTED RIFLES.**			*Howard P	1879
Leek	C	-	r	Founded in 1875 Captain Arbuthnot			Howe	1879
Levey	R	-	r	commanded the unit in Pearson's column.			*Jacobs	1879
Lowe	A	-	r	Strength two troops of 20 each.			*Jackson A.E	1879
Mahomet	J	-	r	**CAPTAIN**			Jacoh	1879
Mahoney	P	1877-8 r		*Addison F		1879	John	1879
Maker	J	1877-8 r		**SURGEON**			*Louw J (Jacob)	1879
Manning	M	-	r	Jones		1879	*Louw J	1879
Mc Kay	R	-		**QUATERMASTER**			Lyle	1879
Meakins	J	1877-8 r		*Knox		1879	*Mc Clintock	1879
Miller	H	-	r	**LIEUTENANT**			Moore	1879
Miller	H	1877-8 r		*Shuter		1879	Neish	1879
Northcote	H	-		*Warren		1879	Phring	1879
O' Conner	P	-	r	**SERGEANT MAJOR**			*Robbins W (Jas)	1879
Peters	H	-	r	*Moore		1879	*Robbins W.C	Not on medal roll
Petersen	A	-1877-8 r		**SADDLER SERGEANT**			*Rogers	Not on medal roll
Pierre	C	-1877-8 r		Rogers		1879	*Toohey	1879
Pitts	W		r	**SERGEANT**			*Warren C	1879
Powell	C	-	r	Brunner		1879	*Warren W	1879
Quiller	H	-		Dinglax		1879	*On 1st December 1878 the following	
Quoine	R	1877-8		*Fayle		1879	members of the corps were mobilized.	
Reardon	J	-	r	**CORPORAL**				
Richardson	B	1877-8 r		*Bumner	Not on medal roll		**STEVENSON'S HORSE.**	
Rodeck	J	-	r	*Davidson		1879	**CAPTAIN COMMANDING**	
Roscoe	J	-	r	Gielink	J	1879	Stevenson J.W	1877-8
Schultz	P	-	r	Robbins		1879	**LIEUTENANT**	
Scott	H	-	r	**TRUMPETER**			Blake W.N	1877-8 r
Scroder	H	-	r	*# Colenbrander J.W		1870	Ranger A.B	1877-8 r
Shaw	N	1877-8		**TROOPER**			Ranger A.H	1877-8
Skelly	E	1877-8 r		*Addison		1879	**TROOP SERGEANT**	
Shields	J	1877-8 r		*Bannik (Bannink)		1879	Lowry J	1877-8
Smith	G	1877-8 r		*Bond		1879	**ACT QUARTER MASTER**	
Smith	J	1877-8 r		*Boyce J		1879	Steiner J	1877-8 r
Smith	W	-		*Boyce L		1879	**SERGEANT**	
Stecley	C	1877-8		*Brown H.M		1879	Gormley F	1877-8
Sullivan	W	1877-8 r		Buckley		1879	Had a medal from an earlier campaign.	
Sylvester	A	-	r	*Burne		1879	No details given.	
Taylor	James	1877-8 r		Burms		1879	Luyt J	1877-8 r
Taylor	Joseph	1877-8 r		Champneys		1879	See also Cpl. J. Luyt, Kaffrarian Rangers.	
Thompson	H	1877-8 r		#Colenbrander		1879	**CORPORAL**	
Tucker	G	1877-8 r		Dickens		1879	Chandlier J	1877-8 r
Van der Plash	J	-	r	Dickson		1879	Leeding W	1877-8 r
Vernon	H	-	r	Dore		1879	Naude C	1877-8 r

Johan Wilhelm Colenbrander born 1856, Pinetown Natal, of Dutch parents who emigrated from Java to Natal in 1854. Their indigo venture failed and the family founded the settlement of New Guelderland near Stanger. Johan married Mollie Mullins in 1883, and after her death, Yvonne Nunn in 1902. His third wife was Catherine Gloster. He founded Kitchener's Fighting Scouts during the Anglo-Boer War. He died in 1918 while crossing the Klip River, near Johannesburg, during the making of the film, The Symbol of Sacrifice.

Stevenson's Horse

Schneider A	1877-8	
TROOPER		
Bergmann T	1877-8 r	
Berndt A	1877-8 r	
Bezuidenhout C	1877-8 r	
Bezuidenhout F	1877-8 r	
Bezuidenhout H	1877-8 r	
Bezuidenhout P	1877-8 r	
Chandlier A	1877-8	
Chandlier C	1877-8	
Churchill A	1877-8	
Clarke J	1877-8	
Delport P.J	1877-8 r	
Dennis F	1877-8 r	
Els J	1877-8 r	
Enevich H	1877-8	
Ferreira P	1877-8-9 r	
Ferreira T.S	1877-8-9 r	
Flowers P	1877-8-9	
Fick G	1877-8-9	
Fick F	1877-8-9	
Goetsch H	1877-8-9	
Goetsch J	1877-8-9	
Goetsch W	1877-8-9	
Grobler J	1877-8-9 r	
Hardle J	1877-8-9 r	
Howard W	1877-8-9 r	
Illgen W	1877-8	
Kleck J	1877-8-9	
Kleck W	1877-8-9	
Kondile J	1877-8-9	
Krull C	1877-8-9 r	
Lentz D	1877-8-9	
Lewis R	1877-8-9 r	
Lindamann F	1877-8-9	
Loeffer C	1877-8-9 r	
Lowman H	1877-8-9 r	
Mackgalogan R	1877-8-9 r	
Marshall C	1877-8-9	
Maurer C	1877-8-9 r	
Noble W.J	1877-8-9 r	
Petzer J	1877-8-9	
Phillipps C	1877-8-9 r	
Ralingson C	1877-8-9 r	
Rennalls S	1877-8 r	
Rouveski F	1877-8	
Rustenberg A	1877-8	
Schneider G	1877-8	
Schneider W	1877-8	
Sents M.G	1877-8 r	
Siebert K	1877-8	
Slater W	1877-8	
Smith G.R	1877-8-9 r	
Spann A	1877-8 r	
Stratham J	1877-8 r	
Tutani W	1877-8	
Vanderwesthuizen C.J	1877-8 r	
Vanderwesthuizen C	1877-8 r	
Vanderwesthuizen N	1877-8 r	
Warneke	1877-8	

STOCKENSTROOM RANGERS.
CAPTAIN
Green J.W	1877-8-9	

LIEUTENANT
Green G	1877-8-9	
Hagelthorn C	1877-8	

SERGEANT
Baker G	1877-8 r	
Shaw J	1877-8	

CORPORAL
Maree S	1877-8	
Taylor M	1877-8	

BUGLER
Dubber J	1879 r	
O'Dell F	1877-8 r	

TROOPER
Arlow M	1877-8-9 r	
Bazuidenhoud G	1877-8 r	
Bazuidenhoud H	1877-8-9 r	
Bazuidenhoud W	1877-8-9 r	
Bernhard N	1877-8 r	
Botha H	1879 r	
Botha J	1877-8 r	
Froneman J	1879 r	
Green C	1877-8	
Green G.H	1877-8	
Herman I	1879	
Herman S	1877-8	
Herman T	1877-8	
Lincoln O	1877-8 r	
Lloyd J	1877-8	
Mann J	1877-8	
Maree D	1877-8 r	
Maree P	1877-8 r	
Mason J	1877-8	
Norman J	1877-8	
Potgieter H	1877-8-9 r	
Raubenheimer N	1877-8 r	
Shaw W	1877-8	
Stuart W	1877-8	
Van der Westhuizen J	1877-8-9 r	
Van der Westhuizen P	1877-8-9 r	
Van Wyk D	1877-8 r	
Van Wyk J	1877-8 r	
Van Wyk H	1877-8 r	
Van Wyk M	1877-8 r	
Van der Merx J	1879 r	
Victor D	1877-8-9 r	
Victor G	1877-8-9 r	
Victor J	1879 r	
Victor R	1877-8	

STOCKENSTROOM RIFLE VOLUNTEERS.
LIEUTENANT
Samuels I	1877-8-9	

SERGEANT
Hoffman D	1877-8-9	
Rooy A	1877-8-9	
Draghonder B	1877-8-9	

CORPORAL
Toots Snr P	1877-8-9	

PRIVATE
Apple P	1877-8-9 r	
Bantam A	1877-8-9	
Bantam P	1877-8-9	
Basson J	1877-8-9	
Crammer E	1877-8-9 r	
Davids Snr D	1877-8-9	
Davids Jnr D	1877-8-9	
Jordan (Jordaan N) M 1877-8-9		
KIA Moirosi's Stronghold.		
Jurie J	1877-8-9	
Pretorious (Pretorius) not on medal roll		
KIA attack on Muntyao's Cave 30/8/1879		
Rensburg K	1877-8-9	
Rooy D	1877-8-9	
Runters A	1877-8-9	
Toots G	1877-8-9	
Turner R	1877-8-9 r	

STOCKENST ROOM VOLUNTEER RIFLES.
CAPTAIN
Green G	1878-9	

LIEUTENANT
Gibb J	1878-9	

SERGEANT
Didloff N	1878-9	

CORPORAL
Stewart J	1879	

BUGLER
Odell F	1878-9	

PRIVATE
Arends J	1878	
Banse F	1878-9	
Banse P	1879	
Basson J	1879	
Berrange C.A.L	1879	
Cramer J	1878-9	
Danster J	1879	
Daveds A	1879	
Dirk W	1878-9	
Fortuin H	1879	
Flanegan J	1879	
Green C	1879	
Green G.H	1878-9	
Groepe J	1878-9	
Groepe J.W	1878 r	
Groepe P	1879	

Stockenst Room Volunteer Rifles

Groepe	S	1878 r	PRIVATE			Forth	M	1877-8
Groepe	T	1879 r	August	G	1878 r	Grunnewald	A	1877-8
Jasson	A	1879	Bandry	C	1878	Hahn	C	1877-8 r
Jonkers	H	1879 r	Birch	J.E	1878	Hansel	F	1877-8
Jurie	J	1878-9	Botcher	H	1878 r	Heuer	C	1877-8
Keane	W	1878-9	Davies	E	1877-8 r	Heuer	G	1877-8
Loots	H	1878-9	Eberhardt	A	1878 r	Heuer	J	1877-8
Loots	J	1879	Friedericks	J	1878 r	Heuer	W	1877-8 r
Loots	P	1879	Frank	W	1877-8 r	Klemp	W.F	1877-8
Nagerman	W	1878-8	Gundinck	H	1878 r	Liebman	J.A	1877-8
Noland	H	1879	Harrison	J	1877-8 r	Lupke	A	1877-8 r
Peffer	H	1879 r	Herb	G	1878 r	Lupke	F	1877-8
Peiters	J	1878-9	Horman	L	1878	Lupke	G	1877-8 r
Prince	H	1878-9	Houth	F	1878 r	Manshe	C	1877-8
Prince	J	1878-9	Jensen	A	1878 r	Muller	A	1877-8 r
Rensburg	A	1878-9	Jorden	L	1878 r	Muller	F	1877-8
Rooy	H	1878-9	Lahner	H	1878 r	Riebow	F	1877-8
Rooy	K	1878-9	Lahner	J	1878	Schemel	H	1877-8 r
Stewart	P	1879	Loscher	E	1878-8 r	Schemel	N	1877-8
Tracey	C	1879	Marcher	F	1878 r	Schwulst	C	1877-8
Tracey	W	1879	Paulson	N	1878 r	Schwulst	C	1877-8
			Rasche	C	1878 r	Schwulst	W	1877-8

STREATFIELDS FINGO LEVIES.
"Streatfeild's Fingoes," the corps retained its name through nearly a year's campaign, was composed of many levies. At one time they were over a thousand strong.

			Rensberg	L	1878 r	Steinhoffel	F	1877-8
			Rohland	E	1878 r	Steinhoffee	G	1877-8
			Russell	A	1878 r	Supra Snr	J	1877-8
			Spann	C	1878 r	Supra Jnr	J	1877-8
			Stafford	S	1878 r	Vogt	G	1877-8 r
			Thomas	N	1878 r			

COMMANDANT
Streatfield F.M 1877-8
CAPTAIN
Aggett T 1877-8
Bradshaw W.F KIA 1877-8
Hoed D 1877-8
Humphrey A 1877-8
O'Connor N 1877-8
Wienand E.D 1878
LIEUTENANT
Cumming R 1877-8
Hamonerland - 1877-8
Kettles R 1877-8
Mabandhla B 1877-8
Marillier G 1877-8
Wienand E 1877-8
PRIVATE
Hawkins J 1877-8

STUTTERHEIM FOOT POLICE.
SERGEANT
Birch D 1878
  Clasp Only
Petzer J.J 1878 r
CORPORAL
Pohlman W 1878

Volga	E	1878 r
Volger	W	1878 r
Whitstock	W	1878 r

STUTTERHEIM LIGHT INFANTRY VOLUNTEER
1ST LIEUTENANT
Belling J 1877-8
2nd LIEUTENANT
Kath F 1877-8 r
COLOUR SERGEANT
Huber A 1877-8
SERGEANT
Hahn C 1877-8
Lukpe G 1877-8 r
CORPORAL
Grunnewald O 1877-8
Kobus M 1877-8 r
PRIVATE
Brandt A 1877-8
Brandt C 1877-8
Bunge F 1877-8 r
Dominec I 1877-8
Ewers J 1877-8 r
Forth C 1877-8

STUTTERHEIM MOUNTED POLICE.
CAPTAIN
Muller C.J 1878-9
LIEUTENANT
Kropf A.E.F 1878
QUARTERMASTER SERGEANT
Kropf P.P.G 1878
Landrey J 1878
See also Captain J.L. Landrey.
Frankfort Burghers & Finges Levies.
SERGEANT
Kumm W 1878
Peters J 1878 r
Wentzler R 1878 r
CORPORAL
Evers V 1878
Ferreira P 1878
Kumm A 1878
Nicholson W 1878
Shewel A 1878-9 r
  KIA Isandhlwana
PRIVATE
Beeling C.T.E 1878-9
See also 1st Cape Mtd Yeomanry.
Belling J.E 1878

Dixons Gazette No13 Spring 1998 Corporal 0. Grunewald, Stutterheim Light Infantry Volunteers.
South Africa Medal 1877-1879, 1 clasp, 1877-8 (Corpl. Stutterheim L.I Vols:); Cape of Good Hope General Service Medal 1880-1897, 1 clasp, Basutoland (Corpl. Stutterheim I. Vol.) (2) Only 7 other ranks on Cape Roll. 40 S.A. medals issued and 13 returned. Stutterheim Light Infantry: an Eastern Province Corps of the Cape, strength three officers and 36 other ranks, raised in 1878 and served in the Basutoland Rebellion of 1880, forming part of the garrison of Maseru. NEF £360.00

See also 1st Cape Mtd. Yeomanry

Brands C 1878
Condon J 1878 r
Demmer J 1878
Durheim F 1878
Ferreira P 1878
Friedrichs P 1878
Goodman C 1878
Hansel F 1878
Heuer A.G 1878
Heuer C 1878
Hove F 1878-9
Hove W 1878-9
Kock L 1878 r
Krempling C 1877-8
Lahner A 1878
Londrey A.E 1878
Maurer C 1878 r
Meggersee C 1878
Opitz T 1878 r
Pagel C.F 1878
Rahn J 1878
Rose W 1878
Ross C 1878-9 r
Schlodder C 1878 r
Schreiber A 1878 r
Schreiber W 1878
Siebert F.H.A 1878 r
Sohnur W 1878-9 r
Spann W 1878 r
Sweet J 1878 r
Thompson P 1978 r
Tiedt J.A.C 1878 r
Untiedt C.W.G No clasp
Venske F.A.A 1878 r
Vogelsang H 1877-8
RANK NOT KNOWN
Barby A.R ????
Sellinh C.A.H 1878

SWAMIES KAFFERS.
Also listed as: Swanies Kaffers.
Siwani Levies and Swains Levies.
CAPTAIN
Clarke J.S 1878 r
LIEUTENANT
Poole T 1878 r
Preston W 1878
QUARTERMASTER SERGEANT
Valentine J 1878 r
SERGEANT
Booth J 1878
Brown P 1878 r
Lambert F 1878
Rawlinson W 1878 r
Sheard H 1878 r
PRIVATE
Brill W 1878 r

SWAZIE CONTINGENT.
LIEUTENANT
Barnett J.C 1879- r
Brecher B.G 1879
Walker A.B 1879
ACTING QUARTERMASTER.
Beitt (Brett ?) E.H 1879
CIVIL COMMISSIONER
Campbell A.H KIA 1879
INTERPRETER
Heilmener A 1879 r
TROOPER
Barron W.J 1879
Medal named 'Woods Irregulars'
Also served in 'Burgher Force'

TAMBOOKIELAND DIVISION.
COMMANDANT
Hemming J 1877-8
DOCTOR
Berry W.B 1877-8
Rhind J 1877-8
See also Queenstown Vol. Rifle Corps.
FIELD ADJUTANT
Hilliard J 1877-8
FIELD CORNET
Thomas J 1877-8

TARKASTAD BURGHER CONTINGENT.
LIEUTENANT AND ADJUTANT
Franken P.F 1878 r

TARKASTAD SOUTH RANGERS.
CAPTAIN
Mundell H.C 1878
LIEUTENANT
Whitehead G.A 1878
SERGEANT
Adams T 1878
CORPORAL
Mundell J.E 1878
PRIVATE
Bezeidenhout H 1878 r
Daval J 1878 r
Ensel S 1878 r
Jordaan J 1878
Jordaan W 1878 r
Klopper A 1878
Klopper S 1878 r
Lombard S 1878 r
Muller W 1878
Mundell E 1878
Prinsloo A 1878
Webster E 1878
Whitehead J 1878
Whitehead J.H 1878 r

TENBU LEVIES.
RANK NOT KNOWN
Elliot H.G 1877-8
Lodar C 1877-8
Read W.H 1877-8
Stanford A.H.B 1877-8
Stanford W.E.M 1877-8

TRANSKEI FINGOES.
COMMANDANT
Rorke R.F 1877-8-9
  Also had medal for 1853 War. He should have been issued the Clasp only.
CAPTAIN
Graham W 1877-8
Holliday C 1877-8-9
LIEUTENANT
Dodd W.H 1877-8
Muller F 1877-8

TRANSKEI (N) FINGO LEVY.
LIEUTENANT
Patterson J.H 1878
Smith A.H 1877-8 r
Thornton G.E 1877-8
NO RANK SHOWN
Tainton L 1877-8

TRANSKEI FINGO MILITIA.
COMMANDANT
Pattle T.P.M 1877-8
CAPTAIN
Austin A.G 1877-8
Bikesha J.V 1877-8
Blakeway W.J KIA 1877-8
Fuller A.W 1877-8
LIEUTENANT
Keyser M.J 1877-8

TRANSKEI RIFLES.
CAPTAIN
Mc Taggart H.E 1877-8
  He had a medal from an earlier campaign. No details. See also Pulleines Rangers and Southeys Rangers.
ADJUTANT
Ellis G 1877-8
LIEUTENANT
Brown G.H 1877-8-9 r
  Had a medal for New Zealand.
SERGEANT MAJOR
Stoneham C 1877-8 r
QUARTERMASTER SERGEANT
Chappelton J 1877-8 r
SERGEANT
Armstrong W 1877-8
  See also Wodehouse True Blues.
De Wet W 1877-8 r

Transkei Rifles

Morden J		1877-8
Williamson D		1877-8 r
CORPORAL		
Austin D		1877-8
Luck (Lack) D		**KIA 1877-8-9 r**
Otter A.H		1877-8
Robinson W		**KIA 1877-8**
Rochfort D		**KIA 1877-8-9**
Russell W		**KIA 1877-8-9 r**
Seager J.W		1877-8 r
Walker J		1877-8-9 r
Walsh T		1877-8-9 r
LANCE CORPORAL		
Stewart J		**KIA1877 r**
BURGLER		
Catchploe W		1877-8-9 r
PRIVATE		
Able J		**KIA1877-8-9 r**
Atkins H		**KIA 1877-8-9 r**
Baker H		1877-8
Barstow T		1877-8 r
Bartram J		1877-8 r
Bartlett J		1877-8 r
Bates ?		1877-8 r
Bennett J		1877-8 r
Beyes ?		1877-8
Brown J.C		1877-8 r
Bryant ?	**KIA**	**1877-8-9 r**
Burk W.H		1877-8 r
Cadevit L		1877-8-9 r
Callow R		1877-8 r
Cameron T		1877-8
Carnie ?		1877-8-9 r
Crawley J		1877-8 r
Cunningham W		1877-8 r
Drescher P		1877-8-9
Dunstan J		1877-8-9
Edwards E		1877-8-9 r
Ellis G.l		1879
Eyre T		1877-8-9 r
Fahrenhiem E		1877-8-9 r
Fowler J		1877-8-9
Fredrickson ?		1877-8-9
Gallacher W		1877-8-9 r
Goudie ?		1877-8-9 r
Harris A		1877-8-9 r
Haywood T		1877-8-9 r
Hayden C		1877-8-9 r
Holmes W		1877-8-9 r
Ingram W		1877-8-9 r
Isherwood J		1877-8-9 r
Jackson J		1877-8 r
Joliffe M		1877-8
Johnson W		1877-8
Jones J		1877-8 r
Kenney T		1877-8
Kent W		1877-8 r
Kirk T		1877-8 r
Kirkron D		1877-8 r
Kitson ?		1877-8-9
Kut J		1877-8 r
Lane J		1877-8 r
Lednan H		1877-8 r
Leek ?		1877-8 r
Legg W		1877-8 r
Le Man H		1877-8 r
Long ?		1877-8 r
Lund A		1877-8 r
Mahoney P		1877-8 r
Meaney J	**KIA**	**1877-8-9 r**
Mone J		1877-8 r
Mugan S		1877-8 r
Muir H		1877-8 r
Neil T		1877-8 r
Nessen ?		1877-8 r
O'Grady J		1877-8 r
Parsons ?		No clasp r
Petersen C		1877-8 r
Quinn M		1877-8-9 r
Rabiet ?		1877-8 r
Renner ?		1877-8 r
Roberts ?		1877-8 r
Robinson T		1877-8 r
Rostell ?		1877-8 r
Schmidt ?		1877-8 r
Shaughnessy J		1877-8 r
Sherman W		1877-8 r
Shipley ?		1877-8 r
Short ?		1877-8 r
Smith (1) G		1877-8 r
Smith (2) G		1877-8 r
Smith H		1877-8 r
Smith H.J		1877-8 r
Smith J		1877-8 r
Smith J.H		1877-8 r
Stapleton ?		1877-8 r
Sullivan C		1877-8 r
Tarbett J		1877-8
Techman M		1877-8 r
Theron G	**KIA**	**1877-8**
Turner G	**KIA**	**1877-8 r**
Villet C		1877-8
Wahl P.l		1877-8 r
White R		1877-8 r
Whittick G		1877-8
Williams T		1877-8-9 r
Willis F		1877-8-9 r
Wilson ?		1877-8-9
Wood ?		1877-8-9 r

TRANSPORT SERVICE DEPARTMENT
NO RANK SHOWN
Mac Gregor C.F.M 1879
Westerton G.P.S 1879

TRANSVAAL ARTILLERY.
COMMANDANT
Knox W.G. (RA) 1879
CAPTAIN
Priedel O.H 1878-9
SURGEON MAJOR
Ellwood O 1879
LIEUTENANT
Eastwood E.D 1879
SUB LIEUTENANT
Barnes G 1879
SERGEANT
Kendal C 1879
Mc Cann W 1878
Russell A.T 1878
Sawyer A 1878 r
CORPORAL
Burke J 1878
Modeste J 1878-9 r
Spence P 1878 r
BOMBARDIER
Schmiderman J 1878-9 r
GUNNER
Berghoom B.S 1879 r
Brown D 1879
Chabrond H 1879 r
Cox T 1879
De Klerk W 1878
See also Tpr. Transvaal Rangers.
Desbrow C 1879
Elie H 1878
Forrett A 1879
Frazer T 1879
Goetz S 1878 r
Green E.D 1879
Krlisy (?) A 1878
Lorimer J 1879
Lynch J 1879 r
Mc Donald J.T 1878
Millar R 1878 r
Moore J 1879
Newington J 1878 r
Nicholson J 1879
Robinson F 1878-9
Sellar J 1879
Thomas G 1878 r
See also Tpr Transvaal Rangers.
Thomas J 1879
Thomas S 1879
Vaughan T 1879 r
Watson R 1879 r
See also Border Horse.

TRANSVAAL BORDER HORSE
Murton(Mouton?) A 1879 r

Transvaal Mounted Rifles

TRANSVAAL MOUNTED RIFLES.
All who were killed in action (KIA) lost their lives at Sekukuni's Kraal 28/11/1879..

COMMANDANT
Macaulay	**J.E**	**KIA**	**1879**

CAPTAIN
Jones	W.A	1877-8
King	W.V	1879

LIEUTENANT
Bates	A	1878
McLachlan	W.J	1879
O'Reilly	J.R.O	1879
Von Brandis	E	1879

LIEUTENANT QUARTERMASTER
Kirby	E	1879

REGIMENTAL SERGEANT MAJOR
Jarvis	H	1879 r

TROOP SERGEANT MAJOR
Doonan	W	1879
Verceuil	P	1879

QUARTERMASTER SERGEANT
Marcellens	B	1879

FARRIER
Francis	C	1879 r

SERGEANT
Bailey	W	1879
Johannes	F	1879 r
Kok	A	1879 r
Minto	S	1879

CORPORAL
Adams	C	1879 r

Severely wounded at Sekukuni's Kraal.
Damon	J	1879
Feeder	P	1879
Hedges	W	1879
Jansen	J	1879 r
Millar	H	1879
Reid	G	1879
Roberts	W	1879

TROOPER
Abner	J	1879 r
Abrahams	B	1879
Abrahams	J	1879
Agnew	J	1879 r
Alems	D	1879
Anderson	J	1879

See also Lydenburg Rifles.
Andries	J	1879
Andries	W	1879 r
Anton	B	1879
Anton	J.P	1879
Apler	A	1879
Apples	M	1879 r
Apraman	G	1879 r
Arends	P	1879 r
Aries	J	No clasp r
Augustin	C	1879 r
Beckhuis	W	1879
Bloem	W	1879 r
Bobbles	P	1879 r
Boone	W	1879 r
# Boshoff	K	(see page 166) 1879
Button	W.H	1879
Cloppers	W	1879
Coburg	D	1879
Coburg	H	1879 r
Corkee	P	1879 r
Crawford	J.P	1879
Crowley	M	1879
Davids	K	1879
De Villiers	M	1879 r
Dick	J	1879 r
Divans	J	1879
Drake	H	1879
Dryer	J	1879
Esau	D	1879
Farnac	C	1879
Farrow	I	1879

Slightly wounded at Sekukuni's Kraal.
Feland	A	1879 r
Feland	D	1879
Foltaine	L	1879 r
Francis	A	1879
Gara	J	1879 r
Gervell	G	1879
Gunas	A	Not on medal roll

Severely wounded at Sekukuni's Kraal.
Gildenhuis	W	1879 r
Gilgower	W	1879 r
Hendricks	A	1879
Hendricks	S	1879
Hendricks	W	1879
Hewitt	W	1879 r
Hogan	T	1879

See also Frontier Light Horse.
Jacobs	P	1879
Jacobus	J	1879 r
Jacomb	A	1879 r
Johannes	H	1879 r
Johannes	J	1879
John	J	1879 r
Julie	H	1879 r
Julius	J	1879 r

Severely wounded at Sekukuni's Kraal.
July	N	1879
Keats	J	1879 r
Kelly	J	1879 r
Kevitt	J	1879 r
Kevitt	K	1879
Kitchee	E	1879
Klaas	I	1879 r
Kok	B	1879 r
Kok	C	1879 r
Kok	James	1879 r
Kok	John	1879
Kok	J.J	1879 r
Kok	S	1879
Koranna	W	1879 r
Kordon	D	1879
Krotz	P	1879 r
Kruils	D	1879
Leho	H	1879 r
Long	J	1879 r
Low	A	1879 r
Lucas	S	1879
Macapan	M	1879 r
Mahlasbla	J	1879
Manuel	C	1879
Martin	W	1879
Mathebis	**P**	**KIA 1879**
Mentor	A	1879

Slightly wounded at Sekukuni's Kraal.
Meyers	J	1879
Millar	H	1879 r
Mont	D	1879
Morgan	G	1879 r
Moses	J	1879 r
Moss	W	1879 r
Nelson	D	1879
Nelson	Jacobus	1879
Nelson	John	1879
Peters	P	1879 r
Phillips	A	1879 r
Pikure	K	1879 r
Plaatjes	H	1879 r
Platt	J	1879 r
Prince	A	1879
Prince	H	1879
Prinsloo	K	1879
Rantje	P	1879 r
Reilly	J.J	1879 r
Reiters	A	1879 r
Rossouw	C	1879 r
Saunders	P	1879
Scanley	D	1879
Schalkwyk	J	1879
September	A	1879
Seves	A	1879 r
Simon	A	1879 r
Simon	P	1879
Smith	C	1879
Smith	S	1879 r
Sowell	P	1879 r
Spoyler	M	1879
Stapely	J	1879
Steyn	J	1879

See also Cpl J Stein Tvl Rangers.

Dixons Gazette No41 Spring 2004
596 1 clasp, 1879, engraved in the correct style. Trooper K. Boshof, Transvaal Mounted Rifles. On roll as Boshoff. VF/GVF £350.00

Transvaal Mounted Rifles

THE LATE COMMANDANT PIET UYS, TRANSVAAL MOUNTED VOLUNTEERS, KILLED IN THE ZULU WAR.

Stighling	P	1879 r
Swanepoel	J	1879
Thomas (1)	J	1879 r
Thomas (2)	J	1879
Vandyze	?	1879 r
Vann	J	1879 r
Van Wyk	F	1879
Van Wyk	M	1879 r
Viljoen	D	1879
Voltein	J	1879
Vries	D	1879
Wiles	C	1879 r
Williams	I	1879
Williams	J	1879 r
Wilson	W	1879
Windvogel	J	1879 r
Yessow	?	1879 r

TRANSVAAL MOUNTED VOLUNTEERS STAFF.
BREVET MAJOR (COMMANDANT)
Carrington F   1879

CHAPLAIN
Law   J.A   1879
   See also under Chaplains.
CAPTAIN
Ritter   A   1879
CAPTAIN & ADJUTANT
Williams   P.T   1879
PAYMASTER
Cumberland G Bentinck 1879
COMMISSARIAT OFFICER
Galloway F Herbert   1879
TRANSPORT OFFICER
Egerton   R   1879
LIEUTENANT INTERPRETER
Tainton   A.B   1879
COMMISSARIAT SERGEANT
Middleton H.B   1879
FARRIER SERGEANT
Hughes   T   1878-9
   See also Transvaal Rangers.

ORDERLYROOM SERGEANT
Jones   ?   1879
PAYMASTER SERGEANT
Edwards   S   1879
   See also Border Horse.
SPECIAL COMMISSIONER
Clarke   M.J   1879
   See also Brevet Major M.J. Clarke
CMG R.A. Staff

TRANSVAAL RANGERS (RAAFS HORSE).
An irregular unit raised by Pieter Raaf with a strength of approximately 140 Note on top of the "rewritten" Roll. "Initials are omitted on manuscript and spelling of names cannot be relied on".
COMMANDANT
Raaff   P.E
CAPTAIN
Jullien   J.G

Dixons Gazette No33 Spring 2003 412 1 clasp, 1878-9. Lieutenant H. Mc.K. Paterson, Transvaal Rangers.
Transvaal Rangers, raised by Commandant Pieter Raaf with a strength of approx 138 and also known as Raafs Horse. Many of its personnel came from Kimberley. It served with Buller's Mounted Force throughout the Zulu War and in the operations against Sekukuni. 243 clasped medals issued, 133 returned. EF £750.00   Editors note: also listed on Ferreiras Horse medal roll,rank Orderly Sergeant.

Transvaal Rangers

The two names above, appeared on the Roll, but were deleted with a remark: "No medal should be prepared, financial transactions unsatisfactory."

COMMANDANT
Rudoloph A 1879

CAPTAIN
Carr J 1879
Carr J.A 1878-9
Hamilton T.R 1879
  KIA Inhlobane 28/3/1879.
On Casualty Roll, Rice-Hamilton, T
Master R.A 1878
  See also TSM R.A. Master, Diamond Fields Horse.
Weldon J 1879 r

LIEUTENANT
Bolger T 1879 r
Fawcus ? 1878-9
Few W 1879
O'Donovan T.H 1878-9
Paterson H.Mc K 1878-9
Raaff G 1879
Silverlocke ? 1878-9 r
White D/W H 1879 r
Wickesson O.S 1878 r

QUARTERMASTER
Boosey ? 1879
Fry E.H 1878

REGIMENTAL SERGEANT MAJOR
Cheffins F.W 1879

TROOP SERGEANT MAJOR
Carighan ? J 1879
Carney J 1878 r
Degenkohl P.J 1879 r
Hagen J 1879

Hill S 1878
Hood ? 1878-9
Martin ? 1879 r
  KIA Inhlobane 28/3/1879.
Rossiter T 1879

SERGEANT MAJOR
Brophy T (Thos,) 1878-9
  KIA Inhlobane 28/3/1879.
Cumming(Cummings) J.W 1878-9
  KIA Inhlobane 28/3/1879.
Lemon S.M 1878
Wilson J.C 1878-9

FARRIER SERGEANT
Hughes T 1878
Jannetsburg H 1879

HOSPITAL SERGEANT
Beagley ? 1879 r

ORDERLYROOM SERGEANT
Chinn J.W 1879
Stanley ? 1879 r
Whittaker F.A 1879

QUARTERMASTER SERGEANT
Paxton W.H 1879 r
Perrott T.W 1878
Stiles R.W 1878
Walker ? 1878 r

SADDLER SERGEANT
Didcott C.W 1879
  See also Border Horse.
Hamilton T 1878-9

VETERINARY SERGEANT
Riordan J 1879 r

SERGEANT
Agers W 1878-9
Cloete H 1879
Druder F 1879 r

Egan J 1879 r
Ellitson E 1878-9 r
Maining M.C 1879
Marsh J 1878 r
Monro W.M 1879 r
Scheepers J.S 1879 r

CORPORAL
Adams T 1878-9
Adler D.J 1878-9
  See also Tpr D Adler Diamond Fields Horse.
Baker ? 1878 r
Bean W 1879 r
Beaty A 1879
Dempster ? 1878 r
Harding W 1879
  See also Tpr W. Harding this roll.
Hayes ? 1878
  See also Farr Sgt N. Hayes Lydenburg Rifles.
Henry J 1879 r
Krige J.S 1879
Nelson J 1878
Newman O 1879 r
Samsons F.H 1879
Smith W 1879 r
Stein J 1878
  See also Tpr J. Steyn Transvaal Mounted Rifles.
Ward T 1879

LANCE CORPORAL
Bryant H 1879 r

TRUMPETER
Carmody R 1879

##Sgt. Maj. C. H. Chinn, Transvaal Rangers. (See previous page) Dix Noonan Web Auction 2 Jul 03 Lot 526, Hammer price £1300 South Africa 1877-79, 1 clasp, 1879 (Sgt. Maj. C. H. Chinn, Transvaal Rangers.) small official correction to one letter of rank and one letter of unit, otherwise nearly extremely fine. Estimate £600-800
Footnote
Civilian Conductor C. H. Chinn was killed in action at Marabastadt on 19 February 1881. He had previously served with the Transvaal Rangers during the Zulu War in 1879, and was present at the engagements at Hlobane and Khambula. He is mentioned in a privately published account of the action at Hlobane Mountain which is taken from The Zulu War. And my part in it, by W. H. T. [probably Trooper W. H. Thomas, Transvaal Rangers]:
'We kept to this position for about twenty or so minutes, thus ensuring the escape of at least some of our comrades. At about this time I briefly looked over at Commandant Raaff and saw him exchange words with an officer of the Frontier Light Horse, whom I did not recognise [probably Lieutenant Everitt] and Serjeant Chinn of our unit. Moments later I watched as this officer moved back towards the Ntendeke Nek until he was out of sight. Once this officer disappeared I commenced my firing again until I felt a tap on my shoulder. I turned around to find Serjeant Chinn standing above me. He leaned toward me so as to be heard above the noise, and told me to follow him. Which I did along with perhaps seven others, from various units, including one man from Bakers Horse... Our group became instantly separated from each other. And although I don't recall many individual instances during the descent, I do recall seeing Serjeant Chinn spin around and fall to one side. I could not get to him for the amount of others between and I felt sure he must be killed or condemned to be so. On this count I am glad to say I was wrong.'
Sergeant Chinn, whose occupation is given as Waggoner, appears to have been discharged from the Transvaal Rangers in August 1879. In October 1880 he was attached to the 94th Regiment as a Civilian Conductor. Prior to the outbreak of hostilities in 1880, two companies of the 94th Regiment were based at Marabastadt. On 23 November, one company was ordered to Pretoria, leaving behind one under-strength company, and approximately 25 civilians under the command of Captain E. S. Brook, of the 94th. This small garrison withstood a three month siege, losing 4 men killed or died of wounds, and 13 wounded. Sold with research.

Transvaal Rangers

TROOPER

Name		Year
Anderson	J	1879
See also Lydenburg Rifles.		
Andrews	C	1878 r
Babington	?	1878
Bankhead	S	1878
Banks	**?**	**1879 r**
KIA Inhlobane 28/3/1879.		
Barkworth	T	1879
Barnard	C.J	1879 r
Bennett	G	1879 r
Medal marked "Barnett"		
Benson	H	1878
Beukes	**J**	**Not on medal roll**
KIA Inhlobane 28/3/1879.unkown rank.		
Blair	A.H	1878 r
Borrobeck	?	1878 r
Botha	J	1878 r
Boyle	J	1878 r
Briancon	A	1879 r
Brick	M	1879
Brown	W	1878 r
Brown	W.S	1878 r
Bryson	?	1878
Butt	F	1878
Callaghan	J	1878 r
Cameron	J	1878
See also Border Horse.		
Campbell	?	1878 r
Cannon (Cameron?)	W	1879 r
Carver	T	1879 r
Christian	J.B	1879 r
Clarke	W	1879 r
Clarkson	R	1878 r
Collins	J	1879
Cooper	A.E	1878
Cooper	D	1878
See also Lydenburg Rifles.		
Cornelissen	?	1878 r
Coyle	E	1879
See also Diamond Fields Horse.		
Crane	P	1878 r
Creagher	?	1879 r
Crives	J	1879
David	P	1879 r
Davies	J	1878 r
Deiring	**J**	**1878 r**
KIA 22/6/1878		
De Jonk	A	1878-9 r
De Klerk	W	1878
See also Transvaal Artillery.		
De Waal	C	1878
Dupuis	?	1878 r
Durning	C	1879 r
Edwards	?	1878 r
Farren	T	1878 r
Faure	M	1879 r
Ferguson	G	1879
Fields	W	1878 r
Flinn	J	1878 r
Foley	**R**	**1879 r**
KIA 22/6/1878		
Ford	W.H	1878
See also Ferreiras Horse.		
Forsyth	D	1879 r
Fraser	J	1878 r
Friend	R	1879
Garner	W	1878
Gerharts	O	1879
Goodinge	J	1879 r
Grandt	A	1879 r
Green	C	1878 r
Greening	?	1878 r
Hagan	J	1878 r
Hagart	C	1879
Haines (Harris?)	J	1879 r
Hall	J	1879 r
Hamilton	J	1879
Harding	W	1879
See also Cpl W. Harding this roll.		
Harman	F	1878-9 r
Harris	J	Not on medal roll
KIA 15th March 1879, Kambula Hill		
Harrison	?	1878 r
Hart	J	1879 r
Hartigan	L	1879 r
Harvey	H.A.F	1878
Harvey	W	1878 r
Henderson	?	1878
See also Arm Sgt K. Henderson		
Lydenburg Rifles.		
Henery	H	1878 r
Henning	A	1879 r
Henning	A	1879 r
See also Ferreiras Horse.		
Hett	J	1878-9
Hill	H	1878 r
Hintze	J	1879
Hood	**A**	**Not on medal roll**
KIA 11/8/1878		
Hogan	J	1878-9
Holloway	R	1878 r
Holtzhausen	H	1878 r
Holtzhausen	T	1878 r
Howardson	J	1878
See also Tpr J Howatson Border Horse.		
Johnson	F	1879 r
Johnson	J	1879 r
Johnson	S	1878 r
Johnstone	J	1879 r
Jordan	C	1878-9 r
Keyser	P	1878
Kirkland	?	1878
Kruger	H	1879
Lawson	J	1878 r
Levitson	J	1878 r
Lillycrap	?	1878
Linstrom	F	1879 r
Lister	?	1878 r
Luther	?	1878 r
Maherry	P.T	1879 r
Malcolm	A	1878 r
Mallow	F	1878 r
Manning	R.H	1879 r
Martin	**W.H**	**Not on medal; roll**
KIA Inhlobane 28/3/1879.		
Mason	J	1879
Masson	G	1879 r
May	J	1878 r
Mayer	E.H	1879
Mc Gonigal	J	1878 r
Mc Master	J.A	1879
Mc Naughten	H	1878 r
Meikle	A	1878
Meister	C	1879 r
Melville	J	1878 r
Miller	H	1879 r
Mills	W	1879 r
Moodie	S	1879
See also Tpr C.S. Moody Lydenburg Rifles		
Muller	J	1878
Murnan	J	1879 r
Nicklinson	V	1878 r
Nickolls	M	1878 r
Oliver	A	1879 r
Oliver	**E**	**1878 r**
KIA 27/5/1878		
Oppel	C	1879 r
Ormond	J	1879 r
Osterlow	E	1878
Osterlow	J	1878
Page	J	1879
Pargeter	F	1878 r
Putchell	T	1879 r
Rayner	S	1879 r
Reaney	J	1878 r
Reynolds	M.S	1878-9
# Richardson	J	1879
Ricketts	A	1879
Ridley	H	1878
Robinson	J	1878 r
Roodman	A	1878 r

Dix Noonan Web Auction Lot 934, 29 Jun 06
Three: Private J. Richardson, Transvaal and Muter's Rangers, later Cape Garrison Railways
South Africa 1877-79, 1 clasp, 1879 (Tpr., Transvaal Rangs.); Cape of Good Hope General Service 1880-97, 2 clasps, Transkei, Basutoland (Pte., Muter's Rangs.); Queen's South Africa 1899-1902, no clasp (J. Richardson, C.G.R.) very fine and better (3) Hammer Price: £1200 Footnote Clasps confirmed.

Transvaal Rangers

Salmonsing ?	Not on medal roll	Zibi	S	1877-8	Mahlanbeza		1877-8 r
Wounded at Kambula		CORPORAL			Maka		1877-8 r
Schroeder T	1879	Maejata	J	1877-8 r	Maketa		1877-8 r
Seitz D	1879	Zono		1877-8 r	Makufula		1877-8 r
Shannon J	1878 r	PRIVATE			Maloza		1877-8 r
Sibbley G	1879 r	April	J	1877-8 r	Marona		1877-8 r
Simon E	1879	Baba		1877-8 r	Mazhiba	A	1877-8 r
Simpson J	1878 r	Banjani		1877-8 r	Matambo	J	1877-8 r
Smith (1) J	1879 r	Bayete		1877-8 r	Matokomo	J	1877-8
Smith (2) J	1879 r	Blewkie		1877-8 r	Matyila		1877-8 r
Sniders J	1879 r	Boko		1877-8 r	Mazwe		1877-8 r
Symes M	1879	Boonla	N	1877-8	Mbi	D	1877-8 r
See also Snyman's Burghers.		Booy		1877-8 r	Mdawo		1877-8 r
Spolander A	1879	Bottle	T	1877-8 r	Mdluva	J	1877-8 r
Stamen H	1879	Bulawa		1877-8 r	Metula	P	1877-8
Stanley Chas Not on medal roll		Bulawa		1877-8 r	Mgogo		1877-8 r
KIA Inhlobane 28/3/1879.unkown rank.		Capukiso		1877-8 r	Mhlambiso		1877-8 r
Stanton J	1879 r	Casambile		1877-8 r	Mijiba		1877-8 r
Stephanus J	1879 r	Cisana		1877-8 r	Mjula	S	1877-8 r
Stewart D	1879 r	Daniel		1877-8 r	Mpambani		1877-8 r
Stock H	1878	Dansley		1877-8 r	Mtyewda		1877-8 r
Stone T	1879	Devana		1877-8 r	Mtuedwa		1877-8 r
Storm P	1879 r	Dingindhlu		1877-8 r	Muki		1877-8 r
Medal engraved W.Storm		Dutyulwa		1877-8 r	Muya		1877-8 r
Synes R.H	1879	Dida	J	1877-8 r	Myikiliso		1877-8 r
Tait H	1878	Faleni		1877-8 r	Mzimjati		1877-8 r
Thomas G	1878	Faleni	J	1877-8 r	Mzini		1877-8 r
See also Transvaal Artillery.		Faxana		1877-8 r	Ncapayi		1877-8 r
Thomas W.H	1879	Feke		1877-8 r	Ndabambi		1877-8 r
Thompson W	1878	Foko		1877-8 r	Ndawo		1877-8 r
See also Diamond Fields Horse.		Ganie		1877-8 r	Ndesi		1877-8 r
Thring W	1879 r	Gamle		1877-8 r	Ndiko		1877-8 r
Tonkien A	**1879**	George		1877-8 r	Ndwana		1877-8 r
KIA Inhlobane 28/3/1879.		Hlesikibokwe		1877-8 r	Nelesi		1877-8 r
Tonkins G	Not on medal roll	Jali		1877-8 r	Nene		1877-8 r
Wounded at Kambula		Jantye		1877-8 r	Ngctsha		1877-8 r
Turner W	1879	John		1877-8 r	Nggandaz		1877-8 r
Ungefroren L	1879	Jonas		1877-8 r	Niukwa		1877-8 r
Va der Venn W	1878 r	Joni		1877-8 r	Nivelo		1877-8 r
Van Leent P	1878 r	Kanazo		1877-8 r	Njoram		1877-8 r
Vivian ?	1878 r	Kanterdi		1877-8 r	Noggaba		1877-8 r
Wade A.H	1878	Katshana		1877-8 r	Nombombo Z		1877-8 r
Walsh J.J	1878	Kebete	K	1877-8 r	Nondlazi		1877-8 r
Watson J	1879 r	Ketani		1877-8 r	Nyahe		1877-8 r
Weeber C	1878 r	Keto		1877-8 r	Nyushu		1877-8 r
Wemmer S	1878	Kilikedana		1877-8 r	Nzabela		1877-8 r
See also Ferreiras Horse.		Klaas		1877-8 r	Oloza		1877-8 r
West W.L	1878 r	Klaas	P	1877-8 r	Pambani		1877-8 r
Williamson W.W	1879	Koyibelo		1877-8 r	Pambani		1877-8 r
		Kutshuman		1877-8 r	Papana		1877-8 r
TSHUNIE VOLUNTEERS.		Kwaiman		1877-8	Pepeta	V	1877-8 r
Also shown as TSHUNIE NATIVE LEVY.		Kwenana		1877-8 r	Peter	B	1877-8 r
CAPTAIN		Lali		1877-8 r	Philip		1877-8 r
Attwell J	1877-8	Lebala	C	1877-8 r	Pinda		1877-8 r
LIEUTENANT		Lendani		1877-8 r	Qeunla		1877-8 r
Dorrington J	1877-8	Londika		1877-8 r	Qonvati		1877-8 r
Francis J	1877-8	Mackinon		1877-8 r	Reid		1877-8 r
SERGEANT		Maclean		1877-8 r	Richard		1877-8 r
Bovula J	1877-8	Maggongonza P		1877-8 r	Sambani		1877-8 r

Crossing the Buffalo River

The Lime juice Parade at Fort Bengough

A Night Alarm at Fort Bengough: "Stand to your Arms", the Zulus are Coming"
THE ZULU WAR - WITH THE NATAL NATIVE CONTINGENT

Capt. C. T. SANER
O.C. Victoria Mounted Rifles 1875–1886

VICTORIA MOUNTED RIFLES

Formed in September 1862 in Victoria County.
On the 1st November 1862 they held their first parade at HQ Verulam. 50 members enrolled. The following officers were appointed:
Geo Adams J.P.- Major, CJ Vacey-Lyle J.P.- Captain,
Henry Binns - 1st Lieutenant and Adjutant,
William Lister - 2nd Lieutenant and
J Stanton - Quartermaster.

The Coronation in September 1873 of the Zulu King, Cetewayo, was associated with pomp and ceremony. A detachment of ten volunteers from the Victoria Mounted Rifles, under Captain Harry **Escombe**, formed part of Theophilus Shepstone's escort to Zululand. Elaborate preparations were made to crown the King of the Zulus in the name of England's Queen. An enormous marquee was erected with a pair of carved oak chairs situated in the centre. A travelling opera company supplied the robe and tinsel crown.

In 1875 Captain Henry Binns, one of the founder members of the Corps, took over command. By the end of 1878 when the Zulu War broke out, Captain Charles Saner* was in command and the VMR received orders to march from their headquarters at Verulam to Pietermaritzburg. Three officers and 42 men left Verulam on 2 December 1878 for the Zululand frontier: The Corps, as part of the Natal Volunteer Force, saw action at the battle of Inyezane on 22 January 1879 and the relief of Eshowe.

In 1886 Captain William R Cowley** took command of the Corps, followed by Captain Harry Sparks in 1887.

* Charles Taylor Saner, born 1850 in Yorkshire, emigrated to Natal in the early 1870s and farmed at Verulam. He married Mary Blaine, daughter of Dr Blaine, magistrate of Verulam. After the Anglo-Zulu War, Saner joined a gold-mining company in the Transvaal and became manager of Van Rhyn Estates. His four sons served in the Anglo-Boer War.
** William Cowley, born 1852 in Fairford England, came to Natal in 1859, and farmed in the Little Umhlanga Valley. He was one of the VMR's best shottists. (The unit produced numerous brilliant marksmen.)

Members provided their own horses, uniforms, saddlery and other equipment. Arms, ammunition and field equipment were supplied by the Government. At first armed with the Terry and Snider carbine, this was replaced in 1875 by the Swinburn-Henry carbine firing a .450 lead bullet. Officers carried swords and revolvers. Ammunition was carried in a pouch slung to a cross-belt, white leather with black pouch for full dress, and brown leather belt for service order. Colonial pattern saddlery was used.
Source:
Early Natal Volunteer Units http://www.genealogyworld.net/azwar/victoria.html
iButho - Anglo Zulu War Group http://www.ibuthu-anglozuluwar.com/
The Washing of the spears
Donald R. Morris.

Officers of the Victoria & Stanger Mounted Rifles

Tshunie Volunteers

Sasa	A	1877-8 r
Sebile		1877-8 r
Sedlooa		1877-8 r
Selwana		1877-8 r
Silwana		1877-8 r
Sinana		1877-8 r
Sirumya		1877-8 r
Skepe		1877-8 r
Swartland		1877-8 r
Sweli	J	1877-8 r
Teji		1877-8 r
Tenti		1877-8 r
Tesi		1877-8 r
Tingatinga		1877-8 r
Tintintinti		1877-8 r
Tolongwana		1877-8 r
Tonga		1877-8 r
Tonise		1877-8 r
Tseto		1877-8 r
Tshandaua		1877-8 r
Tulana		1877-8 r
Twtota		1877-8 r
Umhli		1877-8 r
Umpite		1877-8 r
Umputule		1877-8 r
Umswishwi		1877-8 r
Umzalikazi		1877-8 r
Vebebayi		1877-8 r
Vela	J	1877-8 r
Vetboy		1877-8 r
William		1877-8 r
Zesi	T	1877-8 r
Zumetzweni		1877-8 r

UPINGTON'S FOOT.
CAPTAIN
Eddie C 1877-8
See Grahamstown Volunteer Rifle Corps.
Fitzgerald A.C 1877-8
Upington T 1877-8
SERGEANT MAJOR
D'Arcy J.H 1877-8
SERGEANT
Bowen J 1877-8
CORPORAL
Fulton J 1877-8
PRIVATE
Brown H 1877-8 r
Flisher F 1877-8
Flynn C 1877-8 r
Grant G 1877-8 r

Hoffman	H	1877-8 r
Holborn	E	1877-8 r
Jones	G	1877-8 r
Keenan	J	1877-8 r
Magee	C	1877-8 r
Mahn	J	1877-8 r
Mathew	J	1877-8 r
McEvoy	R	1877-8 r
Nivell	F	1877-8 r
O'Connor	P	1877-8
O'Sullivan	J	1877-8 r
Pollard	J	1877-8
Rhodes	W	1877-8 r
Ryan	S	1877-8 r
Sands	S	1877-8 r
Saunders	G	1877-8 r
Schmidt	C	1877-8 r
Smith	H.E	1877-8
Stevens	F	1877-8 r
Toole	L	1877-8

UTRECHT BURGHERS.
TROOPER
Johnstone W 1879

UTRECHT NATIVE LEVIES.
COMMANDANT
Henderson J.W 1879
CAPTAIN
Hazelhurst E 1879
Henderson L.P 1879
Klopper E 1879
LIEUTENANT
Henderson P.F 1879
INTERPRETER
Lass A.M 1879

VAALHOEK MOUNTED VOLUNTEERS.
CAPTAIN
Fleischer J 1878

VAN DER VENTER'S (Captain) VOLUNTEER. CORPS.
QUARTERMASTER SERGEANT
Rorke T.J 1879 r
TROOPER
Sharpe ? 1879

VICTORIA EAST DIVISIONAL POLICE
RANK NOT KNOWN
Letter W 1878

VICTORIA MOUNTED RIFLES.
Formed in 1861, originally a troop of the Royal Durban Rangers. In 1875 part of the Regiment was formed into the Stanger Mounted Rifles. In 1873 formed part of the force sent into Zululand for Cetewayo's coronation. Commanding the unit in the Pearson's column was Captain Charles Saner, an emigrant Yorkshireman. The Corps, as part of the Natal Volunteer Force, saw action at the battle of Inyezane on 22 January 1879 and the relief of Eshowe.

CAPTAIN
Sauer (Saner) C.T 1879
LIEUTENANT
Acutt 1879
Robarts 1879
QUARTERMASTER
Plant 1879

SERGEANT MAJOR
Armstrong 1879
QUARTERMASTER SERGEANT
Foss 1879
SERGEANT FARRIER
Gove 1879
SERGEANT
Galloway H 1879
Pokingjorne 1879
CORPORAL
Acutt S 1879
Hobday 1879
Knight 1879
LANCE CORPORAL
Todd 1879
TRUMPETER
Lewis 1879
TROOPER
Acutt S 1879
Adams 1879
Armstrong 1879
Blamey A 1879
Blamey J.C 1879
Coates E 1879
Coates L 1879
Dykes E 1879
Dykes J 1879
Fynney H 1879
Galloway F 1879
Garland A.H 1879
Godden H 1879

Charles Taylor Saner, born 1850 in Yorkshire, emigrated to Natal in the early 1870s and farmed at Verulam. He married Mary Blaine, daughter of Dr Blaine, magistrate of Verulam. Saner,f,8-Aug-1875,13-Aug-1875,"At the Gables, St Andrews Street, the wife of Charles T Saner J.P. of Southburn in Victoria county of a daughter" Natal Witness of 1875. Members provided their own uniforms, and horses. Arms, ammunition and field equipment were supplied by the Government. At first armed with the Terry and Snider carbine, this was later replaced by the Swinburn-Henry carbine firing a .450 lead bullet.
After the Anglo-Zulu War, Saner joined a gold-mining company in the Transvaal and became manager of Van Rhyn Estates. His four sons served in the Anglo-Boer War.

NATAL MOUNTED RIFLES

Trooper, later **Quarter Master Alpheus Howe Garland**
Victoria Mounted Rifles/Natal Mounted Rifles
Identified on the reverse by a period inscription as Mr H. Garland this cabinet photograph depicts an officer or senior NCO of the Natal Mounted Rifles. He is in all likelihood the same H. Garland who as a trooper in the Victoria Mounted Rifles was Mentioned in Despatches for actions at Eshowe during the Anglo-Zulu War of 1879 (The London Gazette, 16 May, 1879).

He wears the 1877-79 South Africa Medal (which is often referred to as the Zulu War Medal) with the single clasp awarded for that war. The Natal Mounted Rifles were formed in 1888 from several Zulu War-era volunteer units including the Victoria Mounted Rifles (VMR), the Stanger Mounted Rifles, the Alexandra Mounted Rifles and the Durban Mounted Rifles.

I believe that H. Garland is the same person as Alpheus Howe Garland who enlisted in the Victoria Mounted Rifles in 1877. Nowhere can I find reference to two different troopers by the name Garland serving with the VMR during the period of the Anglo-Zulu War. The son of a prominent Natal resident Thomas William Garland and his wife Henrietta, Garland was born at Verulam, Natal on 24 September, 1854.

He enlisted as a trooper in the VMR in 1877 and served as previously stated in the Anglo-Zulu War of 1879, receiving a Mention in Despatches for actions around the mission station at Eshowe. After the war he continued with the Natal volunteers serving for some 18 years total and eventually rising to the rank of Quarter-Master (30 October, 1885).
This photograph probably shows him while holding that rank. He does not seem to have done any active service during the Anglo-Boer War.

He was active in several other organizations including the Kearsney Rifle Association and the Zulu Border Rifle Association. He made his living in civilian life as an auctioneer. On 7 May, 1881 he married Miss Elizabeth Stanley of Chatham, Kent. He lived to the ripe old age of 85 years, dying on 16 October, 1939 and was buried at the cemetery at Stanger.

A special thanks to Mr. Cameron Simpson for providing additional biographical details on A. H. Garland.

Photograph: Cabinet Photograph William Laws Caney - Photographer
Late of D'Urban & Kimberly, South Africa c. 1890

Mentioned in Despatches for actions at Eshowe
Connected with the vedette duties, I wish to mention a circumstance which I think reflects great credit upon Captain Sherrington, Native Contingent, and the undermentioned men, viz,:- Corporal Adams, Native Contingent, Privates Whale, Robson, Higley and Keys, 99th Regiment, and Trooper Garlands, Victoria Mounted Rifles. The vedettes, shortly after our arrival at Ekowe, were daily annoyed when they patrolled in the morning, before finally taking up their posts, by the fire of a party of Zulus from a high hill. It was believed that this party took up their position very early in the morning, and Captain Sherrington and above party volunteered to go out at night and lie in wait for them behind some rocks near the top of the hill, being utterly ignorant, however, of the number of the Zulus.
I consented, and this little expedition resulted in 3 Zulus being wounded (though not so seriously as to prevent them from making good their escape),and the vedettes never being annoyed from this hill again. In fact, no Zulu was ever afterwards seen there....
I have, &c.C.K.Pearson, Colonel, Commanding No 1 Column.
Ref London Gazette 16th May 1879 page 5.Issue 24723.
http://www.soldiersofthequeen.com/

From Colonel Pearson, Commanding No, 1 Column, to the Military Secretary, &c Durban.
Fort Tenedos, Lower Tugela Drift, Zululand, SIB, April 9,1879. Staff Office, Head Quarters.
I have the honour to furnish the following report relative to the part taken by the mounted troops in the action at the Gingindhlovo on the 2nd instant. At 6 a.m. Captain Nourse reported that some of Thausie's mounted scouts had seen the Zulus crossing the Inyezana, and almost immediately afterwards the attack commenced. I directed the mounted troops to saddle up and stand to their horses for dismounted duty, one man holding four horses, leaving three-quarters in reserve for use in the trenches if required. At 6.40 a.m. I advanced out of the laager by the front face with the Volunteers and mounted Infantry, and opened fire on the enemy who had retired into the long grass out of fire from the laager. At 7. a.m. the rear face of the laager was attacked in force, and I took half squadron of mounted Infantry to observe the movement. **Captain Cook's** troop of Natal Horse, also two squadrons of mounted Natives then advanced out of the laager by the right face.

The enemy then retired -to the low ground below the rear face, and the Natal Horse brought an effective flanklfire on them, assisting in causing the Zulus to break.The dispositions of the mounted troops at this period were as follows:—
Inyezana.
1. Half squadron mounted Infantry, **Lieutenant Sugden**.
2. Volunteer squadron.
3. Half squadron mounted Infantry, **Lieutenant Rawlins**.
4. Natal Horse Troop.
5. Mafunzi's Natal Horse.
6. Thausie's Natal Horse.

At about 7.15 a.m. the Zulus retired from the rear face and the Natal Native Contingent advanced out of the laager. At the same time, accompanied by **Lieut. Courtnay**, I succeeded in making a flank attack
on the retreating Zulus with half a squadron mounted Infantry under Lieut. Rawlins who led his squadron with considerable dash and to my entire satisfaction. The half squadron drew swords and charged the Zulus, who were iu large numbers, but utterly demoralized. The actual number of men killed with the sword were probably few, but the moral effect on the retreating Zulus as the swordsmen closed in on them was very great. In most cases they threw themselves down and showed no fight, and were assegaied by the Natal Native Contingent who were following up. A few Zulus showed fight and assegaied one or two horses, but the majority did not do so. The half squadron then rallied and followed up again up to a distance of 1 1/4 miles from camp,when it was at last checked by a spruit.

The Natal Horse followed up in support, but were unfortunately unable to charge owing to having no arm blanche or revolver. They fired however with effect. I have no hesitation in saying, that had a regiment of English Cavalry been on the field on this occasion scarcely a Zulu would have escaped to the Umisi Hill.

The half squadron mounted Infantry, under Lieut. Sugden, and the Volunteer squadron endeavoured to follow up on the front face, but were unable to close on enemy on account of the boggy ground and the fire of the Natal Native Contingent.

The mounted Natives followed the enemy for some miles towards the Gingindhlovo Kraal and Amatakulu, and Thausie's squadron succeeded in recapturing some 15 head of cattle, which the Zulus had found outside the laager. I think that credit is due to these Native mounted squadrons for advancing out of the laager by the right face when the main attack of the Zulus was being made.

The loss of the mounted troops was as follows:—Mounted Infantry, 2 men wounded severely; 1 man wounded slightly; 2 horses killed; 5 horses wounded. Volunteer Squadron, nil; Natal Horse, nil; Thausie's Native Horse, 1 man killed; Mafunzi's Native Horse, 1 man wounded severely.

The few casualties amongst the horses of the mounted troops, half of whom were outside the laager during the whole action, except the first half-hour, does not say much for the accuracy of the Zulu fire.
P. E. S. Barrow, Major, Commanding Mounted Troops, No, I Column.

Supplementary Return of Wounded in the Action at Zhlobana Hill (Col. Wood's Column) 28th March, 1879. Frontier Light Horse—**Sergeant J. Dews,** severely. Supplementary Return of Wounded in the Action at Kambula Hill (Col. Wood's Column), 29th March, 1879.
1st Battalion 13th foot—**Private J. Cogan**, slightly.

Return of Horses Killed and Wounded in Action at Gingilovo, 2nd April, 1879. Staff, 2 killed, private horse," Lieut.-Colonel Crealock; public do., Capt. Molyneux; Mounted Infantry, 2 killed, wounded, private horse, **Lieut. Courtenay**, 20th Hussars; Transport Department,
1 killed; 5th Battalion Natal Native Contingent, 2 killed, 1 wounded, Capt. Gurney, Lieut. Jay, and Lieut. Thompson. Total, 7 killed, 6 wounded.
J. NORTH CREALOCK, Lieut.-Colonel,
Staff Officer.

Reference: London Gazette Issue 24723 published on the 16 May 1879

J. North. Crealock.Lieut.-Colonel,

Victoria Mounted Rifles

Groome (Groom)	1879	
# Hall	1879	
Hewardine	1879	
Jackson C	1879	
Jackson T	1879	
James	1879	
Johnston	1879	
Lister	1879	
Logan	1879	
Ludeman (Laderman)	1879	
Manning A	1879	
Manning C	1879	
Mc Dermot	1879	
Mellor	1879	
Mitchell A	1879	
Page	1879	
Plant H	1879	
Ramsay	1879	
Ratcliffe	1879	
Rathbone F	1879	
Reed H	1879	
Rumsey J	1879	
Saunders	1879	

VICTORIA WEST VOLUNTEERS.
NO RANK SHOWN
Devenish Wn G   1878

VON SUEENBERG RANGERS
Also shown as Von Suenberg Mtd Police.
LIEUTENANT
Leisfeldt I.B   1877-8
PRIVATE
Eales R.G   1878 r
Lichfieldt J.B   1877-8
Mc Cusker J   1878
Meser C   1878
Olivia P   1878
Selling C.A.F   1877-8

WEENEN YEOMANRY.
MAJOR GENERAL
Lloyd   1879
    See also Colonial Commanders and Levy Leaders
LIEUTENANT
Popham   1879
2ND LIEUTENANT
Lloyd   1879
QUARTERMASTER
Blaker   1879
SERGEANT MAJOR
Trafford   1879
SERGEANT
Guillod   1879

CORPORAL
Lindsay   1879
White   1879
TROOPER
Brandon   1879
Colville   1879
Crouch   1879
Foord   1879
Griffin   1879
Liversage   1879 r
Spilsbury   1879
Starkey   1879
Taylor   1879
Turvin   1879
Wray   1879
No details as to the Clasp issued.
Probably qualified for the 1879 clasp.

WHITTLESEA MOUNTED RIFLES.
CAPTAIN
Leach C.W   1877-8

WINDERBERG GREYS VOLUNTEERS.
CAPTAIN
Sweetnam J   1878
LIEUTENANT
Baker M   1878
2ND LIEUTENANT
Sweetnam J   1878
SERGEANT MAJOR
Sweetnam A   1878
SERGEANT
Mulligan J   1878
Sutton A   1878
CORPORAL
Holmes A   1878 r
TROOPER
Bishop L   1878
Botha T   1878 r
Boucher John   1878 r
Boucher Joseph   1878 r
Brymer W   1878
Erasmus A   1878 r
Erasmus D   1878 r
Holmes G   1878 r
Kirton J   1878
Meyer H   1878 r
Meyer M   1878 r
Muller C   1878 r
Rawstorne L   1878
Rouse J   1878 r
Staples S   1878 r
Sumner H   1878 r
Sutton G   1878
Sutton H   1878 r
Sweetnam C   1878

Sweetnam J.J   1878
Sweetnam T   1878
Thurtell E   1878 r

WODEHOUSE TRUE BLUES.
CAPTAIN
Spillman E   1877-8
LIEUTENANT
De Beer J.J   1877-8-9
Gaz (Gay) P   1877-8-9
KIA Moirosi's Stronghold. See also Pte. P. Gav 2nd Cape Mounted Yeomanry.
Mayes F.W   1877-8 r
Parkes R   1877-8-9
SERGEANT MAJOR
Hutchins A.V.M   1877-8-9
SERGEANT
Allen T   1878-9
    See also Cpt T. Allen 2nd Cape Mounted Yeomanry.
Armstrong ?   1878
    See also Transkie Rifles.
Badgere E   1877-8
See 2nd Lt in 2nd Cape Mounted Yeomanry.
Best J   1878
De Beer A.A   1877-8
Duncombe ?   1877-8
Hulley S.J   1877-8
Mabett C.D   1877-8
Read S   1877-8 r
Taylor W.R   1877-8
Von Hirschbert Count F 1877-8-9
    See also Lt 4th Natal Native Contingent.
CORPORAL
Ballard H.E   1878
Best R   1878
    See also Sgt. R. Best 2nd Cape Mounted Yeomanry.
Brannager J   1878 r
Croll C   1878 r
Howell W   1877-8
    See also Tpr W. Howell 2nd Cape Mounted Yeomanry.
Hunter F   1878 r
Mc Coll J.C   1877-8
    See also Tpr J. Mc Coll 2nd Cape Mounted Yeomanry.
Murray D   1878
Taylor C.J   1877-8 r
TROOPER
Berry J   1878-9
    See also Frontier Light Horse.
Botha P.S   1878 r
Burn ?   1878 r

Dixons Gazette No41 Spring 2004
597 1 clasp, 1879, engraved in the correct style, official correction to 'Rifles'. Trooper Hall, Victoria Mounted Rifles. VF/GVF £350.00

Wodehouse True Blues

Caffyn P.W		1878-9 r
KIA Pirie Bush 8/5/1878		
Catherine W.J.H		1877-8 r
Claassen J (P.F)		1878 r
KIA Pirie Bush.8/5/1878		
De Beer	P.F	1878
De Bruin	D	1878 r
De Lange	P.A	1878 r
Demmer	H	1878
Demmer	J	1878
Develing	A	1877-8
Dicks	C	1877-8 r
Dicks	Jonah	1878 r
Dicks	Joseph	1878 r
Dicks	Josiah	1878 r
Dicks	R	1878 r
Du Preez	J	1878 r
Dyer	J	1878 r
Edgar	S	1877-8-9
Eloff	J	1878
France	Not on medal roll	
KIA Pirie Bush.8/5/1878		
Ferreira	G.M	1878 r
Fincham	C	1878 r
Foster	F	1878
Foster	W	1878
Gradwell	E.J	1878 r
Gradwell	J	1878 r
Haskins	J	1878
Henderson	T.H	1878 r
Heuer	?	1878 r
Higgins	E	1878 r
Holden	J.B	1878 r
Huay	J	1878
Hurley	P	1878 r
Jacobs	?	1878 r
Jenner	H	1878
Johnson	C	1878
Severely wounded Pirie Bush.8/5/1878		
Kearney	R	1878
Kees	?	1878 r
Kelly	W	1878
See also 2nd Cape Mounted Yeomanry.		
Lamnde	J	1878-9 r
KIA at Morosi's Stronghold 8/4/1879		
Mac Mullen	J	1878 r
Marshall	?	1877-8
Meredith	**E.H**	**1878-9 r**
KIA at Morosi's Stronghold 8/4/1879		
Meyburgh	J	1878
See 2nd Cape Mounted Yeomanry.		
Meyburgh	L	1878
Meyer	J	1878
Meyer	M	1878
Nelson	?	1877-8 r
Oelofse	J	1878 r
Murray	J	1878
Murray	L.J	1878
Paech	A	1878-9
See also 2nd Cape Mounted Yeomanry.		
Paech	P	1878-9
See also 2nd Cape Mounted Yeomanry.		
Powell	J	1878 r
Richards	G.W	1878
Rodneck	?	1878 r
Rou r	E	1878 r
Rou r	G	1878 r
Schoff	W	1878 r
Schultz	C.A.W	1878 r
Simon	?	1878 r
Slater	C	1878 r
Steinhofel	G	1878 r
Styles	**R**	**1878-9 r**
KIA at Morosi's Stronghold 8/4/1879		
Thies	C.A	1878
Thompson	?	1878 r
Turner	H	1878 r
Van Niekerk Snr	C	1877-8
Van Niekerk Jnr	C	1877-8
Van Niekerk	F	1877-8
Van Niekerk	P	1878
Van Zijl	**G.M**	**1878 r**
KIA Moirosi's Stronghold with 2nd Cape Mtd Yeo.		
Velleman	P.F	1878
Wakeford	W	1877 r
Walters	S	1878 r
Watkins	C	1878 r
Wentworth	E	1877-8 r
William	T	1877-8
Williams	J	1878

DETECTIVE
Jacob		1878 r
Simon		1878 r

WOODS IRREGULARS. 1ST BATTALION
COMMANDANT
White	T.L	1877-8-9

Wounded at Ulundi 4/7/1879

CAPTAIN
Harber	S.S	1879
Horton, S.S Wounded at Ulundi 4/7/1879		
Macrae	C.D	1879

LIEUTENANT
Cowdell	E.J	1879

Wounded at Ulundi 4/7/1879
Rathbone	C.R	1879

TROOPER
Schaal ? Not on medal roll
Died of Fever 2/3/1879 VanSlanden's Farm another list KIA details as above.

WOODS IRREGULARS. 2ND BATTALION
COMMANDANT
Roberts	R.G	1879

LIEUTENANT
Mulligan	J	1879

ZENTZE MOUNTED CORPS BURGHERS.
CAPTAIN
Hay	C.D	1879

ZOUTPANSBERG NATIVE CONTINGENT.
COMMANDANT
Meyer	W.C	1879

CAPTAIN
Dahl	O	1879
Fourie	B	1879
Nybrea	F.F	1879
Polkinghorne	B.S	1879

Wood's Irregulars Caractacus Reliance Rathbone

Caractacus, Ephraim's fourth son, known as 'Crack' to the family, had a remarkable career in his own right. Born in 1854 in Zululand, he married in 1881 Caroline Magdaline Williams and farmed at 'Tiverton' in the District of Utrecht. In 1870 he went to the Diamond Fields with his brother-in-law John Seymour, and took up claims at Heilbron. After working these for six months he went to Dutoit's Pan in 1871 and then went to New Rush (later called Kimberley), selling out of his claims there in 1872. He then proceeded to Button's Gold Reef near Marabastad, before returning to his farm. He saw service throughout the Anglo-Zulu War 1879 as Lieutenant in Wood's Irregulars, under Sir Evelyn Wood, receiving the campaign medal and bar. In 1880 he served in Basutoland as a Lieutenant in Hanson's Troop, Transvaal Horse, and earned another medal and bar. He was Guide and Interpreter to Colonel Deane OC Natal Field Force in 1881 (First Anglo-Boer War), then transferred to Field Hospital as Officer-in-Charge and Interpreter to Native Stretcher Bearers, under Surgeon-Major Babington.

Colonial Army List July-Aug 1881

Cape of Good Hope.

(Corrected to 18th Feb. 1881.)

Governor and Commander-in-Chief.
Robinson, Sir Hercules G. R., G.C.M.G.

Military Secretary.
St. John, Captain (local Major) E. B., 35 F.

Aide de Camp.

Extra Aide de Camp to H. E. the Governor.
Newton,   Esq.

Commandant General of Colonial Forces.
Clarke, Bt. Col. (local Brig.-General) C. M., C.B., h.p. *late* 57 F.   11June80

Aide de Camp.
Edwards, Lieut. H. H., 23 F. (*temp.*)

Assist. Adj. Gen.
Cochrane, Capt. (local Major) W. F. D., 32 F.   1Sept.79

Paymaster General.
Garcia, A., *Esq.*   1Oct.80

Inspector of Stores & Transport Department.
Nesbitt, C. A., *Esq.*   25Dec.77

Commissary of Ordnance.
Wells, W. H., *Esq.*   25Sept.79

Staff Officers of Volunteers.
Wavell, Col. A. G. (Capt. 9 F.) (*Cape District*)   1Mar.80
Cherry, Capt. and Bt. Maj. C. E. Le M., 32 F. (*Grahamstown Dist.*)   22Jan.80
Deare, Major G. R. (*Port Elizabeth Dist.*)   9Apr.80

Cape Field Artillery.

Head-quarters—Basutoland.

Captain Commanding.
Giles, G. E. (Lieut. R. Art.)   1Oct.80

Lieuts.
Heyman, H. M.   1Nov.80
Whitaker, F. S.   1Dec.80
Lodge, F. W.   1Dec.80

Paym. & Q.M. Best, J.   1Oct.80

Cape Mounted Riflemen.

Right Wing.
Head-quarters—King William's Town.

Lieut. Colonel.
Bayly, Z. S., C.M.G., *late* Lt.9 F.   12June79

Capts.
Baillie, C. C., *hon. m.*   5Aug.78
Goldsworthy, J. W. (*Adj. & I. of M.*)   5Aug.78
Bourne, J. H. W., *hon.m.* 5Aug.78
Maclean, J. K.   5Aug.78
Sprenger, C.   20Nov.79
Blaine, Alf.   16Mar.80

Lieuts.
Fynn, H. W.   5Aug.78
M'Callum, W.   4Mar.79
Goldsworthy, C. L.   4Mar.79
Watson, R.   6Oct.79
Russ, G. F.   6Oct.79
Winslow, L.   6Oct.79
Shortt, F. G.   6Oct.79
Fraser, D.   15Nov.80
Knott, M. E.   15Nov.80
Stewart, R. B.   15Nov.80

Adj. & I. of M. Goldsworthy, J. W., *capt., late* Lt. 86 F.   5Aug.78
Paym. Hutchinson, W. L., *hon. m.*   5Aug.78
Surg. Maj. Hartley, E. B. 5Aug.78
Vet. Surg. Dawkins, T. B. S.   29Aug.79
Q.M. Leatherland, J., *hon. capt.*   3Sept.78

Cape Mounted Riflemen.

Left Wing.
Head-quarters—Basutoland.

Lieut. Colonel.
Carrington, F., C.M.G., Capt. and Bt. Lt. Col. 24 F.   29Jan.80

Captains.
Grant, Jas. M., *late* Lt. 25 F. *hon. m.*   5Aug.78
Waring, J. C.   6Feb.79
Montagu, H. S. M.   8Aug.79
Shervinton, C. R. St. L. 4Mar.80
Hatton, E. F.   24Oct.80

Lieutenants.
M'Mullen, G.   5Aug.78
Cochrane, J. P.   5Aug.78
West, C. S.   1July79
Kennon, R.   8Aug.79
Goldsworthy, H. W.   6Oct.79
Neylan, N.   6Oct.79
Dent, R. B.   29Oct.80
Cruitwell, W.   29Oct.80

Adj. & I. of M. Bowers, J. T., *hon capt., late* Capt. 59 F.   22Mar.80
Paym. M'Cabe, J., *hon. capt.*   15Dec.79
Surg.-Maj. Smith, J.A.J. 5Sept.78
Vet. Surg. Garnett, G.   9May80
Q.M. M'Carter, W. A., *hon. capt.*   15Dec.79

Cape Mounted Yeomanry.

1st Regiment.
Head-quarters—Basutoland.

Colonel.
Brabant, E. Y., C.M.G., *late* Capt. 80 F.   5Aug.78

Capts.
Sansom, J.
Dell, S. W.   10Sept.78
Nettleton, T. S.   10Sept.78
Sprigg, H.   10Sept.78
Purdon, J. T.   10Sept.78
Stone, H. M.   8Oct.79
Mullin, P.   24Dec.79
Vincent, L. L.   12Apr.80
Van Ryneveld, C.   1May80
    18May80

Lieuts.
Brent, T.   1Dec.78
Schaefer, F.   1Dec.78
Gray, J. W.   1Dec.78
Smith, H. M.   1Dec.78
Fletcher, A. A.   6Dec.79
Jones, C. R.   13Dec.79
Girdlestone, C. H.   25Dec.79
White, W. N.   1June80

2nd Lieuts.
Willmore, W. H.   1Jan.80
Marshall, G.   1May80
Krunse, P. M.   1July80
Callender, C. E.   22Sept.80

Adj. & I. of M. Dalgety, E. H., *hon. capt., late* Lt. 21 F.   10Sept.78

Paym. & Q. M. Ellis, G. J., *hon. capt.*   27Jan.79
Surg.-M. McCrea, J. F.   30July80

Cape Mounted Yeomanry.

2nd Regiment.
Head-quarters—Basutoland.

Colonel.
Southey, R. G., Capt. 10 F. 10Oct.78

Capts.
Nesbitt, H., *late* Lt. 12 F.   18Nov.78
White, H.   7Feb.79
Hutchons, A. N. M.   24May79
Barrable, W.   18May80
Kannemeyer, H. M.   22May80
Stretton, J. K.   31July80
Leach, C. W.   11Sept.80
Feathers, T. R.   15Feb.80

Lieuts.
Brady, J.   7Feb.79
Badger, E.   27Oct.79
Schweitzer, C.   1Apr.80
Gan, P.   20Apr.80
Eva, R. G.   11Sept.80
Frost, W. C.   14Nov.80

Cape of Good Hope *contd.*

2nd Lieuts.
Kirkpatrick, W. G. — 20Apr.80
Vice, C. J. — 18May80
Brady, A. R. — 22May80
Stirton, G. — 31July80
Copeland, W. J. S. — 31July80
Staples, E. — 11Sept.80
Pohl, J. — 29Nov.80

Adj. & I. of M. Cooper, E. R., *hon. capt., late Lt. 96 F.* — 12Jan.80
Paym. & Q. M. Davis, C. — 30Jan.79
Surg. Kannemeyer, D. R. — 22Feb.79

Cape Mounted Yeomanry.
3rd Regiment.

Head-quarters—Basutoland.

Colonel.
Minto, T. E. — 11Sept.78

Capts.
Chiappini, A. L. — 18Nov.78
Bowker, J. F. F. — 18Nov.78
Lamb, J. — 18Nov.78
Van Niekerk, C. J. — 8June79
Watermeyer, F. — 26July80

Lieuts.
Hudson, C. R. — 27Jan.79
Syd, T. — 5June79
Heugh, P. R. — 8June79
Raynier, P. G. — 26July80
Sinclair, B. C. R. — 4Dec.80

2nd Lieuts.
Van Niekerk, A. — 8June79
Gibbon, H. J. — 4Dec.80

Adj. & I. of M. Christian, E. J., *hon. capt., late Lt. 91 F.* — 25May80
Paym. & Q. M. Ellis, O. — 1Feb.79
Surg. Lamb, R. G. — 20Nov.78

Northern Border Police.

Head-quarters—Kenhardt.

Inspector.
Mason, G. B. B. — 5May.80

Sub-Inspectors.
Hackenburg, W. C. A. — 25Jan.80
Errington, N. G. — 25Jan.80

Paym. & Q. M. (Hon. Insp.) Blum, ... — 25Jan.80

VOLUNTEERS.

CAVALRY AND MOUNTED INFANTRY.

Adelaide Mounted Infantry.
(Adelaide.)

Capt.
Lee, H. C. — 30Sept.76

Lieuts.
Wood, J. — 12Sept.78
Barnett, C. — 17Jan.80

Surg. Conry, J. — 4July78

Albany Mounted Rangers.
(Salem.)

Captains.
Gardner, J. — 15Oct.78
Shaw, S. B. — 15Oct.78

1st Lieut.
Attwell, W. — 15Oct.78

2nd Lieuts.
Hill, G. — 15Oct.78
Elmslie, W. — 15Oct.78

Beaufort Rangers.
(Fort Beaufort.)

Capt.
Richards, J. — 20Feb.78

Lieut.
Harley, W. — 21July80

2nd Lieut.
Niland, B. — 21July80

Berlin Mounted Infantry.
(Berlin.)

Capt.

Lieuts.
Bauer, C. — 22Mar.79
Linow, A. — 28July79

2nd Lieut.
Rosteberg, T. — 28July79

East London and Chalumna Volunteer Cavalry.
(East London.)

Capt.
Warren, T. H. — 28Mar.76

Lieut.
Forrester, R. W. — 26June80

Cape Town Volunteer Cavalry.
(Prince Alfred's Own.)

(Cape Town.)

Capt.
Wills, P. T. — 20Oct.79

Lieut.
Berrangé, D. F. — 20Oct.79

2nd Lieut.
Hewitt, R. W. — 20Oct.79

Surg. Abercrombie, A. — 26Jan.80

Sidbury Mounted Rangers.
(Sidbury.)

Capt.
Howarth, W. — 27Feb.80

Lieut.
Thomas, W. — 1June80

2nd Lieut.
Daniell, R. H. J. — 1June80

Colonial Army List July-Aug 1881

Cape of Good Hope contd.

Stockenstrom Rangers.
(Balfour.)

Capt.
Green, J. W.   16June77

Lieut.
Theron, J. J.   24July79

2nd Lieut.
Bernard, N.   27Aug.79

Winterberg Greys.
(Blinkwater.)

Capt.
Sweetnam, Jas.   24Feb.78

Lieut.
Baker, M.   24Feb.78

2nd Lieut.
Sweetnam, J.   24Feb.78

ARTILLERY.

Grahamstown Horse Artillery.
(Grahamstown.)

Capt.
Reynolds, G.   5Dec.76

Lieut.
Nelson, A. E.   5Dec.76

2nd Lieut.
Siegert, C. F.   29Sept.79

King William's Town Artillery.
(King William's Town.)

Capt.

Lieuts.
Dyer, F.

2nd Lieut.   4July77

Surgeon.
Piers, C. E.   4July77

Kaffrarian Artillery.
(East London.)

Capt.
Nicholls, C. E.   27July80

Lieuts.

2nd Lieut.
M'Taggart   13Aug.80

Surgeon.
Duminy, B. F.   31May77

Cape Town Volunteer Artillery (Prince Alfred's Own).
(Cape Town.)

Major.
Southey, R., C.M.G.   10Oct.77

Capt.
Inglesby, T. J. C.   10Oct.77

Lieuts.
Stigant, P. J.   13Aug.74
Duff, B.   23Aug.80

Surg. Roux, P. J.   11July61
Q.M. Mutton, T. W.   7Mar.79
Hon. Chapl. Clarke, Rev. C. B. W.   9May78

ENGINEERS.

Cape Town Volunteer Engineers.
(Cape Town.)

Capt.
Tennant, J.   14Oct.79

Lieut.
Stuttaford, W. F.   30Oct.79

2nd Lieuts.
Munks, J. H.   10June80
Serrurier, C. G.   9Aug.80

Surgeon.
Falkiner, T. F.   8Apr.80

INFANTRY.

Beaufort West Volunteer Rifles.
(Beaufort West.)

Capt.
Thwaites, T. A.   8Mar.79

Lieuts.

2nd Lieut.
M'Intyre, W. W.   8Mar.79

Surg. Drew, H. W.   8Mar.79

Q.M. Tripp, H. E.   8Mar.79

Cradock Rifle Volunteers.
(Cradock.)

Capt.
Green, J. E.   28June80

Lieut.
Sykes, W.   28June80

2nd Lieut.
Holmden, W.   27Sept.80

Surgeon.
Fehrsen, J. M.   9Apr.78

Cape Town (Duke of Edinburgh's Own) Volunteer Rifles.
(Cape Town.)

Colonel.
Wavell, A. G., *Capt.* 9 F. 1Mar.80

Majors.
Goodliffe, F. G.   15Apr.78
Jones, H. H.   25July78

Capts.
Buchanan, E. J.   6Mar.78
Jones, T. E.   15Apr.78
Moore, W. E.   15Apr.78
Knox, E. B. J.   13June78
Searle, T.   14June78
Alchin, J.   6Jan.79
Brown, J. L. M.   24Oct.79
Hardey, S.   30June80

Colonial Army List July-Aug 1881

Cape of Good Hope contd.

Lieuts.
Murison, J. — 15Apr.78
Miles, T. P. — 15Apr.78
D'Arcy, E. S. — 15Apr.78
Daniell, H. G. — 25Apr.78
Crowley, W. H. — 14June78
Lawton, T. H. — 24Oct.79
Tennant, H. — 30June80
Durrant, C. H. — 9Sept.80

2nd Lieuts.
Furniss, O. — 15Apr.78
Bell, A. — 15Apr.78
Davis, J. F. — 15Apr.78
Andrews, J. — 25Apr.78
Stevens, G. — 16Nov.78
Barry, J. — 6Jan.79
M'Laren, J. — 24Oct.79
Turner, W. B. — 8July80
Richards, S. — 9Sept.80

Adj. Whindus, E. J., *capt.* — 15Apr.78

Paym. Dickson, C. A., *hon. capt.* — 15Apr.78

Surg. Ross, W. H. — 15Apr.78

Q. M. Roberts, C. J. — 15Apr.78

Commiss. Off. St. Leger, F. Y. — 6June78

Hon. Chapl. The Very Rev. the Dean of Cape Town — 15Apr.78

1st City Volunteers.
(Grahamstown.)

Capt. Commandant.
Cherry, Capt. & Bt. Maj. C. E. Le M., 32 F. — 28Apr.80

Capts.
Sampson, D. — 2Sept.77
Copeland, T. H. — 26May80

Lieuts.
Gowie, C. — 30June78
Galpin, W. H. — 30June78

2nd Lieuts.
Middleton, T. — 30June78
Tillard, R. — 30June78

Adj. Young, G. — 15July76

Keiskama Hoek Volunteers.
(Keiskama Hoek.)

Capt.

Lieut.
Frauenstein, G. — 3Feb.77

2nd Lieut.
Keitzmann, C. — 3Feb.77

King William's Town Rifle Volunteers.
(King William's Town.)

Capt.
Hood, R. — 7Feb.80

Lieut.
Carroll, J. — 7Feb.80

2nd Lieuts.

Port Elizabeth Volunteer Rifles (Prince Alfred's Guard).
(Port Elizabeth.)

Major.
Deare, G. R. — 18May80

Capts.
O'Flaherty, C. R. — 1Nov.77
Gordon, G. — 10Nov.77
Wilmot, A. — 12Apr.78
Stewart, D. S. — 13Nov.78
Little, A. — 12May79
Thornton, H. R. — 9June80

Lieuts.
Tancred, A. F. — 12Apr.78
Birt, E. A. T. S. — 16Nov.78
Spence, M. H. — 13Nov.78
Thornton, J. M. — 9June80
Miles, W. H. — 24Aug.80
Slater, R. — 25Aug.80

2nd Lieuts.
O'Connor, J. — 5Jan.80
Back, W. J. — 9June80
Storey, J. G. — 8Sept.80
Purland, T. C. — 28Sept.80
Young, W. W. — 24Sept.80

Hon. Chapl. Wirgmann, Rev. A. T., M.A. — 30Nov.76

Sprigg's Own Border Rifle Volunteers.
(Aliwal North.)

Captains.

Lieuts.

2nd Lieut.
Knight, T. H. — 5June80

Surgeon.
Zeederberg, R. A. — 5June80

Stockenstrom Rifle Volunteers.
(Balfour.)

Capt.
Green, G. — 24June78

Lieuts.
Samuels, I. — 24June78

2nd Lieut.
Gibb, J. S. — 24June78

Stutterheim Light Infantry Volunteers.
(Stutterheim.)

Capt.
Belling, J. — 29Nov.79

Lieut.
Demmer, I. — 29Nov.79

2nd Lieut.
Hansel, A. — 29Nov.79

CADET CORPS.

Diocesan College Cadet Corps.
(Rondebosch.)

Capts.

1st Lieuts.

2nd Lieut.
Webb, C. D. — 1Feb.80

Cape of Good Hope *contd.*

Grahamstown Public School Cadet Corps.
(Grahamstown.)

Capt.
Templeton, R.   16July79

Lieut.
Walker, J. B.   30Sept.79

2nd Lieut.
Snell, A. L.   30Sept.79

Queenstown Cadet Corps.
(Queenstown.)

Capt.
Cathrine, W.   18Mar.80

Lieut.
Goosen, J.   15Oct.80

2nd Lieut.
Moorcroft, J.   15Oct.80

St. Andrew's College Cadet Corps.
(Grahamstown.)

Capt.
Ross, G. G.   12May79

Lieut.
Mathews, A.   12May79

2nd Lieut.
Rippon, S.   12May79

South African College Cadet Corps.
(Cape Town.)

Capt.
Buchanan, B. R.   2Feb.78

Lieut.
Bowern, A.   1Nov.79

2nd Lieut.
Jones, H.   11Nov.80

Stockenstrom Cadet Corps.
(Seymour.)

Capts.

Lieuts.

2nd Lieuts.

King Williamstown Cadet Corps.
(King Williamstown.)

Capts.

Lieut.
Dix, R.   22Nov.80

Gambia.
West Africa Settlements.
(*Corrected to 10th Feb. 1881.*)

COMBO MILITIA.

Col. Commandant.
The Officer administering the Government.

Capt.
Berkeley, Wm. H.   25Feb.75

Lieut.
Topp, James   14Mar.73

Qua. Mast. & Paym.

Malta.
(*Corrected to 21st Jan. 1881.*)

MILITIA.
Capt. Commandant.

Surgeons.
Cousin, G., *M.D.*
Sammut, E., *M.D.*

Great Harbour Company.

Lieuts.
Sant, F. S.

Adj. Ferro, H. C., *capt.*

Marsamuscetto Company.

Capt.
Olivier, P. Testaferrata.

Lieut.
Zimelli, H.

Ens.
Perret, G.

Floriana Company.

Capt.
Zammit, E.

Lieut.
Spiteri, P.

Ens.
Darmanin, G.

Vittoriosa Company.

Capt.
Pirotti, V.

Lieut.
Bonello, R.

Senglea Company.

Lieut.
Sammut, J.

Gozo Company.

Capt.
Pace, J.

Lieut.
Mallia, R.

Ens.
Monreal, G.

Natal.
(*Corrected to 12th March 1881.*)

Major Commandant Volunteer Force.

Dartnell, J. G., *late* 27 F.

Drill Instructor Volunteer Force.
Davey, N. E.   23Jan.74
   Capt. & Adj. 17Aug.77

Natal Carbineers.

Capt.
Shepstone, T.   16June70

Lieut.
Royston, W.   18Sept.78

2nd Lieut.
MacFarlane, G. J.   7Dec.80
Q.M.
Surg.

Victoria Mounted Rifles.

Capt.
Saner, Chas.   11May77

Lieut.

2nd Lieut.

Alexandra Mounted Rifles.

Capt.
Arbuthnot, W. T.   24Apr.70

Lieuts.
Cooke, W.   24Apr.70
Q.M. Kirkman, T.   22Mar.78

Natal Hussars.

Capt.
Meane, Theo.   16July80

1st Lieut.
Handley, T.   16July80

Adj.
Q.M. Taylor, F.   23Dec.80
Surg. Birtwell, Dr. D.   6Feb.77

Colonial Army List July-Aug 1881

Natal continued.
Durban Mounted Rifles.
Capt.
Shepstone, W. E. — 30 Oct.74
1st Lieut.
Voysey, W. — 16 Sept.80
2nd Lieut.
Addison, W. H. — 16 Sept.80
Q.M. Adams, S. — 15 June 78

Stanger Mounted Rifles.
Capt.
Addison, F. — 4 Nov.78
1st Lieut.
2nd Lieut.
Shuter, H. J. — 5 Dec.78
Q.M.
Surg. Jones, H. W. — 1 Apr.76

Durban Volunteer Artillery.
Capt.
M'Neil, A. — 19 Apr.76
1st Lieut.
Beddoes, G. — 7 Nov.77
2nd Lieut.
Benningfield, R. — 13 Jan.79
Q.M. Holmes, R. — 21 Dec.78

Maritzburg Rifles.
Capt.
Matterson, G. O. — 9 Apr.75
Lieut.
2nd Lieut.
Horsley, R. W. — 26 Nov.75
Q.M. Thring, A. Z. — 16 Feb.80
Surg.

Royal Durban Rifles.
Capt.
Flack, P. S. — 23 May 79
Lieut.
Nolan, J. D. — 16 Mar.76
2nd Lieut.
King, J. F. — 6 Jan.81
Surg. Schultz, J. — 4 Apr.78
Q.M. Woodroffe, W. S. — 6 Jan.81

New Germany Rifles.
Capt.
Freese, F. W. — 26 Aug.71
1st Lieut.
Hilmer, W. — 7 Oct.78
2nd Lieut.
Hilmer, A. — 7 Oct.78
Q.M. Böhmer, W. — 26 Aug.71

Quartermaster-Sergeant J.C Bullock, of the Natal Carbineers

Claiments to Zulu Medal

List of Claimants to Zulu War Medals for whom medals have not been received.
Minute paper dated 21.01.1884 reads:
To Commandant of Volunteers. A list is being prepared of those who have applied to the Natal Government for the S.A War Medal but for whom no medals have been received. Will you kindly look through the enclosed names and inform me if you can give me any information concerning them. You will see that in some cases it is not known in what Corps the applicants served. Can you add the names of #Lieut. Prendergast, Lonsdale's Horse and Lieut. Andrews Natal Native Pioneers. They both sent in applications through the D.A.G soon after the war, their medals have not been received.

No	Date	Name	Address	How disposed of:
4665	13.10.82	de Loval	Junction City U.S America	Name not included in list
4502	22.10.82	??? Neilson	Leeds, England	Medal forwarded
4419	14.10.82	James Hanrahan	Loxford, Ireland	Medal forwarded
3965	14.10.82	G. Eckersley	Victoria ???	Referred to WM Longlands
3723	30.07.82	?.? Highton	London	Medal forwarded
3380	28.07.82	H.Smyth	London	Medal forwarded
3127	12.07.82	M.M.Gandolfe	France	Medal forwarded
3726	07.07.82	T. Linelain?	Ireland	Medal forwarded
3008	28.06.82	M.H.White	England	Medal forwarded
?857	22.06.82	W.H.Smith	Crown Agents	Medal forwarded
2741	12.06.82	J.B. Gilroy?	Scotland	Medal forwarded
2040	25.05.82	James Orr	Winbuy	Referred to S of S for War
1138	10.02.82	W.H.Mumford	???	Referred to King Williamstown
368	26.01.82	A. Beaty	-	Transferred to Wm Longlands
310	01.01.82	W.T.Barrow	???	Informed that medals was not yet ???
302	01.01.82	H.Rock	Durban	Referral to ???? Commandant
211	01.01.82	H.S.Portal	Richmond	Referred to D.C.G
111	06.0182	C.F.Klein	-	Transferred to Longlands
2068	15.05.83	J.H.Macwaite	Bloemhof	Medal forwarded
1866	08.05.83	J Rodgers	Klopperfontein	Informed that Kaffrarian Rifles medals were not ??
1337	08.03.83	W Stapely	England	Medal forwarded
1147	28.01.83	C.E Corleton	??	Informed his name is not upon any list.
856	02.02.83	C.Chandler	??	Informed his name is not upon any list.
804	27.01.83	C.N.Barker	London	Informed his name is not upon any list.
573	12.02.83	? ? Paterson	-	Referred to H.M Commissioner
533	01.02.83	S.Herbert	Griqualand West	Medal forwarded
286	15.01.83	L Moore	-	Informed his name is not upon any list.
287	19.01.83	G.L Mathews	Orange Free State	Informed his name is not upon any list.
271	20.12.83	W.B.Prien	England	Informed his name is not upon any list
257	21,12.83	E.J.Howes	Cape Town	Informed Commisiriat Medals were not

A separate document has the following listed. James Orr - Lonsdale's Horse, W.H Mumford, W.B. Prien, & G.J Matthews - Frontier Light Horse. J Moore - 3/1 Nat.Native,Contingent. C.N.Barker -2nd Batt Nat Native Contingent. H.S.Portal - Dresser Field Hospital Col Durnford's Column. Stapely Trooper - Ferreira's Horse, and two names listed with a corps out C.E.Corleton & C.Chandler

---

Spinks Auction 19 Nov 2009 Lot 51, Four. Major A. Prendergast, Natal Police, Late Lonsdale's Horse
South Africa 1877-79, one clasp, 1879 (Lieut: A. Prendergast. Lonsdales. Horse); Cape of Good Hope General Service 1880-97, one clasp, Basutoland (Cpl. A. Prendergast. Nat. M. Pce), engraved in upright serif capitals; Queen's South Africa 1899-1902, one clasp, Natal (Inspector A. Prendergast. Natal Police.); Natal 1906, with clasp (Major A. Prendergast, Natal Police.), engraved in running script, generally very fine or better, with copied research giving insights into Prendergast's assignments with the Natal Police (4)
Hammer Price £2,200

Major Alfred Prendergast, J.P. (1855-1930); born Thurles, Ireland; served as Lieutenant Lonsdale's Horse during both the Zulu War; enlisted in the Natal Mounted Police, 10.8.1879, and served with them during the First Boer War, 1881; advanced Sergeant, 1883; Sub-Inspector 1894; Inspector 1897; advanced Major and J.P. for the Magistrate Division of Pietermaritzburg; he died residing in Eighth Avenue, Durban.

Provenance: Spink February 1982.

Imperial Troops Medal Summary

THE IMPERIAL and THE ROYAL NAVY	Page	W/M	1877	1877-8	1877-9	1877-8-9	1878	1878-9	1879	No Clasp	TOTAL
(W/M returned to Woolwich Mint)											
STAFF	190			3		8	1	4	27	5	48
AYR & WIGHTON MILITIA	190			1							1
EDINBURGH LIGHT INFANTRY MILITIA	190								1		1
QUEENS ROYAL ANTRIM RIFLES MILITIA	190								1		1
ROYAL ANGLESEY ENGINEER MILITIA	190								1		1
ROYAL EAST MIDDLESEX MILITIA	190								1		1
ROYAL GLAMORGAN MILITIA	190								2		2
ROYAL LANARK MILITIA	190								1		1
ROYAL LANCASHIRE MILITIA	190								1		1
TOWER HAMLETS MILITIA	190								1	1	2
WEST CORK MILITIA	190								1		1
WEST KENT MILITIA	190								1		1
WEST YORK YEOMANRY	190								1		1
4th HUSSARS	193								2		2
7th HUSSARS	193								5		5
9th HUSSARS	193								2		2
13th HUSSARS	193								1		1
14th HUSSARS	193								3		3
19th HUSSARS	193								2		2
20th HUSSARS	193								1		1
21st HUSSARS	193								1	1	2
COLDSTREAM GUARDS	193								5		5
DRAGOON GUARDS 2nd	193								9		9
DRAGOON GUARDS 3rd	193								2		2
DRAGOON GUARDS 4th	193								2		2
DRAGOON GUARDS 6th	193								1		1
GRENADIER GUARDS	193								16		16
1st KINGS DRAGOON GUARDS	194	6							641	78	719
LIFE GUARDS	199								4		4
SCOTS GUARDS	199					2			8		10
5th LANCERS	199								1		1
9th LANCERS	199								3		3
12th LANCERS	199								1	1	2
16th LANCERS	199							1	5		6
17th LANCERS	199	7							599	33	632
2/3rd REGIMENT	208	19						38	892	81	1011
2/4th REGIMENT	214	19							971	28	999
1/7th REGIMENT	222								3		3
8th REGIMENT	222								1		1
1/9th REGIMENT	222									1	1
2/10th REGIMENT	222								1		1
1/11th REGIMENT	222									1	1
1/13th REGIMENT	222	15					38	688	81	226	1033

Imperial Troops Medal Summary

	Page	W/M	1877	1877-8	1877-9	1877-8-9	1878	1878-9	1879	No Clasp	TOTAL
1/16th REGIMENT	229									1	1
1/18th REGIMENT	229								1		1
1/19th REGIMENT	229								1		1
2/21st REGIMENT	229	16							862	153	1015
22nd REGIMENT	236					1			1		2
23rd REGIMENT	236								1		1
1/24th REGIMENT	236	28		157		526	1	24	663	33	1404
2/24th REGIMENT	253	23		55		823			163	290	1331
1/26th REGIMENT	265							1			1
2/26th REGIMENT	265								2		2
27th REGIMENT	265								1		1
29th REGIMENT	265								3		3
30th REGIMENT	265								1		1
31st REGIMENT	265								3	1	4
32nd REGIMENT	265								4		4
33rd REGIMENT	267								1		1
35th REGIMENT	267								1	1	2
38th REGIMENT	267									2	2
39th REGIMENT	267								1		1
41st REGIMENT	267									2	2
45th REGIMENT	267								1		1
47th REGIMENT	267								1		1
49th REGIMENT	267								2		2
52nd REGIMENT	267								3	2	5
53rd REGIMENT	267								2		2
54th REGIMENT	267					1					1
56th REGIMENT	267								1		1
57th REGIMENT	267	44							1034	141	1175
58th REGIMENT	276	62							689	345	1034
60th REGIMENT	284								4		4
3/60th REGIMENT	284	65				1		1	1024	38	1064
61st REGIMENT	291								1		1
70th REGIMENT	291			1							1
71st REGIMENT	291							1	1		2
75th REGIMENT	291								2		2
77th REGIMENT	292								3	1	4
80th REGIMENT	292	7					294	626	198	121	1239
82nd REGIMENT	302								2		2
87th REGIMENT	302								1		1
88th REGIMENT	302	110		252		400			387	35	1074
90th REGIMENT	311	51		72		556	1		388	55	1072
91s REGIMENT	321	41							954	85	1039
93rd REGIMENT	328								2		2
94th REGIMENT	328	80							948	44	992

Imperial Troops Medal Summary

	Page	W/M	1877	1877-8	1877-9	1877-8-9	1878	1878-9	1879	No Clasp	TOTAL
95th REGIMENT	336					1			1		2
98th REGIMENT	336								1		1
99th REGIMENT	336	30							903	31	934
103rd REGIMENT	344								2		2
104th REGIMENT	344					1			1		2
107th REGIMENT	344								1	1	2
108th REGIMENT	344									1	1
109th REGIMENT	344								1		1
RIFLE BRIGADE	344								1	1	2
WEST INDIA REGIMENT	344								1		1
ARMY HOSPITAL CORPS	344	24		11		9	1		249	197	467
ARMY MEDICAL DEPARTMENT	347	3	2	11		4	17	16	78	65	193
ARMY PAY DEPARTMENT	349			8		6			10	16	40
ARMY SERVICE CORPS. COMMISSARIAT	349	4	1	5	1	5	1	1	83	71	168
ARMY SERVICE CORPS. ORDINANCE	350						1	1	36	116	154
ARMY ORDINANCE STORE DEPARTMENT	351			7					23	14	44
ARMY SERVICE CORPS.TRANSPORT	352	6		4		1		1	495	146	647
ARMY VETERINARY CORPS	357							1	14	1	16
CHAPLAINS	357								9	5	14
COMMISSARIAT & TRANSPORT STAFF	357	8		14		9		1	100	37	161
ROYAL ARTILLERY STAFF	358			1					11		12
R.A 2nd BRIGADE L BATTERY	358								1		1
R.A 2nd BRIGADE O BATTERY	358					1			1		2
R.A 4th BRIGADE N BATTERY	358									2	2
R.A 5th BRIGADE B BATTERY	358								1		1
R.A 5th BRIGADE DEPOT BATTERY	358			1					1		2
R.A 5th BRIGADE N BATTERY	359	6		11		124			132	6	273
R.A 6th BRIGADE M BATTERY	361	5							174	2	176
R.A 6th BRIGADE N BATTERY	363	4							173	7	180
R.A 6th BRIGADE O BATTERY	364	2							160	1	161
R.A 7th BRIGADE	365					1					1
R.A 7th BRIGADE 8 BATTERY	365	3		23		12			54	2	91
R.A 7th BRIGADE 10 BATTERY	365	1							60	3	63
R.A 7th BRIGADE 11 BATTERY	366	4		7		40		13	99	11	170
R.A 11th BRIGADE 12 BATTERY	367								1		1
ROYAL ARTILLERY REGIMENT	367					1	2			1	4
ROYAL HORSE ARTILLERY	367								5		5
ROYAL ENGINEERS	367			2		1			12	6	21
ROYAL ENGINEERS C TROOP	367	2							134	43	177
ROYAL ENGINEERS 2nd COMPANY	369	3							141	36	177
ROYAL ENGINEERS 5th COMPANY	370	9							100	39	139
ROYAL ENGINEERS 7th COMPANY	371			28		2		1	14	1	46
ROYAL ENGINEERS 30th COMPANY	371	4							206	6	212

Imperial Troops Medal Summary

	Page	W/M	1877	1877-8	1877-9	1877-8-9	1878	1878-9	1879	No Clasp	TOTAL
ROYAL NAVY	373								1		1
ROYAL NAVY HMS ACTIVE	373			65		108			53	183	409
ROYAL NAVY HMS BODICEA	376			1		3			223	249	476
ROYAL NAVY HMS EUPHRATES	380									261	261
ROYAL NAVY HMS FORESTER	382								76		76
ROYAL NAVY HMS HIMALAYA	383									229	229
ROYAL NAVY HMS ORONTES	385									226	226
ROYAL NAVY HMS SHAH	386	1							394	311	705
ROYAL NAVY HMS TAMAR	393									216	216
ROYAL NAVY HMS TENEDOS	395								57	139	196
		712	3	740	1	2647	357	1421	14952	4486	24607
TOTAL CLASPS AND MEDALS RETRUNED											
TO WOOLWICH/MINT		712									

The Times of February 1879
Woolwich, Feb 18,(The Times, Thursday, Feb 20, 1879)
To the Editor of the Times.
Sir,-I see that officers now proceeding to the Cape have to purchase revolvers from the gunsmiths. Let me urge on them to select the largest bore that is made. All who have had any experience of the race they are going to meet will agree that a Caffre or a Zulu will carry away a lot of lead, and that a too small bore is simply useless. It is not a bad plan to carry a spare cylinder already loaded.
Your obedient servant,
Edwin Litchfield, Assistant Commissary General.

To the Editor of the Times.(The Times, Wednesday, Feb 19, 1879)
Sir, ...The Zulus have no cavalry, and in my time the guns they purchased from traders were more likely to injure themselves than their enemies. They are, however good shots at short ranges, and very expert with their assegais. If they can be lured into open land (and there is plenty between the Tugela and the Inghowie range), I think a charge of cavalry will have a beneficial effect, and perhaps settle the war. The Zulu is perfectly indifferent to pain or death, but is easily panic struck, and as he knows nothing of cavalry warfare, I hope he will be agreeably surprised.
Cetywayo used to be so fat that he could scarcely walk.
Your obediently, S.H.Harford,
late Captain Cape Mounted Riflemen.
Stapleton, near Bristol, Feb 17.

To the Editor of the Times.(The Times, Wednesday, Feb 19, 1879)
Sir,- "Everybody" has been talking for the last few days of the selection of the two cavalry regiments told off for service in South Africa. It is due to the Horse Guards to say that in this, as in other cases, they have avoided selection. The King's Dragoon Guards and the 1/th Lancers are sent to reinforce Lord Chelmsford simply and solely from the fact that they are the "next on the roster" for foreign service- in other words, they are the two corps that have been longest home from India. Both regiments are what is called the "medium" class-that is to say, something as regards size and weight between our heaviest and so-called light Cavalry, but with a distinct inclination towards the former. Those who are well acquainted with Cape warfare say that this class of horse-soldier is but ill-suited to the work to be done, which combines much outpost duty and that kind of fighting that might be most advantageously carried out by "Mounted Infantry - i.e troops who, getting about rapidly on horseback so as to outstrip our active Zulu enemies, would dismount and pepper them well with the carbine.......The only official information before the public tends to show that the King's Dragoon Guards have fallen off within the last few years from their former fair standard. Crime and discontent have certainly increased. The court-martial in the regiment, which were 25 in 1874 and 43 in 1875, rose to 76 in 1876, and in 1877 to 167, a number more than double that of any other cavalry regiment; while the desertions, which were 20 in 1874 and 17 in 1875, became 66 in 1876 and 7e in 1877. The number of trials for desertion in the last year is given as 114. To show how exceptional was the state of things, I may quote the return before me for 1877 of the two regiments standing next in order. Thus, while the King's Dragoon Guards had 167 court-martial and 75 desertions, the 2nd Dragoon Guards (Queen's Bays) had 26 court-martial and 10 desertions, and the 3rd Dragoon Guards 18 court-martial and 13 desertions.
Your obedient servant, X

Staff

STAFF.
COMMANDING OFFICER GENERAL
Wolsely Sir G.L 1879
GCMG KCB
GENERAL
Cunynhame Sir A 1877-8
GCB
Also had China Medal (1841) and British and Turkish Crimea Medals.
MAJOR GENERAL
Chelmsford Lord 1877-8-9
GCB
Clifford Sir H.H 1878
VC KCMG CB
His VC was for an action in the Crimea.
Crealock H.H 1879
CB CMG
Also had medal and clasp for Indian Mutiny.
Marshall F 1879
CMG
Also had British and Turkish Crimea Medals.
Newdigate E 1879
CB
BRIGADIER GENERAL
Wood Sir H.E 1877-8-9
VC KCB
His VC was for an action during the Indian Mutiny. He also had Indian Mutiny and Ashanti War (1873-4) Medals.
COLONEL
Bellairs W 1877-8
CB
Colley Sir G.P 1879
KCSI CB CMG
Also Medal and two clasp for China 1860 and Medal and Clasp Ashanti 1873-4.
Jarvis S.P 1877-8-9
CMG
Pearson Sir C.K 1879
KCMG CB
Rowlands H 1878-9
VC CB
His VC was for an action at Inkerman. Also had British and Turkish Crimea Medals.
LIEUTENANT COLONEL
East C.J 1879
Lonsdale Hale A 1879
BREVET LIEUTENANT COLONEL
Brackenbury H 1879
CB
MAJOR
Butler W.F No clasp
CB
Medal from an earlier War Ashanti.

Clery C.F 1878-9
Wood Hon H.J.L 1879
Ashanti War Medal with clasp Coomassie.
BREVET MAJOR
Poole J.R 1879
INTELLIGENCE OFFICER
Drummond Hon W 1877-8-9
KIA Ulundi
GARRISON SERGEANT MAJOR
Healey T 1877-8-9
COLOUR SERGEANT
Dixon G 1879
Hewerdine G.J.F 1879
Holdgate H No clasp
Keane M.C 1879
KIA Isandhlwana
Mabin G.W 1878-9
Pierson F 1879
Pilcher F.W 1879
Scrivenor H 1878-9
Whiley T.R 1877-8
Wood S 1878
D/S
MILITARY STAFF CLERK
Peacock J.T No clasp
STAFF CLERK
Cooper J No clasp
SUPERINTENDENT CLERK
Newman H 1877-8-9
NO RANK STATED
Dawnay Hon 1879
Russell W.H 1879
LLD
PRIVATE SECRETARY
Herbert St L 1879
GENERAL MANAGER TELEGRAPHS
Sievewright J 1877-8-9
CMG
TELEGRAPH ENGINEERING SUPERINTENDENT
Bayly B 1879
INTERPRETER 1st CLASS
Doyle F 1879
INTERPRETER
Langrest Newby 1879
Lloyd (Mr) L 1879
Roberts (Mr) I 1879
GUIDE
De Haas H.W 1879
REMOUNT DEPARTMENT
Garnett (Mr) G No clasp
CIVILIAN SERVANT
Fricke C 1879
Pearce W 1877-8-9

AYR AND WIGHTON MILITIA.
LIEUTENANT
Dalrymple W.R.E 1877-8

EDINBURGH LIGHT INFANTRY MILITIA.
CAPTAIN
Robertson D.S 1879
Attached 2/21st Regt.

QUEENS ROYAL ANTRIM RIFLES MILITIA.
CAPTAIN
Preston J 1879

ROYAL ANGLESEY ENGINEER MILITIA.
LIEUTENANT
York V.S 1879

ROYAL EAST MIDDLESEX MILITIA
LIEUTENANT
Rushbrook E.R 1879

ROYAL GLAMORGAN MILITIA.
CAPTAIN
Kemys-Tynte? A.M.P 1879
LIEUTENANT
Kemys-Tynte? E.P 1879

ROYAL LANARK MILITIA 2ND
2nd LIEUTENANT
Lumsden D.M 1879

ROYAL LANCASHIRE MILITIA 3RD
LIEUTENANT
Higgins H 1879
attached 2/21st Regt.

TOWER HAMLETS MILITIA.
LIEUTENANT
Fox The Hon. S.L No clasp
#Terry G.K 1879

WEST CORK MILITIA.
CAPTAIN
Cade C.S 1879

WEST KENT MILITIA.
CAPTAIN
Cropper T 1879

WEST YORK YEOMANRY. 1st
LIEUTENANT
Beaumont Lord H.G 1879
Attached to 17th Lancers.

Glendining & Co Auction 18th March 1981, South Africa 1877-9. Clasp 1879, (Lieut G.K.Terry, 2/Tower Hamlet Mil) An offical late issue or replacement. Brilliant extremely fine. Two 1879 clasps issued to Tower Hamlets Militia. Was attached to the 80th Foot at Ulundi.

GENERAL THESIGER AND HIS STAFF
From left to right: North Crealoch, Molyneux, Evelyn Wood, Thesiger, Redvers Buller, Mat Gossett

GROUP OF OFFICERS AND CIVIL SERVANTS AT KING WILLIAM'S TOWN
Back row standing, from left to right: Much, 1/24th; Rainforth, 1/24th; •White, 1/24th; Hillier; Parr; •Pullen, 1/24th; •Porteous, 1/24th; •Pulleine, 1/24th; •Hodson, 1/24th; Walker; Sivewright; •Atkinson, 1/24th; •Wardell, 1/24th
Sitting, from left to right: •Daly, 1/24th; C. Brownlee; Sir Bartle Frere; Sir A. Cuninghame; Glyn, 1/24th; J. X. Merriman
Sitting on ground: Coghill; Littleton
• Killed at Isandlana.

Redvers Buller

Evelyn Wood

Hugh Rudolph Gough

Lord Chelmsford

4th Hussars

4TH (THE QUEENS OWN) HUSSARS.
CAPTAIN
Lawrell　　　　W.G　　1879
　KIA Sekukini's Stronghold 28/11/1879.
PRIVATE
1311 Hayes　　T　　1879

7TH (THE QUEENS OWN) HUSSARS.
CAPTAIN
Mc Calmont　　H　　1879
　Also had Ashanti Medal
　See also Capt Mc Calmont 9th Hussars.
LIEUTENANT
#Byng Hon　　A.J.G　　1879
Jervis Hon　　J.E.L　　1879
St Vincent Lord　　J.E.L　　1879
　Attached 17th Lancers.
PRIVATE
1137 Lees　　W　　1879

9TH HUSSARS. (QUEENS ROYAL LANCERS).
BREVET MAJOR
Mc Calmont　　H　　1879
　See also Capt Mc Calmont 7th Hussars.
PRIVATE
1043 Barford　　H　　1879

13TH HUSSARS.
MAJOR
Baker Russell Sir　　　　1879
　KCMG CB

14TH (THE KINGS) HUSSARS.
MAJOR
Russell　　F.S　　1879
　Also had Ashanti Medal.
CAPTAIN
Gardner　　A.C　　1879
See also Commissiariat & Transport Staff
PRIVATE
1606 Simmonds　　C　　1879

19TH HUSSARS.
CAPTAIN
Barrow CMG　　P.H.S　　1879
SERGEANT
Anderson　　F　　1879

20TH HUSSARS.
LIEUTENANT
Courtenay　　E.R　　1879

21st HUSSARS.
LIEUTENANT
Wyndham　　W.G.C　　1879
FARRIER
1840 Quick　　C　　1878-9
　See also Frontier Light Horse.

2ND BATTALION COLDSTREAM GUARDS.
CAPTAIN
Barton Hon　　R　　1879
　KIA Inhlobane.
Bertie Hon　　G.A.V　　1879
Campbell Hon　　R.C.E　　1879
　KIA Inhlobane
SERGEANT
2941 Johnson　　W　　1879
PRIVATE
3696 Gunning　　H　　1879

2ND DRAGOON GUARDS (QUEEN'S BAYS).
CAPTAIN
Doyle　　F　　1879
LIEUTENANT ADJUTANT
Hippisley　　W.H　　1879
James　　W.C　　1879
LIEUTENANT
Gould　　A.L.G　　1879
See also Commissariat &Transport Staff.
FARRIER
1533 Leader　　E　　1879
PRIVATE
1098 Cooper　　H　　1879
1185 Day　　J　　1879

2273 Forrest　　W.M　　1879
1065 Howard　　J　　1879
　See also Howard No. 2329 17th Lancers.

3RD DRAGOON GUARDS (PRINCE OF WALES'S).
CAPTAIN
Stewart　　H　　1879
PRIVATE
1251 Wood　　A　　1879

4TH DRAGOON GUARDS (ROYAL IRISH).
LIEUTENANT
Wilson　　B.R　　1879
PRIVATE
? Stone　　J　　1879

6TH DRAGOON GUARDS (CARABINEERS).
LIEUTENANT
Pennefather　　E.G　　1879

GRENADIER GUARDS.
COLONEL
Davies　　H.F　　1879
　Also had Baltic & Burma Medals.
LIEUTENANT COLONEL
Needham Hon　　G　　1879
Thynne　　R.T　　1879
Villiers Hon　　G　　1879
LIEUTENANT
Carrington Hon　　R.C.G　　1879
Colville Hon　　C.R.W　　1879
Farrar　　W.D.M.C.P　1879
SERGEANT
4509 Mc Feeters　　R　　1879
　356 Payne　　R　　1879
3054 Pemberton　　T　　1879
PRIVATE
3346 Clay　　D　　1879
4136 Mason　　J　　1879
　? Pauter　　G　　1879
4841 Shore　　J　　1879
4752 Taylor　　H　　1879
4834 Vaughan　　E　　1879

Guards Officers Memorial at the Royal Military Chapel, Wellington Barracks - Zulu War, 1879
Captain the Hon. **Ronald George Elidor Campbell,** Coldstream Guards, March 28th
Captain **Robert Johnston Barton,** Coldstream Guards, March 28th
Transvaal War, 1881
Lieut. **Robert Hamond Elwes,** Grenadier Guards, January 28th

---

Dix Noonan Web Auction Lot 761, 17 Sep 09
South Africa 1877-79, 1 clasp, 1879 (**Lieut: The Hon: A. J. G. Byng,** 7th Hussars) toned, nearly extremely fine and very rare.
Alfred John George Byng was born on 4 May 1851, the son of George Stevens Byng, 2nd Earl of Strafford, and Lady Agnes Paget, daughter of Field Marshal Sir Henry William Paget, 1st Marquess of Anglesey. Gazetted Cornet in the 7th Hussars, by purchase, on 30 October 1869, becoming Lieutenant by purchase in March 1871. Embarked with cavalry drafts in May 1879, served in Natal & Transvaal. He was promoted to Captain in July 1880 and subsequently served as A.D.C. to the Lord Lieutenant of Ireland. He married, 10 January 1887, Lady Winifred Herbert, daughter of the 4th Earl of Carnarvon, but died without issue on 8 November 1887. Hammer price £3300.

1st Dragoon Guards

1ST (THE KING'S) DRAGOON GUARDS.

COLONEL
Alexander H 1879
Also British & Turkish Crimea Medals. and China War 1860, with two clasps.

MAJOR
Marter R.J.C 1879

CAPTAIN
Becher C.A.G 1879
#Benthall J.M 1879
Brownlow W.V 1879
Dickson J.B.B 1879
Douglas-Willan H.P 1879
Gibbings A 1879
##Godson R.G 1879
Lawill W 1879
 KIA (4th Hussars attached).
Thompson W.H 1879
Watson H.J 1879

QUARTERMASTER
Murphy H 1879

LIEUTENANT ADJUTANT
Nicholas R.G 1879

LIEUTENANT
Alexander J 1879
Brewster R.A.F 1879
Burney H.A 1879
Dewar J.C 1879
Lowry R.T.G 1879
Marrow P 1879
Sadlier N.H.H 1879

SUB LIEUTENANT
Harkness W.H 1879

2nd LIEUTENANT
Goold-Adams W.R 1879
###Willett J.S No clasp
Wright E.L 1879

REGIMENTAL SERGEANT MAJOR
875 Lunny J 1879

BANDMASTER
1377 Orton W 1879

PAYMASTER SERGEANT MAJOR
999 Mc Knight J.T No clasp

ORDERLY ROOM SERGEANT MAJOR
819 Bland A.Y 1879

FARRIER MAJOR
685 Knight J 1879

TRUMPET MAJOR
522 Bratby W 1879

TROOP SERGEANT MAJOR
765 Adcock G 1879
837 Byrne J 1879
1502 Dawson G 1879
882 Guthrie R.T 1879
1096 Nix (?) C 1879
907 Pepperday H 1879
1073 Potter G 1879
1260 Pring W.B 1879
234 Tollington E 1879

ARMOURER SERGEANT
1025 Crawshaw S No clasp

QUARTERMASTER SERGEANT
826 Gomersall D/S G 1879

SADDLER SERGEANT
824 Bennett G.H 1879

SERGEANT
2276 Albon A No clasp
856 Baker W 1879
1146 Baker W 1879
832 Bragg H 1879
1239 Carrigan J 1879
2180 Cole A.G 1879
1287 Cooper A.G 1879
1502 Dawson G 1879
778 Etteridge H 1879
1152 Faithorn W 1879
994 Faulkner M 1879
1053 Flint W 1879
1276 Gillispie M 1879
2182 Gunn C 1879
1712 Horsfield T 1879
 No medal Deserted.
362 Hughes R 1879
1280 Ivory G.H 1879
2310 James J No clasp
 No medal tried for embezzlement and desertion.
2181 Mc Gill W 1879
2275 Morris J 1879
1672 Roper R 1879
1437 Shannon J 1879
 No medal Deserted.
1332 Smith R 1879
951 Smith W 1879
284 Snelson F 1879
2179 Tidswell J 1879
1044 Turnley W.H 1879
316 Venables C 1879
1221 Warwick T 1879
629 Williams J 1879

LANCE SERGEANT
1381 Jones A.E 1879
1274 Peacock J.J 1879

CORPORAL
1600 Bentley F 1879
1912 Bonds J 1879
412 Brampton J 1879
1885 Cass C 1879
1136 Daniels W 1879
1536 Drummond W.J 1879
2277 Friais J No clasp
1368 Goodson W 1879
1868 Gough J.A No clasp
1395 Hatton D/S E.C 1879
1331 Hawkes M.B 1879
1406 Herbert W 1879
699 Hickman F 1879
1320 Highnan C 1879
1618 Heodley J 1879
1384 Horace F 1879
1930 Jackson T 1879

Dixon's Gazette No32 Winter 2002. 1 clasp, 1879. Captain J.M. Benthall, 1st Dragoon Guards.
John Matthew Benthall was born at Upton, Torquay, on,6 August 1840. He became an articled clerk at Exeter before purchasing an ensigncy in the Military Train on 20 December 1859. He became Lieutenant, again by purchase, on 30 September 1860, and served with the 1st Battalion in Canada from December 1861 until July 1862. He exchanged into the 1st Dragoon Guards in July 1865, and because Captain by purchase, on 22 July 1868. Benthall served in Natal during the Zulu War of 1879 as Captain of "C Troop being stationed at Conference Hill until employed at the sick horse depot at Landman's Drift. He afterwards served with the regiment in India, becoming Major in July 1881 and Lieutenant-Colonel on 31 December 1884, on which date he retired He lived at his childhood home of Furzewell House, Torquay, and indulged in his hobby of collecting coins and Napoleonic medals. Sold with research. EF £1050.00

##Sotheby & Co auction 27th January 1971 Lot no 92.
South Africa, 1877, 1 bar 1879 (Captn. R.G. Godson, 1st Dragn. Gds.) one or two edge knocks but otherwise almost extremely fine and rare. Captain R.G Godson: "Served at Conference Hill until 25th August when, with his troop, he joined the detachment under Major Marter at Fort Newdigate,relieving Captain Thompson's troop." Godson, with a night patrol, discovered the hiding-place of the Zulu Chief,

Dix Noonan Web Auction Lot 758, 17 Sep 09
South Africa 1877-79, no clasp (2nd Lieut. J. S. Willett, 1st Dragn. Gds.) good very fine . Hammer price £460
With copied roll extracts and other research - listed as a Major in the King's Dragoon Guards 'Old Comrades Dinner of December 1932.

1st Dragoon Guards

Number	Name	Initial	Clasp
1818	Jamieson	W	1879
1465	Lomax	E	1879
1754	Lovett	L	1879
995	Lunny	E	1879
1760	Martin	H	1879
1708	Mills	G	1879
1753	Percival	W	1879
1791	Percy	W	1879
2098	Prisso	J.W	1879
1566	Reid	W	1879
794	Rickman	F	1879
2123	Slack	G	1879
1650	Stone	R	No clasp
1747	Sully	C	1879
1492	Temperley	C	1879

LANCE CORPORAL

Number	Name	Initial	Clasp
2137	Aitken	E.M	1879
2229	Barry	J	1879
2238	Birch	T	1879
2158	Bird	H	1879
1951	Cope	S	No clasp
1822	Cox	J	1879
1289	Evans	R	No clasp
2233	Fawkes	R	1879
1857	Frost	J	1879
2141	Gamble	N	1879
2301	Gough	W.P	No clasp
2093	Grocock	C	1879
1251	Gwillian	J	No clasp
1682	Gyles	J	1879
1900	Howson	W	1879
	No Medal Deserted.		
1663	Joyce	J	1879
2191	Leppard	J	1879
2171	Lush	A	1879
2097	Mortimer	W	1879
1116	Munday	W	1879
690	Painter	W	1879
2200	Pentin ?	A	1879
1436	Pierce	P	1879
2210	Pink	W	1879
2153	Whitehead	S	1879
2292	Williams	G.H	No clasp
960	Wood	G	1879

FARRIER

Number	Name	Initial	Clasp
975	Boylan	M	1879
926	Dancaster	W	1879
1001	Davies	H	1879
1463	Dorricott	J	1879
1357	Hancock	A	1879
1470	Kirby	T	1879
1532	Mc Glinchy ?	C	1879
974	Smeaton	J	1879

SADDLER

Number	Name	Initial	Clasp
1770	Bickerstaff	T	1879
2244	Gillingham	F	1879
618	Johnson	G	1879
830	Spencer	T	1879

SADDLE TREE MAKER

Number	Name	Initial	Clasp
2245	Brown	S	1879
1115	Cutler	C	1879

SHOEING SMITH

Number	Name	Initial	Clasp
2279	Bell	J	No clasp
1061	Carvell	J	1879
1652	Craig	S	1879
1329	Hewitt	G	1879
1270	Little	C	1879
1743	Lomas	J	1879
1063	Osborne	A	1879
1133	Poole D/S	W	1879
2309	Slater	J	No clasp
2147	Standbridge	C	1879
1156	Steanes	T	1879
	No Medal Deserted.		

TRUMPETER

Number	Name	Initial	Clasp
1420	Hayes	W	1879
	No Medal Deserted.		
894	Kearney	W	1879
937	Keys	C	1879
1177	Mallison	A	1879
1273	O'Sullivan	H	1879
941	Sinnett ?	H	1879
1185	Smythe	J.C	1879
1026	Reynolds	G	1879

PRIVATE

Number	Name	Initial	Clasp
2312	Adcock	G.H	No clasp
	No Medal Deserted.		
2165	Alderton	J	1879
1167	Alexander	J	1879
1263	Allen	A	1879
1687	Allen D/S	E	1879
2010	Allen	W	1879
1669	Almond	E	1879
1068	Anderton	W	1879
1729	Asher	G	1879
2136	Ashton	H	1879
2138	Askew	A	1879
1604	Aston	G	1879
1889	Atkins	S	1879
2072	Austin	C	1879
1524	Austin	W	1879
2073	Bagot	J	1879
1635	Bailey	P	1879
2209	Baines	J.T	1879
1918	Baines	W	1879
2079	Baker	A	1879
1861	Baker	E	1879
837	Baker	E	1879
2313	Balcombe	J	No clasp
1958	Balderson	W	No clasp
1964	Bambrick	R	No clasp
1269	Banks	L	1879
582	Barlow	J	1879
2075	Barger	H	1879
2280	Barker	J.E	No clasp
2074	Barker	W	1879
2317	Barrett	E	No clasp
	No Medal Deserted.		
1763	Barratt	T	1879
	No Medal Deserted		
1965	Barrington	P	No clasp
1535	Bass	B	1879
1570	Bates	W	1879
1455	Baxter	J	1879
893	Bedser	W	1879
1639	Beley	A	1879
1752	Bell D/S	J	No clasp
1910	Bell D/S	J	No clasp
2279	Bell	J	No clasp
1330	Bennett	J	1879
2295	Benson	W	No clasp
	No Medal Deserted.		
2076	Bergen	F	1879
2228	Berry	F	1879
1558	Berry	W	1879
1577	Bevan	R	1879
1583	Bickerstaff	W	1879
1091	Birchall	J	1879
1838	Bishop	F	1879
1504	Blackie	W	1879
984	Blake	J.T	1879
2139	Blencce	J	1879
1496	Bobbitt	A	1879
1765	Boggis	H	1879
1213	Bolingbroke	H	1879
	No Medal Deserted		
2294	Bolton	F	No clasp
	No Medal Deserted.		
1742	Bradbury	E	1879
1798	Bradley	P	1879
1767	Bradshaw	J	1879
2315	Brannen	W	No clasp
1444	Branson	E	1879
2077	Breach	W	1879
1736	Brindley	G	No clasp
2126	Briddon	J	1879
1432	Brine	P	1879
	No Medal Deserted.		
2154	Bristowe	A	1879
1298	Brooks	C	1879
2166	Brooks D/S	F	1879
2078	Brown	D	1879
1735	Brown	E	1879
2297	Brown	G	No clasp
	No Medal Deserted.		
2296	Brown	M	No clasp
	No Medal Deserted.		
1229	Brunskill	H	1879
1761	Buckland	G	1879
1247	Buckley	T	1879
1823	Bulmer	C	1879
2298	Butler	S	No clasp
1037	Butterworth	J	1879
1314	Byrne	E	1879

1st Dragoon Guards

Number	Name	Initial	Year/Note
1308	Bryne	E	1879
2079	Byrne	E	1879
1438	Byrne	M	1879
2159	Callaghan	M	1879
2167	Callingham	E	1879
2280	Calton	A	No claps
2190	Calvert	C	1879
1809	Campbell	T	1879
1629	Candelin	J	1879
1923	Carroll	H	1879
2028	Carter	A	1879
2100	Carter	J	1879
	No Medal Deserted.		
1556	Carter D/S	J	1879
2239	Carter	S	1879
1283	Carter	T	1879
1764	Casey	T	1879
1674	Chambers	R	1879
	No Medal Deserted.		
2102	Cheeseman	J	1879
2080	Cheeseman	T	1879
2240	Chester	G	1879
1565	Chisholm	D	1879
1997	Chirell	J	No clasp
	No Medal Deserted.		
474	Churchill	T	1879
2101	Clark	W	1879
1202	Clay	W	1879
	No Medal Deserted.		
	Convicted of Disgraceful conduct.		
335	Clegg	A	1879
1175	Clifton	W	1879
1015	Coles	G	1879
2201	Colgate	H	1879
	No Medal Deserted.		
1180	Collins	C	1879
1255	Collins	W	1879
1863	Concanning	M	1879
2204	Condom	J	1879
	No Medal Deserted.		
2220	Connor	J	1879
2104	Conway	T	1879
	No Medal Deserted.		
2208	Cook	C	1879
2282	Cook	C	No clasp
	No Medal Discharged with ignominy.		
2112	Cook	T	1879
2140	Cook	W	1879
888	Cook	W.H	1879
866	Cooksley	W	1879
317	Cooper	W	1879
1201	Corbitt	W	1879
2219	Cronin	T	1879
2103	Cornish	J	1879
1709	Corthorn	J	1879
1043	Couch	H	1879
2202	Crayford	H	1879
1902	Crew	G	1879
	No medal Deserted.		
1839	Crompton	G	1879
2219	Cronin	T	1879
	No Medal Deserted and rejoined.		
2081	Crossley	A	1879
2111	Croucher	H	1879
1707	Crowder	W	1879
1085	Crow	W	1879
#2190	Crowter	H	1879
1397	Cuming	C.E	1879
1903	Curnock	C	1879
	No Medal Discharged with ignominy.		
1966	Curran	H	No clasp
2283	Curtis	W	No clasp
1172	Daltrey	H	1879
2241	Dann	T	1879
1345	Deacon	J	1879
1158	Dean	J	1879
1472	Death	A	1879
	No Medal Deserted.		
1637	Denning	J	1879
	No Medal Deserted.		
553	Densin	J	1879
2311	Devlin D/S	J	No clasp
2125	Devonshire	J	1879
2196	Dewbury	W	1879
	No Medal Deserted and rejoined.		
2300	Dickenson	J	No clasp
	No Medal Deserted,		
1310	Dicker	J	1879
1749	Dickson	R	1879
2163	Dillon	T	1879
2232	Dobson	F	1879
1654	Dodds	R	1879
1401	Doogan	J	1879
1129	Dorrington	T	1879
2134	Dovey	A	1879
2212	Dovey	F	1879
1859	Doyle	A	1879
2091	Drew	A	1879
2092	Drew	C	1879
1513	Duffy	W	1879
1843	Duffy	W.J	1879
1847	Dunlop	T	1879
1649	Dunn	A	1879
1952	Dunn	D	1879
1943	Dunn	J	1879
	No Medal Deserted.		
1661	Dunn	T	1879
1567	Eastey	P	1879
	No Medal Deserted.		
1521	Edwards	A	1879
	No Medal Deserted.		
1520	Edwards	F.W	1879
1253	Edwards	G	1879
2168	Edwards	J	1879
	No Medal Deserted		
1975	Egan	J.T	1879
2157	Elliott	W	1879
1347	Ellis	B	1879
1503	Emery	J	1879
1034	Etheridge	R	1879
2284	Evenore	C	No clasp
	No Medal Discharged with ignominy.		
2087	Fancourt	W	1879
	No Medal Deserted.		
2083	Farrar	J	1879
2082	Farrell	J	1879
	No Medal Deserted.		
2161	Fawthrop	J	1879
	No Medal Deserted.		
2285	Fenn	R	1879
	No Medal Deserted.		
1670	Ferguson	J	1879
2105	Field	W.H	1879
2169	Fielding	P	1879 r
2126	Finch	G	1879
2247	Finlay	J	1879
1387	Fitzgerald	T	1879
	No Medal Deserted.		
1548	Fitzmaurice	G	1879
2316	Fleming	W	No clasp
1449	Flynn	E	1879
1978	Forrington	J	No clasp
	No Medal Deserted.		
1642	Fraser	J	1879
1551	Fraser	W	1879
1408	Freeman	F	1879
1616	Freeman	F	1879
2113	French	W	1879
1897	Fumallon	D	1879
1507	Gaffey	W	1879
2248	Gaffney	J	1879
885	Gall	W	1879
2144	Gardner	J	1879
1552	Garratt	J	1879
1856	Geo	C	1879
	No Medal Deserted.		
1584	George	T	1879
2213	Geere	G	1879
2106	Gibbs	R	1879
2089	Gilbert	J	1879
1622	Glazebrook	F	1879
1888	Gleave	F	1879
1319	Goldsworthy	J	1879
2286	Goodchild	C	No clasp

Dixons on line Sales List November 2009 http://www.dixonsmedals.co.uk/
South Africa Medal 1877-1879, 1 clasp, 1879. 2190 Private H. Crowter, 1st Dragoon Guards Cost £580.00
Sold with photocopy roll page confirming clasp entitlement.

1st Dragoon Guards

No.	Name	Initial	Year
1638	Gordon	J.H	1879
	No Medal Deserted.		
2096	Grace	E	1879
1807	Grady	J	1879
1354	Grant	J	1879
280	Greaves	G	1879
2320	Griffin	H	No clasp r
2249	Grundy	G	1879
1646	Gunyon	W	1879
	No Medal Deserted.		
1788	Hackin	J	No clasp
2278	Hall	A	1879
2253	Hall	E	1879
2250	Hall	J	No clasp
1675	Hanafin	J	1879
1429	Hanlon	J	1879
1473	Hardy	G	1879
1914	Harrison	A	1879
1614	Harrison	J	1879
1741	Hayman	A	1879
2068	Haystaff	W	1879
2142	Head	C	1879
2252	Heath	W	No clasp
1431	Heathcote	C	1879
1435	Heinsen	C	1879
1040	Hemms	A	1879
2253	Hemes	A	1879
2107	Hemsley	S	1879
798	Hennessey	P	1879
1093	Heppel	J	1879
2114	Heppelstone	J	1879
	No Medal Deserted.		
1074	Heyes	J	1879
	No Medal Deserted,		
1095	Hicks	W	1879
1294	Higgins	M	No clasp
2085	Hills D/S	A	1879
1831	Hills	A	1879
1908	Hill	R	1879
2095	Hillier	W	1879
2287	Hobbs	A	No clasp
1769	Hofland	G	1879
1269	Holdsworth	W	1879 r
1893	Hollingsworth	W	1879
	No Medal Deserted.		
2314	Holmes	G.H	No clasp
542	Holt	T	1879
2230	Howard	H	1879
1571	Howden	A	1879
1195	Howell	H	1879
1016	Hudson	E	1879
2302	Hughes	T	No clasp
2231	Humphrey	E	1879
1485	Hutchinson	J	1879
1493	Hutchinson	J	1879
2164	Ingham	G	1879
2242	Jackson	C	1879
2108	Jackson	W	1879
	No Medal Deserted.		
1534	James	C	1879
2111	James	E	1879
1460	Jarmain	T	1879
	No Medal Deserted.		
2326	Jarvis	R	No clasp
1780	Jessop	A	1879
2194	Johnson	C	1879
329	Jones	C	1879
1886	Jones	E	1879
1704	Jones	J	1879
2094	Jones	J	1879
1499	Jones	J.E	1879
290	Jones	T	1879
2143	Jones	W	1879
	No Medal Deserted.		
1117	Jordan	J	1879
2205	Joyce	T	1879
1479	Keefe	M	1879
1645	Keith	R	1879
1590	Kelly	P	1879
2115	Kelly	W	1879
2254	Kelsey	H	1879
1877	Kelso	J	1879
	No Medal Deserted.		
2303	Kenny	G	No clasp
2322	Kenny	J	No clasp
867	Kerr	J	1879
2162	Kindlin	J	1879
1142	King	H	1879
2116	King	J	1879 r
2114	King	T	1879 r
1722	Kirkwood	W	1879
	No Medal Deserted.		
1318	Kitchenman	W	1879
828	Knight	R	1879
2304	Laming	W	No clasp
1187	Lane	F	1879
1669	Latham	H	1879
2255	Laundry	C	1879
1647	Laurie	A	1879
2256	Lavery	S	1879
2118	Lawless	W	1879
2288	Lee	W	No clasp
1906	Leeson	W	1879
1819	Lever	C	1879
848	Lewington	H	1879
2234	Lewis	P	1879
1785	Littleboy D/S	H	1879
2117	Littler	J	1879
2170	Lockwood	B	1879
1439	Long	W	1879
1598	Loosemore	E	1879
1352	Lowing	J	1879
858	Lunn	J	1879
955	Lush	H	1879
1563	Lynch	C	1879
1762	Lynn	G	1879
2216	Mahon	T	1879
	No Medal Deserted.		
2197	Makepeace	R	1879
2151	Makin	T	1879
2257	Malloy	B	1879
1140	Mangan	J	1879
2172	Marchant	C	1879
2318	Marriott	G	No clasp
2258	Marshall	W	1879
2206	Martin	E	1879
1811	Martin	J	1879
2088	Mate	P	1879
1781	Maunder	W	1879
1529	Matthews	W.R	1879
2260	Mc Alearey	J	1879
1237	Mc Carthy	E	1879
1358	Mc Causland	S	1879
2173	Mc Coy	J	1879
	No Medal Deserted.		
2261	Mc Cutcheon	W	1879 r
2262	Mc Donald	R	1879
2184	Mc Donald	W	1879
2187	Mc Dowell	W	1879
1169	Mc Elroy	C	1879
2156	Mc Gibney	J	1879
2263	Mc Guinness	M	1879
2327	Mc Intyre	S	No clasp
1051	Mc Kay	G	1879
1994	Mc Kenna	J	No clasp
2244	Mc Kenzie	W	1879
1340	Mc Lean	J	1879
2215	Mc Pheley	E	1879
2145	Mc Shea	W	1879
1542	Medhurst	R	1879
1090	Mee	H	1879
1242	Metcalf	H	1879
2306	Micklebore	H	No clasp
1899	Middleton	H	1879
2188	Millar	W	1879
1494	Millfield	A	1879
838	Mimmick	W	1879
2235	Micher	E	1879
338	Mirrin	E	1879
1784	Mitchell	J	1879
980	Moffitt	W	1879
2259	Montgomery	T	1879
2246	Moore	J	1879
2203	Morris	E	1879
2199	Morris	J	1879
	No Medal Deserted.		
1596	Mullins	F	1879
1011	Murdoch	F	1879
1191	Murdoch	W	1879
1771	Murphy	J	1879
	No Medal Deserted.		
393	Musgrove	J	1879
1855	Nailor	J	1879
1917	Neate	L	1879
1568	Newcombe	W	1879
2074	Nicholls	O	1879

1st Dragoon Guards

Number	Name	Initial	Year
1720	Nicholson	H	1879
1949	Norman	C	No clasp
1641	Nurse	W	1879
2227	Nye	A	1879
2246	Nye	C	1879
1808	Ollenrenshaw	J	1879
2146	O'Neill	A	1879
2124	O'Neill	J	1879
	No Medal Deserted.		
1630	Owen	R	1879
1145	Page	G	1879
2243	Pales	G	1879
1125	Pallett	T	1879
1286	Palmer	A	1879
1842	Parker	H	1879
1732	Parker	T	1879
2319	Parks	B	No clasp
901	Paul	A	1879
900	Paul	W	1879
1076	Peacock	F	1879
399	Peacock	J	1879
2152	Pearson	J	1879
1626	Pegram	J	1879
1562	Peirce	J	1879
1446	Penfold	R	1879
1956	Perkins	H.A	1879
1946	Perks	E	1879
1858	Perry	F	1879
1300	Perryman	W	1879
432	Phillips	D	1879
1448	Phipps	T	1879
2134	Pickerell	W	1879
	No Medal Deserted.		
2084	Piek	N	1879
2195	Pithers	E	1879
927	Pilgrim	J	No clasp
1841	Pipper	S	1879
1445	Player	A	1879
2265	Poppleton	S	1879
1443	Porteous	J	1879
1036	Potter	J	1879
1726	Powell	T	No clasp
2119	Power	J	1879
2128	Price	J	1879
2323	Pugh	C	No clasp
1768	Purchase	R	1879
2266	Puttrick D/S	W	1879
1458	Rabbeth	G.W	1879
2217	Redall	J	1879
1605	Redman	E	1879
1482	Reed	J	1879
262	Richards	A	1879
1336	Riley	A	1879
2222	Riley	S	1879
1272	Rixson	R	1879
2321	Robbins	H	No clasp
1066	Roberts	E	1879
2125	Roberts	S	1879
1575	Robinson	J	1879
1415	Ronaldson	A	1879
1651	Royle	J	1879
2226	Salts	T	1879
2183	Sansom	J	1879
	No Medal Deserted.		
1080	Sant	A	1879
2225	Saunders	J	1879
1109	Saunders	T	1879
2281	Saunders	E	1879
2192	Saunders	W.H	1879
936	Sawyer	W	1879
2121	Sayers	W.H	1879
959	Scholes	C	1879
2148	Scott	H	?
2289	Scott	H	No clasp
1909	Seymour	F	1879
2293	Shackle	F	No clasp
	No Medal Deserted.		
1671	Sharples	T	1879
2290	Shaw	W	No clasp
1569	Shipman	H	1879
840	Shorter	C	1879
1453	Shorter	R	1879
1326	Slye	J	1879
	Medal and clasp issued 19/12/1919.		
	He had been convicted of Disgraceful		
	conduct.		
1223	Smillie	W	1879
2308	Smith	E	No clasp
	No Medal Deserted.		
1531	Smith	G	1879
1739	Smith	J	1879
2130	Smith	J	1879
	No Medal Deserted.		
2185	Smith	J	1879
1766	Smith	R	1879
1680	Smith	W	1879
1309	Smith	W	No clasp
	No Medal Deserted.		
1701	Snow	F	1879
2325	Southan	J	No clasp
1495	Speight	W	1879
1549	Spowart	J	1879
786	Spring	C	No clasp
2155	Spurgeon	S	1879
1850	Stacey	W	1879
1416	Stapleton	H	1879
1919	Steele	J	1879
1461	Stevens	A	1879
2223	Stevens	D	1879
1849	Stiff	E	1879
2307	Stovey D/S	H	No clasp
1862	Streatfield	C	1879
	No Medal Deserted.		
2175	Stubbings	T	1879
	No Medal Deserted.		
1725	Stubbs D/S	G	1879
2291	Styche	R	No clasp
950	Styles	W	1879
1097	Sullivan	E	1879
2135	Sullivan	J	1879
1697	Suthers	J	1879
2193	Sutton	H	1879
2224	Syratt	T	1879
	No Medal Deserted.		
1696	Tasker	W	1879
1454	Tatton	S	1879
	No Medal Deserted.		
1694	Tatton	W	1879
1853	Templeton	C	1879
1374	Thomas	A.J	1879
1317	Thompson	H	1879
1505	Till	G	1879
1135	Timbrell	F	1879
1774	Todd	J	1879
2207	Todd	J.H	1879
1302	Townshend	C	1879
1547	Trainer	W	1879
1794	Tratt	W	1879
2176	Turner	T	1879
	No Medal Deserted.		
1608	Tweedie	J	1879
	No Medal Deserted.		
2189	Tynan	J	1879
2177	Vanstone	H	1879
1879	Vaughan	F	1879
1150	Vaughan	H	1879
1182	Veneables	J.D	1879
1500	Vines	C	1879
2237	Vousden	A	1879
2077	Wakeman	J	1879
1801	Walker	C	1879
862	Walker	J	1879
1852	Walters	R	1879
1554	Walton	J	1879
1557	Walton	R	1879
2133	Ward	G.A	1879
1519	Warren	J	1879
1891	Warren	W	1879
775	Washband	T	1879
2149	Watson	H	1879
2186	Watts	R	1879
1079	Way	J	1879
1419	Webb	C	1879
2178	Webb	G	1879
908	Webb	T	1879
1995	Welsh	J	No clasp
	No Medal Undergoing 5 years Penal Sevitude.		
2129	Whaley	J	1879
543	Wheeler	J	1879
1585	Whitehead	A.H	1879
1702	Whitmore	T	No clasp
	No Medal Deserted.		
1792	Wilberforce	C	1879
1186	Wilkens	F	1879
1678	Williams	C	1879
1718	Williams	J	1879

1st Dragoon Guards

1821	Williams	J	1879
1851	Williams	R	1879
1851	Williams	R	1879
	Two Medals to same man.		
1840	Willis	J	1879
1896	Wilson	H	1879
2122	Wilson	W	1879
1892	Wilson	W.G	1879
785	Woodford	J	1879
1080	Woods	C	1879
1954	Woods	W.J	1879
2109	Woolacott	E	1879
2150	Woolford	A	1879
1160	Worrell	G	1879
1334	Worthington	L	1879
307	Wycherley	J	1879
1341	Wye	W	1879

LIFE GUARDS 1st and 2nd.
CAPTAIN
Downe Viscount		H.R	1879
Talbot Hon		R	1879

TROOPER
985	Hammond	L	1879
751	Jestilo?	J	1879

SCOTS GUARDS. 1st and 2nd.
LIEUTENANT COLONEL
Forestier Walker CB	F.W.E	1877-8-9
Montgomery	W.E	1879

CAPTAIN
Cotton Hon		R.S.G.S	1879
Gordon Cumming Sir	W	1879

SERGEANT
2532	Beard	J	1879
1726	Richardson	A	1879

PRIVATE
3288	Cowan	G	1879
2391	Grey	G	1879
1525	Lundry	W	1877-8-9
868	Lyon	D	1879

5th (ROYAL IRISH) LANCERS.
LIEUTENANT
	Morland	H.C	1879

9th (THE QUEENS ROYAL) LANCERS.
MAJOR
Bushman		H A	1879

CAPTAIN
Beresford VC
Lord W.A de la P 1879
His VC was for an action at Ulundi.

PRIVATE
1976	Wright	G	1879

12th (THE PRINCE OF WALES'S ROYAL) LANCERS.
BREVET MAJOR
	Russell	J.C	1879

SERGEANT
1071	Still	A.H	1878-9

16th (QUEEN'S) LANCERS.
MAJOR
Salis-Schwabe		G	1879

LIEUTENANT
Howard		H.R.L	1879
Taaffe		C.R	1879

FARRIER SERGEANT
974	Dyer	H	1878-9
	See also Frontier Light Horse.		

PRIVATE
1182	Allen	H	1879
1454	Cooper	G	1879

17th (THE DUKE CAMBRIDGE'S OWN) LANCERS.
A very difficult roll to read.

COLONEL
Drury Lowe		D.C	1879
CB			

MAJOR
Boulderson		S	1879

CAPTAIN
Alexander		J.F	1879
Belford		E.A	1879
Clark		S.Y	1879
Cooke		T.A	1879
Duke		J.C	1879
Pleydell Bouverie	Hon J	1879
Wyatt-Edgell	Hon E.V	1879
KIA Ulundi.			

QUARTERMASTER
Berryman VC		J	1879

His VC was won at Balaclava. Also has British & Turkis Crimea Medals.

CAPTAIN AND PAYMASTER
Brown J		No clasp	

Also has Britis & Turkish Crimea Medals.

LIEUTENANT & ADJUTANT
Frith		F.J.C	1879

KIA Ezunganyan Hill, 5/6/1979.

LIEUTENANT
Beaumont Lord		H.G	1879
1st West York Yeomanry Attached.			
Fortesque		H	1879
Fortesque Hon		L.H	1879
Herbert		E.B	1879
Jenkins		H.C	1879
Kevill-Davies		W.T.S	1879
Neeld		M.G	1879
Purvis		H	1879
Russell		J.M	1879
Steele		T.A	1879
St. Vincent Lord		J.E.L.	1879
7th Hussars Attached.			
Swaine		C.E	1879
Wood		G.A	1879

2nd LIEUTENANT
Butler		C.H	1879
Anstruther Thomson	C.J	1879
St. Quintin		F.D.H	1879

ORDERLY ROOM CLERK
1278	Whitehead	R.S	1879

REGIMENTAL SERGEANT MAJOR
1251	Coventry	C	1879

TROOP SERGEANT MAJOR
451	Aken	J	1879
1236	Charman ?	H	1879
1157	Davidson	G	1879
1133	Hayton	J	1879
1151	Kennedy	W	1879
1155	Paul	G	1879
992	Ross	W	1879
841	Scarfe ?	G	1879

FARRIER MAJOR
1195	Johnson	J	1879

TRUMPETER MAJOR
1175	Driver ?	J	1879

ARMOURER SERGEANT
425	Bishop	T.K	No clasp

PAYMASTER SERGEANT
1392	Clarr ?	W	No clasp

QUARTERMASTER SERGEANT
989	Williams	W.H	1879

SERGEANT INSTRUCTOR IN FENCING
1550	Hargreaves	W.H	1879

SADDLER SERGEANT
355	Brown	S	1879

SERGEANT
861	Barrett	H.J.S	1879
789	Beaumont	C.J	1879
2180	Blake	V.W	1879
1298	Bolshaw	J.W	1879
1417	Clarke	J	1879
1139	Frim ?	W	1879
1447	Lawrence	A	1879
2195	Lott	W	1879
1485	May	B.A	1879
935	Moss	F	1879
1435	Pilley	W	1879
1372	Reid	F	1879
1388	Sinton ?	F	1879
902	Smith	J	1879
1381	Stamp	G	1879
1194	Stoker	W	1879
1574	Style	F.G	1879
1057	Willding	C	1879
2195	Yeoman	H	1879

LANCE SERGEANT
950	Cowell	C	1879
1529	Clarke	C	1879
1820	Dwyer	P.F	1879

17th Lancers

No.	Name	Initial	Year	No.	Name	Initial	Year	No.	Name	Initial	Year
2250	Forbes	G.W	1879	1927	Pondage	W	1879	1271	Barnard	W	No clasp
2197	Hart	I	1879	1979	Welch	W.C	1879	2253	Barnes	R	1879
1459	Hepburn	W	1879	1528	Woodyard	W	1879	2056	Barnes	R	1879
1054	Mc Kay	W	1879	**SADDLER**				1991	Bartlett	J	1879
951	Parker	C.H	1879	1430	Brown	E	1879	1941	Bartram	A	1879
2251	Symonds	D.A	1879	**FARRIER**				2288	Bartram	J	1879
1521	Whitehill	W	1879	884	Barson	R	1879	2233	Baxter	C	1879
2371	Winship	J	1879	1132	Clarke	J	1879	2298	Bayhoe	W	1879
CORPORAL				1290	Cousins	R	1879	1579	Beane	W.J	1879
1558	Bailey	T	1879	526	Castle	W	1879	2324	Beckett	C	1879
1505	Booth	J.H	1879	2244	Ede	W	1879	1523	Bell	I.R	1879
1178	Cooke	T	1879	2117	Flanagan	P	1879	2170	Bell	R.E	1879
1704	Cotter **KIA**	W	1879	1174	Holmes	S	1879	1828	Bennett	C	1879
1551	Culley	E.A	1879	2054	Ross	M	1879	1501	Bentley	H	1879
2198	Davies	E.G	1879	1302	Taylor **KIA**	J	1879	1590	Beverley	T.C	1879
755	Dawson	T.H	1879	**TRUMPETER**				1051	Bida	A	1879
1201	Evans	C	1879	1225	Brown	T	1879	1495	Biggs	T.H	1879
1210	Goodwin	H	1879	1392	Connor	M	1879	1721	Blake	W	1879
1567	Green	C	1879	907	Duffy	T	1879		No Medal Deserted.		
1980	Harrison	C.W	1879	1428	Dunn	J	1879	1940	Blakewell	S	1879
1850	Kemspton	J.C	1879	1234	Durham	F	1879	2287	Bliss	J	1879
1590	Lee	W	1879	844	Gale	J.H	1879	2210	Bluff	J	1879
1508	Mainstill ?	E.J	1879	1832	Lee	G	1879	2267	Booker	T	1879
1488	Matthews	C.A	1879	1295	Wilde	L.J	1879	1515	Bosworth	H	1879
1476	Powell	H	1879	**PRIVATE**				2211	Bowles	G	1879
1539	Richardson	J.G	1879	1929	Adams	R	1879	1750	Bowers	E	1879
1490	Selwood	G	1879	1541	Adams	T	1879	1732	Bradford	J.L	1879
1078	Smart	H	1879	2081	Aitken	A	1879	1701	Bradley D/S	H	1879
1407	Steward	G	1879	1540	Alcock	T	1879	1892	Bradshaw	J.F	1879
1509	Thomas	J.J	1879	2307	Allen	C	1879	1524	Brian	A.R	1879
1457	Tredgold	F	1879	2205	Allen	E	1879	1193	Brogden	C	No clasp
977	Wilkinson	W.H	1879	1795	Allen	E.C	1879	2101	Brentnall	A	1879
LANCE CORPORAL				2314	Allnutt	C	1879	1702	Brotherstern	G	1879
1654	Alexander	J	1879	2337	Anderson	C	1879	1746	Brown	H	1879
2328	Bruce	A.A	1879	1588	Andrew	J	1879	2071	Brown	S	No clasp
2008	Butler	T.H	1879	2141	Archer	F	1879	2320	Brown	W	1879
1020	Constable	F	1879	1820	Arthur	S	1879		No Medal Deserted.		
2037	Craik	J	1879	2151	Aston	G	1879	2289	Buckley	C	1879
1595	Edwards	J	1879	#2319	Atkings	S	1879	2013	Budd	W	1879
1014	Gunn ?	B	1879	1850	Atkinson	G	1879 r	2312	Bulton	C	1879
2104	Godfray	W	1879		Forfeited. No reason given.			1504	Burton	J.W	1879
2193	Healey	E	1879	1452	Attwell	J	1879	2254	Burton	R.I	1879
1847	Hoffman	H.L	1879	2045	Ault	W	1879	1309	Cain	J	1879
1587	Jenkins	T	1879	2205	Ayres	J	1879	1309	Caldwell	J	1879
1553	King	D.W	1879	1559	Badery	G.W	1879	1744	Cale	F	1879
1705	King	T	1879	2218	Bainbridge	J.J	1879	1395	Calver D/S	E	1879
2074	Lewis	H	1879	1951	Baker	H	1879	2213	Campbell	W	1879
1865	Mansfield ?	W.F	1879	2207	Baker	H.T	1879	1444	Carpenter	H	1879
1758	Mitchell	J	1879	2208	Baker	S.D	1879	2203	Carter	E	1879
1250	Meates ?	W.W	1879	1534	Ballenden	W	1879	1374	Chadwick	M	1879
848	Parsons	G	1879	2209	Barker	H	1879	1551	Chapman	J.B	1879
1953	Payne	T	1879	2235	Barter	J	1879	1203	Chase	H.C	1879

#Historik Orders December 2009 (Editors note; Note different spelling of surname)
ZULU MEDAL NAMED TO: 2319. S. AKTINS. 17th D.C.O. LANCERS. Clasp: 1879. Condition: GVF.
The 17th Lancers Charged at Ulundi the Zlu King's Stronghold. $1,650.00
Spinks - 19 April 2007 Lot 139 South Africa 1877-79, one clasp, 1879 (2319 Pte. S. Atkings. 17th D.C.O. Lcrs.), partly officially corrected, pawn broker's mark to edge, edge bruising, very fine Estimate £ 250-300
2319 Private Samuel Atkings, born St Margaret's, Nottingham; enlisted 5th Lancers, 1878; transferred 17th Lancers, 1879; discharged 1891, after 12 years and 304 days service. Sold for £480

17th Lancers

1254	Chaston	R	1879	2072	Day	W	No clasp	2236	Garner	J	1879
1553	Childs	J	1879	2135	Divine	J	1879	2025	Garnham	W	1879
1350	Chitty	L	1879	2275	Dixon D/S	F.P	1879	2250	Garrate	W	1879
2053	Chouler	T	1879	2091	Douggan	F	1879	1405	Gibbs	J	1879
1327	Church	G	No clasp	2093	Downey	J	1879	1925	Gibson	H	1879
2214	Clarke	E	1879	1352	Drane	F	1879	2094	Gissop	M	1879
1755	Clarke	J	1879	1895	Drew	F	1879	2251	Glud	C	1879
1794	Clarke	R	1879	1528	Duff	W	1879	2268	Godding D/S	H	No clasp
2217	Clifford	J	1879	2310	Dunbar	L	1879	2252	Goodall	W	1879
1704	Cloud	A.S	1879	1854	Duncan	P	1879	1917	Goodman	N	1879
1518	Coates	F	1879	1884	Dundon	M	1879	2322	Gordon	P	1879
1450	Cobley	H	1879	1319	Dwyer	D	1879	897	Gowrie	E	1879
2059	Coldwell	W	1879	2235	Edmonds	A.E	1879	1827	Grant	H.L.H	1879
1889	Coleyran ?	J.W	No clasp	1841	Edmunds	A	No clasp	1512	Grant D/S	J	No clasp
1454	Collins	T	1879	2137	Edwards	T	1879	1995	Gray	C.W	1879
2215	Collins	W	1879	1807	Ellis	M	1879	2190	Gray	W.L	1879
1549	Connor	J	1879	1353	Ellison	W	1879	2122	Greey	F.N	1879
1878	Connor	V.D	No clasp	2222	Elliston	W	1879	1581	Gregg	D	1879
1573	Connolly	J	1879	2245	Evans	G	1879	2308	Grey	A	1879
2282	Cooper	G	1879	1735	Everest	S	1879	2309	Grunt ?	J	1879
2215	Corbett	G	1879	2035	Fairile	T	1879	2022	Gubbins	E G	1879
2045	Costelle	H	1879	1739	Fanning	J	1879	Duplicate Medal & clasp issued 2/6/1914.			
2000	Cotterill	A	1879	1538	Farndest ?	J	1879	1492	Gunnell	E	1879
1954	Cotten	C	1879	1932	Farr	G	1879	1484	Guwer	C	1879
1823	Courts	J	1879	2050	Featherstone	W.T	1879	1912	Hall	H	1879
1575	Cowell	J.C	1879	2157	Ferris	F	1879	2187	Hall	J	1879
2218	Cowley	S	1879	2293	Fisher	E	1879	2253	Hall	J	1879
1944	Cox	H	1879	2252	Flynn	E.J.J	1879	2277	Hall	P	1879
2051	Cox	J	1879	1843	Foley	J	1879	1992	Hallows	W	1879
1222	Cresswell	J	1879	1754	Forster	S	1879	1500	Hammond	R	1879
2295	Crick	W	1879	##1525	Foster	G	1879	1930	Hands	J	1879
1518	Cridland	H	1879	1555	Foster	G	1879	981	Hands	J	1879
1888	Cridland	C	1879	2284	Fox	J	1879	1801	Hanney	H	1879
2219	Crisford	S	1879	1575	Fredericks	W	1879	2015	Hansell	J.B	1879
1545	Crockard	W	1879	1945	Fraser	E	No clasp	1644	Harbiane	A	1879
2220	Crotty	M	1879	1232	French	G	1879	1105	Hardiment	H	1879
1783	Crow	R	1879	###1452	Frost	T.G.H	1879	2011	Harding	H	1879
1845	Crowley	R	1879	1547	Fulton	N	1879	1387	Harding	W	1879
1463	Crowley	R	1879	1367	Gallagher	J	1879	2269	Harman	S	1879
1913	Crutshott	J	1879	2070	Gallon	J	1879	1951	Harold	R	1879
2221	Cull	W	1879	2247	Galpin	W.J	1879	1293	Harper	E	1879
#2073	Cunliffe	H	1879	2158	Gardner	J	1879	2020	Harrap ?	E.W	1879
2005	Cunwold	H	1879	2249	Gardiner	J	1879	2313	Harrison	J	1879
2036	Davies	W.E	1879	1003	Gardner	T	1879	1545	Harsent	J	1879
1832	Davies	W.R	1879	2248	Gardiner	T.H	1879	2254	Hart	J	1879
2234	Davis	J	1879	1183	Gardiner	W	1979	1542	Harwood	G	1879

#Christies 28th Feb 1986, South Africa 1877-79, one clasp, 1879 (2073 Pte. W. Cunliffe. 17th D.C.O.Lrs.), attempted erasure of initial, otherwise nearly extremely fine. On roll, WO 100/46 as Pte H.Cuniliffe. Estimate £ 60-80.

##Spinks - 24 Nov 2005 Lot 312 South Africa 1877-79, one clasp, 1879 (1525 Pte. G. Foster. 17th D.C.O.Lrs.), edge bruise, otherwise good very fine. Estimate £ 440-480 Sold for £550

Ebay - January 2010 Buy it now £1,100 or make an offer Item number: 170428811799 17th Duke of Cambridge's Own Lancers Named to: 1462 Pte F G H Frost 17th D.C.O.Lrs Confirmed on the Forsyth Roll as "1452 T G H Frost, (a notoriously difficult roll to read), but the only Frost on the roll for the 17th. Comes with 6 pages of muster rolls for the period between 1872 and 1880, shows 1452 T G H Frost on the strength for the 17th Lancers, enlisting in Ireland.Mr T Frost was present at the Old Comrades Ulundi Re-Union dinner held at the Holborn restaurant in London on 02.07.1927, one of 30 men present, including the Colonel of the Regiment.
A very nice medal, confirmed to a member of the 17th Lancers who was actually present at the Charge at Ulundi where they routed the Zulu army. Condition: VF

17th Lancers

THOMAS HOLMES, 17th LANCERS

My thanks go to his descendant (Denise Neufeld) for the information on **Thomas Holmes.** The information supplied originated from Denise's mom's brother. He was in his 90s and was the last person alive who remembers Tom who died in 1923. Tom related how tall and well built the Zulu's where, and that they would hide in the long grass and you never knew they were there.

Thomas Holmes son of James Holmes. Despite research it has not been confirmed if James Holmes was in fact the father of Thomas, as Thomas was baptised as Thomas Buy. Young Thomas drifted into trouble in Wandsworth and was jailed more than once. In those days if anyone committed more than one offence they were classed as an habitual criminal.

Despite the uncertainty re his father Thomas kept the name (Holmes) for the rest of his life. Below is an example of his criminal life found in an entry concerning Thomas in Wandsworth prison.

Calendar of Prisoners Wandsworth Prison. Dated 4 March 1872. General Quarter Sessions of the Peace Holden by Adjournment Saint Mary Newington.

No 28 Thomas Holden. Previous Convictions * 14 days 18th Aug 1870, 21 Days 7th Oct 1870,21 Days 3rd May 1871 (2 Months) Criminal Justice Act 13th July 1871.Age 16 Trade or Occupation, Labourer. Committing Magistrate J Bridge Esq. Wandsworth Police Court. Committal date 19th Feb 1872. In Custody 19th Feb 1872.Offence: Feloniously breaking and entering the dwelling house of William Price and stealing therein one pistol and other articles, his property. Tried 5th March 1872 before W Hardman. Pleaded Guilty of Housebreaking and Larceny, after a previous conviction of Felony. Particulars of previous convictions charged in the indictment and proved in Court. Two Calendar months Hard Labour for Larceny, Wandsworth Police Court 13th July 1871. Sentence of Court: 12 Calendar Months hard labour.'

Thomas left Wandsworth Prison on 3 March 1873 and after a few months decided to enlist in the army. This he did on the 2 September 1873, he joined the 17th Lancers, the 'Death and Glory' Regt. By 17 November he had been admitted to hospital with gonorrhoea, during the course of his career he also contracted syphilis. Even on his enlistment details he gave false information, stating he came from Somerset: a check of his papers confirmed it being the right man. Old habits continued and on 9 January 1877 he was in military prison for receiving stolen money, released on 10 Oct 1877. In all he was in the regimental defaulters book seven times and was court martialled once. Thomas saw service in India and in South Africa. In South Africa he took part in the Battle of Ulundi. Thomas stated in his recollections that he was in the party that recovered the body of the Prince Imperial who was killed on 1 June 1879.

Army life especially on horseback did not agree with Thomas and soon he was up before a medical board suffering from varicose veins, so badly that he was discharged from the service on 4 January 1881. He gave as his intended place of residence as his parents' home in Wandsworth. On 17 April 1881 he married Mary Elizabeth SANDHAM.

On 12 October 1889 he was present at the death of his father (?) when in a drunken brawl James Holmes struck his head on a curbstone. One W Chance was charged with manslaughter. Thomas and Mary had four children, twin boys born in 1898; both died shortly after they were born, part of the horrendous infant mortality rate in Victorian London. At the age of 50 he decided to move to Canada: the exact circumstances of this immigration are shrouded in mystery. It was believed by members of his family that he went to Canada c 1907, his wife and daughter following the next year. Both daughters subsequently married but one stayed in England.

The newspapers were full of jobs and opportunities in Canada. Thomas decided to immigrate to Canada. A search revealed that in August 1906 a Thomas Holmes left Liverpool on the SS Lucania arriving in New York on 25 August 1906, passenger Thomas Holmes b 1856 England. It is entirely possible he went to the USA thence to Canada where his wife and daughter followed the next year. Thomas found himself in Oakville, Manitoba, a labourer on a farm. He eventually moved to Oakville as the Canadian census shows. In 1914 despite dyeing his hair he was turned down when trying to re-enlist.

At the time of his death he was a Caretaker in a local bank. Thomas Holmes late 17th Lancers departed this earth on 2 April 1923 in Oakville, Manitoba. Cause of death, Cerebral haemorrhage and Lung abscess aged 66 years 9 months and 7 days. This is his obituary:

At his home last Sunday Mr Holmes passed away and in his passing another of that fast dwindling army, the soldier empire makers of the Victorian era went to his reward. The late Mr Holmes was an ex-member of that very famous regiment the 17th Lancers, the Death or Glory Boys, and with them saw much service. He served with Chelmsford in the Zulu war of 1879, and doubtless took part in most of the big engagements of the campaign, when this was over he accompanied his regiment to India where after several years service he was invalided home. The deceased was born in Wiltshire, England, coming to Canada in 1907 and was followed a year later by his wife and family. He resided in Oakville for many years where he was much loved and respected by members of the community.

Mr Holmes is survived by his wife and two daughters (his twin sons having died a number of years ago), Mrs House of Winnipeg and the other in London (Wandsworth, England). The sympathy of the whole community is with the family in their recent bereavement.'

Sources: Denise Neufeld, & Graham 'Sapper' Mason

17th Lancers

The Ulundi Reunion Dinner held on the 6th July 1929

A Reunion Dinner held at the Great Central Hotel. Survivors of the battle met to celebrate the fiftieth anniversary of the Battle of Ulundi.
Present.—Col. M. G. Neeld, Major C. J. Anstruther, Mr. J. R. Alexander, Mr. J. Clark, Mr. J. Cowley, Mr. E. A. Culley, Mr. J. J. L. Cridland, Mr. F. Douggan, Mr. F. J. Drew, Mr. T. Fairlie, Mr. W. Hands, Mr. W. Hollywell, Mr. T. P. Jones, Mr. F. Langley, Mr. B. A. May, Mr. W. A. Mowatt, Mr. T. Payne, Mr. J. O' Shaughnessy, Mr. J. G. Richardson, Mr. E. C. Smith, Mr. T. Staples, and Mr. W. Woodyard.
Unavoidably absent.—Col. E. A. Belford, Col. H. Fortescue, Col. E. B. Herbert, Mr. W. J. Beane, Mr. C. Burton, Mr. E. Carter, Mr. J. S. Clarke, Mr. C. T. Cridland, Mr. G. Farr, Mr. H. E. Ham, Mr. D. W. King, Mr. W. G. Maddocks, Mr. J. L. Style, Mr. H. Ware, and Mr. L. Wolfe.
Guests.—General the Hon. Sir Herbert Lawrence, G.C.B. (Colonel of the Regiment), Mr. W. D. Blake, Mr. R. E. Doubleday, Mr. E. Scarfe, Mr. —. Drew, jun., Mr. —. Langley, jun., Mr. —. Clark, jun., Mr. —. Jones, jun., Mr T. J. Moore, and Mr. W. Arundel.
The following have joined the ranks of the Old Comrades since our last publication :— Sergt. James, Band Sergt. Woods, Cpl. Fisher, Cpl. Britt, L./Cpl. Hoole, L. /Cpl. C. Brown, L./Cpl. Chapman, Bdsn. Sharpe, Bdsn. J. Brown, Tprs. Wallage, Day, Ive Homewood, Bennett, Coyne, Gater, Hobden, Joyce, Macey, A. Smith, Skipper, Beale, Powell, Reed and L. Osborne, and Cpl. Parks.
The following letters were received in connection with the dinner :—

22 King Street,
High Broughton,,
Manchester.

Dear Sir,
I hope you will excuse me for taking the liberty of writing this letter to you. I happened to read an account in the paper that the survivors of His Majesty's 17th D.C.O. Lancers, to the number of 22, were having a Reunion Dinner at which to celebrate the famous charge which they made on that memorable occasion on July 4th, 1879, at the Battle of Ulundi, South Africa. With me being interested in my late father's Regiment, thought I would write you and give you some interesting particulars as regards my late father, whom I regret to inform you passed away twenty-eight years ago, or otherwise he would have been present on such an auspicious occasion as this one. However, here are the full particulars. My late father enlisted in His Majesty's 17th D.C.O. Lancers at Westminster, being a native of Kingston-on-Thames, Surrey, in the year 1870; for twelve years' Army service, at the age of thirteen years five months. He went into the Royal Military Musical College, Kneller Hall, and was cornet player in the band during the full term of service, which was twelve years twenty-four days. He was trumpeter to the late General Sir Drury Curzon Drury Lowe, and served in the Zulu Campaign, South Africa, 1879, in which he was present at the Battle of Ulundi. I dare- say that Colonel Neeld and a few of the survivors will no doubt remember his name : No. 1334 Trumpet-Major Fred Durham.
After the termination of the Zulu Campaign, my father was drafted with the Regiment from South Africa to Central India and stationed at Mhow, in which he served till he took his discharge in 1882 at Gosport, leaving the Regiment in India. Before taking leave of the Regiment, he was presented with his silver cornet, which was a pocket cornet (specially made) by Lord Fortescue, Colonel Gourie, officers and members of the Regiment.
I have in my possession my late father's Army Book—one of the old originals which you do not see these days, fifty years old, his discharge papers, which are made of a kind of parchment, and his Zulu Medal (1879), with plush case; and I can assure you, Mr. Woodyard, that the medal and case are as perfect as the day they were issued to him in India. I have also in my possession a book* that he wrote of all he saw as regards the Zulu Campaign, giving the names of the officers, men and horses that were casualties, including a 'diary of what he did in India for three years, while he was with the Regiment. I have also a hook that my father wrote himself while he was at the School of Music, at which he was the only boy in the College allowed to use His Majesty's books. He was tutored under Dr. Albert Hartmann. When he left India he was given several Army testimonials by different bandmasters, officers, and one special one from all the members of the Band, autographed by each member, and I have a photograph, taken at Mhow, of the Band in the year 1882.
I am only sorry that I am unable to ask you to inspect these, as we are too far apart, but am proud to know that I have these in my possession after all these years. (continued next page)

17th Lancers

Continued-
I am only sorry that I am unable to ask you to inspect these, as we are too far apart, but am proud to know that I have these in my possession after all these years. If at any time you happen to come into contact or correspond with any of these members, I should be very pleased indeed if you would kindly mention my late father's name to them, especially Colonel Neeld, as they will be pleased to know, I am sure, that his son has not forgotten his father's old comrades. Hoping you are keeping fairly well,
Yours very truly,
Fred Durham.
[* Mr. Durham has been good enough to send us this book, and we are much indebted to him for the very interesting extract from it which appears in this number.—ED.]

Hillside,
Chipping Norton,
Oxon.

Sir,
I have only just seen in Saturday's Morning Post of the Zulu War Veterans' Jubilee.
I was sent out in June, 1879, by the Stafford House South African Aid Committee, as Superintendent Nursing Sister, taking six trained nurses with me, under Surgeon- General Carter Ross, C.S.I. My work was Ladysmith. I believe Capt. Jenkyne was in charge, Major Algoner Somerset was Commandant at Ladysmith, Colonel Bond, Major Foster at Newcastle. I nursed the officer who captured Cetewayo; he belonged to the King's Dragoon Guards. I am so glad so many are alive. I am in my 82nd year, quite strong and well.
Yours faithfully,
EMMA DURHAM (Sister Emma),
P.S.—General Sir H. Lukin was one of my boy patients. I saw him after the Great War. I nursed in the Great War at Mount Stuart Bute and House, and Falkland, Fife.

118 Silver Mere Road,
Catford, S.E

Dear Sir,
Having seen about your Dinner in to-day's News of the World, I regret to say I was not present. I joined the 17th Lancers on December 6th, 1876, at Aldershot. LI was on the march from there to Preston and was present at the Blackburn riots.
I went to South Africa with the Regiment and was at the Battle of Ulundi. I was in " H " Troop (Capt. E. V. Wyatt Edgett's_ Troop) and I remember him being shot in that battle, also Pte. Jones and Farr.-Sergt. Taylor.. came home to Canterbury from South Africa when the Regiment went to India, and was then coachman for two years to Capt. Clarke, also to Surgeon-Major 0. Larie (P.M.O. at Canterbury).
I married off the strength, and on the reduction of the Army was transferred to the Army Reserve. Three months afterwards I was called up again, and I was sent out to Egypt in 1882, and I was in all engagements to Tel-el-Kebir.
I have Zulu Medal and Clasp, 1879, also Egyptian Medal, Clasp and Star. I was 71 last March.
Again regretting I was not present at your dinner,
I remain,
Yours respectfully,
H. C. SKINNER, NO. 1969,
Private," H " Troop, 17th D.C.O. Lancers.
I believe Colonel Neeld was Lieutenant in my Troop, then with Mr. Wood, and I think S.M. Benton was poisoned on the march to Pretoria, through eating a bad sausage roll.

Post Office,
Hapton,
Nr. Burnley

Dear Sir,
Seeing an account of your dinner in London, and request for names of any 17th Lancer men who were at Ulundi, I beg to send in my name : Tpr. Henry Cunliffe, " C " Troop.
I was batman to Capt. Jenkins, of " C " Troop, who was Adjutant after Lieut. Frith got shot farther down the country. I might say I did not go to India, as Capt. Jenkins got leave for me to come home with him. He got badly wounded in the jaw. I am turned 72, and I am pleased to see so many batting with good scores not out.
I am still taking duty as postmaster for this place, where I have been 42 years. With kind regards to all Old Comrades,
Yours truly,
H. CUNLIFFE.

Referance: The White Lancer and the Vedette November 1929.
Editors note: The 17th Lancers received 599 "1879" clasps with 7 medals returned to the mint. Only 285 charged at Ulundi.

17th Lancers

MILES GISSOP, 17th LANCERS

The manuscript of his talk, now in the possession of Mrs. Mary Travers, his granddaughter, has been edited by David Clammer.

The Recollections of **Miles Gissop**: with the 17th Lancers in Zululand. Edited by David Chandler. 14 page article (pages 78 to 92) with portrait included in issue 234 of the Journal of the Society for Army Historical Research.

This photo was taken in Mhow, Central India soon after the 17th Lancers moved there from South Africa following their distinguished service in the Zulu War. Miles Gissop was born in 1858 which makes him 21 at the time of his involvement in the action at Ulundi in 1879. He was born in Leeds and became a cloth-dresser but enlisted in the 17th in 1878. He did not serve for very long, because he left the army some time between 1891 and 1895. The 17th came back from India in 1891. On his return to civilian life he found a job as a Co-operative Society teamster. In November 1899, he was persuaded to give a lecture in the Morley Town Hall describing his experiences in the Zulu War. Transcript of lecture:

"July 4th we were in the saddle 5.30 am and started off at 5.45 the column numbering about 5000 the remainder was left behind to guard the camp, we crossed the White Umfolozi River passed through the remainder of the bush and on to the Plain of Ulundi without seeing a Zulu. The Infantry then formed a hollow square four deep the Artillery inside, the gatling guns in the rear followed by the Native Contingent, the right wing of the 17th Lancers and Bullers Horse, small parties of Bullers Horse and the Native scouts to right and left and the left wing of the 17th Lancers to the rear. We then moved forward past the first Kraal which we set on fire and immediately saw our enemy topping the hill to our left rear. They came down in swarms opening out to right and left and working round us in the shape of a horseshoe then we saw them to our right front performing exactly the same movement until the two parties met on each side and completely surrounded us..... We trotted up to the square when the Infantry stepped on one side to allow us to pass into the square, the right wing of the 17th Lancers, Bullers Horse Mounted Infantry and the Native Contingent doing the same. We dismounted and the Battle commenced in down right earnest. Heavy firing was kept up for a long time when a hearty British cheer (a cheer which I shall never forget) rang out from the mouths of our Gallant British Infantry, who put their helmets on top of there Baynets spinning them as high as they could reach in the air. We knew in a second what this meant. The enemy had turned. It was at this point that my regiment had to do its cruel work. We mounted, were formed up in squadrons, rank entire [?] and charged the retreating foe, who made a Gallant stand at the bottom of a slope, but not sufficient to impede the advance of the dashing 17th. They turned again and ran as fast as there legs would carry them. We were up to them in quick time and our Lances went through them as easy as putting them through a tub of butter. We retired slowly. The enemy having run up a hill which was too steep for us to follow. About 5000 of them squatted themselves at the top. The guns were then brought into range and poured shell amongst them scattering them in all directions, they sloped off and we saw no more of them. Previous to the [?] charge of the 17th Col Drury Lowe was knocked off his horse by a spent bullet. He speedily recovered and about half past nine in the morning received the welcome Order from Lord Chelmsford "Go at them Lowe". In a few moments we were off at a racing speed with lowered Lances, after the flying and disorganised herds of the foe from an unsuspected quarter we were met by a volley which emptied many a saddle, amonst those who fell dead being Captain Hon Wyatt Edgell.

That shot which laid him low was unfortunate for the Zulus, for to the war-like ardour of the men who followed him was added a fierce yearning for revenge. A moment more and the bristling line of steel meets the black and shining wall of human flesh rent and pierced and gashedby a weapon as death dealing and unsparing as their own assegais, still tho' crushed and stabbed by the lances and tho' their fierce array was scattered like sea foam the Zulus fought in sullen knots nor cried for quarter stabbing at the horses bellies as they went down and trying to drag us off them in the melee. The lance was now relegated in most instances to its sling and the heavy sabres of the troops became red with gore. Sir Garnet Wolseley no doubt is a clever experienced General but he could not have moved us in a better manner nor with greater success than did Lord Chelmsford at this memorable Battle.

Reference: Charles Griffin,   http://www.britishempire.co.uk/forces/armyunits/britishcavalry/17thlancersgissop.htm

17th Lancers

No.	Name	Initial	Year	No.	Name	Initial	Year	No.	Name	Initial	Year
1370	Hayden	A	1879	1485	Keen	C	1879	1866	Mc Arthur	D	1879
2159	Hayery ?	H	1879	1855	Kelly	W	No clasp	2223	Mc Clure	R	1879
2039	Head	W.H	1879	1851	Kenney	D	1879	1077	Mc Gowan	E	1879
1409	Heard	H	1879	2299	Kiernan	J	No clasp	2272	Mc Guinness	L	1879
1905	Hedges	T	1879	2273	Killelra	H	1879	1574	Mc Kenna	W.B	1879
2055	Hemlin	J	No clasp	2098	Killick	H	1879	1709	Mc Mahon	R.D	1879
1710	Hicks	H	1879	1102	Kimber	J	1879	1811	Mc Pherson	J	1879
1565	Hill	H	No clasp	2009	King	J.H	1879	518	Mc Sweeney	J	1879
2237	Hill	R	1879	1712	Kirby	A	1879	1034	Medows	C	1879
1999	Hobbs	T.H	1879	1984	Kisbey	A.F	1879	1599	Meagher	W	1879
2323	Hodges	H	1879	1339	Land	W	1879	1445	Meates	C	1879
2079	Hodgson	C	1879	2297	Lane	H	1879	2552	Melville	N	1879
2275	Hoggett	A	1879	2238	Langham	G	No clasp	2049	Merry	W	1879
2255	Holloway	H	1879	2291	Langley	F	1879	1571	Meyrick	F.E	1879
1517	Holywell	W	1879	1345	Large	T	1879	2133	Middleditch	C	1879
2255	Holman	S.V	1879	1925	Layton	J.W	1879	2279	Miller	H	1879
1513	Holmes (page 198)	T	1879	2281	Leach	H	1879	2050	Mills	W	1879
1437	Holt	A	1879	1329	Leamey	J	1879	1673	Milne	R	1879
2329	Howard	R	1879	1780	Leonard	T	1879	2244	Mitchell	B	1879
1897	Hynes	J	1879	2257	Lightfoot	R	1879	1777	Mitchell	G	1879
2019	Howes	T	1879	2033	Lindsay	F	1879	1591	Monteith	R	1879
2201	Huddy	J	1879	1505	Lloyd	T.M	1879	2285	Mooney	J	1879
2033	Hunt	F	1879	2200	Lloyd	W	1879	2565	Morrison	A	1879
2149	Hunt	W	1879	(1)2258	Lorish (Lough)	G	1879		No Medal Deserted.		
1837	Hynes	J	1879	1952	Loval	W	1879	(3) 2305	Moss	W	1879
2124	Icke	F	1879	1548	Ludlow	W	1879	1560	Moulds	J	1879
1859	Ikin	G	1879	1328	Lupton	J	1879	2080	Mowatt	A.W	1879
2095	Ingham	J.L	1879	1382	Mabin	T	1879	2204	Muddle	R	1879
1583	Ingleton	A	1879	(2) 1203	Mack	S	1879	1729	Murphy	E.W	1879
712	Jackson	E	1879	2125	Mackintosh	A.C	1879	1566	Murphy	J	1879
2051	Jamieson	H	1879	1919	Mackrell	J	1879	1800	Murphy	P	1879
1773	Jarvis	T	1879	1587	Mandyan	J	1879	1213	Murphy	I	1879
2302	Jones	A.A	1879	1295	Manning	G	1879	2240	Murphy	J.J	1879
1025	Jones D/S	E	1879	2239	Manning	R	1879	2053	Myers	T	1879
1957	Jones	W	1879 r	2077	Matherson	C	1879	1883	Nelsbold	J	1879
	Forfeited. No reason given			2068	Mapplelick ?	A	1879	974	Nicholls	G	1879
1921	Johnson	A	1879	1558	Marks	J	1879	1877	Nilan	P	1879
1137	Johnson	F	1879	1112	Martin	G	No clasp	2344	Nixson	W.T	1879
1593	Judge	B	1879	2052	Martin	J	1879	2283	Oatley	G	1879
1737	Kavanagh	N	1879	876	Marshall	P	1879 r	1715	Odell	W	1879
2255	Keeble	R	1879	2047	Martinson	W	1879	1774	Odgers	E	1879
1554	Keegan	J	1879	2259	Mash	G	1879	1871	Ogston	W	1879
1570	Keeley	W	1879	2182	Matcham	W	1879	1834	Old	J	1879

(1) Spinks - 01 May 2003 Lot 810 South Africa 1877-79, one clasp, 1879 (2258 Pte G.Lough 17th D.C.O. Lrs), nearly extremely fine Estimate £ 300-340, Sold for £400

(2) Spink & Son Medal Supplement 1987 item No 94
SOUTH AFRICA 1877-9, 1 clasp, 1879 (Pte. S.Mack,17th D.C.O. Lrs) EF £90

(3) Baldwin & Sons Medal List February 1954
17th Lancers SOUTH AFRICA 1877-9, 1 clasp, 1879 (Pte.Gardiner and another Pte Moss, both VF and 18s 6d each

(4) Dixons Gazette No. 50. Summer 2007. Item Number 2531.
1 clasp, 1879. Private J. Ostheirner, 17th Duke of Cambridge's Own Lancers.
Private Ostheirner enlisted into the 17th Lancers in the London recruiting district, on the 4th August 1875, at the age of 22 years. He arrived in Natal with the regiment in early April 1879 and took part with them, as part of the 2nd Division, in the advance into Zululand. He was present at the reconnaissance of the Upoko River, the engagement at Erzungayan, the advance up the Umvolosi Valley and the decisive battle of Ulundi, fought on the 4th July 1879. The charge of the 17th Lancers at Ulundi turned the Zulu defeat into a rout and virtually ended the war. The regiment were then stationed at Mhow in India and it was here that Ostheirner dies, presumably of disease, on the 7th August 1883. Sold with research which includes medal roll page. NEF £700.00

17th Lancers

No.	Name	Initial	Year	No.	Name	Initial	Year	No.	Name	Initial	Year
1835	Orine	J	1879	1249	Rodgers	G	1879	2156	Tait	W	1879
1974	Osborne	G	1879	2315	Rodgers	J	1879	1772	Tanton	W	1879
1857	O'Shaughnessy	J	No clasp	2280	Rogan	S	1879	1574	Taylor	A	1879
(4) 1793	Osthennier	J	1879	2290	Russell	M	1879	2075	Taylor	C	1879
1958	Owens	J	No clasp	1778	Ruth	C	1879 r	1470	Taylor	G	1879
2225	Page	T	1879	1548	Sansom	G	1879	2147	Taylor	O	No clasp
1788	Pannell	J	1879	1498	Savory	J	1879	2174	Taylor	T.P	1879
2057	Parker	J	No clasp	(7) 1757	Scott	A	1879	2092	Taylor	W	1879
870	Parker	W	No clasp	2100	Scott	H	1879		No Medal Deserted.		
1053	Partron	A	1879	2045	Seydin	W	No clasp	2135	Thomas	W	1879
2155	Pattison	J.W	1879	1554	Shakespeare	G	1879	1598	Thompson	C	1879
2305	Paul	J	1879	1932	Sharp	T	1879	2228	Thornton	J	1879
1575	Payne	G	1879	1551	Shaw	A	1879	2229	Tillman	G	No clasp r
1523	Peacock	C	1879	1838	Shaw	H	1879	1411	Tinson	R	1879
1507	Pearce	F	1879	1555	Shelton	F	1879	2173	Tinton	H	1879
1873	Peyton	E.C	1879	2202	Short	H	1879		Replacement Medal issued 29/10/1924.		
1859	Peyton	R	1879	1317	Sibley	C	1879	2155	Tootell	L	1879
1881	Phelan	J	1879	1589	Simon	H	No clasp	1854	Tracey	T	1879
2021	Phillips	A.W	1879	1903	Simpson	J	1879	2230	Tuckwell	C	1879
1595	Pickering	G	1879	2312	Simpson	R	1879	1557	Twinham	G.M	1879
2271	Piper	J	1879	2300	Sinclair	A.C	1879	1915	Underhill	H	No clasp
(5) 1478	Potter	V.D	1879	2301	Sinclair	E.L	1879	2118	Vipond	J.A	1879
2294	Potts	W	1879	1959	Skinner	H	1879	1340	Wade	G	1879
2232	Price	W.F	1879	2037	Smith	E.C	No clasp	2145	Waite	J	1879
1402	Prior	W	1879	(8) 958	Smith	H.G	1879	2243	Walker	W	1879
2241	Purcell	F	No clasp	1281	Smith	Jas	1879	1517	Wallace	J	1879
2004	Pyatt	W	1879	2225	Smith	J	1879	1221	Wallace	H	1879
1295	Pyman	B	1879	1717	Smith	W	No clasp	1595	Wallace	W	1879
2303	Quinn	M	1879	1750	Somerville	G	1879	2270	Walsh	W	1879
1593	Ragin	C	1879	1857	Spall	W.J	1879	(9) 2231	Walters	B	1879
1332	Ransbottom	J	1879	2125	Sparks	C	No clasp		Ware ?	H	1879
1383	Ray	H	1879	1325	Spencer	J	No clasp	2123	Ward	H	1879
1442	Ray	J	1879	2059	Spicer	T	1879	1851	Warren	H	1879
1977	Reaves	A	1879	2227	Staples	T	1879	1318	Wartherby	W	1879
2321	Redfern	R	1879	2087	Starr	G	1879	1799	Waters	H.C	1879
2317	Reid	J	1879	1599	Steele	J	1879	2184	Watson	G	1879
934	Reilly	J	1879	2374	Stephens	L	1879	1782	Watson	J	1879
(6) 2242	Reynolds	L.T	1879	2298	Stewart	H	1879	2005	Watts	J	1879
2053	Rhind	T	1879	2304	Stone	W	1879	1533	Werks ?	G	1879
1955	Richards	C.L	1879	753	Styles	E	1879	2811	White	E	1879
2252	Richmond	A.W	1879	1971	Style	J	1879	847	White	H	1879
	No Medal Deserted.			1351	Sweeney	G	1879	1460	White	Jac	1879
2010	Robbins	S	1879	1503	Syme	W	1879	1377	White	J.F	1879
1849	Robinson	H	1879	2276	Taggart	G	1879	1559	White	J.H	1879

(5) Spinks - 22 Nov 2007 South Africa 1877-79, one clasp, 1879 (1478. Pte. V.D. Potter. 17th. Dco. Lrs.), lacquered, minor edge bruise, otherwise good very fine Estimate £ 380-420 Provenance: Glendinning, 1.8.1934.Sold for £480

(6) Sothebys Lot 136 GVF 6/05/1982
17th Lancers SOUTH AFRICA 1877-9, 1 clasp, 1879, (Pte L.T Reynolds, 17th D.C.O. Lrs) EF £170. (roll confirms)

(7) Glendininings & Co Auction 18th March 1981, Lot 58
17th Lancers SOUTH AFRICA 1877-9, 1 clasp, 1879, (A.Scott, 17th D.C.O. Lrs) VF.

(8) Wallis & Wallis Auction Lot 16 7 July1981
SOUTH AFRICA 1877-9, 1 clasp, 1879 (Blocked engraved 968 H.G Smith, 17th Lancers) GVF and dark toned, in a frame. £130
The 17th Lancers are renowned for their charge at Ulundi.

(9) Glendining's, Auction Lot 223, 7 December 1988 SOUTH AFRICA 1877-9, 1 clasp, 1879 (2231 Pte. **B. Walters,** 17th DCO Lrs), naming engraved in plain upright capitals, upper and lower case on "Pte", "17th and "Lrs". Edge marks, otherwise very fine. Sold for £120. The 17th Lancers are renowned for their charge at Ulundi.

17th Lancers

2nd LIEUTENANT G. R. Evelyn

Number	Name	Initials	Year
1540	White	W.H	1879
1101	Wilkins	T	1879
2040	Wilks	J.H	1879
2030	Williams	D	1879
1792	Williams	H	1879
2274	Williams	R	1879
1256	Williamson	F	1879
1728	Willis	R	1879
1453	Wilson	G	1879
1548	Wilson	H	1879
1799	Wilson	T	1879
710	Wilson	W	1879
1853	Wilberley	B de R	1879
1530	Winder	J	1879
1914	Windon	H	1879
1775	Wolfe	L	1879
1297	Wooden	C.U	1879
2315	Wright	G	1879
2143	Wright	J	1879
1529	Wrightham	G	1879
1158	Wynn	W	1879
1456	Yorston	R.J	1879
2351	Young	A	1879
1225	Young	R	1879

2/3rd (EAST KENT. THE BUFFS) REGIMENT.

The 2nd Buffs served with Pearson's Force, also assisted in construction of Forts Tenedos and Pearson. The regiment distinguished itself in the fighting at Inyezane on the 22nd January 1879. Engaged in operations around Eshowe. Six companies present during Eshowe siege and two in the relief column. Latter present at the battle of Gingindhlovu. Another difficult roll to read.

LIEUTENANT COLONEL
Parnell CB   H   1879

MAJOR
Graves   S   1879
Halahan   H.T   1879
  Also had China Medal with clasp Taku Forts.
Hamilton   C.J   No clasp

CAPTAIN
Alexander   G.A   1879
Forster   J.E   1879
Harrison   H.D   1879
Howarth   W.C   1879
Jackson   A.C   1879
Maclear   H.W   1879
Williams   H.M   1879
  D/S 12/3/1879.
Wyld   W.H   1879

CAPTAIN & PAYMASTER
Gelston   A.W.H   1879
  See also Army Pay Department.

QUARTERMASTER
Morgan   W.G   1879

LIEUTENANT & ADJUTANT
Somerset   H.C   1879

LIEUTENANT
Allen   A.J   1879
Backhouse   J.B   1879
Gordon   C.H   1879
Hughes   J   1879
Knight   H.R   1879
Lewis   D.F   1879
Martin   R.McG   1879
Mason   C.E   1879
  D/S 7/4/1879.
Middleton   H.J   1879
Moody   R.H   1879
Newnham-Davis   N   1878-9

2nd LIEUTENANT
Campbell-Johnston   A.F   No clasp
Evelyn   G.R   1879
  D/S 31/3/1879. No trace of issue
Knight-Bruce   J.C   1879
Tylden-Pattenson   A.H   1879
Vyvyan   C.B   1879

SUB LIEUTENANT
Blackburn   H   1879
Connellan   C   1879

ARMY SCHOOLMASTER
Von Hohnhorst   R   No clasp
Tripper   G   No clasp

SERGEANT MAJOR
999 Murphy   P   1879
  Invalided to England 20/06/1879

BANDMASTER
1445 Quinn   H   No clasp
1248 Sweeney   R   No clasp
  Discharged in Natal

DRUM MAJOR
1376 Dillon   C   1879

COLOUR SERGEANT & ORDERLY ROOM CLERK
1587 Geeland   S   1879

COLOUR SERGEANT
45/113 Derby   F   1879
45/658 Ferguson   J   1879
1649 Foley   F   1879
45/99 Gerrard ?   J   1879
1681 Mc Latter   W   1879
  Issued 7.3.81
1631 Meredith   J   1879
45/273 Slattery   J   1879
45/719 Stacpole   H   1879
2155 Western   W   1879

ARMOURER SERGEANT
1182 Rennie   A   1879

QUARTERMASTER SERGEANT
1740 Fairley   J   1879
814 Flawn   H   No clasp
1335 Groves   J   1879

SERGEANT INSTRUCTOR/ MUSKETRY
944 Norboys   T   1879

SERGEANT
2398 Barret   P   1879
183 Bond D/S   G   1879
1972 Bryant   G   1879
1836 Burt   J   1879
1152 Butler   J   1879
905 Connors   P   1879
1235 Conway   J   1879
2213 Colmer   J   No clasp
1306 Dillon   R   1879
825 Downes   W   1879
506 Downing   J   No clasp
1694 Ellis   R   1879
1200 Guesser ?   M   1879
45/1233 Healey   T   1879
1949 Head   J   No clasp
  No Medal Deserted.
45/267 James   J   1879
2263 Lee   W   1879
2260 Millne   F   1879
1941 Morley   R   1879
45/655 Murphy   J   1879
45/149 Naughton   P   1878-9
285 Norman   P   1879
1807 Pocock   R   1879
1349 Power   L   No clasp
45/1427 Rawlings   J   1879
1553 Reilly   A   1879
1841 Robberts   C   1879
1742 Robinson   G   1879
1724 Robinson   G   1879
1688 Sheppard   W   1879
2394 Smyth   W   1879
45/670 Staines   J   1879
2141 Tilbury   J   1879

2/3rd Regiment

Number	Name	Initial	Year	Number	Name	Initial	Year	Number	Name	Initial	Year
45/339	Vallance	T	1879	45/736	Evans	E	1878-9	1810	Allen	A	1879
2061	Weatherall	R	1879	45/523	Ferris	J	1879	45/1345	Allen	G	1879
2208	Werry	W	1879	45/462	Field	J	1879	45/315	Allison	W	1879
2286	Whitcher	E	1879	2138	Freeman	G	1879	2050?	Anderson	R	1879
2278	Windsor	C	1879	45/1026	Jacobs	J	1879	45/505	Andrews	H	1879
LANCE SERGEANT				1815	Jeans	R	1879	45/1024	Arnold	W	1879
45/379	Bain	H	1879	45/372	Jegers	A	1879	45/1534	Ashworth	W	No clasp
663	Benn	W	1879	1845	Jermer	A	1879	45/1206	Atkins	T ?	1879
45/1291	Caldwell	J	1879	1422	Johnings	J	1879	45/1189	Atkins	G	1879
Issued 2.8.1882				45/1172	Jones	H	1879	2337	Austin	G	1879
45/7	Clover	H	1878-9	45/373	Keeffe	J	1879	45/1118	Ayling	W	1879
45/779	Collingway ?	J	1879	1872	Ker	R	1879	45/479	Bailey	F	1879
45/291	Hall	H	1879	45/1344	King	W	1879	1890	Baldock	G	1879
45/370	Hooper	J	1879	45/1187	Ladlaw	W	1879	45/415	Baldock	W	1879
To England 8.6.1879				45/274	Lovatt	P	1879	45/595	Baldwin	G	1878-9
45/782	Mc Carthy	J	1879	1538	Mc Dowell	W	No clasp	45/500	Ball	E	1878-9
2155	Walton	A	1879	45/1236	Milan	W	1879	1825	Ball	G	1879
CORPORAL				45/649	Miller	J	1879	45/420	Ball	L	1879
2075	Baker	F	No clasp	45/477	Moon ?	J	1879	45/374	Baker	G	1879
1366	Bathurst ?	G	1879	45/707	Murray	E	1879	1797	Baker	H	1879
45/720	Brown	W	1879	45/722	Pickering	J	1879	1932	Baker	J	1879
45/1129	Buck	A	1879	45/1533	Shuckford	T	No clasp	45/282	Bamburg	C	1879
2146	Cardin	T	1879	45/1522	Stock	W	No clasp	45/534	Barham	E	1879
45/1049	Carter	C	1879	2311	Taylor D/S	T	1879	45/352	Barker	A	1879
45/350	Clarke	T	1879	45/717	Terry	W	1879	45/590	Barker	G	1879
45/1317	Coulby	W	1879	2197	Ward	J	1879	45/723	Barkley	J	1879
45/1166	Day	W	1879	45/1154	Wilmot ?	W	1879	45/1175	Barnes	S	1879
1847	Desland	J	1879	**LANCE CORPORAL DRUMMER**				3355	Barnes	W	1879
2071	Dixon	W	1879	45/758	Cole	S	1879	958	Barras ?	G	1879
45/1371	Edgehill	C	No clasp	**DRUMMER**				45/531	Barrett	H	1879
45/491	Evenden	F	1879	45/113?	Barton	W	1879	45/1485	Barrett	W	No clasp
45/504	Ferguson	J	1879	45/575	Bowdidge	J	1879	45/983	Bartlett	W	1879
45/1373	Ganick	P	1879	1580	Cahill	A	1879	45/1115	Bates	G	1879
2301	Green ?	W	1879	45/891	Cornelius	J	1879	573	Batley	R	1879
45/661	Harris	G	1879	45/651	Dundas	J	1879	2432	Batty	F	1879
2292	Harris	J	1879	1703	Hopkins	H	1879	45/410	Beale	W	1879
45/533	Harrison	J	1879	45/268	Jackson	T	1878-9	45/1239	Bean	S	1879
2318	Hurstice ?	D	1879	45/118	Jenkins	P	1879	45/455	Beard	R	1879
45/1521	Jones	W	No clasp	1732	Johnings	T	1879	45/377	Beavitt	W	1879
2102	Kelly	J	1879	432	Mc Clusky	J	1879	45/1120	Becker	L	1879
45/612	Killip	H	1879	*45/223	Mortiner	A	1879	45/759	Beech	W	1879
2226	Maton	F	1879	D/S 6th March 1879 Fort Ekowe				45/1247	Bell	W	1879
45/1001	Medowcroft ?		1879	45/255	Rees	J	1879	45/567	Bellinger ?	H	1879
45/566	Neville	H	1879	2169	Rielly	N	1879	45/840	Bellen	J	1879
45/1028	Pears	A	1879	45/129	Shepherd	G	1879	45/405	Bennett	F	1879
1759	Quinn	J	1879	2105	Synau ?	J	1879	45/488	Bennett	S	1879
2067	Rhind	W	1879	2371	Tapp	R	1879	45/1282	Bennett	W	1879
45/279	Roberts	T	1879	41/171	White	T	1879	45/1235	Bennett ?		1879
45/385	Sandford	B	1879	45/577	Withers	J	1879	45/1159	Bidwell	R	1879
45/1042	Snoshall	H	1879	**PRIVATE**				45/1304	Black	H	1879
2327	Sutton	C	1879	1977	Abel	W	1879	45/581	Bodmer	A	1879
45/856	Wilkinson	G	1879	45/1255	Abell	W	1879	45/1045	Bolton D/S	J	1879
LANCE CORPORAL				3413	Abrahams	F	1879	45/445	Bond	F	1879
2016	Beeching	H	1879	45/553	Abrahams	G	1879	45/1245	Bond	J	1879
1644	Boyce	A	No clasp	45/539	Abrams	A	1878-9	45/754	Boswell D/S	M	1879
45/813	Brady	T	1879	45/752	Acton	G	1879	45/1255	Bough	T	1879
15/1403	Button	E	1879	45/1355	Adams	W	1879	**KIA** Inyanzani.			
45/1025	Dove	H	1879	45/1340	Alfrey	R	1879	45/142	Bowenzer ? D/S	J	1879
2047	Duffin	J	1879	45/1020	Algar	W	1879	1906	Bowden	R	1879

2/3rd Regiment

No.	Name	Initial	Year	No.	Name	Initial	Year	No.	Name	Initial	Year
2184	Bowen	J	1879	270	Carrigh	N	1879	45/839	Courtney	J	1879
45/564	Bowman	G	1879	45/724	Carroll	P	1879	45/1343	Coville	W	1879
45/482	Bowman	T	1879	45/948	Carter	C	1879	45/1197	Cox	R	1879
45/1034	Box	J	1879	583	Carter	J	1879	45/861	Cracknell	T	1879
45/1260	Boxall	W	1879	45/1397	Cardwell	J	1879	45/990	Cramp	W	1879
45/182	Boyce	N	1879	1573	Cardwell	J	1879	2033	Craney	S	1879
2259	Bradley	J	1879	2261	Casey	J	1879	1848	Cressy	S	1879
2349	Brady	J	1879	45/292	Cassidy	P	1879	2342	Criddick	E	1879
45/1292	Bramble	H	1879	2053	Chadburn	F	1879	2334	Crook	J	1879
45/575	Branogan	A	1879	45/1331	Chamberlain	R	1879	45/468	Crocket	G	1879
45/820	Branscombe	M	1879	45/1258	Chance	J	1879	45/1493	Croft	W	No clasp
45/992	Brennan	E	1879	45/1499	Chandler	J	No clasp	45/771	Crompton	J	1879
45/555	Brewer	W	1879	45/685	Chandler	J	1879	45/772	Crowe	W	1879
45/655	Brooke	G	1879	45/1064	Chapman	F	1879	45/757	Crozier	J	1878-9
45/1125	Brooks	J	1879	45/1528	Chapman	J	No clasp	45/542	Culwer	J	1879
45/1355	Brown	A	1879	45/404	Chippendon	F	1879	45/838	Cumming	H	1878-9
45/1386	Brown	A	1879	45/573	Chiswell	E	1878-9	45/287	Curry	A	1879
45/454	Brown	F	1879	45/484	Chiverton	W	1879	45/1204	Currye	G	1879
45/1255	Brown	G	1879	45/575	Clarke	G	1879	2126	Curtis	E	1879
45/558	Brown	G	1879	45/1011	Clarke	J	1879	45/364	Cusack	W	1879
45/1382	Brown	H	1879		No Medal Deserted.			45/863	Dabbage	J	1879
45/1193	Brown	H	1879	45/1298	Clarke	J	1879	45/869	Dadley	F	1879
Deserted.				45/114	Clarke	D/SJ	1879	45/500	Dailey	M	1879
45/1143	Browne	J	1879	45/1421	Clarke	R	1879	45/492	Dale	W	1879
45/537	Brown	M	1879	45/1207	Clarke	W	1879	2325	Daley	C	1879
45/1275	Brown	W	1879	45/580	Clareton	C	1879	45/864	Daley	T	1879
45/375	Brown	W	1879	45/716	Clifford	F	1879	45/757	Daley	T	1879
1822	Brudnell	G	1879	45/1550	Clinton	G	No clasp	45/1347	Dalton	G	1879
1357	Bryant	G	1879		No medal Deserted.			45/1319	Daniels	H	1879
2256	Buck	J	1879	45/878	Cloyne	J	1879	45/1316	Daniels	R	1879
1927	Budgeon	A	1879	2277	Coakly	C	1879	2308	Davas	J	1879
45/495	Bullen	H	1879	45/836	Coakly	H	1879	No trace of issue			
45/140	Bullen	H	No clasp	45/1359	Coats	P	1879	2316	Davis	A	1879
45/483	Bunn	T	1879	45/318	Cocklin	J	1879	45/1323	Davis	A	1879
45/1185	Burch	J	1879	1997	Cole	G	1879	45/486	Davis	D	1879
2370	Burgess	A	1879	45/877	College	R	1879	45/1203	Davis	D	1879
45/551	Burke	J	1879	45/494	Collier D/S	J	1879	45/701	Davis	G	1879
	No Medal Deserted.			45/1128	Collins	J	1879	45/300	Davis	G	1879
45/1050	Burke	P	1879	45/1231	Collings	D	1879	2068	Davis	J	1879
45/459	Burkett	C	1879	45/729	Comeford	T	1879	2017	Davis	W	1879
45/451	Burns	J	1879	45/790	Connelly	H	1879	2221	Dawkins	R	1878-9
1554	Burns	J	1879	45/1196	Connolly	J	1879	45/598	Day	E	1879
45/584	Burns	P	1879	2220	Connor	J	1879	45/770	Day	M	1879
45/1271	Burridge	J	1879	2187	Conner	J	1879	45/578	Dayes	C	1879
45/750	Bury	A	1879	45/784	Connor	P	1879	1987	Dean	H	1879
45/1140	Bush	G	1879	45/1199	Connor	T	1879	2377	Deen	E	1879
45/1290	Bush	T	1879	45/331	Connor	W	1879	45/733	Delaney	N	1879
1075	Bushell	G.H	No clasp	1889	Cook	C	1879	45/392	Denman	J	1878-9
45/1133	Bushell	W	1879	45/1211	Cook	F	1879	1711	Devan	T	1879
45/1408	Butler	J	1879	45/829	Cook	R	1879	45/887	Devlin	O	1879
45/1520	Butler	J	1879		No medal Deserted Oct 1879.			45/469	Devonport	J	1879 r
2408	Byrnes	E	1879	45/458	Cook	W	1879	1244	Dillon	J	No clasp
45/1526	Byrnes	E	No clasp	45/1110	Cooper	T	1879	925	Dillon	M	1879
45/327	Byrnes	J	1879	45/1281	Coopens	J	1879	45/328	Dillon	T	1879
1539	Byrnes	T	1879	45/865	Corbie	J.W	1879	2198	Dixon	J	1879
45/330	Byrnes	W	1879	45/755	Corless	J	1879	45/942	Dixon	J	1879
2326	Cambridge	C	1879	45/1164	Coslin	W	1879	45/876	Dobbs	T	1879
45/536	Carey	T	1879	45/944	Couchman	C	1879	45/743	Doherty	A	1879
45/1032	Carr	C	1879	45/1283	Couchman	D	1879	801	Doherty	J	1879

2/3rd Regiment

45/1170	Dolan	M	1879	45/591	Food	J	1879	45/592	Hall	W	1879
45/1394	Donnelly	D	1879	45/1209	Foster	E	1879	Duplicate Medal and clasp issued			
45/1327	Donovan	C	1879	2358	Foster	J	1879	3/7/1918.			
45/814	Donovan	J	1879	45/525	Fox	S	1879	45/659	Hamilton	E	1879
45/804	Doughty	H	1879	45/1425	Francis	P	1879	45/316	Hammond	W	1879
45/1053	Downs	A	1879	45/525	Fox	S	1879	2300	Hanchett	J	1878-9
550	Downs	C	1879	45/1425	Francis	P	1879	45/1524	Hanley	E	No clasp
45/1171	Downey	T	1879	45/515	Franklin	F	1878-9	45/322	Hanrahan	J	1879
45/297	Dowle	W	1879	45/1030	Franklin	J	1879	45/340	Happe	F	1879
1052	Doyle	J	1879	45/880	Freeborn	J	1879	45/1377	Harding	T	1879
45/708	Doyle	J	1879	45/1021	Freeman	G	1879	45/593	Harlow	H	1879
2258	Drake	J	1879	45/1141	Friar	E	1879		No medal Deserted.		
45/355	Droughton	J	1879	45/573	Friary	T	1879	2302	Harman	W	1879
1766	Duffett	H	1879	3209	Friend	A	1879	45/1124	Harper	W	1879
45/1422	Duffey	J	1879	45/1484	Frogay	G	No clasp	45/522	Harrington	J	1879
45/586	Duignan	D	1879	45/834	Frost	A	1879	45/376	Harrington	R	1879
*??	Dunn	F	Not on medal roll	45/409	Fry	J	1878-9	45/137	Harris	E	1879
D/S 23rd January 1879 Fort Ekowe				45/1175	Fry	T	1879	1780	Harris	T	1879
45/866	Dunne	H	1879	*45/290	Gain	J	1879	45/648	Harris	W	1879
45/127	Dunne	H	1879	290 J.Gavin D/S 16th April 1879 Herwin				No Medal Discharged with ignominy.			
45/1100	Dunne KIA	P	1879	45/689	Galloway	T	1879	45/1194	Harris	W	1879
45/582	Dunkin	E	1879	1390	Galpin	P	1879	45/424	Harrison	G	1879
45/1339	Dunlop	T	1879	45/980	Galvin	J	1879	45/995	Hart	F	No clasp
45/412	Dwyer	P	1879	45/1035	Gardiner	R	1879	45/1530	Hartigan	L	No clasp
45/1088	Edwards	D	1879	45/634	Gardiner	W	1879	45/545	Hatton	W	1879
45/1495	Ellendon	A	No clasp	45/476	Garwood	J	1879	45/588	Hawkes	J	1879
45/394	Elliott	F	1879	45/778	Gascoyne	T	1878-9		No Medal Deserted.		
45/1240	Elms	W	1879	45/1091	Gash	J	1879	45/1078	Hawkins	J	1879
45/1134	Else	T	1879	45/1306	Gately	W	No clasp	45/1165	Hayes	N	1879
2291	Elwell	R	1879		No medal Deserted.			2283	Hayter	A	1879
45/1409	Esmer	F	1879	45/365	Gayner	J	1879	2383	Haywood	H	1879
45/841	Evans	H	1879	45/875	Gee	G	1879 r	45/399	Haywood	W	1879
45/1169	Evans	J	1879	45/1336	George	W	1879	2264	Hazard	W	1879
2305	Everett	S	1879		No medal Deserted.			45/1353	Heresay	A	1879
2241	Eves	J	1879	2017	German	G	1879	2323	Herriott	T	1879
45/824	Eynes	J	1879	45/553	Gerrity	H	1879	1902	Hibbert	G	No clasp
45/1290	Farbrace ?	J	1879	45/1067	Gibbons	W	1879	45/1313	Higgerson	J	1879
2288	Farley	J	1879	45/821	Gibbs	G	1879		No medal Deserted.		
45/527	Farrell	G	1879	2533	Gibbons	T	1879	45/454	Higgins	R	1879
45/5411	Farrell	J	1879	45/833	Gilbert	J	1879	45/335	Hill	J	1879
45/387	Farrell	M	1879	45/579	Godbeher ?G		1879	45/1121	Hillier	J	1879
2320	Farrell	T	1879	45/472	Godfrey	C	1879	45/1158	Holden D/S	J	1879
45/1136	Favell	E	1879	45/1250	Godfrey	T	1879	45/715	Hodges	G	1879
45/1135	Featherstone	H	1879	45/559	Gooding D/S	F	1879	45/1296	Hodges	T	No clasp
45/1059	Fenton	B	1879	45/520	Goodson	W	1879	45/955	Hogan	J	1879
45/314	Ferguson	W	1879 r	45/396	Gough	R	No clasp	45/1554	Hogan	M	No clasp
	Discharged with ignominy.			45/686	Grant	R	1879	45/853	Hole	W	1879
45/319	Field	W	No clasp	45/345	Gray	A	1879	45/985	Holies	M	1879
	No medal. In prison.			45/653	Green	C	1879	45/1356	Holland	J	1879
45/281	Fitzpatrick	W	1879	45/1259	Green	R	1879	45/993	Holland	J	1879
45/795	Flanaghan	B	1879	45/1320	Greenland	T	1879	45/870	Hollingsworth	J	No clasp
45/1150	Flanaghan	H	1879 r	1850	Grimwood	S	1879	No issue. In prison for whole of campaign.			
	Forfeited. Later restored.			45/310	Griffin	P	No clasp	45/879?	Holmes	J	1879
45/1531	Flanaghan	T	No clasp	45/619	Griffiths	J	1878-9	45/718	Holmes	R	1879
*1101	Flannerr D.J Not on medal roll			45/461	Griffiths	W	1879	45/105	Holton	T	1879
D/S 3rd April 1879 Inyenznne				45/158	Groves	H	No clasp	45/1379	Hooks	E	1879
45/1102	Flannery	D	1879	45/254?	Hackett	C	1879	45/1525	Howe	G	No clasp
45/1100	Flannery	D	1879	45/402	Hagger	W	1879	2219	Hoy	J	No clasp
	KIA Gingihlovo.			45/657	Haice	E	1879	45/785	Hughes	D	No clasp

2/3rd Regiment

45/780	Hughes	G	1879	45/786	Kinnisella	G	1878-9	45/641	Mc Carthy	D	1879
2182	Hughes	H	1879	45/712	Kirby	T	1879	45/1188	Mc Carthy	W	1879
45/815	Hughes	J	1879	45/751	Kirkman	T	1879	45/626	Mc Donald	C	1878-9
45/1068	Hughesman	C	1879	1647	Lacey	J	1879	45/763	Mc Donald	J	1879
45/1496	Humphries	S	No clasp	45/816	Laker	C	1879	2304	Mc Evoy	A	1879
45/584	Huxley	D	1878-9	45/1245	Large	W	1879	1140	Mc Evoy	J	1879
45/1117	Hymas	C	1879	45/81?	Larkin	H	1879	45/735	Mc Evoy	P	1879
45/1252	Ives	J	1879	45/1299	Law	A	1879	45/1529	Mc Gann	M	No clasp
45/478	Ives	T	1879	45/528	Lawrence	F	1879	45/1259	Mc Glashan	A	1879
45/505	Jackson	H	1879	1712	Lawrence	S	1879	1307	Mc Grath	J	1879
No Medal Discharged with ignominy.				45/981	Lawson	B	1879	45/1423	Mc Grath	J	1879
2160	Jackson D/S	J	1879	45/1104	Leadbetter	B	1879	45/275	Mc Grath	M	1879
2271	Jacobs	E	1879	45/1127	Leary	C	1879	45/666	Mc Illuriant ?	W	1879
45/825	Jakins	G	1878-9	Deserted. No trace of return of medal.				45/1566	Mc Kendry	A	No clasp
45/312	Jarrett	W	1879	45/872	Leavin	W	No clasp	45/822	Mc King	H	1879
45/1237	Jarvis	H	1879	300	Lee	J	No clasp	45/368	Mc Kinnon	L	1879
45/1153	Jennings	D	1879	45/1123	Lee	T	1879 r	45/1152	Mc Leod	J	1879
45/1214	Jerrald	R	1879	Discharged with ignominy.				*45/1270	Mc Leod	W	1879
No medal Deserted.				45/817	Leighton	W	1879	D/S 13th February 1879 Fort Ekowe			
45/353	Jessup	J	1879	45/353	Leonard	J	1879	45/807	Mc Loughlin	E	1879
2274	Jessup	W	1879	1802	Lewis	J	1879	45/307	Mc Mahon	J	1879
45/1139	Johnston	F	1879	45/754	Lewis	J	1879	45/1555	Mc Millan	J	No clasp
45/1035	Johnston	G	1879	45/1372	Lilly	E	1879	45/1226	Mc Millan	W	1879
1255	Johnston	W	1879	45/989	Lilly	H	1879	45/730	Mc Mullen	R	1879
427	Jones	H	1879	45/501	Lloyd	J	1878-9r	45/747	Mc Nally	J	1879
2339	Jones	J	1879	45/1288	Lloyd	T	1879	45/603	Mc Quillin	R	1879
45/757	Jones	J	1879	628	Lonergan	J	1879	45/1400	Mc Taggert	J	1879
45/1017	Jones	S	1879	45/324	Long	W	No clasp	2386	Mc Stea	H	1879
45/571	Jones	W	1879	45/1079	Loughlin	J	1879	179	Meade	J	1879
45/1324	Joynes	J	1879	45/632	Luhars	B	1879	45/420	Merritt	G	1879
45/306	Kearns	W	1879	45/1107	Lynch	C	1879	*2206	Merritt	G	1879
45/326	Keefe	J	1879	45/618	Lynch	S	1879	D/S 9th April 1879 Lower Tugela			
45/889	Keinan	J	1879 r	2214	Macey	G	1879	45/650	Merritt	W	1879
45/768	Kelleher	R	1879	45/562	Mackie	A	1879	Deserted No Medal.			
KIA Inyezane.				45/629	Mahoney	J	No clasp	2253	Merryweather	R	1878-9
45/738	Kelly	A	1879	45/1180	Mann	A	1879	45/2341	Miller	J	1879
45/765	Kelly	D	1879	439	Marniox ?	M	No clasp	45/546	Miller D/S	G	1879
45/883	Kelly	J	1879	45/818	Maple	J	1879	45/378	Minks D/S	A	1879
45/481	Kelly	M	1879	45/1210	Maple	W	1879	45/1236	Mitchell	J	1879
45/1208	Kelly	M	1879	45/1354	Mara	J	1879 r	45/1009	Moffat	R	No clasp
45/406	Kelly	P	1879	2244	Marley	J	1879	45/1313	Mondin	C	1879
2321	Kennedy	J	No clasp	45/1006	Martin	J	1879	* ???	Monk	J	Not on medal roll
45/881	Kermion	J	1879	2282	Martin	J	1878-9	D/S 4th April 1879 Fort Ekowe			
No medal Deserted.				45/51	Martin	T	1879	45/82?	Moore KIA	C	1879?
45/1011	Kerskey	A	1879	45/939	Martin	W	1879	45/801	Moran	J	1879
No medal Deserted.				45/540	Marsh	G	1879	2345	Moreland	T	1879
45/517	Kerdake	F	1879	45/1051	Marsh	R	1879	45/1023	Morgan	J	1879
2319	Key	J	1879	45/1167	Marshall	R	1879	45/1014	Morley	B	1879
45/702	Kidd D/S	W	1879	45/510	Mathew	C	1879	45/1399	Morley	H	1879
45/806	Kilkenny	J	1879	45/295	Mathews	W	1879	45/585	Morris	A	1879
45/847	Kinchington	J	1879	1793	May	E	1879	45/822	Morris	T	1879
45/1146	King	C	1879	45/1111	May	G	1879	45/224	Mortiner	J	1879
45/1149	King	E	1879	45/1368	May	G	1879	45/567	Moss	W	1879
45/1328	King	G	1879 r	45/1494	May	G	No clasp	45/1230	Moss	W	1879
45/640	King	L	1879	2306	May	P	1879	1562	Mullin	D	1879
45/1294	King	R	1879	45/1297	May	W	1879	45/1428	Mullin	J	1879 r
45/130	Kingdent	G	1879	45/1535	Mc Cabe	J	No clasp	1574	Mullholland	A	1879
*45/1090	Kingston	A	1879	45/741	Mc Cann	J	1879	45/1393	Mullholland	R	1879
D/S 1st February 1879 Fort Ekowe				1588	Mc Cann	R	1879	45/843	Munro	F	1879 r

2/3rd Regiment

No.	Name	Initial	Year
45/138	Munson	W	1879
45/797	Murphy	F	1879
45/846	Murphy	T	1879
45/787	Murphy	W	1879
45/1044	Murray	J	1879
45/417	Muspratt	W	1879
45/788	Neville	E	1879
2346	Nicholls	H	1879
45/1081	Neuman ??	H	1879 r
	Issued in error.		
45/1264	Nickles	H	1879
1897	Nimmo	W	1879
45/1389	Novey	H	1879
	No Medal Deserted.		
45/783	Newman ?	G	1879
45/1369	Nunn ?	H	1879
	No Medal Deserted.		
2299	Newman	G	1879
45/1791	O'Brien	J	1879
45/304	O'Connor	J	1879
1377	O'Connor	M	1879
45/742	O'Doherty	P	1879 r
1345	O'Grady	D	No clasp
45/325	O'Malley	P	1879
45/808	O'Neil	H	1879
1228	O'Neil	H	No clasp
45/1181	O'Sullivan	J	No clasp
*1795	Oakley	E	1879
	D/S 15th February 1879 Fort Ekowe		
45/539	Oates	C	1879
45/397	Orr	G	1879
45/216	Orrigan	W	1879 r
810	Osmond	D	1879
2357	Overy	R	1879
45/1425	Owen	B	1879
1767	Palmer	A	1879
45/366	Palmer	J	1879
1828	Palmer	T	1879
45/343	Parfitt	C	1879
45/850	Parker	A	1879
45/714	Parker	G	1879
45/1168	Parker	H	1879
45/842	Parker	T	1879
45/605	Parnell	E	1879
45/849	Pavey	C	1879
45/1031	Peachey	R	1879
49	Peacock	W	No clasp
45/1004	Pearce	T	1879
45/1003	Pearce	W	1879
1648	Pepper	J	1879
	No Medal Deserted.		
45/991	Perman	T	1879
48/819	Peters	D	1878-9
45/1093	Pethers	G	1879
2382	Petts	A	1879
45/347	Phillip	L	1879
301	Pickering	J	1879
2170	Pierce	D/S W	1879
45/851	Piper	R	1879
45/106	Platford	A	1879
45/991	Poman ?	T	1879
2428	Powell	H	1879
45/1424	Power	M	1879
45/622	Powis	C	1879
1486	Price	E	1879
45/809	Price	T	1879
45/1364	Prior	G	1879
45/568	Purcell	H	No clasp
45/590	Randle	J	1879
2374	Ray ?	T	1879
45/1497	Reeves	H	No clasp r
	Deserted.		
45/943	Reid	H	1879
45/271	Reidy	J	1878-9
45/352	Relin D/S	J	1879
45/1148	Ravello	G	1879
45/1162	Rhodes	J	1879
45/383	Riddle	J	1879
45/755	Roach	J	1879
45/1027	Roberts	W	1879
45/828	Robinson	H	1879
2372	Robinson	J	1879
45/1348	Robinson	W	1879
45/739	Rock	J	1879
45/844	Rodgers	A	1879
45/598	Rodgers	J	No clasp
	No medal Discharged during campaign		
45/525	Rose	D	1879
45/852	Rowe	H	1879
2218	Royle	H	1879
45/124	Ruck	W	1879
714	Rudden	C	1879
45/58	Ruddy	P	No clasp
	No Medal Deserted.		
45/1157	Russell	J	1879
45/946	Russell	W	1879
45/1202	Sabill ?	T	No clasp
	No Medal Deserted.		
45/1098	Sampson	G	1879
45/1191	Saunders	H	1879
1241	Saunders	J	1879
	No Medal Deserted.		
45/675	Savage	W	1879
1441	Saville	F	1879
2166	Scott	B	1879
2162	Scott	I	1879
570	Scott	W	1879
1707	Selfe	E	1879
45/1532	Sharp	D	No clasp
45/810	Shaw	C	1878-9
KIA Isandhwana.			
45/,,??	Shaw	R	1879
45/521	Shaw	T	1879
45/837	Shaw	W	1879
45/550	Shea	J	1879
2343	Shea	T	1879
2331	Shea	M	1878-9
Duplicate Medal and clasp 1878-9 issued 11/7/1918.			
45/793	Sheedy	D	1879
2268	Sheen	J	1879
45/415	Sheppard	F	1879
2183	Sheppard	H	1879
2073	Sheppard	W	1879 r
2234	Sheppard	W	1879
45/795	Sheridan	F	1879
45/1016	Shrubshall	J	1879
45/1334	Shrubsole	S	1879
45/1552	Shruel	J	No clasp
45/1217	Simpson	C	1879
	No medal Deserted.		
45/947	Sinclair	A	1879
45/1178	Sinclair	E	1879
45/1225	Sinclair	J	1879
45/1498	Skells	H	No clasp
	No medal Deserted.		
*45/823	Slack	J	1879
D/S 9h March 1879 Fort Ekowe			
1811	Smith	C	No clasp
	No medal Deserted.		
45/215	Smith	C	1879
45/457	Smith	F	1879
45/624	Smith	F	1879
45/1244	Smith	F	1879
45/502	Smith	F	1879 r
	Deserted.		
45/2176	Smith	G	1879
45/419	Smith	J	No clasp
45/1186	Smith	J	1879
	No medal Deserted.		
45/1318	Smith	J	1879
45/4751	Smith	H	1879
45/1251	Smith	S	1879
45/1019	Smith	S	1879
45/117	Smith	T	1879
45/599	Smith	T	1879
45/811	Smith	W	1879
45/1047	Smith	W	1879
45/119	Smith	W	1879
45/1272	Snaffer D/S	T	1879
45/768	Sothern	W	1879
45/472	Spain ?	W	1879
45/320	Sparks	A	1879
45/1333	Spirit ?	W	1879
45/1105	Spokes ?	J	1879
45/298	Spratt	S	1879
45/1523	Stagg	G	No clasp
45/630	Stansfield	W	1879
45/578	Stanton	P	1879
45/662	Starkey	H	1879
45/664	Steel	J	1878-9
2381	Stephinson	J	1879
45/848	Stevenson	J	1879
45/694	Stirton	T	1879
45/1315	Stone	A	1879

2/3rd Regiment

Number	Surname	Initial	Year/Notes
45/762	Strong	T	1879
45/986	Suckling	T	1879
902?	Sullivan	D	1879
45/1342	Sullivan	J	1879
328	Sullivan	J	1879
45/802	Suswood	J	1878-9
45/1198	Sulton	J	1879
45/1332	Sutton	J	1879
*1274	Swaffu	J	Not on medal roll
	D/S 16th March 1879 Herwio		
45/467	Sweeney	D	1879
45/1267	Swift	J	1879
1132	Sydes	J	1879
2129	Taaffe	P	1879
45/597	Tabran	T	1879
	No Medal Deserted.		
45/1553	Tadd	H	No clasp
2247	Talbto	J	1879
*45/120	Tarrant	A	1879
	D/S 27th March 1879 Fort Ekowe		
45/414	Taylor	E	1879
45/1285	Taylor	J	1879
45/1259	Taylor	J	No clasp
	No medal. In prison during campaign and Deserted.		
*45/1213	Taylor	T	1879
	D/S 21st February 1879 Fort Ekowe		
2333	Taylor	W	1879
2229	Testar ?	T	1879
45/453	Thain	E	1879
45/857	Thom ?	T	1879
2246	Thomas	W	1879
45/1058	Thomerson	W	1879
2269	Thompson	A	1879
45/777	Thompson	G	1879
45/1387	Thompson	J	1879
45/499	Thompson	T	1879
45/344	Thorne	A	1879
45/1314	Thornhill	A	1879
45/604	Thwaltes	S	1879
45/858	Thornton	W	1879
45/557	T ?	J	1879
2362	Tobin	W	1879
45/715	Towers	J	1879
45/1097	Tray	E	1879
2212	Tredgott	J	1879
	No trace of issue		
45/759	Trotter	W	1879
45/740	Trotter	R	1879
45/1070	Tuckett	W	1879
2202	T ?	R	1879
45/1307	Turner	J	1879
45/1155	T ?	J	1879
45/859	Unwin	J	1879
45/951	Vension ?	J	1879
2210	Vile	J	1879
45/830	Wade	W	1879
45/548	Walker	J	1879
1232	Walsh	J	1879
45/533	Walsh	M	1879
45/386	Walsh	T	1879
45/2406	Ward	H	1879
45/609	Ward	J	1878-9
	Deserted. No trace of return of Medal.		
45/369	Warden	J	1878-9
45/627	Warren	H	1879
45/560	Warrington	R	1879
45/812	Watkins	J	1879
45/354	Watson	A	1879
45/1136	Watson	H	1879
45/873	Watson	J	1879
45/447	Watson	P	1879
45/351	Weatherly	H	1879
45/1002	Webb	H	1879
45/401	Welbelove	H	1879
45/1089	Wells	A	1879
45/869	Wells	C	1878-9
45/642	Welch	J	1879
45/709	Wensley	J	1879
2158	Weskon ?	N	1879
45/389	Wheatley	G	1878-9
	KIA Isandhlwana.		
1886	Wheeler	J	1879
45/1537	White	A	No clasp
45/1551	White	G	No clasp
	Invalided to England march 1880		
2188	White	H	1879
45/308	White	J	1879
45/572	White	J	1878-9
45/1274	White	J	1879
45/602	Whitehead	H	1879
45/1538	Whitesner ?	G	No clasp
45/855	Whitnell	H	1879
45/773	Wilday	J	1879
45/984	Wilden	E	1879
45/587	Wilkins	J	1879
45/1092	Williams	E	1879
45/874	Williams	H	1879
45/1527	Williams	J	No clasp
	Deserted		
45/153	Williams	J	1878-9
45/465	Williams	W	1879
45/524	Williams	W	1879
45/1243	Wilson	J	1879
45/574	Wilson	J	1879
45/1485	Wilson	W	No clasp
45/620	Wiltshire	D	1878-9
45/1273	Winder	J	1879
2218	Windus	W	1879
45/1489	Winsley	H	No clasp
1150	Wood	J	1879
2257	Woodhouse	W	1879
45/1054	Woodman	W	1879
45/746	Woods	H	1879
2107	Worsdall	W	1879
45/530	Worsfold	J	1879
2415	Wreach	P	1879
2267	Wright	D	1879
45/628	Wright	G	1879
45/511	Wyles	J	1879
45/489	Wyles	J	1879

* London Gazette 23 May 1879

2/4th (THE KING'S OWN ROYAL) REGIMENT.

Arrived in Durban January 1879, mainly employed on detachment, garrison and escort duties. Embarked for Bombay 8.2.1880. In places a difficult roll to read.

BREVET COLONEL
Bray CB   E.W   1879
Also had medals for Cabul and Abyssinia.

BREVET LIEUTENANT COLONEL
Sykes   W.J   1879

MAJOR
Elliot   J.Mc D   1879
Twentyman   A.C   1879
Also had medal for Abyssinia.

BREVET MAJOR
Blake   W.F   1879
Middleton   O.R   1879

CAPTAIN ADJUTANT
Crofton   N.E   1879

CAPTAIN
Knox   R.A   1879
Laurence   H.B   1879
Leggett   C.G   1879
Moore   H   1879
Sharp   J.R   1879
Stockley   J.C   No clasp
Sutherland   H.B   No clasp
Woodgate   E.R.P   1879
Also had medal for Abyssinia.

QUARTERMASTER
Rowland   H   1879

LIEUTENANT
Elliot   G.H.B   1879
Gawne   J.M   1879
Hay   A.W   1879
Hutchinson   F.M.G   1879
Mac Carthy   R.H   1879
Also had Ashanti Medal.
Matthews   F.B   1879
Ogilby   R.A   1879
Penrose   E.R   1879
Rowlandson   J   1879
Shephard   C.S   No clasp

2nd LIEUTENANT
Bonomi   J.I   1879
Carter   E.A.F   1879
Dolphin   E   No clasp
James   W.L   1879
Ridley   A.B   1879

SCHOOLMASTER
Ireland   F   No clasp

SERGEANT MAJOR
1641   Smith   E   1879

2/4th Regiment

DRUM MAJOR
- 2181 Rafter W 1879

ACTING CONDUCTOR
- 1171 O'Neill J 1879

QUARTERMASTER SERGEANT
- 114 Griffinths R 1879

COLOUR SERGEANT
- 2267 Adams W 1879
- 652 Chapman H 1879
- 1936 Ledsham W 1879
- 202 Martin A 1879
- 1466 Moyens T 1879
- 2088 Parker W 1879
- 1675 Roddis T 1879
- 1928 Ward J.R 1879
- 886 Wardle J 1879

ARMOURER SERGEANT
- 34 Guest J 1879

PAYMASTER SERGEANT
- 2273 Rainsburry A No clasp

PIONEER SERGEANT
- 1240 Gamon A 1879

SERGEANT COOK
- 2642 Langmead H 1879

SERGEANT INSTRUCTOR OF MUSKETRY
- 1677 Musler? A 1879

SERGEANT
- 11/415 Barkey P 1879
- 11/638 Barrington J 1879
- 11/2912 Bishop G 1879
- 1443 Bishop T 1879
- 1899 Burton W 1879
- 613 Cain J 1879
- 11/745 Clancy C 1879
- 2106 Colvin W 1879
- 1234 Cook R 1879
- 11/1208 Costello W 1879
- 621 Darwell B 1879
- 2186 Dean J 1879
- 1379 Fulcher T 1879
- 1940 Gibbons J 1879
- 11/578 Gillett J 1879
- 11/431 Herd J 1879
- 967 Johnson W 1879
- 11/3524 Lacey L.J 1879
- 11/1292 Lee N 1879
- 11/591 Matthews J 1879
- 11/855 O'Brien J 1879
- 11/779 O'Brien V 1879
- 457 Smith F No clasp
- 1759 Stafford J 1879
- 1889 Stalder F No clasp
- 2330 Tood R 1879
- 11/946 Wakefield W 1879
- 11/740 Walsh J 1879

LANCE SERGEANT
- 11/37 Charley R 1879
- 11/2506 Evans J.H 1879

- 11/638 Hogan J 1879
- 11/792 Larkin E 1879
- 11/424 Moore J 1879
- 1887 Oates G 1879
- 11/1130 Radcliffe W.F 1879
- 11/995 Roberts J 1879
- 11/1272 Rowe M 1879
- 11/1694 Slight G 1879

ORDERLYROOM CLERK
- 11/1366 Ryle T.B 1879

CORPORAL
- 2453 Arnold T 1879
- 11/323 Barfield G 1879
- 11/327 Barnes G 1879
- No medal Deserted.
- 11/1130 Bing W 1879
- 11/1119 Binns W 1879
- 11/2187 Casper E 1879
- 11/664 Coote C 1879
- 11/3050 Cowley G 1879
- 11/782 Cullemore T 1879
- 11/668 D'Alton W 1879
- 11/1100 Earle J 1879
- 11/325 Evitt W 1879
- 11/379 Fairplay C 1879
- 11/1241 Fox J 1879
- 11/761 Gall B 1879
- 11/754 Geoghegan M 1879
- 11/1311 Gordon J 1879
- 11/302 Harcourt W 1879
- 11/994 Harris R 1879
- 11/1192 Hemsley W 1879
- 11/715 Kavanagh L.J 1879
- 11/1302 Kercourt W 1879
- 11/1215 Lyons W 1879
- 1594 Madelaine W 1879
- 11/1228 Millett W 1879
- 2014 Morris J 1879
- 11/917 Rogers W 1879
- 11/1062 Smith W 1879
- 11/985 Stamp J 1879
- 11/355 Tyson T 1879
- 11/2180 Webb T 1879
- 11/1198 Windus H 1879
- 11/2474 Wooldridge D 1879

LANCE CORPORAL
- 11/2575 Archer E 1879
- 11/1871 Beckett W 1879
- 11/818 Butler W 1879
- 11/2504 Byrne H 1879
- 1575 Croft J 1879
- 11/2506 Evans J.H 1879
- 1982 Evans T 1879
- 11/2384 Field H 1879
- 2185 Green G 1879
- 2111 Grimmer J.E 1879
- 11/2625 Hayward C 1879
- 11/663 Hogan J 1879
- 11/1021 Johnson W 1879

- 2012 Jones R 1879
- 1790 Kemplin W 1879
- 11/736 Kirwan F 1879
- 11/2494 Mc Lelland D 1879
- 11/715 O'Brien J 1879
- 1888 Penny G 1879
- 11/910 Pompet J 1879
- 11/1272 Rowe M 1879
- 11/2763 Shipp W 1879
- 11/1268 Singleton A 1879
- 11/2798 Trott J 1879

DRUMMER
- 1915 Barry J 1879
- 2237 Brusey J 1879
- 2169 Bucknall C 1879
- 1696 Coleman S 1879
- 11/3051 Ewing H 1879 r
- 11/2900 Gibbs B 1879
- 11/620 Hamblett E 1879
- 2064 Hill H.B 1879 r
- 2170 Hills J 1879
- 1593 Humpries T 1879
- 2165 Hurley A 1879
- 2234 Sherwin J 1879
- 2238 Spooner J.E 1879
- 11/1119 Thorpe W.C 1879
- 2227 Turner W 1879
- 1598 Wilson W 1879

PRIVATE
- 11/1360 Abbott J 1879
- 11/1206 Adams W 1879
- 11/2407 Aithwaite M 1879
- 11/2309 Allen D 1879
- 11/2573 Allen C 1879
- 11/2922 Allen P 1879
- 11/2925 Allen T 1879 r
- 11/31 Anderson J 1879
- 11/2581 Anderson T 1879
- 11/1122 Andrews F 1879
- 11/3136 Armstrong J.A 1879
- 11/2349 Arnold T 1879
- 11/2659 Ashenden F 1879
- 11/1201 Ashworth B 1879
- 11/585 Aspell F 1879
- 11/1141 Bacon T 1879
- 11/2443 Bahan T 1879
- 11/2518 Bailey J 1879
- 11/2464 Baker J 1879
- 11/2584 Baker J 1879
- No Medal Deserted.
- 11/2434 Balman T 1879
- 11/3137 Banks C 1879
- 11/1270 Barber T 1879
- 11/2463 Barley C 1879
- 11/3065 Barnard J 1879
- 11/917 Barnes W 1879
- 11/381 Barnett S 1879
- 11/1588 Barnett W 1879
- 11/1241 Barrett B 1879

2/4th Regiment

Number	Surname	Initial	Year	Number	Surname	Initial	Year	Number	Surname	Initial	Year
11/849	Barrett	D	1879	11/960	Bryan	M	1879	11/2765	Coburn	W	1879
11/785	Barrett	M	1879	11/1195	Buckingham	J	1879	11/3061	Colbert	R	1879
11/2488	Barrett	T	1879	11/2620	Bundle	R	1879	11/1018	Collins	D	1879 r
11/1119	Barron	T	1879	11/2470	Buntin	J	1879	11/1147	Collins	G	1879
11/2561	Barry	P	1879	11/2376	Bunting	T	1879	11/2276	Collins	J	1879
2166	Bartlett	C	1879	11/2537	Burgoine	D	1879	11/373	Compton	J	1879
11/587	Bartlett	W.A	1879		No Medal Deserted.			11/2490	Condon	M	1879
11/2572	Batchelder	W	1879	11/615	Burke	T	1879	11/436	Connell	J	1879
11/2388	Bateman	F	1879		No Medal Deserted.			11/1162	Connor	J	1879
11/290	Baxter	W	1879 r	11/2435	Burness	D	1879	11/1097	Connors	D	1879
11/2957	Beaver	W	1879	11/2739	Burns	T	1879	11/763	Conroy	W	1879
11/803	Bedlington	T	1879		No Medal Deserted.			11/941	Constant	G	1879
11/2924	Belcher	S	1879	11/2353	Burrows	J	1879	11/193	Constant	T	1879
2141	Bennett	A	1879	11/3074	Burton	J	1879	11/446	Constant	W	1879
1663	Bennett	C	1879	11/1044	Butler	G	1879	11/1315	Conway	J	1879
1886	Bennett	F	1879	11/1296	Butterfield	J	1879	11/2803	Cooper	T	1879
11/2718	Bennett	J	1879	11/786	Byrne	B	1879	11/2653	Cooney	J	1879
	No Medal Deserted.			11/2794	Byrne	E	1879	11/674	Cope	A.E	1879
11/776	Bermingham	J	1879	11/642	Byrne	J	1879	11/2380	Cope	R	1879
11/631	Beswick	R	1879	11/660	Byrne	J	1879	11/2489	Corbett	S	1879
11/2756	Bibby	J	1879	11/1842	Byrne	T	1879	11/2562	Corcoran	J	1879
11/359	Bingham	J	1879	11/2799	Byrne	W	1879	11/3039	Corduck	G	1879
11/702	Birch	J	1879	11/1187	Byrne	W	1879	11/966	Cornhill	J	1879
11/2386	Bird	C	1879	11/2757	Callaghan	A	1879	11/2475	Costello	T	1879
11/2406	Bird	J	1879	11/2311	Callaghan	J	1879	11/2061	Cottle	J	1879
1851	Birrell	D	1879	11/671	Callaghan	J	1879	2179	Coughtrey	G	1879
11/568	Blake	J	1879	11/600	Callanan	M	1879	11/396	Court	A.E	1879
2182	Blake	W	1879	11/2758	Calvert	H	1879	11/3057	Coseney	B	1879
11/2423	Boland	J	1879	11/393	Campbell	J	1879	11/2919	Cox	A	1879
11/540	Booth	E	1879	11/3043	Canon	J	1879	11/3047	Cox	C	1879
11/816	Borkin	J	No clasp	11/326	Carberry	C	1879	11/937	Cox	W	1879
11/2408	Borden	J	1879	11/439	Carberry	J	1879	11/2454	Crabtree	W	1879
11/739	Bourke	T	1879	11/780	Carroll	J	1879	11/1274	Cragg	R	1879
11/2501	Bowner	W	1879	11/2798	Carroll	P	1879	11/2566	Craig	J	1879
11/3046	Boxall	E	1879	11/2817	Cartledge	F	1879		No Medal Deserted.		
11/956	Boyce	J	1879	11/2621	Carter	J	1879	11/384	Cramer	E	1879
11/2173	Boyd	R	1879	11/576	Casey	O	1879	11/566	Cravan	J	1879
11/2446	Bradley	J	1879	11/1265	Catterall	J	1879	11/2180	Crawley	W	1879
11/2302	Bradley	J	1879	11/368	Catterall	W	1879	11/1589	Cronin	C	1879
11/1227	Bradshaw	D	No clasp r	11/961	Cawley	T	1879	11/2029	Cronshaw	J	1879
11/2310	Bray	H	1879	11/2894	Chadwick	J	1879	11/2505	Croxford	G	1879
865	Breakwell	S	1879	11/2127	Chadwick	W	1879	987	Cummings	A	1879
11/416	Breen	J	No clasp	11/2233	Chalk	H	1879	954	Cummings	J	1879
11/643	Brennan	C	1879	11/2790	Chapman	G	1879	11/749	Cummings	T	1879
11/405	Brennan	T	1879	11/1994	Chater	A	1879	11/2228	Cunniffe	J	No clasp
11/2589	Brewin	W	1879	11/2661	Chowne	T	1879		No Medal Deserted.		
11/2502	Bridgeman	T	1879		No Medal Deserted.			11/395	Cunningham	J	1879
11/429	Brockbank	J	1879	11/448	Clancy	P	1879	11/729	Curley	J	1879
	No Medal Deserted.			11/2761	Clarke	D	1879	11/2313	Dale	J	1879
11/1036	Brooker	G	1879	11/2659	Clarke	F	1879	11/2424	Darton	W	1879
1897	Brooks	G	1879	11/2382	Clarke	G	1879	11/2389	Davis	D	1879
713	Brophil	W	1879	11/351	Clarke	J	1879	11/2338	Davis	E	1879
11/2503	Brown	J	1879	11/2917	Clarke	T.P	1879	11/2334	Davis	G	1879
11/2619	Brown	T	1879	11/492	Clarkson	W	1879	11/967	Davis	G	1879
	Medal forfeited. No reason given.			11/1034	Cleary	P	1879	11/1970	Davis	H	1879
11/717	Brusey	W	1879	11/2755	Clissold	R	1879	11/1293	Davis	J	1879
11/2286	Bryan	J	1879 r	11/1189	Clough	T	1879	11/2379	Davis	J	1879
	Medal forfeited. No reason given.			11/2647	Clune	P	1879	11/2364	Davis	J	1879
11/768	Bryan	L	1879	11/2312	Coates	S	1879	11/586	Davis	J.G	1879

2/4th Regiment

11/2230	Davis	R	1879	11/1204	Edwards	J	1879	1976	Goston	F	1879
11/341	Davis	R	No clasp	11/2200	Edwards	J	1879	11/2759	Gould	G	1879
11/101	Davis	T	1879	11/2371	Edwards	J	No clasp	11/3048	Goulding	H	1879
11/1110	Davis	W	1879	11/898	Egan	T	1879		No Medal Deserted.		
11/2455	Davis	W	1879	1640	Eggleton	J	1879	11/640	Graham	M	1879
11/1045	Day	W	1879	11/787	Elder	R	1879	2168	Grainger	A	1879
11/2409	Dean	J	1879	11/1277	Elley	E	1879	11/2336	Grant	H	1879
11/2425	Deegan	J	1879	11/2574	Elliott	J	1879	11/2438	Grantham	F	1879
11/1007	Deighton	T	1879	11/714	Ellis	W	1879	11/2570	Gray	H	1879
11/2551	Delaney	D	1879	11/2198	Ellis	W	1879	11/1299	Greaves	J	1879
11/1064	Delaney	K	1879	2236	English	J	1879	11/2485	Green	J	1879
11/762	Delaney	W	1879	11/348	Ettridge	G	1879 r	11/2775	Green	J	1879
11/1085	Dempsey	M	1879		Forfeited. No reason given.			11/644	Green	J	1879
	No Medal Deserted.			11/412	Evans	T	1879	1740	Green	T	1879
2235	Dempsey	J	1879	11/2645	Fall	H	1879	11/2492	Griffiths	A	1879
11/2908	Dennis	A	1879	11/729	Farrell	P	1879	11/2807	Griffiths	D	1879
11/2468	Devine	H	1879	11/2907	Featherstone	C	1879	11/366	Griffiths	J	1879
11/604	Devine	N	1879		No Medal Deserted.				No Medal Deserted.		
11/874	Devison	G	1879	11/2182	Fennelly	J	1879	11/2142	Griggs	J	1879
11/771	Devlin	J	1879		No Medal Deserted.			1792	Griggs	W	1879
11/2636	Dillon	D	1879	1853	Finn	D	1879	11/3044	Grisswood	W	1879
11/2473	Dobbins	C	1879	11/677	Finnegan	J	1879		No Medal Deserted		
11/2770	Dobble	J.H	1879	11/2410	Fitzpatrick	J	1879	11/420	Grundy	T	1979
11/1636	Dobson	J	1879	11/2675	Flaherty	M	1879	11/606	Gunn	J	1879
11/877	Dolan	J	1879	11/1004	Fletcher	G	1879	11/2482	Haggis	R	1879
11/731	Dooley	P	1879	11/741	Flood	J	1879	11/2452	Hainley	J	1879
11/595	Dootson	J	1879	11/489	Flynn	F	1879	11/2447	Hale	W	1879
	No Medal Deserted.			11/3152	Foley	P	1879		No Medal Deserted.		
11/705	Douglas	H	1879	11/2314	Foote	A	1879	11/2469	Haley	T	1879
2072	Douglas	S	1879	11/3040	Foster	J	1879	11/339	Hall	T	1879
11/1048	Dowbiggan	S	1879 r	11/2372	Francis	D	1879	*11/2511	Halliday	B	No clasp
	Forfeited. No reason given.			11/2794	Freeman	M	1879	D/S 16th Mar.1879 GreyTown Pte. H.Halli			
11/629	Dowling	J	1879	11/903	Frew	J	1879	11/3053	Halpin	T	1879
11/662	Downes	G	1879	1642	Furlong	J	1879	11/2897	Hanna	D	1879
11/2771	Downton	S	1879	11/2507	Gale	J	1879	11/1030	Hannaghey	S	1879
11/1038	Doyle	B	1879	11/2357	Gale	W	1879	11/2660	Hannigan	P	1879
11/3068	Doyle	J	1879	11/2315	Gallagher	T	1879	11/2552	Harrington	J	1879
11/1135	Doyle	J	1879	11/472	Garhety	M	1879	11/2155	Harrol	J	1879
11/716	Doyle	M	1879	11/125	Garlick	G	1879	11/2172	Harrold	J	1879
11/2491	Dring	T	1879	11/2373	Garrally	M	1879	11/2318	Hartshorn	R	1879
1879	Duck	J	1879	11/2352	George	E	1879	11/755	Harvey	E	1879
11/2206	Duckworth	M	1879	11/2430	Gibbons	J	1879	11/2888	Harvey	S	1879
11/752	Dunn	J	1879	11/2456	Gibbons	J	1879	11/2921	Harwood	W	1879
11/374	Dunn	T	1879	11/2317	Gibson	T	1879	2228	Hattam	E	1879
	No Medal Deserted.				No Medal Deserted.			11/2585	Hatch	J	1879
11/1022	Dunn	T	1879 r	11/1265	Gibson	W	1879	11/2811	Hathaway	B	1879
	Forfeited. No reason given.			11/2891	Gill	C	1879	11/2493	Hawkey	W	1879
11/632	Dutton	G	1879	11/2411	Gillegan	S	1879	11/2631	Hawkins	W	1879
11/635	Dwyer	J	1879	11/2480	Gillon	M	1879		No Medal Deserted.		
11/2661	Dwyer	M	1879	11/491	Gillson	J	1879	11/721	Hawthorne	W	1879
11/2623	Dyer	J	1879	11/1107	Gladwell	J	1879	11/2354	Hayward	D	1879
11/3045	Ede	A	1879		No Medal Deserted.			610	Heath	J	1879
11/389	Ede	G	1879	11/634	Gleeson	P	1879	11/3077	Hemmings	T	1879
11/1137	Edmonds	W	1879	11/579	Glynn	M	1879	11/2366	Hennessy	J	1879
11/2778	Edwards	C	1879	11/2400	Goddard	J	1879	11/2632	Hennell	E	No clasp
11/2183	Edwards	E	1879	11/2534	Good	D	1879		No Medal Deserted.		
11/259	Edwards	G	1879		No Medal Deserted.			11/2426	Hepworth	J	1879
11/2773	Edwards	G	1879	11/357	Gordon	D	1879	11/2139	Hersey	J	1879
11/2571	Edwards	H	No clasp	11/2339	Gorman	J	1879	11/972	Hessian	J	1879

2/4th Regiment

Number	Name	Initial	Year	Number	Name	Initial	Year	Number	Name	Initial	Year
#11/2512	Hicks	J.M	1879	11/303	Jones	H	1879	11/625	Langdell	H	1879
11/2576	Higgins	J	1879	11/2810	Jones	J	1879	11/291	Langham	W	1879
11/2280	Higgott	I	1879	11/2343	Jones	J	1879	11/3067	Large	C	1879
11/2437	Hill	A	1879	11/2331	Jones	J	1879	11/2793	Lawler	F	1879
11/2573	Hills	G	1879	11/2387	Jones	J	1879	11/2563	Leahy	D	1879
11/2895	Hills	T	1879	No Medal Deserted.				11/609	Lee	F.E	1879
809	Hill	T	1879	11/2792	Jones	J.A	1879	11/2516	Lee	J	No clasp
11/2668	Hinchey	T	1879	11/2375	Jones	W	1879	11/2499	Leggott	J	1879
11/573	Hindle	R	1879	11/3069	Jones	W	1879	11/304	Lennon	R	1879
11/2457	Hobbs	T	1879	11/3064	Jordan	W.C	1879	11/2341	Lewis	J	1879
11/2680	Hobson	J	1879	11/2647	Judge	M	1879	11/2804	Lewis	R	1879
11/2319	Hobson	W	1879	No Medal Deserted.				11/2398	Lewis	W	1879
11/2397	Hogan	C	1879	11/2565	Kehoe	D	1879	2134	Lightburn	T	1879
1313	Holden	H	1879	No Medal Deserted.				11/2517	Liney	H	1879
812	Holditch	B	1879	11/2431	Kehoe	J	1879	11/916	Little	G	1879
11/2487	Holland	F	1879	11/1130	Kellaher	W	1879	No Medal Deserted.			
11/2403	Hollerow	D	1879	11/2413	Kellick	E	1879	11/2531	Llewellyn	W	1879
11/2583	Hollingberry	T	1879	2700	Kelly	C	No clasp	11/2805	Lloyd	T	1879
11/2768	Holloway	F	1879	2050	Kelly	E	1879	2374	Longham	E	1879
2183	Holmes	H	1879	11/1039	Kelly	J	1879 r	11/2458	Lovell	F	1879
11/2404	Horn	J	1879	11/2282	Kelly	J	1879 r	2518	Lovelock	W	No clasp
11/1203	Hornett	R	1879	11/2808	Kelly	J	1879	11/599	Lyons	J	1879
11/2892	Howarth	G	1879	11/2909	Kelly	J	1879 r	11/2776	Lyons	P	1879
11/1242	Howse	C	1879	Discharged with ignominy.				11/1037	Mack	J	1879
11/2626	Howse	R	1879	11/672	Kelly	O	1879 r	No Medal Deserted.			
11/2354	Hoystead	D	1879	11/2760	Kelly	P	1879	11/2915	Maher	J	1879
11/1182	Hudson	J	1879	11/2918	Kelly	T	1879	11/3070	Maher	J	1879
11/2359	Hughes	J	1879	11/2212	Kennedy	E	1879	11/2673	Mahoney	J	1879
11/617	Hughes	P	1879	11/735	Kennedy	H	1879	11/2350	Mahoney	K	1879
11/2462	Humpries	C	1879	11/850	Kennedy	J	1879	11/2558	Mahoney	M	1879
11/1283	Hunt	G	1879	11/3060	Kennedy	T	1879	11/127	Mahoney	W	1879
11/2207	Hunt	W	No clasp	11/3060	Kennedy	T	1879	1118	Maloney	J	1879
D/S 16th April 1879 Pietermaritzburg				Two medals to same man.				1789	Maloney	P	1879
11/3066	Hurden	W	1879	11/996	Keogh	W	1879	No Medal Deserted.			
11/2905	Hurley	S	1879	11/2795	Kernon	L	1879	11/965	Mandsley	T	1879
11/602	Ingle	J	1879	957	Kewell	D	1879	11/2414	Manton	W	1879
11/401	Inwood	I	1879	11/2568	Kiernon	J	1879	1552	Markey	W	1879
11/1176	Irvine	J	1879	11/567	Kilbride	P	1879	11/2495	Marshall	F	1879
11/623	Isherwood	J	1879	11/494	Kilbride	T	1879	11/2606	Martin	G	1879
11/2514	Isles	D	1879	11/2628	King	J	1879	11/2466	Martin	J	1879
2019	Izzard	C	1879	11/2317	Knight	W	1879	No Medal Deserted.			
11/782	Jackson	H	1879	11/2787	Knowles	J	1879	679	Martin	S	1879
11/1063	Jackson	J	1879	11/2530	Knowles	R	1879	11/360	Marvin	J	1879
11/2450	Jackson	J	1879	11/2297	Laffan	G.W	1879	11/2416	Massingham	A	1879
No Medal Deserted.				11/2498	Laing	D	1879	11/2603	Mason	C.W	1879
11/2797	Jarman	J	1879	1767	Laing	P	1879	11/2459	Mason	F	1879
11/2569	Jarvis	E	1879	11/2320	Lambell	E	1879	11/508	Matthews	D	1879
11/2916	Jenkins	J	1879	11/2605	Lamden	G	No clasp	11/889	Matthews	J	1879
11/2577	Jennings	R	1879	11/882	Lancaster	J	1879	11/2520	Matthews	J	1879
11/914	Johnson	J	1879	11/2629	Lane	E	1879	11/1281	Matthews	S	1879
11/2457	Johnson	W	1879	No Medal Deserted.				11/1072	Matthews	J	1879
11/2412	Johnstone	A	1879	11/2132	Lane	T	1879	364	Maxwell	A	1879
11/2612	Jones	A	1879	No Medal Deserted.				11/2567	Mayberry	R	1879
11/2355	Jones	D.E	1879	11/2674	Lane	W	1879	11/2802	Maysbank	J	1879

Dixons on line Sales List November 2009 http://www.dixonsmedals.co.uk/
South Africa Medal 1877-1879, 1 clasp, 1879, (2512 Pte. 2/4th Foot). 2512/2523 Conductor J.M. Hicks, 2/4th Foot Awarded the L.S. and G.C. on 01.07.1907. (2) Sold with photocopy roll pages. Cost £675

2/4th Regiment

No.	Name		Year
11/367	Mc Auley	J	1879
11/2429	Mc Bride	J	1879
11/605	Mc Cann	J	1879
	No Medal. Discharged with ignominy.		
11/2535	Mc Carthy	J	1879
1449	Mc Carthy	J	1879
1601	Mc Carthy	J	1879
	No Medal Deserted.		
11/2342	Mc Carthy	M	1879
11/712	Mc Connell	F	1879
11/670	Mc Cullagh	J	1879
11/343	Mc Donald	P	1879 r
11/2322	Mc Donald	T	1879
11/2500	Mc Donough	J	1879
11/2519	Mc Dowell	S	1879
11/2769	Mc Gowan	D.D	1879
11/675	Mc Gowan	P	1879
1796	Mc Grail	J	1879
11/2914	Mc Graith	D	1879
11/2323	Mc Grath	P	1879
11/2438	Mc Grath	T	1879
11/2428	Mc Innessy	M	1879
11/2637	Mc Kay	N	1879
11/2298	Mc Keog	H	1879
11/2899	Mc Kee	D	1879
11/2564	Mc Kee	E	1879
11/484	Mc Laughlin	J	1879
11/2370	Mc Laughlin	J	1879
11/2195	Mc Leod	A	1879
480	Mc Loughlan	H	1879
2321	Mc Mahon	J	1879
11/636	Mc Mahon	P	1879
11/2672	Mc Mahon	T	1879
	No Medal Deserted.		
11/6809	Mc Nalty	T	1879
11/2484	Machan	M	1879
	No Medal Deserted.		
11/307	Medley	H	1879
11/3071	Menzies	R	1879
2178	Middleton	W	1879
11/1199	Miller	H	1879
11/2393	Mills	W	1879
11/2415	Minggel	J	1879
1246	Mitchell	E	1879
11/2902	Moles	J	1879
11/638	Molloy	H	1879
11/388	Monaghan	G	1879
11/2896	Monaghan	W	1879
11/2440	Montgomery	A	1879
11/2663	Mooney	H	1879
11/904	Moore	J	1879
11/2777	Moore	T	1879
	No Medal Deserted.		
11/2394	Morgan	H	1879
11/2655	Moriarity	J	1879
11/608	Morris	J	1879
11/2772	Morris	J	1879
11/2555	Morrissey	J	1879
11/1243	Moss	M	1879
11/2671	Mottley	J	No clasp
11/1251	Mousley	J	1879
11/2632	Moyniham	C	1879
11/1098	Mulhall	W	1879
1791	Mullans	W	1879
11/2556	Mulverhill	J	1879
11/2670	Murphy	J	1879
11/2325	Murphy	P	1879
	D/S 8th March 1879 Utrcht		
11/2399	Murphy	T	1878-9
11/2448	Murphy	T	1879
11/2667	Murphy	T	1879
11/590	Murray	S	1879
11/658	Murray	W	1879
11/3041	Muzzle	W	1879
11/1217	Nash	F	1879
11/2486	Neil	J	1879
11/2651	Neil	J	1879
11/2522	Nelson	A	1879
	No Medal Deserted.		
11/1193	Newburry	J	1879
11/2890	Newburry	J	1879
11/2594	Newman	W	1879
1483	Nichols	J	1879
11/614	Nicholson	J	1879
11/3078	Nockolds	W	No clasp
11/2788	Noden	S	1879
11/1151	Nolan	D	1879
11/905	Oakley	R	1879
11/2586	O'Brien	J	1879
11/2669	O'Brien	T	1879
	No Medal Deserted.		
11/2650	O'Connell	J	1879
11/692	O'Connor	J	1879
11/2664	O'Dea	P	1879
11/2677	O'Leary	T	1879
	No Medal Deserted.		
11/2367	O'Leary	W	1879
11/2324	O'Keefe	J	1879
11/1124	O'Keefe	H	1879
11/2809	Oliver	C	1879
11/764	O'Neil	J	1879 r
	Forfeited. No reason given.		
11/2422	O'Neill	J	1879
11/2654	O'Shaughnessy	M	1879
11/665	O'Shaughnessy	P	1879
11/2385	Ottoway	W	1879
11/2588	Owens	J	1879
11/3055	Owen	R	1879
11/693	Pallas	T	No clasp
11/2427	Pardoe	T	1879
11/2441	Parry	A	1879
11/957	Parsons	W	1879
11/2587	Pattenden	T.A	1879
11/417	Patterson	A	1879
11/3072	Patterson	G	1879
11/2325	Patterson	J	1879
1903	Paul	J	1879
1831	Paul	T	1879
11/3138	Pearce	J	1879
11/301	Pearce	T	1879
11/2476	Peddison	A	1879
11/690	Pendergast	H	1879
1952	Penn	J	1879
11/2363	Perrett	H	1879
11/2390	Pinkham	P	1879
	No Medal Deserted.		
11/1319	Pinnock	S	1879
	No Medal Deserted.		
11/2634	Pitt	F	1879
11/2423	Pomphery	J	1879
	No Medal Deserted.		
11/2356	Poole	T	1879
11/3076	Pope	J	1879
11/2595	Porter	H	1879
11/2910	Potter	T	1879
	No Medal Deserted.		
11/2348	Powell	M	1879
11/678	Power	J	1879
11/2806	Price	P	1879
11/2243	Price	W	1879
11/682	Purcell	M	1879
11/2596	Quelch	H	1879
11/2181	Quinn	L	1879
	No Medal Deserted.		
11/2378	Rees	D	1879
11/2615	Reeves	A	1879
11/2396	Reeves	J	1879
11/2887	Reeves	M	1879
11/397	Reid	C	1879
11/2405	Reid	S	1879
11/2600	Reilly	H	1879
11/610	Reilly	J	1879
11/653	Reilly	J	1879
11/3054	Reynolds	J	1879
11/2402	Richards	D	1879
11/2326	Richardson	T	1879
11/1369	Ridout	J	1879
11/532	Riordan	D	1879
11/2559	Riordan	J	1879 r
11/533	Riordan	P	1879
11/2327	Rix	J	1879
	No Medal Deserted.		
11/1043	Roach	A	1879
	No Medal Deserted.		
1933	Roberts	C	1879
11/2442	Roberts	R	1879
11/2328	Robey	A	1879
11/3073	Rogers	J	1879
11/2213	Rooney	A	1879
11/2288	Ross	J	1879
11/2417	Rouse	J	1879
	No Medal Deserted.		
11/2467	Russell	J	1879
	No Medal Deserted.		
11/2913	Russell	W	1879
11/2460	Russell	W	1879
11/2679	Ryan	A	1879

2/4th Regiment

Number	Name	Initial	Year	Number	Name	Initial	Year	Number	Name	Initial	Year
11/2665	Ryan	J	1879	11/2579	Steins	W	1879	11/2598	Vincent	H	1879
11/2560	Ryan	P	1879	11/2525	Stevens	J	1879	1870	Wagstaff	T	1879
11/2800	Salter	T	1879	11/2401	Stevens	L	1879	11/2926	Wakely	J	1879
11/612	Saunders	J	1879	11/1114	Stevens	W	1879	11/1245	Walker	P	1879
11/2658	Saunders	R	1879	11/2479	Stokes	H	1879	11/2418	Wallace	W	1879
11/414	Savage	J	1879	11/2329	Stonehouse	D	1879	11/2911	Walliker	G	1879
11/1006	Sayers	A	1879	11/2901	Stubbings	T	1879	11/2419	Wallis	W	1879
11/3056	Schway	C	1879 r	11/2383	Styling	J	1879	No Medal Deserted.			
Medal Forfeited. No reason given.				11/2330	Sugden	B	1879	11/2337	Walsh	D	1879
11/2395	Sears	H	1879	11/422	Sullivan	D	1879	11/789	Walsh	R	1879
11/3056	Selway	C	1879	11/2611	Sullivan	D	No clasp	11/522	Walsh	W	1879
11/2477	Semar	T	1879	11/2643	Sullivan	T	1879	11/2420	Walton	G	1879
11/2232	Seville	J	1879	11/2578	Surry	J	1879	11/1287	Warburton	W	1879
11/2377	Shaw	C	1879	11/2553	Sweeney	E	1879	11/433	Ward	T	No clasp
1877	Shaw	J	1879	11/2649	Sweeney	E	1879	11/770	Ward	W	1879
11/521	Shaw	J	1879	11/2648	Sweeney	J	1879	11/2641	Warner	F	1879
11/2764	Shaw	J	1879	11/1047	Sweetland	R	1879	11/1139	Warnford	F	1879
11/2662	Shea	J	1879	No Medal Deserted.				11/2767	Warrett	R	1879
11/2340	Shea	M	1879	11/2232	Swift	E	1879	11/1191	Watson	J.T	1879
11/2461	Shea	P	1879	11/2779	Swingwood	J	1879	588	Watt	F	1879
11/2681	Short	J.W	1879	11/2346	Taylor	A	1879	11/2496	Watts	J	1879
11/2521	Shuttleworth	J	1879	1715	Taylor	C	1879	11/2527	Webb	A.D	1879
11/2449	Skipper	J	1879	No Medal Deserted.				11/2785	Webster	H	1879
1364	Smith	A	1879	11/1172	Taylor	H	1879	11/618	Wegg	F	1879
11/2478	Smith	C	1879	11/3063	Taylor	J	1879	11/4	Weir	J	1879
11/2465	Smith	C	1879	No Medal Deserted.				11/2481	Wells	H	1879
No Medal Deserted.				11/2225	Taylor	T	1879	11/526	Wells	R	1879
11/2785	Smith	D	1879	829	Teasdale	J	1879	No Medal Deserted.			
11/297	Smith	E	1879	11/646	Tedford	G	1879	11/2666	Whelan	A	1879
11/2444	Smith	F	1879	11/2597	Thomas	D	1879	11/756	Whelan	J	1879
11/506	Smith	G	1879	11/2322	Thompson	A	1879	11/2781	White	C	1879
11/1123	Smith	G	1879	11/1206	Thompson	J	1879	11/2786	White	F	1879
11/2898	Smith	H	1879	11/1202	Thompson	J	1879	11/2762	White	T	1879
11/2523	Smith	H	1879	11/2923	Thompson	S	1879	11/2333	Whitfield	W	1879
11/2680	Smith	H	1879	11/2445	Thompson	T	1879	No Medal Deserted.			
11/613	Smith	J	1879	11/2392	Thompson	W	1879	11/2361	Whitman	A	1879
11/969	Smith	J	1879	11/2345	Thompson	W	1879	11/2360	Whitman	G	1879
11/2408	Smith	J	1879	11/2678	Thrower	J	1879	11/2801	Whittaker	F	1879
11/2524	Smith	J	1879	11/3062	Tilley	W	1879	11/2368	Wignall	W	1879
11/2471	Smith	J	1879	11/780	Timmins	P	1879	11/1153	Wilkinson	T	1879
11/350	Smith	R	1879	11/2580	Todd	T	1879	11/2784	Wilks	W	1879
1546	Smith	S	1879	11/2893	Tonge	T	1879	1975	Wills	E	1879 r
1912	Smith	T	1879	11/501	Toole	J	1879	11/2362	Williams	D	1879
11/1019	Smith	T	1879	11/2676	Tougher	J	1879	11/2547	Williams	E	1879
No Medal Deserted.				No Medal Deserted.				11/2483	Williams	G	1879
11/2331	Smith	T	1879	11/1102	Treadaway	G	1879	11/830	Williams	H	1879
11/499	Smith	W	1879	11/2889	Tripp	H	1879	1380	Williams	H	1879
11/2432	Smith	W	1879	11/418	Troughton	J	1879	11/2766	Williams	J	1879
11/3059	Smith	W	1879	11/3041	Trower	J	1879	185 ?	Williams	T	1879
11/440	Smye ?	L	1879	11/2643	Trusler	J	1879	11/2118	Williams	W	1879
11/765	Smyth	F	1879	11/2365	Tucker	G	1879	11/445	Williams	W	1879
11/1247	Soden	F	1879	11/1236	Tudor	H	1879	11/2334	Williams	W	1879
11/2646	Soley	J	1879	11/2582	Tunbridge	D	1879	1975	Wills	E	1879
11/2244	Sollis	J	1879	No Medal Deserted.				11/338	Wilson	J	1879
11/1033	South	J.W	1879	1019	Turner	H	1879	11/1000	Wilson	J	1879
11/1232	Southgate	T	1879	11/428	Turney	J	1879	No Medal Discharged with ignominy.			
11/2903	Squibb	W	1879	11/1061	Tyson	W	1879	1898	Wilton	F	1879
11/437	Stamper	J	1879	11/719	Villiers	L	1879	2097	Windmill	E	1879
11/2791	Stanley	H	1879	11/2562	Vincent	H	1879	11/227	Winstanley	G	No clasp

Corporal Punishment

During the duration of the War, 545 British soldiers were flogged; the highest number for many years. It was seen as a powerful deterrent The prisoner was given twenty-five lashes for offences ranging from drunkenness and stealing to insubordination, and desertion. The most common offence was "dereliction of duty", which covered those sentries who fell asleep when on guard duty, and merited fifty lashes. After Isandlwana, the Zulus were taken very seriously and any lack of vigilance which jeopardised the security of the camp had to be dealt with severely to "encourage" the other sentries. The most frequent cases were those of the Natal Native Contingent, many of whom were flogged for desertion.

SOLDIERS FLOGGED.

Colonel STANLEY, in reply to Mr HOPWOOD, said he had ascertained that three men of the 1st Dragoon Guards were tried on board the steam transport *Spain*, and sentenced—two of them to receive twenty-five lashes, and the third twenty lashes, and he believed these sentences had been carried out.

Northern Echo, Wednesday, May 21, 1879

1807, 1000 lashes was established as a maximum.
1836 reduced to 200 lashes.
1847 reduced to fifty lashes.
1867 flogging was restricted and replaced by "Field Punishment No. 1, in which a man was tied to the wheel of a gun carriage for a specified period."
1868 an act of Parliament outlawed flogging for troops on home srevice.
1871 The practise of tattooing deserters under the arm with the letter "D" was discontinued.
1879 flogging in war time was suspended in the Royal Navy.
1879 reduced to a maximum of 25 per offence.
1881 flogging in the army was abolished.
Flogging was in use in military prisons till 1907.

A return was issued this morning, which had been moved for by the Earl of Doncaster in the House of Lords, of the number of persons in the naval and military forces who have been punished by flogging during the ten years ending 31st December, 1878, stating the number of lashes in each case, and the crime for which the punishment was inflicted. In the navy during the time mentioned corporal punishment was inflicted in 247 cases for insubordination. The highest number of lashes awarded in any case was 48, and the lowest eight. It must be understood, however, that while the latter punishment was only inflicted once, the former appears to have been adopted in the large majority of cases. It is significant of the effect of public feeling regarding the use of the "cat" that while in 1869 there were 61 men flogged in the navy, the number has been sensibly diminished every year since, until we come to 1878, when there are only eight cases recorded. The return for the army presents rather a striking contrast in this latter respect, for in 1869 there were but 21 soldiers flogged, whilst in 1878 no less than 41 received that punishment, the increase in the ten years being gradual but marked. In more than three-fourths of cases in which the "cat" has been applied in the army, the delinquents were confined in military prisons, and received the punishment for insubordination more or less gross. The return seems to be incomplete, in so far as the names of the regiments to which the culprits belonged are not given, nor the names of the individuals themselves, which, however, is a minor fault.

Flogging Freeman's Journal and Daily Commercial Advertiser (Dublin, Ireland), Wednesday, June 9, 1880

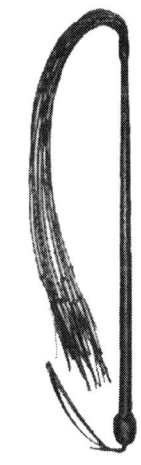

2/4th Regiment

Number	Name	Initial	Year
11/296	Winterton	R	1879
11/2236	Wixon	J	1879
11/3058	Worsley	W	1879
11/1174	Woodman	G	1879
11/2529	Wooley	H	1879
11/3075	Wooster	C	1879
11/605	Wright	J	1879
11/2471	Wright	J	1879
11/2906	Wythe	G	1879
11/2347	Zimmer	F	1879

1/7th (ROYAL FUSILIERS) REGIMENT.
CAPTAIN
    Barton G 1879
Also had Ashanti 1873-4 Medal.
See also 4th Btn Natal Native Contingent.
LIEUTENANT
    Heron Maxwell W.H.S 1879
Attached 4th Kings Own.
    Nicholson G.S 1879

8th (THE KING'S) REGIMENT.
CAPTAIN
    Jocelyn R.J.O 1879

1/9th (EAST NORFOLD) REGIMENT.
CAPTAIN
    Wavell A.G No clasp

2/10th (THE NORTH LINCOLNSHIRE) REGIMENT.
CAPTAIN
    Huntley H.C 1879

1/11th (NORTH DEVONSHIRE) REGIMENT.
CAPTAIN
    Ballantyne J.G No clasp

1/13th (1st SOMERSETSHIRE PRINCE ALBERT'S LIGHT INFANTRY. REGIMENT).
In 1878 engaged against Sekukuni. On the outbreak of the Zulu War joined Sir Evelyn Wood's column. On the 24th January engaged the enemy at Zunguin Nek. The Battalion was reunited at Kambula, were they played a major part in checking the advance of the Zulu left wing. The 13th also occupied the right of the square at the battle of Ulundi on the 4th July 1879
LIEUTENANT COLONEL
    Gilbert CB P.E.V 1878-9
MAJOR
    England E.L 1878-9
    Leet VC W.K 1878-9
VC won at Inhlobane 28/3/79.

CAPTAIN

	Name	Initial	Year
	Allfrey	I.S	No clasp
	Bradshaw	F.B	1878-9
	Cox	W	1878-9
	Evans	W.H	1878-9
	James	J.F	1879
	Kinloch	G.H.A	1878-9
	Otway	R.C	1878-9
	Parr	H.H	1878-9
	Pearsse	D.T	1878-9
	Thurlow	H.H	1878-9
	Waddy	J.M.E	1878-9

PAYMASTER
    Gleig A.C 1879
See also Army Pay Department.

LIEUTENANT

	Name	Initial	Year
	Allen	J.C	1878-9
	Clarke	E.W	1878-9
	Fownes	E.J	1878-9
	Gallwey	E.J	1878-9
	Justice	F.J	1879
	Levinge	R	1878-9
	Pardoe	G.A	1878-9
	D/W Ulundi		
	Pollock	A.W.A	1878-9
	Payne	R.L	1878-9
	Poynton	E.M	1878-9
	Townshead	R.A.H	1878-9
	Walsh	H.A	1878-9
	Wilbraham	A.G	1878-9
	Williams	R.B	1878-9

2nd LIEUTENANT

	Name	Initial	Year
	Hillas	R.W.G	1879
	Lovett	H.W	1879
	O'Donnell	A.C	No clasp
	Snow	T.D'D	1879
	West	J.W.H	1879

SERGEANT MAJOR
368	Headley	G	1878-9
1650	Powis	H	1878-9

SERGEANT MAJOR COOK
1531	Johnson	W	1878-9

BANDMASTER
802	Vivers	J.W	1878-9

COLOUR SERGEANT
1292	Baker	J	1878-9
1863	Bentley	W	1878-9
1264	Burcher	R	1878-9
1821	Chamberlain	T	1878-9

QUARTERMASTER SERGEANT
1117	Doyle	P	1878-9

SERGEANT INSTRUCTOR OF MUSKETRY
1436	Robinson	J.A.L	1878-9

PAYMASTER SERGEANT
36/589	Young	J	1878-9

ORDERLY ROOM CLERK
1719	Huggins	J	1878-9

BUGLE MAJOR
1623	Cockling	P	1879

SERGEANT TAILOR
1760	Bowen	H	1878-9

SERGEANT

Number	Name	Initial	Year
538	Biss	H	1878-9
35/1897	Boshell	J	No clasp
1895	Bright	J	1878-9
1967	Brook	W	1878-9
36/119	Chapman	J	1878-9
1126	Collier	C	1878-9
757	Darling	G	1878-9
1681	Davidson	E	1878-9
1401	Davis	T	1878-9
315	Early	J	1878-9
1331	Fricker	A	1878-9
35/264	Flynn	W	1878-9
360	Grant	H	No clasp
1486	Grant	J	1878-9
36/64	Hargreaves	G	1878-9
35/1880	Harrison	T	No clasp
35/249	Hassett	P	1878-9
35/1911	Hathaway	T	No clasp
1188	Hughes	J	1878-9
1384	Jaques	E	1878-9
702	Kavanagh	R	1878-9
1445	Kendall	J	1878-9
1632	King	R	1878-9
1792	Leach	E	1878-9
1194	Lennon	M	1878-9
1683	Martin	H	1878-9
2033	Ollernshaw	J	1878-9
35/315	Owens	D.C	1878-9
35/235	Owens	J	1878-9
# ?	Pegg	J	1878
950	Quinn	W	1878-9
2013	Rowlands	J	1878-9
1876	Rowley	J	1878-9
1705	Sharpe	R	1879
36/1984	Trimlett	F	1878-9
1530	Watkins	J	No clasp
594	Waud	J	1878-9
1268	Whall	W	1878-9
2014	Woods	J	1878-9

LANCE SERGEANT

Number	Name	Initial	Year
1852	Cooper	A	1878-9
2002	English	W	1878-9
1612	Hawes	W.H	1878-9
1565	Jarvis	R	1878-9
35/158	Ritchie	B	1878-9

CORPORAL

Number	Name	Initial	Year
36/282	Beggs	G	1878-9
1363	Bilborough	J	1878-9
36/276	Boyd	S	1878-9
1202	Burge	B	1878-9
36/1926	Burgoyne	J	No clasp
35/1356	Clarke	J	No clasp
1669	Cooney	A	1878-9
1487	Cudmore	A	1878-9

Casualty Roll 1st Bn. 13th Foot

Casualty Roll for the Zulu and Basuto Wars   South Africa 1877-79   1st Bn. 13th Foot: later the Somerset Light Infantry

Captain
Cox, W. Severely wounded at Kambula 29/3/1879

Lieutenant
Pardoe, G.E. Severely wounded at Ulundi 04/07/1879 D.O.W.

Sergeants
1331 Fricker, A. Severely wounded in head at Ulundi 04/07/1879
     Pegg, J. Mortally wounded at Tolyana Stadt 27/10/1879
2014 Woods, J. Severely wounded at Kambula 29/03/1879

Bugle Major
1623 Cockling, P. Severely wounded in head at Ulundi 04/07/1879

Corporal
296 Minary, C. Wounded whilst on convoy escort 07/10/1878

Lance - Corporal
1362 Walker, C. Slightly wounded at Ulundi 04/07/1879

Buglers
100 Burge, G. Slightly wounded in thigh 27/10/1879
2037 Burns, T. Dangerously wounded at Ulundi 04/07/1879 D.O.W.
91   Cleary, J. Slightly wounded at Kambula 29/03/1879
1769 Cockling, M. Mortally wounded at Ulundi 04/07/1879

Privates
576 Arthur, H. Killed in action at Kambula 29/03/1879
113 Bellamy, W. Slightly wounded at Kambula 29/03/1879
1733 Blakeman, E. Dangerously wounded at Kambula 29/03/1879
1934 Bourne, J. Severely wounded at Ulundi 04/07/1879
172 Bradley, W. Killed in action at Ulundi 04/07/1879
1526 Cogan, J. Severely wounded at Kambula 29/03/1879
87   Collins, J. Killed in action at Kambula 29/03/1879
1399 Davis, G. Severely wounded at Kambula 29/03/1879
1476 Davis, J. Dangerously wounded at Ulundi 04/07/1879 D.O.W.
487 Doherty, J. Wounded whilst on convoy escort 07/10/1878
307 Duff, J. Severely wounded at Ulundi 04/07/1879
168 Duncan, J. Killed in action at Kambula 29/03/1879
1637 Emery, T. Slightly wounded 27/10/1878
1912 Grosvenor, W. Mortally wounded at Kambula 29/03/1879
1164 Harkness, J. Slightly wounded at Kambula 29/03/1879
27   Hart, W. Severely wounded at Ulundi 04/07/1879
426 Hayball, A. Dangerously wounded at Kambula 29/03/1879
277 Hayes, J. Killed in action at Kambula 29/03/1879
1798 Johnson, C. Severely wounded at Ulundi 04/07/1879
1783 McNulty, W. Wounded 02/04/1879
399 Madden, J. Severely wounded at Kambula 29/03/1879
1771 Makin, T. Severely wounded 27/10/1878
29   Medlam, G. Severely wounded at Kambula 29/03/1879
1956 Merryweather, J. Dangerously wounded 27/10/1878
163 Montgomery, S. Mortally wounded at Kambula 29/03/1879
1075 Mooney, P. Mortally wounded at Kambula 29/03/1879
154 Nutt, G. Dangerously wounded at Kambula 29/03/1879
102 Owens, H. Severely wounded at Ulundi 04/07/1879
1145 Redpath, S. Mortally wounded at Kambula 29/03/1879
1875 Roberts, H. Wounded at Kambula 29/03/1879
1811 Sheppard, W. Mortally wounded at Ulundi 04/07/1879
1891 Shipton, W.G. Dangerously wounded at Ulundi 04/07/1879
1919 Smith, F. Slightly wounded 27/10/1878
290 Swain, J. Slightly wounded at Ulundi 04/07/1879
2042 Stokes, T. Slightly wounded at Ulundi 04/07/1879
107 Todd, W.J. Severely wounded at Kambula 29/03/1879
1764 Ward, A. Severely wounded at Ulundi 04/07/1879

Source: Military History Magazine - March 1998,

1/13th Regiment

Number	Name	Initial	Year	Number	Name	Initial	Year	Number	Name	Initial	Year
36/382	Farrell	J	1878-9	36/347	Hunt	T	1878-9	36/1653	Best	H	No clasp
36/36	Gaffney	J	1878-9	1103	Leahy	J	1878-9	36/1499	Bessant	J	No clasp
1661	Graves	E	1878-9	346	Morris	F	1878-9	1894	Bethell	J	1878-9
1767	Guest	R	1878-9	36/591	Stewart	W	1878-9	36/1199	Bevis	T	1879
26/1985	Hadley	C	1878-9	36/24	Thornton	J	1878-9	36/1604	Beinding	H	No clasp
36/1051	Hine	C	No clasp	1477	Webster	P	1878-9	36/200	Bird	J.C	1879
36/145	Hutchinson	S	1878-9	36/177	Wilson	J	1878-9	36/1401	Bird	P	1878-9
36/136	Hutton	S	1878-9	PRIVATE				1891	Birch	T	1878
36/108	Jennings	W	1878	36/1472	Adams	C	1879	1933	Blake	T	1878-9
36/1438	Lewis	W	1878-9	2030	Adams	W	1878-9	36/1733	Blakeman	E	1878-9
36/397	Mc Clenahan	J	1878-9	36/59	Adrain	W.J	1878-9	36/1809	Blair	K	No clasp
1926	Mc Dougal	D	1878-9	36/1550	Ainsworth	C	1879	2028	Blum	J	1878-9
36/117	Mc Gibbon	A	1878-9	36/1762	Ainsworth	J	No clasp	1790	Bolton	C	1878-9
36/296	Minary	C	1878-9	36/72	Allen	A.S	1878-9	262	Bond	T	1878
1183	Morrissey	J	1878-9	36/1136	Allen	J	No clasp	37/370	Bonny	J	1878-9
36/1894	O'Brien	B	No clasp	36/198	Allsworth	J	1878-9	38/142	Bothwell	T	1878-9
1454	O'Brien	P	1878-9	36/286	Anderson	J	1878-9	36/1496	Bough	T	No clasp
36/184	Quial	J	1878-9	36/595	Anderson	W	1878-9	1934	Bourne	J	1878-9
1435	Quinn	P	1878-9	36/126	Andrews	H	1878-9	36/1460	Boyce	W	No clasp
36/430	Parrott	P	1878-9	36/1881	Annesley	E	No clasp	36/109	Boyles	W	1878-9
36/418	Phillips	H	1878-9	36/166	Ardies	D	1878-9	36/464	Bradfield	S	1878-9
35/466	Priddle	J	1879	36/1540	Arnold	G	No clasp	36/172	Bradley	W	1878-9
35/358	Satterly	S	1878-9	36/576	Arthur	H	1878-9	36/199	Brady	J	1878-9
2036	Seale	F	1878-9	36/121	Ashford	A	1878-9	36/274	Brady	J	1878-9
1972	Smith	E	1878-9	382	Atkinson	T	No clasp	36/114	Branchflower	F	1878-9
1838	Smith	G	No clasp	36/469	Austin	T	No clasp	36/1489	Bragg	E	No clasp
2060	Turley	G	1878-9	36/1180	Backhouse	J	1879	1890	Brazzell	T	1878-9
35/1602	Weir	W.C	No clasp	36/584	Bacon	A	1878-9	36/371	Brennan	C	1878-9
1833	Whatley	F	1878-9	36/1574	Bailey	A	1879	36/273	Brennan	J	1878
433	Wilson	J	1878-9	1813	Bailey	F	1878-9	36/1815	Brewer	J	No clasp
570	Wylie	A	1878-9	36/60	Bailey	G	1878-9	1541	Brian	J	1878-9
LANCE CORPORAL				1947	Baillean	T	No clasp	36/1742	Bridgeman	G	No clasp
1504	Buckley	P	1878-9	36/1534	Bailie	F	1879	36/1527	Brimmer	W	No clasp
2041	Clayton	H	1878-9	36/599	Bain	J	1878-9	1212	Broom	W	1878-9
1686	Collins	P	1878-9	36/1954	Barcroft	T	No clasp	1939	Broughton	W	1878-9
36/600	Dimmick	A	1878	36/480	Barnes	C	1878-9	1763	Brown	C	1878-9
36/377	Donaldson	R	1878-9	35/1807	Barnes	D	No clasp	1923	Brown	F	No clasp
1654	Emberson	H	1878-9	35/1808	Barrans	E	No clasp	36/194	Brown	J	1878-9
2017	Gornell	C	1878-9	36/1968	Barry	P	1879	1453	Brown	J	1878-9
2008	Jones	G	1878-9	36/1890	Base	A	No clasp	2045	Brown	M	1878-9
36/243	Kenny	J	1878-9	36/1593	Bartlett	J	No clasp	36/260	Brown	W	1878-9
34/1421	Magill	J	1878-9	36/21	Bartlett	W	No clasp	36/1293	Brown	W	1878-9
36/81	Mc Clory	J	1878-9	1776	Bates	E	1878-9	36/514	Brown	W	1878-9
1913	Mc Gaull	H	1878-9	36/1887	Bates	T	No clasp	2077	Brown	W.T	1878-9
1127	Rawlings	J	1878-9	36/1912	Baxter	J.H	No clasp	36/1544	Bryant	T	No clasp r
1997	Steaggles	R	1878-9	35/1956	Bayles	E	No clasp	35/1884	Buchan	J	No clasp
36/1575	Tobias	T	No clasp	36/458	Beardsell	J	1878-9	36/1656	Budge	T	No clasp
36/1388	Trevelyan	C	No clasp	36/1888	Beckett	W	No clasp	1581	Bull	G	No clasp
1362	Walker	C	1878-9	36/125	Beggs	R	1878-9	35/1482	Bull	W	1879
BUGLER				1662	Belcher	H	1878-9	35/477	Bullock	E	1878-9
36/573	Bernard	C	1878-9	36/113	Bellamy	W	1878-9	1465	Burden	G	1878-9
2037	Burns	T	1878-9	1198	Bellinger	H	1878-9	36/1415	Burford	P	1878-9
36/100	Burge	G	1878-9	36/595	Bendon	J	No clasp	35/266	Burke	J	1878-9
1587	Cannings	H	No clasp	36/319	Benham	W	1878-9	589	Burke	M	1878-9
91	Cleary	J	1878-9	1576	Bennett	A	1878-9	36/127	Burke	M	1878-9
1769	Cockling	M	1878-9	1570	Bennett	C	1878	1564	Burns	D	1878-9
2039	Davis	T	1878-9	1937	Bennett	H	1878-9	36/186	Burt	J	1878
256	Frean	J	1878-9	36/1457	Bennett	J	1878	36/342	Burton	J	1878-9
1825	Halasey	D	1878-9	25	Bent	R	1878-9	35/580	Bush	T	1878-9

1/13th Regiment

1589	Butler	J	No clasp	36/128	Critchard	F	1878-9	36/1427	Duddridge	F	1879
1857	Butler	J	1878-9	1452	Crogs	J	1878-9	36/307	Duff	J	1878-9
36/322	Byrne	T	1878-9	910	Crogs	W	1878	1664	Duffey	W	1878-9
1577	Candeland	A	1878-9	36/955	Cronin	H	1878-9	36/1401	Dunham	J	1878-9
36/1763	Cannon	M	No clasp	2071	Cronin	J	1878-9	36/1484	Dunn	J	No clasp
36/359	Cantwell	E	1878-9	1646	Crowe	W	1878-9		No Medal Deserted.		
36/1564	Cape	G	No clasp	36/478	Crumby	W	1878-9	1159	Dunne	R	1878-9
36/336	Cardwell	W	1878-9	36/106	Cumberland	J	1878-9	1077	Dunne	T	1878-9
36/299	Carrol	W	1878-9	36/492	Cunningham	F	1878-9	36/1461	Durnford	H	1879
2048	Carter	G	1878-9	36/569	Cunningham	J	1878-9	36/1483	Durston	C	1879
1474	Casey	W	1878-9	36/87	Cunningham	R	1878-9	36/339	Dutch	J	No clasp
2009	Cash	G	1878-9	36/1768	Curtis	R	No clasp	36/168	Duncan	J	1878-9
36/170	Cassidy	C	1878-9	36/1756	Curr	F	No clasp	36/1909	Dwyer	W	No clasp
36/1737	Cavanagh	J	No clasp	1836	Dale	J	1878-9	1929	Dymes	S	No clasp
36/579	Cave	J	1878-9	2090	Daley	M	1878-9	36/441	Edmonds	J	1878-9
*36/1497	Charlton	J	No clasp	1277	Daley	M	1878-9	1889	Edwards	J	No clasp
D/S 9th April 1879, Utrecht				1430	Daley	P	1878-9	36/1579	Edwards	J	No clasp
36/467	Chick	R	1878-9	36/1880	Daley	T	No clasp	36/1596	Edwards	S	1878-9
36/46	Chislett	W.G	1878-9	36/1960	Dallas	J	No clasp	36/609	Edwards	W	1878-9
36/1573	Clapp	H	1879	1954	Dalton	C	1878-9	225	Edwards	W	1878-9
981	Clarke	E	1878-9	36/250	Daniels	J	1878-9	1946	Edwards	W	1878-9
36/203	Clarke	P	1878-9	1940	Daniels	T	1878-9	1834	Elgin	C	1878-9
36/258	Clarke	W	1878-9	1644	Darbin	C	1878-9	36/655	Elkins	G	No clasp
36/1413	Clarke	W	1878-9	1603	Darbin	G	No clasp	1969	Eldridge	J	1878-9
2067	Clement	T	1878-9	36/1932	Darling	S	1879	36/61	Elliott	A	1878
1749	Clifford	E	1878-9	36/83	Darragh	J	1878-9	36/447	Elliott	J	1878-9
1526	Cogan	J	1878-9	1399	Davis	G	1878-9	1793	Ellis	T	1878-9
36/1446	Coles	C	No clasp	35/1476	Davis	J	1879	58	Ely	J	1878-9
*36/1481	Coles	E	No clasp	36/1546	Davis	J	No clasp	1637	Emery	T	1878-9
1481 W Coles D/S 9th April 1879, Utrecht				36/1886	Davis	L.C	No clasp	36/1406	England	S	1878
36/40	Coles	J.C	1878-9	36/375	Deacon	T	1878-9	35/330	Ervins	J	1878-9
87	Collins	J	1878-9	1014	Delahunty	P	1878-9	36/1879	Evans	C	No clasp
1971	Collinson	T	1878-9	1352	Delaney	C	1878-9	1900	Everton	J	1878-9
36/1957	Collingford	W	No clasp	1865	Delaney	R	1878-9	36/340	Exton	G	1878-9
36/240	Conlon	T	1878-9	36/1926	Dennard	J	No clasp	1837	Fagan	M	1878-9
272	Connors	M	1878-9	1978	Dennehey	M	1878-9	36/1542	Farmer	J	No clasp
36/257	Connoly	M	1878-9	2091	Devine	M	1878-9	2019	Farnham	A	1878-9
710	Cook	H	1878-9	1680	Dickerson	T	1878-9	1186	Farrand	T	1878
35/1958	Cook	T	No clasp	36/226	Dillon	M	1878-9	36/380	Farralley	C	1878-9
1433	Cook	W	1878-9	69	Dixon	J	1878-9	36/39	Farrar	J.H	1878-9
1953	Cooper	T	1878-9	36/1892	Dobbs	G	No clasp	36/1431	Fear	F	1878-9
104	Copeland	J	No clasp	765	Doble	R	No clasp	36/1988	Featherstone	T	1878-9
1817	Corcoran	P	No clasp	36/487	Doherty	J	1878	36/94	Fee	J	1878-9
36/560	Cordial	J	1878-9 r	36/562	Dolan	B	1878-9	36/334	Ferguson	S	1878-9
	Forfeited.			1013	Dolan	J	1878-9	36/1900	Fiddler	H	No clasp
36/329	Corkan	F	1878-9	36/154	Donnelly	J	1878-9	36/1961	Field	C	No clasp
1853	Cornwall	G	1878-9	36/232	Donnelly	P	1878-9	2073	Findlater	C	1878-9
36/1456	Corps	A	1879	1994	Donohoe	J	1878-9	36/1811	Finnigan	P	1879
1932	Corps	G	1878-9	36/231	Doogan	J	1878-9	1255	Fisher	L	1878-9
36/424	Cotterall	W	1878	36/69	Dougal	A	1878-9	1246	Fitzgibbon	C	1878-9
36/343	Counsell	J	1878-9	46/431	Douglas	J	1878-9	2032	Flanagan	J	1878-9
1766	Coville	A	1878-9	36/1925	Dowden	G	No clasp	35/1946	Flaherty	P	No clasp
557	Cox	A	No clasp	36/1959	Downey	J	No clasp	1667	Flynn	R	1878-9 r
1554	Coxford	T	1878-9	36/1878	Downie	T	No clasp		Forfeited.		
1898	Coyne	J	1878-9	36/37	Doyle	J	1878-9 r	912	Foster	A	1878-9
36/289	Crawley	A	1878-9	36/37	Doyle	J	1878-9 r	36/219	Foster	D	1878-9
36/1628	Creighton	J	No clasp		Also has India 1854 Medal.			36/38	Foster	J	1878-9
1879	Crick	G	1878-9	36/1769	Drummy	M	No clasp	36/1317	Fowles	J	No clasp
1862	Crips	A	1878-9	36/376	Driskill	M	1878-9	36/89	Foye	J	1878-9

225

1/13th Regiment

No	Name	Initial	Clasp	No	Name	Initial	Clasp	No	Name	Initial	Clasp
1963	France	R	1878-9	36/1417	Hart	S	1878-9		Note the Roll here is indistinct. Could be clasp 1879 and not 1878-9.		
36/582	Francis	J	1878-9	36/27	Hart	W	1878-9				
956	Freeman	J	1878-9	36/387	Harwood	J	1878-9	36/1493	Irwin	S	1879
1412	Frith	E	No clasp	1133	Haw	J	1879	2085	Izod	R	1878-9
754	Frost	J	No clasp	36/1398	Hawker	R	1878	36/462	Jackson	J	1878-9
36/1922	Fullard	T	No clasp	36/54	Hawkins	E	1878-9	36/1420	James	J.F	1879
1482	Furlong	T	1878-9	36/1399	Hawkins	F	1878-9	36/1538	Jarrett	W	No clasp
36/44	Gale	T	1878	1217	Hawthorne	E	1878-9	395	Jarvis	C	No clasp
36/1734	Gallagher	T	No clasp	36/426	Hayball	A	1878-9	2056	Jeasons	J	1878-9
1762	Garbett	C	No clasp	36/438	Hayes	C	1878-9	1312	Jenner	D	1878-9
2057	Garden	A	1878-9	1983	Hayes	D	1878-9	36/1404	Jennings	J	1878-9
36/1500	Garland	C	1879	36/262	Haynes	E	1878-9	1798	Johnson	C	1878-9
36/45	Garland	W	1878-9	36/277	Hayes	J	1878-9	1814	Johnson	J.W	1878-9
36/41	Gastion	R	1878-9	1567	Hayes	J	1878-9	36/1812	Johnson	W	No clasp
36/33	Gawthorne	W.H	1878-9	36/1536	Headford	G	No clasp	36/451	Johnstone	J	1878-9
36/176	Gaylard	H	1878	679	Headley	F	1878-9	36/1532	Jolliffe	J	No clasp
36/588	George	H	1878-9	36/1495	Helps	H	1878-9	1909	Jolly	F.A	1878-9
36/1409	Geard	J	1879	36/1924	Henderson	H	No clasp	36/361	Jones	A	No clasp
36/1187	Gibbs	H	1878-9	35/146	Henry	J	1878-9	1827	Jones	H	1878-9
36/633	Gillmore	P	1878-9	1830	Hicks	G	1878-9	1449	Jones	J	1878-9
36/75	Glenfield	J.C	1878-9	36/468	Higgins	E	1878-9	36/1705	Jones	J	No clasp
141	Godwin	J	1878-9	36/99	Higgins	J	1878-9	36/1773	Jones	L	No clasp
1799	Gover	J	1878-9	36/187	Higgins	W	1878	36/1814	Jones	W.W	No clasp
1317	Graham	W	1878-9	1636	Hill	G	1878-9	1090	Keane	H	1878-9
36/1587	Grant	G	1878-9	2062	Hill	J	1878-9	1061	Keane	J	1878-9
36/1429	Greed	J	1878-9	1580	Hill	W	1878-9	*36/171	Kearney	W	1878-9
36/165	Gribben	J	1878-9	36/1763	Hillen	T	No clasp		KIA 1st April 1879, Kambula Hill		
36/1819	Griffiths	W	No clasp	36/1633	Hillman	R	No clasp	36/201	Kearns	J	1878-9
36/123	Grimstead	G	1878	1862	Hinchey	M	1878-9	1892	Keefe	J	1878-9
*1902	Grosvenor	W	1878-9	1238	Hiscox	F	1878-9	1602	Kelly	E	No clasp
	KIA 29th March 1879, Kambula Hill			1576	Holman	T	1879	36/420	Kelly	J	1878-9
36/1624	Hadigate	R	No clasp	36/1467	Holly	F	No clasp	36/1896	Kelly	J	No clasp
1453	Hagan	J	1878-9	36/1575	Holly	N	1879	36/157	Kelly	J	1878-9
760	Halpin	M	1878-9	1905	Hopkins	T	1878 r	36/1817	Kelly	R	No clasp
1855	Hale	F	1878-9	1599	Hopton	D	1878	*36/594	Kennedy	J	1878-9
36/346	Hall	F	1878-9	2084	Horton	J	1878-9		D/S 7th March 1879 Kambula Hill		
36/1393	Hall	H	1878-9	356	Howard	G	No clasp	1619	Keon	H	1879
1538	Hall	J	1878-9	1874	Howard	T	1878-9	36/389	Kernaghan	F	1878-9
36/1885	Hamilton	H	No clasp	1192	Howell	G	1878-9	36/82	Kerr	J	1878-9
2079	Hammill	J	1878	1732	Hughes	J	1878-9 r	36/320	Kinchin	C	1878-9
1889	Hancock	G	1878		Forfeited.			36/48	Kinchin	W	1878-9
2010	Hancock	E	1878-9	36/1947	Hughes	P	No clasp	36/1921	King	J	No clasp
36/460	Handron	J	1878-9	36/443	Hughes	T	1878-9	1271	Kirkland	G	1878-9
36/1883	Hanlon	W	No clasp	36/1479	Huish	A	No clasp	1167	Kithidge	C	1878-9
36/71	Hanna	J	1878-9	2087	Hunt	W	1878-9	36/1597	Knight	T	No clasp
#1164	Harkness	J	1878-9	1652	Husband	J	1878-9		Deserted.		
36/1419	Hardin	G	1878-9	36/1434	Hurley	J	1878-9	36/1903	Knight	W	No clasp
1758	Hardy	H	1878-9	36/209	Hutchinson	S	1878-9	1568	Ladbrook	J	1878-9
36/195	Hardy	T	1878-9	1844	Hyland	J	1878-9	311	Lamb	S	No clasp
1563	Hargrave	J	1878-9	35/227	Hunter	C	1878-9	1835	Lancaster	H	1878-9
36/1658	Harris	J	No clasp	1859	Igo	P	1878-9	36/1131	Lappin	W	1879
36/1471	Harris	T	No clasp	1794	Ingersent	J	1878-9	36/122	Larcombe	W	1878-9
36/1898	Harrison	J	No clasp	36/349	Irvine	J	1878-9	2069	Larney	D	1878-9
36/74	Harrison	S	1878-9	36/1439	Irvine	W	1878-9	36/484	Laughlan	J	1878-9
1428	Hart	G	1878-9	36/300	Irwin	A	1878-9	36/1527	Laver	G	No clasp

#Sotherby's London, Auction Lot 80, 29 October 1987
SOUTH AFRICA 1877-9, 1 clasp, 1878-9 (**Pte. J.Harkness. 1/13th Foot**), edge knock otherwise very fine. Recipient was slightly wounded at Kambula on 29 March 1879, sold with photocopied enistment, discharge papers and P.R.O confirmation on casualty return. (£120-140)

1/13th Regiment

35/1818	Law	S	No clasp	36/440	Mc Annally	J	1878-9	36/1908	Mines	M	No clasp
36/575	Lawrence	A	1878-9	36/149	Mc Areavey	J	1878-9	734	Mitchell	H	1878-9
36/112	Lawrence	W	1878-9	36/143	Mc Caffery	W	1879	36/404	Mitchell	J	1878-9
1911	Lawson	A	1878-9	1283	Mc Callion	G	1878-9	36/1531	Mitchell	T	No clasp
36/1218	Lee	G	1879	36/58	Mc Cann	H	No clasp	1964	Mintern	T	1878-9
	No Medal Deserted.			36/253	Mc Cann	J	1878-9	36/1525	Mintey	T	1879
35/1938	Lee	J	No clasp	36/1877	Mc Carroll	J	No clasp	1548	Monks	J	1878-9
35/1549	Lemmon	T	1879	36/1810	Mc Cartin	C	No clasp	35/163	Montgomery	S	1878-9
1968	Lewis	G	1878-9	36/179	Mc Cartney	P	1878-9	36/267	Montgomery	W.J	1878-9
1948	Lewis	J	No clasp	36/95	Mc Clean	R	1878-9	36/1904	Moody	J	No clasp
36/1541	Light	W	1879	36/67	Mc Cleod	T	1878-9	1075	Mooney	P	1878-9
1888	Linahan	T	1878-9	35/610	Mc Combe	W	1878-9	972	Monorey	P	1878-9
1724	Lipscombe	J	1878-9	36/298	Mc Connell	J	1878-9	36/402	Moore	J	1878-9
36/1895	Little	G	No clasp	36/159	Mc Cormick	H	1878-9	36/183	Moore	T	1878-9
36/246	Little	R	1878-9	36/223	Mc Crory	J	1878-9	35/236	Moore	W.J	No clasp
2065	Lloyd	H	1878-9	36/499	Mc Crudden	F	1878-9	395	Moran	P	1878-9
36/148	Lloyd	T	1878-9	36/222	Mc Crudden	J	1878-9	953	Moreland	W	1878-9
36/590	Lochhead	J	1878-9	434	Mc Cummins	R	1878-9	36/301	Moreland	W	1878-9
1877	Long	J	1878-9	36/167	Mc Donald	R	1879	1961	Morrall	J	1878-9
1190	Longthorne	C	1878-9	36/461	Mc Donough	R	1878-9	36/1256	Morris	T	No clasp
1822	Lovelock	J	1878-9	35/405	Mc Dougal	A	1878-9	1551	Morris	W.J	No clasp
2053	Lowe	J	1878-9	36/295	Mc Gee	J	1878-9	36/593	Morrison	J	1878-9
36/138	Lowery	J	1878-9	36/1910	Mc Gillicuddy	J	No clasp	1635	Morton	G.D	1878-9
36/133	Lowery	J	1878-9	36/169	Mc Gough	C	1878-9	941	Morton	T	1878-9
1845	Lomsden	W	1878-9	36/652	Mc Gourty	F	1879	1670	Mott	J	1878-9
1912	Lyons	J	1878-9	36/1902	Mc Govern	C	No clasp	36/275	Mulholland	B	1878-9
36/218	Macauley	R	1878-9	36/214	Mc Govern	J	1878-9	1565	Mullan	J	1878-9
36/1463	Macey	J	No clasp	36/304	Mc Gregor	C	1878-9	2063	Mumford	G	1878-9
36/217	Macdonald	W	1878-9	36/269	Mc Intyre	R	1878-9	1176	Munroe	J	1878-9
36/399	Madden	J	1878-9r	36/161	Mc Knight	R	1878-9	36/150	Murphy	J	1878-9
36/91	Magill	H	1878-9	35/1736	Mc Larnin	R	No clasp	36/576	Murphy	T	No clasp
36/309	Magowan	A	1878-9	1849	Mc Kay	W	1878-9	36/394	Murrain	M	1878-9
36/398	Maguiness	P	1878-9	36/403	Mc Kelvey	W	1878	36/263	Murray	M	1878-9
36/175	Maguire	A	1878-9	1307	Mc Kenna	T	1878-9	36/77	Murray	S	1878-9
2026	Maguire	J	1878-9	36/393	Mc Keown	W	1879	1999	Murrow	J	1878-9
36/400	Mahoney	M	1878	36/70	Mc Kibbon	J	1878-9	1955	Neal	E	1878-9
37/1716	Mahoney	P	No clasp	36/153	Mc Laughlin	D	1878-9	1882	Neal	T	1878-9
36/116	Mahoney	W	1878-9	36/263	Mc Murray	R	1878-9	2024	Newman	T	1878-9
36/1416	Maidment	H	1878-9		A replacement issued 15/10/1920.			35/1260	Nicholson	A	1878-9
2016	Mair	J	1878-9	36/196	Mc Murry	T	1878-9	938	Nicholson	E	1878-9
36/1771	Makin	T	No clasp	*1783	Mc Nulty	W	1878-9	2075	Nic	W	1878-9
36/137	Malone	J	1878-9		**KIA 2nd April 1879, Kambula Hill**			1329	Nightingale	C	1878-9
1915	Manion	J	1878-9	36/98	Mc Quade	W	1878-9	36/483	Noble	J	1878-9
1629	Mannan	M	1878-9	36/140	Mc Stay	J	1878-9	36/1899	Noonan	P	No clasp r
36/489	Marley	N	1878-9	#1914	Mc Toy	E.D	1878-9	35/1877	Norman	T	No clasp
36/25	Marshman	T	1878-9	36/151	Mc Vicar	G	1878-9	36/160	Norris	A	1878-9
1492	Martin	J	1878-9	36/29	Medlam	G	1878-9	35/1813	Nugent	J	No clasp r
36/1085	Martin	J	1878-9	1956	Merryweather	J	1878	35/229	Nugent	N	No clasp
36/1920	Mason	H	No clasp	608	Miles	W	1878-9	35/1930	Nunn	E	No clasp
36/1313	Masters	C	1879	36/316	Mills	W	1878-9	154	Nutt	G	1878-9
36/118	Matthews	G	1878-9	36/124	Mills	W	1878-9	2064	O'Brien	H	1878-9
36/624	Mathews	H	1878-9	36/1362	Milsome	G	1878-9	1509	O'Connor	E	1878-9
1463	May	J	1878-9	36/1445	Milton	J	1879	35/352	O'Dogherty	P	1878-9

During the first Sekukuni War on the 27th October 1878, Colonel Rowlands with a force of 730 men and three guns attacked one of Umsutu's headmen, at a place called Tolyana Stad. Private McToy in his book "A Brief History of the 13th Regiment (P.A.L.I.) in South Africa", 1880. gives a graphic and exciting account of this action in which Colour Sergeant John Pegg was killed and seven men were wounded. The grave of Colour-Sergeant Pegg can be located on Google Earth not far from the present Steelpoort Station. Reference: http://samilitaryhistory.org/vol026nk.html

1/13th Regiment

No.	Name	Initial	Clasp	No.	Name	Initial	Clasp	No.	Name	Initial	Clasp
1974	O'Farrell	W.F	1879	35/111	Pring	W	1878-9	2012	Shea	J	1878-9
787	O'Flanagan	T	1878-9	2054	Pritchard	F	1878-9	1950	Shea	H	1878-9
35/135	O'Hare	D	1878-9	1214	Purvis	W	1878-9	2066	Sheppard	G	1878-9
1774	O'Keefe	L	1878	35/132	Pyne	J	1878-9	36/314	Sheppard	J	1878-9
35/152	O'Neil	J	1878-9	1866	Pyne	W	1878-9	1811	Sheppard	W	1878-9
1935	Osborne	G	No clasp	35/18	Quinlan	H	1878-9	35/1927	Sherron	J	No clasp
1120	Osborne	J	No clasp	35/55	Quinn	H	1878-9	36/216	Shevlin	R	1878-9
36/1411	Osborne	W	1878-9	1981	Radley	S	1878-9	35/1891	Shipton	W.G	No clasp
35/102	Owen	H	1878-9	35/312	Rafferty	M	1878-9	53	Silk	J	1878-9
35/1764	Owens	J	No clasp	35/1397	Randell	G	1879	879	Sims	J	1878-9
1197	Page	A	1878-9	35/207	Reavey	H	1878-9	1918	Simmonds	C	1878-9
D.C.M	Kambula 29.3.79			*1145	Redpath	S	1878-9	1880	Sipthorpe	S	1878-9
36/1119	Page	W	1879	**KIA 29th March 1879, Kambula Hill**				159	Skews	W	No clasp
2082	Paice	F	1878-9	1469	Reed	J	1878-9	1660	Sligo	J	1878-9
36/1804	Palmer	G	No clasp	36/31	Rendell	T	1878-9	36/411	Sloane	J	1878-9
35/1418	Parish	C	1878-9	36/1916	Rennell	J	No clasp	36/1458	Slowcombe	A	No clasp
35/578	Parkhouse	T	1878-9	97	Reynolds	J	1878-9	36/663	Smart	F	No clasp
36/1949	Parslow	G	No clasp	35/585	Richards	J	1878-9	36/1457	Smart	S	No clasp
36/47	Parsons	J	1878-9	35/1765	Richardson	J	No clasp	36/1950	Smart	C	No clasp
1858	Parsons	J	1878-9	2061	Rielly	P	1878-9	1919	Smith	F	1878-9
35/1494	Parsons	T	No clasp	35/134	Rielly	P	1878-9	35/1524	Smith	G	No clasp
1856	Partridge	E	1878	36/1473	Roberts	A	No clasp	36/204	Smith	H	1878-9
35/57	Patten	J	1878-9	1875	Roberts	H	1878-9	1074	Smith	J	1878-9
35/224	Peacock	J	1878-9	35/479	Robertson	R	1878-9	36/473	Smith	P	1878-9
35/53	Peach	J	1878-9	36/311	Robinson	D	1878-9	36/302	Smith	T	1878-9
1878	Pearman	G	1878-9	1808	Robinson	T	1878	35/85	Smith	W.J	1878-9
2047	Pearman	J	1878-9	36/564	Robinson	T	1878	36/1969	Snelling	G	No clasp
1444	Penaluna	T	1878-9	35/409	Rodgers	N	1878-9	36/1724	Snelling	J	No clasp
779	Peoples	R	1878-9	35/303	Rogan	E	1878-9	239	Snoyd	P	1878
36/1526	Peppin	J	1879	1651	Root	E	1878-9	347	Snook	J	1878-9
35/1605	Perkins	F	No clasp	36/1606	Rossiter	A	No clasp	32	Sparks	J	1878-9
1927	Perrin	G	1878-9	1674	Rourke	J	1878-9	36/1480	Spiller	C	1879
2046	Perry	G	1878-9	1250	Rouse	J	1878-9	35/355	Spiers	W	1878-9
36/1654	Perry	S.J	No clasp	2088	Rowe	W.G	1878-9	2052	Stacey	W	1878-9
36/1400	Pester	R	1878-9	36/456	Russell	B	No clasp	36/1556	Stanbury	W	No clasp
36/110	Phillips	J	1878-9	922	Russell	E	No clasp	36/356	Stephenson	J	1878-9
1206	Phillips	J	1878-9	1288	Russ	R	No clasp	2080	Stevens	J	1878-9
36/1486	Phillis	J	1878-9	1998	Ryan	T	No clasp r	36/180	Stevens	R	1878-9
36/1498	Pike	J	1879	36/1929	Sadler	J	No clasp	35/1681	Stevens	W	No clasp
1467	Pike	W	1878-9	2083	Sainsbury	J.E	1878-9	36/535	Stevens	W	1878-9
35/230	Pinnell	R	1878-9	1578	Sandiford	H.O	1879	36/410	Stewart	J	1878-9
36/1562	Pitcher	F	No clasp	36/256	Salter	F	1879	36/1465	Stokes	E	1879
1832	Pollard	J	1878-9	36/1579	Salter	T	1879	2042	Stokes	T	1878-9
1205	Ponfield	H	1878-9	36/1618	Saturley	W	No clasp	175	Sullivan	T	1878-9
35/1918	Poole	E	No clasp	2050	Saunders	W	1878-9	36/290	Swain	J	1878-9
35/1919	Poole	G	No clasp	36/1652	Savory	H.A	No clasp	36/577	Swam	T	1878-9
36/1462	Pope	F	1879	1796	Savory	J	1878-9	1957	Swanwick	S	1878-9
35/79	Pope	J	1878-9	1959	Scanlon	J	1878-9	36/1457	Sydenham	C	1879
36/1805	Pope	T	No clasp	1551	Scully	M	1878-9	36/488	Sylvester	A	1878-9
210	Pope	W	No clasp	36/321	Scutter	W	1878-9	1645	Tacchi	J	1878-9
36/1917	Potts	C	No clasp	36/328	Seale	J	1878-9	36/1454	Talbot	F	1879
36/889	Power	E	1878-9	35/1466	Sealey	A	1879	35/185	Tanner	G	1878-9
304	Prangley	E	1878-9	213	Searle	S	1878-9	35/1657	Tanton	W	No clasp
16	Pratt	G	1878-9	36/73	Seymour	J.H	1878-9	1638	Tarry	B	1878-9
2057	Preece	J	1878-9	36/536	Sharpe	J	No clasp	36/238	Tatchell	A	1879
36/1331	Prescott	F	No clasp	1782	Sharpe	J.A	1878-9 r	36/115	Tatchell	W	1878-9
35/1448	Priddle	H	1879		Forfeited.			36/1740	Tatterson	J	No clasp
35/1430	Priddle	J	1878-9	36/1586	Shaughnessy	S	No clasp	2622	Tatterson	J	1878-9
35/1578	Pring	H	No clasp	36/130	Shave	H	1878-9	2015	Taylor	J	1878-9

1/13th Regiment

36/287	Taylor	W	1878	36/363	Wells	F	1878-9
35/1758	Thew	A	No clasp	1848	Welling	W	1878-9
36/1601	Thomas	E	No clasp	36/120	Welsh	S	1878-9
36/481	Thompson	J	1878-9	1980	West	J	1878-9
36/1915	Thompson	W	No clasp	36/1635	Whatley	J	No clasp
35/1569	Thorne	G	No clasp	1936	Wheble	J.R	1878-9
36/1607	Thorne	J	No clasp	1419	Wheeler	G	1878-9
36/1928	Till	D	No clasp	1985	Whelan	W.D	1878-9
36/1219	Tilley	H	1879	36/1735	White	D	No clasp
35/107	Todd	W.J	1878-9	1893	White	G	1878
1352	Tons	R	No clasp	1448	White	G	1879
1864	Towers	G	1878	36/413	White	J	1879
35/1585	Towell	W.H	No clasp	1842	White	J	1878-9 r
36/1487	Townsend	H	No clasp		Forfeited.		
36/1459	Triggle	J	No clasp	1366	Whittaker	E	1878-9
36/412	Trotter	R	1878	36/364	Whittaker	G	1878-9
36/470	Trump	W	1878-9	36/261	Whitley	H	1878-9
36/1592	Tucker	G	No clasp	36/1563	Wide	W	No clasp
36/103	Tucker	H	1878-9	1418	Wilborne	W	1878-9
36/1403	Tucker	S	1878-9	36/1760	Wilkinson	W	No clasp
36/1365	Tucker	W	1878-9	36/317	Williams	J	1879
35/1538	Tudball	G	No clasp	36/1914	Williams	R	No clasp
35/228	Tumilty	H	1878-9	2043	Williams	S	1878-9
1233	Turpin	R	1878-9	2044	Williams	T	1878-9
36/634	Twaddle	G	1879 r	36/1953	Willmot	C	No clasp
	Forfeited.			36/1232	Wilmot	G	1879
1952	Tye	W	No clasp	36/78	Wilson	T	1878-9
36/1198	Tyrell	W	1879	1362	Wiltshire	J	1878-9
36/422	Venning	J	1878-9	36/1535	Wingfield	J	No clasp
36/76	Vincent	H	1878-9	36/1474	Witch	J	No clasp r
36/1788	Wadsworth	R	No clasp		Deserted.		
36/448	Walker	G	1878-9	36/415	Wolfe	H	1878-9
36/581	Wall	C	1879	36/1770	Wood	H	No clasp r
36/414	Wall	J	1878-9	36/1426	Wood	H	1878
157	Wallace	W	1878	36/490	Wood	R	1878-9
36/1632	Walsh	J	1879	36/1557	Woodhouse	J	No clasp
1921	Walsh	P	1878-9	36/365	Worth	H	1878-9
1764	Ward	A	1878-9	1461	Worth	J	1878-9
1922	Ward	E	1878-9	1429	Wykes	H	1879
36/265	Ward	J	1878-9	1938	Young	D	1878-9
36/281	Ward	P	1878-9	36/876	Young	E	1879
1771	Ward	R	1878-9	36/1477	Young	E	No clasp
1795	Warren	R	1878-9	1854	Young	J	1878-9
130	Warrin	C	1878-9	36/1959	Young	J	No clasp
36/43	Wasson	W	1878-9	888	Young	W	1878-9
36/1589	Watkins	G	No clasp				
1586	Watson	J	1878-9				
36/647	Watson	W	1878-9				
36/1475	Watts	F	No clasp				
35/425	Waygood	A	1878-9				
36/1889	Weaver	G	No clasp				
36/1807	Webb	J	No clasp				
1990	Webb	J	1878-9				
36/278	Webb	W.J	1878-9				
36/1470	Webber	J	1879				
36/1913	Webster	C	No clasp				
36/884	Webster	P.J	1878-9				
177	Wedlock	V	1878-9				
635	Weightman	D	No clasp				

* London Gazette 23 May 1879

1/16th (THE BEDFORDSHIRE) REGIMENT.
CAPTAIN
Paterson   A.H   No clasp

1/18th (THE ROYAL IRISH) REGIMENT.
LIEUTENANT
Lawrence   W.W   1879
See also Commissariat & Transport Staff.

1/19th (1st YORKSHIRE NORTH RIDING) (PRINCESS OF WALES' OWN) REGIMENT.
CAPTAIN
Oakes   G   1879

2/21st (ROYAL SCOTS FUSILIERS) REGIMENT.
Landed at Durban 23rd March 1879, took part in the battle of Ulundi, where they faced the brunt of the enemy's first attack
BREVET COLONEL
Collingwood   W.P   1879
Also had British Crimea Medal and clasp. The Turkish Crimea Medal and Ashanti Medal.
BREVET MAJOR
Bainbridge   E.T   1879
MAJOR
Hazlerigg   A.G   1879
Also had British Crimea Medal, and clasp and Turkish Medal.
Winsloe   R.V.C   1879
Also had British Crimea Medal and clasp and Turkish Medal.
CAPTAIN
Auckinleck   D   1879
Also had Ashanti Medal and clasp.
Browne   E.C   1879
Burr   F.W   1879
Falls   A.L   1879
Gordon   J.M   1879
Robinson   C.B   1879
Spurgin   J.H   1879
Thorburn   W   1879
Willoughby   R.T   1879
BANDMASTER
2424   Daniels   F.F   No clasp
QUARTERMASTER
Clifford   J   1879
CAPTAIN & PAYMASTER
Tew   J.M   No clasp
See also Army Pay Department
LIEUTENANT ADJUTANT
Chichester   S.F   1879
LIEUTENANT
Alexander   H.R   1879
Browne   P.W   1879
Collings   A.W   1879
Duckett   W.M   1879
Dunn   A.C   1879
Justice   A.S   1879
Lambart   F.R.H   1879
Lindsell   C.F   1879
Scott-Douglas   J.H   1879
KIA Fort Evelyn
Young   W.A   1879

2/21st Regiment

2nd LIEUTENANT
Twistleton-Wykeham Fiennes G.C 1879
Hardinge Hon. A.S 1879
Lean K.E 1879
Stannell H.S. Mc C 1879
Thorneycroft A.W 1879

ATTACHED OFFICERS
CAPTAIN
 Robertson D.S 1879
 (Edinburgh L.I. Militia)
 Woodmas C 1879
 (Cheshire Volunteers)

LIEUTENANT
 Higgins H 1879
 (3rd R. Lancashire Militia)

SERGEANT MAJOR
 1508 Watts F 1879

DRUM MAJOR
 2311 Osborne W.H 1879

PIPE MAJOR
 2422 McGruer S 1879
Also had Medal for North West Frontier of India.

COLOUR SERGEANT
 922 Comrie D 1879
 2613 Cook G 1879
 1982 Finch G 1879
 2037 Hardwick J 1879
 2144 Mc Culloch D 1879
 1528 Martin W 1879
 1388 Williams H 1879

ARMOURER SERGEANT
 111 Everand W.H 1879

BAND SERGEANT
 1027 Shelver W No clasp
 1338 Williams H 1879

COOK SERGEANT
 626 Davies H No clasp

SERGEANT INSTRUCTOR OF MUSKETRY
 1512 Hampson J 1879

PAYMASTER SERGEANT
 1395 Wells G.F.B No clasp

QUARTERMASTER SERGEANT
 575 Gerry J 1879

SERGEANT
 61B/2215 Armstrong D 1879
 2358 Brooks E 1879
 61B/214 Brooks J No clasp
 281 Burns W 1879
 61B/486 Clay W.H 1879
 1775 Egan J 1879
 720 Eycott F 1879
 563 Freeth W No clasp
 2269 Glenallen R No clasp
 2333 Harty J 1879
 61B/2438 Haslam I.R No clasp
 61B/517 Hempseed R 1879
 2228 House J 1879
 61B/404 Hume J 1879
 61B/2493 Hurst J 1879
 327 Joseph O No clasp
 1264 Layland T 1879
 1592 Michell J 1879
 61B/2221 Neffers R 1879
 894 Parker H No clasp
 1547 Pettitt T 1879
 2583 Pettitt W 1879
 2302 Preston M 1879
 1643 Quegan T 1879
 61B/1232 Reynolds H 1879
 1693 Rice J No clasp
 61B/552 Ritchie T 1879
 872 Rosser J 1879
 720 Russell G 1879
 1358 Ryan T 1879
 61B/2434 Standring G 1879
 2725 Troy J 1879
 1121 Turner A 1879
 2590 Turner G 1879
 738 Tweedie D 1879
 1629 Wall W 1879
 61B/2552 Walsh T 1879

LANCE SERGEANT
 2242 Baskett C 1879
 61B/899 Boddy R.J 1879
 2672 Fox H.W 1879
 412 Minto W 1879

CORPORAL
 61B/789 Anderson C 1879 r
 61B/845 Band W 1879
 No Medal Deserted.
 61B/866 Barr J 1879
 2334 Beck G 1879
 2155 Brown G 1879
 61B/989 Byrne M 1879
 1576 Dalton J 1879
 No Medal Deserted.
 61B/2216 Emery W 1879
 61B/120 Forbes A 1879
 61B/926 Grace L 1879
 1348 Hemming I 1879
 2227 Henderson W 1879
 No Medal Deserted.
 61B/2497 Kelly T 1879
 511 Kelly F 1879
 61B/2208 Leadham J 1879
 1291 Locke J 1879
 767 Mahoney J 1879
 946 Marston J 1879
 311 Mc Lean A 1879
 61B/739 Mc Inally P 1879
 61B/914 Mc Quire J 1879
 61B/2359 Morton J No clasp
 2523 Prest W 1879
 1818 Shea D 1879
 2231 Tormey T No clasp
 61B/917 Turner T No clasp
 2671 Walker R 1879
 61B/2225 Walker T 1879
 61B/740 Watt G 1879
 1986 Wheatley W 1879
 2265 White J 1879
 471 Wiggins R 1879
 1655 Woods F 1879

LANCE CORPORAL
 2421 Barnatt E No clasp
 61B/2261 Bayley F.H 1879
 1608 Bell W No clasp
 2309 Birmingham D 1879
 Duplicate Medal and clasp issued. Date unknown.
 2464 Brand J 1879
 2632 Bronson I 1879
 2304 Campbell P 1879
 1827 Clarke W 1879
 2224 Cossar J No clasp
 2070 Dougal J 1879
 1859 Duncan J.B 1879
 61B/2203 Fiddler T 1879
 1507 Hunter R 1879
 61B/1637 Mc Donald D 1879
 1612 Meayers C 1879
 997 Norman R 1879 r
 61B/2280 O'Brien D 1879
 2280 O'Brien D 1879
 Duplicate?
 61B/921 Potts J 1879
 61B/1054 Robertson J 1879
 61B/346 Ross W 1879
 2536 Rotherve J 1879
 61B/562 Seenan P 1879
 501 Strachan G 1879
 61B/2205 Warner J.S 1879
 2631 Wood P.T 1879

ORDERLYROOM CLERK
 2599 Smith C 1879

DRUMMER
 61B/185 Armstrong S 1879
 2630 Byrne R 1879
 141 Clifford T 1879
 2478 Deighton W 1879
 2324 Fivian ? P 1879
 2840 Howard T 1879
 2201 Howarth W 1879
 61B/69 Manley M 1879
 990 Massons J 1879
 61B/39 Mc Grady W 1879
 61B/142 Orr D 1879
 1495 Smith G 1879
 No Medal Deserted.
 61B/291 Sparks A 1879
 2675 Sweeney J 1879
 1408 Tuck J 1879

PIPER
 2367 Cameron J 1879
 No Medal Deserted.

2/21st Regiment

PRIVATE

No.	Surname	Initial	Clasp/Year
456	Adley	T	1879
806	Agnew	W	1879
1076	Aiken	H	1879
1966	Alden	R	No clasp
1758	Allison	J	No clasp
2313	Ambler	R	1879
1865	Anderson	J	1879
2546	Anderson	R	1879
864	Armitage	D	1879
1665	Ash	M	1879
2239	Ashley	C.H	1879
	No Medal Deserted.		
2146	Ashley	C.W	1879
2524	Atkins	J	1879
2589	Attwood	G	1879
	No Medal Deserted.		
2194	Ailtz	C	1879
2242	Axon	J	1879
2609	Badman	H	No clasp
1687	Bain	A	1879 r
1579	Baird	G	1879
898	Ball	T	No clasp
	No Medal Discharged with ignominy.		
439	Ballentyne	H	No clasp
943	Banks	J	1879
2116	Banks	J	No clasp
1000	Banks	T	1879
	No Medal Discharged with ignominy.		
1629	Banks	W	1879
2202	Barker	A	1879
2396	Barlow	G	1879
2455	Barnard	W	1879
2525	Barnes	A	1879 r
2061	Barnett	B.L	1879
2/21 2225	Barnett	J	1879 r
1667	Barry	J	1879
	No Medal Deserted.		
1074	Batchelor	J	1879
2467	Bavister	S	1879
1316	Beavis	J	No clasp
815	Beckett	J	1879
2467	Beavan	W	1879
1680	Bedford	J	1879
	Duplicate Medal and clasp issued. Date unknown.		
1459	Beechgood	N	1879
1086	Belcher	R	1879
694	Bell	D	1879
2352	Bennett	C	1879
1739	Bennis	G	1879
1766	Benson	I	1879
1032	Betten	W	1879
1724	Bevendges	J	1879
2429	Bill	J	No clasp
854	Binnie	A.S	1879
2041	Bishop	J	1879
	No Medal Deserted.		
1710	Black	P	1879
1711	Black	R	No clasp
389	Blair	A	1879
1409	Boleyn	P	1879
2682	Bond	F	1879
952	Boyd	R	No clasp
1739	Boyd	W	1879
	Duplicate Medal and clasp issued.		
1753	Boylan	W	1879
	No Medal Deserted.		
1750	Boyle	F	1879
	No Medal Discharged with ignominy.		
1767	Boyle	J	1879
725	Boyle	W	1879
2465	Brennan	E	1879
	No Medal Deserted.		
692	Bridger	G	1879
2286	Brien	C	1879
2308	Brien	T	1879
	No Medal Deserted.		
2237	Briggs	J	1879
2233	Briggs	W	1879
2378	Bright	T	No clasp
2369	Brisland	J	No clasp
450	Britton	T	1879
2379	Broadbent	G	1879
1513	Brock	A	1879
512	Brown	A	1879
1798	Brown	G	1879
1682	Brown	J	1879
1748	Brown	J	1879
2307	Brown	M	1879
667	Browne	T	1879
	No Medal Deserted.		
2312	Brownbill	C	No clasp
	Duplicate Medal issued. Date unknown.		
980	Brownlee	J	1879
2245	Brucker	E	No clasp
1933	Bull	G	1879
2306	Bullock	W	1879
	No Medal Deserted.		
1621	Burke	J	1879
2504	Burke	J	1879
1836	Burns	G	1879
1029	Burnes	J	1879
702	Burnes	M	1879
2388	Burnes	T	1879
2372	Burton	H	1879
2418	Bush	H	1879
1779	Byrne	C	1879
	Duplicate Medal and clasp issued. Date unknown.		
2305	Byrne	J	1879
1042	Cahill	F	1879
778	Caldow	H	1879
1680	Callaghan	J	1879
2526	Callaghan	R	No clasp
61B/856	Cameron	J	1879
1761	Campbell	A	1879
101	Campbell	G	1879
851	Campbell	H	1879
1572	Campbell	J	1879
1624	Campbell	J	1879
1660	Campbell	J	1879
1740	Campbell	J	No clasp
499	Campbell	O	1879
1715	Campbell	W	1879
1043	Cane	J	1879
2633	Canning	B	1879
2477	Carolan	P	1879
893	Carroll	E	1879
2360	Cartwright	F	1879
1686	Casey	P	1879
2342	Cashman	J	1879
2248	Charlesworth	H	1879
2420	Checkley	S	1879
1803	Cherry	A	1879
1784	Christie	R	1879
1661	Christy	H	1879
1598	Clark	J	1879
61B/2482	Clarke	T	No clasp
2377	Clayton	H	No clasp
318	Cleary	P	No clasp
1923	Clews	G	1879
	No Medal Deserted.		
838	Clynes	J	1879
1821	Cochrane	W	1879
2335	Coleman	J	1879
2348	Collett	W	1879
1073	Collings	W	1879
	Duplicate Medal and clasp issued. Date unknown.		
1648	Collings	W	1879
252	Collins	C	1879
2240	Coltman	R	No clasp
2333	Colvin	W	1879
1668	Cook	G	1879
718	Cook	J	No clasp
1060	Cook	W	1879
684	Cooper	A	1879 r
2303	Connell	D	No clasp
1069	Connolly	J	1879
1725	Connolly	J	1879
888	Conry	T	1879
1597	Conway	J	No clasp
832	Cooney	J	1879
1746	Cooney	T	No clasp
714	Coombs	E	No clasp
2414	Corbishley	J	1879
1829	Corrie	H	No clasp
	Duplicate Medal issued. Date unknown.		
1833	Cox	D	1879
1824	Coyle	J	1879
1061	Craddick	J	No clasp
1620	Craig	D	1879
1758	Craig	W	No clasp
2017	Craigie	H	1879
2340	Crawley	C	1879

2/21st Regiment

1823	Crichton J		1879
1674	Croatt J		1879
178	Croft T		No clasp
2303	Cronan P		1879
1707	Crosbie J		1879
	No Medal Deserted.		
2419	Crowley B		1879
	No Medal Deserted.		
801	Cruickshank J		1879
1762	Cruickshank J		1879
1645	Cruickshank W		1879
1751	Cunnief P		1879
2195	Cunningham C		1879
1734	Cunningham W		1879
2246	Cure R		No clasp
1794	Currie J		1879
1051	Currie J		1879
1019	Curtain J		1879
2406	Dale A		1879
1752	Daley C		1879
1967	Daley P		1879
1926	Dalgleish J		1879
991	Daly H		1879
977	Dalzell W		No clasp
2400	Darlington J		No clasp
1402	Daveney J		1879
1720	Davidson A		1879
2227	Davenport D		No clasp
2206	Davis F		1879
906	Davis G		1879
2193	Davis J		1879
922	Davis W		1879
691	Dawes W		1879
849	Day D		1879 r
2527	Day M		1879
896	Dearn J		1879
2328	Devensy ? I		1879
853	Demey J		1879
	No Medal Deserted.		
1609	Denning A		No clasp
2302	Derby J		1879
2331	Devine M		1879
884	Dewitt P		1879
61B/1678	Diamond D		1879
1628	Dias J		1879
218	Dick J		1879
2511	Dickens H		No clasp
1795	Dignan W		1879
	No Medal Deserted.		
2300	Dinnigan M		1879
2140	Dixon E		1879
	No Medal Deserted.		
874	Dixon T		1879
1808	Dobbs F		1879
	Duplicate Medal and clasp issued. Date unknown.		
944	Donagby F		1879
	No Medal Deserted.		
883	Donagby W		1879
1014	Donald T		No clasp
154	Donaldson R		1879
2299	Donnelly B		1879
857	Donnelly J		1879
940	Donnelly J		1879
1631	Donigan F		1879
2236	Donohoe B	KIA	1879
1785	Doody W		1879
999	Dott J		1879
881	Douce J		1879
1664	Dougal J		1879
671	Downie D		1879
1007	Douvard D		1879
1589	Dowdle M		1879
2440	Dowlen E		No clasp
920	Doyle J		1879
1583	Doyle J		1879
2399	Doyle J		1879
	No Medal Discharged with ignominy.		
2639	Driscoll T		1879
2235	Drummond W		1879
2243	Drury P		No clasp
1702	Dryburgh A		No clasp
2422	Duddy J		1879
2528	Duffey M		1879
1780	Duncan P		1879
	No Medal Deserted.		
1718	Dunbar T		1879
1081	Dunn R		1879
1723	Dunne J		No clasp
2529	Dunne J		1879
2439	Dunning J		1879
907	Durham P		1879
913	Durham W		1879
1603	Eadie J		1879
	No Medal Discharged with ignominy.		
1755	Earlie P		No clasp
	No Medal Deserted.		
699	Easton A		1879
992	Easton J		1879
993	Easton R		1879
2395	Easton W		1879
2087	Edwards W		1879
2395	Edwards W		1879
2503	Edwards F		1879
1657	Elliott J		1879
2200	Ellis M		1879
1577	Emmett G		1879
2500	Evans J		1879
	No Medal Deserted.		
1346	Evans T		1879
2297	Evans G		1879
61B/114	Fackler J		No clasp
1017	Faichen R		1879
465	Fairful J		1879
52	Fallon p		1879
	No Medal Deserted.		
2236	Farr H		1879
989	Farrell M		1879
800	Farrell P		1879
1804	Fegan A		1879
2296	Fennessy J		1879
1652	Fenthry A		1879
2313	Finnigan P		1879
1968	Flaherty T		1879
847	Flynn H		1879
2424	Flynn H		1879
2405	Flynn R		1879
	Duplicate Medal and clasp issued. Date unknown.		
973	Flynn S		1879
2295	Foley T		1879
1806	Ford G		1879
2548	Forscutt H		1879
2258	Foster H		1879
1004	Foster J		1879
2223	Foyster H		No clasp
2517	Francis W		No clasp
1768	Fraser A		1879
	No Medal Deserted.		
2320	Frawley T		1879
2317	Frawley W		1879
859	Frier P		1879
	No Medal Deserted.		
1722	Frith W		No clasp
1816	Gagen F		1879
61B/2260	Galvin B		1879
1036	Gambley R		1879
61B/2169	Gartshore J		No clasp
	Duplicate medal issued. Date unknown.		
2314	Garvey G		1879
2241	Gear F		1879
1756	Getgood G		1879
2432	Gibson C		1879
	No Medal Deserted.		
2448	Gibson J		No clasp
2484	Gifford A		No clasp
61B/1777	Gillies D McG		No clasp
2249	Gilligan J		1879
804	Givens J		1879
817	Glenn R		1879
971	Glendinning D		1879
2496	Godding J		1879
386	Goodwin J		1879
2422	Goose B		1879
	No Medal Deserted.		
966	Gordon J		1879
830	Gorman M		1879
892	Gorne C		1879
2294	Grace J		1879
1074	Graham R		1879
1008	Grahames W		1879
	Duplicate Medal and clasp issued. 24/4/1919.		
2109	Grandage R		1879
1053	Grant W		1879
	Duplicate Medal and clasp issued. Date unknown.		

2/21st Regiment

1763	Gray	P	1879
994	Gray	T	1879
	No Medal Deserted.		
2394	Gray	W	1879
1584	Greer	J	1879
	No Medal Deserted.		
1847	Gribbon	J	1879
2355	Griffiths	B	1879
2409	Griffiths	J	1879
2485	Griffiths	J	1879
2255	Guerin	P	1879
	No Medal Discharged on Conviction by Civil Court.		
2293	Guthrie	J	1879
1829	Guthrie	T	No clasp
2468	Hall	G	No clasp
1275	Hall	H	No clasp
894	Hall	J	1879
2234	Hall	T	1879
74	Hallet	J	1879
2425	Halley	J	1879
837	Halsworth	J	1879
2310	Hamer	J	1879
978	Hamilton	T	1879
2428	Hampton	H	1879
2336	Hansberry	W	1879
2292	Hare	T	1879
819	Harper	A	1879
1035	Harris	G	1879
1886	Harris	J	1879
2362	Harris	W	1879 r
2483	Harrison	H	1879
1811	Hart	E	1879
2393	Harvey	A	1879
61B/2291	Harvey	T	No clasp
954	Hasdell	C	1879
1023	Haughey ?	J	1879
	No Medal Deserted.		
589	Hayhurst	W	1879
1002	Haynes	W	No clasp
2319	Heaps	J	1879
2412	Heavy	T	1879
	No Medal Discharged with ignominy.		
886	Hedger	T	No clasp
2485	Heelahaw	T	1879
885	Hefferman	D	1879
343	Henderson	F	1879
820	Henderson	W	1879 r
2415	Hennessy	J	1879
1039	Heron	D	1879
	No Medal Deserted.		
1637	Hewitt	A	1879
1619	Higgins	J	1879
2572	Higgins	J	1879
938	Higgins	W	1879
2382	Hill	R	1879
2487	Hill	W	1879 r
2450	Hobson	R	1879

2574	Hockaday	C	1879
802	Hodgson	W	No clasp
1040	Hogarth	R	1879
2201	Holden	J	1879
2231	Holderson	T	1879
	No Medal Deserted.		
1704	Holt	H	1879
	No Medal Deserted.		
1759	Hopkins	H	No clasp
2381	Horseman	W	1879
	No Medal Deserted.		
684	Hotchin	T	1879
2144	Hoy	W	1879
	No Medal Deserted.		
2237	Hoy	W	1879
61B/2066	Hudson	J.E	1879
2505	Hugh	T	1879
121	Hughes	J	1879
	No Medal. Discharged with ignominy.		
2290	Hughes	J	1879
1677	Hughes	T	No clasp
924	Hughes	T	1879
2100	Hughes	T	1879
758	Hume	J	1879
951	Hume	W	1879
260	Humphries	J	1879
1625	Humphries	W	1879
2485	Hunt	A	No clasp
1813	Hunter	J	1879
1644	Hunter	T	1879
1786	Irvine	J	1879
1044	Irvine	S	No clasp
696	Jackson	J	1879
1012	Jackson	J	1879
2510	Jackson	J	1879
2561	James	S	1879
1025	Jamieson	W	1879
2363	Jarvis	F	1879
	No Medal Discharged with ignominy.		
2398	Jarvis	F	1879
1814	Jeffrey	J	1879
1005	Jeffrey	M	1879
	No Medal Deserted.		
1653	Jeffrey	W	1879
2431	Jones	C	1879
2515	Jones	H	1879
2495	Jones	J	1879
2289	Jones	R	1879
911	Jones	W	1879
910	Johnson	A	1879
1789	Johnson	P	1879
1341	Jordan	J	1879
	Duplicate Medal and clasp issued. Date unknown.		
2427	Joyce	T	1879
2478	Kane	F	1879
452	Kean	J	1879

1684	Keane	J	1879
	No Medal Deserted.		
2452	Keating	J	1879
2470	Keenan	W	1879
2373	Keenan	W	1879
	Duplicate Medal and clasp issued. Date unknown.		
955	Kelly	J	1879
1647	Kelly	J	No clasp
2472	Kelly	J	1879
2253	Kelly	T	1879
278	Kennedy	D	1879
1839	Kennedy	D	No clasp
	No Medal. Discharged with ignominy.		
792	Kennedy	J	1879
1629	Kennedy	T	1879
2027	Kenny	J	1879
1623	Kernez	R	1879
61B/1692	Kerr	G	1879
841	Kerrigan	W	1879
2441	Kerry	J	1879
	Also had Abbyssinia Medal.		
772	Keulin	B	No clasp
	No Medal Deserted.		
2254	Kieley	J	1879
1913	Kiggens	J	No clasp
	No Medal Deserted.		
2416	King	C	1879
1063	King	E	1879
	Duplicate Medal and clasp issued. Date unknown.		
2251	King	J	1879
2210	King	J	1879 r
1706	King	T	1879
2288	Kinsella	T	1879
1769	Kirk	J	1879
1731	Kirkwood	T	1879
2674	Knight	J	No clasp
2410	Kyneston	J	1879
2287	Lacey	J	1879
2490	Lacey	W	1879
1382	Ladden	W	1879
846	Lafferty	W	1879
818	Laird	A	No clasp
	Duplicate Medal issued. Date unknown.		
1818	Laird	J	1879
1617	Lambert	C	1879
2311	Lambart	P	No clasp
1616	Lamont	A	1879
2586	Lane	J	1879
2354	Lander	S	1879
2330	Lavery	J	1879
	No Medal Discharged with ignominy.		
901	Law	W	1879
2403	Lawler	J	1879
941	Lawrie	G	1879
2424	Lawton	F	1879

2/21st Regiment

Number	Name		Year/Note
2582	Leach	W	1879
2498	Lee	J	1879
1737	Lees	F	No clasp
1047	Leishman	J	1879
	Duplicate Medal and clasp issued. Date unknown.		
2509	Lewis	B	1879
1781	Lions	J	No clasp
	No Medal Deserted.		
2508	Lord	R	1879
1771	Loughlin	R	1879
509	Lounes	R	1879
2048	Lovatt	E	1879
891	Lowndes	F	1879
2489	Luck	W	No clasp
2592	Lycett	D	1879
1784	Lynch	C	1879
872	Lynch	P	1879
2556	Lynn	G	1879
2285	Maher	J	1879
2464	Maley	M	1879
887	Maley	W	No clasp
2259	Maloney	J	1879
1131	Maloney	P	1879
1747	Mann	L	1879
1856	Marsh	A	No clasp
2332	Marshall	T	1879
1026	Martin	D	1879
1614	Martin	D	1879
	No Medal Deserted.		
2173	Martin	F	No clasp
1013	Martin	J	1879
1666	Martin	J	1879
112	Martin	W.J	1879
2481	Matthews	T	1879
1797	Mc Bride	P	1879
678	Mc Cafferty	E	1879
1782	Mc Callum	W	1879
275	Mc Cann	E	1879
1815	Mc Cann	P	1879
1733	Mc Cartney	J	1879
1698	Mc Clanaghan	D	1879
	No Medal Deserted.		
2391	Mc Clean	G	1879
449	Mc Cluskey	J	1879
1822	Mc Connell	G	1879
2237	Mc Conville	A	1879
1841	Mc Cormack	T	No clasp
2469	Mc Crann	T	1879
	No Medal Deserted.		
981	Mc Cullock	A	1879
1730	Mc Dermott	J	1879
1925	Mc Donald	G	No clasp
1609	Mc Donald	J	1879
1641	Mc Donald	J	1879
1643	Mc Donald	W	1879
934	Mc Donough	J	1879
2217	Mc Donough	T	1879
2530	Mc Evan	H	1879
1581	Mc Ewen	J	1879
835	Mc Fadden	J	1879
376	Mc Fall ?	A	No clasp
1605	Mc Gachie	W	1879
1654	Mc Garry	L	No clasp
	No Medal Deserted.		
797	Mc Gee	J	1879
1709	Mc Gibbons	T	1879
717	Mc Gill	J	1879
	No Medal Deserted.		
1699	Mc Gill	Q	1879
	No Medal Deserted.		
867	Mc Gintey	E	1879
1826	Mc Given	P	1879
1612	Mc Govern	P	1879
305	Mc Grady	J	1879
2531	Mc Grath	J	1879
998	Mc Grath	T	No clasp
2337	Mc Greary	O	1879
	No Medal Deserted.		
950	Mc Gregor	J	1879
741	Mc Gregor	M	1879
714	Mc Guinness	J	1879
61B/2367	Mc illroy	T	1879
1049	Mc Intyre	M	1879
1590	Mc Kenna	T	1879
1775	Mc Kenzie	J	No clasp
2238	Mc Kenzie	K	1879
1996	Mc Kenzie	M	1879
1691	Mc Laughlin	J	1879
1697	Mc Laughlin	R	1879
560	Mc Lean	A	1879
166	Mc Lean	J	No clasp
1783	Mc Millen	A	No clasp
2308	Mc Mullen	R	1879
247	Mc Murdy	S	1879
2376	Mc Namara	M	1879
935	Mc Nicholas	E	1879
1779	Mc Onnish ?	P	No clasp
1676	Mc Phee	W	No clasp
1717	Mc Rae	P	1879
503	Mc Roberts	R	1879
1595	Mc Sally	P	1879
1688	Mc Uggan	F	1879
1633	Mc Vey	P	1879
1588	Mc Vicar	J	1879 r
1578	Meers	N	1879
712	Mein	J	1879
2380	Messenger	R	No clasp
932	Middleton	J	1879
1061	Miller	J	No clasp
1642	Miller	T	1879
579	Miller	W	No clasp
115	Milne	T	1879
1880	Milroy	R	1879
982	Minto	J	1879
2402	Mitchell	T	No clasp
	No Medal Deserted.		
2532	Montgomery	J	1879
2204	Moore	J	No clasp
2284	Moore	J	1879
2454	Moore	P	1879
2283	Moore	S	1879
1592	Moran	J	1879
466	Morgan	H	1879
2491	Morledger	W	No clasp
2350	Morris	D	1879
	Duplicate Medal and clasp issued.19/3/1919.		
2502	Morris	D	1879
2073	Morris	J	1879
2244	Morris	J	1879
2282	Morrissey	W	1879
2475	Morrissey	W	1879
865	Morrison	S	1879
1716	Morton	J	1879
2342	Moss	L	1879
1556	Mould	J	1879
2346	Moyles	M	1879
	No Medal Deserted.		
773	Mulholland	C	1879
2463	Mullen	J	1879
	Duplicate Medal and clasp issued. Date unknown.		
22	Murdock	W	1879
2082	Murphy	G	1879
	No Medal Deserted.		
2494	Murphy	J	1879
1713	Murphy	J	1879
61B/2262	Murphy	J	1879
2430	Musgrove	B	1879
	No Medal Deserted.		
756	Muirhead	S	No clasp
1585	Nailor	W	1879
2200	New	C	1879
1818	Nicol	J	1879
2352	Nightingale	D	1879
103	Niven	J	1879
2462	Noble	G	1879
607	Noble	J	1879
1844	Noble	J	1879
	Duplicate Medal and clasp issued. Date unknown.		
1805	Nolan	T	1879
2281	Noonan	T	1879
2199	Norton	G	1879
1585	Nuthall	H	1879
1377	O'Connell	P	1879
1744	O'Donnell	J	1879
	No Medal. Penal Servitude.		
2532	O'Donnell	T	1879
2347	O'Hara	M	1879
1672	O'Keefe	J	1879
1575	Oliver	A	1879
	No Medal Deserted.		
1602	O'Neil	F	1879
2253	O'Neill	P	1879
2252	O'Shea	D	1879

2/21st Regiment

812	Outhwaite	C	1879
2256	Park	J	1879
2401	Parsons	W	1879
2152	Partridge	R	No clasp
1663	Paton	R	1879
2533	Peed	W	1879
2492	Pelling	H	1879
2364	Pemberton	C	1879
2397	Pemberton	E	1879
2506	Pennell	C	1879
2279	Phelan	M	1879
	No Medal Deserted.		
908	Phillips	J	1879
2229	Phillips	T	1879
	No Medal Deserted.		
918	Phillips	W	1879
939	Pickard	S	1879
1084	Piggott	J	1879
2534	Pilgrim	G	No clasp
839	Platt	W	1879
775	Plowman	D	1879
1635	Pollock	W	No clasp
2212	Porter	G	1879
	No Medal Deserted.		
2358	Potts	R	1879
2413	Poval	J	1879
2375	Powell	W	1879
2278	Power	L	1879
	No Medal Deserted.		
2276	Power	M	1879
2277	Power	M	1879
	No Medal Deserted.		
2136	Probart	W	No clasp
2275	Purcell	M	1879
	No Medal Deserted.		
2322	Quinn	E	1879
2274	Quinn	J	1879
1610	Quinn	W	1879
2006	Rae	J	1879
1586	Rae	R	1879
1778	Rainford	D	1879
	No Medal Deserted.		
1785	Rancy	J	1879
2142	Ratcliffe	J	1879
1610	Reddish	J	No clasp
1689	Reed	G	No clasp
2343	Regan	J	1879
2459	Reid	T	1879
1639	Reilly	D	No clasp
513	Reilly	J	1879
1828	Reilly	J	No clasp
	No Medal Deserted.		
2373	Reilly	J	No clasp
2348	Reilly	M	No clasp r
844	Reilly	T	1879
1498	Rex	J	1879
2488	Reynolds	J	No clasp
Duplicate Medal issued. Date unknown.			
2247	Reynolds	W	No clasp
2356	Rhodes	E	1879
609	Rice	P	1879
1606	Richardson	T	1879
936	Riley	P	No clasp
1832	Ritson	J	1879
882	Roach	J	1879
1757	Roach	T	1879
2512	Roberts	C	1879
	No Medal Deserted.		
2513	Roberts	E	1879
2315	Roberts	H	No clasp
2374	Roberts	W	1879
816	Robertson	D	1879
823	Robertson	D	1879
828	Robertson	J	1879
1600	Rodgers	C	1879
2326	Roh	C	1879
2411	Rosbotham	A	1879
1006	Ross	D	1879
1754	Ross	G	1879
1041	Ross	J	1879
1059	Ross	J	1879
2115	Rothwell	W	1879
2590	Rowan	J	1879
2387	Rowley	J	1879r
836	Rutherford	G	1879
2271	Ryan	M	1879
2272	Ryan	M	No clasp
2535	Ryan	M	1879
2246	Sanderson	J	1879
2198	Sanderson	W	No clasp
2353	Saunders	J	1879
2327	Scantlin	W	1879
983	Scott	R	1879
1591	Scott	W	No clasp
1467	Scuffle	E	1879
2417	Seal	H	1879
2321	Selwood	W	1879
2499	Setford	S	No clasp
1695	Shannon	E	1879 r
471	Shearer	A	1879
2408	Sheely	J	1879
2724	Sheppard	S	1879
2383	Shermer	T	1879
1580	Sherrett	A	No clasp
2214	Shields	H	1879
1760	Shields	J	1879
1640	Shields	W	No clasp
61B/544	Short	W	1879
2243	Simms	S	1879
	No Medal Deserted.		
813	Simpson	R	1879
2421	Slack	G	No clasp
1819	Slade	W	1879
2384	Slater	E	1879
2637	Slaughter	J	1879
253	Slaven	J	1879
1995	Slaven	J	1879
306	Slaven	T	1879
1068	Sloan	R	No clasp
2317	Sly	J	1879
2370	Smith	A	1879
2390	Smith	G	1879
569	Smith	J	No clasp
956	Smith	J	No clasp
2676	Smith	J	No clasp
2329	Smith	J.A	1879
1700	Smith	P	1879
1118	Smith	R	1879
860	Stafford	J	1879
2351	Stanton	J	1879
1589	Stephenson	E	No clasp
1817	Stewart	H.I	No clasp
1801	Stewart	James	1879
437	Still	M	1879
2537	Stirling	W	1879
2385	Stokes	J	No clasp
2194	Strainey	E	1879
527	Strong	G	No clasp
1015	Stuart	C	1879
115	Suggell	R	No clasp
2257	Sugure ?	J	1879
1479	Sullivan	D	1879
	No Medal Deserted.		
2263	Sullivan	J	1879
430	Sullivan	J	1879
	No Medal Deserted.		
2501	Sullivan	J	1879
2555	Sullivan	J	1879
	No Medal Deserted.		
972	Sullivan	M	1879
2270	Sullivan	P	1879
470	Surgener	T	1879
434	Sweeney	M	1879
2193	Sykes	R	1879
2361	Sylvester	A	1879
2457	Tallon	C	1879
895	Tauny	O	1879
916	Taylor	B	1879
1659	Taylor	F	1879
2316	Taylor	F	1879
931	Taylor	G	1879
	No Medal Deserted.		
1701	Tennant	J	1879
1028	Thaker	R	1879
927	Thew	T	1879
2675	Thomas	E	1879
2365	Thomas	J	1879
2197	Thomas	J.C	1879
1688	Thompson	G	1879
	No Medal Deserted.		
814	Thompson	J	1879
929	Thompson	J	No clasp
2012	Thompson	J	No clasp
1764	Thompson	W	No clasp
2195	Thornbeck	T	1879
Duplicate Medal and clasp issued. Date unknown.			

2/21st Regiment

No	Surname	Initial	Year		No	Surname	Initial	Year		No	Surname	Initial	Year
2307	Tighe	J	1879		49	White	W	1879		1829	Corrie	Hugh	
1177	Tinker	G	1879		1606	Wightman	R	1879		1808	Dobbs	Felix	
1008	Tobin	D	1879			No Medal Deserted.				1053	Grant	William	
704	Todd	W	1879		790	Wilburn	W	1879		1341	Jordan	James	
2196	Tomlinson	W	1879		2389	Wilkes	G	1879		2405	Flynn	Robert	
2538	Toolan	D	1879		769	Wilkie	J	1879		2373	Kennan	William	
2474	Toole	J	1879		912	Wilkinson	T	1879		1063	King	Edward	
869	Travers	J	1879		2349	Williams	C	1879		818	Laird	Alex	
852	Treaghurst	H	1879		519	Williams	F	1879		1047	Leishman	John	
1726	Tulloch	J	1879		2357	Williams	G	1879		2463	Mullen	James	
823	Turner	J	1879		951	Williams	H	No clasp		1844	Noble	John	
2083	Tweedie	G	No clasp			No Medal Deserted.				2488	Reynolds	John	
843	Upton	J	No clasp		1732	Williams	J	1879		2195	Thornbeck	Thomas	
2000	Vage ?	J	1879		2507	Williams	T	1879		1050	Watson	J.F	
1673	Valleley	M	1879		1776	Williamson	J	1879					
2539	Varley	D	1879		2471	Wilson	A	1879		*Subsequently Found.			
928	Verity	C	1879		2211	Wilson	G	1879					
1066	Waild	B	1879		1062	Wilson	J	1879		**22nd (CHESHIRE) REGIMENT.**			
1555	Walker	C	1879		2219	Wilson	J	1879		CAPTAIN			
1714	Wallace	J	1879		829	Wilson	T	1879			Molyneux	W.C.F	1877-8-9
2269	Wallace	T	No clasp		862	Wilson	T	1879			Woodmas	C	1879
1662	Wallace	W	1879		849	Winterbottom	M	No clasp		See also 2/21st Regt.			
	No medal Deserted.				2230	Witty	H	1879					
61B/2218	Walsh	A	1879		2683	Wood	G	1879		**23rd (ROYAL WELSH FUSILIERS)**			
2323	Walsh	P	No clasp		2386	Woodall	G	No clasp		**REGIMENT**			
2407	Walthoe	C	1879		2428	Woodcock	J	1879		LIEUTENANT			
2590	Ward	J	1879		876	Woods	P	1879			Evans	E.R	1879
2226	Ward	R	1879		1020	Woods	W	1879					
2232	Warren	T	1879		2371	Woodward	W	1879		**1/24 (THE 2nd WARWICKSHIRE)**			
	No Medal. Discharged with ignominy.				2504	Woolnough	F	1879		**REGIMENT.**			
2268	Warren	W	1879		925	Woters	J	No clasp		Those listed as Killed in Action (KIA) lost			
2318	Warrilon	H	1879		2486	Yates	T	No clasp		their lives at Isandhlwana on 22/1/1879.			
840	Watson	J	1879		2541	Young	J	1879		LIEUTENANT COLONEL			
1050	Watson	J.F	1879			No Medal Deserted.				Glynn CB R.T			1877-8-9
	Duplicate medal and clasp				1016	Young	R	1879		Also had British and Turkish Crimean			
	issued. Date unknown.				762	Young	T	1879		Medals and Indian Mutiny Medal.			
1703	Watt	J	No clasp		947	Young	W	1879		MAJOR			
880	Waugh	A	1879		1626	Young	W	1879		Logan	W.B		1877-8
	No Medal Deserted.									Pulleine	H.B	KIA	1877-8-9
1487	Webb	F	No clasp		List of men whose South Africa medals,					BREVET MAJOR			
1065	Webster	A	1879		it is presumed, stolen by the boers in					Much	W.T		1877-8
1067	Webster	J	1879		transit to England.and were replaced at					QUARTERMASTER			
1593	Weir	T	1879		the public expense.					Pullen	J	KIA	1877-8-9
2868	West	W	1879		THESE MEN WERE EITHER KILLED OR					CAPTAIN			
2581	Weston	W	1879		DIED DURING 1880/1881.					Brander	W.M		1879
2209	Wheatley	G	1879							Degacher	W	KIA	1877-8-9
	No Medal Deserted.				No	Rank	Name			Harrison	H.A		1877-8
2267	Wheeler	J	No clasp		2169	Corp. Gartshore	John			Moffatt	H.B		No clasp
2220	Whitburn	T	1879		1680	Pte. Bedford	James			Mostyn	W.E	KIA	1877-8-9
961	White	H	1879		2309	Birmingham	Daniel			Tongue	J.M.G		1877-8-9
2226	White	J	1879		1739	*Boyd	William			Paton CMG	G		1877-8-9
2249	White	P	1879 r		2312	Brownbill	Charles			Rainford	T		1877-8-9
2264	White	R	1879		1779	*Byrne	Charles			Upcher	R		1877-8-9

#Glendining's, Auction Lot 52, 5 March 1986
SOUTH AFRICA 1877-9, 1 clasp, 1879 (Lieut. W. W. Lloyd, 1-24th Foot). Very Fine. Sold £520
Mentioned in "The Road to Isandlwana" by Philip Gon. Many of his drawings appeared in Illustrated London News, including "Defenders at Helpmakaar", and Retreat of Fugitives across the Buffalo River from Isandkvana". He was military illustrator of some note. Photo included of his work with lot.

1/24th Regiment

#Bosleys Auction 14th September 2005 Lot 516 1st Battalion 24th Foot Historical South Africa "Zulu" Isandhlwana Casualty Medal.

An extremely fine and rare boxed South Africa 1879 Medal, awarded to "1881 Sergt J. Edwards l/24th Foot", bearing the clasp "1877-8-9". Near Mint Condition. The medal is contained in the original Royal Mint envelope, this in turn is contained in the original card box. Retaining Paper label seal "South Africa Medal 1877-8¬9". The box with ink inscription "1881 Sergt J. Edwards 1/24th Foot", also the numbers "AG105 27". The box is then contained in the original Registered envelope, this addressed Mrs Edwards Cape Town South Africa. Post mark July 1882. Box in very fine condition, envelope a little delicate. This medal is accompanied by family medals including: Sergeant Edwards son's Queen's South Africa Medal, bearing two clasps "Cape Colony", "Orange Free State"- "385 Corpl J.R. Gardiner Cape Town Highrs". This medal is again in near mint condition and contained in a Royal Mint envelope, which in turn is contained in the original cardboard box. This with typed label "385 Corpl J.R. Gardiner Cape Tn Highrs" also pencil inscription "alas J R Edwards".... Grandsons medals awarded to Sergeant J.R. Edwards South African Forces. Comprising: 1939/45 Star, Italy Star, War Medal, African Service Medal. Medals loose South. African issue named to "614452 J.R. Edwards. Complete with forwarding slip and envelope addressed to Mnr/Mr J.R. Edwards. The groups are accompanied by a number of copy photographs, one showing Sergeant Edwards senior wearing uniform at Gibraltar in 1873, another in civilian cloths dated Cape Town 1875. A photograph of Corporal Edwards of the Cape Town Highlanders wearing Boer War uniform... A number of Sergeant Edwards, South African Forces wearing uniform during WWII. Overall VGC

Estimate (£6,000 - £7,000) Hammer Price £8200

1881 Sergt John Robert. Edwards 1/24th Foot is confirmed as being killed at the disastrous engagement at Isandhlwana on the 22nd January 1879. He joined the Regiment in 1872 and was promoted to Corporal in 1873, whilst the Regiment was serving at Gibraltar. In 1876 he was promoted to Sergeant and with special permission of the Regiment married Sarah Emily White. A copy of this permission is believed to be held at the Regimental museum Brecon. He had two children, a daughter who died in 1878 and a son christened John Robert Edwards, he was destined not to see his father been born two months after his father's death. Serving with the 1st Battalion of 24th Foot in A Company he stood and fell with his Regiment at Isandhlwana. Emily remarried in 1882 to a James Gardiner of the 1st Battalion Argyll & Sutherland Highlanders, young John Robert now carried the name Gardiner and it was to this name he enlisted and was awarded the Queen's South Africa Medal. When he came to marry, he decided to revert to his father's name of Edwards. His son John Robert was born in 1908 and carried on the family military tradition volunteering for military service in WWII.

1881 Sergeant J. R. Edwards, 1st Bn. 24th Foot. Killed at Isandhlwana – Lot 516

1/24th Regiment

Wardell	G.V	**KIA** 1877-8-9		
Younghusband	R	**KIA** 1879		

LIEUTENANT
- Anstey E.O.H **KIA** 1877-8-9
- Atkinson C.J **KIA** 1877-8-9
- Bennett L.H 1877-8-9
- Brown VC E.S 1878-9
  His VC was for an action at Inhlobane 29/3/1879.
- Carrington F 1877-8
- Cavaye C.W **KIA** 1877-8-9
- Clements R.A.P 1877-8-9
- Coghill VC N.J.A **KIA** 1877-8-9
  His VC was for an action at Isandhlwana.
- Connolly J.H 1879
- Daly J.P **KIA** 1877-8-9
- Halliday F.T 1879
- Heaton W 1877-8-9
- Hodson G.F.J **KIA** 1877-8-9
- #Lloyd W.W 1879
- Melvill VC T **KIA** 1877-8-9
  His VC was for an action at Isandhlwana.
- Moore G.K 1879
- Morshead A.A 1877-8-9
- Palmes G.C 1877-8
- Porteous F.P **KIA** 1877-8-9
- Roche the Hon U de R B 1877-8
- Spring W.E.D 1877-8
- Sugden W 1877-8-9

2nd LIEUTENANT
- Birch A.W 1879 r
  See also Lt A.W Birch 2/24th Regt.
- Campbell R 1879
- Dyson E.H **KIA** 1879
- Godfrey W.C 1879
- Phipps A.B 1879
- Scott-Ker R 1879
- Weallens W 1879
- Williams J.D.M 1879
- Yorstown M.E.C 1879

SERGEANT MAJOR
- 671 Gapp F **KIA** 1877-8-9

DRUM MAJOR
- 843 Taylor K R **KIA** 1877-8-9

SCHOOL MASTER
- Moore J 1877-8

COLOUR SERGEANT
- 1125 Ballard J **KIA** 1877-8-9
- 1978 Brown R 1879
- 1118 Brown T **KIA** 1877-8-9 r
- 1257 Cook J 1877-8
- 868 Davison G 1877-8-9
- 1289 Edwards W **KIA** 1877-8-9
- 1789 Fallon A 1879
- 598 Tompkins J.J 1877-8-9
- 1791 Wadly W 1877-8-9
  Also had medal for Abyssinia.
- 1887 Whitfield W **KIA** 1877-8-9
- 617 Wolfe F.H **KIA** 1877-8-9

ARMOURER SERGEANT
- ? Haigs F.G No clasp
- 400 Hayward H **KIA** 1877-8-9

COOK SERGEANT
- 1510 Field A **KIA** 1877-8-9

CANTEEN STEWARD
- ? Seaton W.P **KIA** 1877-8-9

ORDERLYROOM CLERK
- 1850 Fitzgerald G **KIA** 1877-8-9

PAYMASTER SERGEANT
- 896 Mead G **KIA** 1877-8-9
- 1369 North T 1877-8-9

QUARTERMASTER SERGEANT
- 557 Leitch **KIA** T 1877-8-9

SERGEANT INSTRUCTOR OF MUSKETRY
- 1011 Chambers G **KIA** 1879
- 2880 Dredge E.B 1879

TAILOR SERGEANT
- 2578 Chudley W No clasp
- 559 Smedley J **KIA** 1877-8-9

SERGEANT
- 1699 Ainsworth P **KIA** 1877-8-9
- 2078 Aylward J 1879
- 1895 Benneth G **KIA** 1877-8-9
- 1980 Beresford J 1879
- 1790 Bond W 1879
- 520 Bradbury J 1877-8
- 909 Bradley D **KIA** 1877-8-9
- 2079 Butterley J 1879
- 585 Cambrey W 1877-8-9
- 954 Clarkson J **KIA** 1877-8-9
- 1019 Coholan W **KIA** 1877-8-9
- 1313 Cooper T **KIA** 1877-8-9
- 256 Deeming T 1877-8
- #1881 Edwards J **KIA** 1877-8-9
  (see page 237)
- 1880 Emery G 1879
- 1849 Fay T **KIA** 1877-8-9
- 1929 Field J 1877-8
- 945 Fitzmaurice J 1878-9
- 607 Fleming M 1877-8-9
- 315 Fowden J **KIA** 1877-8-9
- 1979 Franklin J 1879
- 570 Gamble D **KIA** 1877-8-9
- 968 Giles E **KIA** 1877-8-9
- 1754 Greatorex J **KIA** 1877-8-9
- 1430 Hart W 1877-8
- 132 Hayward W 1877-8-9
  Also had Indian Mutiny Medal.
- 1806 Hippenstall C **KIA** 1877-8-9
- 1771 Hooton S 1877-8-9
- 824 Hornibrook M **KIA** 1879
- 416 Jamieson R 1878-9
- 1440 Johnston J 1877-8-9
  Duplicate medal and clasp issued 2/2/1918.
- 472 Jones J 1877-8-9
- 1411 Kenny E 1877-8-9
- 1507 Lambert T 1877-8-9
- 2197 Moore J 1879
- 878 Morrissey P 1877-8-9
- 581 Parsons W **KIA** 1879
- 1540 Partis H 1877-8
- 1045 Piall **KIA** A 1877-8-9
- 514 Price J 1877-8
- 332 Richards T 1877-8
- 2080 Sale A 1879
- 1879 Shepherd A.H 1879
- 1982 Skinner T 1879
- 1977 Smith B 1879
- 1370 Smith J **KIA** 1877-8-9
- 1792 Smith W 1879
- 294 Street H 1877-8-9
- 320 Taylor G 1877-8r
- 1881 Thomas J 1879
- 1793 Turner R 1879
- 565 Upton G **KIA** 1877-8-9
- 1290 White J No clasp
- 56 Wilson E 1877-8-9

LANCE SERGEANT
- 917 Betterton J 1877-8
- 1911 Jackson W 1877-8
- 1883 Jones J 1879
- 232 Milner J **KIA** 1879
- 519 Murphy W 1877-8
- 1882 Murray T 1879
- 243 Newman T 1877-8
- 1260 Reardon J **KIA** 1877-8-9
- 2087 Ryan J 1879
- 2082 Wilson F 1879

CORPORAL
- 126 Ball N **KIA** 1877-8-9
- 421 Bell P **KIA** 1877-8-9
- 1415 Bellhouse J **KIA** 1879
- 1798 Bennett G 1879
  Also had medal for Abyssinia.
- 837 Berry H 1877-8
  This medal may have had two clasps viz 1877-8 and 1879.
- 1173 Bickley J 1877-8-9
  Possible two different clasps issued..
  A survivor at Isandhlwana
- 1391 Board A **KIA** 1877-8-9
- 434 Chislett A 1877-8-9
- 335 Collett R 1877-8
- 1694 Corrie J 1879
- 2108 Cotton R 1879
- 622 Darling W 1877-8-9
- 125 Davis R **KIA** 1877-8-9
- 129 Edkins C 1877-8
- 28 Everett E **KIA** 1877-8-9
- 23 Frank J **KIA** 1877-8-9
- 495 Fuller G 1877-8-9
- 175 Geraghty P 1877-8
- 1923 Gillman J.E 1877-8-9
- 328 Godrich W 1877-8-9
- 1853 Green G 1877-8-9

1/24th Regiment

140	Honan	E	1877-8-9	2004	Wolfendale	A KIA	1877-8-9	348	Bennett	G	1877-8-9
2028	Hoole	T	1879	1399	Wolfendale	J KIA	1877-8-9	1670	Bennett	H	1877-8
957	Johnston	F	1877-8-9	PRIVATE				1891	Bennett	J.G	1879
658	Kinlock	J	1877-8-9	1442	Abbott	R KIA	1877-8-9	647	Bennett	R KIA	1877-8-9
1886	Knight	J KIA	1877-8-9	2089	Ackerman	W	1879	643	Benson	R KIA	1877-8-9
415	Lawler	J KIA	1877-8-9	255	Acton	J	1877-8-9	1890	Beresford	R	1879
1931	Lee	A	1879	2091	Adcock	W	1879	316	Bergin	W	1879
1073	Lonergan	J	1877-8-9		Also had medal for Ashanti.			407	Berry	H	1878-9
1842	Lythaby	J	1879	1986	Adds	W	1879 r	1996	Berry	J	1879
356	Maher	W	1877-8-9		Forfeited Subsequently restored.			1738	Berry	T	1879
829	Mangan	P	1877-8-9	1987	Akers	H	1879	2096	Bethell	T	1879
524	Markhan	P KIA	1877-8-9	476	Allingham	T KIA	1877-8-9	1656	Betterton	N KIA	1877-8-9
375	Mc Cann	J	1878-9	1785	Alls	W	1877-8	1804	Bidgood	F	1879
997	Mc Kinnell	G	1877-8-9	394	Appleton	J	1877-8-9	635	Birch	J KIA	1877-8-9
1616	Miller	M KIA	1879	937	Amos	E KIA	1877-8-9	600	Bird	T	1877-8-9
1850	Mooney	J	1879	620	Anderson	J	1877-8-9	154	Bishop	J KIA	1877-8-9
Also had Indian Mutiny Medal and India				2090	Armstrong	R	1879	1681	Blackhurst	R KIA	1877-8-9
General Service 1854 Medal.				1884	Armstrong	S	1879	976	Blount	H	1877-8-9
1904	Naylor	H	1877-8-9	2088	Armstrong	W	?	1474	Blower	J KIA	1879
1548	Noble	C	No clasp r	285	Ashton	W	1877-8	221	Bodman	F KIA	1877-8-9
646	Norman	J Not on medal roll		303	Askew	T	1877-8-9	1679	Booth	H	1879
London Gazette 23 May 1879 listed on				1237	Atkins	A KIA	1877-8-9	1893	Boulger	J	1879
nominal return of Deaths.				1885	August	R	1879	64	Boulton	S KIA	
2081	Ogborne	W	1879	1988	Austin	J	1879	638	Bowe	J	1879
1056	Parker	H	1877-8-9	469	Bailey	A	1877-8	2093	Bowen	W	1879
611	Parry	W	1879	1989	Bailey	J	1879	1749	Bower	N	1879
1736	Richardson	H KIA	1877-8-9	710	Bailey	J KIA	1879	1894	Bowler	R	1879 r
885	Rowden	J KIA	1877-8-9	1886	Bailey	W	1879		Deserted.		
2059	Savage	R	1879	1496	Baker	E KIA	1877-8-9	1905	Bowles	J	1879
784	Scott	T	1877-8-9	1778	Baker	T	1877-8-9	2098	Boyes	T	1879
962	Sharpe	T	1877-8	1990	Baker	W	1879	106	Boylan	J KIA	1877-8-9
2066	Stewart	A	1879	1526	Ball	C	No clasp	2095	Boyle	P	1879
1538	Tarbruck	J KIA	1877-8-9	1991	Ball	G	1879	1997	Bradley	E	1879
1795	Taylor	D	1877-8	1995	Ball	G	1879	1998	Bramble	T	1879
473	Thomas	P	1877-8-9	489	Barnaby	E	1877-8-9	950	Bray	J KIA	1877-8-9
2189	Toomey	D	1879	1887	Barnes	M	1879	99	Brazier	J	1877-8
286	Waddington	H	1877-8-9	1992	Barnett	M	1879	487	Breeze	J KIA	1877-8-9
193	Williams	R KIA	1879	1536	Banyard	G	1877-8	2101	Brennan	O	1879
LANCE CORPORAL				1993	Barrett	E	1879	10	Brennan	P	1877-8-9
2109	Collins	J	1879	422	Barrett	P	1877-8-9	1895	Brereton	E	1879
2067	Sullivan	A	1879	466	Barry	J KIA	1877-8-9		Also had medal for Bhootan.		
DRUMMER				727	Barry	J KIA	1877-8-9	2194	Brett	M	1879
2003	Adams	W.H KIA	1877-8-9	300	Barsley	E KIA	1877-8-9	43	Brew	J.W KIA	1879
267	Andrews	C KIA	1877-8-9	2097	Bartles	C	1879	1805	Brian	A	No clasp
502	Burden	J	1877-8	1476	Bartles	J KIA	1877-8-9	2093	Brian	B	1879
35	Burley	G	1878-9	451	Bastard	C KIA	1879	817	Brian	C	1877-8-9
1786	Dibden	G KIA	1877-8-9	440	Batchelor	J	1877-8-9	2099	Brian	J	1879
205	Hayman	J	1877-8-9	1994	Bates	S	1876	236	Bridgewell	H	1878-9
1829	Hennessey	E	1879	1743	Bates	W	1877-8-9	1770	Bridges	T	1879
2084	Herbert	C	1879	501	Beadon	R KIA	1877-8-9	675	Bridgnall	A	1877-8
1985	Hunt	W	1879	135	Beckett	W	1877-8-9	1637	Brimble	W	1879
2	Orlopp	J.F KIA	1877-8-9	1467	Beebie	J	1879	718	Broderick	J KIA	1877-8-9
1226	Osmond	C KIA	1877-8-9	1607	Beiby	G	1879	1762	Brown	C	1879
1-24/1	Perkins	T KIA	1877-8-9	750	Beilby	J	1877-8-9	1896	Brown	C	1879
1645	Piall	S	1877-8-9	1803	Belcher	C	1879	1999	Brown	C	1879
318	Reardon	T KIA	1877-8-9	1892	Bell	J	1879	1673	Brown	J	1879
248	Sprong	W	1879	2102	Bell	J	1879	1889	Brown	J	1879
1787	Thompson	J KIA	1877-8-9	349	Benham	J KIA	1877-8-9	628	Brown	J KIA	1879
1237	Trottman	D KIA	1877-8-9	1469	Bennett	A KIA	1877-8-9	357	Brown	M	1877-8

1/24th Regiment

313	Brown	M	1877-8-9	2122	Clifton	W	1879	3732	Craddock	W	1877-8
320	Brown	W KIA	1879	724	Clutterbuck	W KIA	1877-8-9		Also had Indian Mutiny Medal.		
1888	Bryan	W	1879	677	Ceate	H	1879	842	Crates	D	1877-8
822	Buckley	C	1877-8	2104	Cochrane	R.N	1879	1429	Craven	W	1877-8
452	Bugby	F.W KIA	1879	2113	Coefar	M	1879	2112	Crawford	D	1879
1875	Bull	J KIA	1877-8-9	1757	Cokeley	J	1879	2116	Crawford	W	1879
1684	Burke	E	1879	334	Cole	A KIA	1879	1811	Crerrys	I	1879
55	Burke	T KIA	1877-8-9	1477	Cole	W	1877-8-9		Duplicate medal and clasp issued		
146	Burke	W	1877-8-9	749	Coleman	J KIA	1877-8-9		14/10/1919.		
176	Burke	W KIA	1877-8-9	1667	Coleman	W	1877-8	1810	Cresswell	J	1879
886	Burke	W KIA	1877-8-9	1662	Colgan	P	1879	622	Cronin	J	1877-8-9
1806	Burnett	G	1879		Deserted. No trace of return of the medal.			301	Crook	C	1877-8-9
71	Burns	J	1877-8	2083	Collingwood	C	1879	2012	Crosby	J	1879
291	Burns	R	1877-8	359	Collins	D KIA	1879	1833	Cross	J	1877-8-9
2000	Burns	W.A	1879	1615	Collins	E No clasp		797	Cullen	M KIA	1877-8-9
166	Burridge	R	1877-8	245	Collins	T KIA	1879	101	Cullenan	J KIA	1877-8-9
2100	Burrows	W.J	1879	242	Collins	W	1877-8-9r	1319	Cummings	H	1877-8
554	Burrows	W	1877-8-9	205	Colston	T KIA	1877-8-9	2117	Dale	G	1879
2001	Burrows	W	1879	2006	Colteman	J	1879	881	Dalton	J	1877-8
1461	Busby	T KIA	1877-8-9	1901	Comberton	G	1879	640	Davis	A KIA	1877-8-9
2103	Bush	W	1879	2110	Commiskey	J	1879	1752	Davis	A	1879
1983	Butchers	W	1879	1424	Conboye	G KIA	1879	401	Davis	B	1877-8-9
481	Butler	W	1878-9	2111	Connah	E	1879	1099	Davis	E KIA	1879
480	Butler	M	1879	38	Connell	D	1877-8	377	Davis	G	1878-9
1908	Butler	W KIA	1877-8-9	170	Connell	T	1877-8	194	Davis	H	1878-9
308	Bye	J	1877-8-9	722	Connolly	C KIA	1879	714	Davis	H No clasp	
494	Cahill	J KIA	1877-8-9	199	Connolly	J KIA	1877-8-9	2013	Davis	J	1879
499	Caine	F	1877-8-9	484	Connolly	J	1879	1592	Davis	T	1879
664	Caine	J	1877-8	2115	Connolly	J	1879	2119	Davis	T	1879
449	Cairns	J	1877-8-9	2007	Connor	J	1879	1042	Davis	W KIA	1877-8-9
2102	Callaghan	O	1879	290	Connors	S KIA	1877-8-9	1639	Davis	W	1879
825	Camp	J KIA	1877-8-9	1809	Conroy	W	1879	1903	Davis	W	1879
2003	Campbell	J	1879	2107	Considine	W	1879	568	Desmond	P	1877-8-9
840	Campbell	M KIA	1879	1898	Cook	G	1879		Forfeited. No reason given. No indication		
1390	Campbell	W	1877-8	112	Cook	J KIA	1879		of the return of medal. (Rorke's Drift)		
358	Canning	E No clasp		2008	Cook	J	1879	1904	Devitt	R	1879 r
713	Cantillon	J KIA	1877-8-9	1808	Cooke	J	1879	184	Diggle	M KIA	1877-8-9
1652	Carmody	T	1877-8	2009	Coombes	J	1879	115	Diggle	T KIA	1877-8-9
648	Carpenter	H KIA	1877-8-9	409	Cooney	M	1879	110	Dillon	E	1877-8-9
337	Carrol	P KIA	1879	1836	Cooper	F	1877-8-9	72	Dillon	W	1877-8
507	Casey	J KIA	1877-8-9	2010	Cooper	H No clasp		395	Dobbin	J KIA	1877-8-9
1902	Cassinells	J	1879	18	Cooper	H KIA	1877-8-9	550	Dobbs	W KIA	1877-8-9
204	Ceily	E KIA	1877-8-9	2011	Copeland	G	1879	715	Dodinead	J	1877-8
406	Chadwick	W KIA	1877-8-9	971	Corby	No clasp		96	Dogherty	J	1877-8
2004	Challis	W	1879	554	Corke	E	1879	961	Doney	E	1878-9
2001	Chalmers	W KIA	1877-8-9	1897	Corney	T	1879	1790	Donohoe	C KIA	1879
1825	Chapman	W	1877-8	1820	Cotter	R	1877-8	242	Doran	M KIA	1877-8-9
421	Charlesworth	W	1877-8	2114	Cotterill	W	1879	1845	Dorman	J KIA	1879
389	Chatterton	J KIA	1877-8-9	1690	Coughlan	R KIA	1879	674	Dowde	P KIA	1879
206	Chepman	W KIA	1877-8-9	1900	Couples	J	1879	1812	Down	J	1879
1842	Chester	J	1879		Number on medal 900.			1905	Doyle	J	1879
1177	Christian	J KIA	1879	505	Cox	J KIA	1877-8-9	2014	Doyle	J	1879
1545	Clarke	A KIA	1877-8-9	927	Cox	J No clasp		235	Dredge	W KIA	1877-8-9
2103	Clarke	G	1879		Deserted. No indication of return of medal			438	Duck	T KIA	1877-8-9
1801	Clarke	M KIA	1877-8-9	1132	Cox	J	1877-8-9	1677	Duckworth	G KIA	1877-8-9
2005	Clarke	W	1879	290	Cox	T KIA	1877-8-9	1491	Duffy	A	1877-8
1807	Clayton	J	1879	1171	Coxall	R	1877-8-9		Also had Indian Mutiny Medal.		
226	Clements	W KIA	1877-8-9	2106	Coyne	J	1879	185	Duffy	J KIA	1877-8-9
1899	Clewlo	S	1879	1572	Crabtree	J	1879	1327	Dugmore	E KIA	1877-8-9

1/24th Regiment

#Haywards List No 11 May 1979 Pair. Private J. Power, 1st Bn. 24th Foot.
D.C.M. (Victoria). South Africa 1877-79, one clasp: "1878-9".
499 Private John Power, 1st Bn. 24th Foot, Mounted Infantry. Public Record Office. Ref. No. W.O./ 146/I. Submission to the Queen for Approval ("Gallant Service performed by him during the Campaign in Zululand.").
Services: "This man was one of a detachment serving under Lieut. N. N. Davis of "The Buffs" against the rebels in GRIQUALAND WEST, in September 1878. He there distinguished himself by being first on the top of a ridge occupied by the enemy, at the concluding affair of "GOBETSEH". At the retreat from the upper portion of the "ZLOBANI", on the 28th March, 1879, his coolness was mentioned with praise by Major Tremlett, R. A. During the action of "KAMBULA" on the 29th March, 1879, he was under his Commanding Officer's observation the whole day, and was most forward during the pursuit that followed. On the 4th July, 1879, in the action, and pursuit following, near "ULUNDI", his conspicuous coolness was again noticed by his Commanding Officer, who speaks highly of the assistance he rendered him, during the reconnaissance of the 3rd July, 1879, in rallying the men and in aiding to cover the retreat to the Laager."
The "Commanding Officer" referred to in the Record of Services is, of course, Lieut. E. S. Browne, V. C. 1st Bn. 24th Foot, who commanded the detachment of Mounted Infantry of that Regiment. He received the V.C. for his gallantry on the 29th March, 1879, one of the dates mentioned in Power's Services.
Extract from "The South Wales Borderers, 24th Foot", by Atkinson.
"By the middle of April the situation had much improved. Substantial reinforcements had arrived. A column under Lord Chelmsford's personal command relieved Colonel Pearson at Etshowe, defeating the Zulus at Ging¬hilovo. Colonel Wood, to whose column Russell's Mounted Infantry, including Lieutenant Browne's detachment of the Twenty-Fourth, had been transferred, beat off an attack on his camp at Kanibula (March 29th) in no uncertain style. His mounted men had on the previous day been sharply and not too successfully engaged on the Inhlobana mountain. This action was, however, memorable for the Twenty-Fourth, as Lieutenant Browne. when the Mounted Infantry were being driven back, saw Zulus closing on a man whose horse had been shot, He galloped back and, though under heavy fire, managed to get the man up on to his horse and bring him out of action from under the very noses of the Zulus, for which act of gallantry he was awarded the V.C. Private Power, who had already distinguished himself on several occasions, was again greatly to the fore in assisting to cover the retirement and was awarded the D.C.M."
During the Zlobani affair, Pte. Power conveyed a despatch from Colonel Russell to Colonel Buller, riding for some eight miles through a country swarming with the enemy.
Only three D.C.M's were awarded to the 24th for Zululand. The other two were awarded for "Rorkes Drift". They are in fact much scarcer for this campaign than the V.C. of which the Regiment received ten for Zululand. Of a total of 16 D.C.M's awarded for the campaign of 1878-79 Pte. Power's is unique, being awarded for Griqualand and the Zulu War, 1878-79. 3 Average V.F. £3000.00

The Bayonet In Zululand.
The Times, Tuesday, Mar 04, 1879; pg. 10; Issue 29506
Sir, We read that at Isandula "the bayonet was found to be no match for the shield and assegai" How was that? We have been led to believe that the bayonet has been generally relied upon to decide almost every engagement. What, then, has caused the change? Breechloaders taking the place of muzzleloaders? Not with regard to the case in point, for it is stated that the heroic, though luckless, 1st Battalion of the 24th, after having expended all their ammunition-viz., 70 rounds- had to depend solely on the bayonet, which however, was found to be no match for the shield and assagai of the Zulu warrior. How, then, is falling off in the practical value of the bayonet to be accounted for in this particular instance? Easily enough, though it does not appear to have ever been pointed out to the authorities. Now, every soldier who has fired from his Martini-Henry (or, perhaps, any other breech loading rifle) only ten rounds, with any approach to the rapidity, knows that the barrel is then so heated that he is unable to grasp his rifle with his left hand round stock and barrel, to bring it to "the charge" If so, what could he do after firing 70 rounds? At best he could only hold his rifle with his right hand round the small", and allow the wood under the barrel to rest on his left, pinching it as hard as possible to keep it steady; but as to using his bayonet with any hope of effect, that is out of the question, for a child could almost knock it out of his hand.....
I have the honour to be, Sir, your obedient servant, February 27 A Sergeant-Major

The Times, Thursday, Jan 28, 1886; pg. 13; Issue 31668;   Defective Bayonets. AN OLD SOLDIER..
Letters to the Editor
Sir,- Has it ever occurred to any one to try what effect about 60 rounds of rapid firing (frequently repeated), with bayonets fixed, has on the temper of the bayonet? I rather suspect that the people who write about bayonets being used as pokers have never paraded for guard-mounting with the fear of a smart adjutant before their eyes. Yours obediently, An old Soldier

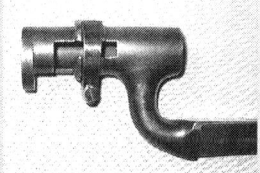

The Times, Wednesday, Oct 20, 1875; pg. 10; Issue 28451;
   The Martini-Henry Rifle. A FIELD OFFICER..
 Letters to the Editor
....that Mr Hardy should pay to the Martini-Henry Committee the compliment of asking the members to reassemble and take evidence as to the failures in the mechanism of the lock. They could also elicit the true history of the Committee which condemned their sword bayonet, the reason why our infantry is now armed with a weapon insufficient at close quarters. A field Officer

1/24th Regiment

#The Medal to 710 Pte. George Lisbeck 24th Regt. Killed Isandlwana January 22, 1879

There is really nothing left today to attest to the life of George Lisbeck killed at the battle of Isandlwana on January 22, 1879. Like most men killed in this disaster all that is left today are names on a roll. However there are some shreds related to the life of George Lisbeck that help a little in piecing together his story.

George Lisbeck was born in England in 1837, the year Queen Victoria took the throne and the start of the Victorian Era. Nothing is sadly known of his family or childhood. In fact a basic search of census records from 1841 onwards turns up no Lisbeck's what so ever; the name is almost unheard of in Great Britain.

George Lisbeck enlisted into the 24th Regiment on July 31, 1858 at the age of 18 years.

The 1861Census finds him at Chatham Barracks, as being with the 1st Depot Battalion. Weather this describes the Chatham depot or that of the 24th, I don't know. Lisbeck gave his place of birth as being 'Hendon, Wilts.' I've not been able to find a Hendon in the county of Wiltshire, although there is a well known Hendon in Middlesex, nowadays north London. Was his birthplace recorded incorrectly, or given falsely, or perhaps mistakenly, we will never know.

Pte. George Lisbeck joined the 24th Regiment after their return home from the Indian Munity. It was at this time a second battalion of the 24th Regiment was formed at Dover in 1858. The first battalion again embarked on foreign service in 1866, and was stationed for some years at Malta and Gibraltar, whence it proceeded to the cape, and was employed in the West Griqualand in 1875, and afterwards on the Eastern frontier, in the Galeka War of 1877-8. The second battalion arrived in South Africa in 1879, and the two battalions served together in Natal and Zululand during the Zulu War of 1879... (24th Regimental History)

Isandlwana, January 22, 1879

The great battle of Isandlwana is well known to most, so I wont try at my own interpretation of things here, except to say the fighting was severe and savage. The where abouts of Pte. George Lisbeck during the desperate fighting at Isandlwana will forever be unknown. What is for sure is Pte. Lisbeck was killed along with 700+ men of his Regiment who fought to the death in an unparallel battle against 15 – 20 thousand Zulu warriors.

Pte. George Lisbeck's South Africa Service Medal was collected by his Next of Kin.

The Medal

The Zulu medal attributed to Pte. George Lisbeck is properly engraved as 710 Pte. J. Lisbeck 1/24th Regt. Foot.

The initial 'J' was engraved in accordance with the original medal roll details for the South Africa Medal that shows Lisbeck's name in error with the initial J. Somebody, a wife or mother obviously cared a great deal for him as the medal has at one time been brooch mounted. The medal had not been brooch-mounted in the usual way by attaching a pin brooch to the obverse or reverse face. It had been placed into what is termed a spinner brooch, a small circular frame with pins through it into the rim of the disc at 12 o'clock and 6 o'clock. Therefore there are no solder 'scar' marks to the surface of the medal. All that is now visible is a slight disturbance to the naming at 6 o'clock where the rim has been plugged between the letters 'E' and 'C' of the recipient's surname LISBECK. There is no doubt another plug at 12 o'clock must exist, but this is of course hidden under the claw of the suspender. A very neat job indeed and one that might be missed if in fact you were unaware that the medal had been reconstituted.

Information supplied by David Bluestein.

1/24th Regiment

No.	Surname	Initial	Notes
446	Dunn	F	**KIA** 1877-8-9
2121	Dunn	J	1879
751	Dunn	W	No clasp r
2118	Dunne	J	1879
146	Durden	R	1877-8
1797	Dust	E	1879
2120	Dwyer	T	1879
215	Fyer	J	**KIA** 1877-8-9
376	Early	W	1877-8-9
2124	Edwards	E	1879
191	Edwards	J	1877-8
562	Edwards	J	**KIA** 1877-8-9
599	Edwards	J	1878-9
1906	Edwards	J	1879
1799	Edwards	W	**KIA** 1877-8-9
66	Egan	T	**KIA** 1877-8-9
1582	Egan	W	**KIA** 1877-8-9
1659	Egan	W	1879
2122	Eichfielder	N	1879
211	Elderington	W	**KIA** 1877-8-9
1318	Elderton	G	**KIA** 1879
695	Eley	J	1879
1161	Elkes	S	1877-8-9
517	Elliott	J	1877-8
312	Ellis	O	**KIA** 1877-8-9
362	Ellis	W	1877-8-9
163	Ellison	H	**KIA** 1877-8-9
450	Ellsmore	J	**KIA** 1877-8-9
979	Ellwood	J	1877-8
614	Evans	C	1877-8-9

This man may have received two clasps viz 1877-8 and 1879.

No.	Surname	Initial	Notes
1678	Evans	C	1879
566	Evans	D	**KIA** 1877-8-9
1608	Evans	G	1879
282	Evans	J	1879
1775	Evans	J	1879
1907	Evans	J	1879
2015	Evans	J	1879
371	Evans	J.E	1877-8-9
109	Evans	J.W	**KIA** 1879
351	Evans	W	1877-8-9
382	Evans	W	1877-8-9

This man may have received two clasps viz 1877-8 and 1879.

No.	Surname	Initial	Notes
2123	Evans	W	1879
518	Evry	T	**KIA** 1877-8-9
2128	Fagan	L	1879
21	Faircloth	J	**KIA** 1879
1813	Fannion	M	1879
178	Farmer	W	**KIA** 1877-8-9
1814	Farrell	P	1879
67	Farren	J	1879
2016	Farrens	J	1879
403	Fay	G.H	**KIA** 1877-8-9
354	Ferris	M	**KIA** 1877-8-9
1737	Finch	B	1877-8-9
1876	Finch	L	1877-8
527	Fitzgerald	D	1877-8
2126	Fitzgerald	D	1879
806	Fitzgerald	E	1877-8-9
2125	Fitzgerald	E	1879
1029	Fitzgerald	G	1877-8
73	Fitzgerald	T	**KIA** 1877-8-9
1815	Fitzpatrick	T	1879
374	Flaherty	J	1877-8
1908	Flaherty	T	1879
2127	Flannigan	R	1879
1879	Flint	E	**KIA** 1877-8-9
1816	Flood	B	1879
1752	Flood	W	**KIA** 1877-8-9
1818	Floyde	H	1879
362	Flynn	F	1877-8-9
1617	Force	F	No clasp
1459	Fortune	J	**KIA** 1877-8-9
1819	Foster	H	1879
1910	Fovey (Fivey)	J	1879
1909	Freeman	G	1879
862	Freeman	W	**KIA** 1877-8-9
1799	Frost	G	1879
1627	Fryher	R	1879
378	Fullerton	J	1877-8-9
2084	Gabbott	W	1879
83	Gadd	J	1877-8-9
795	Gale	J	1878-9

Deserted No trace of the return of medal

No.	Surname	Initial	Notes
2123	Gallagher	C	1879
1755	Gallougher	J	1879
1907	Galloway	W	1877-8
1915	Galpin	J.G	1879
1820	Galvin	M	1879
1611	Gange	T	1879
576	Gardner	J	1877-8-9

Medal roll indicates No Bar

No.	Surname	Initial	Notes
528	Gardner	W	1877-8-9
1800	Gardner	W	1879
1912	Gardner	W	1879
448	Gardner	W.C	1877-8-9
2017	Garnon	I	1879
2018	Garvey	P	1879
122	Gavin	C	1879
1374	Gelsthorpe	G	1877-8-9
1151	George	J	1879
173	Gibbs	T	1877-8-9
2123	Gibbons	J	1879
1305	Gilder	T	**KIA** 1877-8-9
22	Gillan	J	**KIA** 1877-8-9
1722	Gillan	P	No clasp
120	Gilmartin	J	1877-8-9
830	Gingell	J	1877-8-9
1722	Gillan	P	No clasp
120	Gilmartin	J	1877-8-9
830	Gingell	C	**KIA** 1877-8-9
408	Glass	G	**KIA** 1877-8-9
1646	Gleed	A	1879
1365	Gleeson	E	1877-8-9
1826	Gliddon	W	1879
1794	Goathen	O	**KIA** 1877-8-9
863	Goddard	C	**KIA** 1877-8-9
2019	Goldsworthy	G	1879
878	Goodall	G	1879

Deserted No trace of the return of the medal

No.	Surname	Initial	Notes
1872	Goodchild	G	**KIA** 1877-8-9
1744	Goodurn	G	1877-8-9
1822	Gorman	J	1879
1750	Goss	T	**KIA** 1877-8-9
1911	Gould	H	1879
665	Grant	H	1877-8-9

Survivor at Isandhlwana 22/1/1879

No.	Surname	Initial	Notes
2131	Gray	W	1879
1824	Green	H	1879

Deserted No indication of the return of the medal

No.	Surname	Initial	Notes
321	Green	J	1879
724	Green	J	1879
1823	Green	J	1879
1825	Green	N	1879
1854	Green	W	**KIA** 1877-8-9
2020	Greenaway	W	1879
2131	Greenwood	R	1879
1423	Gregg	W	**KIA** 1879
514	Gregson	W	**KIA** 1879
1914	Griffen	W	1879
391	Griffin	C	1887-8
535	Griffiths	G	**KIA** 1877-8-9
1457	Griffiths	T	1879
19	Grindley	J	1877-8-9
1455	Grindy	J	1877-8
2129	Grogan	A	1879
274	Groom	T	1877-8-9
1913	Guare	E	1879
667	Hadden	G	**KIA** 1877-8-9
1981	Hadden	R	1879
1725	Haines	J	1879
153	Hale	I	**KIA** 1877-8-9
264	Haley	J	1877-8-9
633	Hall	J	**KIA** 1877-8-9
588	Hall	S	1877-8
344	Hall	W	1877-8 r
821	Halloran	D	1877-8
2021	Halse	G	1879
231	Hammond	D	1877-8-9
2022	Hanks	R	1879
1661	Hanley	D	1877-8-9
11	Hannaford	J	**KIA** 1879
171	Hardwick	T	1877-8-9
2136	Hardy	T	1879
1656	Harfield	G	1879
1459	Harkin	T	**KIA** 1877-8-9
2023	Harkins	D	1879 r
678	Harman	J	**KIA** 1877-8-9
565	Harney	D	**KIA** 1877-8-9
787	Harrington	D	**KIA** 1877-8-9
2024	Harrington	T	1879

1/24th Regiment

No.	Name		Initial	Year
Boy	Harrington	**KIA**	T.J	1879
433	Harris		E	1877-8
Deserted No trace of the return of the medal				
1773	Harris		G	1879
1827	Harris		G	1879
1292	Harris		J	1877-8
1916	Harris		J	1879
234	Harris	**KIA**	T	1879
392	Harris	**KIA**	W	1877-8-9
29	Harrison		G	1877-8
1747	Harrison		G	1877-8-9
509	Harrison		H	1877-8
1761	Harrison		H	1877-8
2085	Harrison		T	1879
400	Hayden**KIA**		W	1879
1796	Hayes		E	1879
77	Hayes		G	1877-8-9
542	Haynes **KIA**		J	1877-8-9
1704	Healey		T	1879
1917	Healey		W	1879
1819	Heaney		J	1879
1362	Heaton		J	1877-8
30	Hedges **KIA**		J	1879
195	Hedges		T	1879
639	Heggarty		J	1879
696	Hemmings **KIA**		C	1879
1828	Hennessey		C	1879
51	Herridge		E	1878-9
7	Hewitt **KIA**		J	1877-8-9
1295	Hibbard **KIA**		J	1877-8-9
747	Hicken **KIA**		W.H	1877-8-9
1856	Hicks **KIA**		T	1877-8-9
202	Higgans		J	1877-8-9
720	Higgins **KIA**		T	1879
1830	Hill		E	1879
1680	Hillett		W	1877-8-9
1659	Hilton		W	1877-8-9
1857	Hind **KIA**		T	1877-8-9
1831	Hinks		H	1879
2025	Hipkiss		W	1879
776	Hitchene**KIA**		J	1879
1757	Holden **KIA**		W	1879
1780	Holland **KIA**		J	1879
2135	Holland		M	1879
2027	Holland		T	1879
2026	Holland		W	1879 r
736	Holmes		A	1877-8-9
1801	Holmes		W	1879
1218	Holt		C	1877-8-9r
1834	Holt		G	1877-8-9
Died on service prior to Zulu War. Should have had the clasp 1877-8.				
1918	Hopkins		J	1879
1121	Hopwood		I	No clasp r
833	Horgan **KIA**		D	1879
1920	Horlock		W	1879
1673	Horn **KIA**		J	1877-8-9
1501	Hornbuckle **KIA**		C	1877-8-9
495	Horrigan		D	1877-8-9
1861	Horrigan		W	1877-8-9
123	Hough		W	1877-8-9
1444	Hough	**KIA**	J	1877-8-9
1772	Howells		B	1879
251	Howells		W	1879
2092	Howen		J	1879
1832	Howes		R	1879
1921	Hudson		T	1879
533	Hughes **KIA**		E	1877-8-9
2137	Hughes		E	1879
237	Hughes **KIA**		J	1877-8-9
404	Hughes **KIA**		J	1877-8-9
324	Hughes **KIA**		O	1879
1833	Hughes		R	1879
206	Hughes **KIA**		T	1877-8-9
298	Hughes		T	1877-8-9
This man may have received two clasps viz 1877-8 and 1879.				
190	Hulme		J	1877-8-9
586	Hunter		J	1879
736	Hurley		H	1877-8-9
2134	Hurley		P	1879
1892	Iggulden **KIA**		A	1877-8-9
413	Iles		T	1877-8
This man may have received two clasps viz 1877-8 and 1879				
1882	Isley	**KIA**	F.G	1877-8-9
69	Irving		J	1877-8
536	Ivatts	**KIA**	E	1877-8-9
1648	Jackson		G	No clasp
2029	Jackson		J	1879
1475	Jackson		T	1877-8-9
252	Jacobs		P	1877-8-9
1922	James		D	1879
1625	James		H	No clasp
2140	Jaynes		F	1879
2030	Jefferson		G	1879
295	Jenkins		O	1877-8-9
This man may have received two clasps viz 1877-8 and 1879.				
841	Jenkins		J	1879
2139	Jenkins		R	1878
1083	Jenkins**KIA**		W	1879
1767	Jenkins**KIA**		W	1879
86	Jennings		P	1877-8
429	John		O	1877-8-9
581	John	D/S	P	1877-8
825	John		P	1879
1926	Johns		T	1879
553	Johnston **KIA**		G	1877-8-9
1774	Johnston **KIA**		H	1877-8-9
287	Johnston**KIA**		J	1879
2031	Johnston		J	1879
299	Johnston		W	1877-8-9
1449	Johnston **KIA**		W	1877-8-9
1465	Johnston **KIA**		G	1877-8-9
144	Johnston		J	1877-8
381	Johnston**KIA**		J	1877-8-9
633	Johnston**KIA**		J	1877-8-9
1925	Johnston		J	1879 r
1633	Johnston		W	1879
1834	Johnston		W	1879
25B/1	Johnston**KIA**		A	1879
905	Jones		A	1877-8-9
141	Jones		C	1877-8-9
386	Jones		D	1877-8-9
25B/350	Jones **KIA**		E	1877-8-9
1653	Jones		G	1879
76	Jones		H	1877-8-9
220	Jones		J	1879
704	Jones		J	1877-8-9
821	Jones		J	1877-8-9
Deserted No trace of the return of the medal				
1298	Jones		J	1879
1624	Jones		J	1879
1649	Jones		J	1879
1666	Jones		J	1879
1751	Jones		J	1879
1835	Jones		J	1879
2138	Jones		J	1879
360	Jones **KIA**		J	1879
428	Jones **KIA**		J	1877-8-9
1663	Jones		J.E	1879
1924	Jones		P	1879 r
1927	Jones		R	1879
340	Jones		T	1877-8
774	Jones		T	1877-8-9
1923	Jones		T	1879
259	Jones **KIA**		T	1877-8-9
146	Jones		W	1877-8-9
341	Jones **KIA**		W	1877-8-9
1682	Jones **KIA**		W	1879
2032	Joyner		T	1879
647	Kay		A	1877-8-9
680	Kay		J	1877-8-9
1767	Kay		T	1879
88	Keane **KIA**		J	1879
2142	Kearney		J	1879
2141	Keatinge		P	1879
1802	Keatland		J	1879
869	Keefe		J	1877-8
363	Keefe		T	1877-8
1259	Keegan **KIA**		J	1877-8-9
682	Keene		J	1877-8-9
898	Kelcher		D	1877-8-9
432	Kelly	**KIA**	A	1877-8-9
645	Kelly	**KIA**	F	1879
1306	Kelly		J	1879 r
2033	Kelly		J	1879
2143	Kelly		J	1879
520	Kelly	**KIA**	J	1879
789	Kelly	**KIA**	J.F	1877-8-9
90	Kelly		H	No clasp
1890	Kempsell	**KIA**	N	1877-8-9

1/24th Regiment

No.	Name	Init.	Year
883	Kempster **KIA**	J	1877-8-9
224	Kendall	J	1877-8-9
2145	Kennedy	W	1879
1737	Kenworthy	H	1879
1836	Kernick	H	1879

Remarks medal roll Pte R.Kernick "With 32nd Regiment"

No.	Name	Init.	Year
1929	Kerr	J	1878
2034	King	J	1879
2144	King	M	1879
1641	Kiniton	C	No clasp
2035	Kirby	J	1879
1837	Kirby	W	1879
27	Kirk	J	1877-8
392	Kirk	W	1877-8
894	Kisley	W	1877-8-9
2036	Knight	A	1879
1155	Knight **KIA**	J	1879
1928	Knott	J	1879
275	Lamb **KIA**	J	1877-8-9
1873	Lambert	A	1877-8-9
707	Lambert **KIA**	T	1879
1934	Lang	H	1879
1838	Larner	L	1877-8-9
1541	Lawrence **KIA**	J	1877-8-9
1930	Lawson	G	1879
326	Leaver **KIA**	T	1879
1035	Leaver	T	1877-8-9
1936	Lebborn	C	1879
1839	Lee	G	1879
882	Lee **KIA**	J	1879
131	Leach **KIA**	R	1877-8-9
2037	Lemon	R	1879
1614	Lewis	A	1879
703	Lewis	E	1877-8-9
72	Lewis **KIA**	H	1879
790	Lewis	J	1879-8
1932	Lewis	J	1879
2038	Lewis	J	1879
478	Lewis **KIA**	R	1879
2146	Lewis	R	1879
678	Lewis	T	1877-8-9
1933	Lewis	W	1879
1394	Limmington	W	1877-8
1277	Ling **KIA**	J	1877-8-9
531	Linnane **KIA**	J	1877-8-9
133	Lippett **KIA**	S	1877-8-9
#710	Lisbeck **KIA**	J	1877-8-9
(See page 242)			
1840	Livermore	H	1879
1703	Llewellyan	W	1879
1660	Lloyd	D.R	1879
1862	Lloyd **KIA**	J	1879
174	Lloyd	J	1877-8-9
2039	Lloyd	J	1879
162	Llock	T	1877-8-9 r
2040	Lock	T	1879
296	Lockett **KIA**	W	1877-8-9
1838	Lowder	G	1877-8
1841	Lovatt	T	1879
1935	Lovell	A	1879 r
521	Lovell **KIA**	C	1879
1649	Lowe **KIA**	C	1877-8-9
338	Lowe	J	1879
1841	Lowe **KIA**	R	1877-8-9
271	Lucas	R	1877-8-9
272	Lucas	R	1879
268	Lycett **KIA**	J	1877-8-9
863	Lynch	J	1877-8
1720	Lynch	M	1879
2041	Lynch	T	1879
258	Lyons **KIA**	J	1877-8-9
1378	Mack **KIA**	A	1877-8-9
630	Mackenzie **KIA**	J.J	1877-8-9
47	Maer **KIA**	J.R	1877-8-9
2042	Maher	D	1879
503	Maher	L	1877-8-9
1616	Mahon	W	1879
590	Mahoney **KIA**	C	1879
1726	Mahoney	J	1879

Deserted No trace of the return of the medal

No.	Name	Init.	Year
2043	Male	T	1879
2154	Maloney	J	1879
1942	Maloney	M	1879
137	Maloney **KIA**	M	1877-8-9
2044	Manley	J	1879
992	Mann **KIA**	W	1879
203	Marland	J	1877-8
916	Marley **KIA**	L	1879
1348	Marney **KIA**	C	1879
2086	Marsh	E	1879
327	Marsh	H	1877-8
1523	Martin	C.G	1879
1758	Martin **KIA**	D	1877-8-9
1642	Maslen	H	1879
212	Maslen	J	1879
1676	Mason	T	1879

Deserted No trace of return of the medal

No.	Name	Init.	Year
1938	Masterson	P	1879
1943	Maten	G	1879
1571	Matthews	A	1879
1740	Matthews	C	1877-8
1/61	Matthews	C	1879
1891	Maynard	H	1877-8
2150	Mears	W	1879
293	Meredith **KIA**	J.H	1879
828	Meredith	H	1877-8
2047	Merrett	W	1879
508	Miller **KIA**	P	1877-8-9
843	Mills	T	1877-8
36	Mitchell D/S	G	1877-8
708	Mitchell	T	1879

Deserted.No trace of return of the medal

No.	Name	Init.	Year
2160	Moore	J	1879
914	Moore	M	1877-8-9
1398	Moore **KIA**	R	1879
39	Moore	S	1877-8-9
617	Morgan	J	1877-8-9
803	Morgan **KIA**	J	1877-8-9
1609	Morgan	T	1879
490	Morgan **KIA**	W	1877-8-9
2156	Morris	G	1879
610	Morris **KIA**	G	1879
107	Morris	J	1877-8-9
1654	Morris	J	1879
2152	Morris	J	1879
851	Morris	M	1879
2048	Morris	T	1879
859	Morrison	E	1877-8-9
1852	Morrison	R	1879
730	Morse **KIA**	R	1877-8-9
523	Mulcahy	J	1877-8-9

This man may have received two clasps 1877-8 and 1879.

No.	Name	Init.	Year
2153	Mullaly	J	1879
1509	Mullen **KIA**	C	1879
457	Mullins	J	1877-8
475	Muncton	R	1877-8-9
646	Munn	E	1877-8-9
858	Murphy	D	No clasp
1844	Murphy	D	1879
1937	Murphy	D	1879
2147	Murphy	H	1879
2148	Murphy	H	1879
25B/63	Murphy **KIA**	J	1877-8-9
89	Murphy	J	1877-8-9
598	Murphy	J	1877-8-9
1617	Murphy	J	1879
1756	Murphy	J	1879
2149	Murphy	J	1879
1500	Murphy	L	1877-8
862	Murphy **KIA**	P	1879
549	Murphy	W	1877-8-9
2151	Murphy	W	1879
594	Murray **KIA**	J	1877-8-9
1516	Murray	M	1877-8
2159	Murrell	G	1879
1670	Mc Carten	J	1879
1941	Mc Clune	S	1879 r

Forfeited. No reason given.

No.	Name	Init.	Year
1687	Mc Corsack	T	1877-8
1844	Mc Donagh	A	1879
1845	Mc Donagh	J	1879
128	Mc Donald	H	1877-8-9
1863	Mc Donald	I	1877-8-9
1843	Mc Donald	J	1879 r

Discharged as incorrigible.

No.	Name	Init.	Year
663	Mc Donald **KIA**	M	1879
2157	Mc Donald	W	1879
557	Mc Donnell	J	1877-8
1846	Mc Duff	R	1879
1393	Mc Farlane **KIA**	M	1877-8-9
585	Mc Farlane	P	1877-8
538	Mc Foy	J	1877-8-9
2161	Mc Glyn	J	1879
2045	Mc Gregor	D	1879

1/24th Regiment

Num	Name		Year	Num	Name			Year	Num	Name			Year
2046	Mc Guire	J	1879	1677	Parkinson	H		1879	1948	Prince	J		1879
330	Mc Hale	KIA J	1877-8-9	1945	Parry	R		1879	1951	Prior	J		1879
2158	Mc Intyre	T	1879	471	Parry	KIA R		1877-8-9	834	Pritchard	C		No clasp
Also had the Ashanti medal.				572	Parry	T		1877-8-9	615	Pritchard	J		1877-8-9
319	Mc Kenzie	R	1877-8-9	611	Parry	W		1878-9	280	Probert	J		1879
1848	Mc Lean	J	1879	1750	Parsons	W		1879	950	Procter	KIA J		1879
1202	Mc Lorninan	R	1877-8-9	12	Patterson	KIA	H.H	1879	597	Prosser	KIA G		1879
1847	Mc Loughlin	T	1879	1855	Patterson	J		1879	797	Prosser	KIA J		1877-8-9
1939	Mc Meekin	W	1879	2053	Patterson	J		1879	182	Pugh	KIA W		1879
2049	Mc Millan	J	1879	218	Paulden	J		1877-8	260	Pugh	W		1878-9
2155	Mc Namara	J	1879	177	Payne	R		1877-8	856	Pugh	KIA W		1879
1849	Mc Neill	J	1879	372	Payton	T		1877-8-9	2168	Purcell	J		1879
284	Mc Nulty	W	1877-8	116	Pead	J		1877-8-9	2169	Purtell	N		1879
1940	Mc Sweeny	C	1879	1732	Pearce	R		1879	1795	Quaine	M		1879
198	Nally	T	1877-8	1947	Pearce	R		1879	482	Quinall	C		1878-9
399	Nash	KIA P	1877-8-9	2054	Peters	H		1879	1815	Quinn	J		1879
2050	Nash	T	1879	310	Peters	KIA J		1877-8-9	1953	Quinn	J		1879
1064	Neagle	J	1879	483	Phelan	J		1877-8-9	2170	Quinn	T		1879
772	Neagle	P	1877-8-9	1629	Phillips	G		1879	2055	Quinton	J		1879
2162	Neeve	S	1879	1949	Phillips	J		1879	513	Quirk	KIA J		1877-8-9
2163	Neill	T	1879	845	Phillips	KIA J.N		1877-8-9	26	Rafferty	H		1877-8
1944	Nelson	J	1879	237	Phillips	KIA J		1877-8-9	1739	Raftree	J		1879
118	Nevin	J	1877-8-9	1756	Phipps	G		1877-8	1859	Ralph	E		1879
1835	Newall	W	1877-8-9	87	Pickard	KIA J.R		1879	1958	Randall	S		1879
1928	Newberry	KIA A	1877-8-9	258	Pile	B		1877-8-9	1954	Raphael	J		1879
1906	Newberry	KIA T	1879	327	Pindard	J		1877-8	2171	Rathbone	T		1879
2051	Newton	R	1879	587	Plant	H		1878-9	2057	Raynsford	W		1879
625	Nicholas	E	1877-8-9	374	Plant	KIA S		1877-8-9	1860	Ready	E		1879
648	Nicholas	KIA W	1879	1856	Plummer	C		No clasp	2056	Redford	W		1879
78	Nolan	P	1877-8-9	123	Plumpton	G		No clasp	2173	Redmond	M		1879
2164	Nolan	R	1879	181	Plunkett	KIA J		1879	398	Reegan	P		1877-8
61	Nurse	W	1877-8-9	1368	Pollen	KIA A		1877-8-9	650	Rees	J		1877-8
1839	Nye	KIA W.E	1877-8-9	1952	Pollock	S		1878-9	1826	Remmington	KIA E		1879
1178	Oakley	A	1879	670	Poole	H		1877-8	1650	Retford	KIA W.H.		1877-8-9
1245	Oakley	KIA W	1877-8-9	546	Poole	T		No clasp	2058	Richards	D		1879
1853	Oaten	E	1879	1793	Pope	KIA W		1877-8-9	17	Richards	G		1877-8
2165	O'Brien	T	1879	1748	Port	R		1878-9	840	Richards	KIA G		1879
754	Odey	KIA G	1877-8-9	222	Potten	KIA U		1879	1955	Richards	D		1879
2052	O'Donnell	J	1879	164	Potter	W		1877-8	691	Richards	R		1879
2196	O'Donnell	P	1879	1651	Potter	W		1879	54	Richards	W		1877-8-9
1417	Ogden	KIA J	1877-8-9	1744	Pound	R		1879	871	Richardson	KIA M		1879
672	O'Hara	J	1877-8	606	Powell	G		1877-8-9	572	Ricketts	T		1879
216	O'Neill	J	1877-8-9	739	Powell	KIA H		1877-8-9	808	Rignay	KIA J		1877-8-9
179	O'Neill	M	1877-8-9	456	Powell	J		1877-8	396	Ring	P		1877-8-9
1735	Orton	H	1877-8-9	539	Powell	R		1877-8	504	Rittman	KIA J		1877-8-9
This man may have received two clasps viz 1877-8 and 1879.				1602	Powell	T		1879	2172	Roach	J		1879
				1713	Powell	W		1879	2175	Roberts	T		1879
532	O'Shea	J	1877-8-9	499	Power DCM	J		1878-9	311	Roberts	W		1879
1854	O'Sullivan	A	1879	A Kambula,Ulundi Decoration.					355	Roberts	KIA W		1877-8
423	Owen	R	1877-8-9	1857	Pratt	J		1879	532	Robinson	J		1877-8
2167	Owens	O	1879	1671	Preece	J		1879	1505	Roche	M		1877-8-9
1478	Padmore	KIA J	1877-8-9	1783	Preece	W		1879	1231	Roddy	T		1879
1946	Page	A	1879	1776	Preston	G		No clasp	1866	Rodgers	KIA H		1877-8-9
Deserted. No trace of the return of the medal.				1858	Price	E		1879	1956	Rodgers	S		1879 r
				1665	Price	G		1879	1957	Rodgers	W		1879
1781	Page	H	1877-8	437	Price	J		1878-9	187	Rothwell	T		1877-8
980	Painter	KIA T	1877-8-9	693	Price	J		1877-8-9	740	Roubery	KIA P		1877-8-9
402	Palmer	H	1877-8	1774	Price	J		1879	510	Rowan	KIA H		1877-8-9
207	Parkin	J	1877-8	1950	Price	J		1879					

1/24th Regiment

Sub Lieutenant Griffiths T.L

No.	Name		Clasp
1542	Roy DCM	W	1877-8-9
A Rorke's Drift Decoration.			
97	Roydes	R	1877-8
345	Ruck	J	1877-8
548	Rule **KIA**	W	1879
2174	Rushbrook	W	1879
40	Russell **KIA**	F	1877-8-9
567	Russell	J	1877-8-9
1380	Russell	J	1877-8
1687	Russell	W	1879
1452	Rutter **KIA**	T	1877-8-9
2176	Ryan **KIA**	J	1879
909	Ryan	J	1879
2185	Salmons	O	1879 r
488	Salter **KIA**	G	1877-8-9
529	Sarney **KIA**	F	1877-8-9
530	Sarney	F	1877-8-9
25	Sault	J	1877-8-9
1652	Saulter	W	1879
2177	Saunders	J	1879
1861	Saunders	W	1879
579	Scannell	J	1877-8
368	Scapplethorn D/S	T	1877-8
2179	Schnurre	G	1879
492	Schofield	R	1877-8-9
521	Scott	S	1877-8
1592	Scudder	T	1878
1862	Scully	E	1879
601	Seaborne	J	1877-8-9
279	Sears **KIA**	H	1879
1971	Sellwood **KIA**	W	1877-8-9
2183	Sexton	J	1879
147	Sharp **KIA**	F	1877-8-9
2187	Sharples	J	1879
1763	Sharples	W	1879
1863	Sharpley	W	1879
Duplicate medal and clasp issued 13/10/1919.			
200	Shaw **KIA**	R	1877-8-9
497	Shea **KIA**	D	1877-8-9
544	Shean D/S	R	1877-8-9
1130	Sheather **KIA** H		1877-8-9
1741	Sheen	J	1879
1963	Sheldon	B	1879
1964	Shields	J	1879
462	Shipway	E	1877-8-9
1612	Short	T	1879
1396	Shrimpton **KIA**	J	1879
649	Silcock **KIA**	R	1877-8-9
2180	Singleton	P	1879
2178	Sissons	S	1879 r
384	Skelton **KIA** W		1877-8-9
547	Skinner	S	1877-8
2186	Slanson	G	1879
506	Smith **KIA**	C	1879
1867	Smith **KIA**	C	1877-8-9
1047	Smith **KIA**	E	1879
1864	Smith	F	1879
58	Smith **KIA**	G	1877-8-9
414	Smith	G	1877-8
1352	Smith	G	1877-8
148	Smith	H	1879
2062	Smith	I	1879
277	Smith	J	1879
1360	Smith	J	1879
1865	Smith	J	1879
1903	Smith **KIA**	J	1879
1960	Smith	J	1879
1961	Smith	J	1879
2061	Smith	J.B	1879
1575	Smith	R	1879
1610	Smith	R	1879
471	Smith	T	1879
1749	Smith	W	1879
2063	Smith	W	1879
2064	Smuin	C	1879
2060	Snape	A	1879
37	Spaxman	J	1877-8-9
396	Speed **KIA**	T	1877-8-9
1962	Spicer	W	1879
Also had India General Service Medal with clasp Bhootan.			
1959	Spillacey	J	1879
2065	Spillane	J	1879
1227	Spurgin	J	1877-8-9
1866	Spurway	S	1879
1967	Stacey	D	1879
256	Standish	T	1877-8-9
114	Stansfield **KIA**	S	1877-8-9
603	Steed	J	1877-8
213	Stephens	J	1877-8
1376	Stephenson	R	1877-8-9
851	Stevens **KIA** H		1877-8-9
20	Stevens **KIA** W		1879
1965	Stewart	J	No clasp r
1889	Stiles	J	1877-8-9
1742	Stokes	G	1879
2184	Stone	W	No clasp r
1966	Stoops	C	1879
900	Strange **KIA**	E	1879
16	Sturt	C	1877-8
1495	Sullivan **KIA**	J	1877-8-9
1591	Sullivan	P	1879
888	Sullivan **KIA**	P	1877-8-9
2181	Sullivan	T	1879
393	Sullivan	W	1877-8
1867	Summerland	B	1879
1868	Summers	J	1879
66	Surell	R	1877-8
Medal Re-issued in the name of Sewell.			
161	Sutton **KIA**	P	1877-8-9
660	Sweeney	P	1877-8-9
2182	Sweeney	T	1879
2068	Swift	T	1879
664	Swoffer **KIA**	R	1879
1779	Tate **KIA**	R	1877-8-9
1771	Taylor	A	1879
659	Taylor **KIA**	E	1877-8-9
130	Taylor	J	1877-8-9
387	Taylor	J	1877-8
1753	Taylor	J	1879
1869	Taylor	T	1879
1670	Terry **KIA**	J	1877-8-9
1753	Theobald **KIA**	W	1879
1969	Thomas	D	1879
460	Thomas	J	1877-8-9
636	Thomas **KIA**	J	1879
765	Thomas **KIA**	J.B.	1877-8-9
592	Thomas	W	1877-8-9
1717	Thomas	W	1879
664	Thompson	H	1877-8-9
1669	Thompson	J	1879
2188	Thompson	J	1879
2069	Thompson	T	1879
Deserted. No trace of return of the medal			
1711	Thompson	W	1879
34	Thornett **KIA** T		1877-8-9
2070	Thornton	J	1879
6	Thorpe	J	1878-9
33	Throssell **KIA**	C	1877-8-9
317	Tillison **KIA**	H	1877 8 9
383	Tinnery **KIA**	T	1877-8-9
1782	Todd **KIA**	G	1879
2190	Tompkins	J	1879
1310	Toms	A	1877-8
379	Tongue	J	1877-8
209	Townshend **KIA**	J	1877-8-9
190	Trainer	J	1879
1968	Trivett	F	1879
512	Trotman	R	1877-8
543	Trowell **KIA**	W	1879
1870	Tucker	W	1879
16	Tullett **KIA**	J	1877-8-9
276	Turbitt	W	1877-8-9
2071	Turnbull	J	1879
946	Turner **KIA**	E	1877-8-9

LETTERS FROM MERTHYR SOLDIERS AT RORKE'S DRIFT.

By the mail which was delivered at Merthyr on Friday, a number of letters were received from soldiers who are serving in the campaign against the Zulus. The receipt of these letters from the Cape has imparted general joy in the neighbourhood where the young men formerly resided, and which, with a few exceptions, was at Caedraw. There are, however, many families in this district who have suffered bereavement by the affair at Isandula, and the grief of the parents at the loss of their sons is still very great. The letters are throughout of such an interesting nature, and bring the feelings which animate our soldiers so graphically before the reader, that the copies of the letters, some of which were written in pencil on scraps of paper, which our Merthyr correspondent has forwarded to us, cannot but be read with the deepest interest.

The first letter is from Private John Jones, whose mother lives at Caedraw:—

Rorke's Drift, Natal,
January 28, 1879.

My dear Mother,—I now take my pen in hand to write you a few lines, as I daresay you will be anxious to hear from me before you receive this, as you will hear of the disastrous battle which we had on the 22nd of this month with the enemy. But, dear mother, I am happy to inform you that I came through it all right without being touched. The enemy came down on our camp, 20 men to one of us, as the most of our column had gone out 15 miles further up the country, expecting to have an engagement, but they outflanked us and came down on the camp, which was defended by 1,000 men only and two guns, and the enemy's force being over 20,000 strong warriors. They came so numerous that every man in camp was slaughtered, but happily to me I was out with the column, so I was saved, but Billy Terrett, Hughey Perkins, Jamey Cantlon, commonly called "Jimmy knocked the house down," were all killed on the field, as five companies of the 1st Battalion and one company of ours, besides 100 artillerymen, and a great number of mounted volunteers of the colony, in all nearly 1,000, perished at the mercy of the enemy, but we took back our camp by 10 o'clock at night, after marching about 35 miles that day, but mostly everything in camp was lost, lost to us, as the enemy had our valises, blankets, big coats, tents, and, in fact, everything excepting what we stood in. There is no one that knows where James Terrett is. He is supposed to be up in the Diamond Fields with the mounted troops, but they will be called down here now as reinforcements, so I don't know how things will turn out as yet, and no one knows what number of lives will be lost by the time it is finished; but I trust in God to return home safe some day. But this is a fearful war, and the havoc will be great among our troops, as it is such a fearful hilly country for marching; and now, since we lost our camp, we are obliged to sleep on the ground in the best way we can, without anything to cover us, and its very cold and wet here now the rainy season is on, but the heat of the sun is so scorchingly hot in the day that it has already caused a great deal of sickness amongst our troops; but in a few days, as soon as we get reinforcements, we will make a further advance into the country towards the King's kraals, where he is supposed to have about from 40,000 to 58,000 troops, and we expect to have a great engagement when we get there, as no mercy is to be shown them any more, owing to the manner they cut out and mutilated our dead bodies. The enemy has already lost nearly 20,000, and before we finish with them we hope to kill them to the last man. Our loss up to the present is about 1,000. So now I beg to conclude. I shall write again soon with more particulars. Hoping I shall hear from you soon, and hoping also that you are all at home enjoying the best of health, give my best respects to all inquiring friends, and accept my kindest love to all at home. —Believe me to remain your very affectionate son, JOHN.

Please address—No. 970, Private John Jones, B Company, 2-24th Regiment, Rorke's Drift, near Helpmakaar, Natal, South Africa.

The next letter is written by Private Clark, whose mother lives at Middle Taff-street, Caedraw:—

Rorke's Drift, February 1, 1879.

My dear Mother,—I now take the opportunity of writing these few lines to you, hoping to find you and my brother William in good health, as this leaves me at present. Thank God, dear mother, I arrived here on the 2nd of last month. We had a pleasant voyage. About three weeks after we landed there was a fearful disaster happened here. Our first battalion was cut to pieces, and 200 of the second; Wm. Terrett, and Johnny Roach, and Hughy Perkins was shot. I hope you will excuse me not writing before, as we are in a wild country now far away from any town, and cannot get paper or stamps. Let me know if William and Sarah are working. I hope, with the help of God, that I shall come safe out of this affair. Let me know if Phillip is working, and if he is in good health. I have not seen James Terrett since I came here. He is in another part of the country, but he is alive and well. As soon as this affair is over, and we settle down somewhere, I shall send you a few shillings. I don't receive any pay now while we are in the field. Dan Lyons and Thomas Harding is in the same company as me. They send their respects to you and all inquiring friends. Dan Lyons did not like to write to Mrs. Terrett about William, as it might put her about a good deal. Tell her quietly about it. It is very hard here; since I joined the regiment I have not had my clothes off. I sleep every night booted and belted. No more at present, from your affectionate son,

No. 1,550. Private J. Clark, J. CLARK.
A Company, 2-24th Regiment, Natal, South Africa.

The following letter was received from Sergeant Jones, whose mother lives at No. 4, Chapel-street:—

Rorke's Drift, Feb. 3, 1879.

My dearest Mother,—According to promise in the last letter that I did scribble to you with blacklead informing you that I was quite safe. Thank God for His mercy and kindness towards me in keeping me safe through the engagement that we had with the Zulus on the 22nd of January, which I thought that I should not be able to write to you again, as I gave myself entirely up for lost. But God was good, and He has kept me safe through all my trouble so far; hoping, dear mother, that I shall be spared to return to England again. The men that we have lost in our battalion is five officers and 10 sergeants, and 159 privates; the first battalion lost five companies and 17 officers and a great number of artillery and mounted infantry that was left to protect the camp. The number of Zulus killed is about 10,000 to 12,000. As we were advancing up to take our position from the enemy, the bodies were laying so thick that we could hardly put one foot on the ground without treading on bodies. The sight was something awful to witness. On the morning of the 22nd the column left camp at about three o'clock a.m. to attack a large party of Zulus that was seen on the night before. We left a great number of men in the camp to protect it, but the Zulus was too numerous for us that they out-numbered us. After the column leaving camp the enemy turned our flank and got the best of us, and took our camp and everything that was in it, and massacred our men that were in the hospital not able to move their back. The Zulus took and ripped them open with their assegas that they use. It was something horrible to see their bowels hanging out, and some with their legs cut off from their bodies. About three o'clock the general formed us up and said he intended to take the camp back from the enemy, if it cost him half the men he had with him. After shelling the Zulus for some time we advanced up; it was drawing towards dark then. The bodies were lying that thick that the men were tumbling over them at times. About ten o'clock that night, dear mother, we reached our camp, and drove the enemy clean out of the place—the position that the Zulus had taken from us. As soon as we got to our position we all gave three cheers for old England. It is a night I shall never forget the longest day that I live. Next morning we had to retire to Rorke's Drift to get provisions and ammunition. We arrived just in time to reinforce a company of ours that was keeping the Zulus in check. We drove the Zulus back with the loss of about 900 Zulus. Our loss there was only one sergeant and five privates. We have now fortified ourselves by making a kind of fortification with earthworks, strong enough to keep 25,000 Zulus back if they liked to attack us. Dear mother, we have just had a change of clothing sent to us. Officers and men are just the same, bad off for clothing. There is a great number of men from Merthyr killed, that I know quite well, which will be a very heavy blow to their mothers when they hear of the death of their sons. Dear mother, I received the *Graphic* which Miss Lewis was kind enough to send me, which I was very proud to receive, and I can assure you that the paper was very acceptable, as it is very little news we get out here. We get the papers from home. Please tell Miss Lewis that I am thankful to her for the paper. Dear mother, I am enjoying the very best of health at present. . . . You can remember me to Jack and Bill and Tom Stanfield. I was only too glad to hear that they were enjoying themselves on furlough, and it was something great to see three brothers on furlough together. I hope, ere long, that it will come to my turn to come on furlough to Merthyr, and I hope that I shall live long enough to enjoy that we are going to get from this war. My best respects to Mrs. and Miss Lewis, Mrs. Stanfield and family.—Yours, &c.,
E. JONES.

LETTER FROM A PONTYPOOL MAN.

The following letter has been received from William Meredith, a private in the 2-24th Regiment, and will be read with interest by his friends in this district. He dates his letter Rorke's Drift, February 5, 1879:—

Dear Brother and Sister,—I write you these few lines in hopes that you are in good health, as it leaves me at present, thank God, considering we had our second fight, in which we got defeated. At our first fight we gained the day, and took a good many head of cattle. But we are properly defeated now; so we cannot go any further now till we get more troops from England. we lost so many men at the last battle. We lost 500 men from the 1st Battalion and 184 from the 2nd Battalion. The second is the regiment that I am in, so don't make a mistake. These are Pontypool boys that got killed at the battle:—Alf Farr, Dick Treverton, and Charley Long. I expect you, will see more of it in the papers, but they generally print them wrong out here, and so they will at home. I could describe the battlefield to you, but the sooner I get it off my mind the better. It was a pity to see about 800 white men lying on the field cut up to pieces and stripped naked. Even the little boys that we had in the band, they were hung up on hooks, and opened like sheep. It was a pitiful sight. We had to retire, and make the best of our way to where we could get ammunition. Please let me know have you sent more than one letter.

WILLIAM MEREDITH,
2-24th Regiment, Natal, South Africa.

LETTER FROM AN ABERGAVENNY MAN.

The following is a letter from John Powell, private, 1st Company, 2-24th Regiment, Natal, South Africa, to his parents living in Abergavenny:—

Rorke's Drift, Feb. 3, 1879.

Dear Father and Mother,—I received your kind and welcome letter on the 23rd of last month. . . . . We crossed over into Zululand on the 11th of January. We went over on pontoon bridges, and after we crossed we stopped on the other side four days, and we had an engagement on a Sunday. To commence there were 11 wounded on our side, and about 300 of the enemy killed; and we had orders for four companies—the E, F, G, H—to go further up about five miles to the Basshe Valley, and we had to work hard making roads for the other companies to follow us. We was there eight days, and we had orders to go up about six miles to a rock called Isandula. We was 2,500 men in there, the General and all his staff. My company mounted piquet on the night we went in, and the following morning we started out leaving (in charge of the camp) one company of ours (2-24th) behind, and five companies of the 1-24th, and all the servants and cooks, and two big guns and 85 artillery men. And we went out about three o'clock in the morning in search of 7,000 Kaffirs, and they turned our flank, and went on the camp and destroyed everything. But our men (those left in charge of the camp) did fight like lions, hand to hand, but the rebels was too many in number, and only eight men escaped. They killed 184 of our battalion (2-24th), and 600 of the 1-24th, and took everything. We had nothing left. They took our colours, our ammunition, burned down our camp—such a cutting up among British soldiers was never known. We was about 20 miles away from camp when the fight was going on, and we started back and came within three miles of the camp. The general formed us up and told us what had happened, and that we should have to take the camp that night, if it was by the point of the bayonet, and said that he could trust us, the 24th, to do so, and we all gave him three cheers; but we took the camp, and after we took it we gave three cheers. We were all fatigued and tired, and we lay down between the dead, our own men and the Kaffirs all mixed together. They killed about 6,000 Kaffirs. It was a dreadful sight in the morning to see our men cut up as they were—not a man living. We lost the band and the drums, five of our officers killed, and we had to come back to Natal across the river. We could see about 3,000 of the enemy watching us, but we did not stop, because we had no ammunition. We had to come for life, and when we came to where our other company was it was on fire (the hospital at Rorke's Drift). They had a hard fight here, they killed about 560 Kaffirs, and 13 of ours killed and wounded. William Watkins, the baker, of Abergavenny, was killed up there. I saw him in the morning as I passed by. Myself and Patsy Morris, and Murphy, and Jim Berry's son is quite well, thank God for it. . . . So no more from your loving son, JOHN POWELL.

LETTERS FROM CARDIFF PRIVATES.

W. Thomas, a private now serving with the 24th Regiment in South Africa, writes, from Grey Town, to his parents, who reside in Cardiff, giving an account of the disaster at Isandula. In addition to the particulars which have been already published, he asserts that the Zulus "were not satisfied with killing our men, but even burnt them, and cut them to pieces." Another private in the 24th Regiment—M. O'Leary—writes from the Lower Tugela, to his parents in Cardiff, and says, in referring to the losses at Isandula, that "the boys from Cardiff are among the rest of the poor fellows."

Robert Jones VC

Robert Jones VC of **Rorke's Drift** fame was born at Raglan, Monmouthshire in August 1857. He enlisted into 2/24th on 10 January 1876 aged 19.

He was found dead, shot in the head, at the age of 41. He was assumed to have committed suicide, though in fact his shotgun may well have gone off accidentally. Suicide was such a disgraceful act in 1898 that he was buried in a grave in Peterchurch churchyard facing away from his church. the coffin was taken into the grave yard over the wall rather than through the gate. The Coroner heard how he was plagued with recurring nightmares following his desperate hand to hand combat with Zulus.

Privates Robert and William Jones were posted in a room of the hospital facing the hill. They kept up a steady fire against enormous odds. While one worked to cut a hole through the partition into the next room, the other shot Zulu after Zulu through the loopholed walls, using his own and his comrade's rifle alternately as the barrels became too hot to hold from the incessant firing. By their united heroic efforts six out of the seven patients were saved by being carried through the broken partition. the seventh, sergeant Maxwell being delirious, refused to be helped, and on Robert Jones re turning to take him by force he found him being stabbed by the Zulus in his bed.

His Victoria Cross passed out of the family and is now thought to be in the possession of Lord Ashcroft. It was bought in 1996 for £80,000, defeating a bid from the regimental museum.

Brigadier-General Henry Mainwaring's - Visit to the Zulu War battlefields March 1921.

Henry Germain Mainwaring was born in Barrackpore in Bengal on 6 January 1852. He was the son of Maj George Mainwaring (22nd Foot) and his wife, Frances and was commissioned into 24th Foot in September 1872. During the 9th Frontier war and during the Zulu campaign in South Africa he served as a Lieutenant with 2nd Battalion. On 22 January 1879, he was with F (Captain Church) Company with Lord Chelmsford's column and therefore missed the disaster at Isandhlwana. Later, he produced his own sketch maps of Isandhlwana and **Rorke's Drift** which still survive. He later commanded 1st Battalion South Wales Borderers from 1896 to 1901 when the Battalion was in Gibraltar and India. He retired from the army as brevet Colonel in 1905, but was recalled in 1915 to command a battalion of the West Riding Regiment in India. Retiring for the second time as a Brigadier-General in 1918, he died at Hastings in February 1922.

Brig Mainwaring was a noted sportsmen and big game hunter. He was a Fellow of the Royal Geographical Society and in 1920 he published his sporting exploits in 'A Soldier's Shikar Trips' covering expeditions in Somaliland and India. The Himalayan bear now standing guard in the Officers' Mess Brecon Barracks brought back by Brig Mainwaring and many of his other sporting trophies are held by the Brecon Museum. This account of his visit to the battlefields was written nine months before his death in 1922 aged 70 years.Fate ordained that I should after many years once more visit the battlefield of Isandhlwana and I owe this chiefly to the kindness of Mr George Plowman CMG, the Administrator of Natal, who made all arrangements and directed an official to take me over the ground.

At 7.30 am 8th March 1921, I started from Dundee. We crossed the Buffalo by the new Drift - Vansdrift - Here a good bridge has been built. The old Drift at Rorke's Drift is almost unused. The old pontoons in which we crossed have fallen to pieces.

We first stopped at St Augustine's Mission Station. in charge of Archdeacon **Charles Johnson** to whom I had telegraphed the previous week from Pietermaritzburg - stating that I proposed visiting Isandhlwana on the 8th March and hoped to see something of him in passing. Unfortunately the Reverend gentleman was too busy to see me. It seemed a pity, as I told his wife, I could have given him information of the battlefield, which he was never likely to hear again. On our way to the battlefield we went by a road south of the Bashee Valley - different from the old route mentioned in the following account. The sloping ground above Rorke's Drift is now much cultivated, almost entirely mealie fields, but on arrival at Isandhlwana I found it very little changed with the exception of a small mealie crop; on the neck there is little or no cultivation.The stones over the graves are all neatly whitewashed and in good order. I was pleased to see that a cairn of stones that our party made on the ledge of Isandhlwana Rock, and where we found and buried Captain Younghusband, one (other) officer unrecognisable and 60 men, 24th Regiment, was still in a good state of preservation.

The 24th Memorial is in a very good position on the neck - could not be better; next to it is the Memorial to the Natal Police or the Natal Carbineers. The Memorial Chapel (St Vincent's) is situated on the Eastern side of the Rock, and under the Ingutu Range. We had no time to visit it. I climbed to the top of Black's Kopje to take a photograph. When a youngster I thought nothing of it, but now it was a very different matter. It was on the top of this Kopje that, whilst making my survey of the battlefield, in the September following - I found a portion of the Colour pole of one of our colours - the only portion of the two colours ever recovered. The above refers only to the 2nd Battalion Colours. Both Colours were taken. The 1st Battalion took only their Queen's Colour. This was afterwards carried out of camp by Lieutenant Melvill, assisted later by **Lieutenant Coghill**. Both officers lost their lives in saving this Colour, which was afterwards recovered from the river. This portion, about two feet, with brass ferrule at the bottom is now, I believe, at Windsor Castle.

As we were leaving the neck the Provincial War Department official in whose charge the battlefield is and who was conducting me over the ground, remarked with reference to the grave "That is the last", so I replied "What about all those down the Fugitives' track?" He told me he was unaware of any soldiers being buried there. I informed him that when we were camped near the spot the following September we spent from a week to ten days burying the dead, all down to Fugitives' Drift. These included some well-known officers, such as Surgeon Major Shepherd (I think his name was) RAMC, the originator of St John's Ambulance, **Major Smith RA**, **Lieutenant Anstey** 24th Regiment etc., etc. I fear now after so many years it will be impossible to locate these graves. We next went on to Rorke's Drift - a small farm has sprung up on the Zulu side opposite the Drift. We crossed the river in a boat and on the other side found horses waiting for us. Fort Melvill is now nothing but a ruin. We passed on to Rorke's Drift house. Within 300-400 yards of the place I could recognise nothing. The old place, as we who were stationed there remember it, has been swept away. Not a vestige of the old house remains. In its place is a small modern villa of a style to be seen in the suburbs of London, an aggressively red-faced little building with a blue slate roof. The old yard round which our defences were formed is now occupied by a Church, the Hospital has been rebuilt almost the same. The two blue gum trees are still there, but the right hand tree so I was informed is new. The place is now in the hands of a Swedish Missionary who did not seem to bear any particular goodwill to the British. I asked to see the graves of our 24th men, and he took me to a small enclosed graveyard at the back. The obelisk over the graves made by **Bandsman Melsop** 24th Regiment, I found in good order but the graveyard is choked up with bushes. These should be cleared away. The whole of the surroundings of Rorke's Drift and grounds not occupied by buildings is covered with an untidy jungle of fruit trees. I am sorry to say it and regret still more that this historic spot should have passed into alien hands. My intended visit to the graves of **Melvill** and **Coghill** had to be abandoned, as time did not permit.

HG Mainwaring Brigadier General May 1921   Reference: The Journal of the Royal Regiment of Wales Journal 68 Spring 2004

1/24th Regiment

No.	Name	Initial	Years	No.	Name	Initial	Years	No.	Name	Initial	Years
104	Turner	H	1877-8-9	380	Watkins **KIA**	W	1877-8-9	778	Williams **KIA**	E	1879
1871	Twigg	W	1879	1152	Wattey **KIA**	J	1877-8-9	1874	Williams	G	1879
1787	Twycross	W	1877-8-9	1735	Watson	J	1879	139	Williams	J	1879
418	Venables	J	1879	108	Watson	M	1877-8-9	545	Williams **KIA**	J	1879
249	Vickers	J	1877-8-9	1919	Watts **KIA**	H	1877-8-9	582	Williams **KIA**	J	1879
85	Vines **KIA**	G	1877-8-9	697	Webb **KIA**	T	1879	799	Williams	J	1877-8-9
2072	Wakefield	H	1879	2194	Webb	W	1879	868	Williams **KIA**	J	1877-8-9
444	Walker **KIA**	E	1877-8-9	90	Weir	A	1879	288	Williams **KIA**	M	1877-8-9
925	Walker **KIA**	E	1877-8-9	343	Welsh	J	1877-8	1975	Williams	N	1879
110	Walker	J	1879	489	Wetherhead **KIA**	H	1879	193	Williams	R	1877-8-9
2193	Wall	J	1879	2192	Wheeler	W	1879	289	Williams	T	1878-9
1784	Wallis	T	1877-8-9	642	Whelan **KIA**	J	1877-8-9	534	Williams **KIA**	T	1877-8-9
336	Walsh	E	1877-8-9	1184	Whelan **KIA**	T	1877-8-9	624	Williams **KIA**	T	1877-8-9
239	Walsh	G	1877-8-9	270	Wherrell	W	1877-8	169	Williams	W	1877-8
339	Walsh	J	1877-8	1978	White	H	1879	580	Williams	W	1878-9
1873	Walsh	J	1879	2195	Whitfield	J	1879	1613	Williams	W	No clasp r
2073	Walsh	J	1879	560	Whorrall	R	1877-8	1784	Williams	W	1879
2191	Walsh	J	1879	591	Whybrow **KIA**	E	1877-8-9	1875	Williams	W	1879
1971	Walsh	R	1879	1583	Whybrow	J	1879	1973	Williams	W	1879
285	Walsh **KIA**	T	1877-8-9	1972	Wicks	J	1879	698	Williams **KIA**	W.E	1879
385	Walsh	T	1877-8	365	Widdows	J	1877-8-9	1876	Williams	W.P	1879
493	Walsh **KIA**	T	1877-8-9	1976	Wilcox	J	1879	13	Wilson	E	1877-8-9
851	Walsh **KIA**	W	1879	1618	Wilding	W	1879	This man may have received two clasps viz 1877-8 and 1879.			
2074	Walton	G	1879	214	Wilford	J	1879				
596	Walton **KIA**	W	1877-8-9	2076	Wise	W	1879	533	Wilson **KIA**	F	1879
2196	Warburton	A	1879	2077	Withem	E	1879	1267	Wilson **KIA**	J	1877-8-9
31	Ward	G	1877-8-9	Forfeited. No reason given. No trace of the return of the medal.				227	Wisher **KIA**	W	1877-8-9
928	Ward	J	1877-8					1872	Wogden	F	1879
2075	Warner	H	1879	297	Wilkinson **KIA**	A	1877-8-9	495	Wolfenden	J	1879
531	Warner **KIA**	J	1877-8-9	134	Wilks **KIA**	F	1877-8-9	888	Wood **KIA**	J	1877-8-9
447	Waters	J	1877-8-9	1970	Williams	C.R	1879	1877	Wood	W	1879
This man may have received two clasps viz 1877-8 and 1879.				261	Williams	D	1877-8	111	Woodford	W	1877-8-9
748	Watkins	C	1877-8-9	455	Williams **KIA**	E	1877-8-9	1878	Woodward	T	1879

Spink Auction Sale 5019 Lot 133. 24 Nov 2005
An Interesting Zulu War C.M.G. Pair to Lieutenant-Colonel J. Mahoney, who served as Chief Paymaster of the 2nd Battalion 24th Foot during the Zulu War, and who probably had the task of clearing the accounts of those killed at **Rorke's Drift** and Isandhlwana
The Most Distinguished Order of St Michael and St George, Companion's (C.M.G.) breast Badge, gold and enamel, with swivel suspension and top gold riband buckle; South Africa 1877-79, one clasp, 1877-8 (Major. J. Mahoney. C.M.G. A.P.Dept:), nearly extremely fine (2) Estimate £ 1,600-1,800
C.M.G. London Gazette 19.12.1879
Lieutenant-Colonel John Mahoney, C.M.G., served as Paymaster with the rank of Major of the 2nd Battalion, 24th Regiment during the Gaika rebellion 1877-78. Served in the Zulu War of 1879 as Chief Paymaster; acted temporarily as District Paymaster; Lieutenant-Colonel 16.3.1884.
He is shown on the 2/24th Foot Medal Roll as Paymaster and Hon. Major, and his entitlement is confirmed on the Army Pay Department Roll where he is referred to the 2/24th Foot.
The Roll states that he is entitled to the 1877-8-9 clasp, not the 1877-8 clasp.
Sold for £1600

Glendining's Auction 24th June 1992. Lot 167 I clasp, 1877-8.(Major J. Mahoney, C.M.G.,A.P.Dept) very Fine. estimate (£250 - 350)
Army list 1903: Mahoney, J. (Hon Lt Col, Staff Paym ret. pay)- s. African War, 1878-9-Kaffir campaign. Expedition against the Gaikas as Paymaster 24th Foot. Zulu campaign-Acted temporarily as District Paymaster.

1/24th Regiment

1266	Woolley **KIA**	J	1877-8-9
589	Worthington **KIA**	E	1877-8-9
1768	Wright **KIA**	R	1879
210	Wyer	J	1877-8-9
257	Wynne	J	1877-8-9
132	Young	T	1877-8-9
1654	Young **KIA**	T	1877-8-9
1646	Young	W	No clasp r
1132	Young	W	1877-8-9

Died on service 6/3/1878. The clasp should thus be 1877-8.

2/24th (THE 2nd WARWICKSHIRE) REGIMENT.

Those Killed in Action (**KIA**) lost their lives at Isandhlwana 22/1/1979.

LIEUTENANT COLONEL
- Degacher CB H.J 1877-8-9

MAJOR
- Black CB W 1877-8-9

Also had British and Turkish Crimean Medals.
- #Caldwell J.F 1877-8
- Chamberlin W.R.B 1877-8-9
- Church H.B 1879
- Dunbar W.M 1877-8-9

Also had British and Turkish Crimean Medals and Indian Mutiny Medal.

BREVET MAJOR
- Bromhead C.J 1879

Also had Ashantee Medal.
- Bromhead VC G 1877-8-9

VC was for the Defence of Rorkes Drift

PAYMASTER HON MAJOR
- ##Mahoney CMG J 1877-8-9

See also Army Pay Department.

QUARTERMASTER
- Bloomfield **KIA** H.J 1877-8-9

LIEUTENANT ADJUTANT
- Dyer **KIA** H.J 1877-8-9
- Trower C.V 1877-8-9

CAPTAIN
- Banister G.S 1877-8-9
- Glennie F 1877-8-9
- Godwin-Austen A.G 1877-8
- Harvey J.J 1877-8-9
- Surplice R.N 1877-8
- Symons W.P 1877-8-9
- Williams H.M 1877-8-9

LIEUTENANT
- Birch A.W 1879
- Curll C.E 1879
- Dolben H No clasp
- Godwin-Austen **KIA** F.G 1877-8-9
- Lloyd J.D.A.T 1879
- Logan Q.Mck 1877-8-9
- Mainwaring H.G 1877-8-9
- Moore Harper E.T No clasp
- O'Donnell H 1879
- Phipps A.B 1879
- Pope **KIA** C.d'A 1877-8-9
- Smyly F.P 1879
- Worlledge A.C No clasp

2nd LIEUTENANT
- Armitage P.T 1879
- D'Aguilar L.G.H No clasp
- Dobre L.G.L 1879
- Franklin R.W 1879
- D/S 20/2/1879
- Hare T.L No clasp

SUB LIEUTENANT
- Griffith **KIA** T.L 1877-8-9

SCHOOL MASTER
- James J 1877-8

SERGEANT MAJOR
- 765 Hogan W.E 1877-8-9

BAND MASTER
- 1777 Bullard **KIA** H.T 1879

DRUM MAJOR
- 2188 Foote J.P 1877-8-9

COLOUR SERGEANT

2459	Bourne DCM	F	1877-8-9
1480	Byrne	G	1877-8-9
*605	Curthbert	J	1877-8-9

D/S 12th March 1879 Rorke's Drift

2001	Essex	J	1877-8-9 r
2131	Gittins	J	1877-8-9
1677	Hamelin	W	1877-8
2336	Lockyer	G	1877-8-9
2408	Roper	C	1877-8-9
430	Ross	A	1877-8-9
1504	Scott	T	1877-8-9
847	Taylor	W	1877-8-9

ARMOURER SERGEANT
- 2075 Duffield J 1877-8-9

COOK SERGEANT
- 1416 Chew **KIA** C 1877-8-9

PAY SERGEANT
- 1165 Hayler H 1877-8-9

PIONEER SERGEANT
- 2219 Morgan J 1877-8-9

SERGEANT INSTRUCTOR OF MUSKETRY
- 1477 Gromley M 1877-8-9

QUARTERMASTER SERGEANT
- 1689 Davis **KIA** G 1877-8-9

SERGEANT

1619	Allen	H	1879
2371	Burrows	W	1877-8-9
1367	Cann	C	1877-8-9
927	Carse **KIA**	H	1877-8-9
949	Chute	J	1877-8-9
1283	Coffey	J	1877-8-9
2835	Curtis	R	No clasp
2117	Daley	E	1877-8-9
2457	Davis	H	1877-8
582	French	J	1877-8-9
81	Gallagher	H	1877-8-9
1227	Harrison	B	1877-8-9
2055	Henry	T	1877-8-9
1064	Hick	T	1877-8-9
1518	Hicks	G	1877-8-9
1580	Hicks	G.H	1877-8-9
2340	Howes	J	1877-8-9
556	Jones	R	1877-8-9
477	Lacey	P	1877-8-9
2227	Lines **KIA**	J	1877-8-9
623	Maxfield	R	1877-8-9

Killed at Rorkes Drift whilst delirious from fever.

653	Mc Donagh	J	1877-8-9
1440	Mooney	A	1877-8-9
2817	Morley	J	No clasp
1174	Morley	W	1877-8-9
2845	Murray	T	No clasp
1932	Neilson	R.McA	1877-8-9
1502	Nokes	J	1877-8
2670	Redmond	H.F	No clasp
975	Rees	E.L	1877-8-9
1078	Reeves **KIA**	J.W.G	1877-8-9
50	Ross **KIA**	J	1877-8-9
2089	Rouston	W	1877-8-9
2336	Shaw **KIA**	G	1877-8-9
1387	Smith	G	1877-8-9
1680	Stratton	A	1877-8

D/S 3/4/1878.

82	Taylor	G	1877-8-9
2069	Taylor	J	1877-8-9
?	Tigar	J	1877-8-9
2407	Twiggs	C	1877-8-9
2146	Walsh	L	1877-8-9
889	Wilkins **KIA**	G	1877-8-9
735	Windridge	J.L	1877-8-9
1152	Yapp	H	1877-8-9

Dixon's Gazette No41 Spring 2005. I clasp, 1877-8. Engraved in a contemporary style. Captain J.F. Caldwell, 2/24th Foot. Major John Fletcher Caldwell born 5.10.1840 at London. Ensign 28.5.1858; Lieut 15.11.1861; Captain 30.10.1866; Major 23.1.1879; Lieut Col 1.7.1881; Colonel 1.7.1885; Half Pay 12.7.1892. Retired circa 1898. Adjutant 1st Bn 24th Foot 16.1.1866 - 29.10.1866; Commanded 2nd Bn South Wales Borderers 9.6.1882 - 9.6.1886. Commanded 27th Regimental District, Omagh, Ireland 12.7.1887 to 12.7.1892. Served in South Africa 15.2.1878 - 11.1.1879 W076/233, including the Kaffir War 1877-78, present at Perie Bush. Married 5.10.1875 Elizabeth Jane Carter at Dover. EF £2400.00

2/24th Regiment

LANCE SERGEANT

No.	Name	Initial	Clasp
2771	Allen	H	No clasp
1217	Heigh **KIA**	J.S	1877-8-9
763	Hiscock	W	1877-8-9
*1067	Jones	D	1877-8-9
	D/S 10th March 1879. Rorke's Drift		
613	Jones	E	1877-8-9
2389	Key	J	1877-8-9
1755	Mc Caffery **KIA**	P	1877-8-9
1230	Peek	R	1877-8-9
652	Powis	E	1877-8-9
1328	Williams	J	1877-8-9
	D/W 25/1/1879 (Rorke's Drift)		

CORPORAL

No.	Name	Initial	Clasp
958	Adams	E	1877-8-9
1404	Adams	W	1877-8-9
1174	Allridge	J	1877-8-9
1249	Aldridge	W.H	1877-8-9
1240	Allen VC	W.W	1877-8-9
	His VC was for the Defence of Rorkes Drift.		
616	Andrews	H	1877-8-9
2452	Bassage	J	1877-8-9
1807	Beech	W	1877-8-9
2836	Breen	F	No clasp
2683	Bell	J	No clasp
1117	Bonner	A.A	1877-8-9
2039	Brown	H	1877-8-9
2364	Challons	W	No clasp
729	Cleaver	C	1877-8-9
733	Cronin	D	1877-8-9
1237	Davies	G.O	1877-8-9
772	Davis	L	1877-8-9
	D/S 30/4/1878		
1069	Davis	T	1877-8-9
2701	Dixon	T	No clasp
	No medal Deserted.		
595	Donoghue	J	1877-8-9
981	Donoghue	J	1877-8-9
917	Dunsford	F	
	No medal Deserted.		
1691	Ellis	E	1877-8-9
2241	Fowler	C	1877-8-9
661	Friend	G.H	1877-8-9
2717	Frost	E	No clasp
2095	Golding	J	1877-8-9
2762	Goodman	T	No clasp
1268	Greenhill **KIA**	W	1877-8-9
2756	Gully	P	No clasp
	No Medal Deserted.		
1228	Haggatta	W	1877-8-9
1282	Halley	W	1877-8-9r
1323	Harding	J	1877-8-9
1635	Harris	W	1877-8-9
1634	Hayes	R	1879
1248	Henshaw **KIA**	J	1877-8-9
769	Hogan	J	1877-8-9
420	Holland	W	1877-8-9
1244	Ife	T	1877-8-9
2631	Jones	T	No clasp
2118	Knowles	J	1877-8-9r
657	Low **KIA**	J.M	1879
1112	Lyons	J	1877-8-9
1576	Mc Carthy	T	1879
2724	Mc Elligott	J	No clasp
725	Mortlock **KIA**	H	1877-8-9
1970	Neilson	W	1877-8-9
439	Parker	W.C	1877-8-9
1535	Reid	J	1879
849	Saxty	A	1877-8-9
673	Sims **KIA**	G	1877-8-9
2266	Sims	W	1877-8-9
2098	Sinley	W	1877-8-9
1139	Smart	J	1877-8-9
757	Smith	W	1877-8
2399	Smithies	J	No clasp
1841	Supple	W	1877-8-9
1111	Thomas	E	1877-8-9
793	Thomas	E	1877-8-9
1103	Thompson **KIA**	T	1877-8-9
752	Trevethen	R.H	1877-8-9
2396	Vaughan	H	1877-8-9
2638	Vousden	G	No clasp
1936	Wales	H	1877-8
1226	Whitely	T	1877-8-9
2179	Woolley	O	1877-8-9

LANCE CORPORAL

No.	Name	Initial	Clasp
2184	Barnes	H	1877-8-9
2350	Bushe	J	1877-8-9
	Wounded 25/1/1879 (Rorke's Drift)		
2352	Delahunty	P	1877-8-9
2352	Ellsworth	H	No clasp
929	Elvey **KIA**	J	1877-8-9
771	Fortune	N	1877-8-9
*1605	Frowen(Freeman)	C	1879
	D/S 12th March 1879 Rorke's Drift		
*1046	Haslam	T	1877-8-9
	D/S 18th March 1879 Rorke's Drift		
852	Hodgson	F	1879
2805	Jeffreys	J	No clasp
1585	Mason	C	1879
2710	Mc Gregor	D	No clasp
1760	Morton	W	1879
2655	O'Keefe	T	No clasp
2700	Scott	T.M	No clasp
535	Sykes	W	1877-8-9
2251	Webb	H	No clasp
1271	Woodford	A	1877-8-9

ORDERLYROOM CLERK

No.	Name	Initial	Clasp
1153	Sutton	W	1877-8-9

BOY

No.	Name	Initial	Clasp
1491	Gordon **KIA**	O	1877-8-9
1494	Gurney **KIA**	J	1877-8-9
1387	Mc Ewan **KIA**	J	1877-8-9

DRUMMER

No.	Name	Initial	Clasp
2161	Anderson **KIA**	J	1877-8-9
1624	Bicknell	W	1877-8-9
2402	Black	A	1877-8-9
540	Chute	J	1877-8-9
487	Coupe	G	1877-8-9
3	Doyle	G	1877-8-9
1713	Galgey	P	1877-8-9
910	Hale	H	1877-8-9
638	Healey	T	1877-8-9
2153	Holmes **KIA**	J	1877-8-9
1342	Hughes	E	1877-8
1428	Jones	E	1877-8-9
2381	Keefe	J	1877-8-9
1731	Manley	J	1877-8-9
2158	Mc Nulty	J	1877-8-9
2383	Meehan	J	1877-8-9
1068	Murphy	E	1877-8-9
1460	O'Gorman	J	1877-8-9
2387	Stevens	E	1877-8-9
1939	Sweeney	W	1877-8-9
2398	Woods	W.G	1877-8-9

PRIVATE

No.	Name	Initial	Clasp
2735	Abraham	G	No clasp
1492	Adams	G	1877-8-9
2736	Adams	G	No clasp r
987	Adams	R	1877-8-9
	KIA (Rorke's Drift)		
1321	Alabaster	E	1877-8-9
2742	Allen	C	1879
1266	Allen **KIA**		1877-8-9
2258	Allen	M	1877-8-9
911	Allen	W	1877-8-9
2626	Almond	E.J	No clasp
2622	Anderson	A	No clasp
1194	Anderson	P	1877-8-9
2769	Archer	C	No clasp
1229	Argent	H	1877-8-9
913	Ashton	J	1877-8-9
1300	Atkins	A	1877-8-9
2725	Baggs	J	1879
2699	Baigent	H	1877-8-9
2025	Bailey	B	1877-8-9
2830	Bailey	G	No clasp
1711	Bailey	J	1877-8-9
2416	Baker	G	1877-8-9
608	Baker	H	1877-8-9
2733	Baker	T	No clasp
	No Medal Deserted.		
1724	Baker	W	1879
2380	Ball	H	1877-8-9
2660	Banan	H	No clasp
1828	Barber	J	1877-8-9
2681	Barkley	R	No clasp
2366	Barlow	T	No clasp
759	Barnett	J	1877-8-9
2402	Barr	W	No clasp
2718	Barron	A	No clasp
	No Medal Deserted.		
1324	Barry	J	1877-8-9
1381	Barry	T	1877-8-9
1091	Barter	J	1877-8-9
1379	Bartlett	J	1877-8-9

2/24th Regiment

1142	Barton	**KIA**	J.W	1877-8-9	880	Brien	W	1877-8-9	2844	Carmody	A	No clasp
2336	Barton	T		No clasp	2053	Brierly **KIA**	J.P	1877-8-9	609	Carpenter	W	1877-8-9
2846	Beard	W		No clasp	1004	Brind	W	1877-8-9	915	Carr	M	1877-8
1471	Beavan **KIA**	S		1877-8-9	1294	Brindle	G	1877-8-9	No Medal Deserted.			
902	Beecher	J		1877-8-9	895	Brockhurst	G	No clasp	1336	Carrol **KIA**	T	1877-8-9
925	Bell	G		1877-8-9r	960	Broderick **KIA**	M	1877-8-9	2785	Carter	J	No clasp
1566	Bell	J		1879	981	Bromwich	C	1877-8-9	1665	Casey	J	1879
2737	Bell	W.H	No clasp r		1524	Bromwich	J	1877-8-9	412	Cassidy	J	1879
2831	Benford	C.S		No clasp	1271	Bromwich	W	1877-8-9	1317	Catchpole	E	1877-8-9
2651	Bennett D/S	E		No clasp	1536	Brooks D/S	W	1879	1352	Challis	W	1877-8-9
1413	Bennet **KIA**	T		1877-8-9	731	Brooks	W	1877-8-9	1275	Chard	T	1877-8-9
1461	Bennett	T		1877-8-9	2732	Brown	G	No clasp	1510	Charles **KIA**	W	1879
918	Bennett	W		1877-8-9	2772	Brown	G	No clasp	1453	Charten	O	1877-8
No Medal Deserted.					1002	Brown	J		1598	Cherry **KIA**	F	1877-8-9
1559	Beresford	J		1877-8	Forfeited. No reason given. No trace of the return of the medal.				1241	Chester	T	1877-8-9
No Medal Deserted.									1335	Chick	J	1877-8-9
1693	Berry	J		1879	1406	Bryan D/S	J	1877-8-9	**KIA** (Rorkes Drife)			
No Medal Deserted.					877	Bryant	E	1877-8-9	1208	Churchill	J	1877-8-9
1287	Bessell	W		1877-8-9	1177	Bryant **KIA**	W	1877-8-9	1418	Churchill	J	1877-8-9
1003	Biby	W		1877-8-9	1402	Buck	W	1877-8-9	No Medal Deserted.			
1718	Biddle	J		1879	959	Buckley	D	1877-8-9	2183	Chute	R	1877-8-9
2711	Billsborough	T		No clasp	517	Buckley **KIA**	R	1877-8-9	1113	Clarke	G	1877-8-9
1596	Bird	W		1879	2708	Buckley	R	No clasp	1556	Clarke	J	1879
1550	Bishop **KIA**	H		1870	1184	Buckley	T	1877-8-9	1265	Clarke	J	1877-8-9
2099	Blackwell	J		1877-8	Duplicate medal and clasp issued 5/7/1924.				2686	Clarke	J	No clasp
No Medal Deserted.									1716	Clarke	J	1879
2820	Blakemore	A		No clasp	988	Buddell	J	1877-8-9	755	Clayton D/S	T	1877-8-9
2372	Blood	G		No clasp	1622	Bull	J	1879	2712	Cleary	J	No clasp
2731	Blount	W		No clasp	1262	Bull **KIA**	T	1877-8-9	723	Cleary **KIA**	M	1877-8-9
2427	Bly	J		1877-8-9	846	Burgess	G	1877-8-9	835	Cleary	M	1877-8
2658	Blythe	T		No clasp	1675	Burgon	A	1879	1361	Clements	W	1877-8-9
2217	Bolsson	F		1877-8-9	2873	Burgon	S	No clasp	2669	Clifford	R	No clasp
2840	Bolitho	J		No clasp	1246	Burke	P	1877-8-9	2653	Clifford	W	No clasp
2813	Boult	A		No clasp	2344	Burke	T	1877-8-9	No Medal Deserted.			
1451	Boulter	W		1877-8	2802	Burke	T	No clasp	1459	Cole	R	1877-8-9
D/S 20/7/1878.					1220	Burke	T	1879	801	Cole	T	1877-8-9
1277	Bowen	J		1877-8-9	2750	Burns	J	1879	**KIA** (Rorkes Drift)			
2397	Boyd	T		No clasp	602	Burton	J	1877-8-9	2371	Collins	J	No clasp
2697	Boyle	G		No clasp	2691	Burton	J	No clasp	102	Collins	M	1877-8
1144	Boyle	J		1877-8-9	1199	Butler	F	1877-8-9	**KIA** 7/4/1878 Tutu Bush.			
D/S 1878. Should have clasp 1877-8.					2841	Butterly	J	No clasp	1396	Collins	T	1877-8-9
2709	Boyle	J		No clasp	1500	Byard **KIA**	A	1877-8-9	2111	Conboy	E	1877-8-9
2734	Bradbury	A		No clasp	721	Byrne **KIA**	J	1877-8-9	2828	Connell	J	No clasp
No Medal Deserted.					1671	Byrne **KIA**	J	1877-8-9	906	Connolly	J	1877-8-9
2393	Bradbury	A		No clasp	2671	Byrne	J	No clasp	2719	Connolly	T	No clasp
2393	Bradley	J		1877-8-9	2420	Caine	P	1877-8-9	1448	Connolly	W	1877-8-9
831	Bradley	J.L		1877-8 r	1107	Callaghan	J	1877-8-9	2310	Connors	A	1877-8-9
D/S 14/8/1878.					1528	Callan	J	1879	1321	Connors	T	1877-8-9
1264	Brady	J		1877-8-9	1181	Camp	W.H	1877-8-9	1340	Cook	G	1877-8
1048	Brailsford	J		1877-8	2692	Campbell	J	No clasp	No Medal Deserted.			
D/S 28/11/1878.					2652	Campbell	P	No clasp	1125	Cook	J	1877 8 9
854	Bray **KIA**	A		1877-8-9	No Medal Deserted.				1501	Cook	J	1877-8-9
897	Bray	T		1877-8-9	2763	Campion	S	No clasp	1319	Cooper	G	1877-8-9
2758	Braysford	C		No clasp	1343	Cannon	R	1877-8-9	12	Cooper	W	1877-8-9
2677	Brennan	J		No clasp	1189	Canty	J	1877-8-9	2453	Cooper	W	1877-8-9
2829	Brice	W.H		No clasp	1944	Care	F	1877-8-9	124	Coote	E	1877-8-9
768	Bridgeman	A		1877-8-9	1156	Careless	A	1877-8	2384	Cope D/S	F	1877-8-9
1141	Bridgewater **KIA**	F		1877-8-9	D/S 6/6/1878.				1503	Corke	J	1877-8-9
1360	Brien	D		1877-8-9	870	Carey	M	1877-8-9	819	Cornish **KIA**	T	1877-8-9

2/24th Regiment

1048	Cotter	J	1877-8-9	1697	Dick	W	1877-8-9	1012	Evans	D	1877-8-9
2755	Cotter	M	No clasp	1634	Dicks	W	1877-8-9	2259	Evans	D	No clasp
1539	Coughlan	J	1879	1171	Diggins	P	1877-8-9	953	Evans	F	1877-8-9
2812	Cox	J	No clasp	2885	Dillon	J	No clasp	1389	Evans **KIA**	J	1877-8-9
2810	Crane	T	No clasp	1227	Dinelli	R.L	1877-8-9	1582	Evans	J	1879
2811	Cripps	W	No clasp	\multicolumn{4}{l}{No Medal Deserted.}	701	Evans	M	1877-8-9
1149	Cronin	M	1877-8-9	1341	Dixon	J	1877-8-9	936	Evans	P	1877-8-9
1529	Cronin	T	1879	2884	Dodds	D	No clasp	1553	Evans	R	1879
\multicolumn{4}{l}{D/S 24/1/1879.}	1081	Dodds	W	1877-8-9	954	Evans	T	1877-8-9
2661	Crundle	W.H	No clasp	2674	Doherty	P	No clasp	2753	Evans	W	No clasp
2614	Cullen	A	1879	1026	Donegan **KIA**	M	1877-8-9	969	Fagan	J	1877-8-9
732	Culley	F	1877-8-9	2843	Donovan	D	No clasp	\multicolumn{4}{l}{**KIA** (Rorkes Drift)}
1124	Cummins	L	1877-8-9	2695	Donovan	J	No clasp	810	Fagge	E	1877-8-9
2752	Curten	C	No clasp	2371	Donovan	T	No clasp	1041	Farr **KIA**	A	1877-8-9
\multicolumn{4}{l}{No Medal Deserted.}	2759	Doogan	J	No clasp	1407	Farr	J	1877-8-9
2633	Daley	T	No clasp	1930	Doran	J	1877-8-9	\multicolumn{4}{l}{D/S 5/3/1879.}
1477	Dancer	R	1877-8	1544	Dorrell D/S	A	1879	1110	Farr	J	1877-8-9
\multicolumn{4}{l}{No Medal Deserted.}	872	Dowle **KIA**	J	1877-8-9	1408	Farr	W	1877-8-9
2043	D'Arcey	T	1877-8	740	Doyle	C	1877-8-9	2129	Farrell	J	1877-8-9
1714	Darling	J	1879	1966	Doyle	J	1877-8-9	1445	Farrell	P	1877-8-9
1200	Davenport	J	1877-8-9	1275	Drake	W	1877-8-9	1255	Farrow	F	1877-8-9
1290	Davenport D/S	J	1877-8-9	2875	Drane	A.E	No clasp	2766	Fay	J	No clasp
1021	Davies	E	1877-8-9	\multicolumn{4}{l}{No Medal Deserted.}	1278	Featherstone	J	1877-8-9
470	Davies	G	1877-8-9	1533	Driscoll	E	1879	2770	Ferraby	J	No clasp
1031	Davies **KIA**	G	1877-8-9	971	Driscoll	T	1877-8-9	1013	Ferris	T	1877-8-9
1252	Davies	J.R	1877-8-9	1525	Driscoll	T	1879	1877	Finch	G	1877-8
743	Davies **KIA**	J.J	1877-8-9	1114	Driscoll	W	1877-8-9	\multicolumn{4}{l}{No Medal Deserted.}
1164	Davies	W	1877-8-9	2894	Drury	P	No clasp	2394	Finlayson	J	No clasp
965	Davies	W	1877-8-9	\multicolumn{4}{l}{No Medal Deserted.}	2798	Finn	M	No clasp
1492	Davies D/S	W.R	1877-8	2128	Duffy	T	1877-8-9	963	Finn **KIA**	T	1877-8-9
2363	Davis	A	No clasp	1421	Dunbar	J	1877-8-9	2404	Finn	T	No clasp
1414	Davis **KIA**	D	1877-8-9	551	Dunne	J	1877-8-9	\multicolumn{4}{l}{No Medal. Discharged with ignominy.}
1521	Davis	D	1879	2715	Duxbury	J	No clasp	1566	Fisher	W	1877-8-9
121	Davis **KIA**	J	1879	1694	Dwane	D	1877-8-9	1211	Fisher	W	1877-8-9
894	Davis **KIA**	J	1877-8-9	1016	Dwight	W	1877-8-9	2307	Fitton **KIA**	G	1877-8-9
921	Davis	J	1877-8	2729	Eades	W	No clasp	2827	Fitzgerald	J	No clasp
\multicolumn{4}{l}{No Medal Deserted.}	2081	Earish **KIA**	J	1877-8-9	2773	Fitzgerald	M	No clasp
1598	Davis	J	1879	1089	Edmunds	J	1877-8-9	845	Fitzgerald	P	1877-8-9
1555	Davis	J	1879	\multicolumn{4}{l}{No Medal Deserted.}	1519	Fitzpatrick **KIA** M		1877-8-9
1015	Davis D/S	T	1877-8	1397	Edmunds	W	1877-8-9	1369	Flanagan	T	1877-8
833	Davis	W	1877-8-9	1166	Edwards **KIA**	E		\multicolumn{4}{l}{No Medal Deserted.}
1385	Davis	W	1877-8-9	922	Edwards	G	1877-8-9	2615	Flood	J	No clasp
\multicolumn{4}{l}{No Medal Deserted.}	1649	Edwards	G	1879	1600	Flynn	C	1877-8-9
1363	Davis	W.H	1877-8-9	786	Edwards **KIA**	J	1877-8-9	1030	Flynn **KIA**	D	1877-8-9
1178	Daw	E	1877-8-9	1122	Edwards	J	1877-8-9	2222	Flynn **KIA**	J	1877-8-9
2868	Dawson	G	No clasp	2392	Edwards	S	No clasp	1432	Flynn	M	1877-8-9
1489	Day	G	1877-8r	1045	Edwards	W	1877-8-9	1465	Flynn	P	1877-8-9
1611	Day	J	1877-8-9	465	Elliott	T	1877-8-9	1725	Foale	P	1877-8-9
1467	Deacon	G	1877-8-9	926	Ellis	G	1877-8-9	797	Ford D/S	J	1877-8
\multicolumn{4}{l}{No Medal Deserted.}	1534	Ellis	J	1879	1444	Ford	J	1877-8-9
1357	Dean	M	1877-8-9	1302	Ellison	J	1877-8-9	2350	Ford	T	No clasp
\multicolumn{4}{l}{No Medal Deserted.}	1378	Emerson **KIA**	R	1877-8-9	738	Fortune **KIA**	M	1877-8-9
2874	Deighas	T	No clasp	1121	Emmett	R	1877-8-9	1320	Foster	C	1877-8-9
1517	Delaney D/S	G	1877-8-9	1439	English	W	1877-8-9	\multicolumn{4}{l}{D/S 8/3/1879.}
1623	Denman	W	1879	\multicolumn{4}{l}{Deserted but rejoined. No trace of the}	1299	Fowler	P	1879
2809	Devery	J	No clasp	\multicolumn{4}{l}{issue of the medal.}	2877	Fox	J	No clasp
1482	Dew	J	1877-8-9	1577	Enwright	J	1879	1162	Fox **KIA**	T	1877-8-9
\multicolumn{4}{l}{No Medal Deserted.}	822	Etheridge	S	1877-8-9	1450	Francis	J	1877-8-9
1322	Deyene	J	1877-8-9	957	Evans	C	1877-8-9	2642	Freeman	A	No clasp

2/24th Regiment

No.	Name	Initial	Clasp
1274	French	J	1877-8-9
2672	Friar	J	No clasp
2872	Frith	J	No clasp
800	Frowan	J	1877-8-9
2335	Fry **KIA**	J	1877-8-9
1561	Fuge	H	1879
2405	Gearon	W	No clasp
1457	Geaves	B	1877-8
2429	Gee	E	1877-8-9
1771	Gee **KIA**	W	1877-8-9
1588	Gention	G	1879
619	Ghost **KIA**	G	1877-8-9
2714	Gibbins	W	No clasp
1196	Gibbons	W	1877-8-9
637	Gibson	J.P	1877-8-9
2657	Gilbert	G	No clasp
730	Gilkes	H	1877-8-9
2808	Giltings	T	No clasp
1473	Golding	W	1877-8-9
1339	Good	S	1877-8-9
1715	Goodall	H	1879
2768	Goodall	W	No clasp
1251	Gordon	P	1877-8-9
675	Gorman D/S	D	1877-8
1590	Gough	R	1879
1703	Goulding	P	1877-8-9
1116	Grace	D	1877-8-9
2738	Grady	N	No clasp
2781	Graham	W	No clasp
1697	Grainger	W	1879
2730	Grant	T	No clasp
	No Medal Deserted.		
1688	Green	R	1879
1733	Greenwood	H	1879
2623	Grey	P	No clasp r
681	Gribbin	J	1877-8-9
820	Grice	G	1877-8-9
2793	Griffin	D	No clasp
1011	Griffith	D	1877-8-9
1245	Griffith	G	1877-8-9
1702	Griffith	W	1879 r
	See also No. 2439 Pte W. Griffiths 1/29th Rgt.		
1056	Griffiths VC	W.M	1877-8-9
	KIA His VC was awarded for bravery on Little Andaman Island on 7/5/1867.		
2619	Grossart	R	No clasp
773	Groves	J	1877-8-9
1958	Gunning	E	1877-8-9
1767	Guppy	W	1879
2720	Hack	H	No clasp
1272	Hacker **KIA**	S	1877-8-9
735	Hadley	J	1877-8-9
795	Hagan	J	1877-8-9
1258	Haley	P	1877-8-9
1527	Hall **KIA**	B	1879
1636	Hall **KIA**	C	1877-8-9
1260	Hall **KIA**	J	1877-8-9
1297	Hall **KIA**	W	1877-8-9
2775	Halloran	P	No clasp
2848	Hallwood	C	No clasp
1152	Halstead	P	1877-8-9
1310	Hamblin	A	1877-8-9
2685	Hammond	G	No clasp
766	Hancock	J	1877-8-9
1743	Hancock	T	1879
2102	Handley	A	1877-8-9
618	Hankin **KIA**	L	1877-8-9
2695	Hardgrove	E	No clasp
2784	Hardiman	F	No clasp
2747	Harding	A	No clasp
994	Harding	E	1877-8-9
	Duplicate medal and clasp issued 26/1/1925.		
1384	Harding	T	1877-8-9
2627	Harper	D	1879
977	Harrington	T	1877-8-9
1786	Harris	J	1879
2654	Harris	J	No clasp
1062	Harris	J	1877-8-9
1504	Harris	P	1877-8-9
2362	Harrison	C	No clasp
1424	Harrison	W	1877-8-9
1434	Hart	T	1877-8-9 r
1580	Hartley	W	1877-8-9
2632	Hartley	W	1877-8-9
1599	Harnett	W	1877-8-9
2323	Hawkins **KIA**	W	1877-8-9
1769	Hayden	G	1879
	KIA (Rorkes Drift)		
1417	Hayes	J	1877-8-9
2067	Hayes	P	1877-8-9
1447	Hayes	R	1877-8-9
2682	Hayes	S	No clasp
1758	Hayward	T	1879
1219	Healey **KIA**	J	1877-8-9
2370	Healey	T	No clasp
2644	Heath	V	No clasp
2068	Hefferman	J.P	1879
576	Herbert	E	1877-8-9
1309	Herbert	H	1877-8-9
2794	Hewison	J	No clasp
1714	Hewitt	J	1879
1988	Hickey	M	1877-8-9
600	Higgs	H	1877-8-9
2103	Hill	J	1877-8-9
1313	Hill **KIA**	J.E	1877-8-9
1010	Hill	M	1877-8-9
2625	Hill	T	No clasp
1303	Hill	W	1877-8-9
1362	Hitch VC	F	1877-8-9
	VC was for the Defence of Rorkes Drift.		
823	Hitchings	L	1877-8-9
2740	Hobson	T	No clasp
4	Holden	W	1877-8-9
2837	Holland	J	No clasp
1088	Holley	G	1877-8-9
1603	Holloway	W	1879
2496	Holmes	G	1877-8-9
1373	Hook VC	H	1877-8-9
	VC was for the Defence of Rorkes Drift.		
1457	Hope	W.J	1877-8
	No Medal Deserted from 90th Regt. See also 1230 Pte W. Hope 90th Regt.		
1331	Hopkins	J	1877-8-9
887	Hopkins **KIA**	H	1877-8-9
874	Horn	W	1877-8-9
2751	Horn	W	No clasp
866	Horrocks **KIA**	G	1877-8-9
2826	Hourigan	J	No clasp
1633	Houseman	T	1877-8-9
2849	Howell	T.W.A	No clasp
791	Howells **KIA**	R	1877-8-9
1699	Hudson	A	1879
1678	Hudson **KIA**	G	1877-8-9
1546	Hughes	E	1879
1024	Hughes **KIA**	F	1877-8-9
937	Hughes	H	1877-8
1721	Hughes	J	1879
890	Hulse	J	1877-8-9
717	Humphries	G	1877-8-9
1084	Humphries	R	1879
1526	Hunt	J	1877-8-9
1593	Hunt **KIA**	J	1877-8-9
876	Hunt	S	1877-8-9
583	Hurford	J	1877-8-9
1579	Hurlow	T	1879
1698	Hussey	M	1877-8-9
1354	Hynes	J	1877-8-9
2726	Hynes	P	No clasp
1648	Jackson	G	1879
885	Jackson	W	1877-8-9
978	James	A	1877-8-9
1353	James	D	1877-8-9
1710	James	E	1879
2707	James	G	No clasp
	No Medal Deserted.		
1504	James	G	1879
	D/S 23/2/1879.		
1481	James	J	1877-8-9
1201	James	T	1877-8-9
1008	Jarman	J	1877-8-9
1135	Jenkins **KIA**	W	1877-8-9
322	Jenkinson	W	1879
	No Medal Deserted.		
1061	Jobbins	J	1877-8-9
2719	Johnson	W	No clasp
1125	Johnstone **KIA**	W	1877-8-9
928	Jones	A	1877-8-9
1097	Jones **KIA**	A	1877-8-9
1746	Jones D/S	A	1879
940	Jones	A	1877-8
	D/S 24/7/1878.		
1059	Jones	C	1877-8-9
1253	Jones	C	1879
53	Jones	D	1879
983	Jones **KIA**	E	1879

2/24th Regiment

1595	Jones	E	1879	2689	Kinsella	P	No clasp r	541	Lyons	M	1877-8-9
1537	Jones	G	1877-8-9	2786	Kinsey	T	No clasp	2394	Lyons	M	1877-8-9
948	Jones KIA	J	1877-8-9	2392	Kremer	G.F	1877-8-9	2017	Lyons D/S	W	1877-8-9
970	Jones	J	1877-8-9	1386	Kiley	M	1877-8-9	671	Machin KIA	J	1877-8-9
1179	Jones	J	1877-8-9	974	Krinks	R	1877-8-9	1197	Mack KIA	J	1877-8-9
1403	Jones	J	1877-8-9	2673	Kyle	W	No clasp	1327	Maggs	C.H	1877-8-9
1009	Jones	J	1877-8-9	1332	Lacey	C	1877-8-9	2687	Maher	P	No clasp
1762	Jones	P	1879	2806	Lampard	W	No clasp	2892	Mahoney	J	No clasp
716	Jones VC	R	1877-8-9	980	Landdrey	L	1877-8-9	1431	Mahoney	J	1877-8-9
VC was for the Defence of Rorkes Drift.				836	Lane	D	1877-8-9	1050	Malley KIA	E	1877-8-9
844	Jones	R	1877-8-9	2825	Lane	J	No clasp	1551	Manahan	L	1879
1034	Jones	R	1877-8-9	2662	Langridge	G	No clasp	446	Manley	M	1877-8-9
1017	Jones	S	1877-8-9	654	Latham KIA	B	1877-8-9	1376	Mann	J	1877-8-9
976	Jones KIA	T	1877-8-9	2891	Laver	A	No clasp	2694	Mariner	C	No clasp
*1146	Jones	T	1877-8-9	1425	Lawton	J	1877-8-9	1478	Marney	D	1877-8-9
D/S 10th March 1879 Rorke's Drift				1115	Leary	M	1877-8-9		No Medal Deserted.		
1382	Jones KIA	T	1877-8-9	1773	Lee	J	1879	1349	Marsh KIA	J	1879
1511	Jones KIA	T	1879	2640	Lee	J	No clasp	964	Marshall	J	1877-8-9
1513	Jones	T	1879	2629	Lemond D/S	A	No clasp	756	Martin	H	1877-8-9
593	Jones VC	W	1877-8-9	985	Leon	E	1877-8-9	898	Martin	R	1877-8-9
VC was for the Defence of Rorkes Drift.				758	Leonard	G	1877-8-9	1496	Martin	T	1877-8-9
804	Jones KIA	W	1877-8-9	941	Leonard	J	1877-8-9	2434	Martingale KIA	E	1877-8-9
956	Jones	W	1877-8-9	2787	Leonard	P	No clasp	1284	Mason	C	1877-8-9
1549	Jones	W	1879	1259	Lewis	C	1877-8-9	838	Mason	W	1877-8-9
1223	Jordan	L	1877-8-9	963	Lewis	D	1877-8-9	2807	Mater	G	No clasp
1426	Jordan	W	1877-8-9r	1532	Lewis KIA	E	1879	2739	Mathieson	F	1879
2437	Judge	P	1877-8-9	1507	Lewis	E	1877-8-9	1593	Matthews	L	1879
2704	Kaine	F	No clasp	1499	Lewis	H	1877-8-9	1441	Maxwell	J	1877-8-9
156	Kaine	M	1877-8-9r	1957	Lewis KIA	J	1877-8-9	143	Maynard	W	1877-8-9
2134	Kavanagh	M	1877-8-9	626	Lewis	O	1877-8-9	2620	Mc Arthur	D	No clasp
1614	Keall	W	1877-8-9	1087	Lewis	R	1877-8-9	2702	Mc Beth	W	No clasp
1675	Keane	J	1877-8-9	1565	Lewis	T	1879	1225	Mc Caffrey KIA	P	1877-8-9
972	Kears	P	1877-8-9	1562	Lewis	W	1879	2616	Mc Cann	J	No clasp
802	Keating	D	1877-8-9	1337	Lewsly	D	1877-8-9	2727	Mc Carthy	C	No clasp
2801	Keefe	D	No clasp	1560	Libby	T	1879	1548	Mc Carthy	D	1879
1207	Keefe	W	1877-8-9	634	Light	W.H	1877-8-9	2650	Mc Carthy	D	No clasp
832	Kelly	A	1877-8-9	1528	Lines	H	1877-8-9	2276	Mc Cormack KIA	J	1877-8-9
2400	Kelly KIA	J	1877-8-9	1458	Lindsay	W	1877-8-9	1458	Mc Cracken KIA	S	1877-8-9
2757	Kelly	J	No clasp r	2679	Lindsay	W	No clasp	2878	Mc Donald	J	No clasp
901	Kelly	T	1877-8-9	70	Llewellyn KIA	J	1877-8-9	1427	Mc Donald	J	1877-8-9
2406	Kelly	T	No clasp	1409	Lloyd	D	1877-8-9	2893	Mc Donnell	W	No clasp
474	Kelly	W	1877-8-9	984	Lloyd	J	1877-8-9	1221	Mc Doon KIA	G	1877-8-9
2776	Kenealy	T	No clasp	1022	Lloyd	J	1879	1212	Mc Farlane	W	1877-8-9
2367	Kennedy	A	No clasp	2046	Lloyd	S	1877-8-9	2635	Mc Ganley	J	No clasp
2135	Kennedy	J	1877-8	1119	Lloyd	W.J	1877-8-9	2834	Mc Goldrick	J	No clasp
2764	Kennedy	J	No clasp	1176	Lockhart	T	1877-8-9	83	Mc Gowan	L	1877-8-9
1205	Kennedy	T	1877-8-9	896	Lodge	J	1877-8-9	1155	Mc Gowan	T	1877-8-9
1707	Kennedy KIA	T	1877-8-9	1304	Lodge	J	1877-8-9	668	Mc Grath	O	1877-8-9
1764	Kenney	J	1879	1768	Loft	J.C	1879	2202	Mc Guigan	F	1877-8-9
2690	Kerr	A	No clasp	1054	Logan	J	1877-8-9	2369	Mc Guin	J	No clasp
2417	Keurn	R	1877-8-9	762	Long KIA	C	1877-8-9	1388	Mc Guire KIA	J	1877-8-9
1710	Kew	J	1877-8-9	1334	Londsdale	F	1877-8-9	2803	Mc Guire	J	No clasp
2783	Kid	T	No clasp	1466	Lovell	A	1877-8-9r		No Medal Deserted.		
2757	Kielly	J	No clasp	2777	Lucas	W	No clasp	2713	Mc Kenzie	G	No clasp
2890	Kinchenton	D	No clasp	1000	Lye	F	1877-8-9	2703	Mc Lean	T	No clasp
1057	King KIA	J	1877-8-9	942	Lynch	T	1877-8-9		No Medal Deserted.		
2842	King	M	No clasp	1273	Lynch KIA	T	1879	2684	Mc Loughlin	H	No clasp
1516	King	P	1877-8-9	1743	Lyons	A	1877-8-9	2407	Mc Loughlin	J	1879
1224	King	T	1877-8-9	1441	Lyons	J	1877-8-9	2792	Mc Manus	E	No clasp

Letters from South Africa

Letters from South Africa

Editors of newspapers were not always accurate in their printing of soldiers' letters. The Bristol Observer misspelt both Corporal Samuel Wiles and a Sergeant W. Morley of the 2/24th. With Corporal Samuel Miles and Sergeant W Maule, mistakenly transcribed by the editor. They quite often mixed up similar sounding names and also managed to print accounts of some soldiers, who had never been present at Isandlwana or Rorke's Drift. It is important to corroborate such material against other historical sources. The majority of letters were often frank and accurate, and have a part to play in our understanding of conditions, under which they lived, worked, and fought during the arduous campaigns in South Africa. Censorship did not apply to the Victorian soldier, one of their main concerns were to allay any fears that their love ones may have gleamed from the newspapers at home. A.R. Skelley gives some figures about army education in his book 'The Victorian Army at Home' Military sources claim that 42,7 per cent of the rank and file could read and write in 1878. Promotion to corporal required a third-class certificate of education. Soldiers had to attend school for five hours each week in an attempt to improve their education the fourth-class army certificate, was designed to enabled them to draft a letter.

Sir,—Will you kindly publish this letter in your widely circulating paper, trusting it may draw the attention of the postal authorities to their system of charging double rates for postage on all letters delivered coming from troops engaged in the field in South Africa to their friends in England?

Stamps cannot be obtained, and I think it extreme to charge double rates. The Postmaster-General of Cape Colony issued a notice stating all letters coming from troops actually engaged in the field, and being franked by their respective commanding officers, would be free of postage through the colony.

If the Cape postal authorities can do this much for a soldier, I think, at the very least, home authorities could reduce their double rates to single. There was a general order, dated February 16, 1879, stating, "When no stamps are procurable for troops on the field, commanding officers are requested when franking letters to add, 'On active service in the field - no stamps,' as by so doing it is hoped that only single instead of double rates will be charged on delivery."

I feel confident if this matter were fully made known postal authorities would take the intimation, and soldiers' friends at home would be saved great inconvenience during the distressing times.

I am, yours truly,
ONE IN THE FIELD.
Zululand, South Africa, March 18, 1879.

The War in South Africa : Soldiers Letters To the editor of the Daily Post
The Birmingham Daily Post, Tuesday 6th May 1879

Western Mail (Cardiff, Wales), Friday, June 13th, 1879.
House of Commons - Thursday
Letters from Soldiers in South Africa
Mr Oliver Walker asked that letters from soldiers serving in South Africa should not be charged double postage, owing to the difficulty of obtaining stamps at the seat of war.
SOLDIERS' LETTERS.
The public have been gratified with a wry miscellaneous exhibition in our columns of soldiers letters. From the battle field of Isanduls, from Rorke's Drift, from Ekowe. Many are written in blacklead, and, as a correspondent phrased it, on a desk made by a dead Zulu ; and are most of them prefaced with the endorsement, "no stamps ; in the field." They tell of discomforts, of suffering, of clothes and boots unchanged for a month, of no money, of great exposure, of loss of kit. In one respect they all agree—in the feeling of sorrow aroused for the loss of comrades; in one expression of honour they are united—that tensed by the exhibition of death and mangling on the battle. While some of the writers regret most piteously that they ever took the shilling, others agree but one object before them, avenging their comrades. .and sweeping away the stain of defeat from the national banner.

During the British Occupation of 1877 to 1882 South African Republic stamps were overprinted "V.R. Transvaal" or stamps inscibed Transvaal were issued. Stamps of Natal were also issued in Zululand from 1876 till 1st May 1888.

2/24th Regiment

From Private John Morgans, No, 15115, 2-24th Regiment, to his brother.

Natal Colony,
South Africa.
1 February 1879.

.... I am very sorry to tell you that on the 22nd of January 1879 I had a narrow escape of my life, also the regiment. We went out early that morning, before daybreak, to attack the Zulus; we went about sixteen miles from camp and, whilst we were away the Zulus came around the hill and about 7000 of them attacked the camp while we were away looking for them, and they killed about 100 of ours and five companies of the 1-24th Regiment, about 400 men altogether. So when we were coming back to camp, on half way the general came to meet us and he made us to sit down while he was speaking to us. He told us that our camp was attacked by the Zulus and that our men fought like warriors in the camp trying to save it but the Zulus were too strong. ....

1. North Wales Express, 11 April 1879.

From Private Edward Hughes, E Company, 1-24th Regiment, 2nd Division to his parents at 4, Little Crown-street, Caernarvon.

Upoko River.
July 1879

......We have had a very hard time of it but we are now enjoying a few days' ease. We have been up as far as the King's Kraal, Ulundi on the White Umvolosi and after burning all the kraals we came across and knocking the Zulus out of time, have returned to this camp to wait the issue of affairs.

We arrived, after a very hard and tedious march, at the King's Kraal, encamping opposite it on the 1st of July. Nothing of any importance occurred until the 3rd when the Zulus surprised us by opening a smart fire on some of our men who were down at the river getting water. The fire was quickly returned by our men down there on duty. The light cavalry were immediately got ready; 4 nine-pounders were got into position; and it was determined to shift the Zulus out of the place, for as long as they were allowed to remain there, it was evident that we could not get any water without great danger. A couple of shells were, therefore, thrown across the river. This had the effect of making the Zulus scamper off to their kraals at full speed. But our horsemen were waiting for them and chased the enemy as far as their kraals. Our men were obliged, however, to retire for the enemy were reinforced by some thousands. Our loss was slight; that of the enemy considerable. The same night the Zulus kept us awake for nearly two hours singing and shouting in a terrible manner.

Next morning, the 4th, we were all quietly awakened at a very early hour. No bugles sounded and everything was done as quietly as possible. Our men crossed the river and made for the open plain. This movement was quite unexpected by the Zulus, for at seven o'clock about 15,000 of them were seen making for our side of the river; but just at this critical moment our column had reached the open. They were then seen by the enemy who imagined that they had a very easy thing of it. But they calculated wrongly for they were greeted by a tremendous fire from our men as they advanced. Forty-five minutes passed after the first shot, when the Zulus wavered; our men cheered heartily; away went the Zulus as hard as they could run, closely followed by the 17th Lancers who mowed them down like grass.

So ended the battle of Ulundi and with it Cetywayo's power over his people.

Our loss, as near as I can ascertain, was ten men killed and about fifty wounded ....

Source:North Wales Express, 19 September 1879. (25B/2137 Edward Hughes Private in the 1st Battalion)

From Edward Evans of Llawrglyn, near Llanidloes who escaped from Isandula to his mother and brother.

3 February 1879.

You know nothing of the horrors of war and if I was to write from now till Christmas, I could never explain half what I have seen or how I was saved. Myself and two more comrades rode our horses through the centre of their line of fire and hundreds of guns pointing at us; but I can assure you it was a ride for life. Many of our noble heroes that escaped from the hands of the enemy lost their lives in crossing the Buffalo River. Thank God for learning me to swim. My horse fell in the water and both of us went down together and both swam out again---but a very hard struggle. I had to let go my rifle and ammunition and everything I had...

Source: North Wales Express, 11 April 1879.

2/24th Regiment

Letter from an Aberdare Soldier in South Africa. - Western Mail Thursday 27th March 1879
The following letter was received from his son by Mr. Wm. Jones, No. 1a, Albert Street, Aberdare :—
Camp, Lower Tugela, Zululand, Feb. 1, 1879.
Dear Mother and Father,—I now sit down to write you these few lines in answer to your kind and welcome letter which I received from you. I was glad to find that you are all well; thank God for it. Dear mother, I write to tell you that the Zulu war is started, but it has turned out very bad for our troops, for they have fought very bard, and I am sorry to say the Zulus have cut up six companies of the 1-24th Regiment, and one company of our regiment, Poor **Johnny Esley,** he may be cut up for what I know, for it was rumoured it was his company that was cut up. You know Johnny that need to come with me next door to the Crown, and **David Thomas**, of Abernant. Dear mother, I would have wrote to you, only I could not get say paper or stamps, but I got 5s. from my officer to-day. Dear mother, I crossed the Tugela on the 15th of January into the enemy's country, and had a severe engagement on the 22nd, and defeated them, with the loss of 800 of the enemy, who all ran away, and we went after them up country end bivouacked for the night. On the same day the general had another engagement. It was then the British troops were cut up. Dear mother, our column are now at a standstill, waiting for troops from England, before we go any further up into the enemy's country. The troops have built forts and are all in them, waiting for reinforcements; and unless we have more troops sent out soon I think all the men will be killed. Dear Mother, I hope you won't vex for me, because it was my own fault that I came out. If God will spare me—and if not I shall be killed—I will live to come home again. Dear mother, I hope that trade is all right in Aberdare, and that my brothers and sisters are all right. Tell them I hope to see them once again ; if God spares me I will come home after the war is ended. Dear mother, I am a long way from my regiment ; I have not seen my regiment for eight months, and thank God I was from them. I think it was a
Godsend I was from them. I think that Tom Roberts's regiment will Come up here, if it is up to the war strength, and the 4lst will come out, so that they will take part in the war. Give my best respects to little Tom Williams, and to all my comrades. By the time you receive this you will have some severe news in the papers. It would make an Englishman think how Englishmen can fight. There was only 600 English troops to 25,000 of the enemy, and when all our soldiers ammunition was gone, they fought with fixed bayonets, back to back, and never gave in until every man was killed. The Zulus killed 600 soldiers, and before the troops were killed they slew 8,000 of the enemy. It was a fearful sight to see 600 British soldiers lying dead on the plain, killed by savages. get. England will be revenged for all this slaughter, and only think, this is the second time that our regiment has been cut up. Dear mother, when the Commander-in-chief hears this it will make his hair stand. Before the war begun the general sent home for more troops, but he was told that he had enough, and now they find out their mistake, that the Zulus are a stronger and more powerful race of people than they thought. Dear mother, please give my love to Mrs, Williams, Mrs. Roberts, to Edwin and friends, and Mrs. Edmunds, and please give my love to enquiring friends. I will write again soon. Hoping you are well, and may God take care of you is the wish of your loving son,
Joseph Morgan, No 1493, Second Squad mounted Infantry, Col Pearson's Column, Zululand, Natal.   In a following letter the same writer says:- Johnny Esley and Davy Thomas, Abernant, were killed. He himself was in good health and spirits.

Letter from a Pontypool Private - Western Mail Thursday 27th March 1879
Rorke's Drift, Feb. 2nd, 1879.
Dear Father, Sisters, and Brother,- I take the pleasure of writing these few lines to you, hoping to find you all well, as I am, so far, I know what soldering is now. We have marched 200 miles, and haven't had a night's sleep this month. We are in fear every night, and have to fight the Zulus, who came on us and killed 800 of our men. They were about 25,000, and we killed 9,000.
I wish I was back it England again, for I should never leave. It is sad time here, and we are on the watch every night with our belts buckled on and our rifles by our side; It is nothing but mountains, all biscuits to eat. We killed about 10,000 Kaffirs, and they killed about 800 of the 1-24th, and 170 of our men. Dear father, and sister, and brother, good-bye. We may never meet again. I repent the day that I took the shilling. I have seen a bed since I left England. We have only one blanket, and are out every night in the rain - no shelter. Would send you a letter before, but have no time. Good bye, if we never meet again, and may God be with you. Give my kind love to all friends: and how is Billy and Tim?
Yours affectionately,
Henry Moses, Private 24th Regiment.

Ashley Thomas Goatham
A memorial to a young soldier in Bredgar churchyard, Kent "This monument is erected to the memory of Ashley Thomas son of George and Roseanne Goatham who was killed in action 22nd January 1879 aged 24 in the battle of Isandula"

"They stood their ground cool and bold
In that disastrous day
And fought like warriors we are told
Till all were cut away
In memory we shall sacred keep
The men that fell that day
Though far in Zululand they sleep
Their souls have soared away
Upon the golden crowd gazing with eager breath
He fought as one who fain would die
And dying conquered death"

2/24th Regiment

No,1092, Private William Rees Western Mail April 9th 1879   The Letter from another "Missing" soldier
We have received for publication the following letter, which has been received by Mr Hopkin Rees, of Ysyrad Rhondda, from his brother, whose name appeared in the official list of the killed at Isandula :-
Rorke,s Drift, February 20, 1879
Dear Brother, - I now take the pleasure of writing these few lines to you, hoping to find you in good health, as they leaves me at present, thank God for it. Dear brother, I am sorry that I have not write to you before, as I have had not much chance, as we have been on the move ever since we have been in this country. Dear brother, this is to inform you that we have had a very heavy battle, on the 22nd of January, at a place called Isandhl. We were encamped there, and on the morning of the 22nd we marched out to meet the enemy, and we went about ten miles from the camp. We had left five companies 1-24, one company and a half 2-24 and some volunteers to guard the camp, with some of the native infanry, and two guns R.A. About one o'clock we could hear some very heavy firing,and we looked in the direction of the camp. We could see that the enemy had been and attacked it. It lasted for about three hours, and we were ordered into camp about three o'clock. We started at once, and when we were within three miles of the camp the General met us and told us that the enemy had attacked the camp and killed all our men, and distroyed everything, and that we must retake the camp at the point of the bayonet. We reformed up in battle order, and marched on to either take it or fall, and when we came within range the guns started shelling the place, and we took the camp without loss. We stopped there all night, and at daylight next morning I saw one of the dreadfullest sights as ever a man seen. The dead were laying about in all directions, and every white man was cut into pieces, and their intrels cut out. We have heard that the number of the enemy that attacked our camp were between 15,000-16,000, the number of ours was about 900 white men and about 500 blacks, and only about nine white men escaped. The number of our loss is five officers, 10 sergeants, eight corporals, two drummers, 159 privates - total, 184 2-24th; 16 officers, and 403 non-commission officers and men-total, 419 1-24th, and about 69 of the Royal Artillery and two guns, making a total of 672 British soldiers, and about 280 Volunteers and mounted police, and about 350 natives. **Robert Stephens**, from Trealaw, is amongst the dead. Dear brother, please to tell **Rees Evans Cooker** that his son Thomas is alive and well, and sends his best respects to him;and please to give my best respects to Henry Rees and his sons, and Sanders, and all my old friends, and accept the same yourself, from your affectionate brother.
No,1092, Private **William Rees**, F, Company, 2-24th Regiment, Natal, South Africa.
Editors note: 25B/1411 Private William Rees killed at Isandhlwana (Mix up with the names).

Survivors of the 24th Birmingham Daily Post Thursday, February 27, 1879; Issue 6440. The Isandula Disaster,
The following men of the 2-24th Regiment escaped at the battle of Isandula, and are at Helpmakaar :- **Corporal McCann, Bandsman E.Wilson, Privates J.Wilson, W. Parry, J.Power, J.Frances, W.Johnson, H.Grant, and J.Williams,**
Bandsman Bickley also escaped but has since died at Helpmakaar.

Recorded Deaths
Aberdeen Weekly Journal (Aberdeen, Scotland), Monday, February 17, 1879; Issue 7488
Killed in action with the enemy near Rorke's Drift on the Tugela River on the 22 Jan, **Edward Hopton Dyson**, 2nd Lieutenant 24th Regiment, eldest son of Major Dyson, formerly of the 3rd Dragoon Guards.

The Belfast News-Letter (Belfast, Ireland), Tuesday, February 25, 1879; Issue 19804.
Coghill January 22, in the action at Rorke's Drift, South Africa, Nevill Josish Aylmer Coghill, Lieutenant 24th Regiment eldest son of Sir Jocelyn Coghill, Bart of Glen Barrahane, Castletownhend, County Cork, aged 26 years.

The Pall Mall Gazette (London, England), Thursday, February 27, 1879; Issue 4374.
Mostyn, Captain William E, 1st Battalion 24th Regiment, killed in action at Isandula, Tugela River, South Africa, aged 36, Jan 22.

Freeman's Journal and Daily Commercial Advertiser (Dublin, Ireland), Friday, February 28, 1879 William Eccles Mostyn only son of the late Rev. George Thornton Mostyn, M.A, formerly incumbant of St Thomas, St Helen's Lancashire, and also of St John's, Kilburn

The Pall Mall Gazette (London, England), Tuesday, March 4, 1879; Issue 4378.
Degacher, Captain William, 1-24th Regiment, killed in the Battle of Isandula, South Africa, Jan 22,

The Pall Mall Gazette (London, England), Friday, March 7, 1879; Issue 4381
Porteous, Francis P, Lieutenant and Instructor of Musketry, 1-24th Regiment, killed in action at Isandula, S.Africa, aged 31, Jan 22.

Liverpool Mercury etc (Liverpool, England), Friday, March 14, 1879; Issue 9724
Griffith - Jan 22, killed at the battle of Isandula, Zululand, aged 21, Sub-Lieutenant Thomas Llewelyn George Griffith, 2nd battalion 24th regiment, eldest son of the Rev. Thomas Llewelyn Griffith of Penynant, Ruabon, North Wales, rector of Deal, Kent.

Freeman's Journal and Daily Commercial Advertiser (Dublin, Ireland), Friday, March 14, 1879;
Anstey - Jan 22, killed in action at the Battle of Isandula, South Africa, aged 27, **Lieutenant Edgar Olipbant Anstey,** Ist Battalion, 24th Regiment, beloved son of G.A.Anstey, Esq., 103 Harley-Street, Cavendish-square, London, late of Highercombe, South Australia.

2/24th Regiment

Number	Name	Initial	Clasp	Number	Name	Initial	Clasp	Number	Name	Initial	Clasp
1198	Mc Nally	J	1877-8-9	1126	Moss	G.W	1877-8-9	1269	Pitts	W	1877-8-9
1014	Mc Neil	M	1877-8-9	1502	Moulton	E	1877-8-9	2646	Plank	L	No clasp
2774	Mc Shane	C	1879	2782	Mudd	W	No clasp	2639	Polten	E	No clasp
2824	Mc Whinney	A	No clasp	1888	Mulhaney	H	1877-8-9	1731	Ponter	A	1879
1071	Mead	R	1877-8-9	2335	Mullins	T	No clasp	546	Poole	J	1879
1182	Meek	B	1877-8	2360	Mullins	W	No clasp	586	Poole KIA	S	1877-8-9
	D/S 17/6/1878.			1994	Mulroy KIA	P	1879	1669	Poole	W	1877-8-9
1613	Mellsop	J	1877-8-9	1452	Mungeam	J	1877-8-9	1709	Popple KIA	S	1877-8-9
1020	Meredith	W	1877-8-9	1454	Murphy	D	1877-8-9	1463	Potter	R	1877-8-9
1359	Merrick	C	1877-8-9	1068	Murphy	E	1877-8-9	Deserted. No trace of the return of the medal.			
1341	Meskill	J	1877-8	662	Murphy	J	1877-8-9				
Deserted. No trace of the return of the medal.				1977	Murphy	J	1877-8-9	1561	Potter	W	No clasp
				1108	Murphy	J	1877-8-9	2636	Potts	R	No clasp
2491	Midwinter	T	1877-8	1469	Murphy KIA	J	1877-8-9	992	Powell	J	1877-8 r
2754	Miller	L	No clasp	930	Murphy	P	1877-8-9	Forfeited. No reason given.			
737	Mills	G	1877-8	1498	Murray	E	1877-8-9	1309	Powell	J	1877-8
No Medal. Discharged with ignominy.				2833	Mussen	R	No clasp	913	Powell	W	1877-8-9
1527	Minehan	M	1877-8-9	1036	Neagle KIA	T	1877-8-9	2778	Power	J	No clasp
2628	Mitchell	H	1879	2688	Neilson	A	No clasp	2821	Power	J	No clasp
2676	Mitchell	T	No clasp	2645	Newman	H	No clasp	500	Power	T	1877-8-9
1068	Mitchen	J	1877-8-9	809	Neville	T	1877-8-9	1683	Preece	J	1879
1168	Mockler KIA	M	1877-8-9	No Medal Deserted.				860	Prendergast	W	1877-8-9
968	Moffatt	T	1877-8-9	1279	Neville	W	1877-8-9	2400	Preston	E	No clasp
1681	Montgomery	J	1879	991	Niblett	A	1877-8-9	2170	Preston	R	1877-8-9
1128	Montgomery KIA	T	1877-8-9r	1645	Nicholson	B	1877-8-9	945	Price KIA	H	1877-8-9
2634	Monoghan	G	No clasp	1901	Nobes KIA	R	1877-8-9	2163	Price	H	1877-8-9
1748	Monoghan	J	1879	947	Noot	G	1877-8-9	1049	Price	J	1877-8-9
2748	Monoghan	P	No clasp	1314	Norman	T	1877-8-9	1098	Price KIA	J	1877-8-9
2744	Moore	C	No clasp	1257	Norris	R	1877-8-9	1500	Price	J	1877-8-9
726	Moore KIA	F	1877-8-9	2823	O'Brien	M	No clasp	1118	Price	J	1877-8-9
986	Moore	W	1877-8-9	1474	O'Brien	W	1877-8-9	1576	Pritchard KIA	D	1877-8-9
861	Morgan	E	1877-8-9	No Medal Deserted.				822	Probert	J	1877-8-9
1587	Morgan	E	1879	2741	O'Connor	J	No clasp	1586	Probert	L	1879
1606	Morgan	H	1879	1535	O'Connell	M	1877-8-9	1785	Prosser	J	1879
1506	Morgan KIA	J	1877-8-9	2822	O'Dea	P	No clasp	767	Pugh	W	1877-8-9
1101	Morgan	J	1877-8-9	1072	O'Donoghue	J	1877-8-9	No Medal Deserted.			
1515	Morgan	J	1879	1549	O'Keefe KIA	T	1877-8-9	1512	Purnell	G	1879
1079	Morgan	J	1877-8-9	2746	Ormond	W	No clasp	949	Quilford KIA	T	1877-8-9
1493	Morgan	J	1877-8-9	1480	Osborne	W	1877-8-9	1868	Quinn KIA	J	1877-8-9
1589	Morgan	J	1879	2799	Owens	W	No clasp	1419	Quirk	J	1877-8-9
1456	Morgan	L	1877-8-9	69	Pardy	W	1877-8-9	2721	Rankin	W	No clasp
1601	Morgan	T	1879	1722	Parker	H	1879	2816	Rawlings	H	No clasp
1209	Morgan	W	1877-8-9	935	Parker	J	1877-8-9	999	Rawlinson	J	1879
No Medal Deserted.				1263	Parker	T	1877-8-9	2804	Reardon	D	No clasp
788	Morris KIA	A	1877-8-9	2382	Parker	W	1877-8-9	1464	Reardon	J	1877-8-9
1342	Morris	A	1877-8-9	1399	Parry	S	1877-8-9	996	Reddington	P	1877-8-9
525	Morris	F	1877-8-9	783	Parsons	J	1877-8-9	2895	Redmond	J	No clasp
2876	Morris	J	No clasp	693	Partridge	W	1879	1476	Rees	C	1877-8-9
No Medal Deserted.				D/S 3/11/1878.				1032	Rees	J.S	1877-8-9
2788	Morris	J	No clasp	1410	Partridge	W	1879	1447	Rees	R	1877-8-9
631	Morris	M	1877-8-9	1552	Pender	W	1879	1583	Rees	T	1879
1590	Morris	W.H	1877-8-9	1210	Pendred	W	1877-8-9	1567	Rees	W	1879
1412	Morrisey KIA	J	1877-8-9	2398	Perkes	G	No clasp	1092	Rees	W	1877-8-9
1371	Morrison	T	1877-8-9	1134	Perkins KIA	H	1877-8-9	1411	Rees KIA	W	1877-8-9
2668	Morrison	T	No clasp	1509	Petters	W	1879	1674	Reeves	C	1879
1449	Morrissey	J	1877-8-9	1680	Phillips	A	1879	2820	Reeves	J	No clasp
1301	Moreton	R	1877-8-9	1383	Phillips KIA	D	1877-8-9	1782	Regan	J	1879
1740	Morton	A	1877-8-9	2722	Phillips	J	No clasp	2887	Resbridge	F	No clasp
1597	Moses	H	1879	1186	Pitts	S	1877-8-9	692	Rice KIA	W	1877-8-9

2/24th Regiment

Number	Name	Initial	Clasp
2838	Rich	A	No clasp
811	Richards	E	1877-8
D/S 26/6/1878.			
1102	Richards	G.C	1877-8-9
1203	Richards	W	1877-8-9
564	Richards	W	1877-8-9
2850	Richardson	J	No clasp
1222	Ricks D/S	G	1877-8-9
2656	Rigney	J	No clasp
2814	Rimmer	T	No clasp
746	Ritchie	W	1877-8
D/S 12/5/1878.			
781	Roache KIA	J	1877-8-9
1505	Roach KIA	M	1877-8-9
908	Robinson	R	1877-8
D/S 8/7/1878.			
1286	Robinson	T	1877-8-9
2401	Robinson	T	No clasp
2315	Rodley	W	1877-8-9
	No Medal Deserted.		
1018	Rodgers	M	1877-8-9
1682	Rogers	J	1879
2647	Roser	J	No clasp
924	Rosser	D	1877-8-9
815	Rosser	J	1877-8-9
814	Rosser	M	1877-8-9
1402	Rowden	W	1877-8-9
1531	Ruck	J	1879
1065	Ruck	J	1877-8-9
2365	Ruddick	J	No clasp r
Forfeited. No reason given.			
2374	Ruffles	W	No clasp
1333	Rushworth	G.R	1879
1165	Russell	C	1877-8-9
2819	Ryan	T	No clasp
2624	Salley	P	1879
2791	Salmon	J	No clasp
850	Saunders KIA	T	1877-8-9
1298	Saunders	T	1877-8-9
1185	Savage	E	1877-8-9
1074	Savage	M	1877-8-9
2761	Scales	G	1879
1051	Scanlon KIA	J	1877-8-9
KIA (Rorkes Drift)			
2678	Scott	F	No clasp
955	Scott	H	1877-8-9
813	Scott KIA	J	1877-8-9
2867	Scott	J	1879 r
2361	Seagrave	J	No clasp
2404	Sears	A	1877-8-9
1563	Sears	H	1877-8-9
2405	Sears	J	1877-8-9
1770	Semmence	C	1877-8-9
1573	Shallcross	G	1877-8-9
2617	Sharkey	J	No clasp
1267	Sharp	M	1877-8-9
2618	Sharp	T	No clasp
2651	Sharpley	J	No clasp
1293	Shaughnessy	J	1877-8
2144	Shaw	J	1877-8-9
1468	Shaw	W	1877-8
D/S 17/5/1878.			
2723	Sheehan	G	No clasp
779	Sheehan KIA	J	1877-8-9
808	Sheehan	J	1877-8-9
1618	Sherman	G	1877-8-9
2797	Shepherd	A	No clasp
2630	Shepherd	J	1879
914	Shergo	J	1877-8-9
2799	Sheridan	J	No clasp
1508	Sherwood	F	1877-8-9
1169	Sherwood KIA	S	1877-8-9
700	Shewring	W.H	1877-8-9
2847	Shotbolt	C	No clasp
79	Shuttleworth KIA	W	1877-8-9
1338	Silverster	J	1877-8-9
1044	Simpson	R	1877-8-9
	No Medal Deserted.		
895	Slade KIA	H	1877-8-9
789	Slaney	J	1877-8-9
1329	Small	W	1877-8-9
1359	Smart	J	1877-8-9
1487	Smith KIA	C	1877-8-9
1096	Smith KIA	D	1877-8-9
1143	Smith KIA	F	1877-8-9
2745	Smith	G	No clasp
907	Smith KIA	H	1877-8-9
1005	Smith	J	1877-8-9
1056	Smith KIA	J	1877-8-9
1537	Smith	M	1879
912	Smith KIA	P	1877-8-9
1495	Smith KIA	R	1877-8-9
938	Smith	W.H	1877-8-9
1037	Smith	W.P	1877-8-9
1195	Smythe	R	1877-8-9
2767	Southam	F.A	No clasp
2349	Southern	H	No clasp
728	Spiller	T	1877-8-9
1483	Stacey	J	1877-8-9
2888	Stainer	G	No clasp
1075	Stainsby	G	1877-8-9
2004	Stanley	W	1877-8-9
1318	Stanton	A	1877-8-9
2032	Stenton	S	1877-8
D/S 17/4/1878.			
1485	Stevens	E	1877-8-9
D/S 13/4/1878.			
1484	Stevens KIA	R	1877-8-9
777	Stevens	T	1877-8-9
486	Steventon	W	1877-8-9
1423	Stock	W	1877-8-9
2765	Straughan	C	No clasp
	No Medal Deserted.		
1296	Stretch	J	1877-8-9
2779	Strickland	G	No clasp
2649	Strong	T	No clasp
2796	Strudwick	W.H	No clasp
998	Sullivan	D	1877-8-9
1538	Sullivan	J	1879
1558	Sullivan	J	1879
1159	Sullivan	M	1877-8-9
1599	Sullivan	P	1879
1747	Sullivan D/S	T	1879
1693	Sullivan	T	1879
2348	Surridge	H.R	No clasp
990	Sutton	M	1877-8-9r
1028	Tandy	T	1877-8-9
2395	Tarrant	H	No clasp
1812	Tasker	W	1877-8-9
1247	Taylor	F	1877-8-9
973	Taylor D/S	F	1877-8-9
1173	Taylor	J	1877-8-9
1073	Taylor	R	1877-8-9
889	Taylor	T	1877-8-9
719	Taylor	T	1877-8-9
792	Terrett	D	1877-8-9
1392	Terrett	J	1877-8-9
782	Terrett KIA	W	1877-8-9
1059	Thomas	C	1879
1709	Thomas	C	1879
1218	Thomas KIA	D	1877-8-9
847	Thomas	J	1877-8-9
1280	Thomas	J	1877-8-9
1391	Thomas	J	1877-8-9
1415	Thomas	T	1877-8-9
1104	Thomas	T	1877-8-9
939	Thomas	W	1877-8-9
1472	Thomas	W	1877-8-9
Duplicate medal and clasp issued 20/12/1915.			
2643	Thompsett	R	No clasp
1107	Thompson KIA	G	1877-8-9
1394	Thompson	J	1877-8-9
2695	Thompson	W	No clasp
2337	Thompson	W	No clasp
2706	Thompson	W	No clasp
2818	Thornton	T	No clasp
1129	Threlfall	T	1877-8-9
2728	Tillman	J	No clasp
1027	Tinker	T	1877-8
D/S 25/6/1878.			
2698	Tobin	J	No clasp
879	Tobin	M	1877-8-9
641	Tobin	T	1877-8-9
1281	Todd	W.J	1877-8-9
2680	Tolerton	A	No clasp
2373	Tompkins	W	No clasp
2780	Tomlinson	J	No clasp
1315	Tongue	R	1877-8-9
999	Toomey	J	1879
1792	Toomey	T	1877-8-9
951	Treverton KIA	R	1877-8-9
1356	Trotter	J	1877-8-9
2358	Turner KIA	E	1877-8-9
453	Turner	E	1877-8-9
2648	Turner	G	No clasp
1787	Turner	J	1879

2/24th Regiment

1479	Twiggs	E	1877-8-9	1187	Wilcox	W	1877-8-9	* London Gazette 23 May 1879
1581	Tydings	T	1879	No Medal Discharged. Disgraceful				
1057	Vaughan	F	1877-8-9	conduct.				**1/26th (THE CAMERONIAN) REGIMENT.**
2388	Vaughan	G	1877-8-9	1291	Wilkins	C	1877-8 r	
1076	Veale	J	1877-8-9	699	Wilkins	J	1877-8-9	CAPTAIN
653	Vedler **KIA**	T	1877-8-9	537	Wilkinson	J	1877-8-9	Brunker H.M.E 1878-9
2396	Vernon	F	No clasp	2839	Wilkinson	T.W	No clasp	Also had Medal for Abyssinia.
1202	Wade	T	1877-8-9	1085	Williams	C	1877-8-9	
2311	Walker	B	1877-8-9	1243	Williams	D	1877-8	**2/26th (THE CAMERONIANS) REGIMENT**
2038	Walker **KIA**	S	1877-8-9	Deserted. No trace of the return of the				
1497	Wall	J	1877-8-9r	medal.				LIEUTENANT
Convicted of disgraceful conduct.				1462	Williams	D	1877-8-9	Lysons VC H 1879
2815	Wallace	G	No clasp	2368	Williams	E	No clasp	His VC was for Inhlobane 28/3/1879.
744	Walsh	T	1877-8-9	1463	Williams **KIA**	E	1877-8-9	PRIVATE
542	Walton	B	1879	1470	Williams **KIA**	E	1877-8-9	Fowler VC E 1879
No Medal Deserted.				944	Williams	E	1877-8-9	His VC was for Inhlobane 28/3/1879.
2749	Walsh	R	No clasp	1023	Williams **KIA**	E	1877-8-9	
1486	Ward	F.H	1877-8-9	1429	Williams	G	1877-8-9	**27th (INNISKILLING) REGIMENT.**
1035	Ward	G	1877-8-9	987	Williams **KIA**	G	1877-8-9	LIEUTENANT
No Medal Deserted.				1053	Williams	H	1877-8-9	Bayly J.C 1879
1543	Waters **KIA**	E	1879	2637	Williams	H	No clasp	See also Commissariat & Transport Staff.
602	Waters	J	1877-8-9	979	Williams	H.P	1877-8-9	
513	Waterhouse **KIA**	W	1877-8-9	903	Williams	J	1877-8-9	**29th (WORCESTERSHIRE) REGIMENT.**
1123	Watkins	A	1877-8	1594	Williams	J	1879	CAPTAIN
769	Watkins	E	1877-8-9	1430	Williams	J	1877-8-9	Mac Gregor H.G 1879
864	Watkins	G	1879	1374	Williams	J	1877-8-9	Spratt E.J.H 1879
No Medal Deserted.				No Medal Deserted.				See also Commissariat & Transport Staff.
353	Watkins	H	1877-8	1232	Williams	J	1877-8-9	PRIVATE
No Medal Deserted.				1395	Williams VC	J	1877-8-9	2436 Griffiths W 1879
1191	Watkins **KIA**	J	1877-8-9	His VC was for the Defence of Rorkes				See also No. 1702 Pte W. Griffiths
1518	Watson **KIA**	G	1877-8-9	Drift.				2/24 Regt. Medal with no clasp
666	Watts	J	1877-8-9	934	Williams	J	1877-8-9	
No Medal Deserted.				D/S 5/2/1879.				**30th (THE CAMBRIDGESHIRE) REGIMENT.**
1708	Weall	T	1879	1398	Williams	J	1877-8-9	
No Medal Deserted.				**KIA** (Rorkes Drift).				LIEUTENANT
1357	Wearn	W.H	1877-8-9	753	Williams	R	1879	Watson A.G 1879
2641	Webber	A	No clasp	1060	Williams	T	1877-8-9	See also Commissariat & Transport Staff.
1038	Webber	J	1877-8-9	1765	Williams	T	1879	
1163	Weldon	H	1877-8-9	982	Williams	T	1877-8-9	**31st (HUNTINGDONSHIRE) REGIMENT.**
2659	Wells	H	No clasp	1788	Williams	T	1879	
2319	Westbrook	C	1877-8-9	1140	Williams **KIA**	T	1877-8-9	CAPTAIN
2760	Wheller	T	No clasp	1080	Williams	W	1877-8-9	Bayley G No clasp
977	Whetton	A	1877-8-9	1233	Williams	W	1877-8-9	Hart A.F 1879
2621	Whitbread	W	No clasp	2047	Williamson **KIA**	J	1877-8-9	Had Ashanti Medal 1873-4 with clasp
515	White	J	1877-8-9	2254	Willies	M	1877-8-9	Coomassie.
812	White	J	1877-8-9	2596	Wilson	J	No clasp	LIEUTENANT
1132	White **KIA**	J	1877-8-9	1726	Wilson	R	1877-8-9	Reynolds A.S 1879
2795	White	J	No clasp	2234	Windsor	C.E	No clasp	PRIVATE
1466	White	R	1877-8-9	1366	Winters	A	1877-8-9	1259 Hallwood C 1879
794	White **KIA**	T	1877-8-9	508	Winters	E	1877-8-9	
2800	Whitely	R	No clasp	2889	Wittey	T	No clasp	**32nd (CORNWALL) LIGHT INFANTRY REGIMENT.**
2123	Whitmore	W	1877-8-9	1316	Wood	C	1877-8-9	
2705	Whittaker	B	No clasp	2351	Wood	F	No clasp	MAJOR
1178	Whittaker	R	1877-8-9	689	Wood **KIA**	G	1877-8-9	Stabb H.S 1879
D/S 24/1/1879.				1475	Woolley	J	1877-8-9	Had Indian Mutiny Medal
2716	Whitworth	J	No clasp	1070	Worgan	H	1877-8-9	CAPTAIN
1095	Wightman **KIA**	A	1877-8-9	1138	Wright **KIA**	J	1877-8-9	Cherry C.E. de M 1879
2743	Wilden	H	No clasp	1416	Yates	W	1877-8-9	
1312	Wiles	S	1877-8-9	1093	Young **KIA**	E	1877-8-9	

Major-General A.F. Hart-Synnot

465 AN IMPORTANT VICTORIAN C.B., C.M.G. GROUP: **Major-General A. F. Hart-Synnot**, East Surrey Regiment, Commanding Officer of the Irish (or Hart's) Brigade in the Boer War: Nine:
THE MOST HONOURABLE ORDER OF THE BATH (C.B.), Military Division, Companion's breast badge, hallmarked 1887, in gold and enamel, with usual swivel—ring suspension and riband buckle devices, THE MOST DISTINGUISHED ORDER OF ST. MICHAEL AND ST. GEORGE (C.M.G.), Companion's breast badge, in silver-gilt and enamel, with usual swivel- ring and riband buckle devices, Ashantee War, 1873, 1 clasp, Coomassie (Capt., 31st Foot), South Africa, 1877, 1 clasp, 1879 (Captn., 31st Foot), Egypt Campaign, 1882, rev. dated, 1 clasp, Tel-el-Kebir (Major, E. Surr. R.), Queen's South Africa, 1899, 5 clasps, C.C., T. Hts., O.F.S., R. of Lady., Trans. (Maj. Gen., C. B., C.M.G.), King's South Africa, 2 clasps (Maj. Gen., C.B., C.M.G., Staff),. TURKEY, Order of the Osmania, 4th class breast badge, in silver-gilt and enamel and Khedive's Star, dated 1882 (unnamed), the Osmania badge chipped in places but otherwise extremely fine (9)
Estimate; £3,000-3,500

MAJOR-GENERAL ARTHUR FITZROY HART SYNNOT, C.B., C.M.G., the son of Lieutenant-General H. G. Hart (who won fame for establishing 'Hart's Army List'), was born on 4 May 1844 and educated at Cheltenham and the R.M.C. Sandhurst, which he entered in 1858 and from which he was taken away by his father who considered him too young at sixteen. He re-entered in 1864 and passed out again to join the 31st Foot as an Ensign in 1864.

In 1870 he passed first into the Staff College, and two years later passed first out. Fast emerging as a high calibre officer,

Major-General A. F. Hart-Synnot,

he was chosen in 1873 to accompany Sir Garnet Wolseley to the Gold Coast, where he trained up the Sierra Leone Company of Russell's Regiment, which he led throughout the Ashanti War during which he was slightly wounded and was twice mentioned in despatches. In 1874 he was promoted Captain and was present at all the fighting up to the Capture of Coomassie (Medal and clasp). Again on Special Service in 1878-79, he took part in the Zulu War, firstly as Staff Officer to two Battalions of the 2nd Regiment Natal Native Contingent, being present with Pearson's Column at the engagement of Inyezane, then as Staff Officer on the Ekowe relieving column and at the action at Gingindhlovb. Near the Inyezene River on 22 January, as the men of No. 1 Column were finishing their breakfasts, a few Zulus appeared on a spur above Pearson's encampment. Hart and his Company of the N.N.C. was sent after them, but as he reformed his company which had become disordered after crossing a ravine, 'a mass of Zulus suddenly appeared over the crest and began pouring down the spur'. At the sight of the Zulus, Hart's Kaffirs fled into the ravine, 'leaving the European officers and N.C.Os to make a fruitless stand before being swept aside'. Afterwards he served as a Brigade Major and finally as Principal Staff Officer to Clarke's Column. In due course he was again mentioned in despatches and advanced to Brevet Major (Medal and clasp).

He was in South Africa during the First Boer War of 1881 and served on the Staff in Natal. In 1882 he went to Egypt as Deputy Assistant Adjutant and Quarter Master General in the Intelligence Department and took part in the actions of Magfur, Tel-el-Mahuta and Kassassin (9 September), where he was wounded in the arm. He served at the second action of Kassassin and the Battle of Tel-el-Kebir, where he met up with his brother, the Victoria Cross holder, Reginald Hart. He received another mention in despatches and was awarded the Brevet of Lieutenant-Colonel (Medal and clasp; Khedive's Star).

Majia's Hill skirmish - On Wednesday 22nd January A company of Graves' Regiment of Native Contingent was put at the head of the column, and marched from a quarter to half a mile ahead, as part of the advanced guard, and two other companies marched on either side. Hart undertook the direction of these companies. Having stopped the column for Breakfast. Colonel Pearson rode to the head of the Column and noticing Zulu scouts watching from the heights said" Hart, go and make a raid upon those fellows"

The result was an ambush, with **Lieutenants Raines Platterer** and six men dead, and **Lieutenant Webb** and another man wounded. Harts natives had only ten Martini-Henrys between them, and decided to retire.

Pearson on hearing the firing sent **Lieutenant Lloyd** with two guns, a hundred men of the Naval Brigade under **Commander Campbell** and two companies of the Buffs, to help rescue the situation. After a couple of hours of fighting the Zulus dispersed leaving two of the Buffs dead, five more wounded along with seven sailors and two of Barrow's mounted men.

Reference: Letters of Major-General FitzRoy Hart-Synnot : Edited by B.M. Hart-Synnot, The Washing of the Spears, Donald R.Morris

32nd Light Infantry Regiment

LIEUTENANT
Cochrane W.F 1879
See also Natal Native Horse.
PRIVATE
1697 King W 1879

33rd (DUKE OF WELLINGTON'S) REGIMENT.
LIEUTENANT
Jefferson M.D 1879
See also Commissariat & Transport Staff.

35th (ROYAL SUSSEX) REGIMENT.
BREVET MAJOR
Barnes W.R.B No clasp
Also had Medal for S.A. War 1853.
Grattan H 1879

38th (1st STAFFORDSHIRE) REGIMENT.
CAPTAIN
Crofton M.S No clasp
LIEUTENANT
St George A.G No clasp

39th (DORSETSHIRE) REGIMENT
CAPTAIN
Malet T.St L 1879

41st (THE WELSH) REGIMENT.
BREVET LIEUTENANT COLONEL
Wavell A.H No clasp
Also had British and Turkish Crimea Medals.
PRIVATE
2700 Kelly ? No clasp

45th (NOTTINGHAMSHIRE) REGIMENT.
PRIVATE
27B/36 Watson W 1879

47th (LANCASHIRE) REGIMENT
CAPTAIN
Hesketh Sir (Bart) T.G.F 1879

49th (PRINCESS CHARLOTTE OF WALES') (HERTS) REGIMENT.
LIEUTENANT
Heldane H.E 1879
See also Commissariat &Transport Staff.
NO RANK SHOWN
Cloke J 1879
Also had Medal for Crimea.

52nd (OXFORDSHIRE) LIGHT INFANTRY REGIMENT.
LIEUTENANT
Boyle C.J 1879

See also Commissariat & Transport Staff.
Odell W.H 1879
Hutton C.M No clasp
PRIVATE
1181 Flynn J 1879
1558 Wanston R No clasp

53rd (SHROPSHIRE) REGIMENT.
LIEUTENANT
White L.A 1879
See also Commissariat & Transport Staff.
LANCE CORPORAL
Lukin H 1879
(Was Lieut. In Natal Pioneers and 2nd Natal Native Contingent.)

54th (WEST NORFOLK) REGIMENT.
BREVET MAJOR
Gossett M.W 1877-8-9

56th (WEST ESSEX) REGIMENT
MAJOR
Huskisson J.W 1879
Also had Inida General Service Medal (1858)

57th (WEST MIDDLESEX) REGIMENT.
Arrived in Durban on 12th March 1879 and on the 2nd April took part in the defeat of the Zulu at Gingindhlovu, where they helped to repel the first Zulu attack on the right face of the laager. Also took part in the relief of Eshowe, and involved in the occupation of Ulundi, and subjugation of the border tribes of the lower Tugela.
LIEUTENANT
Clarke CB C.M 1879
Also had medal for New Zealand 1861.
MAJOR
Tredennick J.R.K 1879
CAPTAIN
Bicknell H.D 1879
Also had Medal for New Zealand (1863-66)
Collins A No clasp
Dewar G 1879
GiffordLord VC E.F 1879
His VC was awarded in the Ashanti War of 1873-4.
Hughes-Hallett H.F 1879
Hinxman H.C 1879
Marryat H.F No clasp
Matthews C.J 1879
Also had Medal for New Zealand (1865-66)
Moorwood H.F 1879
Weigall A.A.D 1879
CAPTAIN (ATTACHED)
Justice P No clasp
See also 108th Foot.

CAPTAIN & PAYMASTER
Phillips H.W 1879
See also Army Pay Department.
QUARTERMASTER
Wood T 1879
Also had 3 clasp Crimea & Turkish Medal and New Zealand Wars 1860-1866).
LIEUTENANT ADJUTANT
Garstin A.A 1879
LIEUTENANT
Bellers E.V 1879
Bellingham S.E 1879
Blake N.J.R 1879
Graham R.W 1879
Hill A.W 1879
Law R.T.H No clasp
Longe R.D 1879
Lyde M.T 1879
Michel C.B.D 1879
Scott-Moncrieff W.S 1879
Sharpe E.J 1879
Towers-Clark A 1879
Warden C.W 1879
White J.G 1879
2nd LIEUTENANT
Bode L.W 1879
James H 1879
Jones G.G.S 1879
Litton T.E.F 1879
Munro G.T 1879
SERGEANT MAJOR
504 Fillis J 1879
929 Fitzpatrick W 1879
BANDMASTER
50B/624 Coleopy N No clasp
DRUM MAJOR
1145 English J 1879
SCHOOLMASTER
- Eccles J No clasp
COLOR SERGEANT
779 Adair J 1879
566 Allen T 1879
293 Barry M 1879
798 Combie R 1879
1655 Cunningham J 1879
1110 Easter W.R 1879
1187 Farrell J 1879
367 Inglis J 1879
339 Stock E 1879
1475 Wiggington J 1879
1722 Walters A.J 1879
ARMOURER SERGEANT
421 Evans G 1879
215 Glenton T 1879
COOK SERGEANT
378 Golding A 1879
PAYMASTER SERGEANT
1690 Grimsdale H 1879

57th Regiment

PROVOST SERGEANT				50B/116	Driver	J	1879	1321	Murphy	J	1879
50B/115	Spencer	G	1879	1111	Elley	R	1879	1670	Purcell	P	1879
QUARTERMASTER SERGEANT				1732	Fowler	J	1879	50B/281	Sams	G	1879
1132	Miller	S.J	1879	50B/71	Harris	T	1879	PRIVATE			
ORDERLYROOM CLERK				20B/157	Hatton	J	1879	50B/447	Abraham	G	1879
1311	Powles	T	1879	1098	Hill	W	1879	1458	Abrams	C	1879
SERGEANT INSTRUCTOR OF				50B/749	Hurley	W	1879	50B/1928	Acres	C	No clasp
MUSKETRY				50B/737	Lansdowne	H.C	1879	1119	Adams	H	1879
617	Bleet	T	No clasp	1238	Lewis	W	1879	50B/1092	Adlam	A	1879r
SERGEANT				50B/12	Mc Conkey	J	1879	50B/640	Airs	E.W	1879
50B/582	Baty	G	1879	1367	Miller	W.H	1879	50B/176	Alden	W	1879
50B/1922	Bowen	D	No clasp	50B/119	Millward	S	1879	50B/239	Aldersley	P	1879
50B/165	Brind	J	1879	50B/44	Moss	E	1879	50B/193	Alderton	D	1879
1448	Chamberlain	G	1879	50B/220	Nash	E	1879	50B/1300	Aldridge	W	1879
1336	Clark	C	1879	50B/75	Page	S	No clasp	1042	Allam	E	1879
1783	Colborn	H	1879	50B/227	Parsons	H	1879	50B/592	Allen	J	1879
50B/9	Davis	C	1879	50B/191	Perkins	T	1879	50B/1937	Allsop	J	No clasp
810	Deacon ?	J	1879	50B/932	Phillips	H	1879	50B/1859	Ambrose	J	No clasp
50B/166	Dunn	E	1879	50B/235	Phillips	J.R	1879	50B/1233	Anderson	J	1879 r
50B/426	Epps ?	W	1879	50B/255	Reardon	J	1879	Deserted.			
1719	Flan ?	H	1879	50B/492	Roach	M	1879	50B/1833	Angood	C	No clasp
46	Flynn	J	No clasp	50B/280	Roberts	S	1879	50B/1025	Angus	G	1879
153	Fowler	H	No clasp	1731	Rowe	W	1879	50B/1754	Antcliffe	A	1879
50B/201	Grist ?	A	1879	1004	Shaughnefrey	M	1879	1347	Anson	J	1879
1745	Hayes	W	1879	50B/732	Starkey	R	No clasp	50B/195	Appleford	G	1879
50B/396	Howes	R.J	1879	50B/389	West	E.C	1879	50B/422	Archer	G	1879
50B/425	Kelder ?	M	1879	50B/633	White	H	1879	50B/756	Archer	J	1879
Forfeited. No trace of return of the medal.				50B/740	Woollett	W	1879	1825	Archer	R	1879
50B/59	Leask	H	No clasp	LANCE CORPORAL				50B/1944	Armstrong	H	No clasp
50B/184	Mc Gowan	H	1879	50B/793	Bailey	W.B	1879	50B/849	Arnold	R	1879
825	Mc Swiney	J	1879	1729	Barrett	T	1879	50B/395	Arthurs	A	1879
50B/585	Mercer	H.C	1879	50B/617	Bennett	J.R	1879	1182	Arworthy	J.R	1879
1454	Millwood	F	1879	50B/483	Blake	T	1879	50B/893	Ashford	H	1879
50B/357	Morton	J	1879	50B/1016	Chater	W	1879	1495	Atkinson	B	1879
1472	Palmer	F	1879	50B/1126	Daw	T	1879	50B/159	Austin	J	1879
1658	Rigby	J	1879	50B/842	Edwards	W	1879	1425	Austin	J	No clasp
50B/943	Roberts	T	1879	50B/546	Forward	W	1879	50B/1671	Ayliffe	C	1879
912	Rowe	C.J	1879	233	Gatland	A	1879	50B/306	Baggett	C	1879
1650	Smart	J.D	1879	1717	Healey	D	1879	50B/1455	Bailey	F	1879
50B/125	Warren	E	1879	1450	Hick	T	1879	50B/491	Baker	B	1879
621	Walsh	C	1879	1263	Joplin	J	1879	50B/1769	Baker	D	1879
1457	White	H	1879	1171	King	O	1879	50B/1806	Baker	E	No clasp
LANCE SERGEANT				50B/748	Mc Connell	R	1879	50B/914	Baker	J	1879
1799	Burch	J.T	1879	50B/777	Moss	W	1879	50B/473	Baker	W.E	No clasp
50B/148	Cheshire	J	1879	50B/401	Read	G.H	1879	50B/1954	Balbiani	J	No clasp
50B/377	Goud	E.H	1879	1121	Winsor	J	1879	1203	Bale	H	1879
50B/189	Humphrey	E	1879	DRUMMER				1096	Balsdon	J	1879
50B/1	Magin	H	1879	1218	Cast	T.D	1879	1314	Balwin	J	1879
50B/340	Rose	G	1879	1019	Condon	T	1879	1060	Banbury	J	1879r
50B/34	Smart	J	1879	50B/128	Cotton	J	1879	50B/196	Banting	W	1879
50B/602	Warren	E.J	1879	1648	Duff	G	1879	50B/1886	Barber	W	No clasp
CORPORAL				1029	Dyer	J	1879	50B/797	Barham	J	1879
50B/534	Adams	J	1879	50B/558	Ford	P	1879	50B/923	Barker	H	1879
50B/676	Anderson	J.B	1879	50B/657	Gallagher	J	1879	50B/131	Barker	W	1879
50B/315	Brennan	T	1879	50B/268	Kane	J	1879	50B/1742	Barlow	W	1879
50B/238	Cannon	F	1879	1081	Mc Kenzie	J	1879	50B/1327	Barnes	A.W	1879
50B/1963	Coleman	P	No clasp	1407	Moore	M	1879	50B/1871	Barnes	H	No clasp
1068	Copping	H	1879	257	Morley	G	1879	1801	Barrett	T	1879
50B/880	Dampster	J	1879	1038	Morrison	R	1879	50B/237	Barry	J	1879

57th Regiment

497	Barry	R	1879	1764	Buckley	E	1879	50B/230	Claydon	W	1879
1402	Bartlett	C	1879	1436	Bunn	J	1879	1809	Clements	T	1879
50B/169	Bartlett	G	1879	50B/1161	Burke	J	1879r	50B/707	Clench	T	1879 r
Roll shows "Deserted". No trace of				50B/1272	Burke	P	1879	1813	Coffey	J	1879
return of the medal.				1235	Burnell	T	1879	50B/1294	Collins	C	1879 r
50B/1303	Bartley	F	1879	# 333	Burns	E	1879	Forfeited. No reason given.			
50B/555	Barton	S	1879	(see page 270)				1253	Collins	J	1879
1159	Bath	G	1879	1353	Burt	J	1879	1350	Collins	J	1879
20B/136	Bazoni	S	1879	50B/102	Burton	F	1879	50B/258	Collins	P	1879
50B/1283	Beach	E.J	1879	50B/307	Busby	H.E	1879	794	Collins	W	1879
1441	Beaven	S	1879	50B/1208	Butcher	G	1879	50B/1215	Collins	W	1879
50B/1821	Belcher	H	1879	1794	Butcher	T	1879	50B/109	Collinson	B.A	1879
50B/1223	Bell	N	1879	50B/770	Butler	J	1879	50B/149	Collyer	H	1879
50B/1923	Bennett	A	No clasp	50B/495	Byrne	J	1879	50B/944	Comerford	J	1879
50B/112	Bennett	J	1879	50B/279	Cahill	J	1879	No Medal Deserted.			
50B/469	Bennett	W	1879	50B/322	Camp	G	1879	1018	Condon	P	1879
1044	Bennett	W.G	1879	50B/23	Camp	W.F	1879r	50B/1932	Connell	J	No clasp
50B/121	Bignell	W	1879	50B/693	Candelett	T	1879	50B/1933	Connery	J	No clasp
1288	Binnion	G	1879	50B/1766	Cann	J	1879r	900	Connolly	B	1879
50B/898	Bird	T	1879	Deserted.				1718	Connolly	J	1879
Discharged with ignominy. No trace				50B/1062	Cannell	T	1879	854	Connolly	P	1879
of the return of the Medal.				50B/1833	Carberry	J	1879	50B/309	Connolly	P	1879
50B/1053	Birmingham	T	1879	50B/547	Careswell	J	1879r	50B/1330	Connor	F	1879
50B/943	Bishop	W	No clasp	50B/1726	Carmody	A	1879	890	Connor	J	1879
50B/1876	Blady	W	No clasp	50B/1243	Carney	T	1879	50B/905	Connor	J	1879
50B/631	Blay	W	1879	50B/323	Carpenter	D	1879	50B/1805	Conway	J	1879
50B/1248	Bleach	W	1879	50B/856	Carpenter	S	1879	50B/385	Cook	F	1879
50B/358	Bonner	I	1879	50B/7	Carr	A	1879	50B/1901	Cook	G	No clasp
50B/343	Boden	W	1879	738	Carroll	H	1879	1466	Cooper	W.J.J	1879
50B/615	Bocese	T	1879	50B/1890	Carroll	P	No clasp	50B/87	Cooper	W	No clasp
50B/873	Booyshaw	F	1879	50B/72	Carroll	W	1879	50B/983	Copus	J	1879
50B/1817	Bosnan	J	1879	1050	Carter	J	1879	50B/1818	Costello	J	1879r
50B/543	Bourke	J	1879	50B/1900	Carter	J	No clasp	Penal servitude for life.			
50B/232	Bowen	W	1879	50B/779	Carter	W	1879	1673	Cottrell	R	1879
50B/643	Boyd	C.A	1879	Deserted. No trace of return of the medal.				50B/482	Coulson	E	1879
260	Boyle	M	No clasp	50B/1807	Carthy	H	1879	50B/1801	Courtney	P	1879
Landed 10/3/1879. Embarked 16/3/1879.				50B/911	Casey	C	1879	1231	Cowper	G	1879
50B/240	Brace	G	1879	50B/767	Casson	A.J	1879	50B/1335	Cox	T	1879
50B/114	Bradley	J	1879	50B/1307	Cathcart	C	1879	50B/1675	Cox	W	1879
50B/1748	Bradley	W	1879	50B/86	Chambers	J.J	1879	50B/830	Cozens	H	1879
1609	Bradshaw	W	1879	50B/821	Chapman	G	1879	50B/64	Craft	A	1879
50B/1821	Brady	M	1879	50B/1743	Chapman	W.H	1879	50B/511	Cranwell	P	1879
50B/1041	Brand	T	1879	50B/1127	Charlwood	W	1879	50B/1710	Crawford	E	1879
50B/1000	Bray	C	1879	1244	Chillcott	F	1879	1737	Creaney	T	1879
1540	Bridgett	E	No clasp r	1317	Chillary	I	1879	438	Creeman	P	No clasp
50B/772	Britton	A	1879	50B/1795	Christie	M	1879	50B/466	Creigton	W	1879
50B/1897	Brooks	J	No clasp	1145	Christopher	T	1879	50B/548	Crips	G	1879
50B/1898	Broughton	H	No clasp r	1337	Chubb	N.G	1879	50B/1040	Crisper	C	1879
50B/1899	Brown	J	No clasp	50B/256	Clancy	J	1879	50B/110	Crocker	W	1879
50B/1725	Brown	J	1879	50B/822	Clancy	T	1879	50B/884	Crockett	A	1879
789	Brown	W	1879	1261	Clark	C	1879	50B/1093	Crompton	F	1879
50B/70	Brown	W	1879	50B/101	Clark	J	1879	1137	Crook	R	1879
50B/240	Bruce	G	1879	1796	Clark	T	1879	50B/438	Crowley	J	1879
50B/45	Brunsden	J.H	1879	1734	Clarke	E.C	1879	50B/1394	Cunningham	E	1879
50B/608	Bruton	H	1879	50B/760	Clarke	J	1879	1185	Curber ?	J	1879
50B/245	Bryan	J	1879	1219	Clarke	J.J	1879	50B/283	Curran	J	1879
50B/82	Bryant	D	1879	50B/1196	Clarke	W	1879	50B/935	Curran	M	1879r
1292	Buck	J	1879	50B/1206	Clay	H.D	1879	50B/625	Cutts	W	1879
50B/940	Buckley	D	1879	490	Clay	W	1879				

57th Regiment

#**Edward Burns** was born in Manchester, and enlisted at Liverpool in the 57th Regiment (West Middlesex) "The Diehards" on the 16th May 1859 at the age of 20 years. He discharged at Dublin after 21 years service. He was in the possession of four good conduct badges. His service overseas 13 1/2 years. Sold with his original Parchment Certificate of discharge.
Available for sale in January 2010 at £500, http://www.medalcollector.co.uk/

The 800 men of the 57th landed at Durban on March 11th, and on the 17th they moved off for the front. Following a short railway journey, they had a long six days' march before they reached the advanced base at Fort Pearson. The crossing of the Tugela on March 29th was without problems , A message was received from Pearson that a Zulu attack was imminent. The camp was formed, into a laager, with the wagons carefully positioned to create an unbroken wall. Gatling guns where mounted at the angles, with trenches dug in front. On the morning of April 2nd, the Zulus attacked. The Battle of Gingindlovu was to be a turning point in the eventual defeat of King Cetshwayo's 10 000 strong army. The camp was rendered fully defensible in case of sudden attack. The north face of the square was held by the 3rd Battalion, the 60th Rifles; the left by the 99th Regiment and the Buffs (3rd Foot) and the right face by the 57th Regiment. Deadly fire was maintained from the trenches, but again and again they attacked; the first attack on the north-east defences, against the 60th and then on the other sides. But though they advanced with the greatest bravery right up to the trenches, they could never get to close quarters, and after an hour's hard fighting a charge of the mounted infantry completed their rout. British casualties were 6 officers and 55 men; among the dead was Lieutenant Colonel Northey of the 60th Rifles.

On the following day the 57th, 60th, and 91st were sent off in a flying column. With only three days' rations, and after a hard march they reached Eshowe. The 57th remained in laager near Gingindlovu under the command of Major Tredennick for three weeks, when they moved down the Nyezane River to a point where a permanent post was built and called Fort Chelmsford. At the end of the month the 57th formed part of a column under Colonel Clarke, which marched from Port Durnford to Ulundi. Cetshwayo was captured on August 28th. After a short stay at Durban the 57th embarked for England on November 1st. They landed at Kingstown on December 13th 1879.

HANSARD Lords Sitting
SOUTH AFRICA—THE ZULU WAR—THE RE-INFORCEMENTS.—QUESTION.HL 31 March 1879 vol 245 c2 2
EARL DE LA WARR I beg to ask the Under Secretary of State for the Colonies, If he has received any further communication respecting the state of affairs at the Cape?

EARL CADOGAN My Lords, there has been received at the Colonial Office to-day a telegram from Madeira; and I cannot give the noble Earl a better answer than by reading it.

"From High Commissioner, Maritzburg, To Secretary of State.

"March 11.—'Tamar' arrived with upwards of 800 men of 57th Regiment on board, which, with Bradshaw's Naval Brigade from" 'Shah,' a very fine body of men, will, I hope, enable Lord Chelmsford to insure communication with Pearson. Oham has not yet joined Wood, but seems to have effectually broken with Cetewayo—a very important defection."

57th Regiment

50B/242	Daley	J	1879r	50B/200	Elkins	T	r	1062	Freeman	J	No clasp
Forfeited. No reason given.				Medal returned to mint. Landed				50B/577	Freeman	G	1879
50B/1790	Daly	J	1879	10/3/1879. Embarked 16/3/1879.				50B/1955	French	W	No clasp
50B/1170	Dalton	J	1879	50B/741	Elliott	C	1879	50B/816	Fricary	L	1879
50B/301	Darcy	J	1879	50B/1861	Elliott	J	No clasp	50B/655	Friend	G	1879
1782	Darlow	I.G	1879	1281	Ellis	H	1879	1197	Frost	J	1879
50B/25	Davies	G	No clasp	1248	Ellis	J	1879	50B/1888	Frost	R	No clasp
50B/845	Davies	G	1879	50B/1839	Ellis	J	1879	50B/1733	Fuller	T	1879
50B/714	Davies	J	1879	50B/577	Elston	A	1879	50B/1816	Furlong	P	1879
50B/987	Davies	J	1879	50B/1925	Elson	J	No clasp	No Medal Deserted.			
50B/174	Davis	T	1879	1297	Elthorpe	T	1879	50B/703	Gale	W	1879
50B/172	Davis	W	1879	50B/538	Elton	E	1879	50B/564	Gannon	P	1879r
1775	Dawson	B	1879	50B/1373	Elvey	H	1879	50B/502	Gardner	R	1879
1753	Day	J	1879	50B/1047	Emery	W	1879	50B/765	Garlick	J	1879
1241	Day	R	1879	50B/81	Ervine	A	No clasp	1026	Garmson	T	1879
527	Deacon	G	1879	50B/379	Etchells	S	1879	50B/1905	Garrett	J	No clasp
945	Deacon	J	1879	50B/866	Everist	J	1879	1427	Genower	G	No claspr
50B/1954	Denyer	D	No clasp	50B/1964	Eyres	H	No clasp	40B/167	Gibson	J	1879
50B/1956	Denyer	J.S	No clasp	50B/1875	Facey	J	No clasp	50B/1717	Gilbert	C	1879
50B/103	Dickson	J	1879	50B/1870	Fahey	G	No clasp	50B/1118	Gilbert	F.W	1879r
50B/493	Dillon	T	1879	1304	Farley	W	1879	1419	Gilbert	W	1879
50B/1800	Donnelly	J	1879	1763	Farr	J.H	1879	50B/57	Gilding	J	1879
50B/1924	Donnelly	J	No clasp	50B/508	Farrell	J	1879	50B/231	Giles	W	1879
50B/1979	Donnovan	D	No clasp	50B/1778	Farrell	J	1879	1308	Gillam	J	1879
253	Dovity	D	No clasp	50B/814	Faulkner	J	1879	50B/803	Girling	J	1879
50B/1819	Doran	M	1879	1496	Fen	J.F		1082	Glanville	N	No clasp
50B/819	Dorman	H	1879r	Medal not issued. Landed				50B/758	Glazebrook	J	No clasp
1692	Dougherty	A.P	1879	10/3/1879. Embarked 16/3/1979.				720	Gleeson	J	1879
50B/1201	Dowling	J	1879	50B/150	Feenin	T	1879	50B/860	Glover	T	1879
50B/1038	Downs	C.S	1879	50B/542	Fenlow	J	1879	50B/424	Goddard	C	1879
1770	Doyle	J	1879	50B/950	Ferris	J	1879	50B/1721	Gomm	A	1879
50B/1812	Doyle	J	1879	50B/1280	Field	S	No clasp	50B/1235	Gooden	H	1879
50B/1646	Drew	H	1879	1176	Field	S	1879	1420	Goodland	B	1879
1728	Driscoll	J	1879	50B/1814	Fill	A	1879	1810	Goodland	R	1879
1735	Duce	J	No clasp	50B/1176	Fisher	F	1879	50B/1200	Goodleman	G	1879
50B/526	Duce	W	1879	50B/1252	Finlay	J	1879	50B/1770	Goodman	S	1879
50B/221	Dudman	G	1879	1758	Fitch	D	1879	50B/1035	Goodwin	F	1879
50B/1745	Duff	G	No clasp	50B/337	Fitzgerald	J	1879	50B/100	Goodwin	R	1879
50B/530	Duffy	J	1879	590	Fitzpatrick	E	1879	50B/1134	Goose	C	No clasp
50B/1824	Duggan	J	1879	50B/1799	Fitzpatrick	M	1879	50B/1731	Gordon	A	1879
50B/270	Duggan	W	1879	50B/883	Fleet	E	1879	50B/1039	Gosden	G	1879
50B/444	Duke	C	1879	50B/1112	Fleet	W	1879	50B/1862	Goss	C.W	No clasp
50B/1902	Duncan	J	No clasp	50B/368	Flint	G	No clasp	50B/1254	Graddage	H	1879
1194	Dunn	G	1879	50B/1310	Flood	M.J	1879	1398	Grafton	C	1879
50B/1321	Dunn	J	1879	892	Foley	J	1879	50B/1130	Grainger	H	1879
50B/1804	Dunne	T	1879r	887	Foley	P	No clasp	50B/449	Green	E	1879
50B/386	Dupree	J	1879	1158	Foot	C	1879	50B/175	Green	G	1879
50B/327	Dupree	J	1879	50B/621	Forbes	J	1879	50B/1867	Green	J	No clasp
50B/828	Dwyer	P	1879	50B/126	Ford	E	1879	50B/1698	Green	J	1879
440	Dwyer	T	1879	50B/1778	Foster	J	1879	50B/718	Green	W	1879
1903	Dyson	J	No clasp	50B/135	Foster	J	1879	Discharged with ignominy. No trace			
50B/1874	Eastwood	J	No clasp	50B/678	Fountain	T	1879	of the return of the Medal.			
1262	Eden	W	1879	50B/1260	Fowler	G	1879	Restoration refused 7/1/1924.			
50B/1719	Edgar	J	1879	1732	Fowler	J	1879	50B/889	Greengrass	E	1879
50B/55	Edgley	H.C	1879	50B/151	Fox	D	1879	50B/1078	Grew	J	1879
50B/614	Edwards	B.P	1879	50B/1065	Fox	G	1879	383	Griffiths	J	1879
50B/1288	Edwards	W	1879	50B/1123	Francis	A.H	1879	1811	Griffiths	W	1879
50B/1904	Edworthy	W	No clasp	50B/15	Franey	G	1879	50B/809	Griffiths	W	1879
50B/1164	Elkins	E	1879	50B/920	Franks	G	1879	1489	Guerin	D	1879

Communications

The main communication methods used in the field during the campaign were despatch riders or visual heliograph signalling. Poor communications was one of the deciding factors in the defeat at Isandlwana. Members of the 1/24th Regiment stationed at Helpmakaar were trained in the use of heliographs. But the equipment appears to have been in short supply.

The photograph below shows a corporal and privates of the 58th Regiment working a heliograph with the second Division.

With many hills situated in Zululand a chain of heliograph stations was a distinct possibility to establish communications between the different forces in the field. Weather conditions have to be suitable with clear skies and sunshine being a prerequisite.

Below is an extracts from Major Hamilton's report written during the Ulundi Campaign:

"The supply of heliographs at the time of the arrival of the Telegraph Troop in the country was so limited that but little could be effected with them at first; later on, as a larger supply was received, an extensive system of signalling was elaborated, and a very large amount of correspondence was flashed by this means. Up to the time of the battle of Ulundi [4th July], the only instruments in use were a pair of 3", a pair of 6", and a pair of 10" instruments. With these, a chain of stations was established from the advanced positions of the army, where the parties of [17th] Lancers worked the 3" instruments, to Landman's Drift, the terminus of the Military Telegraph. The 6" and 10" glasses were worked by the signallers of 'C' Troop, R.E. "

57th Regiment

Number	Name	Initial	Year	Number	Name	Initial	Year	Number	Name	Initial	Year
50B/431	Gully	E	1879	50B/1122	Hoey	G	1879	50B/1763	Judd	J	1879
50B/1257	Halford	W	1879	50B/1228	Hodder	J	1879	50B/750	Kayser	H.A	1879
Discharge with ignominy. No trace of the return of the medal.				50B/745	Holgate	H	1879	50B/841	Kearney	T	1879
				50B/967	Hone	B	1879	50B/507	Keating	J	1879
50B/393	Hall	G.F	1879	50B/1138	Hopcroft	W	1879	50B/1700	Keeman	J	1879
50B/1268	Halliday	J	1879 r	1214	Hope	G	1879	50B/1829	Kelly	M	1879
Deserted.				1691	Hopkins	E	1879	50B/1802	Kelly	P	1879r
50B/61	Halloran	P	1879	50B/587	Hopkins	G.E	1879	Discharged with ignominy.			
50B/572	Hammond	W	1879	50B/876	Hopkins	S	1879	50B/1918	Kelly	P	No clasp
50B/974	Hamper	A.T	1879	50B/381	Hopkins	W	1879	1494	Kemp	M	1879
50B/1191	Hand	H.J	1879	1385	Horsfall	J	1879r	50B/977	Kemsley	G.J	1879
50B/1755	Hand	J.H	1879	50B/324	Horne	J	1879	50B/269	Kenna	M	1879
531	Hannan	M	1879	50B/439	Hose	J	1879	944	Kennedy	J	1879
313	Hannan	W	1879	50B/874	Hour	W	1879	50B/1838	Kennedy	L	1879
50B/554	Hannigan	P	1879	1078	Howard	L	1879	50B/527	Kennedy	W	1879
50B/1697	Hanratty ?	T	1879	50B/823	Howard	W	1879	50B/1815	Keogh	J	No clasp
50B/735	Harber	W.J	1879	50B/775	Howell	G	1879	1408	Kerslake	T	1879
50B/63	Hardie	J.J	1879	50B/318	Howell	W	1879	50B/338	Ketley	E	1879
50B/392	Harding	I	1879	50B/11	Nuggett	G	1879	50B/1912	Kiddle	F	No clasp
50B/838	Hare	J	1879	1779	Huggins	J	1879	50B/929	Kilburn	A	1879
50B/1018	Hare	W	1879	1806	Hughes	C	1879	50B/1810	King	J	1879
1777	Harney	P	1879	50B/1275	Hughes	J	1879	50B/1398	King	J	1879
427	Harper	G	1879	77	Hughes	H	No clasp	50B/49	King	W	1879
50B/1906	Harper	J	No clasp	50B/1803	Hughes	J	1879	50B/1316	King	W	1879
50B/624	Harris	G	1879	50B/1692	Humphrey	H	No clasp	50B/459	Kirby	M	1879
50B/287	Harris	J	1879	Deserted. No trace of the return of the medal.				50B/1493	Kitchener	W	No clasp
50B/58	Harrison	W	1879					1216	Knight	H	1879
1462	Harrison	W	1879	50B/311	Hyland	J	1879r	50B/190	Knott	S	1879
1784	Harrison	W	1879	Deserted.				50B/811	Lack	D	1879
50B/1927	Hart	F	No clasp	50B/1396	Ingham	F	1879	50B/152	Lacker	H	1879
50B/1796	Hart	J	1879	50B/325	Iveson	T	1879	1326	Ladd	W	1879
50B/1832	Hart	J	1879	50B/913	James	J	1879	50B/627	Lamb	J	1879
1492	Harvey	A	1879	1760	Jarman	H	1879	50B/383	Lambert	F	1879
50B/468	Harvey	G	1879	50B/513	Jarvis	W.S	1879	329	Lambert	J	No clasp
1800	Hawkins	J	1879	1582	Jeffreys	C	1879	50B/158	Lancaster	G	1879
50B/1229	Hawkins	T	1879	50B/734	Jeffreys	T	1879	A duplicate medal and clasp issued 22/10/1923.			
50B/544	Hawkins	T	1879	50B/1190	Jelly	A	1879				
50B/1797	Haydon	P	1879	50B/465	Jelly	E	1879	50B/1117	Landey	F	1879
50B/1245	Hayes	R	1879	1787	Johnson	C.F	1879	50B/488	Lane	J	1879
50B/976	Hayes	S	1879	50B/919	Johnson	F	1879	50B/951	Lane	R	1879
50B/1171	Heather	W.B	1879	50B/1211	Johnson	G	1879	50B/855	Langley	F	1879
50B/1113	Hedyman ?	G	1879	1355	Johnson	G	1879	50B/1274	Larkin	T	1879
50B/1460	Hemley	J	1879	50B/1325	Johnson	P	1879	870	Lawless	J	1879
50B/1418	Hennessey	M	1879	50B/1872	Johnson	S	No clasp	50B/598	Lawless	T	1879r
1786	Herod	H	1879	50B/ ?	Johnson	I	No clasp	50B/1204	Lawrence	J	1879
50B/203	Herrick	J	1879	50B/1364	Johnson	W	1879	50B/1006	Lawrence	W	1879
50B/771	Hickey	W	1879	50B/1803	Johnson	W	1879	No medal Deserted.			
1487	Hickling	J	1879	50B/1691	Jones	A	1879	50B/1153	Lawson	A	1879
50B/620	Higgins	W	1879	50B/1764	Jones	E	1879	828	Lawson	E	1879
50B/1305	Higgs	R.W	1879	50B/467	Jones	F	1879	50B/1935	Lawson	H	No clasp
50B/1806	Higham	J	1879	50B/1908	Jones	J	No clasp	50B/1151	Lawson	R.C	1879
1465	Hill	S	1879	50B/264	Jones	J.W	1879	50B/1386	Leary	D	1879
50B/188	Hills	S	1879	50B/1942	Jordan	W	No clasp	Deserted. No trace of the return of medal			
50B/293	Hinds	W	1879	50B/1887	Jordison	W	No clasp	1792	Leary	J	1879r
50B/766	Hirshfelt	H	1879	50B/1284	Joseph	W.F	1879	50B/1864	Leaver	E	No clasp
50B/1328	Hitchcock	F.C	1879	1715	Joslin	W	1879	1792	Leary	J	1879r
1044	Hobbley	W	1879	50B/345	Joyce	C	1879	50B/1864	Leaver	E	No clasp
1167	Hodge	W.H	1879	50B/776	Joyce	T	1879	50B/97	Lee	J	1879
Forfeited. No trace of return of medal.				No Medal. Discharged with ignominy.				50B/1326	Lee	J	1879r

57th Regiment

50B/1831	Leggett	P	1879r	998	Mc Cormack	J	1879	50B/1008	Murphy	M	1879
50B/1920	Leigh	N	No clasp	957	Mc Crudden	R	1879	50B/92	Murphy	M	1879
1272	Lenton	J	1879	50B/1834	Mc Donald	C	1879	50B/1017	Murray	J	1879
50B/286	Leslie	R	1879	50B/998	Mc Donald	M	1879	50B/696	Murray	R	1879
50B/40	Letch	W	1879	50B/1919	Mc Ewan	J	No clasp	50B/688	Musk	C	1879
50B/445	Levett	J	1879	1422	Mc Fell	W	1879	1727	Musselwhite	W	1879
50B/1182	Lewis	C	1879	272	Mc Garry	J	1879	50B/1146	Myatt	A	1879
1238	Lewis	W	1879	50B/1791	Mc Garry	J	1879	Deserted. No trace of the return of			
50B/1220	Lewis	W	1879	50B/1070	Mc Grath	J	1879	the medal.			
50B/276	Lindsay	N	1879	50B/1271	Mc Guire	P	1879	50B/1323	Neckless	H	1879
926	Lintott	E	1879	50B/1757	Mc Guire	S	1879	Deserted. No trace of the return of			
50B/514	Little	A	1879	50B/886	Mc Guiness	J	1879	the medal.			
50B/1114	Littlewood	T	1879	50B/1736	Mc Kenna	F	1879	452	Neill	W	1879
618	Livesay	T	1879	50B/519	Mc Kenna	J	1879	50B/1724	Neilly	R	No clasp
50B/263	Lloyd	A	1879	50B/1699	Mc Kenna	P	1879	50B/1932	Nelson	P	No clasp
50B/411	Lock	H.J	1879	50B/1395	Mc Lavy	M	1879	50B/1941	Newman	C	No clasp r
50B/717	Logan	G	1879	50B/53	Mc Manus	J	1879r	50B/846	Newman	R	1879
50B/310	Lomax	W	1879	50B/1267	Mc Manus	P	1879	50B/1835	Niland	J	1879
1804	Long	W	1879	50B/1701	Mc Mullen	J	1879	50B/1392	Nimick	G	1879
1713	Longson	H	1879	50B/1458	Mc Namara	J	No clasp	50B/544	Noon	T	1879
50B/206	Love	J	1879	508	Mc Quillan	R	1879	1251	Norris	E	No clasp
50B/207	Love	W	1879	50B/958	Mead	D	1879r	50B/1688	Norton	J	1879
50B/162	Lucas	W	1879	50B/1910	Mealey	A	No clasp	50B/36	Nowlan	E	1879
271	Lucey	J	1879	50B/1746	Medhurst	H	1879	1452	Nutt	J.J	1879
1280	Luscombe	R	1879	50B/1808	Melcady	C	1879	50B/1334	Nuttley	A	1879
50B/177	Luttman	H	1879	943	Mellis	T	1879	50B/1793	O'Brien	P	1879
581	Lynch	J	1879	50B/1143	Meredith	V.H	1879	50B/261	O'Brien	T	1879
50B/532	Lynch	R	1879	50B/1172	Merritt	H	1879	50B/942	O'Callaghan	T	1879
1791	Lynch	T	1879	50B/390	Middleton	J	1879	No Medal Deserted.			
50B/266	Lynes	T	1879	50B/869	Miller	S	1879	50B/933	O'Connell	M.J	No clasp
50B/639	Mackay	T	1879	50B/1911	Millin	D	No clasp	954	O'Connell	R	1879
50B/1813	Mackay	T	1879	50B/1083	Mills	G	1879	50B/1711	O'Hara	R	1879
50B/557	Madden	J	1879	1437	Mills	S	1879	50B/1811	O'Loughlin	J	1879
50B/1530	Maher	J	1879	1252	Milne	G.P	1879	50B/924	O'Neill	E	No clasp
50B/549	Maher	M	1879	50B/952	Minne	G	1879 r	50B/478	O'Regan	P	1879
50B/1794	Mahon	J	1879	Forfeited. No reason given.				50B/265	Osborne	W	1879
50B/1298	Mahoney	D	1879	1172	Mitch	T	1879 r	1381	Overton	G	1879
50B/183	Mallisey	G	1879	50B/1001	Mitchell	T	1879	3477	Page	J	1879
50B/253	Manning	W	1879	50B/241	Mobbs	A	1879	50B/882	Parham	H	1879
50B/1203	Marchant	J	1879	50B/589	Monk	C	1879	50B/1136	Parish	W	1879
1315	Mardling	J	1879	50B/569	Monk	M	1879	50B/1737	Parker	B	1879
221	Markey	L	No clasp	50B/210	Mooney	J	1879	1368	Parker	J	1879
50B/1461	Marler	G	1879	50B/1397	Moore	W	1879	50B/1105	Parker	W	1879
50B/1331	Marmion	J	1879	50B/899	Moran	J	1879	1769	Parson	W	1879
A duplicate medal and clasp issued				50B/1936	Moran	J	No clasp	50B/1212	Partridge	H	1879
on 12/8/1924.				50B/1081	Moran	J	1879	50B/1007	Pearce	F	1879
50B/967	Marney	E	1879	50B/1290	Morgan	J	1879	50B/320	Pearce	H	1879
50B/1034	Martin	J	1879	50B/586	Moriaty	J	1879	50B/107	Pearman	A	No clasp
50B/673	Martin	J	1879	1295	Morland	J	1879	1812	Pender	T	1879
50B/1129	Martin	R	1879	50B/818	Mortlock	J	1879	50B/161	Penfold	J	1879
50B/692	Mason	W	1879	50B/1837	Moyers	F	1879	1135	Penny	W.H	1879
1226	Masters	A	1879	1724	Moylen	P	1879	50B/1221	Perkins	R	1879
50B/1214	Masters	A	1879	No Medal Deserted.				1767	Perkins	T	1879
50B/1202	Maud	W	1879	844	Moynihan	H	1879	50B/375	Perrin	J	1879
50B/1708	Mc Allister	C	1879	50B/247	Mudd	H	1879	1461	Perry	E	1879
50B/356	Mc Callum	H	1879	50B/1827	Mullen	J	1879	50B/1249	Perry	T	1879
50B/1885	Mc Carthy	C	No clasp	202	Murphy	H	1879	50B/1207	Perryman	W	1879
50B/1822	Mc Carthy	P	1879	50B/1820	Murphy	J	1879	1003	Pettit	A.J	1879
50B/541	Mc Carthy	W	1879	50B/566	Murphy	J	1879	50B/212	Phillips	C	1879

57th Regiment

Number	Surname	Initial	Year
50B/1213	Phillips	J	1879
50B/1750	Phillips	R	1879
857	Phillips	T	1879
50B/1985	Philmore	W	No clasp
50B/154	Philpotts	T	1879
50B/1005	Phipps	G	1879
50B/1253	Pink	E	1879
50B/1156	Pinnion	T	1879
50B/1938	Pixley	A.J	No clasp
1057	Pocock	T	1879
50B/1197	Pollard	W	1879
50B/742	Portsmouth	J	1879
50B/313	Poulter	W	1879
1168	Poulton	W	1879
50B/156	Powdersham	G	1879
1780	Price	G	1879
50B/1182	Price	J	1879
1675	Priestman	T	1879
50B/968	Pring	J.W	1879
50B/222	Prior	G	1879
50B/404	Prosser	T	1879
50B/136	Pryer	G	1879
No Medal Deserted.			
1389	Pugsley	J	1879
729	Pullen	D	1879
50B/730	Pullen	W	1879
50B/246	Pusey	A	1879
50B/729	Quinton	W	1879
1275	Rance	A	1879
50B/279	Rawlinson	W	1879
Duplicate medal and clasp issued 31/10/1922.			
50B/746	Read	J	1879
50B/857	Redman	J	1879
50B/1836	Redmond	J	1879
50B/2	Redmond	P	1879
860	Redmond	P	1879
50B/805	Reed	R	1879
200	Reed	S	No clasp
50B/1150	Reed	W	1879
50B/1753	Reid	J	1879
Duplicate medal and clasp issued 31/3/1919.			
50B/1795	Reilly	D	1879
50B/284	Reilly	P	1879
50B/781	Reynolds	W	1879
488	Richards	A.J	No clasp
1268	Richardson	G	1879
50B/248	Ridgway	F	1879
50B/661	Rielly	J	1879
50B/1889	Riley	F	No clasp
50B/1909	Rimes	J	No clasp
50B/1749	Rimhan	G	1879
1393	Rispin	C	1879
50B/373	Rixon	J.E	1879
50B/1929	Roach	T	No clasp
1390	Roberts	E	1879
50B/333	Roberts	W	1879
50B/793	Robinson	H	No clasp r
Deserted.			
50B/506	Robinson	J	1879
Deserted. No trace of return of medal.			
50B/1184	Robson	F	1879
Deserted. No trace of return of medal.			
50B/182	Roe	W	1879
50B/851	Rogers	E	1879
50B/122	Rosbrook	J	1879
1789	Rose	G	1879
50B/147	Ross	W	1879
50B/525	Rowe	P	1879
1702	Rowe	W.G	1879
50B/1725	Ruckman	H	1879
1237	Rugg	A	1879
50B/1135	Ryan	R	1879
50B/399	Sadler	J	1879
1161	Salter	J	1879
50B/496	Sams	B	1879
50B/32	Sarsfield	F	1879
50B/1306	Saunders	A.E	1879
50B/1674	Savory	H.E	1879
50B/1023	Scarsbrook	J	1879
50B/181	Scott	J	No clasp
50B/1051	Sears	T	1879r
50B/10	Seaton	O	1879
50B/1875	Seaward	J	1879
50B/179	Sellars	F	1879
50B/1934	Sexton	G	No clasp
50B/1264	Shanks	J	1879
1183	Sharland	J.J	1879
1201	Shattock	W	1879
941	Shaw	J	No clasp
50B/695	Shay	T	1879
50B/1261	Sheahan	J	1879
1287	Sheldrick	W	1879
50B/649	Shepherd	D	No clasp r
50B/1115	Shepherd	H	1879
50B/314	Shepherd	J	1879
1266	Shepherd	W	1879
309	Siely	J	1879
50B/1178	Sill	E	1879
50B/180	Sills	W	1879
50B/1865	Sillis	R	No clasp
50B/406	Simmonds	G	1879
50B/1020	Simpson	A	1879
50B/864	Singleton	W	1879
50B/802	Sivell	R	1879
50B/1747	Skelly	M	1879
50B/272	Skerrett	H	1879
50B/1162	Skevington	W	1879
50B/808	Skimmings	J.A	1879
50B/1825	Skreen	R	1879
50B/69	Slater	G.W	1879
50B/995	Slater	J	1879
50B/1236	Slater	W.J	1879
50B/1723	Slaughter	W	1879
50B/917	Slimes	J	1879
50B/1876	Sloman	E	No clasp
50B/599	Smart	W.O	1879
50B/894	Smith	B.S	1879
Deserted. No trace of the return of the medal.			
50B/494	Smith	C	1879
50B/1155	Smith	C	1879
50B/1167	Smith	C	1879
1761	Smith	G	1879
50B/1138	Smith	G	1879
1735	Smith	H	1879
1803	Smith	H	1879
50B/437	Smith	H	1879
Deserted. No trace of the return of the medal.			
486	Smith	I	1879r
50B/1913	Smith	J	No clasp
50B/680	Smith	J	1879
50B/50	Smith	J	1879
50B/1147	Smith	J	1879r
50B/904	Smith	R.M	1879
1768	Smith	W	1879
50B/744	Smith	W	1879
50B/1939	Smith	W	No clasp
50B/1027	Smyth	S	1879
50B/38	Southernwood	H	1879
50B/829	Speakman	R	1879
50B/215	Spenser	W	1879
1471	Squires	G	1879
1249	Stanton	J	1879
50B/654	Stanton	T	1879
50B/918	Stanton	T	1879
50B/1877	Starr	W	No clasp
1346	Steel	J	1879
50B/1278	Stelfox	J	1879
1246	Stephens	A	1879
50B/681	Stevens	A	1879
50B/824	Stevens	D	1879
50B/225	Stevens	E	1879
50B/37	Stevens	W.J	1879
50B/1265	Stewart	J	1879
1309	Stones	T	1879
50B/1732	Storey	G	1879
50B/807	Stowe	C	1879
50B/733	Strathdee	J	1879
50B/557	Sullivan	J	1879
50B/762	Sullivan	J	1879
50B/664	Surmon	E	1879
50B/1142	Sutherland	J.H	1879
290	Sweeney	M	No clasp
50B/1752	Sweeney	P	1879
1265	Swift	E	1879
50B/559	Taberman	G	1879
50B/21	Tady	J	1879
50B/1806	Tait	J	1879
1179	Tanner	C	1879
359	Tarbotton	E	1879
50B/944	Taylor	J	1879
50B/578	Taylor	T	1879
1756	Taylor	W	No clasp

57th Regiment

50B/670	Thew	G.H	1879	50B/1930	Ward	J	No clasp	50B/394	Wood	J	1879
457	Thomas	H	1879	50B/1209	Warren	W	1879	50B/432	Wood	J	No clasp
1474	Thompson	E	1879	1697	Watkins	W	1879	50B/853	Wood	W	1879
39	Thompson	G	1879	50B/217	Watmore	J	1879	50B/868	Woodcock	J	1879
50B/36	Thompson	G	1879	50B/831	Watson	J	1879	50B/988	Woodley	W	1879
50B/910	Thompson	G.J	1879	50B/1292	Watts	J	1879	50B/1978	Woods	H	No clasp
50B/1869	Thompson	H	No clasp r	324	Waygood	L	1879	975	Wright	G	1879
50B/400	Thompson	J	1879	50B/728	Weatherall	G	No clasp	50B/1781	Wright	G.E.J	No clasp
50B/35	Thompson	R	1879	50B/1291	Webb	J	1879	50B/1474	Wright	J	1879
50B/1878	Thompson	W	No clasp	880	Weightman	J	1879	1123	Wright	J	1879
50B/1322	Thornett	A	1879	50B/78	Welch	J	1879	50B/1180	Wright	T	1879
50B/1296	Thornton	J	1879	50B/780	Welch	J	1879	50B/1302	Wyatt	F	1879
50B/622	Thornton	J	1879	50B/1225	Weller	A	1879	50B/1940	Wyatt	F	No clasp
50B/85	Thorpe	W	1879	1788	Wells	J.R	1879	1177	Yandle	G	1879
50B/75	Thurlow	J	1879	50B/840	West	J	1879 r	1723	Yeates	E	1879
50B/1809	Tindall	J	1879	Deserted.				50B/186	Young	J	1879
842	Tobin	J	1879	1301	West	J.F	1879				
50B/142	Tomlin	W	1879	50B/1148	West	U.A	1879				
1738	Tooth	J	1879	50B/1866	Weston	W.G	No clasp				
284	Tottan	J	1879	50B/1059	Wheeler	C	1879				
50B/336	Town	T	1879	50B/892	Wheeler	G	1879				
50B/123	Townshend	F	1879	50B/1103	Wheeler	N	1879				
50B/1256	Townshend	W	1879	50B/969	Wheeler	R	1879				
50B/901	Tracey	J	1879	50B/20	White	J	1879				
50B/1926	Tribor	M	No clasp	1728	White	R	1879				
1307	Truelove	J	1879	50B/192	White	T	1879				
1198	Tucker	T	1879	1186	White	W	1879				
1224	Tucker	W	1879	50B/1753	White	W	1879				
50B/1879	Tull	W	No clasp	50B/970	Whitehead	D	1879				
50B/168	Turner	C	1879	50B/1254	Whitehead	E	1879				
50B/79	Turner	C.L	1879	50B/299	Whitehead	R	1879 r				
50B/982	Turner	F	1879	1166	Wickett	W	1879				
1786	Tutt	B	1879	50B/1079	Williams	A	1879 r				
1352	Tyler	D	1879	Forfeited. No reason given.							
50B/985	Tyrrel	H	1879	1729	Williams	G	1879				
50B/727	Upfold	H	1879	50B/1247	Williams	G	1879				
50B/973	Upton	G	1879	50B/1309	Williams	H	1879				
50B/371	Usher	H	1879	Deserted. No trace of return of the medal.							
50B/1325	Uttley	C	1879	50B/1301	Williams	H	1879				
1232	Veal	J	1879	50B/753	Williams	J	1879				
1714	Venus	H	1879	50B/1189	Williams	J	1879				
50B/251	Wade	T	1879	50B/76	Williams	L	1879				
50B/826	Walden	W	1879 r	1175	Williams	S	1879				
50B/143	Wale	W.H	1879	50B/908	Williams	W	1879				
50B/725	Wales	R	1879	1166	Williams	W	1879				
1447	Wall	J	1879	50B/789	Wilson	C	1879				
50B/921	Wallace	W	1879	1921	Wilson	J	1879 r				
50B/799	Walker	W	1879	50B/979	Wilson	J	1879				
50B/1121	Wallingford	J	1879	50B/1917	Wilson	W	No clasp				
50B/1914	Walsh	J	No clasp	50B/1219	Wincey	S.J	No clasp				
50B/1916	Walsh	Z	No clasp	50B/1792	Windsor	P	1879				
300	Walter	J	1879	50B/896	Winker	J	1879				
1170	Walters	F	1879	50B/939	Winterton	C	1879				
50B/249	Walton	T	1879	1277	Winthon	J	1879				
50B/671	Walton	W	1879	282	Wiseman	W	1879				
928	Ward	A	1879	1212	Wiseman	W.W	1879				
50B/565	Ward	G	No clasp	50B/74	Witehall	A	1879				
50B/1915	Ward	G	No clasp	50B/286	Withy	R	1879				
50B/865	Ward	G	No clasp	50B/1084	Wood	C	1879				

58th (RUTLANDSHIRE) REGIMENT.
COLONEL
 Whitehead CB R.C 1879
Also had British Crimea Medal, and Turkish Crimea War Medal.
MAJOR
 Bond W.D 1879
 Hingeston W.H 1879
CAPTAIN & BREVET MAJOR
 Foster C.E 1879
 Hesse J.V 1879
CAPTAIN
 Anderson D.G 1879
 Bowling C No clasp
 Churchill M 1879
 Howley P.A 1879
Also had Medal for Indian Mutiny.
 Morris A.W 1879
 St. John O.B 1879
 Saunders H.M No clasp
QUARTERMASTER
 Lenton C 1879
LIEUTENANT and ADJUTANT
 Lovegrove E 1879
LIEUTENANT
 Dolphin H 1879
 Hornby C.L 1879
 Liebenrood G.E 1879
 Mc Mahon L 1879
 Nuthall H.W 1879
 Power W Le Poer No clasp
 Sandys E.D 1879
 Smyth G.T.V.B No clasp
 Williams C.C 1879
 KIA Inhlobane.
2nd LIEUTENANT
 Bolton A.C 1879
 Collison J 1879
 Compton T.E 1879
 Fawcett W.F 1879
 Hill A.R No clasp
 Morgan H 1879

58th Regiment

The 58th (Rutlandshire) Regiment.
The 58th arrived in South Africa directly from England as part of the reinforcements requested by Lord Chelmsford after the abortive first invasion of Zululand in early 1879.
Colonel. R.C. Whitehead, C.B. Commanded the regiment during the war, including the battle of Ulundi. (Mentioned in despatches.)
At the battle of Ulundi the regiment formed a portion of the right of square, and bore the brunt of the onslaught of the Zulu enemy, large numbers of whom got to within thirty yards of the line before the destructive fire stopped their advance. In the engagement Bt. Lieut. Col. Winsloe and Col. Bond were severely wounded.
From April until the end of the war Captains Libenrood, and Saunders remained on detachment at Durban, in command of a company.
Capts. St. John, Morris, Lovegrove, Nuthall, and Liebenrood served with the regiment during the war, and were present at the battle of Ulundi.
Capt. St. John commanded the company which remained at Victoria on the departure of the HQ in August.
Capt. Howley embarked from Portsmouth and served with the regt. from May till the conclusion of the war.
Capt. Morris relieved with a company of. the 21st Fusiliers at Fort Marshall in Aug.
Capt.Churchill remained from April at Ladysmith. till the conclusion of the war.
Capt. Nuthall served on a detachment of K.D.Gs. which, under Major Stabb, completed the cordon between Fort Victoria and KwaMagwasa, drawn to prevent the King from effecting his escape.
Lieutenant Power remained on detachment at Durban from April till the conclusion of the war.
Lieuts. Dolphin, Sandys, Compton, Fawcett,Collinson, Morgan, and Bolton served with the regt. during the war, and were present at the battle of Ulundi.
Lieut. Collinson was also present with the water picquet which was fired on by the enemy on the 3rd July, and remained at Fort Marshall with Capt. Morris's company from August.
Lieuts. McMahon and O'Donel took part with the regiment in the advance of Newdigate's Div. on Ulundi; and remained on detachment at Fort Evelyn from the date of its construction in June until the conclusion of the war.
Lieut. Smyth remained on detachment at Durban from April till the conclusion of the war.
Lieuts. Hill and Jopp, who joined the regt. at Ladysmith, remained there on detachment from April till the conclusion of the war.
Paymaster and Quartermaster. Minchin, J.W. Paymaster Minchin remained on detachment at Pietermaritzburg from the date of the departure of the regiment from that town in April till the conclusion of the war.
Quartermaster.Lenton, C. Quartermaster Lenton served with the regiment. during the war, and was present at the battle of Ulundi.
The 58th remained in Natal after the end of the Anglo-Zulu War and took part in the Transvaal War against the Boers in 1880-81. It was during this campaign that the 58th became the 2nd battalion of the newly organized Northamptonshire Regiment. During that War the 58th became the last British battalion to carry its colours into battle.

William Bostock 58th Regiment - inquest into his suicide held on the 23rd June 1888
He was married on 2nd July 1882, and was 33 years old when he died.
The 58th stayed on in South Africa after the Zulu war and just a year later were embroiled in the 1st Boer War
He seemed to have had a hard time whilst in the army the notes from his inquest state the following:

Foreman: Has your husband been in the army?
Witness: Yes.
Foreman: Has he been in the Soudan?
Witness: Yes.
I.C. Sullivan Oliver produced the deceased's regimental discharge, which the Coroner read. Bostock had been in the 58th Regiment.
Coroner: He received no pay from the Government, I suppose?
Witness: Eighteen months' and a medal.
Coroner: Not since you have been married?
Witness: No, sir.
Continuing, the wife said: I think his head was affected by having been abroad. He has tried to destroy himself before. Once here and once in London. He said he had had sunstroke.
In reply to the Foreman, witness corrected her statement, and said it was the Zulu War that her husband had been in. He had been in some engagements, and he had a medal. He had received a bullet wound through the right ear; an assegai wound in his hip, and a bullet or assegai wound in the stomach. He also had other wounds. He had had two smashed legs. The bones were smashed and never properly set. He was run over the calf of the two legs by a provision van in the Zulu war. He could walk very well, but he twister the left leg. He received no pension. I don't know how it was he didn't
The coroner: I should advise you to take your discharge to the clergyman. Perhaps he could do something for you at the War Office, as your husband received such injuries, they might do something for you.
It was pointed out to the Coroner that deceased had received eighteen months' pay.

Information supplied by: Rhonda Dudley Great, Great Granddaughter of William
Rhonda. http://www.familyhistoryforum.co.uk/index.php?showtopic=2576&pid=9226&mode=threaded&start=#entry9226

58th Regiment

	O'Donel	C.M	1879
SUB LIEUTENANT			
	Joop	S.J.M	No clasp
SERGEANT MAJOR			
774	Murray	C	1879
BANDMASTER			
1700	Moran	J	No clasp
DRUM MAJOR			
3031	Brown	W	1879
COLOR SERGEANT			
1083	Blencoe	C	1879
1246	Carolan	P	1879
962	Drury	T	No clasp
1671	Evans	E	No clasp
1959	Perrin	J	1879
1196	Phillips DCM	J	1879
871	Piper	J	1879
210	Tuck	T	No clasp
1433	Wallingford	T	1879
ARMOURER SERGEANT			
725	Brown	B	1879
BAND SERGEANT			
1698	Smith	W	1879 r
PAYMASTER SERGEANT			
849	Richardson	W	No clasp
PIONEER SERGEANT			
1937	Goucher	R	1879
QUARTERMASTER SERGEANT			
29B/560	Milliken	J	1879
SERGEANT			
29B/770	Anderson	R	No clasp
29B/2060	Bacon	J	No clasp
1444	Belshan	R	No clasp
957	Brill	C	1879
870	Conway	G	1879
722	Conway	J	1879
733	Cresswell	H	1879
1555	Fowles	S	1879
28B/122	Gallagher	P	1879
29B/383	Goucher	T	1879
29B/660	Grundy	W	1879
2123	Hayward	G	No clasp
1559	Head	G	No clasp
1458	Hussey	C	No clasp
1001	Lawrence	C	1879
858	Leggings	F	1879
1898	Lindsell	E	No clasp
1895	Lindsell	J	1879
761	Lonsdale	A	No clasp
29B/1758	Madden	J	1879
1526	Mc Lure	G	1879
29B/1724	Moreton	J	1879

950	Mulchay	T	1879
1762	Norton	J	1879
2181	O'Reilly	P	1879
564	O'Callaghan	N	1879
2025	Parish	T.R	No clasp
1234	Reynolds	W	1879
1057	Roberts	C	1879
1861	Slattery	J	1879r
2145	Spooner	J	No clasp
1104	Sweeney	J	1879
1201	Thearle	H	1879
2138	Thomas	R	No clasp
LANCE SERGEANT			
29B/317	Bridgstock	W	No clasp
29B/325	Langhorn	J	1879
ORDERLY ROOM CLERK			
1693	Flather	R.A	1879
CORPORAL			
1825	Ashton	H	No clasp
29B/978	Barry	J	No clasp
1837	Bates	E	1879r
29B/861	Berry	W.M	1879
29B/792	Bingley	S	1879
29B/1042	Butler	H	1879
1210	Callan	J	1879
29B/984	Cayley	H	1879
29B/744	Cockerill	F	1879
2163	Cooper	J	1879
29B/672	Creek	J	1879
29B/900	Dennsy	J	No clasp
29B/687	Dowell	M	1879
29B/1111	Farrell	P	1879
1519	Fennell	J	1879
429	Fricker	H	No clasp
29B/862	Giles	F	1879
1812	Goodale	R	1879
29B/750	Harrold	J	1879
29B/329	Holton	T	1879
873	Lowrie	J	1879
29B/345	Mackie	H	1879
1400	Mc Cracken	J	No clasp
29B/380	Morris	W	1879
29B/626	Noon	C	1879
1518	Phillips	W	1879
29B/619	Pollard	H	1879
29B/500	Race	T	1879
29B/612	Rudge	H	1879
29B/245	Singleton	H	1879
Forfeited. No reason given.			
29B/305	Smith	J	1879
29B/126	Speed	H	1879
1598	Thompson	W	1879

693	Ward	J	No clasp
29B/353	Weston	T	No clasp
29B/903	Wigley	C	1879
LANCE CORPORAL			
1087	Matthews	J	1879
DRUMMER			
324	Baker	G	No clasp
29B/542	Carr	W	1879
1881	Courtney	J	1879
1227	Creagan	J	1879
29B/1035	Davidson	G	No clasp
29B/136	Derick	J.T	1879
29B/136	Dolbey	G	1879
29B/582	Flannagan	J	No clasp
2152	Fricker	J	1879
2151	Harvey	W	1879
29B/270	Murphy	P	1879
#421	Murray	B	No clasp
1442	Mc Cully	J	1879
1966	Nicel	P	1879
1480	Thomas	G	1879
PRIVATE			
29B/1858	Abbott	D	No clasp
29B/1633	Abbott	R	No clasp
29B/1908	Abert	J	1879
No Medal Deserted.			
29B/914	Able	J	1879
29B/1064	Adams	W	No clasp
29B/765	Addington	C	No clasp
29B/905	Alberry	W	1879
29B/1787	Alford	C	1879
29B/891	Allen	B	No clasp
29B/68	Allen	R	1879
29B/971	Allen	T	1879
29B/1017	Allen	W	1879
29B/1036	Allington	J	1879
29B/1647	Allinston	T	No clasp
29B/2051	Almonds	H	No clasp
29B/1001	Andrews	J	No clasp r
29B/1793	Arscott	G	No clasp
29B/1086	Ashley	E	1879
No Medal Deserted.			
29B/1650	Aspley	J	No clasp
29B/591	Atkins	J	1879
29B/276	Bacchus	W	No clasp
29B/826	Bachellor	J	No clasp
19B/638	Bailey	C	1879
29B/688	Bailey	J	1879
29B/752	Bailey	W	No clasp
1857	Baker	J	1879
29B/1836	Baker	L	1879
29B/1826	Baker	R	No clasp

Spinks Auction Sale 5012 Lot 372. 21 Jul 2005 South Africa 1877-79, one clasp, 1879 (421. Drumr. B. Murray. 58th Foot.), good very fine. Hammer price £1000
421 Drummer Bernard Murray, born Athlone, West Meath, Ireland; enlisted 58th Foot 1859; Drummer 1866; served in the First Boer War (1880-81), and received a gunshot wound to the right breast and lung at Majuba Mountain, 27.2.1881 (London Gazette 29.3.1881); discharged 1882.

58th Regiment

Number	Surname	Initial	Clasp
29B/1897	Banfield	E	1879
29B/1098	Bannon	T	1879
29B/629	Barber	F	1879
29B/813	Barber	J	No clasp
29B/532	Barber	W	1879
1658	Barden	C	No clasp
175	Bargery	H	1879
1835	Barker	W	1879
29B/1862	Barnes	F	No clasp
29B/883	Barr	J	No clasp
29B/656	Barron	W	1879
29B/1846	Bass	G	1879
29B/1114	Bates	J	1879
29B/964	Bates	J	No clasp
29B/1891	Batters	C	1879
29B/814	Bedford	J	No clasp
29B/607	Bedford	R	1879
29B/1806	Beer	J	No clasp
29B/2059	Behan	J	No clasp
29B/2068	Bendall	W	No clasp
29B/644	Benford	S	1879
29B/967	Bennett	J	No clasp
29B/665	Bennett	W	1879
29B/1051	Bent	J	No clasp
29B/1830	Berry	J	1879
29B/648	Betts	J	1879
1824	Bevan	F	No clasp
29B/968	Biles	S	No clasp
29B/791	Bingley	W	1879
29B/1006	Bird	J	1879r
29B/1050	Black	H	1879
29B/674	Blakemore	W	1879
29B/577	Bland	H	1879
29B/1832	Bliss	T	No clasp
29B/711	Bloomsfield	J	No clasp r
29B/2043	Bond	T	No clasp
29B/788	Bostock	W	No clasp
29B/786	Bothrell	W	1879
1548	Bouerbank	J	1879
29B/785	Boulter	T	1879
29B/965	Bourne	A	No clasp
29B/67	Boyle	F	1879
1002	Boyle	J	1879
29B/95	Bradley	T	1879
29B/1063	Brannon	J	No clasp
29B/1079	Branson	J	1879
1164	Brennan	J	1879
29B/1904	Brennan	J	No clasp
29B/1117	Brennan	M	1879
29B/593	Brightwell	J	1879
29B/568	Brockliss	J	No clasp
29B/1750	Brooks	G	1879
29B/673	Bromley	M	1879
2096	Brown	A	1879
2082	Brown	G	1879
29B/513	Brown	G	No clasp
29B/579	Brown	J	1879
29B/1851	Brown	J	1879
29B/901	Brown	J	1879r
29B/727	Brown	J	No clasp No Medal Deserted.
1395	Brown	M	1879
	Brown		No Medal Deserted.
29B/668	Brown	R	No clasp
29B/1808	Brown	S	No clasp
	Brown		No Medal Deserted.
29B/1103	Brown	T	1879
29B/886	Brown	W	1879
1921	Brown	W	1879
29B/2049	Bryan	J	No clasp
613	Budd	J	1879
29B/966	Bugg	C	No clasp
29B/1841	Buggs	G	1879
29B/449	Burden	S	No clasp
29B/555	Burdett	R	1879
29B/1902	Burke	J	1879
29B/130	Burnell	W	No clasp
1920	Burns	O	No clasp
	Burns		No Medal Deserted.
1639	Burns	P	1879
1596	Burry	H	No clasp
29B/947	Burton	B	1879
29B/798	Burton	W	1879
29B/815	Buswell	J	No clasp
808	Bush	G	1879
29B/382	Butter	W	No clasp
2137	Byrne	O	No clasp r
2142	Byrne	P	1879
1149	Cairns	C	1879
29B/1871	Callaghan	G	1879r
1248	Cardwell	R	1879
29B/915	Carham	W	1879
702	Carmody	E	No clasp
1255	Carpenter	P	1879
1270	Carr	T	1879
29B/637	Carrier	W	1879
1755	Carroll	A	1879
29B/1839	Carter	J	1879
1429	Cartwright	J	1879
29B/2046	Chadwick	J	No clasp
1615	Chalk	C	1879
29B/980	Cheek	W	1879
29B/216	Chetwynd	W	1879
29B/953	Church	J	1879
29B/598	Church	S	1879
29B/678	Churchman	D	1879
29B/587	Clapham	E	1879
29B/1142	Clark	W	No clasp
29B/143	Clarke	A	1879
29B/254	Clarke	B	1879
29B/1760	Clarke	E	1879
29B/710	Clarke	J	1879
29B/1742	Clarke	J	No clasp
29B/580	Class	W	1879
29B/1052	Clayton	J	1879
29B/733	Clements	G	1879
29B/885	Clough	J.T	1879
29B/2063	Cock	R	No clasp
29B/518	Cockerill	J	No clasp
29B/1883	Cockling	D	1879
29B/1882	Cockling	J	1879
29B/1923	Codd	R	1879
29B/954	Coles	F	1879
29B/1831	Coles	H	No clasp
29B/955	Coles	R	No clasp
29B/603	Coles	S	No clasp
29B/704	Coles	T	1879
987	Collins	R	1879
29B/1798	Colwell	T	1879
1186	Condron	M	No clasp
29B/1774	Connar	T	1879
29B/1132	Conroll	M	1879
29B/1817	Conroy	J	1879
29B/63	Conway	W	1879
29B/1737	Coogan	M	1879
29B/698	Cook	C	No clasp
993	Cook	J	No clasp
29B/1732	Cook	J	1879
	Cook		No Medal Deserted.
29B/1007	Cook	T	1879
1669	Cook	W	1879
29B/1107	Cooley	F	1879
29B/180	Coombes	W	1879
29B/916	Copsey	B	No clasp
29B/1060	Corbett	B	No clasp
29B/293	Corby	W	No clasp
29B/2056	Cornerford	P	No clasp
29B/1728	Corrigan	J	1879
582	Corry	J	1879
29B/1757	Cosgrove	J	1879r
29B/564	Cotterill	J	1879
29B/368	Cowley	M	1879
29B/556	Cox	A	No clasp
29B/1112	Cox	E	1879
29B/1754	Cox	G	1879
29B/596	Cox	J	1879
29B/1128	Cragg	J	No clasp
29B/1813	Cramon	W	1879
29B/709	Crawford	J	1879
29B/1045	Crawley	W	No clasp
29B/1833	Croker	T	No clasp
	Croker		No Medal Deserted.
1747	Croker	W	No clasp
29B/691	Crooks	L	1879
1086	Crossey	H	1879
29B/803	Crouch	G	No clasp r
			Forfeited. No reason given.
29B/2048	Crowley	D	No clasp
29B/1780	Cullum	B	No clasp r
29B/1892	Cumber	J	1879
29B/667	Cunningham	C	1879
29B/1023	Curl	W.G	1879
29B/348	Currington	G	No clasp r
1541	Curtain	J	1879 r
			Deserted.
29B/661	Curtes	J	1879
29B/365	Dainty	A	No clasp

58th Regiment

Number	Surname	Initial	Clasp	Number	Surname	Initial	Clasp	Number	Surname	Initial	Clasp
29B/1068	Daley	J	No clasp	29B/1772	Elliott	J	1879	29B/487	Garlick	E	1879
29B/987	Daley	L	1879	29B/666	Ellis	W	1879	29B/758	Garey	A	No clasp
29B/1118	Dardas	P	No clasp	29B/940	England	G	No clasp	29B/1876	Garrity	J	1879
29B/1919	Davidson	W	No clasp	29B/534	Essom	A	No clasp	29B/1120	Gaskill	T	1879
29B/615	Davies	W	No clasp	29B/654	Evans	R	No clasp	29B/760	Gawthorne	J	1879
Deserted.				29B/970	Everest	C	1879	29B/1872	Gaylor	J	1879
29B/1842	Davies	W	1879	29B/1843	Everett	W	1879	29B/1873	Gaylor	J	1879
29B/360	Daws	D	1879	29B/434	Everett	W	1879	29B/1773	Gaynor	T	1879
29B/913	Day	W	1879	29B/561	Farmer	G	1879	29B/267	Gibbons	A	1879
29B/1911	Deacon	S	1879	29B/1661	Farmer	J	No clasp	29B/441	Gibbons	P	No clasp
29B/988	Deakin	T	No clasp	29B/498	Farmer	R	1879	# 29B/624	Gibson	E	1879
1577	Dean	S	1879	No Medal Deserted.				29B/622	Gilbert	C	1879
29B/717	Deeming	T	1879	29B/890	Farrell	J	1879	29B/1230	Giles	N	No clasp r
No Medal Deserted.				29B/350	Farrell	T	1879	Forfeited. No reason given.			
29B/1730	Delaney	H	1879	29B/939	Fayakerley	J	No clasp	29B/1816	Gill	W	1879
970	Delaney	J	1879	29B/1642	Fearn	R	No clasp	29B/809	Gillard	G	No clasp
29B/1731	Delaney	N	1879	29B/1492	Ferguson	D	No clasp	1593	Gillboaley	J	1879
Deserted. No trace of return of medal.				29B/681	Ferrier	C	1879	29B/874	Glover	E.H	1879
29B/1874	Demery	N	1879	1118	Field	G	1879	29B/1727	Godfrey	C	1879
Deserted. No trace of return of medal.				29B/827	Filley	C	No clasp	29B/1920	Golbey	A	1879
29B/1743	Destermall	G	1879	No Medal Deserted.				29B/866	Goode	H	1879
29B/1901	Devitt	W	No clasp	1561	Filoe	J	No clasp r	29B/1666	Goodfellow	A	No clasp
1866	Dewsbury	W	1879 r	29B/927	Fincham	J	1879	29B/822	Goodman	G	No clasp
29B/279	Dickens	H	1879	29B/737	Finlay	J	No clasp	29B/313	Goodman	S	1879
1724	Dickson	J	1879	1821	Fisher	J	1879	29B/1478	Goodwin	T	No clasp
29B/1778	Dillon	T	1879	29B/908	Fisher	T	No clasp	29B/1822	Goss	T	No clasp
29B/1008	Dobbyn	P	1879	1399	Fitzharris	T	No clasp	29B/1898	Grady	J	1879
557	Donelly	E	1879	1720	Flint	J	1879	29B/699	Graham	G	No clasp
463	Donolley	W.J	1879	29B/1763	Flynn	P	1879	29B/1784	Graham	W	1879
29B/1735	Donovan	H	1879	29B/1858	Foley	T	No clasp	2099	Grant	W	1879
1589	Doohig	D	No clasp	29B/1845	Forsman	F	1879	29B/679	Greenfield	J.C	No clasp
1355	Dooley	H	1879	29B/956	Fosh	C	1879	2074	Greer	D	1879
29B/1837	Dougherty	J	1879r	29B/960	Foster	J	No clasp	29B/1669	Gribben	J	No clasp
29B/912	Dougherty	W	1879	29B/703	Foster	J	No clasp	29B/761	Griffiths	A	1879r
29B/50	Douglas	F	1879	29B/973	Franklin	W	1879	29B/1751	Griffiths	C	No clasp
29B/1021	Driscoll	J	1879	29B/524	Freeman	C	No clasp r	29B/1010	Griffin	B	No clasp
29B/297	Crury	T	1879	29B/392	French	W	1879	865	Griggs	W	No clasp
Forfeited. No reason given.				29B/61	Fricker	W	1879	1092	Groves	W	1879
29B/1016	Duff	W	1879	29B/820	Frisby	G	1879	1763	Guerin	P	No clasp
1745	Duffey	J	1879	29B/1747	Frite	J.C	No clasp	No Medal Deserted.			
29B/1798	Dunstan	T	No clasp	29B/2052	Frith	E	No clasp	29B/1635	Gunn	A.E	No clasp
No Medal Deserted.				1838	Fry	W	1879	29B/2089	Hacket	C	1879
1744	Dwane	P	1879	29B/1740	Gadd	J	1879	29B/2075	Hadfield	J	No clasp
29B/1865	Dyer	H	1879	29B/1105	Gale	E	1879	1151	Haggerty	J	1879
29B/1781	Eagan	P	No clasp	29B/697	Gallagher	D	No clasp	1678	Haggerty	M	No clasp
29B/671	Eales	T	1879	29B/511	Gamble	J	1879	29B/490	Hales	J	1879
29B/1032	East	J.F	No clasp	29B/766	Gardiner	A.G	1879	29B/972	Hall	H	1879
29B/896	Edwards	E	1879	29B/1089	Gardner	F	1879	29B/1080	Hall	J	1879
29B/385	Edwards	L	1879	A duplicate medal and clasp issued 30/9/1906.				29B/1672	Hall	J	1879
29B/764	Elderkin	W	1879					29B/932	Hall	R	1879
29B/1864	Eldridge	J	1879	29B/1085	Gardner	H	1879	29B/787	Hallis	S	1879
29B/983	Ellerbeck	G	1879	29B/264	Gardner	J	1879	1560	Halpin	R	No clasp
29B/1827	Elliott	E	No clasp	29B/286	Gardner	R	1879	29B/1825	Halsey	G	No clasp
956	Elliott	G	1879	29B/415	Gardner	W	1879	2136	Hammond	J	No clasp

Zulu Medal to 624 Pte Edwin Gibson 58th Foot, on ebay starting bid £300. September 2009. South Africa Medal with 1879 clasp correctly named to 29/624 Pte E. Gibson 58th Foot. Enlisted in Nottingham on 30 Jun 77, fought in the Zulu War and the First Boer War 1880/81. The medal has been broach mounted at some time but this has been carefully. removed. The suspender has also been reaffixed, there is some contact marks around the rim, but all naming is clearly legible.

58th Regiment

Number	Name	Initial	Clasp/Year	Number	Name	Initial	Clasp/Year	Number	Name	Initial	Clasp/Year
29B/1794	Hammond	J	1879 Deserted.					29B/1069	Kimberley	T	No clasp
2136	Hammond	J	No clasp	29B/627	Horne	A.H	No clasp	29B/1859	King	R	1879
29B/897	Hammond	W	1879	29B/288	Horne	G	1879	29B/684	Knight	E	1879
29B/1815	Hancock	W.H	1879	29B/1867	Houghton	J	1879	29B/1786	Knight	J	No clasp
2054	Hanlon	J	1879	29B/1229	Houldgrave	J	No clasp	1436	Knott	J	No clasp
1681	Hanlon	P	1879	29B/606	Houldsworth	A	1879	29B/898	Knowland	D	1879
29B/1801	Hannigan	P	1879 r Forfeited. No reason given.	29B/1011	Howard	E	No clasp				Deserted. No trace of the return of the medal.
				29B/841	Howard	J	1879				
277	Hannigan	W	1879	29B/1847	Howe	H.W	1879	1786	Lacey	W	1879
29B/1819	Hares	O	1879	29B/1655	Howe	T	No clasp	29B/1321	Lambert	G	1879
29B/1795	Harman	G	1879	29B/1916	Hull	J	No clasp	29B/1829	Lamprey	C	No clasp
29B/576	Harmer	W	1879	29B/1127	Humber	H	No clasp	29B/1809	Lang	G	1879 r
1387	Harper	J	1879	29B/1564	Hurst	J	No clasp				Deserted.
29B/1762	Harper	R	1879	29B/1886	Hurst	R	1879	29B/751	Langan	W	1879
29B/801	Harries	A	1879	29B/447	Hurst	W	1879	29B/653	Langford	A	No clasp
29B/1689	Harrison	T	1879	1147	Hutchinson	J	1879	1514	Langston	J	1879
29B/917	Harrod	W	No clasp	29B/823	Hutton	G	1879	29B/1018	Lawrence	E	1879
29B/869	Harvey	H	1879	29B/1059	Huxley	J	No clasp	29B/544	Law	W	1879 r
29B/1084	Hawkins	O	1879	1790	Hyde	J	No clasp				Deserted.
29B/1083	Hawkins	T	1879		No Medal Deserted.			29B/1756	Lawson	H	1879
29B/749	Hay	W	No clasp	29B/1869	Igo	D	No clasp	29B/1489	Layland	J	1879
29B/1893	Hayes	D	1879	29B/918	Ingledon	W	No clasp	29B/1733	Leahey	M	No clasp
	No Medal Deserted.			29B/562	Ingram	J	1879	29B/1828	Learnan	J	No clasp
29B/880	Hayes	W	1879	29B/1041	Innes	J	No clasp	29B/387	Lee	W.G	1879
29B/721	Healey	J	1879	29B/1639	Irish	J.B	1879		No Medal Deserted.		
	No Medal Deserted.			29B/520	Jackson	E	No clasp	1173	Leeks	W	No clasp
1088	Healey	J	1879	29B/819	Jackson	T	1879	1050	Lennon	P	No clasp
29B/1769	Heaney	D	1879	29B/1094	Jackson	W	1879	1661	Letford	T	1879
29B/1792	Heard	T	1879 r Forfeited. No reason given.	29B/1807	James	A	1879	29B/310	Leverett	W	1879
				29B/887	Jamison	M	1879	29B/1022	#Lewis	P	1879
29B/1818	Hearne	J	1879	29B/448	Jelly	W.T	1879	29B/755	Lewitt	B	1879
29B/657	Heathcote	J	1879	29B/422	Johnstone	C	1879	389	Lex	A	1879
29B/494	Hedge	J	No clasp	29B/1077	Johnstone	J	1879	29B/2066	Lightfoot	W	No clasp
29B/1053	Hedges	C	1879	29B/937	Jones	E	1879	29B/1922	Lisch	H	No claspr
29B/1753	Hennessey	M	1879	29B/192	Jones	G	No clasp r	29B/1913	Lock	B	No clasp
29B/1033	Herron	E	1879		Deserted.			29B/577	Lock	W	1879
1562	Hickey	W	1879	29B/1012	Jones	H	No clasp	29B/2057	Long	J.W	No clasp
29B/676	Hickey	W	1879	29B/963	Jones	J	No clasp		No Medal Deserted.		
29B/2055	Higginbottom	T	No clasp		No Medal Deserted.			1843	Long	W	1879
29B/508	Hight	T	1879	29B/1799	Jones	T	1879	29B/444	Lovell	L	1879
29B/652	Hill	G	1879	29B/1877	Kavanagh	D	No clasp r	29B/952	Lovett	E	1879
29B/817	Hill	J	1879	1925	Keane	T	1879	2089	Lowe	D	1879
29B/1820	Hill	J.G	No clasp	1735	Keane	W	1879	29B/863	Luddington	T	No clasp
29B/175	Hinton	C	1879	1718	Keegan	R	1879	29B/982	Luywyche	J	1879
29B/2072	Hoctor	N	No clasp	29B/1061	Keeling	A	No clasp	912	Lynch	D	1879
980	Hoctor	M	No clasp	29B/1797	Keen	R	1879	29B/1748	Lynch	J	No clasp
29B/421	Holman	J	1879	797	Kelley	E	No clasp	29B/1840	Lynch	J	1879
29B/633	Holmes	G	1879	29B/2061	Kelly	M	No clasp		No Medal Deserted.		
29B/1124	Holt	A	No clasp	29B/1738	Kelly	T	1879	1213	Lynch	P	1879
29B/1821	Holt	J	No clasp	832	Kenealey	J	No clasp	974	Lynham	P	1879
1609	Holt	J	1879	1536	Kennedy	W	1879	29B/873	Lyons	P	1879
29B/1037	Holt	T	1879	29B/1139	Kent	A	No clasp	29B/1020	Mack	L	1879
29B/692	Holyland	S	1879	3612	Kent	E	1879	29B/977	Mack	T	No clasp
29B/876	Hoose	G	1879	29B/1095	Kenyon	E	1879	29B/631	Mackley	A.E	No clasp
29B/1129	Hornby	J	No claspr	29B/1921	Kerwin	M	1879	29B/1675	Maddison	J	1879

Glendinings 22nd June 1988 lot 83, South Africa 1877-79, bar 1879, (29/1022 Pte.P.Lewis, 58th Foot) Edge knocks on reverse rim, otherwise very fine estimate £200-£350. Served in first Boar war, 1880-81. Severely wounded at Lain's Nek, 28th January, 1881. (L.G. 29th March, 1881, p 1434)

58th Regiment

Number	Surname	Initial	Year
923	Major	J	1879
29B/337	Mallard	J	1879
29B/637	Mallard	W	No clasp
29B/1725	Maloney	G	1879
29B/1014	Maloney	W	No clasp
29B/330	Manning	J	1879
29B/906	Manuel	G	1879
29B/1875	Marks	J	1879
29B/1104	Maroney	M	1879
1892	Marshall	S	1879
29B/174	Martin	H	1879
29B/59	Martin	H	No clasp
521	Martin	T	1879
29B/554	Maslin	G	1879
2100	Mason	J	1879r
2000	Mason	J.W	1879
29B/670	Mason	W	1879
1572	Masterman	C	1879
29B/702	Matchin	G	1879
29B/586	Matthews	R	No clasp
29B/2176	Maxim	G	1879
1500	Maxwell	D	1879
29B/1761	May	J	1879
29B/597	Maycock	E	1879
29B/590	Maycock	J	1879
29B/386	Mayes	J	1879
29B/867	Mayne	G	1879
2156	Mc Auliffe	P	1879
1085	Mc Cafferty	P	1879r
29B/2098	Mc Carthy	D	No clasp
29B/2069	Mc Carthy	J	No clasp
29B/658	Mc Carthy	J	1879
29B/1890	Mc Carthy	T	1879
29B/1123	Mc Cormack	J	1879
29B/2076	Mc Cormack	M	No clasp
29B/570	Mc Court	W	1879
524	Mc Cracken	J	No clasp
29B/32	Mc Cracken	W	No clasp
29B/1119	Mc Cullurn	J	1879
29B/1062	Mc Donald	J	No clasp
29B/1779	Mc Donald	P	No clasp
29B/941	Mc Donel	P	No clasp
29B/2071	Mc Donough	W	No clasp
1431	Mc Ewen	P	1879
29B/926	Mc Grath	J	1879
29B/355	Mc Gregor	J	1879 r
Forfeited. No reason given.			
1501	Mc Guiggan	A	1879
29B/1115	Mc Guiness	A	1879
1674	Mc Intosh	W	1879
29B/1121	Mc Iver	J	1879
29B/1767	Mc Kegney	J	1879
1154	Mc Keon	M	No clasp
29B/1879	Mc Killop	P	1879
No Medal Deserted.			
29B/816	Mc Kinley	J	1879
29B/928	Mc Laughlin	J	1879
973	Mc Namara	A.J	No clasp
29B/655	Meacham	G	1879
29B/1026	Meadows	J	No clasp
29B/1914	Meakin	J	No clasp
29B/1766	Midoner	J	1879
29B/1043	Millbank	J	No clasp
1095	Miller	T	1879
29B/1854	Miller	W	1879
1823	Mills	J	No clasp
29B/1903	Mills	W	1879
29B/521	Mobbs	W	1879
29B/2045	Monks	J	No clasp
29B/630	Moore	J	1879r
Forfeited. No reason given.			
29B/975	Mooring	J	1879
29B/1848	Morgan	W	1879
29B/336	Morris	E	1879
29B/176	Morris	F	No clasp
29B/1071	Morris	W	1879
29B/875	Mortimer	E	1879
29B/277	Moss	G.J	1879
29B/1075	Moulton	C	1879
29B/888	Moulton	W	No clasp
29B/2047	Mulkern	T	No clasp
29B/808	Munday	G	1879
29B/236	Murray	B	1879
29B/1853	Mustill	W	1879
29B/1099	Mutton	J	1879
29B/1834	Napper	J	1879
29B/2050	Naylor	J	No clasp
29B/922	Naylor	N	1879
29B/919	Neal	S	No clasp
29B/1122	Nelson	P	1879
29B/747	Newbold	J	1879
29B/376	Newbrook	H	1879
29B/1054	Newman	G	1879
29B/1759	Nolan	J	1879
369	Nolan	J	1879
29B/1002	Norton	H	No clasp
29B/327	Nussey	F	No clasp
1155	O'Brien	E	1879
967	O'Brien	L	No clasp
174	O'Brien	W	No clasp
29B/871	O'Connor	A	1879
29B/842	O'Connor	A.H	1879
29B/929	O'Connor	F	1879
29B/324	Ogden	S	1879
29B/795	Old	W	1879
29B/693	Oldham	J	No clasp
29B/1726	O'Neill	A	1879
No Medal Deserted.			
29B/902	O'Reilly	E	1879
29B/1648	Osborne	C	1879
29B/367	Osborne	F	1879
29B/938	Osborne	H	1879
29B/911	Osborne	J	1879
29B/1789	Osmond	W	1879
29B/1889	Page	J	1879
29B/1749	Palmer	J	1879
No Medal Deserted.			
29B/637	Palmer	J	1879r
29B/1026	Meadows	J	No clasp — Deserted.
29B/621	Parker	R	1879
29B/1046	Parker	W	1879
29B/961	Parker	W	1879
29B/1025	Parkes	J	1879
29B/1790	Parsons	G	1879
29B/716	Parrot	E	No clasp
1239	Parry	R	1879
29B/996	Passingham	J	1879
29B/1039	Pateman	C	1879
29B/291	Peach	G	1879
29B/1040	Pearce	R	1879
Deserted. No trace of the return of the medal.			
29B/2042	Pearson	J	No clasp
29B/1098	Pearson	J	1879
29B/1765	Peck	L	No clasp r
29B/1088	Pedder	T	1879
29B/1791	Pedrick	J	1879
29B/909	Pemberton	C	1879
29B/605	Pentelow	J	1879
976	Perkins	J	1879
29B/1895	Perrigo	J	1879
29B/942	Perring	J	1879
29B/946	Peters	C	1879
29B/1878	Pettit	C	1879
29B/299	Peugh	T	1879
29B/1894	Phillips	G	1879
29B/1880	Phillips	G	1879
29B/1048	Phipps	G	1879
29B/1746	Pickroll	J	No clasp
29B/969	Pigrin	B	1879
29B/408	Pilbrow	P	No clasp
29B/1096	Pillburg	J	No clasp
29B/831	Pinfold	B	1879
29B/1126	Platt	J	1879
271	Pointer	E	1879
29B/1078	Pole	G	1879
29B/1484	Poole	G	1879
29B/730	Potter	J	No clasp
29B/993	Poulden	T	1879
29B/1044	Poulton	J	1879
29B/1776	Powell	J	1879r
29B/1777	Power	M	1879
29B/1782	Power	M	No clasp
29B/1856	Preston	T	1879
29B/1785	Pridmore	J	1879
29B/713	Prince	G	No clasp r
1574	Pryce	J	1879
29B/1090	Pullen	F	1879
29B/1762	Purcell	J	No clasp r
1030	Purcell	H	No clasp
29B/981	Purnell	F	1879
No Medal Deserted.			
29B/1800	Pyke	R	1879
29B/1811	Quick	J	1879
29B/640	Quinn	J	1879
29B/1049	Quintrell	J	1879
963	Quirk	W	No clasp

58th Regiment

1850	Raven	W.E	1879	\multicolumn{4}{l}{No Medal Deserted.}	29B/754	Stone	G	1879
29B/481	Rawlings	R	No claspr	29B/2077	Simmonds	W	No clasp	29B/632	Stone	W	1879
29B/1093	Rawson	W	1879	29B/748	Simpson	H	No clasp	29B/2065	Stonehouse	W	No clasp r
29B/1065	Ray	J	No clasp	331	Simpson	T	No clasp r	29B/1841	Storey	R	1879
29B/838	Reed	H	No clasp	29B/992	Sinnott	W	1879	\multicolumn{4}{l}{No Medal Deserted.}
1202	Reefe	P	No clasp	29B/851	Skuce	H	No clasp	29B/720	Sturdy	H	1879
29B/1860	Reilly	J	1879	\multicolumn{4}{l}{No Medal Deserted.}	29B/1072	Styles	W	No clasp
29B/962	Remnant	J	No clasp	482	Smallbones	J	1879	1356	Sullivan	E	1879
29B/1804	Rew	J	1879	29B/1092	Smeardon	S	1879	29B/546	Sullivan	F	1879
29B/1058	Rhodes	E	No clasp	29B/1131	Smith	D	No clasp	29B/1769	Sullivan	N	No clasp
29B/473	Rice	C	No clasp	29B/2179	Smith	E	No clasp	1527	Sutton	R	1879
29B/1096	Rice	W	No clasp	29B/492	Smith	E	1879	29B/2054	Sutton	W	No clasp
1633	Richards	C	1879	29B/1838	Smith	G	No clasp	29B/1852	Swaine	J	1879
29B/1899	Richardson	J	No clasp r	2031	Smith	G	1879	29B/2058	Swaine	M	No clasp
29B/1076	Richmond	J	No clasp	29B/1100	Smith	G	1879	29B/807	Swinfield	A	1879
1214	Rigney	W	No clasp r	29B/643	Smith	G	1879	29B/497	Swinfield	J	No clasp
29B/1910	Ring	W	1879	\multicolumn{4}{l}{No Medal Deserted.}	29B/830	Sykes	F.G	No clasp r
29B/280	Rixon	H	1879	29B/701	Smith	G	1879	\multicolumn{4}{l}{Forfeited. No reason given.}
1450	Roberts	D	No clasp	29B/1646	Smith	H	No clasp	29B/835	Sykes	G	1879
\multicolumn{4}{l}{No Medal Deserted.}	29B/846	Smith	J	No clasp	29B/1918	Talbot	W	No clasp
29B/1812	Robinson	J	1879	\multicolumn{4}{l}{No Medal Deserted.}	29B/1771	Tansley	J	No clasp
29B/589	Rollings	R	No clasp	29B/1788	Smith	J	1879r	29B/794	Tarry	D	No clasp
29B/893	Ross	J	1879	29B/690	Smith	J	1879	29B/811	Tarry	J	1879
29B/1668	Rowe	A	No clasp r	29B/1900	Smith	T	1879	29B/1055	Taylor	F	No clasp
29B/225	Rowe	W	1879	29B/642	Smith	T	No clasp	29B/725	Taylor	J	1879
29B/1849	Rowlands	A	No clasp	29B/705	Smith	W	1879	1578	Taylor	J.T	1879
\multicolumn{4}{l}{No Medal Deserted.}	29B/581	Smith	W	No clasp	29B/1868	Taylor	W	No clasp
29B/1863	Rurnsey	F	1879	29B/958	Smith	W	1879	29B/328	Tero	F	1879
29B/854	Rush	M	1879	29B/1109	Smith	W	1879	673	Thomas	J	1879
29B/1803	Samson	G	1879	1339	Snell	W	1879	29B/845	Thomas	W	1879
\multicolumn{4}{l}{No Medal Deserted.}	29B/707	Sparkes	T	1879	2187	Thompson	A	No clasp
29B/1745	Saunders	H	No clasp	29B/1223	Speechley	W	No clasp r	29B/1896	Thompson	C	1879
29B/611	Saunders	T	No clasp	29B/999	Speed	C	No clasp	\multicolumn{4}{l}{No Medal Deserted.}
29B/1734	Saxton	J.H	1879	\multicolumn{4}{l}{No Medal Deserted.}	1846	Thompson	G	No clasp
29B/1744	Scott	J	No clasp	29B/1081	Spencer	H	1879	1575	Thompson	T	1879r
29B/1097	Scott	T	1879	29B/2067	Spice	R	No clasp	29B/769	Thompson	W	1879
1217	Scully	J	No clasp	29B/899	Spratt	J	No clasp	1197	Tierney	B	1879
337	Seiler	F	No clasp	29B/1881	Squinds	A	1879	29B/342	Tierney	J	1879
29B/1019	Sergeant	W	1879	29B/1116	Stafford	D	1879	2059	Tighe	T	No clasp
29B/1057	Seymour	T	No clasp	29B/1308	Stanton	C	No clasp	29B/502	Tilley	W	1879
29B/986	Sharp	R	1879	29B/1739	Starke	R	1879r	29B/639	Tipping	A	1879
\multicolumn{4}{l}{No Medal Deserted.}	\multicolumn{4}{l}{Deserted.}	29B/1736	Tobin	D	1879
819	Shears	T	1879r	29B/930	Statham	J	1879	29B/934	Tobin	E	1879
29B/1866	Shears	J	No clasp	29B/244	Steele	T	1879	##29B/1138	Tomkinson	J	1879
29B/1814	Sheat	F.H	No clasp	29B/1912	Steele	T	No clasp r	29B/933	Tomlinson	J	1879
29B/677	Sheffield	T	No clasp	\multicolumn{4}{l}{Deserted.}	29B/997	Tongs	S	No clasp
29B/510	Shepherd	J	1879	29B/1855	Steer	E	1879	29B/868	Toohey	T	1879
29B/646	Shore	G	1879	29B/1915	Stephens	C	No clasp	29B/1810	Tovell	W	1879
29B/1805	Short	C	1879	\multicolumn{4}{l}{No Medal Deserted.}	29B/1135	Truswell	R	No clasp
29B/1034	Short	J	1879	29B/2044	Stephens	J	No clasp	29B/96	Tuck	M	1879
29B/418	Simmonds	A	No clasp	#29B/81	Stewart	A	1879	29B/1884	Turner	T	1879
29B/976	Simmonds	L	1879	29B/1887	Stewart	H	1879	29B/2053	Tysoe	J	No clasp

#Glendining's 13th December 1989, Auction Lot 142, Estimate (£300-350) nearly EF
SOUTH AFRICA 1877-9, 1 clasp, 1879 (29/81 **Pte. A.Stewart**, 58th Foot), Pte Stewart served in the Zulu Campaign and was later severely wounded during the First Boer War in the disaster at Laing's Nek, 28th January, 1881.

##Christie's London, Auction Lot 80, 19 July 1988
SOUTH AFRICA 1877-9, 1 clasp, 1879 (1138 **Pte. J.Tompkinson. 58th Foot**), suspension re-affixed, contact marks otherwise very fine 1138 **Private**. J.Tompkinson. was killed in action at Ulundi on 4th July 1879. Estimate £200-£250

58th Regiment

No.	Name	Init.	Notes
	No Medal Deserted.		
29B/261	Underwood	J	1879
29B/789	Vandry	H	1879
29B/1824	Vardy	S	No clasp r
Forfeited. No reason given.			
29B/249	Vaughan	C	No clasp
29B/1013	Vaughan	G	1879
29B/647	Veayey	G	1879
29B/1228	Viles	S	No clasp
282	Vincent	T	No clasp r
29B/1783	Viveash	G	No clasp
29B/812	Walker	J	1879
	No Medal Deserted.		
1011	Walker	R	1879
29B/1752	Walker	W	1879
29B/714	Wall	T	1879
29B/793	Wallace	J	1879
29B/1964	Wallace	J	1879
29B/1764	Wallace	T	1879
29B/145	Waller	T	1879
29B/1729	Walsh	P	1879
29B/1906	Walsh	T	1879
29B/974	Warby	W	1879
29B/746	Ward	G	1879
29B/857	Ward	T	1879
29B/507	Ward	W	1879
29B/898	Warner	J	1879
29B/1136	Warner	T	No clasp
29B/501	Warwick	F	1879
29B/439	Waterfield	J	1879
29B/1056	Waterton	T	No clasp
29B/1091	Waterworth	J	1879
29B/283	Watkins	S	1879
29B/1047	Watson	F	No clasp
29B/614	Watson	J	1879
29B/951	Watson	T	1879
29B/958	Watson	W	No clasp
29B/535	Watts	A	1879
29B/558	Watts	H	1879
29B/266	Watts	J	1879
29B/852	Watts	J	No clasp
Deserted. No trace of return of the medal.			
790	Webb	R	1879
29B/1888	Wederdown	W	1879
29B/849	Welch	M	1879
29B/663	Wells	C	No clasp
830	Welsh	P	No clasp
29B/762	West	B	1879
29B/662	Weston	S	1879
29B/1917	Whelan	E	No clasp
No Medal Deserted.			
29B/1870	Whelan	R	1879
29B/1227	White	J	1879
29B/489	White	J	1879
No Medal Deserted.			
29B/1775	White	J	1879
	No Medal Deserted.		
29B/1631	White	W	No clasp
#29B/1073	Whitehouse	J	1879
29B/2064	Whiteman	A	No clasp
29B/1015	Whitburn	F	1879
29B/1102	Whitfield	W	1879
29B/855	Whitmore	W.J	No clasp r
29B/821	Wilcox	H	No clasp
29B/904	Wilcox	J	No clasp r
29B/547	Wildman	G	No clasp
29B/1907	Wilkens	T	No clasp r
29B/858	Williams	G	No clasp
1054	Williams	J	1879r
878	Williams	J	1879
418	Williams	J	1879
29B/959	Williams	W	1879
29B/557	Williams	W	1879
29B/689	Willis	G	1879
29B/512	Willis	W	1879
2104	Wilson	J	1879
29B/733	Wilson	J	No clasp
29B/1110	Wilson	T	1879
1121	Wingfield	J	No clasp
29B/998	Winkworth	A	No clasp
29B/2073	Wood	H	No clasp
29B/259	Wood	J	No clasp r
Deserted.			
29B/1074	Wood	T	1879
29B/1225	Wooding	H	No clasp
1328	Woods	P	1879r
1107	Woods	P	1879
29B/910	Woodrow	T	1879
29B/1909	Woolf	H	No clasp
No Medal Deserted.			
29B/829	Wootan	B	1879
29B/828	Wootan	C	No clasp
29B/722	Wormwold	J	1879
29B/516	Wright	C	1879
29B/417	Wright	J	1879
29B/2052	Wright	J	No clasp
No Medal Deserted.			
29B/1741	Wright	W	No clasp
29B/636	Wykes	O	1879
29B/715	Yeomans	G	1879
29B/287	Young	E	1879

60th (THE KING'S ROYAL RIFLE CORPS REGIMENT.

BREVET MAJOR
Fryer E.J 1879
Also had Indian Mutiny Medal.

CAPTAIN
Byng G.S 1879
Also had Indian Mutiny Medal with clasp Lucknow.
Lane R.B 1879

LIEUTENANT
Frere B 1879

3/60th (THE KING'S ROYAL RIFLE CORPS) REGIMENT

Present at Gingindhlovu and the relief of Eshowe; two companies acted as escort to the Zulu king after his capture.

LIEUTENANT COLONEL
Pemberton CB W.L 1879
Also had Indian Mutiny Medal.

BREVET LIEUTENANT COLONEL
Grenfell F.W 1877-8-9
Northey F.V 1879
D/W 6/4/1879 Ginghilovo.
Robinson C.W 1879

MAJOR
Ogilvy W.L.K No clasp
Tufnell A 1879
Terry A.F 1879

CAPTAIN & BREVET LIEUTENANT COLONEL
Buller R.H 1878-9
VC CB CMG Also had China Medal (1860) with two clasps and Ashanti War Medal 1873-4. His VC was for Inhlobane.

PAYMASTER
Haynes E.C 1879
See also Army Pay Department.

QUARTERMASTER
Ireland J 1879

CAPTAIN
Bircham A.H 1879
Cramer C.P 1879
Dickenson F.B.N 1879
Fraser E.L 1879
Morris A 1879
Also had China Medal (1860) with two clasps.
O'Brien A.V 1879
Robinson R.C 1879
Smith C.H 1879
Thurlow E.H 1879
Turnour Hon K 1879

LIEUTENANT ADJUTANT
Wilkinson E.O.H 1879

LIEUTENANT
Allfrey H 1879
Astell G 1879
Cotton C.S 1879
Farmer H.L 1879
D/S 20/9/1879.
Featherstonhaug R.S.R 1879
Gunning R.H 1879

Glendinings 22nd June 1988 lot 84, South Africa 1877-79, bar 1879, (29/1073 Pte.J.Whitehouse, 58th Foot) very fine estimate £250-£320. Served in first Boar war, 1880-81. Killed in Action at Majuba Hill, 27th February, 1881.

3/60th Regiment

	Name	Initials	Year								
	Herbert	E.W	1879	QUARTERMASTER SERGEANT				2966	Pettifer	J.C	1879
	Hutton	E.T.H	1879	3935	Gaffney	J	1879	3257	Polkinhorne	E.J	1879
	Michell	C	1879	SERGEANT INSTRUCTOR OF				247	Reid	E	1879
	# Miles	A.E	1879	MUSKETRY				3202	Roberts	A	No clasp
	Nevill	H.J	1879	1951	Langhorne	J	1879	2811	Ward	G	1879
	Thorne	C.R.B	1879	SERGEANT				3230	Williams	O	1879
	Wells	G.H	1879	652	Armstrong	J	1879r	LANCE SERGEANT			
2nd LIEUTENANT				3001	Barton	H	1879	1029	Harrison	J	1879
	Baker	G.C.B	1879	2927	Batchelor	W	No clasp	CORPORAL			
	Crawley	A.P	1879	2314	Blake	W	1879	1069	Barfield	D	1879
	## Garrett	J.R	1879	53	Bowers	J	1879	341	Barrett	R	1879
	Lysley	W.D.V	1879	3046	Britton	J	1879	2728	Caffrey	J	1879
	Markham	W.H	1879	2236	Chambers	G	1879	1520	Clements	G	1879
	Myers	W.J	1879	35	Checkley	J	1879	835	Clifton	E	1879
	Mynors	S.E.B	1879	2978	Chester	H	1879	2046	Codd	A.E	1879
D/S 25/4/1879.				3806	Churches	C.F	1879	995	Critchfield	J	1879
	O'Connell	M	1879	2123	Collyer	A	1879r	774	Crook	G	1879
	Pigott	C.B	1879	1846	Coombe	F.J	1879r	1335	Davis	R	1879
	Ryder	D.G.R	No clasp	62	Cooper	W	1879	1874	Drury	T.H	1879
SERGEANT MAJOR				1074	Cooper	W	1879	1898	Edridge	H	1879
2322	Wilkins	J	1879	3133	Cowan	G	1879	1113	Fanthorpe	W	1879
BAND MASTER				3271	Durrant	G	1879	1115	Fox	C	1879
1595	Walker	A	No clasp	670	Fogg	G	1879	237	Gardener	C	1879
BUGLE MAJOR				259	Freeman	H	1879	978	Healey	L	1879r
2009	Aylett	C	1879	3174	Franklin	H	1879		Deserted.		
COLOR SERGEANT				2299	Gilbert	A	1879	1682	Heath	G	1879
2378	Brown	T	1879	463	Grainger	J	No clasp	2375	Hill	J	1879
3077	Burke	J.W	1879	3035	Hamilton	W.H	1879r	878	Johnson	C.H	1879
2315	Dallon	E	1879	224	Harrington	A	1879	2696	Lambert	W	1879
3030	Dickaty	J	1879	3011	Lovett	T	1879	2634	Leslie	J	1879
1584	Foster	J	1879	2993	Lyons	R	1879r	1412	Leslie	T	1879
2349	Overton	E	1879	2748	Marks	H	1879r		No Medal Deserted.		
2451	Palmer	T	1879	2862	May	H	1879	1064	Malkin	J.W	1879
3044	Shippan	A	1879	2939	Merchant	J	1879	248	Miles	C	1879
ARMOURER SERGEANT				1926	Merriman	J	No clasp	1381	Nixon	F	1879
2419	Proctor	H	1879	2963	Millman	W	1879	805	Orbell	S.J	1879
PAYMASTER SERGEANT				2755	Morrison	W	1879	2235	Payne	A	1879
2586	Fraser	A	No clasp	2638	Nash	W	1879	3028	Peak	R	1879
				2213	Nix	W	1879	1125	Prince	A	1879
				2242	Pemberton	C	1879	3015	Probyn	F	1879

\# Liverpool Medal Company Ltd on Line Sales List, November 2009   http://www.liverpoolmedals.com/
South Africa clasp1879 (Lieut 3/60th Foot) Egypt, 2 bars, The Nile 1884-85, Abu Klea, (Lieut. 2/ K.R.R.C.) to Capt. A.E. Miles, K.R.R.C. Ashanti Star 1896 (unnamed) From Harts 'Served with the 3/60th Rifles in the Zulu War from April to September (medal and clasp). Also served in the Boer War in 1881. Served in the Nile Expedition 1884-85 with the Mounted Infantry Camel Corps, actions of Abu Klea and Gubat - wounded (medal and clasps). Later served with the Wiltshire Yeomanry Cavalry. (3) Cost £3400

\## Buckland Dix & Wood Auction 4th December 1991. Lot 38 The South Africa medal awarded to Lieutenant John Raymond Garrett, 3rd Battalion 60th Regiment, who was killed in action at Ingogo River during the First Boer War
SOUTH AFRICA 1877-9,1 clasp, 1879 (2nd Lt. J. R. Garrett, 3/60th Foot), nearly extremely fine
John Raymond Garrett was born at Crakehall, Yorkshire, son of the Reverend William Thomas Garrett, M.A., J.P., and was educated at Eton College. First commissioned as 2nd Lieutenant with the 11th (Devonshire) Regiment of Foot, he transferred to the 60th on 30 November 1878, and served with them during the campaign against the Zulus in 1879, and subsequently on Special Service. During the action at Ingogo River on 8 February, 1881, Sir George Colley sent one of his staff, Captain McGreggor, R.E., to Colonel Ashburnham with a message that he was to send a company out to the left, as he thought the Boers were going to rush the position. Colonel Ashburnham sent 'I' Company, under Lieutenat Garrett, his only reserve. This side of the position was the one with the least cover, being bare grass, while the rest of the position was mostly covered with rocks and boulders. Captain McGreggor went with them, mounted, to show them where to go. He seems to have gone farther than was intended. He was killed at once and Lieutenant Garrett very soon afterwards. Hammer price £1500

3/60th Regiment

Num	Name	Initial	Year	Num	Name	Initial	Year	Num	Name	Initial	Year
3286	Rogers	W	1879	2584	Applegate	H	1879	1576	Booth	G	1879
617	Stonestreet	N	1879	460	Applin	H.W	No clasp	1734	Boswell	H	1879
2089	Tilbury	D	1879	2218	Archer	W	1879	1670	Bowers	F	1879r
3369	Veitch	J.S	1879	2253	Arnold	W	1879	849	Bowles	W	1879
2954	Ventham	H	1879	3217	Arter	T.J	1879	788	Boyd	T	1879
3200	Wardle	F	1879	3409	Arthur	T	1879	3232	Brain	G	1879
3187	Warner	C	1879	3374	Ashworth	J	1879r	2170	Bramhall	G	1879
252	Watson	J	1879	1784	Aspinall	S	1879	2219	Brewer	G	1879
997	Webb	W	1879	875	Astle	J	1879	913	Brewer	W.H	1879
3048	Wright	S	1879	3386	Attenborough	G	1879	He may have been the recipient of two awards.			
LANCE CORPORAL				No Medal Deserted.							
2742	Cartwright	J	1879	1895	Austin	C	1879	733	Bristow	F	1879
2205	Clifton	J	1879	1825	Austin	H	1879	976	Britton	J	1879
1332	Constantine	E	1879	1150	Auty	J	1879	2101	Brock	J	1879
3618	Jones	P.E	1879	3210	Axelby	W	1879	1941	Brocker	C	1879
2950	Kelleher	T	1879	2143	Ayers	H	1879	1957	Brook	W	1879
2325	Legge	R	1879	1221	Aylott	F	1879	2127	Brooker	A	1879
114	Mills	W.F	1879	858	Babbington	R	1879	834	Brooker	G	1879
1160	Moloney	W.J.D	1879	3247	Bailey	W	1879	2022	Brooks	A	1879
1259	Mudd	J	1879	2062	Bailey	W	1879	1026	Brooks	W	1879
242	O'Brian	J	1879	2128	Bailey	W.J	1879	1018	Broughton	C	1879
2193	Ryan	M	1879	204	Baker	A	1879	856	Brown	E	1879
764	Scurfield	C	No clasp	1941	Baker	C	1879	2239	Brown	G	1879r
1444	Sherman	A	1879	1055	Ballington	A	1879	Deserted.			
215	Sherwood	F	1879	1077	Balls	W.J	1879	2089	Brown	T	1879
3111	Smith	G	1879	175	Bargery	H	1879	1816	Brunt	J	1879
2336	Wickenden	T	1879	145	Bargery	W.J	1879	1802	Bryant	G	1879
2980	Wise	D	1879	783	Barker	J	1879	897	Bryant	J	1879
LANCE CORPORAL BUGLER				1696	Barlow	A	1879	2103	Buckett	A	1879
350	Daniels	G	1879	3530	Barnard	G.J	1879	2116	Buckley	N	1879
ORDERLYROOM CLERK				3349	Barnes	W	1879	2207	Buckley	W	1879
1166	Reid	J.J	1879	2247	Barrett	J	1879	3079	Bull	G	1879
2027	Allen	J	1879	1990	Barrett	J	1879	2940	Bunny	T	1879
2130	Allsop	C	1879	1515	Barry	T	1879r	3086	Burke	M	1879
815	Broomfield	J	1879	Deserted.				891	Burn	E	1879
446	Brennan	P	1879	770	Bartell	W	1879	2873	Burn	G	1879
981	Coleman	T	1879	2197	Barton	W	1879	2105	Burns	J	1879
1198	Dawkins	J.W	1879	1545	Bassham	J	1879	2212	Burnett	W	1879
1942	Fryer	C	1879	1567	Bateman	W	1879	1958	Burrows	D	1879
1943	Gibson	E	1879	2164	Baumann	A	1879	2770	Burrows	J	1879
43	Howe	S	1879	290	Beale	J	1879	No Medal Deserted.			
228	Milledge	J	1879	3330	Bean	J	1879	1577	Burt	J	1879
1169	Oakley	J	1879	190	Belcher	J	1879	3514	Burton	E	1879
2091	Parsons	W	1879	1345	Bellinger	C	1879	1939	Burton	W	1879
788	Plover	W	1879	2100	Bellinger	F	1879	3616	Bushlan	M	1879
1636	Richards	F	1879	2439	Belmore	E	1879	3848	Butler	C	1879
1410	Such	A	1879	2148	Benn	S	1879	1863	Butler	F	1879
3203	Wyatt	C	1879	339	Bennett	W	1879	742	Butler	T	1879
3847	Youart	W	1879	1821	Berry	A.H	1879	293	Calthorpe	C	1879
PRIVATE				1225	Berry	F	1879	2512	Cannon	G	1879
3147	Abbennett	W	1879	3104	Berry	J	1879	3489	Care	K	1879
3304	Adams	W	1879	759	Berry	J	1879	1049	Carroll	F	1879
751	Allen	H	1879	2996	Best	W	1879	2973	Carter	H	1879
3371	Allen	T	1879	2040	Birch	B.H	1879	2331	Carter	H	1879
3432	Allen	W.H	No clasp	3235	Blackmore	W.J	1879	1249	Carter	R	1879
1896	Ambrose	H	1879r	1790	Blanchard	H	1879	3192	Carton	A	1879
Deserted.				2642	Bolwin	G	No clasp	866	Castle	H	1879
1971	Anderson	H	1879	1011	Bond	W	1879	1557	Caswell	J	1879
1454	Andrews	C	1879	1353	Bone	H	No clasp	2288	Cattle	W	1879

3/60th Regiment

Number	Name	Initial	Year
1516	Chalk	C	1879
561	Champion	C.H	1879
2063	Chapman	D.W	1879
1262	Chapman	W	1879
3332	Chappell	J	1879
3467	Cheser	H	No clasp
974	Chipp	R	1879
1196	Chittenden	J	1879
1764	Cills	J	1879
2285	Clapp	F.G	1879
1983	Clarke	J	1879
426	Clarke	J	1879
2087	Clarke	J.W	1879
1949	Clarke	J.W	1879
3074	Clay	P.J	1879
1104	Clementson	W	1879r
1906	Clifton	H.A	1879
425	Coates	J	1879
3343	Coates	J	1879
1934	Coe	C	1879
2121	Coffman	G	1879r
Deserted.			
1740	Cole	A	1879
3488	Cole	D	1879
4211	Coles	G	1879
2138	Coleman	C	1879
2737	Coleman	R	1879
1617	Collins	H	1879
2248	Collins	J	1879
2098	Collins	J	1879
255	Collis	W	1879
1375	Connolly	P	1879
3397	Connolly	T	1879
994	Connors	J	1879
3383	Connors	T	1879
3180	Conway	P	No clasp
3323	Cook	A.G	1879
1207	Cook	C.E	1879
621	Cooke	F	1879
986	Coomber	F	1879
790	Cooper	C	1879
1870	Cooper	E	1879
2269	Cooper	G	1879
1498	Cooper	J.G	1879
2170	Cooper	T	1879
3056	Corbett	D	1879
1838	Cordery	G.J	1879
3850	Corin	F	1879
245	Costin	H	1879
3208	Courtney	G	1879
3425	Cox	C	1879
2070	Cox	E.J	1879
822	Cox	J	1879
3490	Cox	J	1879
1889	Cox	W	1879
1947	Crabb	G	1879
809	Crabbe	J	1879
1663	Crawley	E	1879
1729	Crawley	J	1879
127	Crayford	J	1879
789	Crocker	W	1879
3430	Crofts	C	1879
2294	Crofts	G	1879
3107	Crofts	T	1879
2703	Crofts	W	1879
3279	Crowdson	T	1879
208	Culley	G	1879
3212	Cullum	R	1879
1168	Cummings	W	1879
3662	Curd	G	1879
712	Curel	W	1879
1780	Curtis	W	1879
3310	Daniels	G	1879
1628	Darley	C	1879
1691	Davis	C	1879
2700	Davis	E	1879
1067	Davis	E	1879
3366	Davison	J	1879
1745	Dawkins	C	1879
1207	Dawson	R.C	1879
1540	Dellar	J	1879
912	Denny	J	1879r
2070	Dent	R	1879
2118	Diamond	H	1879
2251	Dixon	G	1879
780	Docking	W	1879
1358	Dooley	?	1879r
Forfeited. No reason given.			
1778	Dooley	M	1879
1746	Douglas	W	1879
2072	Dowdall	J	1879
2299	Dowling	W	1879
2266	Downer	G	1879
2371	Draper	G.W	1879
1233	Driscoll	J	1879
1107	Driver	M	1879
2194	Duck	F	1879
2372	Duffin	H	1879
1415	Duffin	T	1879
1649	Duffy	C	1879
2319	Eales	J	1879
1678	Eames	J	1879r
Deserted.			
3363	Eaton	J	1879
768	Edwards	G	1879
1061	Edwards	J	1879
165	Edwards	J	1879
1040	Edwards	T	1879
1106	Eighteen	J	1879
3285	Elliott	J.W	1879
3370	Ellis	J	1879
1139	Ellis	R	1879
3320	Emmerson	T	1879
3330	Emmett	J	1879r
Deserted.			
1991	Emsley	W	1879
792	Evans	C	1879
36	Everest	J	1879
3244	Farley	J	1879
3548	Farley	T	1879r
Forfeited. C.M. Prisoner.			
1433	Farmer	W	1879
1645	Farnham	G	1879
2190	Farrant	W	1879
2039	Farrell	T	1879
1728	Faulkner	G	1879
1951	Fawcett	J	1879
3396	Felton	H	1879
1753	Field	J.W	No clasp
2912	Field	T	1879
539	Filby	J	1879
3188	Finn	A	1879
2540	Fitzgerald	G	1879
3379	Flanagan	M	1879
306	Floodgate	G	1879
3489	Flynn	D	1879
2184	Flynn	H	1879
2136	Flynn	S	1879
2813	Forkgen	T	No clasp r
2345	Forsyth	T	1879
3327	Foulkes	W	1879
3	Fox	W	1879
907	Foxwell	J	1879
1495	France	E	1879
1873	Franey	J	1879
2894	Franklin	B	1879
3852	Franklin	G	1879
1552	Fraser	A	1879
3410	Freeman	T	1879
3486	Fribbans	D	1879
1913	Gale	G	1879
733	Gamble	W	1879
1494	Garrett	E	1879
320	Gastelow	J	1879
2222	Geddes	D	1879r
3465	Gentry	G	1879
3495	German	D.W	1879
1532	Gescoyne	F	1879
2550	Gibbs	H	1879
250	Gilchrist	H	1879
1994	Gilford	F	1879
327	Gilman	T	1879
968	Gilman	T	1879
1871	Gilroy	P	1879r
3493	Ginn	J	1879
709	Goddard	C	1879
1599	Goddard	G	1879
2034	Goodson	T	1879
2176	Goodwin	J	1879
154	Grant	H	1879r
Two awards possible to this man.			
547	Grant	J	1879
3309	Grave	W	1879
2197	Green	C	1879
667	Green	W	1879
3314	Green	W	1879
No Medal Deserted.			

3/60th Regiment

92	Greenaway	A	1879	59	Healey	T	1879	3199	Ireland	W.H	1879
643	Greenaway	W	1879	1862	Heath	G	1879r	1585	Irwin	I	1879
1773	Greening	J	1879		Forfeited. No reason given.			871	Jacques	E	1879
958	Gregory	T	1879	1439	Heath	W	1879	3354	Jakes	J	1879
1480	Grey	R	1879	2138	Heather	H	1879		No Medal Deserted.		
1554	Greystone	E	1879	901	Herbert	T	1879	2140	James	H	1879r
1882	Grimsley	T	1879	1716	Herridge	W	1879		Forfeited. No reason given.		
3858	Grove	C	No clasp r	2156	Hewitt	J	1879r	1490	James	J	1879
1880	Groves	H	1879		Deserted.			3460	Jarvis	D	1879
2215	Gruncell	C	1879	1828	Hicks	F	1879	882	Jeal	J.W	1879
3319	Grundy	W	1879	1217	Hill	G	1879	615	Jenkins	T	1879r
1510	Gurney	J	1879	1578	Hill	I	1879	1772	Jenkinson	H	1879
	No Medal Deserted.				1416	Hill	J	1879	2125	Jerome	W	1879
2110	Guthrie	J	1879		No Medal Deserted.			2530	Johnson	C	1879
2956	Guyatt	J	1879	3429	Hill	R	1879	3498	Johnson	J	1879
414	Gwynn	J	1879	178	Hill	T	1879	2283	Johnson	J	1879
39	Haggis	J	1879	1186	Hillier	J	1879	3128	Johnson	W	1879
2119	Hailstone	E	1879	1362	Hines	W	1879	183	Jones	D	1879
1902	Hailstone	F	1879		Duplicate medal and clasp issued			2806	Jones	H	1879
659	Haines	R	1879		10/11/1917.			1124	Jones	J	1879
1157	Hall	F.R	1879	2181	Hodson	J	1879	1472	Jones	J	1879
1076	Hall	J.H	1879	1518	Hodges	H	1879	869	Jones	R	1879r
1060	Hall	W	1879	1743	Holley	W	1879	881	Jones	T.A	1879
1861	Hallett	C	1879	1400	Holloway	T	1879	2130	Jones	W	1879
1414	Ham	E	1879	823	Holman	J	1879	1724	Jones	W	1879
1266	Hambling	W.B	1879	2988	Holmes	J	1879	1116	Jordan	W	1879
3347	Hamilton	L	1879	950	Holmes	J	1879	3315	Judge	T	1879
2139	Hampton	G	1879	3246	Holmes	P	1879r	1355	Kane	P	1879
2089	Hand	J	1879	1174	Holton	W	1879	1437	Kearns	T	1879
348	Hankey	E	1879	1383	Hones	C	1879	1153	Keefe	H	1879
104	Hannis	G	1879	2104	Hooper	G	1879		No Medal Deserted.		
3506	Hanson	T	1879	2111	Hopkins	H	No clasp	2097	Kelly	J	1879
3316	Hare	S	1879	1093	Hopson	W	1879	3345	Kelly	J	1879
	No Medal Deserted.				814	Horne	A	1879	2172	Kelly	N	1879
1912	Hargreaves	J	1879	2896	Horne	G	1879r	2159	Kelly	R	1879
1541	Harmer	R	1879	2270	Horner	J	1879	1417	Kelly	N	1879
1129	Harrabin	E	1879	980	Horton	R	1879	3434	Kempshall	H	1879
2013	Harradine	G	1879	3564	Hounsell	H	1879	949	Kennedy	T.V.P	1879
244	Harrington	W.C	1879	778	Howe	F	1879r		No Medal. C.M. Prisoner in England.			
2578	Harris	E	1879	1588	Howes	S	1879	3612	Kent	E	1879r
631	Harris	J.C	1879	2275	Howse	G	1879	969	Keogh	W	1879
1537	Harris	T	1879	1572	Howse	J	1879	1768	Kerrigan	T	1879r
896	Harris	T	1879	2410	Hudson	R	1879r	1878	Kevill	H	1879
1978	Harris	W	1879		Forfeited. No reason given.			3019	Kilpin	E	1879
1955	Harrison	F.G	1879	2323	Hughes	G.H	1879	1932	Kingston	G	1879
3400	Harrison	H.H	1879r	1499	Hughes	J	1879	752	Knight	G	1879
1606	Harrison	S	1879	939	Hughes	T	1879	962	Knight	J	1879
1058	Harrod	T	1879	2066	Humberstone	W	1879	1899	Knowles	T	1879
990	Hart	F	1879	2281	Humphrise	W.H	No clasp	2188	Ladley	G	1879
3491	Hartney	J	1879	2099	Hunt	J	1879r	1316	Lahiff	H	1879r
824	Harton	R	1879	2045	Hunt	S	1879		Deserted.		
2282	Harvey	H	1879	3356	Hunter	G	1879	3611	Lamb	D	1879
1455	Harvey	W	1879	2025	Hurdus	J.S	1879	3031	Lambden	A	1879
3525	Hasted	W.R	1879	1493	Hurley	M	1879	1982	Lambert	F	1879
2210	Hawkins	T	1879	2057	Hurley	P	1879	3449	Lane	J.P	No clasp
3867	Hayes	R	1879	1601	Hurn	J	1879	1375	Lang	J	1879
2784	Hayman	T	1879	2453	Illsley	G	1879	1837	Langley	G	1879
2902	Hayter	J	1879	2453	Irman	G	1879	2241	Larcombe	W	1879

3/60th Regiment

49	Larkins	W	1879	3403	Masterson	J	1879r	226	Nice	F	1879
3500	Lattice	J	No clasp r	Forfeited. No reason given.				2910	Nicholas	A	1879
Deserted.				889	Matthews	J	1879	1809	Nicholls	G	1879
1788	Lavis	T	1879	2983	Mayo	T	1879	393	Nicklefs	H	1879
2074	Leadley	H	1879	1618	Mc Cabe	P	1879	No Medal. Discharged with ignominy.			
2550	Leahy	D	1879	#1965	Mc Cann	J	1879	3075	Nixey	J	1879
150	Leahy	J	1879r	138	Mc Carthy	J	1879	1167	Noakes	C	1879
2239	Legg	W.C	1879	1715	Mc Cullough	R	1879	1034	Norris	C	1879
1797	Leggett	R	1879	3358	Mc Farlane	W	1879	1033	Norris	W.J	1879
1144	Letchford	S	1879	3346	Mc Gann	J	1879	2130	North	G	1879
2598	Lewis	F	1879	3277	Mc Glocking	C	1879	2883	North	J	1879r
2611	Lewis	W	1879	3401	Mc Grane	C	1879	3034	Nortley	W	1879
1812	Lift	R	1879	3402	Mc Grane	M	1879	1061	Nunn	J	1879
1642	Linscott	T	1879	841	Mc Manus	F	1879	1442	Nutt	J.B	1879
1886	Livesay	J	1879	1884	Mc Namara	J	1879	No Medal Deserted.			
2183	Lock	H	1879	3361	Mc Nulty	E	1879	1213	O'Connor	F.P	1879
3321	Lockett	J	1879	2538	Meaghan	W	1879	922	O'Connor	M	1879
2342	Loftus	J	1879r	857	Medwell	C	1879	3496	Odell	W	1879
806	Lomas	F.J	1879	No Medal Deserted.				3193	Ogden	T	1879
?	Lomas	I	1879	2149	Mefsenger	W	1879	278	Ogden	T	1879
Servant to Prince Imperial.				2123	Merchant	C	1879	1851	O'Hara	J	1879
2426	Lovelock	E.C	1879	3087	Merchant	F	1879r	30	Oliver	A	No clasp
722	Lovelock	H	1879	2006	Merrills	J	1879	1550	O'Meara	J	1879
1765	Lovelock	H	1879	No Medal. Discharged with ignominy.				3858	Orchin	H	1879r
336	Lovick	G	1879	599	Merry	G	No clasp r	52	Osborne	J	1879
2020	Lowe	J	1879	2120	Miles	G	1879	814	O'Shaughnysy	T	1879
1219	Lynam	T	1879r	No Medal Deserted.				1267	Page	G	1879
2348	Lynch	J	1879	1128	Millard	T	1879	2206	Page	G	1879
2911	Lyons	T	1879	1484	Millard	W	1879	3427	Paintin	S	1879
1875	Macrow	H	1879	1963	Miller	J	1879	1373	Palmer	A	1879
2173	Madigan	T	1879	1579	Mills	W	No clasp	1581	Palmer	C.H	1879
3241	Maggs	J	1879	2227	Monger	D	1879	50	Palmer	J	1879
923	Major	J	1879	3485	Monk	S	1879	2082	Pankhurst	J	1879
1974	Maldon	A	1879	3436	Moore	J	1879	944	Parker	C.J	1879
2193	Manley	C	1879	2399	Moore	J	1879	929	Parker	J.H	1879
3325	Mann	J	1879	3313	Moore	M	1879	2252	Parkins	J	1879
335	Manners	W	1879	3373	Moreton	A	1879	Deserted. Issued 3/11/1911.			
1070	Manning	J	1879	2982	Morgan	C	1879	3482	Parr	T	1879
2036	Manning	J	No clasp	2255	Morgan	F	1879	3355	Parr	W	1879
2221	Mannion	M	1879r	241	Morgan	H	1879	862	Parry	P	1879
Deserted.				1807	Morgan	H	1879	4227	Parsons	E	1879
598	Maple	A	1879	1041	Morris	H.G	1879	469	Parsons	F	1879
2369	Marritt	G	1879	3378	Morris	J	1879	2353	Partridge	A	1879
630	Marshall	D	1879	3196	Mullins	F	1879	1647	Patterson	F	1879
1056	Marshall	F.C	1879	1256	Mullins	J	1879	3388	Pattison	T	1879
3394	Marshall	H	1879	3002	Mullins	L	1879	2408	Pauling	G	1879
2156	Martin	E	1879	776	Murphy	W	1879	3278	Pedder	W	1879
1761	Martin	G	1879	1850	Murray	J	1879	1776	Pelliseur	A	1879
194	Martin	J	1879	1964	Murray	J	1879r	2488	Penfold	W	1879
2135	Martin	J	1879	1222	Myers	J.N	1879	2005	Perkins	W	1879
2064	Martin	J.J	1879	1265	Nash	W	1879	2318	Perry	G	1879
2276	Martin	R	1879	3376	Naylan	E	1879	3317	Perry	H	1879
1231	Martin	T	1879	890	Neal	R	1879	1091	Perry	W	1879
1131	Martin	W	1879	3368	Newman	C	1879	141	Petherwick	R	1879
3262	Mason	F	1879	2205	Newman	T	1879	1188	Pheby	G	1879
992	Mason	G	1879	1832	Newton	A	1879	1600	Phillips	E	No clasp

#Glendining & Co Auction Lot 539, 28 September 1972
SOUTH AFRICA 1877-9, 1 clasp, 1877-8-9 (**Pte. J. McCann 3/60th Foot**),Very Fine.   Killed at the Ingogo RiverUlundi

3/60th Regiment

Num	Name	Init	Year	Num	Name	Init	Year	Num	Name	Init	Year
1411	Phillips	H	1879	3459	Roberts	J.F	1879	2460	Shrimpton	W	1879
2112	Phillips	P.D	1879	3372	Roberts	S	1879	2160	Siggers	F.H	1879
1756	Pickett	C	1879	811	Roberts	T	No clasp	2059	Sillett	W	1879
951	Pigrem	C	1879	3431	Robinson	A	1879	840	Simmonds	H	1879
1441	Pike	F	1879	943	Robinson	J	1879	3519	Simmonds	T	1879
2240	Pippler	J	1879	1546	Robinson	J	1879	3322	Simpson	G.H	No clasp
3557	Pocock	J	1879	2166	Robinson	W	1879	1785	Simpson	J	1879
3570	Pocock	T	1879	2256	Rockeli	T	1879	2019	Singleton	M	1879
2171	Pope	T	1879	3143	Roden	P	1879	3225	Slade	E	1879
1926	Poplett	W	1879	1952	Rogers	J	1879	2264	Small	J	1879
3204	Pore	G	1879	2243	Rogers	T	1879	3438	Smewin	R	1879
2159	Porteous	R	1879					411	Smith	A.G	1879
807	Potkins	W	1879	2072	Roggers	G	1879	914	Smith	C	1879
2615	Powell	C.W	No clasp r	251	Romer	H	1879	915	Smith	C	1879
937	Pratley	C	1879	3142	Rooney	J	1879r	3061	Smith	E	1879
1747	Pratt	J	1879					2480	Smith	G	1879
1793	Preston	J	1879	1235	Rowley	G	1879	2234	Smith	G	1879
1881	Price	S.S	1879	1507	Roysence	J	1879				
3267	Priest	W	1879	3341	Rozier	H	1879	1202	Smith	H	1879
2289	Prior	W	1879r	985	Rumney	A	1879	2260	Smith	J.H	1879

No Medal. Discharged with ignominy. (after 2159 Porteous)
Forfeited. No reason given. (after 1747 Pratt)
Deserted. (after 2289 Prior)
No Medal. Discharged with ignominy. (after 985 Rumney)
No Medal Deserted. (after 2260 Smith J.H area)

Num	Name	Init	Year	Num	Name	Init	Year	Num	Name	Init	Year
955	Punter	H	1879	1598	Russell	C	1879	1962	Smith	J.J	1879
715	Purcell	W	1879	2258	Russell	F	1879	3860	Smith	M	1879r
3523	Puzey	G	1879	2273	Russell	M	1879	474	Smith	M	1879
1395	Pyatt	F.J	1879	938	Rutter	A	1879	3292	Smith	P.J	1879
1176	Pyle	A	1879	3324	Saich	W	1879	2556	Smith	P.J	1879
2337	Pysing	G	1879	2180	Sainsbury	E	1879	1080	Smith	S	No clasp
2065	Quade	J	1879	1891	Salter	J	1879	2930	Smith	T	1879
766	Quarterman	W	1879	1774	Sartin	A	1879	3367	Smith	T	1879
1864	Quinn	S	1879	2574	Savory	A	1879				
638	Radford	W	1879	2100	Sawyers	J	1879	2340	Smith	W	1879
3392	Ramsey	J	1879	1374	Say	S	1879	2855	Smith	W	1879
44	Randall	W	1879	2870	Sayers	R	1879	2310	Smith	W	1879
1523	Range	R	1879	1089	Scholey	H	1879	289	Smowton	I	1879
2678	Rankin	P	1879	1234	Scott	C	1879	529	Snashall	R	1879

Deserted. No trace of the return of the medal. (after 2678 Rankin)
No Medal Deserted. (after 3367 Smith T)

Num	Name	Init	Year	Num	Name	Init	Year	Num	Name	Init	Year
				3298	Searle	J	1879	2948	Snell	A.W	1879
1565	Ransley	W	No clasp	868	Selby	F.W	1879	1897	Somerville	C	1879
846	Rayner	J	1879r	2227	Sexton	H	1879	2030	Sopp	H	1879
2203	Readings	J	1879	1230	Seymour	F	1879	945	Spanton	J	1879
1986	Reardon	A	1879	2209	Seymour	J	1879	1112	Sparrow	J	1879
2120	Reddy	R	1879	2856	Seymour	W	1879	565	Spearing	C	1879
3300	Reeves	A	No clasp	1409	Sharpe	H	1879	953	Springall	W	1879
(Alias John Hope)				2262	Sharpe	H	1879	1803	Squires	F	1879
				1360	Sharpe	J	1879	1046	Squirrell	A	1879
2282	Reeves	J	1879	538	Sharpe	W	1879r	3457	Standish	G	1879
1639	Reid	W	1879	2021	Sharpe	W	1879				
1633	Richards	C	1879r	852	Shaw	S.H	1879	298	Stanley	C	No clasp
1636	Richards	F	1879	2107	Shean	J	1879	3191	Stanley	J	1879
2004	Richards	R	1879	2158	Shearman	T	1879	879	Stanley	T	No clasp
1336	Richardson	E	1879	1200	Shears	F	1879	1073	Stanley	W	1879
1083	Richardson	R	1879	987	Sheldrake	E	1879	1822	Starks	E	1879
1808	Richings	J	1879	3297	Shepherd	A.H	1879	2384	Starman	W	1879
1005	Ricketts	J	1879	3555	Shepherd	G	1879	964	St Clair	E	1879
3418	Ridley	T	1879					1024	Steer	E	1879

Deserted. No trace of the return of the medal. (after 3418 Ridley)
No Medal Deserted. (after 3555 Shepherd G)
No Medal Deserted. (after 2021 Sharpe W)

Num	Name	Init	Year	Num	Name	Init	Year	Num	Name	Init	Year
				1402	Shergold	H.J	No clasp	3404	Steer	G	1879
				1608	Sherwood	G	1879	2587	Stewart	W.O	1879
3484	Rigg	J.N	1879	928	Shingleton	D	1879	2220	Still	T	1879
151	Roach	J	1879	1054	Shirley	J	1879	1071	Stimson	G	1879
2415	Roberts	F	1879	1806	Shreeves	E	1879	1482	Stokes	B	1879

3/60th Regiment

Captain D.B. Moriarty (Page 292)

No.	Name	Init	Year
	No Medal Deserted.		
999	Strange	G	1879
184	Strickett	G	1879
1361	Stringer	E	1879
1917	Stuckey	H	1879
2246	Stunt	W.G	1879r
762	Sturgeon	A.R	1879
1406	Styles	W	1879
3164	Suckling	S	1879
2105	Sulin	J	1879
1232	Sullivan	E	1879
611	Sullivan	J	1879
970	Sutton	G	1879
661	Sutton	G	1879
3062	Swain	J	1879
1160	Swan	E	1879
	No Medal. Discharged with ignominy.		
3464	Tarbotton	J.H	1879
1119	Tarry	W	1879
1330	Taylor	C	1879
1248	Taylor	F	1879
3504	Taylor	J	1879
2552	Taylor	J	1879
1810	Taylor	R	1879
2861	Terry	W	1879
747	Thomas	A	1879
3160	Thomas	J.W	1879
1135	Thomas	W	1879
3315	Thomas	W	1879
1170	Thompson	G	1879
2143	Thompson	J	1879
3619	Thompson	J	1879
2166	Thorne	G	1879
2555	Threadgold	G	1879
3364	Tinley	P	1879
3411	Toop	C	1879
353	Townsend	R	1879
2270	Troy	C	1879
	Deserted.		
1453	Trueman	W	1879
2126	Tucker	G	1879
3311	Turfrey	J	1879
55	Turner	A	1879
2230	Turner	H	1879
3476	Turner	J	1879
3360	Turner	T	1879
942	Turrell	C	1879
3615	Twigg	J	1879
2280	Twyman	H.J	1879
3554	Tyler	J	1879
34	Uhrmacher	W	No clasp
1833	Underhill	J	1879
988	Underwood	A	1879
415	Usherwood	T	1879
3458	Vale	H	No clasp
	No Medal Deserted.		
2167	Vale	M	1879
2274	Verney	T	1879r
1051	Vice	S	1879
3512	Vile	W	1879
1845	Vincent	H	1879
3268	Virgin	J.G	1879
57	Wade	J.W	1879
3451	Wagstaff	E	1879
3515	Waite	A	1879
2381	Wait	J	1879
623	Walker	W	1879
1424	Wall	D	1879
2225	Wallace	F	1879
3212	Warburton	J	1879
1787	Ward	H	1879
3487	Ward	J	1879
	No Medal Deserted.		
2185	Ware	W	1879
2402	Wareham	H	1879
1751	Wareham	R	1879r
557	Waterage	J	1879
2502	Waterhouse	W	1879
2132	Watkinson	W	1879
3614	Watson	C	1879
3190	Watson	J.H	1879r
800	Watts	W	1879
804	Webb	D	1879
2137	Webb	H	1879
2944	Webb	W	1879r
1258	Wells	A	1879
3042	Townsend	W	1879
1888	Wells	J	1879
1813	Wells	W	1879
1743	Wells	W	1879
1523	Wells	R	1879
1505	Welsh	T	1879
1393	Welsh	W	1879
680	Wesley	W.H	1879
1630	West	C	1879r
1918	Wheeler	E.R	1879r
2093	Wheeler	H	1879r
131	White	H	1879
2048	White	M	1879
	No Medal Deserted.		
755	Whitehead	T	1879
2157	Whittaker	F	1879
1927	Williams	G	1879
3318	Williams	H	1879
2228	Williams	J	1879
	No Medal Deserted.		
1623	Williams	R	1879
1824	Williamson	H	1879
769	Willsher	F	1879
3606	Wilson	J	1879
2416	Winehouse	A	1879
2033	Winter	R	1879
1396	Winter	W	1879r
2103	Wiseman	G	1879
2981	Wood	J.N	1879
2365	Woodcock	E	1879
2957	Woodford	E	1879
347	Woodgate	W	1879
734	Woodward	W.H	1879
1713	Wornham	H	1879
2094	Wright	T	1879
746	Young	T	1879
3382	Young	W	1879
1098	Young	W.J	1879

61st (SOUTH GLOUCESTERSHIRE) REGIMENT.
CAPTAIN
    Murray C.W 1879

70th (SURREY) REGIMENT.
LIEUTENANT
    Boyle H.R 1877-8
Also had Ashanti Medal.

71st (HIGHLAND LIGHT INFANTRY) REGIMENT
CAPTAIN
    Braithwaite E.L 1879
    Harvey C.L 1878-9
Also had Bavarian Order of Merit and Silver Medal from Royal Humane Society.

75th (STIRLINGSHIRE) REGIMENT.
CAPTAIN
    # Essex E 1879
LIEUTENANT
    Baynes D.L 1879

3/60th Regiment

77th (EAST MIDDLESEX) REGIMENT.
MAJOR
    Bengough H.M 1879
See also 2nd Battalion Natal Native Contingent.
CAPTAIN
    Marryat H.Fz R 1879
LIEUTENANT
    Law R.T.H 1879
    Westmacott R.F No clasp

80th (STAFFORDSHIRE VOLUNTEERS) REGIMENT.
Prior to serving in No5 Column during the invasion of Zululand, the 80th saw a great deal of arduous service in the frontier wars of 1877-78. On the 12th March 1879, one company was attacked by the Zulu whilst on convoy escort duties over the Intombi River, 64 Officers and men were killed; the remainder 45 in all, fought their way back to Luneberg. Present at the Battle of Ulundi on the 4th July.
Those Killed in Action (**KIA**) lost their lives at Intombi River 11/3/1879.
LIEUTENANT COLONEL
    Tucker CB C 1878-9
Also had Medal and Clasp for Bhootan 1865.
MAJOR
    Creag C.A.F 1878-9
Also had Medals for Crimea and New Zealand.

    Tyler C.J.R 1878
Also had Medal and Clasp for Crimea. The Turkish Crimea War Medal and China Medal and Clasp Taku Forts 1860.
BREVET MAJOR
    Bradshaw J.L 1878-9
CAPTAIN and BREVET MAJOR
    Huskisson S.G No clasp
QUARTERMASTER
    Pendery J 1878-9
CAPTAIN
    Anderson W.T 1878-9
    Cole C.C 1879
    Howard W 1878-9
Also had medal and clasp for Bhootan 1865.
    Johnson H.J 1878-9
    Moriarty KIA D.B 1878-9
Also had medal for N.W. Frontier 1868.
    Potts L.C 1878-9
    Prior J.E.H 1878-9
    Roworth C.E.W 1878-9
    Saunders A 1878
    Sherrard J.O 1878-9
LIEUTENANT ADJUTANT
    Griffin T.E 1878
LIEUTENANT
    Cameron S.W 1878
    Chamberlain T.J 1878-9
    Harward H.H 1878-9
    Hast A.W 1878-9
    Horsbrugh A.B 1878-9
    Lindop A.H 1878-9
    Lyons F.W 1878-9
    Moore W 1878

    Raitt H.A 1878-9
    Savage H.C 1878
2nd LIEUTENANT
    Daubeney E.K 1878-9
    Marshall F.M.H 1878
    Ussher B.W.R 1878-9
    Williams G.A 1879
CIVIL CONDUCTOR
    Whittington J 1879
Employed as wagon conductor. See also Army Service Corps Transport.
SERGEANT
4202 Allen J 1878
BANDMASTER
2109 Frayling W.W 1878
DRUM MAJOR
692 O'Day O 1878-9
SCHOOLMASTER
    Bird H.J 1878
COLOR SERGEANT
919 Booth VC A 1878-9
His VC was awarded for an action at Intombi River.
1048 Day H 1878-9
895 Else W 1878-9
459 Fredericks **KIA** H 1878-9
918 Machin F 1878-9
201 Norton W 1878-9
2098 Richardson W 1878-9
No Medal Deserted.
3124 Shore E 1878-9
336 Waters J 1878-9
1965 Woods A.H 1878
ARMOURER SERGEANT
149 Smallwood S 1878

Battle of Intombe
Before dawn on the 12 March 1879, a shot was heard close to the camp, Moriarty decided that it was nothing. the men returned to their beds. A short time later, a sentry on the far bank saw to his horror, through a clearing in the mist, a huge mass of Zulus advancing. 'He at once fired his rifle and gave the alarm,' Tucker recorded. 'The sentries on the other side did the same. Of course the men were up in a moment, some men sleeping under the wagons and some in the tents; but before the men were in their positions the Zulus had fired a volley, thrown down their guns... and were around the wagons and on top of them, and even inside with the cattle, almost instantly. So quickly did they come, there was really no defence on the part of our men; it was simply each man fighting for his life, and in a few minutes all was over, our men being simply slaughtered.'
Moriarty was the first to die struck in the back with an assegai as he charged out of his tent, not before shooting dead three Zulus with a revolver. His last words were 'I am done; fire away, boys.' However, few managed to put up any resistance, sharing a similar fate. Those who survived fled into the river, the troops on the far bank providing as much covering fire as possible, **Lieutenant Henry Harward,** Moriarty's second-in-command, gave the order to withdraw upon seeing several hundred Zulus crossing the river. No sooner had he done this, when he grabbed the first horse he spotted and fled, abandoning his men.
Colour-Sergeant Anthony Clarke Booth now found himself in command. For three miles, the Zulus pursued the group of around forty survivors. Whenever they drew closer, several of the bolder troops, along with Booth stopped to deliver a volley, which dispersed their pursuers. Four men who split up from the group were killed. The others made it to Raby's Farm, around two miles from Lüneberg where the Zulus broke off pursuit. The wagons were looted and all the ammunition and supplies were carried off by the Zulus or destroyed. Booth was rewarded with the Victoria Cross.
Source: History of the Zulu war and its origin. London: Chapman and Hall. 1880. pp. 348, http://en.wikipedia.org/wiki/Battle_of_Intombe
The Washing of the Spears, Donald R. Morris, 1998, p.474, gives 80 killed: 62 British soldiers, 3 European conductors and 15 natives.

Edward Essex, attached transport officer from the 75th regiment, was an Isandlwana survivor. His medal is held in the regimental museum of the Gordon Highlanders in Aberdeen. There were only two South Africa medals awarded to the 75th, the other being to Lieutenant D.L.Baynes, who was also a transport officer. With an accompanying photograph.

80th Regiment

ORDERLYROOM CLERK
1500	Mc Guinness	C	1878

PAYMASTER SERGEANT
854	Grantley	T	1878

QUARTERMASTER SERGEANT
2003	Thompson	J	1878-9

SERGEANT INSTRUCTOR OF MUSKETRY
366	Jones	N	1878-9
	No Medal Deserted.		

SERGEANT
894	Allen	C	1878
1968	Attride	G	1878-9
36	Beverley	J	1878
1387	Brown	T	1878-9
98	Butler	J	1878
603	Byrne	C	1878-9r
995	Cameron	H	1878-9
1044	Carter	S	1878-9
2026	Clarke	O	1878
222	Cleaver	W	1879
3244	Collins	J	1878
2101	Davis	C.G	1878
909	Davis	J	1878
947	Davis	P	1878
488	Dickey	W	1878
1076	Dollin	R	1878-9
1804	Duncan	J	1878
1383	Enion	G	1878-9
570	Evereth	W	1878-9
1362	Faulks	J	1878-9
3	Hancox	S	1878
#2107	Jennings	E	1878-9
442	Jervis	J	1879
1271	Johnson	W	1878-9
	KIA Isandhlwana.		
668	Kelly	P	1878-9
1567	King	J	1878
2065	Lawrence	R	1878-9
1321	Lynch	T	1878
416	Markwell	T	1878
1525	Mc Cready	R	1878-9
1761	Mc Donald	N	1878-9
124	Mc Mullen	J	1878-9
1249	O'Neill	T	1879
1257	Penketh	J	1878-9
98	Perkins	B	1878-9
1863	Searl	H	No clasp
1503	Stevenson	J	1878-9
2081	Thompson	H	1879
	KIA Isandhlwana.		
63	Trott	C	1878
	No Medal Deserted.		
1665	Walker	H	1878-9
##1217 (1212)	Ward	H	1878-9
1630	Watts	H	1878-9
	KIA 4/7/1879 Ulundi.		

LANCE SERGEANT
1054	Beal	W	1878-9
1389	Carter	H	1879
889	Horton	T	1878-9
1627	Sansom KIA	G	1878-9

CORPORAL
1822	Allen	A	1879
93	Arthurs	W	1878
200	Bailey	J.J	1879
1103	Baxter	J	1878
276	Bebbington	W	1879
762	Brew	G	1878-9
1340	Carey	F	1878-9
1497	Clarke	T	1879
1241	Comaskey	J	1878-9
545	Constable	T	1879
966	Cooper	A	1879
1063	Cox	G.W	1878-9
1115	Delaney	M	1878-9
900	Duggan	M	1878
143	England	W.H	
1045	Fallon	J	
1439	Garner	G	1878-9
	See also 1429 Pte Garner G. Could be same man.		
1297	Grant	J	1878-9
1915	Green	H	1878-9
1671	Guilfoy	J	1878
	See also 1671 Pte Guilfoy J. Could be same man.		
288	Hammer	G	1879
1646	Harcourt	F	1878-9
1802	Hopkins	H	1878
890	Horn	W	1878
544	Johnson KIA	E	1878-9
1833	Lewis	W	1878
2066	Little	W	1878-9
1990	Loage ?	J	No clasp
374	Lockett	J	1879
999	Lovegrove	R	1878
999	Lovegrove	R	1878
	Apparently two awards to same man.		
185	Lowbridge	D	1879
1487	Major	R	1878-9
2000	Martin	C	1878
714	Maynard	W.J	1878-9
733	Mc Coy KIA	J	1878-9
303	Mc Donald	J	1878-9
1618	Mc Mullen	H	1879
1867(8)	Mellon	J	No clasp
1867	Moon	R	No clasp
1372	Moore	G	1878
1555	Newman	J	No clasp
784	Pendergast	H	1878-9
1401	Prichard	S	No clasp
1108	Rickman	G	1879
2062	Stephens	E	1878-9
1776	Sterling	H	1879
1163	Tolley	W	1878-9
1320	Weldon	P	1878-9
515	Wood	J	1878-9
2062	Woolcot	H	1878

DRUMMER
1188	Appleby	J	1879
2038	Barnwell	W	1878
301	Collier	A	1878-9
1769	Cunningham	T	1878-9
594	Donovan	W	1878-9
1917	Ferguson	D	1878
	No Medal Deserted.		
1892	Floyd KIA	J	1878-9
595	Lawrence	C	1878
1647	Leather KIA	J	1878-9
110	Lewis	J	1878-9
596	Maker	J	1879
1767	Mc Quillan	J	1878-9
1336	Moran	W	1878-9
555	Nicholls	B	1879
1757	Terry	A	1878-9
540	Vyse	J	1878-9
1320	Weldon	P	1878
1006	Wilkinson	W	1879

PRIVATE
304	Abbott	J	1878
1505	Adair	H	1878-9
1856	Adams	G	No clasp
704	Adams	R	1878-9
546	Adey KIA	J	1878-9
976	Adey	W	1878-9
1916	Aher	J	No clasp
1206	Ainsworth	H	1878
1822	Allen	A	1878

#Sold on ebay 23 Sep, 2009 Winning bid: £561.00, only three bids. A genuine zulu war medal.south africa medal with 1878-1879 clasp,named to 2107,Sergt.E.Jennings,80th.foot. Edgar Jennings was from Hyton near Liverpool. This a very nice genuine medal.the 80th foot were engaged in some heavy fighting at the Intombi River VC action and at Ulundi.This medal was sold by Spink a few years ago. Enlisted at Liverpool on 05/02/73, Aged 24 years10 months. Ht 5ft 8 1/2 ins, Trade Clerk. Transfered to Army Reserve 04/10/7. In Robert Hopes book Jennings is listed as Corporal.

ebay 4th November 2009, Victorian campaign medal for South Africa, named to 1212 SERGT. H. WARD. 80TH. FOOT, It has a few minor contact marks, and the silver is toned, small portion of ribbon and this has a bar marked 1878-9. Winning bid £809.99 with 9 bids

80th Regiment

No.	Name	Init	Year	No.	Name	Init	Year	No.	Name	Init	Year
1850	Allen	F	1878	1520	Baskoth	T	1879	1664	Broadhurst	A	1878-9
1968	Allen	J	No clasp	1038	Bateman	W	1878-9	745	Broughton **KIA**	G	1878-9
1444	Allen	V	1878	1259	Baverstock	G	1879	576	Brown	E	1878-9
1283	Allison	J	1878-9	865	Baxter	S	1878	1914	Brown	G	No clasp
1236	Allport	C	1879	349	Baxter	W	1878-9	48	Brown **KIA**	J	1878-9
1017	Allsopp	J	1878-9	1358	Baxter	W	1878-9	122	Brown	J	1878
231	Anderson	F	1878-9	1145	Bayless	J	1879	542	Brown	J	1878-9
573	Andrews	W	1878	1535	Beamer	J	1878	1553	Brown	W	1878
1916	Annals	A	1878	1110	Beatson	M	1878	488	Brownson **KIA**	H	1878-9
1817	Ansell	J	No clasp	1028	Beaumont	A	1878-9	659	Buckler	T	1878-9
585	Anthony **KIA**	J	1878-9	276	Babbington	W	1878	1134	Bullock	G	1879
1521	Appleton	T	1878-9	1164	Bedwith	A	1878-9	907	Bullock	W	1879
1058	Archer	H	1878-9	636	Beecroft	A	1878-9	1172	Bunday	D	1878
857	Archer	R	1879	736	Bell	J	1878-9	1728	Bunday	H	1878-9
922	Archer	T	1879	1070	Bellerson	T	1878-9	2004	Burden	J	1878
1970	Archer	W	No clasp	680	Bennett	W	1878-9	2054	Burgess	W	1878-9
1437	Arkell	J	1878-9	105	Bentley	J	1878-9	169	Burgwin	W	1878-9
441	Armstrong	J	1878	275	Bentley	J	1878-9	2055	Burke	D	1878-9
7	Armstrong	T.W	1878-9	975	Benton	S	1878	1856	Burnett	J	1878-9
1055	Armstrong	W	1878	513	Betts	H	1878-9	736	Burns	H	1878
108	Arthurs	M	1878-9	1687	Bickerton	J	1878-9	79	Burns	H	1879
2033	Atkins	C	1878	1081	Biddle	J	1879	323	Burns	H	1879
1452	Atkinson	J	1878-9	280	Biernes	T	1878	1078	Burnes	W	1879
1874	Atkinson	S	No clasp	\multicolumn{3}{c|}{No Medal Deserted.}		2071	Burnett	W	1878
1918	Attwater	J	No clasp	1076	Billingham	T	1878-9	1922	Bursnell	J	No clasp
1907	Austin	E	1878	\multicolumn{3}{c|}{No Medal Deserted.}		1609	Burtenshaw	H	1878
759	Backett	J	1878-9	1251	Bills	T	1879	99	Burton	A	1878-9
1065	Bagnall	J	1878	1174	Birch	J	1879	1737	Burton	J	1878
779	Bagnall	T	1878-9	29	Birch	W	1878-9	1984	Burton	T	1878-9
1998	Bailey	F	1878-9	109	Bird	F	1878-9	1936	Bush	J	1879
1199	Bailey	J.D	1879	1854	Blackham	W	No clasp	278	Butler	F	1878-9
200	Bailey	J.J	1878	412	Blakeway	J	1878-9	574	Butler	J	1878-9
1788	Bailey	R	1878	719	Boden	J	1878-9	1139	Cairns	E	1879
1223	Bailey	T	1879	16	Bond	W	1878	1222	Callaghan	M	1879
577	Baker	J	1878-9	1015	Bond	W	1878	159	Callaghan	P	1878-9
397	Baker	P	1879	1897	Booker	A	1878-9	1129	Cameron	F	1878-9
560	Baker	W	1878-9	1155	Booth	E	1878-9	1938	Camp	D	No clasp
22	Bale	R	1878	766	Booth	F	1878-9	406	Carbery	R	1878-9
1870	Ball	J	No clasp	265	Bourn	W	1878-9	112	Carpenter	J	1878-9
2056	Balshaw	A.E	1878	1138	Bow	S	1878	2100	Carr	J	1878
\multicolumn{4}{l|}{No Medal. Discharged with ignominy.}	519	Bowen	T	1878-9	1578	Carroll	J	1878-9
202 ?	Banks **KIA**	A	1878-9	1277	Bowker	R	1878	18	Carroll	J	1878-9
1049	Banks	T	1878-9	\multicolumn{3}{c|}{No Medal Deserted.}		\multicolumn{3}{c|}{No Medal Deserted.}	
1086	Banks	W	1879	534	Bown	E	1878-9	986	Carter	C	1878
943	Banner **KIA**	J	1878-9	349	Boyd	T	1879	387	Carter	J	1879
1883	Bannon	P	No clasp	489	Boyle	M	1878-9	1140	Cartwright	S	1879
1448	Barber	A	1878-9	2102	Boyle	T	1878-9	818	Cash	W	1879
1382	Barcklie	M	1878-9	1564	Bradshaw	W	1878-9	1913	Cassidy	W	No clasp
1908	Bargery	H	No clasp	1919	Brady	R	No clasp	387	Cater	J	1878-9
1935	Barker	W	No clasp	567	Bramill	W	1878-9	1656	Chadwick	H	1878-9
\multicolumn{4}{l|}{No Medal Deserted.}	1877	Braze	T	1878-9	1290	Chadwick **KIA**	J	1878-9
1514	Barnes	J	1878-9	273	Brereton	T	1878-9	1974	Champion	J.R	No clasp
531	Barnett	R	1878-9	722	Brew	G	1878	287	Chair	C.E	1878-9
1928	Barr	T	1878	415	Bridgewood	W	1878	1914	Chase	R	1878
2053	Barrett	D	1878	633	Brindley	A	1879	1944	Cherrie	W	1878-9r
1591	Barron	A	1878	647	Brindley	W	1879	\multicolumn{4}{l}{Forfeited. No reason given.}
1872	Barsby	T	1878	1381	Brisbane	W	1878	1043	Cheshire	J	1878
1634	Barter	R	1879	\multicolumn{3}{c|}{No Medal Deserted.}		1377	Chesterton	J	1878-9
1859	Bartley	M.H	No clasp	1556	Britton	E	1879	\multicolumn{4}{l}{**KIA** Isandhlwana.}

80th Regiment

No.	Name	Initial	Clasp/Year	No.	Name	Initial	Clasp/Year	No.	Name	Initial	Clasp/Year
1906	Childerstone	S	No clasp	1169	Corry	J	1879	1202	Dutton	N	1879
2171	Childs	E	1878	1029	Costelo	S	1879	1900	Dyball	W	1878
1797	Christie **KIA**	J	1878-9	502	Cowdrell	R	1878-9	8	Dyer	G	1878
1967	Cinamond	T.E	No clasp	601	Cox	J	1878		No Medal Deserted.		
1884	Clarke	A.G	1878	1966	Cox	W	No clasp	794	Eady	J	1878-9
507	Clarke	J	1878-9	1874	Coy	W	1878-9	1876	Eaton	W	No clasp
1052	Clarke	J	1879	123	Coyne	J	1878-9	1973	Ede	T	No clasp
1911	Clarke	J	No clasp	499	Crawford	W	1879	713(8)	Edwards	E	1878-9
2026	Clarke	O	1879	1904	Creagh	W	No clasp	379	Edwards	E	1878-9
1014	Clarke	T	1878-9	194	Crudington	R	1879	1554	Edwards	E	1879
1497	Clarke	T	1878	1198	Cruise	S	1879	1094	Edwards	M	1879
983	Clarke	T	1878-9	1111	Cruite	G	1878	1624	Edwards	R	1878-9
94	Clarke	W	1878	232	Cullen	M	1878-9	1035	Edwards	W	1878-9
1934	Clarke	W	No clasp	1523?	Cullen	P	1878-9		No Medal Deserted.		
1827	Clay	I	1878	1650	Culley	F	1878	1141	Edwards	W	1878-9
1982	Clayton	G	1878	1889	Cullum	J	No clasp	750	Egerton	S	1879
1658	Clayton	H	1878-9	631	Curtin	J	1878-9	421	Eley	F	1878-9
487	Cleaton	W	1878-9	465	Dabbs	R	1878-9	1543	Ellis	G	1878
2	Cleaver	J	1878	1272	Dagger	H	1878-9	376	Ellis	G	1878
551	Cluit	J	1878-9	78	Dailey	J	No clasp	1162	Ellis	H	1878
413	Clulec	T	1878	1158	Dakin	G	1879	84	Ellison	R	1878-9
2044	Colbridge	W	No clasp	410	Dale	H	1879	1003	Evens	E	1878-9
755	Colclough	G	1878-9	1364	Daniels	G	1878	214	Evens	G	1878-9
1550	Cole	C.C	1879	1728	Daniels	S	1879	713	Evens	H	1878-9
	No Medal Deserted.			209	Daniels	W	1878-9	1074	Evens	J	1878-9
298	Cole	F	1878	1213	Darby	W	1879	1026	Fallon	J	1878
561	Cole	W	1878-9	614	Davis	J	1878		No Medal Deserted.		
1969	Coleman	J	No clasp	846	Davis	S	No clasp	1830	Farmer	W	1878
485	Coleman	T	1878-9	1312	Davis	W	1878-9	1028	Farnall **KIA**	W	1878-9
1478	Collier	W	1878-9	1042	Day **KIA**	A	1878-9	2019	Farrell	P	1878-9
1324	Collinson	R	1878-9	1930	Day	W	1878		Note on Roll: "No Medal."		
1989	Colyer	W	1878-9	1119	Deacon	W	1878-9	1643	Faulkner	W	1878
1240	Comaskey	J	1879	1623	Delaney	M.J	1878	467	Fawcett	T	1878-9
1098	Concaly	J	1879	1464	Dempsey	A	1878-9	877	Feighney	R	1878-9
314	Conlon	J	1878-9	1361	Dermot	J	1878	1884	Feltwell	J	No clasp
739	Connell	J	1879	256	Dobson	E	1878		No Medal Deserted.		
690	Connell	J	1878-9	953	Dodd **KIA**	J	1878-9	2052	Ferris	J	1879
1221	Connolly	W	1879	1971	Doe	J	1878	1114	Field	E	1878
545	Constable	T	1878	1071	Done	B	1878-9	222	Findley **KIA**	W	1878-9
988	Convey	J	1878-9	1271	Donnelly	P	1879	520	Finn	J	1878-9
1935	Cooke	A	1878	1879	Donohoe	M	No clasp	1860	Finnegan	P	1878
1371	Cooke	C	1878	101	Donovan	T	1878	1228	Fisher	J	1878
82	Cook(e)	G	1878-9	1901	Double	C	No clasp	230	Fisher	J	1878-9
1913	Cook(e)	G	1878-9	1330	Doyle	A	1878-9	1947	Fisher	T	1878-9
1232	Cook	T	1879	243	Drinkwater	E	1878-9	1857	Fitton	J	No clasp
966	Cooper	A	1878	2005	Dudley	A	1878	1286	Fitzmorris	T	1878-9
2072	Cooper	E	1878	274	Dudley	J	1878-9	604	Fitzpatrick	T.P	1878-9
1245	Cooper	J	1879	1231	Dudley	T	1879	1512	Fletcher	A	1879
696	Cope	S	1878	1219	Dudwell	J	1879	233	Fletcher	J	1878-9
736	Cope	T	1879	1616	Duffy	M	1878-9	1695	Flewitt	J	1878
1051	Corbett	D	1878-9	2079	Dumbleton	B	1878-9	701	Flint	J	1878
18/1	Corbett	T	No clasp	507	Dunn	C	1878-9	1895	Floyd **KIA**	J	1879
753	Corns	J	1878-9	#260	Dutton **KIA**	J.H	1878-9	**KIA** 4/7/1879 Ulundi.			

Spinks Auction 5th December 2002 Lot 40
An Intombi River Casualty Pair to Private J.R.Dutton, 80th Foot. India General Service 1854-95, one clasp, Perak (260 Pte J.R.Dutton. 80th Foot), South Africa 1877-79, one clasp, 1879 (260 Pte J.R.Dutton. 80th Foot), minor edge bruising, alteration to "6" on second medal, otherwise very fine. Private J.R.Dutton was killed in action on the Intombi River 12.3.1879. Hammer price £1900.

80th Foot Casualty Roll

Casualty Roll for the Zulu and Basuto Wars South Africa 1877-79 80th Foot
Killed in action at Intombe River 12 March 1879 (unless stated otherwise)

459 Colour Sergeant Henry Fredericks - Missing in Action
1271 Sergeant W. Johnson - killed in action at Isandhlwana 22 Jan 1879
2081 Sergeant H. Thompson - killed in action at Isandhlwana 22 Jan 1879
1630 Sergeant H. Watts - killed in action at Ulundi 4 July 1879

Privates:
546 Jonah Adey
585 John Anthony
203 Arthur Banks
943 John Banner - Missing in Action
745 George Broughton
48 James Brown
488 Henry Brownson
1290 John Chadwick
1377 J. Chesteron - killed in action at Isandhlwana 22 January 1879
1797 James Christie
1042 Alfred Day - Missing in Action
953 John Dodd - Missing in Action
260 J.H. Dutton
1028 William Farnell - Missing in Action
222 William Findlay - Missing in Action
1892 Joseph Floyd - killed in action at Ulundi 4 July 1879
1465 William Fox - Missing in Action
1925 John Furniaux - Missing in Action
500 Edward Gittings
1696 Joseph Green
526 George Hadley - Missing in Action
227 George Haines
2008 Julian Hart - Missing in Action
999 Eli Hawkes - Missing in Action
783 Thomas Healey
1021 Henry Hill
709 Thomas Hodges
1433 E. Holman - killed in action at Isandhlwana 22 January 1879
1499 John Hughes

1627 Lance-Sergeant G. Sansom
544 Lance-Corporal E. Johnson
733 Lance-Corporal John McCoy
1647 Drummer John Leather

Privates:
1919 Henry Jacobs
1865 John Lafferty
996 Ralph Leese
1931 Henry Lodge - Missing in Action
559 W. McDonald - killed in action at Isandhlwana 22 January 1879
1378 Bernard McSherry
590 Henry Meadows
2063 Arthur Middow
1976 George Mitchell
2048 Robert Moore
1032 William Moran
1926 Henry Night
220 William Phipps
2085 Charles Pritchard
1163 Arthur Pummell
1974 F. Ralphs
259 John Robinson
2070 Henry Ruffle
695 William Seymour
615 Michael Sherridan - Missing in Action
1770 Joseph Silcock - Missing in Action
510 Henry Smith - Missing in Action
587 Joseph Tibbott
1291 Richard Tomlinson - Missing in Action
1705 George Tucker - Missing in Action
104 Thomas Tucker
370 Joseph Vernon
60 J. Whitehouse - killed in action at Isandhlwana 22 Jan 1879
1605 Herbert Woodward - Missing in Action

Biddle & Webb Auction March 2005 South Africa medal with 1879 clasp, Private H Brownson 80th Foot. Killed in Action. Hammer Price £2700

A detachment of the 80th Regiment joined Col H. Rowlands, No 5 Column Three Gunnersubalterns were selected, to train and command some of the gun detachments provided by infantry. They were Lt's Bigge and Nicolson, Lt F.G. Slade. His two 6 pr Armstrongs were handed over to men of 80th Regiment.

80th Regiment

176	Flyfield	**KIA** W	1878-9	1671	Guilfoy	J	1878-9	783	Healey **KIA**	T	1878-9
785	Flynn	R	1878	1999	Gutterege	A	1878-9	871	Heath	R	1879
490	Foden	J	1878-9	1031	Gutteredge	P	1878	599	Heath	W	1878-9
613	Follows	G	1878-9	1034	Guy	P	1878	1576	Heavey	B	1878
812	Ford	J	1878-9	368	Guy	W	1878-9	No Medal. Discharged with ignominy.			
1342	Ford	P	1879	1176	Hacker	W	1878-9	1906	Herman	G	1878-9
340	Ford	T	1878-9	820	Hackley	J	1879	167	Herriman	E	1878-9
303	Foreman	H	1878	1502	Hackman	S	1878-9	1868	Hickey	J	No clasp
1866	Foster	B	No clasp	526	Hadley **KIA**	G	1878-9	604	Hickson	H	1879
1820	Foster	R	1878	1518	Hadley	W	1879	1848	Hill	J	1879
754	Foster	T	1879	227	Haines **KIA**	G	1878	1021	Hill **KIA**	H	1878-9
778	Foster	W	1878-9	538	Hale	C	1878-9	721	Hill	T	1878-9
1597	Foulkes	J	1878-9	539	Hale	W	1878-9	256	Hill	T	1878-9
1030	Fox	J	1878-9	580	Halford	J	1878-9	1068	Hill	T	1878-9
1465	Fox **KIA**	W	1878-9	No Medal Deserted.				207	Hince	T	1878-9
2080	Francis		1878	1777	Hall	J	1878-9	737	Hing	T	1878-9
1552	Frayne	J	1879	1937	Hall	J	No clasp	2047	Hippenstall	J	No clasp
1918	Fricker	J	1878-9	957	Hall	W	1878-9	604	Hixon	H	1878
151	Fryer	W	1878-9	1812	Halligan	J	1878	881	Hockley	P	1878-9
1449	Fulton	W	1878-9	1539	Halligan	T	1879	740	Hogan	M	1878-9
2089	Furness	A	1878	1853	Hamilton	J	No clasp	709	Hodges **KIA**	T	1878-9
679	Furness	R	1878-9	1859	Hammerton	T	1878-9	498	Holden	S	1878-9
1925	Furniaux **KIA**	J	1878-9	1513	Hammonds	F	1878-9	1032	Holman	C	1878
1196	Gallagher	J	1879	1891	Hammonds	W	1879	1433	Holman	E	1878-9
1544	Gallagher	P	1879	281	Hancox	J	1878-9		**KIA** Isandhlwana.		
2015	Gardner	C	1878-9	492	Hands	W	1878-9	97	Holmes	A	1878-9
1429	Garner	G	1879	937	Hanes	E	1879	29	Holmes	J	1878-9
1024	Garford	E	No clasp	1558	Hankinson	P	1878	894	Hope	J	1879
No Medal Deserted.				288	Hanmer	G	1878	820	Hopkins	G	1878
1813	Garvey	T	No clasp	702	Hannon	J	1878-9	1994	Hopkins	J	1878
925	Gibbons	J	1879 r	No Medal Deserted.				1994	Hopkins	J.T	1878
469	Giblin	O	1878-9	1368	Hanson	W	1878	2094	Hopkins	W.F	1878-9
173	Gibson	J	1878-9	512	Harbattle	G	1878-9	979	Hopley	W	1878-9
700	Gillham	J	1878	1880	Harbridge	G	No clasp	2083	Hopson	J	1878-9
1335	Gilligan	W	1878-9	1325	Hardy	W	1878	1522	Hough	J	1878-9
500	Gittings **KIA**	E	1878-9	121	Harper	J	1878-9	129	Hoult	E	1878
1261	Gilinnon	T	No clasp	643	Harris	H	1878-9	1720	Howard	C	1878-9
1390	Goddard	W	1878	1824	Hart	G	1878	1945	Howard	F	1878
1901	Godden	T	1878	1253	Hart	J	1879	543	Howard	H	1878-9
699	Godwin	W	1878-9	2008	Hart **KIA**	J	1878-9	1721	Howard	O	1878-9
1184	Goulden	P	1879	135	Hartrick	W	1878-9	2067	Howes	J	1878-9
3642	Graham	E	1878	1816	Harvey	J	1878	1933	Hoyle	J	No clasp
936	Granger	T	1879	1231	Harvey	W	1878	495	Hughes	B	1878-9
1182	Grant	J	1878-9	1562	Haslam	R	1878	525	Hughes	G	1879
603	Gratton	J	1878	1073	Hatton	F	1878-9	552	Hughes	J	1878-9
743	Greatback	J	1878-9	1864	Haven	J	No clasp	1499	Hughes **KIA**	J	1878-9
1131	Greatrix	B	1879	134	Hawkes	C	1878	1589	Hughes	J	1878-9
1696	Green **KIA**	J	1878-9	999	Hawkes **KIA**	E	1878-9	1814	Hughes	R	No clasp
1800	Gretton	W	1878	147	Hawkins	W	1878-9	1060	Hughes	T	1879
239	Grey	W	1878	1129	Hawksworth	G	No clasp	1132	Hughes	W	1879
1851	Griffin	G.W	No clasp	1951	Hayden	G	1878-9	1898	Hunt	F	1878-9
1463	Griffiths	E	1878-9	1975	Hayelton	W	1878	925	Hunt	J	1878
1550	Griffiths	H	1878	1966	Hayes	D	1878	1900	Hunt	W	No clasp
1538	Griffiths	J	1879	1818	Hayes	E	No clasp	1072	Hurd	W	1878-9
639	Griffiths	T	1879	1268	Haynes	J	1879	945	Hussell	W	1878-9
835	Griffiths	W	1879	921	Haywood	C	1879	535	Husselbee	J	1878-9
836	Gubbins	N	1878	1267	Haywood	H	1879	1142	Husselbee	T	1879
1044	Guest	J	1878	235	Haywood	J	1878-9	229	Hutchinson	T	1878
1239	Guest	T	1879	761	Hayward	M	1878-9	1887	Hyem	H	1879 r

80th Regiment

No.	Name	Init.	Clasp		No.	Name	Init.	Clasp		No.	Name	Init.	Clasp
902	Ingham KIA	J	1878-9		1907	Keen	J	No clasp		1351	Manning	S	1878-9
1838	Irvine	W.T	1878		115	Keenan	W	1878-9		963	Mannison	M	1879
1965	Jackman	E	No clasp		2045	Kelly	J	No clasp		181	Manson	A	1879
1509	Jackson	B	1879		682	Kelly	P	1878-9		1927	Mantell	H	1878-9
566	Jackson	J	1878		1477	Kelly	T	1878-9		1161	Marlow	J	1878
272	Jackson	T	1878-9		1711	Kelly	T	1878-9		No Medal Deserted.			
742	Jackson	T	1878		578	Kesterton	W	1878-9		1890	Marsdin	M	1878
					1357	Kettle	J	1878-9		2046	Marshall	H	No clasp
					526	Kilbride	J	1878-9		2103	Marson	W	1878
					1344	Kilsill	H	1878-9		206	Martin	F	1878-9
					914	King	C	1879		1909	Martin	T	1878-9
					456	King	J	1878		1397	Martin	W	1879
					1217	King	P	1879		588	Mason	E	1878-9
					1632	Kitchen	J	1878		1522	Mason	J	1879
					No Medal Deserted.					1712	Massey	T	1878-9
					182	Knowles	H	1879		732	Mastersib	P	1878-9
					461	Kynaston	J	1878-9		1933	Matthews	A	1878-9
					1376	Lacey	J	1878		170	Matthews	C	1878-9
					1865	Lafferty KIA	J	1878-9		1846	May	J	1878-9
					393	Lawley	H	1878		1801	Mayfield	F	No clasp
					No Medal. Discharged with ignominy.					2108	Mc Auliffe	E	1878-9
					357	Lawrence	W	1878-9		300	Mc Caffery	H	1878-9
					1885	Lawson	J	No clasp		2007	Mc Call	M	1878
					1902	Lawton	H	1878		2017	Mc Cann	P	1878
					632	Leek	J	1878-9		No Medal Deserted.			
1919	Jacobs KIA	H	1878-9		996	Leese KIA	R	1878-9		62	Mc Cleary	D	1878-9
823	James	J	1879		1795	Leigh	R	1878		1253	Mc Clennon	J	No clasp
1083	Jefferson	W	1878-9		1029	Lewis	H	1878		1314	Mc Cormack	M	1878
285	Jenkins	H.C	1878-9		1506	Lewis	P	1878-9		1120	Mc Cue	J	1879
1059	Jenkins	R	1879		1958	Lineham	J	No clasp		1349	Mc Cullough	J	1878-9
241	Jennings	G	1878-9		1625	Linkston	R	1878-9		765	Mc Dermott	J	1879
223	Jennings	T	1879		1834	Linnett	J	1878-9		559	Mc Donald	W	1878-9
1005	Jobbourn	H	1878-9		No Medal Deserted.					KIA Isandhlwana.			
776	Johnson	H	1878		267	Linskey	P	1878-9		1858	Mc Gillan	T	1878
653	Johnson	H	1878-9		27	Lloyd	W	1878-9		1975	Mc Glockin	J	No clasp
No Medal Deserted.					1990	Loage	J	1878		1799	Mc Gookin	J	1878
1723	Johnson	J	1878-9		917	Locker	G	1879		1972	Mc Grath	D	No clasp
1679	Johnson	J	1878-9		374	Lockett	J	1878		1875	Mc Grath	W	No clasp
2058	Johnson	W	1878-9		1931	Lodge KIA	H	1878-9		1719	Mc Guirk	P	1878-9
891	Johnson	W	1879		1903	Loney	T	No clasp		2282	Mc Kee	E	1878-9
226	Jones	C	1878-9		583	Longstaff	G	1878-9		1546	Mc Kee	W	1878-9
1819	Jones	D	No clasp		1863	Loomes	R	1879		1775	Mc Kenny	E	1878-9
240	Jones	H	1878-9		1657	Lord	W	1878-9		1040	Mc Kennon	J	1879
997	Jones	J	1878		185	Lowbridge	D	1878		309	Mc Kenzie	J	1878-9
437	Jones	J	1879		1230	Lowder	J	1879		1960	Mc Loughlin	J	No clasp
1619	Jones	J	1878		271	Lowe	S	1878		1159	Mc Mahon	R	1878
155	Jones	J	1878-9		1653	Lowrie	J	1878-9		77	Mc Neal	M	1878-9
1961	Jones	S	No clasp		1532	Luck	J	No clasp		1177	Mc Nichols	M	1879
1260	Jones	T	1879		773	Lunn	J	1878		1378	Mc Sherry KIA	B	1878-9
1214	Jones	T	1879		1213	Lunt	W	1878-9		1580	Meachin	A	1878
1391	Jones	W	1878-9		1645	Lynch	W	1878		1010	Mead	I	1878
1814	Jones	W	1878-9		1771	Lyons	T	1878		1983	Mead	T	1878-9
1488	Jones	W.J	1878-9		305	Mace	J	1879		590	Medows KIA	H	1878-9
1964	Jones	W.J	1878-9		1012	Machin	J	1878		1025	Meekin	E	1878-9
1976	Joyce	E	No clasp		1981	Macklin	J	1879		1492	Meers	E	1878-9
1251	Joyce	M	1878-9		2092	Maden	G	1878-9		432	Melsop	J	1878-9
1783	Joyce	W	1878-9		1426	Makepeace	J	1878-9		1683	Mercer	G	1878
589	Judd	T	1878-9		1568	Malloy	J	1878-9		344	Merrill	T	1879
418	Keats	J	1878-9		879	Manning	J	1879		No Medal Deserted.			

MOFFATT
IN MEMORY OF
THOMAS J.
WHO SERVED IN THE ZULU WAR
AT RORKE'S DRIFT
1855 – 1936
AND HIS DEAR WIFE
MARTHA
1877 – 1941
ALSO JOSEPH
SON OF THE ABOVE
1897 – 1972
ALSO THEIR GRANDSON
BRIAN McCALLION
1940 – 1945
R.I.P.

80th Regiment

678	Merryman	J	1878-9	161	Morris	W	1878	1566	Nunnerly	J	1878-9
83	Middleton	E	1878	768	Morris	W	1878-9	119	Oakley	T	1878
2063	Middow KIA	A	1878-9	1920	Morris	W	No clasp	1117	O'Brien	R	1878-9
1910	Midgley	J	No clasp	315	Mountford	W	1878-9	478	O'Gera	W	1878
49	Millar	J	1878	1904	Muddell	C	1878	1812	O'Gilvie	J	No clasp
851	Millership	W	1879	1678	Mulgrew	J	1878-9	1456	O'Neil	J	1878-9
586	Millington	T	1878-9	1579	Mulholland	J	1878	166	Owens	E	1878-9
1109	Mills	H	1879	2043	Mulligan	J	No clasp	1162	Owen	G	1878
1976	Mitchell KIA	G	1878-9	127	Mullins	T	1878-9	2087	Owens	H	No clasp
268	Moffatt	J	1878-9	1534	Murch	S	1878-9	1840	Owen	J	1878
1057	Moffatt	J	1878-9	1964	Murphy	P	No clasp	1240	Owens	R	1879
1083	Moffatt	T	1879	1501	Murphy	W	1878-9	1858	Owens	T	No clasp
2106	Monaghan	P	1878-9	1226	Musson	W	1879	165	Owens	W	1878-9
1033	Monckton	E	1878	1962	Nash	G	No clasp	1736	Owens	W	1878-9
1372	Moore	G	1879	157	Navan	J	1878-9	582	Page	A	1878-9
554	Moore	G	1878-9	1493	Naylor	G	1878	1147	Parker	T	1879
1319	Moore	H	1878-9	984	Neale	J	1878-9	1027	Parkes	C	1878-9
2048	Moore KIA	R	1878-9	958	Newman	A	1879	1256	Parkes	H	1878-9
924	Moran	J	1879	1963	Newman	E	No clasp	1885	Parrott	G	1878
310	Moran	M	1878-9	758	Newry	W	1878-9	172	Parry	H	1878-9
1032	Moran KIA	W	1878-9	1868	Newton	H	1878-9	1903	Parson	J.W	No clasp
1397	Moreton	W	1878	555	Nichols	B	1878	719	Parsons	R	No clasp
787	Morgan	B	1878-9	1508	Nicholl	G	1879	1160	Patey	J	1878-9
1084	Morley	M	1879	468	Nicklin	T	1878-9	527	Payne	E	1878
873	Morris	A	1879	1926	Night KIA	H	1878-9	971	Payne	T	1878-9
2049	Morris	G	No clasp	263	Nixon	J	1878-9	698	Pearce	C	1878-9
1821	Morris	J	1878-9	2023	Nolan	J	1878	805	Pemberton	H	1878-9
180	Morris	J	1878-9	548	Nolan	P	1878	399	Pepper	J	1878-9
476	Morris	J	1878-9	1339	Nolan	P	1878	685	Perkins	A	1878
504	Morris	J	1878-9	1681	Nolan	T	1878-9	No Medal. Discharged with ignominy.			
681	Morris	M	1878-9	772	Noonan	T	1878-9	662	Perkins	J	1878-9
964	Morris	T	1878-9	1062	Norton	J	1878-9	116	Perkins	J	1878

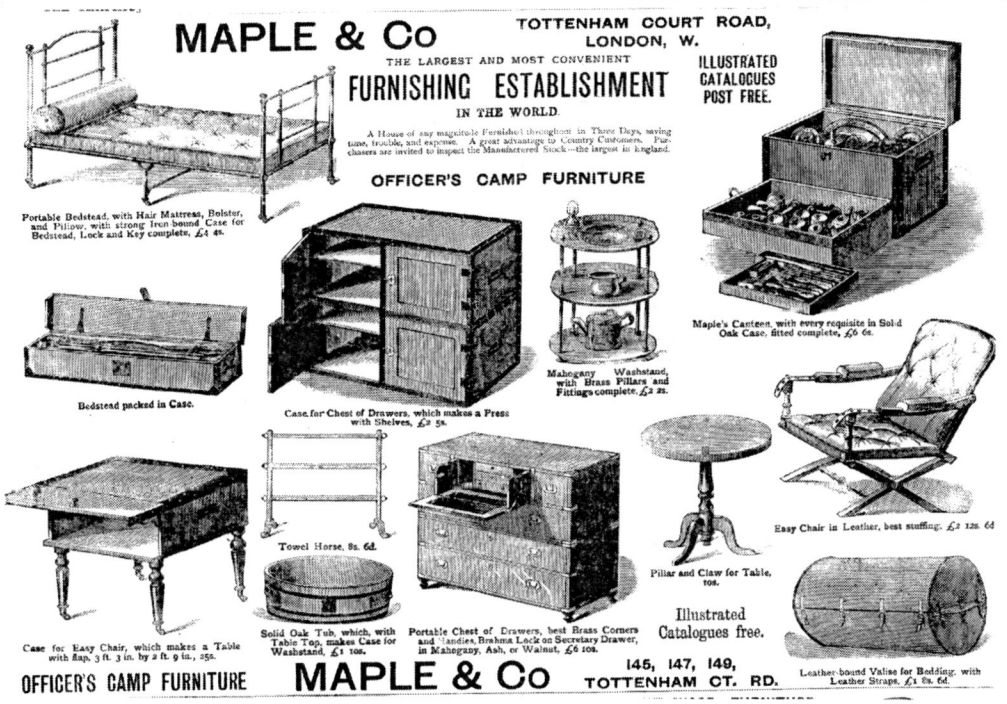

80th Regiment

No.	Name	Initial	Clasp	No.	Name	Initial	Clasp	No.	Name	Initial	Clasp
92	Peters	F	1878-9	1393	Rochell	H	1878-9	324	Simcock	J	1878-9
246	Phillips	A	1878-9	1296	Rodgers	J	1879	819	Simpson	A	1878
477	Phillips	T	1878-9	965	Rodgers	S	1878-9r	511	Simpson	W	1878-9
612	Phillips	T	1878-9	1881	Roe	J	No clasp	607	Sinclair	W	1878-9
220	Phipps KIA	W	1878-9	486	Rohen	P	1878-9	378	Sivorns	W	1878-9
649	Picken	G	1878-9	1540	Rollason	H	1879	1864	Skellan	T	1878-9
1225	Picken	J	No clasp	1811	Rose	W	No clasp	610	Slack	E	1878
286	Pitcher	J	1878-9	358	Rouse	W	1878-9	1557	Slater	J	1879
360	Plant	H	1878-9	744	Rowan (Rowe)	T	1878-9	608	Sleigh	W	1878-9
1604	Plant	W	1878-9	975	Rowe	J	1878-9	684	Smallman	J	1878
1917	Plummer	P	No clasp	1573	Rowe	J	1879	376	Smith	C	1878-9
1549	Poole	J	1878-9	853	Rowley	G	1879	893	Smith	D	1879
904	Potts	J	No clasp	663	Rowley	T	1878-9	386	Smith	D	1878-9
706	Powell	E	1878-9	1337	Rubie	G	1878	1018	Smith	D	1878-9
1234	Powers	J	1878-9	1085	Rubie	R	1878	1171	Smith	G	No clasp
1852	Powis	N	No clasp	2070	Ruffle KIA	H	1878-9	1048	Smith	G	1878-9
717	Powis	S	1878-9	711	Rush	F	1878-9	646	Smith	H	1878
186	Preece	G	1878-9	2010	Russell	J	1878-9	510	Smith KIA	H	1878-9
1909	Preston	J	No clasp	1923	Rutledge	J	No clasp	479	Smith	H	1878-9
1265	Price	J	1879	1254	Ryan	D	1878-9	725	Smith	H	1878-9
1816	Price	J	No clasp	1912	Ryan	H	1878-9	424	Smith	J	1878-9
2031	Prince	J	1878-9	1263	Ryan	J	1879	1063	Smith	J	1878-9
757	Prince	J	1878	1423	Ryan	J	1878	1350	Smith	J	1878-9
2085	Pritchard KIA	C	1878-9	1971	Ryan	J	No clasp	1948	Smith	J	1878-9
1053	Proud	P	1878	1878	Ryan	R	No clasp	144	Smith	J	1878
1163	Punnell KIA	A	1878-9	1007	Ryder	T	1878	1050	Smith	J	1878-9
645	Quenney	O	1878-9	375	Salt	G	1878-9	1523	Smith	J	1879
2047	Quick	J	1878	1889	Salter	C	1878	258	Smith	J	1878-9
824	Quinn	J	1879	1873	Sample	T	No clasp	657	Smith	J	1878-9
829	Rafferty	J	1879	439	Sands	W	1878-9	61	Smith	M	1878-9
1974	Ralphs KIA	F	1878-9	968	Sergeant	H	1878-9	1240	Smith	N	1878-9
201	Ramsey	G	1878-9	1553	Satterley	W	1878-9	705	Smith	T	1878
414	Randall	H	1878-9	972	Saunders	J	1878-9	664	Smith	T	1878
1094	Ratcliffe	G	No clasp	1017	Savage	J	1878-9	1494	Smith	W	1878-9
1953	Raymond	C	1878-9	962	Saville	E	1878-9	200	Snape	J	1878
533	Reid	G.F	1878-9	670	Saxton	J	1878-9	2027	Soan	B	1878-9
869	Reilly	M	1879	2074	Scott	E	1878-9	1902	Southworth	B	No clasp
158	Renfrey	A	1878-9	1253	Seddons	T	1878-9	1805	Speers	J	1878-9
1183	Reeves	J	No clasp	377	Sedgeley	W.H	1878-9	729	Spence	R	1878-9
1541	Reynolds	J	1879		No Medal Deserted.			1077	Spencer	H	1878
609	Rhoades	R	1878-9	1888	Selby	G	No clasp	746	Spink	J	1878-9
1894	Rhoades	T	1878	262	Senior	J	1878-9	2009	Stabbs	J	No clasp
1093	Rice	A	1879	650	Sergeant	J.W	1878-9	1526	Stacey	A	1878-9
1108	Rickman	G	1878	1904	Sewll	J	No clasp	2016	Stanley	A	1878-9
528	Richardson	C	1878-9	695	Seymour	W	1878-9	1776	Sterling	H	1878
2012	Richardson	G	1878-9		KIA 22/1/1879.			1107	Stevenson	G	1878
1099	Richardson	R	1879	484	Shapcott	H	1878-9	1137	Stevenson	T	1878
933	Riley	A	1879	970	Shaw	F	1878-9	473	Stokes	D	1878
995	Riley	M	1878-9	1535	Shaw	J	1879	138	Stokes	F	1878-9
1963	Ring	E	1878-9	1534	Shaw	R	1879	1067	Stokes	J	1878
878	Roach	T	1879r	1165	Shaw	S	1878		No Medal Deserted.		
	Forfeited. No reason given.			1810	Shaw	W	No clasp	1987	Storas	W	1878
578	Robbins	W	1878-9		No Medal. Discharged with ignominy.			225	Storer	W	1878-9
1960	Roberts	H	1878-9	323	Shea	C	No clasp	229	Street	W	1878
1959	Robertson	S	No clasp	2035	Shellock	J	1878	1792	Sturges	W	1878
259	Robinson KIA	J	1878-9	615	Sherridan KIA	M	1878-9	1376	Sugden	R	1878-9
1483	Robinson	R	1878-9	514	Shirley	H.W	1878-9	2042	Sullivan	M	1878-9
1000	Robinson	S	1878	508	Sigley	J	1878-9	1274	Summers	J	1879
1047	Robson	J	1878-9	1770	Silcock KIA	J	1878-9	2060	Summersby	H	1878

80th Regiment

1988	Sutton	J	1878-9	1546	Walker	G	1879	247	Wiley	C	1878-9
120	Tallice	G	1878-9	563	Walker	T	1878-	137	Wiley	T	1878
No Medal Deserted.				124	Walkley	T	1878	1555	Wilkes	W	1879
1245	Tansley	J.F	1879	549	Walsh	A	1878-9	24	Wilkins	H	1878-9
630	Tarver	J	1878	219	Walsh	J	1878-9	815	Wilkinson	D	1879
1244	Taylor	A	1879	803	Walsh	J	1878	791	Wilkinson	S	1879
No Medal Deserted.				1495	Walsh	W	1878-9	1006	Wilkinson	W	1878
720	Taylor	J	1878-9	No Medal Deserted.				1549	Wilks	J	1879
1207	Taylor	J	1879	1851	Ward	I	No clasp	450	Willings	E	1878
735	Taylor	J	1878-9	1530	Ward	J	1879	991	Williams	C	1878-9
1121	Taylor	J	1879	1921	Ward	J	No clasp	1876	Williams	G	1878
1330	Taylor	R	1878	62	Ward	W	1878	691	Williams	H	1878-9
1895	Taylor	T	1878-9	1144	Ware	W	1879	1915	Williams	J	No clasp
368	Taylor	W	1879	204	Warner	C	1878-9	997	Williams	S	1878-9
1536	Taylor	W	1878	1092	Washington	W	1879	361	Williams	T	1878-9
255	Taylor	W	1878-9	1016	Wassall	C	1878-9	573	Williams	T	1878
373	Teehan	J	1878-9	427	Wassall VC	S	1878-9	1809	Williams	T	No clasp
435	Terry	J	1878	His VC was awarded for an action at				617	Williams	W	1878-9
No Medal Deserted.				Isandhlwana.				1037	William(s)	W	1878-9
816	Tetlow	E	1878-9	1924	Waxham	T	1878-9	442	Williamson	F	1878
162	Thirley	T	1878-9	730	Weaver	B	1878-9	2013	Wilmoth	W	1878-9
No Medal Deserted.				606	Weaver	J	1878-9	1896	Wilson	C	1878
1511	Thomas	D	1879	1289	Weaver	J	1878-9	627	Wilson	F	1878-9
1794	Thompson	A	1878	716	Weaver KIA	J		1175	Wilson	H	1878-9
2096	Thompson	E.G.A	1878-9	605	Webster	J		1375	Wiltshire	B	1878-9
1957	Thompson	R	1878	1009	Wedge	H	1878	No Medal Deserted.			
811	Thompson	T	1878-9	1704	Wells	E	1878	686	Winter	J	1878-9
2002	Thompson	W	1878-9	1905	Wells	J	1878	1020	Winwood	J	1878-9
587	Tibbott KIA	J	1878-9	987	Welch	J.H	1878	295	Wood	C	1878-9
1011	Tidball	H	1878-9	1495	Welch	W	1879	446	Wood	D	1878-9
1061	Tilley	G	1878-9	No Medal Deserted.				1535	Woodford	J	1878
1826	Toal	J	1878	1002	West	E	1878-9	1486	Wooding	I	1878-9
649	Tomlin	T	1878-9	1815	Westcoth	J.R	No clasp	1605	Woodward KIA	H	1878-9
1291	Tomlinson KIA	R	1878-9	990	Western	C	1878-9	724	Woodward	J	1878
1529	Tomlinson	W	1878-9	1269	Weston	P	1879	977	Woodward	J	1878
329	Topp	C	1878	294	Westwood	J	1878-9	980	Woodward	J	1878
1108	Toy	J	1879	228	Westwood	T	1878-9	1394	Woolcott	H	1879
1705	Tucker KIA	G	1878-9	1506	Wheat	C	1879	1871	Woollams	F	1878
104	Tucker KIA	T	1878-9	1097	Wheeler	R	1878-9	1551	Worrolls	H	1879
669	Tulley	P	1878-9	752	While	W	1878	1912	Worth	R	No clasp
487	Tully	C	1878	1069	Whitby	C	1878	2098 ?	Worty	J	1878-9
1091	Tunstall	A	1879	2061	White	G	1878	2048	Wrick	W	No clasp
1887	Turner	C	1878-9	624	White	J	1878	598	Wright	F	1878-9
459	Turner	E	1878-9	1536	White	J	1879	564	Wright	G	1878-9
782	Turnor	W	1878	752	White	W	1879	2051	Wright	J	1878-9
1322	Tydesley	T	1878	1095	White	W	1878	1882	Wright	J	No clasp r
501	Tyler	J	1878-9	769	Whitehead	R	?	1023	Wright	W	1878-9
188	Upperdine	J	1878-9	See R. Whitehouse below				566	Wroe	J	1878-9
1872	Upsdale	H	No clasp	1041	Whitehouse	D	1878-9	1972	Young	H	1878
902	Upton	H	1879	60	Whitehouse	J	1878-9	No Medal Deserted.			
993	Vanston	F	1878	KIA Isandhlwana.				1888	Young	T	1878
423	Varley	J	1878-9	769	Whitehouse	R	1878-9	1013	Youxall	F	1878
1516	Vaughan	F	1879	See R. Whitehouse above.							
1941	Vaughan	H	1878	774	Whitehouse	W	1878-9				
1046	Vaughan	J	1878-9	1250	Whittaker	D	1879				
370	Vernon KIA	J		2097 ?	Whittaker	W	1878				
1080	Vickery	S	1878-9	2097 ?	Whyman	T	1878-9				
1911	Wakeling	G	1878-9	A duplicate medal and clasp 1879 was							
530	Walker	E	No clasp	issued 24/9/1919.							

82nd Regiment

82nd (THE PRINCE OF WALES' VOLUNTEERS REGIMENT.
CAPTAIN
    Cardew F 1879
Also had Medal and clasp for North West Frontier 1863.
LIEUTENANT
    Hall R.W 1879

87th (ROYAL IRISH FUSILIERS) REGIMENT.
    Martin E.C 1879
See also Commissariat & Transport Staff

88th (CONNAUGHT RANGERS) REGIMENT.
The 88th went out to the Cape in 1877, and served in the Kaffir War of 1877-8, and in the Zulu War of 1879. From South Africa it went on to India in 1880, and returned home in 1891.
LIEUTENANT COLONEL
    Lambet CB W 1877-8-9
Also had British and Turkish Crimea Medals and Indian Mutiny Medal.
MAJOR
    Hopton E 1877-8-9
Also had British and Turkish Crimea Medals and Indian Mutiny Medal.
    Owen A.A 1877-8
BREVET MAJOR
    Dalrymple W.L 1877-8-9
Also had medal and clasp for Ashanti War 1874.
CAPTAIN and BREVET MAJOR
    Fry J.W 1877-8
    Moore VC CB H.G 1877-8
His VC was for an action at Draaibos 29/12/1877, attempting to save the life of a Cape policeman. Had medal and clasp for Central India, and Medal and clasp for Ashanti War 1874.
CAPTAIN
    Acklom S 1877-8
    Baldwin F.C 1877-8-9
    Benn M No clasp
    Bowen H.G 1879
    Brind E.A 1879
    Curran J.P 1877-8-9
    Jeffreys P.D 1879
    Kell W.C.F 1877-8 r
    Larpent Sir G.deH 1877-8-9
    Penton C.T.W 1879
QUARTERMASTER
    Cousins S 1877-8-9
Also had British and Turkish Crimea Medals & Indian Mutiny Medal and clasp.
LIEUTENANT and ADJUTANT
    Hammond D.T 1877-8-9
LIEUTENANT
    Gardner S.H 1879
    Maher V.H 1877-8
    Mann H.B 1877-8
    Moore M.G 1877-8-9
    Thirkill J 1877-8-9
D/S 22/4/1879
    Webb D.J.M 1877-8-9
    Wood A.H 1877-8
2nd LIEUTENANT
    Acton J.L.C 1877-8-9
He appears to have received clasp 1877-8 and 1879.
    Barton N.A.D 1879
    Elton A.G.B 1877-8-9
    Freckleton G.W 1877-8
    Heldane E.H.V 1879
    Rickards F.S.H 1879
    Wyncoll C.E 1877-8-9
On the 15th August, 1877, he was gazetted to the 88th Connaught Rangers
SERGEANT MAJOR
1083 Morrison C 1877-8-9
COLOR SERGEANT
1382 Barnes T 1877-8-9
1281 Bowen B 1877-8-9
1390 Clancy H 1877-8
471 Davin J 1877-8-9
548 De Lapoer J 1877-8-9
1519 Dinnage W 1877-8-9
1545 Farrell M 1877-8-9
720 Gorman T 1877-8-9
693 Hynard S 1877-8
1574 Mc Mahon T 1879
ARMOURER SERGEANT
387 Morrison J 1877-8-9
COOK SERGEANT
15 Chapman S 1877-8-9
PAYMASTER SERGEANT
605 Canty J 1877-8-9
PIONEER SERGEANT
643 Mitchell A 1877-8-9
QUARTERMASTER SERGEANT
13 Pullen B No clasp
SERGEANT INSTRUCTOR OF MUSKETRY
5108 Denness G 1877-8-9
SERGEANT
1026 Adams T 1877-8-9
24 Baker R 1879
17 Bowen T 1877-8
752 Brady T 1877-8
2999 Brereton W 1877-8
39 Brooks J 1877-8-9
530 Butler F 1877-8-9r
536 Butler J 1877-8
1468 Christie P 1877-8-9
1464 Connor E 1877-8-9
1027 Connors J 1877-8-9
1561 Coogan T 1877-8
738 Davin T 1877-8-9
370 Duffy F 1879
1033 Furey T 1877-8
1625 Harrington J 1877-8-9
Duplicate medal and clasp issued 8/1/1919.
269 Hickey T 1877-8
400 Hogan P 1879
248 Horan O 1879
739 Kelly L 1877-8-9
1480 Lowe M 1877-8-9
1584 Masterson J 1879
1374 Mc Bride R 1879
601 Mc Bride T 1877-8
91 Mc Cormack J 1879
181 Mc Guigan T No clasp
1512 Milligan J 1879
1650 O'Neill J 1877-8-9
1550 Purtrill J 1879

Spinks Medal Supplement 1989.
South Africa Medal 1877 bar 1877-8-9 (Cr. Sergt. B. Bowen, 88th Foot). EF £150
The relevant roll, WO 100 47, shows COLOUR SERGEANT BARTHOLOMEW BOWEN (sic) No. 1281, as engaged against the Gaikas, Galekas and other Kaffir Tribes 1877-78; also engaged against the Zulus in 1879. The roll was signed at Mooltan on 22nd January, 1881. Muster rolls of the 1st Bn. Connaught Rangers in India: 1281 Colour Sergeant BARTHOLOMEW BOWEN, placed on the married roll 12th April, 1880. Wife, HESTER: She died sometime in the period Oct-Dec 1881, no children of the marriage being recorded. BOWEN embarked for England 21st April, 1882.
Depot, Connaught Rangers, Galway: 1281 Colour Sergeant BARTHOLOMEW BOWEN, from Netley 23rd June, 1882. Wife recorded as JOANNA from October, 1883 (presumably he remarried). At the school of musketry from 18 Aug.-Dec. 1887. Regimental Number changed to 470 as from April, 1884. Transferred to 2nd Bn Connaught Rangers at Portsmouth from 1st Dec. 1887 and to 1st Bn. from 31st Dec., 1887. 1st Bn. the Connaught Rangers in India: Jan.-Dec. 1888: 470 Colour Sergeant BARTHOLOMEW BOWEN, from Home Bn. 5th Jan., 1888: Wife JOHANNA (sic), one child aged three years. Placed on married roll 21-2-1884.

88th Regiment

Officers of the 88th Connaught Rangers with the First Division Back Row - Left to Right
Quartermaster S. Cousins, Captain H.G. Bowen, Surg. Captain Harding, Lt C.F. Wyncoll
2nd Lt F.S.H. Rickards, Lt.M.G. Moore
Centre Row
Captain John Philpot Curran, Lt E.H.V. Haldane, Captain E.A. Brind
Front Row
Captain Chevenix Baldwin, Lt & Adj. D.T. Hammond, Lt Col E. Hopton, 2nd Lt N.A.D. Barton, Captain C.T.W. Penton

1315	Richards	E	1877-8-9	610	Freeman	J	1877-8-9	1029	Murphy	J	1877-8-9
1518	Scanlon	T	1877-8-9	1125	Gordon	W	1877-8-9	1661	Murphy	M	1877-8
1486	Simmonds	A	1877-8-9	1507	Hale	A	1877-8-9	771	Murphy	W	1879
1075	Spiers	J	1879	770	Henry	J	1879	412	Murray	J	1877-8
292	Tope	T	1877-8-9	508	Hill	R	1877-8-9	718	Murtogh	P	1877-8-9
129	Wright	S	1879	696	James	R	1877-8-9	1248	Nixon	P	1877-8-9
CORPORAL				713	Jones	J.R	1877-8-9	1194	Notley	J	1879r
1316	Allen	T	1877-8-9	682	Jones	R	1877-8-9	822	O'Dowd	J	1879
985	Darry	J	1877-8-9	543	Kavanagh	L	1877-8	788	O'Farrell	C	1879
1093	Boyde	T	1877-8	1523	Kelly	M	1879	1021	Slattery	W	1879
828	Brown	J	1877-8-9	1275	Kenny	M.J	1877-8-9	334	Smith	J	1877-8-9
390	Charlton	E	1879	410	Kenny	W	1879	233	Springett	C	1877-8-9
402	Clarke	H	1877-8-9	810	King	J	1877-8	1376	Twohey	J	1879r
640	Connor	M	1879	1209	Leonard	M	1877-8r	749	Waters	T	1879
75	Cooper	J	1879r	522	Leviston	J	1877-8-9	See also Royal Horse Artillery.			
823	Corbett	W	1877-8	1479	Lyss	H	1877-8	88	Wood	J	1877-8
255	Cunningham	J	1877-8	875	Mc Dermott	J	1877-8-9	ORDERLYROOM CLERK			
457	Daly	W	1877-8	1111	Mc Grath	M	1877-8-9	1615	Mc Crohon	J	1877-8-9
573	Develin	J	1877-8	1284	Mc Lachlan	D	1879	DRUMMER			
1322	Flanagan	P	1879	792	Meaney	L	1877-8	1347	Connor	M	1877-8-9
484	Flynn	H	1879	1557	Moore	J	1877-8-9	1635	Connors	P	1877-8-9
555	Folan	C	1877-8-9r	1210	Moran	P	1877-8	136	Cook	J	1879
1256	Ford	J	1879	392	Mulreonan	M	1877-8r	957	Farrell	J	1879

88th Regiment

No.	Name	Init.	Clasp	No.	Name	Init.	Clasp	No.	Name	Init.	Clasp
1149	Fury	F	1877-8	354	Bodkin	J	1877-8-9	704	Byrne	J	1877-8-9
1121	Gallagher	J	1877-8-9	927	Boland	P	1877-8r	620	Byrne	J	1877-8
There is a query on the roll as to this clasp for he left for Mauritius in 1878, and India in 1879. He appears to be entitled to clasp 1877-8.				979	Boothman	G	1877-8-9	694	Byrne	J	1877-8-9
				2107	Borkin	P	1879	862	Byrne	J	1877-8-9
				1102	Bourke	E	1877-8	704	Byrne	J	1877-8-9
				821	Bowen	P	1877-8-9	He appears to have received clasps 1877-8 and 1879.			
722	Griffin	R	1879	259	Bowers	H	1877-8				
963	Hanlon	F	1877-8	7	Boyde	J	1879	1433	Byrne	M	1877-8-9
470	Hatch	L	1879	379	Boyde	J	1877-8-9	688	Caddell	R	1877-8-9
1505	Heath	J	1877-8-9	681	Boyde	W	1877-8	550	Caffrey	J	1877-8-9
348	Long	T	1877-8-9	1013	Boyle	J	1877-8-9	He appears to have received clasps 1877-8 and 1879.			
4272	Martin	J	1877-8	861	Boyle	J	1877-8				
394	O'Gorman	J	1877-8-9r	1274	Boyton	S	1877-8-9	1484	Cahill	C	1879
1523	Payne	C	1877-8-9	944	Boyton	T	1877-8-9	525	Cahill	J	1879
1025	Rynhart	J	1877-8	2018	Boyle	E	1879	270	Cahill	M	1879
1657	Trouse	F	1877-8-9	1298	Brady	J	1877-8-9	901	Cain	P	1879
1506	Vincent	J	1877-8-9	He appears to have received clasps 1877-8 and 1879.				572	Callaghan	E	1879
1522	Young	J	1877-8					993	Callaghan	J	1877-8
PRIVATE				1055	Brady	J	1877-8	272	Callery	E	1879r
1061	Ahern	W	1877-8r	1147	Brady	M	1877-8-9	1382	Brown	J	1879
1106	Aldridge	R	1877-8-9	644	Breheny	T	1877-8-9	481	Callery	M	1879
764	Allen	J	1877-8-9	1154	Brennan	J	1877-8	1245	Canning	J	1877-8-9r
1176	Alley	J	1877-8	556	Brien	J	1877-8	994	Cannon	J	1877-8-9
1238	Alson	S	1877-8	849	Brien	J	1879r	631	Carberry	A	1877-8-9
648	Anderson	C	1879	711	Broderick	J	1879	He appears to have received clasps 1877-8 and 1879.			
1045	Anderson	G	1877-8-9	1023	Broderick	J	1877-8-9				
1448	Andrews	T	1879	629	Broderick	P	1879	1024	Carberry	J	1877-8
1146	Armstrong	W	No clasp	2147	Brogan	A	1879	1262	Carberry	J	1877-8
No Medal. Discharged with ignominy.				1233	Bront	R	1879	1014	Carney	T	1877-8-9
343	Ashe	J	1877-8-9	1232	Bront	T	1879	2075	Carroll	E	1879
1082	Askew	J	1877-8-9	873	Brown	F	1877-8	1336	Carroll	M	1879
156	Atkinson	J	1879r	557	Brown	J	1877-8-9	902	Carroll	P	1877-8-9
470	Aughey	J	1877-8-9	675	Brown	R	1877-8-9	866	Carthy	J	1877-8
1283	Auldridge	T	1877-8-9	No Medal Deserted.				No Medal Deserted.			
69	Baker	C	1879r	856	Brown	W	1877-8-9	1487	Carty	M	1879
2037	Baldwin	D	1879	He appears to have received the clasps 1877-8 and 1879.				568	Carty	P	1877-8-9
1062	Baldwin	F	1877-8-9					1432	Cartwright	J	1877-8-9
974	Ball	J	1877-8	623	Bruen	B	1879	2032	Casey	E	1879
1327	Bambrick	L	1879	1116	Bruen	J	1877-8	870	Casey	E	1877-8r
1251	Banks	P	1879	727	Brunt	J	1877-8-9	863	Casey	J	1877-8
532	Bannon	W	1877-8-9	571	Bryan	D	1877-8-9	2133	Casey	P	No clasp
634	Barnes	T	1877-8-9	1083	Buckley	J	1877-8-9	1348	Casey	T	1879
1397	Barrett	J	1879	838	Bulman	J	1877-8-9	1358	Cassels	T	No clasp
1189	Barrett	M	1877-8-9	1163	Burke	J	1877-8-9	1312	Cassidy	A	1879
1488	Barrett	P	1879	280	Burke	J	1877-8-9	661	Cassidy	J	1879
1144	Barron	J	1877-8	624	Burke	J	1877-8-9	958	Cassidy	M	1877-8-9
765	Barry	M	1877-8-9	1345	Burke	J	1879	1035	Cassidy	P	1877-8-9
2078	Beattie	J	1879	373	Burke	M	1877-8	1181	Caufield	J	1877-8
1654	Beattie	W	1879	No Medal. Discharged with ignominy.				1135	Caufield	T	1877-8
379	Beckett	J	1877-8-9	1429	Burke	M	1879	1585	Cavanagh	P	1879
166	Bennett	A	1877-8-9	885	Burke	T	1877-8-9	1236	Chalk	J	1879
1072	Berry	J	1877-8-9	616	Burke	T	1877-8-9r	1237	Chalk	S	1879
273	Berry	W	1877-8r	268	Burke	W	1877-8-9r	1238	Chambers	M	1879
1270	Bevine	P	1877-8-9	2086	Burns	A	1879	829	Champney	T	1877-8r
1658	Birchill	W	1877-8-9	1140	Burns	J	1877-8	441	Chapman	C	1879
1630	Birmingham	J	1877-8-9	1117	Burns	P	1877-8-9	702	Chiney	H	1877-8-9
1258	Birmingham	W	No clasp	654	Burns	P	1879	544	Clarke	M	1879
515	Bishop	A	1877-8-9	907	Butler	M	1877-8	1664	Clarke	P	1879
961	Bishop	W	1877-8r	1150	Butler	P	1877-8-9	366	Clarke	T	1877-8-9

88th Regiment

No.	Name	Initial	Clasp	No.	Name	Initial	Clasp	No.	Name	Initial	Clasp
168	Cleary	J	1877-8-9r	899	Corcoran	M	1877-8-9	148	Davis	W	1879
1637	Cleary	J	1879	1190	Corley	T	1877-8	469	Dawson	T	1877-8r
791	Cleary	P	1879	913	Cormack	F	1877-8	772	Deegan	E	1879
864	Clements	W.G	1877-8-9	566	Corrigan	J	1877-8-9r	617	Delaney	M	1877-8
1003	Clifford	W	1877-8	2091	Cosgrove	M	1879	1532	Dempsey	C	1879
Deserted. No trace of the return of medal.				1306	Cosgrove	T	1877-8-9	859	Dempsey	M	1877-8
302	Cloherty	P	1877-8	2129	Cosgrove	T	1879	636	Dennison	T	1879
266	Clough	F	1877-8-9	1016	Costello	J	1877-8-9	2083	Devaney	C	1879r
142	Coady	T	No clasp	896	Coughlan	M	1877-8	783	Devaney	P	1877-8-9
1435	Coen	J	1879	1026	Cox	G	1877-8-9	391	Devine	J	1877-8-9
1414	Coen	M	1879	1300	Cox	M	1877-8	No medal. Discharged with ignominy.			
842	Coghlan	P	1877-8	562	Cox	M	1877-8	266	Devine	L	1877-8
1534	Colligan	J	1877-8-9	2123	Cox	O	1879	428	Devlin	F	1877-8r
455	Collins	C	1877-8-9	747	Coyne	M	1877-8-9	95	Devlin	J	1879
1631	Collins	H	1877-8-9	Deserted. No trace of the return of the medal.				1359	Dillon	J	1879
183	Collins	J	1879					1406	Dobson	G	1879
1041	Collins	M	1877-8-9	1088	Coyne	T	1877-8-9	1148	Dolan	D	1877-8-9
2140	Collins	M	1879	712	Cremen	B	1877-8-9	152	Donald	C	1879
677	Collins	P	1879	1311	Creighton	J	1879	1285	Donegan	T	1877-8
294	Collins	T	1877-8-9	331	Crilly	E	1877-8-9	1140	Donegan	W	1879
632	Condon	J	No clasp	906	Cronin	J	1879	510	Donelan	M	1879
453	Conma	P	1877-8-9	778	Cronin	M	1877-8-9	878	Donnell	E	1877-8
502	Connallon	J	1879	892	Cronin	T	1879	1371	Donnelly	J	1879
1295	Connaughton	M	1879	1036	Crowley	J	1877-8-9	2046	Donnelly	P	1879
2020	Connell	O	1879	448	Crowley	J	1877-8r	346	Donoghue	D	1877-8
1406	Connell	T	1879	276	Cryan	M	1877-8	786	Donohue	P	1877-8
602	Connell	W	1877-8	1017	Cuffe	C	1877-8-9	569	Donovan	M	1879
1396	Connery	T	1879	663	Cuffe	M	1879	577	Donovan	T	1877-8-9
972	Connier	P	1879	760	Cuffe	P	1877-8-9	395	Doolan	J	1877-8-9r
905	Connolly	E	1877-8-9	321	Cullen	E	1879	969	Dooley	J	1877-8-9
1160	Connolly	P	1879	809	Cullen	J	1879	1119	Dooley	W	1877-8
1004	Connolly	P	1879	1050	Cullen	M	1877-8	1475	Doran	T	1879
396	Connolly	W	1877-8-9	611	Cullinan	M	1877-8	1290	Dorrill	H	No clasp
1230	Connors	C	1879	1056	Cummings	M	1877-8-9	1301	Dowd	L	1877-8-9
1461	Connor	L	1877-8-9	537	Cunningham	P	1877-8-9	2126	Dowd	P	1879
1042	Connor	M	1877-8-9	404	Curran	T	1877-8-9	164	Dowdle	M	1879
1009	Connor	P	1879	1289	Curtis	F	No clasp	766	Dower	J	1877-8-9
1138	Connors	P	1877-8	1243	Daftery	D	1877-8-9	920	Dower	M	1877-8
1659	Connors	P	1877-8-9	1176	Dally	T	1877-8r	814	Dowling	E	1877-8-9r
He appears to have received the clasps 1877-8 and 1879.				549	Dalton	M	1877-8-9	Forfeited. No reason given.			
				1587	Daly	C	1877-8-9	1480	Dowling	J	1879
1105	Connors	W	1877-8-9	612	Daly	J	1877-8-9	104	Dowling	W	No clasp
301	Conroy	J	1877-8-9	1375	Daly	L	1879	No Medal. Discharged with ignominy.			
265	Conroy	P	1879r	869	Daly	P	1877-8r	706	Downes	J	1877-8-9
298	Conroy	T	1877-8	874	Daly	P	1877-8-9	8	Downes	P	1879
2112	Conroy	V	1879r	1216	Daly	P	No clasp	1314	Dowson	J	1877-8
263	Conway	C	1879	1261	D'Arcy	P	1877-8-9	1362	Doyle	A	1879
898	Conway	J	1877-8	434	Darragh	H	1879	550	Doyle	A	1879-8r
182	Coogan	P	1879	641	Davidson	J.T	1877-8-9	781	Doyle	J	1879
1299	Cooney	P	1877-8	685	Davis	J	1877-8-9	1094	Doyle	J	1877-8
364	Corbett	W	1877-8-9	1393	Davis	J	1879	1089	Doyle	M	1877-8
No Medal Deserted.				261	Davis	W	No clasp r	No Medal Deserted.			

> The Times, House of Commons debate Tuesday 4th March 1879.
> "Many of the men recently sent out were well grown and fairly good soldiers but it could not be denied that, as a whole, the infantry sent out were far too young for the work they had to do. It could not be denied by any competent authority that the 88th Regt. when last sent out was composed mainly of boys. It was mentioned in a recent despatch as to their gallant conduct in the field that Major Moore at the head of 44 of these boys engaged and defeated a detachment of the enenmy 600 strong; and Major Moore speaking himself of the engagement said he "drove off the enemy with a small party of young soldiers imperfectly aquainted with their weapons"

88th Regiment

371	Doyle	P	1877-8	297	Finnigan	P	1877-8-9r	1319	Geraghty	J	1879
1294	Doyle	P	1877-8-9	colspan="3"	Reissued 1882 and again returned this	909	Geraghty	J	1879
1156	Doyle	W	1879	colspan="3"	time to the mint in 1897.	1211	Geraghty	P	1877-8-9
2092	Drury	J	1879	1070	Fitzgerald	J	1879	1271	Gibbons	J	1879r
1057	Duane	J	1879	941	Fitzgerald	M	No clasp	275	Gildea	J	1877-8-9r
176	Duddy	M	1879	890	Fitzgerald	P	1877-8-9	1279	Gill	H	1877-8
337	Duff	W	1877-8	429	Fitzgerald	T	1877-8	1416	Gillespie	P	1879
2125	Duffy	J	1879	889	Fitzgerald	W	1877-8-9	540	Gilligan	E	1877-8-9
colspan="4"	No Medal. Discharged with ignominy.	1090	Fitzharris	J	No clasp	242	Gillmartin	P	1879
1084	Duffy	M	1879	1064	Fitzpatrick	B	1877-8-9r	1239	Gilroy	T	1879
1095	Duffy	T	1879	883	Fitzsimmons	T	1877-8-9	1493	Gleeson	J	1879
1166	Duggan	T	1877-8	1504	Flaherty	P	1879	1379	Gleeson	J	1879
1296	Duignan	P	1879	585	Flaherty	T	1877-8-9	1254	Glynn	P	1879
599	Dullard	E	1877-8-9	916	Flanagan	J	1877-8-9	762	Gogan	T	1877-8-9
1217	Dunleavey	J	1877-8r	1109	Fleming	E	1877-8-9r	367	Goggins	J	1877-8-9
1499	Dunleavey	D	1879	497	Flinter	W	1877-8-9	462	Gohery	T	1879
968	Dunn	D	1879	1133	Flynn	J	1877-8-9	1452	Golden	M	1879r
1032	Dunne	P	1877-8	1096	Flynn	J	1877-8-9	1207	Golden	M	1877-8
830	Durcan	T	1877-8-9	1114	Flynn	P	1879	1106	Golden	T	1877-8
322	Durnin	D	1877-8r	356	Flynn	P	1879	1307	Gorman	J	1877-8
954	Durville	J	1879	735	Fogarthy	T	1877-8-9	438	Graham	J	1877-8-9
2039	Edwards	P	No clasp	1157	Folan	M	1877-8-9	663	Gray	P	No clasp
colspan="4"	No Medal Deserted.	669	Foley	J	1879	976	Green	I	1877-8
1120	Edwards	T	1877-8	996	Ford	J	1877-8-9r	1520	Green	J	1879
1277	Egan	J	1877-8	colspan="3"	Forfeited. No reason given.	626	Green	T	1879
570	Egan	M	1877-8r	938	Ford	M	1877-8-9		Deserted. No trace of return of the medal.
1241	Egan	P	1879	2131	Ford	P	1879	851	Greenhalgh	J	1879
460	Egan	P	1877-8r	1110	Ford	T	1877-8-9	1052	Greenwood	W	1877-8-9
1656	Elliott	F	1879	1398	Forder	J	1877-8-9	776	Greham	N	1879
# 835	Elliott	T	1877-8-9	1097	Foster	J	1877-8-9r	1091	Grennon	M	1879
1063	Ennis	M	1877-8-9	colspan="3"	Forfeited. No reason given.	1006	Griffin	M	1877-8-9
58	Evans	G	1879	382	Fox	J	1879	882	Grime	H	1877-8
474	Fagan	W	1877-8-9	816	Fox	J	1877-8-9	2081	Grogan	J	1879
1206	Faherty	S	1877-8-9	2090	Fox	J	1879	1267	Grogan	J	1879
393	Fahey	P	1877-8-9	804	Foy	J	No clasp	1085	Guiry	M	1879
769	Farrell	E	1879	1365	Frean	H	1879	1386	Guiry	P	1879
2127	Farrell	F	1879	1509	Freeman	J	1877-8-9	1185	Haddock	J	1877-8-9
741	Farrell	J	1877-8	942	French	J	1877-8	106	Haggan	S	1879r
908	Farrell	J	1877-8-9	372	Fuller	G	1877-8	1037	Hall	A	1877-8
1246	Farrell	J	1877-8-9	colspan="3"	No Medal. Discharged with ignominy.	9	Hall	J	1877-8
1018	Farrell	R	1877-8-9	2063	Fury	J	1879	700	Halliday	A	1877-8
1019	Farrell	T	1877-8-9	1027	Gahon	J	1877-8-9	1490	Halpin	M	1877-8-9
1051	Farrelly	J	1877-8	colspan="3"	He appears to have received clasps	2155	Hamilton	J	1879
683	Feeney	T	1877-8	colspan="3"	1877-8 and 1879.	945	Hamilton	R	1877-8-9
1108	Fegan	P	1879	2042	Gallagher	A	1879	217	Handel	A	1877-8
128	Finegan	P	1879	484	Gallagher	J	1877-8-9	1291	Hards	W	No clasp
1005	Finegan	P	1877-8-9	409	Gallagher	P	1877-8r	921	Hardy	W	1877-8-9
colspan="4"	He appears to have received the clasps 1877-8 and 1879.	1171	Gallagher	T	No clasp	405	Harrington	J	1879r
				824	Ganley	F	1877-8-9	73	Hart	T	1879
989	Fineran	J	1877-8-9	252	Gannon	B	1879	1137	Harvey	J	1877-8-9
580	Finerty	T	1877-8-9	231	Gant	S	1877-8r	349	Hassett	T	1877-8
629	Finn	J	1877-8	479	Gavagan	T	1879r	1486	Haverty	T	1879
1195	Finn	J	1877-8-9	1244	Gavin	J	1879	926	Hayden	J	1877-8-9
				495	Gavin	M	1877-8	519	Hayes	J	1877-8-9
				1405	Gavin	T	1879	818	Hayes	P	1877-8-9

Ebay Item number: 190369333504 Zulu War Medal 1879, 4 bids sold for £365 6th February 2010.
Zulu War Medal 1879, This medal is correctly named to: 835 Corpl. T. Elliott. 88 th Foot (88th Foot = The Conaught Rangers) The medal is in excellent condition with good definition, originally bought from Raymond Holdich Medals. Editors note; No clasp on medal?

88th Regiment

No.	Name	Init.	Date	No.	Name	Init.	Date	No.	Name	Init.	Date
951	Healey	J	1877-8-9	1151	Keavney	B	1879	831	Magee	J	1877-8-9
657	Healey	P	1879	1157	Kelleher	M	1877-8-9	1059	Magrath	J	1877-8-9
950	Healy	C	1877-8-9	924	Kelly	H	1877-8		Deserted. No medal.		
934	Hefferman	H	1879	586	Kelly	J	1877-8	1065	Maguire	J	1877-8-9
230	Hennesy	M	1877-8-9	1305	Kelly	J	1879-8r	253	Mahon	J	1879
422	Hennety	J	1877-8	490	Kelly	P	1877-8	1395	Mahony	J	1879
437	Henry	W	No clasp r	795	Kelly	W	1877-8	893	Malley	J	1877-8
1334	Hester	P	1879	1115	Kelly	W	1877-8	1044	Malley	P	1877-8
997	Hewson	J	1877-8-9	936	Kennedy	A	1877-8	1142	Mannion	J	1877-8-9
386	Higgins	J	1877-8-9	1098	Kennedy	J	1877-8-9	1179	Mannion	J	1877-8
19	Higgins	J	1879	751	Kennedy	J	1877-8-9	1175	Mannix	J	1879
1124	Higgins	P	1877-8	1064	Kennedy	J	1877-8	1661	Mansell	T	1879
984	Higgins	W	1879	195	Kennedy	M	1879	588	Markey	M	1877-8
656	Hinchey	P	1877-8-9r	1250	Kenny	J	1879	1038	Marsh	R	1877-8-9
653	Hines	P	1879		No Medal Deserted.			1201	Martin	P	1877-8-9
543	Heare	G	1879	1167	Kenny	J	1877-8-9	1186	Martin	S	1877-8-9
1302	Hoare	M	1877-8	1263	Keogh	P	1879	699	Maxwell	A	1877-8-9
931	Hoare	T	1877-8-9	846	Keoghery	T	1877-8	1224	Mayart	E	1879
1075	Hobson	J	1877-8	1099	Kerrins	J	1877-8-9	146	Mc Affee	J	1879
485	Hodges	J	1877-8-9	895	Kilgallon	J	1877-8-9	2052	Mc Andrews	J	1879r
527	Hogan	J	1877-8	939	Kilgallon	J	1877-8	487	Mc Bride	J	1877-8-9
1191	Hogan	J	1879	1310	Killalea	J	1879	652	Mc Cann	J	1877-8-9
840	Hogan	P	1877-8	914	Killalea	J	1877-8-9	1578	Mc Cann	M	1877-8
642	Holden	W	1879	178	Killeen	J	1877-8r	440	Mc Carroll	A	1877-8
931	Holian	J	1879	819	Kinsella	P	1877-8-9	407	Mc Carroll	P	1877-8-9r
1453	Holland	P	1879		No Medal Deserted.				D/S 3/12/79.		
686	Holloran	P	No clasp	998	Knott	J	1877-8-9	202	Mc Carthy	A	1879
1177	Howard	G	1879	787	Lahon	J	1877-8	558	Mc Carthy	J	1879
103	Hughes	H	1879	1247	Laney	J	1877-8-9	1549	Mc Carthy	M	1879r
755	Hughes	P	1877-8-9	2166	Larkin	B	1879	1219	Mc Cormack	J	1877-8
1074	Hughes	T	1877-8	797	Larkin	W	1877-8-9	667	Mc Cormack	J	1877-8-9
1154	Hurley	J	1877-8	987	Lavelle	M	1877-8-9	1076	Mc Cormack	T	1877-8
33	Isles	W	No clasp	1347	Lawless	J	1879	488	Mc Crann	F	1877-8
56	Jackson	G	1879	2141	Lawless	J	1879	1280	Mc Cusker	J	1877-8
1331	Jennings	J	1879	1303	Layden	T	1877-8-9	1482	Mc Daid	J	1879
	No Medal Deserted.			801	Leary	M	1879	2049	Mc Dermott	P	1879
521	Jennings	P	1877-8	486	Leddy	M	1877-8-9	879	Mc Dermott	P	1879
2048	Johnstone	J	1879	1308	Lee	E	1877-8-9	1200	Mc Dermott	P	1877-8-9
2128	Johnston	R	1879	982	Lewis	C	1879	500	Mc Donald	C	1877-8
812	Johnston	T	1877-8-9	192	Linnel	J	1877-8r	991	Mc Donald	M	1877-8
714	Jones	H	1879	144	Livingston	J	1879	1172	Mc Donald	P	1877-8
	Discharged with ignominy. No trace of the return of the medal.			1444	Lloyd	J	1879	1320	Mc Donnell	P	1879
				426	Lockhart	H	1879	540	Mc Donnell	P	1877-8
1028	Joyce	G	1877-8-9	1403	Logan	M	1879	1260	Mc Donough	J	1877-8-9
1081	Joyce	J	1877-8-9	952	Looby	T	1877-8	1128	Mc Donough	P	1877-8
659	Joyce	M	1877-8-9	621	Luddy	P	1877-8-9	695	Mc Donough	P	1877-8-9
271	Judge	C	1877-8-9r	1315	Ludlow	S	1877-8-9	922	Mc Donough	P	1877-8-9
1640	Judge	J	1877-8-9	781	Lych	R	1877-8-9	493	Mc Fadden	J	1879
1010	Kane	B	1877-8-9	2139	Lyden	J	1879	218	Mc Garry	F	1879
748	Kane	M	1877-8	756	Lyden	M	1877-8-9	960	Mc Garry	P	1877-8
1125	Kavanagh	J	1877-8	1100	Lynam	P	1877-8-9	2144	Mc Garry	P	1879
929	Kavanagh	M	1877-8-9	?	Lyons	D	No clasp	1192	Mc Gee	E.J	1877-8
1450	Kavanagh	P	1879	1218	Lyons	J	1877-8	701	Mc Gee	P	1877-8-9
196	Kavanagh	T	1879	507	Lyons	P	1877-8-9	82	Mc Gee	R	1879
1492	Kavanagh	W	1877-8	98	Mabett	G	1877-8	1101	Mc Gerety	J	1877-8
1253	Keane	M	1877-8		Discharged with ignominy. No trace of the return of the medal.			1490	Mc Glew	J	1879
708	Kearns	N	1877-8-9					2076	Mc Glone	B	1879
695	Kearney	P	1879r	1241	Madden	T	1877-8-9	406	Mc Gough	B	1879
171	Keating	T	1879r	933	Madden	T	1879	143	Mc Gough	B	1879

88th Regiment

No.	Surname	Initial	Clasps
184	Mc Gowan	J	1879
387	Mc Gowan	T	1877-8-9
383	Mc Granagan	P	1877-8
811	Mc Grane	J	1879
1329	Mc Grath	J	1879
1430	Mc Grath	M	1879
970	Mc Grath	P	1877-8-9
1178	Mc Grath	P	1877-8-9
911	Mc Grath	T	1877-8
876	Mc Grath	W	1877-8-9r
	Deserted.		
1349	Mc Greal	J	1879r
891	Mc Greevy	T	1877-8
445	Mc Guigan	A	1877-8
	No Medal. Discharged with ignominy.		
160	Mc Guire	P	1879
528	Mc Hale	M	1877-8-9
885	Mc Hugh	E	No clasp
325	Mc Hugh	J	1879r
135	Mc Intosh	H	1879
90	Mc Kee	W.J	1879
929	Mc Kenna	W	1877-8-r
1352	Mc Keon	P	1879
424	Mc Kernon	B	1879
964	Mc Loughlin	F	1879
1411	Mc Loughlin	J	1879
897	Mc Loughlin	J	1877-8-9r
	He appears to have received clasps 1877-8 and 1879.		
910	Mc Loughlin	J	1877-8-9
1498	Mc Loughlin	P	1879
87	Mc Loughlin	P	1879
	Note on role: "Medal and clasp issued 5/8/1914."		
608	Mc Loughlin	T	1877-8
1278	Mc Mahon	G	No clasp
732	Mc Mahon	J	1877-8-9
1636	Mc Mahon	J	1877-8
1240	Mc Mahon	J	1877-8
1443	Mc Mahon	P	1879
999	Mc Mahon	P	No clasp
1417	Mc Morrow	E	1879
1077	Mc Nally	J	1877-8-9r
1354	Mc Namara	T	18789
367	Mc Nulty	W	1877-8-9r
489	Mc Sharry	M	1877-8
405	Mc Vay	J	1877-8-9
208	Mc Vee	J	1879r
1012	Meehan	J	1877-8
1309	Melia	A	1877-8
784	Melia	E	1879
1020	Merrigan	P	1877-8
833	Merriman	P	1877-8-9
345	Mighton	J	1877-8-9
1180	Mitchell	J	1877-8-9
2124	Mitchell	P	1879
1066	Moat	W	1877-8-9
2101	Mochan	J	1879
	No Medal Deserted.		
518	Molloy	T	1877-8
673	Moloney	M	1877-8-9
1489	Moloney	R	1879
1134	Monaghan	P	1877-8
799	Montgomery	H	1877-8
1575	Mooney	F	1877-8
832	Mooney	J	1877-8-9
777	Mooney	T	1879
1193	Moran	D	1877-8
529	Moran	J	1877-8-9
	He appears to have received clasps 1877-8 and 1879		
1008	Moran	T	1877-8
1173	Morgan	T	1877-8
20	Moriaty	J	1879r
1187	Morrison	F	1877-8
2121	Morrison	J	No clasp
2152	Morrisroe	M	1879r
177	Morrison	W	1879
700	Moughan	J	1877-8
494	Moughan	M	1879
359	Mounds	R	1879
1389	Mulcahy	M	1879
1320	Mulanny	J	1879
805	Mullany	J	1879
900	Mullaney	P	1877-8-9r
436	Mullen	J	1877-8-9r
384	Mullens	M	1879
1028	Mullen	P	1877-8
503	Mullett	M	1877-8-9
	Deserted. No trace of medal return.		
1269	Mulligan	J	1877-8-9
267	Mulvene	M	1877-8-9
444	Murdick	J	1877-8
1662	Murphy	J	1877-8-9r
499	Murphy	J	1877-8-9
1215	Murphy	J	1877-8
1502	Murphy	J	1879
1337	Murphy	J	1877-8-9
1047	Murphy	J	1879r
1060	Murphy	J	1877-8-9
2021	Murphy	J	No clasp
940	Murphy	M	1877-8-9
788	Murphy	M	1877-8
837	Murphy	M	1877-8
1530	Murphy	M	1879
1413	Murphy	M	1879
1264	Murphy	P	1877-8-9
741	Murphy	T	1877-8
794	Murphy	T	1877-8
250	Murphy	T	1879r
1116	Murphy	J	1879
575	Murray	J	1877-8-9
1067	Murray	M	1877-8-9
313	Murray	P	1877-8-9
245	Murray	P	1879r
1127	Murray	T	1877-8-9
854	Murray	T	1877-8
1153	Murtagh	T	1879
564	Murtogh	R	1877-8-9
1139	Naughton	F	1879
2069	Naughton	M	1879r
1264	Naughton	P	1877-8-9
658	Naughton	P	1879
2170	Nee	M	1879
1039	Neeley	A	1879 r
	Discharged with ignominy.		
379	Neill	J	1877-8-9
800	Neill	P	1877-8
1342	Nicholson	A	1877-8
2153	O'Boyle	T	1879
1497	O'Brien	D	1879
1068	O'Brien	G	1877-8-9
374	O'Brien	P	1877-8-9
	No Medal. Discharged with ignominy.		
2026	O'Brien	P	1879r
	Forfeited. No reason given.		
2071	O'Brien	T	1879
376	O'Brien	T	1877-8-9r
	Forfeited. No reason given.		
1034	O'Connor	J	1879r
1333	O'Connor	P	1879
1203	O'Donnell	A	1877-8
1129	O'Donnell	P	1879
680	O'Donnell	T	1879r
502	O'Farrell	H	1877-8-9
582	O'Farrell	W	1879
771	O'Keefe	P	1877-8-9
41	O'Keefe	W	1879r
1660	O'Meara	T	1877-8-9
449	O'Neill	H	1879
1503	Ormsby	J	1879
512	O'Rourke	T	1879
754	O'Shea	T	1877-8-9
758	O'Toole	J	1877-8-9
759	Page	T	1877-8-9
1346	Parker	M	1879
1512	Parker	T	1879
725	Patterson	J	1879
16	Payne	W	1877-8-9
498	Pendergast	T	1877-8-9
1196	Persse	J	1877-8
2	Peters	W	1877-8-9
	Deserted. No trace of the return of the medal.		
477	Phillips	A	1877-8
1092	Power	J	1877-8
1363	Power	J	1879r
	Forfeited. No reason given.		
1165	Preston	J	1879
303	Pringle	R	1877-8-9
378	Pugh	J	1877-8r
1119	Purcell	C	1879
928	Purcell	W	1877-8
328	Pyne	P	1877-8-9
1441	Qualters	W	1879r
2122	Queenan	J	1879
1304	Queeny	T	1877-8-9

88th Regiment

No.	Name	Initial	Clasps
	No Medal. Discharged with ignominy.		
387	Quinn	J	1877-8-9
1174	Quinn	J	1877-8-9
767	Quinn	M	1879
1030	Quinn	M	1879
2115	Quinn	P	1879
1033	Quinn	P	1877-8r
	Forfeited. No reason given.		
1313	Quinn	S	1879
372	Rafferty	T	1879
670	Reddican	P	1879
365	Reid	J	1879r
111	Reilly	J	1879
31	Reilly	M	1877-8-9
279	Reilly	P	1879
	No Medal Deserted.		
630	Rennick	J	No clasp
2145	Reynolds	H	No clasp
871	Reynolds	S	1879
1169	Rigney	J	1879
789	Roache	J	1877-8
1437	Roache	J	1879
552	Roache	R	1877-8-9
1146	Roberts	J	1879
887	Rodgers	J	1877-8-9r
975	Ronan	J	1877-8
775	Rowe	E	1879
296	Russell	J	1877-8-9r
2161	Rush	P	1879
12	Rush	W	1879
1253	Rutledge	J	1877-8-9
2130	Ryan	D	1879
411	Ryan	J	1877-8
1657	Ryan	J	1879
576	Ryan	J	1877-8r
350	Ryan	T	1877-8-9
1130	Ryan	T	1879
213	Ryan	W	1879
843	Ryanhart	M	1877-8
1249	Saint	E	1877-8-9
1055	Salmon	J	1877-8-9
1047	Saxon	G	1877-8-9
1271	Scahill	J	1879
439	Scott	W	1877-8-9r
13	Scully	M	1879
	No Medal. Discharged with ignominy.		
998	Scully	P	1877-8-9
1422	Seavers	R	1877-8
	"He got a bullet through the head. It went in his mouth and came out under his ear and took a piece of his tongue away. He will be dumb for life." Letter John McCusker, dated March 1878. Ref http://www.rootschat.com/forum/i		
1455	Shanley	J	1879
1355	Shanley	T	1879
1429	Shannon	M	1879
1297	Shannon	P	1877-8
1356	Shannon	T	1879
2108	Sharp	T	1879
1103	Shea	P	1877-8
806	Sheridan	J	1879
1533	Simmonds	J	1877-8
1104	Skehan	J	1877-8-9
1276	Smith	E	1877-8-9r
690	Smith	J	1879
	No Medal Deserted.		
888	Smith	J	1877-8-9
893	Smith	J	1877-8
260	Smith	J	1879
798	Smith	M	1877-8
959	Smith	W	1877-8-9
105	Spence	J	1879
380	Sproule	C	1877-8-9
1481	Stanton	J	1879
565	Stapleton	F	1877-8-9
311	Sterrett	D	1897
578	Stevens	D	No claspr
1265	Stokes	M	1877-8
454	Stothers	P	1877-8-9
1495	Stringer	J	1879
1507	Stringer	M	1879
530	Sullivan	D	1877-8
841	Sullivan	J	1877-8r
76	Sullivan	J	1879
1054	Summers	T	1879
1323	Sweeney	E	1877-8-9
1204	Sweeney	J	1879
583	Sweeney	J	1877-8
631	Sweeney	M	1877-8r
1220	Sweeny	P	1877-8
726	Swift	N	1877-8-9
74	Symonds	F	1879
793	Tallon	C	1877-8
2039	Tarpey	J	1879
191	Thake	W	1877-8-9
1581	Theress	C	1877-8-9
1292	Thirkettle	A	No clasp
415	Thompson	G	1877-8
1078	Thompson	J	1877-8-9
172	Thompson	J	1879
1079	Thompson	W	1877-8
2103	Thompson	W	1879
596	Thumpkin	L	1877-8-9
884	Timlin	H	1879
1376	Tisdale	W	1877-8
418	Tobin	J	1877-8r
421	Toohey	A	1877-8
967	Toole	E	1877-8-9
1159	Treanor	J	1877-8r
930	Troy	J	1877-8-9
826	Troy	J	1877-8-9
1259	Troy	J	1877-8-9
277	Troy	R	1879r
299	Tully	J	1879
703	Tully	J	1879
1002	Turner	M	1879
1377	Twohey	J.F	1879r
1105	Twohey	M	1877-8
919	Vale	P	1879r
1462	Valentine	C	1877-8-9
872	Walle	R	1879
1031	Walsh	G	1877-8
569	Walsh	J	1877-8
1112	Walsh	J	1878-9
773	Walsh	J	1879
637	Walsh	M	1877-8-9
	He appears to have received the clasps 1877-8 and 1879.		
1459	Walsh	M	1877-8-9r
516	Walsh	P	1877-8
750	Walsh	P	1879
1205	Walsh	T	1877-8
524	Walsh	T	1879
1483	Walsh	T	1879r
2143	Ward	A	1879
1266	Ward	C	1879
1242	Ward	P	No clasp
	No Medal. Discharged with ignominy.		
1148	Ward	P	1877-8r
	He appeared to have received the clasps 1877-8 and 1879.		
949	Ward	T	1877-8-9
1022	Ward	T	1877-8-9
1209	Wardlow	T	1879
817	Warren	J	1877-8
55	Watson	J	1879
535	Watters	J	1877-8
1354	Whelan	J	1877-8-9
289	Whelan	P	1877-8-9
584	White	J	1877-8
774	Whitelaw	J	1879
45	Wilkie	S	1879r
427	Williamson	A	1877-8-9
742	Wilson	M	1877-8-9r
	He appears to have received the clasps 1877-8 and 1879.		
645	Wilson	J	1877-8-9
1282	Wilton	J	1879
1539	Witten	H	1877-8-9
2051	Wogan	J	1879
561	Worsford	W	1877-8-9
844	Wright	W	1877-8
2016	Wynne	M	1879

90th Regiment

Spinks 19 April 2007 Sale 7012 Lot 1017
An Important Kambula Casualty South Africa 1879 Medal to Second **Lieutenant A.T. Bright,** Who Lost His Life at the Head of his Men Counter Attacking the Zulu Impi at the Point of the Bayonet
South Africa 1877-79, one clasp, 1879 (2nd Lieut: A.T. Bright. 90th Foot.), virtually mint state, with original named lid of card box of issue, and registered envelope addressed to next of kin, and photographic image of recipient
Hammer Price £10,000
Second Lieutenant Arthur Tyndall Bright, of Woodcote, Aigburth, Liverpool; born 1857; educated under the **Reverend T. Browning**, at Thorpe Mandeville and thence to Eton 1870-75; his Head of House upon hearing of his death wrote of him, 'his principles were high, his sense of honour unblemished, and his love for liberty that he knew was given to him to use and not abuse unbounded.... For two years a member of the eight, second to none as a foot-ball player, a keen and excellent volunteer officer..... Eton was as dear to him as he was to Eton'; entered Sandhurst, February 1877, and passed out the following December once again drawing praise this time from Major Williams of the College, 'When Colonel, now **General Sir Evelyn Wood** asked me one day if I could name to him a lad for his regiment, then about to sail for the Cape, whose characteristics should be 'perfect gentleman and keen soldier', I could and did without a moment's hesitation answer, 'Yes Arthur Tyndall Bright''; commissioned Second Lieutenant 90th Light Infantry, January 1878, and a month later embarked for the Cape; arrived in South Africa and joined his corps in the Perie bush, twenty miles north of King William's Town and on termination of the hostilities with the Gaikas Bright proceeded with the headquarters and five companies under the command of Colonel Evelyn Wood to march overland to Natal; the force arrived in Maritzburg ten weeks later and remained there until the 20th October 1878, when they were ordered to Utrecht, Transvaal, the future base of operations for Wood's column; Bright, a talented artist was initially employed in the weeks leading up to the outbreak of the Zulu War to sketch certain positions and in the successful expedition undertaken by Colonel Wood into Zululand, for the purpose of affording protection to a tribe which had declared for British rule, Bright was selected to accompany Wood and to sketch the Zlobane Mountain stronghold; the column attacked the latter on 28.3.1879, resulting in an enemy counter attack on Wood's men at their camp in Kambula the following day; due to casualties suffered from the attack on the 28th Bright was elevated to the command of "G" Company, 'The enemy flushed with their recent success, made the most determined onslaught, approaching again and again to within a few yards of the position held by the column. When for three long hours the defenders of the laager had stoutly resisted them, and dense masses still congregating in the valley beneath showed that a final effort would yet be made, Wood decided on making a counter attack. For this purpose two companies of the 90th were ordered to advance, and at the point of the bayonet force back the threatening impi. One of these two was the G Company , and those who knew Arthur Tyndall Bright can realize with what pride he placed himself in front of the advancing line. It was in this position, while gallantly leading and cheering on his men, that he received his death wound. Though he was tenderly watched and cared for by the medical attendants, and by his faithful servant, he only lingered for a few hours, his name being added, ere the day was quite spent, to the glorious roll of those who have rendered up their lives for Queen and country."
The Washing of Spears adds further detail 'A shot drilled through Arthur Bright's thigh, missing the bone but drenching him in blood'.
General Sir Evelyn Wood, writing upon the life of Arthur Bright, says:-
"Arthur Tyndall Bright was a beautiful character, wrote a former comrade, when he heard that the brave young life had been given up on the very threshold of manhood. It was given up in the light of victory. He had sought the post of danger with honourable eagerness, and his unstained past fitted him to encounter sudden death, but it was hard for his surviving friends to realize that he was gone, for he was lively in the best sense of the word. His high spirit, ballasted as it was by a conscientious firmness of mind not common at his age, his cheery grace of manner, his vigour in manly sports, all combined to make him one of those foremost figures in life's groups that seem alike to impress and attract friends. He excelled, too, in the lighter accomplishments, and his sweet, clear voice was greatly appreciated by the soldiers, who used to take especial pleasure in hearing him sing such ballads as 'Nancy Lee' and 'Far Away', for soldiers on active service delight in pathetic music, perhaps because there is a sense of impending farewell in times when no one knows what a day may bring forth. And when the day came that abruptly stilled the voice of the singer, everyone who had known, and therefore loved him, felt that the loss of Arthur Bright was not the loss only of his country, nor even of his personal friends, but that it was, too, a loss to everyone who had been brought into contact with him.' (The South African Campaign of 1879, Mackinnon and Shadbolt, refers).

90th Regiment

Officers of the 90th. The officer with the beard in the centre is Major R.M. Rogers V.C

90th (PERTHSHIRE VOLUNTEERS LIGHT INFANTRY) REGIMENT
A difficult roll to read. Probable errors.

LIEUTENANT COLONEL
    Palmer CB H.W   1877-8
Had a medal for an earlier campaign.

BREVET LIEUTENANT COLONEL
    Cherry A   1877-8-9
Had Indian Mutiny Medal.

MAJOR
    Rogers VC R.M   1879
Had medals for Crimea and China. His VC was awarded for action at Taku Forts China 21/8/1860.

BREVET MAJOR
    Hackett **KIA** R.H   1877-8-9

CAPTAIN
	Hamilton	W.S	1879
	Hutchinson	C.W	1879
	Lawrence	R	1877-8-9
	Laye	J.H	1877-8-9
	Lethbridge	E	1877-8-9
	Sandham D/S	G	1877-8-9
	Stevens	S.J	1877-8
#Ward		R.I	No clasp

Also had British and Turkish Crimea War Medals.
    Wilson W.F   1879

QUARTERMASTER
    Newman J   1877-8-9
Served in the Indian Mutiny as a Sergt.

ADJUTANT
    Lomax S.H   1877-8-9

LIEUTENANT
	Campbell	H.M	1877-8-9
	Gordon	A	1877-8-9
	Heathcote	G.R	1877-8-9
##	Lysons	H	1879

V.C won at Hlobane.

Lieutenant Henry Lysons

	Maude	A.M	1879
	Rawlins H de C		1877-8-9

Saltmarche	H		1877-8
Sheehan	P.E.C		1879
Smith	F		1877-8-9

2nd LIEUTENANT
# Bright	D/WA.T.		1877-8-9
Fell	R.B		1879
Hotham	H.E		1877-8-9
Hopkins	C.H.J		1879
Ross	J		1877-8-9
Strong	S.P		1877-8-9
White	A.O		1879

SERGEANT MAJOR
1087 Cousins E 1877-8-9

BANDMASTER
N/N Brandes C.E.W 1877-8

BUGLE MAJOR
1006 Courtney ? J 1877-8-9

COLOR SERGEANT
436	Baster	W	1879
1184	Daborn	C	1879
616	Darling	W	1877-8-9

Duplicate medal and clasp issued 19/7/1927.
1081	Dean	W	1877-8-9
1249	Gill	W	1877-8-9
164	Jeffs	M.A	1877-8-9
626	Mc Allson	T.H.E	1877-8-9
1190	Pickett	D	1879

Bosleys Auction December 2nd 2009. Lot 536 An enigmatic group Crimean War Medal clasp Sebastopol, South Africa Medal 1877 (without clasp), Turkish Crimea Medal to Randall Ironside Ward, Royal Navy and 90th Foot. Ward served as a Midshipman on Hannibal in the Crimea, later transferring to the Army, and becoming (as a Captain) the only officer of his regiment to receive the medal without clasp during the Zulu War. The top estimate of £1,200 was beaten, the lot achieving Hammer Price £1,438.

90th Regiment

Number	Name	Initial	Clasp
330	Ratcliff	T	1877-8-9
993	Smith	C	1879
705	South	S	1877-8
D.C.M Tutu Plateau 30.9.78; £10 annuity			
ARMOURER SERGEANT			
951	Whiteman	F	1877-8
ORDERLYROOM SERGEANT			
852	Rose	T	1877-8-9
PAYMASTER SERGEANT			
499	Conwood	C	1877-8
QUARTERMASTER SERGEANT			
858	Duckworth	J	1877-8-9
SERGEANT INSTRUCTOR OF MUSKETRY			
1912	Wishart	G	1879
SERGEANT			
709	Allen	W	1879
1362	Attwood	C	No clasp
1219	Barnes	J.S	1877-8-9
1010	Bennett	G	1877-8-9
2080	Bentall	J	1877-8-9
587	Boyd	J	1877-8-9
2026	Brown	G.S	1879
593	Brown	J	No clasp r
830	Burford	J	1879
514	Clinch	C	1879
3035	Cooper	G.W	1879
1301	Darling	A	1877-8
567	Fogarty	J	1877-8-9
108	George	G	1879
1887	Gilbert	W.H	No clasp
871	Hawton	J	1877-8-9
1383	Hyland	P	1879
465	Jarvis	E	1879r
2062	Jelliff	B	1879
1437	Jones	C	1877-8-9
1555	Kelly	F	1877-8-9
1239	Keysell	W	1877-8-9
1617	Lyons	W.N	1877-8-9
393	Mc Cae	T	No clasp
825	Morgan	J.R	1879
726	Morris	D	1877-8-9
1619	Nicol	G	1877-8
1015	Norris	R.H	1877-8-9
1048	Parkinson	C	1877-8-9
No Medal. Deserted.			
1239	Reysell	W	1877-8-9
1963	Richardson	H	1879
925	Russell	W	1877-8
1588	Scott	J	1877-8
1678	Simmon ?	W	1877-8-9
1768	Thomson	R	1877-8-9
1677	Titman	J	1877-8-9
729	Wood	S	No clasp
LANCE SERGEANT			
159	Layfield	R	1877-8-9
1011	Reddon	M	1879
807	Roy	F.E	1877-8-9
556	Russell	J	1879
1597	Stewart	W	1877-8-9
CORPORAL			
1649	Ansy ?	W	1877-8-9
N/N	Arnold	H	No clasp
1600	Barker	F	1877-8
267	Barraclough	H	1879r
2086	Baxter	C	No clasp
1532	Brookfield	W	1877-8-9
1128	Byrne	M	1877-8-9
60B/1601	Cave	H	1877-8-9
1409	Currie	H	1879
420	Delaney ?	C	1877-8-9
1399	Easton	J.H.A	1879
1298	Edgerton	W	1879
1181	Evans	F.W	1879
595	Ewing	J	1877-8
1551	Finlay	R	1879
3030	Fox	W.G	1877-8-9r
Deserted.			
1655	Gould	J	1877-8-9
1487	Grace	A	1879
1123	Graham	J	1877-8-9
815	Grant	F.G	1877-8-9
825	Gray	R.L	1877-8-9
1632	Guthrie	B	1877-8
53	Hall	R	1877-8
2100	Hambridge	F	1879
264	Hayward	M	1877-8-9
2003	Hillier	W	1877-8
1390	Jelliff	G	1879
1119	Martin	T	1877-8-9
1069	Mc Carthy	D	1877-8-9
631	Mc Crea	H	1877-8-9
513	Mc Lies	J	1877-8-9
1041	Newsham	S	1877-8
1109	Norton	C	1877-8-9
1367	Orton	G	1879
1507	Rawlinson	E	1879
778	Robinson	A.K	1877-8-9
955	Smith	G.W	1877-8-9
1266	Smyth	L.J	1879r
547	Smith	J	1877-8-9
1409	Sparling	G	1879
373	Spiers	T	1877-8-9
874	Suregeonor ?	A	1879
495	Waterson	J	1879
1229	Williams	J	1879
1288	Wood	A.J	1877-8-9
1269	Wright	W	1877-8-9
LANCE CORPORAL			
561	Blair	W	1879
597	Blue	J	1879
966	Burnley	F	1879
1444	Everest ?	C	1879
436	Fearnley	J	1879
1666	Guyatt	H	1877-8-9
1161	Haywood	T	1877-8-9
1310	Hefferman	J	1879
No Medal. Deserted.			
739	Henderson	J	1879
5	Hogg	J	1879
918	Morison ?	W	1879r
1605	Peake	J	1877-8
541	Steer	C	1879
1307	Taylor	W	1877-8-9
1197	West	F	1879
568	White	J	1879
CANTEEN STEWARD			
N/N	Mc Partland	M	1877-8-9r
BUGLER			
1628	Arnett	J	1877-8-9
145	Bamrick	F	1879
1166	Bramley ?	J	1877-8-9
70	Cook	W	1877-8-9
1596	Coote	H	1877-8-9
1415	Flin	T	1877-8-9
940	Ford	L.H	1877-8
842	Helps	J	1877-8-9
72	Herne	W	1877-8-9
1312	Jenkins	W.J.S	1877-8-9
1408	Kelly	C	1877-8
442	Lusk	H	1877-8
213	Noon	P	1877-8-9
1848	O'Neil	H	1877-8-9
N/N	Pollard	W	1878
He also received clasp 1879. The latter clasp was returned on 22/5/1885.			
116	Styles	S	1879
837	Watson	J	1877-8-9
PRIVATE			
392	Adams	J	1879
1366	Aderman	C	1879
947	Allen	A	1879
1471	Allen	C	1877-8-9
1178	Allen	G	1877-8-9
1040	Allen	J	1877-8-9r
Deserted.			
789	Allen	J	1877-8-9
1592	Allen	J.H	1877-8-9
1102	Amos	J	1877-8-9
1343	Amos	W	1877-8-9
1792	And	D	1879
1763	Anderson	C	1879
486	Anderson	J	1879
1703	Andrews	J	1879
1241	Arkinstall	H	1877-8
1155	Armstrong	J	1879
1679	Arney	J	1877-8-9
1165	Ashton	E	1877-8-9
1563	Atherton	R	1877-8-9
767	Atkinson	C	1879
1476	Bailey	W	1879
1679	Baldock	J	1877-8-9
956	Ball	T	1877-8
1383	Ballard	T	1877-8-9
1159	Balshaw	W	1877-8-9
1726	Banks	F	1877-8-9
1158	Banks	J	1879

90th Regiment

1447	Banks	W	1877-8-9	1355	Boyle	H	1879	477	Brown	J	1877-8-9
1241	Barclay	J	1877-8	No Medal. Deserted.				1749	Brown	W	1877-8-9
532	Barclay	N	1877-8	930	Boyle	J	1877-8-9	1445	Bryson	C	1877-8-9
1359	Barclay	T	1877-8-9	1086	Boyle	S	1877-8-9	627	Buchanan	J	1877-8-9
1056	Barefoot	J	1879	785	Boyle	W	1879	1899	Buckland	R	1877-8-9
1650	Barker	F	1877-8-9	886	Braden	J	1877-8-9	181	Buckley	J	1877-8-9
1179	Barlow	T	1877-8-9	No Medal. Deserted.				1196	Buckley	S	1879
596	Barnes	F	1879	1889	Bradley	W	1877-8-9	1628	Buddle	W	1877-8-9
1564	Barnes	J	1877-8-9	610	Bradshaw	J	1877-8-9	71	Bullen	W	1877-8-9
1758	Barrett	J	1879	1446	Brady	H.J	1877-8-9	257	Bunce	M	1879r
514	Barry	H	1879	N/N	Branch	J.R	1877-8-9	1505	Bungry ?	G	No clasp
1755	Barry	J	1879	731	Bray	J	1879	269	Burke	P	1879
1130	Bass	J	1879	1175	Bray	T	1877-8-9	1600	Burns	J	1877-8
1667	Baxter	W	1879	2065	Brechin	H	1877-8-9	1510	Burns	J	1879
984	Beatty	J	1877-8-9	1477	Brett	H	1879	467	Burns	W	1877-8-9
1547	Beckett	R	1877-8-9	1855	Brett	S	No clasp	1448	Burrows	J	1877-8-9
743	Beham	P	1877-8-9	N/N	Brewster	C	No clasp	1461	Butler	H	1877-8-9
1163	Bell	T	1879	1532	Brien	T	1879	961	Butler	J	1879
1614	Bellany	H	1877-8-9	No Medal. Deserted.				221	Butterworth	J	1879
1240	Bellinger	G	1879	1584	Brigg	F	1877-8-9	1464	Butt ?	J	1877-8-9
1412	Bellis	T	1879	1169	Brimmer	T	1877-8-9	772	Byers	A	1879
1466	Betts	G	1877-8-9	1570	Broadhurst	G	1877-8-9	1652	Byrne	C	1877-8-9
1771	Bindy	J	1879	1122	Broderick	P	1879	1247	Byrne	J.B	1879
1384	Bishop	B	1879	1364	Broderick	R	1877-8-9	1038	Byrne	R	1877-8-9
613	Black	C	1879	1859	Brooks	J	1879r	1635	Byrne	J	1879
960	Blakes	J	1879	412	Brophy	J	1879	1695	Cahill	J	1879
1720	Blaney	A	1879	1492	Brothers	J	1879	Two identical medals and clasps appear			
1387	Bolton	J	1879	1335	Brown	G	1877-8-9	to have been issued to this man.			
1064	Bonnett	W	No clasp	No Medal. Discharged with ignominy.				1519	Campbell	D	1877-8-9
1395	Bonskill	J	1877-8-9	826	Brown	J	1877-8-9	1732	Campbell	P	1879
1208	Boulton	W	1877-8-9	1127	Brown	J	1877-8-9	894	Campbell	W	1879
732	Bowsher	J	1877-8-9	1408	Brown	J	1879	1569	Cannon	P	1877-8-9
2008	Boyce	W	1879	No Medal. Deserted.				934	Cantwell	W	1877-8-9

90th Foot Casualties

2003	Corpl W. Hillier - wounded at Intaba Ka'Udoda 30 April 1878. died of wounds
1421	Pte. H. Arkinstall - wounded at at Intaba Ka'Udoda 30 April 1878. died of wounds
1635	Pte. J. Byron - wounded at Kambula 29 March 1879. died of wounds
1570	Pte. G. Broadhurst - killed in action at Isandhlwana 22 January 1879
1669	Pte. J. Chapman - wounded at Kambula 29 March 1879. died of wounds
1183	Pte H. Edwards - killed in action at Isandhlwana 22 January 1879
1580	Pte. J. Fairclough - killed in action at Kambula 29 March 1879
1330	Pte. H. Gilbert - wounded at Kambula 29 March 1879. died of wounds
1593	Pte. W. Healey - killed in action at Isandhlwana 22 January 1879
900	Pte. J. McLean - killed in action at Kambula 29 March 1879
985	Pte. R. Murphy - killed in action at Kambula 29 March 1879
1739	Pte. W. Pack - wounded 27 October 1878. died of wounds
1231	Pte. H. Pallert - killed in action at Intaba Ka'Udoda 30 April 1878
1610	Pte. D. Pattrick - killed in action at Isandhlwana 22 January 1879
1509	Pte. W. Peace - killed in action at Kambula 29 March 1879
1512	Pte. J. Richardson - killed in action at Kambula 29 March 1879
945	Pte. P. Ryan - wounded at Kambula 29 March 1879. died of wounds
1071	Pte. H. Silvester - killed in action at Intaba Ka'Udoda 30 April 1878
907	Pte. J. Slowey - wounded at at Intaba Ka'Udoda 30 April 1878. died of wounds
1347	Pte. W. Spence - killed in action at Kambula 29 March 1879
1474	Pte. T. Walsh - killed in action at Isandhlwana 22 January 1879
1668	Pte. C. Wickham - killed in action at Isandhlwana 22 January 1879

90th Regiment

1541	Carey	J	1877-8r		No Medal. Deserted.			388	Doherty	J	1879r
973	Carlisle	W	1877-8-9	1770	Connolly	D	No clasp	1002	Donaldson	D	1877-8-9
	No Medal. Deserted.			1735	Connolly	J	1879	1385	Donigan	J	1877-8-9
780	Carter	J	1877-8-9	1688	Connolly	J	1877-8-9	1144	Donnelly	P	1879
747	Carorran?	J.N	1879	11	Connolly	O	1877-8-9	1017	Donerson?	P	1879
1348	Carney	W	1877-8-9	1403	Connolly	P	1877-8-9	1654	Dorley	J	1877-8-9
1291	Carr	J	1877-8-9	730	Connor	J	1877-8-9r	1423	Dowd	J	1877-8-9
1237	Carracher	M	1877-8-9	1263	Connors	J	1877-8-9		No medal. Deserted.		
1279	Cass	G	1877-8-9	903	Coogan	J	1877-8-9	1389	Downey	M	No clasp
1595	Cass	W	1877-8-9	1463	Cooke	S	1877-8-9	1290	Doyle	J	1879
1853	Cassidy	B	No clasp	1262	Cooney	E	1877-8-9	1737	Doyle	M	1877-8-9
1851	Cavahon?	T	No clasp	1058	Cooper	C	1879		No medal. Deserted.		
1575	Chalmers	T	1879	1549	Copeland	G	1879	1373	Dring	F	1877-8-9
1975	Channer	T	1879	1550	Cotton	J	1879	1521	Duckworth	H	1877-8-9
861	Chapman	A	1877-8-9	1516	Couglan	D	1877-8-9	1721	Duffy	P	1877-8-9
1669	Chapman	J	1877-8-9	1641	Courtney	A	1879	993	Duffy	P	1879
1488	Chapman	W	No clasp	669	Cousins	M	1879	941	Duffy	T	1879
1433	Charlton	T	1879	2097	Cracknell	G	1879	1785	Duke	J	1879
1479	Chatham	H	1879	964	Craig	A	1877-8-9	1548	Dunkeld	J	1877-8-9
1660	Chignall	W	1877-8	1185	Cramb	H	1877-8-9	1428	Dunn	H	1877-8-9r
1826	Christie	A	No clasp	1514	Crapper	F	1879	1114	Durham	J	1877-8-9
1554	Church	W	1877-8-9	813	Crawford	J	1877-8-9	1183	Edwards	H	1877-8-9
1449	Cinnamond	J	1877-8-9	1760	Crawford	T	No clasp	1567	Eggelton	J	1877-8-9
1029	Clarke	G	1879	470	Creehan	A	1877-8	1312	Eldon	M	1877-8-9
1595	Clarke	G.H	1877-8-9	1469	Cripps	J	1877-8-9	1350	Ellie	S	1877-8
				770	Cross	G	1879	1962	Elliott	G	1877-8-9
				1004	Crouch	G	1879		No medal. Deserted.		
				891	Crowel	P	1877-8-9	1392	Emms	J	1877-8-9
				906	Cruickshank	G	1879	1687	Entwistle	D	1877-8-9
				1438	Cryne	J	1879r	1557	Essington	T	1877-8-9
				675	Cummings	J	1879		No medal. Deserted.		
				1698	Currand?	F	1879	215	Eyre	W.H	1879
				51	Curran	H	1877-8-9	1653	Faby	J	1877-8-9
				1177	Curtis	H	1877-8-9	1580	Fairclough	J	1877-8-9
				1244	Daly	J	1879	1581	Fairclough	W	1877-8
				1520	Darling	G	1877-8	733	Farrell	D	1877-8-9
				1315	Davey	L	1879	1681	Farrell	F	1877-8-9
				832	Davidson	W	1879	552	Farrell	J	No clasp
				1182	Davis	A	1877-8-9	1223	Farrell	J	1879
				680	Davis	W	1879	1638	Feather	J	1879
				1302	Davis	W.L	1877-8-9	1146	Feely	B	1879
					No medal. Deserted.			860	Ferguson	H	1877-8-9
				1311	Dawson	J.H	1879	1619	Fielding	J	1877-8-9
				1260	Deane	W	1877-8-9	1164	Fisher	F	1877-8-9
1616	Clarke	I	1877-8	1467	Dean	W	1879	1858	Fisher	J	No clasp
1143	Clarke	J.H	1877-8	1453	Dean	W.H	1877-8-9	917	Fisher	W	1879
1135	Clarkson	T	1877-8-9	648	Deegan	W	1879	1320	Fitzgerald	R	1877-8-9
542	Clifton	J	1877-8-9	1466	Delaney	T	1877-8-9	830	Fitzpatrick	W	1877-8-9
N/N	Clinton	W	No clasp	1696	Dellar	G	1877-8-9r	188	Flaherty	P	1877-8
1374	Cloe	H	1877-8-9	1253	Dennehy	E	1879	1259	Flannery	P	1877-8-9
390	Codlon	P	1877-8-9	536	Denny	J	1877-8-9	1501	Flannigan	W	1879
1663	Cole	H	1877-8-9	1003	Denver	F	1877-8-9	1377	Fletcher	F	1877-8-9
928	Colgahown?	J	1877-8-9	413	Devanney	C	1877-8-9	1304	Fletcher	T	1879
1515	Collier	R.P	1877-8-9		Two identical medals and clasps appear				No medal. Deserted.		
996	Collins	P	1879		to have been issued to this man.			1212	Fletcher	W	1877-8-9
864	Collins	R	1877-8-9	1339	Devanney	T	1877-8-9	1127	Flood	J	1879
214	Collins	T	1879	1713	Devans	A	1879	1517	Flynn	F	1877-8
1478	Condon	T	1879	1496	Dixon	P	1879	94	Forbes	J	1877-8-9
799	Condon	T	1879	824	Dobson	J	1877-8-9	1055	Fordham	C.W	1879

#Private E.J Fowler

90th Regiment

953	Fordham	H	1877-8-9	1317	Gray	E	1877-8-9	528	Howes	G	1877-8
418	Fordham	J	1877-8-9	1590	Gray	G.W	1877-8-9	1494	Hubbard	W	1879
1566	Foster	W	1877-8-9	1575	Grayham	W	1877-8-9	1365	Huggett	F	1877-8-9
1090	Foweraker	F	1879	997	Green	H	1879	2057	Huggett	W	1877-8
#1317	Fowler	E	1877-8-9	1209	Green	J	1877-8-9r	788	Hughes	F	1877-8-9
V.C won at Hlobane				978	Green	T	1877-8-9	1498	Hughes	H	1879
1430	Fox	C	1877-8-9	1311	Greegan	W	1879r	22	Hunter	J	1877-8-9
119	Foy	J	1877-8r	1246	Gregg	G	1879	1380	Hunter	J	1877-8-9
1651	Foy	T	1877-8-9r	1020	Griffin	W	1877-8-9	1762	Hurst	J	1879
954	Franklin	R	1877-8-9	1695	Gurnbridge	H	1877-8-9	1134	Hussey	E	1877-8-9r
1702	Fraser	H	1877-8-9	843	Gaag	A.E	1877-8	1277	Hutchinson	T	1877-8-9
1791	Freeman	T	1879	617	Hagerty	J	1877-8-9	437	Hutchinson	W	1879
1336	Fryer	J	1877-8-9	36	Hagins	J	No clasp	1344	Huxter	T	1879
1214	Fuller	H	1877-8-9	1633	Hale	R	1877-8-9	178	Ikin	J	1877-8-9
781	Gains	J	1877-8-9	1450	Hall	A	1877-8-9	1475	Innes	J	1877-8
679	Gallagher	J	1879	481	Hamilton	W	1877-8-9r	1499	Irvine	J	1879
766	Gallagher	J	1879	1292	Handy	B	1877-8-9	1717	Irvin	J	1879
1767	Gallagher	J	1879	866	Hardy	G	1877-8-9	1995	Izzard	A.J	1877-8-9
No medal. Deserted.				No medal. Deserted.				735	Jarard	J	1877-8-9
1660	Gallagher	M	1877-8	224	Hardy	J.A	No clasp	498	Jervis	J	1877-8r
1243	Gashercole	J	1879	1701	Hardwicke	A	1879	565	Jeffes	C	1879
No medal. Deserted.				1870	Harford	J	1877-8-9	1667	Jeffries	J	1877-8-9
1625	Gedding	E	1877-8-9	1156	Harper	J	1879	1414	Johnson	E	1879r
1432	Geraty	G	No clasp	883	Harper	W	1877-8-9	741	Johnston	J	1877-8-9
406	Giblin	J	1877-8-9	1400	Harris	S	1879	1957	Johnston	J	1877-8
496	Giblin	L	1877-8-9	No medal. Deserted.				?	Johnson	J	No clasp
1369	Giblin	W	1877-8-9	1111	Harris	T	1879	912	Johnston	R	1879
1454	Gibson	J	1877-8-9r	1513	Harrison	J	1879	743	Johnson	W	1879
1369	Gibson	W	1877-8-9	1275	Hartley	A	1877-8-9	1576	Jonhson	F	1877-8-9
1106	Giddings	A	1879	1397	Hazelwood	W	1879	1631	Jones	D	1877-8-9
1330	Gilberts	H	1879	1018	Heagney	P	1879	1854	Jones	J	No clasp
1486	Giles	L	1879r	1627	Heagnon	O	1877-8r	1475	Jones	J	1877-8
911	Gillie	G	1879	1515	Heald	J	1879	1294	Jones	J	1877-8r
1133	Gilligan	J	1877-8-9	1593	Healey	W	1877-8-9	1044	Jones	J	1879
804	Gillon	J	1879	1537	Hearn	M	1879	1647	Jones	W	1877-8-9
1096	Gilmour	H	1879	1085	Heath	B	1879	1176	Jones	W	1877-8-9
1055	Gladwell	J	1879	1527	Henry	G	1879	1194	Jones	W	1877-8-9
943	Glass	H	1879	1611	Herridge	W	1877-8	1536	Jordan	W	1879
397	Glynn	P	1879	1966	Higgins	J	1879	1325	Kavanagh	J	1877-8-9
1683	Gobie	T	1877-8-9	1237	Hill	J	1879	1372	Kearney	B	1877-8-9
198	Golding	J	1879	731	Hilliard	J	1877-8-9	Deserted. No trace of the return of the medal.			
1401	Golding	M	1877-8-9	1382	Hinde	R	1879				
1586	Goodfellow	J	1877-8-9	1677	Hitcher ?	F	1877-8-9	1139	Kearney	W.J	1877-8-9r
550	Goodyear	F	1877-8-9	1556	Hogan	T	1877-8-9	81	Keating	J	1879
614	Gordon	W	1879	844	Hogg	J	1877-8-9	1072	Keeble	A	1877-8-9
851	Gorman	J	1879	1589	Holbert	J	1877-8-9	1167	Keeling	J.H	1877-8-9
796	Gorman	J	1879	1362	Hollingwood	J	1879	1704	Kehoe	W	1879
1388	Gould	J	1877-8-9	1521	Holloway	R	1879	1613	Kelly	G	1877-8
1421	Gouldie	C	1877-8-9	925	Holmes	J	1879	1200	Kelly	J	1879
551	Gouldie	W	1877-8-9	1230	Hope	W	1877-8-9	1283	Kelly	J	1879
1417	Graham	J	1879	1558	Hopkins	J	1877-8-9	1422	Kelly	D	1877-8-9r
897	Graham	J	1877-8-9	No medal. Deserted.				644	Kelly	T	1877-8-9
1622	Graham	R	1877-8-9	1538	Hornshaw ?	J	1879	1054	Kelly	W	1879
No medal. Forfeited for disgraceful conduct.				1162	Horton	J	1877-8-9	1656	Kenney	J	1877-8-9
				3092	Hotson	H	1877-8	936	Keogh	J	1877-8-9
1588	Grainger	J	1877-8-9	398	Houze	J	1879r	1273	Kerr	E	1877-8-9
1747	Grant	D	1877-8-9	Re-issued 15/4/1910 with Egypt 1885 medal.				1000	Kerr	J	1877-8-9
1533	Grant	J	1879					1534	Kidd	H	1877-8-9
No medal. Deserted.				1853	Howes	G	1877-8-9	1451	Killean	J	1877-8

90th Regiment

No.	Name	Initial	Years
716	Kilrey	B	1877-8
1456	Kilshaw	J	1877-8-9
1672	King	H	1877-8-9
1844	King	J	1879r
1521	Kingston	M	1879
1648	Kingswell	J	1877-8-9
999	Kinnon	S	1879
	No medal. Deserted.		
1671	Kirby	R	1877-8-9
764	Kirwan	J	1879
1585	Knight	J	1877-8-9
1472	Label	J	1877-8-9
428	Ladd	T	1877-8-9
913	Lamb	R	1877-8-9
748	Landy	R	1879
N/N	Lane	T	No clasp
454	Lapsley	D	1877-8-9
1367	Law	P	1877-8-9
957	Lawrence	T	1877-8-9
1118	Laws	W	1877-8-9
637	Leacy	J	1879
1218	Leake	J.T	1879
1150	Lees	W	1877-8-9
1316	Lehaney	P	1879
939	Le Lore	A	1879
1179	Leonard	C	1877-8-9
1512	Lenderyon	T	1879
307	Lennon	R	1877-8-9
492	Leslie	W.J	1879
1229	Lewis	G	1877-8-9r
1284	Lewis	H	1879
1110	Lewis	W	1879
1497	Ley	H	1879
1646	Light	J	1879
833	Livingston	J	No clasp r
1640	Long	J	1877-8-9
1778	Longland	D	1879
1748	Lonic	A	1877-8-9
1065	Looby	J	1877-8-9
99	Lott	W	1877-8-9
1497	Lowrey	T	1879
1508	Lynch	C	1879
1559	Lynch	M	1877-8-9
973	Lynch	T	1879
1607	Lyon	P	1877-8-9
1594	Lyons	T	1879
1670	Mackie	J	1877-8-9
1424	Mackin	H	1877-8-9
1189	Macvicar	T	1877-8-9
1124	Madden	T	1877-8-9
	No Medal. Deserted.		
1354	Madigan	E	1877-8-9
1328	Madigan	J	1877-8-9
98	Maidment ?	C	1877-8
1360	Mains	J	1879
1322	Maloney	P	1877-8-9
1723	Maloney	W	No clasp
	No medal. Deserted.		
1104	Manion	J	1877-8-9r
	Deserted.		
1261	Manning	M	1877-8-9
1315	Marks	T	1877-8-9
1196	Martin	J	1879
1493	Martin	R	1879
	Forfeited for Desertion. No further service. Application refused on 18/9/1917. Found that he had joined 7th Regt. Fusiliers. Medal and clasp subsequently reissued.		
52	Martin	T	1877-8-9
1074	Martin	T.W	1879
	No medal. Deserted.		
1733	Martin	W	1879
1332	Mason	J	1879
203	Masterson	F	1877-8-9
1270	Masterson	H	1877-8-9
147	Mathews	J	1877-8-9
1370	Mathews	P	1877-8-9
1001	Mathews	P	1879
626	Maxwell	R	1877-8-9
1149	Mayne	J	1879
867	Mc Arthur	A	1877-8-9
1347	Mc Arthur	C	1877-8-9
1598	Mc Cahill	T	1877-8-9
1375	Mc Cairns	T	1877-8-9
1225	Mc Call	D	1879
1187	Mc Callow	J	1877-8-9
1727	Mc Carron	P	1879
857	Mc Cartney	C	1877-8-9
1126	Mc Claren	W	1877-8-9
632	Mc Clelland	H	1879
890	Mc Claskey	J	1877-8-9
1257	Mc Cormack	D	1877-8-9r
896	Mc Comb	H	1879
801	Mc Conville	H	1877-8-9
608	Mc Crea	R	1879
594	Mc Culloch	A	1879
816	Mc Culloch	H	1877-8-9
1775	Mc Cue	J	1879
1520	Mc Dermott	T	1877-8-9
1874	Mc Devitt	J	1879
1136	Mc Donald	J	1879
1152	Mc Evoy	O	1879
1160	Mc Ewan	J	1879
1783	Mc Farlane	J	1879
1356	Mc Farlane	J	1877-8-9
1788	Mc Ghey	J	1879
1457	Mc Gill	J	1877-8-9
1368	Mc Ginley	C	1879
875	Mc Ginth	W	1879
1662	Mc Ginty	J	1877-8-9
1716	Mc Gonegal	J	1879
1264	Mc Govern	P	1877-8-9
1485	Mc Gowan	J	1879
988	Mc Gowan	J	1879
402	Mc Gowan	J	1877-8-9r
	Deserted.		
797	Mc Guinn	W	1877-8-9
926	Mc Guire	P	1877-8-9
1746	Mc Ilwain	C	No clasp
846	Mc Intyre	J	1879
1659	Mc Kendry	W	1877-8-9
272	Mc Kenna	J	1879r
811	Mc Kenzie	W	1877-8-9
1228	Mc Kie	F	1879
186	Mc Kirney	S	1877-8-9
1309	Mc Kirwan	D	1877-8-9
1093	Mc Lachlan	J	1877-8-9r
	Deserted.		
1872	Mc Laren	D	No clasp
1692	Mc Laren	P	1879
1076	Mc Laughlin	J	1877-8-9
	No medal. Deserted.		
549	Mc Laughlin	F	1877-8-9
629	Mc Laughton	H	1877-8-9
900	Mc Lean	?	1877-8-9
1699	Mc Many	M	1877-8-9
1202	Mc Monmony	J	1879
901	Mc Miller	J	1877-8-9
525	Mc Millan	J	1879
67	Mc Neil	J	1877-8
	No medal. Deserted.		
873	Mc Phail	H	1877-8-9
1726	Mc Phie	R	1879
1602	Mc Queen	J	1877-8-9r
1632	Mc Shane	H	1879
965	Mc Sweney	W	1879
676	Mc Veeney	F	1879
1506	Meade	J	1879
1579	Mealey	T	1877-8-9
1613	Meehan	J	1877-8-9r
816	Meehan	J	1877-8-9
	Deserted. No trace of medal return.		
1224	Middleton	J	1879
1512	Milburn	J	1877-8-9
1037	Miller	J	1877-8-9
1037	Miller	J	1877-8-9
	Duplication		
1414	Miller	W	1877-8-9
624	Miller	W	1879
1504	Milling	J	1879
1710	Mitchell	R	1879
1426	Monaghan	P	1877-8-9
55	Monk	G	1877-8-9
1652	Montague	F	1879r
	Discharged with ignominy.		
1465	Mooney	A	1877-8-9
1145	Mooney	C	1877-8-9
1138	Mooney	J	1877-8-9
681	Moore	J	1879
1697	Moore	J	No clasp
1750	Moore	J	No clasp
1529	Moran	A	1877-8
944	Moran	P	1877-8-9
1271	Moreland	W	1877-8-9

90th Regiment

1534	Morgan	D	1877-8-9	1680	Pannett	N	1877-8-9	1523	Rixon	C	1877-8-9
649	Morris	C	1879	217	Patrick	W	No clasp	1548	Roach	J	1877-8-9
714	Morris	J	1879	1714	Patterson	A	No clasp	522	Roberts	E	1877-8
1800	Morris	J	1879r	2070	Patterson	W.J	1879	557	Roberts	E	No clasp
Deserted.				1610	Pattrik	D	1879	779	Roberts	J	1877-8-9
1125	Morrisey	J	1877-8-9	1568	Paxton	H	1877-8-9	1879	Roberts	T	No clasp
1068	Muir	J	1877-8-9	1509	Peace	W	1879	535	Robertson	A	1877-8-9
740	Muihead	J	1877-8-9	1589	Peacock	G	1877-8-9	1536	Robertson	D	1877-8r
1685	Mulholland	?	1877-8-9	1604	Peake	J	1877-8	771	Robertson	W	1879
448	Mullanay	?	1877-8-9	1665	Pearce	C	1877-8-9	501	Robinson	J	1879
1154	Mullen	D	1879	Note on Role "Not issued Sent to Mint."				1529	Robinson	W	1877-8-9
1021	Mullins	M	1877-8-9	1045	Pearce	W	No clasp	641	Robson	W	1877-8-9
1452	Mullins	M	1877-8-9	1674	Pearce	W	1877-8	1414	Rogers	D	1877-8-9
1678	Mullis	J	1877-8-9	1617	Peplar	A	1877-8-9	1591	Rosendale	N	1877-8-9
1287	Murfin	C	1879	884	Pettigrew	G	1877-8-9	No medal. Deserted.			
1462	Murphy	F	1877-8-9	1029	Petts	S	1877-8-9	1349	Ross		1877-8-9
1856	Murphy	J	1877-8-9	1255	Phelan	R	1879	1530	Ross	P	No clasp r
817	Murphy	P	1879	1643	Phillips	F	1877-8-9	Deserted.			
985	Murphy	R	1879	1170	Phillips	G	1877-8-9	581	Ross	T	1877-8-9
492	Murray	J	1877-8-9	849	Phillips	J	1877-8-9	No medal. Deserted.			
96	Murray	P	1877-8-9	1709	Phillips	W	No clasp	1781	Ross	W	1879
371	Murray	P	1879	No Medal. Deserted.				1707	Ross	W	1879
1675	Myers	W	1877-8-9	1871	Piritt	T	No clasp	1441	Rone ?	F.E	1877-8
1555	Myers	W	1877-8-9	1684	Pitman	S	1877-8	1764	Rousby	M	1879
204	Myles	W	1879	100	Pordage	E	1877-8-9	1540	Rundle	S	1877-8-9
1135	Mynott	T	1879	1249	Prescott	W	1877-8-9	650	Russell	G	1877-8-9
1592	Needham	J	1877-8-9	1421	Preston	J	1877-8-9	1222	Russell	H	1877-8-9
1612	Neil	J	1877-8-9	1334	Price	J.H	1877-8-9	799	Russell	W	1877-8-9
727	Neil	J	No clasp	1870	Pritchett	A	No clasp	1644	Rustick	J	1877-8
1637	Neil	T	1877-8-9	1857	Proud	J	No clasp	Note on Roll. "Not issued – to Mint."			
1796	Neilson	J	1879	1352	Proudfoot	L	1879	1219	Rutter	J	1879
1047	Newby	J	1879	777	Purvis	H	1877-8-9	1538	Ryan	J	1877-8-9 r
1709	Newhall	P	1879	672	Quinn	M	1877-8-9	Discharged with ignominy.			
1459	Newham	?	1877-8-9	1544	Quinn	P	1877-8-9	715	Ryan	J	1879
1664	Nestor	P	1877-8-9r	1747	Raay	R.J	1879	945	Ryan	P	1877-8-9
Deserted.				831	Randall	G	1879	728	Ryan	P	1877-8-9
1597	Nicholas	C	1877-8-9	1100	Randall	T	1879	1624	Salvage	G	1877-8
1711	Nicholson	?	1879	818	Randall	W.E	1877-8-9	967	Saul	D	1877-8-9
1605	Nixon	G	1877-8-9	1192	Rands	R	1877-8-9	511	Saunder	J	1879
1531	Nixon	J	1879	856	Rankin	G	1879	1326	Scabill	W	1877-8-9
1116	Norton	J	1877-8-9	1195	Ratcliffe	W	1879	674	Scott	J	1879
No medal. Deserted.				1712	Ratcliffe	J	1879	2022	Seabrook	J	1879
1006	Oakes	S	1879	1030	Read	A	1877-8-9	1437	Searle	R	1879
1752	O'Brien	P	1879	1081	Reason	W	1879	1049	Seed	J	1879
845	O'Connor	T.D.R	No clasp	1171	Reed	C	1879	1798	Sellars	W	1879
1143	O'Donnell	F	1879	1232	Reeve	H	1877-8-9	1107	Sellick	G	1879
935	O'Donohue	P	1877-8-9	1091	Reeve	J	1879	1042	Shannon	J	1877-8-9
1473	O'Hara	J	1877-8-9	1518	Reid	T	1877-8-9	1274	Shannon	J	1877-8-9
929	O'Hara	J	1877-8-9	1810	Reilly	J	1879	1806	Sharkey	J	No clasp
368	O'Hara	T	1879	1871	Reynolds	J	1877-8-9	1303	Shaw	R	1877-8-9
1629	O'Leary	W	1877-8-9	1686	Reynolds	J	1877-8	1641	Shea	J	1879
1634	Oldham	J	1879	No medal. Deserted.				1173	Shears	C	1877-8-9
530	O'Neil	D	1877-8-9	1458	Ricaby	R	1877-8-9	1780	Shehan	M	No clasp
872	O'Neil	J	1877-8-9	1597	Rice	T	1877-8-9	1358	Sheldon	J	1877-8-9
190	O'Neil	S	1877-8-9	1615	Richardson	J	1877-8-9	1731	Sheridan	M	1879
1059	Osborne	H	1879	1512	Richardson	J	1879	493	Sherry	P	1877-8-9
N/N	Pack	W	1877-8-9	1092	Richardson	S	1879	1525	Shirley	J	1879
1205	Pagett	J	1877-8-9	1765	Richmond	G	1879	1071	Silverster	H	1877-8
1231	Pallert	H	1877-8	1518	Rispin	P	1877-8-9	1562	Simpson	A	1877-8

90th Regiment

No.	Name	Initial	Years
1689	Singer	A	1877-8-9
1014	Skehan	M	1879
1075	Slater	J	1877-8-9
622	Slater	W	1879
907	Slowry	J	1877-8
1553	Small	G	1877-8-9
	No medal. Deserted.		
983	Smith	A	1877-8-9
972	Smith	A.T.G	1877-8-9
1642	Smith	C	1877-8-9
1626	Smith	C	1877-8-9
1098	Smith	G	1879
1700	Smith	G	1879
1872	Smith	G	1877-8-9
1379	Smith	J	1877-8-9
1046	Smith	J	1879
1095	Smith	J	1879
1024	Smith	J	1877-8
1560	Smith	J	1877-8-9
1371	Smith	J	1877-8-9
1225	Smyth	T	1879
1782	Snow	J	1879
1534	Sollitt	J	1879
1542	Sowerbutts	H	1877-8-9
160	Sparks	T.H	1879
1702	Spearing	W	1879
	No medal. Deserted.		
1332	Spencer	H	1879r
1052	Spencer	T	1879
1142	Spencer	W	1877-8-9
1491	Stakin	J	1879
1877	Standing	J	No clasp
909	Stanton ?	G	1877-8-9
1565	Stanton ?	W	1877-8-9
1480	Starks	G	1879
931	Stars	W	1879
	No medal. Deserted.		
1391	Steel	H	1879
1546	Steel	J.H	1877-8-9
1005	Steer	F	1879
1320	Stenning	T	1877-8-9
1199	Stevens	J	1879
1638	Stevens	T	1877-8-9
1729	Stevens	T	1879
10	Stevens	W	1879
20	Stevenson	J	1877-8-9
1694	Stevenson	J	1879
	No medal. Deserted.		
834	Stevenson	R	1879
1583	Stevenson	W	1877-8
	No medal. Deserted.		
1188	Steward	J	1877-8-9
825	Stockey	L.J	1877-8-9
952	Stringer	A	1877-8-9
431	Stringer	G	1877-8-9
1639	Sullivan	T	1879
1682	Summersall	A	1877-8-9
1606	Sweals	J	1877-8-9
1468	Swindell	J	1877-8-9
1193	Tappy	H	1877-8-9
1569	Tate	J.W	1877-8-9
1577	Taylor	A	1877-8-9
1673	Taylor	H	1877-8-9
1571	Taylor	J	1877-8-9
	No medal. Deserted.		
1293	Taylor	R	1879
	No medal. Deserted.		
1661	Taylor	W	1877-8-9
1117	Teece	J	1879
1670	Terry	C.H	1877-8-9
1609	Terry	W	1877-8-9
1410	Thistle	T	1879
980	Thomas	J	1877-8-9
1847	Thomas	S	No clasp
	Deserted. No trace of the return of the medal.		
1442	Thompson	G	1877-8
683	Thompson	J	1877-8-9
1786	Thompson	J	1879
1481	Thompson	W	1879
1582	Tierney	M	1877-8-9
1552	Timbers	G	1879
1572	Timperley	T	1877-8-9
91	Tinsley	J	1879
1398	Todd	W	1877-8-9r
	Note on role: "This man served in S.A. 11/1/78 to 18/10/79. Not entitled to 1877-8-9 clasps, but 1878-9". Deserted.		
N/N	Toolom	H	1879
1195	Truelove	E	1877-8-9
1353	Tucker	W	1877-8
1077	Urrell ?	J	1877-8-9
1708	Vale	J	1879
1522	Vest	J	No clasp
1502	Vickery	C	1879
1573	Waddle	T	1877-8-9
914	Wade	J	1877-8-9
1470	Waldron	T	1879
1806	Wales	J	1879
1272	Walker	H	1877-8-9
1561	Walker	T	1877-8-9
#104	Walkinshaw	A	1877-8-9
814	Wallace	A	1879
464	Walls	A	1879
1645	Walsh	D	1877-8-9
1540	Walsh	E	1877-8-9
	No medal. Deserted.		
1022	Walsh	J	1879
1157	Walsh	P	1879
1539	Walsh	R.B	1877-8-9
	No medal. Deserted.		
1474	Walsh	T	1877-8-9
1267	Walsh	W	1879
1397	Warbuton	J	1877-8-9
732	Ward	C	1877-8-9
1495	Ward	R	1879
1251	Ward	W	1877-8-9
1389	Warner	J	1877-8-9
1582	Warroll	R	1879
170	Watson	A	1877-8-9
619	Watson	D	1879
447	Watson	W	1879
963	Webber	E.H	1877-8-9
1574	Webster	J	1877-8-9r
1236	Weedon	F	1877-8-9
1578	Welsh	T	1877-8-9
1210	Wenlock	J	1877-8-9
1082	West	A	1877-8-9
	No medal. Deserted.		
1537	Whelan	J.W	1879
167	Whelan	M	1879
1668	Whickham	C	1877-8-9
1482	White	A	No clasp
	No medal. Deserted.		
2372	White	J	1879
1019	White	M	1877-8
1690	White	W	1879
2081	Whitely	T	1877-8-9
1306	Whittaker	W	1877-8-9
1620	Williams	A	1877-8-9
1607	Williams	B	1879
N/N	Williams	L	No clasp
812	Willis	T	1877-8-9
1174	Wilson	G	1877-8-9
968	Wilson	J	1877-8-9
987	Wilson	J.H	1877-8-9
1489	Wilson	R	1879
1929	Wilson	W	1877-8-9
590	Winslow	A	No clasp
1636	Winters	T	1877-8-9
1050	Witham	T	1879
N/N	Withers	R	No clasp
1522	Wood	G	1879
1730	Wood	R	1879r
1338	Woodruffe	G	1879
1088	Wollard	J	1879
1204	Woolridge	S	1877-8-9
969	Yeadon	W	1879
459	Yeoman	W	1877-8
1120	Yeomans	W	1877-8-9
2076	Yetman	W	1877-8-9

Distinguished Conduct Medal. Pte A.Walkinshaw 90th LI (later 58th Foot and 2 Northampron Regt); SQ 25.3.82; Hlobane Mountain 28.3.79; orderly bugler to Brigadier-General (later Field Marshal) H.W.Wood; details WO 32/7834. Ref P.E.Abbott

C. W. SMART (late A. H. BEARD), Port Elizabeth.

Two Zulu Chiefs in Leopard Skin and Plumed Headresses with Assegais and Hide Shields.

Zulu Warrior with Hide Shield

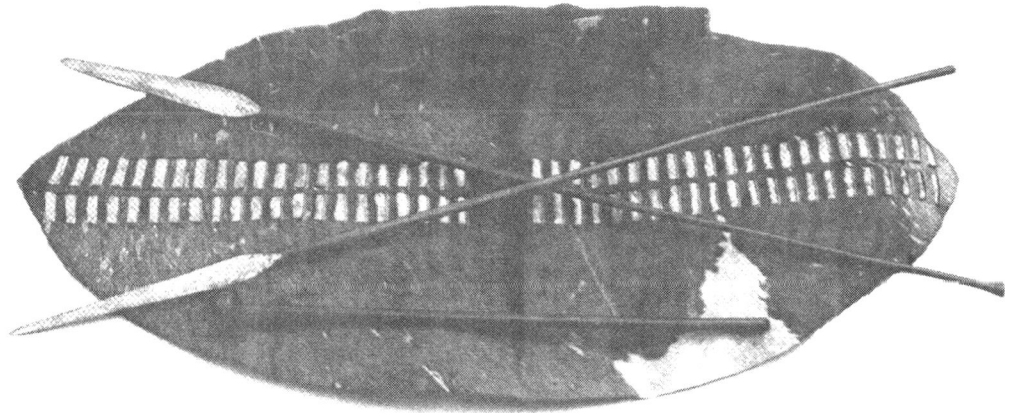

Zulu shield, assegais and knobkerrie.

91st Regiment

Battle of Gingindlovu

On the 2nd April 1879 the 91st Foot fought in the battle of Gingindlovu, which was a part of the Eshowe Relief Column under Lord Chelmsford. All 8 companies of the 91st Foot were present. They formed the southern face of the British Laager and repulsed a determined Zulu attack during the day, killing approximately 250 of the enemy. Casualties for the 91st Foot were 1 killed and 8 wounded.

Christie's Auction 27th November 1990, had the following lots for sale:

514 SOUTH AFRICA, 1877-79, one clasp, 1879 (2nd. Lieut. T. Fraser. 91st. Foot.), edge bruise, otherwise good very fine
Captain Thomas Fraser entered the 91st. Highlanders as a Second Lieutenant, 1879; served during the Zulu War of 1879 and was present at the Battle of Ginginhlovo where he carried the Queen's Colour on the last occasion in which it was taken into battle; took part in the Relief of Eshowe and subsequent operations in Zululand; served on detachment in Mauritius, 1879-81; Lieutenant 1880; Captain 1885; placed on half-pay, 1888 and subsequently served with the Shropshire Light Infantry; Captain Fraser died in London, 11th. January, 1908.
Estimate £200-250

Captain Thomas Fraser (seated left) with other officers, serving with the 'Kandy Detachment' circa 1885.

515 SOUTH AFRICA, 1877-79, one clasp, 1879 (2), both to the 91st. Foot (Sergt. J. Lahey.; Pte. G. Allan), last medal brooch mounted and claw replaced, otherwise good fine and better (2)
Colour Sergeant James Lahey, born in Dundee, Forfar; joined the 58th. Brigade at Falkirk, aged 23, 1876 and was posted to the 91st. Regiment later that year; Corporal 1876; Sergeant 1878 but reduced to the ranks the following year; Corporal 1880; Sergeant 1882; Colour Sergeant 1888; discharged to pension, 1896.
Private George Allan, born, Aberdeen; joined the 58th. Brigade at Aberdeen, aged 20, 1878 and was posted to the 91st. Regiment later that year; served in South Africa, February 1879 to January 1880 and St. Helena, January to October, 1881, discharged 1890.
Estimate £120-140

516 SOUTH AFRICA, 1877-79, one clasp, 1879 (2), both to the 91st. Foot (Cook Sergt. G. Ainslie; Pte P. Savage.), contact marks to first medal, good fine; second medal with edge bruise, good very fine (2)
Colour Sergeant George Ainslie joined the 58th. Brigade at Stirling, aged 18, 1874 and was posted to the 91st. Regiment later that year; Corporal 1874; Lance Sergeant 1877 and promoted Sergeant the same year; Colour Sergeant 1878; Acting Paymaster Sergeant, 1879.
Estimate £120-160

512 Family Pair:
SOUTH AFRICA, 1877-79, one clasp, 1879 (Captn. W. Prevost. 91st. Foot), nearly extremely fine
QUEEN'S SOUTH AFRICA, 1899-1902, two clasps, C.C., O.F.S. (Lieut. E. de W. T. Prevost. Rl. Lanc: Rgt.), edge bruising, good fine (2)
Major William Prevost entered the 91st. Regiment as an Ensign, 1867; Lieutenant 1870; Captain 1878; served during the Zulu War of 1879 and was present during the Battle of Ginginhlovo and the Relief of Eshowe; Major 1882; Major Prevost died in Hong Kong, 16th. January, 1889.
Second Lieutenant Edward de William Tessier Prevost, entered the 3rd. Battalion, King's Own (Royal Lancaster) Regiment, 1901; served during the South African War, 1901-02 as a Press Censor; was present during operations in the Orange River Colony, March to September, 1901 and served in the Cape Colony, September 1901 to January 1902; resigned with the rank of Honorary Second Lieutenant, 1903.
Estimate £300-350

513 SOUTH AFRICA, 1877-79, one clasp, 1879 (Lieut. D. G. M. Fowler. 91st. Foot.), nearly extremely fine
Captain Donald George Mackay Fowler, entered the 91st. Regiment as a Lieutenant, 1874; served during the Zulu War of 1879 and took part in the Battle of Ginginhlovo, the Relief of Eshowe and the subsequent operations in Zululand; Captain 1884; retired 1893.
Estimate £200-250

91st Regiment

91st (PRINCESS LOUISE'S ARGYLLSHIRE HIGHLANDERS) REGIMENT.

Landed in Natal on the 17th March 1879, formed part of the advance guard of the Eshowe Relief Column. At the battle of Gingindhlovu on the 2nd April they held the rear face of the laager and repelled the second attack by the zulu.

LIEUTENANT COLONEL
	Bruce	CB A.C.	1879

MAJOR
	Gurney	W.P	1879

CAPTAIN
	Boulderson	J	1879

Also had Indian Mutiny Medal and clasp & Medal for North West Frontier 1863.

	Chater	V	1879
	Craufurd	W.R.H	1879
	Fallowfield	H.G	1879
	Mills	W.S	1879
	O'Sullivan	G.L	1879
	#Prevost	W	1879
	Rogers	J.T	1879
	Stevenson	G.U	1879

PAYMASTER CAPTAIN
	Candwell	W.D	1879

See also Army Pay Department.

QUARTERMASTER
	Gillies	J	1879

LIEUTENANT ADJUTANT
	St Clair	J.L.C	1879

LIEUTENANT
	Collings	G.D	1879
	Cookson	F	1879
	Fowler	D.G	1879
	Goff	G.L.J	1879
	Johnston	H.F.C	1879
	MacDonald	D.J McG	1879
	Robbins	G.B	1879
	Schank	H.A	No clasp
	Tottenham	A.E.H	1879

2nd LIEUTENANT
	Dickson	D.J.A	1879
	Fox-Pitt	W.A.L	1879
	Fraser	T	1879
	Richardson	C.J	1879
	Wilson	A	1879
	Wyllie	F	1879

SERGEANT MAJOR
928	Nowell	H	1879

BANDMASTER
2282	Kelly	P	No clasp

DRUM MAJOR
1138	Kelly	J	1879

PIPE MAJOR
1186	Campbell	R	1879

COLOR SERGEANT
232	Ainslie	G	1879
1415	Bethune	D	1879
905	Cameron	D	1879
1436	Clayton	C.F	1879
774	Denholm	J	1879
384	Downs	J	1879
318	Pearce	E	1879
911	Scott	W	1879
353	Somerville	W	1879
1166	Wark	J	1879

ARMOURER SERGEANT
431	Robinson	W	1879

QUARTERMASTER SERGEANT
432	Mc Quirk	C	1879

SERGEANT INSTRUCTOR OF MUSKETRY
1407	Moore	D	1879

SERGEANT
1323	Baylis	T	1879
1196	Cahill	E	1879
1664	Campbell	H.M	1879
2242	Connolly	M	1879
768	Crawford	J	1879
192	Crooks	M	1879
444	Cunningham	J	1879
938	Dechon	J	1879

No medal. Discharged with ignominy.

565	Douglas	W.M	1879
397	Giles	L	1879
2324	Golling	R	1879
647	Keen	G	1879
564	Kelly	J	1879
551	Kelly	J	1879
415	Kelly	R	1879
798	Lahey	J	1879
1274	Lindsay	W	1879
2248	Martin	H	1879
2094	Maunsell	F.C	1879
1480	Mc Cauley	J	1879
549	Mc Donald	A	1879
813	Mc Innes	J	1879
728	Mc Intyre	J	1879
334	Mc Kay	J	1879
554	Mc Quann	J	1879
1531	Muir	R	1879
547	Patterson	R	1879
844	Pirie	J	1879
470	Redmond	R	1879
714	Renwick	J	1879
924	Robertson	T.H	1879
785	Walls	J	1879
630	Wright	H.G	1879

No medal. Deserted.

LANCE SERGEANT
274	Allen	E	1879
1089	Beattie	C	1879
943	Finnie	A	1879
689	Lawonan ?	J	1879
4110	Marsh	G	1879
1048	Noble	W	1879
1800	Patterson	J	1879
1056	Smith	J	1879
1788	Williamson	R.C	1879

CORPORAL
471	Anderson	W	1879
749	Barrett	T	1879
739	Boyd	J	1879
836	Burns	P	1879
2181	Crichton	W.McK	1879

Deserted. No trace of the return of the medal.

2286	Davis	W	1879
1095	Foster	H	1879

Deserted. No trace of the return of the medal.

953	Gray	W	1879
1044	Green	T	1879
2587	Hoare	R	1879
625	Home	R	1879
931	Johnstone	E	1879
2250	Kennedy	P	1879
2218	Leach	W	1879
1034	Liddle	C	1879
1013	Mack	G	1879
757	Magilton	H	1879
1043	Mc David	G	1879
528	Mc Kay	A	1879
959	Mc Kee	R	1879
978	Mc Nab	J.N	1879
658	Mefser	D	No clasp r
2246	Minihan	D	1879
2416	Morgan	F.E	1879
2228	Murray	J	1879
786	Parsons	C	1879
588	Ramsay	H	1879
1041	Robinson	J.W	1879
2288	Rogers	G.A	1879

Deserted. No trace of the return of the medal.

975	Ross	J	1879
1021	Sawers	T	1879
1022	Scott	J.J	No clasp
1035	Sellars	M	1879

Spinks Auction 5th December 2002, Lot 46 South Africa 1877-79, one clasp 1879 (Captn W. Prevost. 91st Foot.), nearly extremely fine, with a small portrait photograph of recipient Hammer Price £1050.
Major William Prevost, commissioned into the 91st in 1867, was promoted to Lieutenant 1870 and Captain 1878. He was present at the battle of Gingindhlovu and relief of Eshowe. Promoted Major, 1882, he died in Hong Kong in 1889.

91st Regiment

1858	Sheedy	J.T	1879	786	Parsons	C	1879	845	Auld	W	1879

Deserted. No trace of the return of the medal.

				1986	Paterson	A.G	1879	Deserted. No trace of the return of the medal.			
296	Steel	J	1879	397	Polwarth	E	1879				
2161	Stevenson	F	1879	2595	Saunders	T	No clasp	2343	Baddeley	J	1879
308	Stewart	D	1879	2311	Savin	J	1879	1670	Bain	A	1879
4053	Wale	A.C	1879	1863	Smith	W	1879	1698	Bain	J	1879
2106	Wetherll	J	1879	2413	Sumner	T	1879	2387	Baker	J	1879

LANCE CORPORAL

				2399	Sweeney	J	1879	2188	Baldwin	H	1879
2594	Atkinson	J	No clasp	621	Syncox	J.H	No clasp	1105	Barker	O	1879
1752	Auld	W	1879	1751	Thom	W	1879	2189	Barker	W	1879
2134	Baggott	P	1879	2289	Tomalin	G	1879	2095	Barlow	M	1879
2409	Baskerville	F.S	1879	2407	Wood	J	1879	2629	Barns	J	No clasp

ORDERLY ROOM CLERK

1903	Black	J	No clasp	295	Jeal	G.J	1879	2190	Bate	A	1879
371	Burns	T	1879					1012	Beattie	T	1879

DRUMMER

								734	Beattie	W	1879
2139	Butcher	H	1879	496	Ashley	S.E	1879	1773	Bee	J	1879
1889	Cameron	W	1879	2292	Baker	J	1879	2115	Beesley	J	1879
227	Campbell	M	1879	3763	Bruce	H	1879	1697	Bell	A	No clasp
1170	Chetham	M.P	1879	881	Campbell	G	1879	772	Bell	T	1879
615	Cowan	M	1879	1254	Clark	J	1879	2420	Bennett	S	1879
478	Cowan	W	1879	1004	Dean	E	1879	Deserted. No trace of the return of the medal.			
1025	Craig	J	1879	616	Duncan	W	1879				

No medal. Deserted.

				1027	Elliott	H	1879	1078	Bern	P	No clasp
1506	Cumming	W	1879	1253	Hackshaw	G	1879	2295	Best	G	1879
848	Dickson	S.H	1879	996	Henderson	W	1879	1131	Bingham	J	1879
2174	Doyle	G.W	1879	1207	Holmes	J	1879	1885	Binnie	G	1879
1917	Faith	G	1879	662	Hutton	L	1879	2365	Birchall	H	1879

Deserted. No trace of the return of the medal.

				679	Marshall	J	1879	Deserted. No trace of the return of the medal.			
				1291	Parker	G	1879				
1973	Foster	C	1879	1289	Stanridge	H	1879	593	Black	A	1879
759	Fraser	D	1879	1052	Sutton	W	1879	1059	Black	R	1879
1454	Grant	J	1879	908	Thomas	J.J	1879	1777	Bealson	A	1879
1804	Green	J	1879	709	Ward	G	1879	1790	Black	S	1879
2092	Hanson	H	1879					2359	Blackburn	E	1879

PIPER

Deserted. No trace of the return of the medal.

				894	Adams	J	1879	2169	Blackburn	J	1879
				624	Malcolm	A	1879	2191	Boardman	J	1879
2630	Harrison	W.H	No clasp	718	Young	H	1879	2179	Bodkin	S	1879

PRIVATE

537	Higgins	D	1879					2097	Bolt	W	1879
1152	Hollinger	J	1879	2616	Adams	J	No clasp	2129	Bolton	J	1879
1959	Hoy	W	1879	1743	Aird	W	1879	2377	Booth	J	1879
2103	Ince	W	1879	1142	Aitken	J	1879	2090	Boots	E	1879
2592	Kane	J	No clasp	555	Aitken	R	1879	2170	Bonds	W	1879
682	Kearney	J	1879	1738	Akers	H	1879	2618	Bowers	W	No clasp
1496	Law	J	1879	1852	Allan	G	1879	2125	Bowman	J	1879
1910	Lindsay	J	1879	2364	Allen	R	1879	851	Boyd	R	1879
2398	Lyons	J	1879	1747	Allerton	J	1879	1766	Boyle	P	1879
1116	Mason	J	1879	821	Anderson	H	1879	Duplicate medal with clasp issued 4/7/1918.			
2249	Mc Carthy	D	1879	2114	Anderson	J	1879				
730	Mc Ewan	J.C	1879	1721	Anderson	J	1879	1053	Bradley	J	1879
961	Mc Kenzie	J	1879	1821	Anderson	J	1879	2613	Brady	J	No clasp
2593	Mc Nally	J	No clasp	2609	Anderson	J	No clasp	1112	Brady	M	No clasp
618	Mc Naughton	A	1879	1143	Andrews	A	1879	2350	Bramwell	J	1879
2309	Millen	J	1879	769	Armstrong	R	1879	1722	Brennan	J	1879
2049	Milton	J	1879	2155	Arthurs	R	1879	1807	Brennan	J	1879
2416	Morgan	F.E	1879	2371	Ashton	F	1879	2325	Brennan	M	1879
792	Muir	G	1879	1287	Atkinson	J	1879	2278	Brian	J	1879
2228	Murray	J	1879	2112	Atkinson	T	1879	1071	Brimer	R	1879r
840	Nash	M.F	1879	2335	Atwood	C.W	1879	Forfeited. No reason given.			
1137	O'Flaherty	M	1879					2258	Broad	T	1879

91st Regiment

Number	Surname	Initial	Year
1811	Brodie	F	1879r
1994	Brodie	J	1879
2192	Brogan	M	1879
683	Brooks	J	1879
1183	Brown	A	1879
917	Brown	J	1879
1072	Brown	J	1879
1781	Brown	J	1879
1184	Brown	J	1879
2408	Brown	J	1879
2245	Brown	R	1879
2330	Brown	T	1879
	Deserted. No trace of the return of the medal.		
2193	Brown	T	1879
2620	Brown	W	No clasp
1546	Brownlie	R	1879
997	Buchannan	A	1879
1094	Buchannan	T	No clasp r
1164	Bunce	W.G	No clasp
2159	Bunting	F	1879
1283	Burke	J	1879
2301	Burnard	J	1879
2383	Burne	H	1879
461	Burtonskin ?	J.E	1879
#2156	Butler	J	1879
498	Butt	J	1879
	Deserted No trace of medal issue.		
325	Cain	J	1879
2427	Cain	F	1879
2087	Cain	P	1879
1826	Cairns	H	1879
1758	Cairns	J	1879
1068	Cale	T	1879
1786	Callaghan	J	1879
1745	Callanin	T	1879
2194	Cambers	A	1879
932	Cameron	D	1879
2381	Cameron	G	1879
1246	Cameron	J	1879
1837	Campbell	D	1879
2615	Campbell	J	No clasp r
134	Campbell	J.S	1879
2042	Campbell	N	1879
1901	Campbell	W	1879
2195	Cannon	J	1879
1829	Carlane	J	1879
1820	Carmichael	J	1879
1688	Carr	H	1879
1730	Carriban	F	1879
2013	Carson	A	1879
2279	Casey	J	1879
2606	Cassidy	H	No clasp
2410	Cassidy	J	1879r
2034	Cassidy	P	1879
	Deserted. No trace of the return of the medal.		
668	Castles	H	1879
2247	Chambers	G	1879
	No medal. Deserted.		
2196	Cheetham	W.T	1879
117	Chevers	W	1879
2167	Chowney	W	1879
1826	Christy	A	No clasp r
2602	Chrystal	J	No clasp
2461	Clarke	W	1879
2171	Clayton	T	1879
2632	Clifford	M	No clasp
849	Coates	R	1879
1818	Cochrane	J	1879
1785	Cochrane	W	1879
289	Cole	C	1879
2316	Coleman	T	1879
2280	Collins	B	1879
2056	Collins	J	1879
1384	Committee	J	1879
955	Connachan	J	1879
1754	Connell	J	1879
1801	Conolly	E	1879
	Discharged with ignominy. No trace of the return of the medal.		
2176	Connolly	J	1879
2147	Connor	B	1879
1793	Connor	J	1879
545	Conroy	J	1879
1771	Conway	H	1879
1936	Conway	M	No clasp
2086	Cook	G	1879
2281	Cooke	C	1879
1844	Cooney	T	1879
	No medal. Deserted.		
2319	Cooper	A	1879
2127	Cooper	J	1879
723	Corbet	J	1879
1797	Cormack	S	1879
2317	Corry	J	1879
2612	Cosgrove	T	No clasp
2083	Cotton	J	1879
2197	Coulthard	W	1879
2093	Court	H	1879
1298	Covell	J	1879
892	Cowden	W	1879
1119	Cowie	J	1879
497	Cox	E.C	No clasp
	Deserted. No trace of the return of the medal.		
2625	Coyne	E	No clasp
1950	Craig	R	1879
2462	Cree	J	1879
1173	Crichton	L	1879
1247	Croker	T	1879
123	Cronin	D	1879
2307	Crowl	R	1879
1874	Cumming	S.E	1879
2199	Cuniff	M	1879
2259	Cunningham	J.H	1879
2437	Cunningham	P	1879
	No medal. Deserted.		
2598	Cunningham	R	No clasp r
2430	Curran	E	1879
2200	Curry	T	1879
2201	Curtain	S.T	1879
1964	Cuthill	P	1879
1109	Dalziel	J	1879
2283	Carling	J	1879
2064	Davies	D	1879
	Deserted. No trace of the return of the medal.		
2057	Davies	T	1879
2073	Davies	W	1879
2282	Davis	G	1879
2290	Dawes	E.W	1879
2376	Dawson	R	1879
	Deserted. No trace of the return of the medal.		
2345	Dean	J	1879
2338	Dempsey	J	1879
2019	Dennington	J	1879
2260	Devers	J	1879
672	Devine	E	1879
1054	Devitt	J	1879
1010	Dewitt	P	1879
1869	Digan	J	1879
1159	Dillon	H	1879
	Discharged with ignominy No trace of the return of the medal.		
1798	Docherty	J	1879
1045	Docherty	R	1879
	Deserted. No trace of the return of the medal.		
754	Donnelly	D	1879
2373	Doran	C	1879

Spinks Auction 5th December 2002.
South Africa 1877-79, one clasp, 1879 (2156. Pte J. Butler. 91st Foot.) nearly EF. Hammer Price £300.
Private John Butler, a tailor from Edinburgh, enlisted in the 26th Foot in 1864 and served with them in Abyssinia in 1868, receiving the medal, which was "left with his kit at Durban". His character was indifferent "on account of absences and drunkernness". He transferred into the 91st in February 1879, but was discharged with heart problems and general debility "after dysentery contracted on the march to relieve Eshowe and attributed to bad water and exposure" He was discharged in September 1879 as a "prematurely broken down, worn out old soldier probably just able to earn a very small livelihood, a very precarious one"

91st Regiment

No.	Surname	Init	Year	No.	Surname	Init	Year	No.	Surname	Init	Year
560	Douglas	E	1879	2096	Eshdale	E	1879r	2206	Ford	J	1879
963	Douglas	W	1879	2419	Etchells	W	1879	1156	Forrest	G	1879
460	Dow	C	1879	2202	Evans	G	1879	2166	Foster	J	1879
2297	Down	T	1879	1833	Evans	S	1879	2080	Forthergill	G	1879
1830	Downie	A	1879	2067	Evans	W	1879	2313	Foulds	H	1879
1842	Downie	H	1879	2240	Everden	G	1879	1157	Franklin	G	1879
2075	Drane	H	No clasp	599	Fairley	J	1879	Deserted. No trace of the return of the medal.			
1847	Duckworth	D.G	No clasp	1856	Fallon	J	1879				
537	Duff	P	1879	2203	Fallon	P	1879	2443	Fraser	J	1879
1001	Duffy	E	1879	1834	Farley	C	1879	810	Fraser	J	1879
2403	Duffy	J	1879	2379	Feeley	J	1879	1848	Fraser	J	1879
Deserted. No trace of the return of the medal.				2204	Feran	J	1879	1502	Fraser	W	1879
				1783	Fiddes	W	1879r	2183	French	G	1879
2136	Duffy	J	1879	Forfeited. No reason given.				2154	Gaffey	M	1879
Deserted. No trace of the return of the medal.				2344	Fielding	J.T	1879	1780	Gaffney	J	1879
				No medal. Deserted.				1861	Gallacher	D	1879
1151	Duffy	T	1879	1860	Findlay	J	No clasp	1716	Gallocher	J	1879r
2131	Duke	F	1879	1024	Findlay	P	1879	2207	Gardiner	W	1879
1839	Duncan	T	1879	2262	Fisher	A	1879	991	Gardner	J	1879
2182	Dunneworth	J	1879r	1787	Fisher	D	1879	2332	Gardner	J.J	1879
363	Dutton	W	1879	2312	Fisher	J	1879	2208	Garner	E	1879
				2263	Fisher	W	1879	2209	Garrity	J	1879
#927	Eadie	A	1879	1897	Fitton	A	No clasp	2603	Gartland	T	No clasp r
1109	Easton	A	1879	No medal. Deserted.				1992	Gaynor	R	No clasp
698	Eden	C	No clasp	1091	Fitzgerald	J	1879	No medal. Deserted.			
2261	Edwards	G	1879	2264	Fitzjohn	J	1879	1449	George	E	1879
2342	Edwards	J	1879	2077	Fitzsimons	C	1879	Deserted. No trace of the return of the medal.			
2611	Egan	M	No clasp	2138	Flanigan	J	1879r				
2133	Egan	T	1879	2389	Fleming	J	1879r	2210	Getliffe	G	1879
1080	Elliott	T	1879	2205	Fletcher	G	1879	1133	Gillan	C	1879
1190	Elliott	T	1879	2402	Flood	B	1879	2211	Gillispie	P	1879
1197	Ellis	W.J	1879	2347	Flynn	J	1879	1909	Glasgow	R	1879
2382	England	W	1879	1065	Flynn	T	1879	2621	Glass	J	No clasp
601	Erskine	J	1879	1776	Foley	M	1879	2070	Goat	W	1879

```
# 927 Alex Eadie 91st Foot/1st Bn. Taken from Muster Rolls WO16/2029, 2033, 2039, 2035
19-05-1877            Enlists at Belfast in 91st Foot number 927 from 58 Brigade Depot.
10-09-1877            Fined 7s 6d for drunkenness
17-01 to 26-02-1878   Furlough
14 to 15-08-1878      Dublin. Imprisoned in military goal stopped 2 days pay.
April-September 1878  Five entries for being drunk, fined 2s 6d then 10s each time.
22-11 to 06-12-1878   Furlough
09-01-1879            Imprisoned for drunkeness fined 7s 6d
07 to 18-02-1879      Imprisoned 12 days pay forfeited
01-04 to 30-06-1880   Begins duty on detachment at Mauritius during this period
26-06-1880            Fined 7s 6d for drunkenness
29 to 30-06-1880      Imprisoned 2 days pay forfeited
01 to 05-07-1880      Imprisoned 25 days pay forfeited for this and subsequent imprisonment
11 to 30-09-1880      Imprisoned
14-09-1880            Fined 10s by courts martial for drunkenness
01 to 04-10 1880      Imprisoned 4 days pay forfeited
23-04 to 15-05-1881   Imprisoned 23 days pay forfeited
28-04-1881            Fined £1.0.0 by Courts Martial for drunkenness
16-05-1881            Returned from Mauritius to Cape Town
03-08-1881            Drunk fined 5s by officer commanding
01-10 to 30-09-1882   No entries in defaulters list.    13-06-1883 Discharged to depot Gosport

The above medal was for sale via Military Antiques, in 2004 some edge bruises and a small scratch to the Queen's cheek otherwise VF
condition. Cost £385   One can only assume the edge bruises where caused when he fell over.
```

91st Regiment

2340	Godfrey	J	1879	452	Hemblen	E	1879	2421	Kelly	M	1879
2150	Goldsmith	A	1879	1713	Henderson	J	1879	778	Kelly	P	1879
661	Gore	T	1879	686	Hendry	D	1879	1731	Kelly	W	No clasp
1170	Gorman	O	1879	2406	Henighan	J	1879	1093	Kennedy	D	1879
708	Gourlay	J	1879	2341	Hennessey	J	1879	231	Kennedy	J	1879
1908	Gowans	D	1879	No medal. Deserted.				2261	Kennedy	J	1879
2423	Graham	C	1879	2417	Henry	J	1879	Forfeited. No reason given. No trace of the return of the medal.			
2386	Graham	J	1879	2039	Heron	A	1879				
2597	Graham	R	No clasp r	930	Heron	W	1879	2153	Kennedy	J	1879
1750	Grant	B	1879	2214	Hindley	J	1879	1893	Kennedy	N	1879
1146	Grant	J	1879	156	Hoines	C	1879	Forfeited. No reason given. No trace of the return of the medal.			
1853	Gray	A	1879	2284	Holmes	W	1879				
220	Gray	T	No clasp	882	Hood	W	1879	2401	Kennedy	P	1879
1898	Greenhalg	W	No clasp	1707	Hope	W	1879	2178	Kennington	S	1879
Deserted. No trace of the return of the medal.				2336	Horrocks	J	1879	2424	Kinceale	J	1879
				2363	Houlikan	M	1879	1180	Kinmond	W	1879
2041	Greenwood	J	1879	Deserted. No trace of the return of the medal.				2215	Kirby	R	1879
2368	Greer	R	1879					1700	Kirk	P	1879
2060	Griffiths	D	1879	2370	Hughes	E	1879	802	Kirk	R	1879
2349	Griffiths	J	1879	1162	Humphrey	R	1879	1098	Kirkwood	J	1879
Discharged with ignominy. No trace of the return of the medal.				1761	Hutcheson	A	1879	1163	Lacey	E.C	No clasp
				1669	Hutchison	A	1879	2357	Ladds	C	1879
2212	Grimes	C	1879	2326	Hyde	T	1879	No medal. Discharged as incorrigible and worthless.			
2361	Grindrod	J	1879	2141	Hyland	T	1879				
559	Guttridge	A	1879	2591	Icombe	T	No clasp	1768	Lafferty	J	1879
1029	Hall	R	1879	1315	Inglis	W	1879	1126	Laing	D	1879
2327	Halliday	J	1879	985	Irvine	J	1879	2314	Lambert	J	1879
832	Halliday	R	1879	1665	Izatt	A	1879	2108	Lambert	J	1879
2339	Hamer	G	1879	1862	Jack	J	1879	2146	Langan	H	1879
204	Hamill	H	1879	2266	Jackson	B	1879	2122	Langhorn	R	1879
404	Hamilton	C	1879	2333	Jackson	D	1879	2216	Lavin	O	1879
1104	Hamilton	G	1879	1135	Jackson	J	1879	905	Law	J.S	No clasp
1805	Hamilton	J	No clasp	1906	Jackson	T	1879	2217	Lawrenson	J	1879
Forfeited. No reason given. No trace of the return of the medal.				1746	James	W	1879	No medal. Deserted.			
				Deserted. No trace of the return of the medal.				2071	Lawson	S	1879
2157	Hammond	T	1879					2062	Lee	D	1879
2102	Hancock	E	1879	1779	Jardine	W	1879	294	Lindsay	J	1879
2362	Hanlon	P	1879	1696	Jeffrey	R	1879	1757	Linton	G	1879 r
1134	Hardie	G	1879	2298	Jenkins	C	1879	2455	Lister	J	1879
983	Hardy	G	1879	1887	Jephcott	G	No clasp	1918	Livingston	J	1879
2418	Harris	J	1879	2633	Johnston	J	No clasp	2050	Llewellyn	J	1879
182	Harris	J	1879	2374	Jolley	J	1879	2162	Lockwood	J	1879
2390	Harrison	T	1879	517	Jones	R	1879	91	Lofkrig	W	1879
1899	Harrison	J	No clasp	2300	Jury	W	1879r	Deserted. No trace of the return of the medal.			
2213	Harrison	T	1879	2128	Kaylor	W	1879				
2367	Hartley	F	1879	2322	Kearns	P	1879	1760	Logie	J	1879
No medal. Deserted.				1418	Kealing	W.J	1879	2219	Lomax	W	1879 r
1944	Hasall	A.A.F	No clasp	Deserted. No trace of the return of the medal.				Forfeited. No reason given.			
2404	Hasting	T	1879					2220	Loney	J	1879
Note on roll: "I & W. No medal."				2385	Keegan	M	1879	1013	Lorrimer	S	1879
2265	Hatfield	J	1879	1028	Keegans	J	1879	1767	Lothian	T T	1879
2590	Hayton	J	No clasp	2117	Keenan	O	1879	2268	Lowe	F	1879
No medal. Deserted.				2414	Keenan	W	1879	1803	Lowden	W	1879
1166	Hazlett	T	1879	1720	Kelly	J	1879	1049	Lumsden	T	1879
Deserted. No trace of the return of the medal.				1066	Kelly	J	1879	2123	Lymen	W	1879
				No medal. Deserted.				2610	Lynch	J	No clasp
2397	Heavy	R	1879r	2172	Kelly	J	1879r	965	Lynch	S	1879
Forfeited. No reason given.				1778	Kelly	M	1879r	2113	Lynn	J	1879
1875	Heggie	J	1879	Deserted. No trace of medal return.							

91st Regiment

No.	Name	Initial	Year/Note
543	Lyons	N	1879
	Discharged with ignominy. No trace of the return of the medal.		
2184	Macartney	F.A	1879
2166	Maguire	J	1879r
2430	Malie	J	1879
2346	Malley	J	1879
725	Malone	M	1879
1825	Mann	D	1879
2608	Manton	T	No clasp
2223	Mantle	T	1879
1816	Marks	T	1879
400	Marshall	J	1879
2135	Marshall	KIAR	1879
2251	Martin	J	1879
2257	Martin	J	1879
1717	Martin	R	1879
2321	Maslin	W	1879
1077	Mason	T	1879
1495	Massie	J	1879
740	Matheson	J	1879
1204	Maune	R	1879
1048	Mc Cabe	J	1879
1796	Mc Callum	J	1879
	No medal. Deserted.		
2143	Mc Cann	M	1879r
	Forfeited. No reason given.		
2148	Mc Carbrey	P	1879
3911	Mc Carten	F	1879
1509	Mc Carten	J	1879
2059	Mc Carthy	J	1879
2145	Mc Carthy	J	1879
1989	Mc Clifferty	J	1879
1704	Mc Cluskey	J	1879
	Deserted. No trace of the return of the medal.		
818	Mc Cluskey	T	1879
1734	Mc Colligan	D	1879
	Deserted. No trace of the return of the medal.		
1103	Mc Cord	R	1879
1819	Mc Cormack	J	1879
1775	Mc Cormick	D	1879
1124	Mc Cowan	R	1879
1900	Mc Crystal	W	1879
	Forfeited. No trace of the return of the medal.		
1691	Mc Culloch	A	1879
1881	Mc Culloch	G	No clasp
1036	Mc Culloch	H	1879
2017	Mc Culloch	J	1879
2110	Mc Culloch	T	1879
1087	Mc Dermid	P	No clasp
1113	Mc Devitt	J	1879
	No medal. Deserted.		
2617	Mc Diarmid	A	No clasp
976	Mc Donald	A	1879
1108	Mc Donald	J	1879
1850	Mc Donald	J	1879r
	Forfeited. No reason given.		
1928	Mc Donald	N	No clasp
1101	Mc Dougall	D	1879
902	Mc Dowall	J	1879
2098	Mc Evoy	J	1879
1092	Mc Ewan	J	1879
791	Mc Ewen	T	1879
1443	Mc Fadyen	J	1879
1845	Md Fadyen	W	1879r
1086	Mc Farlane	J	1879
1980	Mc Gee	D	1879
2604	Mc Gee	P	No clasp
531	Mc Gill	J	1879
1982	Mc Ginlay	J	1879
1769	Mc Ginlay	P	1879
	Deserted. No trace of medal return.		
1117	Mc Glone	H	No clasp
1530	Mc Gowan	D	1879
	Deserted. No trace of the return of the medal.		
1841	Mc Gregor	J	1879
1855	Mc Guire	P	1879
2221	Mc Hale	J	1879
2222	Mc Hugh	T	1879
2607	Mc Hugh	T	No clasp
693	Mc Innes	A	1879
1310	Mc Intyre	C	1879
834	Mc Kaig	T	1879
1031	Mc Kay	C	1879
	No medal. Discharged with ignominy.		
1171	Mc Kay	F	1879
1915	Mc Kay	J	1879
	No medal. Deserted.		
1865	Mc Kay	P	1879
1136	Mc Kelvie	D	1879
854	Mc Kendrick	J	1879
1890	Mc Kendrick	J	1879
535	Mc Kenna	W	1879
901	Mc Kenzie	A	1879
1666	Mc Kenzie	J	1879
	Deserted. No trace of the return of the medal.		
735	Mc Kenzie	J	1879
1914	Mc Kenzie	T	1879
1822	Mc Kenzie	W	1879
2296	Mc Kinney	J	1879
	Deserted. No trace of the return of the medal.		
773	Mc Kinney	R	1879
1026	Mc Kinnon	C	1879
	Deserted. No trace of the return of the medal.		
1174	Mc Laren	T	1879
2355	Mc Laughlin	J	1879
1975	Mc Laughlin	J	1879
2253	Mc Laughlin	W	1879r
2405	Mc Laughlin	W	1879
926	Mc Lean	R	1879
334	Mc Leod	D	1879
2605	Mc Leod	D	No clasp
2396	Mc Leod	J	1879
1712	Mc Lucas	D	1879
2378	Mc Mahon	P	1879
532	Mc Nair	J	1879
966	Mc Naughton	G	1879
2433	Mc Phee	J	1879r
336	Mc Pherson	D	1879
2621	Mc Partland	?W	No clasp
1138	Mc Shane	P	1879
1463	Mc Williams	J	1879
142	Meadows	W	1879
2352	Meaney	J	1879
	Deserted. No trace of the return of the medal.		
2104	Mellaney	M	1879
	Forfeited. No trace of the return of the medal.		
2600	Menzies	R	No clasp
1941	Menzies	T	1879
910	Mencer	D	1879
1178	Mill	W	1879
1755	Miller	D	1879
	Deserted. No trace of the return of the medal.		
1055	Miller	J	1879
1188	Miller	W	1879
	No medal. Deserted.		
2306	Mills	E	1879
	Deserted. No trace of the return of the medal.		
2356	Miners	J	1879
1147	Mitchell	A	1879
646	Mitchell	A	1879
817	Mitchell	J	1879
1161	Mitchell	J	1879
2337	Mencrieff	H	1879
2358	Moore	J	1879
316	Moore	W.W	1879
2132	Moran	J	1879
2422	Moran	T	1879
2303	Moren	C	1879
2065	Morgan	D	1879
	Deserted. No trace of the return of the medal.		
2076	Morgan	W	1879
2224	Morris	W	1879
	No medal. Deserted.		
1871	Morrison	A	No clasp
	Deserted. No trace of medal return.		
2052	Morrissey	J	1879
2225	Mortimer	W	1879
1946	Muir	W	1879
2392	Mullarkey	W	1879
1983	Mullen	A	1879
2226	Mullen	G	1879

91st Regiment

No.	Name	Initial	Year/Note
1933	Mullins	D	1879
2227	Murphy	J	1879
2596	Murphy	J	No clasp
2175	Murphy	T	1879
	Deserted. No trace of the return of the medal.		
2375	Murphy	T	1879
2354	Murphy	P	1879
	Deserted. No trace of the return of the medal.		
2255	Murphy	W	1879
724	Murray	J	1879
1160	Murray	J.A	1879
2074	Murray	P	1879
2091	Murrell	H	1879
527	Naughton	M	1879
2126	Nelson	J	1879
1052	Newall	T	1879
2163	Newport	H	1879
1718	Nisbett	R	No clasp
1118	Niven	R	1879
2254	Nolan	D	1879
2393	Nolan	J	1879
	Discharged with ignominy. No trace of the return of the medal.		
2149	Norman	J	1879
2302	Northcott	G	1879
831	Nowell	L	1879
2269	Oakes	J	1879
2079	Oakley	R	1879
2121	O'Brien	T	1879
1749	O'Brine	T	1879 r
	Forfeited. No reason given.		
941	O'Connor	D	1879
1155	O'Donnell	J	1879
	Deserted. No trace of the return of the medal.		
2360	Ogden	R	1879
1765	O'Hara	E	1879
1065	O'Neil	J	1879
1137	O'Neill	P	1879
1189	O'Neil	W	1879
2229	O'Reilly	C	1879
1694	Orr	J	1879
1122	Orr	W	1879
2061	Owen	R	1879
2622	Page	G	No clasp
2270	Palmer	S	1879
1802	Park	J	1879
	Deserted. No trace of the return of the medal.		
2160	Parker	T	1879
2230	Parsons	H	1879
2130	Partridge	G	1879
2143	Pateman	J	1879
1081	Paton	A	1879
	No medal. Deserted.		
1849	Patterson	J	1879
1877	Patterson	W	1879
2085	Payn	J	1879
1203	Payne	P	1879
2626	Peacock	A	No clasp
2458	Pendrigh	W	1879
	No medal. Deserted.		
1145	Penman	A	1879
1740	Pickring	F	1879
2075	Poole	E	1879
1954	Poots	T	1879
2152	Porter	M	1879
2244	Power	T	1879
2185	Proctor	H	1879
2120	Quinn	C	1879
2180	Rains	T	1879
1809	Railly	J	1879
1906	Ralph	J	1879
1770	Ramage	J	1879
1792	Rankeillor	J	1879
2271	Ranson	C	1879
2623	Ranson	H	No clasp
2627	Reed	G	No clasp
1959	Reid	A	1879
1001	Reid	J	1879
1690	Reid	J	1879
2318	Reidy	M	1879
1135	Reilly	O	1879
2595	Reilly	O	No clasp
2144	Rennix	J	1879
1411	Richards	M	1879
860	Reach	J	1879
2384	Roach	J	1879
2048	Roberts	J	1879
2334	Roberts	W	1879
1957	Robertson	A	1879
2456	Robertson	J	1879
1736	Robertson	R	1879
1689	Robertson	W	1879
2299	Robinson	J.J	1879
1940	Robinson	J	1879 r
	Forfeited. No reason given.		
1891	Ross	J	1879
2099	Ross	J	1879
1060	Ross	W	1879
1158	Ross	W	1879
2310	Rowe	F	1879
2119	Rush	W	1879
2619	Ryan	G	No clasp
2412	Ryan	J	1879
2272	Ryder	J	1879
1724	Sands	C	1879
1823	Sangster	T	1879
2078	Satterthwaite	B	1879
647	Savage	P	1879
2329	Scholey	G	1879
1728	Shanley	F	1879
	Deserted. No trace of the return of the medal.		
1799	Sharp	J	1879
	No Medal. Deserted		
1756	Sharp	W	1879
2100	Sheridan	J	1879
1120	Shields	R	1879
1824	Shiels	J	1879
	Discharged with ignominy. No trace of the return of the medal.		
2256	Short	M	1879
2118	Shutler	F	1879
829	Silcock	A	1879
1709	Simpson	C	1879
	No medal. Deserted.		
2128	Simpson	G	1879
2028	Simpson	J	1879
	Deserted. No trace of the return of the medal.		
1708	Simpson	W	1879
2231	Sims	G	1879
1744	Slane	W	1879
1187	Sleder	D	1879
2124	Slocombe	W	1879
520	Smail	G	1879
1794	Small	D	1879
255	Small	M	1879
2047	Smith	C	1879
1782	Smith	H	1879
1107	Smith	J	1879
2273	Smith	J	1879
2252	Smith	J	1879
2177	Smith	J	1879
	Discharged with ignominy. No trace of the return of the medal.		
2348	Smith	J	1879
1719	Smith	J	1879 r
	Deserted.		
921	Smith	P	1879
2315	Smith	R	1879
1789	Smith	R	1879
2173	Smith	S	1879
2353	Smith	T	1879
1851	Smith	W	1879
1168	Smullen	T	1879
1854	Sodden	A	1879
214	Speddy	J	1879
1149	Stark	A	1879
1735	Stark	W	1879
344	Steel	E	1879 r
1945	Stephenson	G	1879
	No medal. Deserted.		
2293	Stevens	A	1879
2395	Steward	E	1879
1181	Stewart	G	1879 r
	Forfeited. No reason given.		
2614	Stewart	G	1879
467	Stewart	H	No clasp r
	Forfeited. No reason given.		
1172	Stewart	T	1879
1008	Stewart	W	1879
	Deserted. No trace of the return of the medal.		

91st Regiment

1742	Stirrat	W	1879	2328	Walsh	R	1879	1073	Wright	G	1879
837	Stocker	A	No clasp	2237	Warburton	T	1879	2109	Wright	J	1879
697	Stokes	H	No clasp	2305	Ward	O	1879	1727	Wright	R	1879
1832	Stoney	T.G	1879	2331	Ward	T	1879 r	2369	Yates	J	1879
2274	Stump	H	1879	2628	Warren	E	No clasp		No medal. Deserted.		
2275	Sugden	C.W	1879	1846	Waterhouse	J	No clasp	2415	Yates	W	No clasp r
2168	Sullivan	D	1879	1741	Waterson	J	1879	2084	Yaw	W	1879
1140	Summers	J	1879	2111	Watmore	A	1879	700	Yellands	A	1879
	Convicted under Section 18. No trace of the return of the medal.			1097	Watson	D	1879	733	Young	A	1879
				2631	Watson	J.M	No clasp r	809	Young	D	1879
423	Sunderland	A	1879	567	Watson	R	1879	2840	Young	H	1879
1912	Sutherland	G	1879	1009	Watson	R	1879	2058	Young	J	1879
2232	Sutton	R	1879	1808	Watt	D	1879	1872	Young	J	1879
	No medal. Discharged with ignominy.			1069	Watt	J	1879	2388	Young	J.T	1879 r
1535	Sweenie	R	1879	2137	Watts	J	1879	504	Young	R	1879
2164	Tait	H	1879	2051	Wells	J	1879	1716	Young	W	1879
	Deserted. No trace of the return of the medal.			1836	Welsh	W	1879				
				2291	West	G	1879				

93rd (SUTHERLAND HIGHLANDERS) REGIMENT.

CAPTAIN

Elliot	Hon W.F	1879
Hannay	O.C	1879

603	Tait	R	1879	2088	West	H	1879
2233	Taylor	J	1879	2054	Westbrook	E	1879
2186	Taylor	R	1879	2238	Whell	J	1879
2234	Taylor	T	1879	2165	Whelpton	C	1879
2285	Temple	R	1879	181	White	J	1879
2142	Thomas	G	1879	2372	White	J	1879

94th REGIMENT.

LIEUTENANT COLONEL

Malthus CB	S	1879

2081	Thomas	J	1879
2072	Thomas	J	1879

Deserted. No trace of the return of the medal.

MAJOR & BREVET LIEUTENANT COLONEL

Murray CB	J	1879

2063	Thomas	W	1879	2277	White	W	1879
2053	Thomas	W	1879	2239	Whittaker	T	1879
57	Thomas	W.J	1879	2089	Whitwood	C	1879

MAJOR

Anstruther	P.R	1879

1919	Thompson	G	1879	2391	Wickstead	P	1879
2304	Thompson	W	1879 r	1810	Wilkieson	D	1879

Reissued 4/4/1882.

CAPTAIN & PAYMASTER

Elliott	J.M	1879

2082	Thorley	J	1879	2634	Williams	W.H	No clasp
1692	Thornton	J	1879	2380	Williams	G	1879

See also Army Pay Department.

Forfeited. No trace of the return of the medal.

QUARTERMASTER

Lacey	P	1879

880	Threw	A	1879
2411	Tickle	P	1879

CAPTAIN

2107	Toomey	C	1879	2066	Williams	J	1879

Bowlby	G.R.S	1879

Discharged with ignominy. No trace of the return of the medal.

2240	Williams	J.S	1879
2294	Williams	R	1879
1705	Williams	J	No clasp

Brook	E.S	1879
Brooke	L.G	1879

2351	Travers	P	1879	1838	Williamson	A	1879
1192	Tulley	J	1879	1723	Williamson	D	1879

Browne	J	1879
Campbell	F.B	1879

51	Turner	F	1879	1935	Wilson	A	1879
2366	Turner	J	1879		Deserted. No trace of the return of the medal.		
2624	Upton	F	No clasp				

Froom	G	1879
Montague	W.E	1879
Nairns	S.N.McL	1879

Discharged with ignominy. No trace of the return of the medal.

1806	Wilson	G	1879
1498	Wilson	H	1879

Poe	J.H	1879

1828	Vallance	A	1879 r

Deserted. No trace of the return of the medal.

LIEUTENANT ADJUTANT

Harrison	H.A.C	1879

Forfeited. No reason given.

1063	Wilson	J	1879

LIEUTENANT

2308	Vanner	H	1879	1774	Wilson	J	1879
2105	Vincent	J	1879	2101	Wilson	T	1879 r

Campion	H.F.G	1879
Carroll	F.H	No clasp

2235	Waite	G	1879	2394	Wire	T	1879
2276	Wakeling	J	1879	2069	Wood	A	1879
2236	Wakerley	W	1879	1484	Wood	D	1879 r
1002	Walker	J	1879	2055	Wood	J	1879
981	Wallace	D	1879	1176	Wood	J	1879

Mac Swiney	J	1879
O'Grady	J.deC	1879
Spooner	H.W.W	1879
William	C.H.B	1879

Deserted. No trace of the return of the medal.

1201	Woods	J	1879

2nd LIEUTENANT

869	Wallace	M	1879	2320	Woodward	G	1879
804	Walls	J	1879	2241	Worswich	G	1879

Campbell	A.D	1879
Cowper	H	1879
Gordon	R.G.W	1879

94th Regiment

	Harding	E	1879	65B/213	Morrow	R	1879	684	Connor	J	1879
	Hume	J.J.F	1879	1506	Naylor	R.C.W	1879	1783	Cooper	S	1879
	Maclean	A.W.D	1879	912	Newton	H	1879	1386	Coward	C	1879
	Massy	G.L.E	1879	65B/396	Pearce	J	1879	65B/1895	Crothers	J	1879
	Nicol	L.L	1879	902	Pears	J	1879	2328	Davis	J	1879
SERGEANT MAJOR				65B/2688	Percival	W	No clasp	1085	Dennis	F	1879
1010	Fox	G	1879	1325	Podd	G	1879	65B/2159	Dixon	J	1879
DRUM MAJOR				65B/895	Popple	R	1879	65B/2389	Doyle	W	1879
600	Naughton	J	1879	1559	Small	C	1879	65B/1315	Esdale	J	1879
ORDERLY ROOM CLERK SERGEANT				768	Small	R	1879	65B/1939	Farley	M	1879
1441	Maister	H	1879	65B/69	Stanton	J	1879	65B/2232	Foord	R	No clasp
COLOR SERGEANT				1209	Tomlinson	G	1879	65B/800	Gaffney	J	1879
1874	Freeth	J	1879	**LANCE SERGEANT**				65B/2405	Godward	A	1879
900	Gladwin	J	1879	65B/255	Boshell	J	1879	65B/780	Graves	C	1879
2506	Hogan	W	1879	65B/194	Cummings	C	1879	65B/1790	Haigh	A	1879
1104	Hume	E.W	1879	65B/2191	Hunt	E	1879r	65B/722	Halligan	R	1879
1190	Payne	D	1879	1993	Philpotts	W	1879r	65B/2141	Harrington	J	1879
1459	Smith	J	1879	1081	Rooker	A	1879	65B/966	Holmes	H.W	1879
65B/859	Stratford	H.deA	1879	65B/208	Rooney	P	1879	65B/2406	Howard	E	1879
1032	Wright	T	1879	65B/206	Ryan	T	1879	65B/2370	Jarvis	H	1879
ARMOURER SERGEANT				1831	Stokes	S	1879	65B/1115	Jobling	W	1879
360	Devlin	A	1879	**CORPORAL**				65B/2682	Jones	T	1879
BAND SERGEANT				1542	Asling	J	1879	65B/962	Lemon	G	1879
3327	Tovell	H	No clasp	65B/767	Balderson	J	1879	1099	Marwood	G	1879
COOK SERGEANT				2025	Blight	S	1879	65B/955	Mc Gilton	J	1879
1637	Stacey	W	1879	1088	Briggs	F.G	1879	65B/2301	Mount	G	1879
PAYMASTER SERGEANT				1246	Fitzgerald	J	1879	65B/2419	Mowatt	D	1879
65B/454	Mc Clelland	T	1879	65B/788	Fogarty	P	1879	1962	Price	W	1879
PIONEER SERGEANT				1388	Godfrey	A	1879	65B/1934	Raper	J	1879
929	Marsh	G	1879	893	Hassett	J	1879	65B/2338	Rourke	J	1879
QUARTERMASTER SERGEANT				65B/483	Howell	T	1879	65B/2429	Scott	M	1879
1182	Earle	C	1879	65B/904	Hunter	J	1879	65B/2403	Stanway	C.W	1879
SERGEANT INSTRUCTOR OF MUSKETRY				65B/350	Kelly	J	1879	65B/2368	Taylor	W	1879
				1561	Lockington	J	1879	65B/1777	Walstow	F	1879
813	Dunne	W	1879	967	Loughens	J	1879	65B/2327	Wardman	J	1879
SERGEANT				65B/673	Mc Allister	P	1879	65B/1901	Winwood	J	1879
1660	Babbington	W	1879	65B/458	Mc Crea	R	1879	**DRUMMER**			
1379	Badger	W	1879	65B/740	Millar	J	1879	65B/355	Bell	G	1879
1192	Burgess	H	1879	1638	Pay	J	1879	1387	Bland	J	1879
Two awards may have been made to this man.				981	Porter	J	1879	1736	Eley	J	1879
				65B/732	Sharkey	P	1879	1746	Evans	J.F	1879
1193	Burgess	R	1879	65B/401	Sloane	T	1879	No medal. Deserted.			
65B/266	Cowdy	J.L	1879	65B/750	Smith	D	1879	65B/280	Gardner	J	1879
1095	Cummings	G	1879	65B/335	Smyth	J	1879	1594	Haynes	R	1879
9/1	Donaldson	E.E	1879r	65B/402	Spence	A	1879	65B/377	Hunter	A	1879
1947	Edwards	W	1879	65B/2143	Starrett	W	1879	1089	Jenkins	W	1879
65B/151	Gladwin	W	1879	65B/491	Stevenson	R	1879	65B/525	Keough	A	1879
1791	Godfrey	A	1879	65B/1900	Stockton	J	1879	65B/68	King	M	1879
1458	Gordon	R	1879	1548	Sullivan	J	1879	1530	Mason	O	1879
65B/2156	Gribbon	E	1879	1205	Thorpe	F	1879	1080	Meadows	R	1879
65B/2186	Hook	J.R	1879	65B/1833	Webb	W	1879	65B/74	Reddick	J	1879
65B/289	Jamieson	C	1879	65B/1846	White	H	1879	65B/400	Wall	J	1879
1938	Jones	T	1879	65B/244	Wilson	S	1879	1202	Watson	C.B	1879
65B/2337	Lyndhurst	E	1879r	**LANCE CORPORAL**				65B/477	Wilson	W.J	1879
1869	Martin	J	1879	65B/2205	Baxter	G	1879	**PRIVATE**			
65B/564	Mc Nally	J	1879	673	Bradley	J.T	1879	65B/2243	Adams	J	1879r
1745	Mc Rae	J.L	1879	65B/2432	Brown	W.J	1879	Deserted.			
1248	Mc Swegan	H	1879	65B/1861	Byrne	J.A.D	1879	65B/2418	Adams	W.G	1879
633	Moloney	T	1879	65B/734	Clarke	W	1879	No medal. Deserted.			

94th Regiment

	1275	Addison	R	1879	65B/846	Breheney	T	1879	65B/1965	Carter	W	No clasp
65B/1916	Aird	J	1879	65B/2333	Brennan	P	1879	No medal. Deserted.		
65B/956	Alcock	S	1879	No medal. Deserted.				65B/2155	Cassidy	E	1879
	1604	Alexander	W	1879	65B/2072	Breslin	W	1879	65B/412	Cassidy	F	1879
65B/2357	Allen	C	1879	65B/2397	Brian	J	1879	65B/1920	Cathcart	T	1879
65B/1959	Allen	D	1879	65B/2315	Brickley	E	1879	65B/2127	Chamberlain	C	1879
65B/910	Allen	G	1879r	65B/2051	Briggs	W	1879	65B/976	Charteris	H.V	No clasp
Deserted.				65B/2279	Brown	A	1879	65B/2207	Chatterly	G	1879r
	1378	Andrews	N	1879	65B/993	Brown	A	1879	1661	Cheesman	C	1879
	1228	Ansell	J	1879	65B/193	Brown	C	1879	1875	Chipps	H	1879
65B/2361	Anthony	G	1879	65B/473	Brown	J	1879	65B/1905	Clarke	H	1879
65B/2420	Arthur	A	1879	No medal. Deserted.				65B/1995	Clarke	J	1879
65B/1997	Ashenden	W	1879	65B/2061	Brown	J	1879	65B/776	Clarke	W	1879
65B/2286	Atkinson	G	1879	65B/370	Brown	T	No clasp	65B/2154	Cleary	N	1879
65B/1024	Atkinson	J	1879	65B/711	Brown	T	1879	65B/971	Clements	J	1879
65B/2379	Ault	J	1879	No medal. Deserted.				65B/2138	Clewly	G.A	1879
	1553	Ayres	R	1879	65B/2010	Brown	W	1879	65B/900	Clinton	J	1879
	1879	Baker	A	1879	65B/1837	Bruton	W	1879	65B/2015	Coates	G	1879
65B/2444	Baker	H	1879	65B/2421	Bryan	T	1879	65B/644	Cochrane	T	1879
65B/2468	Baker	J	1879	65B/887	Buchanan	R	1879	65B/843	Colgan	T	1879
	956	Baker	J	1879	1832	Buckley	T	1879	65B/1978	Collins	J	1879
65B/949	Banahan	M	1879	65B/2355	Buckley	J	1879	1930	Collins	J	1879
65B/2672	Banks	J	No clasp	65B/2287	Bull	J	1879	65B/2271	Collins	T	1879
65B/2282	Barrett	J	1879	65B/2185	Bullock	J	1879	1882	Collins	T	1879
65B/2158	Barron	B	1879	65B/2464	Burke	P	1879	65B/2364	Collity	P	1879r
65B/306	Barry	J	No clasp	65B/386	Burns	A	1879	Deserted.		
65B/2438	Bartle	J	1879	65B/974	Burns	J	1879	65B/1860	Collyer	C	1879
65B/2288	Basford	G	1879r	65B/1814	Burns	P	1879	65B/2360	Condon	J	1879
Deserted.				65B/672	Burnistone	J	1879r	65B/2181	Condon	J	1879
65B/2452	Bates	J	1879	Deserted.				1078	Condron	J	1879
65B/2445	Baxter	R	1879	65B/1843	Burrows	A	1879	65B/2433	Conduct	J	1879
65B/773	Bebb	W	1879	65B/1913	Butcher	S	1879	2008	Connell	J	1879
65B/710	Beckett	C	1879	65B/2269	Butler	J	No clasp	65B/2077	Connell	J.P	1879r
65B/1876	Bell	J	1879	65B/828	Byers	S	1879	Deserted.		
65B/2065	Bell	T	1879	65B/1999	Byrne	E	1879	65B/957	Connell	W	1879
65B/2320	Bell	W	1879	65B/2453	Byrne	J	1879	65B/798	Connelly	J	1879
	1448	Belsey	G	1879	885	Byrne	J	1879	65B/392	Connelly	M	1879
65B/205	Belsey	S	1879	65B/1794	Byrne	J	1879	65B/2272	Connor	J	1879
65B/2267	Bennett	G	1879	65B/2246	Byrne	J	1879	65B/835	Conroy	T	1879
65B/1948	Bennett	J	1879	65B/2130	Cahill	T	1879	65B/2201	Conway	P	1879
65B/2339	Bew	J	1879	65B/726	Cain	J	1879	65B/1931	Cook	J	1879
65B/1023	Bill	R	No clasp	65B/969	Cain	W	1879	65B/2454	Cook	J.S	1879
65B/2206	Bingham	H	1879	Deserted. No trace of the medal return.				65B/1791	Corcoran	J	1879
65B/1821	Blake	G	1879	65B/2256	Caine	E	1879	65B/704	Cornfield	P	1879
	1304	Blake	R	1879	65B/1007	Caine	E	1879	65B/991	Cosgrovoe	P	1879
65B/428	Bishop	G	1879	65B/877	Callaghan	J	1879	1528	Costello	D	1879
65B/2229	Bolton	A	1879	65B/2348	Callaghan	J	1879	1427	Cotterill	H	1879
65B/2123	Boyland	J	1879	65B/2049	Callaghan	T	1879	65B/1953	Coyle	F	1879
65B/996	Boyle	F	1879 r	65B/736	Campbell	D	1879	65B/854	Coyle	J	1879
Discharged with ignominy. Restored as an act of grace on 25/7/1924. Duplicate then issued.				65B/489	Campbell	M	1879	65B/972	Coyle	J	1879r
				65B/295	Campbell	R	1879	Deserted.		
				65B/2363	Cane	J	1879	65B/699	Coyles	M	1879
65B/2280	Brady	J	1879	65B/2366	Care	E	1879	Also known as No. 5922 M. Leeson 4th Rifle Bde.		
65B/2153	Brady	J	1879 r	65B/302	Carey	J	1879		
Forfeited. No reason given.				65B/2142	Carlin	H	1879	65B/849	Craig	T	1879
65B/387	Brady	M	1879	65B/2680	Carroll	E	No clasp	65B/1818	Craig	T	1879
65B/2270	Bradley	J	1879	65B/935	Carry	J	1879	1971	Crane	W	1879
65B/1796	Brannigan	J	1879	65B/2402	Carter	E	1879	1402	Crann	T	1879r
65B/1114	Brazier	C	1879	65B/938	Carter	G	1879	Discharged with ignominy.		

330

94th Regiment

65B/2200	Crawford	J	1879r	65B/781	Dorrington	J	1879	No medal. Deserted.			
65B/2455	Crawford	P	1879	65B/2067	Downer	T	1879	65B/2164	Foy	M.J	1879
65B/2108	Crawford	W	No clasp	65B/951	Doyle	P	No clasp	65B/797	Foy	P	1879
65B/2345	Crawley	J	1879	65B/1912	Doyle	W	1879	65B/2041	Francey	S	1879
65B/2299	Cribbin	R	1879	65B/2359	Driscoll	D	1879	65B/2456	Francis	A	1879
1593	Crick	F	1879	65B/2006	Duffy	H	1879	1569	Frankum	F	1879
65B/1909	Crisp	J	1879	65B/1902	Dugdale	W	1879	1666	French	W	1879
65B/2412	Cronin	P	1879	575	Dunham	H	No clasp	65B/2150	Frewen	F	1879
65B/925	Crooks	G.J	1879	65B/2052	Dunlop	J	1879	65B/2233	Foster	H.C	1879
65B/725	Crooks	W	1879	65B/801	Dunn	M	No clasp	65B/1872	Fyfield	J	1879
65B/2226	Croombes	J	1879	65B/2139	Dunne	J	1879	65B/899	Gallagher	J	1879
65B/814	Croxford	A	1879	65B/837	Dunning	S	1879	65B/2189	Gamble	M	1879
65B/1946	Crozier	W	1879	65B/2209	Dyche	A	1879	65B/992	Garden	W	No clasp
65B/2054	Cruddas	J	1879	65B/2394	Edwards	J	1879	No medal. Deserted.			
65B/1908	Cull	J	1879	65B/2346	Egan	B	1879	65B/1779	Garmony	J	1879
65B/2104	Cullen	J	1879	No medal. Deserted.				65B/885	Garring	A	1879
65B/1987	Cummings	C	1879	65B/2352	Eley	J	1879	65B/2268	Garrity	J	1879
65B/2194	Cummings	J	1879	65B/811	Ellender	G	1879	65B/2671	George	C	No clasp
65B/1823	Cunningham	T	1879	65B/1886	Elliot	J	1879	65B/2071	Gerrity	J	1879
65B/844	Curran	J	1879r	65B/742	Elliot	R	1879	65B/2303	Gibbon	C	1879
Deserted.				65B/794	Elliott	W	1879	No medal. Deserted.			
65B/276	Cush	F	1879	1614	Emery	P	1879	65B/1907	Gibbon	J	1879
65B/2351	Dagnall	P	No clasp	65B/810	Entwistle	J	1879	65B/224	Gibson	J	1879
65B/1001	Daley	P	1879	65B/2177	Fallon	W	1879	65B/2223	Giles	J	1879
65B/2283	Darling	P	1879	65B/2227	Farrell	T	1879	65B/231	Gilmore	A	1879
65B/1851	Davies	F	1879	65B/2335	Farrelly	M	1879	65B/2325	Gillespie	W	1879
No medal. Discharged with ignominy.				65B/2249	Ferran	J	1879	65B/2247	Gleeson	D	1879
65B/2208	Davis	W	1879	65B/2210	Fiddler	J	1879	1220	Glenn	J	1879
65B/2241	Davies	W	1879	65B/654	Finn	J	1879	65B/2413	Godden	G	1879
65B/795	Davison	J	1879	65B/1000	Finn	T	1879	65B/2211	Godfrey	T	1879
65B/2373	Dempsey	J	1879	65B/964	Finncane	C	1879	1552	Godfrey	W	1879
65B/2446	Dempsey	J	1879	65B/757	Finnegan	J	1879	65B/2314	Godridge	F	1879r
1728	Dennis	G	1879	65B/930	Finnegan	L	1879	Deserted. Restored 6/10/1925.			
656B/2408	Desmond	D	1879	65B/2195	Fisher	G	1879	65B/847	Goodwin	J	1879
65B/2074	Devlin	J	1879	65B/2237	Fisher	G	1879	65B/1845	Goodwin	G	No clasp
65B/875	Devlin	M	1879	1608	Fisher	J	1879	65B/2163	Gorman	T	1879
No medal. Deserted.				1188	Fitchett	P	1879	3169	Gormley	M	1879
65B/2131	Dicken	W	1879r	65B/926	Fitzgerald	J	1879	65B/2365	Gould	W	1879
65B/2313	Dickinson	J	1879	65B/439	Fitzpatrick VC	F	1879	65B/2212	Graham	G.H	1879
65B/2673	Diddle	M	1879	His VC was for an action against				65B/1906	Gray	J	1879
65B/2681	Dillon	J	1879	Sekukuni's Town 28/11/1879.				65B/683	Greacey	G	1879
65B/2273	Dillon	M	1879	65B/1028	Fitzpatrick	M	1879	65B/720	Green	T	1879
65B/2234	Dimmock	M	1879	No medal. Deserted.				65B/712	Greenan	J	1879
65B/2255	Dinan	M	1879	65B/2284	Flannagan	J	1879	#65B/832	Greenwood	E	1879
65B/2340	Dinwoodie	W	1879	65B/2423	Flawn VC	T	1879	65B/2290	Gregory	E	1879
65B/912	Dixon	J	1879	His VC was for an action against				1412	Grey	F	1879
665B/701	Doherty	J	1879	Sekukuni's Town 28/11/1879.				65B/2167	Griffin	S	1879
65B/1879	Doherty	J	1879	65B/2674	Fleming	A	1879	65B/2222	Griffin	W	1879
65B/1006	Doherty	T	1879	65B/361	Flood	J	1879	1940	Griffith	W	1879
65B/1015	Donnelly	J	1879	2049	Flynn	J	1879	65B/2196	Griggs	A	1879
65B/2422	Donovan	J	1879	65B/2289	Foster	J	1879	707	Grimes	T	1879
65B/1947	Donovan	J	1879r	65B/745	Fowler	W	1879	65B/103	Grimley	J	1879
Deserted.				65B/1844	Fox	H	1879	65B/2334	Grogan	M	1879
1345	Donovan	M	1879	65B/2182	Fox	J	1879	65B/2242	Gunter	J	1879

#Christie's, Auction Lot 50, 21 Oct 1991
SOUTH AFRICA 1877-9, 1 clasp, 1879 (Pte. **E. Greenwood.**, 94th Foot), extremely fine. Sold for £308
Private Ellis Greenwood was wounded in the chest, 8th February, 1881 during the defence of Lydenburg(Jan 6th-Mar 30th) one of the beleagured Transvaal garrisons in the 1st Boer War of 1880-81.

94th Regiment

65B/1858	Gurney	J	1879	65B/2146	Hogan	P	1879	1663	Kent	S	1879
65B/2260	Gwynne	J	1879	65B/2390	Holden	G	1879	65B/1820	Kerr	H	1879
65B/440	Hagan	J	1879	65B/2375	Holland	G	1879	65B/879	Kincade	J	1879
65B/2462	Hagan	P	1879	65B/2318	Holmes	T	1879	65B/891	Kinsella	J	1879
65B/2457	Haley	J	1879	65B/1862	Holt	H	1879	65B/2336	King	P	1879
65B/2274	Halford	H	1879	65B/2374	Horner	A	1879	65B/2068	Kisner	P	No clasp
No medal. Discharged with ignominy.				65B/2265	Hougham	W	1879	No medal. Deserted.			
65B/2439	Hall	C	1879	1616	Howard	G	1879	1994	Kitching	G	1879
65B/1824	Hall	J	1879	65B/2447	Howard	J	1879	65B/1850	Knight	J	1879
65B/1928	Halliday	W	1879	65B/2434	Howell	F	1879	65B/2458	Knott	G	1879
65B/908	Halligan	W	1879	65B/2435	Howett	F.M	1879	65B/1955	Lackey	J	1879
65B/1864	Hamilton	J	1879r	65B/2341	Howes	J	1879	65B/2307	Landers	J	1879r
Deserted.				65B/2396	Howick	T	1879	65B/1936	Lane	H	1879
65B/2008	Hamilton	J	1879	65B/1802	Huddelstone	J	1879	65B/2220	Larkin	F	1879
65B/1817	Hamlin	W	1879	65B/578	Hughes	H	1879	65B/813	Larkin	T	1879
65B/822	Hammil	D	No clasp	65B/2170	Hughes	J	1879r	65B/2425	Latham	W	1879
64B/1826	Hancock	W	1879		Later reissued.			65B/2032	Lawlor	W	1879
65B/1899	Hancock	W.A	1879	65B/2393	Hughes	J	1879	65B/753	Lee	G.H	1879r
65B/641	Hannon	D	1879r	1939	Humbley	G	1879	65B/2160	Lee	P	1879
Deserted.				65B/2275	Hurley	D	1879	65B/2380	Lee	W	1879
65B/2297	Harden	J	1879	65B/888	Hurley	J	1879	65B/2145	Lee	W	1879
65B/1008	Hanlon	J	1879	65B/2276	Hurne	J	No clasp	65B/2028	Lemon	J	1879
65B/2066	Hardy	J	1879	No medal. Deserted.				65B/2347	Lemon	S	1879
65B/755	Hare	T	1879	65B/2037	Hutchings	W	1879	65B/990	Leonard	P	1879
65B/2029	Harmer	T	1879	65B/851	Irvine	A	1879	65B/2149	Lidyard	J.L	1879
65B/2291	Harrington	D	1879 r	65B/403	Irvine	W	1879	471	Littler	W	1879r
Deserted.				65B/526	Irwin	J	1879	65B/2376	Lloyd	J	1879
1525	Harris	W	1879	65B/2133	Jackson	W	1879	65B/1932	Lloyd	W	1879
65B/747	Harrison	G	1879	1727	James	H	1879	65B/2426	Lockwood	W	1879
65B/2240	Harrison	J	1879	65B/695	Jameson	J	1879	65B/724	Loney	F.J	1879
65B/2039	Harrison	M	1879	65B/1986	Jenner	W	1879	65B/2169	Looby	P	1879
65B/2424	Hart	E	1879	65B/1832	Jennings	W	1879r	65B/2193	Loughlan	P	1879r
2012	Hasgate	W	1879	65B/808	Johnstone	H	1879	Deserted.			
65B/2224	Hatterell	G	1879	65B/2414	Johnstone	J	1879r	65B/744	Love	W	1879
1389	Hawkins	J	1879r	65B/730	Jones	E	1879	65B/413	Ludlow	P	1879
65B/2407	Hawkins	T	1879	65B/901	Jones	J	No clasp r	66B/589	Lynch	J	1879
1430	Hawthorne	M	1879	65B/1992	Jordan	A	No clasp r	65B/2152	Lynch	J.A	1879r
1987	Hayleby	W	No clasp r	65B/2165	Jordan	J	1879	Deserted.			
1990	Hayward	E	1879	2036	Jordan	W	1879	65B/855	Lynch	P	1879
65B/2259	Healey	D	1879	65B/2323	Joy	P	1879	65B/466	Lynch	T	1879r
65B/2264	Healey	D	1879	65B/2245	Juniper	E	1879	65B/2675	Lyons	E	1879
65B/532	Heaney	J	1879	65B/2122	Judd	P	1879	65B/865	Mahoney	J	1879
65B/2228	Hearns	J	1879	1598	Jupp	H	1879	65B/2219	Maley	J	1879
65B/2151	Heath	E	1879	65B/2035	Kairns	J	1879r	65B/504	Mallon	J	1879
65B/756	Hefferman	J	1879	65B/749	Kavanagh	J	1879	65B/2168	Mann	J	1879r
2021	Hefferon	T	1879	65B/886	Kavanagh	J	1879	Deserted.			
658	Herbert	W	1879	65B/2277	Keane	A	1879	65B/1898	Mann	T	1879
65B/2409	Hetherinton	T.G	1879r	65B/336	Kearney	J	1879	65B/1983	Manners	J	1879
65B/802	Hickey	P	1879	65B/2278	Keating	J	1879	65B/2292	Mannion	E	1879
65B/587	Higgins	C	1879r	1350	Keeling	W	No clasp	65B/595	Marron	F	1879
Deserted.				65B/2326	Kelly	J	1879	65B/2124	Marron	F	1879
65B/2198	Higgins	H	1879	65B/2173	Kelly	M	1879	65B/805	Marron	P	No clasp
65B/748	Higgins	W	1879	65B/2683	Kelly	M	1879	65B/2459	Marshal	H	1879
65B/1927	Hill	J	1879	65B/2045	Kelly	P	1879	1610	Martin	C	1879
1612	Hill	J.T	1879	65B/2262	Kelly	R	1879	65B/2031	Martin	D	1879
65B/467	Hill	T	1879	65B/932	Kelly	T	1879	65B/2353	Martin	J	1879
1563	Hissey	R	1879	65B/799	Kennedy	J	1879	65B/2416	Mattison	S	1879
65B/1866	Hodgen	W	1879	65B/2252	Kennedy	P	1879	65B/1827	Maynard	J	1879
65B/839	Hogan	M	1879r	65B/845	Kennedy	T	1879	65B/2046	Mayors	F	1879

94th Regiment

65B/384	Mc Ardle	D	1879		65B/2676	Mc Gee	J	1879		65B/2377	Miles	W	1879
65B/1013	Mc Bennett	J	1879		65B/823	Mc Gee	P	1879		1607	Millard	S	1879
65B/875	Mc Bride	J	1879		65B/297	Mc Givern	J	1879		65B/2331	Miller	C	1879
65B/291	Mc Bride	J	1879		65B/1804	Mc Glone	F	1879		65B/819	Miller	H	1879
65B/965	Mc Bride	P	1879		65B/2076	Mc Guirk	F	1879		1978	Miller	J	1879
65B/936	Mc Bryde	B	1879		65B/1811	Mc Guirk	J	1879r		65B/1892	Miller	S.D	1879
65B/425	Mc Caffrey	H	1879		Deserted.					65B/2174	Meade	M	1879
65B/451	Mc Cann	J	1879		65B/903	Mc Hugh	J	1879		65B/241	Miskimmin	S	1879
65B/1005	Mc Cann	P	1879r		65B/465	Mc Kee	W	1879		65B/1889	Mitchell	J	1879
Deserted.					65B/2069	Mc Kee	W.J	1879		65B/34	Molly	J	1879
65B/694	Mc Cann	W.H	1879		65B/2106	Mc Kenna	M	1879		No medal. Deserted.			
1970	Mc Carthy	J	1879		65B/2199	Mc Keown	J	1879		65B/524	Molloy	J	1879
65B/2684	Mc Carthy	J	No clasp		65B/1021	Mc Keown	P	1879		65B/2322	Monaghan	P	1879
2026	Mc Carthy	J	1879		#65B/1025	Mc Kew	J	1879		65B/2404	Monk	J.J	1879
65B/2383	Mc Carthy	J	1879		65B/723	Mc Kew	W	1879		65B/2399	Montgomery	J	1879
					65B/569	Mc Kinney	S	1879		65B/909	Mooney	W	1879
65B/2415	Mc Carthy	M	1879r		65B/1894	Mc Kitterick	P	1879		65B/953	Moore	J	1879
Deserted.					65B/2436	Mc Lennan	W	1879		65B/2030	Moore	W	1879
65B/2176	Mc Carthy	T	1879		65B/2171	Mc Loughlan	M	1879r		65B/2677	Moreland	W	1879
65B/848	Mc Conville	C	1879		Deserted.					65B/2686	Morgan	P	1879
65B/690	Mc Conville	W	1879		65B/747	Mc Mahon	E	1879		1702	Morris	J	1879
65B/363	Mc Coo	J	1879		65B/739	Mc Manus	J	1879		65B/751	Morris	W	1879
65B/1018	Mc Coo	S	1879r		65B/1904	Mc Nair	A	1879		65B/1984	Morris	W	1879
Deserted.					65B/2388	Mc Namara	M	1879		65B/2372	Mulgrew	J	1879
65B/2367	Mc Cormack	J	1879		65B/915	Mc Namee	F	1879		65B/2350	Mullheran	J	1879r
65B/187	Mc Cormick	J	1879r		65B/766	Mc Parland	P	1879		Deserted.			
Deserted.					65B/697	Mc Phillips	P	1879		65B/921	Mulholland	J	1879
65B/960	Mc Cormick	W.J	1879		65B/737	Mc Quaid	P	1879		65B/999	Mulholland	R	1879
65B/2000	Mc Court	J	1879		65B/1026	Mc Shane	B	1879r		No medal. Deserted.			
65B/2190	Mc Culla	D	1879		Deserted.					65B/2324	Mullhall	L	1879
874	Mc Culloch	J	1879		1711	Mc Shane	J	1879		No medal. Deserted.			
65B/1089	Mc Dermot	H	1879r		65B/830	Mc Veigh	J	1879		65B/820	Mullen	H	1879r
65B/2329	Mc Donald	H	1879		65B/2685	Meade	W	1879		Deserted.			
65B/558	Mc Donald	J	1879		65B/2461	Meek	F	1879		65B/2285	Mullen	P	1879
65B/2121	Mc Donald	M	1879r		65B/2401	Meek	T	1879		65B/852	Mullin	R	1879
65B/2192	Mc Donald	M	1879		65B/793	Megaw	S	1879r		65B/2440	Munro	J	1879
65B/2266	Mc Donald	T	1879		Deserted.					65B/989	Murphy	B	1879
65B/344	Mc Donnell	R	1879		65B/998	Mera	W	No clasp		1461	Murphy	E	1879
65B/934	Mc Dowell	A	No clasp r		65B/952	Mercer	J	1879		65B/804	Murphy	J	1879
65B/2281	Mc Fall	R	No clasp		65B/771	Mercer	R	1879		65B/1027	Murphy	J	1879
65B/98	Mc Gahegan	J	1879		65B/1836	Merrick	E	1879		65B/961	Murphy	J	1879
65B/995	Mc Gann	J	1879		65B/2001	Michan	E	1879r		65B/2427	Murphy	J	1879
65B/372	Mc Gaughey	A	1879		Deserted.					65B/2175	Murphy	J	1879

Glendinings Auction 7th Junce 1989 - Lot 172. - A South African 1877-79 (Zulu War) Medal awarded to a private in the 94th Foot, who was killed later in action in the first Boer War. South Africa 1877-79, one bar, 1879 (1025 Pte. J. McKew, 94th Foot). Better than very fine. (£200-300)

K.I.A. Bronker's Spruit, 20th December, 1880.

Upon receiving orders from Sir Owen Lanyon to concentrate his forces in Pretoria, Col. Anstruther set out to march the 180 miles from Lydenburg with two companies of the 94th. With them went three women and two children, plus a baggage train.

On the 20th December, at Bronker's Spruit, some 38 miles from Pretoria, 500 mounted Boers appeared before him. A Boer approached with a white flag and Col. Anstruther went out to parley. He was handed a letter declaring the establishment of the South African Republic and that until the Boers there knew if war had been declared or not the British could not proceed further. Col. Anstruther replied that he was under orders to march to Pretoria and this he would do.

During the parley the Boers had used the cover provided by trees and rocks to surround the British. Before the colonel could rejoin the column the Boers opened a fusilade on the troops and the strung-out baggage train. A short exchange of fire followed, in which the Boers picked off seven out of the nine British officers, and after a brief time Col. Anstruther, himself mortally wounded had to surrender.

Of the British, 56 were killed and 101 wounded. It would appear that some of the wounded were subsequently shot by the Boers. This incident marked the beginning of open warfare in the First Boer War.

NAMING ON THE SOUTH AFRICA 1877-79 MEDAL

Naming is usually engraved, in sloping or upright capitals, both styles can appear in medals to the same regiment. As a general rule all original issue medals are engraved, it is possible that later issue medals could be impressed, in whatever style was in use at the time of issue. The sloping capitals has a number of variations, it must be appreciated that not all the 37,000 medals where engraved by the same person, so styles will change.

94th Regiment

65B/211	Murphy	M	1879	65B/2147	Preston	C	No clasp	65B/2050	Sheals	J	No clasp
65B/2093	Murphy	M	1879	65B/2298	Price	J.A	1879	65B/1842	Sheals	P	1879
65B/2254	Murphy	W	1879	65B/1915	Price	W	1879	65B/2053	Sherrey	B	1879
65B/833	Murray	J	1879r	#65B/2312	Price	W	1879	65B/803	Shiels	P	1879
65B/2253	Murray	J	1879	65B/1880	Pugh	T	No clasp	65B/2395	Shephard	W	1879
65B/792	Murtha	P	1879	65B/821	Quail	W	1879	65B/2184	Shimmell	M	1879
65B/2354	Myles	J.N	1879	65B/1952	Quilton	B	1879	65B/2378	Siddall	B	1879
65B/2187	Nagle	M	1879	65B/2330	Quinn	L	1879r	65B/2136	Simmons	W	1879
65B/2148	Narbeth	A	1879	Deserted.				65B/2295	Simpson	A	1879
65B/2079	Naughton	P	1879	65B/670	Reaney	R	1879	65B/2258	Siviter	S.H	1879
65B/2371	Neland	M	1879	No medal. Deserted.				65B/727	Skehan	T	1879
65B/229	Nery	P	1879	2004	Reardon	S	1879	65B/2310	Slater	S	1879
65B/447	Nesbitt	I	1879	65B/1863	Reavy	F	1879	65B/2400	Smith	A	1879
65B/2687	Nicoll	D.M	1879	65B/2293	Redfern	J	1879	1426	Smith	F	1879
65B/2311	Norman	F	1879	65B/1859	Reid	R	1879	1633	Smith	H	1879
65B/1839	Norton	E	1879					65B/2306	Smith	J	1879r
65B/937	O'Brien	M	1879	65B/927	Reid	W	1879	65B/2203	Smith	J	1879
65B/1813	O'Brien	P	1879	No medal. Deserted.				65B/2316	Smith	J	1879
65B/658	Ogle	J	1879	65B/831	Reilly	J	1879	No medal. Deserted.			
65B/2057	O'Hara	P	1879	65B/850	Reilly	J	1879	65B/806	Smith	J	1879r
65B/2321	O'Kelly	J	1879	65B/1829	Reilly	J	1879	Deserted.			
65B/2358	O'Neal	T	1879	65B/2202	Reilly	M	1879	65B/1780	Smith	W	1879
65B/834	O'Neill	W	1879	65B/2385	Ribbands	E	1879	65B/2025	Smith	W	1879r
65B/2411	Organ	C	1879	65B/2075	Rice	J	1879	Deserted.			
1224	Ovens	T	1879	65B/2308	Richards	H	1879	65B/2678	Sprouled	J	1879r
65B/2225	Overton	S	1879	65B/2463	Richardson	W	No clasp r	Forfeited. No reason given.			
1540	Palfrey	G	1879	65B/2362	Riley	J	1879	65B/2128	Stanton	W	1879
65B/2261	Parker	J	1879	65B/1012	Robinson	J	1879	1187	Starkie	J	1879
65B/1903	Parks	A	1879	65B/2263	Robinson	J	1879r	65B/2231	Stead	W	1879
1674	Parsons	W	1879	Deserted.				65B/2140	Stephens	H	1879
65B/1011	Patterson	F	1879	65B/221	Robinson	J	1879	65B/951	Stephenson	M	1879
65B/853	Patterson	J	1879	65B/294	Robinson	W.J	1879	65B/2178	Stevens	J	1879
65B/2236	Paycock	R	1879	65B/469	Rochford	T	1879	65B/2144	Stevens	L	1879
65B/2302	Pemberton	T	1879	65B/2059	Roden	N	1879	65B/1840	Steveton	W	1879
65B/2239	Penfold	C	1879	65B/783	Rodgers	G	1879	65B/2448	Stewart	A	1879
65B/1870	Perkes	G	1879	65B/2230	Rodgers	W	1879	1629	Stiff	C	1879
839	Peters	A	1879	65B/1914	Rogers	W	1879	65B/973	Stinson	P	1879
65B/2441	Phelan	J	1879	65B/2250	Rooney	J	1879r	No medal. Deserted.			
65B/2428	Phillips	G	1879r	65B/761	Rooney	J	1879	65B/2317	Stokes	J	1879
65B/2244	Phillips	P	1879	65B/784	Rowan	S	1879	983	Strain	J	1879
65B/2467	Phillips	R	1879	65B/2460	Rowan	C	1879	65B/2157	Street	J	1879
2043	Piercy	J	1879	65B/2442	Rowley	G	1879	65B/2386	Sullivan	D	1879
65B/2183	Pitt	S	1879	65B/2387	Ryan	P	1879	65B/2248	Sullivan	D	1879
65B/2392	Pocklington	H	1879	65B/1980	Sampson	W	1879	1549	Sullivan	E	1879
65B/406	Pond	F	1879	1588	Sawyer	T	1879	65B/2382	Sullivan	J	1879
65B/2689	Potter	G	1879r	65B/577	Scarlett	D	1879	65B/2213	Sullivan	J	No clasp
65B/1963	Potter	S	1879	619	Schofield	H	1879	No medal. Deserted.			
65B/407	Potter	S	1879	65B/646	Scott	J	1879	65B/2443	Sweeney	J	1879
65B/2437	Potterton	W	1879	65B/2398	Scullion	P	1879	65B/2251	Sweeney	J	1879
65B/2161	Potts	G	1879	65B/2197	Scully	P	No clasp	65B/829	Synnot	W	1879
65B/2342	Powell	D	1879	65B/1849	Selby	T	1879	65B/2344	Taylor	J	1879
65B/1853	Powell	W	1879	65B/2134	Sharman	R	1879	65B/2215	Taylor	W	1879
65B/2343	Power	J	1879	65B/2305	Shaw	S	1879	65B/2238	Thomas	A	1879
65B/911	Power	J	1879	65B/2137	Shaw	W	1879	65B/2214	Thomas	J	1879
65B/2369	Pressley	W	1879	65B/2172	Shea	M	1879	65B/2257	Thomas	W	1879

Glendinings 19th September 1989 lot 248 South Africa 1877-79, bar 1879, (2312 Pte.W.Price, 94th Foot) N.EF estimate £220-£250. Served in first Boar war, 1880-81. Killed in Action at Bronkhorst Spruit.

94th Regiment

65B/2294	Thompson	H	1879r	65B/2300	Wigmore	R	1879	
65B/590	Thompson	S	1879	65B/1940	Wild	J	1879	
65B/818	Toal	W	1879	No medal. Deserted.				
65B/882	Tolan	J	1879r	65B/2466	Wildsmith	W	1879	
65B/2319	Toomey	P	1879	65B/2180	Wilkinson	G	1879r	
65B/2384	Toomey	P	1879	Deserted.				
65B/2179	Toplis	G	1879	65B/1893	Williams	J	1879	
65B/2349	Tougher	M	1879	65B/1835	Williams	J	1879	
65B/2135	Towle	S	1879	1391	Williams	J	1879	
65B/721	Travers	F	1879	65B/2417	Williams	J	1879r	
65B/1815	Traynor	M	1879	65B/2162	Williams	W	1879	
65B/2438	Trott	H	No clasp	65B/2217	Williamson	G	1879	
65B/2465	Troy	G	1879	65B/840	Wilson	A	1879	
No medal. Deserted.				65B/227	Wilson	D.S	1879r	
65B/1993	Troy	J	1879 r	65B/2235	Wilson	F.S	1879	
Deserted.				65B/2451	Wilson	R	1879	
65B/779	Turner	M	1879	65B/2431	Witch	F	1879	
No medal. Discharged with ignominy.				992	Woollard	L	1879	
65B/1004	Turner	W	1879	65B/2218	Wolstenholme	T	1879	
65B/2132	Tyers	C	1879	65B/2125	Woods	J	1879	
65B/2356	Tyghe	J	1879	65B/2679	Woods	P	1879	
65B/2449	Valentine	G	1879	1880	Woods	S	No clasp	
65B/2204	Waldron	P	No clasp	Discharged with ignominy. No trace of the return of the medal.				
65B/2381	Walker	J	1879r					
Deserted.				65B/1778	Wright	A	No clasp r	
65B/2332	Walker	T	1879	65B/645	Wright	W	1879	
792	Wallace	G	1879	65B/259	Wylie	J	1879	
65B/500	Wallace	W	1879r	1236	Wynn	J	1879	
65B/785	Walsh	J	1879	65B/2309	Young	H.W	1879	
65B/2221	Warbrick	J	No clasp	65B/884	Young	J	1879	
65B/817	Ward	D	1879	65B/987	Young	S	1879r	
65B/1977	Ward	J	1879	Deserted.				
65B/2166	Ward	J	1879					
65B/2126	Ward	J	1879	**95th (DERBYSHIRE) REGIMENT.**				
65B/790	Warren	M	1879r	LIEUTENANT COLONEL				
65B/1917	Warren	W	1879		Crealock CB	J.N.	1877-8-9	
65B/2430	Watkins	E	1879	Also had Medal and clasp for Indian Mutiny.				
65B/2296	Watkins	R	1879					
No medal. Deserted.				LIEUTENANT				
65B/741	Watson	J	1879		#Smith-Dorrien	H.L	1879	
65B/2410	Watson	W	1879r					
65B/1571	Watts	D	1879r	**98TH (PRINCE OF WALES') REGIMENT.**				
65B/270	Watts	J	1879	LIEUTENANT				
65B/1996	Way	E	1879		Carey	J.B	1879	
1729	Waston	H	1879					
65B/2129	Whalen	M	1879					
65B/2304	Wharton	J	1879r					
65B/2216	Whetton	W	No clasp					
65B/2450	White	W	1879					
65B/2188	Whitstone	N	1879					
65B/2391	Whittaker	T	1879					

99th DUKE OF EDINBURGH'S (LANARKSHIRE) REGIMENT.
Arrived in South Africa early in January 1879 and served in the actions on the Inyezane on 22nd January and at Gingindhlovu on 2nd April.

LIEUTENANT COLONEL
    Welman CB W.M.D.R 1879

BREVET LIEUTENANT COLONEL
    Ely H.F.W 1879
Also had medal and clasp for China 1860.

MAJOR
    Coates C 1879
    Walker A.L 1879
Also had medal and clasp for China 1860.

CAPTAIN
    Cotton R.B 1879
    Hanson J.M 1879
    Kennedy C.H.S 1879
    Macklin G.R.W 1879
    Moir A.McA 1879
    #Nevile C.C 1879
    Story F.L 1879
    ##Wayman G.A 1879

QUARTERMASTER
    Bateman J 1879

LIEUTENANT ADJUTANT
    Davison A.S.F 1879
D/S 27/3/1879.
    Harford H.C 1879

LIEUTENANT
    Alexander C.H 1879
    Johnson G.C.J 1879
KIA Ginghilovo 2/4/1879
    Johnson T.G 1879
    Jones W.D 1879
    Payne A.V 1879
    Rowden H.W 1879
    Turner A.W 1879

2nd LIEUTENANT
    Cockburn F.P 1879
    D'Arcy W.I 1879
    D/S 23/9/1879
    Elderton A 1879
    Gavin M.W 1879
    Guille J.S 1879
    Justice C.leG 1879
    Welman C.F.G 1879

For Sale March 2010 HISTORIK ORDERS, LTD
ZULU MEDAL NAMED TO: CAPTAIN. C. C. Nevile. 99th. Foot. Clasp: 1879. Condition: VF with a minor bruise 4 o'clock on the reverse. Both Captain Nevile and Wayman are named on a regimental memorial in St. James' Parish Church Comes with research and a photo of the memorial to the Wilts in St. James' Parish Church. $3,495.00 (US$)
##ZULU MEDAL NAMED TO: CAPTAIN. G.A. WAYMAN. 99th. FOOT. Clasp: 1879. Condition: GVF..
Wayman reached the rank of Major. $3,495.00 (US$)

Horace Smith-Dorrien

The Zulu War Hairbreadth Escape from Isandula. Story of a Survivor.
Northern Echo Saturday March 8th 1879
Lieutenant Dorien, who was in the fighting of Isandula, has written a letter describing the struggle, in which he never mentions any lack of ammunition, nor does he say that any troops were cut off from the camp. He says:-
"At about 1.30 the Zulus were seen coming over the hills in thousands. They were in most perfect order, and seemed to be in about twenty rows of skirmishers one behind the other. They were in a semi-circle round our two flanks and in front of us, and must have covered several miles of ground. The Zulus nearly all had firearms of some kind and lots of ammunition. Before we knew where we were they came right into the camp, assagaing everybody right and left. Everybody then who had a horse turned to fly. The enemy were going at a kind of very fast half-walk and half-run."
Lieut. Dorien, galloped headlong over broken ground as follows:-
"I jumped off and led my horse down. There was a poor fellow of the mounted infantry (a private) struck through the arm, who said as I passed that if I could bind up his arm and stop the bleeding he would be all right. I accordingly took out my handkerchief and tied up his arm. Just as I had done it **Major Smith**, of the artillery, came down by me wounded, saying, "For God's sake get on man; the Zulus are on the top of us" I had done all I could for the wounded man, and so turned to jump on my horse. Just as I was doing so the horse went with a bound to the bottom of the precipice being struck with an assegai. The Zulus were all round me finishing off the wounded, the man I had helped and Major Smith among the number. I rushed off on foot and plunged into the river, which was little better than a roaring torrent. I was being carried down the stream at a tremendous pace, when a loose horse came by me and I got hold of his tail and he landed me safely on he other bank; but I was too tired to stick to him and get on his back. I got up again and rushed on and was several times knocked over by our mounted niggers, who would not get out of my way, then up a tremendous hill, with wet clothes and boots full of water. About twenty Zulus got over the water and followed us up the hill, but, I am thankful to say they had not their firearms. Crossing the river, however, the Zulus on the opposite side kept firing at us as we went up the hill, and killed several of the niggers round me.I was the only white man to be seen until I came to one that had been kicked by his horse, and could not mount.I put him on his horse, and lent him my knife." Lieutenant Dorien reached Helpmakaar in safety.
From thence he went to Rorke's Drift. He says:- "I am there now in a laager. We are expecting pestilence to break out here, as there were about 850 Zulus killed here, and some are buried in the ruins.
Editors note: Lieutenant Horace Lockwood Smith-Dorrien had been forced to continue his journey on foot after crossing the Buffalo river. By the time he arrived at Helpmekaar, after running and walking over 20 miles he was close to collapse: -
"I got into Helpmekaar at sundown, having done twenty miles on foot from the river, for I almost went to Sandspruit. At Helpmekaar I found Huntley of the 10th, who had been left there with a small garrison, and also Essex, Cochrane, Curling and Gardner, from the field of Isandhlwana, all busy placing the post on a state of defence Acting Control Officer "
It was J.Hamer, who had been found exhausted in the Buffalo river by Lieutenant H. Smith-Dorrien, he then found him a horse and helped him on his way.
Ref: Horace Smith-Dorrien Memories of forty-eight years Service.

99th Regiment

SERGEANT MAJOR
1897	Strachan	D	1879

SERGEANT MAJOR TAILOR
2321	Fuller	S	1879

BANDMASTER
917	Burton	J	1879

COLOUR SERGEANT
1796	Barnett	J.J	1879
1952	Dowding	F.M	1879
1994	Farquhar	J.M	1879
1575	Green	J	1879
1018	Mc Mullen	D	1879
2112	Mankelow	H	1879
2109	Wigmore	C	1879
2129	Wilson	H.J	1879

STAFF SERGEANT
1881	Tumbelty	H	1879

ARMOURER SERGEANT
?	Beeton	J.W	1879

PAYMASTER SERGEANT
2058	Pepper	G	1879

PIONEER SERGEANT
2334	Bell	D	1879

QUARTERMASTER SERGEANT
782	Farrell	P	1879

SERGEANT INSTRUCTOR OF MUSKETRY
1875	Webster	J.F	1879

ORDERLY ROOM CLERK
1580	Robinson	G	1879

SERGEANT
1482	Anderson	J	1879
1968	Atkinson	R	1879
824	Bennett	W	1879
551	Boyle	P	1879
1262	Creed	M	1879
1737	Doyle	W	1879
2059	Gillett	J.H	1879
1974	Greer	H	1879
388	Hancock	J	1879
1931	Heming	A	1879
1959	Henning	J	1879
1819	Hill	J	1879
710	Holland	F	1879
1064	Holsgrove	J	1879
2026	Kennell	W	1879
1889	Lambert	A	1879
862	Marsh	R	1879
1689	Matthews	W	1879
475	Mc Carragher	R	1879
1269	Mullen	M	1879
1650	Peat	J	1879
1900	Pendlebury	R	1879
2177	Rhodes	J	No clasp r
Forfeited. No reason given.			
1222	Rose	R.F	1879
619	Saunders	H	1879
771	Selfe	E	1879
2324	Smith	D.S	1879

1138	Speed	W	1879
1902	Stay	J	1879
2049	Thompson	G	1879
1272	Watson	W.S	1879r
371	Watt	W.S	1879
1742	Whelan	J	1879
1924	Whitcombe	T	1879
1609	Wilson	T.J	1879
1821	Wyatt	F	1879

CORPORAL
987	Angell	T	1879
1877	Ball	E	1879
1886	Ball	G	1879
2150	Ball	W.J	1879
1082	Beaven	W	1879
1882	Bennett	H	1879
1326	Bilton	G	1879
2040	Budd	W	1879
445	Carson	S	1879
902	Church	F	1879
1188	Crumplin	R	1879
1301	Dellar	H	1879
1316	Farley	R	1879
782	Fielding	H	1879
1199	Fisk	R	1879
953	Flynn	D	1879
336	Gasson	F	1879
2382	Gavin	R	No clasp
1091	Haddrell	F	1879
1475	Haskell	W	1879
2189	Hawkins	J.H	1879
2038	Henderson	W	1879
2104	Holgate	W	1879
1827	Kelly	R	1879
1182	King	H	1879
695	Laverick	A	1879
2377	Lynch	W	No clasp
801	Mahon	H	1879
1470	Mahoney	D	1879
507	Mc Callum	J	1879
1873	Mc Leod	J	1879
901	Mould	W	1879
567	Newberry	W	1879
1012	Peake	W.J	1879
1087	Piggott	E	1879
758	Rickards	W	1879
1929	Smoker	C	No clasp
2246	Sparry	J	1879
1308	Spencer	T	1879
1003	Sweetzer	W	1879
1229	Talbot	J	1879
898	Towers	J	1879
1107	Weddap	C	1879
No medal. Discharged as incorrigible.			
812	Wildgoose	A	1879
719	Wilkins	T	1879

DRUMMER
1077	Clarke	S	1879
1893	Couchman	F	1879
355	Cooper	W	1879
370	Dobie	T	1879
609	Fallowfield	T	1879
855	Flowers	A	1879
1899	Glover	A	1879
1903	Holden	B	1879
1895	Hunter	J	1879
1962	Lawlor	J	1879
#1894	Quinn	J	1879
753	Thompson	G	1879
1086	Tomlin	W	1879
854	Walliker	W	1879
1904	Whiley	G	1879

PRIVATE
1094	Abraham	E	1879
2135	Adams	D	1879
897	Adams	W	1879
1044	Agar	C	1879
2389	Aldridge	S	No clasp
469	Alexander	H	1879
1015	Allen	T	1879
2120	Amos	E	1879
1005	Amos	J	1879
2013	Andrews	A	1879
1276	Andrews	J	1879
1328	Annable	W	1879
2136	Aoten	W	1879
775	Archer	R	1879
2014	Armstrong	G.F	1879
1912	Armstrong	P	1879
942	Ashby	J	1879
1220	Ashley	T	1879
2137	Astle	G	1879
1118	Atkins	J	1879
1744	Atkinson	C	1879
*859	Baden	C	1879
D/S 2nd March 1879 Fort Pearson			
2138	Bagley	E	1879
1854	Bailey	J	1879
1025	Bailey	T	1879
1052	Bailey	T	1879
1017	Bailey	W	1879
720	Bailey	W	1879
1929	Baker	F	1879
767	Baker	F	1879
1251	Baker	G	1879
2093	Baker	T.G	1879
1867	Ball	J	1879
1252	Ballard	W	1879
2015	Barnes	H	1879
988	Barnett	G	1879
1792	Barnett	H	1879
1853	Barrett	R	1879
1309	Barry	W	1879
2139	Barter	J	1879r
2140	Bartley	P	1879
805	Batchelor	G	1879
1919	Batha	J	1879
545	Beaven	A	1879

99th Regiment

#Drummer J Quinn 99th Foot

One of the Zulu medals in my collection to Drummer J Quinn 99th Foot has special significance, because of he documents that accompanied the medal. Including:

1. Army form B 2077. Waterproof Parchment Certificate of Character on Discharge (Describes his character as Good.Gives a physical description of him including a tattoo on his left forearm of a serpent, and the right Peacock.A5 sized folded into four and printed on the reverse is information and bonus payments paid to Recruiting Agents .A job that discharged soldiers could do. The whole of the reverse is covered with this information.
2. Army Form B.128 Certificate of Discharge. This certificate details his place of birth, (Chatham) enlistment (Rochester age 14 years), service, and physical description on discharge.
3. A letter dated 11.01.1921 from Wiltshire regiment old comrades association.
4. A Soldier's Farewell typed document of his farewell.

Extract from A Soldier's Farewell:

A most pleasing event happened at Fort George last evening, though not without a touch of sadness. Sergt J.Quin had completed his 21 years of service in the regiment and his comrades bade him farewell at a smoking concert in the mess. Sergt-Major Grant presided and the first part of the evening was given over to harmony, the following being a list of the singers :- Sergt. Neale "Safe in his father's home, "Sergt Light "Mary Maloney", Sergt Smith "Nora O'Grady, Segt Cook "I do believe", Sergt- Major Grant "Jolly Smiths", Mr Fuller "Off to sleep" the Quarter-Master-Sergeant "Charge of the Light Brigade," Sergt. Jacobs "Sucking Cider." Sergt Worsan "Honest Heart," Sergt. Smith "Deal Old Pals," Mr Smythson "On the Ice."

During the eveng Sergt-Major Grant rose and propsed the health of Sergt. Quin, a very old comrade and member of the mess, whom they were all very sorry to lose. He had had a very honourable military career, having enlisted in May 1878, in the same year he went to South Africa, and served through the Zulu Campaign........

Drummers formed part of the rank and file but were normally paid more than privates, reflecting the skill in their job. Drummers had to be able to play as many as 150 different drum signals plus music. Some signals were for daily routines such as reveille and taptoo while others were for assembling, or summoning specific groups such as sergeants or officers.

And your duties didn't end there, at least in the army. As well as carrying and playing the drum, you were expected to carry ammunition supplies on the battlefield and act as a stretcher bearer. Sixteen drummers formed the corps of drums and were detailed two per company when operating in the field. Rifle regiments and Light Infantry had bugle corps.

99th Regiment

433	Beaven	G	1879	1031	Burke	M	1879	2155	Cook	T	1879
1067	Beckingham	T	1879	1198	Burrows	J	1879	1319	Cook	T.W	1879
1039	Behan	A	1879	1225	Burton	J.H	1879	999	Coombes	C	1879
2141	Belcher	C	1879	874	Burton	W	1879	977	Cooper	W	1879
1257	Bell	G	1879	968	Busby	A	1879	942	Cornish	J	1879
2142	Bell	T	1879	432	Burcher	C	1879	941	Cosh	H	1879
2261	Belt	J	1879	912	Butler	J	1879	1274	Costello	M	1879
2046	Bennett	A	1879	794	Byrne	D	1879		No medal. Penal servitude.		
2016	Bennett	G	1879	2147	Byrne	J	1879	419	Cox	J	1879
411	Bennett	H	1879		Discharged as incorrigible. No medal.			2098	Craig	D	1879
2017	Bernardi	G	1879r	2148	Caffull	R	1879	949	Craig	W.R	1879
2018	Berridge	G	1879	1164	Calnan	C	1879	2032	Creasey	F	1879
2262	Bestwick	W	1879	472	Cameron	A	No clasp	2157	Cronan	J	1879
2040	Bevis	R	1879	1901	Camille	H	1879	895	Crook	J	1879
1013	Biddle	W	1879	1148	Camille	J	No clasp	2158	Crowe	W	1879
2019	Bingham	C	1879	2013	Campbell	A	1879	1206	Cunningham	F	1879
2121	Birch	F.A	1879	2095	Campbell	C	1879	2033	Cunningham	W	1879
2143	Birmingham	J	1879	1134	Campbell	J	1879	1300	Curd	J	1879
2094	Black	H	1879	2096	Campbell	P	1879	2159	Cureton	J	1879
1880	Blackman	S	1879	1906	Carey	F	1879	716	Curnick	J	1879
2263	Blackwell	J	1879	1030	Carlton	A	1879	2099	Curran	J	1879
2021	Blagden	J	1879	2149	Carroll	J	1879	2160	Curtis	G	1879
1171	Blakely	H	1879	1147	Carroll	J	1879	2100	Cuthbert	A	1879
899	Blick	F	1879	707	Carter	H	1879	2161	Dale	F	1879
783	Bodman	J	1879	808	Carter	J	1879	321	Daley	J	1879
974	Bolwell	E	1879	1101	Cassin	J	1879	2034	Dance	T	1879
1152	Boot	T	1879	2025	Cavey	W	1879	2074	Darling	S	1879r
1054	Bowley	E	1879	2097	Chambers	S	1879	423	Dark	J	1879
983	Bowsher	S	1879	971	Champion	F	1879	887	Davis	C	1879
1071	Bowsher	W	1879	2026	Chapman	C	1879	2267	Davies	D	1879r
992	Box	J	1879	455	Chequer	G	1879	2269	Davies	H	1879
1223	Boyden	T	1879	853	Cherry	J	1879	2163	Davis	G	1879
1203	Brace	E	1879	2027	Chinery	F	1879	2268	Davis	G	1879
1050	Bradley	W	1879	785	Chivers	G	1879	2123	Davis	S.G.B	1879
774	Breech	A	1879	2265	Chivers	J	1879	1226	Dawson	E	1879
424	Brewer	F	1879	2028	Cirteene	D.A	1879	926	Day	J	1879
1934	Brewer	J	1879	2029	Clark	B.A	1879	1472	Deal	J	1879
580	Brewer	R	1879	1029	Clarke	G	1879	2164	Deboard	E	1879
1313	Bridgland	W	1879	2150	Clarke	G	1879	1657	Dee	T	1879
2144	Brindle	J	1879	2381	Clarke	J	No clasp	2035	Dennis	J	1879
936	Brinsden	D	1879	1344	Clarke	J.H	1879	2036	Denny	W	1879
2145	Brooks	W	1879	2122	Clarke	T	1879	2165	Depper	W	1879
2264	Brown	C	1879	2151	Clarkson	W	1879r	1905	Deverill	T	1879
2022	Brown	G	1879r	2030	Clay	W	1879	2162	Devenport	E	1879
	Forfeited. No reason shown.				1855	Cleary	J	1879	1237	Dewberry	A	1879
2146	Brown	H	1879	1202	Clements	J	1879	1241	Dine	R	1879
684	Brown	J	1879	2152	Clifford	R	1879	2073	Dixon	I	1879
2023	Brown	J	1879	2031	Clifton	W	1879	2166	Dolphin	F	1879
2385	Brown	J	No clasp	1997	Cochrane	J	1879	1038	Donohoe	C	1879
1040	Brown	W	1879	945	Cole	G	1879	2037	Donovan	E	1879r
2120	Brown	W	1879	1065	Cole	H	1879r	1921	Doughty	J	1879
2380	Buckingham	W	No clasp	1059	Collins	H	1879	946	Dredge	W	1879
2390	Buckland	W	No clasp	1024	Commane	W	1879	1911	Drew	J	1879
1201	Bunker	J	1879	2266	Concannon	C	1879	2101	Dungey	T	1879
2024	Burden	W	1879	2383	Connolly	J	1879	1258	Dunkerley	J	1879
1021	Burford	J	1879	920	Connor	A	1879	2167	Durbin	W	1879
650	Burge	J	1879	2153	Connors	J	1879	1179	Durnford	J	1879
1343	Burgess	J	1879	2154	Cook	C	1879	1721	Dwyer	C	1879
519	Burke	J	1879	2156	Cook	H.J	1879	2168	Dyson	B	1879

99th Regiment

2102	Eastwood	R	1879	1110	Godwin	W	No clasp r	1315	Hembrey	J	1879
697	Eatwell	A.W	1879	1019	Gough	J	1879	1112	Hempstead	A	1879
935	Eavis	J	1879	715	Gray	J	1879	2090	Herring	J	1879
956	Ebsworth	J	1879	1001	Green	C	1879	1000	Heslop	A	1879
1207	Eden	E	1879	2042	Green	E	1879r	970	Hicks	E	1879
1942	Edge	I	1879	2180	Greening	A	1879	993	Highman	J	1879
1278	Edgerton	R	1879	2181	Gregory	W	1879	1286	Higley	T	1879
1908	Edwards	J	1879	961	Griffin	W.T	1879	2047	Hill	F	1879
1196	Edwards	W	1879	1144	Groom	G	1879	1922	Hill	J	1879
867	Edwards	W	1879	1178	Guest	G	1879	2191	Hill	J	1879
1008	Elliott	E.F	1879	2043	Gudgeon	A.S	1879	1280	Hindley	J	1879
516	Elliott	F	1879	369	Gunn	P	1879	1479	Hislop	T	1879
2039	Elliott	R	1879	No medal. Deserted.				Discharged with ignominy. No trace of			
826	Ellis	J.C	No clasp	1322	Guy	J	No clasp	return of medal.			
No medal. Discharged with ignominy.				2182	Gwinn	W	1879	1266	Hockley	H	1879
2038	Ellis	J	1879	2273	Gwither	A	1879	2192	Hodges	J	1879
777	Elmes	J	1879	1035	Hacking	A	1879	896	Hodges	W	1879
2124	Embley	W	No clasp	1982	Hackwell	G	1879	1874	Hoeck	C	1879
990	Etheridge	G	1879	1333	Haddrell	A	1879	2193	Holland	T	1879
947	Evans	E.J	1879	975	Haddrell	W	1879	2048	Hollis	W.J	1879
1279	Evans	J	1879	764	Haines	J	1879	1166	Hopkins	A	1879
2169	Farmer	F	1879	765	Haines	J	1879	2049	Hopkins	J	1879
1230	Farrell	J	1879	2275	Haire	J	1879	2194	Hook	W	1879
523	Farrell	N	No clasp	913	Hale	H.J	1879	1129	Horner	W	1879
2170	Farrell	T	1879	2276	Hales	F	1879	1092	House	A	1879
2171	Farrell	W	1879	2044	Hall	J	1879	2159	Howell	J.P.E	1879
2270	Farrissey	T	1879	1063	Halliday	T	1879	2195	Howells	W	1879
2172	Faulkner	W	1879	1855	Hams	J	1879	1221	Hoyle	H	1879
768	Fell	H	1879	2183	Hancock	J	1879	1304	Hubbard	H	1879
964	Feltham	H.J	1879	2103	Handley	F	1879	2050	Hudson	W	1879
1909	Ferris	H	1879	2157	Hankins	G	1879	1097	Hughes	J	1879r
937	Ferris	J	1879	2125	Hanks	J	1879	1907	Hulbert	D	1879
2173	Finney	T	1879	2045	Harding	G	1879	1111	Humm	F	1879
2174	Fippins	G	1879	1170	Harper	A	1879	2091	Humprey	F	1879
2041	Fisher	J	1879	A duplicate medal and clasp issued to				718	Humphries	L	1879r
2040	Fisher	J	1879r	him as a Sergeant.				769	Hunt	J	1879
1270	Flanaghan	M	1879	2184	Harper	W	1879	2278	Hunt	W	1879
2175	Fletcher	E	1879	2185	Harper	W	1879	1194	Hunter	W	1879
511	Fletcher	G	1879	1020	Hartland	J	1879	2277	Hutchinson	J	1879
1159	Foster	G	1879	2188	Hartland	W	1879	1022	Hutton	C	1879
950	Fox	H	1879	1150	Harrison	T	1879	2196	Hyman	H	1879r
914	Frayling	T	No clasp	2186	Harris	A	1879r	2127	Ivey	J	1879
2271	Freeman	C	1879	Convicted of willful murder.				736	James	H	1879
2272	Garlock	J	1879	1177	Harris	C	1879	949	James	J	1879
1342	Garney	J	1879	2046	Harris	J	1879	2197	James	T	1879
2176	Garrish	H.W	1879	2187	Harris	J	1879	1242	Jarman	A	1879
2177	Gavan	J	1879	669	Harvey	J	1879	2198	Jarman	G	1879
940	Gibbons	C	1879	1047	Harwell	E	1879	995	Jefferies	W	1879
2179	Gibbons	T	1879	1200	Harwood	J	1879	2199	Jenkins	G	1879
2178	Gibbs	A	1879	1002	Hethersmith	L	1879	2200	Jenkins	W	1879
2051	Giblin	P	1879	1186	Hawkett	J	1879	2201	Jennings		1879r
1290	Gill	J	1879	1190	Hawton	J	1879	2128	Johns	A	1879
1214	Gilligan	J	1879	2126	Hayes	T	1879	389	Johnson	J	1879
1292	Glasoon	G.H	1879	1302	Haylor	G	1879	2051	Johnson	W.J	1879
1048	Glen	H	1879	1240	Haylor	R	1879	900	Johnston	C	1879
2274	Glennon	J	1879	2027	Haynes	J	1879r	878	Johnstone	G	1879
1069	Godden	J	1879	1291	Healey	J	1879	1289	Jones	D	1879
929	Godwin	G	No clasp	894	Hedges	W	1879	2202	Jones	G	1879
No medal. Discharged with ignominy.				2190	Heeks	W	1879	2052	Jones	H	1879

99th Regiment

1124	Jones	H	1879	1912	Long	W	1879	2283	Morgan	D	1879
2204	Jones	J	1879	1168	Longhurst	J	1879	909	Morris	H	1879
*908	Jones	J	1879	667	Love	P	1879	2110	Morris	T	1879
D/S 3rd March 1879 Fort Pearson				2260	Lowe	J	1879	907	Mould	E	1879
2203	Jones	J	1879	1162	Lyons	J	1879	1246	Mulcahy	J	1879
1158	Jones	P	1879	2213	Mack	J	1879	1058	Mulcahy	J	1879r
1308	Jones	R	1879	2058	Makings	W	1879	1092	Muldoon	J	1879
2279	Jones	W	1879	2059	Mann	D	1879	2111	Mullen	J	1879
2105	Jordan	J	1879	1234	Manning	G	1879r	508	Munday	F	1879
1061	Joyce	P	1879	1006	Manning	H	1879	2061	Munn	C	1879
1468	Keefe	O	1879	1125	Mansbridge	J	1879	1046	Munn	J	1879
1231	Kelly	J	1879	2384	Markey	F	No clasp	2221	Murphy	D	1879
2122	Kelly	J	1879	546	Marks	G	1879	1011	Murphy	J	1879
666	Kelly	T	1879	2214	Mason	J	1879	2054	Murphy	P	1879
2053	Kempton	D	1879	2215	Matthews	G	1879	1296	Murphy	T	1879
2205	Kenealy	M	1879	1227	Matthews	J	1879	668	Murphy	W	1879
1282	Kennedy	J	1879	2109	Matthews	J	1879	No medal. Deserted.			
2280	Kennedy	T	1879	2107	Mc Allister	W	1879	787	Nally	J	1879
948	Kent	J	1879	1216	Mc Carroll	R	1879r	628	Nash	E	1879
2028	Kent	W	1879	789	Mc Carney	J	1879	693	Nash	G	1879
1009	Keyes	E	1879	1016	Mc Carthy	J	1879	1883	Neate	H	1879
2106	Keyes	T	1879	2282	Mc Carthy	J	1879	1253	Needham	W	1879
1909	Kimber	J	1879	1249	Mc Cauley	M	1879	1027	Neven	J	1879
1109	Kimber	J	1879	386	Mc Donald	J	1879	518	Newell	J	1879
1790	Kimber	J.M	1879	747	Mc Donnell	P	1879	1310	Newman	C	1879
1930	King	D	1879	1023	Mc Donnell	W	1879	1173	Newman	F	1879
967	King	G	1879	2212	Mc Dowell	H	1879	735	Newman	J	1879
1183	King	G	No clasp	1232	Mc Garrey	T	1879	2222	Newstead	J	1879
889	King	J	1879	1213	Mc Gowran	F	1879	1908	Nicol	A	1879
1865	King	J	1879	794	Mc Guinness	J	1879	963	Nicholas	T	1879
2056	King	W	1879	799	Mc Guire	J	1879	1986	Nicholson	J	1879
2206	Kings	M	1879	2108	Mc Laughlin	J	1879	1281	Nunnerley	J	1879
2055	King	W	1879	724	Mc Laughlin	P	1879	1174	Nye	H	1879
996	Kirby	H.S	1879	1060	Mc Nally	P	1879	1205	Oakley	C	1879
2387	Kirby	J	No clasp	436	Mc Pate	J	1879	1244	O'Brien	J	1879
1331	Knee	W	1879	482	Mc Taggart	J	1879	1197	O'Connor	D	1879
2207	Knott	J	1879	1261	Mead	G	1879	1218	O'Leary	D	1879r
2208	Lacey	T	1879	1167	Medhurst	J	1879	Medal forfeited. No reason shown.			
A duplicate medal and clasp issued on 12/1/22.				1960	Melville	J	1879	361	Orchard	T	1879
				2216	Middleton	S	1879	2223	Orchard	W.H	1879
771	Lake	W	1879	2391	Mildon	T	No clasp	*866	Painter	W	1879
1254	Lane	T	1879	2217	Miller	W	1879	86 D/S Pte W Paynter Fort Pearson.			
1076	Lannan	J	1879	2218	Millicheap	T	1879	624	Parker	J	1879
1263	Large	T	1879	2060	Millings	J	1879	1180	Parsons	W	1879
1932	Lawrence	J	1879	1172	Mills	E.J	1879	2224	Patchett	E	1879
2035	Leary	J	1879	1923	Minety	E	1879r	1132	Paul	J	1879
841	Lee	T	1879	1050	Minshall	G	1879	1068	Payne	C	1879
1332	Lee	T.H	1879	962	Mizen	W	1879	1153	Payne	F.W.E	1879
1330	Lee	W	1879	502	Molloy	J	1879	2225	Payne	G	1879
1915	Lemon	E.J	1879	No medal. Deserted.				966	Payne	J.P	1879
872	Leonard	E.J	1879	1175	Moloney	P	1879	2226	Paynter	J	1879
2386	Lever	H	No clasp	1295	Moloney	W	1879	938	Pearce	A	1879
61	Lewis	B	1879	2219	Montgomery	J	1879	2062	Pearce	A	1879
2057	Lewis	H	1879	1010	Montgomery	R	1879	1937	Pearce	H	1879
2210	Lewis	T	1879	1074	Moore	G.J	1879	2063	Pearson	J	1879
2281	Leyshon	D	1879	1139	Moore	J	1879	712	Peirce	J	1879
2211	Linnett	T	1879	2220	Moore	J	1879	780	Percey	J	1879
1268	Littlewood	H	1879	1037	Moran	M	1879	2064	Pepper	E	1879
1106	Long	R	1879	1163	Moran	M	1879	980	Perrett	J	1879

99th Regiment

No.	Name	Initial	Year	No.	Name	Initial	Year	No.	Name	Initial	Year
2066	Peterson	P	1879	1228	Ryan	P	1879	2068	Stanton	R	1879
1176	Phelan	G	1879	2852	Ryan	T	1879	2076	Steel	E	1879
1072	Phillimore	W	1879	887	Sadler	J	1879	1026	Stevens	A	1879
1287	Phillips	D	1879	2129	Sadler	J	1879	834	Stevens	J	1879
788	Philpott	C	1879	2238	Sadler	T	1879	2393	Stevens	T	No clasp
1321	Pickett	F	1879	2112	Sampson	S	1879	1189	Stiff	J	1879
1088	Pickett	W.J	1879	2287	Samuel	T	1879	1299	Still	F	1879
414	Pinchin	F	1879	2239	Sankey	J	1879	1079	Stocks	W	1879
2388	Pinfold	J	No clasp	2240	Saunders	H	1879	1062	Stone	D	1879
1157	Pike	J	1879	1041	Saunders	S	1879	1034	Stroad	G.D	1879
919	Plank	A	1879	2286	Savage	T	1879	1081	Stroad	J	1879
973	Plank	G	1879	1664	Scandlin	J	1879		Duplicate medal and clasp issued		
979	Polden	J	1879	1884	Screech	J	1879		17/5/1926.		
965	Poolman	A	1879	2069	Score	W	1879 r	773	Stroad	T	1879
984	Poolman	C	1879		Medal forfeited. Convicted by Court			2247	Styles	C.J	1879
2227	Potter	F	1879		Martial.			1793	Sullivan	C	1879
1918	Pound	C	1879	1191	Seamons	W.J	1879	792	Sullivan	E	1879
2284	Power	F	1879	714	Selman	L	1879	2248	Sullivan	J	1879
1243	Prendergast	M	1879	1307	Sergeant	T	1879		No medal. Discharged with incorrigible.		
2228	Price	G	1879	2070	Sewell	W	1879	1085	Summers	J	1879
2229	Price	J	1879	994	Seymour	J	1879	1154	Swann	H	1879
2230	Price	L	1879	681	Shanley	B	1879	1320	Swann	J	1879
1285	Price	R	1879	2241	Share	W	1879	2077	Swann	P	1879
2065	Prior	J	1879	1014	Sharp	J	1879	1306	Tamsett	T	1879
2231	Pugh	E	1879	45	Shaw	J	1879	1303	Tanner	C	1879
	Forfeited. No trace of return of the medal.			2242	Shaw	J	1879	1239	Taylor	J	1879
888	Pullen	F	1879		Deserted. No medal.			1318	Taylor	S	1879
1797	Pursey	R	1879	1536	Shay	J	1879	1869	Teeder	T	1879
2379	Quinn	J	No clasp	1032	Shaylor	A.B	1879	1861	Thomas	J	1879
1264	Rackstraw	J	1879	2071	Shephard	F	1879	1163	Thompson	J	1879
2392	Rand	J	No clasp	2243	Shephard	J	1879	1323	Thompson	W	1879
1195	Ratcliff	W.J	1879	1497	Shields	J	1879	2078	Thorburn	W	1879
2232	Raybould	H.F	1879	1149	Sibley	S	1879	883	Tombs	G	1879
2061	Read	J	1879	1064	Simmons	F	1879	2115	Trennam	A	1879
2234	Reading	T	1879	2072	Simpson	T	1879	833	Trimby	J	1879
2233	Reaney	J	1879	1192	Singleton	H	1879	400	Trottmann	T	1879
2092	Reddin	J	1879	989	Slade	J	1879	1057	Tubb	J	1879
1871	Redman	J	1879	1133	Sloane	G	1879	742	Tucker	W	1879
1145	Rees	W	1879	2073	Smart	J	1879	2249	Tully	R.W	1879
916	Reeves	A	1879	2288	Smith	A	1879	1176	Turner	F	1879
1004	Reid	G	1879	2074	Smith	F	1879	757	Turner	J	1879
2067	Rey	J	1879	2075	Smith	F	1879	1210	Turner	T	1879
2235	Rhodes	S	1879	1879	Smith	G	1879	2131	Turner	W	1879
2236	Rice	P.G	1879	329	Smith	H	1879	2076	Twine	W	1879
481	Rigsby	J	1879	1102	Smith	J	1879	1870	Underwood	E	1879
985	Robins	W	1879	1245	Smith	J	1879	397	Uphill	H	1879
698	Robbins	W	1879	2244	Smith	J	1879	2161	Upson	W	1879
1156	Robinson	E	1879	2289	Smith	J	1879	2079	Varley	H	1879
1590	Robson	J	1879	1633	Smith	R	1879	1288	Venn	T	1879
2285	Robson	T	1879r	1056	Smith	T	1879	2116	Vickers	J	1879
982	Roche	J	1879	2245	Smith	T	1879	1939	Vickery	F	1879r
1283	Roden	J	1879	2290	Smith	T.A	1879	2080	Vickery	G	1879
884	Rogers	C	1879	890	Smith	W	1879	2250	Wakeman	G	1879
1070	Rogers	D	1879	1933	Spackman	A.W	1879	1910	Waldron	A	1879
1857	Rothwell	W	1879	986	Spackman	H	1879	957	Walker	G	1879
1136	Rowan	P	1879	2013	Spain	J	1879	470	Walker	T	1879
2237	Rowberry	T	1879	1888	Spanner	A	1879	2251	Wall	J	1879
1151	Rumbelow	H	1879	2114	Spencer	F	1879	2081	Waller	G.E	1879
1005	Ryan	J	1879	2120	Stagg	J	No clasp	2252	Walliker	F.W	1879

99th Regiment

2253	Walsh	P	1879	2133	Wood	J	1879	
1459	Walsh	R	1879	2134	Wood	P	1879	
1045	Walter	E	1879	\multicolumn{3}{l	}{No Medal. Deserted.}		
2082	Warder	W	1879	2259	Woodhouse	J	1879	
309	Warry	E	1879	1146	Woodlock	J	1879	
1868	Warwick	G	1879	2292	Worthington	T	1879	
891	Watkin	J	1879	1127	Wren	T	1879	
2254	Watton	F	1879	2089	Wright	G	1879	
2132	Weadon	J	1879	1925	Wright	R	1879	
784	Webb	F	1879	918	Wright	T.J	1879	
1856	Webb	F	1879	1075	Yeates	H	1879	
927	Webb	G	1879	1881	Young	C.R	1879	
2255	Webber	T.W	1879	2090	Young	J	1879	

No medal. Deserted.

2092	Webster	U	1879
1209	Weir	H	1879
1816	Weir	H	No clasp
#1260	West	C	1879
906	Westover	G	1879
539	Whale	J	1879
673	Wheeler	F	1879
2291	Wheeler	R	1879r
1018	Whiley	T	1879
1940	White	J	1879
750	White	W	1879
2083	White	W	1879
2084	White	W	1879
1314	Whitehead	E	1879
1236	Whitehead	M	No clasp
2256	Whitehead	W	1879
2085	Whiteway	H	1879
2117	Whitfield	J	1879
2086	Whitwell	J	1879
1298	Wickenden	T	1879r
1979	Wilkins	W.G	1879
2378	Wilkinson	T	No clasp
1273	Williams	E	1879

No Medal. Discharged as incorrigible.

1083	Williams	H	1879
2257	Williams	H	1879
1108	Williams	J	1879
2258	Williams	S	1879
1089	Williams	T	1879
944	Williamson	F	1879
535	Willmott	J	1879
1204	Wilson	J.R	1879
2118	Wilson	W	1879
2087	Wilson	W	1879r
976	Witshire	C	1879
664	Wise	E	1879
2119	Wise	J	1879
2088	Wood	H	1879

* London Gazette 23 May 1879

103rd (ROYAL BOMBAY FUSILIERS) REGIMENT.
CAPTAIN
Pally-Clarke E.L 1879
See also Commissariat & Transport Staff.
LIEUTENANT
Dick J.R 1879

104th (BENGAL FUSILIERS) REGIMENT.
CAPTAIN & DAA & QMG
Spalding H 1877-8-9
Also had Indian Mutiny Medal.
CAPTAIN
Liptrott J 1879
Also had Medal for Ashanti War 1874.

107th (BENGAL INFANTRY) REGIMENT.
CAPTAIN
Cavaye W.F 1879
PRIVATE
1545 Bronkhurst J No clasp

108th (MADRAS INFANTRY) REGIMENT.
CAPTAIN
Justice P No clasp
See also 57th Regiment.

109th (BOMBAY INFANTRY) REGIMENT.
CAPTAIN
Vanrenen E 1879

RIFLE BRIGADE (THE PRINCE CONSORTS OWN)
CAPTAIN
Somerset A.H.T.H No clasp
Also had Medal for Ashanti 1874 with Clasp Comassie.
LIEUTENANT
Hardy D/S 1879

WEST INDIA REGIMENT 1st
CAPTAIN
Ellis A.B 1879

ARMY HOSPITAL CORPS
LIEUTENANT OF ORDERLIES
Cox C.A 1879
Also had medal and clasps for Taku Forts and Pekin and medal for Long and Meritorious Service.
Gorman L No clasp
Also had British and Turkish Crimea medals.
Hall A.W 1879
KIA Isandhlawana.

	Horn	J	1879
	Johnson	H	No clasp
	Marshall	J.D	No clasp
	Mc Greal	F	1879
	Mc Intyre	D	No clasp

Also had Abyssinia Medal 1867-1868.

	Pike	W	1879
	Sylvester	H.J	1877-8
	Troy	J	1879

D/S 8/10/1879.

COLOUR SERGEANT

2315	Campion	W	1879
2311	Daxon	E	1877-8
2926	Lally	T	No clasp
1328	Maltby	S	No clasp
2470	Nolan	W	No clasp
1273	Woodhouse	S	1879

SERGEANT

3591	Bampton	J	No clasp
1608	Barnes	H	1877-8
2040	Barry	R	No clasp
2051	Bateman	J	No clasp
3551	Brake	T	1879
2900	Broughton	J	1879
2577	Colston	H	No clasp
3408	Cox	J.T	No clasp
2111	Dear	C.F	No clasp

\# Dixons on line Sales List November 2009 http://www.dixonsmedals.co.uk/
South Africa Medal 1877-1879, 1 clasp, 1879. 1260 Private C. West, 99th Foot Cost £460
The Regiments most notable action was when the Headquarters and three companies were besieged by a large force of Zulus at the fortified Mission Station at Eshowe from Thursday 23rd Jan to Thursday 3rd April 1879

\#\# Lieutenant of Orderlies Arthur William HALL - Army Hospital Corps killed at Isandlwana, 22nd January 1879. Aged 37. Son of Joshua Hall, of Norwich.

Army Hospital Corps

Number	Surname	Initial	Clasp
1789	Douche	M	No clasp
2039	Dowling	E	1879
3530	Eastbourne	P	1879
2312	Fawell	J	No clasp
1874	Glynn	W.P	No clasp r
	Forfeited. No reason given.		
2274	Gurney	J	No clasp
2175	Haymes	R	No clasp
2701	Hewitt	M.J	No clasp
559	Hunt	D	1877-8
?	Marshall	A	1879r
?	Mc Gill	J	1879
3523	Melville	J.H	No clasp
2678	Merritt	G	No clasp
3169	Miller	R.H	No clasp
2687	Milner	W.E	1879
3088	Moore	H	1879
2494	Morris	J.H	1879
3303	Raworth	W	1879
2101	Smith	E.B	1877-8-9
2284	Thurgood	J	1879
2060	Thurston	F	No clasp
3020	Walter	A	1879
3700	Welford	W	1879
2132	West	R	1879
2047	Wood	H.F	1879
2693	Wright	G	No clasp

LANCE SERGEANT

| 1692 | Baker | J | 1877-8 |

CORPORAL

2738	Allen	T	No clasp
3180	Bannister	W	1879
2382	Carrusthers	R	No clasp
3597	Cross	J	No clasp
2334	Douglas	W	1879
3415	Foote	C	1879
3925	Harris	C	1879
3521	Hassell	H	1879
3021	Jackman	C.H	No clasp
2946	Jackson	R	No clasp
2393	Lee **KIA**	J	1879
2540	Marston	T	1879
3712	Mathews	J	No clasp
2793	Mc Leod	H	No clasp r
2664	Mc Nulty	J	No clasp
3221	Murray	J	1879
2809	Osborne	C	1879
3511	Pollock	R	No clasp
2536	Reilly	J	No clasp
3670	Sellex	G	1879
3571	Smith	F	1879
3453	Voss	G	1879
3446	Watkins	J.C	1879
2986	Watts	T	No clasp
3909	Welch	A	1879
3689	Whitehead	J	1879

2nd CORPORAL

2440	Addicutt	J	1879
3332	Bell	R.A	1879
3534	Brodie	W	1879
1524	Brown	G	1879
3311	Clarkson	L	No clasp
1573	Dillingham	J	1879r
3371	Ennis	J	1879
1514	Fearn	R	1879
3077	Green	W	1877-8
1906	Humphries	J	No clasp
3037	Luddington	T	1879
#3359	Mc Mahon	M	1879
	No medal. Deserted.		
3563	Mehern	T	No clasp
2648	Nock	G	1879
2307	Penny	G	No clasp
2149	Reid	J	No clasp
1298	Stevens	E	No clasp
1957	Thatcher	J	No clasp
3257	Thompson	J	1879
840	Turner	H	No clasp r
2164	Walker	F	No clasp
2336	Warman	J	No clasp
2415	Warren	A	No clasp
2169	Wheeler	G	No clasp
3071	Whitehorn	C	No clasp
1862	Whitehorn	J	No clasp
2712	Witherow	S	1879
2568	Woods	T	No clasp

LANCE CORPORAL

2622	Amor	J	1877-8-9
3269	Brigham	J	1877-8-9
3031	Brown	J	No clasp
2075	Cripps	J	No clasp
2365	Davies	M	1879
2392	Garner	T	1879
2330	James	H	No clasp
2496	Mitchell	J	1879
2851	Page	W	No clasp
?	Ransley	J.H	1879
2260	Shanley	M	1879
2568	Woods	T	No clasp

PRIVATE

3896	Allen	C	1879
3639	Allwright	W.L	No clasp
	No medal. Discharged with ignominy.		
2938	Ambrose	C	No clasp
3795	Andus	H.J	No clasp
1879	Angell	W	1879
3609	Annis	E.K	1879
3703	Arnold	A	1879r
3191	Ashall	T	1879
3919	Austin	S	1879
3456	Avery	J	No clasp
3305	Bagley	J	1879

3917	Bailey	J	No clasp
3941	Bailey	R	No clasp r
	Forfeited. No reason given.		
3148	Baker **KIA**	G	1879
3769	Baker	H	1879
3532	Ballentine	J.R	No clasp
3361	Bamford	J	No clasp r
3159	Barentyen ?	P	1879
2518	Barker	W	1879
4010	Barnes	D.R.B	1879
3728	Barrett	C	1879
3094	Beale	T	No clasp
3434	Bennett	C	1879
3977	Benson	J	1879
	Forfeited. No reason shown. No record of medal being returned.		
2588	Berry	W	No clasp
3508	Bibby	E	No clasp r
3654	Blackman	E	1879
3122	Boal	T	No clasp
3500	Bogie	N.L	No clasp
3504	Bonny	W	1879
3790	Bowden	J.A	1879
3897	Bowles	W.J	1879
2595	Bradley	J	1879
3316	Brocklesby	J	1879r
3170	Brooks	J	1879
3244	Broomhead	J	1879
2833	Broughton	P	No clasp
2787	Brunning	J	No clasp
3801	Bryant	W	1879
1955	Burfoot	J	No clasp
2245	Burke	U	1879
3895	Burley	A	No clasp
3463	Burrows	H	1879
	Deserted. No trace of return of the medal.		
3848	Butcher	T.J	1879
3201	Cain **KIA**	A	1879
3952	Cain	J	No clasp
2771	Callard	W.H	1879
3906	Campbell	J	1879
2641	Cann	S	1879
2726	Canning	C	No clasp
3920	Cannon	W	1879
3324	Cantwell	M	1879
3177	Canute	S	1879r
2090	Carpenter	F	1879
3396	Chapple	C	No clasp
2659	Cherrington	G	1879
3612	Chipperfield	E.W	1879
3539	Christie	R.J	No clasp
3413	Clarke	J	No clasp
3912	Clarke	R	1879
3824	Clarke	S	1879
3684	Codd	H	1879

3359 Michael McMahon - Award of Distinguished Conduct Medal; SQ 15.1.80; Rorke's Drift 22-23.1.79; award cancelled SQ 29.1.80 (absence without leave and theft) Ref P.E.Abbott

Army Hospital Corps

3400	Colley	J	1879	2675	Ginn	F.W	No clasp	No medal. Deserted.			
3246	Collins	C	1879	3890	Girling	J	1879	3666	Keefe	J	1879
3231	Connell	E	No clasp	3913	Gladson	H	No clasp	3358	Kelly	J	1879
3442	Conroy	J	1879	4003	Godfrey	G	No clasp	2665	Kelly	R	No clasp
3713	Coombs	H	No clasp	3193	Goldby	C	No clasp	3552	Kennedy	G	1879
2224	Cope	G.J	No clasp	3949	Gordon	E	No clasp	2543	Keyse	J	1877-8
3904	Cope	T	No clasp	3454	Gorman	T	No clasp	3815	Kiernan	O	1879
3135	Cornish	H	No clasp	3908	Grafton	H	1879	3697	Killian	E	No clasp
2888	Cornwell	E	No clasp	3967	Grant	J	1879	3796	King	W	1879
3768	Cottie	G	1879r	2859	Gray	F	1879	2925	Kings	H	No clasp
3804	Cox	C.H	No clasp	3321	Green	T	No clasp	2666	Kingsland	J	No clasp r
3136	Cox	G	1879	2488	Grieve	G.J	No clasp	3930	Kirkham	A	1879
2083	Cremer KIA	A	1879	3259	Grimes	M	1879	2642	Lakey	W	No clasp
4011	Crofton	G	No clasp	2038	Grist	P	1877-8	3667	Lane	J	No clasp
3308	Crook	A	1879	3383	Grogan	J	1877-8-9	2625	Lanning	G.E	1877-8-9
3709	Crosby	J	1879	3681	Guess	F.C	1879	3788	Laurie	P	No clasp
3329	Curran	J	No clasp	2765	Guilfoyle	E	1879	3665	Lawrence	A	No clasp r
3557	Curtis	J	1879	2692	Hackett	D	No clasp	Forfeited.			
3968	Dales	G	1879	3475	Halfpenny	J	No clasp	3905	Lawrence	P	1879
3256	Daley	J	No clasp r	3112	Halker	C	No clasp	3574	Lawrence	W.T	1879
4037	Dalton	G	No clasp	3119	Halkett	D	No clasp	3938	Leatham	J	1879
1956	Davies	E	1879	3301	Halls	J	1879	2695	Lewis KIA	H.W	1877-8-9
2671	Davies	G	No clasp	3380	Handcock	W	1879	3879	Lima	F.W	No clasp
4095	Dawson	J	1879	3636	Hanson	S	No clasp	3623	Linnett	J	1879
3147	Deane KIA	J	1879	3564	Harber	W	No clasp	3873	Linsell	G	No clasp
3548	Dickson	S.C	No clasp	3291	Harding	C	1879r	No medal. Deserted.			
3990	Dobson	H	No clasp	2656	Harding	E	1879	3946	Linton	J	1879
3086	Dolphin	W	No clasp	2956	Hargreaves	W	1879	3976	Lloyd	J	1879
2865	Dove	H	No clasp	3575	Harlow	F.H	1879	3282	Lock	W	1877-8-9
3588	Drage ?	G	No clasp	3653	Harris	H	1879	3841	Logan	G	No clasp
3736	Drury	R	1879	3128	Harris	J	1879	3427	Lovell	W	1879
3625	Eckhoff	H	No clasp	3733	Harrison	T	No clasp	3281	Lowe	A	1879
2176	Edge	F	1879	4002	Haselton	G	No clasp	3168	Ludwig	E.A	1879
3355	Edge	J	No clasp	3800	Hawkins	J	No clasp	3460	Lynch	J	1879
2932	Edgcombe	T	No clasp	3515	Hayling	T	No clasp	3152	Lynch	J.J	1879
3138	Edwards	J	1879	3239	Heasell	T	No clasp	3568	Madigan	P	1879
3931	Edwards	T	1879r	3045	Heath	S	No clasp	3812	Mahon	T	No clasp
3544	Ellingwood	L.C	1879	3746	Heenan	J	1879	3394	Manning	F	1879
2965	Ellis	R	1879	3487	Hefferman	E	1879	3661	Mansell	J	1879
3426	Elphick	W	1879	3679	Hodgson	W	1879	3846	Marlow	T	1879
3621	Emery	R	1879	3290	Hogan KIA	J	1879	3833	Martin	W.H	1879
3871	Fagan	T	1879	3960	Hopson	A	1879	3097	Maxwell	J	No clasp
3910	Fairbairn	J	No clasp	3330	Howell	W	1879	3205	Mayell	G	1879
2821	Farrelly	J	No clasp	3139	Howes	J	1879	3747	Maythorn	E	No clasp
4030	Farmer	J	No clasp	3345	Howick	G	No clasp	2598	Mc Cann	N	1879
3518	Fawcett	J	1879	2215	Hudson	A	1879	3978	Mc Connon	R	No clasp
3965	Fisher	H	No clasp	3421	Hughes KIA	J	1879	2796	Mc Donald	J	1878
3326	Fitzgerald	J	No clasp	2269	Humprey	W	1879	3971	Mc Dowell	J	1879
3425	Fivey	G	No clasp	3934	Hustwick	T	No clasp	3847	Mc Dowell	p	No clasp
3005	Flanagan	J	No clasp	2872	Hyland	J	No clasp	3438	Mc Garvey	W	1879
2884	Francis	W	No clasp	4094	Inge	W	1879	3422	Mc Gill	J	1879
2827	Franks	J	No clasp	3822	Jackson	J	No clasp r	2376	Mc Govern	J	No clasp r
3581	Fraser	H	1879	Deserted.				3558	Mc Leod	N	No clasp
3155	Frizzel	P	No clasp	3664	Jackson	T	No clasp	3859	Mc Pherson	J	No clasp
3878	Frost	J.W	1879	3356	Johnstone	H	No clasp	4033	Mc Williams	D	1879
3627	Futcher	E	1879	3711	Jones	A	1879	2667	Medler	A	No clasp
3791	Gardner	G	No clasp	3233	Jones	T.H	1879	3513	Meredith	J	No clasp
3719	Gillispie	R	1879	2367	Jordan	S	1879	2279	Merrill	H	No clasp
2852	Gillman KIA	J	1879	3710	Joyce	S.J	1879	2063	Middlebrook	J	1879

Army Hospital Corps

Number	Name	Initial	Year
3688	Miller	J	1879
3185	Miller	T	1879
3600	Mills	J	No clasp
3828	Mitchell	H	1879
3644	Mitchell	W	No clasp
3827	Money	L	1879
3214	Monaghan	P	1879
4015	Moore	A	1879
3918	Mower	T	1879
3891	Muldowney	H	1879
3354	Munn KIA	G.G	1879
3146	Munro	N	1879
4098	Murphy	E.A	No clasp
3845	Neill	H	No clasp
3634	Nicholson	T	No clasp
3360	Oakley	G	1879
2331	O'Callaghan	P	1879
3131	O'Neill	D	No clasp
3381	Page	W	No clasp
3350	Painter	W.H	No clasp
3258	Pattenden	E	1879
3686	Peel	G.B	No clasp
3198	Pearce	J	1879
4014	Penfold	G	No clasp
3836	Petherwick	J	1879
3783	Phillips	W	1879
3837	Piggott	R	1879
3154	Pike	J	No clasp
3677	Pimlott	H	No clasp
3406	Pollard	J.F	No clasp
2650	Pottle	T	1879
3223	Powell	G	1879
3114	Powell	G	1879
3973	Purtell	J	No clasp
3976	Quelch	T.J	No clasp
4012	Raymond	A.E	1879
2205	Read	C	1879
2069	Read	H	1879
3346	Reardon	J	1879
3496	Redding	T.J	1879r
3322	Reid	J	1879
3395	Reilly	P	1879
3843	Rendle	F	1879
3834	Richards	F	1879
3369	Richards	J	1877-8-9
3200	Rogers	J	1879
1915	Rose	T	No clasp
2448	Ryan	J	1879
3261	Ryan	T	No clasp
2313	Salmon	G	No clasp
3348	Saunders	W	No clasp

A duplicate medal issued 23/5/22.

Number	Name	Initial	Year
2873	Saunders	W	No clasp
3051	Sayer	J	1879
3474	Sayers	W	1879
3771	Sealey	G	No clasp
3489	Senior	C	1877-8r
2242	Shea	M	?
3786	Sheldrick	C	No clasp
2149	Smith	H	No clasp
3865	Smith	J	No clasp
3092	Staaer ?	T	1879
2971	Stacey	J	1879
3610	Stanton	E	1879
4004	Stevenson	A.G	1879
3864	Stevenson	J	1879
3565	Stock	A	No clasp
3418	Stokes	T	1877-8
2619	Stonehill	E	1877-8
3141	Stubbersfield	J	1879
3466	Sutton	G	No clasp
3226	Sweeney	J	1877-8-9
3980	Swift	W	1879
3888	Talbot	W	1879
3922	Taylor	A.K	1879
4006	Taylor	E	No clasp
3732	Taylor	J	1879r
3151	Thompson	T.J	No clasp
3762	Thornton	T	1879
3182	Tilly	J	No clasp
3832	Turner	E	1879
3809	Turner	F	1879
3903	Turner	F	1879
3618	Tyler	J	No clasp
2524	Underwood	G	1879
3911	Vale	W	1879
3404	Veir	F	1879
3985	Wadhams	N.J	1879
3659	Wadley	F.C	No clasp
3055	Wallace	F.W	No clasp
3704	Wallace	R	1879r Deserted.
2338	Waller	T	No clasp
3660	Weston	T	1879r
4009	Whelan	T	1879
2994	White	J	No clasp
3265	White	J	1879
2278	White	R	1879
3648	White	S.J	No clasp
3125	Whitehorn	G.W	1879
3536	Wilkenson	R	1879
2094	Williams	A	1879
4013	Williams	J	1879
3085	Willmott	J	1879
3866	Wilson	G.C	No clasp
4031	Wilson	J	1879
3268	Wilson	J	1879
2848	Wilson	N	No clasp
3585	Winchester	E.W	1879
3776	Wolfe	F	No clasp
2940	Wood	E.J	1879
3498	Woods	J	No clasp
3196	Woods	S	No clasp
3440	Wright	W	No clasp
2725	Wyatt	J	1879

ARMY MEDICAL DEPARTMENT
SURGEON GENERAL
Rose CIE J.T.C No clasp
Woolfryes CM CMG J.A 1877-8-9
Also had medal and clasp for Ashanti War 1873-4.

DEPUTY SURGEON GENERAL
Holloway CB J.L No clasp

SURGEON MAJOR
Name	Initial	Year
Alcock	N	1878
Ashton	G	1879
Babington	T	No clasp
Boulton	E.J	1879
Bourns	D.C.G	1879
Burnett	W.F	1879
Comerford	H	1879
Cuffe CB C. Mc D		1877-8-9
Dobson	G.E	No clasp
Dudley	W.E	1879
Edge MD	J.D	1879
Elgee	W	1879
Fitzmaurice	J	1878-9
Giraud	C.H	1879

Also had Baltic Medal 1855 and China medal and clasp Taku Rofts 1860.

Name	Initial	Year
Hare	R.W	No clasp
Hector	J	1879
Hickson	R.C.C	1877-8
Hodgson MD	D.F. de	1879
Hunt	J.H	1879
Ingham	W.J	No clasp
Jackson CB	R.W	1879

Also had British Crimea Medal and clasp, Turkish Crimea Medal, Indian Mutiny Medal and 3 clasps and Ashanti Medal 1843-4 and clasp.

Name	Initial	Year
Jennings MD	V.A	1879
Johnson	W	1878-9
Kerr MD	B.C	1879
Kilroy	P.L	1879
Lamb	H	No clasp

Also had medal for New Zealand 1863-65.

Name	Initial	Year
Leslie MD	D.A	No clasp

Also had medal and clasp for Bhootan 1865.

Name	Initial	Year
Mally	R.N	1879
Murphy	R	No clasp
Renton MD	D	1879
Reynolds VC	J.H	1877-8-9

The VC was awarded for Rorkes Drift.

Robertson VC J.H 1877-8-9
Also medal and clasp for Indian Mutiny.

Name	Initial	Year
Robinson	A.B	1879
Scott	F.B	1879
Semple	A	1879
Shepherd	P	1879

KIA Isandhlwana.

Army Medical Department

	Skeen	W	No clasp	Ward	E.C.R	No clasp	Woods	A.A	1879
	Smith	W.P	1879	Wilson MD	J.B	1879	**CIVIL PRACTITIONER**		
	Stafford	P.W	1879	Young	A.P	1877-8	Batchelor	?	1877-8

Also had medal and clasp for Ashanti War 1873-4.

				CIVIL SURGEON			Beviss	C	No clasp
	Stock	J.N	1879	Apthorp	F.W	1879	Campling	W.J.B	1877-8
	Townshead	E	1879	Beresford	W.H	1878-9	Chadwick	?	1878
	Tarrant MD	T	1878-9	Birdwood	R.A	1878-9	Clinton	S.A	1877-8

Also had British Crimea medal and clasp. Turkish Crimea Medal and Indian Mutiny Medal.

				Boomer	J.M.W	No clasp	Cumming	?	1877-8
				Brannigan	H.C	1879	D'Uminy	B.F	1877-8
	Wallace	J	No clasp	Burton	J.R	No clasp	Glanville	W.G.D	1879
	Ward	E	No clasp	Busby	A.R	1878-9	Gordon	J	No clasp

Also had medal for Ashanti War 1873-74.

				Cheyne	W.R	1879	Gunn	C	1879
				Clubbe	C.P.B	No clasp	Hall	B.W	1878
	Wills CB	C.S	No clasp	Cobbin **KIA**	W.J	1878-9	Hartley	A	1878

KIA Intombi River 12/3/79 attached 80th Regt.

SURGEON

							Hepworth	W.H	1878
	Anderson MD	J.A	1879				Hyde	S.C	No clasp
	Ash	R.V	No clasp	Connolly	P.B	1878-9	Jones	W.H	No clasp
	Brown	A.L	1878-9	Duncan	A.S	1879	Kay	J.A	1879
	Brown	D.B	1879	Garland	G.H	1878	Lindley	C.L	No clasp
	Bushe	C.J.L	1879	Giles	B.F	1878-9	Matthews	J.W	1878
	Connolly	B.B	No clasp	Giles	G.M	1878	Paley	J.H	1877-8

Also had German Steel War Medal for the Sedan 1870-71.

				Gill	J	No clasp	Palmer	?	1878
				Gordon	S.F	No clasp	Pearson	J.C	1877
	Cross	H.R.O	1879	Greer	T	1879	Peters	J	1877-8
	Dowman	J.F	No clasp	Gubbins	C.O'G	1879	Pope	C.E	1878
	Drury MD	R	1879	Hare	E.H	1879	Reed	S.C	1879
	Falvey	J.J	1879	Hartley	W.D	1878	Scott	W.J.S	No clasp
	Fraser	J	1879	Hayes	T.E.D	1878	Smith	F.A.A	1879
	Gasteen	W.C	No clasp	Heath	J.L	1879	Squire	?	1878
	Geoghegan	W	No clasp	Hebb	R.G	No clasp	Stevenson	E.S	1877
	Harding	A	1879	Illingworth	C.R	1879	Stoker	G	1879
	Heather	D.C.W	No clasp	Jennings	E	No clasp	Roll shows him as Doctor.		
	Jagoe	H	1879	Johnston	R.C	1879	Wilson	?	1878
	Jennings	C.B	1878	Jolly	R.W	1878-9	Young	J.W.S	1878
	Landon	A.J	1879	Jones	J.M	1879	# Zeederberg	?	1877-8
	Leake	G.D.N	No clasp	Leslie	A	No clasp	Ziervogel	J.F	1878
	Lloyd	O.E.P	1879	Lesslie	R.B	1879	**SUPERINTENDENT OF NURSES.**		
	Maartney	J	1877-8	Lewie	C.B	No clasp	Duble Mrs	J.C	No clasp
	Martin	J.W.O'M	1879	Linden	H.C	1879			
	Mc Gann	J	1879	Mansell	E.R	1878-9	**NURSE**		
	O'Reilly	J	1877-8-9	Mc Donald	W.C.C	No clasp	Armfield	M	No clasp
	Parkinson	R.C	No clasp	Moir	J.H	1878-9	Crips	A	No clasp
	Ring MD	J	No clasp	Mulligan	E.J	No clasp	Durham	E	No clasp
	Ritchie	J.L	1879	O'Callaghan	G.H.K	1879	Gray	J	No clasp
	Ryan	G	No clasp	O'Neill	J.G	1879	Hawkey	A	No clasp
	Saunders	W.E	No clasp	Reynolds	L.M	1878-9	Horner	E.A	No clasp
	Stokes	A.H	No clasp	Roberts	F.J	No clasp	Jerrard	J	No clasp
	Stokes	H.H	1879	Roe	C	No clasp r	King	E	No clasp
	Thornton	D	1879	Ryley	J.R	No clasp r	Ray	A	No clasp

Also medal and clasp Ashanti War 1873-74.

				Thrupp	J.G	1878-9	Selby	M	No clasp
				Twiss	G.E	1879	Strickland	M.A	No clasp
				Wardrop	D	1878-9	Wells	J	No clasp
	Usher	J.H	No clasp	Wilson	E.M	1879	Williams	H.W	No clasp

Also had medal and clasp for Ashanti War 1873-74.

				Wood	R.E	1879	**HOSPITAL DRESSER**		
				See also 2nd Battalion Natal Native Corps.			Armitage	G.F	1879
	Wallis	K.S	1879				Boyd	R.I	1879

Glendining's 19th March 1997 Lot No 53 South Africa 1877-1879, one bar, 1877-8 (Civil, Practr. **Zerderburg**, Very fine.(£300-400), Together with a passenger ticket dated 18 July 1911, no 136, for C.H. Zeederberg's Passenger and Parcel Service.

Army Medical Department

	Chevers	V.B	No clasp		Minchin	J.W	No clasp	C/1343	Craft	E	1877-9
	Gausseu	C.H	1879r		O'Brien	J.A.B	No clasp	C/3482	Eastland	W	1879
	Kennedy	R.L. de V	1879		Phillips	H.W	1879	C/3465	Finch	C.H	No clasp
	Portal	H.J	No clasp		See also 57th Regt.			C/3409	Fry	J	No clasp
	Schulz	A	1879		Ryders	H.C	No clasp	C/1084	Hibbert	F.W	No clasp
	Smith	W.N	No clasp		Stockley	J.C	1879	C/2465	Hinton	E	1877-8-9

1st CLASS INTERPRETER
Lantman J 1879
Nunn H.J 1879

Taylor F.N.J 1879 — C/2760 Hornblower W 1879
Tew J.N 1879 — C/951 Kelly W.J No clasp
See also 2/21st Regt. — Forfeited. No reason shown. Medal does not appear to have been returned.

INTERPRETER
Hollowell T 1879
Mc Alister J 1879

ACCOUNTANT
Brown E.N No clasp

ASSISTANT PAYMASTER
Addis J.E 1879 — C/1514 Lathey G 1877-8-9
Burgess H.W.K 1877-8-9 — C/1311 Pearson A 1879
Gleig A 1879 — C/2786 Peathers T.H No clasp
See also 1/13th Regt (A.C. Gleeg) — C/2631 Petty W 1879
Hardwick J 1879 — C/2490 Pilcher C 1877-8-9
Kaye W.R 1877-8 — C/3437 Robinson H No clasp
Williams R.K 1877-8 — C/1223 Rollings W.E 1879

ACTING PAYMASTER
Collins C.L.S 1877-8-9 — C/2639 Smith H 1879

TEMPORARY CLERK
Barnes F.E 1879
Collins E.L.S 1877-8-9
Kay H.D 1877-8
Page H.A 1879
Ross H.L 1877-8-9

ARMY PAY DEPARTMENT
The names seem to indicate that the roll is incomplete. Only Officers (apart from the temporary clerks) are listed. No WO's, NCO's or men appear; the roll is not complete.

LIEUTENANT COLONEL
Ball CB W.C No clasp

MAJOR
Forbes C.D.O 1877-8
Mahoney CMG J 1877-8-9
Also had China medal. See also 2/24 the Regt.
Morris M.K No clasp
Also had medal for Gwalior Campaign 1843.
White F.F 1877-8-9
KIA Isandhlwana. Also had medal for India.

CAPTAIN
Bacon T.W No clasp
Also had Crimea War Medal.
Balders C.M No clasp
Brockman W.L No clasp
Candwell W.D No clasp
See also 91st Regt.
Coppinger T.S No clasp
Dawson H.C No clasp
Drage T.W 1877-8
Elliott J.M No clasp
See also 94th Regt.
Elliott J.G No clasp
Gelston A.W.H 1879
See also 2/3 Regt. Also had Crimea Medal.
Gorges E.H 1877-8
Haye W.R 1877-8
Haynes E No clasp
See also 3/60th Regt.
Kaye W.R 1877-8
Mc Donald A.L No clasp

ARMY SERVICE CORPS.
COMMISSARIAT.

1st CLASS STAFF SERGEANT
C/1155 Hewish C 1879
C/1479 Jebb J.G 1879
C/3131 Mc Gonagil J No clasp
C/2459 Theobalds W No clasp

2nd CLASS STAFF SERGEANT
C/1448 Hibberd J 1877-8

3rd CLASS STAFF SERGEANT
C/2705 Allen W 1879
C/1251 Booth G No clasp
C/1968 Coombs T No clasp
C/3056 Gow A No clasp
C/2752 Heaney R No clasp
C/3410 Henderson J No clasp
C/1207 Hodgkins G.F 1879
C/1983 Mc Innes W No clasp
C/2665 Mc Lernon E 1879
C/2478 Sharpe J.L 1879
C/2840 Wallace W 1879

SERGEANT
C/2469 Attwood F 1879
Cpl Attwood ASC, DCM Rorke's Drift
C/1266 Broomhead H No clasp
C/3425 Cottle L.G No clasp

CORPORAL
C/2501 Coombs W 1879
C/1211 Cox S.W 1877-8
C/1315 Cryer F.P No clasp
C/1991 Dean A 1879
C/2634 Freeman H 1878-9
C/1387 Hunter H No clasp
C/3633 Johnson W 1879
C/3283 Mc Allister J 1879
C/1305 Nicol A No clasp
C/3383 Pointer J 1879
C/1562 Tull F.K No clasp

2nd CORPORAL
C/1748 Baker W.J 1879
C/1500 Breuer J 1877-8
C/1001 Day W 1879
C/1443 Dodd A No clasp
C/1873 Ferry W.A 1879
C/1188 Forsdick R 1879
C/958 Gleeson A.F 1877-8-9
C/1427 Golding W 1879
C/1434 Ivory H.J No clasp
C/2875 Mannings G 1879
C/2925 Rawlings W No clasp
C/1698 Shaughnessy M No clasp
C/1328 Smith W 1879
C/1912 Soane G 1879
C/2001 Tate G 1879
C/1599 Taylor H No clasp
C/1534 Welch A 1879
C/1297 Williams C No clasp

LANCE CORPORAL
C/1642 Allfree G No clasp
C/1517 Bailey J 1879
C/1626 Banks F.J No clasp
C/1964 Box W.F 1879

In 1869 the first Army Service Corps was formed from the Military Train, but was without its own officers, commanded firstly by the Control Department,, and then by the Commissariat and Transport Department. The first Army Service Corps was formed in 1888 and for the next seventy-seven years the transport and supply functions were to remain together and provide a vital service to the Army.

Army Service Corps Commissariat

Number	Name	Initial	Clasp/Year
C/3448	Bunton	J	1879
C/1854	Gibbs	W	No clasp
C/3634	Green	A.H	No clasp
C/1955	Harbinson	W.J	No clasp
C/1235	Horohan	H	No clasp
C/3417	Howard	F	No clasp
C/1406	Horley	J.T	No clasp
C/1593	Hunkittrick	W	1879
C/1149	Penton	E	No clasp
C/1536	Rice	C.W	1877-8
C/1473	Shepherd	H.J	No clasp
C/1824	Smith	A.J	1877-8-9
C/2017	Taylor	H	No clasp r

No Medal. Deserted.

BUGLER

C/1887	Clarke	J.C	No clasp

No medal. Discharged Bad Character

C/1700	Mc Cormick	W	No clasp

PRIVATE

C/1773	Aldrich	R	1879
C/1855	Aplin	W.H	1879
C/2002	Armstrong	J	1879
C/1848	Barnett	W.E	1879

No medal. Deserted.

C/1648	Beldham	T	1879
C/2381	Bishop	E	No clasp
C/3386	Bittle	H	1879
C/2007	Bodmer	J.J	1879
C/1635	Bonnett	J	1879
C/1615	Bourner	G	1879
C/1326	Brown	C.R	No clasp
C/1804	Butterfield	T	1879
C/1847	Buxton	E.J	1879
C/2851	Buxton	R	1879
C/3203	Carter	J.W	No clasp
C/2207	Chillcott	W	No clasp
C/1111	Clarkson	E	No clasp
C/952	Clegg	W	1879
C/1794	Cole	J	1879
C/1757	Cooper	J	1879
C/3382	Coppin	W	1877
C/1342	Craddock	R	No clasp r
C/1684	Dabbs	W	No clasp
C/1904	Darling	W	No clasp
C/2008	Edwards	G	1879
C/1478	Evans	T	1879

Duplicate Medal and clasp issued on 9/2/1927.

C/1717	Field	H	1879

Duplicate medal and clasp issued 10/11/1922.

C/1451	Filling	C.J	No clasp
C/1859	Fletcher	J	No clasp

Deserted. No indication of the withdrawal of the medal.

C/3614	Forsyth	A	1879
C/1705	Furbank	J	No clasp
C/1320	Gill	C.E	1879
C/1528	Gleeson	P	No clasp
C/1953	Gourlay	J	1879
C/1623	Gray	J.A	1879
C/1571	Grayland	R.G	1879
C/948	Guerin	P.J	1877-8
C/1133	Hambridge	W	1879
C/980	Hamilton	J	No clasp
C/1504	Harrison	C.J	No clasp
C/3221	Hartgrove	J	1879
C/1909	Hewson	H.J	No clasp
C/1026	Hunt	R	No clasp
C/3164	Jackson	W	1879
C/2691	Jarvis	G	No clasp
C/1923	Kelly	D	1879
C/1844	Kennedy	J	1879
C/1467	Kent	W.J	1879
C/1840	Leahy	E	1879
C/1975	Leslie	A	No clasp
C/956	Liston	D	1879
C/3330	Loader	G	No clasp

No medal. Deserted.

C/1201	Maile	W	No clasp
C/1112	Mallage	H	1879
C/1914	Mills	W.J	1879
C/1656	Montgomery	W.C	1879
C/1215	Moss	T	1879
C/2014	Nelson	F	1879
C/1875	Ovington	T	1879
C/1563	Page	H.J	1879
C/1646	Payne	J	1879
C/1299	Philpott	S.H	No clasp r
C/1385	Poynter	G.S	No clasp
C/2820	Read	D	No clasp
C/1814	Robertson	J	No clasp
C/1714	Robertson	J.J	No clasp r
C/1702	Sears	W	No clasp
C/3187	Skehan	T	No clasp
C/2464	Skelding	W.H	No clasp
C/1750	Smith	F	1879
C/1683	Smith	G	1879
C/1720	Smith	S	No clasp
C/1591	Sparke	P.R	1879
C/1866	Staff	F.W	No clasp
C/2015	Stephens	G	1879
C/3348	Styles	G	1879
C/955	Sutton	J	1879
C/1873	Taylor	J	1879
C/3397	Thomas	W	1879
C/2454	Thorpe	J	1879
C/1826	Wade	J	1879

No medal. Deserted.

C/1915	Ward	C.H	1879
C/1523	Watson	F	1879
C/2420	White	H.H	1879
C/2844	Wilkinson	C	No clasp

ARMY SERVICE CORPS. ORDNANCE.

DEPUTY COMMISSARY

	Cooke	W.B	No clasp

SUB ASSISTANT COMMISSARY

	Johnson	W	No clasp

2nd CLASS STAFF SERGEANT

1397	Gane	R	1879
1690	Salter	G	No clasp

3rd CLASS STAFF SERGEANT

1222	Anderson	T	1879
1724	Bishop	W	No clasp
1178	Callaby	J	1879
2131	Emberton	F	No clasp
2508	Johnson	C	1878-9
1522	Lee	J.S	1879
2488	Pank	R	?

SERGEANT

1132	Barnhurst	J	No clasp
2579	Baskett	H	No clasp
1272	Brown	J	No clasp
2676	Cusik	J	1879
1387	Flynn	W	No clasp
1433	Hardy	G	No clasp
3375	Ingle	G	No clasp
1902	Mathews	J	No clasp
2605	Scott	G	No clasp
1703	Shotton	P	No clasp
1647	Robinson	J	No clasp
1749	Sweeney	A	No clasp
3226	Wheeler	W	1878

LANCE SERGEANT

3427	Mc Kenzie	G	No clasp

1st CORPORAL

3308	Bedford	C	1879
3276	Croose	S	No clasp
1047	Giles	G.S	No clasp
1945	Jones	H	No clasp

CORPORAL

1262	Bridge	J	1879
1041	Sanderson	J	No clasp

2nd CORPORAL

2575	Browne	T	1879
1950	Buckley	R	No clasp
1264	Davies	J	No clasp
1022	Deeves	J.G	No clasp
1096	Dennis	C	No clasp
1057	Gough	S	No clasp
1054	Jones	E	No clasp
1038	Lowe	J	1879
942	Plummer	W	No clasp
1089	Saunders	J	No clasp
2738	Smith	E	No clasp

LANCE CORPORAL

1576	Mc Lean	J	1879
1288	Rooke	J	No clasp

PRIVATE

1210	Allen	J	1879
1136	Barber	A	No clasp
1409	Bartholomew	E	No clasp

Army Service Corps Ordnance

No.	Name	Init.	Clasp
1158	Bedford	C.F	No clasp
2698	Bloomfield	W.J	No clasp
1890	Booker	W	No clasp
1197	Bor	J	1879
1341	Bradbury	A	No clasp
1438	Briggs	F	No clasp
1231	Bruden	H	1879
1374	Bruton	J.N	No clasp
1284	Carey	W	No clasp
1344	Carey	W	No clasp
1346	Carr	J	1879
1369	Carter	G	No clasp
1214	Cheeseman	A	No clasp
1291	Clarke	C	No clasp
1312	Clarke	F	No clasp
1321	Collins	J	No clasp
1206	Cooper	C.J	1879
1185	Cooper	W	No clasp
1109	Crofts	T	No clasp
1021	Cronin	J	No clasp
1078	Deane	E	No clasp
1075	Delavigne ?	F	No clasp
1280	Dewhurst	W	No clasp
1334	Dillon	J	No clasp
1238	Dodkins	G	No clasp
1368	Drummond	J	1879
2598	Duffy	P	1879
1174	Dundas	J	No clasp
1429	Dyer	J	1879
1431	Ekins	W	No clasp
1430	Francis	A	No clasp
1277	Fuller	J	No clasp
1098	Gale	A	No clasp
1278	Gardener	F	No clasp
977	Garnett	W	No clasp
2592	Gillibrand	E	1879
3220	Gray	E	No clasp
996	Griffin	H	No clasp
1229	Griffin	J	1879
973	Guvite	G	1879
1318	Hammerstone	H	No clasp
1289	Harding	W	No clasp
1159	Harris	J	No clasp
]1290	Harrison	H	No clasp
1116	Hayman	J	1879
1140	Hennson	G	No clasp
3223	Herbert	S	No clasp
1123	Hogan	M	1879

The clasp was a late issue. It could be loose on the ribbon.

No.	Name	Init.	Clasp
1372	Hood	E	No clasp
2604	Howard	H	No clasp
1065	Howlett	G	No clasp
1395	Hudson	W	No clasp
1142	Ives	W	No clasp
1106	James	C	No clasp
1379	Jarvis	R	No clasp
1186	Kelly	M	No clasp
1153	King	J	No clasp

Deputy Commissary S. T. Phillmore

No.	Name	Init.	Clasp
965	Lingfield	W	1879
1160	Loader	H	No clasp
1535	Lynn	S	No clasp
1570	Magall ?	R	1879

The clasp was a late issue. It could be loose on the ribbon.

No.	Name	Init.	Clasp
1310	Maye	J	No clasp
1117	Mayne	W	No clasp
1237	Montague	E.L	1879
1282	Morley	J	1879
994	Morse	C	No clasp
1137	Mundy	W	No clasp
1156	Oldfield	J.B	No clasp
1234	Parsons	J	No clasp
3594	Paton	G	No clasp
1647	Piper	E	No clasp
1074	Relfe	H	No clasp
1357	Rich	F	No clasp
1154	Robinson	T.B	No clasp
1398	Russell	G	1879
1393	Saul	W H	No clasp
1131	Saunders	C	1879

The clasp was a late issue. It could be loose on the ribbon

No.	Name	Init.	Clasp
1339	Searle	J	1879
1025	Simons	E	1879
1350	Skinner	W	No clasp
1155	Slymey	J	No clasp
1213	Spence	A	No clasp
3278	Spencer	S	No clasp
1442	Staples	W.A	1879
2610	Stone	R	1879

The clasp was a late issue. It could be loose on the ribbon.

No.	Name	Init.	Clasp
1302	Sullivan	J	No clasp
1091	Sussams	W	No clasp
1060	Taylor	F	No clasp
1150	Tribilcock	E	1879b medal Deserted.
1355	Tritton	G	No clasp
1090	Turner	C	1879
3544	Vale	J	No clasp
1371	Vant	H	No clasp
1309	Vaughan	H	No clasp
1088	Waller	J.W.B	No clasp
1257	Waller	S	No clasp
1390	Waller	W	No clasp
1463	Ward	C.J	No clasp
1801	Watson	J	No clasp
1049	Webb	A	No clasp
2924	Weller	H	No clasp
1166	Whatley	T	1879
1228	White	C	No clasp
1145	Wood	C	No clasp
1122	Worthington	A	No clasp
1175	Young	E	No clasp

ARMY SERVICE CORPS. ORDINANCE STORE DEPARTMENT

DEPUTY COMMISSARY GENERAL

Name	Init.	Clasp
Wright CB	W.F	1879

COMMISSARY

Name	Init.	Clasp
Angell	J.C	No clasp
March	G.E	1879
Moors	H.P	No clasp

Also had medal for North China 1860.

DEPUTY COMMISSARY

Name	Init.	Clasp
Campbell	C.G.L	1879
Gordon	W.C	1879
Hillier	H	1877-8
#Phillmore	S.T	1877-8

D/S 7/4/1879.

Name	Init.	Clasp
Wyon	H.T	No clasp

ASSISTANT COMMISSARY

Name	Init.	Clasp
Appelbe	E.B	1879
Barrett	H.W	1879
De Ricci	R.S	No clasp
Heron	T	1879
Hobbs	G.R	No clasp
Hunt	R.P	1877-8
Markwell	E.E	No clasp
(Markwick	?)	
Mulcahy	F.E	No clasp
Sadler	A	No clasp
Steevens	J	1879
Wainwright	E.C	1879

SUB ASSISTANT COMMISSARY

Name	Init.	Clasp
Carlin	H	No clasp
Cox	W.S	1879
Sparks	G	1879
(Spinks	?)	

ACTING COMMISSARIAT OFFICER

Name	Init.	Clasp
Durnbreck	F.T	1879
Norton	R.A	1877-8

Army Service Corps Ordnance Store Dept.

ACTING TRANSPORT OFFICER
	Wickham	E	1879

CONDUCTOR
	Aggett	T	1877-8
	Cox	W	No clasp
	Harris	G	No clasp
	Hewlett	A	1879
	Longbotham	J	No clasp
	Petuntze ?	J	1879
	Tims	F	No clasp
	Walround ?	G	1877-8
	Warnes	T.J	No clasp

CIVILIAN CONDUCTOR
	Fritto	A.H	1879

1st CLASS STAFF SERGEANT
1031	Mc Cauley	T	1877-8

CLERK
	Boyle	J	1879
	Brailsford	F	1879

TEMPORARY CLERK
	Pooley		1879

PRIVATE
1123	Hogan	M.F	1879
?	Howes	B	1879
1570	Magall	R.J	1879
2610	Stone	R	1879

ARMY SERVICE CORPS. TRANSPORT
SUPERINTENDENT OF TRANSPORT
	Ball	C.M	1879

Also had New Zealand Medal 1863-4

TRANSPORT OFFICER
	Baxter	H	1879
	England	T.H	1878-9
	Hicks	G	1879r
	Struben	F	1879r

HEAD CONDUCTOR
	Kirby	F	1879

CIVIL CONDUCTOR
	Bibbs	C	1879
	Mittens	G	1879
	Ward	W.M	1879
	Whittington	J	1879

See also 80th Regt.

CIVILIAN
	Garden Mr	D.D	1879

COMPANY SERGEANT MAJOR
T/3013	Farmer	G	1879
T/3516	Kimber	J	1879
T/1298	Watson	W	1879
T/3570	White	J	1879

COLOUR SERGEANT
T/1288	Collins	D	1879
T/3579	Collins	G	1879
T/2546	Cook	H	1879
T/2138	Curry	J	1879
T/1402	Dilley	A	1879
T/976	Dunsford	W	1879
T/1211	Field	G	1879

T/197	Lunn	J	1879
T/2285	Morley	G	1879
T/1185	Nicholls	J	1879
T/1305	Simmonds	J	1879
T/967	Stocker	G	1879
T/210	Taylor	W	No clasp

1st CLASS STAFF SERGEANT
T/603	Ayres	T	1879

2nd CLASS STAFF SERGEANT
T/2105	Battman	W	No clasp
T/301	Bennett	T	1879
T/665	Blake	J	1879
T/2246	Brown	F	1879
T/2566	Cooper	A.C	1879
T/516	Coxon	J	1879
T/1836	Fellowes	H	1879
T/577	Goldsmith	G	1879
T/2371	Hellyer	H	No clasp
T/691	Hopkins	H.M	No clasp
T/2066	James	R	No clasp

3rd CLASS STAFF SERGEANT
T/435	Baker	J	1879
T/2005	Bartlett	H.G	1879
T/1843	Bigg	W	1879
T/2110	Birch	R	1879
T/1873	Blakey	G	No clasp
T/240	Chambers	C	1877-8
T/632	Chambers	S	No clasp
T/405	Connors	T	1879
T/182	Coopey	W	No clasp
T/163	Cowdry	J	No clasp
T/3060	Crapp	J	1879
T/1217	Crees	J	1879
T/3346	Cushing	J	1879
T/2288	De Lancey	J	1879
T/464	Eycott	H.C	1879
T/530	Fillmore	J	1879
T/330	Garside	T	No clasp
T/3261	Granger	W	No clasp
T/221	Hall	S	1879
T/332	Hill	H	1879
T/2145	Hiscocks	S	1879
T/2312	Howe	C.F	1879
T/3177	Howes	W	1879
T/2827	Mason	J	No clasp
T/569	May	F	No clasp
T/1952	Rogers	W	No clasp
T/2365	Scudmore	T	1877-8
T/801	Strong	W	No clasp
T/106	Sullivan	W	1879
T/622	Tribbeck	H.C	1879
T/383	Turner	E	No clasp
T/2855	Turner	J	1879
T/2790	Vine	H	No clasp
T/1911	Watson	T	No clasp
T/2361	Wilson	J	No clasp

SERGEANT
T/368	Andrews	J	1879
T/2378	Andrews	T	No clasp

T/3430	Batho	W	1879
T/2357	Biddulph	W	1879
T/1165	Brag	J	1879
T/238	Brooks	J	1879
T/3325	Cusack	P	1879
T/3434	Davis	J	1877-8
T/321	Dean	A	No clasp
T/389	Deegan	R	1879
T/3562	Elliott	J	No clasp
T/2756	Ellis	W.J	No clasp
T/580	Freestone	S	1879
T/2747	Gibbs	G	1879
T/481	Hayter	J	No clasp
T/3568	Hollick	J	No clasp
T/3244	Hubbard	D	No clasp
T/503	Jackson	W	1879
T/2693	James	J	1879
T/2343	Johnson	W	1879
T/941	Kearns	T.J	1879
T/1953	March	J	1879
T/2500	Mulholland	J.H	No clasp
T/3460	Newton	C	1879r

Medal forfeited. No reason shown.

T/1033	Owers	J	No clasp
T/2400	Page	J	1879
T/2892	Palmer	J	1879
*T/540	Potter	W	1879

D/S 27th March 1879 Pietermaritzburg
* London Gazette 23 May 1879

T/1116	Reid	A	No clasp
T2149	Reigate	A	No clasp
T/1085	Sanders	F	1877-8
T/965	Shepheard	R.W	1879
T/1065	Smith	G.F	1879
T/2718	Stephens	H	1879
T/1957	Swaffield	H.J	1879
T/874	Thompson	W	No clasp
T/2777	Walter	V.B	1879
T/711	Weston	O	1879
T/3489	Williams	W	No clasp

LANCE SERGEANT
T/2364	Blinco	A	1879
T/2344	Howgill	W	No clasp
T/959	Mc Bride	T	No clasp

CORPORAL
T/1026	Aggett	H	1879
T/100	Angell	W	1879
T/151	Barriball	A	1879
T/3207	Bates	W.H	1879
T/1383	Bennett	F.T	No clasp
T/1471	Bennett	T.W	No clasp
T/1011	Beal	W	1879
T/3439	Bleach	G	1879
T/3927	Brooker	J	1879
T/3301	Chard	J	No clasp
T/1123	Chambury	T.A	1879
T/2175	Clackson	W	1879
T/39	Clarke	R	No clasp
T/1049	Clay	G.H	1879

Army Service Corps Transport

Number	Name	Initial	Year/Note
T/1060	Cockell	W	1879
T/3072	Croasley	W	1879
T/2836	Downer	W	1879
T/113	Dumphy	W	1879
T/1181	Eades	J	1879
T/3326	Elam	E	1879
T/690	Elsey	A	No clasp
T/3507	Farley	W	No clasp
T/3260	Flower	G	1879
T/2904	Gambling	R	1879
T/1031	Goddard	G	1879
T/1839	Hearsey	J	No clasp
T/2887	Hoctop	T	1879
T/3247	Howe	W	1879
T/2675	Hughes	J	1879
T/3485	Ivatts	T	No clasp
T/1955	Jones	W	1879
T/1881	Kelly	E	1879
T/1370	King	W.W	1879
T/3434	Mc Mahon	T.J	1879
T/1999	Mayo	H	1879
T/596	Offord	J.P	1879
T/3461	Organ	J	1877-8-9
T/3488	Ormes	A	1879
T/1316	Palmer	A	No clasp
No medal. Discharged with ignominy.			
T/2196	Parker	H	1879
T/3088	Phillips	W.M	1879
T/297	Pott	W	1879
T/2654	Pritchard	J.J	1879
KIA Isandhlwana.			
T/3569	Quick	J	1879
T/1134	Rodgman	E	1879
T/2402	Salmon	G	1879
T/2360	Savell	C	No clasp
T/949	Skuse	T	1879
T/544	Smart	R	1879
T/1187	Smith	H	No clasp
T/1104	Spragg	A.C	1879
T/2689	Stewart	W.A	No clasp
T/991	Summers	C.M	1879
T/1994	Tyrrell	J	1879
T/2407	Webb	G	1879
T/3141	Wright	A	1879
2nd CORPORAL			
T/1045	Bexley	H	1879
T/3249	Boby	J	1879
T/1284	Burton	J	1879
T/2280	Carr	J	1879
T/1202	Covey	H	No clasp
T/2700	Crawford	G	1879
T/1450	Figgins	C.J	1879
T/1089	Frances	R	1879
T/1354	Mainwaring	W.H	No clasp
Forfeited. No trace of return of the medal.			
T/1155	Murphy	H	No clasp
T/1180	Purkiss	B	No clasp
T/1050	Purvey	W	1879
T/2154	Turner	W	No clasp
T/2919	Webster	W	1879
T/1238	White	W	No clasp
LANCE CORPORAL			
T/1166	Angus	W	1879
T/1469	Banks	S.J	1879
T/1300	Barry	W	1879
T/3030	Bunce	A	1879
T/1235	Burgess	C	No clasp
T/317	Campbell	D	1879
T/1048	Cheesman **KIA** R		1879
T/1971	Cook	C	1879
T/1410	Coombs	J	No clasp
T/1996	Crow	W	1879
T/1486	Eisele	G.R	1879
T/753	Fisher	J	1879
No medal. Deserted.			
T/2320	Gibson	W	1879
T/952	Johnson	J	1879
T/1290	Lisney	W	No clasp
T/1419	Marshall	H.F	1879
T/1857	Riddle	G	1879
T/209	Salway	L	1879
T/1048	Summers	T	1879
T/1497	Tanner	F	1879
T/2995	Whitmore	R	1879
BUGLER			
T/2416	Bamford	C.W	1879
T/3605	Buckley	P	1879
T/2415	Flynn	J	No clasp
T/1923	Mc Cann	W	No clasp
T/1302	Orr	C.T	No clasp
T/2413	Pountney	F	No clasp
PRIVATE			
T/1722	Abbey	T	1879
T/2739	Able	J	1879
T/1586	Addis	J	1879
T/1651	Aldridge	J	1879
T/1685	Anderson	A.C	1879
T/3104	Anderson	T	1879
T/1663	Andrews	H	No clasp
T/2982	Andrews	J	No clasp
T/1716	Annison	G	1879
T/1656	Apps	A	1879
T/1677	Archer	A	1879
T/2104	Archer	H	1879
T/2101	Arnett	J	1879
T/1986	Aylward	T	1879
T/1701	Ayton	A	No clasp
T/1425	Baker	J	1879
T/746	Baker	J	1879
T/2788	Baldwin	R	1879
T/1254	Bangs	H.W	1879
T/2393	Barber	H	1879
T/1149	Barker	J	1879
T/1694	Barlow	F	No clasp
T/1665	Barnes	A	1879
T/3392	Barnes	J	No clasp
T/1418	Barron	W	1879
T/1242	Bartlett	G.W	1879
T/1548	Bayes	F	1879
T/1208	Bayes	H	1879
T/1075	Beard	F.C	1879
T/2869	Beach	C	1879
T/776	Beeston	A	1879
T/2171	Belcher	J	1879
T/1207	Benn	J.F	1879
T/960	Berry	H.W	No clasp
T/1420	Beverly	J.W	1879
T/1035	Bigwood	E	1879
T/1012	Billington	W	1879
T/1539	Birch	A.G	1879
T/1785	Bishop	E	No clasp
T/1103	Bishop	H	1879
T/3169	Bishop	T	1879
T/1817	Blake	G	1879
No medal. Deserted.			
T/3000	Bottle	E	1879
T/1067	Bourne	W	1879
T/1618	Bradley	J	1879
T/1613	Bradley	H.J	1879
T/1424	Brien	J	1879
T/1005	Brister	H	1879
T/3236	Brown	A	1879
T/1376	Brown	A.H.C	No clasp
T/3035	Brown	H	1879
T/1807	Brown	J	1879
T/1729	Brown	T	No clasp
T/1158	Brown	W	1879
T/1916	Bryan	J	1879
T/1637	Bunney	G	1879
T/3237	Burch	S	No clasp
T/1052	Burnett	W	1879
T/3379	Butt	R.G	1879
T/181	Cameron	T	1879
T/3543	Carr	Z	1879
T/1907	Carroll	C	No clasp
T/1760	Chad	J	1879
T/2412	Chalk	J	1879
T/2410	Chantry	R	1879
T/2996	Chapman	C	1879
T/1226	Chapman	R	1879
T/1108	Chapman	W	1879
T/2276	Church	J	1879
T/1371	Churcher	C.W	1879
T/1177	Claret		No clasp
T/179	Clark	A	No clasp
T/974	Clements	W	1879
T/108	Cole	I	1879
T/1240	Coleman	G	1879
T/1206	Coles	F.T	1879
T/2267	Colley	T.W	No clasp
T/1686	Cook	E.J	1879
T/1621	Cooper	H	1879
T/1770	Cooper	T.F	1879
T/2746	Cooper	W	1879
T/1751	Cordeary	J	1879
T/1088	Coulter	S	1879

J.N. Hamer Deputy Commissioner

James N Hamer 1888

I would like to thank Pete Jaggard for the following information concerning his step great grandfather James Nataniel Hamer. He was acting Commissary officer to Col. Durnford's column and somehow managed to survive the battle. Hamer is mentioned in several books about the Zulu Wars. James's handwritten account of the action at Isandlwana is in the National Army Museum, of which this is an extract:

"Very soon after the mounted native horse had arrived they were sent out to some hills on the left of the camp. **Captain George SHEPSTONE** in command. I went along with him, and after going some little way, we tried to capture some cattle. They disappeared over a ridge, and on coming up we saw the Zulus, like ants in front of us, in perfect order as quiet as mice and stretched across in an even line. We estimated those we saw at 12000. After his having given orders to the Captain of the Native Horse to retire gradually, Geo SHEPSTONE (& myself) rode as hard as ever we could back to the camp and reported what we had seen. A company of the 1/24 foot was sent to back up our horsemen who by that time had retired down the hill towards the camp. (I sent you a plan of the camp - which being the first I made out is slightly incorrect - I made out two other plans which have been sent to England to the War Office). We left our horses (for Geo SHEPSTONE (& myself) had rejoined the men) at the bottom of the hill, and went up and attacked the Zulus on foot, we drove them back at first, but after retiring over a ridge they were reinforced and came on in overwhelming numbers and we had a sharp run for it to our horses, which were some little distance away. We retreated towards the camp. Up to that time I had only had a revolver, so I rode into the camp and got a carbine. I then joined some soldiers in front of the camp and fired away as fast as possible, but we had to run for the Zulus came on us like ants on all sides, I had the greatest difficulty in finding my horse but got him and galloped through the camp, the Zulus being within 200 yards and then our company of the 24th with poor **Colonel DURNFORD** making a heroic and most gallant stand to cover the retreat. The scenes at the top of the camp baffles description, oxen yoked to wagons, mules, sheep, horses and men in the greatest confusion, all wildly trying to escape. I saw one gun brought over the neck of the hill, but it stuck fast among the stones. We had a very bad country to go over, large rough boulders and stones. Some distance from the camp is a small ravine which was hid by bushes, the greater part of the fugitives fortunately went above it, but several (with myself) went too low down, and met it at the center. We could not go above as the Zulus were too near, and we had to go to the end of it before we could cross. The Zulus saw this and in large numbers tried to cut us off, I and four others were the last to get round, and we had to use our revolvers very freely, for the Zulus followed us up quickly, the ground being very bad for horses, and footmen had not the ghost of a chance. Several even were stabbed on their horses. My horse (Dick) had had a great deal of work that day and with tracking over the stones he got completely done and would not move a step further. I was in jolly predicament when (thank God) a man of the Rocket Battery galloped up with a led horse and let me have it. I had just taken the saddle off poor Dick when a bullet struck him dead and the poor fellow who gave me the horse had only ridden ten yards when I saw him fall killed from his horse. The animal I was now on was a splendid beast, but the girth of the saddle was not strong enough and when I had galloped another two miles it burst and I came down on the stones, luckily I stuck like mad to the bridle and quickly rigged up a girth by passing the neck rein through the D of the saddle, and thereby saved myself as the Zulus were by this time close upon me. I managed all right till I got to the Buffalo River which was very difficult to cross. I myself saw several men swept down and drowned or killed. The Zulus charged us down to the river but they took care to cross lower down where it was safer. I had a dreadful ride to Helpwakaar half insensible and wet through. We got in about 6pm to Helpwakaar and were up all night making (...?) and keeping guard. We four volunteered to go with Major SPAULDING next morning to Rorke's Drift. Where as I had lost everything I possessed horse (and my cash went down the river in my saddle bags (where I had another spill getting out) ......

He appears on Forsythe's roll as J. H. Hamer and was an Acting Commissary Officer. This suggests that he wasn't a civilian at the time. He also served in the same capacity during the Basuto War including the operations in the Transkei 1880-81.

J.N. Hamer is listed on the Cape of Good Hope medal rolls as such: "J.N. Hamer, Deputy Commissioner, Ordinance Department with bars for Basutoland & Transkei."

Hamer travelled to New Zealand from South Africa, and married in 1888. Sadly his wife and only child died the following decade and the widower went back to SA in 1901 as a Lieutenant in the 7th New Zealand contingent. Hamer returned to the UK soon after and in 1902 married Beatrice Taylor, herself a widow with two children. My great aunt has left a description of meeting her step father for the first time "We only remained at the old home for another three years, because during that time my mother re-married a captain in the South African war. I remember being decked out in a new green suit and hat, and my brother in a Norfolk suit, so that we could go to meet him. We were rather dubious as to what he would be like as we had heard terrible stories about stepfathers. He looked every inch a military man with his waxed mustache, as he whisked us away in a cab to go to the London Zoo, which was a great event for us. He was very kind, I guess he thought he had better make a good impression, which he did, and all through the years he lived, I must say he was always very kind to me"......

James Nathaniel HAMER   Account of the fight at Isandluana

Army Service Corps Transport

T/1241	Cousins	W	1879	T/1100	Figgins	G.T	1879	T/1061	Higgins	J	1879
T/2825	Coutts	W	1879	T/1449	Fletcher	F	No clasp	T/1554	Hill	A.J	1879
T/2244	Cox	G	1879	T/940	Flynn	T	1879	T/2034	Hill	C	No clasp
T/1296	Crandle	W.R	1879	T/2824	Ford	G	1879	T/1456	Hill	H	1879
T/1748	Crich	E.C	1879	T/2329	Forman	H	No clasp	T/1706	Hill	H	1879
T/1579	Cross	A	1879	T/3105	Forris	J	1879	T/1493	Hill	J	1879
T/1028	Crouch	J	1879	T/3032	Fox	G	1879	T/1705	Hill	J	No clasp
T/957	Crowe	H	1879	T/1691	Francis	R	1879	T/1460	Hillsdon	J	No clasp
T/975	Crush	C	1879	T/159	Franklin	B	1879	T/1726	Hinson	W	1879
T/1367	Crute	D	1879	T/2100	Frost	G	1879	T/122	Hiscock	W	1879
T/3045	Cuff	C	1879	T/1992	Froud	T	No clasp	T/1162	Hodge	W	1879
T/3046	Cuff	J	1879	T/2290	Froud	W	1879	T/2019	Holloway	H	1879
T/3374	Cunningham	S	1879	T/1399	Fruen	C	1879	T/1530	Hollowell	G	1879
T/2126	Cushing	T	1879	T/1261	Fullick	W	1879	T/3090	Holmes	T	1879
A duplicate medal and clasp was issued on 26/4/1971.				T/1812	Fyffe	E	1879	T/1080	Houghton	G	1879
				T/3602	Galway	J	1879	T/1610	Hunt	W	1879
T/1581	Dady	J.H	No clasp	T/2141	Garrick	W	1879	T/2539	Hunter	W	1879
T/1228	Dance	F	1879	T/328	Gay	W	No clasp	T/1740	Hurley	J	1879
T/860	Dare	G	1879	T/3229	Gayden	J	1879	T/1629	Hutchings	H	1879
T/1042	Davey	J	1879	T/2268	Gibson	D	1879	T/2065	Hutchins	J	1879
T/1572	Davies	W	1879	T/3339	Giles	H	1879	T/2282	Inwood	J	1879
T/1178	Davis	A	1879	T/2022	Gillard	W	1879r	T/1509	Jackson	A.T	1879
T/1523	Davis	F	1879	Medal forfeited. No reason given.				T/1599	Jacques	A	1879
T/1255	Davis	W	1879	T/1422	Goodman	J	1879	T/1531	James	C	1879
T/1167	Davis	W	No clasp	T/1476	Gould	C.H	No clasp	T/2067	Jenkins	A	1879
T/2025	Day	W	1879	T/2179	Granger	T	No clasp	T/2816	Johns	J	No clasp
T/1481	Deer	A	No clasp	T/2017	Gray	C	1879	T/1733	Keane	T	No clasp
T/1702	Delaney	C	1879	T/349	Grayden	T	1879	T/3262	Keen	W	1879
T/1090	Dennett	T	1879	T/2108	Green	F	No clasp	T/2266	Kelly	G	1879
T/1939	Dennison	W	1879	T/1732	Green	J	1879	T/2069	Key	S	1879
T/1620	Dew	E	1879	T/3298	Green	W	No clasp	T/1660	Kilroy	J	1879
T/1313	Dew	J	1879	Killed.				T/1755	Kimplon	F	No clasp
T/1522	Dickerson	J	1879	T/1121	Greenlees	J	1879	T/2272	King	H	1879
T/2652	Dickings	H	1879	T/2534	Gribben	C	1879	T/984	Kinsella	A	No clasp
T/2248	Diggens	J	1879	T/2029	Griffin	J	1879	T/1542	Kitchen	G.A	1879
T/1365	Dobrey	W	1879	T/421	Grundy	H	1879	No medal. Deserted.			
T/1584	Donovan	C	1879	T/3355	Grunsell	W	No clasp	T/1728	Knight	E.A	1879
T/3097	Doran	W	1879	T/2278	Gunner	C	1879	T/3472	Last	J	1879
T/1752	Dorrell	W	1879	T/1369	Hall	F	1879	T/1536	Law	F.J	1879
T/1183	Downey	J	1879	T/1397	Halls	R	1879	T/133	Leahy	W	1879
T/1943	Doyle	V(?)	1879	T/1299	Hampton	C	1879	T/1630	Lee	G	1879
T/1253	Drayton	J	1879	T/1725	Hanson	R	1879	T/1250	Leggate	R.J	1879
T/1215	Duncan	J	No clasp	T/1220	Hanvey	B	1879	T/1713	Leggett	T.F	1879
T/1224	Dunn	S	1879	T/1490	Hardstone	W	1879	T/1375	Leslter	G	1879
T/1009	Eales	T	No clasp	T/54	Harris	G	No clasp	T/3478	Lewis	C	1879
T/1474	Edwards	E	1879	T/2265	Harvey	A	No clasp	T/1516	Lewis	D.W	1879
T/3573	Edwards	E	1879	T/1574	Harvey	A	1879	T/1794	Litson	W	No clasp
T/1123	Edwards	J.J	No clasp	T/1517	Harvey	F	1879	T/1248	Long	G	No clasp
T/1736	Eldridge	F.S	1879	T/2757	Hawkins	C	1879	T/2072	Lorimer	R	No clasp
T/1761	Elliott	J	1879	T/1720	Hawkins	G.J	1879	T/2185	Lovell	W	No clasp
T/3454	Elliott	R.J	No clasp	T/338	Hayward	T	1879	T/2024	Lovett	E.A	1879
T/1768	Evans	C	1879	T/948	Hearn	H	1879	T/1987	Lucas	C	1879
T/1374	Evans	J	1879	T/1357	Heartfield	A	1879	T/1763	Lusher	W	1879
T/3028	Everis	J	1879	T/3519	Hedger	A	1879	T/1099	Mack	C	1879
T/1372	Eyles	H	1879	T/1094	Hedley	J	1879	T/1714	Mann	W.J	1879
T/1435	Fall	H.A	No clasp	T/3572	Henman	F	1879	T/1735	Manning	F	No clasp
T/1199	Farmer	E	1879	T/2397	Hickman	C	1879	T/1356	Marshall	W.R	1879
T/284	Ferguson	G	1879	T/1414	Hicks	W	1879	T/1687	Mathieson	A	1879
T/1308	Field	A	1879	T/2382	Higgs	D	1879	T/1321	May	C	1879

Army Service Corps Transport

No.	Name	Init.	Year	No.	Name	Init.	Year	No.	Name	Init.	Year
T/3292	May	H	1879	T/1921	Purnell	A	1879	T/3578	Stanley	D	1879
T/201	Maynard	F	1879	T/1161	Purnell	H	1879	T/2800	Steedman	W	No clasp
T/1423	Mc Cormack	F.R	1879	T/1777	Purvey	A	1879	T/1480	Stokes	C	1879
	No medal. Deserted.			T/1317	Purvey	J	No clasp	T/1385	Stroud	J	No clasp
T/1592	Mc Kenzie	J	1879	T/3070	Pyne	F	1879	T/1326	Sullivan	J	1879
T/1047	Mc Manus	H	1879	T/1484	Quinton	C.H	1879	T/1148	Swaffield	A	No clasp
T/1466	Mead	S	1879	T/2307	Ratcliffe	J	No clasp r	T/256	Symes	J	No clasp
T/1140	Messer	H.M	1879		No medal. Deserted.			T/1636	Symes	J.J	1879
T/1871	Mew	J	1879	T/622	Reeves	H	1879	T/1139	Symons	S	No clasp
T/1457	Millard	C	1879	T/2369	Reynolds	G	1879	T/1711	Talbut	R.H	No clasp
T/987	Millard	W	No clasp	T/3082	Ricketts	T	1879	T/1569	Tanner	A.W	1879
T/1502	Mills	H	1879	T/1068	Ricketts	W	1879	T/2560	Tasker	D	No clasp
T/1717	Mills	R	1879	T/1021	Riddle	J	1879	T/1160	Taylor	C	1879
T/2821	Mitchell	E	No clasp	T/1709	Ridge	W.R	1879	T/951	Taylor	J	1879
T/1258	Mitchell	G	1879	T/1764	Rivett	T	1879	T/1352	Thompson	H	No clasp
T/199	Morris	J	1879	T/1565	Roberts	G	1879	Deserted. Medal does not appear to			
T/1421	Morton	T	1879	T/2381	Roberts	W.T	No clasp	have been withdrawn.			
T/677	Moss (?)	J.W	1879	T/1487	Rush	J	No clasp	T/2983	Tims	S	1879
T/1571	Mulkern	W.F	1879	T/3086	Russell	C	1879	T/1915	Tisdale	W	1879
T/1513	Murray	T	1879	T/1247	Rydon	G.R	1879	T/2301	Tree	G	1879
T/1645	Myers	J	No clasp	T/65	Salter	A	1879	T/1657	Turner	J	1879
T/1439	Neal	D	No clasp	T/1127	Sampson	J	No clasp	T/1697	Underwood	W	1879
T/2823	Nealis	L	1879	T/1200	Savage	A.J	1879	T/2192	Vaughan	J	1879
T/3487	Nevill	G	1879	T/1262	Savigar	F	1879	T/2168	Vickery	W	1879
T/1721	Newby	R.D	1879	T/1507	Saville	H	1879	T/1661	Waknell	W.R	1879
T/1118	Niblett	W	1879	T/2664	Saxby	T	1879	T/3178	Waldock	T	1879
T/1712	Nice	G	1879	T/1626	Scanlan	J	1879	T/3255	Walford	A	1879
T/2914	Nicholls	A	No clasp	T/1612	Scanlan	M	1879	T/2113	Ward	F.W	1879
T/352	Nicholls	E	1879	T/1980	Scriven	E	1879	T/365	Ward	P	1879
T/1347	Nichols	G	1879	T/1615	Seghers	A	1879	T/600	Watkins	T	No clasp
T/1362	Nichols	P	1879	T/1758	Sewell	E	1879	T/1230	Wearne	J	1879
T/964	Noel	T.E	No clasp		No medal. Deserted.			T/1251	Webb	C	1879
T/944	Norman	W	1879	T/3391	Shannon	R	1879	T/2392	Webb	D	1879
T/1037	Norris	W	1879	T/2426	Sharp	G	1879	T/1727	Webb	H.W	1879
T/3171	Norton	T	No clasp	T/1243	Shepherd	D	1879	T/2808	Webb	J	1879
T/355	O'Bryan	J	1879	T/2374	Shellis	H	1879	T/1688	Westfoot	T.G	1879
T/1485	O'Callaghan	T	1879	T/3631	Shelliss	W	No clasp	T/1051	Weston	C.W	No clasp
T/2091	O'Hanlon	B	1879	T/1951	Shelton	G	1879	T/2124	Weston	H	1879
T/1904	O'Reilly	C	1879	T/2812	Shortland	A	No clasp	T/1117	Wheeler	G	No clasp
T/2408	Osbourn	J	1879	T/1429	Sidwell	S	No clasp	T/2340	Whitehead	H	No clasp
T/1447	Painter	J	No clasp	T/1724	Simpson	T	1879	T/1693	Whitehead	P	No clasp
T/1920	Palmer	J.W	No clasp	T/2405	Skinner	G	1879	T/260	Wilcock	J	No clasp
T/1737	Pamenter	C.W	1879	T/1470	Slingsby	H.G	1879	T/2033	Wilkinson	F	No clasp
T/1501	Parker	C	1879	T/1146	Smith	A	No clasp	T/3787	Williams	F	1879
T/1525	Parson	H	1879	T/2080	Smith	A	No clasp	T/1154	Williams	G	1879
T/1388	Parsons	J	1879	T/1219	Smith	B.T	1879	T/1756	Williams	G	1879
T/3539	Pender	J	1879	T/1084	Smith	C	1879	T/1405	Williams	L.C	1879
T/3479	Penny	T	No clasp	T/1291	Smith	C.H	1879	T/1442	Willis	A	1879
T/1628	Perryer	J	1879	T/1739	Smith	J	No clasp	T/1231	Willis	C	1879
T/1463	Perryman	H	1879	T/2352	Smith	J	No clasp	T/2784	Willis	D	1879
T/1605	Pike	T.A	1879	T/2411	Smith	J	1879	T/1058	Wilson	G	1879
T/1606	Pittard	J	1879	T/1364	Smith	J	1879	T/1174	Wilson	G	No clasp
T/1560	Plant	C.A	No clasp	T/1500	Smith	R	1879	T/1309	Wilson	F	1879
T/3269	Pollard	J	1879	T/1635	Smith	S	1879	T/1272	Wiltshire	F	1879
T/2947	Powell	E	1879	T/1350	Smith	S	1879	T/1373	Windett	J	1879
T/1426	Pratt	J	1879	T/1723	Sparke	R	1879	T/1260	Wing	W	No clasp
T/1673	Prestridge	S	1879	T/2102	Spencer	G	1879	T/1556	Wisby	W	1879r
T/1252	Pritchett	H.C	No clasp	T/1361	Spencer	J	No clasp	Forfeited. No reason given.			
T/1039	Punter	J	1879	T/1345	Spraggon	W	1879	T/1576	Wood	J	1879

Army Service Corps Transport

T/2211	Woodman	J	1879
T/1538	Wright	H.W	1879
T/1524	Yates	W	1879
T/1800	Young	F.G	1879
T/217	Young	S	1879

ARMY VETERINARY CORPS.
PRINCIPAL VETERINARY SURGEON
Gudgin T.P 1879

Also had British Crimea medal with 3 clasps. Turkish Crimea Medal and Indian Mutiny medal and clasp.

VETERINARY SURGEON 1st CLASS
Burt	W	1879
Duck	F	1878-9
Healy	M	1879
Lambert	J	1879
Walters	W.B	1879
Wiltshire	S	No clasp

VETERINARY SURGEON
Fenton	G.H	1879
Glover	B.S	1879
Hagger	W.R	1879

See also N. Battery 6th Bde R/A.

Killick	F.W	1879
Longhurst	S	1879
Morgan	J.W.A	1879
Moore	R	1879
Phillips	C	1879
Raymond	F	1879

CHAPLAINS
SENIOR CHAPLAIN
Coar C.J 1879

3rd CLASS CHAPLAIN
Vandelrur G.O No clasp

4th CLASS CHAPLAIN
Bellord	J	1879
Corbett	R.A	1879
Foran	T	No clasp
Kirkwood	G	1879
Law	J	1879
Ritchie	G.M	No clasp

ACTING CHAPLAIN
Bandrey	A	1879
Goodwin	T	1879

Possible duplicate medal issued

Mactaggart	J	No clasp
#Smith	G	1879
Walsh	A.F	1879

Possible duplicate medal issued

Wilkin T.H No clasp

COMMISSARIAT & TRANSPORT STAFF.
DEPUTY COMMISSARY GENERAL
Long	J	No clasp
Morris CB	E	1879
Palmer	C	?

In possession of a medal from an earlier S.A. War. Also had British and Turkish Crimea Medals.

Strickland KCB Sir E 1877-8-9

Also had British and Turkish Crimea Medals and New Zealand 1864-66 medal.

ASSISTANT COMMISSARY GENERAL
Brownrigg H.J 1879

Also had British Crimea Medal and 3 clasps and Turkish Crimea Medal.

Healy R.C 1879

Also had medal for Ashanti 1874.

Pennell	C.L.B	1877-8
Phillips	G.H	1877-8

COMMISSARY
Cheetham F.G 1879

He may also have had a medal with clasp 1877-8.

Elmes	J.W	1879
Furse	P.G.F	No clasp
Hughes CMG	E	1879
Le Mesurier	T.A	1877-8
Manning	J.F	1877-8
Reeves	H.S.E	1879
Webb CB	E.W.H	1877-8

DEPUTY COMMISSARY
Bridgman	F.H	1877-8
Bridgman	W	1879
Coates	G	1879

Also had Ashanti Medal and clasp 1874.

Granville	S.G	1877-8
Noake	R.D	1879
Ramsey	G	No clasp

Also had British Crimea Medal with four clasps and Turkish Crimea Medal.

Rushton	M.W.R	1877-8
Walton	C.E	1879
Warneford	W.J.J	1877-8-9

ASSISTANT COMMISSARY
Alderton T.G No clasp

Drowned 5/4/1879. aged 45

Bamfield	W.J.B	No clasp
Boyd	J.A	1879
Carter	E.T.S	1879
Chermside	R.A	1879
Cousins	H.J	1879
Dunne	W.A	1877-8-9

Fagan T St J		1879
Grattan	E	1879
Heygate	B	1879
Hope	L.A	1879
Kevill-Davis	E.L.B	1879
Laurence	W.M	No clasp
Loney	J	1877-8
Mc Murray	E.S	1879
Richardson	W.D	1877-8
Santi	C.H	No clasp
Stanley	G	1879
Whitley	J	1879
Wilson	J.G.Y	1879
Winspar (Winspear ?)	W.H	1879
Young	J.S	No clasp

SUB ASSISTANT COMMISSARY
Armstrong	J	1879
Barrell	W.J	1877-8-9
Battersby	F	1879

The clasp was a late issue. Could be loose on ribbon.

Bolton	G	1879
Collett	W	No clasp
De Lisle	F	1879
Grier	G.R	No clasp
Howland	J	1879
Joyce	H	1879
Ledsham	W	1879
Mc Caffery	J	No clasp
Mc Loughlin	J	No clasp
Mc Veigh	W.E	No clasp
Myers	G.L	1879
Nichols	R	1879
Phillips	E	1879
Stead	J	1879

ACTING COMMISSARY OFFICER
Dalton VC J.L 1877-8-9

His VC was for an action at Rorkes Drift. A photograph of him shows his S.A. Medal with two clasp 1877-8 and 1879.

Deare	C.W	1877-8
Findlay	D.L	1879
Hamer	J.H	1879
Hunter	J.H	1879
Munro	R.R	1877-8-9
Murray Mc Gregor	C.A	1879
Tarleton	E	1879
Thompson	?	1879

ACTING TRANSPORT OFFICER
Harrell	J.W	1879
Holt	W.G	1879

#George Smith, promoted to Chaplain to the Forces 3rd Class on 10th February 1890, and 2nd Class whilst in Malta in 1895. Previously had served as acting Chaplain to the Forces in the Zulu War of 1879, present at Rorke's Drift and Ulundi. (Medal and clasp). Served throughout the Egyptian War of 1882. (Medal and Khedive's Star). Served in the Sudan Expedition in 1884 at the engagement in El Tab. (Mentioned in Despatches, two clasps). Served in the Nile Expedition of 1884 -1885 (Clasp). Died 26th November 1918, aged 73 years, buried in Preston Cemetery, Lancashire. His biography 'Padre George Smith of Rorke's Drift' written by Canon William Lummis.

Commissariat & Transport Staff

	Jones	P	No clasp
CONDUCTOR			
	Bussey	F.H	No clasp
	Curle	H	1879r
	Dorman	M	1879r
	Finch	E.W	1879
	Francis	L	1879r
	Hazelhurst	E	1879r
	Henwood	J	1879r
	Keirghry	J	1877-8-9
	Lambert	J	1879
	Page	T.A	No clasp
	Phillips	W.F	1879
	Phillips	W.J	1879
	Rabe	C	1879r
	Rensky	T	1878-9
	Rorke	J	1879r
	Symonds	H	No clasp
	Trevor	H.H	1879
	Usokerman	?R.F	1879r
	Wilkinson	W.P	1879
CIVILIAN CONDUCTOR			
	Emerson	S.A	1879
CONDUCTOR OF SUPPLIES			
	Arthur	J	1879
	Barrett	J	1879
	Brooks	A	1879
Cassell	F		No clasp
	Champion	H.E	1879
	Cleghorn	R	1879
The clasp was a late issue. Could be loose on ribbon.			
	Duncan	H	1879
	Egerton	R	1879
	Field	F.H	1879
	Fletcher	J	1879
	Hatton	J	1879
	Hickie	H	1879
The clasp was a late issued. Could be loose on ribbon.			
	Jewell	A.C	No clasp
	Latten	L	No clasp
	Lemon	G	No clasp
	Luck	E	1879
	Marshall	H	1879
	Miller	D	1879
	Murdoch	D	1879
	O'Loughlin	D	1879
	Parsons	W	1879
	Reid	S	1879
	Reilly	G.S	1879
	Sexton	J	1879
The clasp was a late issue. Could be loose on ribbon.			
	Sidmouth	G	1879
	Stott	E.S	1879
	Turner	H	No clasp
	Wagner	J.R	1879
	Ward	H.S	No clasp
	Watts	C	No clasp
	Wishart	W	1877-8-9
COMMISSARIAT STOREKEEPER			
	Black	J	1877-8
	Drake	S.F	1879
	Kuhlman	W.E	1877-8-9
The clasp was a late issue. Could be loose on ribbon.			
	Sissing	W.F	1877-8
ASSISTANT STOREKEEPER			
	Holton	G	1877-8
Had a medal for a previous campaign.			
DRIVER			
	Almeyda	E	No clasp
INTERPRETER			
	Fynney	F.B	1879
	Phillips	E.T.S	1879
CAPTAIN			
	Gardner	A.C	1879
See also 14th Hussars.			
	Pelly-Clarke	E.L	1879
See also 103rd Regt.			
	Spratt	E.J.H	1879
See also 29th Regt.			
LIEUTENANT			
	Bayly	J.C	1879
See also 27th Regt.			
	Boyle	C.J	No clasp
See also 52nd Regt.			
	Dick	J.R	1879
See also 103rd Regt.			
	Gould	A.L.G	1879
See also 2nd Dragoon Guards.			
	Haldane	H.E	1879
See also 49th Regiment.			
	Jefferson	M.D	1879
See also 33rd Regt.			
	Lawrence	W.W	1879
See also 18th Regt.			
	Martin	E.C	1879
See also 87th Regt.			
	Mitchel	C.B.D	No clasp
	Odell	W.H	1879
See also 52nd Regt.			
	Watson	A.G	1879
See also 30th Regt.			
	White	L.A	1879
See also 53rd Regt.			
	Williams	P.G	1879
SUPERIOR BARRACK SERGEANT			
	Campbell	W	No clasp
BARRACK SERGEANT			
	Baines	H	No clasp
	Brown	P	1879
	Daly	J	No clasp
	Haigh	J	No clasp
	Nolan	C	No clasp
	Sambels	J	No clasp
	Smedley	J	No clasp
	Walter	J	No clasp
	Wilton	T	No clasp
RANK NOT KNOWN			
	Howes	E.J	????
ROYAL ARTILLERY STAFF			
COLONEL			
	Reilly CB	W.E.M	1879
LIEUTENANT COLONEL			
	Brown CB	J.T.B	1879
BREVET MAJOR			
	Clarke CMG	M.J	1879
CAPTAIN			
	Bouwens	L.H	1879
	Knox	W.G	1879
Had medal for an earlier campaign. See also Transvaal Artillery.			
	Maurice	J.F	1879
	Robinson	J.C	1877-8
	Yeatman-Biggs	A.G	1879
LIEUTENANT			
	Williams	W.H	1879
BATTERY SERGEANT MAJOR			
457/DS	Liddy	G	1879
GUNNER			
3799	Beal	W	1879
2860	Knight	H	1879
ROYAL ARTILLERY. 2nd BRIGADE.			
L BATTERY			
LIEUTENANT			
	Creagh	A.G	1879
ROYAL ARTILLERY. 2nd BRIGADE			
O BATTERY			
FARRIER SERGEANT			
2099	James	Mc A	1877-8-9
4389	Smith	S	1879
ROYAL ARTILLERY. 4th BRIGADE			
N BATTERY			
SERGEANT			
4/6530	Chalmers	W	No clasp
GUNNER			
4447	Davies	C	No clasp
ROYAL ARTILLERY. 5th BRIGADE			
B BATTERY			
CAPTAIN			
	Vaughan	H	1879
ROYAL ARTILLERY. 5th BRIGADE			
DEPOT BATTERY			
FARRIER SERGEANT			
2242	Osborne	G	1877-8
DRIVER			
2024	Shepherd	C	1879

Royal Artillery 5th Brigade

\# Brevet Major Stuart Smith, RA

ROYAL ARTILLERY. 5th BRIGADE.
N BATTERY
Those Killed in Action (**KIA**) lost their lives at Isandhlwana on 23/1/1879.

BREVET LIEUTENANT COLONEL
Harness CB A 1877-8-9

BREVET MAJOR
\#Smith **KIA** S 1877-8-9

CAPTAIN
Vibart F.M.E 1879

LIEUTENANT
Curling H.T 1877-8-9
Fowler W.J 1877-8-9
Parsons C.B 1877-8-9
Rundle H.M.L 1879
See also Gattling Field Bty.

SERGEANT MAJOR
41 Cunningham F 1877-8-9

QUARTERMASTER SERGEANT
176/6 Garbutt 1879
No medal. In prison.
*48 Cook J 1877-8-9
D/S 16th March 1879 Helpmakaar

FARRIER SERGEANT
4781 Watson T 1879
841 Whinham **KIA** R 1879

SERGEANT
\# 216 Costellow J 1877-8-9
(see page 360)
7432 Davis G 1879
3483 Edwards **KIA** W 1877-8-9
392 Garnett H 1877-8-9
4757 Hyatt J 1879
215 Kenyon T 1877-8-9
1864 Toole T 1877-8-9
644 Warren W.E 1877-8-9

CORPORAL
1119 Bailey **KIA** H 1877-8-9
4758 Bendall J 1879
2176 Brown J 1877-8-9

2721 Cooper **KIA** W 1877-8-9
4756 Kelvington J 1879r
1872 Langridge **KIA** J 1877-8-9
4740 Meecham J 1879
4700 Stevens C 1879
1080 Smith J 1877-8-9

BOMBARDIER
1568 Brierley W 1877-8-9
4731 Copsey E 1879
926 Cox W 1877-8-9
817 Manns I 1877-8-9
3592 Stubbs G 1879
54 Sime R 1877-8-9
758 Warner W 1877-8-9
1871 Walters D/S G 1877-8

ACTING BOMBARDIER
1882 Aylett **KIA** J 1877-8-9
147 Boswell **KIA** T 1877-8-9
2989 Creswell C 1879
4710 Ganley T 1879
1538 Godden D/S J 1877-8
4702 King W 1879
No medal. Deserted.
3481 Leguay **KIA** J.L 1877-8-9
2196 Mc Donnel **KIA** J 1877-8-9
1763 Nash **KIA** T 1877-8-9
746 Parker **KIA** J 1877-8-9

GUNNER
4701 Anderton J 1879
4732 Ashton J 1879
922 Barrett T 1877-8
4741 Beybutt H 1879
No medal. Deserted.
1883 Beech **KIA** F 1877-8-9
4766 Benham J 1879
655 Berry **KIA** T 1877-8-9
4742 Blakemore G 1879
4712 Bowen H 1879
4771 Buffery W 1879
4733 Bull B 1879
1885 Burk **KIA** J 1877-8-9
2189 Byrne **KIA** J 1877-8-9
157 Caldow J 1879
3760/9 Cantwell J 1877-8-9
2076 Gnr John Cantwell DCM
516 Cochrane **KIA** S.J 1877-8-9
1311 Collins **KIA** R 1877-8-9
1082 Connelly **KIA** J 1877-8-9
4743 Conboy P 1879
8401/3 Connel M 1877-8-9
3992 Conroy M 1879
2757 Corser J.A 1879
4734 Copsey H 1879
1637 Davis **KIA** I 1877-8-9
2732 Davis D/S J 1879
3484 Dickins **KIA** W 1877-8-9
4735 Dickson C 1879
4015 Digney T 1879
4745 Eite W No clasp

1462 Elliot **KIA** T 1877-8-9
1643 Evans A 1877-8-9
1868 Farndell H No clasp
No medal. Deserted.
4768 Fitzgerald T 1879
2292 Gurnett W 1877-8-9
4737 Gaswell J 1879
2766 Goff G 1877-8-9
No medal. Deserted.
665 Green W 1877-8-9
246 Hales A 1877-8-9
1231 Hallaghan T 1877-8-9
669 Halnon J 1877-8-9
1772 Harper R 1877-8-9
No medal. Deserted.
4837 Harris G 1879r
668 Harrison **KIA** T 1877-8-9
2770 Hawker W 1877-8
2741 Henry E 1877-8-9
A replacement issued 17/1/1921.
1412 Hicks **KIA** J 1877-8-9
1632 Hillard G 1877-8-9
1413 Hills D/S S 1877-8
2077 Howard A 1879
3102 Jackson W 1879
1773 James **KIA** E.G 1877-8-9
4738 Jones D 1879
4709 Jones E 1879
4736 Keefe J 1879
1834 King **KIA** C 1877-8-9
4366 King C 1879
1133 Lamb **KIA** J 1877-8-9
4696 Lead R.L 1879
2776 Larkin P 1879
4748 Lloyd T 1879
4767 Lord J 1879
4747 Luckman W 1879
4749 Martin T 1879r
1683 Marshall **KIA** W 1877-8-9
2945 Mc Gregor **KIA** M 1877-8-9
2781 Mc Intyre R 1879
1655 Mead **KIA** J 1877-8-9
4842 Merridan H 1879
2783 Miller J 1079
2630 Miller **KIA** T 1877-8-9
1826 Morris M 1877-8-9
957 Mullaney J 1877-8-9
4708 Mycock W 1879
4770 Nickolas A 1879
2633 O'Neil **KIA** D 1877-8-9
2322 Page **KIA** H 1877-8-9
1774 Page J 1877-8-9
1294 Perrin J 1877-8-9
No medal. Deserted.
4750 Price F 1879
3129 Pyne F 1879
1438 Redmond **KIA** A 1877-8-9
692 Reede **KIA** J 1877-8-9
2460 Regan **KIA** J 1877-8-9

Royal Artillery 5th Brigade

Buckland Dix & Wood Auction 4th December 1991. Lot 30
An important medal awarded to Sergeant John Costellow, N Battery, 5th Brigade, Royal Artillery, who was one of the few to survive the massacre at Isandhlwana
SOUTH AFRICA 1877-9, 1 clasp, 1877-8-9 (216 Sergt. J. Costellon (sic), R.A.), small edge nick, otherwise good very fine Hammer Price £3000.

Sergeant John Costellow is confirmed as one of the four survivors of the battery in a letter written six days after the battle by Elias Tucker, a Driver of N battery, to his mother. His letter was published in the Western Morning News (Plymouth) on 28 March 1879. Interestingly he gives the spelling Costellan whereas the medal rolls consistantly show Costellow, albeit with the same regimental number. Tucker's letter reads:

Battle-field, Helpmakaar, Jan 28th, 1879

'Dear Father and Mother,—It gives me great pleasure to think that I am alive to write to you. We had a severe cutting up on the 22nd of January. Lord Chelmsford went out with the column about three o'clock in the morning; he went about 15 miles from camp to attack the Zulus—to Isinlonana or the Lion's Mane. They left 2 guns and 65 artillery, 6 companies of the 24th Regiment, in all about five hundred men. The Zulus watched the column out of the camp, and then attacked the camp; they came into the camp like wild beasts, which they are.

'We played well on them with the two guns, and the infantry fought well, cutting roads through them. We held the field from half past eleven in the morning until three o'clock in the day. We killed twelve thousand Zulus, but they were too strong for us. They came right round us, and massacred every one; there are only twelve left to tell the tale. Out of sixty-five artillery only four remain, and I am one of the four— Sergeant Costellan (sic), Lieutenant Curling (that's my master), and myself and Gunner Green. We four had a horse each, and we charged right through the Zulus and cut our way out. I was in my shirtsleeves carrying ammunition to the guns.

'We lost everything in camp; they burnt everything that would burn. All our waggons and carts we had for ammunition they filled up with dead white men. They cut everyone up, and took his heart and laid it on his breast, and put his right hand in where they took his heart from, and put all the skulls in a heap. I expect you will see the massacre in the papers before you receive this. I could not write before. We rode a hard gallop from the time we cut our way out of camp until four next morning, and we found ourselves in sight of Helpmakaar, and that gave us fresh strength, hoping to find some help there; but when we got there there were only six men on guard belonging to the 13th Regiment. We frightened them out of their lives. There is only one store in Helpmakaar, and that was filled with stocks of corn. We got that out and barricaded all the doors, and cut some loopholes through the sides and ends to fire through. We were afraid they would attack us here, but they have not been.

The Gatling guns of the Royal Artillery 7th Brigade Number 10 Battery

'Dear mother, still there is hope for us, for our relief came his morning. A lot of Engineers and the 4th (King's Own) Regiment marched in here; we gave them three hearty cheers. Dear mother, I must now conclude, as they are sending out a mounted orderly tonight, and I want these few lines to go with him. I have not received any letters from England since October. The Zulus have taken possession of all the houses on the road and burnt them down. ... Please drop a few lines to London to Tim and my sister to let them know that I am living and well, for I cannot get paper to write on.

'I gave a shilling for this envelope and paper, and it is cheap at that. We can not get paper or envelopes for love or money here in the midst of a wilderness and savages. Please give my kind love to all inquiring friends and tell them all I am alive and well, only a slight wound on the back of the hand. So, good-bye, and God bless you all. They have sent to England for more troops, and we shall pay the Zulus out for this yet.

'Elias Tucker, Driver, N Battery, Royal Artillery,
'Colonel Glyn's Column'

Royal Artillery 5th Brigade

No.	Name		Years
2166	Reynolds	G	1877-8-9
1775	Ridgway	D/SA	1877-8
1605	Roach	P	1877-8
No medal. Deserted.			
1437	Rolls	J	1877-8-9
2183	Roscoe **KIA**	W	1877-8-9
1066	Rowley	T	1877-8-9
3842	Smythe **KIA**	J	1877-8-9
2807	Snowling	G	1877-8-9
4739	Stratton	R	1879
1833	Stevenson **KIA**	R	1877-8-9
1067	Thompson	J	1877-8-9
4769	Todd	W	1879
1832	Walters	J	1877-8-9
4128	Webater	J	1879
1324	White	A	1877-8-9
2652	Williams **KIA**	R	1877-8-9
2819	Wilson **KIA**	T	1877-8-9
1626	Wilson **KIA**	W	1877-8-9
704	Woolacott **KIA**	A	1877-8-9
DRIVER			
1471	Adams **KIA**	W	1877-8-9
715	Allen **KIA**	H	1877-8-9
1687	Baggley	J	1877-8-9
No medal. Deserted.			
5166	Bailey	C	1879
707	Barron **KIA**	W	1877-8-9
1723	Bennett	W	1879
1524	Bishop **KIA**	C	1877-8-9
1033/6	Boswell	J	1879
1310	Boyle	M	1877-8-9
*3520	Bracken	T	No clasp
D/S 9th March 1879 Helpmakaar			
3520 Drummer J Brackan			
2174	Brooks **KIA**	J	1877-8-9
4705	Brown	J	1879
4838	Briggs	A	1879
No medal. In prison.			
4705	Brown	J	1879
1961	Bruce **KIA**	T	1877-8-9
1954	Burchell	J	1879
2826	Burke	T	1879
4774	Child	R	1879
4760	Chilton	F	1879
1598	Clarke **KIA**	T	1877-8-9
4779	Clements	H	1879
No medal. Deserted.			
4725	Coglan	J	1879
No medal. Deserted.			
5280/5	Collins	J	No clasp
4703	Conaidine	J	1879
5167	Cook	E	1879
No medal. Deserted.			
4778	Cording	J	1879
4726	Coughcliffe	T	1879
3480	Cowley **KIA**	H	1877-8-9
5168	Crannes	W	1879
4763	Crowley	C	1879
5169	Cunningham	J	1879
No medal. Deserted.			
1185	Dailey **KIA**	J	1879
2185	Danniher	J	1877-8
4706	Day	W	1879
3154	Denyer	J	1879
No medal. Deserted.			
718	Ellis	E	1877-8-9
1526	Everett	A	1877-8-9
4761	Foster	G	1879
8402/5	Galphin	F.H	1879
4707	Gee	W	1879
4780	Gibson	R	1879
5134	Green	C	1879
4775	Griffin	R	1879
1797	Grimes	P	1877-8-9
4011/6	Grist	W	1879
4727	Grogan	A	1879
4776	Grubby	P	1879
1978	Halbrow	D/S J	No clasp
729	Hatson	G	1877-8-9
727	Hiatt **KIA**	W	1877-8-9
5170	Hitchman	J	1879
4752	Hunt	G	1879
5287/5	Hunt	W	1879
723	Hutchings **KIA**	J	1877-8-9
178/6	Hyde	R	1879
4783	Hydes	I	1879
1843	Jarvis	R	1877-8-9r
No medal. Deserted.			
1999	Jones	E	1877-8
2178	Jones **KIA**	J.W	1877-8-9
1435	Jones	W.J	1877-8-9
1997	Joyce **KIA**	L	1877-8-9
2846	Lane	G	1879
4772	Leeson	G	1879
4753	Lewis	J	1879
458	Lewis	T	1877-8-9
2082	Luford	J	1877-8-9
No medal. Deserted.			
4704	Mahar	J	1879
741	Marchant **KIA**	J	1877-8-9
4751	Marks	A	1879
No medal. Deserted.			
4180	Martin	A.E	No clasp
51/1	Martin	H	1879
2687	Martin	S	1879
4728	Mass	S	1879
2119	Mc Keown **KIA**	G	1877-8-9
2015	Murphy **KIA**	F	1879
5172	New	C	1879
4754	Pead	A	1879
750	Pitt	T	1877-8-9
2086	Potter	J	1877-8
891	Press	B	1877-8-9
2023	Price	E	1879
5164	Rastin	E	1879
2078	Richardson	J	1877-8-9
4755	Roberts	T	1879
468	Rowlands	J	1879
5173	Simpson	J	1879
No medal. Deserted.			
?	Smith	B	1879?
3822	Smith	R	1879
4773	Soutar	W	1879
No medal. Deserted.			
648	Spread **KIA**	C	1877-8-9
4762	Stevens	G	1879
5174	Stevens	J	1879
4729	Surmon	G	1879
No medal. Deserted.			
2031	Sutherland	A	1879
3031	Trainer	P	1879
1204	Trapp	W	1877-8-9
1387	Tucker	E	1877-8-9
484	Underhill	G	1879
5175	Unsworth	R	1879
4764	Walsh	J	1879r
5176	Warden	G	1879
5177	Watkins	H	1879
5165	Woods	D	1879
3912	Wood	S	1879
759	Wood	T	1877-8-9
760	Wood	W	1879
1599	Wood	W	1877-8-9
5178	Wright	C	1877-8
4765	Wright	E	1879
765	Wyatt	A	1877-8-9
482	Wyblin	G.H	1879
COLLAR MAKER			
944	Joy	R	1877-8-9
4723	Lewis	J	1879
697	Sloane	T.W	1877-8-9r
753	Shepherd **KIA**	T	1877-8-9
SHOEING SMITH			
4782	Cahill	W	1879
4730	Kearns	P	1879
1142	Steer	J	1877-8-9
361	Townshead	G	1877-8-9
TRUMPETER			
1561	Martin	N.H	1877-8-9
1343	Neary	P	1879
WHEELER			
1254	Etherington D/S	R	1879
4783	Nightingale	B	1879
* London Gazette 23 May 1879			

ROYAL ARTILLERY. 6th BRIGADE
M BATTERY
MAJOR

	Sandham	W.H	1879
CAPTAIN			
	Legard	J.D	1879
LIEUTENANT			
	Jervis-White Jervis	J.H	1879
	Shiffner	J	1879
	Thomson	J.H	1879
SERGEANT MAJOR			
311	Craig	T	1879

Royal Artillery 5th Brigade

QUARTERMASTER SERGEANT				4042	Curry	J	1879	3221	Clarke	J	1879
580	Hicks	J	1879	1557	Dacey	T	1879	4040	Cole	H	1879
FARRIER SERGEANT				683	Darnyon	J	1879	?	Collins	T	1879
1628	Fisher	T	1879	1634	Dean	C	1879	1088	Cook	W	1879
SERGEANT SERGEANT				923	Dean	J	1879	1647	Creighton	M	1879
666	Sullivan	G	1879	4090	Dougherty	J	1879r	1281	Dels	R	1879
SERGEANT				735	Downtraw ?	J	1879	1564	Doyle	H	1879r
892	Aldis	F	1879	920	Duffy	P	1879r	3373	Earle	T.W	1879
852	Hall	S.W	1879	737	Fairn	J	1879	722	Fairbrother	G	1879
170	Johnson	W	1879	3347	Field	F	1879	1453	Farrant	E	No clasp
326	Keefe	H	1879	3111	Garvey	H	1879	1311	Finnis	A	1879
421	Purdy	H	1879	739	Gerrish	J	1879	3225	Fyles	J	1879
678	Shorbridge	G	1879	4382	Gillman	C	1879	1404	Gill	J	1879
CORPORAL				1431	Graley	J	1879	720	Griffiths	C	1879
103	Bennett	W	1879	741	Grant	F	1879	3913	Hardwick	T	1879
547	Clarke	G	1879	742	Grimes	J	1879	1291	Harris	J	1879
691	Couchman	F	1879	8110	Hart	C	1879	1008	Hastings	J	1879
734	Douglas	J	1879	3118	Harvey	W	1879	709	Head	J	1879
4375	Huft	W	1879	938	Henry	A.F	1879	720	Hill	I	1879
4207	Mason	W.C	1879	721	Holt	J	1879	1645	Jackson	J	1879
BOMBARDIER				3941	Hopewell	G	1879	1276	Johnson	G	1879
616	Barker	W	1879	3113	Horsley	T	1879	1649	Kilbride	H	1879
254	Bush	C	1879	940	Jackman	G	1879	2732	Lane	T	1879
687	Quin	T	1879	1700	James	E	1879	3320	Langley	T	1879
341	Skudder	W	1879	1287	Jary	W	1879	667	Livermore	R	1879
BOMBARDIER COLLAR MAKER				7428	Kemp	F	1879	2007	Lord	A	1879
259	Childs	E	1879	8111	Kimber	J.R	1879	1816	Mc Caslin	F	1879
BOMBARDIER WHEELER				1360	Knappet	C	1879	631	Mc Keown	E	1879
1429	Creek	S	1879	1667	Knight	C.F	1879	715	Moulson	S	1879
ACTING BOMBARDIER				4383	Knight	H	1879	1562	Munro	W	1879
978	Byrnes	J	1879	3207	Leefe	T	1879	4206	Munt	E	1879
3110	Carmody	F	1879	1331	Long	J	1879	1183	Neilson	R	1879
686	Donnelly	T.F	1879	4377	Mc Carty	J	1879	681	Nye	H	1879
1677	Frost	H	1879	3064	Mc Ilveen	F	1879	1111	Rafferty	F	1879
3390	Jonas	W	1879	1445	Mulherne	J	1879	1648	Roberts	J.B	1879
1673	Tuffrey	H	1879	1438	Murphy	T	1879	1563	Robertson	T	1879
3399	Vizer	T.W	1879	1450	Murray	T	1879	1139	Roles	P	1879
GUNNER				657	Mythen	J	1879	3311	Roser	A	1879
1534	Addison	C	1879	695	O'Connor	J	1879	1185	Ryan	J	1879
646	Addy	D	1879	1670	Parker	S	1879	1026	Sears	A	1879
690	Bailey	G	1879	1428	Peck	I	1879	723	Shearing	R	1879
743	Baker	J.C	1879	3201	Pryke	J.B	1879	3374	Stewart	C	1879
3182	Ballantyne	H	1879	3952	Salmon	J	1879r	1182	Thompson	G	1879
No medal. Deserted.				4043	Smith	W	1879	1188	Toner	D	1879
3249	Barr	A	1879	3944	Tait	J	1879	1489	Turthill	G	1879
4049	Barrowcliffe	G	1879	961	Tompkins	G	1879	484	Underhill	G	1879
1337	Bedingfield	R.H	1879	4098	Townrow	C	1879	1293	Walker	J	1879
729	Bee	E.C	1879	663	West	W	1879	6897	Walker	J	1879
1448	Bibby	W	1879	3763	Whittaker	T	1879	1320	Warwick	W	1879
3099	Bould	J.E	1879	1674	Williams	A	1879	670	Watts	J	1879
3156	Briggs	N.J	1879	**DRIVER**				4062	Wilks	A	1879
1440	Brown	W	1879	680	Atkins	R	1879	660	Williams	S	1879
918	Cameron	J	1879	1303	Baldwin	J	1879	3912	Wilson	J	1879
3389	Carpenter	W	1879	6896	Bennett	J	1879	No medal. Deserted.			
4381	Chapman	W	1879	649	Brisley	W	1879	3797	Woods	F	1879
671	Clawe	L	1879	3945	Bugden	W	1879	457	Woodward	W	1879
8100	Conlon	J	1879	1950	Burrough	J	1879	**COLLAR MAKER**			
6893	Cranmer	J	1879	?	Cartwright	T	1879	3313	Thomas	G.W	1879
733	Cross	S.W	1879	?	Childs	C	1879				

Royal Artillery 5th Brigade

SHOEING SMITH

Number	Name	Initial	Year
629	Carroll	P	1879
3348	Foley	J	1879
3825	Harding	W	1879
1329	Solly	W.T	1879

TRUMPETER

Number	Name	Initial	Year
178	Holliday	A	No clasp r
	Deserted. No medal.		
1342	Lynch	J	1879

ROYAL ARTILLERY. 6th BRIGADE
N BATTERY

MAJOR

	Le Grice	F.T	1879

CAPTAIN

	Crookenden	N.N	1879

LIEUTENANT

	Elliott	E.H	1879
	Trench	F.J.A	1879
	Wodehouse	J.H	1879

VETERINARY SURGEON

	Hagger	W	1879

See also Army Veterinary Corps.

SERGEANT MAJOR

758	Rutherford	H	1879

COLLARMAKER SERGEANT

769	Groves	S	1879

QUARTERMASTER SERGEANT

754	Cox	J.H	1879

FARRIER SERGEANT

773	Gill	W	1879
3050	Heathcote	H	1879?

See also 11th Bde. No. 11 Bty. RA.

SERGEANT

1633	Archer	J	1879
4556	Gall	J	1879
176	Garbett	J.H	1879
206	Green	M	1879
934	Harper	R.H	1879
767	Rooney	H	1879
645	Whittle	H	1879

CORPORAL

824	Adams D/S	J	No clasp
779	Boyd	J	1879
3915	Chapman	J	1879
178	Hyde	R	1879
1048	Jelly	J	1879
756	Lauder	J	1879
1709	Pinchen	W	1879
3709	Ward	R	1879
4146	West	J.A	1879

BOMBARDIER

790	Feenan	B	1879r
1445	Holland	H	1879
1212	O'Connell	J	1879
1110	Pearce	J.G	1879
1635	Ricketts	J.T	1879
876	Salter	W	1879
425	Howland	G	1879
3313	Thomas	G	1879?

BOMBARDIER WHEELER

4282	Emery	F	1879?
3224	Kinnear	W	1879

ACTING BOMBARDIER

813	Raison	R	1879
1030	Whent	G.H	1879

GUNNER

4040	Anderson	J	No clasp
1573	Armistead	J	1879r
4063	Baker	A	1879
4016	Beharrell	S	1879
1577	Bennett	G	1879
3133	Bradbeer	W	1879
1688	Brady	J	1879
3823	Brett	C	1879
4081	Brown	J	1879
	No medal. Deserted.		
458	Burke	D	1879
4082	Carthy	H	1879
	No medal. Deserted.		
2609	Charles	F	1879?
785	Conboy	M	1879
1588	Curtis	J	1879
1572	Cutler	F	1879
1512	Davenport	S	1879
157	Dawson	W	1879
3190	Dryland	T	1879
3195	Dunn	T	1879
1685	Folks	W	1879
3822	Gascoigne	W.H	1879
1576	Hammond	R	1879
1432	Hayward	W.H	1879
1408	Hopkins	W.H	1879
1317	Howard	J	1879
1157	Hudson	J	1879
1533	Humphrey	J	1879
	No medal. Deserted.		
4170	Hunt	W	1879
3877	Jackson	R	1879
	No medal. Deserted.		
19	Johns	J	1879
1294	Jones	F.A	1879
4092	Jones	G	1879
1109	Jones	J.J	1879
1361	Leggett	A	1879
1496	Long	J	1879
1497	Lovering	J	1879
1300	Lyons	B	1879
1536	Marmont	J	1879
1161	Maxwell	J	1879
1213	Mc Grath	J	1879
803	Mc Leary	A	1879
1148	Morris	H	1879
72	Nahill	J	1879
	No medal. No reason given.		
4039	New	C	1879
3086	Nickolls	J	1879
1537	O'Connor	J	1879
1636	Owens	D	1879
	Medal forfeited. No reason given.		
4171	Peskett	C	1879
1705	Philpot	H	1879
869	Pierce	W	1879
3163	Pratt	J	1879
2534	Radcliffe	W	1879
1419	Radcliffe	J	No clasp r
3074	Raymond	J	1879
1962	Raymond	W.H	1879
3208	Reid	E	1879
1641	Roderick	T	1879
3122	Rogers	W	1879
3189	Ruder	H	1879
1359	Scott	W	1879
4166	Shelford	B	1879
1163	Shields	A	1879
817	Swift	H	1879
1405	Tanner	W	1879
1248	Tapp	C	1879
3209	Towell ?	H	1879
1152	Towner	E	1879
1107	Watson	W	1879
3305	Watton	W	1879
3472	Wilkins	G	1879
1147	Williams 1st	W	1879
1963	Williams 2nd	W	1879

DRIVER

963	Allen	W	1879
1411	Aubrey	E	1879
1092	Barker	A	1879
828	Barnett	C	1879
3411	Barrett	J	1879
	Deserted. No indication of the return of the medal.		
984	Beer	C	1879
3690	Blake	M	1879
831	Bloomfield	E	No clasp
832	Bolston	C	1879
983	Bolton	R	1879
1033	Boswell	J	1879
833	Bourne	G	1879r
1582	Brennan	D	1879
1390	Clarke	W F	1879
3016	Collins	J	No clasp
835	Crane	J	1879
837	Crook	E	1879
1118	Crowley	M	1879
843	Donnelly	M	1879
1111	Donoghue	J	1879
993	Donovan	P	No clasp
1911	Evans	D	1879
1244	Fean ?	J	1879
183	Field	H	1879
1940	Finnimore	J.P	1879
1351	Gooderham	C	1879
3247	Gray	W	1879
4011	Grist	W	1879
1913	Hale	W	1879

Royal Artillery 6th Brigade

4010	Harris	T	1879	**FARRIER SERGEANT**				4237	Keer	W	1879
4045	Hayter	A	1879	4667	Brewer	W	1879	4222	Mason	T	1879
1581	Hillear	R.G.M	1879	902	Nicol	J	1879	828	Millgrove	J	1879
854	Holdaway	W	1879	**SERGEANT**				4054	Minks	W	1879
2347	Hunt	W	1879	845	Edge	J	1879	4018	Moore	J	1879
3407	Johnson	T	1879	3433	Mc Donald	W.J	1879	3117	Muxlow	N	1879
4146	Kent	S	1879	4298	Roushaw	E.J	1879	1936	Northcott	P	1879
1430	Knott	G	1879	4299	Shute	T.C	1879	4246	Penney	E	1879
1950	Lewis	H	1879	8028	St Ledger	B	1879	4224	Prosser	W.C	1879
1141	Mc Cartney	W	1879	3042	Wilson	J	1879	4008	Savage	H	1879
1143	Moore	C	1879	**CORPORAL**				4225	Shannon	D	1879
4048	Moore	F	1879	4374	Bampton	J	1879	3206	Sharmon	F	1879
861	Nash	A	1879	4234	Byrne	J	1879	1531	Smith	W	1879
1452	Northcott	W	1879	4588	Campbell	J	1879	963	Thomas	H	1879
1502	Nunn	C	1879	4325	Jarvis	J	1879	4231	Tomlinson	C	1879
3286	Nunn	W	1879	5252	Melody	H	1879	**DRIVER**			
867	Page	A.G	1879	1715	Pearse	T.A	1879	4303	Anderson	W	1879
1907	Patterson	W	1879	**BOMBARDIER**				3025	Ashmore	W	1879
584	Price	L	1879	1003	Harris	J	1879	985	Baird	W	1879
3091	Pryke	W	1879	766	Phillips	J	1879	4322	Bamping	E	1879
1023	Randall	E	1879	4283	Prouter	C.W	1879	4321	Barker	J	1879
1467	Regan	J	1879	905	White	W	1879	4302	Brian	P	1879
1275	Rouse	W.E	1879	1614	White	W	1879	4304	Bridgewater	W	1879
1339	Ruddeck	J	1879	**ACTING BOMBARDIER**				4338	Brown	W	1879r
874	Ruddock	W	1879	3853	Curtis	F.H	1879	4211	Callan	W	1879
1589	Rundle	P	1879	935	Hird	C	1879	1313	Chappel	S	1879
1295	Smith	B	1879	1362	Light	P	1879	4214	Chatfield	W.H	1879
4027	Smith	T	1879	950	Newson	W	1879	4287	Cook	A	1879
1542	Sear	A	1879	1368	Ormond	J	1879	8109	Cook	J	1879
818	Spink	W	1879	4245	Simons	E	1879	4320	Cox	T	1879
1164	Staples	C	1879	4289	Skilton	H	1879	1318	Curtis	F	1879
3824	Sutton	W	1879	**GUNNER**				4293	Darby	J	1879
1315	Tucker	C	1879	908	Bartlett	E	1879	641	Davis	R	1879
1031	Wilding	W	1879	4041	Bowers	J	1879	4339	Dixon	P	1879
1914	Wilson	J	1879	7461	Buckingham	J	1879	990	Dowden	G	1879
SHOEING SMITH				8113	Caffery	F	1879	1312	Elviston	W	1879
1264	Beckett	A	1879	4297	Cooke	B	1879	4291	Freer	J	1879
801	Lloyd	S	No clasp	4232	Cook	T	1879	4323	Gall	H	1879
1642	Main	J	1879	915	Corham D/S	T.J	1879	1901	Gallant	E	1879
3304	Swan	G	1879	Accidently shot.				4344	Glover	T	1879
TRUMPETER				913	Cowley	H	1879	828	Hafford	J	1879
775	Little	J	1879	916	Crook	R	1879	4305	Handley	C	1879
				4589	Crudgington	S	1879	4366	Harries	H	1879
ROYAL ARTILLERY. 6th BRIGADE				1478	Crushell	C	1879	4367	Hemmings	R	1879
O BATTERY				4219	Dalton	L	1879	4212	Herridge	T	1879
MAJOR				4220	Davey	A	1879	4306	Hilliard	G	1879
	Duncan	A.W	1879	4240	Davis	W	1879	4307	Humphreys	J	1879
CAPTAIN				4241	Delsey	M	1879	4318	Jackson	R	1879
	Alexander	R	1879	4215	Donovan	H	1879	4084	James	W	1879
	Bally	J.F	1879	924	Dutton	G	1879	566	Johnson	T	1879
LIEUTENANT				4094	Egginton	D	1879	4313	Jones	H	1879
	Anderson	W.C	No clasp	4228	Elliott	P	1879	6895	Kemp	R	1879
	Douglas	J.S	1879	3191	Futter	J	1879	8115	Kennedy	J	1879
	Taylor	W.H.F	1879	4238	Graham	J	1879	2649	Lewis	G	1879
BATTERY SERGEANT MAJOR				3124	Granger	W.H	1879	756	Lewis	J	1879
1149	Riches	F	1879	4230	Groves	J	1879	4368	Lock	H	1879
BATTERY QUARTERMASTER SERGEANT				4235	Hall	W	1879	4346	Marshall	F	1879
				4243	Hunt	J	1879	4341	Milton	T	1879
1082	Evans	J	1879	4221	Kerney	J	1879	4369	Morris	R	1879

Royal Artillery 6th Brigade

Number	Name	Initial	Year
4290	Murray	E	1879
4347	Nelms	T	1879
4215	Newman	J	1879
1019	O'Donnell	J	1879
6898	Overett	H	1879
4309	Papp	J	1879
2261	Pike	A	1879
4213	Plunkett	W	1879
1886	Podd	A	1879
6891	Prior	F	1879
1476	Pryke	C	1879
4370	Pullen	F	1879
4285	Purse	J	1879
4310	Ringwood	G	1879
4342	Roberts	G	1879
4371	Russell	D/S H	1879
4343	Samuels	J	1879
4311	Scriven	T	1879
4350	Senior	L	1879
1951	Settle	H	1879
4316	Sibun	G.F	1879
4348	Skiddle	C	1879
4349	Smith	J	1879r
4216	Stace	G	1879
4284	Steel	W	1879
1028	Theobald	J	1879
3024	Tillbrook	T	1879
1367	Turner	M	1879
4312	Tyler	S	1879
1388	Underhill	C	1879
4351	Vintiner	R	1879
4318	Webster	C.E	1879
4286	Welsby	T	1879

COLLAR MAKER

506	Lineham	J	1879
6988	Murphy	W	1879

SHOEING SMITH

2328	Green	J	1879
4382	Mc Donald	R	1879
5419	Stoot	S	1879
4373	Tennison	E	1879

TRUMPETER

3994	Mc Pherson	E	1879
1308	Spinks	F.W	1879

WHEELER

904	Andrews	J.W	1879
4282	Emery	F	1879

ROYAL ARTILLERY. 7th BRIGADE
LIEUTENANT COLONEL

	Law CB	F.T.A	1877-8-9

Also has medals British Crimea
Turkish Crimea and China

ROYAL ARTILLERY. 7th BRIGADE
NUMBER 8 BATTERY
MAJOR

	Ellaby	H.L	1879

CAPTAIN

	Cooke	T.C	1879
	Maclean	A.H	1879

LIEUTENANT

	Mc Lish	F.J	1879

BATTERY SERGEANT MAJOR

1675	Sym	R	1879

SERGEANT

1903	Allard	A	1877-8
1694	Mc Clustin	I	1879
1847	Owen	J	1877-8
1605	Winlock	H	1879

CORPORAL

1784	Oldin D/S	G	1879
1820	Parfitt	H	1877-8-9

BOMBARDIER

1888	Borderer	J	1879
3111	Griffiths	R	1879
452	Knight	C.H	1879
1777	Painter	J	1879
1721	Thompson	J	1877-8

ACTING BOMBARDIER

1778	Harper	J	1879
2511	Mun	F	1879
2022	Teiling	C	1877-8
2540	Wooding	T	1879

GUNNER

2545	Aulb	J	1879
1872	Batchelor	A	1877-8
1630	Batchford	R	1877-8
2534	Beaumont	C	1879
2674	Bird	J.W	1879
1895	Black	R	1879
1914	Bradish	J	1877-8-9
1966	Brown	F.W	1879
1944	Brown	T	1877-8
1916	Burk	D	1877-8-9
1853	Burk	T	1879
2763	Butler	J.H	1879
1852	Byron	E	1877-8
1978	Campbell	B	1879
2620	Carr	R	1879
2609	Charles	F	1879
2041	Cef	F	1879

No medal .Discharged with Ignominy.

1631	Conway	W	1879
1959	Cotter	J	1877-8-9
1961	Dodwell	I.J	1877-8
1945	Donovan	J	1877-8-9
1937	Donovan	P	1877-8
1651	Dunwoody	W	1879
1962	Ewir ?	A	1877-8
2585	Flanagan D/S	E	1879
2057	Flowers	C	1877-8
2151	Gosney	J	1877-8
1770	Hart	J	1877-8
1922	Hathaway	C	1879
1921	Higgins	J	1877-8
1972	Hellis	W	1877-8
1943	Hutchinson	T	1879
1617	Hyde	H.H	1879
2591	Jerrum?	A	1879
2784	Jones	T	1879
2588	King	T	1879
1939	Kingham	C	1879
1625	Lanch	R.J	1879
2025	Mc Aura	I	1879
2697	Mc Cannon	W	1879
1653	Mc Elroy	E	1879
2035	Mc Nisby	H.J	No clasp
1875	Mc Rae	A	1877-8
1712	Meredith	C	1877-8
1779	Moses	W`	1879
2010	Munro	M.	1877-8-9r
1918	Oswald	W	1879
1716	Passmore	H	1879
2113	Pearl	R	1877-8-9
1587	Phelan	R	1879
1638	Potter	W	1879
3112	Preator	H	1879
2640	Reardon	P	1879r
2109	Roffey	R	1877-8-9
1602	Rogers	C	1879
1620	Scott	J	1877-8
2110	Shalis	J	1877-8
1538	Sharman	A	1879
2032	Slack ?	A.G	1877-8
1590	Smith	J	1877-8-9
2789	Smith	W	1879
1963	Story	R	1877-8-9
1658	Sturgeon	T	1879
1780	Telford	J	No clasp

No medal .Deserted.

1713	Tuck	S	1877-8-9
2048	Welsh	A.E	1877-8-9
2783	Welsh	J	1879

No medal .Deserted.

1654	White	S	1877-8

TRUMPETER

2031	Forsyth	W.H	1879r
1874	Wilson	J	1879

No medal .in prison.

ROYAL ARTILLERY. 7th BRIGADE
NUMBER 10 BATTERY. (GATTLING FIELD BATTERY)

The Anglo-Zulu War of 1879 was the first time that the British Army had used the Gatling Gun against an enemy.

MAJOR

	Owen	J.F	1879

CAPTAIN

	Evans	E.B	1879

LIEUTENANT

	Rundle	H.M.L	1879

See also Lt H.B.L Rundle
N Battery 5th Bde RA.

Royal Artillery 7th Brigade

No.	Name	Initial	Clasp
BATTERY SERGEANT MAJOR			
1671	Whiteman	W	No clasp
FARRIER SERGEANT			
1130	Shepherd	W	1879
SERGEANT			
1623	Blanche	W	1879
1676	Burnett	J	No clasp
1740	Childs	E	1879
1848	Wilkinson	J.J	1879
CORPORAL			
1718	Balley	D	1879
4588	Campbell	J	1879
4134	Jarvis	J	1879
1833	Nerson?	D	1879
BOMBARDIER			
1591	Butcher	W	1879
1735	Clarke	J.R	1879
1995	Harris	G.R	1879
BOMBARDIER WHEELER			
8472	Fullerton	E	1879
GUNNER			
2097	Allender	T	1879
2094	Benneth	C	1879
2658	Bowe	P	1879
4840	Buchan	J	1879
1952	Carbary	M	1879
1982	Carter	J	1879
1985	Cooper	G	1879
1809	Croucher D/S	C	No clasp
2634	Dennison	H	1879
2341	Dumpleton	E	1879
1741	Edwards	J	1879
2736	Elliott	S.A	1879
1738	Franklin	A	1879
1806	Henley	H	1879
2618	Hensly	C	1879
1992	Homer	L	1879
1719	Jefferies	W	1879
2098	Johnston	A	1879
1742	Lewis	E	1879
2800	Lowe	C	1879
2100	Mansergh	T	1879
1610	Mc Clelland	R	1879
2173	Miller	G	1879
2349	Morton	S	1879
1782	Morton	T	1879
2348	Moorhead	W	1879
DCM Ulundi 4.7.79			
2755	Murray	M	1879
1808	Moon	P	1879
1734	Ormond	S	1879
2617	Schutte	T	1879
1739	Sharratt	B	1879
1898	Smart	T	1879
4559	Smith	W	1879
2661	Stephens	J.W	1879
2105	Stoker	T	1879
1664	Symes	W	1879
2571	Thompson	J	1879
2310	Tighe	R	1879
1783	Worsley	J	1879
1877	Wyatt	C	1879
COLLAR MAKER			
3543	Trigg	J.A	1879
SHOEING SMITH			
3541	French	R	1879r
3536	Reading	R	1879
TRUMPETER			
1838	O'Neill	E.E	1879

ATTACHED FROM ROYAL HORSE ARTILLERY
GUNNER
| 6977 | Edis | C | 1879 |

See also Royal Horse Artillery.
DRIVER
| 455 | Willis | H | 1879 |

See also Royal Horse Artillery.
MULE DRIVER
| | Smithdorf | J | 1879 |

ROYAL ARTILLERY. 7th BRIGADE
NUMBER 11 BATTERY
MAJOR
| | Tremlett | E.G | 1877-8-9 |

CAPTAIN
| | Browne | H.R.Y | 1879 |
| | Russell | F.B | 1879 |

KIA Isandhwana.
LIEUTENANT
	Bigge	A.J	1877-8-9
	Davidson	W.L	1879
	Lloyd	W.N	1877-8-9
	Nicolson	F	1879

D/W 30/3/1879.
| | Slade | F.G | 1877-8-9 |

MILITARY STAFF CLERK
| | FitzPatrick | J | 1879 |

BATTERY SERGEANT MAJOR
| 1640 | Orson | R | 1879 |

SERGEANT
135	Barlow	R	1879
1834	Bartz	E	1879
1585	Edwards	J	1877-8-9
4538	Galb	J	1879
1786	Glen	J	No clasp
1627	Sharp	A	1877-8-9
1698	Thomas	J	1879
1855	Walden	T	No clasp
1736	Webster	J	1879

FARRIER SERGEANT
| 4677 | Brewer | W | 1879 |
| 4666 | Heathcote | H | 1879 |

See also 6th Bgde N Battery RA.
SADDLER SERGEANT
| 1637 | Sharpe | A | 1877-8-9 |

CORPORAL
238	Adams	R	1879
1697	Carter	C	1879
1603	Cox	J	1879
1855	Eilbech	H.G	1879
2187	Mc Askill	N	1877-8-9

BOMBARDIER
| 1711 | Adams | M | 1879 |
| 1715 | Elvin | R | 1879 |

No medal. Deserted.
8113	Fraser	J	1879
1844	Haggarty	J	1877-8-9
2193	Hubber	J	1877-8-9
1687	Quiley	E	1878-9

BOMBARDIER WHEELER
| 7170 | Robinson | A | 1879 |

ACTING BOMBARDIER
2000	Pawlesland	G	1878-9
1818	Tamsley	J	1877-8-9
1996	Waddell	R	1879

GUNNER
2045	Amy	C	1879
243	Apsley	J	1879
287	Band	E	1879
2127	Banks	G	1878-9
1930	Belos	E	1877-8-9
2361	Blakey	F	1879
9502	Boyle	B	1879
1789	Bradley	W	1877-8-9
1756	Branch D/SW		1879
2387	Broomhead	C.J	1879
2171	Brinklecombs?F		1877-8-9
2120	Brunitt D/S	G	1877-8
8189	Bundy	R	1879
2060	Burke	P	1877-8-9
?	Burslow	G	1877-8-9
1644	Butcher	G	1879
1608	Campbell	G	1879
2050	Carlton	H	1879
1757	Carly	J	1878-9
4381	Chapman	W	1879
1579	Chester	F	1879
1613	Church	W	1879
2119	Clegg	J	1877-8-9
1856	Clemson	J	1879
1668	Collins	A.P	1877-8-9
2116	Connor	J	1879
437	Connor	T	1879
1762	Cooney	J	1879
2315	Coots	T	1877-8-9 r
508	Corcoran	J	1879
2316	Cornelius	H	1877-8-9
1667	Crew	W	No clasp
2048	De la Cour	F.A	1877-8-9
1702	Doherty	R.A	No clasp
1415	Dunn	J	1879r
1751	Dutch	W	1879
316	Fear	J	1877-8-9
1625	Fielding	H	1878-9

Royal Artillery 7th Brigade

Number	Name	Initial	Year
531	Flanagan	G	1879 r
574	Gibson	M	1879
4382	Gilman	C	1879
2121	Gordon	R	1878-9
1795	Graham	T	1879
2031	Gorman	J.H	1878-9
393	Grant	C	1879
3103	Grant	J	1879
	No medal. Deserted.		
1586	Green	J	1877-8-9
1989	Hall	J	No clasp
1792	Harmer	B	1879
1752	Harvey	J.T	1877-8-9
1699	Hill	J	1878-9
2309	Hedder	M	No clasp
1704	Horton	W	1879
1791	Hunt	W	1879
2195?	Jones	T	1879
1723	Kenny	J	1878-9
2360	Kynastow	J.S	1878-9
2318	Laughlin	J	1877-8
2459	Law	J	1879
2118	Ledger	F	No clasp
2197	Maguire	C	1877-8-9
1865	Mahoney	E	1879
1866	Mc Caan D/W	H	1879
356	Mc Kenna	B	1879
2047	Mc Kerney	W	1878-9
1642	Mc Laren	J	1879
2046	Miller	J.T	1879
1594	Montague	C	1877-8
2317	Mothensole?	T	1879
1753	Morland	A	1879
2188	Murphy	J	1877-8-9
2130	Nolan	M	1879 r
1588	O'Donnel	J	1879
2122	O'Kane	J	1879
2135	Patterson	A	1879
1787	Pinkerton	J	1879
2380	? Price	W	1877-8-9
2117	Rankin	J.A	1877-8-9
	No medal. Convicted.		
1724	Rees	T	1877-8-9
2133	Riley	W	1879
2194	Rochford D/W	D	1877-8
2321	Robinson	W	1877-8-9
1999	Rowe	J	1879
1755	Saunders	D	1879
2322	Shea	J	1877-8-9
2319	Sheehaw?	J	1877-8-9
1785	Shufflebathaw?	T	1879
2646	Smith	C	1879
2325	Smith	H	1877-8-9
2428	Smith	T	1879
177	Southgate	J	1877-8-9
2323	Staines	T	1877-8-9
2326	Stirk	J	1877-8-9
2408	Tattersall	W.H	1879
2134	Taylor	G	No clasp
2134	Taylor	G	No clasp
	Two medals to same man.		
2191	Taylor	W	1879
2201	Thatcher	G	No clasp
1596	Thompson	G	1878-9
2199	Thompson	W	1879
1597	Walker	E	1877-8
2327	Wardle	J	1877-8-9
2324	Webster	J	1879
2328	White	J	No clasp
1997	White	R	1879
1998	Yarnold	A	1879

DRIVER

5166	Bailey	C	1879
2276	Bilton	C	No clasp
5167	Cook	E	1879
	No medal. Deserted.		
5168	Cranness	W	1879
5169	Cunningham	J	1879
2279	Green	C	1879
4686	Hastler	A	1879
5170	Hitchman	J	1879
5171	Martin	H	1879
2315	Newall	T	1879
5172	News	C	1879
8879?	Peck	J	1877-8
5164	Rastin	H	1879
5173	Simpson	J	1879
	No medal. Deserted.		
2333	Stevens	J	1879
2608	Toohey?	J.H	1879
2272	Thompson	W.J	1877-8
5175	Unsworth	R	1879
5176	Warden	G	1879
5177	Watkins	H	1879
5165	Woods	D	1879
5178	Wright	C	1879

PRIVATE

80/1836	Burnett	J	1878-9

COLLAR MAKER

2286	Taylor	H	1879

SHOEING SMITH

3684	Felstead	C	1879

TRUMPETER

1915	Durham	G.H	1879
1947	Lees	E	1879

ROYAL ARTILLERY. 11th BRIGADE
NUMBER 12 BATTERY

CAPTAIN

	Brackenbury	E.F	1879

ROYAL ARTILLERY REGIMENT

COLONEL

	Elgee	C.W	1878

CAPTAIN

	Fox	W.R	No clasp

LIEUTENANT

	Giles	G.E	1877-8-9

GUNNER

4579	Brailey	W	1878

ROYAL HORSE ARTILLERY

CAPTAIN and ADJUTANT

	Alleyne	J	1879

CORPORAL

749	Waters	T	1879
	See also 88th Regt		

DRIVER

2378	Brown	C	1879
455	Willis	H	1879

See also 10th Bty 7th Bde RA

ROYAL ENGINEERS

Prior to 1879, the 7th Field Company were the only resident Royal Engineer unit in South Africa. Two field companies of the Engineers (the 2nd and the 5th) embarked for South Africa on December 2nd, 1878, and landed at Durban on January 4th, 1879.

COLONEL

	Hassard CB	F.C	1877-8

LIEUTENANT COLONEL and BREVET COLONEL

	Durnford	A.W	1879

KIA Isandhwana.

LIEUTENANT COLONEL

	Steward	E.H	No clasp

MAJOR and BREVET LIEUTENANT COLONEL

	Harrisson CB	R	1879
	Warren	C	1877-8-9

MAJOR

	Moysey	C.J	1879
	Webber	C.E	1879

Also had Indian Mutiny Medal.

CAPTAIN

	Anstey	T.H	1879
	Bell	W	1879
	Heneage	F.W	1879
	Hime	A.H	1879

LIEUTENANT

	Baxter	J.C	No clasp
	Clarke D/S	J	No clasp
	James	W.H	1879
	Mc Dowel	F.H	1879

KIA Isandhwana.

	Penrose	C	No clasp
	Watkins	F.W	No clasp

QUARTERMASTER SERGEANT

9921	Bingham	D	1877-8
8933	Passmore	J	1879

SERGEANT

5894	Dadswell	H.I	No clasp

2nd CORPORAL

8867	Docherty	W.H	1879

Royal Horse Artillery

ROYAL ENGINEERS. C TROOP

MAJOR
	Hamilton	A.C	1879

VETERINARY SURGEON
	Walters	W.B	No clasp

LIEUTENANT
	Bond	F.G	1879
	Hare	J	1879
	Rich	H.B	1879

TROOP SERGEANT MAJOR
7388	Lewis	A	1879

TROOP QUARTERMASTER SERGEANT
5947	Scrimshaw	T	No clasp

TELEGRAPHER SERGEANT
8215	Middlemost	J	1879

FARRIER SERGEANT
8214	Hamhlin	F	1879

SERGEANT
10691	Graham	W	1879
9823	Kimber	F	1879
8984	Morgan	D	1879
6382	Osmond	W	No clasp
10473	Waters	F.G	1879

COLLAR MAKER CORPORAL
9642	Morris	G.H	No clasp

TELEGRAPHER CORPORAL
10968	Urguhart	R	No clasp
9948	Wooldridge	H	1879

WHEELER CORPORAL
10367	Tizard	L	No clasp

CORPORAL
10675	Attwood	A	1879
10687	Butler	H	1879
11060	Gibbons	T	No clasp
10715	Scott	W	No clasp
11011	Wainwright	W	1879

2nd CORPORAL
13494	Hamilton	J	No clasp
11000	Jarratt	W	1879
13625	Macdonald	S	1879
11934	Miller D/S	J	No clasp
13379	Seggie	W	1879
12748	Stead	E	1879
12130	Stead	E.G	1879

LANCE CORPORAL
13001	Appleton	W	1879
13371	Charman	J	1879
13649	Fairchild	W	1879
11814	Feist	J	1879
14424	Harrison	W	1879
13739	Jervis	E.H	No clasp
13892	May	I.	No clasp
13496	Oakman	J	1879
13487	Searle	C	1879

TRUMPETER
13872	Evans	W	1879
14393	Kerr	H	No clasp

SAPPER
12751	Allen	J	No clasp
10683	Baker	G	No clasp
10823	Ball	C	1879
7780	Barber	H	1879
11055	Barnecutt	W	1879
11013	Carter	W	1879
13624	Collis	C	1879
13744	Cooper	T	1879
14161	Darnill	A	1879
7784	Darnell	H	1879
13891	Fegan	V	1879
14395	Fowler	W	1879
13502	Gamester	G	1879
13225	Gilshan	H	1879
15619	Harvey	H	1879
13884	Heslop	A	1879
13368	Hogan	D	1879
12118	Howard	H	1879
11043	Jarratt	L	1879
13006	Jones	H	1879
13875	Kent	J	1879
14406	Lawrence	J	1879
14184	Messenger	G	1879
13760	Morris	R	1879
11012	Mould	G	1879
13382	Nickolls	D/SD	No clasp
15592	O'Leary	J	No clasp
13498	Palin	F	1879
13010	Palmer	G	1879
14420	Parker	W	No clasp
12990	Phillips	F	1879
13504	Roe	D	No clasp
11672	Rogers	J	1879
13894	Slee	A	1879
14187	Sturdy	C	1879
12747	Sullivan	D	No clasp
13888	Trayhorn	C	No clasp
10815	Walker	G	No clasp
11003	Warner	J	No clasp
14408	Watmore	D/S W	1879
14415	Wedge	J	1879
11024	Wells	H	No clasp
14658	Weston	W	1879
13754	Winslade	W	1879
14413	Woodward	H	1879
14399	Wooley	J	1879

No medal. Deserted.

13753	Wyatt	J	1879

DRIVER
12453	Aldridge	J	No clasp
15539	Beardmore	C	1879
14405	Blackman	C	1879
14377	Blackwell	H	1879r

Medal forfeited. Application for restoration of medal and clasp refused 12/5/1932.

10777	Blay	R	No clasp
7625	Bristowe	H	No clasp
13877	Burton	E	1879
15563	Byers	J	1879
14683	Carter	H	No clasp
14168	Christian	W	1879
15519	Clatworthy	J	1879
14376	Colcomb	T	No clasp
14680	Collett D/S	T	No clasp
14402	Collins	T	1879
15636	Copeland	H	1879
12121	Cotterell	G	1879
15541	Cox	F	1879
15670	Crack	F	1879
15030	Dawes	T.H	1879
15595	Derrick	A	1879
15657	Drew	T.H	1879
13007	Elderfield	H	1879
15064	Evans	E	1879
13492	French	B	1879
13626	Fussell	H	1879
13215	Haines	H	1879
13206	Halsey	H	No clasp
14191	Harper	J	No clasp
15099	Heath	T	1879
13896	Hedgecock	W	1879
13383	Hollands	W	1879
15602	Houlston	J	1879
13380	Hughes	G	1879
13087	Hurn	T	1879
10694	Hussey	J	1879
13205	Hutton	A	1879
15505	Jackson	J	1879
14412	Kale	C	1879
15066	Lewis	D	1879
13629	Lindsay	J	1879
11673	Marriott	W	1879
10958	Marsh	H	1879 r
14942	Miller	R	No clasp
14378	North	E	No clasp
10822	O'Brien F (or E.T)		No clasp
13375	O'Neill	J	1879

DRIVER
12755	Parker	W	1879
13207	Pepperell	H	1879
13881	Pawling	T	1879
12086	Pearson	J	1879
15495	Player	C	1879
14911	Powell	J	No clasp
15498	Redwood	T	1879
13392	Rogers	C.C	1879
15564	Sexton	J	1879
12444	Simpson	W	1879
13736	Slade	J	1879
15518	Solley	J	1879
15454	Sparks	J	No clasp
13755	Spry	J	1879
13751	Stevens	W	1879
14665	Stripe	G	1879
15061	Strong	W	No clasp
13880	Sutton	J	1879

Royal Engineers C Troop

10774	Taylor	C	1879	12100	Penney	F.W	1879	13979	Cooksey	G	1879
15674	Tibbitts	A	1879	12350	Smith	A.H	1879	13863	Coxhead	G	No clasp
15027	Titcomb	W	1879	8420	Wickens	J	1879	14590	Crawley	J	1879
11010	Turner	W	1879	**2nd CORPORAL**				14479	Crocket	J	1879
14670	Welfare	J	1879	9913	Batter	C.F	1879	11455	Cronk	G.W	1879
15535	Werrall	W	No clasp	12680	Buckwell	A	No clasp	13834	Cullerne	T.H.G	1879
	No medal. Deserted.			12326	Ferguson	R	1879	13992	David	C	1879
14185	Winson	W	1879	12363	Johnson	E	1879r	14545	Davies	D	1879
13089	Wise	W	1879	13268	Licence	F	1879	14330	Davis	C	No clasp
15491	Younger	W	1879	13500	Robinson	J	1879	14421	Davis	C	1879
COLLAR MAKER				13269	Savage	H	1879	14524	Delany	J	1879
11030	Collett	H	1879	13132	Smith	H	1879	14224	Dixon	J	No clasp
SHOEING SMITH				9858	Smith	J	1879	14363	Dixon	J	1879
7769	Brian	O	No clasp	10504	Veller	A	No clasp	14948	Eather	J	1879
15548	Dawkins	C	1879	**LANCE CORPORAL PAID**				13964	Eden	C	No clasp
13234	Massey	B	1879	14267	Berry	T	1879		No medal. Deserted.		
TELEGRAPHER				13016	Middleton	J	1879	14410	Fahy	J	1879
12416	Burgess	E	1879	**LANCE CORPORAL UNPAID**				14427	Ferguson	D	1879
14383	Concannon	R.A	1879	14598	Allen	J	1879	14537	Flynn	J	1879
13388	Irvine D/S	J	No clasp		No medal. Deserted.			13950	Galgarni	G	1879
8396	Jones	R.E	1879	13849	Banks	R	1879	12946	Garland	R	1879
14192	Richardson	J	1879	10322	Ferrer	T	1879	14281	Gibson	G	1879
10597	Smith	W	1879	13845	Hulbert	C.J	1879	11913	Gillispie	D	No clasp
13878	Splane	T	1879	13011	Jefferies	H	1879	12928	Glazebrook	C.T	1879
13092	Tyrell	W	1879	14010	Pass	G.H	No clasp	11162	Godfrey	B	1879
8842	Wheeler	J	No clasp	13070	Stow	F	No clasp	14480	Gould	G	1879
WHEELER					No medal. Deserted.			14539	Gowdy	J.W	1879
11810	East	S	1879	14040	Wise	J	No clasp	14303	Green	B	1879
10975	Furze	W.H	No clasp	**BUGLER**				14636	Griffiths	J	No clasp
14394	Humphreys	H	1879	13414	Harrod	J	1879	13938	Grimwood	R	No clasp
				13108	Mitchell	H	1879	11332	Haggerty	J	No clasp
ROYAL ENGINEERS.				**SAPPER**					No medal. Deserted.		
2nd COMPANY				14336	Armitstead	W	No clasp	14548	Halliday	S	1879
CAPTAIN				14322	Armstrong	W.A	No clasp	13656	Harding	C	1879
	Courtney	D.C.	1879	14366	Ascott	W	1879	13037	Harding	G	1879
	Wynne	W.R.C	1879	13256	Bailey	C	No clasp	13822	Harper	J	1879
	D/S 9/4/1879			13139	Baskerville	J	1879	14500	Harrison	W	1879
LIEUTENANT				13076	Beard	J	1879	14391	Hill	W	1879
	Brotherton T de la	H	1879	14316	Bell	R	1879	14452	Hodgson	T.T	1879
	Conneline	C.E	1879	12943	Beswarrick	J.T	1879	13731	Hookey	E	1879
	Haynes	C.E	1879	10051	Bingham	E	1879	14446	Hopson	J	1879
	Mac Gregor	J.C	1879	14302	Binmore	W	1879	14384	Humphries	H	1879
	Willock	H.B	1879	13716	Boozer	J.E	1879		No medal. Deserted.		
COMPANY SERGEANT MAJOR				13620	Boyd	W	1879	14583	Humphries	J	1879
7466	Fraser	R	1879	13685	Brennen	W	1879	14011	Ivens ?	C	1879
SERGEANT				14513	Brotherton	R	1879	14237	Johnes	W	1879
8780	Campbell	J.R	1879	14471	Brown	H	1879	12724	Johnston	A	1879
10037	Day	T	1879	13127	Brown	S.J	No clasp	14174	Jones	T	1879
7711	Dutton	C	1879	12700	Candler	H	1879	13652	Kipps	E	1879
9652	Swindon	H	1879	14512	Carline	F	1879	13265	Knee	J	No clasp
10102	Titchener	J	1879		No medal. Deserted.				No medal. Deserted.		
11900	Tuckett	W	1879r	11714	Champion	H.J	No clasp	14079	Lang	A	1879
11346	Webb	J.R	No clasp		No medal. Deserted.			13384	Ledger	J	1879
CORPORAL				14535	Charles	P	1879r	14158	Lewis	J	1879
11240	Bridges	T.W	1879	13376	Childs	H	No clasp	14437	Longbottom	J.R	1879
10529	Garner	W	1879	14570	Church	G	1879	14702	Mahen	W	No clasp
13584	Hills	E.B	No clasp	13116	Clack	J	No clasp	13836	Mansfield	R	No clasp
9415	Orchard	G	1879	14546	Cogan	J	1879	13080	Mc Credie	W.S	No clasp
11195	Parton	C	1879	14002	Cole	T	1879	13524	Medews	F	No clasp

Royal Engineers 2nd Company

Number	Surname	Initial	Clasp
14274	Mitchell	T	No clasp
14109	Newell	W	1879
14561	O'Brien	J	1879
14156	O'Donnell	J	No clasp
13081	O'Leary	W	1879
13987	Osborn	A	1879
13534	Osborne	H.J	1879
13706	Parker	J	1879
13217	Pethers	S	1879
13916	Pinchen	S	1879
14489	Redmond	L	1879
13764	Romain	H	1879
14306	Ruane	P	1879
13612	Schwiseo	J	1879
14012	Scott	C	No clasp
13391	Simmons	J	1879
14460	Smith	H	1879
13211	Smith	J	1879
14245	Spring	J	1879
14651	Staines	J	1879
14300	Stanton	J.S	No clasp
14946	Wallis	C	1879
14172	Walters	T	No clasp
13791	Wear	G	1879
13887	Westfold	A	No clasp
11486	White	G.A	No clasp
13469	Woods	T.A	1879
14758	Wright	W	No clasp
11131	Yelland	J	1879
12645	Young	H	No clasp

DRIVER

Number	Surname	Initial	Clasp
10980	Barwell	A	1879
13900	Brand	E	1879
14180	Cannon	A	1879
14173	Carpenter	T	1879
7994	Chapman	J	1879
13899	Corder	A	1879

No medal. Deserted.

13009	Davis	D	1879
10613	Day	E	1879
15478	Feeney	M	1879

No medal. Deserted.

12134	Fluter	C	1879
13201	Lacey	J	1879
14659	Lane	W	1879
10728	Marshall	G	1879
12133	Misselbrook	T	1879
10712	Nutley	W	1879
12624	Robinson	J	1879
13750	Spiers	F	1879
13088	Sprong	W	1879
13632	Standing	S	1879
13095	Stone	G	1879
14668	Wilson	J	1879
13746	Wood	C.H	1879

ROYAL ENGINEERS. 5th COMPANY

CAPTAIN

	Jones	W.P	1879

Had a medal from an earlier war. No details.

LIEUTENANT

	Chard VC	J.R.M	1879
	Porter	R daC	1879

SERGEANT

8218	Davey	W	No clasp
4592	Down	J.G	1879
8481	Ellis	J	1879
8146	Mc Donald	J	1879
8378	Milne	J	1879
7993	Woolnough	J	No clasp
10555	Wright	R.J	1879

CORPORAL

11428	Cahill	D	No clasp
10750	Dinner	C	1879
10300	Fashain	J	No clasp
7100	Gamble KIA	W	1879
8475	Godfrey	P.B	No clasp
11636	Higgins	G	1879
10392	Isaac	D	No clasp
9856	Peters	J	1879
11773	Stewart	C.E	1879

CORPORAL UNPAID GUNNER

10528	Hooper	J	1879
14443	Langmead	H	1879
13830	Mc Kay	A	No clasp
14488	Parsons	W	1879
13847	Pierce	H	1879

2nd CORPORAL

9114	Callingham	G	1879
12877	Crosoer	A	1879
12566	Fuller	F	1879
13160	Howe	P	1879
14076	Parker	F	No clasp
13821	Salkeld	F	1879

LANCE CORPORAL

15011	Gibson	F	1879
12462	Hills	H	1879
14051	Reid	S	1879
12212	Tindall	H.F	1879

BUGLER

13274	Campbell	J.U	No clasp
13585	Harvey	W.H	1879

SAPPER

14135	Ardron	M.A	1879
13702	Bailey	W.R	1879
14141	Betts D/S	F	No clasp
14222	Borthwick	J	1879
13486	Brain	E	1879

No medal. Deserted.

14277	Bray	W.O	No clasp
14000	Brazendale	J	No clasp
14208	Brittain	T	1879
12219	Carrick	C	1879

14250	Chimes	G.M	No clasp
13232	Christian	H	No clasp
11429	Cotton	T	No clasp
14006	Coyle	A.J	No clasp
9312	Cuthbert KIA	H	1879
14476	Dennis	G	1879
14435	Drislan	T	1879r
11985	Driver	J	1879
14282	Eady	J	1879
13416	Evans	G.H	1879
8198	Fairfoul	A	No clasp
14508	Foley	T	1879
14468	Ford	J	1879
14129	Frost	H	1879
10524	Fullalove	B	1879
12073	Gibbs	E.W	1879
10070	Gibbs	J	1879
14441	Gibson	J	1879
14338	Gibson	R	No clasp
11629	Grace	T.J	No clasp
14440	Graham	J	1879
12239	Grandin		No clasp
14310	Haytread	J.B	1879
13838	Herbert	G	No clasp
13977	Higgs	H.T	1879
14340	Hocking	P	No clasp
14519	Hyland	D	1879
14497	Jenkin	E	1879
14496	Jones	H	1879
14494	Lamsley	A.E	1879
7737	Leahy	M	1879
14323	Lillicrap	F	1879 r
13923	Marshall	F	1879
14463	Martin	F	1879
12472	Mc Bain	W	1879
13805	Mc Laren KIA	J	1879
14470	Meredith	J	1879

No medal. Deserted.

12677	Molloy	T	1879

Lieutenant Chard VC

Royal Engineers 5th Company

				ROYAL ENGINEERS 7th COMPANY			ROYAL ENGINEERS 30th COMPANY			
14368	Moir	J	1879	**CAPTAIN**			**CAPTAIN**			
14226	Moore	T	No clasp		Nixon	F.W	1877-8		Blood	B	1879
14374	Munro	T	No clasp	**LIEUTENANT**			**LIEUTENANT**			
14472	Newman	S	1879		Cameron	J	1877-8		Littledale	R.P	1879
14475	Norton	J	No clasp r		Main	T.R	1877-8-9		Mackean	K	1879
14721	O'Brien	J	No clasp	**SERGEANT**				Sherrard	C.W	1879
14354	Parr	T	1879 r	6245	Watkins	H	1877-8	**COMPANY SERGEANT MAJOR**			
14450	Phillips	J	No clasp r	7427	Whenman?	H	1879	7597	Lucas	M	1879
14009	Roberts	W	No clasp	9471	Wood	R	1879	**SERGEANT**			
13946	Rolph	W	1879	**CORPORAL**				8177	Blight	J	1879
14491	Russell D/S	F.W	No clasp	8911	Kemp	G.W	1877-8	7405	Clean	A	1879
13064	Rushbrook	W.S	No clasp	9032	Mansfield **KIA**	H	1879	7982	Harding	A	1879
14454	Saunders	H.R	1879	10869	Moat	J	1877-8-9	7123	Mc Sullivan	A	1879
14477	Scriden	J	1879	**LANCE CORPORAL**				11506	Kennedy	J	No clasp
13154	Shrubsole	G	No clasp	11791	Bettison	R	1879	8404	Sorgatz	E	1879
14515	Smith	J	1879	12588	Hart	W	1877-8	8276	West	G	1879
14429	Stevens	C	1879	7887	Lavender	J.W	No clasp	**CORPORAL**			
13993	Stewart	H	1879	11386	Mc Intyre	A.H.L	1879	11544	Burton	J	1879
13140	Taylor	W	1879	11641	O'Connell	J	1877-8	9265	Clarke	J	1879
14461	Thompson D/S	H	No clasp	10212	Parker	H	1877-8	12135	Goldsmith	G	1879
12720	Turner	J	1879	10182	Pollard	A.J.F.W	1877-8	9349	Hawkins	H	1879
14511	Vosper	S	1879	8880	Williams	T	1878-9	11790	Hillman	R	1879
14650	Ward	J	No clasp r	12842	Williamson	F	1877-8	7160	Hopkins	T	1879
14031	Warnicker	C	No clasp	**BUGLER**				11567	Trout	A.V	1879
13405	Watkins	J	1879	11986	Pryce	D.R	1877-8	6681	Wihigan ?	J	1879
14505	Watling	J	No clasp	**SAPPER**				10720	Woodeson	F	1879
13703	Weston	G	1879	9963	Bellam	J	1879	**2nd CORPORAL**			
12812	Wheatly **KIA**	M	1879	11385	Budge	W	1877-8	13577	Hunter	H.J	1879
13113	Williams	A	No clasp	13285	Burgess	W.J	1877-8	9562	Hutchens	H	1879
13781	Williams	H	1879	11603	Bush	S	1879	9358	Marriott	J	1879
14257	Yates	W.J	1879	9150	Cameron	J	1877-8	11386	Mc Intyre	A.C	1879
14434	Young	F	1879	12081	Evans	R	1877-8	12781	Ralph	M	1879
DRIVERS				11781	Flatman	W	1877-8	10608	Robb	D.M	1879
15094	Addicott	W	1879	9326	Gass	H	1879	12702	Whittaker	W	1879
15068	Attwell	F	1879	11786	Griffiths	J	1877-8	**LANCE CORPORAL**			
13086	Batten	G	1879	11669	Hickmoth	E	1877-8	14614	Douglas	R	1879
8279	Beckett D/S	W	No clasp	6873	Hughes	E	1877-8	12745	Golding	C	1879
12988	Carter	G	1879	8582	Hunter	J	1877-8	14639	Heaysman	H	1879
12053	Church	G	1879	9588	Kahoe ?	F	1877-8	14071	Howard	R	1879
14175	Flynn	T	1879	11533	Little	W	1877-8	8531	Mc Intyre	M	1879
14183	Foster	G	1879 r	8959	Luff	H	1879	12526	Mc Mullen	J	1879
14677	Kennard	T	1879	12226	Mc Adam	A	1877-8	13122	Morgan	W	1879
10761	Leverno	J	1879	9175	Mc Donald	P	1877-8	12931	Read	W	1870
10949	Mandy DS	F	No clasp	9614	Meredith D/S	B	1877-8	13673	Sampson	W	No clasp
13394	Matthews	F	1879	13292	Munnion	H	1877-8	13843	Seale ?	G	1879
10738	Miles	W	1879	9215	Munro	K?	1879	13557	Spender	J	1879
10951	Munro	R	1879 r	13231	Page	F	1877-8	12504	Tennent	T.F	1879
15018	North	C	1879 r	11824	Paine	A.H	1879	13747	Watson	J	1879
13506	Pearose	J	1879	9034	Pettitt	G	1879	14585	Watt	D	1879
13515	Roake	S	1879	11413	Powell	A	1877 8	13523	Wood	H	1879
13366	Roberts	D.E	1879	6178	Smith	S	1879	**BUGLER**			
12046	Robson	C	1879	11605	Till	J	1877-8	13973	Mc Elwee	J.T	1879
12938	Roots	H	No clasp		No medal. Deserted.			**SAPPER**			
13226	Smith	R	1879	8825	Turner	W	1879	14628	Adcock	R	1879
13516	Upton	W	1879					14569	Atkins	J	1879
MULE DRIVER								12952	Bardsley	T	1879
	Fisher	F	1879					14499	Barrow	W	1879
	Hudson	E	1879					13690	Bateman	G	1879

Royal Engineers 30th Company

14609	Batten	J	1879	13454	Hughes	J	1879	**DRIVER**			
13671	Beight	H	1879	14762	Hurn	J	1879	15744	Andrews	G	1879
13599	Bell	R	1879	14617	Hyland	T	1879	10705	Atkins	J	1879
13520	Benford	C	1879	9632	James	W	1879	14396	Berryman	J	1879
14444	Benton	H	1879	14605	Johns	G	1879	15667	Bowyer	H	1879r
14744	Bryson	T.H	1879	14708	Jones	W.B	1879	8273	Burdett ?	C	1879
13182	Bulley	R	1879	8105	Keegan	G	1879	14667	Chandler	J	1879
18550	Chandler	G.H	1879	14638	Kelly	J	1879	13890	Collis	J	1879
13336	Clarke	W	1879		No medal .Deserted.			13203	Cooke	H	1879
13350	Clayton	A	1879	14753	Kenney	H	1879	13374	Cooper	J	1879
14613	Clynch	J	1879	12721	Langford	W	1879	14654	Cox	G	1879
13577	Collins	A	1879	13613	Mann	G.R	1879	14700	Crowe	J	1879r
13317	Connors	M	1879	13079	Martin	J	1879	12036	Davey	E	1879
14621	Conroy	J	1879	13547	May	W	1879	14164	Ellis	J.R	1879
14640	Crawford	J.A.P	1879	13553	Mc Bude	J	1879	14919	Giles	J	1879
14641	Crawford	W	1879	14632	Mc Cann	P	1879	13219	Gunner	W	1879
14528	Davis	G	No clasp	14602	Mc Cann	W	1879	10700	Hall	W	1879
14527	Davis	H	1879	12870	Mc John	J	1879	15015	Hicks	J	1879
14509	Davis	J	1879	10160	Mc Kay	C.M	1879	13003	Hopson	J	1879
14719	Dawson	T	1879r	14644	Mc Laren	A	No clasp	15678	Judge	J	1879
14581	Delaware	W	1879	13941	Mogridge	J	1879	12992	Liddiard	W	1879
10217	Donohoe	M	1879	14622	Moore	P.D	1879	15085	Lowe	G	1879
10181	Dowling	R	1879	13840	Murray	R	1879	15067	Mason	A	1879
14514	Dowsing	D	1879	14606	Musgrove	T	1879r	15683	Petherick	E	1879
13578	Dyer	J.S	No clasp	7460	Nias	W	1879	14913	Pole	A	1879
13429	Eddy	F.R	1879	14534	Nichol	C	1879	14673	Ponsford	R	1879
12974	Evans	C	No clasp	14629	Norman	H.J	1879	12120	Ramsey	W	1879
13339	Flinders	E	1879	13568	Norster	H	1879	12458	Rance	E	1879
14552	Foan	C.C.J	1879	14481	Nudd	W	1879	12449	Rogers	H	1879
14601	Ford	A	1879	13532	Nuttle	W	1879	13220	Rout	G	1879
13121	Forgie	P	1879	14458	Oldham	A	1879	14935	Simkin	H	1879
14769	Gallagher	T	1879	14710	Palmer	H	1879	14652	Small	J	1879
	No medal .Deserted.			14572	Pearce	E	1879	15002	Snoswell	J	1879
14530	Gapp	A	1879	13837	Phasey	W	1879	13757	Stretton	R	1879
14706	Gavin	D	1879	8813	Pitter	F	1879	15082	Stuckey	R	1879
12011	Gibbs	W	1879	13153	Rare ?	F	1879	14945	Taylor	J	1879
8885	Gilchrist	D	1879	13445	Reid	J	1879	15452	Thorogood	H	1879
10084	Gillispie	J	1879	14615	Rogers	W	1879	13882	Tinson	S	1879
13473	Goodrick	H	1879	14624	Ruxton	J	1879	15546	Trew	W	1879
10177	Gray	G.A	1879	14520	Shuring	T	1879	14943	Turner	G	1879
14361	Graham	E	1879	14633	Simmons	G	1879	12129	Turner	W.J	1879
11927	Green	J	1879	14438	Simpson	J	1879	12998	Tyler	G	1879
10057	Griffin	J.W	1879	10373	Smallic	W	1879	14388	Vaughan	F	1879
11878	Haison	W?	1879	14953	Stanley	J	1879	14921	Watkins	W	1879
13826	Hall	E.H	1879	14154	Stokes	S	1879	12746	White	H	1879
12940	Hands	W	1879	13558	Stone	W	1879	15515	Whitfield	C	1879
9903	Handsford?	J	1879	14610	Thomas	W	1879	15687	Winfield	S	1879
14616	Hardwick	G.E	1879	13560	Tobin	P	1879	15003	Wood	J	1879
14563	Harris	J	1879	13589	Tucker	L	1879	14678	Woodham	J	1879
13331	Heald	J	1879	13969	Tyrrell	W	1879				
11666	Healey	H.B	1879	14645	Vaughan	J.F	1879				
13324	Hegarty	J	1879	11665	Voss	T	1879				
14634	Higgs	J	1879	13435	Walsh	J	1879				
14592	Hill	J	1879	14591	Waterson	P	1879				
14637	Hindby	J	1879	11225	Watson	C	1879				
14612	Holmes	J	1879	14600	White	J.T	1879				
14603	Horn	J	1879	14436	Williamson	J	1879				
5680	Howard	W	1879	14620	Woods	S.I	1879				
14648	Hoy	W	1879								

Royal Navy

ROYAL NAVY
Ship not stated
LIEUTENANT
  Legh   N.E.C   1879

ROYAL NAVY. HMS ACTIVE
Certain medals to this ship were without a clasp.
COMMANDER
  Campbell CB   H.J.F   1879
  Wright CB CMG H.T 1877-8
COMMODORE
  Sullivan   F.W   -
CHAPLAIN
  Berry Revd   J.H   -
STAFF SURGEON
  #Norbury CBH.F 1877-8-9
SURGEON
  Thompson   W   1879
  Triggs   J.B.B   -
NAVIGATING LIEUTENANT
  Robinson   C.R.H   -
LIEUTENANT
  Craigie   R.W   1877-8-9
  Hamilton   W.deV 1877-8-9
  Jackson   H.B   -
  Marrack   W   -
  Milne   A.B   1879
NAVIGATING SUB LIEUTENANT
  Hugh   J.G   1879
SUB LIEUTENANT
  Barnes-Lawrence L.A.W 1877-8

  Fraser   T.G   1879
  Loring   A.H   1877-8
  Pitt   S.T.D -
MID SHIPMAN
  Coker   L.C   1879
  D/S 16/3/1879
  De Lisle   F.G   -
  Thierens   H.W   -
PAYMASTER
  Pooley   J   -
ASSISTANT PAYMASTER
  Trew   W   -
CHIEF ENGINEER
  Shearman J.G   -
  Ward   J   -
ACTING CHIEF ENGINEER
  Willey   E.H   -
ENGINEER
  Thompson J.C   -
ASSISTANT ENGINEER
  Agnew   J.W   -
  Donohue   D   -
  Watch   J.S   -
CHIEF ENGINEROOM ARTIFICER
  Barnes   R   -
ACTING ENGINEROOM ARTIFICER
  Cooper   H.S   -
  Fox   C   -
  Green   G   -
  Pleasance C.T   -
SKILLED SHIPWRIGHT 3rd CLASS
  Nichols   R.H   1877-8-9

SHIPWRIGHT
  Carter   R   -
  Hawton   T.B   1877-8
CLERK
  Marwood   R.B   1877-8
  Riches   J   -
WRITER 2nd CLASS
  Williams   W   -
WRITER 3rd CLASS
  Carson   W   -
CAPTAIN OF HOLD
  Dawes   F   1877-8
MASTER AT ARMS
  Harris   J   -
SHIPS CORPORAL CLASS 1
  Triggs   W   -
SHIPS CORPORAL CLASS 2
  Symons   R   -
PETTY OFFICER CLASS 1
  Baker   W   1877-8
  Bateman J   -
  Buxey   F   -
  Castle   J   1879
  Davey   C   -
  Edwards R   -
  Faux   J   1877-8
  Gill   B.J   -
  Hackett S   1877-8-9
  Herbert T   1877-8-9
  Mills   J.M   -
  Nagle   H   1877-8-9
  Oranje   W   -
  Pankhurst T   -

Spinks 19 April 2007 Sale 7012 Lot 1015
The South Africa 1877-79 Medal to Staff Surgeon Sir H.F. Norbury, Later Director General of Naval Medical Services [K.C.B.], Honorary Surgeon to Their Majesties King Edward VII and King George V
South Africa 1877-79, one clasp, 1877-8-9 (H.F. Norbury, Staff Surgn. R.N., H.M.S. "Active"), toned, extremely fine, and a rare clasp to Royal Naval personnel, with photograph of recipient
Hammer Price £3,600
Sir Henry Frederick Norbury, K.C.B., M.D., F.R.C.S., R.N. (1839-1925); educated at Oundle School; studied medicine at St. Bart's, London and the University of Malta; M.R.C.S 1860; appointed Surgeon in the Navy, 1860; M.D. 1870; Staff Surgeon 1872; appointed to the corvette H.M.S. Active on the Cape and West Africa stations, October 1876; and whilst on her books he was landed in Medical charge of the Naval Brigade during the Kaffir War, 1877-78; served in the Transkei as Senior Medical Officer of six different columns of troops and was present in numerous skirmishes and in action at Quorra River and the Battle of Quintana (M.I.D. and strongly recommended for promotion); during the Zulu War of 1879 he was again landed and in charge of the Active's Naval Brigade and served as Principal Medical Officer of Colonel Pearson's Column being present at the Battle of Inyezane, January 1879, and the relief of the garrison of Ekowe (M.I.D. several times); joined General Crealock's Columns as Principal Medical Officer to the entire Naval Brigade and advanced to Port Durnford (Twice M.I.D.); Fleet Surgeon, July 1879 (C.B. July 1879; he also won the Gilbert Blane Gold Medal); appointed in charge of the Naval Hospital at the Cape of Good Hope, August 1879; he held the latter position for three years, during which time he was made M.D. of the University of the Cape; after a brief period at Impregnable training ship for boys, he was promoted Deputy Inspector-General of Hospitals and Fleets, April 1887; transferred to the department of the Director General to assist the then incumbent, Sir James Dick, 1890; Norbury spent five years in this capacity before being promoted Inspector General of Hospitals and Fleets, 1895 (Knight of Grace of the Order of St. John); he succeeded Sir James Dick as Director General of Naval Medical Services, 1898 (K.C.B.); elected Honorary Fellow of the Royal Naval College of Surgeons, 1900; retired 12.11.1904, having been Honorary Surgeon to both King Edward and King George and having written The Naval Brigade in South Africa (a photocopy of which is included with the lot).
Approximately 5 medals with '1877-8-9' clasp awarded to Naval Brigade Officers (Norbury, Lieutenant Craigie, Lieutenant Hamilton - all on Active and Commander E.H. Davis and Lieutenant Cockran on Bodicea. Approximately 111 '1877-8-9' clasp award to the Royal Navy.

HMS Active

	Pearce	J	1877-8	**SIGNALLER CLASS 1**			Caylay	J	1879
	Porteous	J	1877-8-9	Aynsley	W.H	1879	Clapperton	A	1877-8
	Smithers	G	1877-8-9				Clarke	J	1877-8-9
	Stevens	T	-	**SIGNALLER CLASS 2**			Collins	J	-
	Turner			Atkinson	A	-	Cook	W	1877-8
	Turner	C.E	1877-8-9	**SIGNALLER CLASS 2**			Coombs	E	1877-8-9
	White	E	1877-8-9	Butler	T	1879	Cooper	C	1877-8-9
	White	W.T	1877-8	Coglan	P	1879	Creer	C	1877-8-9
	Willcox	E	1877-8	Gostling	J.E.R	1877-8-9	Cross	J	1879
PETTY OFFICER CLASS 2				Hill	T.H	1879	Darlow	G	1879
	Bamford	T	-	**SIGNALLER 3rd CLASS**			Dobbs	H	1877-8-9
	Debell	H	1877-8-9	Heppel	A.J	-	Dove	E	1877-8-9
	Edwards	J.E	1877-8	Mc Donald	J	-	Downay	S	1879
	Futcher	E	1877-8-9	Rowland	C	1877-8-9	Filtness	H	1879
	Gale	W	1877-8-9	Smiley	J	-	Fleming	F.W	1879
	Pearce	A	1877-8-9	**SIGNAL BOY**			Francis	E.R	1879
	Sime	J	1879	Daffey	F	-	Gibbons	V	1877-8-9
COMMANDERS COXSWAIN				**GUNNER**			Gill	J	1879
	Carey	M	-	Bags	H	1877-8	Glesson	T	1877-8-9
LEADING SEAMAN				**ACTING GUNNER**			Gosling	M.D	1877-8-9
	Chantry	F	1877-8-9	Johnson	F	-	Harde	H	1877-8-9
	Cook	G	1877-8-9	Mitchell	J	1877-8	Harding	T	1877-8-9
	Duffet	E	1877-8-9	**BANDSMAN**			Hardwidge	T.G	-
	Kenney	J	1877-8	Goff	H	-	Harper	W	1877-8-9
	#Leal	G.E	1877-8	Harris	J.C	-	Harris	D	-
	Perrins	R	1877-8-9	Mc Cann	F	-	Harvey	C	1877-8-9
	Radford	E	1877-8-9	Medhurst	W	-	Hayman	J	1877-8-9
	Selwood	R	1877-8-9	Rennie	W.A	-	Hillier	C	1877-8-9
	Smith	G	1877-8-9	Riley	T	-	Hoare	A	1879
	Ulmer	W	1877-8	William	T	-	Hunt	J.T	1877-8
LEADING STOKER				**BANDSMAN CLASS 2**			Hunter	T	1877-8
	Avery	W	1879	Boustead	W	-	James	J	1879
	Aylmer	G	-	Hayes	J	-	Jamison	A	1877-8-9
	Hewson	A	-	White	T	-	Jasper	G	1877-8
	Holloway	W	-	**BOATSWAIN**			Le Corney	J	1877-8-9
	Horam	H	-	Cotter	J	1879	Lee	H	1879
	Mills	J	-	**ABLESEAMAN**			Mace	G	1879
	Newing	E	1877-8-9	Agnew	G	-	Maddon	C.F	1877-8
	Smith	H	-	Badge	J	-	Martin	D	1877-8-9
	Summers	F	-	Bartlett	F	1877-8-9	Milden	W.H	1877-8-9
YEOMAN OF SIGNALS				Bearryman	G	1879	Mitchell	W	1877-8-9
	Farleigh	F	-	Boakes	J.W	1877-8	Moore	G	1877-8-9
SIGNALLER				Broomfield	A.J	1877-8	Morgan	H	1879
	Moore	E	1877-8	Brown	J.E	1879	Murrant	A	1877-8-9
	Rogers	E.C.A		Burke	J	1877-8-9	Orrell	T	1877-8-9

Neate Auctions 19 Apr. 2009
South Africa Medal 1877 - 79 Bar: 1877 - 8
G. E. LEAL. LG. SEAN. H.M.S. "ACTIVE".
On 15 December 1877 a small Naval Brigade from HMS Active, under Commander T. Wright, RN, was landed in East London to provide artillery support for the Army. They took with them six 12 pounder guns, one Gatling gun and two 24 pounder rockets and over the next twelve months took part in a number of actions.
The Brigade fought alongside Colonel Glyn commanding the 24th Regiment against Chief Pokwane at the Battle of Quintana and in the action at Peri Bush. They were also present during the smaller actions against the Gaikas and Galikas tribes.
Towards the end of 1878 the Naval Brigade returned to their ship. Their service ashore earned them entitlement to the South Africa Medal with bar 1877 - 8 of which only 76 were issued. The Royal Navy received just 53 medals and bars, the Royal Marines 13 and Native Kroomen 10. With verification and copy of certificate of service. Born Portsmouth, Hampshire. Enlisted as Boy 2nd class, aged 15 on 1/10/1868 and retired as Gunners Mate 25/1/1881. Rare (NEF) Sold GBP 675.00

HMS Active

Name		Years	Name		Years	Role / Name		Years
O'Sullivan	M	1879	Neville	W	-	**ARMOURER**		
Newman	A	1877-8-9	Page	J	1877-8	Essery	A	1877-8-9
Newstead	J	1877-8	Rawlings	H	1877-8	**BLACKSMITH**		
Nops	J.G.S	1877-8-9	Sandercock	W	1877-8-9	Morris	S	1877-8
Page	W	1877-8-9	Sewell	H.A	-	**BLACKSMITHS CREW**		
Page	W	1877-8-9	Smith	W.C	-	Hutchens	D	-
Palmer	G	1877-8-9	Stansbury	J	1879	**BUTCHER**		
Parrington	H	1877-8-9	Sturgess	J	1877-8	Andrews	C	1877-8
Peel	W	1877-8	Thomas	A	-	**CARPENTER**		
Phillips	C	1877-8-9	Walker	S	-	Roff	W	-
Plascett	H	1877-8-9	Walsh	G.M	1879	**CARPENTERS MATE**		
Poole	W	1877-8-9	Ward	H	1877-8-9	Jope	J	1877-8
Rogers	C	1877-8-9	Ward	W	-	Reed	D	-
Rogers	R	1877-8-9	Weeks	W.H	-	**CARPENTERS CREW**		
Rowe	C	1877-8-9	**ORDINARY SEAMAN CLASS 2**			Clarke	W.C	-
Scrivener	W	1879	Bower	C	-	Gibes	R.J	-
Short	S	1877-8-9	Boyce	W	-	Parnell	G	1877-8
Smith	A	1877-8-9	Glazier	W	1877-8	Williams	J.C	-
Smith	J	1877-8	Glover	W	1877-8	**CARPENTERS CREW CLASS 2**		
Spiers	F	1877-8-9	Henley	W	1877-8-9	Cooke	S.J	-
Sprake	W	1877-8	Pride	C.S	-	**CAULKER**		
Stanbury	J	1877-8	**STOKER**			Renton	W	-
Stubbs	J	1879	Barrett	H.M	-	**CAULKERS MATE**		
Sullens	W	1879	Bourgess	L	-	Hamilton	W	-
Swayne	A	1877-8	Bramble	J	-	**SHIPS COOK 1st CLASS**		
Wade	H	1879	Butler	T	-	Thompson	C	-
Wagstaff	G	1877-8-9	Buxey	W	-	**COOKS MATE CLASS 1**		
Walters	J.G	1877-8-9	Cawdry	C	-	Constable	T	-
Williams	G	-	Davis	E	-	**COOKS MATE**		
Woodford	T	1879	Dyer	J.E	-	Pilley	H	-
ORDINARY SEAMAN			Elliott	J	-	**COOPERS CREW**		
Ashton	T	1877-8	Forder	J	-	Hamerston	J	-
Banks	J	-	Fowler	J	-	Pursell	J.H	1877-8
Blane	T	1877-8-9	Jacobs	J	-	Sheehy	R	1877-8
Brint	J	1877-8	King	J	-	**LAMPTRIMMER**		
Brown	J	1877-8	Male	S	-	Evans	J	1877-8
Burfitt	W	-	Maney	G	-	**MUSICIAN**		
Cacutt	J	-	Martell	G	-	Littlejohns	E.S	-
Dobear	R	1877-8	Mitchell	R.W	-	O'Brien	T	-
Doran	G	1879	Nobbs	H	-	**NAVAL SCHOOLMASTER**		
Falconer	A	-	Randle	J	-	Gibson	J	-
Field	H.J	-	Redman	G	-	**PAINTER CLASS 1**		
Handsom	W	1877-8	Tucker	W	-	Derrick	A	-
Hawes	J	-	Wallace	R	-	**PLUMBER**		
Howard	H	-	Ward	M	-	Rimington	F.R	-
Jackson	W	1877-8-9	Williams	J	-	**ROPEMAKER**		
Kerridge	W	1879	**STOKER CLASS 2**			Pailsky	T	-
Lang	J	1879	Bollan	C	-	**SAILMAKER**		
Linscott	H	-	Mead	H	-	Head	J	-
Lowman	G	-	Nash	D	-	**SAILMAKERS MATE**		
Mathews	H	-	Payne	W	-	Entwhistle	J	1877 8
May	C	1877-8-9	Sheir	A	-			

Memorial at Victoria Park, Portsmouth - "Erected by the officers and men of H.M.S. Active. Late flag-ship West Coast of Africa. Kaffir War, 1877-78, Zulu War, 1879. Lower Tugela: A. Pearce (Cox. Cutter), D. Martin (Able Seaman), N. Scandon (Gunner RMA). J. Walsh (Ordinary Seaman) & T. Liverpool (Krooman). Transkei: F. Daffey (Signalman) & A. Mabey (Drummer RM) Fort Ekowe: L. C. Coker (Midshipman), J. Moore (Shoemaker). J. Radford (Leading Seaman), A. Smith (Able Seaman), W. Stagg (Private RM) Isandhlwana: W. Aynsley (Signalman)."

HMS Active

SAILMAKERS CREW
Tutton	H.W	1877-8

SHIPS STEWARD CLASS 2
Martyn	W.M	-

SHIPS STEWARD ASSISTANT
Johns	W.H	1877-8

SHIPS STORES ASSISTANT
Ching	J.E.P	-

SHOEMAKER
Moore	J	1877-8-9

SICKBERTH ATTENDANT
Barrett	C.H	1877-8-9
Budd	A	-
Dingley	J	-

BOY CLASS 1
Bean	W.J	-
Lawrence	C.H	-
Lennard	J	-
Little	W.H	-
Ruse	E.H	-
White	E	-

DOMESTIC CLASS 1
Crew	L	-
Lake	E	-
Mayell	F	-
Saxty	G	-
West	H	1879

DOMESTIC CLASS 2
Cowan	G	-
Grigg	G.J	-
Hall	H	-
Harrison	H	1879
Jarret	A	-
Medding	W	-
Matthew	E.J	-
Phillips	G	-
Rice	G	-
Solomon	M.M	-
Stanley	R	1877-8
Vine	W.H	-
Walker	F	-

DOMESTIC CLASS 3
Brownlow	W	-
Harvey	J.W	-
Hooper	W	-
Month	C	-
Newgent	J	-
Nicholls	T	-
Penn	F.J	-
Wright	W	-

ROYAL MARINES
Including ROYAL MARINE ARTILLERY and ROYAL MARINE LIGHT INFANTRY

LIEUTENANT
Dowding	T.W	1877-8-9

SERGEANT
Blackman	W.T	1877-8-9
Hollis	A	1879
Lewis	J	1877-8

CORPORAL
Botwood	J	1879

BOMBARDIER
Trenchard	B	1877-8-9

GUNNER
Brown	W	1879
Carroll	J	1877-8-9
Dale	J	1877-8-9
Free	E	1877-8
Kilshaw	T	1877-8-9
Lemon	W	1877-8-9
Marshall	A	1877-8
Seddon	W	1877-8-9
Shields	R	1877-8-9
Taylor	J	-

BUGLER
Cook	T.H	1879
Le Delaney	J	-
Maby	A.J	1877-8

PRIVATE
Ansell	J	-
Arnott	J	1879
Barratt	J	1877-8
Bates	J	1877-8-9
Bigwood	W	1877-8-9
Burdekin	G	1877-8
Burke	P	1877-8
Cardell	C.H	1879
Cassell	W	1877-8
Chapple	W	1879
Cook	J	1877-8-9
Davies	C	1877-8-9
Devaney	T	1877-8
Ellard	W	1877-8-9
Fleming	C	1877-8-9
Harding	H	-
Holbrooke	E	-
Iggalden	S	1877-8-9
King	G	1877-8
Marshall	W	1877-8-9
May	C	1877-8-9
Melluish	F	1877-8-9
Netyard	E	1877-8-9
Neale	W	1877-8-9
Pearce	R	1877-8
Penketh	L	1877-8-9
Pepperell	W	1877-8-9
Pickering	G	1877-8
Alias C.G.W Case		
Pratt	H	1879
Rayner	W	1877-8-9
Reed	C	1877-8
Scanlan	J	1877-8-9
Shepherd	W	-
Smith	J	1877-8-9
Smith	T	1877-8-9
Smith	W	1879
Stagg	W	1877-8-9
Viney	G	1877-8-9
Warren	T	1879
Whitnell	C	-
Williams	U.H	1879
Wilson	E	1877-8-9
Woolfenden	J	1877-8-9

In addition to the above names, the names of 42 Krooman (West African Native Rating) had been listed, many with clasps, but the names were deleted and medals were not issued.

ROYAL NAVY HMS BODICEA

She was a 16-gun screw corvette, launched at Portsmouth in 1875 and was of 4,140 tons, 5,290 horsepower and 14.9 knots speed. Certain medals to this ship were without a clasp. The body of the Prince Imperial was carried to England aboard H.M.S. Boadicea.

CAPTAIN
Twiss	G.O	1879

COMMANDER
Davis	E.H.M	1877-8-9
Romilly	F	1879

COMMODORE
Richards	CB F. W	1879

CHAPLAIN and NAVAL INSTRUCTOR
Nicolls	Rev A	-

FLEET SURGEON
O' Malley	J.N.J	

STAFF SURGEON
Martin	J.H	1879

SURGEON
Grant	R	1879
Mahon	E	-
Pollard	E.R.H	1879
Vasey	S.W	1879

NAVIGATING LIEUTENANT
Hatch	H.G	

LIEUTENANT
Benett	J.G	1879
Caffin	C	1879
Carr	F.R	1879
Cockran	R.P	1877-8-9
Hobkirk	E.C	1879
Masterman	J	-
Preedy	H	1879
Smythies	P.K	1879

SUB LIEUTENANT
Cotesworth	H	1879
Lyon	H	1879
Scott	A.L	-
Valentine	F.A	-

MIDSHIPMAN
Bolders	H.S	-
Cawston	A.G	-
Crookshank	A.F	1879
Colville	Hon S.C.J	1879

HMS Bodicea

	Eyre	F.G	-	ASSISTANT ENGINEER			PETTY OFFICER CLASS 1		
	Gleig	C.H.A	-		Biddick	C.H	-	Allen	J	1879
	Hewitt	W.W	1879	SKILLED SHIPWRIGHT			Alridge	W	-
	Hewell	C.A	-		Lovett	S	-	Argue	G	-
	Warrender	G.J.S	1879		Turner	R	-	Bunting	D.S	-
NAVAL CADET				SHIPWRIGHT			Coleman	J	1879
	Boys	W.H	-		Berriman	C	-	Drover	W	1879
	West	G.R	-		Blackwell	J	-	Fox	C	-
PAYMASTER				ENGINEROOM ARTIFICER			Fryer	G.I	1879
	#Dawson	C.T	-		Clinch	J	1879	Hanmer	M	1879
	Ramsey	W.B	-		Day	W	1879	Hawkins	W.C	-
ASSISTANT PAYMASTER					Horder	J.R	-	Hughes	J	1879
	Hale	F.H	-		Norman	C	-	Mazula	A	-
CLERK					Phillips	J	-	Morris	T	1879
	Cleveland	H	-		Wilkins	T	-	Mortimer	D	1879
SECRETARY				TORPEDO ARTIFICER			Ransome	H	1879
	Carlisle	J	1877-8-9		Mitchell	R	1879	Spear	E	1879
WRITER CLASS 1				YEOMAN OF SIGNALS			Stevens	C	1879
	Thompson	W.H	-		Soper	W.D	-	Smith	W.H	-
WRITER CLASS 3				YEOMAN OF STOREROOMS			Sulllvan	J	1879
	King	W	-		Barnes	W	-	Thomas	T	-
CHIEF ENGINEER				BOATSWAIN			Witheridge	S	1879
	Dark	W	-		Killbery	J.W	-	PETTY OFFICER CLASS 2		
ENGINEER				MASTER AT ARMS			Bennett	C	1879
	Brown	W.J.C	-		Mason	J	-	James	W	1879
	Coombes	J.T	-	SHIPS CORPORAL CLASS 1			Laming	C	-
	Couper	I.A	-		Frampton	J	1879	Low	J	-
	Williams	S.I	-					Roach	J	1879

Spinks Auction 5th December 2002, Lot 51 South Africa 1877-79, no clasp (C.T.Dawson, Payr R.N. H.M.S "Boadicea"), toned, very fine Hammer Price £280. Charles Todd Dawson, Paymaster, commissioned as Assistant Clerk in 1854, advanced to Clerk in 1855, Assistant Paymaster 1859, Paymaster 1865 and Fleet Paymaster 1886. Dawson was Clerk aboard Ardent in anti-slaving patrols off West Africa, 1857-59, and was present on that ship in operations against the Sooroo tribes along the Scarcies River in 1858; he was Paymaster of Boadicea during the Zulu War and was Mentioned in Despatches. He retired as Chief Paymaster in 1892 and died in 1897 at Southsea, Hampshire, aged 59 years.

HMS Bodicea

LEADING SEAMAN

Chapell	E.P	1879
Clarke	A	1879
Cotton	W	-
Cranch	W	-
Elliott	W	1879
Enderby	J	1879
Gillis	R	-
Hall	E.T	-
King	C	1879
Lloyd	T	-
Plastine	W.T	1879
Rich	J	1879
Webb	H.W	1879

LEADING STOKER

Cashman	J	-
Harris	J	-

Also had Abyssinia medal.

Hobbs	J	-
Luff	W	1879
Moore	A	-
Newans	J.T	-
Peppernell	J	-
Walsh	D.C	-

GUNNER

Roberts	A.J	-

BANDSMAN

Carter	G	-
Henwood	A	-
Lardiard	H	-
Rossi	L	-
Scott	G	-
Spencer	J	-
Stander	O	-
Wright	H	-

BUGLER BOY

Hinchley	J	1879

dangerously wounded at Gingindhlovu 2/4/1879

Temlett	W.H	-
Wadling	C.L	-

SIGNALMAN

Pyer	T	1879

SIGNALMAN 2nd CLASS

Smith	W.C	1879

SIGNALMAN 3rd CLASS

Perry	E.I	1879
Reid	W.F	1879

Died of Fever In Zululand May 1879

VOLUNTEER ABLE SEAMAN

Jennings	R.V	1879
Ogilvie	P.A	1879

These Seamen served on "THE FLORENCE"

ABLE SEAMAN

Armstrong	H	-
Atkins	A.J	-
Barnard	W	1879
Bickford	J	-
Bone	D	1879
Boniface	W	1879
Charles	J	1879
Childs	J	1879
Clark	W.E	1879
Cleall	E	1879
Clements	C.H	-
Coleman	G.S	1879
Cook	G	1879
Cox	J	1879
Croft	H	1879
Crossby	G	-
Cunningham	W.T	-
Dare	W	1879
Donovan	J	1879
Dunkason	W	1879
Evans	J	-
Flynn	J	1879
Foley	J	-
Gannaway	R	1879
Garn	G	1879
Gibbs	J	-
Greenaway	W.G	1879
Hand	J	1879
Hannon	M	1879
Hawkins	A	1879
Harris	C	1879
Hill	T	1879
Hughes	F	1879
Hurlock	H.T	-
Kelly	T	1879
Knight	W.T	1879
Leggett	J.E	1879
Lloyd	J	1879
Mackley	C	1879
Malby	H.W	1879
Marshall	J	-
Martin	T	1879
Mc Intyre	A	-
Merritt	J	1879
Mitchell	J	-
Moray	W	1879
Perry	F	1879
Porter	E	1879
Robins	G	-
Rose	W	1879
Salter	A	1879
Sismey	J	1879
Taylor	C	1879
Thomas	J	1879
White	J	1879
Whitefield	C	1879
Woods	W	-

ORDINARY SEAMAN

Abram	R	1879
Allen	J	-
Baker	G	-
Barrett	A	1879
Barry	H	-
Bateman	G.E	-
Beaton	R	-
Bentley	T	1879
Birch	W	-
Bohanna	T	1879
Bottomley	A	1879
Boxall	S	1879
Brazier	J	1879
Burns	M	-
Bunn	J	1879
Burton	G	-
Butler	G	1879
Challen	G	-
Collett	W	-
Cox	T	-
Creamer	H.C	-
Cross	F	1879
Dalton	J	-
Dodd	J	1879
Dodds	T	1879
Dowling	J	1879
Downing	P	-
Edwards	H	-
Fabian	W.F	-
Fleming	A	1879
Furneaux	W	-
Gamble	J	1879
George	C.J	1879
Goodall	R	1879
Green	F	1879
Habgood	W	1879
Hanley	E	1879
Hayden	G	-
Hodges	A	1879
Hollands	A	-
Holliday	W	-
Humphries	T	1879
Hunter	E	1879
Jenkins	G	1879
Jennings	H.W	-
Jones	J	-
Kelley	W	-
Keap	W.H	1879
Laing	J	1879
Lee	W.C	1879
Lockley	H	-
Loveless	J	-
Love	J	1879
Lynn	J	-
Martin	E	1879
Martin	F	1879
Mason	J	-
Mc Carthy	D	1879
Mc Cullum	D	-
Mc Gourlick	O	-
Mc Grath	W	1879
Meades	E	-
Marlow	G	-
Murray	C	-

HMS Bodicea

Nightscales	B	-		Stevens	J	-	Wilkins	J.H	1879
Norrie	T	1879		Sutton	W	1879	**SAILMAKERS MATE**		
Pafford	J	-		Sydenham	J	-	Langley	H	-
Passingham	W	-		Thomas	L	-	**SAILMAKERS CREW**		
Payne	H	1879	**STOKER 2nd CLASS**				Maynard	J.H	1879
Philpott	H	1879		Baker	J	-	**SCHOOLMASTER**		
Plaice	R.H	-		Bennett	A	1879	Felton	C	-
Pragnell	T	1879		Eastwood	G	1879	Quick	W.I	-
Quayle	E.A	-		Foley	M	-	**SHIPS COOK**		
Reid	F	-		Harwood	J	1879	Fowler	W.J	1877-8
Richardson	W.H	1879	*Died of Fever In Zululand May 1879*				Mills	G.A	-
Roche	J	-		Hayter	G	-	**COOKS MATE**		
Russel	F	1879		Hilton	J	-	Jessop	G	-
Salmon	D	-		Hughes	H	-	**SHIPS STORES BOY**		
Scrivens	A	1879		Mack	D	1879	Duesbury	H.S	-
Seal	G	1879		Mayers	J	-	**SHIPS STEWARD**		
Sellers	J.W	-		Merritt	J	1879	Curzon	R.W	-
Silk	F.E	-		Russell	J	-	**SHOEMAKER**		
Snell	G	1879	**ARMOURER**				Hellyer	R	-
Speak	J.L	-		White	H	1879	**SICKBERTH STEWARD**		
Sponder	G	-	**ARMOURERS CREW**				Crane	H.J	-
Turner	D	1879		Green	J	1879	**ASSISTANT SICKBERTH ATTENDANT**		
Warton	G	1879	**BARBER**				Bevis	W	-
Whitmore	B	-		Chalkley	W.E	-	**TAILOR**		
Woodard	W.I	1879	**BLACKSMITH**				Neck	H	-
Woods	H	1879		Gilbert	H.T	1879	**BOY CLASS 1**		
ORDINARY SEAMAN 2nd CLASS			**BLACKSMITHS CREW**				Beddell	H.G	1879
Bowler	W.A	-		Squibb	H	-	Bignell	A	-
Brazier	H	-	**BUTCHER**				Briggs	G.H	-
Bull	G	1879		Mills	H	1879	Chapman	W	-
Hall	W.T	1879	**CARPENTER**				Clark	F	-
Holiday	W	-		Cockburn	J.D	-	Cleave	R	1879
O'Connor	C.I	1879	**CARPENTERS MATE**				Coles	E.I	-
Rockall	H	1879		Conday	P	1879	Coles	J.H	1879
Tylee	W	1879	*Dangerously wounded at Gingindhlovu 2/4/1879*				Croucher	A	1879
Woodrow	F	1879					Davis	J	-
STOKER				Seger	J	-	Dooley	J	-
Baker	W	1879	**CARPENTERS CREW**				Elliott	T	-
Brockway	J	1879		Brown	J.E	1879	Foster	F	-
Brooks	E	-		Cue	J	-	Fry	W.R	1879
Brooks	J	-		Hayes	P	1879	Gilbert	G	-
Castle	G	-		Oliver	T	1879	Harkins	H	-
Dalton	J	-		Wellstead	C.H	1879	Harris	T	1879
Downton	A	1879	**CAULKER**				Holland	J	-
Fabery	E	-		Brett	H	-	Hoyle	W.T	-
Fisher	F	-		Stewart	W	-	Langford	E.I	-
Freeman	T	-	**COOPER**				Lefevre	J.T	-
Gray	W	1879		Morris	H.T	-	Lintern	H	-
Guyett	S	-	**COOPERS CREW**				Lush	H	-
Hudson	C	-		Campbell	W.J	1879	Mc Clure	J	-
Lock	W	-	**LAMPTRIMMER**				Mc Grath	R	-
Lynch	W	-		Cotton	J	-	Mould	W	-
Malam	G	-	**PAINTER**				Murphy	W	-
Mathison	J	-		Hill	R	-	Newbury	A	-
Mercy	P	-	**PLUMBER**				Parker	G	-
Ponsford	F	-		Taylor	C	1879	Payne	C.A	1879
Potts	T	1879	**ROPEMAKER**				Phillips	A	-
Saunders	C	1879		Green	T.H	-	Phillips	A.E	-
Stephens	J	1879	**SAILMAKER**				Philpott	C	1879

HMS Bodicea

	Pocknell	E	1879
	Rees	D	-
	Reid	J	-
	Riley	R	1879
	Rockett	J.I	-
	Sampson	J	1879
	Scott	J.W	-
	Thomas	R	-
	Upton	E	-
	Vernon	W	-
	Warren	S	-
	Way	J	-
	Whitton	A	-
	Wise	S	-
	Wiseman	J.G	-
	Wolstenholme	H	-
DOMESTIC CLASS 1			
	Formosa	P	1879
DOMESTIC CLASS 2			
	Adshead	W.H	-
	Bennett	G	-
	Carty	J	-
	Hagan	J	-
	Hyde	T	-
	James	J	-
	Montague	F	-
	Musselwhite	W	-
	Thorne	S	-
	Walker	S	-

Also had Ashanti Medal 1873 – as J.W.I Walker

DOMESTIC CLASS 3			
	Binell	G.T	1879
	Day	R	-
	Figg	H	1879
	Wilks	H	-

ROYAL MARINES.
Including the Royal Marine Artillery.

LIEUTENANT			
	Robyns	J.W	1879
SERGEANT			
	Pawsey	C	1879
	Slugg	R	1879
CORPORAL			
	Field	W	-
	Heazle	J	1879
	Saunders	G	-
BOMBARDIER			
	Crockett	C	1879
	Cropp	J	1879
	Mc Cartan	M	1879
GUNNER			
	Griffiths	T	1879
	Heald	W	-
	Low	T	-
	Maddox	J	1879
	Marshall	E	1879
	Parfit	F	1879

DRUMMER			
	Larkyus	J.W	1879
PRIVATE			
	Allsop	H	-
	Ambrose	J	1879
	Ault	T	-
	Bates	J	1879
	Bird	M	1879
	Bracegirdle	J	-
	Burns	J	-
	Clayton	T.C	-
	Cook	J	-
	Coombes	C	-
	Coy	G	1879
	Daniels	T	-
	Davies	T	1879
	Davis	W	1879
	Deniery	J	1879
	Farmer	H	-
	Finnigan	W	1879
	Foster	J	1879
	Foy	P	1879
	Green	J	1879
	Harding	G	1879
	Helbert	H	1879
	Horn	J	1879
	Hill	W	1879
	Likemon	W	1879
	Matthews	J	1879
	Monaghan	J	-
	Meyer	J	1879
	Parfitt	G	1879

Dangerously wounded at Gingindhlovu 2/4/1879

	Pearse	H	1879
	Phillips	T.T	-
	Stamp	T	1879
	Styles	W	1879
	Waskett	G	-
	White	F.G	1879
	Wilkins	T	-
PRIVATE			
	Wright	S	-

ROYAL NAVY. HMS EUPHRATES
The medals to this Ship were without a clasp.

CAPTAIN			
	Brownrigg	C.J	
CHAPLAIN			
	Gunter Revd	W	
FLEET SURGEON			
	Connolly MD	W	
SURGEON			
	Collot	J.A	
NAVIGATING LIEUTENANT			
	Moore	G.K	
LIEUTENANT			
	Bailey	A.R.F	
	Cotton	N	
	Harris	H.P	
	Young	J.B	
SUB LIEUTENANT			
	Rolfe	H.N	
PAYMASTER			
	Herbert	E.D	
ASSISTANT PAYMASTER			
	Inch	W.W	
	Lyon	J	
WRITER CLASS 2			
	Faulkner	G	
CHIEF ENGINEER			
	Hill	J	
ENGINEER			
	Hobbs	J	
	Maudling	W.J	
	Nicklin	W	
	Stansmore	H.F.C	
ENGINEROOM ARTIFICER			
	Frampton	G.J	
	Gillham	G	
	Metcalf	T	
	Sawyer	W	
	Sweetlove	J	
ACTING ENGINEROOM ARTIFICER			
	Bassam	J.F	
	Carter	J.H	
	Findon	H	
	Schischkar	W	
CAPTAIN Of THE HOLD			
	Korton	T.P	
	Scrivens	J.W	
CAPTAIN COXSWAIN			
	Saunders	D.G	
BOATSWAIN			
	Adams	J	
	Baker	J.R	
	Casey	J	
	Cobby	J.V	
	Doidge	J	
	Wells	J	
MASTER AT ARMS			
	Beckley	W	
SHIPS CORPORAL CLASS 1			
	Donsberry	F.H	
	Luff	J.H	
	Setford	J.S	
CHIEF PETTY OFFICER			
	Stein	C	
ACTING CHIEF PETTY OFFICER			
	Florence	G.H	
PETTY OFFICER CLASS 1			
	Bennett	R	
	Bishop	J.J	
	Cooter	W.F	
	Cox	T	
	Grevatt	W	
	Jones	T.G	

HMS Euphrates

Lee	A
Naish	J
Perry	H
Pool	H
Purfield	R
Robinson	J
Selway	W
Sparkes	W

PETTY OFFICER CLASS 2

Beckett	W.T
Garrett	F
Nicholls	T
Reynolds	T

YEOMAN OF STORES

Chambers	C.J

LEADING SEAMAN

Beard	G
Moore	W.T
Redding	R
Rooke	D
Swayne	H
Thomas	G
Trigwell	W

LEADING STOKER

Bath	J
Bushell	H
Hatfield	G
Massey	A
Payne	C
Potter	G
Pratt	J
Prince	H.R
Tredgold	G

SIGNALMAN CLASS 2

Bratt	W.H

ABLE SEAMAN

Alexander	W
Baker	G
Boland	W
Boles	L
Bridger	A
Budd	R
Carven	J
Castellano	A
Collins	C
Collis	C
Connell	D
Costick	E.J
Eades	W
Esmonde	H
Glamlyn	W.F.H
Goodrich	G
Grinwood	H.L
Hagarty	M
Hoare	C
Horsham	W
Jacobs	P
Kay	J
Matthews	C
Moore	E
Moore	J
Page	C
Pierce	W
Phillips	T
Pudge	J
Russell	A
Self	G
Smith	H
Smith	T.W
Spencer	H
Sullivan	J
Taylor	E
Walters	W
Wheeler	J
Wild	J
Wyatt	E.G

ORDINARY SEAMAN

Attrill	A
Blackford	T
Burnscome	E
Hall	J.R
Hampton	C
Hawkins	J
Law	J
Lawes	H.R
Parker	J.W
Patterson	A
Smith	J
Somers	J.E
Vidler	H.J
Waddups	G.E
Wearn	E
Wells	G.F
Wookey	J

STOKER

Bartlett	W.J
Beck	R
Bricknell	J.A
Clanford	S
Cole	J
Cook	J
Finn	J.J.P
French	E
Gibbs	T.G
Halsey	W
Henwood	W
Hooper	J.T
Hosgood	R.G
Jeffery	J
Jesson	J
Keene	P
Kingswell	H
Little	W
Luff	J.W
Martin	W
Matson	J
O'Keefe	J
Poniton	R
	Alias Porrington.
Pope	W
Robinson	J
Sainsbury	W
Sammuels	J
Travener	F
Welch	W
Wingate	C

STOKER CLASS 2

Burton	S
Cook	H
Hibberd	C
Hinde	G
Jacobson	I
Mc Dermott	T
Mc Nally	J
Nugent	J
Seel	Z
Shirkey	J
Spencer	W

BAKER

Brassey	A
Moore	E

BLACKSMITH

West	S

BUTCHER

Richards	J

BUTCHERS ASSISTANT

Good	W

CARPENTER

Pink	W.J

CARPENTERS MATE

Hobbs	S.G
Lawrence	F

CARPENTERS CREW

Furman	W.H.B
Hall	R
Lynch	F
Mc Duff	F.J
New	C.W

CAULKER

Bone	G

COOPER

Roach	W

LAMP LIGHTER

Bernard	W
Howe	B
Newland	J
Walker	G.F
Way	G

MUSICIAN

Swan	S

PAINTER

Holt	R.J

PLUMBER

Gardner	F.E
O'Brien	D

PLUMBERS MATE

Harris	C

HMS Euphrates

SAILMAKERS MATE
- Thomas H.J.R

SHIPS COOK
- Collins H

SHIPS COOK GENERAL MESS
- Veryard T.E

COOK CLASS 1
- Symons S

COOKS MATE CLASS 1
- Flower W

COOKS MATE 1st CLASS FOR CREW
- Hendy E

SHIPS STEWARD CLASS 1
- Leggett J.H

SHIPS STEWARD GENERAL MESS
- Wilkins C.P

SHIPS STEWARD ASSISTANT
- Evered J
- Smith J

SICKBERTH STEWARD
- Grey C.J

DOMESTIC CLASS 1
- Barrett S.A
- Carnon D.S (Alias Carnochern)
- Scott H

DOMESTIC CLASS 2
- Adams T
- Alten W
- Chapman E
- Hales S
- Houncell W
- Lawrence H
- Miller E.W
- Sherwin M
- Smith C
- Smith H.J
- Spencer F.A
- Squibb W
- Startling J.R
- Stevens J.J
- Whittle T
- Williams J
- Wyatt R.E

DOMESTIC CLASS 3
- Bartlett G
- Black C.L
- Coke C
- Duddleston W
- Fry W
- Johnson R.C
- Prince J
- Wallace A.W.J
- West W.G

ROYAL MARINES

COLOUR SERGEANT
- Rust J

ACTING CORPORAL
- Radford B

PRIVATE
- Baston J
- Cameron G
- Chandler I
- Creswell S
- Honeybun J
- Jackson A
- Jones R
- Mc Gregor J
- Moody I
- Newman J
- Robb J.B
- Sillence J
- Sparey H.W
- Tiller T
- Usher E
- Walker F
- Williams F

ROYAL NAVY. HMS FORESTER

LIEUTENANT
- Smith S.G 1879

SUB LIEUTENANT
- Theed J.H.W 1879
- Wrey R.B.S 1879

SURGEON
- Boyle W.P.M 1879

PILOT
- Le Clercq J.J 1879

ENGINEER
- Bowman J 1879
- Marsh E.W 1879

ENGINE ROOM ARTIFICER
- Murray D 1879

ACTING ENGINE ROOM ARTIFICER
- Fitzjohn J 1879

WRITER CLASS 1
- Pepperell E 1879

WRITER CLASS 2
- Ireland G.W 1879

ASSISTANT PAYMASTER
- Osborn R 1879

PETTY OFFICER CLASS 1
- Godden H 1879
- Hammond G 1879
- Jordan J 1879
- Share C 1879
- Tucker R 1879

PETTY OFFICER CLASS 2
- Streeter W 1879
- Twoney G 1879

ARMOURERS CREW
- Raddon H.L 1879

SAILMAKER'S CREW
- Skinner T.R 1879

YEOMAN OF SIGNALS
- Cleary J 1879

ASSISTANT SICK BERTH ATTENDANT
- Wood H 1879

LEADING SEAMAN
- Butler J 1879

LEADING STOKER
- Moxley J.J 1879

SKILLED CARPENTERS MATE
- Hicks H 1879

SHIP'S STEWARDS ASSISTANT
- Hine H.T 1879

ABLE SEAMAN
- Adams H.T 1879
- Barnes T 1879
- Barry E 1879
- Day J 1879
- Hodskins W.H 1879
- Paley H 1879
- Walker A 1879
- Wills T 1879
- Wolseley R 1879

ORDINARY SEAMAN
- Beatly H 1879
- Cardwell F 1879
- Gore W 1879
- Graham R.J 1879
- Parramore T.A 1879
- Paton J 1879
- Smith J.H 1879

ORDINARY SEAMAN 2nd CLASS
- Roberts G 1879

GUNNER
- Manley G 1879

BOY 1st CLASS
- Hines F.J.W 1879

SIGNALLER 2nd CLASS
- Carroll W 1879

SIGNALLER 3rd CLASS
- Tinsley J 1879
- Carrick E 1879

SIGNAL BOY
- Cooper A 1879
- Sewell J.L 1879

SHIPS COOK 2nd CLASS
- Hardy G 1879

STOKER
- Broad W 1879
- Creeber R 1879
- Connolly D 1879
- Keast S 1879
- Perry H 1879
- Quance J.T 1879
- Reardon W 1879

DOMESTIC CLASS 1
- Western R 1879

DOMESTIC CLASS 2
- Barry M 1879

HMS Forester

Hicks	W	1879	**ROYAL NAVY. HMS HIMALAYA**			SHIPS CORPORAL CLASS 2	
Johns	R	1879	LIEUTENANT			Brown	J.H
Ledlum	I	1879	Law	E.G.F		Hall	J.R
			Neale	C.B			
DOMESTIC CLASS 3			Riddell	D.M.H		BOATSWAIN	
Thomas	Z	1879	Wright	D.		Bloomfield	J
Whitelock	G	1879	SUB LIEUTENANT			Mc Gregor	A
Smith	H.J	1879	Lang	E.L		Pound	W.H
			CHIEF ENGINEER			Trice	G

The names of 33 Krooman (West African Native Rating) were deleted from this roll.

ROYAL MARINES.
CORPORAL
  Billington T 1879
PRIVATE
  Birch J 1879
  Coen J.J 1879
  Cummings R 1879
  Fife F.J 1879
  Griffin T 1879
  Harrison J.C 1879
  Hooper W 1879
  Stratton J 1879

ROYAL NAVY. HMS HIMALAYA
The medals to this ship were without a clasp.
CAPTAIN
  White E
CHAPLAIN
  Cananagh Rev J
FLEET SURGEON
  Wilson D
SURGEON
  Wood MD J
NAVIGATING LIEUTENANT
  Greel W.F.A

CHIEF ENGINEER
  Mather J
ENGINEER
  Douglas O
  Grice T.S
  Robins S.J
ASSISTANT ENGINEER
  Trivess A.M
SKILLED SHIPWRIGHT
  Mitchell G
SHIPWRIGHT
  Chapman A
ENGINEROOM ARTIFICER
  Hooper W
  Pawley R
ACTING ENGINEROOM ARTIFICER
  Mackinnin W.H
  Park A
  Wildish H.R
  Wilson J.A
PAYMASTER
  Dinnis T.R
ASSISTANT PAYMASTER
  Andrews W.S
WRITER CLASS 3
  Prideaux J.H
MASTER AT ARMS
  James J.H
SHIPS CORPORAL
  Carveth W.T

  Vincent W
ACTING BOATSWAIN
  Metters J
YEOMAN OF STORES
  Sheehan D
CHIEF PETTY OFFICER
  Bowie R
  Patey S
PETTY OFFICER CLASS 1
  Alway B
  Berridge T
  Clarke E
  Dearlove W
  Doyle J
  Farr J
  Hampton J.E
  Holland D
  Jacob R
  Mason W.F
  Parr G
  Phillips J
  Pridham S
  Shears W
  Smith J
  Wellman W
PETTY OFFICER CLASS 2
  Brook E.J
  Endacott A

HMS Forester

	Hambly	R		Wakeham	J	**CARPENTERS MATE**	
	Neill	T		Warren	W.H	Hicks	S.G
	Stonelake	M		Wheeler	R		
LEADING SEAMAN				Wingett	R		
	Baker	R		Young	G	**CARPENTERS CREW**	
	Cealing	N		Young	W	Clarke	F.W
	Knowles	G	**ORDINARY SEAMAN**			Mc Kay	A
	Morrow	T		Farley	T.S	Withers	G
LEADING STOKER				Hosking	H	**CAULKER**	
	Gardener	J		Palmer	W	Mc Ilwic	C
	Low	J		Steel	T	**COOPER**	
	Rogers	R		Taylor	J	Mangan	T.G
	Sampson	J		Walker	J	**LAMPTRIMMER**	
	Sutton	J.H		Wingett	G	Martinelli	G
	Walker	J		Winter	J.T	Perry	J
SIGNALMAN			**STOKER**			**MUSICIAN & BARBER**	
	Donovan	D		Allen	A.W	Sullivan	M
	Peter	W.J		Bailey	C	**PAINTER CLASS 1**	
SIGNALMAN 2nd CLASS				Barkell	S	Jope	C.M
	Lawrence	J.B		Bisgrove	W.R	**PLUMBER**	
	Pink	H		Blake	J	Attwell	S
	Thornton	J		Bowhay	W	**SAILMAKERS MATE**	
ABLE SEAMAN				Connox	M	Roncke	J
	Ahern	T		Donovan	D	**SHIPS COOK CLASS 1**	
	Bendy	B		Ferrell	A	Luff	C.T
	Blacke	W		Flynn	J	White	G
	Brookshaw	W		Ford	G.E	**SHIPS COOK**	
	Brodbent	F		Forrester	J	Hawkins	F
	Boyston	C		Gearey	G	**SHIPS STEWARD**	
	Clock	A		Guest	J	Bloomfield	J
	Compton	J		Harris	H	Goodman	G
	Coles	W.P		Harris	W	**SHIPS STEWARD ASSISTANT**	
	Darby	JW		Harvey	W.H	Snowdon	F.A
	Haley	J		Horswell	J	**SHIPS STEWARD BOY**	
	Hallet	W		Jackson	W	Geary	M
	Hawkins	W.H		Leonard	J	**SICKBERTH STEWARD**	
	Hillman	G		Lucks	J.S	Sisne	R.J
	Hogben	G.W		Miners	W.H	**ASSISTANT SICK BERTH ATTENDANT**	
	Hoskings	J.S		Newban	G	Joyce	H
	Jackson	J		Northmore	J	**DOMESTIC CLASS 1**	
	James	G		Palmer	J	Bedison	E
	Keohane	M		Parsons	W	Tellerfield	C
	Lambel	J		Salter	W	World	H
	Langman	W		Trahar	W	**DOMESTIC CLASS 2**	
	Luxton	W.J	**STOKER CLASS 2**			Brown	G
	Norton	F		Brooks	J	Canavas	F
	O'Brien	J		Elley	C	Correschi	E
	Pudner	R		Hall	F	Grills	J
	Pullen	E		Lathrope	J	Matthews	J
	Reid	W		Ryan	T	May	W
	Rooney	D		Truscott	P	Mortimere	J
	Ryder	C.E	**BAKER**			Pearce	G.W
	Salt	W.H		Turner	R	Prow	H
	Searle	R	**BLACKSMITHS CREW**			Purkis	J
	Skinner	E		Greenaway	G	Richards	J
	Symons	G.H	**BUTCHER**			Stuckey	H
	Tamlin	W		Hale	H	West	J
	Thompson	A	**CARPENTER**			**DOMESTIC CLASS 3**	
				Sammels	B	Bickley	S

HMS Forester

Bignell C
New C

ROYAL MARINES
COLOUR SERGEANT
　　Pongelley M
CORPORAL
　　Hunt J
PRIVATE
　　Burgess W
　　Claridge H
　　Davies S
　　Desmond W
　　Dymond J
　　Gray J
　　Gullick W
　　Gunningham S
　　Harwood W
　　Holmes G.H
　　Husson C
　　Jeffery B
　　Lacey M
　　Lane W.H
　　Lucas H.T
　　Miller W
　　Norgrove C
　　Norris P
　　Pickering H.D
　　Scaife T
　　Sharpe A
　　Smith A
　　Smith W
　　Toms C
　　Weaver W

ROYAL NAVY HMS ORONTES
The medals to this ship were without a clasp.
CAPTAIN
　　Kinaken R.G
CHAPLAIN
　　Garrison MA C.E Revd
STAFF SURGEON
　　Magill MD M
SURGEON
　　Cross H.E.F
LIEUTENANT
　　Elton F
　　Greenhow J.E
　　Greaves E.E
　　Hungerford S.A
　　Targell H.W
PAYMASTER
　　Bavertock F.B
ASSISTANT PAYMASTER
　　Dymott R.L
SUB LIEUTENANT
　　Robinson H.R

CHIEF ENGINEER
　　Bannerman J
ENGINEER
　　Aborn G
　　Mather J.R
　　Paterson G.F
　　Swiney G
SKILLED SHIPWRIGHT
　　Jamieson D
　　Reeves G
ENGINE ROOM ARTIFICER
　　Sargeant D
ACTING ENGINE ROOM ARTIFICER
　　Boulton J
　　Brown W
　　Campbell A
　　Day M
WRITER CLASS 1
　　Blake G.S
MASTER AT ARMS
　　Woodhouse H.R
SHIPS CORPORAL 1st CLASS
　　Carter G
SHIPS CORPORAL 2nd CLASS
　　O'Neill M
　　Suttle R
CHIEF PETTY OFFICER
　　Martin H.W
ACTING CHIEF PETTY OFFICER
　　Turner C
PETTY OFFICER CLASS 1
　　Cooper J
　　Collins A
　　Drayson A
　　Douglas W
　　Ewens E
　　Forty A
　　Gable H
　　Grevatt F
　　Hearne T
　　James A
　　Miller D
　　Newman J.R
　　Nutter J
　　Thompson H
　　Whiller J
　　Walpole D
PETTY OFFICER CLASS 2
　　Brown J
　　Bailey M
　　Devereux E
　　Exeter C
　　Hamerton E
YEOMAN OF STORES
　　Wilson T
BOATSWAIN
　　Leech J
　　Slocomb T

ASSISTANT BOATSWAIN
　　Cowdrey J.C
　　Harris R
　　Mc Carthy T
　　Platt W
SIGNALMAN
　　Knight A.J
SIGNALMAN 2nd CLASS
　　Chambers J.G
　　Hodge C
SIGNAL BOY
　　Aunger F
　　Fortune H.J
LEADING SEAMAN
　　Bree J
　　Jones E
　　Mayner J
　　Stewart W
LEADING STOKER
　　Burr G
　　Carpenter W
　　Downer H
　　Dampier J
　　Foote H
　　Langrish J
　　Marguerie J
　　Moore J
ABLE SEAMAN
　　Bridger C
　　Brown R
　　Barton C
　　Brown H.E
　　Briant F
　　Coakley J
　　Coombs J
　　Dabbs W
　　Dobson T
　　Edwards H
　　(Alias Bruton)
　　Fox W
　　Fury J
　　Gaskell W
　　Harvey W
　　Horder A.C
　　Hamilton J.H
　　Harris J
　　Hinks C.G
　　Irish C
　　Joy W
　　Lloyd C.R
　　Lowin W.B
　　Malley M
　　Manns G
　　Martin S
　　Robinson W
　　Staker H.J
　　Smith J
　　Squires C.J
　　Short H

HMS Orontes

	Thomas	D
	Talbot	H
	Walker	E.J
	White	J
	Wooder	J
ORDINARY SEAMAN		
	Beckingham	J
	Bennett	J.J
	Briggs	T
	Crook	W
	Darvill	W
	Dear	W
	Gager	A.G
	Gardiner	S
	Huntley	R
	Knight	H
	Phillips	J
	Spencer	H.T
	Waterman	G
	Wingate	J
STOKER		
	Andrews	H
	Allen	T
	Bath	A
	Bloomfield	W.R
	Baker	F.G
	Burnett	J
	Curling	H.D
	Feast	D
	Ford	J
	Glanville	R.H
	Gray	H.R
	Green	H.C
	Jones	C
	Jones	G
	Kinch	J.H
	Kirton	G
	Kimber	G
	Les	T.S
	Leitch	A
	Lloyd	T.H
	Martin	A.H
	Monday	W
	Marshall	C
	Marsh	J
	Rusbridge	T
	Schecori	P
	Sladdon	W
	Thornton	T
	Tibbles	R
	Webster	W
STOKER 2nd CLASS		
	Kelly	J
BAKER		
	Blake	J.G
ASSISTANT BAKER		
	Batchelor	G
BARBER		
	Rogers	W

BLACKSMITH		
	White	C.G
BUTCHER		
	Bender	L
CARPENTER		
	Hove	D
SKILLED CARPENTERS MATE		
	Stewart	G.K
CARPENTERS CREW		
	Heard	J
	Pollard	E
	Williams	H
CAULKER		
	Wilson	J
COOPER		
	Hawkins	J
LAMP TRIMMER		
	Hall	J
	Tizzard	H
PAINTER 1st CLASS		
	Hay	J
ARTIFICER PLUMBER		
	Chiswell	J.H
SAILMAKERS MATE		
	Gaskin	F
SHIPS COOK		
	Baker	S
	Holmes	R
COOK CLASS 2		
	Bolton	W.H
SHIPS COOK ASSISTANT		
	Cropp	C.J
SHIPS STEWARD		
	Child	T
ASSISTANT SHIPS STEWARD		
	Seaward	T.B
SHIPS STEWARD CLASS 2		
	Blowey	W.H
SHIPS STEWARD BOY		
	Burtenshaw	A.W
SICKBERTH STEWARD		
	Willcocks	E
ASSISTANT SICKBERTH ATTENDANT		
	Mc Bain	H
DOMESTIC CLASS 1		
	Quarrel	R
	Stares	G
DOMESTIC CLASS 2		
	Doughty	W.G
	Douglas	J
	Duke	W
	Dean	E
	Leonard	C.B
	Lakerman	J
	Medland	R.I
	Pearce (a)	J
	Price	F
	Slaman	W.G
	Tewsbury	F

	Tresias	W	
DOMESTIC CLASS 3			
	Crute	C	
	Richards	J	
ROYAL MARINES			
COLOUR SERGEANT			
	Ballantyne	J	
CORPORAL			
	Gosney	D	
PRIVATE			
	Bateman	O	
	Burbage	D	
	Burr	W	
	Burston	C.T	
	Cross	J	
	Diaper	C	
	Ellis	W	
	Fudge	W	
	Harrington	M	
	Hayward	T	
	Hutchings	W	
	Linsky	T	
	Michell	R	
	Morritt	G	
	Hullarkey	O	
	Newton	L	
	Phillips	G	
	Reed	J	
	Richards	J	
	Russell	D	
	Shirkey	J	
	Stamp	W.J	
	Tolhurst	O	
	Upton	T	
	Wagstaff	J	

ROYAL NAVY HMS SHAH
Certain medals to this ship were
Issued without a clasp.

CAPTAIN			
	Bradshaw	CB R	
	Burrows	A.L.S	1879
COMMANDER			
	Brackenbury	CMG J	1879
STAFF COMMANDER			
	Jackson	B.S	
CHAPLAIN			
	Lodge BA Revd H.B		
FLEET SURGEON			
	Willis MD	S.A	
SURGEON			
	Connell MD	J.J	1879
	Sibbald	T.M	1879
PAYMASTER			
	Horniman	W	

HMS Shah

ASSISTANT PAYMASTER
- Terry H.G.W

LIEUTENANT
- Abbott T.F 1879
- Drummond M.H 1879
- Gardner A
- Hamilton F.T 1879
- Holy-Hutchinson Hon P.M 1879
- Henderson G.P 1879
- Lindsay C 1879
- Rainer G.H
- Smith-Dorrien A.H 1879

SUB LIEUTENANT
- Hewitt G.H
- Martin G.W.H
- Patey G.E

CHIEF ENGINEER
- Fillmore J.W
- Sagar T

STAFF ENGINEER
- Shields J 1879

ENGINEER
- Mc Quire W
- Redgrave J
- Senders J.S
- Wilson J.O

ASSISTANT ENGINEER
- Andrew W.J
- Pibworth W.H

CHIEF ENGINE ROOM ARTIFICER
- Randall J.W

ENGINE ROOM ARTIFICER
- Avis J
- Fuller B
- Jager E 1879
- Wells J.R.H

SHIPWRIGHT
- Body W 1879
- Goodman F 1879
- Lage E
- Worley W.A 1879

YEOMAN OF STORES
- Adrian W
- Kearney J
- Murray J
- Weaver A

SHIPS STORES ASSISTANT
- Murphy D.J
- Roberts T
- Smith E.J 1879

MASTER AT ARMS
- Banks J

SHIPS CORPORAL 1st CLASS
- Bouts S
- Bridgwater J
- Chadder G

- Endacott E
- Westbrook J 1879
- Wilson W.D.G

CLERK
- Chapple J.H.G 1879

WRITER CLASS 3
- Haynes F.K
- Maddock C r

BOATSWAIN
- Bumpus J 1879
- Crocker J
- Hammett T 1879

BOATSWAINS MATE
- Flowers G

CHIEF PETTY OFFICER
- Barry J 1879
- Brunnen J
- Eason H.W 1879
- Freeman J
- Knowler W.H 1879

PETTY OFFICER CLASS 1
- Bacon R
- Bacon R.S
- Bonniface M 1879
- Bowen A 1879
- Burnham F 1879
- Burroughs A 1879
- Butler P
- Carter J
- Cookson J 1879
- Day R 1879
- Dennett A
- Edgell W.S
- Eyles W 1879
- Finchett S
- Gedley G
- Hammond G
- Hannan R 1879
- Hennessey T 1879
- Hookway S
- Hope G 1879
- Jenkins W 1879
- Judd J 1879
- Langford J.W 1879
- Lemon C
- Le Nourry J 1879
- Mase S
- Montgomery J.H 1879
- Morris W 1879
- O'Brien W
- Parker J 1879
- Payne S
- Pellows W
- Petts G.T
- Reardon G 1879
- Richardson E 1879

- Robinson H 1879
- Savery F 1879
- Taylor J.W 1879
- Tope E
- #Turner T 1879
- Walsh W 1879
- Wills J 1879

PETTY OFFICER CLASS 2
- Allchin A.W 1879
- Abbott S 1879
- Baines F
- Barron J.P 1879
- Botley W 1879
- Brampton R 1879
- Buxey G
- Croucher W 1879
- Deans J 1879
- Fitzgibbons P 1879
- Ford S 1879
- Harris H
- Hayes T 1879
- Hicks J 1879
- James F
- Leadbeter S.F.G 1879
- Martin W 1879
- Neill E 1879
- Oates J.F 1879
- Pyburn E
- Raby J 1879
- Ratsey G 1879
- Robinson T.W
- Tomkins W
- Turner I 1879
- Woolett W.H 1879

COXSWAIN OF CUTTER
- Marshall T.A

LEADING SEAMAN
- Arney A 1879
- Banham J 1879
- Castellano E 1879
- Clark W.F 1879
- Clarke W 1879
- Corcoran E 1879
- Cruford J 1879
- Davis G 1879
- Doe H.T 1879
- Fletcher W 1879
- Frampton R 1879
- Jeffery W.T 1879
- Knight T.G 1879
- Marchant S.T 1879
- Mc Quvie W 1879
- Mines T.J 1879
- Morgan D 1879
- Morgan J 1879
- Newell B 1879

On Ebay 14th January 2010. This auction is for a South Africa Medal 1877-79 with "1879" clasp to PO1 Thomas Turner HMS Shah. The actual edge reads "Shah T Turner PO 1st Cl HMS". The smallest of edge knocks at the 9 o'clock, 15 bids in all Sold for £575.00

HMS Shah

Name	Initial	Year	Name	Initial	Year	Name	Initial	Year
Rolfe	W	1879	Coombs	J		Ingram	J	
Warren	C	1879	Cooper	O	1879	Isaacs	C.H	
Wilkins	T	1879	Crocker	W.H		Isaacs	J	1879
Wood	C	1879	Crook	W.J	1879	James	J	1879
LEADING STOKER			Cusens	J.E		Jarman	S.B	1879
Aitken	D		Cutler	J		Jennings	A.B	1879
Bath	G.H		Davies	W		Johnson	A	1879
Carter	R		Davis	P	1879	King	G	1879
Gwillin	S		Dawe	G.H	1879	Kirkaldie	G.T	1879
Hewett	J		Dawson	S	1879	Kirkaldie	W.W	1879
Holmes	W		Denbow	R		Knott	W	
Pinkney	W		Dentram	C		Knowlton	W.S	
Pollard	G		Dickenson	J.G		Lamont	W	1879
Stanley	B		Dinan	D		Lansdown	F.E	1879
Wood	J		Douglas	M	1879	Laycock	J.S	1879
ABLE SEAMAN			Drew	S.T		Lee	E.G	1879
Arnold	G	1879	Dunn	E		Lee	J	1879
Arscott	W.J	1879	Eades	W.E	1879	Lewis	T	
Atkins	G.M	1879	Eager	T.S	1879	Lewis	W	
Babb	C	1879	Edwards	J.H	1879	Liles	W.G	1879
Bagshaw	J		Ellis	F.W	1879	Linton	G	1879
Bailey	G	1879	Evans	J	1879	Little	G	1879
Barge	T.W	1879	Fairfield	T.D		Littlejohn	J.A	1879
Barnard	A	1879	Finckin	W	1879	Lloyd	J	1879
Barnes	E	1879	Florance	J		Locock	J	1879
Barwick	W	1879	Flynn	H		Long	A	
Baverstock	W.J	1879	Ford	M		Lonnon	G.F	1879
Beck	F.J	1879	Foster	E		Loveridge	J.W	1879
Bird	E	1879	Fraser	S		Luke	G.E	1879
Bishop	E.J	1879	Freeman	F		Maguire	P	
Bishop	J	1879	Gallagher	W	1879	March	C	1879
Blackman	A		Gay	W.J		Marshall	B.B.R	
Blake	C	1879	Gemmell	J		Martin	T	1879
Bourne	A.P	1879	George	C	1879	Martin	T.J	1879
Bowles	J	1879	Gillingham	J	1879	Maunder	N.K	
Brice	H	1879	Goddard	T	1879	Mc Adams	T	1879
Brooking	J.E	1879	Greenwell	J.H	1879	Mc Cade	R	1879
Brown	A.J	1879	Griffen	J	1879	Mc Carthy	D	
Brown	W	1879	Grinter	G	1879	Mc Carthy	E	1879
Bulger	J	1879	Gulvan	W.J	1879	Middleton	S	
Burger	A.	1879	Haddon	E	1879	Miller	W.J	1879
Burgess	A.E		Haines	J	1879	Mitchell	J	1879
Burrows	R.J.F	1879	Haines	J.A	1879	Mitchell	J.H	1879
Butcher	G.E	1879	Hardy	W	1879	Moore	W	1879
Caddick	C.W	1879	Hardy	W.M		Morris	J	1879
Carter	C		Harris	E	1879	Morris	W.P	1879
Castles	T.H	1879	Hartley	W	1879	Morrish	H	1879
Caton	J	1879	Hatcher	G	1879	Moyse	T	1879
Chandler	T.J	1879	Haynes	J	1879	Muldrew	J	1879
Chapman	C	1879	Heath	T.J	1879	Mullett	W.J	
Chard	J	1879	Helyer	W	1879	Mullins	J	1879
Chavfield	J	1879	Highman	E	1879	Murray	D	
Chivers	T	1879	Hill	J	1879	Nash	J.J	1879
Chubb	S.P	1879	Hill	W		Negus	J.F	1879
Cleveland	A		Hine	H.G	1879	Nelmes	G	
Clevely	W		Holder	R	1879	Newberry	H	1879
Cloudsley	W		Hollbrook	F	1879	Nicholls	W.H	1879
Cogram	W	1879	Huggins	W	1879	Nightingale	J	
Collier	R	1879	Hussey	H	1879	Norris	W.F	1879

Casualty Roll Naval Brigade

Extracts from the London Gazette 7th November 1879 - Issue number: 24780

Table of Killed and Wounded of Naval Brigade.

Isandlhwana.
W. Aynsley, signalman,"Active," killed.

Ulundi
Lieut. A. Milne, R.A., "Active," slightly wounded.

Inyezana.
G. Bearyman, O.S., "Active," severely wounded.
G. Doran, O.S., "Active," dangerously wounded.
H. Gosling, A.B.,"Active," severely wounded.
E. White, Capt. Forecastle, slightly wounded.
J. Butler, signalman, slightly wounded.
J. Ropeyarri, krooman, slightly wounded.
J. Lewis, krooman, slightly wounded.
Giuginlhovo. — J. Porteous, Capt. foretop," Active," slightly wounded.
F. Parfitt, gunner,KM.A., u Boadicea," 'dangerously wounded,
P.Gorday, Captain's Mate, " Boadicea," dangerously wounded.
W. Hinchley, .bugler, " Boadicea," dangerously wounded.
J. Bird, A.B., "Shah,"severely wounded.
J. Bugler, A.B., " Shah," severely wounded.
Mr. W. Longfield, staff surgeon, " Tenedos," dangerously wounded.

All the above wounded officers and men recovered, most of them sufficiently to return to duty, the remainder to be sent home in a transport ship. From the effects of disease there were 17 deaths, including one officer, Mr. L. Coker, Midshipman, H.M.S. *' Active," and one man, also of the " Active," was drowned in the Tugela when attending to his duties on board the pont. Of those who died from disease nine belonged to the *' Active," and five of them occurred during the occupation of Ekowe; three to the " Boadicea;"four to the " Shah," and one to the " Tenedos." Two succumbed to pneumonia, six to dysentery, three to enteric fever, three to remittent fever, one to peritonitis, one to continued fever, and one to sunstroke.

(Signed) HENRY F. NORBURY,

Date: 7 November 1879 Issue number: 24780

A Return of the Naval. Forces landed for Service in Zulu War.

H.M.S. "Active".—Date of landing. 19th November, 1878. Date of embarkation, 21st July, 1879.
Time landed, 8 months.' - Died, 11. Officers, 10, men, 163. Total 173.

H.M.S. " Tenedos "—Date of landing, 1st January, 1879. Date of embarkation, 8th May, 1879.
Time landed, 4 1/4 months. Died, 1. Officers, 3 ; men, 58 Total, 61.

H:M;S: " Shah ".-Date of landing, 7th March,1879.. Date of embarkation, 21st July, 1879.
Time landed, 4 1/2 months. Died, 4. Officers, 16, men, 378. Total, 394.

H.M.S. " Boadicea".—Date of landing, 18th March, 1879. Date of embarkation, 31st July, 1879.
Time landed, 4 1/2 months. Died, 3.Officers, 10, men, 218. Total, 228

H.M.S. "Flora".—Date of landing, 20th April,1879."- Date of embarkation, 31st July 1879.
Time landed, 3 1/2 months. Officers, 2. Total, 2.

By order,

('Signed). G. .POMEROY COL'LEY, Staff Officer, . ..

From the despatches of my predecessor, Commodore Sullivan, which I observe have been duly published in the London Gazette, I haveseen that he has done full justice to the good services performed by Captain (then Commander) Campbell, and the officers and crew of H.M.S. "Active," and of the gallantry displayed by them at the action on the Inyzane on 22nd January, and also to the services of the officers and crew of the " Tenedos," from the date of their first landing in Natal, the "Active" on 19th November 1878, and the "Tenedos" on the 1st January, 1879, to the 17th March, when he resigned the command of the squadron to me.

As their Lordships are aware, the " Shah " arrived at Natal with reinforcements on the 6th March, and the " Boadicea" on the 15th, and contingents from these vessels were immediately landed and pushed forward to the Lower Tugela, where they arrived in time to take part in Lord Chelmsford's advance for the successful relief of Ekowe, in which the "Tenedos" contingent took part also My despatches of 11th April, Nos. 18 and 19, with enclosures, have acquainted their Lordships with the particulars of that expedition, and of the 'part taken by the Naval Brigade in the action at Ginginhlovo.

On the 4th April, at Ekowe, I appointed Acting Captain Campbell, of the " Active," to the command of the United Naval Brigade in the field, a force numbering over 800 men; he retained command until re-embarked at Port Duraford on the 22nd July.

In my despatch of the 11th April, I mentioned the name of Commander Brackenbury (and enclosed the report of that officer, who commanded at the action of. Ginginhlovo) of Lieutenants Carr,. Lindsay,.and Kingscote, R.N., and of Captain Phillips, who commanded the marines of the brigade, and who was ably seconded by Captain Burrowes, R.M.A., and'the other officers of the Royal Marine Regiments.

(Signed) FREDK. W. RICHARDS, Commodore. The Secretary of the Admiralty, Whitehall.

Naval Brigade

Extracts from the London Gazette 11 March 1879 Issue number: 24693
FORWARDING REPORTS ON THE ENGAGEMENTS AT INYEZANE AND ISANDHLWANA.
"Active," off Natal,
SIR,   February 3, 1879.
I have the honour to forward herewith the report of Commander Campbell on the engagement with the enemy of the column under Colonel Pearson, on 22nd ultimo, at Inyezane. . t

2. Their Lordships will learn with pleasure the distinguished part taken by the Naval Brigade in this action, and the gallant behaviour of Commander Campbell, Lieutenant Hamilton, and other officers mentioned in the report.

3. I beg to recommend Commander Campbell to the especial consideration of their Lordships. His zeal and energy are ever conspicuous ; and I learn from unofficial but reliable sources that his skill and courage on this occasion were remarkably so.

4. Lieutenant Craigie has rendered good service both during the late war in the Cape Colony, when his services were brought to their "Lordships' notice, and again during the present war ; he but narrowly escaped with his life a few weeks ago, being swept into river when working the pontoon at the limo D. Martin, A.B., was drowned.

5. Lieutenant Hamilton's gallantry has before been brought to their Lordships' notice, and was by all accounts I have received especially conspicuous on this occasion. I rely with confidence on his merits being duly appreciated by their Lordships.

6. Sub-Lieutenant Fraser is mentioned as having done good service.

7. Lieutenant Dowding, Royal Marine Light Infantry, appears to have handled his men with skill, and to have shown here, as he did in the late war in the Cape Colony, all the attributes of a good soldier.

8. Mr. L. Coker, Midshipman, under considerable difficulties, brought his gun into action with promptitude, gallantry, and skill, and I learn by reliable sources did considerable execution with the Gatling under his charge.

9. Mr. Cotton, Boatswain, also, as stated by Colonel Pearson in his despatch " contributed to the success of the day with the rocketo under his charge." He id an old and valuable officer, and did good service with the pontoons at the Tugela drift. He also served in the trenches during the Crimean war before Sevastopol. I commend him to their Lordships' favourable consideration.

10. Commander Campbell has also brought to my notice the gallantry of Thomas Harding, Ordinary Seaman, H.M.S. " Active," who was the first unmounted man in the enemy's position. (I may here. remark that I have seen by letters from persons present that Commander Campbell himself and Captain Hart, Staff Officer to Natal Native Contingent, both being mounted, were together the first in .I have in consequence rated him A.B. from the date of the action, but 1 venture to recommend -him for some special mark of Her Majesty's favour,

11 I beg also to recommend to their Lordships' favourable notice E. White, P.O, . and E Fufcher, P.O. 2 Cl., H.M.S. "Active" under the circumstances mentioned in Commander Campbell's Despatch. -(Signed) F. W. SULLIVAN, Commodore.

Ehwoe, January 28, 1879.
Sir In continuation of my letter No. 13, of 24th instant, I have to report that no change has taken place in the distribution of the Naval Brigade. Roughly speaking, nearly one-half of No. 1 column is employed, escorting convoys from the Tugela, and the other half, the largest, fortifying this place and preparing it for the depot by which the whole fore in Zululand are in future to be supplied ; a hospital is also to be established here. Until a considerable quantity of stores, &c., are collected here, it is not intended that this column should advance further ; this will perhaps occupy ten days more. We are in constant expectation of a night attack, the alarm being given every night as well as the usual muster of everyone at the " alarm posts " two hours before day break. No enemy have been seen since the battle of 22nd instant.

It seems the number of the enemy killed and wounded at the battle of Tnyezana was underestimated, some of the convoys have passed over the ground since and found more bodies, which leads to the supposition that the killed-must have been at least 400, and the wounded to double that amount. Two of the wounded on our side have since died making our total loss as follows :— Europeans—Killed 10 ; wounded 6 ;' total 16.Seven of the Europeans killed belong to the Native Contingent.

The wounded of the naval brigade are "progressing favourably.
George Doran, bullet in thigh, bullet cannot be found, but he suffers no pain and seems doing well.
George Berryman, bullet in thigh, doing well.
H. Gosling, A.B., wounded in hand, doing well.
Thomas Butler, sergeant, second class, slightly wounded, doing well.
Edmund White, petty officer, first class, slightly wounded, doing well.
Jack Ropeyarn, Krooman, slightly wounded, doing well.
Jack Lewis, Kroomau, slightly wounded,. doing well.
In addition to above two oxen drawing the rocket cart were wounded.
G. Berryman was knocked down by a bullet through his helmet just before being struck in the thigh. George May, ditto.
The five white men were wounded on the hill when the Zulus were being driven back along the path by the A Company of Naval Brigade, and the right half of B Company ; it will be observed that four men out of the five wounded belong to A Company which led the advance through. Colonels Pearson and Parnell both had their horses shot under them as well as one of the mounted orderlies. Ammunition expended bj the naval brigade at battle of Inyezane. 11 Rockets ; 2,400 rounds Martini-Henry ; 300 rounds Gatling.
I regret not .having been able to inform you -of the battle by the first messenger, but was unaware of his being sent.

(Signed) H. FLETCHER CAMPBELL, Commanding Naval Brigade.
(Signed) F. W. SULLIVAN, Commodore. also details added from: Return of Wounded in Action at Inytzane, January 22, 1879.

HMS Shah

Name	Initial	Year	Name	Initial	Year	Name	Initial	Year
North	W	1879	Thompson	N	1879	Lowin	G	1879
Oliver	R	1879	Thompson	R	1879	Manning	L	
Palmer	W	1879	Thurston	H.T	1879	Mc Indoe	J	1879
Paples	T.D	1879	Tooner	H		Miller	H.G	
Parrick	B	1879	Tozer	T	1879	Nisbet	A	1879
Parsons	J	1879	Trevena	W.J	1879	Parker	R	
Partridge	C		Tucker	G		Parkhouse	J	1879
Pearson	G	1879	Turtle	F		Phillpott	J	
Pearson	J	1879	Upsall	R		Phillpott	J.E	
Pidgeon	H	1879	Voysey	A	1879	Protor	T	1879
Pitman	J	1879	Waite	N.J	1879	Read	G	
Pitter	W	1879	Ward	W		Reynolds	M	
Pleass	W	1879	Warner	H	1879	Roberts	T	1879
Poore	A	1879	Warner	R.H	1879	Robinson	G	1879
Price	W		Watson	H.T	1879	Rogers	Jos	1879
Pride	J.L.G	1879	Webber	H	1879	Rowe	A.J	1879
Prior	H	1879	Webber	T	1879	Savage	F.H	1879
Radmore	G.A	1879	Weston	W	1879	Scott	E.S	
Reed	R		Wheadon	J	1879	Sergeant	G.E	
Rennison	H.C	1879	Whittenham	G	1879	Sims	W	1879
Renyard	G	1879	Williams	R.H	1879	Standidge	R.W	
Rickman	A	1879	Williams (1)	T		Stewart	A	1879
Rogers	J	1879	Williams (2)	T	1879	Troop	W	
Rogers	T.W	1879	Wilshire	T	1879	Wallace	H.J	
Saunders	H.J	1879	Wood	C		Walsh	W	
Sellis	E	1879	Woolger	T	1879	Walters	W.R	
Shehan	J		Wotton	H	1879	Wrigley	A	
Shellard	H	1879	**ORDINARY SEAMAN**			**ORDINARY SEAMAN 2nd CLASS**		
Sheppard	E	1879	Adams	G	1879	Lee	F	
Short	S	1879	Aspile	P		**SIGNALMAN**		
Simms	E	1879	Batt	A		Sherlock	W.T	1879
Simpson	W		Beer	W.H		**SIGNALLER 1st CLASS**		
Sinnock	J	1879	Blick	C		**PETTY OFFICER CLASS 2**		
Slapye	F.A	1879	Box	P		Weston	G	
Small	F.D		Brabazon	J		**SIGNALLER 1st CLASS**		
Smith	A.L	1879	Broderick	T	1879	Tyson	G	1879
Smith	C	1879	Brown	P	1879	**SIGNALLER 2nd CLASS**		
Snare	W	1879	Buckler	E.G		Hancock	G	
Soper	G	1879	Bullen	T	1879	Jullien	G	
Spanner	F	1879	Butt	L.A		Slapp	J.H	1879
Sparks	J.G	1879	Cleeve	W		Track	F	1879
Spicer	C	1879	Colwell	R		**SIGNALLER CLASS 3**		
Spicer	J		Connor	M		Pointing	G	1879
Spratt	F	1879	Cox	W	1879	Wearn	.I	1879
Stevenson	J		Crowley	M	1879	**STOKER**		
Stone	J	1879	Dunglison	E.F	1879	Baker	P	
Stowar	T	1879	Fenge		A	Barber	W	
Stroud	A.J	1879	Franklin	G	1879	Barden	J	
Sweetenham	W	1879	Gardiner	F		Barnard	J	
Symons	W.H	1879	Girault		H	Blake	R	
Tamlyn	C	1879	Glascoe	W	1879	Blako	W	
Taylor	G	1879	Goldthorpe	D.A	1879	Burgess	C	
Taylor	G		Grogan	C	1879	Burrow	J.J	
Taylor	H		Hassell		H	Carpenter	A	
Taylor	S.A		Hewett		A	Challen	T	
Tee	W	1879	Hill	J	1879	Chapman	T	
Terry	W	1879	Hunter		J	Crowther	H	
Thomas	A	1879	Lapham	R.W	1879	Dunstane	J	
Thomas	W.J	1879	Lightfoot	H.J	1879	Emmett	C	

HMS Shah

	Ferguson	E	
	Flew	G	
	Giles	T	
	Golding	G	
	Gould	W	
	Harding	H	
	Hart	J	
	Hewett	A	
	Holloway	R	
	Holman	W.E	
	Johnson	J	
	Lewis	E	
	Mayhead	J	
	Morrison	H	
	Oakley	J	1879
	Reid	J	
	Robbins	J	
	Robertson	J	
	Smith	A	
	Smith	W	
	Tomlin	G	
	Townsend	H	
	Truscott	T	
	Veck	F	
	Walton	C	
	Waters	T	
	Wilson	S	
	Winter	T	
	Withers	W	
	Wyld	T	
STOKER CLASS 2			
	Baugust	S.F	
	Wise	E	
GUNNER			
	Bate	H	1879
	Cook	J	1879
	Hutson	R	
	O'Neill	D	1879
GUNNERS MATE			
	Judd	R.H	1879
ARMOURER			
	Buckland	E	1879
ARMOURER			
	Carey	C.L	
CHIEF BANDSMAN			
	Tesco	A	
BANDSMAN			
	Bartlett	F	
	Connell	J	
	Ford	W.G	
	Holland	E	
	Lambert	E.G	
	Lloyd	G	
	Martin	F	
	May	F	
	Murphy	J	
	Platt	H	
	Spicer	A	
	Thompson	H	

MUSICIAN			
	Roper	C	1879
BARBER			
	Mannering	E	
BLACKSMITH			
	Bunce	T	1879
BLACKSMITHS CREW			
	Day	G	
BUTCHER			
	Parlett	A	
CARPENTER			
	Whitford		
CARPENTERS MATE			
	Bennett	A.A	
	Roads	R	
	Snook	J	1879
CARPENTERS CREW			
	Bishop	J	
	Campbell	W	
	Hutchings	F	
	Lynch	J	1879
	Perkins	G	
	Young	J	1879
CHIEF CARPENTERS MATE			
	Deacon	R	
CAULKER			
	Late	J	
COOK 1st CLASS			
	Horswell	O.H	
COOKS MATE 1st CLASS			
	Male	J	
COOKS MATE			
	Holloway	H.R	
SHIPS COOK 1st CLASS			
	Kneebone	W	
SHIPS COOK 2nd CLASS			
	King	R	
COOPER			
	Ferguson	J	
	Montgomery	D	
	Symonds	J.E	1879
COOPERS CREW			
	Ahearn	J	
LAMPTRIMMER			
	Fry	R	
NAVAL SCHOOLMASTER			
	Sandercombe		
PAINTER CLASS 1			
	Cruze	H	
	Fudge	W	
PAINTER CLASS 2			
	Stacey	G	
PLUMBER			
	Mason	G	
SAILMAKER			
	Bury	J.A	1879
	Wills	T	1879
SAILMAKERS MATE			
	Cook	C	

	Halloran	J	
	Higgins	J	
SAILMAKERS CREW			
	Andrews	T	1879
	Gilchrist	C	1879
	Millson	F.W	1879
	Twine	T.E	1879
SHIPS STEWARD CLASS 1			
	Marshall	J	
WARDROOM STEWARD			
	Moyse	J	
SHOEMAKER			
	Lillington	W	1879
SICK BERTH ATTENDANT			
	Bedford	T	1879
	Gamblin	H	
	Pugh	H	
ASSISTANT SICK BERTH ATTENDANT			
	Deer	D.S	
TAILOR			
	Barth	L	
TINSMITH			
	Savell	C.A.G	
DOMESTIC CLASS 1			
	Bailey	W	
	Dalistors	S	
	Hyland	H	
	Selden	C	
DOMESTIC CLASS 2			
	Coleman	R.J	
	Farr	T	
	Freeman	W	
	Frost	W.G	
	Glazbrook	J	
	Trinder	F	
	Williams	W	
DOMESTIC CLASS 3			
	Bolwell	J	
	Day	J.W	
	Frost	G.W	
	Matthews	H	
	Newman	J.C	
	Ramsay	T.S	
	Sleeman	W.H	
	Wassell	C	

ROYAL MARINES
BEING THE ROYAL MARINE LIGHT INFANTRY and the ROYAL MARINE ARTILLERY.

CAPTAIN			
	Philips	J	1879
COLOUR SERGEANT			
	Whittaker	H	
SERGEANT			
	Foxwell	H	
	Gane	J	1879
	Shill	D	1879

HMS Shah

CORPORAL
- Breakspeare G 1879
- Banger A 1879
- Humm S 1879
- Williams J 1879

GUNNER
- Bourton T 1879
- Collins G
- Cottis T 1879
- Crumption P 1879
- Dolman E 1879
- Edgson G.E 1879
- Garrett R
- Gordon G
- Parish A
- Redding W 1879
- Saunders G 1879
- Walker F 1879
- Webster G 1879

DRUMMER
- Hart J

PRIVATE
- Alsop J.I 1879
- Ambrose G
- Arnold J 1879
- Asquith H 1879
- Bailey J 1879
- Betts J 1879
- Binnie J 1879
- Briant W 1879
- alias Bryant G
- Briscoe J 1879
- Bristow J
- Byrne J 1879
- Clooney J 1879
- Collins S
- Coombes G 1879
- Couzens J 1879
- Davis A 1879
- Deacon F 1879
- Duncan J
- Ellis W
- Elvin R 1879
- Francis A 1879
- Gibson A 1879
- Grist C 1879
- Harvey G 1879
- Holley J 1879
- Hopcroft R 1879
- Hulans G
- Hurley J 1879
- Jones J
- Killiard J
- Leech J 1879
- Little S
- Masding J 1879
- Maule H.W.C 1879
- Millbanks J 1879
- Moger J 1879
- Motley D 1879
- O'Brins P 1879
- Payne L 1879
- Payne W 1879
- Pritchard L
- Proctor W
- Rhodes J 1879
- Rick J 1879
- Roberts D 1879
- Rowlett J 1879
- Riley J 1879
- Sampson G 1879
- Simmonds W
- Stevenson G 1879
- Summers J 1879
- Swainston R 1879
- Walker E 1879
- Walker I 1879
- Walsh J 1879
- Ward E 1879
- Watson W 1879
- Wheeler R 1879
- White A 1879
- White C
- Williams C 1879
- Wilson J 1879
- Woodlands J 1879

ROYAL NAVY. HMS TAMAR
Medals to this ship were without a clasp.

CAPTAIN
- Liddell W.H

CHAPLAIN
- Shone LLD BA Revd S.A

STAFF SURGEON
- Lucas L

SURGEON
- Volatti W.J

NAVIGATING LIEUTENANT
- Brown J

LIEUTENANT
- Brietzcke E.R
- Coote J.P.P
- Evans R.W
- Warren H.B

NAVIGATING SUB LIEUTENANT
- Maclean T

CHIEF ENGINEER
- Hull H

ENGINEER
- Earl R.J.W
- Grant J.B

SHIPWRIGHT
- Full J.H

ASSISTANT ENGINEER
- Cook J.A
- Webby T

ENGINE ROOM ARTIFICER
- Cann W.H
- Naylor B

ACTING ENGINEROOM ARTIFICER
- Blackhurst H
- Caldwell A
- Spiers J

PAYMASTER
- Kelly W.E

ASSISTANT PAYMASTER
- Snowden H.G

YEOMAN OF STORES
- Kennacott C

WRITER CLASS 3
- Cocks C.H

BOATSWAIN
- Dawson B
- Fudgelow N
- Hurrell R
- Milton A
- Vickery G.B

ACTING BOATSWAIN
- Easton W.H

MASTER AT ARMS
- Strath F

SHIPS CORPORAL CLASS 1
- Collett T

SHIPS CORPORAL CLASS 2
- Honey J
- White R

CAPTAIN OF THE HOLD
- Morris T.W
- Reardon G

CHIEF PETTY OFFICER
- Lane J

ACTING CHIEF PETTY OFFICER
- Hurst C.E

PETTY OFFICER CLASS 1
- Allen J
- Bennett R
- Benorthan J
- Bradford A
- Deeble W
- Feabes H
- Forrester T.H
- Hancock W
- Lamerton J
- Lee W
- Mc Carthy F
- Patterson D
- Pile G
- Sheils M

PETTY OFFICER CLASS 2
- Gardiner W.S
- Kenshole T
- Morris J
- Penman J.J
- Sowden W
- Usher C

LEADING SEAMAN
- Harwood J

HMS Tamar

Hill	R.C
Hiscock	J
Walker	W
Wilson	G

LEADING STOKER

Cook	R
Handlin	J
Pasker	C
Reeves	T
Smyth	T
Stephens	W

SIGNALMAN

Julian	G

SIGNALMAN 2nd CLASS

Kimins	J
Thorburn	W.E

SIGNALMAN 3rd CLASS

Butland	J.G

ABLE SEAMAN

Aggar	E.J
Bartlett	T.G
Bennett	W.H
Cammack	W
Collier	H
Down	W
Edwards	H
Evans	R
Evans	W
Gawler	S
Hegarty	J
Hurrell	J
Hynes	J
Knight	J.C
Mason	W
May	A
Miliken	J
Northmore	W
Roberts	N
Roche	R.W
Selley	T
Slaughter	C
Stevens	H
Sweeney	M
Timmins	J
Turner	T.R
White	W

ORDINARY SEAMAN

Benham	T
Buckley	J
Bunt	J
Colenso	W
Cross	W
Donovan	W
Fitzjohn	J
Floyd	W.H
Foxford	R
Green	S
Isaac	J
Isaac	John
Jones	J.A
Major	B
Mc Cally	F
Mc Grath	J
O'Connor	F
Rayner	J
Staines	G
Stokes	H
Thomas	W
Wand	I
Whitford	W.H

ORDINARY SEAMAN CLASS 2

Trathaway	R

STOKER

Adams	R
Blackler	D
Clathworthy	J
Clavell	W
Graham	W
Hallett	R
Hamilton	J
Hicks	J
Hudson	T
Lynch	D
Manley	R
O'Neil	E
Parker	T
Pearce	J
Quance	A
Rose	J
Rundle	S
Small	W.T
Thomson	R
Vogwill	J
Williams	J
Wills	J

BAKER

Thoumaine	A

ASSISTANT BAKER

Barrett	W.H

BLACKSMITH

Vosper	G

BUTCHER

Sadler	J

CARPENTER

Turner	H.S

CARPENTERS MATE

Carr	E

CARPENTERS CREW

Carpenter	J
Webb	W

CAULKERS MATE

Gayler	W.C

COOK CLASS 2

Brice	E

GUNROOM COOK

Darby	J.J

SHIPS COOK CLASS 2

Grounsell	J

HMS Tamar

COOKS MATE CLASS 1
- Meech J

COOPERS CREW
- James J

LAMPTRIMMER
- Rickard W
- Thomas H

PAINTER CLASS 1
- Grant F.A

PLUMER
- Short J

SAILMAKERS MATE
- Smith A

SHIPS STEWARD
- Mallon E

SHIPS STEWARD CLASS 2
- Tuck F

SHIPS STEWARD ASSISTANT
- Kirby J.T

SHIPS STEWARD BOY
- Constantine D

ASSISTANT SICKBERTH ATTENDANT
- Sladden W

SICKBERTH STEWARD
- Webb G.A

DOMESTIC CLASS 1
- Crabbe F
- Davey W

DOMESTIC CLASS 2
- Batchelor F
- Corlett W.P
- Loader C
- Medland T
- Murphy C
- Roe H
- Sullivan C.E
- Trout J
- Waters F.A
- Williams C

DOMESTIC CLASS 3
- Geary T
- May W
- Waters F.A
- Woodhead E

ROYAL MARINES

COLOUR SERGEANT
- Dickson R

CORPORAL
- Hannan R

PRIVATE
- Allen J
- Clarke T
- Cole J
- Edney T
- Hawkins C
- Holmes J
- Jones F
- Jones R
- Kane M.O
- King H
- Lewis R
- Male J
- Mantle T
- Milne A.T
- Morle G
- Parkin E
- Polwin E
- Price F.A
- Redford W
- Richards J
- Selby F
- Shutt W
- Smith J
- Stanyon W
- Wolfe R
- Wright G

ROYAL NAVY. HMS TENEDOS
Certain medals to this ship were issued with a clasp.

CAPTAIN
- Adeane E.S

NAVIGATING LIEUTENANT
- Drake C.E

LIEUTENANT
- Bird H.G
- Forlong C.A
- Kingscote A

STAFF SURGEON
- Longfield W.D 1879

SURGEON
- James C

SUB LIEUTENANT
- Ryan J.J.F
- Startin J 1879

CHIEF ENGINEER
- Whitting G

ENGINEER
- Brand J
- Ball H.S

ENGINE ROOM ARTIFICER
- Lakerman G

ACTING ENGINE ROOM ARTIFICER
- Booth J.C
- Hearne J

PAYMASTER
- Grandy M.B
- Sharpe E.V

SHIPWRIGHT
- Bricknoll W
- White R.C

YEOMAN OF STORES
- Rudlands W.H 1879

ACTING CLERK
- Leonard W.V.T

ACTING BOATSWAIN
- Springall G

SHIPS CORPORAL 1st CLASS
- Boone C.H

SHIPS CORPORAL
- Polley J

PETTY OFFICER CLASS 1
- Bartlett J.A
- Bennett S.J
- Brander W
- Coleman J
- Hicks J.B
- Howse J.W 1879
- Keefe D 1879
- Kingston T 1879
- Martin S.T
- Mann W.B 1879
- Powe J.H
- Rendle C.M.C 1879
- Reynolds D 1879
- Smith G

PETTY OFFICER CLASS 2
- Bonallo D
- Harding T
- Mc Namara J 1879
- Perry J.W

LEADING SEAMAN
- Cronin E 1879
- Fitzgerald T 1879
- Mtichell E 1879
- Spencer G

LEADING STOKER
- Bamsey F.J
- Bendle T.J
- Chandler W
- Medland W

GUNNER
- Palmer G

SIGNALMAN
- Mitchell J.J 1879

SIGNALLER CLASS 2
- Palmer W.H

SIGNALLER CLASS 3
- Howie A

ABLE SEAMAN
- Barnett W
- Blacker E.H
- Blake G.H 1879
- Bond G
- Bush H 1879
- Down W.H 1879
- Evans A.A 1879
- Jones J 1879
- Lawrence J
- Mann R.W
- May F.H 1879
- Paltridge T
- Pamfleet E
- Percy T.N 1879
- Ryan J 1879
- Solomon R 1879

HMS Tenedos

	Surname	Initial	Year
	Synes	C	1879
	Thom	W.B	1879
	Trist	S.J	1879
	Wilson	C	
ORDINARY SEAMAN			
	Barton	J	
	Butler	J	
	Chesterman	G.H	
	Chard	A	
	Coombe	T.H	
	Cox	J.T	
	Donovan	J	
	Farmer	E	
	Fitzgerald	E	1879
	Foram	M	
	Gallerfing	G	
	Godbold	W	
	Grant	A	
	Grant	E.R	1879
	Green	W.T	
	Hoff	A	1879
	Leary	J	
	Lloyd	R	1879
	Luckridge	W	
	Mahoney	J	1879
	Maloney	P	
	Mc Connachie	W	1879
	Mc Inally	J	
	Mearns	S	
	Murphy	M	
	Newton	W	
	Parkins	J.T	
	Ramsay	J	1879
	Rice	R	
	Satterley	R	
	Smith	G	1879
	Staddon	W	
	Steel	C.W	
	Titchmarsh	J.H	1879
	Webber	W.W	
	Young	H	
ORDINARY SEAMAN CLASS 2			
	Goodman	G.H	
	Hames	W	
	Jackson	J	
	Jones	T	
	Mc Callum	M	
	Mould	F.J	
	Pearson	A.W	
	Porter	G.H	
	Richardson	S	
	Roberts	J	
	Wilkinson	V	
STOKER			
	Baker	A	
	Bray	F	
	Croyden	J.C	
	Davey	J.E	
	Ferns	J	
	Foote	J	
	Gilbert	R.J	
	Honley	J	
	Hodge	R	1879
	King	J	1879
	March	R	
	Mc Lean	J.C	
	Mullaney	E	
	Tremblett	J.S	
	Warner	W	
	Wheeler	W	
ARMOURERS CREW			
	Knowles	J	1879
BLACKSMITH			
	Watts	W	
CARPENTER			
	Denbow	W	
CARPENTERS MATE			
	Nichols	T	
CARPENTERS CREW			
	Barbour	J	1879
COOPER			
	Sweeney	J	
LAMPTRIMMER			
	Silver	E.J	
MUSICIAN			
	Choake	J	
PAINTER CLASS 1			
	Tucker	F	
PLUMBER			
	Driscoll	J	
SAILMAKERS CREW			
	Finnis	R	
	Hingston	J	
SHIPS COOK CLASS 1			
	Richardson	M	
SICK BERTH ATTENDANT			
	Cole	G.H	1879
SHIPS STEWARD CLASS 2			
	James	R	
BOY CLASS 1			
	Cracknell	A.J	
	Gill	G	
	Hubbard	W.H	
	Jackson	J	
	Kerswell	R	
	Smith	F	
	Suett	F.M	
	Ware	J	
	Webb	A.E	
	Yeo	F	
DOMESTIC CLASS 1			
	Baker	H	
DOMESTIC CLASS 2			
	Huskin	T	
	Long	W	1879
	Potham	W	
	Quintal	J.G	
	Solomon	C	
	Stanley	J	
	Steinhausen	F.F	
	Viant	W.J	
DOMESTIC CLASS 3			
	Saunders	C.A	
	Seldon	W.H	
ROYAL MARINES. Including the ROYAL MARINE ARTILLERY			
COLOUR SERGEANT			
	Pardon	J	1879
CORPORAL			
	Armstrong	J	1879
GUNNER			
	Jones	J	1879
	Kennally	M	
	Payne	R	1879
	Phillips	E	
	Sivter	J	
DRUMMER			
	Black	J	1879
PRIVATE			
	Andrews	J	1879
	Brooks	C	1879
	Chard	T	1879
	Clapp	J	1879
	Davis	J	1879
	Furness	A.A	
	Knowles	W.F	
	Lotey	J	
	Lovegreen	J	
	Lumar	W.J	1879
	Monk	G	1879
	Mooney	P	1879
	Sandercock	R	1879
	Sawyer	H	
	Sweeting	H	
	White	F	1879

Zulus And Kaffirs of South Africa

War Service Imperial & Colonial Units

War service of Imperial and Colonial Units 1877-1879

The 9th Kaffir War, August, 1877, to August, 1878. (Gaika / Galeka War)
An attempt by the amaXhosa tribe returning from the diamond fields to regain control of their land. The following took part in the campaign: Albany Fingo Levy, Albany Mounted Rangers or Rifles, Albert Burghers, Alexandria Mounted Rangers, Aliwal North Mounted Volunteers, Baker's Horse, Beaufort Rangers, Bedford Rifle Volunteers, Berlin Light Infantry, Bolotwa Tembus, Bolotwa Volunteers, Bowker's Rovers, Brabant's Horse, Buffalo Rifle Volunteers, Buffalo Volunteer Engineers, Buffalo Volunteer Horse, Cape Field Artillery, The Prince Alfred's Own, Chalumna Volunteer Cavalry, Clanwilliam Volunteers, Colesberg Light Horse, Colesberg Volunteers, Cradock Mounted Volunteers, Cradock Rifle Volunteers, Diamond Fields Horse, Duke of Edinburgh's Own Volunteer Rifles, East London Burghers, East London Cavalry, East London Engineers, First City Volunteers of Grahamstown, Fort Beaufort Burghers, Frontier Light Horse, George Town Volunteers.

Second Sekukuni War 1878/1879
In the first campaign detachments of the 80th Regiment -- 2nd Battalion, supplemented by 200 men of the Frontier Light Horse under Major Redvers Buller. Fort Weeber detachments of 1/13 Regiment and 80th Regiment, sixty mounted volunteers. Forts Mamalube and Faugh-a-ballagh fifty men of 1/13 Regiment and fifty volunteers at each fort. Detachments of 1/13 Regiment and 80th Regiment present at Krugers Post. Also involved in the 2nd campaign, 2/21st Regiment, 94th Regiment, Four mountain guns under R.A. Officers, Royal Engineers, Ferreira's Horse, Border Horse, Transvaal Mounted Rifles, Transvaal Artillery and Bantu levies.

Relief of Griquatown 22 May 1878.
A large body of Griquas under their leader, Moses Moos, threatened to capture Griquatown if it did not surrender. The Frontier Armed Mounted Police and Diamond Fields Horse took part in the campaign. All the rebels were killed or captured with 43 dead. Our casualties numbered nine and the enemy about 100.

The Northern Border War, May, 1878, to July, 1879.
Barkly Rangers, Cape Field Artillery, The Prince Alfred's Own Cape Field Artillery, Carrington's Horse, Colesberg Light Horse Diamond Fields Horse, Grahamstown Volunteer Horse Artillery

1st Invasion 11th January 1879 (see page 403)
The plan was to invade Zululand using five columns and to converge at Ulundi the Zulu King's homestead. Chelmsford's No 3 coumn with two battalions of the 24th Regiment, the 1st composed of battle-hardened troops, whilst the 2nd consisted of younger, less experienced men. A masterpiece of British imperial mismanagement, with poor communications, inadequate intelligence with no idea of the Zulu dispositions, and the preconceived idea that the Zulus where Stone Age tribesmen, all added to the total disregard for the enemy.
With only one Royal Artillery battery of 7-pound guns at his disposal and having no regular cavalry support, the support of the Natal Native Contingent (NNC), was vital. With the column weakened by being divided, the result a massacre. (see page 406)

The Battle of Inyezane - 22nd January, 1879, and the Siege of Eshowe
A Zulu force attempted to bar Pearson's No.1 Column on its journey to Ehowe. The following took part in the campaign: 2nd Battalion of the East Kent Regt (the 'Buffs'), the 99th Regt (the Duke of Edinburgh's Lanarkshire Regt), Naval Brigade from H.M.S. Active, and H.M.S. Tenedos (the latter anchored off the mouth of the Tugela), 2 guns from the Royal Artillery, 2 seven-pounder guns with the Naval Brigade, a Gatling gun, the Alexandra Mounted Rifles (30), Barrow's Horse, Durban Mounted Rifles, Natal Hussars, Stanger Mounted Rifles and the Victoria Mounted Rifles. After the disaster at Isandhlwana the Natal Hussars and most of the Colonial Units returned back to Natal, to be employed in the defence of the border against Zulu attacks. There were also some 2 200-odd Natal Natives formed into two battalions of the 2nd Regt., Natal Native Contingent and a company of Durnford's Natal Native Pioneer Corps. Colonel Charles Pearson was besieged at Eshowe for two months by the Zulus. many of the garrison died of dysentery, enteric, and other fevers.

Intombi River: 12 March 1879,
The Battle of Intombe fought, between Zulu forces and British soldiers defending a supply convoy.
80th Regiment. (140)

Moirosi's Mountain campaign in Basutoland, 25th March - 20th November 1879 (see page 414)
Basutoland Mounted Police, Cape Mounted Riflemen, Frontier Armed & Mounted Police, Royal Artillery Troop, Cape Mounted Yeomanry Fort Beaufort Burghers, Fort White Mounted Volunteers, Stockenstroom Volunteer Rifles

Hlobane Mountain, 28th March 1879
February saw Wood receive much needed reinforcements in the form of Transvaal Rangers, mounted troops, a troop of German settlers and five companies of the 80th Regiment of Foot.
Seven companies of the 1st Battalion, 13th (Prince Albert's Own Somersetshire) Light Infantry took part in this battle. Names mentioned are Major William Knox Leet, Captain William Cox, Private William Grosvenor, Colour Sergeant Arthur Fricker, Private Albert Page DCM, Captain John Miller Waddy, Private John Snook (whose letter was published in the North Devon Herald on May 29, 1879).

War Service Imperial & Colonial Units

Continued from previous page.
Chelmsford told Sir Evelyn Wood's troops to attack the Zulu stronghold. Lieutenant Colonel Redvers Buller, led the attack. The Zulu main army arrived to help their besieged tribesmen and the British soldiers were scattered.
1st Squadron, Mounted Infantry, 13th Regt.
Rocket detail of the Royal Artillery.
Kaffrarian Rifles, Edendale Troop of the Natal Native Horse, Border Horse, Frontier Light Horse, Weatherley's Border Horse
British casualties on Hlobane numbered 17 officers and 82 enlisted men killed, along with some 100 irregular and native troops. One officer and seven other ranks were wounded.

The Battle of Khambula 29th March 1879
Khambula: the battle at which Evelyn Wood's column heavily defeated a Zulu army in the opening stages of the war.
Royal Artillery, 11th Battery, 7th Brigade.
1st Battalion of the 13th Light Infantry: later the Somerset Light Infantry and now the Light Infantry.
90th Perthshire Light Infantry: later 2nd Battalion the Scottish Rifles; disbanded in 1966.
Mounted Infantry about 400 mounted men in all.
Border Horse
Boer Commando, Petrus Lafrus (Piet) Uys commanded about 40 scouts, including two of his sons.
Cape Colony volunteers of Bakers Horse (80)
Frontier Light Horse under Lieutenant Colonel Buller (156 men)
Transvaal Rangers (70 men)
Native Contingent of Swazis warriors & 277 native troops of the 2nd Battalion of Wood's Irregulars.

The Battle of Gingindlovu and the Relief of Eshowe - 2nd April 1879
The Battle of Gingindlovu was fought between a British relief column sent to break the Siege of Eshowe, and the Zulus. The new force totalled over 3300 whites and over 2300 native troops. The Zulu's attacked Chelmsford's laagered position, the charge faltered because of constant gunfire and the support of the Gating guns. 700 Zulu bodies were counted on the outside of the laager and 300 more were killed in the mounted chase of the retreating warriors. British Casualties eleven dead, including a Lieutenant-Colonel, and 48 wounded.
The following took part in the campaign:
Natal Native Contingent, Natal Native Horse, Diamond Fields Horse. A naval company and two companies of Buffs with a Gatling gun and 7-pounders. (Two Naval companies took part one each from H.M.S Boadicea and H.M.S Shah).
57th Regiment: later the Middlesex Regiment and now the Princess of Wales's Royal Regiment.
3rd Battalion, 60th Rifles, Brvt Lt-Col Northey was killed : later the King's Royal Rifle Corps and now the Royal Green Jackets.
91st Highlanders: now the Argyll and Sutherland Highlanders.
99th Regiment: later the Wiltshire Regiment and now the Royal Gloucestershire, Berkshire and Wiltshire Regiment.
On 3 April, the relief column entered Eshowe, led by the pipers of the 91st Highlanders.

2nd Invasion 27th May 1879
After reinforcements arrived Chelmsford. could proceed with his second attempt to defeat the Zulu Nation. He had a pressing reason to proceed with haste Sir Garnet Wolseley was being sent to replace him, and he wanted to inflict a defeat once and for all on Cetshwayo's forces The second invasion of Zululand consisted of the 1st Division of 7,500 troops under Maj Gen Henry Crealock who advanced along the coast, the Flying Column Wood's force of 8, 000 troops, and the centre column or 2nd Division of 8, 000 troops under Maj Gen Frederick Marshall, accompanied by Chelmsford.
One of the early casualties was the exiled heir to the French throne, Imperial Prince Napoleon Eugene, who had volunteered to serve in the British army and was killed on 1 June while out with a reconnoitering party.
Crealock was in command of the coastal column, it included the 88th, 2/3rd, 3/60th, 57th, 91st and 99th regiments, a naval brigade, mounted volunteers and artillery. The headquarters where located at Fort Pearson, Major General Henry Hope Crealock was ordered to advance into Zululand and establish a base with supplies to last for two months. The 88th lost Lieutenant John Thirkill and four men to fever. Charles Wyncoll, who had been transferred to "F" company under the command of **Captain F.C. Baldwin**, received promotion to Lieutenant on the 17 May 1879. He was disappointed by the unattractive role allotted to his battalion and later wrote:- "We had a deal of hard work but no fighting, having the misfortune to be in Crealock's division".
Duties consisted of providing escorts to the ox wagon convoys, The column soon began to be called "Crealock's crawlers".. With the unhealthy climate, disease continued to plague the troops as they advanced and constructed forts along the way.
Provisions were stored in the Forts Tenedos, Crealock, Chelmsford and Napoleon. The oxen were barely able to pull the wagons and could only manage an advance of about five miles a day. With numerous rivers to cross progress was slow. The 88th reached Fort Chelmsford on the 19 June, where four companies were ordered to remain behind to guard the supplies. By the 22 June, the remaining two companies of the 88th had reached Fort Napoleon.
Linking up with Wood, Chelmsford continued his advance to the Zulu capital. The final battle took place at Ulundi on 4 July.

War Service Imperial & Colonial Units

The Battle of Ulundi, 4th July 1879
Ulundi: the final battle of the Zulu War at which the army of Cetshwayo was destroyed. By 1st July 1879, the British were encamped by the White Mfolozi River. On the morning of the 4th, the bulk of the column, had formed into a a fortified square, Buller's horse and the 1st Dragoon Guards acted as skirmishers, scouting the surrounding countryside. The royal kraal of Ulundi was burnt to the ground and by the end of August Cetewayo was a prisoner of the British.

Royal Artillery
17th Lancers: now the Queen's Royal Lancers.
1st Battalion, 13th Light Infantry: later the Somerset Light Infantry and now the Light Infantry.
2nd Battalion, 21st Royal Scots Fusiliers, now the Royal Highland Fusiliers.
58th Regiment: from 1882 the Northamptonshire Regiment, now the Royal Anglian Regiment.
80th Regiment: from 1882 the South Staffordshire Regiment, now the Staffordshire Regiment.
90th (Perthshire) Regiment: from 1882 the Scottish Rifles (Cameronians), disbanded in 1966.
94th Regiment: from 1882 the North Staffordshire Regiment, now the Staffordshire Regiment.
Bettingtons Horse (16) Frontier Light Horse.

The royal kraal of Ulundi was burnt to the ground Chief Cetewayo had not stayed to watch the defeat of his army.
In defeating the Zulu army at Ulundi. Chelmsford had regained his dignity On 9th July he telegraphed Wolseley his resignation. And on the 27th he sailed out of Durban for England with Evelyn Wood and Redvers Buller accompanying him.
Cetewayo was captured on 28 August and exiled to London.

Battle Honours
On the 25th July 1882 a total of fourteen Infantry Regiments and two Cavalry Regiments were awarded a Battle Honour for the campaigns in South Africa

South Africa 1877-78-79

24th (2nd Warwickshire) Regiment of Foot; post 1881, The South Wales Borderers; from 1969, the Royal Regiment of Wales (24th/41st Foot)
90th (Perthshire Volunteers) Light Infantry; post 1881, The 2nd Cameronians (Scottish Rifles) - disbanded in 1968
88th (Connaught Rangers) Regiment of Foot; post 1881, 1st Battalion Connaught Rangers – disbanded in 1922
94th Regiment of Foot; post 1881, 2nd Battalion Connaught Rangers – disbanded 31st July 1922

South Africa 1878-79

13th (1st Somersetshire) Light Infantry or Prince Albert's Light Infantry Regiment; from 1968, The Light Infantry
800th (Staffordshire Volunteers); post 1881, 2nd Battalion, The South Staffordshire Regiment; from 1959, The Staffordshire Regiment (the Prince of Wales's)

South Africa 1879

1st Dragoon Guards (The King's); from 1959, 1st The Queen Dragoon Guards
17th Lancers (Duke of Cambridge's Own); from 1922, 17th/21st Lancers
3rd (East Kent) Regiment of Foot (Buffs); post 1881, Buffs (Royal East Kent); from 1966, The Queen's Regiment
4th (The King's Own Royal) Regiment of Foot; post 1881, The King's Own Royal Lancasters and from 1959; The King's Own Border Regiment
21st (Royal Scots Fusiliers); post 1881 The Royal Scots Fusiliers and from 1959, Royal Highland Fusiliers
57th (West Middlesex) Regiment of Foot; post 1881, 1st Battalion The Duke of Cambridge's Own (Middlesex Regiment), after 1966; The Queen's Regiment
58th (Rutlandshire) Regiment of Foot; post 1881, 2nd Battalion Northamptonshire Regiment; after 1964, The Royal Anglian Regiment
60th (The King's Royal Rifle Corps); post 1881, The King's Royal Rifle Corps; after 1966, The Royal Green Jackets
91st (Princess Louise's Argyllshire Highlanders); post 1881, The 1st Argyll and Sutherland Highlanders, (Princess Louise's)
99th (The Duke of Edinburgh's – {Lanarkshire}) Regiment of Foot; post 1881, 2nd Battalion Wiltshire Regiment; after 1959 The Duke of Edinburgh's Royal Regiment

References
Cook, H C B The Battle Honours of the British and Indian Armies 1662-1982 Leo Cooper, London 1987

Galekas Revolt September 1877-June 1878

Galekas Revolt September 1877 - June 1878
There was a serious rebellion in 1877 between the Galekas and the Gaikas which required a considerable force of imperial and colonial troops in order to put down the uprising. A large contingent of 7,500 men were sent into Galekaland and the war was subsequently known as the Ninth Xhosa War.
Extracts from THE SOUTH AFRICAN WAR OF 1877-8.
Sir Barde Frere, sent a message to Kreli, chief of the Galekas, to keep quiet, as any disturbance would be punished. Kreli replied that he could not restrain his young men, upon which the Governor gave orders for the Frontier Mounted Police to assemble as rapidly as possible under **Commandant Griffith** on the borders of and between Fingoland and Galekaland... On September 27th 1877 the Galekas attacked the Fingoes. On September 30th Commandant Griffith with a force of two hundred Europeans and two thousand Fingoes was attacked by several thousand Galekas; the enemy was in the end defeated, but it became evident that the revolt was spreading....By December, 1877, there were three tribes in revolt, but all the fighting up to that time had been in independent Kaffraria, the boundary of British Kaffraria being the River Kei.
Commandant Griffith, with Police, Volunteers, and Fingoes, swept Galekaland with several columns, and by the middle of November had driven the insurgents over the river Bashee into Pondoland, where it was not thought politic to pursue them....
In the new year fights came fast and furious. **Sir Arthur Cunynghame** had moved to Ibeka in the Transkei, and had assembled a force, in four columns to sweep Galekaland, the regular troops being the 1st batt. 24th, who had been quartered at King Williams Town, and part of the 88th with Blue-jackets and Marines from the Active, the flagship on the Cape station ; there were also Police, Volunteers, and Fingoes. The line of communication with King William's Town, by way of Butterworth, Kei Drift, Komgha, and Draiibosch, was kept open by posts of the 88th, while to overawe the Gaikas and keep them from their old battleground among the Amatola Mountains, posts were established in a north-west direction from King William's Town to Cathcart. There were skirmishes every day, and important fights at Draiibosch (where **Major Hans Garrett Moore** of the 88th won his Victoria Cross*),near Komgha, at Quintana Mountain, at the Chichaba Valley, at the Kabousie River and other places on both sides of the Kei ; and about the end of January the Tambookies, under Gongabele, threw in their lot with the rebels, which resulted in more fighting near Queenstown and in the valley of the Thomas River.
The imperial forces had been strengthened. In the middle of February the 90th Light Infantry from England had relieved the detachments of the 88th, who had returned to garrison Cape Town, except their mounted infantry which remained at the front.
The 90th had been sent to Fort Beaufort to operate against **Tini Macomo** in the Waterkloof. The colonial forces were decreasing, six months being the time for which Volunteers and Burghers had engaged ; such as remained were being instructed to take orders from the Lieutenant-General, but isolated cases still existed where local forces preferred to look after their own districts....
The weapons of the Kafir are one short broad bladed stabbing-assegai, half-a-dozen long, tapering, throwing-assegais, a knobkerrie, or club, and now generally a gun ; perhaps an old Tower musket... The throwing-assegai of the Kafir will wound seriously at forty yards ; the coup de grace is given with the stabbing assegai in the abdomen so that the corpse shall not swell, it being their belief that if a body swells the hand of the slayer will suffer also......

*Hans Moore was born in Dublin on the 31st March 1834. He joined his father's regiment, the 88th Connaught Rangers, that landed in Cape Town in 1877 and which was then sent to serve on the Eastern Frontier. On 29 December 1877 near Komgha, South Africa, during an action with the Gaikas, Major Moore saw that a **Private Giese** of the Frontier Mounted Police was unable to mount his horse and was left at the mercy of the enemy. Realising the danger, Major Moore rode back alone in the midst of the enemy, and continued in his efforts to save the man's life until the latter was killed. The major shot two and received an assegai in the arm during this gallant attempt. He retired in 1888 and drowned when sailing off Dromineer Bay off the coast of Ireland

Galekas Revolt September 1877-June 1878

General contemporary map of the Eastern Cape frontier and Kaffrarian area

1st Invasion 11th January, 1879

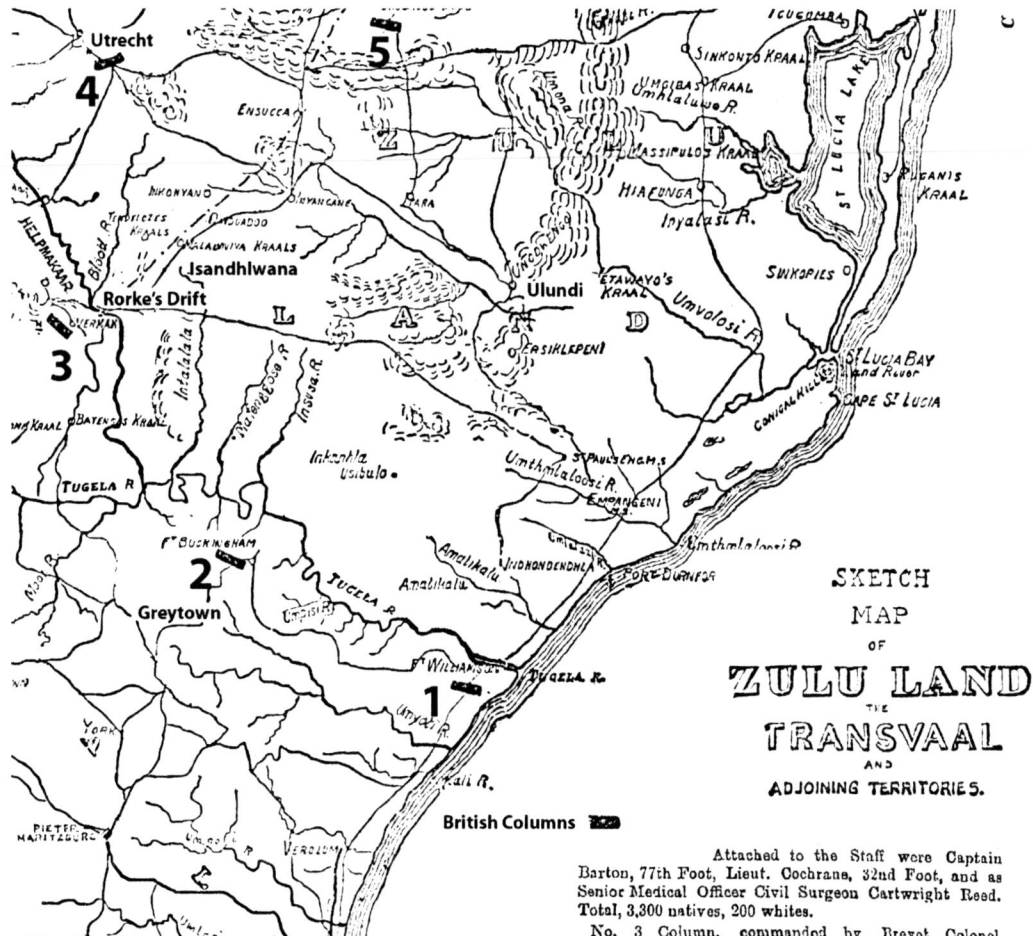

The invading force, under the command of Lieutenant General Lord Chelmsford, K.C.B., was divided into five columns, composed as under:—

No. 1 Column, under the command of Colonel Pearson, consisted of Royal Artillery, two 7-pounders, Lieutenant Lloyd; Royal Engineers, No. 2 Company, Captain Wynne, R.E.; 2nd and 3rd Foot, Brevet Lieutenant-Colonel Parnell; 99th Foot, six companies, Lieutenant-Colonel Welman; Naval Brigade, Commander Campbell, R.N.; Mounted Infantry, No. 2 Squad, Major Barrow; 12th Hussars, Natal Hussars, and Durban Mounted Rifles, Alexandra Mounted Rifles, Stanger Mounted Rifles, Victoria Mounted Rifles, 2nd Regiment Native Cavalry, 1st Battalion, Major Graves, 3rd Foot (commanding); 2nd Battalion, Commandant Nettleton; No. 2 Company Natal Native Pioneer Corps. Total, 1,650 whites and 2,000 natives.

No. 2 Column, Lieut.-Colonel Durnford, R.E., commanding, consisted of a Rocket Battery, Captain Russell, R.A.; 1st Battalion, 1st Regiment Natal Native Contingent, Commandant Montgomery; 2nd Battalion ditto, Major Bengough; 77th Foot, 3rd Battalion, 1st Regiment Natal Native Contingent, Captain Cherry, 32nd Foot; Sikali's horse; No. 3 Company Natal Native Pioneers, Captain Allen.

Attached to the Staff were Captain Barton, 77th Foot, Lieut. Cochrane, 32nd Foot, and as Senior Medical Officer Civil Surgeon Cartwright Reed. Total, 3,300 natives, 200 whites.

No. 3 Column, commanded by Brevet Colonel Glyn, C.B., 24th Foot, consisted of N Battery, 5th Brigade Royal Artillery, Lieut.-Colonel Harness; Royal Engineers, No. 5 Company, Captain Jones, R.E; 24th Foot, 1st Battalion, Brevet Lieut.-Colonel Pulleine; 2nd Battalion, Lieut.-Colonel Degacher, C.B.; No. 1 Squad Mounted Infantry, Lieut.-Colonel Russell, 12th Lancers; Naval Mounted Police, Major Dartnell; Natal Carabineers, Captain Shepstone; Newcastle Mounted Rifles, Captain Bradstreet; Buffalo Border Guard, Captain Smith; 3d Regiment Natal Native Contingent, Commandant Lonsdale; 2nd Battalion ditto, Commandant Cooper; No. 1 Company, Natal Native Pioneer Corps, Captain Nolan. Attached to the Staff were Lieutenant Coghill, 24th Foot, Major Clery, Captain Gardner, 14th Hussars, Captain Essex, 75th Foot, Senior Commissariat Officer Dunn, A.C., Captain Elliot, Paymaster, and Surgeon-Major Shepherd, Senior Medical Officer. Total—100 whites, 2,000 natives.

No. 4 Column, Brevet Colonel Evelyn Wood, V.C., C.B., 90th Foot, commanding, consisted of Royal Artillery, six seven-pounders, Major Tremlett, R.A.; 1-13th Foot, Lieut.-Colonel Gilbert; 90th Foot, Brevet Lieut.-Colonel Cherry; Frontier Light Horse, Brevet Lieut.-Colonel Buller, C.B.; 60th Foot; Wood's Irregulars, Commandant Henderson. Total, 1,800 whites.

No. 5 Column, under Colonel Rowlands, V.C., C.B., consisted of 80th Foot, Eckerly's Contingent, Raaff's Corps, Ferreira's Horse, Weatherly's Border Lancers, Transvaal Rangers, Cape Mounted Riflemen, one Krupp gun, and two Armstrong six-pounders.

1st Invasion - British Forces 11th January 1879

1st Invasion of the Anglo-Zulu War - British Fighting Forces in Klip River County 11 January 1879, Klip River county the territory between the Buffalo and Tugela Rivers

NO. 3 COLUMN — Col. R.T. Glyn, 1/24th

Position	Force	Commander	Strength
Rorke's Drift	N Battery, 5th Brig., Royal Artillery (6 7-pdrs)	Lt-Col. A. Harness	(abt.132)
	1st Battn, 24th (2nd Warwickshire) Regt: 5 companies.	Lt-Col. H.B. Pulleine	419
	2nd Battn, 24th Regt: 8 companies.	Lt-Col. H.J. Degacher	(abt.580)
	3rd Regt, Natal Native Contingent	Cedt. R. la T. Lonsdale	2,566
	No. 1 Company, Natal Native Pioneer Corps	Capt. W.J. Nolan	(abt.80)
	No. 1 Squadron, Mounted Infantry	Lt-Col. J.C. Russell, 12th Lancers	
	Buffalo Border Guard	Lt. W.C.Smith	22*
	Natal Carbineers	Capt. T. Shepstone, Jr.	320
	Natal Mounted Police	Maj. J.G. Dartnell	10*
	Newcastle Mounted Rifles	Capt. R. Bradstreet	30*
Helpmekaar	1st Battn, 24th Regt: 2 companies	Maj. R. Upcher	(abt.150)

COLONIAL DEFENSIVE DISTRICT NO. I — Resident. Magistrate (Newcastle) W.H. Beaumont

Position	Force	Commander	Strength
Border	Native Border Guard (in process of formation)		
	Bomvu levies	Mr. R. Du Bois	150
	Bekeni and Mabaso levies	Mr. J. Frankish	(abt.300)
	Ngabayena and (Mhlalenil levies	Mr. J.L. Knight	(abt.300)
	Nxumalo, Nongamulana, Zimelana	Mr. J.S. Allison	(abt.660)
	Nkonza and Zinzele levies		
	Mangwe and Theebu levies, Mnyembe's levy	Mr. J.J. Gregory	346
Buffalo River line		Field Cornet J.S. Robson	10
Newcastle Division	Border Police	Res. Mag. H.F. Fynn, jr.	(Abt 60)
Umsinga Division			
Ermelo Fort (near Dundee0	Burghers formed into Town Guards	Unknown	Unknown
Fort Pine	-	-	-
Pieters' Laager	-	-	-

Notes :
1.*Official letters had been despatched all over the district ordering the Volunteers to meet on 3rd December.
2. Lord Chelmsford plan was to send five invading columns into Zululand on 11th January 1879. Chelmsford accompanied column No: 3 or the centre column in all 4,659 officers and men. Col Richard Glyn crossed into Zululand at Rorke's Drift. Evelyn Wood Northern Column also crossed the Buffalo River some 50 miles to the North. Colonel Charles Pearson in command of No: 1 column invaded along the coast,. Colonel Charles Pearson in command. No: 2 column under Col Anthony Durnford RE was positioned South of No: 3 column and was expected to provide assistance to No: 3 column on the way to Ulundi—the kings royal homestead.
3. Col R.T. Glyn,was supported by several staff officers, namely, Lieutenant N.J.A. Coghill, orderly officer; Major C.F. Clery, principal staff officer; Captain A.C. Gardner, general duties; Captain E. Essex, transport; Assistant Commissary, W.A. Dunne; Paymaster Elliot and Surgeon Major P. Shepherd.
4. Eight Border Police posts were located along the Buffalo River with Field Cornet J.S. Robson in charge of operations.
5. Four companies of the 2nd Battalion of the 4th King's Own Royal Regiment, formed the lines of communication back to Greytown under the command of Col. E.W. Bray,
The column was accompanied by Lieut-General Lord Chelmsford and his staff, In all, 4 659 officers and men.
6. In order to transport and supply services to this large force there were 220 wagons, 82 carts, 1 507 oxen, 49 horses (excluding those of the cavalry) and 67 mules controlled by 346 conductors, drivers and voorlopers.

Battles of the Zulu War 1879

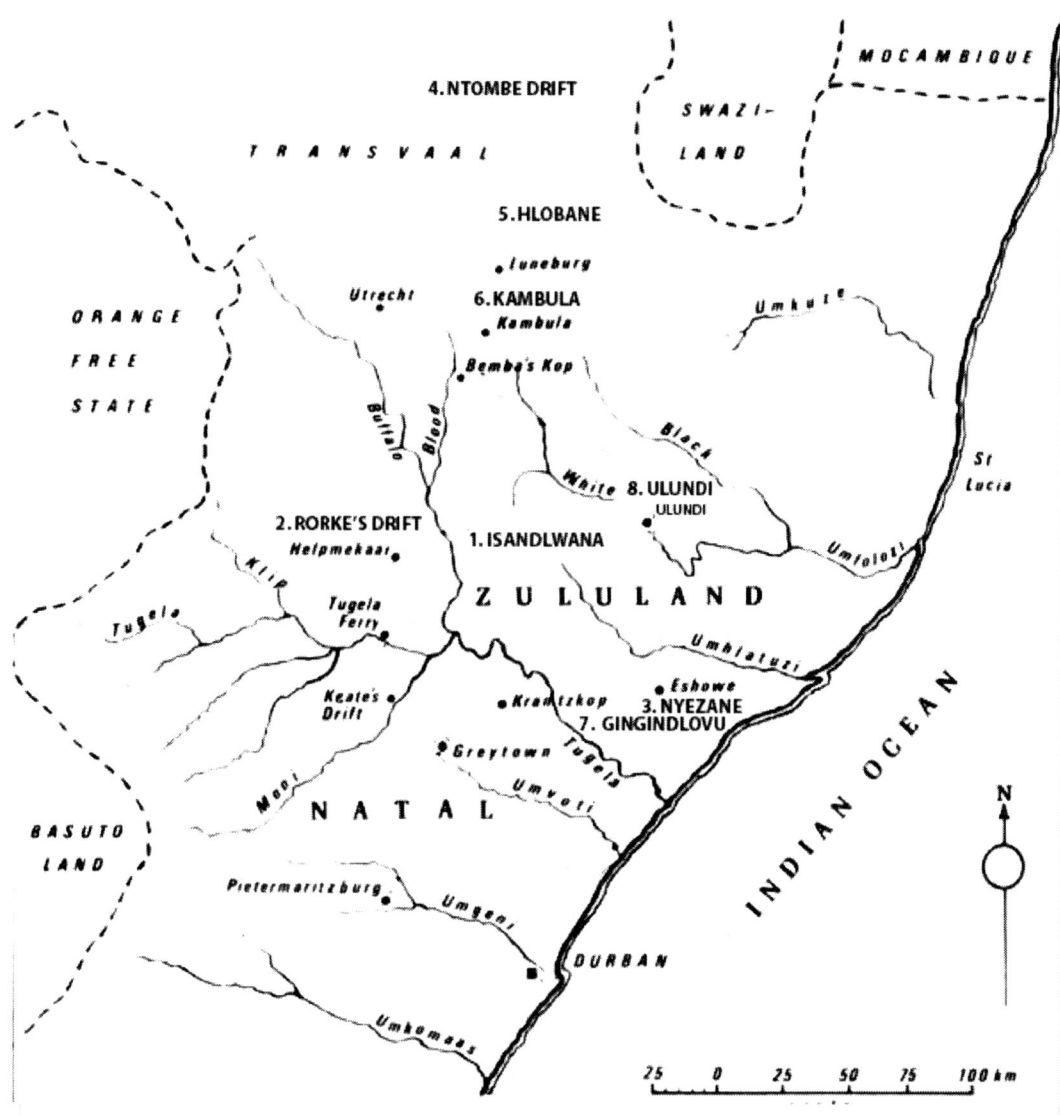

1. **ISANDLWANA**, 22 January 1879. British defeat by 20,00 Zulu warriors. Lord Chelmsford divided his army (No3 Column) and set out to find the Zulus. He left the 1st battalion of the 24th Regiment behind to guard the camp, under the command of Colonel Henry Pulleine. The Zulu attacked and the rest is history. Fatalities 950 Europeans & 400 African auxiliaries; 2,000 Zulus.
2. **RORKE'S DRIFT** 22/23 January 1879. Heroic defence of No 3 Column's supply depot by 140 men. Fatalities 17 Europeans; 1,000 Zulu.
3. **NYEZANE**, 22 January 1879, Colonel Pearson's No1 Column defeats an attack by 6,000 Zulus. Fatalities 14 Europeans; 400 Zulu.
4. **NTOMBE DRIFT**, 12 March 1879. Zulus ambushed a supply column, under command of Capt. Moriarty, that was heading for Khambula to replenish Col Sir Evelyn Woods No 4 Column. Fatalities 73 Europeans; Zulu casualties were negligible.
5. **HLOBANE**, 28 March 1979. Attack on mountain stronghold by mounted troops and African auxiliaries of Brigadier Wood's No 4 Column. Buller's attacking force where surprised by the sudden appearance of a massive Zulu impi the result a spectacular running battle which lasted the entire day. Fatalities 93 Europeans and 100 African auxiliaries; 100 Zulu
6. **KAMBULA**, 29 March 1879. Colonel Evelyn Wood's forces prepared to receive an attack on its heavy fortified position. Never again would an impi fight with such ferocity and resolution, their morale sapped by heavy losses. Fatalities 29 Eurpeans; 2000 Zulu
7. **GINGINDLOVU**, 2 April 1879. The Zulus fail to get within 50 yards of the relief force and its heavily fortified wagon laager. The following day Pearson relieved Eshowe. Fatalities 13 Europeans; 1000 Zulu
8. **ULUNDI**, 4th July 1879. The Zulus make an attempt to defend their capital by attacking the square formed by Lord Chelmsford's column. The lancers seal their fate in the final charge of the campaign Fatalities 13 Europeans; 1500 Zulu

Isandhlwana - 22 January 1879

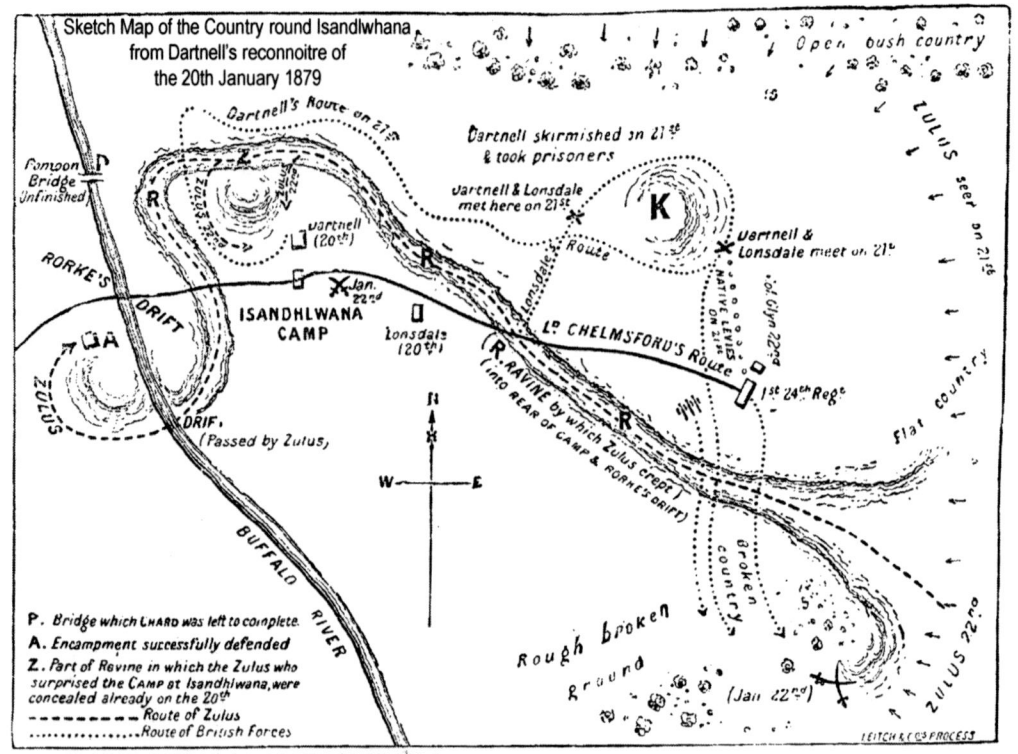

THE BATTLE OF ISANDLWHANA

The camp was placed on the southern slope of the Isandlwhana Hill, which in itself is a peculiar feature. It rises almost as a precipice to the west, where may be said to be the head of the crouching animal it resembles in shape, and then after forming the back, it again abruptly descends to the east. At either end is a neck connecting it with smaller ridges of undulating hills, of which the more level portion of the country is composed.

On the 22nd of January the General, Lord Chelmsford, advanced with a large portion of the main column to attack the enemy on his front, leaving behind him a sufficient body of men to guard the camp. Very soon after the departure of the column bodies of the enemy were reported to the left, and about 6 A.M. a company of the Natal Native Contingent were ordered in that direction. There seems to have been nothing of any consequence for several hours beyond reconnoitring, which only resulted up to 9 A.M. in discerning small bodies of the enemy. At that hour an officer of the Native Contingent returned, and reported that the Zulus were in immense force (probably 20,000 or 30,000 men) and advancing, driving the pickets and scouts before them. By this time Colonel Durnford, R.E., with 300 mounted natives, a rocket battery, under Captain Russel, R.A., had arrived from Rorke's Drift, making up the force in the camp to some 700 Europeans and 600 natives. In round numbers these consisted of 335 men of the 1st Battalion of the 24th Regiment; 90 men of the 2nd Battalion, 24th Regiment; 80 men of the Royal Artillery; 30 men of the Natal Carabineers (Volunteers); 35 Mounted Natal Police; 35 Mounted Infantry (Regulars); 20 Buffalo Border Guard and Newcastle Rifles. This estimate is rather under than over the mark, and does not include the numerous non-combatants always to be found in a camp.

As soon as it was understood that the Zulus were advancing in force, Colonel Durnford's mounted men divided into three bodies, and commenced the attack. Those sent out to the left were immediately engaged, and firing was soon after heard all along the crest of the hill.

Shortly after this they had to retreat, closely followed by the Zulus, who were described as swarming over the centre ridge like bees. Meanwhile the Zulu left was being rapidly pushed forward, driving everything before them in spite of the heavy artillery fire which was opened on it, and on the more slowly advancing centre. On seeing the left wing of the Zulus menacing the camp, the officer commanding in all probability ordered the troops to take up the following ground. On the left of the Native Contingent, and facing the hill over which the Zulu army was pouring, was a body consisting of three companies of the 24th Regiment, the Native Contingent on their right front, and immediately to their right were three guns, and the right camp consisted of two companies of the 24th Regiment and the Mounted Corps.

The infantry now came into action all along our line, and from every account their fire was said to be steady and rapid, the enemy fell in hundreds, mowed down by the "Martini-Henry," but still came on in apparently undiminished numbers.

Nothing seems to have deterred them, as rank after rank of the foremost fell, others pressed forward steadily and quickly. They do not appear to have made much use of their guns, but to have depended on their numbers to bring them at last to within such distance of our men that they could use their assegais. Young and old, regulars and volunteers, alike fought as gallantly as ever British soldiers did, side by side, but the overwhelming numbers were too many for them, and they died like heroes, sticking to their posts to the very last. Out of the whole number of men engaged, only some nine men escaped, who themselves looked upon their escape as miraculous.

DIGBY WILLOUGHBY
Captain, Natal Native Contingent.

"The Battle of Isandlwhana" is furnished by
Capt. Digby Willoughby, Natal Native Contingent.
The Graphic: March 29th, 1879; P.139

Isandhlwana - 22 January 1879

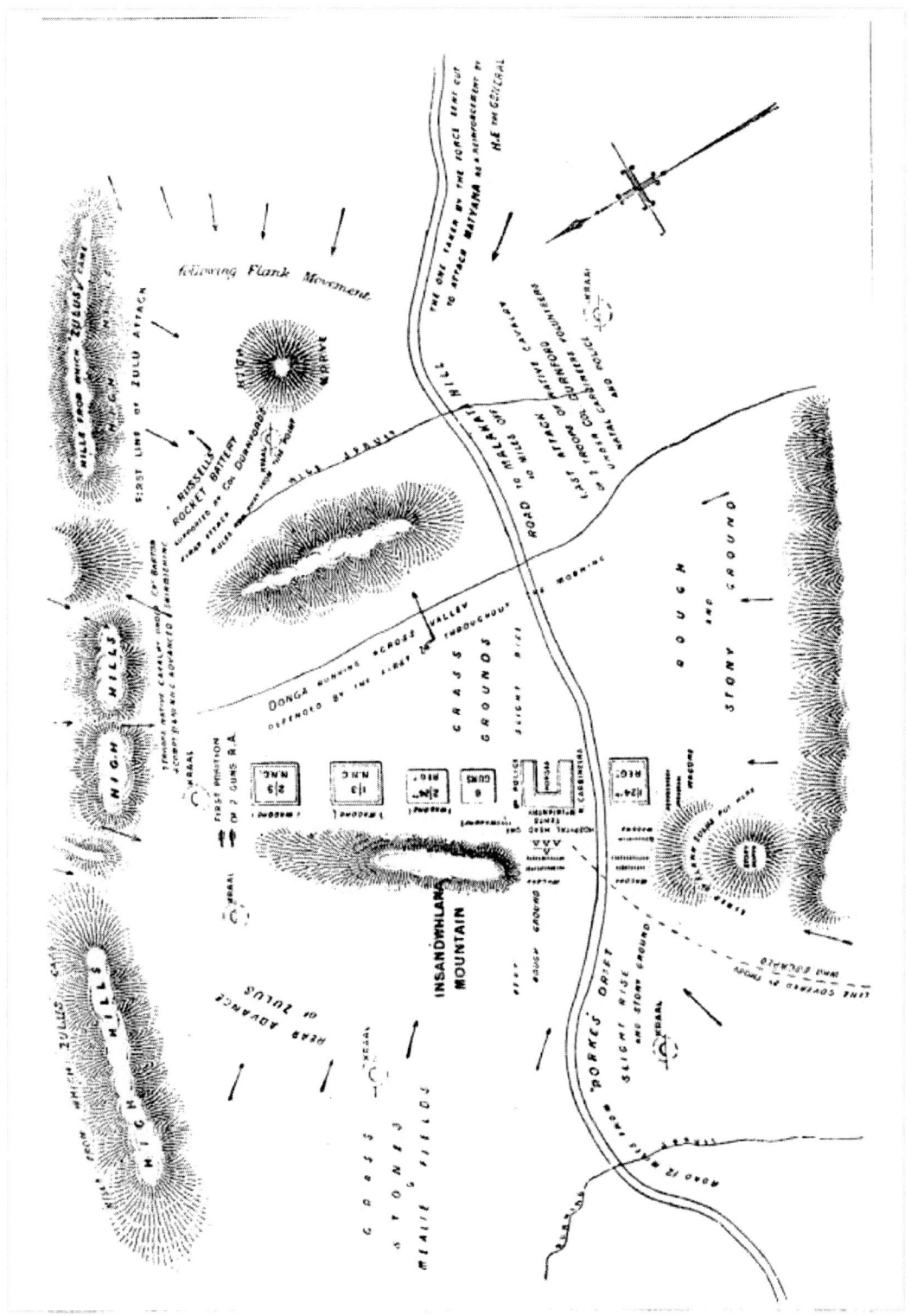

Isandhlwana - 22 January 1879

THE BATTLE OF ISANDLWHANA

The camp was placed on the southern slope of the Isandlwhana Hill, which in itself is a peculiar feature. It rises almost as a precipice to the west, where may be said to be the head of the crouching animal it resembles in shape, and then after forming the back, it again abruptly descends to the east. At either end is a neck connecting it with smaller ridges of undulating hills, of which the more level portion of the country is composed.

On the 22nd of January the General, Lord Chelmsford, advanced with a large portion of the main column to attack the enemy on his front, leaving behind him a sufficient body of men to guard the camp. Very soon after the departure of the column bodies of the enemy were reported to the left, and about 6 A.M. a company of the Natal Native Contingent were ordered in that direction. There seems to have been nothing of any consequence for several hours beyond reconnoitring, which only resulted up to 9 A.M. in discerning small bodies of the enemy. At that hour an officer of the Native Contingent returned, and reported that the Zulus were in immense force (probably 20,000 or 30,000 men) and advancing, driving the pickets and scouts before them. By this time Colonel Durnford, R.E., with 300 mounted natives, a rocket battery, under Captain Russel, R.A., had arrived from Rorke's Drift, making up the force in the camp to some 700 Europeans and 600 natives. In round numbers these consisted of 335 men of the 1st Battalion of the 24th Regiment; 90 men of the 2nd Battalion, 24th Regiment; 80 men of the Royal Artillery; 30 men of the Natal Carabineers (Volunteers); 35 Mounted Natal Police; 35 Mounted Infantry (Regulars); 20 Buffalo Border Guard and Newcastle Rifles. This estimate is rather under than over the mark, and does not include the numerous non-combatants always to be found in a camp.

As soon as it was understood that the Zulus were advancing in force, Colonel Durnford's mounted men divided into three bodies, and commenced the attack. Those sent out to the left were immediately engaged, and firing was soon after heard all along the crest of the hill.

Shortly after this they had to retreat, closely followed by the Zulus, who were described as swarming over the centre ridge like bees. Meanwhile the Zulu left was being rapidly pushed forward, driving everything before them in spite of the heavy artillery fire which was opened on it, and on the more slowly advancing centre. On seeing the left wing of the Zulus menacing the camp, the officer commanding in all probability ordered the troops to take up the following ground. On the left of the Native Contingent, and facing the hill over which the Zulu army was pouring, was a body consisting of three companies of the 24th Regiment, the Native Contingent on their right front, and immediately to their right were three guns, and the right camp consisted of two companies of the 24th Regiment and the Mounted Corps.

The infantry now came into action all along our line, and from every account their fire was said to be steady and rapid, the enemy fell in hundreds, mowed down by the "Martini-Henry," but still came on in apparently undiminished numbers.

Nothing seems to have deterred them, as rank after rank of the foremost fell, others pressed forward steadily and quickly. They do not appear to have made much use of their guns, but to have depended on their numbers to bring them at last to within such distance of our men that they could use their assegaies. Young and old, regulars and volunteers, alike fought as gallantly as ever British soldiers did, side by side, but the overwhelming numbers were too many for them, and they died like heroes, sticking to their posts to the very last. Out of the whole number of men engaged, only some nine men escaped, who themselves looked upon their escape as miraculous.

DIGBY WILLOUGHBY
Captain, Natal Native Contingent.

THE BATTLE OF ISANDLWHANA, JANUARY 22, 1879

Isandhlwana - 22 January 1879

THE UNBURIED DEAD AT ISANDLWANA

Henry Francis Fynn and **Thomas Munro Carbutt**, who was his friend, took a prominent part in burying the dead at Isandlwana. In February, both of them had accompanied Major Black in the tracks of the fugitives, to find the bodies of Melvill and Coghill, and to retrieve the colours of the 24th. In March and May they gained the field of Isandlwana and were able to piece together the fate of some of their friends.

Some local men had escaped. **William Craighead Smith** of the Buffalo Border Guard had been sent to buy and returned the day after. Young Brickhill, the interpreter from Umsinga, was safe, and so was Jackson. **Martin Foley** of Greytown was another; he fled about one o'clock after seeing the Union Jack outside the General's tent torn to pieces. Seeing the regulars hemmed in, and **Smith-Dorrien** desperately battling to open ammunition cases, Foley had ridden off and forced his way through the melee beside Melvill, whom he last saw struggling to hold on to the colours as they swam through the Buffalo. Foley escaped to Helpmekaar and the following day, with Captain Stafford, carried the news of the disaster to Greytown.

Dugald Macphail, Q.M. of the Buffalo Border Guard, managed to scramble out the same way and to get to Newcastle with Donald Moodie. But Malcolm Moodie had died. Sick on the day of the battle, he had been seen coming out of his tent, firing his revolver: then had been seen no more. On May 21st, Fynn and Carbutt found his body, with that of another Carbineer trooper, Jackson, four hundred yards further back than the body of their unit. They had made a brave last stand.

Dubois had died within sight of freedom. After a frantic search for a horse on the battlefield, he had fought his way down to the Buffalo, had swum it, and was scrambling out when he was felled by a shot in the head — aimed at another man! His body, too, was found by Carbutt and taken for burial to the family farm "Giba," at Helpmekaar.

Fynn came across the bodies of two Buffalo Border Guards that were unrecognisable. Fighting their way down the ravine towards the river, they had been pushed over a cliff and were only found in the undergrowth months later. In the four months, however, before Carbutt's Rangers led in General Marshall's cavalry and volunteers to bury the dead, the ghosts of Isandlwana haunted the melancholy and forlorn frontier, and local families were deeply grieved by the disrespect of their dead.

Colour-Sergeant M.C. Keane

Remains of British soldier who died at the Battle of Isandlwana, have been identified after 130 years - by his tunic button. In the casualty lists he is described as........."staff clerk to military secretary".

Colour-Sergeant M.C. Keane was just 24 on January 22, 1879 when he fell during the battle when 1,350 British redcoats were slaughtered by 22,000 Zulu warriors.

The metal badge was discovered with Colour-Sergeant Keane's skeleton in April during excavations by Amafa, the heritage organisation responsible for protecting the historic battle field 100 miles north of Durban. Historian Arthur Konigkramer said the distinctive metal badge was that of the General Staff Corps - and the only soldier from that regiment who fought at Isandlwana was Colour-Sergeant Keane.
Source 17th June 2009 Daily Mail

Extract from: MEMORIES OF WAR AND PEACE   Forbes, Archibald, 1838-1900

I accompanied the first party that visited that Aceldama, and the spectacle which it presented I can never forget. A thousand corpses had been lying there in rain and sun for four long months. The dead lay as they had fallen, for, strange to relate, the vultures of Zululand, that will reduce a dead ox to a skeleton in a few hours, had apparently never touched the corpses of our ill-fated countrymen. In the precipitous ravine at the base of the slope stretching down from the crest on which stood the abandoned waggons, dead men lay thick mere bones, with toughened discoloured skin like leather covering them and clinging tight to them, the flesh all wasted away. I forbear to describe the faces, with their blackened features, and beards blanched by rain and sun. The clothes, had lasted better than the poor bodies they covered, and helped to keep the skeletons together. All the way up the slope I traced, by the ghastly token of dead men, the fitful line of flight. It was like a long string with knots in it, the string formed of single corpses, the knots of clusters of dead, where, as it seemed, little groups must have gathered to make a hopeless, gallant stand, and so die.

Still following the trail of dead bodies through long rank grass and among stones, I approached the crest. Here the slaughtered dead lay very thick, so that the string became a broad belt. On the bare ground, on the crest itself, among the Avaggons, the dead were less thick ; but on the slope beyond, on which from the crest we looked down, the scene was the saddest, and more full of weird desolation than anything I had ever gazed upon. There was none of the stark, blood-curdling horror of a recent battle-field ; no pools of yet wet blood; no torn flesh still quivering. Nothing of all that makes the scene of a yesterday's battle so repulsive shocked the senses. A strange dead calm reigned in this solitude of nature. Grain had grown luxuriantly round and under the waggons, sprouting from the seed that had dropped from the loads, fallen on soil fertilised by the life-blood of gallant men. So long in places had grown the grass that it merci- fully shrouded the dead, who for four long months had been scandalously left unburied.

As one strayed aimlessly about, one stumbled in the grass over skeletons that rattled to the touch. Here lay a corpse with a bayonet jammed into the mouth up to the socket, transfixing the head and mouth a foot into the ground.

There lay a form that seemed cosily curled in calm sleep, turned almost on its face ; but seven assegai stabs had pierced the back. It was the miserablest work wandering about the desolate camp, amid the sour odour of stale death, and gathering sad relics, letters from home, photographs, and blood-stained books. After many delays the day at length came when, as our little army camped on the White Umvaloosi, there lay on the bosom of the wide plain over against us the great circular kraal of Ulundi, King Cetewayo's capital....

Isandhlwana - 22 January 1879

Probably the final chapter in this dreadful affair took place in February 1883 almost four years after the massacre of our forgotten heroes. Mr Boast a civilian contractor was given the task of the burial of their remains.

The Hon Colonial Secretary
Sir,
    I have the honour to report that I reached here on Saturday evening with the party. I have inspected the neighbourhood of Isandhlwana and hope to have all the bones buried in three weeks from this date.
I have the honour to be, Sir
Your obedient Servant Alf Boast   (Isandhlwana February 12th 1883)

From the Colonial Secretary
25th February 1883

Dear Mr Boast,
    I write you a line privately to impress upon you the importance of you being able eventually to report that the burials at Isandhlwana have been thoroughly effected and that there has been nothing of a perfunctory nature in the discharge of the duties entrusted to your party. His Excellency is anxious that the thing should be very thoroughly well done and I think it as well to let you know this as I have been a little surprised at your stating that you expect to have it completed in as short a time as three weeks. No part of the neighbourhood must be left unexplored, and each grave must be made as nearly as possible in accordance with your instructions. Remember that there will be nothing satisfactory in completing the work within a short time, if it is afterwards found to have been inefficiently done, and that there is no occasion for hurry. I shall be glad to receive for his Excellency's information a short ad interim report saying what progress has been made to date, and you have been able in every case to adhere strictly to your instructions.
Signed Haden
Isandhlwana
28th February 1883

The Honourable Colonial Secretary
Sir,
    I have the honour to report for his Excellency's information, that up to this date, two hundred and forty three (243) graves have been dug and built over with stone in the shape of a cairn, according to your instructions.
I find there very little rock to make it difficult for digging graves. The shale which is about the deck of Isandhlwana, is normally soft, and easy to dig. I have only used about half a dozen charges of dynamite supplied to me, and this I could have done without.
I conclude the work will be thoroughly well done by the end of this week. After that I intend to keep the men for two to three days, to explore the ground we have been working on, as well as the neighbourhood.
In the discharge of my duties I have adhered diligently to my instructions and that the two Europeans and natives under my orders have been working unaccountably well.

I have the honour to be Sir Your obedient Servant
Alf Boast   (Isandhlwana 28th February 1883)

Alfred Boast Final Report 13th March 1883. Map of Grave Locations
I commenced operations on the 12th of February on the battlefield and carefully interred the bodies of the volunteers and Mounted police, at a spot marked by a monument marked in memory of Mr Hitchcock and in the immediate neighbourhood of Mr Blailie's tombstone at this spot there were about 30 graves and nearly all of them had been poached upon by the weather that the remains were exposed from this spot. I proceeded to where the camp had stood and was occupied for some days in searching for and committing to earth the skeletons of who had fallen in their advance to meet the enemy in an easterly direction. Having completed this position I returned to the "Nek" and proceeded to perform this duty to those who had fallen at the base of the Isandlhwana mountain. On the Northern side of it and close to Mr Geo Shepstone's tombstone. Hence I searched between that spot and the stream and afterwards crossed the Wagon Road and searched between the Wagon Road and Donga which runs almost parallel to the road. On completion of my duty there I followed the line to Fugitives Drift. Altogether 298 separate graves were dug and usually from 2-4 skeletons or remains were deposited in each. In all cases where any single grave was marked with a cross or other token, whereby it could hereafter be identified, care was taken to preserve that identification. The rough sketch of the country traversed by me, shows as near as possible the position, and number of the different graves. The duty was completed on the 8th March and I returned homewards on the following morning. Each grave was dug three feet deep and one foot six inches wide. The graves were carefully and sufficiently filled in and there locality marked by a cairn of stones built over each grave with the largest obtainable to the height of not less than 3 feet. Every precaution was taken by me not to offend the prejudices of the natives under my directions but of their own free will, they collected and handled the scattered remains and altogether they worked readily.......
Alfred Boast Greytown 13th March 1883.
Pietermaritzburg Archive Depot NAB Referance 1883/867 & 1883/580: A. Boast report on burying the dead at Isandlwana

Isandhlwana - 22 January 1879

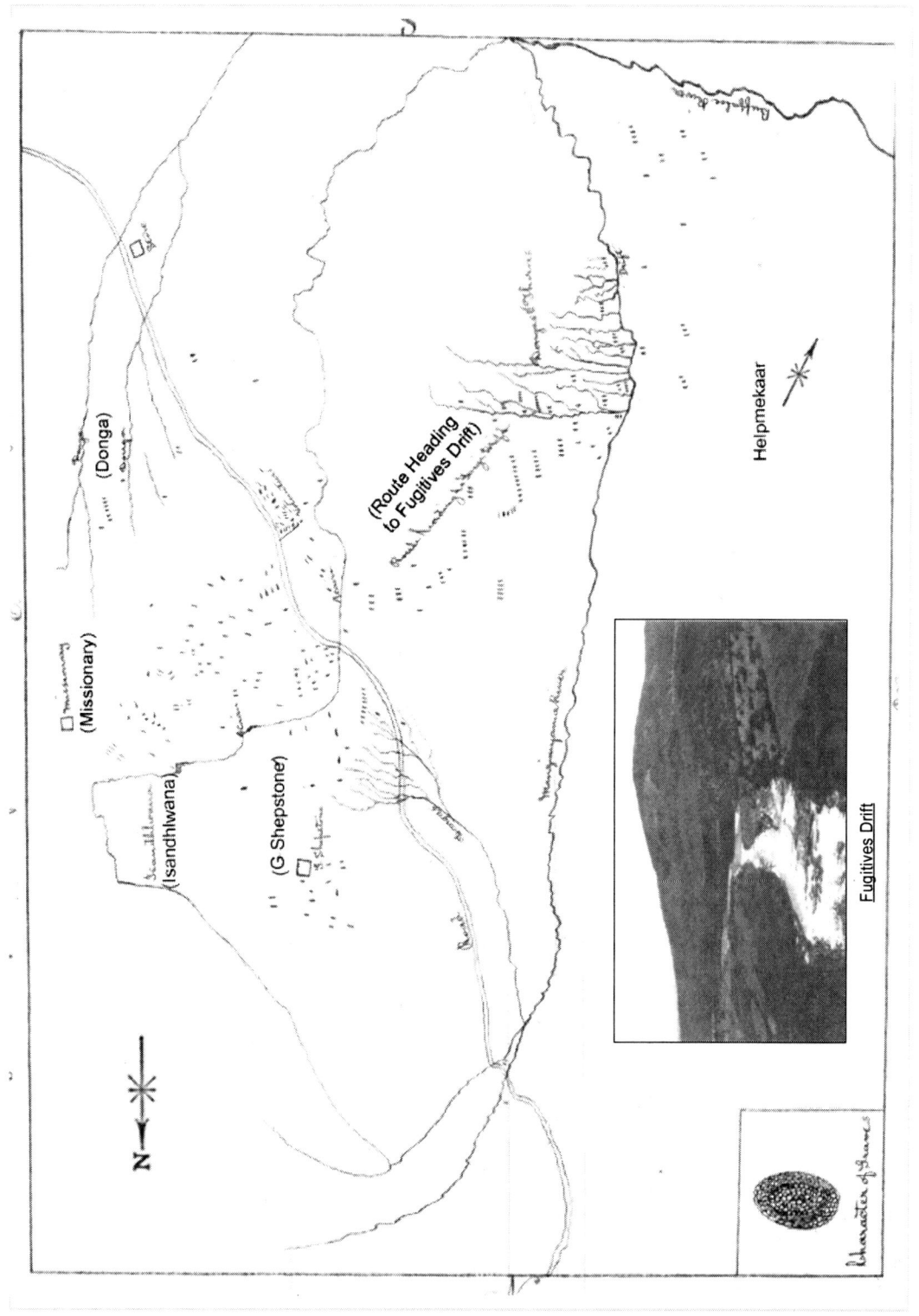

Rorke's Drift 22-23 January

The Defence of Rorke's Drift

In 1936 BBC Radio broadcast the personal accounts of the survivors who witnessed extraordinary moments in history as part of the series 'I was there'. This is the talk given by Lieutenant Colonel Frank Edward Bourne OBE DCM in which he describes his experiences as Colour Sergeant during the defence of Rorke's Drift on the 22nd and 23rd January 1879 in the Anglo Zulu War.

A transcript of the recording was printed in the weekly journal 'The Listener' in December 1936. Extracts below:

"In December 1872, when I was 18 years old, I enlisted in the 24th Regiment and received the princely pay of 6d a day, of which 3.5d was deducted for messing and washing, leaving 1s. 5.5d a week - for luxuries. I went to bed every night hungry but quite happy, and it made a man of me.....

.The Kaffir War ended in June 1878 and we were moved to Pietermaritzburg, Natal, to assist in raising the curtain on the Zulu drama. On January 11 (1879) we crossed the Buffalo river at Rorke's Drift - into Zulu country. Our Commander-in-Chief was Lord Chelmsford. Our strength was four thousand five hundred men, including thirteen Companies of my Regiment, the 24th, now the South Wales Borderers. One company was left behind at Rorke's Drift, to guard the Hospital stores, and the Pontoons at the Drift on the Buffalo River. This was my Company, and at the time I was bitterly disappointed. We saw the main Column under Lord Chelmsford engage the enemy at once, and I watched the action, along with my four Sergeants, from a little hill by Rorke's Drift. Then we saw them move on again, and they disappeared.

And now I must tell you what happened to them during the next ten days......

Shortly after 3.30 an Officer commanding a Troop of Natal Light Horse arrived, having got away from Isandhlwana, and asked Lieutenant Chard for instructions. He was ordered to send detachments to observe the Drift and Pontoons, and to place outposts in the direction of the enemy to check his advance.

About 4.15 the sound of firing was heard behind the hill on our front; the Officer returned and reported the enemy close upon us. He also reported that his 100 men would not obey his orders and had ridden off. About the same time another detachment of 100 men belonging to the Natal Native Contingent bolted., including their Officer himself. I am glad to say he was brought back some days later, court-martialled and dismissed from the service. The desertion of these detachments of 200 men appeared at first sight to be a great loss, with only a hundred of us left, but the feeling was that we could not have trusted them, and also that our defences were too small to accomodate them anyhow.

We knew now that whatever might happen we had to fight it out alone, and about 4.30 the enemy, from 500 to 600 strong, came in sight round the hill to our south, and driving my thin red line of skirmishers, made a rush at our south wall. They were met, and held, by a steady and deliberate fire for a short time, then, being re-inforced by some hundreds, they made desperate and repeated attempts to break through our temporary defences, but were repulsed time and again. To show their fearlessness and their contempt for the red coats and small numbers, they tried to leap the parapet, and at times seized our bayonets, only to be shot down. Looking back, one cannot but admire their fanatical bravery. About 7 o'clock they succeeded, after many attempts, in setting fire to the Hospital. The small number we were able to spare defended it room by room, bringing out all the sick who could be moved before they retired. Privates Hook, R. Jones, W. Jones and J. Williams were the last to leave, holding the door with the bayonet when all their ammunition was expended. The Victoria Cross was awarded to these men, and they fully deserved it.

The Zulus had collected the rifles from the men who they had killed at Isandhlwana, and had captured the ammunition from the mules which had stampeded and threw their loads; so our own arms where used against us. In fact, this was the cause of every one of our casualties, killed and wounded, and we should have suffered many more if the enemy had known how to use a rifle. There was hardly a man even wounded by an assegais - their principle weapon.

The attack lasted from 4.30 p.m. on the twenty-second to 4.00 a.m. on the twenty-third - twelve exciting hours - and when daybreak occurred, the enemy was out of sight. About 7 o'clock they appeared again to the south-west. But help was at hand; Lord Chelmsford with the other half of his original force was only an hour's march away. On the previous afternoon he had learned of the destruction of his camp at Isandhlwana. A certain Commandant Lonsdale had chanced to ride back to the Camp and had been fired at by Zulus wearing our men's uniform. He escaped by a miracle and was able to report the news to Lord Chelmsford.

Lord Chelmsford at once addressed his men and said: 'Whilst we were skirmishing ahead the Zulus have taken our Camp; there must be ten thousand in our rear, and twenty thousand in front, we must win back our Camp tonight and cut our way back to Rorke's Drift tomorrow'.'All right sir, we'll do it'.

They got back to camp that night, but they found a grim and silent scene as they cautiously approached. The next day they resumed their march and appeared at Rorke's Drift, and our enemy retired.

In his dispatch afterwards, Lord Chelmsford said: 'To our intense relief the waving of hats was seen from the hastily erected entrenchments, and information soon reached me that the garrison...had for twelve hours made the most gallant resistance I have ever heard of against the determined attack of some 3,000 Zulu's, 350 of whose dead bodies surrounded the post.' Our losses were 17 killed and 9 wounded. Theirs 351 killed that we buried. Their wounded must have been 400 to 500, which they removed under the cover of night.

There are two things which I think have made Rorke's Drift stand out so vividly after all these years. The first, that it took place on the same day as the terrible massacre at Isandhlwana, and the second, that Natal was saved from being overrun by a savage and victorious foe.

Seven VC's were awarded to this one Company of the Regiment which is now the South Wales Borderers. I have told you the names of the four men who won the VC; the other three were Lieutenant Bromhead, Corporal Allen and Private F. Hitch. The Victoria Cross was also awarded to Lieutenant Chard, Royal Engineers, Surgeon Reynolds, and Corporal Schiess, but not one, I regret to say, of those VCs is alive today. In fact, there are only six survivors of Rorke's Drift alive today: Ex-Privates W. Cooper, G. Edwards, H. Martin, W. Owens, H. Williams, and myself.

Action at Gingihlovo - 2 April 1879

Action at Gingihlovo
SOUTH AFRICA—THE ZULU WAR—Despatches.—Questions in the house. HC Deb 22 April 1879 vol 245 cc833-5 833

§ MR. W. E. FORSTER
I hope, Sir, I may be allowed to anticipate the usual order of the Questions, and ask the Secretary of State for the Colonies, Whether he can satisfy the anxiety of the House by giving us the actual official information received by the Government to-day from the Cape?

§ SIR MICHAEL HICKS-BEACH
The telegram has already been published in the Press this afternoon by my right hon. and gallant Friend the Secretary of State for War; but probably the House will desire me to read it. I have also a telegram addressed to myself from Government House, Capo Town, giving information on other points. I will read it first, as it is the shorter one. It is dated Cape Town, April 7th, 1879— No news from High Commissioner's camp since last mail. Postmaster at Pietermaritzburg telegraphed to Under Colonial Secretary, Cape Town, 4th April: High Commissioner and Staff 30 miles beyond Newcastle, on road to Standerton, 31st March; all well. Lord Chelmsford has successfully relieved Ekowe, and brought away garrison safely. Relieving force under Lord Chelmsford left Fort Tenedos 29th March. Attacked by enemy, about 12,000 strong, at Gingihlovo, 2nd April; completely defeated them. General continued march to Ekowe with part of column; reached it 3rd April. I understand particulars of engagement have been telegraphed by Sir Henry Bulwer.
That telegram I will read shortly— Colonel Hopton, Fort Tenedos, telegraphs to me, 6th April—General and Staff all well. Pearson and Ekowe garrison now encamped 15 miles hence, and will come here to-morrow. Transport Clyde wrecked off Dyer's Island and sunk; all on board safe and unhurt; troops taken on board Her Majesty's ship Tamar; proceed to Durban to-day; all other Infantry re-inforcements landed at Durban; also 17th Lancers by England. Loss of Puller's men at Hlobane less than newspapers reported. Telegram from Maritzburg, 3 p.m. to-day, states: General, Commodore, and Staff arrived at Fort Pearson noon to-day. Then there is a telegram from the Colonial Secretary, Cape Town, to myself, dated 7th April 1879— The Lieutenant Governor of Natal, Sir Henry Bulwer, desires me to communicate the following message, which he has received from Colonel Hopton, at Fort Pearson, Tugela River:—'I am directed by Lord Chelmsford to send the following communication:—The relieving column under Lord Chelmsford formed laager near Gingihlovo on the afternoon of the 1st April. Very heavy rain throughout evening and night. At 6 a.m. on the 2nd, Zulus attacked laager, on each side in succession—two distinct forces employed. Enemy advanced in most courageous manner, but never got within 20 yards of shelter trench. At 7.30 a.m. the attack was repulsed, and the enemy retired precipitately, followed for some miles by mounted Infantry and Natives under Barrow and Barton, and Nettleton's regiment of Natal contingent. Sabres of the mounted Infantry did great execution. The fight was witnessed from Ekowe, and Colonel Pearson, flashing signals, congratulated General on success. Casualties—Lieutenant Johnson, Privates J. Smith and Lawrence, 99th, Private R. Marshall, 91st, and Private J. J. Pratt, 60th Rifles, killed. Colonel Northey, 60th Rifles, and Dr. Longfield, of Her Majesty's ship Tenedos, dangerously wounded. Major Barrow, of the 19th Hussars, and Captain Hinxman, 57th, slightly wounded. Twenty soldiers and sailors wounded; one Native killed, and 10 wounded. There were 471 bodies of Zulus counted within 1,000 yards of the laager. The long grass and bushes helped their approach and assisted their retreat. Total loss must have been double. Portions of 11 regiments are known to have taken part—viz., Ngoxamonosi, Uvemmsityu, Unambonambu, Zulwana, Nokenka, Nodwena, and others. Prisoners state that 195 companies were engaged, which, at 60 men each, would give 11,000. Dabulmanzu, mounted, led the final attack. Somapo was in chief command. Lord Chelmsford intends to abandon Ekowe, both roads being very difficult of approach. He will establish a permanent post on the coast road. Gingihlovo laager will be reduced to permit its being held by a garrison. The General goes to Ekowe to-morrow with three regiments and carts. Prisoners state that messengers arrived yesterday with news of Colonel Wood's victory on the 29th. Since the foregoing message was received, further intelligence has arrived from the Natal Government that Lord Chelmsford has relieved Colonel Pearson at Ekowe, and has returned with the whole garrison to his camp.

§ COLONEL STANLEY
said: With the permission of the House, I would wish 835 to supplement the statement of my right hon. Friend (Sir Michael Hicks-Beach). I was under the impression that the telegram I received was the same as that sent to the Colonial Office; but I find this is not so. I have received this morning from Colonel Bellairs, the Deputy Adjutant General at Durban, the following telegram:— Intelligence of important victories gained by Lord Chelmsford and Colonel Wood having reached me, have taken it upon myself to arrange for mail to leave Cape Town one day earlier, and to call specially at St. Vincent, enabling you to receive the news earlier than viâ Madeira. Colonel Wood's despatches state that on the 29th Inhlobani successfully attacked. Some thousand cattle taken by mounted Corps and Natives; but Zulus, 20,000 strong, coming up, we suffered considerable losses, and cattle were re-taken. Weatherley's corps cut up and all killed, with the exception of Captain Denison and a few men; also three fives Frontier Horse, under Captain Barton, Coldstream Guards, only seven escaping. Eleven officers and 80 men are returned killed, including Captains Campbell and Barton, Coldstream Guards; Lieutenant Williams, 58th; Colonel Weatherley, Captain Rice Hamilton, Lieutenants Von Steiten, Cronlys, Pool, and Weatherley; and Messrs. Piet Uys and Lloyd, of Colonial Corps. Colonel Wood's horse killed under him on 29th. The Zulu Army, the regiment of which had come from Ulundi, attacked Kambulama camp. Action commenced 1.30 p.m.; lasted four hours; enemy driven off, and pursued by mounted troops seven miles. Their loss very heavy, 500 bodies lying close into camp; 300 fire-arms, including several Martini-Henry rifles, picked up. Enemy advanced close up, some even penetrating into cattle laager. Our casualties, 80 killed, two wounded. Lieutenants Nicolson, R.A., and Bright, 90th, killed; Major Hackett and Lieutenant Smith, 90th, dangerously wounded; Captains Gardner, 14th Hussars, Cox and Persse, 13th Foot, slightly wounded. Natives nearly all deserted. Unymana, King's Minister, and chief commander, did not come under fire. The remainder of the telegram is what my Right Hon Friend has read.

Morosi War 25th March to 20th November 1879

THE MOROSI WAR

Morosi, chief of the Baphuti, committed various acts deemed to be hostile to the Cape Colonial administration of Basutoland late in 1878, including the forcible release of his son, Doda, from jail.

Refusing to surrender Doda, Morosi and his tribe withdrew to a mountain in the Drakensberg southern Basutoland in the Quthing District, which had been fortified over a period of years, and there defied the Colonial government.

A Cape Colonial force under **Col C. D Griffith**, with Basuto support was mobilized, and, reaced the mountain on 25 March, 1879. Reinforcements arrived in early April with two 7-pounder guns and some rockets. After an artillery bombardment on the 8th of April the Colonial forces made an assault. This failed.

Further reinforcements under Col E Y Brabant, and a 12-pounder field gun arrived after the first assault Brabant, who took over command from Griffith, ordered a second assault on 5 June. This also failed. All this time the Colonial forces had maintained a blockade of the mountain. Colonel Brabant has under his command a force of about 200 Europeans, Cape Mounted Rifles and about 500 Hottentots, Fingos and Basutos. In October **Col Z S Bayly** relieved Brabant, and after training his men thoroughly, ordered an assault on the night of 19/20 November. This succeeded, the mountain was taken, and Morosi and most of his men killed. During the siege three Victoria Crosses were awarded to British troops: **Peter Brown, Edmund Hartley** and **Robert Scott**.

Ref: Journal Vol 8 No 3. South African Military History Society http://samilitaryhistory.org/vol083jh.html.

THE FRONTIER ARMED & MOUNTED POLICE

Braine,	Pte.	8/4/1879	1st Assault
Cole, W. F.	Sgt.	8/4/1879	1st Assault
Edwards, J.	Sgt.	8/4/1879	1st Assault
Jones, A.	Cpl.	5/6/1879	2nd Assault
Martindale, C.	Cpl.	8/4/1879	1st Assault
Paskie,	Pte.	8/4/1879	1st Assault
Peterson, R.	Pte.	6/5/1879	
Schwartz,		20/11/1879	Final Assault
Surmon, J.	Capt.	8/4/1879	1st Assault

1ST REGIMENT, CAPE MOUNTED YEOMANRY

Toomey, E.	Trooper	5/6/1879	2nd Assault

2ND REGIMENT, CAPE MOUNTED YEOMANRY

Muldoon, T.	Sgt.	23/3/1879	During the approach
Robinson, J.	Sgt.	5/6/1879	2nd Assault
Vice, A. J.	Trooper	5/6/1879	2nd Assault
Wyk, S. van	Trooper	5/6/1879	2nd Assault

FORT BEAUFORT BURGHERS

Sluyter, W.	Trooper	5/6/1879	2nd Assault
Kay, W.	Trooper	29/5/1879	Night Attack
King, W.	Trooper	No date	

3RD REGIMENT, CAPE MOUNTED YEOMANRY

Reed, N. A.	Lieut.	8/4/1879	1st Assault
Muldoon, T.	Sgt.	23/3/1879	During the approach
Ferreira, P.S.	Trooper	29/5/1879	Night Attack
Hannon, W. E.	Trooper	5/6/1879	2nd Assault
Hastings, A.	Trooper	29/5/1879	Night Attack
Johnstone, A.	Trooper	29/5/1879	Night Attack
Johnstone, Thomas	Trooper	29/5/1879	Night Attack
Laurens, T. P.	Trooper	29/5/1879	Night Attack
Leonard, H.	Trooper	5/6/1879	2nd Assault
Lourens, Cornelius	Trooper	29/5/1879	Night Attack
Mason, C.	Trooper	29/5/1879	Night Attack
Meyer, Fred	Trooper	29/5/1879	Night Attack
Thornton, C.	Trooper	29/5/1879	Night Attack
Warren, R.	Trooper	No date	

STOCKENSTROOM VOLUNTEER RIFLES

Jordaan, N.	Trooper	5/6/1879	2nd Assault
Pretorius,	Trooper	5/6/1879	2nd Assault

Note: The casualties, copies by the late Major Deare from the Government Gazettes of the Cape of Good Hope.

MR. A. M'ARTHUR asked the Under Secretary of State for the Colonies, whether he will inquire into the truth of a statement made in the "Christian Express," published at the Lovedale Institution in South Africa, that the body of the Chief Moirosi had been dreadfully mutilated, and his head carried off for scientific purposes by a Negro attached to the Cape Mounted Rifles.

MR. GRANT DUFF, in reply, said, that it was quite clear that the body of Moirosi was buried the day after his mountain was taken; but, so far back as January last, a statement came to the knowledge of the then Secretary of State to the effect that his head had been removed for anatomical purposes. He immediately, of course, gave orders by telegraph that the head should be decently interred with the other remains, and soon afterwards a telegram was received stating that the order had been carried into effect. HC Deb 29 June 1880 vol 253

Morosi War 25th March to 20th November 1879

Natural Embrasure on the Summit of the Saddle Rock - A Colonial Soldier in Hiding.
The Siege of Morosi's Mountain

Officers Left to Right - Mr. Herbert - Gen. Colley - Sir. G. Wolsely - Col. Brackenbury - Mr. T. Shepstone - Gaon.
Zulu chiefs signing the peace stipulations, Ulundi, Sept 1.

Basuto War 1880-1881

THE BASUTO WAR Gun War
The Basutos rebelled when the Government tried to disarm them. Fighting took place on several fronts, with the main engagements taking place around Mafeteng, just across the Orange Free State border, where Colonel Carrington was besieged with 200 Cape Mounted Riflemen. The relieving force, which included the CMY, was surprised by a mounted Basuto force at Kalibani. Conflict in the British territory of Basutoland (present-day Lesotho)
Extracts taken from: "Among Boers and Basutos and With Barkley's Horse, the Story of Our Life on the Frontier." by Fanny Alexandra Barkly, London: Roxburghe. 1893. 257p.

Letter dated September 8th, 1879 :
A camp guard who was just on the bank of the Quithing saw a black mass rush along under the bank of the river towards the camp; he ran into the camp about fifteen or twenty yards-followed by the enemy, who gave a yell as they came on. The sentry woke **Captain Chiappini**, who came out to get his men together. On coming out he saw the enemy round two tents silently cutting the guy-ropes and stabbing through the canvas with their assegais. The men out of the other three tents were quickly rallied behind the stone wall, that is between the wall and the Quithing. There they remained till daybreak. The enemy, who thus had full possession of the camp, made use of their time by sacking and pulling everything upside down in the tents. The Burghersdorp (G) Troop, 2nd Regiment, which is stationed across the Orange River, in charge of one of the guns, heard the frightful noise occasioned by the firing, shouting for help, and Kaffir yells of triumph, and running to the river, cheered away as hard as they could. One of the enemy was heard to say in Sesuto, "Listen, the bugle is blowing, and they are coming, let us go." They then retreated, carrying their dead and wounded with them. Before they went they had made one or two attempts to take the party behind the wall on either flank, but fortunately did not
succeed. A couple of bugles had been got out of one of the tents, and on these the men were making as much noise as possible. At daybreak an awful sight presented itself. Everything was in the utmost confusion. Tents simply cut to shreds by the assegais, great pools of blood, assegais, guns, blankets, bodies of the dead and wounded, and in one place a lot of human teeth, evidently belonging to one of the enemy, and all the various little necessities of camp life, were lying about in all directions. On following the path the enemy had taken-for they were easily traced by the blood of their wounded -they were found to have returned back to the mountain.
Casualties:- **J. Kannemeyer**, bullet in left eye, dangerous; **P. L. Mair**, two assegai wounds, slight; **T. Laurence**, four bullet and eleven assegai wounds, dangerous; **W. Parkes**, two assegai wounds, slight; **P. Ferreira**, twenty assegai wounds, doing well; **A. Mansfield**, two loopers in left arm, slight; **A. Johnson**, one bullet wound, since dead. Three others slightly wounded.
The subsequent siege of Moirosi's Mountain dragged on and on until November 1879, when the Baphuti, who still kept their positions in the caves and rocks of this terrible mountain, were actually starved out, and the mountain was taken.

Letter dated November 25th.
Morale's Moirosi's Mountain has fallen at last, and the old fellow himself; also his sons Setuka and Motsap were shot by the C.M.R. (Cape Mounted Rifles), who stormed the stronghold. He had apparently been deserted by most of his people, or starvation had compelled them to leave the mountain. The attack was made at 4.15 A.M. on the 20th in five different places with scaling ladders.
The defence was feeble compared with what it was in the two former attacks. In fact there were not men enough on the mountain to defend it properly, and it was taken as soon as the first body of C.M.R. got up the ladders, as they did with no loss, though one man had his cap shot off as he put his head over the rock. He, however, shot the Baphuti dead who did it, and though he got another shot through his coat, jumped up, followed by his comrades, who fixed bayonets (they had long sniders), and charged right across the top of the mountain, driving the enemy before them. At this the defence ceased. At the other points attacked our men came swarming up on every side, and all was over.
The rebels fought to the death; three chiefs were wounded and one killed, and the same number of Fingoes were knocked over. Of the Baphuti, excepting some eight or ten, all were killed and among them the old chief Moirosi himself, who was killed on the top by a soldier servant of ours who had been in the "Blues," and accompanied me to the mountain, who afterwards received £20 as a reward for his conduct on the occasion. 'Some Baphuti took refuge in a cave, but in the evening a charge or two of dynamite was thrown in, and several more of the enemy were killed. Two rushed out, one of them believed to be the chief Doda, and sliding down a krantz some thirty-five feet high, escaped under a heavy fire. 'The whole thing was well planned and well carried out, but the weakness of the enemy made it easier.
'Moirosi's son Doda escaped untouched to the inner depth and fastnesses of the Quithing.'

Basuto War 1880-1881

Letter dated 12th October 1880, Mafeteng, Camp Cape Mounted rifles.
We are going to try and send in a messenger to Wepener, to-night, so I write in the hope that he will get in safely, the last one who came out was nearly caught. **Clarke**, now a. local Brigadier General, with **Southey**, and about four hundred yeomanry, and C.M.R. with two guns, are encamped at Wepener, waiting for reinforcements before coming in, as the enemy are very strong. We are meanwhile, living chiefly on horse, which is not particularly bad eating, we have, however, plenty of flour, groceries, etc., and we can hold out, if necessary, for a fortnight or more on short rations. We have been having floods of rain, lately, which makes life a burden, but is useful to us in many ways, keeping the rebels from crossing the river, and making the grass grow for the horses, which would otherwise have starved. The rumor we hear now, is, that the enemy's plan is to mass all the force that can be collected to attack us again, and when we are disposed of, to go for Maseru. This design is impracticable at present owing to the rivers, and if they do come, they will be beaten, as before, only a great deal worse, for we have improved our defences since the last attack, but it would take six thousand or seven thousand men (Europeans) with a good strong native levy, to bring this war to an end in any reasonable time. Brabant is expected with about two hundred yeomanry, and one hundred or so infantry volunteers. Willoughby's Horse are coming later, and the Diamond Fields' Horse, two hundred strong, are on their way with them. **Captain Shervington** and Lieutenants **Carstensen, Clarke,** and **M'Mullen** Leading in the skirmishes which took place. on the 17th of September, a vedette named **Bernard White** was killed, and in another **Lieutenant Clarke** C.M.R., fell. The latter must not be confused with Brigadier Clarke C.B., the Commandant-General of the Colonial Forces.Lieutenant Clarke was sent out with reinforcements to cover some of Captain Shervington's men, who were in danger from a force of 1200 rebels surrounding them. In covering their retreat, the horse of one of the Riflemen, Private **Magee** was killed, and he himself wounded, whereupon **Lieutenant Clarke**, although closely pressed by the enemy, stopped and dismounted, placing the wounded man upon his horse, which, however, threw them both and broke away, and he and Magee being left in the midst of the rebels were immediately surrounded and cut to pieces. Clarke was seen to make a desperate resistance, killing three or more of the enemy. The bodies of the dead were afterwards recovered. These were our only causalities; while the rebels had from 40 to 50 killed and wounded. After this the Basutos seemed to have determined on a simultaneous attack upon the garrisons at the Magistracies of Maseru, Mafeteng, and Mohalie's Hoek; but Mafeteng and a neighbouring trading station, (Diphering) bore the brunt of it,
Lerothodi himself, with a following of about five thousand men, well armed and mounted, leading the assault. The defending force consisted only of two hundred Cape Mounted Rifles, one hundred and twenty natives and a few volunteers; but they had made preparations for the attack; as on reconnoitering Lerothodi's kraal the previous evening it was observed that large reinforcements had arrived there, and an attempt on the camp was therefore expected.

Colonel Carrington reporting to the Commandant-General the particulars of this engagement which occurred on the 21st of September,
The three schantses (temporary fortifications with high walls and a traverse) above the court-house were commanded by Mr **Barkly**. The main schantse was held by fourteen Cape Mounted Rifles and two volunteers with Mr Barkly. No. 2 schantse by thirteen Cape Mounted Rifles and twelve natives. No. 3 schantse by eight Mounted Rifles, fifteen natives and Mr Mallraison. Diphering, Mr Fraser's store, was held by twenty-five Cape Mounted Rifles, twentyfive volunteers, and **Captain Montague**.The entrenchment, stone horse-~raal and Mr Barkly's house and hospital all adjoining, were held by one hundred and thirtysix Cape Mounted Rifles, waggon drivers, and a few natives; the house and hospital A tremendous fire was at once opened upon their retreating, they continually dismounted and picked up their dead and wounded. Fifty-nine dead horses and some seven to eight bodies lay round the schantse.
Captain Shervington, by my orders, did not pursue, as the reserves in masses came down at once. A very large number of dead and wounded were lying behind a sod wall, but they were carefully covered by a large reserve, and most of them carried away after dark. Our casualities were of the Cape Mounted Riflemen, **Corporal W. Brownlee** and Privates **S. Meyer, J. Bevan,** and **W. Curran**, gunshot wounds, and one of the Basuto police also wounded. The smallness of the list was owing to the fact that every man was under cover, erected with the greatest care by Lieutenant Carstensen, Cape Mounted Rifles, a young officer formerly in the Prussian Army. The enemy were well armed with Martini-Henry and Snider rifles, as was proved by the large number of cartridge cases found. Their loss was estimated at a hundred and fifty killed and incapacitated, and the ground around the camp was strewn with dead and wounded horses. **Dalgety** is field-adjutant, and had a very narrow escape yesterday, a bullet going through his sleeve and a silk handkerchief which he had tied round his wrist. He is a very smart and plucky young fellow, and we were delighted to find that

Basuto War 1880-1881

Continued from previous page.
he wasn't hurt at all, nor even grazed by the bullet. '
Meanwhile the forces were gradually assembling from the Colony, but the numbers were very small in comparison to the rebels whom they were to conquer.
On the 12th October, 1880 Brigadier General Clarke, with Colonel Southey and about four hundred yeomanry, and Cape Mounted Rifles, with two guns, were encamped at Wepener, waiting for reinforcements before coming into Basutoland, as the enemy was very strong. The little garrison at Mafeteng were reduced to short rations, and living chiefly on horse flesh, no vegetables, nothing to drink but tea.
On the 19th of October, 1880, Brigadier General Clarke, Commandant-in-chief of the colonial forces, succeeded in relieving Mafeteng. The rebels made their "assegai charge" and caught two or three troops of the 1st Yeomanry extended in skirmishing order, and killed thirty two, wounding eleven. They were, however, severely punished, and over thirty cut to pieces.
Cape Mounted Rifles, a very fine Corps, composed chiefly of the sons of gentlemen.

Extract from the Times, Friday, November 19, 1880.
Cape Town October 26th.
When I last wrote there was little relief to the dark clouds which hung loweringly over our position in Basutoland. The rebels were testifying by revolt and rapine their ingratitude for the efforts of our government and people to protect them and assist them in their progress from barbarism towards civilisation. Three of the seats of magistracy were closely invested by overwhelming numbers who repeatedly made enraged rushes upon their small bands of gallant defenders and only at two places, Leribe and Quithing, were the loyal people and the representatives of government holding their position undisturbed. Since then the colonial government has been able to muster its forces, to equip its men and to march some of them over a distance of one thousand miles to the scene of rebellion.
The besieged garrisons of Mohale's Hoek and Mafeteng have been relieved, and they, together with our troops, are now able to take the offensive against the enemy, and have indeed, already inflicted upon them a telling defeat in the capture and destruction of the Chief Lerothodi's stronghold. Brigadier-General Clarke, the commandant-general of the colonial forces, effected the relief of Mafeteng on the 19th of October. His column consisted of one thousand seven hundred men with field guns and mortars, and upwards of forty wagons and ambulances, besides spans of slaughtered oxen for the garrison, as it was known Mr Barkly's gallant band and Carrington's force were in want of provisions, having been for several days on rations of horse-flesh. They formed a considerable train as they marched from their camp on the Free State border. The 1st Cape Mounted Yeomanry under Colonel Brabant, being the advance guard and supports; the 2nd Yeomanry, under Colonel Southey and Cape Mounted Rifles flanking detachments; and the 3rd Yeomanry Kimberley Horse, and Captain Hunt's Volunteers the rear guard. The 1st City Rifles, (Graham's Town), Prince Alfred's Guard (Port Elizabeth), and the Mohale's Hoek contingent marched on the left of the column, and the Duke of Edinburgh's own Volunteer Rifles (Cape Town) at the right. Mafeteng being the key of the military position in Basutoland, the general commanding threw up a small fort between that place and Diphering and made the position of his camp secure, while he, with an escort, reconnoitered towards Lerothodi's stronghold. On the 22nd of October this place was gallantly taken, with very slight loss on our side, and a severe defeat inflicted upon the rebels. General Clarke, in the following official despatch to the Premier, details the operations:......

The Zulu War : Lancers returning from burning kraals.

Appendices

Page	Appendix	Title
420	Appendix 1	Anglo-Zulu War Memorial, Pietermaritzburg
422	Appendix 2	Memoriam Tablet Maritzburg College
429	Appendix 3	Colonial Troops Zulu War 1879
432	Appendix 4	Casualty Roll 9th April to 3rd May 1878
435	Appendix 5	Medal Awards the 24th Foot
438	Appendix 6	Medal Awards- Killed in Action Isandhlwana
449	Appendix 7	Survivors of Isandlwana
453	Appendix 8	Rorke's Drift
454	Appendix 9	The Victoria Cross

ROSS & CO.,
MANUFACTURING OPTICIANS,
164, NEW BOND STREET, W.

COLT'S REVOLVERS AND SHOT-GUNS.

COLT'S *double-action Army Revolver, as supplied to H.M.'s War Department.*

COLT'S *single-action Army Revolver, as adopted by the United States Government.*

COLT'S *double-action ·380 cal. Revolvers for travellers and house protection.*

COLT'S *Pocket Pistols, ·380 and ·410 cal.*

COLT'S *Deringers, for the vest pocket.*

COLT'S NEW DOUBLE-BARREL BREECH-LOADING SPORTING GUNS

Now Ready. Each Gun is London proved and carefully tested before it is sent out, and its performance is guaranteed.

PRICE LIST FREE.

COLT'S Fire Arms Company, 14, Pall Mall, London, S.W.

Anglo-Zulu War Memorial

The unveiling ceremony took place on Thursday 11 October 1883 during a humid and rainy day. As luck would have it, a brake in the weather allowed the event to proceed. Dignitaries present included the Lieutenant-Governor, Sir Henry Bulwer, Theophilus Shepstone, Dean Green and Archdeacon Colley. There were addresses by Sir Henry Bulwer and the mayor of Pietermaritzburg, Mr H Griffin.

The military contingent included the 2nd Battalion 58th (Northamptonshire) Regiment under the command of Captain Dickinson. The Natal Carbineers under the command of Captain William Royston and a small Natal Mounted Police detachment, also present the Maritzburg Rifles (Captain Birkett), accompanied by the Edendale Horse contingent (Captain Wyatt Vause).

The Natal Witness, commented on a disappointing turnout which was explained as follows: 'The residents of Pietermaritzburg are not, as a rule, so demonstrative as their more lively coast neighbours. Events which in Durban would cause quite an hysteria are treated very nonchalantly in the capital. It may be that the pomp of gubernatorial movements is so much part of our everyday life, that there is not the novelty in them that there is to the Durban people.'

The Memorial depicts on each corner four life-size figures, representing the participants in the campaign Facing Church Street stood a Natal Carbineers officer; a British soldier-of-the-Line faced the corner of Church Street and Commercial Road; a sailor of the Naval Brigade faced Commercial Road; and a levy of the Natal Native Contingent (NNC), facing the gardens. Unfortunately the monument was vandalised on the 14 April 1994 with one of its life-size statues falling to the ground which shattered the marble. It has since been repaired.

References: http://samilitaryhistory.org/vol101mc.html

Unveiling of the Anglo-Zulu War Memorial 11th October 1883

Anglo-Zulu War Memorial

Anglo-Zulu War Memorial, Pietermaritzburg

Front side
In memory of Honour and in hope of Peace
This Monument
inscribed with the names
of Natal Colonists
who fell during the Zulu War
Is erected
by
Public Subscription
They being dead yet speak

Second side

Name	Corps	Place
Capt G Shepstone	N N Horse	Isandlwana
Lieut F J D Scott	Natal Carbineers	Isandlwana
Q/Master W London	Natal Carbineers	Isandlwana
Trooper J Blaikie	Natal Carbineers	Isandlwana
Trooper G Bornin	Natal Carbineers	Isandlwana
Trooper I C Bullock	Natal Carbineers	Isandlwana
Trooper G C S Christian	Natal Carbineers	Isandlwana
Trooper J Deane	Natal Carbineers	Isandlwana
Trooper J Lumley	Natal Carbineers	Isandlwana
Trooper W Mendenhall	Natal Carbineers	Isandlwana
Trooper J Ross	Natal Carbineers	Isandlwana
Trooper E Tarboton	Natal Carbineers	Isandlwana
Trooper H Davis	Natal Carbineers	Isandlwana
Trooper H Dickenson	Natal Carbineers	Isandlwana
Trooper W Hawkins	Natal Carbineers	Isandlwana
Trooper C Hayhow	Natal Carbineers	Isandlwana
Trooper C Haldane	Natal Carbineers	Isandlwana
Trooper R Jackson	Natal Carbineers	Isandlwana
Trooper G Macleroy	Natal Carbineers	Isandlwana
Trooper M Moodie	Natal Carbineers	Isandlwana
Trooper W Swift	Natal Carbineers	Isandlwana
Trooper J Whitelaw	Natal Carbineers	Isandlwana
Trooper J B Hay	Natal Carbineers	Helpmekaar
Trooper Eary	Buffalo Border Guard	Isandlwana
Trooper Guttridge	Buffalo Border Guard	Isandlwana
Trooper Wehr	Buffalo Border Guard	Isandlwana
Capt R Bradstreet	Newcastle Mtd Rifles	Isandlwana
Q/M G F Hitchcock	Newcastle Mtd Rifles	Isandlwana
Sgt A Swan	Newcastle Mtd Rifles	Isandlwana
Trooper J W Barnes	Newcastle Mtd Rifles	Isandlwana
Tpr G Greenbank	Newcastle Mtd Rifles	Isandlwana
Tpr A Macalister	Newcastle Mtd Rifles	Isandlwana
Tpr J Dinkelman	Newcastle Mtd Rifles	Isandlwana
Trooper A E Dixon	Newcastle Mtd Rifles	Isandlwana
Cpl Lally	Natal Mounted Police	Isandlwana
L/Cpl Campbell	Natal Mounted Police	Isandlwana
Trooper C H Bango	Natal Mounted Police	Isandlwana
Trooper H Berr	Natal Mounted Police	Isandlwana
Tpr F Blakeman	Natal Mounted Police	Isandlwana
Trooper H S Capps	Natal Mounted Police	Isandlwana
Trooper T Clark	Natal Mounted Police	Isandlwana
Trooper S Daniel	Natal Mounted Police	Isandlwana
Trooper C Doury	Natal Mounted Police	Isandlwana
Trooper J Eason	Natal Mounted Police	Isandlwana
Trooper W Fletcher	Natal Mounted Police	Isandlwana
Trooper H S Lloyd	Natal Mounted Police	Isandlwana
Trooper T Macrae	Natal Mounted Police	Isandlwana
Trooper C Mears	Natal Mounted Police	Isandlwana
Trooper H Neil	Natal Mounted Police	Isandlwana

Source: The Natal Witness, Friday 12 October 1883

Fourth side
In grateful recognition of succour rendered in a time of doubt and peril, the names of the Imperial and other Regiments that took part in the Zulu campaign are here recorded

Regiments	Killed officers	Killed NCOs and men
Staff	3	10
17th Lancers	2	2
Royal Artillery	2	69
Royal Engineers	2	4
Coldstream Guards	2	-
2nd Bn, 3rd Regiment	-	3
Ist Bn, 13th Regiment	1	10
2nd Bn, 21st Regiment	1	-
1st Bn, 24th Regiment	16	404
2nd Bn, 25th Regt	5	187
58th Regiment	1	1
3rd Bn, 60th Rifles	1	1
80th Regiment	1	61
90th Regiment	1	13
91st Regiment	-	1
94th Regiment	-	2
99th Regiment	1	2
Mounted Infantry	-	15
AS Corps	-	4
AH Corps	1	10
A M Department	2	-
Frontier Light Horse	3	28
Transvaal Rangers	2	6
Border Horse	5	39
Burgher Force	1	-
Shepstone's Native Horse	-	2
Baker's Horse	-	8
TOTAL	**53**	**882**

Third side
Inyezane
Isandlwana
Rorke's Drift
Hlobane
Kambula
Etshowe
Gingindlovu
Ulundi

Appendix 2 - Memoriam Tablet Maritzburg

The tablet being placed in the entrance hall of the College, was unveiled on the 28th April, 1882, in the old High School by His Excellency Sir Henry Bulwer, K.C.M.G,, etc., the then Governor of the Colony, Sir John Akerman, K.C.M.G., the Mayor of Maritzburg, and many other officials being present.

The Story of an African City. 139

unto death, is placed here in the trust that it will not speak in vain to the generations of schoolboys who may sit in their places, but that it may be the means of helping to noble thoughts, and to the formation of manly, brave, and duty-loving lives.

His Excellency at this stage unveiled the tablet, which bears the following inscription :—

"DULCE ET DECORUM EST PRO PATRIA MORI."
IN PIAM MEMORIAM
HUJUS SCHOLÆ ALUMNORUM
QUI UT OLIM PUERI INTER STUDIA LUDOSQUE
ÆMULI FUERANT
SIC JUVENES CONTRA BARBAROS PRO ARIS ET FOCIS
ALIUS ALIO FORTIUS
PUGNANTES
MORTEM OPPETIVERUNT
HOC MONUMENTUM
ICTI DESIDERIO CONDISCIPULI MAGISTRIQUE
HIC ERIGENDUM CURAVERUNT.
R. H. ERSKINE, N.C., APUD "BUSHMAN'S PASS,"
PRID: NON: NOV., MDCCCLXXIII.

J. P. ARCHBELL, N.N.C.
J. A. BLAIKIE, N.C.
H. W. DAVIS, N.C.
F. G. DOYLE, L.H.   APUD "ISANDHLWANA,"
F. J. D. SCOTT, N.C.   XI. KAL. FEB.,
G. T. MACLEROY, N.C.   MDCCCLXXIX.
G. J. P. SHEPSTONE, N.N.C.

C. A. POTTER, W.N.C., APUD "HLOBANE," V. KAL.
APRIL, MDCCCLXXIX.
J. FERREIRA, C.D., APUD "KAMBULA," IV. KAL.
APRIL, MDCCCLXXIX.
C. MEARS, APUD "SECOCOENI," FINES IV. KAL.
DEC., MDCCCLXXIX.

PIETERMARITZBURGII, MENSE JANUARIO,
MDCCCLXXXII.

We may add that the inscription was written by Mr. Clark, Headmaster of the School, and the tablet has been erected by Messrs. Jesse Smith & Son.

Appendix 2 - Memoriam Tablet Maritzburg

140   *The Story of an African City.*

The following brief sketch of the lives of those referred to in the foregoing function will be of interest :—

ROBERT HENRY ERSKINE,

son of the Honourable Major Erskine, for many years Colonial Secretary of the Colony of Natal, was born in India on the 26th July, 1846. He was one of the foundation boys

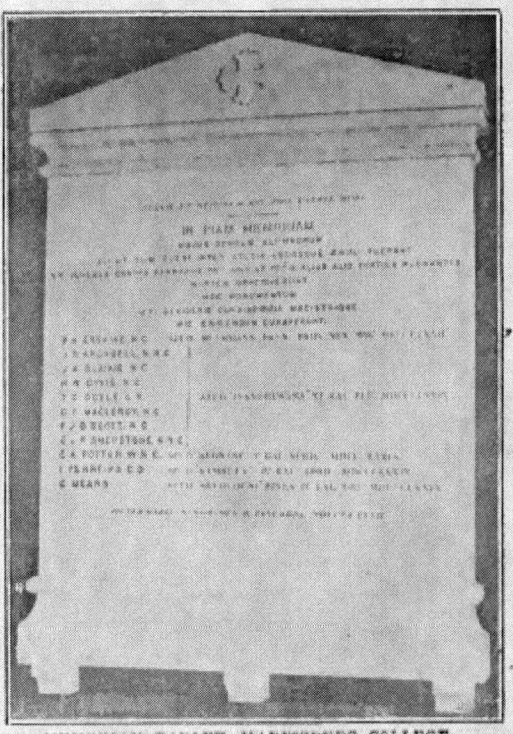

MEMORIAM TABLET, MARITZBURG COLLEGE.

of the High School, Pietermaritzburg, where he won for himself the esteem of his fellow-scholars. After leaving school, he became Private Secretary to His Excellency R. W. Keate, Esq., Lieutenant-Governor of the Colony, and was subsequently admitted as an Advocate of the Supreme

Appendix 2 - Memoriam Tablet Maritzburg

The Story of an African City.

Court. He joined the Natal Carbineers, in which corps he served as a trooper, meeting his death on the 4th November, 1873, at the age of 27, at Bushman's Pass, when one wing of that corp was exposed to the fire of the escaping Amahlubi, in what is known as the Langalibalele expedition.

JAMES PHILIP ARCHBELL

was born on the 13th October, 1853, at Pietermaritzburg. He studied at the High School during the years 1863 and 1864, and twice obtained the Good-Fellowship Prize by the vote of his school-fellows. After leaving school, he first became a clerk in Pietermaritzburg, and subsequently engaged in agricultural pursuits. He volunteered as a non-commissioned officer in the Natal Native Contingent, raised for the defence of the Colony during the Zulu war. As Colour-Sergeant of the 1st Native Contingent, he fell at Isandhlwana, 22nd January, 1879.

JAMES ADRIAN BLAIKIE

was born at Aberdeen, Scotland, on 2nd March, 1859. He entered the High School, June, 1869, remaining until December, 1872, when he had risen to a high position in the school. He then went to Fettes' College, Edinburgh. Returning again to the Colony, he first entered the Civil Service, and then a solicitor's office, where he was long remembered for his remarkable intelligence. During this time he joined the Natal Carbineers as a trooper, and lost his life on 22nd January, 1879, on the field of Isandhlwana. His remains were identified as amongst those who fell surrounding their leader.

HARRY WILLIAM DAVIS,

son of Mr. Peter Davis, one of the oldest colonists of Natal, was born at Pietermaritzburg on the 26th November, 1859. He was at the High School for five years, from 1873 to Christmas, 1877. When he left he had attained the position

Appendix 2 - Memoriam Tablet Maritzburg

of third in the First Class. He entered a merchant's office in this City, and became a trooper in the Natal Carbineers, falling at Isandhlwana on 22nd January, 1879. With Blaikie, his body was found close to that of the noble Durnford.

THOMAS GERALD DOYLE,

son of Mr. P. Doyle, was born on the 22nd March, 1859, and studied at the High School during 1871 and 1872, when he was in the Second Division. After leaving school he entered a solicitor's office in Pietermaritzburg, and subsequently went to Kokstadt, where he gained a very good name. At a later date he entered the service of the Railway contractors. He became a Conductor in Lonsdale's Horse, and was killed at Isandhlwana on 22nd January, 1879. His body was found by his father near those of Captain Bradstreet, (B.B.G.), Lieutenant Hitchcock, and S. Grant. They had evidently made a stand together, and fallen fighting. Four months later his remains were interred by his father.

GEORGE THOMSON MACLEROY,

son of the late Mr George Macleroy, for many years General Manager of the Natal Bank, was born at Pietermaritzburg on the 7th November, 1856, and entered the High School about the year 1867 He remained at the school for six years, occupying, when he left, a prominent position in the Upper Room. During this period he won for himself many friends, and on more than one occasion was awarded the Good-Fellowship Prize by them. He was greatly esteemed for his kind and genial disposition, and will long be remembered for his wit and humour; as a caricaturist, also, he was much appreciated. On leaving school he entered into commercial life, and by close attention to duty gave promise of a successful future. Shortly before the Zulu War he joined the Natal Carbineers, and, like so many of his comrades, did not survive the action at Isandhlwana, 22nd January, 1879. At a subsequent date his remains were removed to the City cemetery by his sorrowing parents.

FREDERICK JOHN DURRANT SCOTT,

son of Mr. D. B. Scott, one of the early settlers in the Colony, was born at Pietermaritzburg on the 19th April, 1851. He was a foundation boy of the High School, and continued there until 1866, when he occupied the second place in the school, and then left to finish his education at Godolphin School, Hammersmith. There he not only passed through his curriculum with much credit, but distinguished himself in athletic exercises—in 1868 winning a medal as the best athlete in the school, and in the same year the average bat. In after years he maintained this character, and was ever distinguished for his prowess in sports. Returning to the Colony, he first filled the position of a clerk in a merchant's office, and subsequently became a partner in the firm of Messrs. Mason & Scott. He joined the Natal Carbineers in 1874, and rose to the rank of second Lieutenant. He marched to the front in December, 1878, and was in command on the 22nd January, 1879, when he fell at Isandhlwana by the side of Colonel Durnford. He left behind him the name of a brave Volunteer, esteemed and beloved by his men.

GEORGE JOHN PALMER SHEPSTONE,

son of Sir Theophilus Shepstone, K.C.M.G., was born at Pietermaritzburg on the 11th June, 1849. After studying at the High School, he went to Capetown to finish his education. On his return he successively held the appointments of Secretary to the Chief Justice and Registrar of the Supreme Court, and thereafter was admitted as an Advocate. Subsequently he entered into commercial life, and became a partner of the firm of Messrs. Henderson & Co.

He joined the Natal Native Horse raised at the commencement of the Zulu War, and became Staff Officer of the late Colonel Durnford, with the rank of Captain On the 22nd January, 1879, the Natal Native Horse were hurried up to support the camp at Isandhlwana. No record remains of the circumstances under which he met his death. Of a friendly disposition, and universally popular, he was deeply lamented by a large number of friends and companions.

CHARLES ALFRED POTTER

was born on the Berea, Durban, on the 29th July, 1853, and entered the High School in August, 1864, remaining until June, 1868. He passed through most of the classes of the school, and each year carried off prizes, the last being December, 1867, when he was head boy of the Second Class. The reports of his attendance showed that he valued his privileges, as the records remaining show that he was never late nor absent for the period to which they refer. Genial, kind, and benevolent, he was beloved by all his companions. On leaving school he went into the Transvaal trading with his father, and was also occupied part of his time as a book-keeper. When the Zulu War commenced he joined Major-General Wood's First Native Contingent, under Major Leet, which followed the General to Kambula. He was Interpreter and Guide to Colonel Rowland's Column, on the Amaswazi border, and was selected on several occasions as special messenger to the Swazi King. He had before been repeatedly employed by the Transvaal Government as confidential messenger to Cetywayo. On the 28th March, 1879, he left Kambula Camp with Major-General Wood, and was amongst the ill-fated on the Hlobane Hill who could not make good their escape. He was on several occasions mentioned in despatches, and was referred to by name by Sir E. Wood in his public speeches on his return to England. Wherever he moved he sustained the character of an upright

Appendix 2 - Memoriam Tablet Maritzburg

The Story of an African City. 145

gentleman, kind and courageous, beloved by his comrades in arms.

IGNATIUS FERREIRA

(familiarly known as Jonkey), son of Mr. Philip Ferreira, a pioneer in the Colony of Natal, was born at Pietermaritzburg on the 8th February, 1850. He was several years at the High School, where he became known as one always to the front in athletic sports and manly exercises. After leaving school he entered the Master of the Supreme Court's Office, remaining there for two years; afterwards he assisted his father in the business of auctioneer. Whilst living in Maritzburg he joined the Natal Carbineers, of which Corps he continued to be a member till he left the City for the Diamond Fields, where he lived several years. On the commencement of the Zulu War he went to the front as a civilian, in the capacity of Contractor's Agent, and there accepted a special temporary appointment, and attached himself to the Commissariat Department. He took part in the gallant defence of Kambula on the 29th March, 1879, when the camp was attacked by the full strength of the Zulu army, and at the close of the day was found amongst the dead.

CHARLES MEARS

was one of the first boys who attended the High School. On leaving he went to live in the Transvaal, and fell in the service of the Republic at the storming of Mathebi's Kop (Secocoeni Campaign) in the year 1878.

The Council of Education, immediately after its formation in 1878, took steps for complying with the law regarding the establishment of two Model Schools in Pietermaritzburg, one for boys and one for girls. These were termed model schools, because it was intended that they should train pupil teachers, and employ only the most modern methods of instruction.

Appendix 3 - Colonial Troops Zulu War

APPENDIX D.

Volunteer and other Corps called out during the Zulu War of 1879.

Names.	Raised.	Disbanded.	Men.	Horses.	Remarks.
Alexandra Mounted Rifles	Nov., 1878	Aug., 1879	20	27	At first employed with No. 1 Column; afterwards with the IInd Division.
Buffalo-Border Guard	Ditto	July, 1879	38	38	At first with No. 3 Column; afterwards in Natal.
Durban Mounted Rifles	Ditto	Ditto	64	72	At first with No. 1 Column; afterwards with the 1st Division.
Natal Carabineers	Ditto	Aug., 1879	25	35	At first with No. 3 Column; afterwards in Natal.
Natal Hussars	Ditto	July, 1879	38	46	At first with No. 1 Column; afterwards with the 1st Division.
Natal Mounted Police	Ditto	Sept., 1879	80	83	At first with No. 3 Column; afterwards in Natal; a portion joined Col. Baker Russell's Column.
Newcastle Mounted Rifles	Ditto	July, 1879	16	16	At first with No. 3 Column.
Stanger Mounted Rifles	Ditto	Ditto	40	40	No. 1 Column and 1st Division.
Victoria Mounted Rifles	Ditto	Ditto	51	51	No. 1 Column and 1st Division.
Amangwani Scouts	April, 1879	Aug., 1879	37		Attached to Cavalry.
Amatonga (or Amabonu)	Feb. and Mar., 1879	Ditto	71	71	Attached to 17th Lancers.
Baker's Horse		Ditto	236	224	Served with Wood's Flying Column.
Border Horse [Weatherley's]	Ditto		61	108	" "
Burgher Force [Piet Uys']			45		With General Wood. Not regularly engaged.
Dunn's Scouts	Jan., 1879		244		Served with 1st Division.
Fereira's Horse		Sept., 1879	115	114	Raised by Colonial Government; served with Wood's Column.

Appendix 3 - Colonial Troops Zulu War

Unit	Raised	Disbanded	Strength	(col)	Remarks
Frontier Light Horse	1877	...	216	278	With General Wood's Column; afterwards to Baker Russell's Column; name changed to Natal Light Horse.
Jantzi's Native Horse	Feb. and Mar., 1879	Sept., 1879	68	83	At first with No. 2 Column; then with the 1st Division; afterwards with Clarke's Column.
Kaffrarian Rifles [Schermbrucker]	Feb., 1879	June, 1879	42	42	With General Wood.
Lonsdale's Mounted Rifles	Feb. and Mar., 1879	Aug. and Sept., 1879.	236	234	Raised principally at Cape Town; served with 1st Division; afterwards with Clarke's Column (two troops), and with Baker Russell's Column (one troop).
Mafunzi's Mounted Natives	Ditto	Sept., 1879	73	80	With 1st Division and Clarke's Column.
Natal Horse, No. 1 Troop [de Burgh]	Feb., 1879	Ditto	48	55	Composed of N.C.O.'s of 3rd N.N.C.; with 1st Division and Clarke's Column.
" No. 2 Troop [Cooke]	Ditto	July, 1879	50	18	Composed of N.C.O.'s of 3rd N.N.C.; with 1st Division.
" No. 3 Troop [Bettington]	Ditto	Oct., 1879	60	67	Composed of N.C.O.'s of 3rd N.N.C.; with IInd Division.
Natal Light Horse	Mar., 1879	Ditto	138	161	Originally a troop of Frontier Light Horse; served with Baker Russell's Column.
Natal Native Horse [Cochrane]	Feb. and Mar., 1879	July, 1879	129	159	At first with No. 2 Column; afterwards with Wood's Column.
Natal Native Pioneers, No. 1 Company [Nolan.]	Nov. and Dec., 1878	Oct., 1879	80	...	Served with No. 3 Column; afterwards with Wood's Column.
" No. 2 Company [Beddoes.]	Ditto	Ditto	104	...	Served with No. 1 Column.
" No. 3 Company [Allen.]	Ditto	Ditto	89	...	Served with No. 2 Column.
Native Zulu Carriers	July, 1879	Sept., 1879	2,000	...	Carried stores between Port Durnford and St. Paul's.
Shepstone's Native Horse	Feb. and Mar., 1879	Ditto	180	212	Served with IInd Division and Baker Russell's Column.
Transvaal Rangers [Raaf's]	April, 1879	...	138	168	Served with Wood's Flying Column; afterwards with Baker Russell's Column.
Wood's Irregulars	Dec., 1878	July, 1879	400	10	With Wood's Column.

Appendix 3 - Colonial Troops Zulu War

Original Title.		Commanding Officer.	New Title.	Commanding Officer.	Raised.	Disbanded.	Strength.	Remarks.
1st Regt. Colonel Durnford	1st Batt.	Comdt. Montgomery	1st Batt.	Comdt. Montgomery	Nov. and Dec., 1878	Sept., 1879	960	Remained at Krans Kop; a detachment was at Isandhlwana.
	2nd Batt.	Major Bengough	2nd Batt.	Major Bengough	Ditto	Ditto	1,066	Served with the IInd Division; three companies left in posts on line of advance, remainder went on to Ulundi.
	3rd Batt.	Captain Cherry	3rd Batt.	Captain Cherry	Ditto	Ditto	879	Remained at Kraus Kop.
2nd Regt. Major Graves	1st Batt.	Major Graves	4th Batt.	Captain Barton	Ditto	Ditto	1,134	Served with No. 1 Column; 1st Division and Clarke's Column.
	2nd Batt.	Comdt. Nettleton	5th Batt.	Comdt. Nettleton	Ditto	Ditto	887	Served with No. 1 Column and 1st Division; afterwards at Forts Crealock and Chelmsford, and Port Durnford.
3rd Regt. Comdt. Lonsdale	1st Batt.	Comdt. Brown	...	...	Ditto	...	...	These two battalions served with No. 3 Column, but after Isandlwana they ceased to exist. The European N.C.O.'s formed the Natal Horse.
	2nd Batt.	Comdt. Cooper	...	...	Ditto	...	...	

NOTE.—When these troops were first raised, 10 per cent. of the rank and file were armed with fire-arms. Afterwards they were armed nearly entirely with fire-arms, the 4th Battalion receiving Martini-Henrys, and the 3rd Battalion Sniders and muzzle-loaders.

Frontier light Horse

The Frontier Light Horse had earned a reputation for hard riding and tough fighting raised by Lieutenant F.Carrington of the 2nd/24th Regiment at Kingwilliamstown, Cape Colony, in 1877, it was eventually commanded by Major Redvers Buller.

During September and October, 1878 the Regiment saw service against Sekukuni, and in November returned to Natal. Its strength in the Zulu War was 216. On 28 March, 1879, the unit, acted as a rearguard during the disastrous withdrawal from Hlobane Mountain. Following the disaster at Isandlwana the Zulus had increased their fire power by adding many hundreds of breech-loading rifles and ammunition to their arsenal.

British casualties numbered 17 officers and 82 enl sted men killed, along with some 100 irregular and native troops.. The Regiment's Commanding Officer in the column, Captain Robert Barton of the Coldstream Guards, was also killed, and was succeeded by Captain Cecil D'Arcy.

There had been no shortage of bravery on either side. Five Victoria Crosses were awarded for extraordinary valor at Hlobane--to Browne, Buller, Fowler, Leet and Lysons--as well as five Distinguished Conduct Medals. For their role in the day's victory, the young bachelor zulu warriors added personal honors to those already won at Isandlwana--and with them, the eligibility to marry, if they survived the war.

Two members of the Frontier Light Horse, Captain D'Arcy and Sergeant Edmund O'Toole were awarded the Victoria Cross for their acts of valour in endeavouring to save the lives of soldiers during the reconnaissance made before the Battle of Ulundi on 3 July 1879

Appendix 4 - Casualty Roll 9th April to 3rd May 1878

NOMINAL RETURN OF KILLED AND WOUNDED from 9th April to 3rd May 1878.

Corps.	Regimental No.	Rank and Name.	Killed.	Wounded. Dangerously.	Wounded. Severely.	Wounded. Slightly.	Remarks.
Ayliff's Fingos	–	Fingo Body	–	1	–	–	Gun shot, left leg, bone splintered; gone home.
			11th April, at Peri.				
Davis's Fingos	–	Fingo Sondaga, B.	–	–	1	–	Gun shot near ankle joint.
			11th April, at Buffalo Point.				
Frontier Light Horse	–	Trooper Smith, H.	–	1	–	–	Gun shot, left arm, bone much splintered; amputation.
			11th April, at Izedingi.				
2/24th	–	Captain Glennie, F.	–	1	–	–	Gun shots, 2, thigh (accidental).
			20th April, at				
90th Light Infantry	–	Captain Stevens, T.J.	–	1	–	–	Gun shot, left upper jaw.
90th Light Infantry	–	Lieut. Saltmarshe, A.	1	–	–	–	Gun shots, 2, chest.
90th Light Infantry	2,003	Corporal Hillier, W. H.	–	1	–	–	Gun shots, 2, shoulder, penetrating chest.
90th Light Infantry	1,071	Private Silvester, H.	1	–	–	–	Gun shot, penetrating left chest (accidental).

NOMINAL RETURN OF KILLED AND WOUNDED.

Corps.	Regimental No.	Rank and Name.	Killed.	Wounded. Dangerously.	Wounded. Severely.	Wounded. Slightly.	Remarks.
D. F. Horse	–	Trooper Bamberg	–	–	–	Slightly	At Debe Neck, 5th April 1878. Assegai wound, right thigh.
Ayliff's Fingo Levies.	–	Lieut. Webster	Yes	–	–	–	At Ioda Induda, 6th April. Gunshot of head.
	–	Fingo Tekesi	–	Yes	–	–	Gunshot of arm and abdomen, since dead.
	–	Fingo Unanzaniso	–	Yes	–	–	Gunshot of abdomen.
	–	Fingo Nobanizma	–	Yes	–	–	Gunshot of shoulder.
	–	Fingo Jadezelo	–	Yes	–	–	Gunshot of leg.
	–	Fingo Somsom	–	–	Yes	–	Gunshot of arm.
	–	Fingo Stofill	–	Yes	–	–	Gunshot of chest.
	–	Fingo Evondana	–	Yes	–	–	Gunshot of back and arm.
	–	Fingo Gomive	–	–	Yes	–	Assegai wound of hip.
	–	Fingo Kupiso	–	Yes	–	–	Gunshot wound of neck.
	–	Fingo Mbenya	–	–	Yes	–	Gunshot wound of arm.
	–	Fingo Zuzura	–	–	Yes	–	Assegai wound of back.
	–	Fingo Togi	–	Yes	–	–	Gunshot wound of abdomen.
2/24th	102	Private Collins, J.	Yes	–	–	–	At Bailie's Grave, 8th April. Gunshot wound of head.
George volunteers.	–	Lieut. Belling	–	–	Yes	–	Gunshot wound of shoulder and arm.
Stutterheim.	–	....	–	–	–	–	No medical report received.

Appendix 4 - Casualty Roll 9th April to 3rd May 1878

Corps.	Regimental No.	Rank and Name.	Killed.	Wounded. Dangerously.	Wounded. Severely.	Wounded. Slightly.	Remarks.
90th Light Infantry	1,231	Private Pallett	1	–	–	–	Gun shot, penetrating left chest.
90th Light Infantry	1,185	Private Cramb, H.	–	–	–	1	Gun shots, 2, chest and left hand.
90th Light Infantry	907	Private Sloney, J.	–	1	–	–	Gun shot, left chest and left arm; since dead.
90th Light Infantry	188	Private Flaherty, P.	–	–	1	–	Gun shot, left elbow joint.
90th Light Infantry	728	Private Ryan, P.	–	–	–	–	Gun shot, left temple.
30th April, at Taba Ka'Udoda.							
Alexander Maclean's Fingos.	–	Fingo Silvana	–	–	–	1	Assegai wound of leg.
	–	Fingo Utuka	–	–	–	1	Assegai wound of buttock.
	–	Fingo Madosal	–	1	–	–	Gun shot penetrating chest; since dead.
	–	Fingo Murray	–	–	–	1	Gun shot, right leg.
	–	Fingo Celana	–	–	1	–	Assegai wound, left knee.
	–	Fingo Antooka	–	–	1	–	Assegai wound, left hip.
2nd May.							
Commandant Von Linsingen.	–	Fingo Sergt.; name unknown	1	–	–	–	Reported by Commandants, nature of wounds therefore not known.
	–	Fingo; name unknown	1	–	–	–	
	–	Fingo; name unknown		*One wounded.			
Siwani's Kafirs	–	Fingo; names unknown	2		1	–	
	–	Fingo; names unknown		*Two wounded.			
2nd May.							
Capt. Develing's Alice Fingos.	–	Names unknown	–	–	–	4	Reported by Commandant, nature of wounds not known.
	–	Names unknown	–	–	–	4	
	–	Names unknown	–	–	1	–	
		Total	8	7	4	13	

* And 3 natives of wounds unknown at present.

The Deputy Adjutant-General,   (Signed) J. A. WOOLFRYES,
King William's Town.   Deputy Surgeon-General, P.M.O.

F. COLONIAL and IMPERIAL TROOPS.

Losses known to have been inflicted on the Rebels between 9th April and 3rd May 1878.		List of Killed and Wounded between 9th and 3rd May 1878.							
		Killed.			Wounded.				
					Severely.			Slightly.	
		Officers.	Men.	Natives.	Officers.	Men.	Natives.	Officers.	Men.	Natives.
Killed	302									
Wounded	40									
Prisoners	9									
Approximate number of women surrendered	500	1	2	5	2	4*	8†	–	2	11
Cattle taken (about)	240									
Sheep	300									
Horses	10									

*Two since dead.
†Since dead

Appendix 4 - Casualty Roll 9th April to 3rd May 1878

RETURN OF KILLED AND WOUNDED.

Regiment.	No.	Rank and Name.	Killed.	Wounded. Dangerously.	Wounded. Severely.	Wounded. Slightly.	Remarks.
	At Peri Bush, on 8th May 1878.
Frontier Light Horse.	–	Captain Macnaghten	1	–	–	–	Gun shot wound; chest.
Frontier Light Horse.	–	Captain Whalley	–	–	–	1	Contused wound; abdomen.
Frontier Light Horse.	–	Corporal McCabe	1	–	–	–	Gun shot wound; head.
Frontier Light Horse.	–	Private Davis	1	–	–	–	Gun shot wound; head.
Frontier Light Horse.	–	Private Gilbert	–	1	–	–	Gun shot wound; chest.
Wodehouse Contingent.	–	Private Klassen	1	–	–	–	Gun shot wound; abdomen.
Wodehouse Contingent.	–	Private Johnson	–	1	–	–	Gun shot wound; left arm shoulder joint.
Wodehouse Contingent.	–	Private France	1	–	–	–	
Lonsdale's Fingos	–	Private Tapité	–	–	1	–	Gun shot wound; upper jaw.
Lonsdale's Fingos	–	Private Mountewa	1	–	–	–	Gun shot wound; head.
	At Mount Kempt, 9th May 1878.
2/24th Regiment	–	Captain Austen	–	–	–	1	Gun shot wound; back.
	At Tab Indoda, 12th May 1878.
Lonsdale's Fingos	–	Hendrick	–	1	–	–	Gun shot wound; thigh; fracture of femur.
Lonsdale's Fingos	–	Quaba Manego	–	–	1	–	Gun shot wound; leg; fracture of tibea.
Lonsdale's Fingos	–	Quebeso	–	–	1	–	Gun shot wound; back.
		Total	6	3	3	2	

The Deputy Adjutant-General,   (Signed) J. A. WOOLFRYES,
King William's Town,   Deputy Surgeon-General.
May 14, 1878.

Losses known to have been inflicted on the Rebels between 7th May and 12th May 1878.			List of Killed and Wounded between 7th and 12th May 1878.						
Killed 138			colspan="3"	Killed.	colspan="6"	Wounded.
Prisoners 3									
Approximate number of women and children surrendered ... 118			Officers.	Men.	Natives.	colspan="3"	Dangerously or Severely.	colspan="3"	Slightly.
Cattle taken 8			1	4	1	Officers.	Men.	Natives.	Officers.	Men.	Natives.
						–	2	–	2	1	5

One horse killed and two wounded.

Appendix 5 - Medals Awards to the 24th Foot

Medals awarded to the 24th Foot

The following pages contain information on the award of medals to the 24th foot, this has been an interest of mine since I started collecting medals over 40 years ago. Watching the trends over the years you find the same medals do re-surface from time to time. But it is still quite amazing how rare these medals really are, they do not come up for sale very often.

I include past Auction medal prices, which show the price trends and help to prove the provenance. Unfortunately the early catalogues in my collection show few details of the ordinary soldier, and just group the medals together. For example a pre war Glendining's auction catalogue "Lot 34 - two medals to the 1/24 foot and another 2/24th all fine." Only officers were named. This trend was put in reverse by the publication of The Gazette produced by John Hayward in October 1966. The Gazette gave details of the awards including biographical and service details of the medal recipients. The very first Gazette contained as its main item the Zulu Victoria Cross pair to Private Thomas Flawn, Connaught Rangers for the action on the 28th November 1979 at Sekukuni's Town which was offered at £865.

Some years later the actor Stanley Baker, who played Chard in the film Zulu, successfully bid at Auction for Chard's medal, which sold for £2700 with John Hayward as the under bidder. At the time a record braking price for any VC. John's business was to close in June 1979. He his now employed as the Executive Consultant in the Medal Department at Spink.

Together with the award of campaign medals The Zulu War saw the award of twenty-three Victoria Crosses and 15 Distinguished Conduct Medals. The defence of Rorke's Drift on the evening of the Isandlwana disaster was marked by the award of no less than 11 Victoria Crosses and 5 Distinguished Conduct Medals, an all-time record for a single action. A premium is normally associated with medals to the 24th, quite often this is not justified, the majority of the 24th foot with the 1879 clasp or no clasp medals, did not arrived in Natal until after the Isandhlwana and Rorke's Drift events of the 22-23rd January 1879. The 1st Battalion was part of the second invasion, but were stationed in forts built for supply and communications purposes. And the 2nd Battalion remained in Natal. The majority of soldiers saw no action.

During the first invasion the 2nd Battalion if not being annulated at Isandhlwana were part of Chelmsford's reconnaissance. A safe bet is to purchase a medal with the 1877-8-9 clasp, but always check the service papers and muster rolls.

The 1st Battalion of the 24th foot were awarded a total of 1404 medals, while the 2nd Battalion were awarded 1331 of which 290 medals had no clasp. Many no clasp medals sell for over £500 which makes little sense when they did not fire a shot in anger.

	1877-8	1877-8-9	1878	1878-9	1879	no clasp	total
1st Battalion	157	526	1	24	663	33	1404
2nd Battalion	55	823			163	290	1331

Chelmsford's 1st Invasion of Zululand in January 1879 consisted in the main of two battalions of the 24th Regiment, the 1st battalion composed of battle-hardened troops involved in earlier campaigns in the Eastern Cape whilst the 2nd consisted of less experienced men, also one Royal Artillery battery of 7-pound guns and a poorly equipped Natal Native Contingent. By the 23rd of January, after disaster struck, all that was left of the 1st battalion were the three companies in Natal. The medal collector is faced with a problem in trying to establish the participation of an individual in a particular action, and will in most cases require research, unless the recipient is mentioned in a casualty roll, a reference in a letter or diary, Regimental histories, Press reports, and memorials can sometimes be the only clue.

Bandsman G. Conboy 24th Foot,
Spink Auction Sale 4020 Lot 332 30th November 2004
The 'Isandhlwana' Cornet Used by Bandsman G. Conboy 24th Foot, recovered from the Battlefield
A brass Cornet, numbered '19405' made by 'F. Besson', Brevetee, 188 Euston Road, London', engraved 'Found at Isandhlwana, Farrier Sgt. J. Dorricott K.D.G. 13th June 1879', additionally engraved in a different hand 'Found whilst burying the dead. Presented at Rorkes Drift to E. Conboy by the Commd. Officer of 24th Regt. it being the instrument his brother (G. Conboy) used who was killed at Isandhlwana.', an emotive artefact in relatively good condition considering the find spot.
Estimate £ 500-1,000

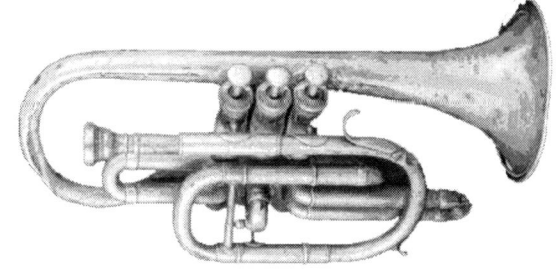

1-24/1424 Private George Conboy was killed in action at Isandhlwana 22.1.1879 and his effects including his South Africa Medal with clasp 1879 were claimed by his father.

A small number of musical instruments belonging to members of the Band of the 1st Battalion 24th Foot recovered from Isandhlwana, are displayed in the South Wales Borderers Museum, Brecon.

The Isandhlwana Cornet Used by Bandsman G. Conboy 24th Foot, recovered from the Battlefield. PRA brass Cornet, numbered 19405

Appendix 5 - Medal Awards, 24th Foot

Summary of Medals - awarded to the 24th shown in date order

	Name	Rank	Clasp	Regiment	Comments	Date	Price
	T Carmody	Pte	1877-8	1/24th Foot	Glendinings Lot 228 Fine	9-12 June 1913	
	H Mulhaney	Pte	1877-8-9	2/24th Foot	Glendinings Lot 228 Fine	9-12 June 1913	
	M.Macdonald	Pte	1879	1/24th Foot	Glendinings Lot 228 Fine	9-12 June 1913	
	E Fitzgerald		1877-8-9	1/24th Foot	Glendinings Lot 229 Fine	9-12 June 1913	
	G Scales	Pte	1879	2/24th Foot	Glendinings Lot 229 Fine	9-12 June 1913	
	A.A.Morshead	Lieut.	1877-8-9	1/24th Foot	Baldwin & Sons sales List V F	July 1948	£1.17s 6d
	Burnaby	Pte	1877-8-9	1/24th Foot	Baldwin & Sons sales List F	July 1948	10s 6d
	W. Richards	Pte	1877-8-9	1/24th Foot	Baldwin & Sons sales List E. F	July 1948	15s
	Mussen	Pte	No Clasp	2/24th Foot	Baldwin & Sons sales List E.F	July 1948	8s 6d
	Etheridge	Pte	1877-8-9	2/24th Foot	Baldwin & Sons sales List E F	July 1948	15s
	P. Harris	Pte	1877-8-9	2/24th Foot	Baldwin & Sons sales List V.F	July 1948	12s 6d
	Sears	Pte	1877-8-9	2/24th Foot	Baldwin & Sons sales List V.F	July 1948	12s 6d
	J. Gorman	Pte	1879	2/24th Foot	Baldwin & Sons sales List V.F	July 1948	12s 6d
	M. Fannion	Pte	1879	2/24th Foot	Baldwin & Sons sales List V.F	July 1948	12s 6d
	Fannion	Pte	1879	1/24th Foot	Baldwin & Sons sales List V.F	July 1955	£1.2s 6d
	J Manley	Pte	1879	1/24th Foot	Baldwin & Sons sales List V.F	July 1955	£1.2s 6d
	J Gorman	Pte	1879	1/24th Foot	Baldwin & Sons sales List Mint	July 1955	£1.7s 6d
	T.James	Pte	1877-8-9	2/24th Foot	Baldwin & Sons sales List V.F	July 1955	£1.2s 6d
	W. Richards	Pte	1877-8-9	2/24th Foot	Baldwin & Sons sales List V.F	July 1955	£1.2s 6d
	J.McNulty	Drum	1877-8-9	2/24th Foot	Baldwin & Sons sales List V.F	July 1955	£1.2s 6d
	J.Golding	Cpl	1877-8-9	2/24th Foot	Sothebys lot 164 GEF	05/03/1980	(£150-180)
	J Preece	Pte	1879	1/24th	Sotherbys lot 69 renamed	02/07/1980	
	W. Thompson		No Clasp	2/24th Foot	Glendinings Lot 43 VF	18/03/1981	
	T. Parry		No Clasp	2/24th Foot	Glendinings Lot 43 EF	18/03/1981	
220	J.Jones	Pte	1879	1/24th Foot	Wallis & Wallis Lot 12 GVF	10/03/1981	£140
	P.Regan		1877-8		Sothebys Lot 130 GVF	6/05/1982	£190
	J.Hurford		1877-8-9	2/24th Foot	Sothebys Lot 130 GVF	6/05/1982	£230
	W.W Lloyd	Lieut.	1879	1/24th Foot	Glendinings Lot 52 VF	05/03/1986	£520 Note 1
1332	C.Lacey	Pte	1877-8-9	2/24th Foot	Glendinings Lot 60 VF	26/11/1986	£210 Note 2
	A. Cole	Pte	1879	1/24th Foot	Spinks Medal Supplement	1987	Sold
728	T.Spiller	Pte	1877-8-9	2/24th Foot	Glendinings Lot 91 VF	04/03/1987	£190
351	W. Evans	Pte	1877-8-9	2/24th Foot	Glendinings Lot 359 VF toned	02/03/1989	(£100-120)
2158	J. McNulty	Drum.	1877-8-9	2/24th Foot	Glendinings Lot 360 AEF	02/03/1989	(£110-130)
1461	T.Bennett	Pte	1877-8-9	2/24th Foot	Glendinings Lot 120 NEF	28/03/1990	(£100-150)
284	W.McNulty	Pte	1877-8	1/24th Foot	Glendinings Lot 255 NVF	28/03/1990	(£120-180)
2161	J. McGlyn	Pte	1879	1/24th Foot	Glendinings Lot 602 VF	20/06/1991	
1126	G.W. Moss	Pte	1877-8-9	2/24th Foot	Glendining's Lot 260 F	16/09/1991	(£120-180)
	W.Sykes	Lce	1877-8-9	2/24th Foot	DNW Lot 166 NVF	06/05/1992	£300
	W. Lindsay	Pte	No Clasp	2/24th Foot	Glendinings Lot 324 EF	27/05/1992	£180
	J.Pritchard	Pte	1877-8-9	1/24th Foot	Glendinings Lot 329 EF	27/05/1992	£250 Note 3
1071	R.Mead	Pte	1877-8-9	2/24th Foot	Glendinings Lot 169 VF	24/06/1992	(£120-180)
1073	R.Taylor	Pte	1877-8-9	2/24th Foot	Glendinings Lot 170 VF	24/06/1992	
	J Burns	Pte	1877-8	1/24th Foot	Glendinings Lot 211 VF	23/06/1993	£250
	J George	Pte	1879	1/24th Foot	Glendinings Lot 641 VF	27/06/1994	
	H.Naylor	Cpl	1877-8-9	1/24tn Foot	DNW Lot 160 VF	08/12/1994	£280
	W.Alls	Pte	1877-8	1/24th Foot	Glendining's Lot 101 GVF	5/07/1995	(£150-180)
	S.Hall	Pte	1877-8	1/24th Foot	Glendining's Lot 101 VF edge knock	5/07/1995	(£140-180)
	G.Mitchell	Pte	1877-8	1/24th Foot	Glendining's Lot 108 GVF died in service	26/03/1998	(£240-280)
	T.Richards	Sergt	1877-8	1/24th Foot	DNW Lot 583 EF	09/12/1999	£380
	E.Barnaby	Pte	1877-8	1/24th Foot	DNW Lot 437 GVF	04/04/2001	£270 Note 4.
	G. Grindy	Pte	1877-8	1/24th Foot	DNW Lot 127 NEF	04/12/2001	£420 Note 5
374	J. Flaherty,	Pte	1877-8	1/24th Foot	DNW Lot 287 EF	27/06/2002	£460 Note 6
847	W. Taylor,	Cr Sergt	1877-8-9	2/24th Foot	DNW Lot 295 VF	27/06/2002	£880 Note 7
1785	W. Alls	Pte	1877-8	1/24th Foot	Dixons No 36 NEF	Winter2003/4	£800 Note 8
2055	T.Henry	Sergt	1877-8-9	2/24th Foot	Spink Lot 68 (2 medals)	30/04/2004	£1500 Note 9
647	J Dodiread	Pte	1877-8	1/24th Foot	DNW Lot 730 NEF	17/09/2004	£650 Note 10

Appendix 5 - Medal Awards, 24th Foot

Summary of Medals - awarded to the 24th shown in date order

	Name	Rank	Clasp	Regiment	Comments	Date	Price	Page
1785	W. Alls	Pte	1877-8	1/24th Foot	Dixons No 36 NEF	Winter 2003/4	£800	Note 11
303	T. Askew	Pte	1877-8-9	1/24th Foot	Spink Lot 369 EF	21/07/2005	£980	
486	W.Steventon	Pte	1877-8-9	2/24th Foot	Dixons claw tightened AVF	Autumn 2005	£685	
1848	J.McLean	Pte	1879	1/24th Foot	Spink Lot 314 GVF	24/12/2005	£680	
1836	R.Kernick	Pte	1879	1/24th Foot	Bosleys (with 32nd Regt)	1309/2006	£650	
1508	F.Sherwood	Pte	1877-8-9	2/24th Foot	Spink Lot 1144 GVF	19/07/2007	£1100	
2796	W.H Strudwick	Pte	No Clasp	2/24th Foot	Wellington Postal Auctions NEF	April 2008	(575-650)	Note 12
1011	D.Griffith	Pte	1877-8-9	2/24th Foot	Spink Lot 559 AEF	23/07/2009	£850	Note 13
831	J.L Bradley	Pte	1877-8	2/24th Foot	Spink Lot 242 AEF	23/07/2009	£800	Note 14
1535	M O'Connell	Pte	1877-8-9	2/24th Foot	Bill Friar Medals VF	Dec 2009	£1125	Note 15
2744	C.Moore	Pte	no bar	2/24th Foot	Dixons	Dec 2009	£450	Note 16
	M.Sullivan	Pte	1877-8-9	2/24th Foot	Historik Orders	Nov 2009	$2675 Sold	
1848	J.McLean	Pte	1879	1/24th Foot	Historik Orders GVF	Dec 2009	$2500	
1688	R.Green	Pte	1879	2/24th Foot	Historik Orders VF	Dec 2009	$2400	
1117	A.A.Bonner	Corpl.	1877-8-9	2/24th Foot	Historik Orders VF	Dec 2009	$2500	
1788	T.Williams	Pte	1879	1/24th Foot	Historik Medals GVF	Dec 2009	$2500	
	G.Doyle	Drum.	1877-8-9	1/24th Foot	Historik Medals GVF	Dec 2009	$2950	

Note 1 one bar, 1879 (Lieut. W. W. Lloyd, 1-24th Foot). Very fine. Mentioned in "The Road to Isandlwana" by Philip Gon. Many of his drawings appeared in the Illustrated London News. He was military illustrator of some note. Photo included of his work with lot.

Note 2 Private Charles Lacey, no 1332, 25th Brigade. Born in the parish of St Paul's, Greenwich, Kent. Enlisted 2.3.1877, aged 20 years and 7 months at Wolverhampton. By trade a Tinman. He could not write his own name which is shown by his attestation papers. In confinement, 28.6.1879 for being drunk on duty. Tried and sentenced to 35 lashes. Discharged at Brecon 6.3.1889, having completed 12 years service. Conduct given as indifferent. service at Home and Abroad:- England 3rd Mar 1877 to 31st Jan. 1878. South Africa, 1st Feb. 1878 to 12th Jan 1880. Meditterranean, 13th Jan 1880 to 11th Aug 1880. India 12th Aug. 1880 to 27th May 1883 (wounded 2.9.1880) Home 28th May 1883 to 6th Mar. 1889. Entitled to South African Medal and clasp.

Note 3 J.Pritchard Medal Minor edge bruising and pawnbroker's mark lightly scratched into obverse field, otherwise better than very fine

Note 4 South Africa 1877-79, 1 clasp, 1877-8-9 (489 Pte. E. Barnaby, 1/24th Foot) naming engraved in a slightly later style, lacquered, otherwise good very fine. Edward Barnaby enlisted at Oswestry, Shropshire, on 24 November 1874, aged 19 years 7 months. He transferred to Army Reserve prior to November 1880. Another medal named to this recipient in the collection of the regimental museum at Brecon.

Note 5 Died of disease in South Africa during 1878

Note 6 Two edge bruises,John Flaherty enlisted Burnley, Lancashire,13 /07/1874, aged 20. Transferred to the 1st Class Army Reserve in 1880. The same medal also sold on the 23 Sep 2005 for £350.

Note 7 William Taylor was promoted to Colour Sergeant on 23 October 1878. He lost his kit at Isandhlwana, he himself having left with Lord Chelmsford's Force before the fatal Zulu attack. Discharged sometime in 1880 also received the L.S. & G.C. medal in December 1880.

Note 8 William Alls i Continued service with the rank of Cpl. in the South Wales Borderers from 1.7.1881. Discharged 29.10.1882.

Note 9 India Genral Service 1854-1895, one clasp, Burma 1885-7 (2055 Pte. T. Henry 2nd Bn. S. Wales Bord.); South Africa 1877-79, one clasp, 1877-8-9 (Sergt.), nearly extremely fine (2) Estimate £ 700-800 Sold for £1500
Sergeant Thomas Henry deserted at Pietermaritzburg, Natal, 24.8.1878; rejoined two days later; confined 11.1.1879, tried two days later, and reduced to Private; Sergeant Henry appeared to have a drink problem.

Note 10 William Dodiread (medal roll gives initial as J.) was born at Warminster, Wiltshire. He enlisted at Monmouth on 7 January 1876, aged 20 years, his trade at the time being given as a labourer. He died of disease on 19 April 1878, and his name is commemorated on a memorial at St Pauls' Churchyard, Komgha, Eastern Cape.Same medal also sold DNW on 19th Sep 2003 Lot 608 for £720.

Note 11 William Alls is confirmed on the medal roll of the 1/24th Foot for the S.A.War medal with clasp 1877-8. Continued service with the rank of Cpl. in the South Wales Borderers from 1.7.1881. Discharged 29.10.1882.

Note 12 South Africa Medal 1877-79, no clasp, named to 2796 Private W.H. Strudwick, 2-24th Foot. Confirmed on roll as no clasp medal. With service details imprisoned by civil power. 17-12-1879. NEF Estimate £575-650

Note 13 South Africa 1877-79, one clasp, 1877-8-9 (1011. Pte. D. Griffith. 2-24th. Foot.), about extremely fine
1011 Private David Griffith, born Llanally, Breconshire, 1850; enlisted December 1876; served in South Africa, February 1878- February 1880; in India, August 1880- January 1883; transferred to the Reserve March 1883, Discharged 25.01.1889.Sold for £850

Note 14 South Africa 1877-79, one clasp, 1877-8 (831. Pte. J.L. Bradley. 2/24th Foot.), remnants of lacquer, small test mark to edge at 11 o'clock, good very fine 831 Private John L. Bradley served with the 2nd Battalion 24th Foot in South Africa and died of disease at Pieter-maritzburg, 14.8.1878. Published transcription of roll records South Africa Medal with 1877-8 clasp as being issued for recipient and being returned to the Mint, 17.9.1885. The medal was subsequently re-issued, probably to the next of kin.Sold for £800

Note 15 Faint pawnbrokers mark on obverse.

Note 16 Private C. Moore, Enlisted Norwich 24.8.1876. 1/ 9th Foot. Norfolk Regiment. 1877 joined the 104th Foot. Joined the 2/24th Foot in Natal from 104th Foot, 17.7.1879. Gib. January- August 1180. India October 1880 – January 1883
Sold with photocopy Pay Lists and roll page, confirming medal with no clasps.

Appendix 6 - Medal Awards, Killed in Action Isandhlwana

Summary of Medals - Killed in Action at Isandhlwana medals shown in date order

	Name	Rank	Clasp	Regiment	Comments	Date	Price
	J. Bray	Private	1877-8-9	1/24th Foot	A.H Baldwin Medal list	July 1948 Mint	£1.15s
	W.E Mostyn	Captain	1878-9	1/24th Foot	Glendining's	14 Dec 1951	£12.10s
718	J. Broderick	Private	1879	1/24th Foot	J.B Hayward & Son	June 1972	£120
446	F. Dunn	Private	1877-8-9	1/24th Foot	J.B Hayward & Son	June 1972	£125
677	G. Hadden	Private	1877-8-9	1/24th Foot	J.B Hayward & Son	June 1972	£125
1444	W. Hough,	Private	1877-8-9	1/24th Foot	J.B Hayward & Son	June 1972	£150
350	E. Jones,	Private	1877-8-9	1/24th Foot	J.B Hayward & Son	June 1972	£125
87	J.R Pickard	Private	1877-8-9	1/24th Foot	J.B Hayward & Son	June 1972	£120
504	J Rittman	Private	1877-8-9	1/24th Foot	J.B Hayward & Son	June 1972	£125
34	T. Thornett	Private	1877-8-9	1/24th Foot	J.B Hayward & Son	June 1972	£125
642	J. Whelan	Private	1877-8-9	1/24th Foot	J.B Hayward & Son	June 1972	£125
	Glennie	Captain	1877-8-9	2/24th Foot	Sotheby's	5 Mar 1980	
	Moor	Sergeant	1879	Natal Md Police	Glendining's	30 June 1982	
87	J.R. Pickard	Private	1879	1/24th Foot	Glendining's	25 Nov. 1987	Unsold
320	W. Brown	Private	1879	1/24th Foot	Glendining's	28 Sep 1988	
285	T. Walsh,	Private	1877-8-9	1/24th Foot	Christies	22 Nov 1988	
34	T. Thornett	Private	1877-8-9	1/24th Foot	Christies	22 Nov 1988	
536	E. Ivatts,	Private	1877-8-9	1/24th Foot	Glendining's	7 Dec 1988	£800
	W. Russell	Sergeant	1877-8-9	1st Btn.Nat.Congt	Glendining's	28 Mar 1990	
550	W. Dobbs	Private	1877-8-9	1/24th Foot	DNW Auction	12 June 1991	£1,000
1627	R. Fryher	Private	1879	1/24th Foot	Glendining's	16 Sep. 1991	
1634	T. Young	Private	1877-8-9	1/24th Foot	Christie's	21 Oct 1991	£1,078
216	J. Costellon	Sergt.	1877-8-9	R. A.	DNW Auction	4 Dec 1991	£3,000
722	C. Connolly	Private	1877-8-9	1/24th Foot	DNW Auction	4 Dec 1991	£950
895	H. Slade	Private	1877-8-9	2/24th Foot	DNW Auction	28 July 1993	£1,100
1444	W. Hough,	Private	1877-8-9	1/24th Foot	DNW Auction (sold 06.72)	1 Dec 1993	£1,380
954	J. Carkson	Sergeant	1877-8-9	1/24th Foot	Glendining's	5 July 1995	
1758	D. Martin,	Private	1877-8-9	1/24th Foot	DNW Auction	25 Feb 1998	£1,700
668	T. Harrison	Gunner	1877-8-9	N/5 Royal Artillery	Dixons	Spring 1999	£2,400
299	W. Johnson,	Private	1877-8-9	1/24th Foot	DNW Auction	9 Dec 1999	£3,500
1763	T. Nash	Bombardier	1877-8-9	Royal Artillery	Dixons	Summer 2000	£2,650
718	J. Broderick,	Private	1879	1/24th Foot)	DNW Auction (sold 06.72)	15 Dec 2000	£2,300
692	W. Rice	Private	1877-8-9	2/24th Foot	DNW Auction	4 April 2001	£1,950
293	J. H. Meredith	Private	1877-8-9.	1/24th Foot	DNW Auction	4 July 2001	£2,600
341	W. Jones	Private	1877-8-9	1/24th Foot	DNW Auction	4 July 2001	£3,300
193	R. Williams	Corporal	1879	1/24th Foot	Dixons	Winter 2000/01	£2,800
1906	T. Newberry	Private	1879	1/24th Foot	Dixons	Winter 2000/01	see below
1928	H. Newberry	Private	1879	1/24th Foot	Dixons (Pair sold together)	Winter 2000/01	£5,600
428	J. Jones	Private	1877-8-9	1/24th Foot	DNW Auction	28 March 2002	£3,600
1459	T. Harkin	Private	1877-8-9	1/24th Foot	DNW Auction	27 June 2002	£3,500
185	J. Duffy,	Private	1877-8-9	1/24th Foot	DNW Auction	27 June 2002	£2,900
147	T. Boswell	Ag Bombr	1877-8-9	Royal Artillery	Spinks	5 Dec 2002	£3,300
841	R. Whinham	Farr Sert	1877-8-9	Royal Artillery	Spinks	5 Dec 2002	£3,400
1491	D. Gordon	Private	1877-8-9	2/24th Foot	Bonhams	17 Dec 2002	
1673	J. Horn,	Private	1877-8-9	1/24th Foot	DNW Auction	2 July 2003	£3,700
1777	H.F. Bullard	Bandmaster	1879	2/24th Foot	Dixons	Summer 2004	£6,500
521	C. Lovell	Private	1879	1/24th Foot	Spink Auction	30 Nov 2004	£4,500
1654	T. Young,	Private	1877-8-9	1/24th Foot	DNW Auction	17 Sep 2004	£5,800
	T. L. G. Griffith,	Sub. Liet.	1877-79	2/24th Foot	DNW Auction	1 Dec 2004	£13,000
535	G. Griffiths,	Private	1877-8-9	1/24th Foot	DNW Auction	1 Dec 2004	£4,000
642	J. Whelan,	Private	1877-8-9	1/24th Foot	DNW Auction	23 June 2005	£5,500
521	C. Lovell,	Private	1879	1/24th Foot	DNW Auction (sold 30.11.04)	23 June 2005	£5,500
1881	J. Edwards	Sergeant	1877-8-9	1/24th Foot	Bosley's Auction	September 2005	£8,200
285	T. Walsh,	Private	1877-8-9.	1/24th Foot	DNW Auction (sold 22.11.88)	23 Sep 2005	£4,200
1465	G. Johnston	Private	1877-8-9	1/24th Foot.	Dixons	Autumn 2005	£6,000
360	J. Jones,	Private	1879	1/24th Foot	DNW Auction	7 Dec 2005	£4,500

Appendix 6 - Medal Awards, Killed in Action Isandhlwana

Summary of Medals - Killed in Action at Isandhlwana medals shown in date order

	Name	Rank	Clasp	Regiment	Comments	Date	Price
536	E. Ivatts,	Private	1877-8-9	1/24th Foot	DNW Auction (sold 7.12.88)	7 Dec 2005	£7,000
114	S. Stansfield	Private	1877-8-9.	1/24th Foot.	Dixons	Spring 2006	£4,950
93	R. Williams	Corpl.	1879	1/24th Foot	DNW Auction	March 2007	£7,800
1097	A. Jones	Private	1877-8	2/24th Foot	Warwick & Warwick (clasp?)	9 May 2007	£4,000
722	C. Connolly,	Private	1879	1/24th Foot	DNW Auction (sold 4.12..91)	27 June 2007	£4,200
	W.H.J. Barnes	Trooper	1879	Newcastle M.R	Spink Auction	19 July 2007	£2,400
1047	E. Smith	Private	1879	1/24th Foot	Wellington Auctions	January 2008	£7,000
797	J. Prosser	Private	1877-8-9	1/24th Foot	Wellington Auctions(Late issue)	April 2008	£2,800
235	W. Dredge	Private	1877-8-9	1/24th Foot	DNW Auction	17 Sep 2009	£5,500
1857.	J. Hind.	Private	1877-8-9	1/24th. Foot	Historik	October 2009	$9,995 (US)
285	T. Walsh	Private	1877-8-9	1/24th Foot	Dixons	December 2009	£6,950

Short Summary of the involvement of the 24th in the South African Campaigns

In January 1875 the 1st Battalion of the 24th Regiment of Foot (The Warwickshire Regiment) landed at Cape Town.
From early 1877 the 1st Battalion had been involved in campaigns against the Gaikas and the Galekas in the Eastern Cape. Hence the clasps 1877-8 and 1877-8-9. When the hostilities ceased, orders where received at King William's Town that five companies of the 1st Battalion 24th Foot, were to move into Natal at the same time reinforcements were requested from England. Leaving one company at Durban, the other seven marched to Pietermaritzburg where they arrived on the 6th August.
Fort Napier a prominent structure south-west of Pietermaritzburg overlooking the city, was to become the home of the Regiment for the next three months, with intense training, half lived in tents, and the other half occupying the barracks inside the Fort.
Early in November the regiment. marched to Greytown and then advanced to Helpmaker. An ultimatum had been sent to Cetewayo, which demanded, virtually, the breaking up of the Zulu army. No answer came from the Zulu king.
The 2nd Battalion arrived in 1878, they received the incorrect clasp on their medals 1877-8-9 instead of 1878-9. The second battalion of the 24th Regiment arrived at Helpmakaar on the 31st December 1878

From Private Ellis (son of Mr. Thomas Ellis, 1 Cross Keys Court, Caernarvon) to his father and family

1st Battalion 24th Regiment,
Helpmakaar, Cape Colony,
31 December, 1878.

..........The second battalion of the 24th Regiment arrived here about 4 o'clock on Sunday afternoon. They came from Grey Town and the first battalion welcomed them by treating them to tea and bread and meat. There are also here three companies of the Cape mounted police and many volunteers ...

(Extract from North Wales Express, 21 February 1879.)

On the 7th January 1879 they marched to Rorke's Drift then on the 11th crossed into Zululand with the remainder of the ill fated 3rd Column. Lieut Bromhead and one company of the 2nd Battalion were left behind at Rorke's Drift to defend the post and the line of communications. Three companies of the 1st Battalion were left behind two at Helpmakaar and one on the south coast of Natal.
After the disaster at Isandhlwana on the 22nd the battalion lost 5 officers and 173 men., with just six survivors from the 1st Battalion. The majority of the 2nd Battalion survived because they had the good fortune to accompany Lord Chelmsford on his advance, on the very day the camp was annulated. After suffering considerable hardships they were not permitted to join the advance, but were scattered along the border to protect the lines of communication. Later they were employed in completing the burial of the dead at Isandhlwana. The two companies of the 1st Battalion moved from Helpmekaar to Dundee, and were joined by 15 officers and 526 men sent from England, to make good the 1st Battalion losses. The remaining four companies of the 2nd Battalion were garrisoned at Fort Melvill. The 1st Battalion took part in the final assault on Ulundi. The majority of the men that have the 1879 clasp or no-clasp medals arrived in Natal after the 23rd January. The 1st Battalion had 663 1879 awarded clasps and the 2nd 163 clasps. The battallion eventually embarked for Gibraltar in January 1880.
The premium asked for medals to the 24th has to be put in context. It can be argued that the vast majority of men with the 1879 clasp belonging to the 2nd Battalion saw no action.
Together with the no-clasp medals which were reinforcements arriving after January 1879. It is vital to do your research before you purchase a medal with such a high premium, reference to the soldier's service papers and muster rolls held at the National Archives are a must.

Appendix 6 - Medal Awards, Killed in Action Isandhlwana

Appendix 6 - Medal Awards, Killed in Action Isandhlwana

J.B Hayward & Son, Medal Sales Catalogue June 1972, a collection of KIA South African Medals for sale.
The recipients of the following nine medals were killed in action at Isandhlwana.

S.A 49	Clasp "1879"	718 Pte J **(Jeremiah) Broderick**	E.F	£120
S.A 50	Clasp "1877-8-9"	446 Pte F **(Francis) Dunn** Enlisted at Portsmouth 25.6.61	E.F	£125
S.A 51	Clasp "1877-8-9"	677 Pte **G (George) Hadden**	E.F	£125
S.A.52	Clasp "1877-8-9"	1444 Pte **W. (William) Hough** (Colonel Glyn's cook)		

The following is an extract from the statement of 139 Pte John Williams 1/24th Foot who survived Isandhlwana. "While there was very heavy firing on the left and left centre. I myself and Private Hough, the Colonel's cook, went to the left beyond the General's tents where we were joined by three of the General's servants and began to fire from the left of No 5 Coy, 1/24th Regt - we fired 40 or 50 rounds and the native contingent fell back on the camp and one of their officer's pointed out to me that the enemy were entering the right of the camp. We then went to the right - No 5 Coy still holding its position and fired away the remainder of our ammunition"   EF   £150

S.A.53	Clasp "1877-8-9"	350 Pte **E. (Evan) Jones**. Enlisted at Monmouth on 6.7.74 aged 19 years 9 months. Served in "H" Coy	EF	£125
S.A 54	Clasp "1879"	87 Pte **J.R(Jabez R.) Pickard**. Enlisted at Ashdon on 17.3.74 aged 22 years Served in "H" Coy	E.F	£120
S.A.55	Clasp "1877-8-9"	504 Pte **J. (John) Rittman**.	E.F	£125
S.A 56	Clasp "1877-8-9"	34 Pte **T. (Thomas) Thornett**.	E.F	£125
S.A 57	Clasp "1877-8-9"	642 Pte **J. (John) Whelan**	E.F	£125

Glendining's 2nd March 1988 Lot 142 One bar, 1879 (87 Pte.J.R.Pickard, 1/24th Foot) ribbon fitted with ornately engraved pin brooch. Nearly extremely fine, estimate (£800-1,000) Killed in action Isandhlwana.

South Wales Borderers Museum Collection
The medals are named to the following all killed at Isandhlwana:

1/24th
Lt Col. H.B.Pulleine. (centre)
Pte 628 Joseph Brown
Pte 749 James Coleman
Sgt 1313 Thomas Cooper
Pte 290 Thomas Cox
Drmr 1786 George Dibden
Pte 438 Thomas Duck,
(shown as 2/24th)
Pte 66 Thomas Egan
Pte 403 George Henry Fay
Pte 131 Robert Leach
Pte 147 Frederick Sharp
Pte 161 Patrick Sutton
Pte 1753 William Theobald

2/24th
Pte 1272 Samuel Hacker
Drmr 2153 John Holmes

The Royal Regiment of Wales was formed in 1969 by the amalgamation of two of Wales' most distinguished regiments, namely The South Wales Borderers (24th Foot) and The Welch Regiment (41st/69th Foot). The South Wales Borderers distinguished themselves in many campaigns. Perhaps best remembered, for the tragic Isandhlwana and the glorious Rorke's Drift in the Anglo-Zulu war of 1879.
The museum contains many pictures and paintings, drums, assegais, ammunition, buttons, badges, medals and uniforms which all combine to form a vivid image of life as a Victorian soldier.
One of the the main attractions in the museum is the Zulu War Room. The exploits of the 24th Regiment during the 1879 Anglo-Zulu War are legendary. Queen Victoria referred to her gallant soldiers as 'The Noble 24th'. The Zulu War Room tells the compelling story of the defence of Rorke's Drift by B Company, second battalion of the 24th in the Zulu war of 1879. And contains a fascinating display of artefacts. All brought to life in Sir Stanley Bakers 1964 film Zulu.

Appendix 6 - Medal Awards, Killed in Action Isandhlwana

Sotheby's Auction Lot 163, 5th March 1980
SOUTH AFRICA 1877-9, 1 clasp, 1877-8-9 (Capt. F. Glennie 2-24th foot), Good Very Fine. recipient (later brevet Colonel) served in the Kaffir War, 1877-78, and was present at the engagement of Taba Ka Udoda where he was dangerously wounded; also served in the Zulu War of 1879..Estimate £300-350 List of prices realised not available.

Glendining's, Auction Lot 82, 30 June 1982
SOUTH AFRICA 1877-9, 1 clasp, 1879 (Sergt. Moor Natal Md Police), Very Fine. K.I.A. Sergt. G.Moor Natal M.P. Attchd, N.N.C, Killed Isandhlwana 22nd January 1879, only 110 men in entire Regt. 26 killed at Isandhlwana. See book "Washing of the Spears" D. Morris. Roll I.E Sgt Moor was attached to the 2nd Bn., 3rd Regt. N.N.C.. List of prices realised not available.

Glendining's, Auction Lot 94, 25 November 1987
SOUTH AFRICA 1877-9, 1 clasp, 1879 (87 **Pte. J.R Pickard**, 1/24th Foot), Ribbon fitted with ornately engraved pin brooch. Nearly extremely fine. Killed at Isandhlwana. Estimate £1000-£1200. Same withdrawn or unsold. Probably too high a reserve.

Glendining's, Auction Lot 94, 28 September 1988
SOUTH AFRICA 1877-9, 1 clasp, 1879 (320 Pte W. Brown, 1/24th Foot), Nearly extremely fine. Killed at Isandhlwana. Estimate £800-£1000.

Christie's London, Auction Lot 32, 22 November 1988
SOUTH AFRICA 1877-9, 1 clasp, 1877-8-9 (34 **Pte. T.Thornett**, 1/24th Foot), good very fine
Private. T.Thornett was killed in action at Isandhlwana on 22 January, 1879. Estimate £900-£1000

Glendining's, Auction Lot 256, 28 March 1990
SOUTH AFRICA 1877-9, 1 clasp, 1877-8-9 (Sergt. **W. Russell,** 1st Btn. Nat. Congt.), Signs of brooch marks on reverse. Nearly very fine (£500-700) Recipient killed in the disaster at Isandhlwana.

Dix Noonan Webb, Auction Lot 33, 12 June 1991
SOUTH AFRICA 1877-9, 1 clasp, 1877-8-9 (550 **Pte. W. Dobbs**, 1/24th Foot), small edge bruise, othe wise good very fine
Private William Dobbs was killed in action at Isandhlwana on 22 January, 1879. He attested for the 24th Foot at Monmouth on 1 February, 1875, aged 21 years. His effects were claimed by his mother, brothers and sisters.

Glendining's, Auction Lot 176, 16 September 1991
SOUTH AFRICA 1877-9, 1 clasp, 1879 (1627 Pte **R.Fryher** 1/24th Foot), Slight edge bruising but better than very fine. (£150-200) Sold with the medal is a statement that Fryher was an Isandhlwana casualty as verified by Lt. Col. Jarman, S.W.B. Regt Museum; this is not however confirmed by either Forsyth's or Tavender's rolls.

Christie's, Auction Lot 50, 21 October 1991
SOUTH AFRICA 1877-9, 1 clasp, 1877-8-9 (1634 **Pte. T. Young**, 1/24th Foot), extremely fine. Sold for £1078
Private Thomas Young was killed in action at Isandhlwana on 22 January, 1879.

Dix Noonan Webb, Auction Lot 37, 4 December 1991
SOUTH AFRICA 1877-9, 1 clasp, 1879 (722 Pte. **C. Connolly,** 1/24th Foot), official correction to 'Foot,' light surface scratching, otherwise very fine Private Cornelius Connolly was killed in action at Isandhlwana on 22 January 1879, as also was his brother 199 John Connolly. Born in 1854, he enlisted at Brecon on 22 January, 1876, and left England almost immediately with the lst/24th Foot for service in Africa where he arrived on 15 May 1876. Hammer Price £950
Same medal Sold again Lot 238, 27 June 2007 DNW Auction, Hammer Price £4200.

Dix Noonan Webb, Auction 28 July 1993
SOUTH AFRICA 1877-79, 1 clasp, 1877-8-9 (895 **Pte. H. Slade**, 2/24th Foot) some light surface marks but generally good very fine and a scarce casually to the 2nd Battalion 895 Private Henry Slade was killed in action at Isandhlwana on 22 January, 1879. He had served in 'D' company, 2nd Bn. 24th Foot and his medal was issued to his next of kin on 29 August, 1882. Hammer Price £1,100

Appendix 6 - Medal Awards, Killed in Action Isandhlwana

Dix Noonan Webb, Auction Lot 53, 1 December 1993
SOUTH AFRICA 1877-79, 1 clasp, 1877-8-9 (1444 Pte. **W. Hough,** 1/24th Foot) nearly extremely fine
Private William Hough was Colonel Glyn's Cook and was killed in action at the battle of Isandhlwana. He is mentioned in the account of one of the survivors of the battle, 139 Private John Williams, 1/24th Regiment, Colonel Glyn's Groom: 'Meanwhile there was very heavy firing on the left and left centre. I myself and Private Hough, the Colonel's Cook, went to the left beyond the General's tents where we were joined by three of the General's servants, and began to fire from the left of No. 5 company, 1/24th Regiment. We fired 40 to 50 rounds each when the Native Contingent fell back on the Camp and one of their officers pointed out to me that the enemy were entering the right of the Camp. We then went to the right, No. 5 company still holding their position, and fired away the remainder of our ammunition, the Kaffirs turned the left of No. 5 company by coming over a high rock. The firing at this point still continuing very heavy.' William Hough was born at Manchester and was a striker by trade. He attested at Lichfield on 13 August, 1867, aged 19 years, and served in 'H' company at St. Helena during 1876-77. For further details see 'The Silver Wreath' by Norman Holme..

Glendining's, Auction Lot 103, 15 July 1995
SOUTH AFRICA 1877-9, 1 clasp, 1877-8-9 (954 Sergt. **J. Carkson,** 1/24th Foot), Extremely fine. (£1200-1400) note spelling of surname.
Sergeant **John Clarkson** was killed in action at Isandhlwana, attested 21.4.1864, aged 18 years; promoted Corporal 1873; Sergeant 1874; effects claimed by his father.

Dix Noonan Webb, Auction Lot 123, 25 Febuary 1998
South Africa 1877-79, clasp, 1877-8-9 (1758 **Pte. D. Martin,** 1/24th Foot) attractively toned, extremely fine £1600-1800
David Martin attested on 23 August, 1870, aged 21 years. He re-engaged at King William's Town on 20 September, 1878, and was killed in action at the battle of Isandhlwana on 22 January, 1879. Hammer Price: £1700

Dixon's Gazette, No17 Spring 1999
1 clasp, 1877-8-9. 668 Gunner **T. Harrison,** N/5 Royal Artillery.
The gun detachments of N/5, with the limber gunners running behind, fought their way through the camp, losing fifty men in an attempt to save the guns. 'They paused on the Nek long enough to confer with Coghill about what hope there was of making a stand, and decided it was futile. Major Smith, who was wounded, felt that his first duty was to save the guns.The rock-strewn slope behind the stony kopje was near impossible for any wheeled conveyance; and the spectacle of the big guns in flight acted as an incitement to the warriors behind Isandlwana. Slowed by the broken ground and by stragglers clinging to the traces, the teams were quickly overtaken. Drivers were pulled off their horses and gunners from their seats. The unattended horses, crazed by noise and stab wounds, broke into a wild, headlong gallop that took them to their destruction over the edge of a boulder-strewn ravine. The only survivors were the two independently mounted artillery officers. Gunners and stragglers were hacked to pieces.' From 'The Road to Isandlwana' by Philip Gon. Gunner T. Harrison was killed in action at Isandhlwana on 22 January 1879.   Almost Mint £2400.00

Dix Noonan Webb, Auction Lot 973 15 December 2000
South Africa 1877-79, clasp, 1879 (718 **Pte. J. Broderick,** 1/24th Foot) extremely fine. Hammer Price £2,300
Jeremiah Broderick enlisted at Newport, Monmouthshire, on 13 January 1876, just three days after 716 Robert Jones who went on to win the Victoria Cross at Rorke's Drift. Broderick was posted to the 1st Battalion and was killed in action at Isandhlwana. The South Africa Medal Roll records him as entitled to the clasp dated '1877-8-9', however, the medal was issued in error with the '1879' clasp. Ex Norman Holme collection and sold with a letter from him dated 18 September 1974.

Dix Noonan Webb, Auction Lot 438, 4 April 2001
South Africa 1877-79, 1 clasp, 1877-8-9 (692 **Pte. W. Rice,** 2/24th Foot) clasp and carriage buckled, small edge bruise, otherwise nearly extremely fine. Hammer Price: £1950 Walter Rice enlisted at Newport, Monmouthshire on 1 December 1875, at the age of eighteen. He served in 'G' Company and was killed in action at the Battle of Isandhlwana on 22 January 1879.

Dix Noonan Webb, Auction Lot 437, 4 July 2001
South Africa 1877-79, 1 clasp, 1877-8-9 (293 **Pte. J. H. Meredith,** 1/24th Foot) single edge bruise, otherwise good very fine.
John H. Meredith enlisted at Manchester, Lancashire on 17 June 1874, aged 19 years. He was killed in action at Isandhlwana on 22 January 1879. According to The Noble 24th, by Norman Holme he was entitled to the clasp with date for 1879. Hammer Price: £2600

Dix Noonan Webb, Auction Lot 437, 4 July 2001
South Africa 1877-79, 1 clasp, 1877-8-9 (341 **Pte. W. Jones,** 1/24th Foot) extremely fine. Hammer Price: £3300
William Jones enlisted at Monmouth on 6 July 1874, aged 19 years 9 months. He was killed in action at Isandhlwana on 22 January 1879.

Dixon's Gazette, No 24 Winter 2000/01
1 clasp, 1879. 193 Corporal **R. Williams,** 1/24th Foot. Robert Williams enlisted at Wrexham, Denbighshire 16.5.1874. Killed in action Isandhlwana. Age 19 years 6 months. Effects claimed by his mother, brother and sister. GVF £2800.00

Appendix 6 - Medal Awards, Killed in Action Isandhlwana

Dixon's Gazette, No24 Winter 2000/01
Pair of Medals   1 clasp, 1879, 1906 Private **T. Newberry**, lst/24th Foot.
                                 1 clasp, 1877-8-9, 1928 Private **H. Newberry**, lst/24th Foot.
A very rare family pair to the Newberry brothers who were both killed in action at Isandhlwana 22nd January 1879. Thomas Newberry joined the 25th Brigade Depot when it was formed 1873. Posted to 1/24th 15.11.1874. Promoted Corporal 5.7.1876; reduced to Private 24.11.1877. Alfred Newberry joined the 25th Brigade Depot when it was formed 1873. Posted to 1/24th 15.11.1874. The effects of both brothers claimed by their father.   EF £5600

DNW Auction Lot 100, 28 March 2002
South Africa 1877-79, 1 clasp, 1877-8-9 (428 Pte. **J. Jones**, 1/24th Foot) extremely fine. Hammer Price £3600
Private John Jones was killed in action at Isandhlwana on 22 January 1879. He had enlisted at Brecon on 29 August 1874, aged 19 years 6 months, and proceeded to South Africa early in 1875. During his short career he was repeatedly fined and imprisoned for drunkenness. His effects were claimed by his father.

DNW Lot 297, 27 June 2002
South Africa 1877-79, 1 clasp, 1877-8-9 (1459 Pte. **T. Harkin**, 1/24th Foot) some nicks and marks, otherwise better than very fine Hammer Price: £3500
Thomas Harkin was killed in action at Isandhlwana on 22 January 1879. He had attested for the 24th Foot on 29 August 1867, aged 21, and re-engaged at Cape Town on 19 December 1876. His effects were claimed by his father.

DNW Auction Lot 296, 27 June 2002
South Africa 1877-79, 1 clasp, 1877-8-9 (185 Pte. **J. Duffy**, 1/24th Foot) suspension slack, edge bruising and polished, therefore good fine and better £1800-2200
Private John Duffy was killed in action at Isandhlwana on 22 January 1879

Bonhams Auction   17 Dec 2002
South Africa 1877-79, 1 clasp, 1877-8-9 (1491 Pte D.Gordon 2/24th) Extremely fine. Band Boy Gordon, attested December 1877 aged 13 and was probably the youngest casualty at Isandhlwana. Sold with an article from Seaby's Bulletin July 1978.

DNW Lot 318, 2 July 2003
South Africa 1877-79, 1 clasp, 1877-8-9 (1673 Pte. **J. Horn**, 1/24th Foot) good very fine. Hammer Price £3700
John Horn enlisted in the 24th Foot in Preston District in June 1869, aged 18 years. He subsequently served with the regiment on Malta from 1870-72, in Gibraltar from 1872-74, in Cape Town from 1875-76, on St. Helena from 1876-77, and thereafter back in South Africa, where he was killed in action at Isandhlwana on 22 January 1879. His effects were recorded for claim by his next of kin.

Dixon's Gazette, No 38 Summer 2004
1777 Bandmaster **H.F. Bullard**, 2/24th Foot. 1 clasp, 1879, suspension claw refixed.
Ex Watts Collection March 1964. Bandmaster Bullard is listed in the Silver Wreath as 'Staff. Harry T. Ballard was K.I.A. at Isandhlwana on 22nd January 1879, his effects were claimed by his mother-in-law. NEF £6500.00
Comment with the medal when purchased by Dixon's: Norman Holmes credits Bullard with the '1877-8-9' clasp in The Noble 24th and given the above medal's refixed suspension claw, it seems more likely a member of the late Bandmaster's family at sometime exchanged this with the single-dated '1879' clasp to commemorate the actual year of his death. anomalies like this, some of which were in there boxes of issue. NEF £6500.00 Same medal sold by DNW Lot No75 16th December 2003 Hammer price £4400

Spink Sale Sale 4020 Lot 331. 30 November 2004
South Africa 1877-79, one clasp, 1879 (521. **Pte. C. Lovell**). Hammer Price £4500
25B/521 **Private Charles Lovell** enlisted 18.12.1874 1st Battalion 24th Foot, aged 18 years; killed in action at Isandhlwana 22.1.1879. Same medal sold again Lot 117 23 June 2005 DNW 'Effects recorded for claim by next of kin' (The Noble 24th refers). He had enlisted at Northampton in December 1874, aged 18 years. Hammer Price £5,500

DNW Lot 318, 17 September 2004
South Africa 1877-79, 1 clasp, 1877-8-9 (1654 Pte. **T. Young**, 1/24th Foot) some minor marks, otherwise nearly extremely fine Hammer Price £5800
1654 Private Thomas Young, 1st Battalion, 24th Foot, was killed in action at Isandhlwana on 22 January 1879.

DNW Lot 448, 1 December 2004
South Africa 1877-79, 1 clasp, 1877-8-9 (535 Pte. **G. Griffiths**, 1/24th Foot) fitted with silver ribbon brooch, extremely fine £4000-4500
George Griffiths enlisted at Brecon on 21 December 1874, aged 21 years. He was killed in action at Isandhlwana on 22 January 1879, his effects being claimed by his mother, brothers and sister.

Appendix 6 - Medal Awards, Killed in Action Isandhlwana

DNW Lot 117, 23 June 2005
South Africa 1877-79, 1 clasp, 1877-8-9 (642 Pte. **J. Whelan**, 1/24th Foot) extremely fine Private John Whelan was killed in action at Isandhlwana on 22 January 1879. He had attested at Brecon on 24 September 1875, aged 23 years.

Bosley's Auction September 2005.
1879 medal Sgt **John Edwards** 24th Foot who was killed at Isandhlwana. It is described as being a pristine example complemented by the Royal mint packet and box of issue the latter with ink written details and contained in the forwarding registered envelope it is the first time it has been put up for sale. £8,200

DNW Lot 526, 23 September 2005
South Africa 1877-79, 1 clasp, 1877-8-9 (285 **Pte. T. Walsh**, 1/24th Foot) fitted with silver ribbon brooch, two edge bruises, otherwise good very fine Hammer Price: £4200 Thomas Walsh enlisted at Manchester on 15 June 1875, aged 19 years. He served with the 1st Battalion, 24th Foot, and was killed in action at Isandhlwana on 22 January 1879. His effects were claimed by his mother and sister. Same medal sold Christies 22 November 1988 Lot 33 Estimate £800 -£1000

Dixon's Gazette, No 43 Autumn 2005
1 clasp, 1877-8-9. 1465 Private **G. Johnston**, 1/24th Foot. George Johnston was posted to Service Companies 27/4/1868. Promoted Corporal, date unknown; returned to Private 26/1/1874. K.I.A. at The Battle of Isandhlwana. 21.1.1879. No trace of claim for effects. Sold with photocopy page from the casualty roll in the publication The Nobel 24th and copy SA 1879 medal roll page. First time on the market. NEF £6000.00

DNW Lot 573, 7 December 2005
South Africa 1877-79, 1 clasp, 1879 (360 Pte. **J. Jones**, 1/24th Foot) nearly extremely fine. Hammer Price £4500
25B/360 Private John Jones, 1st Battalion, 24th Foot, had enlisted at Cardiff on 8 July 1874, aged 24 years. He was killed in action at Isandhlwana, 22 January 1879. His effects were claimed by his brothers.

DNW Lot 570, 7 December 2005
South Africa 1877-79, 1 clasp, 1877-8-9 (536 **Pte. E. Ivatts**, 1/24th Foot) nearly extremely fine.   Hammer Price £7000
Ernest Ivatts was killed in action at Isandhlwana on 22 January 1879. He enlisted at Abergavenny, Monmouthshire in December 1874, aged 18 years, and served in South Africa from the summer of 1875 until his death - 'Effects recorded for claim by next of kin' (The Noble 24th refers). Also sold at Glendining's 7 December 1988 for £800.

Dixon's Gazette, No 45 Spring 2006
1 clasp, 1877-8-9. 114 Private **S. Stansfield**, 1/24th Foot. Verified on roll for medal and clasp as Drummer. Initial 'S' rubbed. Pte Stansfield enlisted in Manchester 6.4.1874 aged 18 years 11 months. He was K.I.A. at Isandhlwana 22 January 1879. The medal roll lists his initial as 'S' but Holmes (The Noble 24th' p.241) records Stansfield with Christian name Michael. Sold with photocopy roll page confirming K.I.A.. VF £4950.00

DNW Lot 570, 7 March 2007
South Africa 1877-79, 1 clasp, 1879 (193 Corpl. **R. Williams**, 1/24th Foot) minor marks, nearly extremely fine Hammer Price: £7800
Corporal Robert Williams was K.I.A at Isandhlwana. Enlisted at Wrexham, Denbighshire, on 16 May 1874, aged 19 years 6months.

Warwich & Warwick Auction 9th May 2007.
1 clasp, 1879. (1097 Pte A. Jones 2/24th Foot) Extremely fine. Pte Abraham Jones was killed in action on 22nd January 1879 at Isandhlwana while serving with Lt Pope's G Company, the only Company of the 2/24th present at the battle. 176 members of the 2/24th were killed. He enlisted at Pontypool on 20th January 1877 his effects were claimed by his family. Medal roll states clasp 1877-8-9.

Spink Sale 7022 Lot 1362. 19 July 2007
The Isandhlwana Casualty Zulu War Medal to Trooper W.H.J. Barnes, Newcastle Mounted Rifles.
South Africa 1877-79, one clasp, 1879 (Tpr. W.H.J. Barnes. Newcastle M.R.), officially impressed in medium sans-serif capitals, extremely fine. Hammer Price £2400 **Trooper W.H.J. Barnes** was killed in action at the Battle of Isandhlwana, 22.1.1879

Wellington Auctions January 2008 Postal Auction South Africa General Service Medal 1877-79 - bar '1879', named to 1047 Private Edwin Smith,1/24th.Foot Edwin Smith- Attested 14 January 1877. Killed in action Isandhlwana 22 January 1879,
Effects claimed by next of kin. Sold with verification, Original ribbon toned Extremely fine Sold for £7000

Wellington Auctions April 2008 Postal Auction Lot No 60. South Africa Medal 1877-79, with bar 1877-8-9, named to 797 Private J. Prosser, 1/24th Foot. A late issue medal on a slightly smaller flange. Enlisted at Monmouth, 23rd March 1876, aged 18 years and 4 months. Effects claimed by his mother and brother. Prosser was Killed at Isandlwana. GVF sold for £2800

Appendix 6 - Medal Awards, Killed in Action Isandhlwana

DNW Lot 584, 9 December 1999 Collection: SOUTH WALES BORDERERS (9 December 1999)
The Zulu War Medal awarded to Private **William Johnson,** 1st Battalion, 24th Foot, one of the few survivors of the massacre at Isandhlwana, later Sergeant-Major and Drill Instructor to 7th T.F. Battalion Liverpool Regiment
South Africa 1877-79, clasp, 1877-8-9 (299 Pte. W. Johnson, 1/24th Foot) extremely fine and very rare Hammer Price: £3500
The statements, held in the Regimental Museum, of the six private soldiers of the 1st Battalion, 24th Regiment, who escaped from the battlefield of Isandhlwana, 22nd January, 1879, were published for the first time in Medal Rolls of the 24th Regiment of Foot, South Wales Borderers by Norman Holme (J. B. Hayward & Son 1971) and subsequently in The Silver Wreath by Norman Holme (Samson Books 1979), to whom acknowledgement is hereby given for that reproduced here. The following is the statement of 299 Private William Johnson, 1/24th Regiment:
'I was one of the Rocket Battery under command of the late Captain Russell, R.A., which was attached to Colonel Durnford's Column. We got to Isandhlwana Camp about 11 a.m. on the 22nd January 1879. We halted there about 10 minutes when Colonel Durnford came down from the Camp of the 1/24th Regiment and gave orders that, as the Zulus were retiring fast, the mounted men should advance up a hill about two and a half miles from Camp, and that the Rocket Battery supported by the Infantry of the Native Contingent should follow in rear of the Mounted Basutos. About two miles out we met a 'vidette' of the Natal Carbineers who reported that the Mounted Basutos were heavily engaged on the opposite side of a hill on our left, at the same time offering to show us a short cut to the place where the engagement was going on. The Captain galloped up the hill and before he returned to us shouted 'Action front'.
While we were getting into action the Zulus kept coming out of a kloof on our left, which the big guns had been shelling from the Camp. We had time to fire our rocket when they came over the hill in masses, and commenced to fire on us. As soon as they opened fire the mules carrying the rockets broke away. The Native Contingent, who were in the rear of us, after firing a few shots ran away. I observed that a great number of them were unable to extract the empty cartridge cases after firing, and offered to do so for some of them but they would not give me their rifles. Before this the horses had broken away and I tried to help Captain Russel from the field, but he was shot before we had gone many paces. I made my escape to a donga held by some of the Police, Mounted Infantry and Carbineers. On my way to this place I met Colonel Durnford and he asked me where my battery was; I told him that the battery was cut up and the Captain shot, when he said you had better go back and fetch him. I then pointed out to him that the enemy had already nearly surrounded us. At this time he was mounted as well as his orderly who had a spare horse, and he retired with a few Basutos towards the left of the Camp. Just below the Camp I met Privates Trainer and Grant with Bombardier Gough, they gave me a horse. We then went up to the Camp and found the Police extended in front of it and they were shortly afterwards driven in. The Camp was now almost completely surrounded and I made for the Buffalo following some of the Police and other mounted men, and crossed it below Rorke's Drift. I afterwards met Major Spalding on the road to Helpmakaar, and turned back and joined the Companies of 1/24th under Major Upcher. We met a lot of natives on the left of the road to the Drift but could not make out what they were for certain.'

DNW Lot 447, 1 December 2004
The South African campaign medal to **Sub-Lieutenant T. L. G. Griffith**, 2nd Battalion, 24th Foot, youngest of the battalion's five officers killed at the battle of Isandhlwana. South Africa 1877-79, 1 clasp, 1877-8-9 (Sub-Lieut. T. L. Griffiths, 2/24th Foot) brilliant extremely fine and very rare. Hammer Price: £13000
Ex Spink auction 28 March 1995 and formerly in the collections of Dr S. Z. Ross and Norman Holme.
Thomas Llewelyn George Griffith was born at Chadlington, Oxfordshire, on 8 October 1857, eldest son of the Reverend **Thomas Llewelyn Griffith**, M.A., of Pen-yNant, near Ruabon, North Wales, and Rector OD Deal, Kent, and Mary Moncrieff, his wife, daughter of **Brevet Major George St Vincent Whitmore**, Royal Engineers. He was educated at Marlborough College and at the Priory at Croydon, passing his Army examination as well as those at Sandhurst and Edinburgh, where for a period he was attached to the 78th Highlanders. On 14th August 1877 he was gazetted as a Sub-Lieutenant into the 2nd Battalion, 24th Foot, his commission being antedated to 11 November 1876. He joined the battalion at Chatham in October 1877, and on 1 February 1878 embarked with the regiment for the Cape of Good Hope. In November 1878, he joined the force preparing for the invasion of Zululand, and took part in the subsequent advance into that country, being present at the storming of Sirayo's stronghold in the Bashee Valley, afterwards proceeding to Isandhlwana. On the morning of 22nd January 1879, Griffith left Isandhlwana with the main body of the column under **Lord Chelmsford,** but subsequently rode back on special service with **Major Smith, Captain Gardner** and **Lieutenant Dyer**, to convey the General's orders to advance the camp. Colonel Black, visiting the battlefield five months afterwards, for the purpose of burying the dead, found the bodies of some sixty officers and men lying in a group, giving evidence of their having gathered together and fought desperately to the last. Among them were the remains of **Captain Wardell**, Lieutenant Dyer and a captain and subaltern of the 2-24th, the latter, it is believed, being the body of young Griffith. A memorial lectern in the parish church of St Leonard's, Deal, marks the estimation in which he was held by those round his own home, having been placed there by friends in his father's parish and the neighbourhood. His South Africa medal with clasp 1877-8-9, incorrectly named 'Griffiths', was issued on 30 June 1882. The above information was extracted from The South African Campaign of 1879, by J. P. Mackinnon and S. H. Shadbolt, and The Noble 24th, by Norman Holme.

Bosleys Military Auctioneers 3 March 2010 Lot No 516
24th Foot The South Wales Borderers South Africa Zulu Isandhlwana Casualty Medal.. A rare example, awarded to 1267 Pte J. Wilson 1/24th Foot . Bearing the clasp 1877-8-9 . Near VGC. Private John Wilson joined the 1st Bn of the 24th Foot on the 12th June 1866 at the age of 17. He saw service in Malta and Gibraltar, before embarking for South Africa during December 1874. It was here that the Regiment was garrisoned until the the start of the Zulu War. He had reengaged at Cape Town during October 1876 and the last Regimental Muster Roll available for him is dated September 1878 showing him serving at King William s Town in the Cape. He is confirmed as being Killed in Action on the 22nd January 1879 at the action at Isandhlwana.

Appendix 6 - Medal Awards, Killed in Action Isandhlwana

Spink Sale Sale 4020 Lot 331. 30 November 2004
South Africa 1877-79, one clasp, 1879 (521. Pte. **C. Lovell**).
Hammer Price £4500
25B/521 **Private Charles Lovell** enlisted 18.12.1874 1st Battalion 24th Foot, aged 18 years; killed in action at Isandhlwana 22.1.1879.

HISTORIK ORDERS, LTD Sales List November 2009
Zulu Medal Named To: 1857. **Pte. J. Hind.** 1/24th. Foot.   Clasp: 1877-8-9. Condition: GVF. SOLD US $9,995.00

Dixons Medals, December 2009 South Africa Medal 1877-1879, 1 clasp, 1877-8-9. 285 Private **T. Walsh**, 1/24th Foot .Minor edge bruise 3.0 obverse, 5.0 reverse otherwise. EF Thomas Walsh enlisted at Manchester on 15 June 1875, aged 19 years. He served with the 1st Battalion, 24th Foot, and was killed in action at Isandhlwana 22.1.1879.   £6,950.00

DNW Auction 4 December 91 Lot 30,   (AA Upfill-Brown Collection)
An important medal awarded to Sergeant John Costellow, N Battery, 5th Brigade, Royal Artillery, who was one of the few to survive the massacre at Isandhlwana SOUTH AFRICA 1877-9, 1 clasp, 1877-8-9 (216 Sergt. **J. Costellon** (sic), R. A.), small edge nick, otherwise good very fine Hammer Price: £3000
Sergeant **John Costellow** is confirmed as one of the four survivors of the battery in a letter written six days after the battle by Elias Tucker, a Driver of N battery, to his mother. His letter was published in the Western' Morning News (Plymouth) on 28 March 1879. Interestingly he gives the spelling Costellan whereas the medal rolls consistantly show Costellow, albeit with the same regimental number. Tucker's letter reads:
Battle-field, Helpmakaar, Jan 28th, 1879.
' Dear Father and Mother-It gives me great pleasure to think that I am alive to write to you. We had a severe cutting up on the 22nd of January. Lord Chelmsford went out with the column about three o'clock in the morning; he went about 15 miles from camp to attack the Zulus- to Isinlonana or the Lion's Mane. They left 2 guns and 65 artillery, 6 companies of the 24th Regiment, in all about five hundred men. The Zulus watched the column out of the camp, and then attacked the camp; they came into the camp like wild beasts, which they are.
'We played well on them with the two guns, and the infantry fought well, cutting roads through them. We held the field from half past eleven in the morning until three o'clock in the day. We killed twelve thousand Zulus, but they were too strong for us. They came right round us, and massacred every one; there are only twelve left to tell the tale. Out of sixty-five artillery only four remain, and I am one of the four- Sergeant Costellan (sic), **Lieutenant Curling** (that's my master), and myself and Gunner Green. We four had a horse each, and we charged right through the Zulus and cut our way out. I was in my shirtsleeves carrying ammunition to the guns.
'We lost everything in camp; they burnt everything that would burn. All our waggons and carts we had for ammunition they filled up with dead white men. They cut everyone up, and took his heart and laid it on his breast, and put his right hand in where they took his heart from, and put all the skulls in a heap. I expect you will see the massacre in the papers before you receive this. I could not write before. We rode a hard gallop from the time we cut our way out of camp until four next morning, and we found ourselves in sight of Helpmakaar, and that gave us fresh strength, hoping to find some help there; but when we got there there were only six men on guard belonging to the 13th Regiment. We frightened them out of their lives. There is only one store in Helpmakaar, and that was filled with stocks of corn. We got that out and barricaded all the doors, and cut some loopholes through the sides and ends to fire through. We were afraid they would attack us here, but they have not been.
'Dear mother, still there is hope for us, for our relief came his morning. A lot of Engineers and the 4th (King's Own) Regiment marched in here; we gave them three hearty cheers. Dear mother, I must now conclude, as they are sending out a mounted orderly tonight, and I want these few lines to go with him. I have not received any letters from England since October. The Zulus have taken possession of all the houses on the road and burnt them down.... Please drop a few lines to London to Tim and my sister to let them know that I am living and well, for I cannot get paper to write on. 'I gave a shilling for this envelope and paper, and it is cheap at that. We can not get paper or envelopes for love or money here in the midst of a wilderness and savages. Please give my kind love to all inquiring friends and tell them all I am alive and well, only a slight wound on the back of the hand. So, good-bye, and God bless you all. They have sent to England for more troops, and we shall pay the Zulus out for this yet.
'Elias Tucker, Driver, N Battery. Royal Artillery,

Editors comment:
Section N/5 Battery had at its disposal at Isandhlwana ,two 7 prs, Rocket Battery and three rocket troughs
The guns opened fire, on the approach of the Zulus and quickly changed to case shot, to inflict maximum damage on the advancing hordes. The two 7 prs were incapable of stopping the Zulu advance. To prevent the guns from being overwhelmed, the order was given to retire. to take up a position on higher ground. **Major Stuart Smith** was wounded along with several of his men. The men were forced to run alongside the guns. but the Zulus were there first. The guns changed direction and went straight through the camp, losing more men on the way, before coming to an abrupt halt stuck in a ravine, the drivers were pulled off their horses and killed. There was not even time to spike the guns.
N/5 Battery had lost Major Stuart Smith, 61 NCOs and men, two guns, 24 horses, 30 mules and 534 rounds of ammunition. The Rocket Battery lost Major Russell, six men and all its equipment.

Appendix 6 - Medal Awards, Killed in Action Isandhlwana

DNW Lot 70, 25 February 1999 The Zulu War medal awarded to **Lieutenant A. F. Henderson,** Commanding the Hlubi Troop, Natal Native Horse, one of the few survivors of the massacre at Isandhlwana, later awarded the C.M.G. for services during the Siege of Ladysmith, and commanding the Estcourt Militia Reserves during the Natal Rebellion 1906
South Africa 1877-79, clasp, 1879 (Lieut. A. F. Henderson, Natal Native Horse) extremely fine and very rare Hammer Price: £5400
Alfred Fairlie Henderson was born sometime in1854 and educated at Heidelberg in Germany, returning to Natal in 1872 where he began farming and prospecting for gold. Of his fortunate escape from the battlefield of Isandhlwana, the following details appeared in the Natal newspapers at the time of his death: "With the passing of Mr. Henderson, Natal has lost a soldier whose experiences in the Zulu and Anglo Boer Wars were probably more trying than any other men who survived them. In 1879 he was one of the very few to escape the massacre of Isandhlwana...... At the outbreak of the Zulu War in 1879 Mr. Henderson was placed in command of a big batch of natives recruited from Edendale under Captain George Shepstone. This contingent was amongst those surrounded but with one or two others Mr. Henderson broke through the weakest spot in the Usutu circle and effected a narrow escape. Having come through such a slaughter with his own life one would have expected that he would have moved on to safety as quickly as possible, but he did not, and in his actions at this juncture one can read the bravery, unselfishness and hardiness which combined to form a noble character. One of the very few Natal Carbimeers who escaped was **Trooper Barker** whose narrative of the battle was taken as an official one. In Barker's description one reads that he (Barker) escaped and was riding away when he came across Lieutenant Higginson who was running away having lost his horse in crossing the flooded river. Barker gave his horse to Higginson and continued on foot. It appears that Mr. Henderson saw Higginson riding and recognised Barker's horse, so promptly discovered that Barker was left behind unmounted, fleeing from a horde of blood-thirsty Zulus. It was riding to a possible death but Mr. Henderson did not waver. He collected another horse and rode back to meet Barker. In company with other men they escaped to Helpmekaar."
Three days after the disaster at Isandhlwana Henderson wrote to his father from Helpmekaar, "You will have heard before this reaches you of the fight and massacre in Zululand. I would have written you yesterday only I wanted to try and hear something about George [Capt. G. J. P. Shepstone, Natal Native Horse, killed - Alfred's brother-in-law]. I am afraid there is no hope for him. Colonel Durnford we think was killed as he has not turned up. The kaffirs surrounded us in thousands. We were fighting from about 9.30 a.m. until about 2 p.m. when the Zulus drove us into the camp. Our kaffirs fought well and stood their ground until we were surrounded. I never saw George all through the fight as he was with another part of our mounted men. There must have been about five hundred of our men killed. Twenty-two of the Natal Carbineers are killed. I don't know what they are going to do with us just now. We have lost everything belonging to us. We may have to go down to town to fit out again then I will be able to give you more particulars."
Alfre wrote again three days later with further details: "I wrote you the other day to say that I had got out of the fight the other day. I have not as yet heard anything about George. If I had known what sort of a man Durnford was (when he got into action) I don't think I would have gone with him. He was close to me during most of the fight and he lost his head altogether in fact he did not know what to do. The General was (I think) a good deal to blame as he left the camp in such a bad place to defend. As far as I can make out there are about 700 killed white and black. They say there were about 20,000 Zulus and I think there must have been quite that number. We shot hundreds of them but it seemed to make no impression they still came on. Here we are now with nothing, all I saved was my mackintosh which was on the saddle. I have got one shilling left today. We have got to patrol the country with my troop and the Edendale troop, the only ones left..."
It is curious that Henderson makes no reference in his letters to the remarkable defence of Rorke's Drift, for, at about 3.30 p.m. he arrived there from Isandhlwana with some one hundred men of the Hlubi and Edendale troops, Natal Native Horse. Lieutenant Chard, no doubt grateful for some reinforcements in light of the disturbing news that Henderson carried with him, put them out as a mounted screen to observe the Drift and the reverse slope of the Oskarberg. Several more survivors from Isandhlwana arrived and attempted to impress upon the garrison the futility of a defence, but Chard's resolve could not be altered. These survivor's, however, having seen the horror of Isandhlwana, and believing the same fate would surely befall Rorke's Drift, continued their flight. At about 4.20 p.m. sporadic gunfire was heard behind the Oskarberg, and the Natal Light Horse galloped past the mission station in the direction of Helpmekaar. Lieutenant Henderson, pausing only to report that his troops refused to obey orders, took off in pursuit of them.
Henderson shortly afterwards contracted typhoid fever and returned to his home where he was nursed back to health in time to be in at the kill when the Zulu power was crushed at the battle of Ulundi. For the next twenty years Alfred was engaged in business with interests in several mining concessions amongst other enterprises. In the Boer War Henderson again came to prominence and received high commendation from the Director of Military Intelligence: "Mr. Alfred Fairlie Henderson, Field Intelligence Department, took part in the Defence of Ladysmith and was present at the operations near Helpmekaar and the actions at Alleman's Nek and Bergendal and the advance on Lydenburg. Mr. Henderson's services were invaluable. Mentioned in despatches, London Gazette 8th February, 1901." For his scouting services throughout the defence of Ladysmith, Henderson was created a C.M.G.
Alfred subsequently served through the Zulu Rebellion of 1906 in the Helpmekaar Field Force under Colonel Mackay of Estcourt and was Chief Leader of the 1st Estcourt Militia Reserves. In a newspaper report of the 1st June, 1906, a correspondent with this force wrote that it seems a strange coincidence so many years after Isandhlwana that the Carbineers should camp on the scene of the calamity which had taken place twenty-seven years earlier. He added that it seemed even stranger since, with the Carbineers in the person of Mr. Henderson, chief leader of the Estcourt, Mooi River and other reservists, there should be one of the survivors of the fight. "A hale hearty old Gentleman, Mr. Henderson despite his years is as eager now as he was in the full vigour of his youth in pursuing the work he has taken up."Much of the information given above has been taken from the history of the Henderson Family by Peter Hathorn (privately published, Pietermaritzburg, 1973) which includes a full chapter on Alfred Henderson. Relevant copies are sold with the lot.

Appendix 7 - Survivors from Isandlwana

Isandlwana survivors who reached Helpmekaar.

Name	Regiment
Brevet Major H.Huntley	Staff
Captain. Edward Essex	Staff
Captain Alan Gardner	Staff
Lieutenant Francis Cochrane	Staff
Lieutenant Horace Smith-Dorrien	Staff
Mr Brickhill	Staff
Martin Foley (Civilian)	Conductor
James Hamer (Civilian)	Transport Officer
Lieutenant Henry Curling	Royal Artillery
Sergeant John Costellow	Royal Artillery
Act. Bombardier George Goff	Royal Artillery
Driver Elias Tucker	Royal Artillery
Gunner William Green	Royal Artillery
Sergeant Patrick Naughton	Imperial Mtd Infantry
Corporal John McCan	Imperial Mtd Infantry
Private Henry Davis	Imperial Mtd Infantry
Private Edwards	Imperial Mtd Infantry
Private William Parry	Imperial Mtd Infantry
Private John Power	Imperial Mtd Infantry
Private Samuel Wassall	Imperial Mtd Infantry
Private Thomas Westwood	Imperial Mtd Infantry
Private James Bickley	1/24th Regiment
Private Hector Grant	1/24th Regiment
Private William Johnson	1/24th Regiment
Private James Trainer	1/24th Regiment
Private John Williams	1/24th Regiment
Private Edmund Wilson	1/24th Regiment
Quartermaster Dugald McPhail	Buffalo Border Guard
Trooper John Adams (Senior)	Buffalo Border Guard
Trooper John Adams (Junior)	Buffalo Border Guard
Trooper Lennox	Buffalo Border Guard
Trooper C.Stretch	Buffalo Border Guard
Trooper William Barker	Natal Carbineers
Trooper William Edwards	Natal Carbineers
Trooper C.Fletcher	Natal Carbineers
Trooper W.Granger(Grainger)	Natal Carbineers
Trooper Andrew Muirhead	Natal Carbineers
Trooper W.Sibthorpe	Natal Carbineers
Trooper W.Tarboton	Natal Carbineers
Corporal G.Collier	Natal Mtd Police
Corporal G.Collier	Natal Mtd Police
Corporal D.Doig	Natal Mtd Police
Corporal W.Dorehill	Natal Mtd Police
Lance Corporal Robert Eaton	Natal Mtd Police
Trumpeter Richard Stevens	Natal Mtd Police
Trooper William Hayes	Natal Mtd Police
Trooper Robert Kincade (Kincaid)	Natal Mtd Police
Trooper R.Shannon	Natal Mtd Police
Trooper Charles Sparks	Natal Mtd Police
Captain Cracroft Nourse	Natal Native Contgt
Captain D. Smythe	Natal Native Contgt
Captain Walter Stafford	Natal Native Contgt
Lieutenant Adendorff	Natal Native Contgt
Lieutenant Higginson	Natal Native Contgt
Lieutenant Wallace Erskine	Natal Native Contgt
Lieutenant Vaines	Natal Native Contgt
Sergeant-Major J.Williams	Natal Native Contgt
Lieutenant G.F Andrews	Natal Native Pioneers
Captain William Barton	Natal Native Horse
Lieutenant Harry Davis	Natal Native Horse
Lieutenant ? Henderson	Natal Native Horse
Lieutenant Charles Raw	Natal Native Horse
Lieutenant Richard Vause	Natal Native Horse
Sergeant Walsh (Welsh)	Newcastle Mtd Rifles
Trumpeter J.Horne	Newcastle Mtd Rifles
Trooper John Berning	Newcastle Mtd Rifles
Trooper Thomas Brown	Newcastle Mtd Rifles
Trooper Burne	Newcastle Mtd Rifles
Trooper Donald Moodie	Newcastle Mtd Rifles
Trooper Hendrick Parsons	Newcastle Mtd Rifles

Newspaper article published on the 31st January 1879.
Men of the 1/24th regiment known to have escaped on the 22nd and to be at Helpmakaar

	Rank & Name	Comp.	
1173	Private James Bickley	F	Band
13	Private Edmund Wilson	B	Band
375	Corporal J.McCan	E	Mounted Infantry
194	Private H.Davis	D	Mounted Infantry
611	Private W.Parry	D	Mounted Infantry
499	Private J.Power	B	Mounted Infantry
196	Private J.Trainer	C	Rocket Party
299	Private W.Johnson	C	Rocket Party
665	Private H.Grant	C	Rocket Party
139	Private J.Wiliams	D	Colonel Glyn Groom

They Fell Like Stones by John Young includes the additional survivors: 1st Batt. 1st Reg. Natal Native Contingent, Captains: C.Nourse; D.M.Smythe ;W.H.Stafford. Lieutenants;C.Raw; R.W.Vause;A.F.Henderson; H.D.Davis. 2nd Batt 3rd Reg. Lieutenant H.Fairclough. Also "N" Battery, 5th Brigade, Royal Artillery; Trumpeter N Martin, Shoeing-Smiths: J.Steer; G.Townsend; Drivers J.Baggeley; J.Burchell; E.Price. 2nd Batt. 3rd Foot (The Buffs) Sergeant P.Naughton; Private E.Evans. 1st Batt 13th Light Infantry Private D.Whelan. 80th (The Staffordshire Volunteers) Reg. of foot Privates: S.Wassall, VC; T.Westwood.

Apart from the named individuals above there are several accounts that have 17 men from the No1 Squadron of Imperial Light Infantry who escaped.6 unnamed Infantrymen from the 1/13th regiment. There are also numerous letters and accounts which cannot be collaborated.

J.Frances of 2/24th Regiment listed as a survivor arrived at Helpmakaar, article in Birmingham Daily Post, February 27, 1879; Issue 6440. Editors comment; Pte 1450 J Francis 2nd Battalion 24th Regiment, medal with clasp 1877-8-9.

Reference: The Red Book - Ron Lock and Peter Quantrill   Page 57 & 63. The Defence of Helpmakaar by Graham Alexander

Appendix 7 - Survivors from Isandlwana

The Aberdeen Journal - Monday March 10th 1879

The *Natal Mercury*, dated Durban, February 3, says the following non-commissioned officers and men of the 1-24th Regiment are known to have escaped from the action of the 22nd January, and to be at Helpmakaar :—

Regimental No.			Remarks.
1173	Private	James Bickley...	Band.
13	,,	Edmund Wilson	do.
315	Corporal	J. M'Cann......	Mnted Inftry.
184	Private	H. Davis	do.
611	,,	W. Parry	do.
499	,,	J. Power	do.
196	,,	J. Trainer	Rocket Party.
299	,,	W. Johnson......	do.
665	,,	H. Grant	do.
139	,,	J. Williams......	Groom to Col. Glyn.

The following list of names of those who have turned up since the last list was posted on Wednesday night at the Colonial Office, having been received by the Greytown cart that evening :—

Natal Carabineers.—Muirhead, Edwards, Tarboton, Barker, Fletcher, Grainger, Sibthorpe.

Buffalo Border Guard.—McKrail, Lennox, Adams (2), Stretch.

Newcastle Mounted Rifles.—Bentley, Moodie, Walsh, Brown, Berning, Horn, Parsons.

Mounted Police.—Sparks, Stevens, Hayes, Dohill, Colner, Kincade, Eaton, Shannon, Doig.

Spinks Auction 5th December 2002, From the collection of Keith Harvie Lot No 5.
An Extremely rare and Emotive Medal to an Isandhlwana Survivor.
South Africa 1877-79, one clasp, 1877-8-9
(665. Gunr W. Green, 5th Bde R.A.) nearly extremely fine   Hammer Price £7400.
665 Gunner William Green, born in Tewkesbury, initially attested for the 29th Regiment in 1863 but transferred into the Artillery later that year, he served in the Zulu War with N/5 R.A and his presence at the battle of isandhlwana is stated in his discharge papers.
The following is an extract from a letter by Driver Elias Tucker, another survivor of N/5 Battery, written to his parents a few days after the battle: The Zulus watched (Chelmsford's) column out of the camp and then attacked the camp. We played well on them with the two guns and the infantry fought well, cutting roads through them. We held the field from half past eleven in the morning until three o'clock in the day. We killed twelve thousand Zulus but they were too strong for us. They came right round us and massacred every one there are only twelve left to tell the tale. Out of sixty-five artillery only four remain and I am one of the four - Sergt Costellan (sic). Lieutenant Curling (that's my master) and myself and Gunner Green. We four had a horse each and we charged right through the Zulus and cut our way out"
(See article by P.E.Abbott, Journal of the Society of Army Historical Research, vol,56, p95 and vol.59, p.47)

Charles Lennox Stretch (born 22/9/1830 in Uitenhage; died 10/5/1896 in Vryheid). in the Natal Government Gazette for 1880, where claims and awards of compensation were posted. Trooper Stretch claimed £36.10s in respect of the loss of his horse, saddle and kit at the battle of Isandlwana, awarded £7.2s
Referance: Victorian Wars Forum. Brett Hendey & Phillip A Gill

On the 22nd December 1909 C.L Stretch applied for Financial Assistance to the Colonial Secretary. of the Colony of Natal.. In his application he states that he is one of the few survivors of Isandhlwana. He served in the Buffalo Border Guard which was later confirmed.
"I was born in Durban on the 28th March 1852. As a trooper in the Buffalo Border Guard I was in the battle of Isandulwana on the 22nd January 1879 and one of the few, who escaped with their lives......The Commandant General on the 8th January 1910 requested a Police report from Standerton.. The report came back stating that his case was deserving "He is really too infirm to do hard work...... I am also satisfied of his identity." Signed Sub Inspector Kennedy.
In his written testament dated 13th January 1910."I am 58 years of age next March. I was married in 1872. I have had ten children. Four are alive six are dead. All those alive are daughters, one is still at home she is 19. Goes on to state he is in debt to the tune of £40, and is unable to work, also reaffirms his claim to be a survivor from Isandhlwana His request was turned down on the 8th February.
Pietermaritzburg Archive Depot NAB Referance 1909/7237 C L Stretch Survivor of Isandhlwana applies for financial assistance.

TROOP SERGEANT MAJOR SIMEON KAMBULA, DCM Natal Native Horse by Dr F K Mitchell, JCD
Simeon knew the country, and avoiding the Zulus force, made, by paths known to himself, to what afterwards became known as "The Fugitive's Drift". It is a ford over the Buffalo River. Before they reached the Drift, they heard the yells of men, the neighing of horses, and the bellowing of cattle. When they arrived upon the banks above the Drift they found it choked with men and beasts. On every rock stood two or three Zulus, stabbing every man they could reach, while on the Natal bank of the river a large body of Zulus waited to dispatch every man who escaped from the river.
Simeon dismounted his men. They were all good shots. Short and sharp he gave his orders. A volley was sent into the centre of the Zulu line on the opposite bank of the river. They closed in, and with wild yells, hurled a cloud of assegais, which, however, did but little harm, as the distance was too great. Three times the Edendale men fired their deadly volleys across the river, and then the Zulus broke and fled. Instantly Simeon rode down to the Drift.' Owen Watkins went on to record that calling other fugitives to cling to the stirrups of his men, Simeon led his Contingent through the fast-flowing river, then formed them up on the far bank to fire a final volley at the pursuing Zulus. Their ammunition exhausted, he then led them off to Helpmekaar, the only group to maintain their cohesion through the great Zulu victory of Isandlwana. There was grief in Edendale over their many young men who did not come home, but volunteers came forward immediately to replace the fallen, and the Contingent was soon off to war again, this time under command of Capt Cochrane, 32nd Regt, to operate with Col Evelyn Wood VC in the North, at Fort Kambula. They served with Wood - in the final advance as part of his 'Flying Column' - until the final defeat of Cetshwayo at Ulundi on 4 July 1879. Ref: Military History Journal - Vol 7 No 6

Appendix 7 - Survivors from Isandlwana

Extracts from Memories of Forty-Eight Years Service by **Smith-Dorrien**

" It was about this time, too, that a Colonial named Du Bois, a wagon-conductor, said to me, " The game is up. If I had a good horse I would ride straight for Maritzburg." I never saw him again. I then saw Surg. Major Shepherd, busy in a depression, treating wounded. This was also the last time I saw him. To return to the fight. Our right flank had become enveloped by the horn of the Zulus and the levies were flying before them. All the transport drivers, panic-stricken, were jostling each other with their teams and wagons, shouting and yelling at their cattle, and striving to get over the neck (see sketch) on to the Rorke's Drift road; and the red line of the 24th, having fixed bayonets, appeared to have but one idea, and that was to defeat the enemy. The Zulu charge came home, and, driven with their backs to the rock of Isandhlwana, and overpowered by about thirty to one, they sold their lives dearly..... When this final charge took place, the transport which was in-spanned had mostly cleared the neck, and I jumped on my broken-kneed pony, which had had no rest for thirty hours, and followed it, to find on topping the neck a scene of confusion I shall never forget, for some 4,000 Zulus had come in behind and were busy with shield and assegai. Into this mass I rode, revolver in hand, right through the Zulus, but they completely ignored me. I heard afterwards that they had been told by their King Cetywayo that black coats were civilians and were not worth killing. I had a blue patrol jacket on, and it is noticeable that the only five officers who escaped—Essex, Cochrane, Gardner, Curling, and myself—had blue coats. The Zulus throughout my escape seemed to be set on killing natives who had sided with us, either as fighting levies or transport

drivers. After getting through the mass of Zulus busy slaying, I followed in the line of fugitives. The outer horns of the Zulu Army had been directed to meet at about a mile to the south-east of the camp, and they were still some distance apart when the retreat commenced. It was this gap which fixed the line of retreat.....

Again I rode through unheeded, and shortly after was passed by Lieutenant Coghill (24th), wearing a blue patrol and cord breeches and riding a red roan horse. We had just exchanged remarks about the terrible disaster, and he passed on towards Fugitives' Drift. A little farther on I caught up Lieutenant Curling, R.A., and spoke to him, pointing out to him that the Zulus were all round and urging him to push on, which he did. My own broken-kneed transport pony was done to a turn and incapable of rapid progress.

The ground was terribly bad going, all rocks and boulders, and it was about three or four miles from camp to Fugitives' Drift. When approaching this Drift, and at least half a mile behind Coghill, Lieutenant Melvill (24th), in a red coat and with a cased Colour across the front of his saddle, passed me going to the Drift. I reported afterwards that the Colour was broken; but as the pole was found eventually whole, I think the casing must have been half off and hanging down. It will thus be seen that Coghill (who was Orderly Officer to Colonel Glynn) and Melvill (who was Adjutant) did not escape together with the Colour. How Coghill came to be in the camp I do not know, as Colonel Glynn, whose orderly officer he was, was out with Lord Chelmsford's column"....

I got into Helpmakaar at sundown, having done twenty miles on foot from the river, for I almost went to Sandspruit. At Helpmakaar I found Huntley of the 10th, who had been left there with a small garrison, and also Essex, Cochrane, Curling, and Gardner, from the field of Isandhlwana, all busy placing the post in a state of defence. We could see that night the watchfires of the Zulus some six miles off, and expected them to come on and attack, but we knew later they had turned off to attack Rorke's Drift.

I at once took command of one face of the laager, and shall never forget how pleased we weary watchers were when, shortly after midnight, Major Upcher's two companies of the 24th, with Heaton, Palmes, Clements, and Lloyd, came to reinforce. These two companies had started for Rorke's Drift that afternoon, but had been turned back to Helpmakaar by Major Spalding, a Staff Officer, as he said Rorke's Drift had been surrounded and captured, and that the two companies would share the same fate. Luckily, his information proved to be wrong.

Such is briefly my story of the 22nd January 1879, and I have endeavoured to avoid personal incidents as far as possible, though I should like my boys to know that on the evidence of eye-witnesses I was recommended for the V.C. for two separate acts on that day. These recommendations drew laudatory letters from the War Office, with a regret that as the proper channels for correspondence had not been observed, the Statutes of the Victoria Cross did not admit of my receiving that distinction, and having no friends at Court the matter dropped.

With the outbreak of the First World War Smith-Dorrien, who was a veteran of Isandhlwana and the Second Boer War, was given command of II Corps of Sir John French's British Expeditionary Force (BEF). He was praised for his conduct during the Battles of Mons and Le Cateau in August 1914, and was given command of Second Army from December 1914 to April 1915.

Smith-Dorrien fell foul of Sir John French, whom he little respected, during the Second Battle of Ypres, when he recommended a strategic withdrawal closer to Ypres, feeling that nothing short of a major counter-offensive was likely to regain the ground taken by the Germans during their offensive. French disagreed, dismissing Smith-Dorrien home to England upon the pretext of ill-health, and replacing him with Herbert Plumer, who ironically also recommended a withdrawal upon taking up his position; French accepted Plumer's advice.

Reference: http://www.firstworldwar.com/bio/smithdorrien.htm

Appendix 7 - Survivors from Isandlwana

ESCAPES FROM ISANDULA.
A TERRIBLE NARRATIVE.

A correspondent sends to a London contemporary the following copy of a letter sent home by his brother, a young man twenty years of age, who only recently joined the Natal Police, and who had a miraculous escape from the terrible conflict at Isandula:—

"HELPMAKAAR, January 27.

"I cannot find words to thank God for His merciful guidance in sparing me to be able to write to you. I am almost afraid to tell you all the dreadful news I know, but I think it is best to let you know all. I will commence from our entrance into Zululand. It took two or three days for the whole of the column to cross the river. There was not a Zulu to be seen for some distance. Patrolling parties were sent out, and came back with a lot of cattle, and said there was no 'niggers' to be seen. We pitched camp over the river, and stayed there some time. On Sunday, the 19th January, the outposts reported the enemy in great force on a big hill in the distance. We all turned out, but only saw a few of them. The infantry halted on one side of the hill, and we went to the other. Then we saw them following us, but thinking they did not mean to fight we went quite close to them and when we were about 100 yards off they fired on us, and we all dismounted and let them have it. They bid away in the stones, but we turned them out and killed most of them; that is the greater part of that affair. I must now go on to the more dreadful occurrence. We were ordered to move the camp further in the country; so we advanced about 10 or 12 miles and pitched camp again. The next day the greatest part of the column was ordered out. I could not go as my horse was sick; by and by a message came in to say that they had seen the enemy, and were going so stop out all night; so we sent food and greatcoats to them. The next morning our camp outposts came in and reported the enemy in sight again; we had only about 600 men in camp altogether. Well, we all formed up ready for action, and at that time seven or eight Zulus came in and gave up their arms. The colonel let them go. Soon after that we saw the hill black with them, coming on in swarms, estimated at 20,000. We held a ditch as long as possible, but being outnumbered the order was given to get into camp. Well we got there. I went all over the place for a gun, but could not get one. My revolver was broken; so I stopped in camp as long as possible, and saw one of the most horrid sights imaginable.

"The Zulus were in the camp ripping our men up, also the tents and everything they came upon, with their assegais. They were not content with killing, but mutilated the bodies afterwards. Never has such a disaster befallen the English army; there was no means of sending to the General, who was out with the column. Now about myself. I got out of camp on a horse somehow —I do not know how—and went through awful places to reach the drift, where my horse was taken away from under me, and I was as nearly drowned as possible, but I just managed to catch hold of the tail of another horse, which pulled me through. I have since managed to reach this place, where, thank the Almighty, I am all safe. There were 537 of the 24th Regiment killed in camp, and 26 of ours, besides several others; so you can imagine what it was. The Zulus have all our waggons, with stores and ammunition. I have not told you all yet, as I have neither time nor paper, but will write on the first opportunity."

Bosleys Auction, 13th December 2006 Lot No 613. £14,000. An important Battle of Isandhlwana Officer Survivor's 1879 South African Medal.--

Awarded to Captain William Barton an Irish soldier of fortune who commanded the Sikali Squadron Natal Native Horse part of Number 2 Column and witnessed the action which resulted in the award of the Victoria Cross to Private Samuel Wassall of the 80th Foot. South African 1879 Medal with clasp "1879" named to "Capt W. Barton Natal Horse". Slight correction to rank, otherwise near VGC. Captain William Barton was an Irish soldier of fortune who had previous fought the Indians in South America. He arrived in South Africa and raised over 200 Basutos, who were formed into a irregular cavalry unit. He volunteered his services to the Natal Horse and was given command of the Sikali Squadron. He is confirmed as being present at the Battle of Isandhlwana. During the early stages of the engagement he was ordered to take two troops onto the plateau to investigate the sighting of Zulus and clear them. Barton is later quoted as saying "My mounted men really fought well at their first charge and until all their ammunition was exhausted, they were then compelled to fall back on the camp, where they sought a fresh supply of ammunition". Seeing that the overall situation was deteriorating, he ordered his men to make a fighting retreat towards the Buffalo River. He was now on the flank and moved his men to cover the river crossing, he then retired firing and was the last man to cross. Many of the retreating men owing their lives to Barton 's actions. The following is Barton's own account and statement that led to the award of the Victoria Cross to Private Wassall of the 8th Foot. The original hand written report is held in the National Archives. "On the 22nd January 1879 when the camp of Col Glyn 's column had been taken by the enemy, I was retreating towards the Buffalo River to cross into Natal. As I approached the river, a man of the mounted Infantry was riding in front of me (This was Pte Wassall) and I also saw at the same time another man of the mounted infantry struggling in the river and he called out his comrades name, he was apparently drowning. The Zulus were at this time firing at our people from above us, others were down on the river stabbing others of our people on both sides of where I was. The man of the mounted infantry who rode down in front of me dismounted left his horse on the Zulu side and sprang into the river to save his comrade. I consider this man to have performed a most gallant and courageous act, in trying to save his comrade at the almost certain risk of his own life. I crossed the river myself about the same time and I did not think that it possible that either of these 2 men could have escaped alive. Indeed I spoke some days afterwards, to Lieut Walsh of the mounted infantry of the circumstances which I had witnessed and spoke of it to him, as evidence of my seen two of his men lost at the Buffalo River. I have this day identified in the Hospital here, the man whom I saw struggling in theriver, and I have also given Lieut Walsh a description of the horse which I saw the other man of the mounted infantry riding in front of me and from which he dismounted to save his comrade". Signed by Wm Barton Captain dated 11th February 1879. Captain Barton had been engaged on a 6 month contract which was common to all Officers of the Natal native contingent and in May appears to have slipped away once more into obscurity, unlike many of his fellow survivors who were keen to publish their accounts. Barton get a number of mentions. This medal was issued on the 10th March 1882.

Appendix 8 - Rorke's Drift

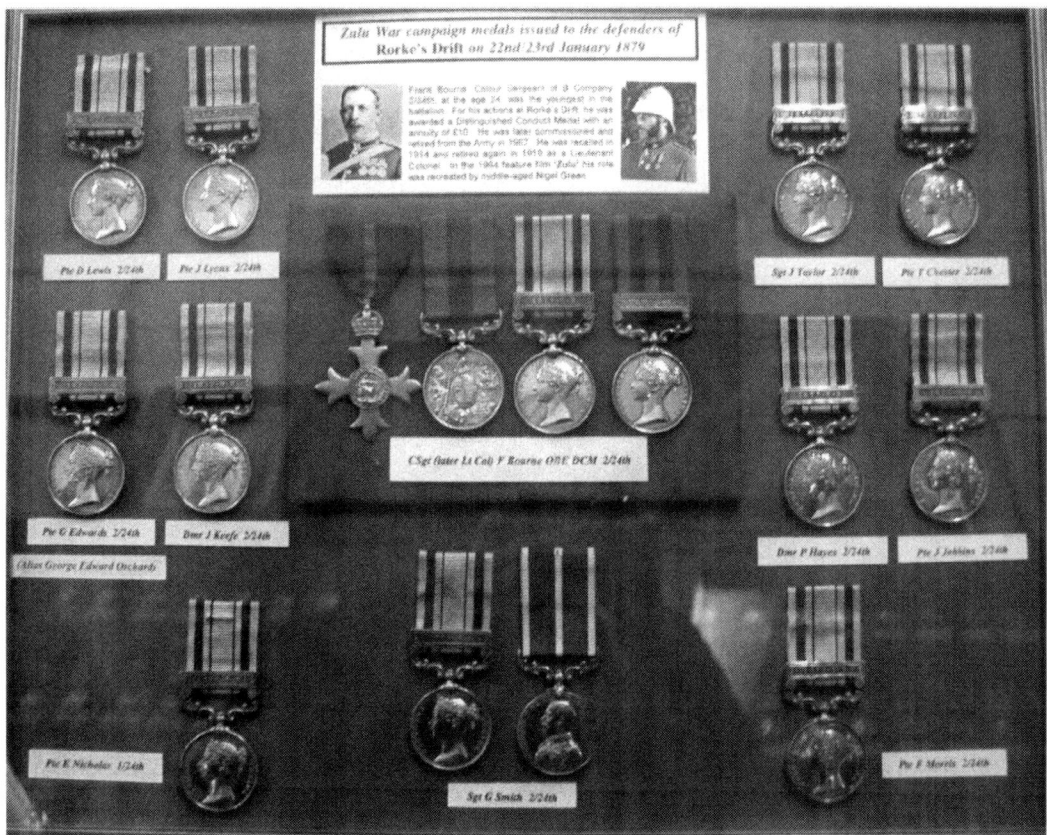

The above is part of the Medal Collection held at South Wales Borderers Museum to Defenders of Rorke's Drift.

Private **David Lewis**. 25b/963. Born at Swansea, Glamorgan ; trade tin worker.Posted to 24th foot 22/1/1877. Discharged 4/8/1879. Character indifferent.Died 1/7/1938 Brynmill, Swansea.

Private **John Lyons**. 2-24/1441. Born at Kallaloe, Ireland; trade labourer. Transferred to 24th foot 1/7/1861. Discharged as unfit 4/8/1879. Character very good. Died 2/1/1900, probably Manchester.

Private **George Edwards**. 25B/972. Born at Bristol; employed as a shoemaker's apprentice. Posted to 2nd Bn 24th Foot at Brecon 15/12/1876. Discharged 1889. Died 14/2/1940 Bristol.

Drummer **James Keefe**. 2-24/2381. Born at St. Clement's London; trade none. Enlisted for the 24th at London 3/3/1871 age 14 years 10 months. Permitted to continue in the service beyond 21 years. Died 18/9/1893.

Private **Edward Nicholas** 25B/625. Enlisted at Newport 30/7/1875 age 18 years, recorded in the records as E.Nicholls.

Colour Sergeant **Frank Bourne** DCM, 2-24/2459. Born in Balcombe, Sussex in 1854. He enlisted at Reigate on 18 December 1872 aged 18 years 8 months. He was the last defender to die on VE Day 1945 - 8 May - he was aged 91.

Sergeant **George Smith** 2-24/1387. Enlisted 29/5/1860 age 18 years, served a total of 23 years 63 days.

Lance Sergeant **James Taylor**, posted to 2nd Bn 24th Foot at Brecon 18/3/1874, died 15/11/1919

Private **Thomas Chester**. 25B/1241. Born at Calthorpe near Rugby; trade labourer, posted to 2nd Bn 24th Foot 21/2/1877. Discharged 19/2/1889. Character very good.

Drummer **Patrick Hayes**. 2-24/2067. Born Newmarket, Ireland; trade labourer. Enlisted at Ennis 8/9/1868 age 14 years.Discharged on 30/11/1892, became a civilian workman at the barracks at Brecon, until well over the age of 60. Died at London 4/10/1940.

Private **John Jobbins**. 25B/1061. Enlisted at Pontypool 12/1/1876. Described the battle in a letter to his father who was then working at the Crown Hotel, Pontypool. Returned to England from India on 29/1/1983. Buried with full military honours 26/9/1935 at Treveth churchyard, Pontypool.

Private **Frederick Morris**. 5B/525. Enlisted at Liverpool 4/12/1874. Died in service at Secunderabad, India 26/9/1883.

Appendice 9 - The Victoria Cross

The above is part of the Victoria Cross Medal Collection held at South Wales Borderers Museum.
Sergeant **William Wilson ALLAN**. Victoria Cross. South Africa Medal 1877-79 1 clasp: "1877-8-9" (Rorke's Drift)
Major **Gonville BROMHEAD**. Victoria Cross. South Africa Medal 1877-79 1 clasp: "1877-8-9" India General Service Medal 1854-95 2 clasps: "Burma 1885-87" - "Burma 1887-89" (Rorke's Drift)
Brigadier General **Edward BROWNE.** Victoria Cross Companion, Order of the Bath (CB) South Africa Medal (1877-79) 1 clasp: "1878-9" Queen Victoria Jubilee Medal (1897) (13th October, 1900, at Geluk,)
Lieutenant **Nevill Josiah COGHILL**. Victoria Cross. South Africa Medal 1877-79 ,1 clasp: "1877-8-9" (Isandhlwana)
Private **Frederick HITCH**. Victoria Cross. South Africa Medal 1877-79 1 clasp: "1877-8-9" (Rorke's Drift)
Sergeant **Alfred Henry HOOK**. Victoria Cross . South Africa Medal 1877-79 1 clasp: "1877-8-9" (Rorke's Drift)
Private **William JONES.** Victoria Cross .South Africa Medal 1877-79 1 clasp: "1879" Long Service & Good Conduct Medal (Rorke's Drift)
Private **Robert JONES.** Victoria Cross . (Rorke's Drift) Orginal medal in the possession of Lord Ashcroft, bought in 1996 for £80,000.
Lieutenant **Teignmouth MELVILL.** Victoria Cross South Africa Medal 1877-79 1 clasp: "1877-8-9" (Isandhlwana)
Sergeant **John WILLIAMS**. Victoria Cross .South Africa Medal 1877-79 1 clasp: "1877-8-9" (Rorke's Drift)

Appendice 9 - The Victoria Cross

The Victoria Cross (VC) was awarded to 23 members of Colonial and Imperial Armed Forces for action during the Zulu War of 1879. Prince Albert, the Prince Consort was much involved in the decision to institute the Victoria Cross The Victoria Cross was instituted by Royal Warrant on 29 January 1856 for award to both officers and non-commissioned ranks of the Royal Navy and the Army who, in the presence of the enemy 'shall have performed some signal act of valour...'. The first VC was awarded to Sergeant L O'Connor, 23rd Regiment (later Royal Welch Fusiliers), Battle of Alma, 20 September 1854, Crimean War.

Under the original Royal Warrant, the VC could not be awarded posthumously. Between 1897 and 1901, several notices were issued in the London Gazette regarding soldiers who would have been awarded the VC had they survived. In a partial reversal of policy in 1902, six of the soldiers mentioned were granted the VC, but not "officially" awarded the medal. In 1907, the posthumous policy was completely reversed and medals were sent to the next of kin of the six officers and men; Nevill Coghill and Teignmouth Melvill were two of the soldiers who were decorated thus. A total of eleven Victoria Crosses were awarded for the action at Rorke's Drift. Seven to the 2nd Battalion, 24th (2nd Warwickshire) Regiment of Foot, one each to the Royal Engineers, Army Medical Department, Commissariat and Transport Department and the Natal Native Contingent. Twenty-four VCs where awarded for the second relief of Lucknow, 16 November 1857 the largest number of VCs awarded on a single day(This figure includes 5 VCs awarded under Clause 13 of the 1856 warrant during the period 14-22 November 1857).

Name	Unit	Date of action	Place of action
William Allen	24th Regiment of Foot	22-23 January 1879	Rorke's Drift, Zululand
William Beresford	9th Lancers	3 July 1879	Ulundi, Zululand
Anthony Booth	18th Regiment of Foot	12 March 1879	Intombi River, Zululand
Gonville Bromhead	24th Regiment of Foot	22-23 January 1879	Rorke's Drift, Zululand
Edward Browne	24th Regiment of Foot	29 March 1879	Battle of Hlobane, Zululand
Redvers Buller	60th Rifles	28 March 1879	Battle of Hlobane, Zululand
John Chard	Royal Engineers	22-23 January 1879	Rorke's Drift, Zululand
*Nevill Coghill	24th Regiment of Foot	22 January 1879	Battle of Isandhlwana, Zululand
James Dalton	Commissariat & Transport Department	22-23 January 1879	Rorke's Drift, Zululand
Henry D'Arcy	Frontier Light Horse	3 July 1879	Ulundi, Zululand
Edmund Fowler	26th Regiment of Foot	28 March 1879	Battle of Hlobane, Zululand
Frederick Hitch	24th Regiment of Foot	22-23 January 1879	Rorke's Drift, Zululand
Alfred Hook	24th Regiment of Foot	22-23 January 1879	Rorke's Drift, Zululand
Robert Jones	24th Regiment of Foot	22-23 January 1879	Rorke's Drift, Zululand
William Jones	24th Regiment of Foot	22-23 January 1879	Rorke's Drift, Zululand
William Leet	13th Regiment of Foot	28 March 1879	Battle of Hlobane, Zululand
Henry Lysons	26th Regiment of Foot	28 March 1879	Battle of Hlobane, Zululand
*Teignmouth Melvill	24th Regiment of Foot	22 January 1879	Battle of Isandhlwana, Zululand
Edmund O'Toole	Frontier Light Horse	3 July 1879	Ulundi, Zululand
James Reynolds	Army Medical Department	22-23 January 1879	Rorke's Drift, Zululand
Christian Schiess	Natal Native Contingent	22-23 January 1879	Rorke's Drift, Zululand
Samuel Wassall	18th Regiment of Foot	22 January 1879	Battle of Isandhlwana, Zululand
John Williams	24th Regiment of Foot	22-23 January 1879	Rorke's Drift, Zululand

* Awarded posthumously

Reference:
http://www.nationalarchives.gov.uk/documentsonline/victoriacross.asp
Victoria Cross Register, Volume 2, 16 August 1864 - 31 January 1900 (WO 98/4)

Spinks Auction 5th December 2002 Lot 83.
The South Africa Medal to Lieutenant A.M.Smith, Frontier Light Horse, whose rescue on Hlobane Mountain led to the award of the Victoria Cross to Major W.Knox Leet of the 13th L.I. South Africa 1877-79, one clasp, 1879 (Lieut:A.M.Smith,Frontr. l. Horse), very fine, Hammer Price £6,500
During the debacle following the engagement on Hlobane Mountain, Smith was part of one group of refugees which was closely pursued by the Zulus in its attempt to descend from the ridge. Smith, whose horse had been shot and who had defended himself with his revolver, was unable through exhaustion to continue any further and "intended to sit down and give up all chance of saving my life" With the Zulus only yards away, Major Knox Leet stopped and dragged Smith onto his horse and carried him safely down the mountain, amidst a shower of spears and bullets.

Bibliography

Abbott P.E	Recipients of the Distinguished Conduct Medal	1975
Army Records Society	Lord Chelmsford's Zululand Campaign	1994
Ashe Major & Wyatt-Edgell Capt.	The Story of the Zulu Campaign	1880
Barthorp, Michael	The Anglo-Boer Wars	1987
Bellairs, Lady Blanche	The Transvaal War 1880-81	1885
Castle, Ian	Majuba 1881	1996
Churchill, Sir Winston	The River War	1899
Drooglever, R.W.F	The Road to Isandhlwana	1992
Emery, Frank	The Red Soldier	1977
Farwell, Byron	For Queen and Country	1981
Farwell, Byron	Queen Victoria's Little Wars	1973
Featherstone, Donald	Colonial Small Wars	1973
Forsyth D.R	South african War Medal 1877-8-9	1978
Gardyne, Ltn Col	The life of a Regiment – Vol 2	1929
Giddings, Robert	Imperial Echoes	1996
Gon, Philip	The Road to Isandlwana	1979
Gordon L.L. Major	British Battles and Medals	1947
Grierson, Ltn-Col J. Moncrieff	Scarlet into Khaki	1899
Hamilton, Ian	Listening for the Drums	1944
Hattersley, Alan F.	The History of the Royal Natal Carbineers	1950
Holme, Norman	The Noble 24th	1999
Hurst, G.T.	Short History of the Volunteer Regiments of Natal	1945
Jackson F.W.D	Hill of the Sphinx - the battle of Isandlwana	2002
Judd, Denis	Someone has Blundered	1973
Knight, Ian & Castle, Ian	The Zulu War Then and Now	1993
Knight Ian	Great Zulu Battles 1838-1906	1998
Laband, J & Thompson, P	Illustrated Guide to the Anglo-Zulu War	2000
Laband P.S Thompson, S. Henderson	The Buffalo Border 1879	1983
Lehmann, Joseph	The First Boer War	1972
Lock Ron & Quantrill Peter	The Red Book Natal Press Reports	2000
Mackinnon, J.P. & Shadbolt, S.H.	The South African Campaign of 1879	1882
Marling, Percival Scrope	Rifleman and Hussar	1931
Morris, Donald R	The Washing of the Spears	1965
Norris-Newman, Charles	In Zululand	1880
Rider Hagard, Sir H.	The Days of my Life	1926
Rider Hagard, Sir H.	The Last Boer War	1899
Rogers, H.C.B.	Weapons of the British Soldier	1960
Skelley, Alan Ramsay	The Victorian Army at Home	1977
Smith-Dorrien, H.	Memoirs of forty-eight years service	1925
Tomasson W.H	With the Irregulars In the Transvaal & Zululand	1881
Wilkinson-Latham, Christopher	Uniforms & Weapons of the Zulu War	1978
Wilmott, A	A History of the Zulu War	1880
Wood, Henry Evelyn	From Midshipman to Field-Marshall	1906
Whybra, Julian	England's Sons – A casualty and survivors roll of British combatants	2004
Young P.J	Boot & Saddle	1955
Young, John	They Fell Like Stones	1991

London Gazette. Casualty rolls 23 May 1879 Issue number: 24725 Page number: 3541
Journals, Manuscripts, Newspapers and Magazines
Blue Books For the period 1879 – 1881   H.M.S.O.
Narrative of the field operations with the Zulu war   H.M.S.O.   1881
South Africa Correspondence relative to the military affairs in Natal H.M.S.O.   1879
The Journal of Edward Essex (D.A.A.G) Staff Officer – Boer War 1881   National Army Museum
Regiment magazine The Highlanders   June - September 1999
The Journal of the Anglo Zulu War Historical Society   1997 – 2002
The South African Military History Society Journal   Volume 5 No 2 & No 5 , http://samilitaryhistory.org/vol014jh.html
The Times, The Graphic & Illustrated London News, and local newspapers. From Micro film records, and the British Library digital archive, with over two million pages of 19th century newspapers,. A truly fantastic resource.

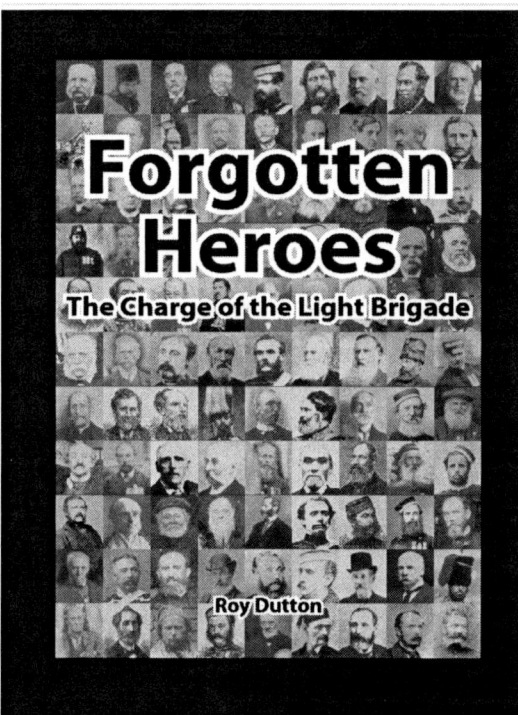

First in the series of Forgotten Heroes, The Charge of the Light Brigade. The book contains first hand accounts of the men who took part in the heroic and tragic Charge at the Battle of Balaclava on the 25th October 1854.

Previously unpublished biographies of the men and photographs bring their stories to life. What became of our heroes? Some died penniless while others found fame and fortune.

Set within an unrelenting and cruel military campaign, where many would perish, unravelling the myths to find many of the missing Chargers was a massive undertaking.
With an a additional 47 Chargers identified, bringing the total number of known Chargers to 562 and 29 marked as "Possibily rode in the Charge"

This book is about the ordinary people that made an Empire and gave the World a Legacy.

(ISBN: 0955655401) 420 pages. Hardback.
(800 b/w photos, illustrations & tables)
First Edition

The Charge of the Heavy Brigade at Balaclava on the 25th October 1854, is one of the most neglected events in the annals of British military history. Against all odds they attacked a Russian force which outnumbered them 5:1.
On the day in question the Heavy Brigade were involved in two separate charges.
The first was the successful charge of the Brigade on the advancing Russian cavalry, who were intent on capturing the over crowded port of Balaclava, the main supply point for the British army.
The second was in support of the Light Brigade on their unsuccessful attack on the Russian artillery. Raglan's real intention was to prevent the Russians from removing the British guns situated in the redoubts along the Causeway heights, but the orders were confused. As the Light Brigade advanced down the valley the Heavies followed in support. Lord Lucan had sufficient foresight to halt the advance which had come under heavy bombardment, to prevent the brigade from being annihilated in the same fashion as the Light Brigade.

To date no book has ever been written on the subject. With over 1300 men listed, with numerous biographical details A truly inspirational undertaking.

(ISBN: 0955655425) 375 pages. Hardback.
(600 b/w photos, illustrations & tables)
First Edition

Index

Regiments

13th Foot Casualty Roll, 223
17th Lancers, Reunion Dinner, 203
24th Officers at King William's Town 190
24th Foot Medal Awards, 435
58th (Rutlandshire) Regiment. 277
80th Foot Casualty Roll, 296,
88th Officers, 303
90th Foot Casualties 313
90th Officers, 311
91st Officers 320

A

Abingdon Works Co. 113
Adams, Corporal, Native Contingent, 175
Adams, Major George, 173
Addison, Captain Friend, 12
Addison, Trooper, Durban Mounted Rifles 72
Ainslie, Cook Sergt. G. 91st Foot, 320
Aktins, Pte S. 17th Lancers, 200
Alexandra Mounted Rifles, Officers, 145
Allan, Pte. G. 91st Foot, 320
Anderson,Tpr. W. Cape Mounted Yeomanry, 57
Andrews, Lieut. 139
Anglo-Zulu War Memorial, 420, 421
Anstey,Lieut. Edgar Olipbant, 24th Foot, 251, 262
Arbuthnot, Captain, Alexandra Mounted Rifles, 23, 145
Archbell, James Philip, 424
Army Service Corps. 349
Aswegen, Captain J. Van, 20

B

Baird, Sir David, 5
Baker,Major J.F. 12
Baker, Trooper W.W. 128
Baldwin,Captain Chevenix, 88th Regt. 303, 399
Balfour, Pte. E. C.M Rifles, 46
Barker, Sergt. W. Natal Carabineers, 145
Barker, Trooper, Natal Carbineers, 448
Barkly, Governor, 49
Barnes, Lieut. U.M.R 145
Barnes, Trooper W.H.J. 143, 445
Barnett, 122
Barrow, Major, P. E. S. 176
Barry, Metcalfe, 81
Barton, 2nd Lieut N.A.D. 88th Regt. 303
Barton, Captain, Natal Horse 452
Barton, Captain, Coldstream Guards, 91, 193, 413
Basuto Police, 159
Basuto War 1880-1881, 3, 416, 417, 418
Battles of the Zulu War 1879, 405
Baudoin, Cramazan, 34

Bayly, Colonel, 29, 414
Baynes, Lieut. D.L. 292
Bayonets, 241
Beachcroft, Levy Leader R.A. 64
Beaconsfield Town Guard, 68
Beaumont, William Henry, 143
Beddoes, Captain, 142
Benthall, Captain John Matthew, 194
Bethune's Mounted Infantry 141
Bettington, Captain R. 12
Bevan, Pte J, CMR. 417
Bickley, Bandsman, 24th Foot, 262
Bigge, Lieut. 80th Foot, 296
Binns, Lieut. & Adj. Henry, 173
Birbeck, Sgt-Major T., 47
Birdekin, Pte. F. 155
Black, Lieut. Norman Lister, 123, 139
Blackbeard, Trooper C.A. 68
Blaikie, James Adrian, Trooper 123, 128, 424
Blake, Lieut. V.W.L. 145
Blane, Lt. Alfred 25
Boast, Alf. 410
Boast, Trooper, 143
Booth, Colour-Sergt. Anthony Clarke, 290
Borain, Trooper, 70
Boshof, Trooper K. 167
Bostock, Pte. William, 58th Regt. 277
Bourchier, Lieut. C.L.J. 120
Bourne, Lieut. Colonel Frank Edward, 412
Bowen, Captain H.G. 88th Regt. 303
Bowen, Cr. Sergt. B. 88th Foot, 302
Bowker, Commandant, 47, 49
Boyd,Lance-Corporal W. 85
Brabant, Colonel, 28, 40, 53, 414, 418
Bradstrret, Captain C.R. Newcastle Mounted Rifles 123,143
Brady, Captain H.J. 22
Bremer, Pte H.N. 156
Brewer, Corpl H.M. 156
Brewer, Sergt H. Natal Carabineers, 128, 145
Bright, 2nd Lieut. A.T. 90th Foot, 310
Brind, Captain E.A. 88th Regt. 303
Brissenden, O.R Sergt. F.D. 125
Broderick, Pte. J. 1/24th Foot, 443
Brook, Captain, E. S. 169
Brown, Peter, 414
Brown, Pte W. 1/24th Foot, 442
Brown, Trooper R. Frontier Light Horse, 91,123
Brown, Trooper T. Frontier Light Horse, 91
Brownlee, Corpl W. CMR. 417
Brownson, Pte. H 80th Foot, 296
Bru de Wold, Captain, H.T. 145
Bullard, Bandmaster, H.F. 2/24th Foot, 444
Buller, Brevet Major, R. Henry, 25, 32, 34, 81, 82, 84, 89, 192
Bullock,Quartermaster-Sergeant J.C. 184
Burghersdorp Troop, 416
Burns, Pte. Edward, 57th Regt. 270
Butler, Pte J. 91st Foot, 323
Byng, Lieut: The Hon: A. J. G. 193

C

Caldwell, Captain J.F. 2/24th Foot, 253
Camp, Edwin, 134
Camp, Fred. 134
Camp, Pte. W. 100
Campbel, Hon. Captain Ronald George Elidor, 34, 193
Campbell, 122
Campbell, Commander, 266, 390
Campbell, Lieut. Alister R.N. 122
Cantwell, Lieutenant-Colonel R.F. 79
Cape Garrison Railways 170
Cape Mounted Riflemen 45
Carbutt's Border Rangers 11, 158
Carbutt's Volunteers 61
Carbutt,Q.master, T. Munro, 61
Carbutt, Thomas Munro, 61
Carey, Lieut. 98th Foot, 30
Carkson, Sergt. J. 1/24th Foot, 443
Carrington, Lieut. Frederick, 77, 91
Carstensen,Lieut. Adolf Heinrich 18
Carstensen, Lieut. Diamond Fields Horse, 417
Casualties, Basutoland Rebellion, 47
Casualty Roll 9th April to 3rd May 1878 432, 433, 434
Casualty Roll for 80th Foot, 296
Casualty Roll Morosi War, 414
Casualty Roll Naval Brigade, 389, 390
Casualy Roll Inhlobani, 413
Cetewayo 34
Chalmers, Inspector, 49
Chard, Lieut. VC. 61, 370
Chelmsford, General Lord 33, 88, 137, 143, 189, 192, 404, 445
Chiappini, Captain 416
Chinn, Sgt. Maj. C. H. 169
Chipps, Pte, 122
Christian, Trooper C.S. 91
Claiments to Zulu Medal 185
Clarence, Corp. 72
Clarence, Trooper B.C. 128
Clarke, Brigadier General, 417, 418
Clarke, Lieut, C.M.R, 417
Clarke, Lieut. Colonel, 41
Clarke, Lieut. Diamond Fields Horse, 417
Clarke, W.J. 134
Cocker, Mr. J.R. 56
Cogan, Pte. J, 13th Foot, 176
Coghill, Lieut.Nevill Josish Aylmer, 262
Coker, Midshipman L. 390
Colenbrander, Johan Wilhelm, 162
Colonial Army List July-Aug 1881 3, 179, 180, 181, 182, 183, 184
Colonial Forces 115
Colonial Medal Summary 3, 13, 14, 15, 16, 17, 18
Colonial Troops 12, 429, 430, 431
Colt's Revolvers 418
Comley, Captain, 84
Comrie, Sergt 128
Conboy, Bandsman G. 24th Foot, 435
Connolly, Pte. C. 1/24th Foot, 442
Conolly, Surgeon Paul Bennett, 91
Cook, Captain, 176
Cook, Trooper J. 91
Cooke, Captain J.W. 138
Cooke, Sergt. 128
Cooker, Rees Evans, 24th Foot, 262
Corrie, Capt. E. V. 121, 122
Costellan, Sergt. 447
Costellon (Costellow), Sergt. J., R. A, 360, 447
Cotton, Boatswain, 390
Court, Corp. John Markham, 49
Courtenay, Lieut. 176
Cousins, Quartermaster S. 88th Regt. 303
Cowley, Captain William R. 173
Craft, E. Sergt. 8
Crealock, Lieut.-Colonel, J. North. 77, 120, 138, 176
Crowter,Pte H. 196
Cunliffe, Tpr. Henry, 17th Lancers, 201, 204
Cunningham, T.H, N.M.R. 41
Cunnynghame,Sir Arthur, 49, 401
Curling, Lieut. R.A, 447, 451
Curran, Captain John Philpot, 88th Regt. 303
Curran, Pte. W, CMR. 417

D

D'Arcy,Captain Cecil 25, 91, 92, 123
Dalgety, Field-adjutant, 417
Dalgety,Lieutenant-Colonel, 79
Dalton, Assistant Commissary J. L. 8
Darcy, Trooper, 156
Dartnell, Levy Leader, J.G. 64
Dartnell, Major, 114, 124, 127
Davies, Commandant 29
Davies, Lt.-Colonel H.L. 28
Davis, Gunner, 71
Davis, Harry Willam, 424
Dawson, PayMaster C.T. H.M.S Boadicea, 377
Degacher, Captain William, 262
Demmer, Inspector, 47
Denys, Lieut. Jacob Peter, 146
Dews, Sergt J. Frontier light Horse, 176
Diamond, Trooper F.W, 70
Dinkelman, John, 143
Dobbs,Pte. W. 1/24th Foot, 442
Dobson, Trooper Arthur, Frontier Light Horse 86, 87, 88, 89
Doig, Trooper, Natal Mounted Police, 131
Donahoe, Pte H. 122
Donovan, Captain Joseph, 66
Dorien-Smith,Lieut. Horace, 337
Dowling, Lieut. 66
Doyle, Thomas Gerald, 425
Duffy, Pte. J. 1/24th Foot, 444
Durban Mounted Reserve, 11
Durban Mounted Rifles 12, 71, 72, 73, 115, 144, 175, 398
Durban Volunteer Artillery, 11
Durham, Fred, 17th Lancers, 204
Durham, Sister Emma, 204
Durnford, Colonel, 81, 137, 139
Dutton, Pte J.R. 80th Foot, 295

Dyason, Adjt W. W. 146
Dyer, Lieut. 446
Dymes, Capt. H. Natal Native Contingent, 139
Dyson 2nd Lieut. Edward Hopton, 262

E

Eadie, Pte. Alex. 91st Foot, 324
Earle, William Trooper, 8
Eary, Trooper, 38
Eckersley, George, 122
Edwards, Corpl. T. 145
Edwards, Sergt. John. I/24th Foot 237, 445
Edwards, Sergt. W. 145
Elliott. Corpl. T. 88th Foot, 306
Ellis, Pte 1/24th Foot, 439
Elwes, Lieut. Robert Hamond, 193
Escombe, Captain Harry, 173
Eshowe 114, 138, 173, 174, 175, 208, 267, 270, 284, 320, 321, 323, 344, 398, 405
Esley, Johnny, Pte. 24th Foot, 261
Essex, Edward, 75th Regt. 292
Evans, Pte. Edward, 24th Foot, 260
Evans, Sergt. 72
Evelyn, 2nd Lieut. G. R. 208
Everson, G.R. 76
Evezard, Pte. E.H, 51

F

Ferreira, Colonel Ignatius, 77, 428
Ferreira, Trooper P.S. Corp. Cape Mounted Yeomany 59
Ferreira P, Burghersdorp Troop, 416
First Boer War. 333
Flogging 221
Forbes, Archibald, 409
Forster, Mr. W. E. 413
Forsyth. D.R 4
Fort Pearson, 153
Foster, Pte. G. 17th Lancers, 201
Fowler, Lieut. D. G. M. 91st. Foot 320
Fowler, Pte. E.J, 90th Foot, 314
Foxon, Sergt. 128
Frances, Pte. J. 24th Foot, 262, 449
Frankish, Levy Leader J. 64
Frank Long, 8
Fraser, Captain Thomas, 91st Foot, 320
Frere, Sir Barde, 401
Frost, Pte F.G. H. 17th Lancers, 201
Fryher, Pte R. 1/24th Foot, 442
Fufcher, P.O. 2 Cl., E H.M.S. Active 390
Fynn, Levy Leader H.F. 64

G

Galekas 3, 6, 125, 141, 157, 302, 401, 438
Gardiner, Pte. 17th Lancers, 206
Gardner,Captain 20, 446
Garland, Quarter Master Alpheus Howe, 175
Garrett, Lieut. John Raymond, 285

General Order 5
Gibson, Lieut. Arthur, 132
Gibson, Pte Edwin, 58th Foot, 280
Gierke, Pte. C., Buffalo Md. 39
Giese, Pte, Frontier Mounted Police, 77, 401
Gifford, Trooper, 156
Gilliat, Edward, 81
Gingindlovu 12, 138, 211, 270, 320, 398, 399, 421
Gissop, Pte. Miles, 17th Lancers 205
Glanville, Dr. Doyle, 159
Glennie, Captain F. 2-24th, foot 442
Glynn, Brigadier- General, 49
Goatham, Ashley Thomas, 261
Godson, Captain G.G. 194
Gordon, Pte D. 2/24th Foot, 444
Goss, Captain Michael, 49
Gosset, Captain Albany Rangers, 20
Gough, Hugh Rudolph, 192
Graham, Trooper J. Frontier Light Horse, 91
Grainger, Tropper W. Natal Carabineers, 128
Grandier, Trooper Ernest 34
Grant, Inspector J.M, 47
Grant, Pte. H. 24th Foot, 262
Green, Staff-clerk Gus, 70
Green, Trooper, Natal Mounted Police, 131
Greene, Regt. Sergt-Major E.M. 145
Greenwood, Pte. E. 94th Foot, 331
Griffith, Charles Duncan, F.A.M.P. 49, 77, 401, 414
Griffith,Sub-Lieut. Thomas L. George, 2/24th Foot, 247,262,446
Griffiths,Pte. G. 1/24th Foot, 444
Grix, Trooper F, Durban Mounted Reserve, 70
Groves, Trooper E. Durban Mounted Reserve, 70
Grunewald,Corpl. 0. 164
Gurney, Captain,Natal Native Contingent, 176
Gutridge, Trooper 38

H

Hagen, Trooper A Von, 91
Hair, Sergt. A. 128, 145
Haldane, Lieut E.H.V. 88th Regt. 303
Hall, Lieut. of Orderlies Arthur William, 344
Hall, Trooper,Victoria Mounted Rifles 177
Hamer, Commissary Officer James Nataniel 354
Hamilton, Captain T.R. 124
Hamilton,Major, 272
Hamilton-Brown, Major, 66
Hammond,Lieut. & Adj. D. T. 88th Regt. 303
Hanch, Trooper, 156
Hancock, Lieut H. 138, 142
Hannon, Trooper W. E. 59
Harber, Sergt. Dan, 49
Harding, Ord. Seaman,Thomas HMS Active, 390
Harding,Surg. Captain 88th Regt. 303
Harford, Captain S.H. 189
Harford, Colonel Henry Charles, 134
Harkin,Pte. T. 1/24th Foot, 444
Harkness, Pte. J. 1/13th Foot 226
Harris, Lieut. Col. David, 66

Harris, Trooper W.H. 156
Harrison, Gunner T. N/5 Royal Artillery, 443
Hart, Captain, 390
Hart, Reginald VC, 266
Hart-Synnot, Major-General A. F. 266
Harvey, Lieut, 47
Harward, Lieut. Henry, 290
Hastings, Trooper A. 59
Hay, Lieut. A.B. 141
Heliograph signalling, 272
Helpmekaar 38, 61, 134, 337, 404, 409, 421, 439, 448, 449, 450
Henderson, Lieut A. F. 448
Henderson, Mr. Alfred Fairlie, 448
Henderson, Mrs Sheila, 38
Henwood, Trooper, 72
Hicks, Conductor J.M. 2/4th Foot, 218
Hicks-Beach, Michael Sir, 413
Higginson Lieut. W.R. N.N.C. 139
Highton, Captain E.C. 138, 140
Higley, Pte. 99th Regiment, 175
Hind, Pte. J. 1/24th. Foot. 447
Hitchcock, Edward, 143
Hlobane Mountain 91, 169, 318, 399, 431, 455
Hodgkinson, Trooper T. 62
Hoffmeister, Trooper G. 54
Holdich, Laurance, Maydwell, 84
Holdich, TSM Laurence Maydwell, 91
Holmes, Pte Thomas, 17th Lancers, 202
Hook, Inspector 49
Hooker, Trooper E. 156
Hopton, Lieut Col E. 88th Regt. 303
Horn, Pte. J. 1/24th Foot, 444
Hough, Pte. W. 1/24th Foot, 443
Howe, Pte. W. 99
Hughes, Pte. Edward 1-24th Foot, 260
Hunter, Trooper, Natal Mounted Police, 131
Huntley, 10th, 337
Hutchinson, Trooper R. 156
Hutton, Paymaster, 89
Hutton, Sergt. 128
Hyde, Lieut.Dr G. Clarence, 61

I

Imperial, Prince, 30, 131, 134, 138, 202, 289, 376
Imperial Troops Medal Summary 186, 187, 188, 189
Intombi River 290, 292, 293, 295, 348, 455
Isandlwana survivors who reached Helpmekaar. 449
Isandlwhana 406, 409
Ivatts, Pte. E. 1/24th Foot, 445

J

Jackson, Noomi, 136
Janssens, Lt General Jan Willem, 5
Jay, Lieut. Herbert Valentine, Natal Native Contingent, 138, 176
Jennings, Sergt. E. 80th.Foot, 293
Johnson, A. Burghersdorp Troop, 416
Johnson, Private A Royal Durban Rifles, 156
Johnson, Pte William 1/24th Foot, 262, 446

Johnston, Pte G. 1/24th Foot, 445
Johnstone, Trooper A. Cape Mounted Yeomany, 59
Johnstone, Trooper Thomas, Cape Mounted Yeomany, 59
Jones, Pte. J. 1/24th Foot, 444, 445
Jones, Pte. W. 1/24th Foot, 443
Jones, Pte A. 2/24th Foot, 445
Jones, Robert VC, 250
Jones, Trumpeter 47
Jonsson, Trooper I .Y, 70

K

Kambula, Troop Sergt. Major Sieon, 450
Kannemeyer J. Burghersdorp Troop, 416
Kay, Trooper W. 59
Keane, Colour-Sergeant M.C. 409
Kennedy, Trooper, Durban Mounted Rifles, 72
Kerr, Lord Mark, 82
Keys, Pte, 99th Regiment, 175
King, Trooper W. Cape Mounted Yeomany, 59
Kirby, Levy Leader H.E. 64
Kirkman, Qr. Mr. Thos. 23
Kitchener's Fighting Scouts 162
Knight, Levy Leader J.L. 64
Knott, Major William, 131
Kock, Trooper. J.D. 54
Kock, Trumpeter, 47

L

Laasen, Trooper L. 159
Lahey, Sergt. J. 91st Foot, 320
Lane, Sergt. T. 129
Lanyon, Sir Owen 333
Laurence T. Burghersdorp Troop, 416
Laurens, Trooper T. P. Cape Mounted Yeomany, 59
Lawrell, Captain W. G. 122
Leal, Leading Seaman, G.E, HMS Active, 374
Leet, Major William K. 81, 82
Lehmann, Joseph 122
Leonard, Trooper H. Cape Mounted Yeomany, 59, 60
Lerothili, Chief 28
Leslie, Trooper J, 90
Letters from South Africa, 259
Lewis, Pte. P. 58th Foot, 281
Linsingen, Captain Von, 40
Lisbeck, Pte. George, 24th Foot, 242
Lister, Lieut. William 173
Litchfield, Edwin 189
Lloyd, Lieut. 266
Lloyd, Lieut. W. W. 1-24th Foot, 236
Lloyd, Mr 34
Long, Frank Trumpeter 8
Long, Lieut. Walter, 121
Lonsdale, Captain J.F. 125
Lonsdale, Commandant , 134
Lotz, Trooper W. 156
Lough, Pte G. 17th Lancers 206
Lourens, Trooper Cornelius, Cape Mounted Yeomany, 59
Lovell, Pte. C. 1/24th Foot, 444, 447

Lucas, Stanley, 41
Luck, Inspector, 47
Lugg, Henry Natal Mounted Police, 131, 134
Lugg, Lieut. H, U.M.R. 145
Lumley, Trooper Joseph, 129
Lydenburg Rifles 122
Lysons, Lieut. Henry, 90th regt. 311

M

M'Mullen, Lieut. Diamond Fields Horse, 417
Macaulay, Captain J. E. 122
Mack, Pte S. 17th Lancers 206
Mackay, Trooper, 122
Maclean, Allan, 84
Macleroy, George Thomson, 425
Macnaghten,Captain Elliot, 84, 91
MacNally, Cpl P. 122
Macomo, Tini, 401
MacPhail, Dugald Quartermaster, Buffalo Border Guard, 38
Macphail, Ian Quartermaster, Buffalo Border Guard, 38
MacPherson,Sergt. C. G., 46
Mafunzi's Natal Horse 176
Magee, Pte, CMR. 417
Mahoney, Lieut.-Colonel J. 252
Mainwaring Brigadier-General Henry, 251
Mair, P. L. Burghersdorp Troop. 416
Majia's Hill skirmish 266
Major Dennison, 32
Makar, Trooper J. 156
Manderson, Bugler E. 156
Mann, Trooper C.S, 70
Mansfield, A. Burghersdorp Troop, 416
Mansfield, Trooper A.J. Cape Yeomanry, 60
Maple & Co, 299
Margetson, Mr. B. P. 122
Marshall, Robert 38
Martin, Pte. D. 1/24th Foot, 443
Martingale, 49
Martini-Henry 113, 114, 115, 241, 413, 417
Mason, Trooper C. Cape Mounted Yeomany, 59
Matibe, Trooper P. 122
Maxwell, Major T. 66
Mayer, Corporal, 139
Maytham, Alfred Trooper 8
Maytham, Mathew Trooper 8
McCann, Corporal, 24th Foot, 262
McCann,Pte. J. 3/60th Foot, 289
McCarthy, M 41
McColl, John Trooper 8
McCormack, Quartermaster J.R. 124
McGonigle, C. Sergeant, 8
McKenzie, Corpl. D. 145
McKew, Pte. J. 94th Foot, 333
McLean, Captain 28
McLeod, QMS N. Border Horse 122
McMahon, Michael, Army Hospital Corps, 345
Mears, Charles, 428
Medal Awards, 24th Foot 436, 437

Medal Awards, Killed in Action Isandhlwana 438, 439, 440, 441
Medal Design 6
Medal Naming 334
Medals Rorke's Drift 453
Melsop, Bandsman 24th Foot, 251
Melvill, Lieut. 451
Memorial at Victoria Park, 375
Meredith,Pte. J. H. 1/24th Foot, 4423
Metcalfe-Smith, Lieut. A, 25
Meyer, Pte.S CMR. 417
Meyer, Trooper Fred. Cape Mounted Yeomany, 59
Miles, Capt. A.E. 285
Millais, J.G. 136
Millar, Alice, 143
Miller, Trooper, 128
Minto,Lieut Col T.E. 53
Misplon, Trooper, 156
Mitchell, Cpl E. 122
Moffatt, Thomas .J. 298
Molyneux, Captain, 176
Molyneux, R-S Major, 128
Molyneux, Tpt-Major A.J. 128
Montague, Captain, CMR. 417
Moor, Sergt. Natal Md. Police, 442
Moore, Lieut.M.G. 88th Regt. 303
Moore, Major, 49
Moore, Major, 88th Regt. 305
Moore, Major Hans Garrett, VC. 77, 401
Morgan, Joseph Pte. 24th Foot, 261
Morgans, Pte. John 2-24th Foot, 260
Moriarty, Captain D.B. 291
Morosi's Mountain 29, 47, 55, 59, 79, 414
Moses, Henry Pte. 24th Foot, 261
Mossop,Sergt. George 25
Mostyn, William Eccles, 262
Muir, Sergt. 128
Muirhead, Trooper A. 128
Muldoon, Sergt. T. Cape Mounted Yeomany, 8, 55, 59
Mullins, Mollie, 162
Mundy, Lieut.R. 75
Murray's Orange Rovers 126
Murray, Captain. G. 126
Murray, Drummer. B. 58th Foot, 278
Murray, Lieutenant-Colonel John, 77

N

Natal Carbineers 144, 145
Natal Horse 176
Natal Mounted Police 132
Natal Mounted Rifles 132
Natal Native Contingent 138, 176
Natal Volunteer Units 173
Nel, Carl Trooper 8
Nesbitt, Major R.C. 56
Nettleton, Capt., 40
Neumann, Captain A.H. 136
Nevile, Captain C. C. 99th Foot, 336
Newberry, Pte H. 1/24th Foot, 444

Nicolson,,Lieut, 80th Reg. 296
Norbury, Staff Surgeon Sir H.F. 373
Norris-Newman, Charles, 81
Northend, Gunner, 71
Norton, Lieut. 98
Nourse, Captain, N.N.C, 139, 176
Nourse, Lieut. Henry, 77

O

O'Neill, Lieut. F.A.M.P 77
O'Toole, Sergt. Edmund, V.C 91
Officers Killed in the Transvaal 92
Ostheirner, Pte J. 17th Lancers, 206

P

Parkes W, Burghersdorp Troop, 416
Parkin,Lieut H. 100
Parminter, Major W. G. 25
Parry, Pte. W. 24th Foot, 262
Parson, Trooper, 143
Paterson, Lieut H. Mc.K. 168
Pearson, Colonel Charles Knight, 114, 176, 266
Pegg, Colour-Segt. 13th Foot, 227
Penton, Captain C.T.W. 88th Regt. 303
Phillmore, Deputy Commissary S. T. 351
Pickard, Pte. J.R. 1/24th Foot, 442
Pietermaritzburg Rifles, 11
Pike, Stephen, 61
Plante, Horace P, 84
Platterer, Lieut. 266
Plowman, Mr George, 251
Poole, Lieut. J. 124
Porteous, Lieut. Francis P. 262
Potter, Charles Alfred, 427
Potter, Pte. V.D. 17th Lancers, 207
Powell, Sergt. 128
Power, Pte. J. 24th Foot, 241, 262
Prendergast, Major A. 185
Prevost, Captain. W. 91st. Foot, 320, 321
Price, Pte.W. 94th Foot, 335
Private J. Schwitzer,Pte J., 40
Prosser, Pte J. 1/24th Foot, 445
Prozesky, Rev. Mr, 143
Purvis, Lieut. T. Natal Native Contingent,139

Q

Quinn, Drummer J. 99th Foot, 339

R

Raaff, Lieut. P, 77
Raines, Lieut. J. 124, 266
Rampton, Sgt. Maj: J. 119
Rapson,Corpl. J. 156
Rapson, Trooper T. 156
Rathbone, Caractacus Reliance, 178
Raw, Captain Charles, 81
Rawlins, Lieut. 176

Ready, Sergt. S, 53
Reed, Lieut. N.A Cape Mounted Yeomany, 59
Rees, Pte William, 2-24th Foot, 262
Reston, Pte Wm. 122
Rethman, Lieut. F. 145
Returned Medals 9
Reyner, Pte. H. 112
Reynolds, Levy Leader,T.H. 64
Reynolds, Pte L.T. 17th Lancers, 207
Rice, Pte. W. 2/24th Foot, 443
Richardson, Pte J. 170
Rickards, 2nd Lieut. F.S.H. 88th Regt. 303
Robertson, Trooper J.L. 156
Robinson, Levy Leader, N.H. 64
Robinson, Sergt. J. 55
Robson, Pte. 99th Regiment, 175
Rogers, Major R.M. V.C 90th Regt. 311
Rorke's Drift 88, 114, 115, 131, 134, 135, 137, 250, 251, 252, 259, 261, 262, 337, 345, 354, 357, 404, 412, 419, 421, 435, 439, 441, 443, 446, 448, 451, 453, 454, 455
Rose, Trooper, 156
Ross, Sergt. Geo. 145
Rowlands, Colonel, H 87, 227,296
Royal Artillery 262
Royal Durban Rifles 11, 156
Royston, Lieut. W. 127
Russell, Captain R.A. 446
Russell, Lt Colonel Baker, 120
Russell ,Major R.A. 139
Russell, Sergt. W. 1st Btn. Nat. Congt. 442

S

Sampson, Lieut. 122
Saner, Captain Charles Taylor, 173, 174
Sangmeister, Lieut. W. 145
Sansom's Horse 157
Sansom, Captain, 157
Sansom, Pte J.E. 112
Savage,Pte P. 91st Foot, 320
Scheiss, Corporal, 139
Schermbrucker, Commandant, 159
Scott, Captain J. 76
Scott, Frederick John Durrant, 125, 144, 426
Scott, Pte A. 17th Lancers, 207
Scott, Sgt Major D. 144
Scott, Trumpeter C. 144
Secocosni, 86
Seely, Major 9
Shannon, Trooper, Natal Mounted Police, 131
Sharp, Lieut. Thomas, 137
Shepherd, Surgeon Major, 251
Shepherd, Trooper C.S. 91
Shepstone, Captain T. 127
Shepstone, Captain W.E, 72
Shepstone, George John Palmer, 354, 426
Sherrington, Captain, 175
Shervington, Captain, Diamond Fields Horse, 417
Sir David Baird 5

Skinner, Pte H.C. 17th Lancers, 204
Slade, Lieut. F.G. 80th Foot, 296
Slade, Pte. H. 2/24th Foot, 442
Smith, Brevet Major Stuart RA. 359
Smith, Capt. Tom 38
Smith, Chaplain George, 357
Smith, Edwin, 1/24th Foot, 445
Smith, Lieut. A. M. 82
Smith, Lieut. William Craighead, 38
Smith, Major Stuart, RA 251, 337, 446, 447
Smith, Metcalfe 81
Smith, Pte H.G. 17th Lancers, 207
Smith, Trooper J. 156
Smith-Dorrien 451
Southey's Rangers, 11
Southey, Lieut. Col. R.G. 53
Spaulding, Major, 354
Sprenger, Major 79
Stafford, Captain W.H. N.N.C 139
Stainbank, Captain 12
Stamp, Trooper G. 91
Stanford, Robert William 31
Stanley, Lord 9
Stansfield, Pte S. 1/24th Foot, 445
Stanton, Quartermaster J, 173
Stephens, Robert 24th Foot, 262
Stevanus, Trooper O. 91
Stevenson, Captain, N.N.C. 139
Stewart, Pte. A. 58th Foot, 283
Stirton, Corpl. H. 128
Stirton, Sergt H. 145
Stretch, Charles Lennox 450
Sugden, Lieut. 176
Survivors from Isandlwana 449, 450
Swinburn Henry 113, 114, 115, 128, 174

T

Tarte, Captain Edward F. 72
Tatham, Trooper C. 128, 145
Terry, Lieut G.K. Tower Hamlet Mil. 190
Thausie's Natal Horse. 176
Theis, Corpl. C.A. 85, 91
Thesiger, General and Staff 190
Thesiger, General Frederick A. 135
The Victoria Cross 454, 455
Thirkill, Lieut. John 88th Regt. 400
Thomas, Pte. David, 24th Foot, 261
Thompson, Lieut. Natal Native Contingent, 176
Thompson, Trooper A.H. 62
Thornett, Pte. T. 1/24th Foot, 442
Thornton, Trooper C 59
Tilney, Sergt. 128
Tomasson, Lt. & Adt. William H. 25
Tompkinson, Pte. J. 58th Foot, 283
Townsend, Major 10
Transvaal Rangers 11, 12, 35, 66, 68, 69, 73, 74, 121, 124, 125, 126, 160, 166, 168, 169, 399, 421
Tremlett, Major R. A. 241

Tucker, Driver Elias, 360
Turner, Thomas, P.O HMS Shah. 387
Tutton, Pte W.R., 40
Tweedie, A Trooper 8

U

Umzimkulu Mounted Rifles, 145
Uys, Piet, 41, 91, 168

V

Vacey-Lyle Captain, C.J. 173
Vause, Lieut R. 145
Venter, Private W. 27
Verkker, Lieut. Hon. Standis W.P, 81, 91, 94, 125, 132
Vice, Trooper A. J. 55
Victoria Cross 412, 454, 455
Victoria Mounted Rifles 144, 173
Vinnicombe, Trooper W.D. 91
Voysey Lieut. 72

W

Walker 122
Walkinshaw, Pte A. 90th Foot, 318
Walsh, Lieut. 452
Walsh, Pte. T. 1/24th Foot, 445, 447
Walsh, Trooper, 143
Walters, Pte. B. 17th Lancers, 207
Ward, Captain, 66
Ward, Captain Randall Ironside RN & 90th Foot, 311
Ward, Lieut. G.Walter, 66
Ward, Sergt. H. 80th Foot, 293
Wardell, Captain, 446
Warner, Levy Leader W.C. L 64
Warner, Private G. 22
Warren, Lieut.-General Sir Charles 65
War service of Imperial and Colonial Units, 398
Wassail Pte. 8th Foot, 452
Watts, Corp. 72
Wayman, Captain, G.A. 99th Foot, 336
Weatherhead, George James Trooper 8
Weatherley, Lieut.-Colonel Frederick 32, 36, 123
Weatherley, Trooper J 36
Webb, Lieut. 266
Welch, Pte C. 157
West, Pte C. 99th Foot, 344
Weston, Pte W. 122
Whale, Pte. 99th Regiment, 175
Whalley, Captain George Hampden, 84
Wheeler, Levy Leader T. 64
Whelan, Pte. J. 1/24th Foot, 445
White, Bernard, CMR. 417
White, P.O, E. HMS Active, 390
Whitehead, Colonel. R.C. 277
Whitehouse, Pte.J. 58th Foot, 284
Whittaker, Sergt. 128
Willett, 2nd Lieut. J. S. 194
William, Captain, 49

William, Captain E. 262
William Earle, 8
Williams,Corpl. R. 1/24th Foot, 443, 445
Williams, Lieut. G. 124
Williams, Pte J. 24th Foot, 262
Williams, Sgt Major, 81
Willoughby, Captain Digby, 138
Wilson,Bandsman E. 24th Foot, 262
Wilson, Pte. J. 24th Foot, 262, 446
Wilson, Sgt-Maj. R. 122
Wollaston, Captain, 66
Wood's Irregulars, 178
Wood, Colonel 34
Wood, General Sir Evelyn, 82, 114, 178, 192, 222, 310

Worman,Sergt. 128
Wright,Commander T. RN, 374
Wyk, Trooper S. Van 55
Wyncoll, Lieut C.F. 88th Regt. 303

Y

Young,Pte. T. 1/24th Foot, 442, 444
Younghusband, Captain, 251

Z

Zeeman, Gunner, 71
Zerderburg, Civil, Practr. 348
Zulu Warrior 319

Victorian obsession with collecting artefacts and souvenirs of the Zulu war was so strong that life was almost put at risk to secure pieces.

Lightning Source UK Ltd.
Milton Keynes UK
23 June 2010

155953UK00001B/13/P